By the same author

Supertips to Make Life Easy
Supertips 2
Pasta for Pleasure
Enquire Within Upon Modern Etiquette

Publisher's Note

Changes to UK Telephone Dialling Codes

Telephone dialling codes are changing on 16 April 1995. These changes were announced too late to be incorporated in this edition, but readers can continue to use the telephone numbers given throughout the book by remembering three main changes:

- all UK area codes will start 01 instead of 0. Thus the area code for Oxford will change from 0865 to 01865, and the code for Liverpool will change from 051 to 0151.

- five cities will receive completely new codes and an extra digit in front of each local number.

Leeds	0532 xxxxxx	becomes	0113 2xx xxxx
Sheffield	0742 xxxxxx	becomes	0114 2xx xxxx
Nottingham	0602 xxxxxx	becomes	0115 9xx xxxx
Leicester	0533 xxxxxx	becomes	0116 2xx xxxx
Bristol	0272 xxxxxx	becomes	0117 0xx xxxx

- the international dialling code will start 00 instead of 010.

Both old and new codes can be used from 1 August 1994 to 16 April 1995.

The changes apply only to geographical codes. Service codes, such as free phone services 0500 or 0800, remain the same. Operator services and emergency numbers 999 and 112 also remain the same.

ENQUIRE
within
UPON EVERYTHING

THE COMPLETE HOME REFERENCE BOOK

ENQUIRE

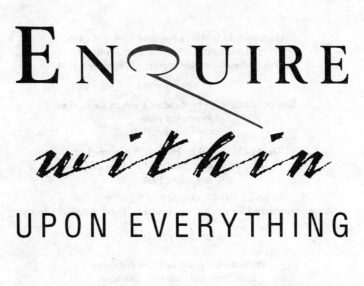

within

UPON EVERYTHING

MOYRA BREMNER

Helicon

To H.R.H. with love

Text copyright © Moyra Bremner 1988, 1990, 1994
Illustrations and Enquire Within title
copyright © Helicon Publishing Ltd 1988, 1990, 1994

First published 1988 by Random Century Group Ltd
Reprinted 1988
Second Edition 1990

Third Edition 1994 by Helicon Publishing Ltd,
42 Hythe Bridge Street, Oxford OX1 2EP

Reprinted 1995

British Library Cataloguing in Publication Data
A catalogue record for this book is available from the British Library

ISBN 0 09 177641 4

Printed and bound in Great Britain by
Bath Press Colourbooks, Glasgow

CONTENTS

Where to Find More Information

At the ends of chapters you will find the addresses, and other details, of all the useful organizations referred to in that chapter (those already in other chapters have page numbers in the text). You will also find suggestions for books which cover the topics in detail.

INTRODUCTION

Enquire Within is a title with a curious history. The first book by that name was published in 1856. It was a runaway bestseller and, between 1856 and 1976, ran to 126 editions – claiming to be 'the most famous book of domestic reference in the world'.

Its author – an anonymous man who wrote of 'my wife's little suppers' – had created a quirky, highly individual and delightful hotch-potch. It covered everything a Victorian family needed to know: from the making of 'mouth glue' (presumably the kind you licked) to 'hints for wives' – on tolerance towards their husbands.

Unfortunately, 120 years of revising and updating left it full of good details but like a suit which has been altered so often it isn't quite sure what fashion it represents. So I was asked to write a totally new book, starting from scratch, which would have the same title as the old one and solve the daily problems of the 1980s and 1990s as effectively as the first edition solved those of the 1850s.

We don't need to make our own 'mouth glue' but most domestic chores loom as large as they ever did. We may have washing machines but self-removing stains and trouble-free pets and children are not yet available. So this book has had to cover almost all the domestic topics covered by the old one: but does it in totally modern terms.

However, life today is infinitely more complex than it was for the Victorians. We can no longer sit back, as our ancestors could, certain that the world we confront today is much as it was yesterday and that we know how to deal with it. Since my first edition of this book there have been major changes in law, social security, and the educational system. And the financial world has been both shaken and stirred to produce a cocktail unlike anything that has ever existed before.

To keep abreast of such changes we need to be better informed than we have ever been. For example, to a Victorian we would seem positively swaddled in consumer protection, but the law only protects us *if* we know and use it.

Our grandmothers had a simple choice over where to put their earnings or their savings: the bank, the teapot, or a sock under the bed. Today we face choices our parents would not have dreamt of: and people are falling over themselves to lend you money. But choices cut both ways and every year ordinary people lose their homes because they don't know enough to make the right decision. Similar opportunities and pitfalls can be found in almost any area of modern living.

So I decided that, for the 1980s and 1990s, *Enquire Within Upon Everything* would need to take on every aspect of modern living, guiding readers through the maze, explaining what to do and where to go for help with the problems that beset private life. The result is a survival guide for life today.

Where organizations are given, you will find a briefing on what they offer either in the main text or with their addresses, which you will find grouped together between chapters. With the addresses I have also recommended books which expand the facts I have given on many topics. Often they are the latest books, but I believe that a first-rate book from a library is worth two second-rate ones from a bookshop, so not all the recommended books are in print.

To find the very latest facts in every field, I have sifted through not only a substantial range of books but also drawn on almost three-quarters of a ton of letters and leaflets which arrived in reply to over 2,000 letters I sent out asking for information. But this is not a book written simply from theory. Having brought up three children, alone, for over 21 years, I have had first-hand experience of almost every area I cover. And where my personal life left gaps I have found my professional experience has stepped in. In fact, part of the pleasure and excitement of writing this book has been the satisfaction of seeing the varied threads of my life all adding to some aspect of it.

However, despite its name, it makes no claim to say everything about everything; that would take a library. Instead it is a first source which gives the key facts and provides pointers to where to find out anything else you want to know.

It is organized into sections and alphabeticized subsections. For example, the section on law is sub-divided into consumer law, criminal law and so on.

Within each sub-division the headings are usually in alphabetical order. But a natural order sometimes overrules that. In First Aid, for example, it was safest to start with the emergency procedures which must be done first, and work through the correct stages in saving life. Basic tasks like making a curtain or cooking a chicken also have their own overriding order which has been followed in preference to the alphabet. I suspect that these deviations will seem as natural to you as they do to me, and make the book even easier to use. For those who like to go straight to the page, with no browsing on the way, there is also a detailed index. I hope you will turn to it even when you seem to have found what you need. Often topics overlap and useful information could appear in more than one place.

Not being sexist, yet equally reluctant to distort the English language, hims appear randomly in some paragraphs and hers in others and I hope readers will assume that what is written applies equally to both sexes – unless logic dictates otherwise.

The author of the 1856 *Enquire Within* ended his introduction with the words: 'Our Interviews [paragraphs] will be varied, genial, and entirely original in their arrangement. The pleasure of your company is earnestly solicited.'

I hope you will find my paragraphs just as 'varied and genial'. Having little time for useful books which aren't interesting, I have woven into its pages curious facts, quotations from far and wide, and extracts from the first *Enquire Within*, so you can pick it up from time to time for nothing more serious than a contented browse. In this, most of all, the pleasure of your company is indeed most earnestly solicited.

ACKNOWLEDGEMENTS

The anonymous author of the Victorian edition of *Enquire Within* said he compiled his book with the help of his friends and quaintly directed his readers to find 'a schoolmaster at [paragraph] 1925', 'a surgeon at 2186' and so on. I have continued his tradition and my first thanks must go to my friends. It is no exaggeration to say that this book could not have been written without them. They have given me inside information which I could have found in no other way. Their generosity in sharing their knowledge is something for which I am more grateful than I can express.

To keep this book totally up to date it has been necessary to draw most of my information from people rather than from books. So I have also been helped by an army of experts, officials, and press officers in almost every major organization in Britain; to them I also owe a great debt. Their kindness in answering endless queries, reading my text and correcting my errors, has been extraordinary, and many went well beyond the call of duty to assist me. I would like to name them all, but that would be a book in itself, so I can only name a selection of those to whom I owe a particular debt or whose organizations do not appear in the book. I hope that all those who do not appear below will feel no less warmly thanked. I will long remember with gratitude the many individuals who gave me so much help and encouragement.

My particular thanks go to the following (in random order):
Bruce and Amanda Weatherill
Dr Graham White
Imperial Chemical Industries
The Health and Safety Executive
Metropolitan Police
David Butcher
Nella Opperman
Ian Wood
Deborah Carnworth
Corinne Julius
Anne Beeching
Jennifer Bonner
Alison Bonner
Pat Buckingham
The London Fire Brigade
Black & Decker
Barbara Davies
Paint Research Association
Slumberdown
Harrods
Bud Henson
Lever Bros
Michael Simmons and Emma Lodge-Patch of Malkin Cullis and Sumption
The Worshipful Company of Goldsmiths
Caroline Hunt
Kim Bertram
Melvin Brown
Doyin Lawumi
Paul Newman
Automobile Association
Brian Davis
British Agrochemical Association
Christopher Peel
Laura Ponsonby
Safeway
Banking Information Service
British Insurance Association
National Westminster Bank
Barclays Bank
Moypark Chickens

Midland Bank
Nicholas Carew Hunt
The Stock Exchange
Rosemary Burr
Phillida Dally
National Consumer Council
British Farm Produce Council
Dornay Foods
Sea Fish Industry Authority
Shellfish Association of Great Britain
H.J. Grimes
Rex Thomas
Sharp Electronics
J. Sainsbury
Whitworth's Foods
Cherry Valley Ducks
Meat and Livestock Commission
Jenny Salmon of The Food Dimension
Diane Roberts of the Public Health Laboratories
Tony Hein
David Cossart
Wine of Australia
Italian Trade Centre
Bulgarian Vintners Co
German Wine Information Service
Food and Wine from France
The Sherry Institute of Spain
Wines from Spain
Portuguese Government Trade Office
Wine Institute of California
Tim Stanley-Clarke
William Warre
Stanley Holland
American Airlines
Penny and Roger Holland
Graham Marr
Smith Brothers
Digital Equipment Corporation
Zena Edmunds
Tesco
Paton & Baldwin

H. Milward & Sons
Waitrose
Peter Jones
Donald Wadsworth
Bradley Viner
J.R. Bainbridge
Chrissie Nicholls
British Equine Veterinary Association
The Zoological Society
The Natural History Museum
Coral Bazaar Aquariums
Dr J. Brett
Dr Emond
David Simpson
Dr Stephen Inman
Dr Ione Inman
Dr Victoria Murday
Dr Richard Cotterell
Kate Start (Chief Paediatric Dietician, Guy's Hospital)
Professor J.R. Mitchell
Dr Ilya Kovar
Dr Bronwyn Hughes
Dr Sheena Sutherland
Dr C. Robinson
Dr Lynda Howard
Dr Tony Martin
Dr David Barlow
Dr Clarke of the London School for Hygiene and Tropical Medicine
Dr E.L. Rhodes
Rand Rocket
J. Cork of St John Ambulance
Mr Peter Diggory
Lorraine Hewitt of the Standing Conference on Drug Abuse
Marks & Spencer
Sainsbury
Dr Jon Darius
Cassandra Darius
J.C. Wells (Reader in Phonetics, London University)
Collins Publications
Oxford University Press

BBC Pronunciation Department
Rowena Gedye
Adam Leyland
Sophie Bennett
Andy Smith
Donatella Rovera
Simon and Esther Herrtage
Monique Sandoz

Smythson of Bond Street
Lars Gorton
Liz Filippini
Ian Hope Morley
Fiona Hunter
Pat Verity
Deborah Cullen
Dr A. Martin

The Science Museum
The Royal College of Physicians
Suzanne Tarlin
Felise Tucker
The Electricity Council
English Abrasives
GKN

My thanks also go to my original editors Gail Rebuck, Sarah Wallace and Valerie Buckingham, without whose support and patience this book could not have been completed, and to Julian Holland and my illustrators who have so excellently converted by works into a book. I particularly want to thank Sarah Riddell and Mary Remnant who edited by words with a sensitive and restrained pencil, and showed such great understanding of what I was trying to achieve.

Finally, there are no words for the debt I owe to my children, Siobhan, Fergus and Rory, who endured with infinite tolerance and understanding my preoccupation, the massive invasion of paper, and the domestic chaos which writing a book of this diversity inevitably caused; and who also helped me in my research and lent me their knowledge in their own special fields.

Key to the Symbols Used with Addresses

This key explains the symbols used after organizations throughout this book. But most are constantly developing and may now be offering services or facilities which were not on offer when I contacted them. Also I noted the points they emphasized. So if an organization told me they specialized in giving advice on the telephone I put 'Tel Ad' – but that doesn't mean that all the organizations without 'Tel Ad' *don't* give advice on the phone. So please take my summaries as a broad indication of what is being offered, rather than as a hard and fast guide which allows no change or deviation.

M£L	membership fee low – under £10 pa
M£M	membership fee moderate – £10–20 pa
M£H	membership fee high – over £20 pa
M£var	membership fee variable
M£Vol	at your discretion

Children, OAPs and other special categories are often much less, and most charities provide free basic help and information to non-members.

A	activities are organized
Ad	advice is given on the subject in question
B	book list or books on mail order
C	career advice is available
CC	credit card orders accepted
Cl	runs clinics
Comp	competitions/shows organized
CS	for children with the complaint
Disc	membership provides certain discounts
E	sells equipment
Ed	educational facilities or information
EI	information on equipment
Ex	exhibitions run or visited
F	sells or hires films on the topic
F&F	for the family and friends of sufferers
Fest	members take part in festivals
G	there are local groups or clubs which can be contacted and/or joined, these may be branches of the main body or loosely affiliated
GP or Dr	referral from a doctor needed
H	holidays are offered
HC	holiday or residential courses run
HD	the handicapped are catered for
Inf	information provided
Ins	insurance cover via the organization
Int Comp	international competitions arranged
Jun	junior section for children to join
L	they have leaflets on the topic
Lec	lectures are given on relevant topics
Leg	offers relevant legal advice
Lib	members may use a special library
M	magazine or news sheet sent to members
O	older people (i.e. elderly) catered for
RC	registered charity
Res	respite care – of sick/old/handicapped to give relative a rest
Rg	regional centres
S	for sufferers from this condition
sae	send a stamped, self-addressed envelope with any query
T	travel opportunities for members
Tel:	telephone number as follows
Tel Ad	telephone advice
Th	therapy offered
TR	hires or sells tape recordings on the topic
V	sells or hires videos on the topic
vg	very good, shows I am most impressed
Vis	visits to relevant places of interest

SOCIAL BEHAVIOUR

Social behaviour is decided by conventions of manners and etiquette which are such minefields of prejudice and misconception that I am tempted to open by saying 'Abandon hope all ye who enter here'. For a start, you cannot discuss either without class raising its unfashionable head. But unfashionable I shall have to be.

Etiquette is the conventional code of behaviour within a particular group or class – embellished, of course, with regional or national variations. It is a behavioural uniform by which people tell the world the social group to which they belong – or aspire to belong. The British make a habit of asserting that England is the most class-conscious country in the world. In fact, class consciousness exists everywhere (even in communist countries), and most of the foibles and snobberies which we think of as distinctly English are found in every sophisticated country in Europe.

Good manners, on the other hand, are barrier breakers, based on consideration for others. They involve adapting to make others feel comfortable. So good manners tell you a lot about someone's character, while etiquette tells you a lot about someone's class.

I would prefer to write only about good manners. But etiquette has to be covered because there are still situations in which not knowing what to wear or do, in a group other than your own, can be a disadvantage. So this chapter concentrates on the established form. It isn't *the* correct way to behave; it is *a* correct way to behave. Some of it may sound both bossy and snobbish. But it is impossible to write about rules of any kind without laying down the law and, for example, nobody needs to know how to dress to go and stay in ordinary houses: it only becomes a problem if those you are visiting live rather more grandly than you do.

However, bossiness and encouragement of snobbery are not my intention. So far as I am concerned the best social behaviour is what comes naturally to people who are gentle and genuinely considerate, and social niceties are unimportant in comparison. But not everyone would agree with me, and the trivial points of etiquette can still *be* hidden traps for people in both their career and their social life. It therefore seems essential to include them.

However, nobody should imagine for a moment that I am suggesting people should alter their ways to those I outline. If any of my readers choose to do things differently that is their right. I don't always follow all these rules either. Those who want to know about general points not covered here should read Debrett's *Etiquette and Modern Manners*, or turn to Debrett's *Correct Form* for the details on how to address, either in speech or writing, every kind of dignitary.

Accidents and Breakages

If someone breaks or damages something belonging to someone else, the first step should be to try to put it right, or help the owner or hostess to put it right. If food or drink has been spilt, mop it up – but if you are inexperienced at such jobs ask her how she would like it handled. If an item needs to be cleaned or replaced offer to pay for it (unless it is so expensive that this would be ridiculous). Whatever happens, there should never be any attempt to conceal the accident. Concealing it is a form of lie.

The person whose property has been damaged should always try not to embarrass their guest further by making much of it. Whether or not the offer to pay for the cleaning or repairs is accepted is a matter of their relative situations.

General Courtesies

The first edition of *Enquire Within* enjoined its readers to: 'Be polite. Politeness is the poetry of conduct – and like poetry it has many qualities. Let not your politeness be too florid, but of that gentle kind which indicates a refined nature.'

At that time the gestures of courtesy tended to be a one-way traffic; from men to women, young to old. Now things are far more flexible. Those with the best manners extend their consideration in all directions. So a woman will open a door for a heavily laden man, or give her seat up for a younger woman who is pregnant or carrying a child, just as much as for someone elderly. But she in turn should have a seat given to her or the door opened by any child or man, unless they are more heavily laden than she is.

The bonus of teaching such manners to children is that it sets a pattern for thoughtfulness within the family too.

ENTERTAINING

Buffet Meals

With a buffet meal almost anything goes. Buffets usually start with the main course (which is generally cold), move on to pudding and may include cheese and fruit. If you care for your guests at all try to have food which can comfortably be eaten with just a fork. This applies not only to the type of food but to how it is prepared. Lettuce torn into sizeable pieces is nothing but a nuisance, but chop it finely as they do in Arab salads and it is perfect for fork meals.

The organization of any buffet can be adapted to fit the household, but here are some points to bear in mind.

- There are always laggards. If you can arrange things so you don't have to clear the main course in order to serve the pudding and cheese you do both them and yourself a favour.
- The placing of the table should make it easy for people to queue to get at the food and encourage them to leave the room afterwards.
- If you have people helping on one side of the table it is fastest to have one serving the meat or fish and another the salads, rather than both serving everything. This keeps people moving along.
- Put the plates at the entry but the forks at the far end to move people away.
- If someone is around to usher them to where they can sit down, they won't stand by the food and stop others getting at it.
- If you have the drink well away from the food it makes people circulate.
- Avoid all foods which stain badly – beetroot, purple fruits and curry are among the worst.
- Remember some guests feel compelled to open bottles – even if plenty are already open. So only bring them out as the others run low, or you'll be left with a mass of half-empties.
- Expect drink to be spilt – so choose colourless drinks if you can.
- Have white paper napkins. Someone is bound to mop up spilt drink with their napkin, and the dye from coloured ones will ruin your carpet.

★ Small French polished tables which would be marked by glasses can be covered with cling film. Carefully stretched it is invisible in low light.

It is, incidentally, perfectly good form for guests at a buffet meal to return for second helpings once everyone else has been served. They don't have to wait to be asked.

Cocktail Parties and Drinks Parties

A formal 'At Home' invitation can be issued for any type of drinks party and they normally start at 6.00 or 6.30 pm. Usually, they only last two hours and the leaving time is often given on the invitation. Drinks parties can also start closer to 9 pm and be designed to go on all evening – often with dancing. For these no end time is given.

The drink can range from champagne, through spirits to cheap wine cup, according to the occasion. Cocktails are rarely served. The food is scanty – nuts, crisps and dips predominate, and canapés are served by those who use caterers. For late evening drinks parties buffet food or a substantial selection of cheese is often offered. In this case, the invitation should make it clear by saying 'Buffet Supper' or 'Wine and Cheese'.

The host and/or hostess should keep moving people round and introducing them. This doesn't mean breaking up groups or couples who are clearly having a great time together, but it does mean having an eagle eye for the simulated interest of someone who has been stuck for too long. Take someone who is at a loose end to join some others, introduce them and then extract a guest you want to move. Having taken that person on to the next group you can extract someone else from there – and so on.

However, guests don't have to be dependent on the host or hostess; anyone can introduce themselves to anyone else, and it makes the party go a lot better if they do. It is everyone's responsibility to see that no stranger is left standing by themselves.

If you have been stuck with a group for too long, you can either melt out of a large group without comment, or openly excuse yourself saying there is someone you have to go and talk to (even if there isn't), then vanish from sight. If you are stuck with one person take him or her to meet someone else and then excuse yourself. If you know nobody, manoeuvre him or her into a crowd – via getting a drink or food – then excuse yourself and head for the loo.

Formal Lunches and Dinners

Advance Planning

The secret of enjoying one's own entertaining is to do as much as possible well ahead. It always seems to be the so-called 'little jobs' which take the time. So it helps to have a running 'battle plan' permanently on file giving a countdown on what needs to be done on each of the days that lead up to the event.

Ideally, the battle plan enables you to do all the little jobs at least 24 hours ahead, and your choice of foods lets you have no more than one course which needs to be cooked on the day. That way you should still be ready by a whisker even if – as tends to happen – the cat is sick, the phone never stops ringing and a child throws the tantrum of its life.

Planning is very much easier if you keep a note of any previous entertaining. It is useful to jot down who came, what you gave them to eat, how much was made of each dish and how much was left, any foods they said they disliked or obviously avoided, any foods they obviously loved, and whether they drank coffee, or something else. This means you don't keep bringing the same groups of people together, give pâté to the same couple three times running, or foist fish on someone who clearly loathes it.

All this may sound like a system for those with leisure. Far from it. It's those who have the most work who find systems most useful.

Addresses and suggestions for further reading are at the ends of chapters.

HOSPITALITY

Arriving

Lunch invitations are usually for between 12.30 and 1 pm, and dinner/supper invitations for half an hour before the time when you plan to serve dinner. As dinner tends to start between 8 pm and 9 pm, people are usually invited for 7.30 pm, 8 pm or 8.30 pm. In picking the time, thoughtful hosts and hostesses take account of how late the guests may have to work and how far they have to come.

In Britain guests are expected to arrive 15 to 20 minutes late for dinner, but be rather more punctual for lunch. Some countries have very different rules of punctuality (page 24).

Presents from Guests

It used to be unusual for guests to arrive with presents for their host. They are still not essential, and it is perfectly all right to arrive empty-handed. But the younger the group the more likely it is that people will bring a bottle. And, at all age groups, more and more people take flowers, or after-dinner chocolates if not a bottle of wine. It all depends on who is at the receiving end. Flowers, rather than wine, are taken to the well-off but those on a small budget may particularly welcome wine to eke out what they have bought for the meal – and friends can offer to bring a bottle, when they are invited.

It is tactful for the hostess to show her appreciation by using the present at the meal. The exception to this is a fine bottle of wine which will not be at its best after a journey; ask the guest whether he or she thinks it can be drunk immediately or whether it should be allowed to rest until another day. If it is mainly for their own delectation the guests will opt for drinking it immediately (however ill-advised this is). But if they have brought it for your pleasure they will tell you to keep it.

Canapés Before Meals

Those who enjoy making fiddly canapés to munch with the drinks will probably find their guests fall on them with shouts of glee, but they aren't essential. Small bowls of nuts or crisps are fine, and some people offer nothing at all. Alternatively, those who hate washing up can dispense with a first course by having some interesting and substantial dips which guests eat with their drinks. This is an unconventional ploy, but I find it works. And if anyone is particularly late, or you have worked all day and are late cooking the meal, it salves your guests' impatience.

Drinks Before Meals

Drinks are usually served in the sitting room before both lunches and dinners; if the weather is hot few places are better than a garden. Pimms and Kir are the garden drinks par excellence, but inside or out anything goes, provided it suits the occasion, from beer before an impromptu barbecue to champagne before a black-tie dinner. Nowadays wine is often served. But a guest should never ask for wine as an aperitif unless it has been offered – the host (or hostess) may have no wine which is suitable, or too little to go round at dinner if it is drunk before. Offering a guest a choice of specific drinks guards against this, as well as making it easier for the guest. The usual selection is gin, whisky and sherry or vermouth plus, perhaps, campari. There should also be at least one enjoyable, not too sweet, non-alcoholic drink clearly on offer: drivers don't necessarily have a passion for tap water.

Laying the Table

There used to be a lot of debate over whether mats or a cloth should be used when laying a table. Now you can use either, provided the cloth is a plain colour. If the table has a lovely surface it may be a shame to cover it, but a tablecloth conceals a multitude of sins and allows you to cover the surface with a protective undercloth. There are two kinds: bulgomme and heat-resistant felt. Both are sold by the yard in good furnishing fabric departments. You can also use a layer or two of blanket, if the cloth will conceal it. The padding gives a hospitable softness to the table as well as protecting it.

Knives and All That

The rules for table laying are the same for both lunch and dinner. The places are set so that the guests are evenly spaced round the table. Knives and spoons go to the right of each place and forks to the left, arranged in the order in which they will be used – with those which will be used first on the outside. Apart from the small knife for buttering bread, everything is laid in pairs. So the large knife should be there, with its blade facing the mat, even if the food only needs to be eaten with a fork, and the small fork should be there even if the pudding does not need a fork. Whether it is or is not correct to put the pudding spoon and fork head to tail above at the top of the mat is a matter of dispute, but it is never wrong to put them at the side.

An ample number of serving spoons should be on the table, unless they are to be put in each dish as it comes to the table. There should also be a knife (or knives) for the butter, plus suitable spoons for mustard, bread sauce, whipped cream and so on.

The normal order of courses is:

First course   soup, pâté or some other light starter

Second course   fish – this is often omitted or eaten instead of a first course

Main course   meat, or a major fish, usually with hot vegetables

Fourth course   green salad – very optional but increasingly popular, though the French deplore a vinegar dressing when wine is drunk

Fifth course   pudding

Sixth course   cheese

Seventh course   fresh fruit

Eighth course   coffee sometimes accompanied by chocolates and/or liqueurs.

At home people rarely have more than three or four courses, plus coffee, even when giving a formal dinner; and at lunch three courses are ample. This means you can start either with the main course and have both pudding and cheese, or have a first course and forget the cheese.

Whatever the meal, the fourth, fifth and sixth courses are very flexible. Fresh fruit is often eaten with cheese and, at an informal meal, this combination may take the place of pudding. Equally, at a formal meal, at which a dessert wine will be served, it may be better to have cheese before pudding – as the French do.

Glasses
The glasses go above the spoons and knives. At most meals only one wine will be served, but provide two glasses and have water on the table as well. If you have more than one wine there should be a fresh glass for

Tumbler   Brandy
        Sherry

White wine
Champagne   Red wine

each. There are no rules for how these should be arranged, provided it looks good, but there are rules on the size of glass.

To wine lovers tulip-shaped glasses are best. This is because the in-curving rim holds the scent of the wine, which is a large part of its pleasure.

★ Storing glasses is tricky as they easily pick up the smell of a cupboard – especially if stored upside down on a wood shelf. So, if the glasses aren't used daily, keep smells out by standing them upright with a piece of cling film covering each one.

Napkins and Plates
The classic system is to have a dinner service with matching plates for every course. But matching isn't essential; one of the prettiest dinner services I know consists entirely of unmatched antique plates, of similar styles, picked up in junk shops. Failing such originality, anyone buying a dinner service might consider plain white, which shows off food extremely well. For large numbers you can also add any other white china you like and, by candlelight, only your most critical guests will notice the mismatch.

A small plate, for bread, goes to the left of the forks (even if you don't intend to serve bread) and the table napkin goes on it. If you enjoy napkin origami, do it; but there is really no need and very elaborate napkins call for food which lives up to them. Double damask dinner napkins (as in the tongue-twister) are ideal for formal meals, but any fabric napkin can be used, and nowadays large soft paper napkins, in a colour which suits the table setting, are perfectly good for many occasions.

Making Serving Easier
Have all the plates which will be used cold – and even the hot ones if you have a warmer – already in the dining room before the meal. Medium-sized plates are used for first courses, such as pâté, and for puddings. They can also be put under small containers, such as cocotte dishes, small soup bowls or glasses of sorbet. So, when buying a dinner service, it is worth getting twice as many of these as of the meat plates.

At an informal meal, you can let guests eat a salad course from their meat plate. But it does depend on the food. The juices of some meat are delicious with lettuce; but fish juices can be vile, so it is useful to have a separate salad plate. This can be a crescent shaped plate, but is more often a middle-sized plate or a small bowl. Equally, cheese should really have a separate plate – but by this stage hostesses are often running out, so people often use their bread plates.

Pepper, Salt and All That
There are all kinds of extras which people may need with their food – pepper, salt, butter, sauces, mustards and so on. Ideally, everyone passes these to everyone else. In reality, nobody passes anything. So put as many on the table as you can muster. The butter can stay on until after the cheese, but every pepper, salt and sauce container should be removed after the main course – or the salad, if you are having one.

Addresses and suggestions for further reading are at the ends of chapters.

Decorating the Table

Except for occasions like Christmas, tables don't really need much decorating – the food and the guests provide the colour. The main point is not to let any central flowers create a hedge between the two sides of the table; nothing dampens cross-table conversation quite like shouting through foliage.

Lighting the Table

Bright light is a great conversation-stopper and can reduce a party of friends to stilted small talk. But put even strangers in the cosy softness of candlelight and the shy unwind and the confident become garrulous which is just what makes an evening go. But the light shouldn't be so dim that you are left fumbling for your fish bones.

If you dislike candles use low lamps or dimmed lights which don't point directly at the table. And if you want the conversation to keep flowing when everyone returns to the sitting room its lighting must be equally dimmed.

Seating People at Table

Hostesses usually decide who will sit where. At a large or formal gathering there can be a name card at each place. At smaller gatherings she can tell each person where to sit. But even for quite small groups it can be useful to draw a plan: a good arrangement is not as easy as it seems.

There are three standard rules for seating. First, men and women should alternate. Second, husbands and wives (or couples of less classic mould) should not be next to each other. Third, the most important man should sit on the hostess's right, and the most important woman (often the important man's wife) should sit on the host's right. This last is often abandoned (as is the charming tradition of giving a new bride priority among the women). But it is a rule worth observing if there is any guest sufficiently old, or eminent, to be offended by having less than the best place.

It's also worth pairing people who will get on well together, and placing anyone shy and silent near a good talker who will keep that part of the table going. (The malicious use the vengeance system, and place the most boring person next to whoever they like least.)

Strictly speaking, each man should pull back the chair of the woman on his right and push it in as she sits down. It's charming when men do.

If it's a large group, someone is bound to wish they were next to someone who is just out of reach. So I like to ask all the men to move round two male places after each course – taking their glass and napkin with them. This is not conventional and doesn't suit a *very* formal meal but people do seem to enjoy having two new people to talk to at each course – and the 'Mad Hatter's Tea Party' air it gives tends to help things go.

Serving Food

If there are staff the food should be served to the most important woman first, then to the other women in order of importance (for formality) or simply according to where they are sitting. Then this pattern repeated with the men. For the main course, the plate of meat or fish should be put in front of each person and the vegetables then offered separately, so everyone can help themselves to what they want. If two people are serving it is quickest to have two sets of vegetables and let them each offer them down one side of the table. All plates and dishes are served from the left of each guest – to avoid a raised glass and a proffered plate colliding.

If you yourself are serving, adopt the order of precedence staff would use, but simply pass the plates down the table. Or, if there is plenty of room to move round the table, it may be easier to have one member of family serve and the other take the plates to each person. The vegetables and other extras should be on the table and it is up to the guests to offer these to the person on their right and hold the dish while they take what they need.

Serving Wine

Wine is served from the right of the diner, and a wine glass should never be more than half full: to fill it further is to leave no room for the bouquet. If (as usually happens) there is only one wine, and it will go with the first course, it is served from the start of the meal. But if the flavours will clash it can be held back until the main course.

At a very formal meal the staff serve each guest and stay in the room to refill glasses as necessary. More often, the wine is served, and then put on the table so guests may top up their glasses as they wish. The host should make sure that they do and pour more if necessary. At informal meals the host may ask guests to help themselves from the start – in which case the men should pour the wine for the woman on their left.

Empty bottles should be taken from the table, and if there is more than one wine, each wine is removed before the next is served. If port is served, it arrives with the cheese. Tradition has it that the host pours port only for the person on his right, he then helps himself and passes the port to his left, and it then continues to progress clockwise.

Clearing the Table

One of the worst developments in modern restaurants is that waiters often take people's plates away as soon as they finish – even though others at the table are still eating. This should never happen – nor should hosts permit it. It makes those who are slow feel guilty that they are holding other people up. No plate should ever be removed until the last person has finished – and even then, not until a few minutes after.

To Stack or Not to Stack

In the early 1950s there was a Punch cartoon of a wife at a dining table turning to her husband and saying 'Do we stack or are we gentry?' An allusion to the fact that, lacking staff, only those who clung very determinedly to their pre-war standards continued to carry the plates off one at a time after family meals. However, it is correct and there is an argument for doing so when entertaining.

Serving Coffee

Some people serve coffee at the dinner table, so the flow of conversation is uninterrupted. Others go to the sitting room. In this case, the hostess often removes the women from the table slightly earlier to allow time for loos and retouching make-up. But the days are long gone when men could tell stories over the port, while the women talked about babies over coffee.

As fewer people are drinking coffee, more smart hostesses are offering a choice of coffee, an after-dinner tea or herbal tisane. This is still unusual, but perhaps worth considering. It doesn't matter whether the hostess asks each guest if they want sugar or cream and puts it in, or lets them do it themselves, but there should be a coffee spoon on every saucer, whether or not people take sugar.

Leaving

Urban (if not urbane) lunch parties usually end at about 3.00 pm – though business lunches are usually shorter. In the country at weekends lunch may flow into a walk and then tea (in which case the hosts should indicate that this will be the form). Dinner parties usually end between 11 pm and 12 pm, although they can last into the small hours if the hosts look as if they want everyone to stay and the guests are keen to do so.

If guests have a special reason for needing to leave early (for example, to catch an early plane next morning) it is tactful if they tell the hosts about this when they accept the invitation – then there won't be doubts about whether they enjoyed themselves. Normally, guests say good-bye (without formalities) to other dinner guests, but when leaving early it may be best to leave inconspicuously. Then they won't spoil the party by starting a general exodus.

Guests should take their cue for leaving from what they know about the host and hostess. If someone is an early riser it's thoughtful to leave early. If they like nothing better than to talk into the small hours, early leaving (unless you have to) is spoiling their fun.

Hosts should accept that not going to bed at the usual time is a price they pay for the pleasure of having guests, and if guests outstay their welcome there is no *good* way to get them to go. However you wrap it up, making someone leave before they choose to is saying you have tired of their company or that you care more about your comfort than their pleasure – and neither is very hospitable.

On leaving, guests should thank the hosts, and the hosts should accompany them to the door and wait as they go to the street. If a woman is leaving alone at night the host should walk with her to her car, or see that she has other transport.

Tea

Tea, as I remember it from childhood, with meltingly wonderful home-made cakes, is, sadly, a vanishing tradition. But, laden as it is with forbidden fruits – fats, sugar and bread – it is an occasional delight which is worth maintaining.

Except for children's parties, invitations to tea are seldom written. Unless the tea is mainly for the benefit of young children, it is eaten in the sitting room, not at a table. Each person has a cup and saucer, with a teaspoon, and a small plate with a small knife. Neither doilies nor cake forks should be used – if a cake is too messy to eat with the fingers the pundits say it should not be served.

The hostess pours the tea for each person and, if you are bothered about such things, the tea goes in first. The up-market tea is China, drunk with a thin slice of lemon and no milk, but Indian is more popular. Lump sugar can be added to either. The usual food is sandwiches, cake(s) and possibly biscuits. The hostess should at first offer the food to guests, but this is one meal at which people may help themselves, within reason, as the meal progresses.

The official method of drinking tea is to hold the saucer just above the knees and lift the cup to the mouth – head ducking and little finger crooking are out. When eating, the cup and saucer are put down on a side table (there should be one close to each chair) and the plate is held like the saucer or put on the lap. Small cakes are eaten as they are. Large slices of cake may be eaten in sections which you cut off, and small napkins aren't essential unless the cakes are sticky.

Teenage Parties

At an informal party there is, in my view, only one rule: don't go out and leave teenagers alone in your home. I know this is contentious, and it would be a shame to hover about and spoil their fun, or embarrass them to bits by trying to join in. But it is one thing to keep out of their hair, and another to give them totally free rein. When drink is poured into inexperienced and undisciplined heads there is always a risk that some of their friends will try to take things too far. If that happens they need an adult within call. Today there is also the risk of violent gate-crashers to be considered.

Weekends and More

It is said that in-laws should live far enough away to have to put their hats on, but not so far that they have to stay the night. But friends are a different matter provided everyone sticks to the ground rules.

The respective roles of the host and his or her house guests are summed up in the anonymous quote: 'The perfect host makes his guests feel at home; the perfect guest never behaves as if he *is* at home.' But achieving this ideal state of affairs demands a lot from both sides especially from the host and hostess, for it is up to them to express welcome and attentiveness, while subtly conveying enough house rules to let guests fit in smoothly. This latter is essential, as much for the guests as for themselves: it is impossible to feel at home when you don't know what to expect next.

Issuing Invitations

Most invitations to stay are issued on the phone or informally in a letter. If you are inviting guests for a particular date you should say when you expect them to arrive. The best way is to indicate the time of the first meal for which they are expected, for example, 'Do come

---

Addresses and suggestions for further reading are at the ends of chapters.

for dinner on Friday night. We usually eat at about 8 o'clock, so we'll expect you sometime after 6.' This gives them decent leeway for hold-ups on a long journey, but makes it clear that arriving at 8 would be too late. It is also wise to indicate a departure time. Again, meals are a good reference point. You can easily say, 'We do hope you'll stay for Sunday lunch', whereas you can't say, 'We do hope you'll go after Sunday lunch' – which is what it means.

The Length of the Stay

How long friends should stay is really a matter of how far away they live and how well you know them. A rough guide is one night for every 1 to 1½ hours of travel to reach you. So if you live 3 hours' drive away you can't decently invite them for less than 2 nights.

The same rule applies when inviting yourself to stay with someone who has issued an open invitation. But a week is about the maximum – even if you fly round the world – unless you are genuinely pressed to stay longer. Be specific about the time you'd like to arrive and depart and, unless an invitation includes pets and/or children, they should not be taken.

If guests are arriving by train the host(ess) usually tries to meet them at the station. Those who invite themselves shouldn't expect this consideration, but a good host (or hostess) will give it.

Briefing Guests on Clothes

Guests should be casually briefed on whether they need to bring special clothes. So tell them if you have a swimming pool, or tennis court, or if you are going to a point-to-point on Saturday, or usually change for dinner, or even if you want them to help with DIY. If a host (or hostess) forgets to do this a guest can always ask.

House Rules

Once guests arrive they need to be kept briefed on the form for the house – the times of meals, whether they can have a bath whenever they want, plus the quirks of difficult taps and lavatories. They also need to know the rules on getting up. Some people insist that their guests are on parade for breakfast at set hours, but if you are happy to let them get up at any time, say so – making it clear whether or not food will still be available for latecomers. It is not unreasonable to say, 'Breakfast is sometime between 8 and 9, but if you want to skip breakfast and sleep late you can just make yourself a cup of tea whenever you get up.' This absolves you from the duty to fry eggs all morning and lets guests get a rest – and a sleeping guest is never any bother. But some people can sleep like the dead, so tell them if they need to be up by midday – and offer to wake them.

Conversely, guests who wake early and hungry should conceal this and not sit around waiting to be fed, like a family dog. Unless there is clear evidence to the contrary, they should also assume everyone is fragile and needs quiet at breakfast time.

Privacy

Unless two people are married or you are *certain* they sleep together, give them separate rooms – preferably close enough for them to creep across surreptitiously. All guests need hangers, and towels; Americans may expect a face flannel too, and flowers in the room make up for a multitude of shortcomings.

Once guests are in their room hosts should regard it as private. To knock and walk in, even with cups of early morning tea is to invite embarrassment. Instead, knock and say you are leaving the tea outside the door.

Bedtime and Waking

It is up to the guests to go to bed first (just as it is up to them to leave a party). Not all guests know this, so there can be a stalemate as each side sits waiting for the other to make the first move. Once a reasonable hour has been reached the hosts can cure this by offering a nightcap or hot drink 'before bed'.

Before saying good-night hosts should check that guests have enough blankets on their beds, and brief them *fully* on any alarm system. It is all too easy to tell them not to go downstairs but to forget to tell them not to go upstairs, or not to let the dogs out.

As people often wake early and thirsty in a strange house it is also a good idea to show guests where they can make themselves tea or coffee early in the morning. If an alarm system prevents this they can at least be given a thermos of boiling water, and what they need to make instant coffee, or even a jug of orange juice to cheer the early hours. To lie awake unable even to make a drink is miserable.

If guests are able to go down to the kitchen hosts needn't take the odd clink as a signal to leap up and start breakfast. This will only make the guests feel guilty. Equally, guests should avoid clattering about 'helpfully' preparing breakfast – it will only make the hosts feel they should have risen earlier. The only thing worse than a guest who does nothing is one who does too much.

Gifts on Arrival

It's conventional to arrive bearing gifts when going to stay with people. This can be anything you choose, but food and drink are the most usual. Or, you can take flowers, or send them afterwards. The size of the present should suit the length of your stay.

Food and Drink

Anyone who has any serious food allergy should warn the hostess – no one wants to make guests ill. A hostess should also try to ask about food likes and dislikes, if only to spare herself the depressing sight of guests picking at her food.

Some households tell guests to help themselves to any food or drink they feel like. Guests should use this privilege with great moderation. If that invitation isn't issued they should always ask before taking anything, and keep their asking to a minimum.

Helping

The main role of any guest is to be good company but that isn't quite all.

Unless there are staff, good guests should look to see

what needs to be done and either do it unobtrusively or offer to do it: vague offers of help are simply annoying. However, there are limits to how much work a guest should do. Nobody wants a guest to turn into a demon cleaner in the middle of a sociable visit, and a quick way to have the hostess smiling through gritted teeth is to clean things far more thoroughly than she does. The matter of contributing to the food budget also needs tact. Money, in any form, should *never* be handed to the hostess (unless perhaps to split a specific bill when you are shopping together), but contributions in kind are always welcome and may be expected if someone is staying several days.

On leaving ask the hostess if she would like the beds stripped. But *only* do it if she says yes. Underblankets are not always designed for guests' eyes.

The Host's Children and Animals

Unlikely as it may seem to devout child and animal lovers, some perfectly civilized people regard both as they regard adults – they like some and dislike others. Liking the parents or owners does not guarantee any affection for their offspring and pets. So little darlings, of both kinds, should be prevented from molesting the guests. By the same token, guests must do all they can to treat them well and deflect them tactfully.

Staff

If there are staff one of them may well unpack a guest's suitcase – so consider before you pack anything embarrassing. On leaving, guests should tip any members of staff who have helped them – including the daily woman who has cleaned their room during the stay. It is always wisest to ask your host or hostess how much you should give.

EVENTS

Christenings

Parents who want their child christened should ring the clergyman, priest or appropriate official of their church, and make an appointment to discuss the arrangements. Some Church of England clergymen prefer to make christenings part of the morning service, but it is normally possible to have it as a separate service especially if you offer to bring the child for a blessing with the whole congregation at another time.

The exact forms of service vary with each branch of the Church, but they are all easy to follow and need no advance preparation. One difference, however, is that in the Church of England the godmother usually holds the child before baptism; in the Roman Catholic Church the mother holds it.

Announcing the Christening

Christenings can be announced in the court and social pages of *The Times* and the *Daily Telegraph* and should be submitted to the social editor in writing. Just give the parents' names, the name of the clergyman, what the child was christened, the date and place and who the godparents were.

Choosing Godparents

The parents usually select two godfathers and two godmothers. They are normally expected to be baptized, confirmed and practising Christians – though this is usually taken for granted without questions being asked. The idea is to give the child an even better extended family, and more loving (and Christian) guidance than nature provided.

It is an honour to be asked to be a godparent, but it carries long-term responsibilities and it is unfair to the child if you accept when you really don't feel inclined to carry these out. If you want to refuse a good excuse is needed. One possibility is to say you have so many godchildren already that you don't feel it would be fair to take on another – much as you'd like to. The important thing is to give no hint to parents that you don't like their child – which may well be the truth.

Godparents are expected to give the child presents and so are the immediate family. The presents should be something lasting – jewellery or small items of silver are traditional. Godparents can make life easier for themselves if they choose something to which they can add at every birthday. Then the problem of what to give is solved for years ahead. Others who are invited to the service have no obligation to give anything, but they may feel more comfortable giving at least a token unless they visited the mother in hospital and gave her something for the baby then.

The Occasion

Dress is very much like a wedding so far as women are concerned, but men wear dark suits. The baby traditionally wears a white christening robe – but any good white garment is suitable.

Everyone who attends the christening usually goes back to the parents' house for a small party. It could be a lunch, tea or evening drinks – depending on the time of the christening – but, whatever the hour, it is traditional to have a special cake (rather like a wedding cake) and perhaps champagne. A godfather usually proposes a toast to the baby.

Funerals

The formalities which used to surround death dwindled almost to nothing during the two World Wars, but there are certain conventions which remain. There are also legal requirements and these can be found in the section under Law.

Announcing a Death

When someone dies relatives and close friends should be notified immediately. This can be done in person, by telephone or by letter. An announcement can also be put in the papers, and *The Times*, the *Daily Telegraph* and the *Scotsman* all have deaths columns. Some regional papers, like the *Yorkshire Post*, and some local papers, do too. The announcement should briefly give the name of the deceased, the date and place of death, and the date, time, and location of the funeral. If flowers are not welcome it should say so. For example:

> **PETRIE** – On 5 April at Great Ormond Street Children's Hospital, Anne-Marie, darling daughter of John and Isobel Petrie. Funeral the Brompton Oratory 4 pm, 10 April. No flowers please, donations to the Leukaemia Research Fund if desired.

Dress

People no longer go into mourning by wearing black, but a man should wear a dark suit and white shirt, and a woman a dark dress, suit or coat. A hat isn't essential, but it is preferable, especially for women, and showy jewellery shouldn't be worn. The only exception is if a widow wants to wear clothing or jewellery which her husband loved to see her in. If his favourite colour was red, then red she can wear.

There is no longer any need to wear black in the weeks which follow, although if people feel they want to make this visual expression of their sense of loss it would be cruel to try to jolly them out of it. A time for mourning is needed if the bereaved are to recover fully in the long run, and to hurry people into some phoney 'normality' is to paper over cracks which are best left to heal in their own time.

Letter Writing

It is still customary to write a letter of sympathy to friends and relatives, when they are bereaved. These should be written swiftly, as the whole purpose is to give support to the bereaved during the difficult and lonely days immediately after the death, but those who are less close to the family may prefer to write in the second week.

It can be hard to know what to write, but this shouldn't put you off writing. You only have to say how very sorry you are to hear of the death. Offer your sympathy and let them know that they are being thought of, and are not alone in their grief. The simplest and most genuine words are the best.

Letters of condolence should always be answered, unless the writer says there is no need for a reply – and clearly means it. All that is needed is one sentence saying how much their kind and understanding letter was appreciated, another saying something about the deceased – for example, that mercifully they died very peacefully – and perhaps a final sentence saying that you are sure they understand that you are not able to write more, but that you hope to be in touch before too long. If there are a lot of replies to write the whole family can share the task, making it clear that they are writing on behalf of the chief mourner. Nowadays ordinary writing paper and envelopes, not mourning paper, are used.

The Flowers

Flowers from either family or friends are sent to the funeral director, so they can be put with the coffin on its journey. Those who wish to send flowers should ask the family where to send them. It is possible to have a tree planted in memory of someone who has died (see page 377)

Undertakers/Funeral Directors

Undertakers are called undertakers because they undertake all the arrangements for a funeral, though they now like to be called funeral directors. Most operate a 24-hour service and will collect a body as soon as the death has been certified by a doctor. From then on the relatives need only tell the funeral director what they wish to have arranged and he does everything for them.

Funerals are expensive and made more so by the fact that only complete packages are available. You can expect to spend over £400, and the price will rise with extra options, such as an elaborate coffin or a headstone. But prices also vary considerably from one company to another for exactly the same 'package'. The costs come out of the dead person's estate (see under Law). So if someone would have resented his or her savings being spent on inflated funeral costs you should ring round and ask for comparative prices. But this must be done *before* the body is collected. Once any company has collected the body there is, effectively, no changing. (See also under Law). The most basic package usually includes:

- the collection of the body from the home or hospital
- keeping the body in a chapel of rest
- all arrangements – phoning the crematorium, church, minister etc., a simple coffin
- taking the body to the cemetery or crematorium
- the staff required for this
- It may also include one car for the family on the day, and more can be provided at extra cost.

If the family wants to view the body it will normally be embalmed – possibly at extra cost. But some funeral directors embalm *every* body they handle – unless you ask them not to.

The costs don't end there. In cities, obtaining a plot and having the grave dug costs several hundred pounds, and in some places the bill is close to a thousand pounds (but see under Law). Although the undertaker makes the arrangements for the crematorium, the fees involved are *not* included in his charges. There will be fees for the extra medical certificates needed for a cremation, and there will also be a fee for the use of the crematorium and possibly for an officiating minister.

Most good funeral directors belong to the **National Association of Funeral Directors** which will deal with any complaints which you can't resolve with the company concerned.

The Funeral

The date and time of the funeral may depend on what the officiating priest can manage, but the family should tell the undertaker their preferences. Occasionally, people put requests regarding the service in their will, and in religions and denominations that allow variations the family usually discuss their special requirements with the priest and, choose the hymns.

The chief mourners are usually collected from the deceased's house, and the funeral cars take them both to and from the service. Other mourners should arrive about 15 to 20 minutes before and there should be a verger or family friend there to see the correct pews are filled and that enough space is left for the family at the front.

If the body is being buried the coffin will be carried out to the grave after the service and the family will lead the mourners out to the graveside for the final moments.

Cremations

Cremation is becoming more popular and crematoriums permit services of all religions and also non-religious services – such as those of the humanists. If the body is to be cremated, there are two possibilities. The service can be held in the non-denominational chapel at the crematorium, with the dead person's local priest or someone on the crematorium roster officiating. Alternatively, the service can be at the deceased's usual place of worship and the coffin taken to the crematorium afterwards. In this case, it is usually only accompanied by the family. The crematorium will need to know what should be done with the ashes.

What Happens After the Funeral

After the funeral, the relatives and close friends usually return to the house of whoever has died for some kind of food and drink. Often this is prepared by friends or relatives and brought along in advance, to spare whoever is in mourning the work involved. If food and drink is available anyone who would be welcome to return for it should be told in advance – there is no need for a proper invitation – and anyone who turns up unexpectedly at the funeral and would be welcome can be invited too.

Weddings

Engagement rings were once part of an intricate system of ring signals. In the first (1856) edition of *Enquire Within* I found these signals described in a section called 'Love's Telegraph', which explained:

> If a gentleman wants a wife, he wears a ring on the first finger of the left hand; if he is engaged he wears it on the second finger; if he is married on the third; and on the fourth if he never intends to be married. When a lady is not engaged she wears a hoop or diamond on her first finger; if engaged, on her second; if married, on her third; and on the fourth if she intends to die a maid.

This subtle signalling didn't stop at a ring, for the writer continues:

> When a gentleman presents a fan, flower, or trinket, to a lady with the left hand, this, on his part, is an overture of regard; should she receive it with the left hand, it is considered as an acceptance of his esteem; but if with the right hand, it is a refusal of the offer. Thus by a few simple tokens, explained by this rule, the passion of love is expressed: and, through the medium of the telegraph, the most diffident man may, without difficulty, communicate his sentiments of regard to a lady, and, in case his offer should be refused, avoid experiencing the mortification of a refusal.

It seems rather a pity that we have retained the engagement ring, and discarded all the other useful signals. It

might save a lot of heartbreak if those who had no intention of marrying announced it on their hands.

Even without these aids some 400,000 people get married in Britain each year. Although Church of England weddings predominate, there are numerous other forms and even the C of E conventions vary with the region. Much as I would like to include traditions of Scots Presbyterians, Bah'ais or Buddhists, I am limited for space and can only cover the classic Church of England conventions. The civil requirements are covered opposite.

Church of England Weddings

For most Church of England marriages the civil preliminary is the calling of the banns, but there are other options (see below).

The Banns

A Church of England wedding can only take place if the banns have been called on three Sundays. For this, the bride and groom each visit their own parish priest, ask for banns to be called and pay a statutory fee. Some clergy like seven days' notice before the first banns are called. If the couple is marrying at a church which isn't in either of the parishes the banns must normally be called there too. The banns involve asking the congregation if they know any reason why these two people should not be married, and the clergyman will usually talk to the couple and check this.

Common Licence

For a common licence to get married one of the couple must have lived in the parish for 15 days before applying. Together they then apply for the licence to whoever represents the bishop in that area. If it is granted the couple can get married the next day.

Special Licence

It is a legal requirement to get married in either your own parish or that of your fiance. If you want to get married anywhere else you need a special licence from the Archbishop of Canterbury which allows a wedding to take place anywhere – for example, in a hospital. You get an application from the **Registrar** at **The Faculties Office**.

Church Weddings Not in the Church of England

All weddings not conducted by the Church of England must be preceded by the preliminaries needed to obtain either a certificate or a licence for a registry office wedding (see below). That doesn't necessarily mean that there has to be a registry office wedding as well as a religious service. Once the Superintendent Registrar has issued an authorization for the wedding to take place the marriage can often be conducted in the place of worship.

Some priests and ministers are registered as 'authorized persons' and allowed to register a marriage; others are not. This is not a matter of some denominations or religions being registered, but of some individuals being registered. So the fact that one Catholic priest registers marriages doesn't mean the next one necessarily can. If whoever conducts the service is not authorized, a registrar of marriages may be able to come to the place of marriage and register the wedding. Only when this is not possible is it necessary to have a registry office ceremony as well as a religious ceremony.

Civil Weddings

For a marriage to be valid it must be registered – any religious service is, from the legal point of view, just icing on the cake. Registration can either take place in a Registry Office or in a building which is authorized by the state – such as most of the Christian churches.

If a marriage is purely in a registry office there are two options – a certificate or a licence. To obtain either the bride or groom must live in the area of the registry office being used. For a **certificate** each takes their birth certificate and a fee to the registry office in the area where they live (those who have been married before must also take a decree absolute or a death certificate). If they live in two different areas one registry office just accepts notification that the person intends to marry, and a booking is made at the other. This must all be done not more than 3 months and not less than 21 days before the day they wish to marry. The couple book a definite time and day – book early for Saturdays. It is also worth asking how many guests may come and whether a photographer will be allowed in; some registry offices are very small.

For a **licence** the documents and fees for both the bride and groom are taken to the registry office where they intend to marry. This must be done at least one clear working day before the wedding, and both of them must have been living in the area of the registry office for at least 15 days.

On the day they must bring a further fee (it is considerably more for a licence than for a certificate) and two witnesses. They exchange vows, in a ceremony lasting about 10 minutes, and sign the register. A ring isn't a legal requirement, though most couples use one. If there is a reception afterwards it is often paid for by the couple, especially if it is a second marriage. Invitations can be issued in exactly the same way as for a church wedding and the reception can follow the same formula if they wish.

Scottish Civil Weddings

In Scotland the procedure is very similar. It's a myth that you can just run away to Gretna Green and get married. Only in an emergency can you have a sheriff's licence which allows the wedding almost immediately. Normally, even to apply for a civil wedding in Scotland one of you must have lived there for the past 15 days. You then have to sign application forms in the presence of two local householders and the forms must be displayed for seven days before a Certificate is issued; the marriage can take place within the next three months.

> There is a special form of licence which allows someone to be married anywhere – for example, in hospital – if he or she is too ill to be married in any of the usual places.

Second Marriages

Second marriages present no legal problems. So any couple free to marry can have a registry office marriage without question. The same is true of religious ceremonies if both their previous partners are dead. But problems arise if one or other of them is divorced – even if he or she was the 'innocent' party. Some branches of the Christian Church do permit second marriages in certain circumstances but not all. Those who care deeply about this, and have been barred from a service in their own church, can contact the main offices of other denominations (see Organizations) and ask if a marriage service would be possible.

Where a second church marriage is possible the bride can still wear white, but there are usually no bridesmaids; she may be given away by a male relative if she wishes or she can dispense with this. Unless she is a young girl and her family want to give her a second reception she normally pays the wedding expenses which fell to her parents the first time round.

Planning a Wedding

A wedding is the largest, and most expensive, festivity that most families ever arrange, and to make it a success takes a great deal of planning. It needs to be regarded as a military operation, for which every move is planned as far ahead as the length of the engagement allows.

At one time weddings followed set rules. Today most weddings keep fairly close to them, but there is far more variation than there used to be. What follows is the classic format, but couples can have anything they want. It is, after all, their big day and if the bride wants to wear puce and turn the reception into a disco she has a perfect right to do so.

Who Decides What

Most of the work of planning a wedding falls to the bride and her mother. Both should remember that for weddings everything is priced individually: the reception food doesn't include the cake, the church music doesn't include the bells, the bride's bouquet doesn't include a buttonhole for her father etc. So bills can escalate alarmingly. The decision making divides like this:

Wedding invitation printing	Bride's family
Wedding service printing	Bride's family
Whether there will be carpet and an awning to the church	Bride's family
Where the wedding presents will be displayed (if at all)	Bride's family
Wedding service details	Bride and groom
Wedding present list	Bride and groom

Bridesmaids'/pages' outfits	Bride
Bridesmaids' and bride's flowers	Bride
Reception details	Bride's family
Flowers for the church	Bride – but if others are being married there the same day it is wise to agree one lot of flowers for all the weddings – and much cheaper.
Guest list	Whoever is paying for the reception decides how many will be invited. Then each family lists about half that number with names and addresses. The groom's list is then given to the bride's family, and they send the invitations.

Bride's father usually pays for:
Press announcements of the engagement and
    wedding
Printing wedding invitations
Flowers in the church
Flowers for the reception
Wedding dress and trousseau
Music in church
Carpet and awning at church (if used)
All costs related to the reception
The photographer
Cars apart from those for the groom and best man
Printing the service sheet

Groom usually pays for:
Engagement ring
Fees for licence or banns
Bride's and bridesmaids' flowers
Buttonholes for himself and best man
Cars for himself and best man
Wedding ring
A present for the bride
Church expenses other than music or flowers
(e.g. bells, banns)
A present for each bridesmaid
A present for best man and possibly for each usher
The honeymoon

There is so much to consider that you may want to read the chapter on weddings in my book, *Modern Etiquette and Successful Behaviour* which includes not only Church of England weddings but those of other denominations and faiths, such as Roman Catholic, Quaker and Jewish weddings. **Brides and Setting Up Home** will answer all queries personally and if you send an sae will supply a list of shops which hire wedding dresses. Other magazines for brides have useful information if you can't find something you need. Some, however, are not reliable in their information on etiquette – but not everyone wants to observe it anyway.

Who Pays for What
Weddings now cost so much that the old rules about who pays for what are often ignored. The main expense is the reception, and the bride, the groom and even the groom's family may well contribute to it. However, the conventional division of costs makes a good starting point for discussion.

The bride chooses the bridesmaids' and pages' outfits, but they or their parents usually pay for them. So it's considerate to consult them and try to choose dresses they will like and be able to wear on other occasions.

Some magazine articles imply that you not only need to have printed invitations but also printed table napkins, book matches and so on. If this is all the rage in your area you may want to go along with it, but it is most certainly not the standard form and is one expense which can be avoided.

Preparations
How far in advance you need to book anything depends on the time of year. In peak wedding periods everything gets booked up months in advance, while in the low season you can get away with less forethought. It looks as if the saying that 'in spring a young man's fancy lightly turns to thoughts of love' is very true: most engagements are 3 to 6 months long and the peak-months for weddings are always July, August and September, with April, May and June being runners up. Whereas January to March has only a fraction of the nuptials.

Invitations
As the bride's father usually pays for the reception, the wedding invitations are normally worded to show that the bride's parents are the hosts. This can be the case even if they are divorced – provided they themselves are happy with this. But if, for example, the father is dead and the mother and an uncle are giving the reception, or the bride and groom are giving their own reception, the wording will reflect this.

People are normally invited to both the service and the reception, but for a registry office wedding the invitation can be simply to the reception. When inviting guests of another faith, who may feel unable to attend the service, one solution is to enclose a note saying that they will be most welcome at the reception if they are not able to be at the service, and say when the reception is expected to start.

Planning a Wedding

As Early as Possible

- [ ] Make a guest list.
- [ ] Find out the dates on which both the church and a good venue for the reception are available *before* deciding the date of the wedding.
- [ ] Book the church.
- [ ] Book wherever you will hold the reception (or a marquee).
- [ ] Book the caterers, a cake maker and staff, if the reception will be in a private house.
- [ ] Book music for the reception if you want it (most weddings don't have it, but if you want a string quartet in the garden or a disco for dancing don't delay).
- [ ] Book a photographer or a video company – the best get *very* booked up.
- [ ] Book cars for the bride, bridesmaids and her family and for the groom and best man.
- [ ] Book a toastmaster (page 38-39) – if one is being used.
- [ ] Book the honeymoon, and plan clothing.
- [ ] Ask the best man, bridesmaids etc. as soon as possible.
- [ ] Find, or order, a wedding dress, and headdress and bridesmaids'/pages' clothes.
- [ ] Decide on the service and the hymns you want.
- [ ] Order the wedding invitations (printing usually takes 2 to 4 weeks).

Well in Advance

- [ ] Arrange a wedding list at a suitable shop.
- [ ] Talk to florists, get comparative prices and ideas, and book your choice.
- [ ] All men involved must book morning dress if they need to hire it (allow 6 weeks).
- [ ] Confirm with the minister the dates of the banns and the details of the wedding.
- [ ] Order the service sheets for the wedding.
- [ ] Agree the food and drink with the caterers.
- [ ] Buy a wedding ring.
- [ ] Get suitable luggage for going away – if you don't have it.
- [ ] Buy shoes for the wedding and wear them round the house so they are comfortable on the day.
- [ ] Get a passport or check your passport (you can't have it put into your married name until you have a marriage certificate to show them). Apply for visas, if needed.
- [ ] Have any immunizations needed for the honeymoon (if they last long enough). Some make you feel rough so *don't* leave it to the last minute.
- [ ] Get family planning advice.
- [ ] Send out invitations 6 to 9 weeks before.
- [ ] Check off each acceptance or refusal.
- [ ] Start a wedding present list and note who gives you what *as you open it*. Then if you get behind on letters you still know

The Last Month

- [ ] Check that guests who have failed to reply have received their invitations.
- [ ] Arrange accommodation for guests travelling long distances, if needed.
- [ ] Book a hair appointment for the day.
- [ ] Make final arrangements for the flowers for: the reception, the church, the bride, the bridesmaids and buttonholes for the bride's father, the groom and ushers.
- [ ] If you are having a sit-down meal make a seating plan.
- [ ] Give the final numbers to the caterers 2 weeks before the wedding.
- [ ] Book a hotel for the first night if you will need it.
- [ ] Arrange the incidental music with the organist.
- [ ] Prepare a newspaper announcement of the wedding and submit it.
- [ ] Make arrangements for any stag (or doe) nights – preferably not the night before.
- [ ] Bride buys presents for pages; groom for the bridesmaids.
- [ ] Bride and groom buy presents for each other.
- [ ] Bride's parents buy a present for the groom.
- [ ] Groom's parents buy a present for the bride.

The Last Week

- [ ] Rehearse the wedding ceremony.
- [ ] Confirm or double check any arrangements not yet totally certain.

The name of each guest is hand-written at the top left-hand side of their invitation, and if children are welcome at the wedding their names should be with those of the parents. If they aren't, the parents should assume they won't be welcome. As many guests may be coming to an unknown place it can also be useful to enclose a map or diagram showing how to find the church and/or reception.

Presents

Everyone who accepts the invitation is expected to send a present in advance, and relations and very close friends usually give presents whether or not they accept. The couple often put a list of what they would like in a department store – or in several. The list(s) should be reasonably long and include items to suit every pocket. They can be quite specific, and even give the design of dinner service wanted. This allows guests who can't get to the shop to do the whole business by phone and still know they are giving something which will be enjoyed.

The presents are sent to the bride's home before the wedding – or elsewhere if the couple prefer – with a card bearing good wishes and the full name of the sender. At one time it was traditional for the presents to be displayed at the reception, but the practice is almost dead.

The Best Man and Bridesmaids

The groom picks one of his closest friends as best man who then has a key role in the proceedings. He normally knows all the plans and his duties usually include the following:

● discussing the timing of events in the reception with the toastmaster if one is being used
● organizing the ushers
● arranging for the church fees to be paid before the wedding
● making sure the groom's clothes and luggage for going away are in place on the day
● arranging the groom's stag night
● getting the groom to the church (accompanying him in a car or driving him) and taking him in through a side entrance
● standing beside him before the ceremony on his right in the front right-hand pew
● handing the wedding ring to the minister
● accompanying the chief bridesmaid into the vestry when the register is signed and down the aisle at the end
● being the timekeeper who gets the bride and groom into place at each stage of events at the reception
● being master of ceremonies and introducing the speakers if there is no toastmaster
● proposing the speech to the bridesmaids
● making sure the bride and groom leave on time. There are no rules about how many bridesmaids a bride can have, and both they and pages are entirely optional, but it may be useful to have one good friend to help with getting in and out of the wedding dress.

Giving the Bride Away

The bride is normally escorted to the church by her father and he stands beside her and gives her away. If there is no father she can be escorted by another male relative and he can give her away, or her mother can step forward for the giving away.

Dress

A formal wedding invitation indicates that guests are expected to dress formally too. This means women wear smart day clothes. Anyone in white or cream should relieve it with black or a strong colour so as not to steal the bride's thunder. Men traditionally wear morning dress (see page 22) for a church wedding, but a dark suit is sometimes substituted and is worn at most registry office weddings and receptions.

The Wedding Ceremony

● The best man makes sure the groom gets ready and gets to the church on time, and he has charge of the wedding ring.
● Ushers arrive at a wedding 40 minutes before it is due to start; it is their job to hand out service sheets and show people to their seats.
● The organist plays and the bells peal for 30 minutes before it starts.
● The groom and best man should be seated 20 minutes before the start.
● Guests arrive *at least* 15 minutes before the service starts. The bride's relations and friends sit on the left of the aisle (as you look at the altar), the groom's relations and friends on the right.
● The bride's mother should be the last person to take her seat, 5 minutes before the bride arrives. This acts as a signal that the bride is on her way.
● The bridesmaids and pages arrive 5 minutes before the bride and get in position near the main door.
● The priest and choir then wait, ready to process up the aisle before the bride.
● The bride arrives and once she has adjusted her veil, and possibly posed for photographs, processes up the aisle on her father's (or a substitute's) right arm.
● After the wedding the bride and groom leave first.

Confetti

Confetti is almost universally hated by church wardens and hoteliers. In theory, it can be thrown either as the couple leave the church or as they leave on honeymoon. But permission should be asked of the church or hotel beforehand. It is best avoided in the rain as some confetti is not colour-fast and can ruin a light dress.

The Reception

The loveliest wedding receptions are often those in a private house with a beautiful garden. And the home of a relative or friend may be borrowed to provide one. But, given the risk of a deluge, it must have enough flat lawn to take a marquee. As most people don't have the space the reception is usually in a hotel or a suitable club, but you can also hire stately homes, or anything from an island to a swimming pool for a wedding reception. For

Addresses and suggestions for further reading are at the ends of chapters.

likely addresses you could try your local tourist board or Chamber of Commerce. But beware, many places only allow you to use a set list of caterers and some of these can be expensive. For other suggestions see page 38. The reception can take any form you wish – the most usual is probably a stand-up affair with champagne and canapés which may perhaps lead on into tea when the cake is cut. But fashions are changing. More and more people seem to be going for a sit-down meal either at lunchtime or in the evening, with dancing to follow. But the sit-down meal need not be formally served; it can equally well be a beautifully presented buffet, or there may be simply a meal with no dancing. The essence of a wedding is that it delights those concerned. There are no absolute rules

Food and Drink

Champagne is the stuff of which weddings are made. Non-vintage is usual but many people use a good méthode Champenoise to save money. And there is often a back-up of white wine for those who don't like fizzy drinks. It is also essential to serve non-alcoholic drinks. If the reception runs into tea-time, tea is usually served towards the end of the reception.

Though some people do have a sit-down 'wedding breakfast', the classic format is still for everyone to stay standing and be offered light buffet food. In choosing it, the appetites of guests who have driven a long way without eating should be borne in mind.

It should be delicious, festive, easy to eat with the fingers when smartly dressed. So ban anything with deep-fried crumbs which could leave a greasy trail down dresses. Ideally, some of the food is laid out on tables and some circulated on trays, so even guests who get stuck with deaf Aunt Amy will get a morsel.

Avoid the paddling pools on stems which caterers may offer as champagne glasses. The tall glasses called flutes are far less likely to spill.

Arriving at the Reception

The receiving line which traditionally greets guests as they arrive at the reception is: the bride's mother and father, groom's mother and father, bride and groom – in that order – and the guests shake hands with each as they enter. This can lead to a very tedious delay, and even queueing in the rain.

Before the last war the bride's mother, as hostess, was the only person to greet guests, so the receiving line is not sacrosanct, and some stylish weddings have abandoned the formal line-up; instead its members circulate more freely during the reception, which is much more enjoyable for the guests.

Speeches

Speeches are traditional but it's a rare bride whose menfolk are all entertaining speakers. The speech-makers should make it easy for themselves – and everyone else – by remembering the dictum that 'brevity is the soul of wit', unless, of course, *other people* rate them as wits.

Normally, the best man urges the bride and groom into position at a pre-arranged time (about an hour after the reception starts, or later if there has been a long lineup). The best man or toastmaster (see pages 38-39), then asks for silence, and the bride's father (or an old family friend chosen by him) makes a speech proposing the health and happiness of the bride.

Next the bridegroom makes a speech in which he thanks the bride's parents for letting him marry their daughter and for the reception, and thanks the guests in general – *not* individually – for their presents. Finally, he proposes a toast to the bridesmaids.

The best man replies on behalf of the bridesmaids and may read out a *few* telegrams and greetings cards provided they really are entertaining and if most of the guests know the people concerned.

Cutting the Cake

The cake is cut after the speeches. The bride and groom jointly use a knife (or service sword) to cut one slice while guests stay silent. The other slices are then cut by the caterers, and the cake is passed round to all the guests.

Leaving the Reception

The bride and groom always leave first, driving off in their going-away clothes. The timing is up to them, but the other guests are expected to follow very soon afterwards.

If it is raining the ushers should be armed with umbrellas to hold over the bride and groom and over guests as they leave.

At one time it wasn't only those in the forces whose path was lined with symbols of their profession – though a guard of honour might not like to *be* called that. In country districts wood shavings would be strewn for a carpenter, cloth for a tailor and so on. It would be amusing to see this revived with computer chips and dummy share certificates strewing the path.

What Happens Next

What happens next is beyond the scope of this chapter but the Victorian edition of *Enquire Within* gave clear guidelines for how to live happily ever after:

HOW TO TREAT A WIFE. – First, get a wife; secondly be patient. You may have great trials and perplexities in your business with the world, but do not carry to your home a clouded or contracted brow. Your wife may have many trials, which, though of less magnitude, may have been hard to bear. A kind, conciliating word, a tender look, will do wonders in chasing from her brow all the clouds of gloom . . . oh! bear with her; she has trials and sorrows to which you are a stranger, but which your tenderness can deprive of all their anguish. Notice kindly her little attentions and efforts to promote your comfort. Do not treat her with indifference, if you would not sear and palsy her heart, which, watered by your kindness, would, to the latest day of your existence, throb with sincere and constant affection. Sometimes [!] yield your wishes to hers. Do you find it hard to yield sometimes? Think you it is not difficult for her to give up always? If you never yield to her wishes there is a danger that she will think you are selfish, and care only for yourself, and with such feelings she cannot love you as she might.

While the 'Advice to Wives' reads as follows:

. . . She must study never to draw largely on the small stock of patience in a man's nature, nor to increase his obstinacy by trying to drive him; never, never if possible, to have scenes . . . If irritation should occur a woman must expect to hear from most men a strength and vehemence of language far more than the occasion requires. Mild, as well as stern men, are prone to exaggeration of language; let not a woman be tempted to say anything sarcastic or violent in retaliation. The bitterest repentance must needs follow if she do. Men frequently forget what they have said, but seldom forget what is uttered by their wives. They are grateful, too, for forbearance in such cases; for whilst asserting most loudly that they are right, they are often conscious that they are wrong. Give a little time, as the greatest boon you can bestow, to the irritated feelings of your husband.

Needless to say, the author of *that* edition of *Enquire Within* was a man.

Wedding Anniversaries

The only anniversaries which are usually celebrated with presents and parties are the silver, ruby, golden and diamond wedding anniversaries. By tradition, silver presents are given for a silver wedding, gold for a gold and so on, but this can be expensive. Happily, the tokens associated with other anniversaries have charm without great cost.

1st	Paper	9th	Pottery	25th	Silver
2nd	Cotton		or willow	30th	Pearl
3rd	Leather	10th	Tin or	35th	Coral
4th	Fruit or		flowers	40th	Ruby
	flowers	11th	Steel	45th	Sapphire
5th	Wood	12th	Silk or	50th	Gold
6th	Iron		linen	55th	Emerald
7th	Wool or	13th	Lace	60th	Diamond
	copper	14th	Ivory		
8th	Bronze or	15th	Crystal		
	pottery	16th	China		

MANNERS AND DRESS

General Table Manners

In France, at one time, socially selective mothers would vet prospective sons or daughters-in-law by serving raw peaches at dinner. Anyone who failed to eat one with due elegance – and a knife and fork – was unlikely to gain acceptance. Such deliberate testing has surely died out, but good table manners still make an impression – and the more so as they become rarer.

The details vary from country to country, but the underlying aim is usually to avoid eating in a way which is an eyesore and look after other people's needs as well as your own. This leads to certain do's and don'ts. You may think them too obvious to mention. For, in this era of fast food, it's easy to forget the niceties of behaviour and it may be useful for parents to have a check list to wave at children who insist that *nobody in the world* really expects the manners their parents are trying to instil.

Do's for Good Guests

Be guided by the behaviour of your host and hostess. Do as they do, not as you do at home – unless their manners are so dreadful that you can't go quite that far. It is far better manners to drink beer from a can, when the host is serving it that way, than to discomfort everyone by finding a glass. As with any manners the touchstone is consideration for others. So the rules are these – and, of course, they aren't limited to social occasions.

- Look to see who needs something passed to them, and pass it. If it is on a dish, hold it while they help themselves.
- Look to see how many helpings will be needed from a dish before helping yourself, and adjust your portion accordingly – though without looking as if you are *counting* the peas, however few there are.

- Avoid the temptation to take all the best bits, or most luscious cakes.
- Avoid taking more than you need, want or will eat.
- If you discover you have been given food you hate there is a dilemma. At one time you had to eat everything on your plate, however much you loathed it. Few people keep to this now. But, if a hostess's feelings matter to you, leave only a *very* little.
- If *offered* a food you dislike ask for a smaller than average portion, giving some plausible excuse – for example, the previous courses were so delicious you hardly have room for more. *In extremis* you can even claim an allergy to it.
- If you have to get rid of a bone, or other debris raise your fork or spoon to your mouth and *discreetly* eject the offending morsel. Then slip it neatly on to the side of your plate – tucking it under other leftovers if it is something which might embarrass the hostess. When eating fruit with your fingers, a stone can be ejected into the hole formed by the thumb and forefinger of a lightly clenched fist, then placed on the plate.
- Spare any slow eater the embarrassment of eating alone by dawdling a little yourself, so you finish only just before them.
- Make sure that nobody is left out of the conversation for any length of time.

Don'ts for Good Guests

- Don't reach across other people to get what you need, ask if they can pass it.
- Never start eating until the last person at the table has been served (unless the hostess tells you to). With central heating food only gets cold if the numbers are immense and, unless there are people waiting at table, it is essential that guests pass things to others instead of eating. Starting immediately also leaves the poor

host and hostess, who are served last, eating alone when others have long finished.

- Don't put your own knives, forks or spoons into serving dishes.
- It's 'not done' to handle food which others are going to eat – so don't check the peaches for ripeness or pick up hard cheese to cut it.
- There is a story that a woman was once so used to feeding children that at a formal dinner she automatically turned to the man next to her and cut all his food into tiny pieces – while he looked on aghast. Perfectly possible. It's amazing how many women play 'mother' at other people's dinner tables and 'helpfully' serve other people with food. *Don't* unless they ask you to. They are adults able to choose how many potatoes they have, not children who need it decided for them.
- Don't eat so fast that you finish before everyone else. Someone who wolfs their food neither talks nor listens – which makes them a poor guest.
- Don't make noises or chew food with your mouth open – half-chewed food looks awful. The worst example I have seen of this was someone who put whole baby crabs into his mouth and extruded the shells on to his plate, in a continuous stream as he munched.
- Don't even attempt to smoke between courses. The smell of smoke in a room can ruin many people's enjoyment of food. In France, in a famous Normandy restaurant called 'La Mère Corbeau', those who lit cigarettes while waiting for their meal to arrive would instantly be presented with coffee and the bill. If they protested the patron would explain that since they had no palate left there was no point in cooking for them.
- Never start clearing before the hostess does so – she may want to offer second helpings and you can ruin her plans. This includes buffet meals.
- Don't automatically stack plates to help the hostess clear away. Look to see what she does. If she takes the plates off individually do the same.
- Don't insist on getting up to help a hostess unless she looks as if she wants (as opposed to needs) the help. Getting up breaks the conversation, so it may be far more helpful to keep the conversation flowing and allow her to take her time in the kitchen.
- Don't reach for more drink, unless you have been told to help yourself, and *never* put the bottle on the floor beside you.
- Don't insist on helping to wash up. Offer, if it's appropriate, but listen to the reply. If the 'no' sounds as if the host or hostess is sure leave it there. Guests charging round the kitchen when the cook is dying just to sit and talk are trying, not helpful.
- Don't push your chair back from the table during the meal or rock on its two back legs – it may break.

The Details of Table Manners

The general table manners I've given above apply almost everywhere. But the details of table manners are like pronunciation: there is a 'correct' form – equivalent to standard English. If anyone is being vetted for a job, or even a marriage, they are the ones which those who care about such things will be looking for. But people can eat tidily, and give no offence to anyone, without following them.

Which Knife and Fork to Use

A correctly laid table should make the choice of cutlery easy. The rule is: start at the outside and work in. If the order looks wrong remember that the largest fork and knife will be for the meat, and the smallest spoon and fork for the pudding – you may then be able to decide when to use the rest. There may or may not be fish knives and forks – they were considered rather 'lower class' for many years and fish was eaten with normal forks and knives. But recently fish knives have begun to become fashionable again. The rules for wielding them are:

- take food up to your mouth; don't duck your mouth down to it
- manoeuvre the cutlery while keeping your elbows close to your sides, so as not to nudge your neighbour
- when not actively in use, rest any cutlery on your plate with the handles apart, in an upside-down V.

- (The handles shouldn't ever rest on the table). If you are holding cutlery, keep it low, with the tips lower than the handles
- you show you have finished by placing the cutlery side by side close together, with the prongs of the fork pointing up and the blade of the knife facing towards it.

Finger-Bowls

These are placed above the forks when food is eaten with the fingers. You dip the tips of your fingers in the water, brushing them across the lemon if there is some, and discreetly dry them on your napkin. If a finger bowl arrives on your fruit plate you put it in position yourself, usually with the lace mat it is sitting on.

Forks

When a fork is used without a knife, a right-handed person holds it in the right hand with the prongs pointing up, and food may be cut by turning it on its side and pressing down with its inner edge. It is used like this for fork suppers and for food which needs no knife – pasta, and rice dishes like risotto or pilaff. In Britain, when a knife is added, the knife and fork form a marriage: once you have picked up both they have to work together. You cut one mouthful at a time and use the knife to press the food on to the fork, which is held with its tines pointing *down*. But the difficulty of balancing peas on that side of a fork means that forks are turned over more and more. This is now almost acceptable, provided it is done elegantly and the food pushed on to the inner edge. But many people still regard it as 'kitchen manners' to be used only within the family – if then.

Knives

The correct way to hold a knife is to grasp it so the top of the handle lies *inside* the palm of the hand, and the forefinger lies along the top of the knife, without resting on the blade. It shouldn't be held so it rests between the thumb and first finger, like a pen.

Napkins

You unfold a napkin to make a long strip and place it across the knees (never tucked into your front). Apart from wiping drips from your chin (which shouldn't be necessary), it stays there until you dump it unfolded on the table at the end of the meal. It is only folded if you are a house guest and napkin rings have been provided.

Spoons

Spoons are one of the big catches: a soup spoon, unlike a knife, should be held rather like a pen, but the wrist turned so the spoon faces across the body and is parallel to the table. The soup is then quietly sipped from the *side* of the spoon as you tilt it towards the mouth. You don't blow on it, nor do you put the spoon in your mouth. Then, as the soup gets low in the bowl, tilt it away from

you, and if you cannot lift a spoonful to your mouth without dripping, lightly brush the drips from the back of the spoon against the farther edge of the bowl, before lifting it to your mouth.

A pudding or cereal spoon is used in rather the same way. But if a pudding is served on a plate, a small fork must *always* be used to help the food on to the spoon. You only omit the fork for mousses and creams in small containers, and for these a teaspoon may be used instead of a pudding spoon.

Problem Foods

A Victorian book of etiquette warned its readers to 'avoid embarking on an orange, as it requires long experience, a colossal courage, any amount of cool self-possession and great skill to attack and dispose of one without harm to yourself or your neighbours.' A warning anyone who has been squirted in the eye would endorse. But happily, with most foods, it is just a matter of knowing what to do, and today few people mind if the style is unconventional provided the spectacle isn't unpleasant. If in doubt the golden rule is: watch everyone else and do as they do. But for those who like to know in advance the conventions are these.

Artichokes (Leaf)

If you are offered sauce, put some on the side of your plate – unless the centre of the artichoke has been removed to take it. Pull off the leaves with a finger and thumb, one at a time, starting at the outside. Dip the fat base of the leaf into the sauce and place it between your teeth. Then pull the leaf out as you bite hard enough to squeeze out the flesh from the base without biting through the skin. Stack the bitten leaves neatly on the side of your plate or they will fall off on to the table. Near the centre the leaves become papery and not worth eating. Under them is the choke, a tight cluster of fibrous seeds rather like those of a dandelion. Pull, or cut, these off in neat lumps to reveal the delicious fleshy base which you eat with a small knife and fork.

Asparagus

This is a real test of dexterity if the asparagus is thin and floppy. Pick up the spears, one at a time by the base, with your fingers. Dip the tip in the sauce on your plate and bite it off; dip it in sauce again and bite some more. If the skin is tough, you may press the flesh out from inside it with your teeth instead of biting right through. You only eat the part which is tender; the rest is stacked neatly at the edge of the plate. The art is neither to expose your teeth while biting nor to drip the sauce on your chin.

Bread and Rolls

With rolls or French bread you break off one bite-sized piece at a time, butter it and eat it, and slices of bread for breakfast or tea, or with cheese, pâté or smoked salmon, should be cut into quarters, not just halves.

Butter should be taken from its container with a butter knife (not your knife) and marmalade or jam with a jam

Addresses and suggestions for further reading are at the ends of chapters.

spoon – and put on the side of your plate. Only then do you apply them to the bread, a little at a time – not spread right across the slice, except perhaps at breakfast.

Though some sauces beg to have bread dipped in them, almost the only time you can correctly use your bread to mop up the juices from food is when eating snails.

Cheese or Pâté
Serve yourself from a wedge of cheese so that you take the rind as well as the middle – don't cut the point off and leave the less moist bit for everyone else. Put the wedge on your plate and eat it by cutting off a small piece, placing it on your buttered biscuit, or on a small piece of bread (see Bread, above) and eating the two together. Do the same with pâté.

Stilton buffs insist that Stilton should be cut from the round in thin wedge-shaped portions, but those who have a whole round still tend to scoop it out in large crumbs.

Crab
Crab is usually served already dressed (see under Food) and is easily eaten from the shell. But if it is served whole you scoop the flesh out of the red, upper part of the body. Then crack the legs with nutcrackers; the flesh can be taken from them with a special implement made for the purpose which has two little hooks on the end. The white under-section of the body also contains a good deal of meat which can be hooked out with the same implement. It is always messy food and finger bowls are needed.

Fish
It is best to lift fish from its skin and bones a little at a time, as you eat it, rather than fillet it. Otherwise your plate immediately becomes littered with unsightly bones.

Fruit
If a table is laid with a fruit knife and fork you don't touch the fruit with your hands at all (except to help yourself). Instead you use them to cut the fruit into quarters, and peel it (if appropriate). Then cut off small slices and eat them on the fork. If there is only a fruit knife cut the fruit in quarters, peel it if you wish (holding it close to the plate) cut off a small section at a time and eat it in your fingers. Small fruit, such as cherries or plums, are simply eaten in the fingers.

Lobsters
Lobsters are no problem, as the flesh is usually served in a halved shell, to be eaten with a knife and fork, or fork alone. Claws are treated like crab claws (see above).

Mussels
The British usually pick up a mussel in their fingers and remove the contents with a small fork. The empty shells are either put in a separate dish or neatly stacked round the edge of the plate. Many mussel recipes have liquid which can be spooned up and drunk like soup.

Oysters
As Jonathan Swift wrote, 'He was a bold man that first ate an oyster.' But if you are feeling bold lift the raw oyster from its half shell with a fork, while you hold the shell down. Having eaten it, you then drink the juice from the shell.

Pasta
Pasta is never cut up. To eat long pasta, such as spaghetti, stick your fork into the edge of the pasta, so only two or three strands are caught within the prongs, then twist the fork so the pasta is wound into a neat bundle with a minimum of trailing ends. The trick is to get it to your mouth before it undoes.

Prawns
Prawns have to be shelled with the fingers. Hold the body while you pull off the head. Pull the under edges of the shell so they open out and release the body. Remove this main shell and then pull off the tail. Place the prawn on the plate and eat it with a knife and fork, or fork alone, according to what accompanies it.

Snails
Snails are held with a pair of tongs designed for the purpose and the flesh lifted out with a small, sharp fork. Dip each in the sauce before eating it.

Restaurant Manners

If you are going to entertain someone give them as much consideration as possible. Ring and reserve a table. If it's winter and you really want to please your guest, ask for a table well out of the draught; in hot weather ask for one by a window or in the garden. Having made your reservation keep to it, or ring the restaurant and cancel the booking.

Arriving
A host should always arrive before his or her guests – unless he or she accompanies them – and use the time to make sure the table is correct, to arrange the method of paying (if there might be problems) and make tentative decisions about the wine.

If a woman arrives at a restaurant with a man she should enter before him but then allow him to draw abreast, or even ahead, so that he can ask for a table or confirm his booking. He should then stand aside to let her walk ahead of him to the table. If a waiter does not pull out a chair for her the man should do this. Continental manners, however, dictate that the man enters the restaurant first.

Choosing Food and Ordering
The food-conscious choose the main course first, and then pick other courses to balance the meal. All ordering should be done through the host, and the host should ask his or her guest what they want before the waiter arrives. So another advantage of choosing the main course first is that you can tell your host what this will be and wait to see if you are asked to choose a first

course too. Which gets you over the dilemma of not knowing what is expected of you.

The first two courses are usually ordered together, but the choice of pudding or cheese is left until after the main course is finished. Coffee or liqueurs are then ordered later – if you are having them. Offering coffee is basic, offering liqueurs is a luxury extra. Although ordering tea after lunch or dinner used to be bad, it is gradually becoming more acceptable – provided it is a smart tea such as a tisane.

If you order anything which can be served in more than one way – for example steak well done, medium or rare – a good waiter will ask how you want it cooked. If he forgets, tell your host how you would like it *before* the waiter leaves.

All that is fine if you can understand the menu. If you can't don't let it bother you. When a menu is in a foreign language nobody should be afraid to ask what the names of the dishes mean. Some names may be well-known dishes, but an inexperienced diner can avoid showing ignorance by asking the waiter to explain how they cook dish X or Y 'here' – thus implying familiarity with the normal way of making it. But avoid wording it like this if the dish says *à la maison* or *dans notre façon* – which indicate a recipe created by the restaurant. If you ask a waiter if the steak is good or the melon ripe 'today', a good waiter will tell you the truth. But beware of asking his advice over what dish to have. Many managers instruct waiters to suggest any dishes which are selling poorly on that particular day.

Whatever you choose, avoid the most expensive dish unless you are paying or your host urges you to have it. Any host who is planning to splash out should let guests know – by picking out some of the more expensive dishes and suggesting they might like them.

In restaurants where the guest is given a menu with no prices it's best to ask hosts who don't have bottomless pockets, which dishes they recommend.

Ordering Drink

The choice of drinks is up to the host, who should bear in mind the food the guests have chosen (see under Drink). When the wine is brought the waiter will pour some for the person who ordered and wait while it is tasted. In fact, your nose should tell you if wine is all right or not, and if it isn't say so. But don't make the common mistake of saying wine is 'corked' because bits of cork float on the top.

A considerate host should also ask if guests want water with their meal. Failing that a guest can ask if some can be ordered. Heavy advertising means that in many restaurants 'water' means Perrier unless you ask for something else, but Badoit, which is less gassy, goes better with many foods. Or ask for tap water and let water snobs be damned.

Attention During a Meal

It is up to the host to see that his or her guests have what they ordered. If someone ordered a rare steak the host should ask if it is how the guest likes it, and *look* to see if it *is* rare – the guest may be embarrassed to admit it

isn't. If anything isn't right the host should calmly ask for the problem to be corrected. There's no need to make a song and dance about complaining, but neither is there any need to eat anything which is not right. When the food returns check it again: some restaurants just rearrange the plate and send it back.

If a host needs to call a waiter during a meal raising the head and looking questioningly should work. If it doesn't, a small indication with the hand should attract attention. Only when these fail is it permissible to call 'waiter'.

To call a waiter over if you are a guest is to imply that the host isn't looking after your needs. So, if you are a guest and need something during the meal, the correct form is to ask the host if you may have whatever is needed (say a glass of water) and let him call a waiter. But if this is impractical wait until a waiter passes very near and then quietly make your need known to him.

Whenever a waiter serves food or drink it is usual to say thank you, speaking quietly enough not to interrupt the conversation. If you are being spoken to at the time, just glance at the waiter and nod or smile slightly to indicate your thanks silently. The same holds true when being served by staff in a private house.

Going Dutch

How a bill is divided between friends can be a very sore point. Traditionally, if people agree to 'go Dutch' everyone splits the bill. Fine, provided they all eat and drink much the same amount. But if anyone wants to eat or drink conspicuously more than the rest that person should be sure to chip in with more than his or her basic share, so the others don't have to pay for somebody else's indulgence.

Obtaining and Paying the Bill

A small writing movement in the air is an international signal for a waiter to bring the bill. But sometimes, even asking for the bill brings no results and you are left marooned and unable to leave. If need be, the swiftest course is for the whole party to get up, as if to leave, and walk towards the manager. It galvanizes even the slowest waiter.

Tipping

If service is included in the bill there is no need to leave a tip in Britain unless you feel the waiter has been exceptional. But small change is left if you pay in cash. When service is not included a 12 per cent tip is average, and 10 per cent is enough for below average service, but give 15 per cent (or more) if it was especially good. The tip can be included in a cheque or credit card payment or given as cash. The same tips apply in bars where drinks are brought to the table. If you need a copy of a bill ask for it as you pay.

What to Wear When

Dress is a tribal matter. I say tribal because the purpose of tribal dress is to celebrate certain rituals or to show which group of people you identify with, and want others to know that you belong to. Whether by the

Addresses and suggestions for further reading are at the ends of chapters.

studded jacket of a Hell's Angel, or a businessman's dark suit, we are all, whether we realize it or not, walking around in uniform, with our garments proclaiming our tribe to everyone we meet. We all conform, even if we conform by a particular style of rebellion – as do the punk rockers.

Nobody needs this book to tell them how to dress as they please. The only time when reading about dress is any use is when you need to take part in a tribal ritual (such as Ascot) which is new to you or to camouflage yourself as belonging to some other 'tribe'. So, while there's no need for anyone to conform to the following rules, they can be useful.

Formal Dress for Men

The 1856 edition of *Enquire Within* instructed men to:

> *Dress well but not superfluously. Be neither like a sloven, nor like a stuffed model. Keep away all uncleanly appearance from the person. Let the nails, and teeth, and, in fact, the whole system receive SALUTARY rather than STUDIED care. But let these things receive attention in the toilette – not elsewhere.*
>
> *Avoid displaying excess of jewellery. Nothing looks more effeminate upon a man.*

Very little has changed in over two hundred years. Jewellery, apart from a signet ring, is still frowned on and the essence of a man being well dressed is still immaculate cleanliness and understatement. Not even the smallest spot is permissible. But, true to not looking like a 'stuffed model', nothing must look too new or too carefully arranged. An appearance which suggests a total lack of effort is the keynote. An attitude which Dorothy Sayers caught perfectly when, in one of the Lord Peter Wimsey books, Lord Peter turns to his valet and says, 'How do I look?' The valet replies, 'Perfect. That is to say, slightly flawed – the sign of a true gentleman'.

For business and formal occasions the essential garments for this look are a dark suit in a good wool cloth, without a conspicuous pattern in the fabric, worn with a white, pastel-coloured or discreetly striped shirt, plain dark socks and a good quality tie which does not draw attention to itself. There are also a host of details which make the difference between looking 'right' or just missing the look. For example:

- the lowest button on a waistcoat should be left undone
- the top and bottom buttons of a single-breasted jacket are undone
- a wallet goes in the inside jacket pocket not in the trousers
- the outside breast pocket of a jacket is left empty
- the socks never show when standing
- with a black, grey or navy suit the shoes are always black – never grey – and the ornamentation should be minimal, unless they are brogues.

Some of the rules for correct formal dress spill over into informal and evening occasions and among the points which conventional bosses and mothers-in-law might especially frown on, at any time, are:

- ready-tied ties (though ready-tied bow ties are creeping in)
- ties with very large knots
- ties of organizations to which the wearer does not belong
- very dark shirts with suits
- frilly or embroidered shirts – even in the evening
- dinner jackets decorated with braid
- white socks, except for sport
- suits, trousers or jackets in strong colours or very conspicuous checks (Prince of Wales check apart)
- shirt collars smoothed out over the jacket collar, when tieless
- socks which allow the skin of the ankle to show when seated.

Of course, it is all a matter of personal preference and there are always exceptions. For example, Prince Charles breaks the rule about breast pockets. But that, it seems, is no criterion. For when I pointed out this fact, to a very elegant Old Etonian, he remarked, 'But, my dear, the royals never *did* have any style'. So those who find themselves breaching the sartorial code can comfort themselves that they are, at least, in good company.

Dress for Women

Since women are always more individualistic in their dress than men, there are fewer rules and a woman can usually get away with whatever she can carry off. Mercifully, thanks to the Princess of Wales, the old rule that it was suspect to be glamorous is beginning to disappear. But there is also an international 'Sloane Ranger' uniform to be found among established families whether in London, Paris or seemingly egalitarian Amsterdam. It neither follows fashion nor totally ignores it and, as in the male equivalent, minute details are important. As it changes fractionally from year to year it is almost impossible to pin down except to say that good quality is essential.

How far anyone follows fashion, or seeks to conform to a social group, is simply a matter of taste, but on occasions, such as interviews when making an impression counts, it is hard to go wrong with the following:

- natural fibres (or blends which look natural)
- well-cut shirts in plain colours
- well-cut suits or skirts
- understated make-up
- accessories which match each other – but not too emphatically particularly if you avoid wearing:
- white shoes with dark stockings
- exotically patterned fabrics – except Liberty prints
- ankle chains
- imitation anything
- clothes so tight they have a VPL (visible panty line)
- clothing that is rampantly sexy
- very decorated shoes.

As with men, everything must be immaculately clean and perfectly pressed – someone can look well-dressed with only one good garment in their wardrobe, if it is always pressed before wearing, or look a mess with a wardrobe full of model clothes, if they are uncared for.

When in doubt, it is considered correct to be underdressed rather than overdressed. Neither too smart, too fashionable nor too conspicuous. The classic rule for jewellery, for example, is to put on as much as looks exactly right, and then remove one piece. This ultradiscretion is not simply a British foible; I have observed it in other European drawing rooms as well. But my personal sympathies are with the splendidly outrageous older wife of a young academic who once told me, 'Darling, I always put on what looks exactly right – and then *add some.*' She looked marvellous and knew it. Such flamboyance is no good at all as social camouflage – which is what a lot of dressing is about – but it has an indiscreet charm.

Dressing for a Country House Weekend

For anyone not brought up in an English country house, dressing for the country is one of the hardest tasks. Country-house dwellers seem blissfully unaware of the huge range of clothes which their seemingly casual lifestyle demands. The list varies with the people and the season, but might include:

● wellingtons – for walks in the wet
● jeans – clean but with a decidedly lived-in look
● inconspicuous shirt(s) and jumper(s) to go with the jeans
● something suitable for going to church (if they do)
● cords for a man, plus V-neck pullover, shirt and possibly a casual cravat for neater wear – such as informal drinks with neighbours
● smart trousers or skirt, shirt and jumper for a woman
● a black-tie outfit or a dress formal enough to pass muster if they decide to dress up for dinner – still not uncommon in large country houses (but anyone who doesn't own one can always ask if there will be changing for dinner, and only acquire one if it's needed)
● a dark suit or dress which is suitable for an ordinary dinner party
● tennis clothes in summer, if there's a tennis court
● if there may be shooting it's essential to have really warm waterproof clothes which are dark enough not to scare the birds. The ideal for a woman is a Puffa (a waistcoat mated with an eiderdown) and/or the dark-green waterproof jacket called a Barbour (pronounced barber). A new Barbour is almost a contradiction in terms, so anyone who doesn't want to look like a new boy in school should try to wear it while gardening or pushing through woods
● possibly clothes for a point-to-point or racing.

If that list seems daunting and expensive don't worry. Wearing the right clothes may make you feel more 'in' but, unless you are being summed up for a job or marriage, or wear bright clothes to a shoot, nobody will care a hoot what you wear. Only those who are socially fragile themselves are critical of other people's lapses in clothing conformity. In some country houses jeans, a jumper and wellingtons are all you need in a week.

To Dress or Not to Dress

For most invitations people blithely insist that dress is casual. And casual is whatever the speaker chooses to make it from cocktail dress to track suit.

However, saying dress is casual or informal is at least better than saying it is 'optional'. That means so little that one friend of mine, with a quirky sense of humour, punished his hosts for such an invitation by taking it literally, and arrived stark naked – upon which, they turned the tables by making him stay that way all evening.

Given the immense variation in what people mean, hosts owe it to their guests to give them some guidance over what to wear. This doesn't mean you have to push them around It's perfectly easy to say, 'It's just an informal evening, so I'll probably wear jeans but do dress up if you feel like it', or vice versa. When hosts don't do this it is perfectly reasonable to ask how casual it is going to be. If you can't do that the correct form is to underdress rather than overdress. But this can be taken too far: as a friend of mine wisely remarked, 'How you dress reflects your opinion of what your hostess is inviting you to.'

White Tie

Men
The full evening dress implied by 'white tie' is seldom worn, except for very formal occasions. Men are expected to conform to a formula of black trousers with braid at the sides, black tail coat, waistcoat, stiff-fronted white shirt with stiff detachable wing collar, and white pique (Marcella) bow tie. Gold or mother-of-pearl studs and cufflinks fasten the shirt and black silk socks are worn with plain shoes in either black patent leather or fine calf. Dandies can even add a black cloak, black silk top hat, white kid gloves and a black, silver-topped cane – and go looking for Scarlett O'Hara if they wish.

Women
A white tie invitation opens the door to the grandest ballgown you can muster and, unless long dresses are totally out of fashion, most women wear long rather than short. If you have gems prepare to show them now. Long gloves, of the sort which open at the wrist and roll up, used to be essential for white-tie evenings. They aren't absolutely essential for balls – though they have recently had a considerable come-back – but they are needed for royal and diplomatic occasions on which evening dress is worn. Bracelets go over them and rings go under, and they are kept on for shaking hands and dancing but removed for eating. If they have buttons at the wrist they are not removed entirely but the hands are slipped out and the hand part rolled neatly inward so it tucks under the wrist section. They can be any colour which suits the dress.

Morning Dress

Men
Morning dress is the daytime equivalent of white tie. It is used for weddings, Royal Ascot, state openings of

parliament and other elegant occasions. It consists of black or dark-grey trousers, with a fine stripe, a dove-grey waistcoat and a black or dark-grey morning (tail) coat. For very formal occasions, such as Ascot and the smartest weddings, there must also be a grey top hat – correctly called a 'white hat' – but for ordinary weddings fewer and fewer men bother with them. Either way, classic black calf shoes are worn, plus a white shirt usually with a stiff collar, and a light-grey silk tie or cravat. This is one of the few occasions on which a man may be dandified and wear a tie pin. Creamy yellow chamois gloves are also correct, though very little used. (See page 39 for hiring.)

Women

The female counterpart is a really smart dress in summer – often in silk – or an elegant suit, or coat. If you are buying something for a morning dress occasion a suit is the best buy, as it can be adapted to any weather, whereas a dress just looks chilly on a bad day. Strictly speaking, morning dress means a hat should be worn, and they are one of the features of Ascot, but at weddings the young increasingly flout this convention.

Black Tie

Men

The words 'Black Tie' are an invitation for both sexes to dress up. For a man it's easy. The set formula is a dinner jacket with matching trousers (on braces not a belt) which usually have a single strip of black braid down

① Fold the right half at mid-bulge and hold it where the tie should be.

② Double the other end at the bulge and push the fold through the loop behind the rest of the bow. Tighten by alternately pulling both folded ends then both single ends.

the outer seam. This is worn with a white evening shirt and a formal black bow tie, of a kind designed to go with the shirt and jacket. The shirt usually has a pique or finely pleated front, and sleeves with double cuffs and cufflinks. A single-breasted suit may have a matching waistcoat but is more often worn without one and with a cummerbund in black or dark-red silk. Double-breasted suits don't need a waistcoat or a cummerbund (but they are less often in fashion). In hot climates the black jacket is replaced by a white one. The footwear used to be patent leather shoes, but these are only worn now by those who have clearly had them for years. To wear new patent is just not done, and fairly plain black calf shoes are the usual footwear, plus black socks (ideally in silk). In winter the whole lot can be topped by a black overcoat, and a long white silk scarf.

If a man doesn't want to wear the classic outfit he can simply wear a dark suit (a pity, as almost every man looks more handsome in evening dress). Alternatively, he can wear a more original version of black tie by sporting a dark velvet jacket with evening trousers instead of a matching jacket.

Conventional bow ties come in two kinds: single-ended and double-ended. The single-ended is worn with wing collars, the double-ended with turn-down collars. They are tied as in the diagram on the left.

Women

For women it is less easy. At one time when full evening dress of white tie and tails was the form a long dress was needed, and a black tie invitation indicated that a short evening dress would almost certainly do. Now white tie is very little used and black tie spans both occasions – even when a long dress would be preferable for a woman. One guide to what to wear is the type of people who will be there. Another rough guide is the place where the event is being held. If it is somewhere grand then there is a good chance that you are being offered an excuse to wear a long evening dress, though a short one will probably be fine. It's worth thinking about coverage as well as mere length. A seductive dress which would be perfect for a film première may be not be the thing for a black-tie dinner at the rotary club or an Oxford college.

Scottish Formal Dress

If you are wearing a kilt there is no sharp distinction between black tie, white tie and morning dress. There are two styles of jacket which can be used for either: a black barathea (Prince Charlie) with silver buttons, or a black velvet (Montrose). The Prince Charlie is usually worn with an evening shirt and black bow tie, the Montrose with a softer shirt and a lace jabot. In both cases, a man wears either cream knee socks or dark socks to pick out a dark tone in the tartan. The shoes are either heavy leather shoes called gillie brogues, or black patent with cross-over straps. Whatever the occasion, a man does not wear a dress tartan. Dress tartans are said to be one of Queen Victoria's inventions and are strictly reserved for women to wear on evening occasions.

Clothes for Early Evening Parties

Standard clothing is a dark suit, a plainish shirt and darkish tie for a man, with black shoes. Women wear cocktail dresses, evening suits, or evening trousers and tops. Adjust the clothing to your hosts – in some circles anything goes and no man would dream of wearing a jacket; in others he wouldn't be allowed through the door without one.

Point-to-points and Races

At point-to-points the chief aim is to keep warm and dry so the clothes are the same as for shooting (see page 22). The races are a different matter. They vary considerably in smartness but – Ascot aside – men tend to wear dark suits and women elegant tweeds. Trilbys are often sported by men and elegant hats with a country air by women, which – when they are in fashion may well be a female trilby. This is an occasion on which the classic Englishwoman's shoes, with heels which are not particularly high or narrow, come into their own for walking on grass. Ascot is an occasion for morning dress and women dressed up to the tens – be warned.

Some of the companies which hire morning dress and other clothes for special occasions are on page 39.

OVERSEAS MANNERS

Foreign manners can be perplexing and the nuances often elude the visitor. Here are just a few of the pitfalls.

Arriving

It's easy to assume that everyone does it the British way, arriving 10 to 15 minutes late to allow for a host or hostess who isn't quite on time. This isn't the case. The French expect their guests within 15 minutes of the invited time, in southern Italy they expect them to be on time – knowing they will be late – while Scandinavians, northern Italians and some Germans, expect guests to be perfectly punctual. The Dutch take it even further: in Holland the time you are invited for is the *latest* you can arrive and in courtesy you should be 10 to 15 minutes early. Which would make for disaster if the Dutch invite the Portuguese. In Portugal you should be at *least* half an hour late and an hour late is quite normal.

Encounters between the Japanese and the Dutch may be no easier. The Dutch never arrive empty-handed and it is considered very rude for the person receiving the present to fail to open it immediately and express appreciation. The Japanese also take presents but in Japan the present must *never* be opened while the giver is there. The idea is that it cannot possibly be good enough, so the giver will be embarrassed that it isn't better.

Swedes may arrive bearing flowers or chocolates, but don't expect the French or Italians to do this. In both these countries it is thought more considerate to send flowers the next day, though the ultra-thoughtful guest may send them on the morning before.

In most of Europe shaking hands on first meeting is essential. But in Thailand and Japan they prefer not to shake hands, and use a traditional half bow as greeting. In the Middle East people go to the other extreme and often shake hands *every* time they meet, not just on the first occasion of the day. This may not apply to greetings between the sexes; some Arab women may touch no man except their husband.

Kisses on greeting have an etiquette all of their own. For example, few people know that in France hand-kissing is strictly for the ungloved hand of a married woman. Or that cheek-kissing between close friends is limited to two kisses in France and Italy and three in Belgium, while the Scandinavians hardly kiss (in that sense) at all – though this is changing in the younger generation. However, in Japan social kissing is totally taboo and considered most upsetting behaviour.

At Table

In all Muslim countries the left hand must never be used to touch food. Muslims aren't the only people to have hand conventions. In Italy, home of the Borgias, it is essential to keep your hands in sight throughout the meal. They should rest lightly on the edge of the table, never on your lap. In France you may put your hands where you like, but to put salt or pepper on food without tasting it (and even then) is to insult your host, and anyone who drinks anything but water with salad is thought to show a total lack of palate. Another sidelight on French meals is that, since crests are put on the underside of the handles, spoons and forks are usually laid with the bowl or prongs towards the tablecloth.

There are few rules on second helpings, but in France they will be offered first to the most senior woman and she should always accept, even if she only toys with the food, or other guests may feel compelled to follow her lead and refuse too.

At social functions in Sweden it is traditional to 'skala'. This involves a man raising his glass to one of the women and saying 'Skala Anna' (or whatever her name is). Then both drink from their own glasses while keeping eye contact. To drop the eyes is considered rude. The skala must also be returned soon after, and nobody may skala the hostess unless there are fewer than six guests.

Functions do not always end when you might expect. In both the Arab world and among the Chinese in Hong Kong guests are expected to leave almost as soon as the coffee has been drunk. To linger and talk is not polite.

Naming Names

Most of northern Europe has caught the British and American habit of using first names almost immediately, even in business situations. Not so the French. The young may switch quickly to first-name terms and use *tu*, but the older generations still stick to *vous*, and *Monsieur*, *Madame* or *Mademoiselle* and the surname until they are invited to use the first name and *tu*. Foreigners should do the same, for *tu* used in the wrong place can be a sign not of friendship but of contempt. In talking, they also refer to their friends and acquaintances as *Monsieur* or *Madame* plus the surname, and in Portugal it is correct to apply this same formality, using Don or Donna when speaking to, or about, anyone older than oneself, which lends a certain period charm to conversation in both countries.

Body Language

Quite apart from the hazards of uncovering too much flesh in regions where flesh is considered indecent, the ways in which the body is used can also be considered insulting. For example, to cross your legs in the company of Arabs in such a way that the sole of the shoe even slightly faces towards someone is to say, 'You are lower than the sole of my shoe.' In Thailand not only is the sole of the foot considered so low that it is insulting even to stand so that your toes point towards somebody, but also the top of the head is the highest point and must be respected. So ruffling a child's hair affectionately is a serious breach of respect for the child and its family.

Praising

I once made the mistake of telling a Japanese that he had a very beautiful wife, only to be astonished at his assertions that she was a 'very ugly and horrible wife'. It is not polite for a Japanese to admit to having a lovely wife because a wife is considered part of the husband and he is therefore bound to be modest. In Arab countries it is even worse. If you admire an object the owner may feel obliged to give it to you. This can, in some circumstances, extend to women even today.

At the Cinema

The French and Italians will all make their way to an inside seat facing the screen. But in Germany or Sweden it is considered insulting to pass another person with your behind pointing towards them.

Language

Words don't always mean quite what they seem to mean in translation – which is perhaps one reason why British prime ministers tend to avoid speaking in foreign languages. Americans are not always so cautious. After a visit to a foreign country one American president made a farewell speech in which he expressed his great pleasure at having had the opportunity to 'get to know' so many of the people of that country. His speech caused quite a stir: his speechwriter had unfortunately used the verb which in that language meant to 'know' in the purely carnal sense.

There is also the pitfall of the double meaning. President Kennedy made a famous speech in Germany at the climax of which he proclaimed *'Ich bin ein Berliner'*. Everyone roared their approval but what he had said could be translated not only as 'I am a Berliner' but also as 'I am a doughnut' (a *Berliner* being a type of doughnut).

Anyone setting forth for the Middle East should read *Manners and Correct Form in the Middle East* by Sir Donald Hawley KCMG, MBE, Debrett.

WRITING AND SPEAKING

Rules of English

As recently as 1965, that highly respected work, *Fowler's Modern English Usage*, could say, 'Received Pronunciation is the pronunciation considered correct for an educated Englishman.' Today that statement is unacceptable: 'education' is no longer thought to be limited to those with a particular background and accent. That doesn't alter the fact that it is necessary to define a standard pronunciation which can be given in dictionaries, taught *to* foreigners, and so on.

Today's Received Pronunciation (RP), or Standard English, is almost literally 'the Queen's English' – for it is very close to her style of speech. This means it is fundamentally the pronunciation which comes naturally to those who were born into the landed gentry and the professions, and educated at public schools, though they are by no means the only people to speak the 'Queen's English'.

Its official position doesn't mean that Received Pronunciation is 'right' in any absolute sense. But, since it has been chosen as the benchmark, it does mean that words should be pronounced that way unless the speaker has a regional or national accent which overrides it. But Received Pronunciation isn't fixed for ever. Language is a living thing and the accepted patterns of speech gradually change, rather as hairstyles do. Today's Received Pronunciation is not the same as it was in our mother's day, still less our grandmother's time. Even if your dictionary is only 20 years old it may not be right to settle an argument by referring to it.

The Maverick H

One of the classic changes in pronunciation concerns the letter 'h', which has always been a vexed letter. When the first edition of *Enquire Within* came out in 1856 the author wrote, 'Few things point so directly to a want of CULTIVATION as the misuse of the letter "h" by persons in conversation.' He told his readers, 'H should always be sounded except in the following words':

A heir, honest, honour, hour, hostler

B herb, hospital, humble, humour and words made from them.

He could have added hotel, and history from which the 'h' was also dropped in correct speech at that time, as was the g in huntin', shootin' and fishin'.

The interesting thing is the way these words have changed. In correct British speech, the g is now sounded on all 'ing' words; the 'h' is still not sounded on the words in list A, but *is* sounded in list B, and in hotel and history. In other parts of the English-speaking world the changes have not been the same: for example, Americans still pronounce herb as 'erb, just as the Victorians did.

None of this would matter were it not for the confusion which it creates over whether to use 'a' or 'an' before such words. The rule, of course, is that 'a' is used before words starting with a consonant, while 'an' is used before vowels. But words beginning with 'h' are sometimes one and sometimes the other. Despite what you may see in conservative publications, the top authorities on pronunciation say it is now correct both to say *and* write 'a' before words like humble, hospital, and hotel in which the 'h' is sounded.

The 'h' also causes trouble in words beginning with 'wh'. The Victorians used to pronounce the 'h' before the 'w', saying h-wite, and h-wen. But correct speech has changed: as the 'h' isn't *written* before the 'w', in Standard English the 'h' is simply left out altogether.

Simple Speech

Many of the greatest writers in the English language have commented on the power and excellence of plain words. Yet, on television, you can often hear nervous spokesmen using long words which clearly aren't those they would use at the breakfast table. They obviously feel their ordinary speech isn't good enough, or impressive enough. They are quite wrong: most of Shakespeare's greatest speeches, and those of any great orator, are written in words anyone could say at breakfast. Saying utilize, for example, when you mean 'use' diminishes rather than enhances the strength of a phrase.

Nor is it only in the choice of general vocabulary that simplicity is best. Understatement rules at every level. So a car is called a car, even if it's a Rolls-Royce, and a mink is just a coat. And if you spent the weekend at Great Grandure Castle with Lord Havealot you either don't mention it at all or you say you were at Great Grandure visiting Jim Havealot.

Singulars and Plurals

It can sometimes be difficult to tell a singular from a plural – which makes it hard to use a verb correctly after it. The United States is a good example – it ends in an s, and refers to a collection of states, so it could well be a plural: it isn't, it is a united country. So you would say 'The United States *is* going to declare war . . .' The same holds true of group nouns – like the government or the committee – which usually take the singular, so 'the committee is in session.' The exception comes when the members of the group are clearly acting as individuals. So you would say 'The committee are in the garden having drinks' – to use 'is' would suggest they had one drink between the lot of them. The rule for getting this right is mentally to replace the noun with 'it' or 'they', and let whichever sounds right dictate the rest of the sentence.

Split Infinitives

Splitting infinitives is a fault schoolteachers love to point out. The perfect example came in the opening words of the television series Star Trek – 'To boldly go where no man has gone before.' The word 'boldly' splits the 'to' away from 'go' – which is the infinitive form of the verb. (Infinitives are all the basic verbs as you'd see them listed in a grammar book – to run, to sit, and so on.) So the sentence should have been, 'Boldly to go where no man has gone before.'

However, sometimes it is better to deliberately split an infinitive, and have the emphasis right rather than stick

to the rule and sound flat. That sentence is an example. Putting 'deliberately' before the 'to' gives it far less emphasis yet it is the key word in that sentence, so there is an argument for having it right where it is.

Subject or Object

People sometimes agonize over whether they should say I or me in sentences like 'Harry and I went to Ascot.' There is a very simple rule: use the form which would let you drop the other person from the sentence and still allow it to sound correct. You can shorten 'Harry and I went to Ascot' to 'I went to Ascot', but you couldn't say 'Me went to Ascot', so I is correct there. But though 'Pass it to Harry and I' may sound reasonable, it is shown to be wrong the moment you drop Harry. 'Pass it to me' works; 'Pass it to I' doesn't.

The Written Word

Capital Letters

There has been a trend towards the effusive capital. That is, capitals used just because the writer feels the word is important, as in 'my Boss'. This seventeenth-century practice is not really correct today, but the correct use of capitals isn't as obvious as it may seem. In some instances there are rules on the use of capitals; in others it is a matter of taste, but the current guidelines are these.

- Although capital letters start each new sentence, and so follow full stops, they don't always come after exclamation marks.
- Capital letters are always used for the initials of people or organizations, e.g. J. B. Priestley.
- Capitals start each major word of the name of a person, place, official position, organization or creative work, e.g. Mrs Hippy, Loch Ness, Lever Bros, *Gone With The Wind*.
- Capitals are used for full titles, so you write 'the Duke of York'. You may write either 'the Duke' or, 'the duke' – though the first has the edge.
- Some words have two meanings – in one case it is used as the shortened name of an organization, in the other as a basic noun. Only the shortened name takes a capital letter. So you would write, 'I am going into the church' but, 'The Church still forbids the ordination of women.
- The capital is always dropped if the word doesn't mean one particular person, organization, etc. So you would write, 'I would like to be a managing director', but 'Ian Kairn, Managing Director of Kairn Industries'.
- When it comes to place names associated with objects you write 'french windows' and 'Cheddar cheese'. This is not consistent.
- On the points of the compass and the seasons of the year it is up to you.

Punctuation

I write about punctuation with some trepidation, since to do so is to throw every stop and comma in this book open to criticism – and in a book this long there are bound to be misplacements.

Though it's easy to get it wrong when in a hurry,

punctuating is much easier than people think. After all, most punctuation is just designed to indicate the position and length of the pauses you would leave if you were talking. So, the first rule is to read the words with as much expression as possible (gabbling won't work) and listen to where the natural pauses come. When you know where they *feel* right you can then decide how big each pause needs to be, and choose the punctuation mark accordingly.

The remaining punctuation marks are a kind of shorthand to tell people the things they would know automatically if the words on the page were a live scene which they could watch. For example, speech marks tell you someone is speaking, and an exclamation mark tells you someone is speaking with force. To put those in you only have to decide what is happening.

The only tricky punctuation marks are colons and semi-colons. Even the greatest experts are not entirely agreed about the finer points of their use, but you can write perfectly clear English without ever using them – as most newspapers show.

The following list is in order of the length of the pause – except where two marks have much the same length, but are used in different situations.

Punctuation for Pauses

comma
Commas are used for the shortest pause and are the Swiss army knife of the writer's tools – they can be used for almost everything. In modern writing, of the less literary kind, they are even used instead of the slightly longer pause correctly indicated by a semi-colon. But the correct uses of commas are as follows.

1 To separate items in a list (e.g. The thieves stole rubies, emeralds, and diamonds). People sometimes argue over whether there is a comma before the 'and' in such a list. If you read the list you will hear it is there in speech. However, some authorities feel that in lists the 'and' provides the pause and no comma is needed before it.
2 Before and after a word or phrase which is added to the main sentence but is not essential (e.g. The Prime Minister, unfortunately, lost his voice . . .). In this situation it must be possible to remove the words inside the commas without altering the sense. If you can't you have put the commas in the wrong places.
3 Between two adjectives describing the same noun (e.g. A long, dark night).
4 To divide direct speech from the words introducing or explaining it (e.g. 'I'm going out,' she said).
5 To separate the main part of a sentence (which makes sense by itself) from a less important section – which doesn't – (e.g. She didn't eat her potatoes, because she was slimming).
6 After 'Dear John', or whoever, when starting a letter and after the final phrase – 'Yours faithfully,' etc.

dash
This gives almost the same length of pause as a comma but is used in slightly different situations.

1 Like the commas in (2) above, dashes mark off words inserted in the middle of a sentence. But you put them before and after words which interrupt the flow of the sentence (e.g. She was immensely beautiful – though I know you, Susan, disagree – and her charm was extraordinary.) They can also be used to draw attention to the words within them.
2 A dash can also be used to divide two contradictory sections of a sentence (e.g. I will meet you at the station – unless you prefer to come by car).
3 In direct speech, a dash is used to indicate that someone has been interrupted in mid-sentence (e.g. 'I was only –')
'Don't give me any excuses.').

semi-colon
This is a longer pause than a comma and suggests a slightly heavier style of speech or writing. It is used between two statements which are too closely linked to be separate sentences but need a decided pause between them. Often the two have very similar structure and counterbalance one another, as if on scales, with the semi-colon as the fulcrum. The classic example is: 'To err is human; to forgive divine.'

colon
A colon is a slightly longer pause than a semi-colon but very similar.

1 Like the semi-colon, it divides two sections of a sentence, but the colon is mainly used if what follows it extends and elaborates the idea set up in the first half, as in examples of cause and effect. Nancy Mitford used it perfectly when she wrote, 'An aristocracy in a republic is like a chicken whose head has been cut off: it may run about in a lively way, but in fact it is dead.'
2 It introduces a list of any kind (e.g. There was a cast of three: James Mason, Anna Neagle and Cary Grant).
3 It is used after these words: to sum up, for example, namely, the following.

full stop
This is the longest pause of all.

1 It ends all sentences that don't end in an exclamation mark or a question mark. But if there is a sentence within another sentence, as can happen with a quotation you only use the full stop at the end of the main sentence.
2 Full stops follow some abbreviations.
3 Initials of people have full stops, e.g. F.E. Smith, whereas organizations which are pronounced as a name do not, e.g. NATO.

Tradition has it that full stops can never be used before an 'and' or a 'but'. Popular journalism has thrown that rule away. Inelegant as it may seem, this only reflects how people speak – 'ands' often do follow long pauses, and semi-colons and colons are not always appropriate.

Punctuation for Explanation

apostrophe

1 This shows that at least one letter has been missed out, and replaces the vanished letters (e.g. do not becomes don't; he will becomes he'll).
2 It is also used to show that something belongs to someone (or to a group of people) and it comes after the main word and before the final *s* which is used to make the possessive (e.g. the dog's dinner, women's rights). It is a touch trickier when a word already ends in *s*:
   a after singular words ending in *s* the possessive is still *'s* (e.g. Queen Bess's soldiers, Charles's children). The only exceptions to this are words pronounced *iz* at the end (e.g. Moses' son), classical names (e.g. Herodotus' books) and long words like Nicholas which can take the apostrophe or *'s*.
   b after plurals ending in *s* or *es* the apostrophe is added *without* an extra *s* (e.g. a girls' school).

brackets

1 They are used to insert a little comment directed at the reader: e.g. James (more often known as Tubby) sat down heavily.
2 They contain an explanation, reference note or translation.
3 Square brackets contain additional information which was not put in by the original writer. So they are often used in translations and edited diaries (e.g. 'My darling Pebbles [Jane Seymour], how I have missed you . . .').

exclamation mark

An exclamation mark is only needed when the words before it are an exclamation (e.g. Damn! Good Heavens! Ow!) and occasionally in novels to show that someone is saying something seemingly mild with more than usual emphasis (e.g. 'What a horrid day this is!' is quite different from 'What a horrid day this is').

In all other situations if a sentence is well worded it doesn't need an exclamation mark; the words say it all. It is the punctuation equivalent of a nudge and a wink – and just as unnecessary if the joke or remark made the point. The sole exception is perhaps a letter between close friends.

hyphen

Hyphens are used when you need to split a word in writing it, because it won't fit on to the line. In this case split the word where the syllables break naturally. It can also link two words and replace a word like 'to' (e.g. The London to Brighton express could be written as the London-Brighton express). It is also used to link nouns, more neatly than words could manage (e.g. 'the Anglo-French agreement' is much neater than 'the agreement between the English and the French').

question mark

Obviously, this shows that someone is asking a question. It is always used, even when the words clearly indicate a question without it.

inverted commas, quotation and speech marks

There are two kinds – single ' and double " – and either can be used in the following situations.

1 At each end of words which are spoken, e.g. 'I love you,' he said and the punctuation relating to the spoken words goes *inside* the marks. Only the words showing who is speaking stay outside.
2 Inverted commas go round quotations of all kinds when the words are *exactly* what was said or written, or where any omissions are indicated by . . . but don't go round compressed extracts, or inexact quotes.
3 Inverted commas go at each end of any quoted titles but not round the name of any book of the Bible. (Italics are usually used for titles of books, films and plays.)

Although there are no fixed rules about when to use double inverted commas, and when single, the most usual convention is to use single ones as much as possible. This means speech is in single marks, and if someone uses a quotation in the course of speaking the quotation is in double marks to distinguish it from the rest.

Job Interviews

An interview is a situation in which every aspect of someone's social behaviour is being looked at, and looked at critically. Those who are experienced at being interviewed have probably developed a technique for handling it. So what follows is mainly intended for those new to the game.

The time leading up to the interview should be used for careful preparation. This starts with taking all the focus *off* yourself. Instead of thinking about how you feel about the interview, put yourself in the shoes of the interviewer. Bear in mind the sort of job it is and the type of person who will be interviewing you (if you know) and what they will want to know. Interviewing people is tough, and often boring, work. Think how you'd like a good interviewee to be and then work out how to be like that.

> Almost any interview boils down to three issues:
> Why do you want this job?
> Why do you want to work for this company?
> Why are *you* right for the job?

Why Do You Want this Job?

Decide why you do want that particular job. The fact that you haven't got another and need work is not enough. You have to seem as if their particular job is the very one you want. If you don't know enough about the job to sound convincing *find out*. Then work out some good reasons *why* it really appeals to you. If you want the job enough to apply there must be things you genuinely like about it. Don't down-play them.

Why Do You Want to Work for this Company?

Showing an interest in a company is one of the most vital aspects of an interview and one of the most neglected. Yet even those applying for senior jobs in management

Addresses and suggestions for further reading are at the ends of chapters.

sometimes fail to take this basic step. So find out all you can about this particular company and think of some good reasons why you would like to work for it. Good reasons mean reasons which will seem good to *them*. You may be applying because they have a great pension scheme, but *they* may be more impressed if you say you are excited by their latest business activities.

To find out about a public company just ring its head office and ask for the latest report and accounts to be sent to you. If it's a small firm all you may be able to find out is what they do in general. In that case, just work out the questions you need to ask.

Why Should They Employ You?

There are several aspects to this and you need to think about each of them.

What qualifications do they want?

If there was an advertisement this will tell you. Decide the best way of talking about your qualifications. They should already have the bald facts in writing, but was some aspect of your training angled in the perfect direction? If so, prepare to tell them about it.

What previous experience would they like someone to have?

Decide which aspect of your previous work or school provides the best springboard for the job you are applying for. Then decide how best to bring this out. You should be able to sound as if you enjoyed your other work and took an interest in it.

What sort of personality are they likely to want for the job?

The ideal salesman has a very different personality from the ideal bank manager. Work out how you can bring out the aspects of yourself which most suit the job.

What are your hobbies and interests?

If you have a hobby prepare to answer questions about why you took it up and why you enjoy it. Watch yourself. If you are applying for a job which means you have to be with people, don't say you like bird-watching because you prefer to be alone. If you have no real hobbies or interests *find at least one*. Then learn enough about it to answer a question on it. For most jobs it doesn't matter whether you say it is disco dancing or backgammon, but admitting to spending every evening in front of the television is like admitting you have brain death – even if you only watch serious documentaries.

Other Questions to Prepare For

There are obviously no rules about which questions will be asked, but the following are some others which are most likely to crop up. So plan your answers.

- In your last job/in school what were you best at?
- Have you ever lost your job? And why was that?
- If you get the job how long do you plan to stay?
- Tell me about yourself.

- If we can't take you for this job but can offer you one at a lower salary will you take it?
- What are your ambitions/goals in life (or in your career)?

Whatever you do don't try to write down the answers you will give and learn them up, as it will leave you totally tongue-tied if the question isn't worded as you expect or you forget your lines.

What Do You Need to Know?

When you have found the best answers to all those questions you will have a very good idea of how to show you are right for the job. Having seen it from their point of view, you can now see it from your own.

What do you want to know about the job?

You may only have time to ask one question, and you are very unlikely to have time for more than three. So work out what you want to know and be ready to put your questions in the order of importance to you; then think what impression your questions will make on that particular company. The best questions are the ones which suggest you are really interested in the job – not the perks.

How Will They Expect Someone in that Job to Dress?

Packaging counts. If you have to wear a city suit to work, you need to turn up in a city suit – if that means borrowing or hiring it, do so. Equally, if it's a job where casual clothes are the rule wear something appropriate. The role of your clothes is to make others feel you are one of them, that you will fit in. Make it easy for them to think that (see page 20).

On the Day

The rules on the day are very simple:

- Before going for the interview read the copy you kept of your letter or application form and memorize what you said on it.
- Make sure you look right for the job.
- Take with you everything you have been asked to take.
- Be early – not hours early, but have time to spare so you can go in five minutes ahead of time without rushing.
- Take something to do while you wait; they may run behind time and if you sit doing nothing the nerves may mount.
- When you enter the interview be guided by the interviewer as to whether you shake hands or not. If you do so make it firm (but not gripping) and decisive, and look at the person you are greeting.
- Follow the plan you have worked out above but listen carefully for any cues the interviewer gives. The way a question is worded will often suggest the answer which is wanted.
- Look at the interviewer.
- Don't smoke unless the interviewer invites you to.
- Never criticize a previous employer.

After the Interview

Some people suggest that you should write a pleasant businesslike letter to the interviewer the next day – you should have made a note of his or her name and initials. In it you should:

- thank them for the interview
- say how much you appreciated the chance to learn more about the job
- say how interesting you found it
- tell them briefly anything *vital* you omitted from the interview if really necessary
- let them know that you do want the job and are looking forward to hearing from them.

This does have the advantage of allowing you to say something vital which you forgot in the interview, but to some people it could seem pushy. So the situation needs to be judged carefully.

Making Conversation

I have to confess that I simply cannot tell anyone how to make small talk. It is not one of my skills and, like origami napkin folding, I have always left it to those who do it better. As with origami, it is quite extraordinary the lengths to which some take it. Some people have talk that is both so small and so incessant that listening to it is like being choked to death with talcum powder. Mercifully, now that women are allowed to have brains, small talk is getting bigger.

Opening Gambits

There are books which give you all kinds of advice on how to start conversations with people. But there is only one rule: it doesn't matter what you say so long as you take an interest in *them*. As the 1856 edition of *Enquire Within* put it:

> The true art of being agreeable is to appear well pleased with all the company, and rather to seem well entertained with them than to bring entertainment upon them.

Avoid talking about yourself; praising your own works; and proclaiming your own deeds. If they are good, they will proclaim themselves; if bad, the less you say of them the better.

Ask them a question about themselves which is likely to produce an interesting answer. Listen very attentively to the answer, pick up a point from it, and ask another question – the more flattering, the better. Given an attentive ear almost anyone will find something interesting to say, in time. It's a technique with which you can't go wrong: the unimportant and shy are flattered that, for once, someone is listening to them; the important and self-opinionated are getting what they regard as their due. Even the shyest person can adopt the tactic with ease, as it involves deflecting attention away from oneself.

Topics of Conversation

The basic rule is never to talk about anything which will upset anyone else who is present. Nor should you say anything which is likely to stop the conversation dead with surprise. So what you say at a Hampstead drinks party is rather different from what you say at a tea with a country vicar. Religion and politics are no longer banned – but they do have to be carefully handled if they are not to touch anyone on a sensitive spot. Sex is rather the same. General comments are now acceptable at many tables, but the personal or anatomical usually brings conversation to a halt.

The permissible level of debate is a matter of taste and nationality. The British tend to be more afraid of debate than other Europeans, but restrained arguments are tolerated, provided they are intellectual, not personal. The old *Enquire Within* put it rather well:

> Avoid Disputation, for the mere sake of argument. The man who disputes obstinately and in a bigoted spirit, is like the man who would stop the fountain from which he should drink. Earnest discussion is commendable; but factious argument never yet produced a good result.

Once anyone starts to get heated the host or hostess should deflect the conversation towards something less controversial. Whatever the topic, anyone who has not spoken for a long while should be brought into the conversation by a direct question and not left out in the cold.

Making Introductions

Introductions are an essential oil in the wheels of social encounters. Whenever anyone finds themselves with two acquaintances who don't know each other, he or she is duty-bound to introduce them. It makes no difference whether the meeting was engineered or a chance encounter in the street.

If the two people are more or less equal in age, sex and standing you can introduce either to either. If you need to bring them together across a room, and there is any inequality, you always take the less important person to meet the more important one – therefore, given equal status, you take a man to meet a woman, not vice versa, and you introduce them on the same basis.

When making the introduction the counsel of perfection is to work a few words into the introduction which allow them to start a conversation easily. So look for something which they have in common. For example, to introduce a medical student to a doctor, the format would be 'John' (assuming you are on first name terms) 'I'd like you to meet Dr Scapula. Dr Scapula (or his first name if you normally use it), John Sternum is studying medicine at Barts – that's your old hospital, isn't it?' (assuming it is).

The issue of how to introduce someone with a title is a vexed one. If the title owner is likely to be offended at it not being used then it must be used. But it may put both sides at a disadvantage, so since good manners should never make anyone feel uncomfortable, the title can often be omitted. There are no rules; you can only judge each situation as it comes.

If people don't appear to be linked, but are – such as wives who keep their maiden name, and lovers – it is useful to introduce them both at the same time and throw in some phrase which clearly tells the rest of the

Addresses and suggestions for further reading are at the ends of chapters.

room that they are a couple. It doesn't matter whether it's that they have enchanting children or have just got back from a holiday in Casablanca; it saves the rest of the room wondering.

Children tend to get left out of such courtesies. They shouldn't be. A child deserves an introduction just as much, and they tend to behave better if they are treated with a touch of formality.

When introducing a person or a couple to a large group of people the usual method, unless one of the people is particularly important, is to start off by giving the names of the newcomer(s) and then to name all the others going round the group. It is convenient to go round the circle in the order that people are standing, but some still introduce all the women before the men. Whether you use Christian names or surnames or whether people shake hands on introduction will depend on the formality of the occasion and the age of the guests.

On the Telephone

According to Debrett, the correct way to answer a private telephone is simply with the word 'Hello'; 'Hello, this is 2346789' or 'Hello, Susan Selby [or whoever] speaking' should be reserved for work. I disagree. Good manners are about making things easier for other people. Only if you give your number or name do callers know if they have got through to the right number. It also gives them a chance to realize who has answered – so they don't launch into a long conversation only to find they are talking to the daughter, not the mother.

Stopping people talking is a common problem. The classic British solution is to express your pleasure at having talked to them but say you mustn't keep them. If they ignore this go for a range of excuses – you'd love to go on talking but . . ., you can smell something burning in the kitchen, or your husband/wife/boss/mother/child is calling you about something urgent.

Answering Machines
Many owners make it almost impossible for their callers to leave a message by failing to say whether their particular machine will only take a brief message or gives unlimited time. When recording the message to callers:

- tell them your number
- ask them to leave a message
- tell them how long the message can be (some machines have unlimited time, others only 30 seconds)
- ask them to wait for the tone before speaking.

It is then basic politeness for the caller to leave a message, and not let the poor machine owner return to the tantalizing series of burrs and clicks which show someone rang and left no message.

Ringing Up
Telephones are extraordinary: dial someone and you walk right into their life – interrupt them in mid-sentence, get them out of the bath, or wreak havoc with their love-making. Thoughtful telephoners start by trying to avoid times which won't suit other people.

Next, let them know who you are: it's amazing how many people ring and say 'Hi, it's me' or 'Hello, it's Susan', forgetting that there are an awful lot of mes and Susans around. And whether telephoning an office or a home, it's considerate to ask if it is a good moment to talk, or would they rather you rang later (even, or perhaps especially, if you are a relative) – it is surely presumptuous to suppose anyone, however close, is free to talk to you at any minute you choose. If you are busy when the phone goes you are perfectly within your rights to say so and ask if you can call them back later – but some people are reluctant to do this. If it's a business call keep it very much to the point – so decide exactly what you want to say before you ring.

Paying for Calls
Whether one should or should not pay for calls made on a friend's telephone is a tricky matter. Some people are insulted at being offered money; others are upset if calls aren't paid for. So, avoid phoning long distance or overseas and be brief. But if you have to make a long or expensive call you can see that a proud friend isn't out of pocket by putting money to cover it beside the telephone. Then, as you leave you can mention that you put it there. Alternatively, scribble a note and put it with the money, saying you've done so because it was a rather long call.

Public Speaking

Being a first-rate public speaker is an ability which, like that of being a racing driver, is inborn as much as learnt. However, almost everyone can get from A to B as a speech maker, just as they can as a driver. It is a matter of knowing what to do.

Introducing a Speaker
Someone who introduces a speaker simply has to be the oil which eases the speaker into place. You don't have to be clever or witty, just pleasant and competent and keep it short.

1 Say how pleased you are to be able to welcome the speaker. And if you are an official of the organization to which the speech is being made, say you are delighted to be able to welcome the speaker on behalf of that organization. (You can also add that it is a personal pleasure, if there is some reason why that is true.)

2 Introduce the speaker by name and give an indication of their position. Make sure you include any qualifications relevant to the subject to be spoken on.

3 If the speaker has spoken to your organization before say something to indicate that he or she is particularly welcome because everyone enjoyed his or her last speech so much.

4 Give an indication of the subject the speaker has come to speak on. *Only* do this if you have had a chance to find out beforehand what the speaker's subject *is*. He or she may have changed the speech in the train, and it is embarrassing if you announce that the subject is

flower arrangement and the speaker launches into the mating habits of the mongoose or vice versa.

5 Finish with 'Ladies and gentlemen' (or whatever is appropriate), and the person's name, then start the applause, and sit down when it ends.

Thanking the Speaker

This should be *very* brief – people's patience wears a bit thin after a speech. Just say a few very warm words of praise about what you have just heard. Sound really appreciative, however awful the speech was. For someone who is bad at speaking to have made a speech at all was probably an immense effort which deserves thanks. Try to pick out a particularly memorable point which the speaker made and remark on it. Then say where everyone should go from there. It may be that the speaker was speaking on behalf of a charity – in which case you will be expected to urge people to make donations. On the other hand, if the talk was just for everyone's pleasure and the next move is a cup of tea or a drink announce it, or nobody will know when they can get up.

If the applause at the end of the speech failed to materialize, or was less than enthusiastic, you can smooth this over by saying something like, 'But before we all go to tea I'm sure we'd all like to give [the speaker's name] a *big* round of applause.' Then lead the applause loudly, egging the others on with your example.

Making a Speech

Most people who have to give a speech are worried sick about what they are going to say. That is totally unnecessary. Talking is rarely a problem. What does matter is getting together *thoughts* which will make a talk worth listening to. The bad speaker is someone who says what everyone has heard before, in words which are all too familiar.

The other route to a bad speech is (in most cases) to write it out. Actors, professional broadcasters and a few politicians apart, very few people can read a speech so that it sounds alive and immediate. Usually the written word becomes a barrier between the speaker and the audience. Only by picking your words as you go along can you be certain to speak *to* people not *at* them, and so hold their attention.

Nobody can teach anyone how to be witty or charming, but the following method should allow anyone to create a speech which is well organized and has a chance of being effective, and perhaps original. Yet it relies entirely on notes which will fit on a series of postcards, and is extremely easy to use.

Preparing a Speech

In the early stages of preparation the essential thing is not to try too hard. Relax and let your mind wander over the topic you have to speak on. Each time you think of something connected with it write it down in just *one* or *two* words each. It should be a disordered jumble of ideas, let them be as crazy and far-fetched as you like. Give your imagination free rein, don't sit there being critical. Ideas are shy things: your brain only has to sense

you criticizing one of its suggestions and, like a criticized person, it will stop being original and interesting and start coming up with the safe and the boring.

When you run out of ideas, go through what you have written down and pick out the three key areas, or topics, which your jumbled notes suggest to you. They may be there as words already, or you may see several patterns in what you have written down and think of a heading for each. (If your words are really dreary have another go from the beginning.)

Make these the three main headings for your talk (you could pick out five for a very long speech). Put each one at the top of a separate sheet of paper.

Under each heading write down any relevant ideas and points you would like to make on that particular aspect of the subject. Don't worry about structure; write things down just as they come into your head.

Look at what you have written down in the light of the type of speech you are wanting to make. Cross out the things you don't want to say on this particular occasion. Leave in those that you do want to say. For example, suppose you are making a wedding speech. You have chosen three headings: The Past, The Present and The Future. You find that under 'The Future' your random jottings include 'One marriage in three ends in divorce', so you cross it out. But if you were making a speech in a debating society and the motion was 'Marriage has no future in our society', you would certainly keep that statistic in.

Having sorted out which ideas you will use, decide the order in which your three headings should go, and mark them A, B and C. Remember that your speech should build to some sort of climax, not shoot its bolt in the early minutes and go downhill from there.

Once you know the order of the main headings you can start to arrange the order of the ideas within them. They need to lead easily from one to another within a section, and they also need to be planned so the last idea in each section takes you easily into the next heading. Once that is done you have the backbone of what you will say. The invariable structure of all but the frothiest speech is this:

1 Your introduction gets the audience interested and outlines what you will talk about.

2 The body of your speech is made by building point on point or witty remark upon witty remark, according to the nature of the subject.

3 You summarize what you've just said and round the speech off smoothly.

You now need to decide on an attention-catching opening, and find an entertaining way to summarize all the main points of the speech. Then flesh out the bones of section 2 with clever comparisons, examples, statistics, jokes or anything else that will give interest to what you have to say. This is the bit you have to work at and polish until you are sure that every idea can be made really interesting. But don't try to be precise about the words you will use. Keep noting your ideas in one or two words beside the point they relate to.

When that is done take five postcards. Write the notes

Addresses and suggestions for further reading are at the ends of chapters.

for the introduction on one, and the headings and summary on the other four. Under each heading list the one or two word reminders of the points to be made – in the order you have decided – plus a memory jogger for anything you need to flesh each out. Your speech is now ready.

★ The technique of jotting down random ideas and then organizing them under headings is one worth practising. Once you get the hang of it there is no faster way of preparing an examination answer and making sure it reads well.

Debating
Each debating society tends to have small variations on the rules of debating, but the basics are very simple. First, a motion is formulated as a statement; for example, the motion on one radio debate in which I took part was 'Women aren't funny'. There then have to be four speakers:

- one to propose the motion
- one to second (agree with) the motion
- one to oppose the motion
- one to second the opposition motion

There must also be a chairman, and a 'house', which is a participating audience. In some debates there are six speakers, each side having an extra seconder.

Each of the speakers prepares a speech, the length being set beforehand so they all speak for the same time – 10 to 15 minutes is average. At the start of the debate the chairman announces the motion and calls on the first speaker to propose the motion. The proposer then puts forward an argument in favour of the motion, producing as many persuasive points as possible, and trying to win the audience over to agreeing.

Next the chairman calls on the other side to oppose the motion. This should be an equally persuasive argument against it.

After that the seconders alternate in the same way, putting forward new arguments and ideas for their side. They are allowed to refer to what the other side has said and point out how their arguments refute it.

When all four have spoken the debate is normally 'thrown open to the floor'. At this stage anyone can catch the chairman's eye – usually by raising a hand and the chairman can call on that person to speak from the floor. He or she will then put points on either side but always addressing the chairman, not the speakers, so the opening words must be 'Mr Chairman' or Madam Chairman'.

Nobody should interrupt anyone else or speak unless the chairman has called on them to do so. But there are two exceptions. Anyone on the floor can leap to their feet and say, 'On a point of fact/information, Mr Chairman . . .' and go on to correct a factual inaccuracy by any speaker or by anyone else on the floor. They can also leap up and say, 'On a point of order, Mr Chairman . . .,' and point out how someone has broken the rules of debate.

Good chairmen will not allow speakers from the floor to go on for more than three minutes and will cut them off sooner if they are boring. They allow a set amount of time for the debate on the floor, after which they first call on the opposer to sum up his or her argument and then on the proposer to do the same. After that the motion is put to the vote. Only those on the floor vote, not the chairman or speakers.

Running a Meeting
The chairman's job is to make sure that everyone gets a fair chance to put his or her point of view, that the meeting proceeds at a decent pace and that decisions get taken. To do this he or she must start by making it clear that the meeting will be held with a certain degree of formality. This doesn't have to mean the elaborate pseudo-parliamentary protocol which is still used by the highly traditional. It just means being businesslike. However, a degree of protocol does bring it home to people that chatting is out of order. So the most basic procedure is given below.

The Agenda
It is usually helpful to have an agenda listing the topics which will be discussed and voted on. It can be drawn up by the chairman on the basis of topics which other members of the committee ask him or her to include.

The agenda should have attached to it the minutes of the last meeting. These are brief but accurate notes on every decision which was taken and on who agreed to do what. So at every meeting someone must take these down, even if there is no official secretary. If this doesn't happen there will be decisions but no action.

The agenda and the minutes of the last meeting should be circulated, in advance, to everyone who will be coming to the meeting and they should read them before they come.

At the Meeting
The chairman should sit at the head of the table or in a dominant position. He or she should check that everyone is present and allow only a brief grace for late arrivals. From that point on every comment should be addressed to the chair. So 'Mr Chairman' or 'Madam Chairman' will precede each person's opening words.

The chairman should then outline the purpose of the meeting, and perhaps check that everyone has an agenda, with the minutes. He or she will then ask the secretary to read any apologies for absence. The minutes of the last meeting are then gone through, point by point.

If a decision for someone to take action was minuted, the chairman should ask that person what was done and what the outcome was.

He or she should make his or her reply short and to the point. If people ramble in reply the chairman should bring them gently to the nub of the matter. If this part of the proceedings is allowed to drag there will be no time to discuss any fresh issues or make new decisions.

If any action decided on in the last meeting is completed it is said to be 'adopted'. If it needs further action it is re-minuted so it will be brought up again at the next meeting. This proceeds until all the minutes have been dealt with.

Next the points on the agenda are considered one by one. Each point is discussed in detail and the chairman can call on whoever put an item on the agenda to speak first. It is the chairman's job to keep things moving forward and decide when any point has been discussed for long enough. He or she then sums up the general mood of the meeting and steers people firmly towards a decision. For example, 'Are we all agreed that there should be a cake stall at the Bring and Buy?' If everyone agrees, there is no problem. If they don't, the chairman asks for a vote. The decision is taken on a majority vote, through a show of hands, and the chairman votes last, making the final decision if an equal number are for and against.

> Things go more smoothly if decisions are kept simple. Decide to have a cake stall; *then* decide who will run it. Once any point has been voted on the topic is closed. If anyone tries to take the discussion back to it the chairman should intervene at once, or the meeting will get nowhere.

When all the points on the agenda have been dealt with, the last item is usually 'any other business'. This is a chance for people to raise issues which failed to get on the agenda and need to be dealt with. The chairman then closes the meeting – having, of course, arranged the date of the next one, if this is appropriate.

Business Letters

The best letter is the one which expresses what you have to say simply and clearly. Just write as you would speak. It is far better to say, 'If you need more information please let me know', than to use the cliche, 'If you need more information do not hesitate to contact me. Hesitation about business matters went out years ago.

However, there are a couple of special rules. Business letters should have the address of the person to whom the letter is being sent written at the top left-hand corner. If your letter is a reply your first sentence must also give the date and reference number (if there is one) of the letter you are replying to. The simple form is:

Dear. . . . . .
In reply to your letter of (date), reference number (quote the reference numbers or letters on their letter).

Then say what you want to say. Time is money – sometimes it's their money, but if you are consulting professionals it is your money. They need only the key points (don't be embarrassed by bare paper). If you need to give more than a few facts, it can often be useful to split the information. Suppose you have an appointment with a lawyer, write confirming the appointment and say what you are consulting him about (problems with a neighbour, a divorce or whatever) and what help you hope to get from him. Then say the background facts are enclosed, and on the separate sheet give all the main facts he might need to know to advise you. Giving him a chance to read a clear outline can save you a lot of time and money when you actually see him.

Spend time deciding which facts really *are* relevant and important. He doesn't need to know that it was your

birthday when the neighbour's tree fell, breaking your fence, but he will need to know who is legally responsible for the fence.

Keep a copy of every business letter you send or receive, and only destroy them when they could be of no possible use. The same holds good for all documents and evidence – guarantees, receipts and so on – never post them without keeping a copy, or better still, keep the original and send the copy. If there is any chance that someone may say you did not write, pay a bill or return goods at an appointed time, ask the post office for a free certificate giving proof of posting.

Complaining

The golden rule for complaints is to praise first. If you have usually had satisfactory service from the company start by saying so. Then explain what was wrong. Ask them for whatever redress you feel is appropriate (see Consumer Rights) and either tell them what evidence you are enclosing or ask them to arrange to see the problem (you could not after all post a faulty sofa). If you are sending items by post remember to get proof of posting

Most big businesses have Customer Relations Departments which deal with complaints. But if in doubt write to the Managing Director – complaints, like water, filter down very easily, but if you send them to somebody too low down the ladder they never rise to the level of someone who can deal with them.

Job Applications

When applying for a job bear in mind that you are advertising yourself. A good advertisement gives the key facts, briefly and cleverly, and says no more than is needed to get the reader interested. The aim is to get them to take a look at the product – and this time the product is you. So don't be tempted to go on and on: instead give the full details in a curriculum vitae (CV, see below). If the job needs you to apply by phone, make a note of what you will say before you phone. If the application must be in writing, plan the letter carefully.

Start by saying which job you are applying for and how you knew it was available. Briefly say why you are especially qualified for the job and sound as if you are genuinely interested in work of its type. Finally, tell them about any enclosures and politely show that you expect a reply. For example:

Dear. . . . . . .
I am writing to apply for the job of senior crocodile keeper, which was advertised in The Animals' Friend of Saturday 25 September.
For the past three years I have been assistant reptile keeper in Animal Haven, a large private zoo in California, and have had special responsibility for crocodiles and alligators.
Crocodiles have always been my special interest, and I have studied and applied the latest developments in their care and handling. Last year, for example, I attended an advanced course on the subject at Las Bestas State Zoo where, as I am sure you know, they have pioneered captive breeding of the more difficult crocodile species.

Addresses and suggestions for further reading are at the ends of chapters.

A curriculum vitae, giving full details of my qualifications and experience is enclosed, and I will be glad to supply references from my two previous employers if you need them.

I believe that I have both the qualifications and the experience which are needed for the post you advertised, and I am greatly attracted by this opportunity to work in an operation which is so dedicated to conservation and research.

I very much look forward to meeting you and learning more about what sounds like a most interesting job.

Yours faithfully,

Needless to say, a job application must never go on to a second page, should be totally free from errors of spelling, punctuation and grammar, and be typed, or written in good hand-writing. The managing director of one dynamic company told me he always rejects, without further reading, an application – for a post at *any* level – if he finds even one small error in it. In his view, 'If someone can't be bothered to check that everything is absolutely correct, when *their* future and income are at stake, what chance is there that they will take trouble over details which matter to the company?'

Curriculum Vitae (CV)

A CV lists all the background details a prospective employer might need to know. But it must be carefully selected and compressed into no more than two sides of A4 paper. The key facts are:

- schools/colleges/universities attended
- all exams passed, plus the standard achieved if it was good
- all special awards
- special achievements – head boy/girl, captain of cricket and so on
- any further training you received
- every job or position held unless you are so senior that only recent experience is relevant
- key hobbies and interests in private life.

Select hobbies to suggest abilities which could be useful in the job – working in a team, being creative and so on.

The dates go, in exact sequence, down the left-hand side. Some people write CVs starting with their most recent job and working *back* to their birth; others start at their birth and work through. Start with whichever end of your life is most impressive – if you sound dull at the start of the CV the prospective employer may not bother to read to the end.

The CV is your one chance to reveal yourself, and you should be very careful about what you reveal accidentally. There is a difference between the person who writes:

1981-85   Export Manager for YT Industries PLC. The need to pull out of South Africa made this a difficult time for the company. However, by working on our existing markets in the Far East I was able to minimize the impact of this and maintain profits.

and the one who writes:

1981-85   As Export Manager for YT Industries PLC I faced the challenge of restructuring the company's export strategy. By moving strongly into new markets it was possible substantially to increase the company's profits from exports, despite the fact that key markets had to be dropped by the board for political reasons.

It isn't just a matter of giving the facts but of giving the facts in a way which sounds appealing. So work out what the prospective employer is looking for – using the advertisement as guidelines, and then write a CV which combines the two. Some employers frown on CVs prepared by agencies, as they simply don't reveal enough about the real person to show whether they are worth interviewing.

As employers are usually suspicious of those who take time off to do nothing, and seem to fear it may be a recurrent disease, there should be no unaccounted-for years. But be careful, if you are someone who feels the need to account for idle years, never to claim to have done something which you haven't done at all. Anything in a CV is open to questions at the interview and you can't be sure that the interviewer won't have been to the place you claim to have visited or done what you claim to have done.

Invitations

Sending Invitations

The etiquette of invitations is a legacy from the days when, instead of directly inviting people to your house, you let them know that you regarded them as worthy of your acquaintance and would be 'at home' on a certain day if they called. This curious wording is still the classic style of invitation to send out for almost all occasions except weddings or children's parties. A typical invitation would read:

If the event is to take place at a country house, but the hosts find it more convenient to receive replies at their London address, they would put 'at Grandthorpe Manor, Little Airs, Buckinghamshire' under the date, and the RSVP address would remain at the bottom left-hand corner. Strictly speaking, the words 'At Home' can only be used when a *woman* is sending out the invitations. So a wife issues the invitations in her name only. Stiff white card, 4 x 6¾ in (10 x 17 cm), is traditional. The name and address, and the words 'At Home' should be printed. But the time and date can be either printed or hand-written, and the names of the guests are then hand-written at the top left-hand corner.

One of the hazards of the basic wording is that the poor benighted guests are left wondering just what sort of a party they are being invited to. So drinks or dinner (or whatever) is usually written or printed above the time. If there is a special reason for the party this should also be given. So if parents are giving a party for one of their children they will put 'For John' or 'For Miss Susan Bold' – according to how formal they wish to be (the latter is more correct) – under the date.

If a man is giving a party or a couple wish to use their joint names on an invitation, the words 'At Home' are replaced by 'request(s) the pleasure of your company'. These words can also be used if the party is not being held at the hostess's home.

Other Parties
Invitations to casual parties and parties for the young can take any form you like, from bought cards to felt-pen writing on balloons, and be varied according to the age of those concerned. For children's parties put the time the party ends. After entertaining a hoard of children that will be the time you really care about.

Accepting Invitations
The convention for answering invitations is to repeat the wording of the invitation. A reply to the invitation by Miss Jane Austen (see above) should read:

> *Mr Darcy thanks Miss Jane Austen for her kind invitation to dinner and dancing on Friday 14th May, from 8 to 12 pm, and has much pleasure in accepting.*

or

> *– very much regrets that he is not able to accept as he will be abroad/has a prior engagement/* (or whatever).

It looks minimal but it says all that needs to be said and, well placed, on the smallest size of writing paper it is perfectly adequate. Nothing further is added and it is not signed.

A solo guest bringing a partner should include his or her name in the reply – it may be someone the hostess already knows, or the ex-husband or ex-wife of one of her other guests, and she needs to be forewarned.

Inviting People to Dinner
There are no rules for how far ahead anyone should be invited to dinner – or any other social event. People who lead dynamic social lives are best invited a month beforehand, while most people are perfectly content with two to three weeks' notice.

As dates may need to be juggled, the initial invitation, to anything but a very formal dinner party, is usually by phone. If the arrangements are at all vague, it is then

wise to drop the guests a short note confirming the date and time. For a more formal occasion, Debrett suggests sending an At Home card with the RSVP crossed out and 'To Remind' written above. I personally prefer 'To Confirm' which smacks less of the suggestion that the recipient is absent-minded.

Those who follow in the footsteps of Pussy Gladstone, as she was known (Lord Gladstone's wife), and invite people and then forget they have done so, can even send one to themselves.

Inviting Single Guests
The days when guests had to arrive and go into dinner, two by two, like animals entering the ark, are long gone. But some hostesses still feel awkward on behalf of a single person. There is no need to. In general, only the very newly bereaved or divorced find it embarrassing to be solo. And, though a great excess of either sex can be difficult, it is insulting to someone of either sex to suppose that he or she is not worth inviting without a partner, or that a partner *has* to be produced.

Guests may, however, have an 'opposite number' they would like to bring with them. It's tactful to make it clear, by a telephone call or a note with the invitation, that they are invited solo, but that if *they* particularly want to bring someone, they are welcome to do so. That way, a guest who lacks a suitable partner won't feel that he or she has to scrape around to find someone to bring. Putting 'and guest' on an invitation, though kindly meant, can make solo friends feel that if they can't bring a guest they won't be welcome, which can be hurtful.

Stationery

Paper and Envelopes
Today there is nothing to stop you having purple writing paper ornamented with puce kisses, if you want to. But, as with clothes, there are certain conventions, which apply if someone wants to make a particular type of impression. Colours are more flamboyant than they used to be – but the more striking the choice, the harder it may be to carry off. Those who want to impress would-be employers or parents-in-law should bear in mind that a gentleman's (or woman's) writing paper should be rather like a classic suit: good quality and understated, with discreet details. That means good quality unlined paper in white or pale-blue in any size, with matching envelopes. The address can be printed at the top in a neat, unshowy typeface, either in the centre or at the right-hand corner. Failing that, it is hand-written at the top right. Printed addresses usually include the telephone number (not preceded by the word 'tel:' on private stationery); hand-written ones do not.

Notes and Cards
It is conventional to use plain postcards with your address printed or handwritten along the top edge. Christmas cards always used to have the sender's address printed inside at the bottom-right hand corner, but nowadays many people avoid this expense, except for

business. However, only the address should be printed, not the name, and each card must be handsigned.

Business Cards

Today's business cards sprang from the days before telephones when, to make contact without intruding, people would visit the house and leave a card to show they had called. Flurries of excitement were created when the local big-wigs condescended to leave their card on a newcomer. Today cards are mainly used for business, but in some parts of the world failing to exchange business cards is like failing to return a greeting.

Engraving v Printing

The best cards, business cards and other stationery are engraved and the letters feel raised, whereas ordinary printing feels flat. Engraving is undoubtedly more elegant, but today few people recognize engraving and although, in some people's eyes, the niceties of engraving versus printing, and of good quality card versus light card, are a matter of status, there is now a printing process which mimics engraving.

Social Letters

Writing or Typing

Typing used to be reserved for business letters, and type-written social letters were considered cold and unfriendly, at best. In America this view has long since died out. As hand-writing has deteriorated and type-writers and computers have entered more homes, type-written social letters have become acceptable here too. But a hand-written letter, in good hand-writing, still makes a better impression especially in ink not biro and a type-written one should still contain a sentence excusing the type-writing. Business letters can be hand-written or typed – but the latter looks rather more efficient and makes it easier to keep a duplicate copy.

How to Start Letters

The etiquette of how you start and end letters, and address an envelope to those with ranks or titles is so complex that I cannot cover it here. But Debrett's *Etiquette and Modern Manners* gives every nuance.
For ordinary situations:

- 'Dear Sir,' or 'Dear Madam,' is the correct business opening if you know the sex but not the name.
- 'Dear Sir/Madam,' is now used, if you don't know the name or sex.
- If you know the name 'Dear' followed by Mr or Mrs (or Dr) and the surname is the correct business opening.
- 'Dear' followed by the first name is increasingly used between those on first-name terms either in business or socially.
- Nowadays 'Dear' plus first name and surname seems to be creeping in, when people are not on first name terms but Mr or Mrs might seem too deferential.
- For letters to those close to you any variation goes – My Dear, Dearest, Darling, as you will.

- On postcards use no opening at all, but go straight into the message.

How to End Letters

There is a simple hierarchy of friendliness for the endings to letters. Starting with the coolest, this is:

Yours faithfully,	For formal business letters, especially to someone you have not met, or when starting with Dear Sir – or Madam.
Yours sincerely,	For business letters to those you know (e.g. your bank manager) or for social letters when you wish to show a fair amount of distance and respect.
Yours truly,	Slightly dated, but useful for acquaintances.
Yours,	A neutral ending, neither very formal nor affectionate, useful when you don't want to define the closeness – for example, when writing to a friend's husband or wife.
With very best wishes, Yours	Like this 'Yours' can remain non-intimate but you express more warmth. And the wishes can be extended to a particular person.
Yours affectionately,	Affectionate but slightly distant – say to a relative who is not close enough for 'With love', or to someone for whom you feel real affection but not intimacy.
Yours ever,	A slightly dated ending between friends.
With love, All my love, Much love	At one time these endings were little used. Today they are used, not only between relatives and lovers, but between friends of the opposite sex (who won't misunderstand), and between women friends.

Thank-yous

Nowadays thank-yous are often overlooked entirely, but it is correct to thank people after any major hospitality – lunch, dinner, going to stay or a party. You don't, however, send thank-yous after cocktails, weddings, funerals or royal garden parties.

If a letter can't be written then a quick, enthusiastic telephone call will do – unless it was a long visit or a formal occasion. And many hostesses actually prefer a phone call, which allows them to mull over the evening's events, to a letter, which allows no chance to gossip.

When writing the rules are the same whether you have been entertained or received a present:

1 Thank them for the dinner/party/present and say how much you enjoyed/like it, etcetera.
2 Pick out one or two reasons why you enjoyed/like it so much. If the evening was boring, or the present ghastly, be creative; thank-yous are about making

other people feel good, not a game of truth. But keep within the bounds of reason; if the food was a disaster, praise the flowers or the choice of guests. If the object is terrible, there are plenty of complimentary adjectives you can use without lying about *liking* it. Then say how very kind they were to invite you/give it to you.

3 End with some good wishes, such as that you hope to see them again soon.

If you have large writing paper this may leave a lot of blank space but there is no need to pad thank-you letters with chat.

Styles for Envelopes

It is not just what you call someone on an envelope that matters but how you place the writing on the paper. The name and address should start about half-way down and not threaten to embrace the stamp. They are *only* preceded by 'To' on a parcel address, when there could be confusion between to whom it's addressed to and to whom it's from.

A woman with no special title can be Miss, Mrs or Ms. But Miss and Ms are followed by her first name or initials, then surname, whereas Mrs is followed by the husband's first name or initials. On widowhood, and often on divorce, the husband's initials or name are replaced by her own. Dr is always followed by the woman's first name or initials as the qualification belongs to her not her husband.

The use of Master for young boys is outdated and the first name and surname will do until late adolescence. For a man, the first name or initials (one initial will do) and surname are used. If you don't know his initial, and can't discover it, there is no convention on what to do. Nancy Mitford used to resort to the Greek letter θ (theta) instead of an initial; I myself simply put A.

The classic form of address is to put Esq after the man's name, so it will read A. E. Jones Esq. Mr is used when both the husband and wife are being written to, as in Mr and Mrs Gettogether, or when writing to a surgeon, in which case Mr is – confusingly the correct title. But, under American influence, more and more people are writing Mr for any man, and I fear that Esq will eventually pass into history. It is not, however, there yet and there is still a certain prestige in using it. If a husband and wife are doctors you put Dr John and Dr Joan Cutabout, or whatever. But, strictly, if a letter is intended for both husband and wife it should be written and addressed solely to the wife.

USEFUL ADDRESSES AND BOOKS

Stationery

Conservation Papers, 228 London Road, Earley, Reading RG6 1AH Tel: 0734 668611, offers stationery from recycled paper, plus readdress stickers with a reminder to save trees (which makes re-using envelopes look like virtue not parsimony). (P.36)

Conservatory, 109 Upper Woodcote Road, Caversham Heights, Reading, Berks RG4 7JZ Tel 0734 479120, sells office and personal stationery from recycled paper, and offers a design and printing service too. (P.36)

Frank Smythson Ltd, 44 New Bond Street, London W1Y 0DE Tel: 071 629 8558, is one of the smartest stationer's in Britain – and priced accordingly! (P.36)

Funerals

National Association of Funeral Directors, 618 Warwick Road, Solihull, W. Midlands B91 1AA Tel: 021 711 1343. Its members operate a code of practice agreed with the Office of Fair Trading. (P.8)

Job Interviews

Companies House, 55-71 City Road, London EC1Y 1BB Tel: 071 235 9393, holds the details of every registered company. Anyone can check them during working hours. Alternatively, you can have a postal search done for a small fee by ringing the Cardiff office Tel: 0222 380801/380691. Details of Scottish companies are held separately Tel: 031 225 5774. Companies Registration Office, Crown Way, Maindy, Cardiff. (P.28)

Weddings

Barnums, 67 Hammersmith Road, London W14 8UZ Tel: 071 602 1211, is a shop for carnival and party novelties (also mail order) such as masks, disguises, glow in the dark make-up, wedding bunting and balloons printed to order. (P.10)

Brides and Setting Up Home, Vogue House, Hanover Square, London W1R 0AD Tel: 071 499 9080, has an information service on all aspects of weddings and will supply list of wedding dress hirers, sae. (P.10)

London Convention Bureau, 26 Grosvenor Gardens, London SW1W 0DU Tel: 071 730 3450, is not just a convention centre: it covers a number of unusual locations, within a 25-mile radius of London, which you can hire for every type of occasion. The places offered by its members range from discos to castles and other members provide all the services. The finding service is free to the enquirer, as is their publication *Convention and Exhibition Venues*. (P.15)

The National Association of Toastmasters, Albany House, Albany Crescent, Claygate, Esher, Surrey RT10 0PF Tel: 0372 468022, will put people in touch with toastmasters in their own area. (P.15)

The Registrar, The Faculties Office, The Sanctuary, Westminster, London SW1P 3JT Tel: 071 222 5381, will consider applications for a special licence to get married outside your own parish. (P.10)

Ivor Spencer School of Butlers (See Domestic Matters, 214).

Hiring Clothes for Special Occasions

Costume Call, 158 Munster Road, London SW6 5RA Tel: 071 371 7211, hires out fantasy fancy dress and period costumes and will make one to order.

Moss Bros, 26-27 King Street, London WC2E 8JD Tel: 071 240 4567, has branches, in many towns, which hire formal clothes for men. (P.21)

One Night Stand, 44 Pimlico Road, London SW1 Tel: 071 730 8708 (and in NW1), hires out evening dresses from cocktail frocks to ball gowns. (P.21)

Youngs Formal Wear for Men, Metcalf Drive, Altham, Accrington, Lancs BB5 5TV Tel: 0282 772577, also has branches around Britain which hire formal clothes for men. (P.21)

Useful Books

BBC Pronouncing Dictionary, OUP.

The Oxford Guide to English Usage, OUP.

Moyra Bremner, *Modern Etiquette and Successful Behaviour*, Century; Helicon pbk.

Sir Donald Hawley, *Manners and Correct Form*, Debrett.

Historic Houses, Castles and Gardens, British Leisure Publications, lists wedding venues county by county, and says what type of function each will take.

Debrett's Information Service, 73 Britannia Road, London SW6 Tel: 071 731 4221.

Food

Additives and Labelling • Dairy Products • Eggs • Fish and Shellfish • Food Hygiene • Frozen Food and Freezing • Fruit and Nuts • Game and Poultry • Grains • Herbs, Spices and Flavourings • Meat • Methods and Problems • Pulses • Quantities and Temperatures • Special Cooking Methods • Storage Times • Vegetables

ADDITIVES AND LABELLING

Food Additives

There have always been additives, and we are lucky to have been spared some of those experienced by our ancestors. A hundred years ago milk was watered, tea and flour adulterated and wine, beer, cheese and oil debased. Sugar was as much as 50 per cent sand, causing the popular jingle:

> Little bags of sugar
> Little grains of sand
> Make the artful grocer
> The richest in the land.

Sand was one of the more harmless additives of the time – others were outright poisons, like red lead and verdigris. No wonder it wasn't considered respectable to be 'in trade'.

Reformers fought, and won, a battle for stricter controls. Yet today our food contains more additives than it has ever done. Some do stop food going bad, and a tiny minority improve its flavour. But most simply make food look more appealing than it really is, or are just a modern version of the grocer's old trick of increasing profits by making a small quantity of food go farther.

There is also a new phenomenon. A hundred years ago even the most adulterated food had *some* real food in it. This is no longer true. Today more and more 'food' is totally a laboratory creation: 'fruit' drinks which haven't even had the fruit in question waved over them, snacks which haven't a genuine food element in them, instant desserts – the list is endless.

Never in the history of the world have human beings consumed such vast numbers of chemicals which do not occur naturally in food. Moreover the safety of many of them is just not proven. All that has been established is a *lack of evidence* of them being *un*safe. But if manufac-

turers have a right to make these phoney products, we have an equal right to avoid them. And the failure of such products to sell will make them vanish from the shops far more swiftly than any government legislation. Several organizations concerned with allergic reactions, eczema, and similar conditions, have information of companies producing food free of dubious additives. Their details are given in the address lists of In Sickness, and of In Health.

Defining

Not all additives are bad, some are old friends like salt, sugar and vitamins. But the term also covers the whole caboosh of artificial colourings, flavourings, flavour enhancers, emulsifiers, thickeners, sweeteners, bleaches, antioxidants, anti-foaming agents (yes, in food not detergent), humectants, propellants, solvents and preservatives. Some 6,000 different chemicals all told, and almost *a quarter of a million tonnes* of them are added to British food each year. That means each of us consumes 8 to 10 pounds of additives per year – whether we want to or not.

We tend to assume that if something is permitted it must be safe. This is not true where additives are concerned. The E in E numbers may not stand for Evil – in fact, it shows that the additive is permitted in the EC – but many permitted additives produce ill effects in *some* people.

For example, as I write, tartrazine (E102) – which may cause asthma, hayfever and hyperactivity – is used in 2,995 different products including:

17 types of sausages	59 canned vegetables
21 toppings and sauces	64 preserves
24 milky desserts	86 ice cream products
26 frozen desserts	104 dessert mixes
32 coatings	109 toffees and caramels
48 types of chocolate	188 soft drinks
49 confectionery fillings	201 gums, jellies and
49 soups	pastilles
50 jellies	301 boiled sweets

> Those figures came, not from some pressure group trying to make much of the over use of additives, but from a report by the Ministry of Food and Agriculture in 1987.

Interactions

It is not simply a matter of a single additive being bad for us. There is also the question of interaction. As additives are seldom used singly, we are being exposed to unpredictable chemical cocktails. With over 6,000 additives being added to food, in different combinations it is mathematically impossible for the food industry or any government organization to test *even a useful fraction* of the possible combinations to see if any dangerous by-products are produced. Maybe the additives now in our food do most people no harm. However, since the potential for interactions makes it impossible to prove either way, it is wise to limit our intake.

Government Restrictions

The use in food of substances of no nutritional value is restricted by the Ministry of Agriculture, Fisheries and Food and the Ministry of Health, jointly, Their decisions are curious. For example, they say the British food industry 'needs' food dyes which the rest of the EC does very well without. They allow the use of flavourings which have never been tested for safety. And they allow the general use of additives which are banned from baby foods as unsafe.

Hazards from Additives

People vary enormously in their sensitivity to certain additives, so that something which will be safe for 9 people out of 10 can produce an acute reaction in the tenth. Whether it is foolish to ban something which seems to do most people no harm, or whether 1 in 10 people should not be put at risk by using a chemical which has no food value is a matter of debate.

Each consumer should be able to decide whether to take this risk or not. Current labelling means that most food additives have to be listed on most labels – but not all. The exceptions are additives used in manufacturing processes – for example, to stop food sticking to a mould – and those used in alcoholic drinks, vinegar, butter, milk, cream, cheese, chocolate and some confectionery. And that's an awful lot of food.

The Good Es

There is no need to be alarmed if you see the following Es on food labels. They are either harmless or positively good for you.

Number	Name
E101	Vitamin B2/riboflavin
E101a	riboflavin/5'-phosphate
E140/1	chlorophyll/chlorophyllins
E160a,c,e,f	extracts of plant colourings
E170	calcium carbonate
E172	iron oxides & hydroxides

E260	acetic acid
E261	potassium acetate
E262	sodium hydrogen, acetate, sodium diacetate
E300	vitamin C & l-ascorbic acid
E301/2	sodium l-ascorbate/calcium l-ascorbate
E304	6-0-palmintoyl-l-ascorbic acid
E306	vitamin E (natural tocopherols)
E307/8/9	vitamin E (synthetic tocopherols)
E322	lecithin
E330	citric acid
E331/a-c	sodium citrates and other citrates
E332/3	potassium and calcium salts of citric acid
E334	tartaric acids
E335/6/7	various salts of tartaric acid
E339a-c	derivatives of phosphoric acid
E340a-c	as E339
E350/1/2	derivatives of malic acid
E353	metatartaric acid
E355	adipic acid
E375	nicotinic acid/niacin
E400	alginic acid
E401	sodium alginate
E406	agar
E410	carob gum
E415	corn sugar gum
E440a-b	pectin
E518	magnesium sulphate
E526	calcium hydroxide
E540	calcium hydrogen phosphate
E552	calcium silicate
E553a	magnesium silicate
E570	stearic acid
E576	sodium gluconate
E903	carnauba wax
E920	l-cysteine hydrochloride
---	glycine
---	nitrogen

The Bad Es

Some people would say that any E that isn't a good E is a bad E. But some additives are only bad in high doses or to a small minority who are sensitive to them while others may possibly affect many of us. These latter I term the bad Es, though maybe I should call them the very bad Es. The following are those to which quite large numbers of people are sensitive and which may carry a risk for the rest of us – or on which there is concern as I write. Possible reactions include: hay fever, blurred vision, breathing problems, skin rashes, swollen blood vessels, vomiting, gastric trouble, hyperactivity, asthma, swelling, damage to an unborn child, possible cancer risk, sensitivity to light and blood pressure changes. Yet many of these additives are widely found in basic manufacturers' foods, especially in those such as sweets, cakes and fast foods – which we are likely to give to children. And some are banned in other countries. The EC can ban or allow additives at any time. As I write, there are plans to allow 100 more. So the following list may not cover all those which merit caution.

Number	Name
E102	Tartrazine
E104	quinoline
E107	yellow G2
E110	sunset yellow FCF
E120	cochineal red
E122	carmoisine
E123	amaranth
E124	ponceau 4R
E127	erythrosine
E128/9	red 2G/allura red AC
E131	patent blue V
E132	indigo carmine
E133	brilliant blue FCF
E150	caramel
E151	black PN
E153	carbon black
E154	brown FK
E155	brown HT
E161	canthaxathin
E210	benzoic acid
E211/2/3/4/5/6/7/8/9	various benzoates
E220	sulphur dioxide
E221/2/3/4/6/7	various sulphites
E230/1/2	various phenols
E236/7/8	formic acid variants
E239	benzene derivatives
E249 E250/1/2	various nitrites & nitrates
E280/1/2/3	propionic acid & other propionates
E310/11/12	various gallates
E320	butylated hydroxyamisole (BHA)
E321	butylated hydroxytoluene (BHT)
E336i/ii	monopotassium & dipotassium tartrate
E407	carrageenan, seaweed extract
E413	tragacanth gum
E420/1	sorbitol/mannitol
E430/1	various stearates
E432/3/4/5/6	sorbitol derivatives
E450a-c	various phosphates
E466	carboxymethyl/cellulose sodium salt/CMC
E493	sorbitol derivative Span 20
E513	sulphuric acid
E535	sodium ferrocyanide
E536	potassium ferrocyanide
E553(b)	talc
E621	monosodium glutamate (MSG)
E627	guanosine 5'-disodium phosphate
E631	inosine 5'-disodium phosphate
E635	sodium 5'-ribonucleotide
E907	micro-crystalline wax
E924	potassium bromate
E925/6	chlorine & chlorine dioxide
E954	saccharin
---	aspartame
---	dichloromethane
---	dioctyl sodium sulphosuccinate
---	hydrogenated glucose syrup
---	isomalt
---	nitrous oxide
---	extract of quilaia
---	xylitol

Hyperactivity, often coupled with asthma and/or eczema, is one of the main problems which occur when children react badly to additives. The Hyperactive Children's Support Group (see In Sickness) suggests that the parents of hyperactive children should avoid giving them synthetic colours (E100 – 180 are colours) and flavours, glutamates, nitrates, nitrites, BHA, BHT and benzoic acid. In addition to the list above, anyone with asthma or eczema may find it useful to contact the organizations in In Sickness for information on the additives which most aggravate those conditions.

Paradoxically, medicines do not have to declare the colourings used in them and some children's medicines use colourings which are among the bad Es. It may be worth querying the colouring agent with your pharmacist.

Additive Free Food

Many products are additive free, but most fresh foods have been sprayed with chemicals or grown on land fertilized by man-made fertilizers. If you want to know that food reaches you without the addition of any man-made chemicals at all you will have to buy organic produce. This is being sold more and more widely and now reaches the shelves of supermarkets. 'Organic' is now defined in EC law and may only be used on foods which meet strict standards of production. These are defined in EC law and inspected by a number of regulatory bodies, such as the Soil Association. If you want to know more, MAFF (page 694) has leaflets on this, and on additives and food labelling.

Protection Against Additives

It would be nice if we could totally avoid all potentially harmful additives. The truth is we can't. Even if we cut them out of our own shopping – which is well nigh impossible – we are bound to encounter them if we ever eat out. Happily, studies in animals have shown that a diet rich in vitamins and fibre helps to minimize the ill effects.

Understanding Food Labels

The usefulness of any label depends on whether you can decode the curious, if not misleading, language which is defined by law.

Addresses and suggestions for further reading are at the ends of chapters.

What's in a Name

Flavour: The word 'flavour' is code for a total lack of the natural ingredient which would provide that flavour. So the word flavour in 'Blackcurrant Flavour Dessert' shows it is a complete fake and hasn't even looked at a blackcurrant. The manufacturer does not have to say 'imitation flavour', or 'synthetic flavour'. Flavourings are not regulated as colourings are – even though some, such as caramel made by modern processes, may possibly be health hazards (see page 41).

Flavoured: The 'ed' at the end of flavoured in 'Blackcurrant Flavoured Dessert' tells you blackcurrants were involved in its making – but just how many is the manufacturer's secret. He doesn't have to say.

Blackcurrant dessert: Tells you real blackcurrants played a reasonable part in the process.

Natural flavourings: This may also be written as 'free from all artificial flavourings', which sounds good, but the food industry is allowed to define as 'natural' man-made flavourings whose chemistry mimics natural ones – though they are no more natural than a china monkey. But full details of flavourings do not have to be given.

Added vitamins: Most products which have added vitamins are made with ingredients which had their natural vitamins removed – or are made of such unnatural ingredients that they never had any in the first place. What's more, manufacturers don't always add as many vitamins and minerals as the food would contain naturally. So those which proclaim 'added vitamins' may not be the best for you.

'Health' food or drink: It is perfectly legal to call a product a 'health food' or a 'health drink' without any evidence that it is especially good for you.

Contents

Food manufacturers are only obliged to list the contents of food if it claims to be 'low fat', 'high fibre' or have 'no added sugar'. Those apart it can be label-less. But there are plans to extend contents labelling to other claims such as 'low salt'. When contents are listed they must be in order, starting with the ingredient which the food contains most of. But this can be misleading. If food contains three different types of sugar, for example, they will be listed separately. So, even if put together they would make sugar the largest ingredient, this may not be clear from the label.

Watch out for meat products doctored with polyphosphates which make them mop up water – bad from your point of view but money for old water for the manufacturer. Water only has to be listed in the ingredients if it is more than 5% of the total weight.

All pre-packed foods must show any food additives by serial number, E code, or their full name, plus a descriptive term – such as 'stabilizer'.

Freshness

There are two terms in use:

A **Use by** date must be given on food which might be unsafe after a certain date. It is illegal to sell such food after that date.

Best before is used on food which becomes less enjoyable after a certain date, without becoming dangerous, e.g., biscuits.

If food bought within the given date has gone off you can expect a refund from the shop. This applies even if it was sold at a reduced price just before the date. If the shop refuses, contact your local Trading Standards Officer (listed in the telephone book under your local council), or write to the manufacturer giving all the facts and enclosing a sample – if this is possible.

DAIRY PRODUCTS

Butter v. Margarine

There is growing evidence that some margarine may not be as good for you as it has been cracked up to be. In making it, healthy unsaturated fats, such as sunflower oil, are often changed into hydrogenated fats. And some research suggests that hydrogenated fats may be bad for the arteries. So, it may be safest either to eat butter in small quantities and cook with oil, not animal fats, or to buy one of the new breed of non-dairy spreads, such as Superspread, which say they contain *no* hydrogenated fat.

Cheese

We have little choice about the age of our cheese. According to Cooper's *Thesaurus* of 1565 we should be thankful, for he informed his readers that:

> *new, sweet, and fresh Cheese, nourisheth plentifully; middle-aged Cheese nourisheth strongly, but old and dry Cheese hurteth dangerously: for it stayeth siege* [constipation?], *stoppeth the Liver, engendereth choler, melancholy, and the stone, lieth long in the stomack undigested, procureth thirst, maketh a stinking breath, and a scurvy skin...*

Look at the surface of cheese before buying; the cut face should be moist and fresh. If a cheese looks dry or sweaty avoid it. Check Brie and Camembert carefully – especially in cold weather. If they have a white chalky slab in the centre, and runny layers top and bottom they are not worth buying. This is the sign that they have been over-chilled in transit; after that the cheese will never ripen evenly. If, however, there is a thin white line through the middle and a firm but creamy layer above and below you can expect it to ripen well at room temperature. But don't expect all soft cheeses to run. The more fatty they are, the less likely they are to run. So Brie labelled 62 per cent *matier gras* will keep its shape, while one in the 40 per cent range will ooze.

Safeway now numbers its cheeses from 1-5 to show their strength of flavour – very useful when choosing cheddar or putting together a varied cheese board – and other supermarkets may follow. They are also stocking good farm-produced local British cheeses and these are well worth trying. And, if you want to learn about British cheese, or see it made, see page 124.

A letter to *The Times* once claimed that the writer had kept a piece of cheddar under a glass for 41 years, and found it to be still good 'but rather hard'. Curious but not to be recommended. The ideal place for cheese is a larder which keeps below 10°C (50°F). Failing that a refrigerator at 5°-10C (40°-50°F). It needs to be closely wrapped to prevent it losing moisture or taking up the smell of other food and put it at room temperature 2 hours before eating it.

Cream and Milk

Anyone who has been lucky enough to taste milk straight from the cow is all too aware of the processing our pintas are subjected to. It may all be commendably healthy, but what exactly are we getting for our money? The table below shows you.

First, to explain how milk and cream are treated. The typical processes are these (though there are others):

- For **pasteurization** they are heated to 63°-71.7°C (145°-161°F) for not less than 15 seconds. This kills all the major bacteria.
- For **sterilization** they are homogenized, sealed and heated to 108°-130°C (226°-266°F) for at least 10 to 45

Facts about Cream

Types of cream	Calories per ¼ pt	Calcium mg per ¼ pt	Percentage fat	Treatment	Flavour
Clotted cream	693	54	55	Scalded to above pasteurization	
Double cream	657	73	48	Pasteurized	
Whipping/whipped cream	546	90	35	Pasteurized	
Sterilized cream	355	126	23	Homogenized and heat treated	Distinct smoky taste very
Sterilized half-cream	241	145	12	and may have additives.	unlike fresh cream.
Cream/single cream	288	133	18	Homogenized to stabilize	
Half-cream	241	145	12	Homogenized	

Facts about Milk

Top style	Calories per pt	Calcium mg per pt	Percentage fat	Character	Result
Gold	445	702	4.8	Rich milk from Jersey and Guernsey cows. Pasteurized: see below.	Food values scarcely changed
Silver	380	702	3.8	Pasteurized by heating to 71.7°C then rapid cooling.	Food value almost unchanged.
Red	380	702	3.8	Homogenized to break down fat globules, and pasteurized.	Food value scarcely changed but 'smoky' taste.
Metal style blue	380	702	3.8	Sterilized at 115° to 130°C.	Distinctly cooked taste. Slight vitamin reduction.
Red stripe	263-280	729	1.5-1.8	Semi-skimmed, pasteurized.	Slightly less vitamins A & D but calcium & other vitamins unchanged.
Blue check	195	761	0.1	Pasteurized, skimmed milk, not for young children or babies.	No vitamins A or D, but other vitamins and calcium retained.
UHT carton	380	702	3.8	Homogenized and heated to 132.2°C +.	Food value hardly changed, but slightly altered taste.
Calcia	227	783	2.35	Pasteurized.	Calcium enriched.
Vital	197	978	0.47	Pasteurized.	

Milk and cream vitamins A, D, B1, B12, B2, protein and fat. In addition to calcium, milk contains most other minerals, including about a third of our daily requirement of zinc.

Addresses and suggestions for further reading are at the ends of chapters.

minutes; this destroys bacteria more thoroughly than pasteurization.

- Under **Ultra Heat Treatment** (UHT) they are taken to 132.2°-140°C (270°-284°F) for not less than 1 to 2 seconds. This is slightly more sterilized.

Those processes are to kill off bacteria. **Homogenization** is different – the liquid is forced through an extremely small hole to create uniform fat globules and make them distribute themselves evenly throughout the liquid.

Whipping Cream

Cream can be whipped if its fat content is between 30 to 42 per cent, but whips best above 38 per cent. This means you can whip double cream, whipping cream and also equal amounts of single and double cream mixed together. Cream must be fridge cold when you whip it. If it is warm it rapidly goes grainy.

Whipping cream doubles its volume when whipped, but double cream is denser and only increases by 1½ times. To give it greater bulk, stir 1 to 1½ tablespoons of milk into 125 ml (¼ pt) of double cream before beating. If you add ½ teaspoon of lemon juice per 125 ml (¼ pt) cream it will whip faster. However, *extra thick* double and spooning cream, which have been thickened by homogenization, won't whip. If you want even thicker, clotted cream you can get it by post (page 123).

Curd Cheese

To make curd cheese: Heat 1 pt of milk to 38°C (120°F). Remove from the heat and add the juice of 1 lemon *or* 1 tsp of rennet (as for junket). Leave for 15 minutes (if lemon) or 20 minutes (if rennet). Transfer the curds to a colander lined with a large square of muslin. Tie the corners of the muslin together diagonally and hang it to drip for 1 hour. Turn out, season to taste and eat.

Yoghurt

Yoghurt can be made with no more equipment than a thermos flask, but if you prefer it set, use a yoghurt maker.

1 Heat 1 pt of milk to 43°C (110°F) or bring it to the boil and cool it to that temperature. (At this temperature your finger should be able to stay in it comfortably for at least 10 seconds.)
2 Stir in 1 level tablespoon of any plain yoghurt.
3 Pour into a pre-warmed vacuum flask, close and leave for 7 hours.
4 Turn it into a basin and cool by standing the basin in cold water and stirring the yoghurt.
5 Refrigerate for 4 hours to let it thicken slightly more.

At stage (2) you can make the yoghurt richer and thicker by adding 50g (1¾ oz) of dried skimmed milk powder or whole milk powder. You can make yoghurt with any type of milk, including UHT, or with diluted evaporated milk instead of part of the milk.

Be warned: the following can make yoghurt go wrong.

- adding extra yoghurt to start it
- disturbing it before the time is up

- leaving it in the warm for longer than recommended.

But yoghurt is temperamental; it can sometimes fail for no obvious reason. Don't let that put you off. Use scrupulous hygiene in making it. Sterilize the flask with Milton, the solution for sterilizing babies' bottles.

EGGS

The size of egg you use in a recipe really only matters in mixtures like cakes and soufflés where the right balance of ingredients is important. The British Egg Information Service tells me that when a recipe says 'take one egg' it means a size 3 egg.

Brown v White

I'm sorry to have to tell you, but brown eggs are not better for you. The only difference between brown and white is the type of chicken which lays them or the chicken's diet. But her diet makes no difference to the food value of the eggs.

Large	SIZE 1	70 g or more	Grade A eggs are perfect.
	SIZE 2	65-69 g	
Standard	SIZE 3	60-64 g	Grade B eggs may have to be cleaned or have a crack, or oversized air cell
	SIZE 4	55-59 g	
Medium	SIZE 5	50-54 g	Grade C eggs cannot be sold to the public, only as broken eggs to the trade.
	SIZE 6	45-49 g	
Small	SIZE 7	under 45 g	

Egg Safety

All eggs should be well cooked if there is a possibility that they are contaminated with salmonella bacteria. This is always important with those of birds other than chickens. Duck eggs easily become contaminated, for example, because the shell on a duck egg forms late, and gull's eggs need 15 minutes despite their diminutive size, and the government now warns against raw or undercooked chickens' eggs too.

Testing for Freshness

If you have put eggs into the egg compartments and aren't sure which are the freshest there is a simple test. Put an egg in a jug with about 10 cm (4 in) of water and watch how it behaves. If it lies on the bottom it is fresh. If one end tilts up it is beginning to age. If it floats to the top it is either bad or only fit for omelettes in which its slackness will not be noticed.

If you crack an egg its freshness is easily judged. A very fresh egg has a ring of *firm bulgy* white around the yolk. The older the egg is, the wider and thinner the white spreads, and the slacker the casing of the yolk. Old slack eggs are almost impossible to whip – even when they are perfectly good to eat – and will spread everywhere if you try to poach them. Very fresh and very old eggs peel badly when boiled.

Baked Eggs
The most foolproof method of cooking eggs looks the most sophisticated: it's baking. Just put the egg in a buttered cocotte dish and bake on a high shelf in a pre-heated oven for 15 minutes at gas no 5 or (190°C) 375°F.

Beating (or Whipping) Eggs
Beating eggs correctly is the secret of so many delicious dishes that it is well worth mastering. And it isn't difficult. Start with a reasonably fresh egg; slack watery ones can be almost impossible to beat. If possible have the egg at room temperature: the proteins which stabilize the foam work best when not chilled.

Egg whites won't beat properly if there is any grease present. To an egg white, a drop of yolk is grease and can reduce the volume of the foam by two-thirds. Egg white also objects to traces of fat on the bowl, and beats less well in plastic bowls (or with plastic beaters), since plastic is oil-based.

If a white is chilled, adding just under a tablespoon of warm (not hot) water is useful in increasing the volume. You can also increase the volume by standing the bowl over gently simmering water as you beat – as Italians do for making zabaglione (but don't overdo the heat). Traditionally, chefs have always used a copper bowl for this job and science has just proved they were right: copper helps egg whites to foam.

The great thing is to know when to stop. Egg white is like a rubber band: you can pull it so far, but go that bit further and it snaps. And when an egg white snaps it won't hold air. If a recipe says 'beat the whites until very stiff' it usually means until the bowl can be turned upside down without the froth falling out. 'Stiff peaks' means the point of a peak sticks straight up; 'soft peaks' means that the tops just turn over.

Once the eggs begin to stiffen keep stopping to test the stiffness of the peaks at regular intervals – lest you over-beat. Once they are perfect use them immediately: eggs go flat again quite quickly and, once flattened, it is much harder to get them to stand well again.

★ If you are short, put the bowl in the sink, to make it lower, while beating.

Boiling Eggs
Curiously, the secret of good boiled eggs is not to boil them. Boiling makes the albumen in egg go rubbery, so they should be simmered. A medium-sized, fresh shop egg, straight from the fridge, put into boiling water for 4½ minutes will have a white which is just set and a runny yolk. In 6 to 6½ minutes it will reach the stage

the French call *oeufs mollets*, when the white is firm enough for you to peel the egg, but the yolk is still runny in the middle. Large or very new eggs will need longer.

For hard-boiled eggs at their best put them into boiling water, simmer for 5 minutes, remove from the heat, and leave them in the water to cool. But if speed is needed simmer them for 10 minutes.

★ Pierce the round end of each egg with a drawing pin before boiling it, so that the air can escape, as it heats and expands, without breaking the egg.

★ To shell hard-boiled eggs easily hold them under a cold tap, and let the water run under the shell.

★ Hard-boiled eggs cut most easily with a wet knife.

★ Only a hard-boiled egg can spin in an even circle, raw eggs have a lolloping motion.

★ It is easier to grate a hard-boiled egg for sandwiches than to chop it.

Omelettes
For a good omelette eggs should be lightly beaten with pepper and salt and a dessertspoonful of water for each egg. Over-beating makes them rubbery. It is also best to cook omelettes in ½ tbsp oil and ½ tbsp of butter – so you get the taste of butter but it won't burn easily.

Poaching Eggs
The rules for poaching eggs successfully are very easy.
● Have a fresh egg broken into a cup.
● Have a dash of vinegar in the boiling water (it helps the egg solidify).
● Stir the water into a whirlpool and slide the egg into the centre.
● Turn the heat down and simmer *very* gently.
● Drain briefly on kitchen roll.

Scrambled Eggs
There are five secrets to good scrambled eggs: use only a dessertspoonful of milk per egg; beat only lightly; use lots of butter; stir all the time; and stop cooking the egg before it is how you like it – it always goes on cooking as you serve it.

Separating Yolks from Whites
Tap the centre of the egg firmly on the edge of a pan. Cup it between eight finger-tips and – with the bowl underneath – gently insert both thumb nails into the crack and pull *slightly*. As the white trickles into the bowl through the crack, tilt the egg on end and pull off the top. The yolk can now be juggled between the two halves while letting the white trickle out. For safety crack your eggs into an empty bowl and transfer each one to whatever you will cook them in. Then an accident won't ruin them all.

★ If you can't manage that crack it on to a plate, cover the yolk with a glass, allowing a tiny gap, and tip the plate up.

★ Separated whites or yolks will keep several days in a refrigerator. Simply cover them closely, or drop a little water on unbroken yolks to stop them drying up.

Addresses and suggestions for further reading are at the ends of chapters.

FISH AND SHELLFISH

There is something special about picking at the succulent white flesh of a fresh crab in a summer garden. But since the early 1970s the trend has been away from fresh shellfish and towards frozen. So much so that, sadly, the humble winkle is now the only shellfish to escape the freezer.

Most taste very much better fresh. So, the chart on the right shows when you ought to be able to obtain fresh ones, though price and availability are greatly influenced by the weather – something you can buy in May one year may not arrive until August in another. However, most fish is now deeply chilled or frozen and the general quality has become sadly poor. So the first task is to find a really good fishmonger.

If you can get it, the best months to buy fresh fish are when summer turns to autumn, around September/October, when they are fat and plentiful from the summer warmth. But the price per pound may be lowest earlier on, when the numbers are ample but the proportion of flesh to bone on any fish is less good. Many fish are unobtainable from March to May.

Buying Wet Fish

Fish is not a food to buy passively, by just asking for it. More than any other fresh food, it needs to be carefully looked at and checked. Most fish are not bred as meat is, so they are far more variable. And there are no rules of organic production for those which are 'farmed' so colorants, for example, are often put into feed. You must pick and choose to get the best – and the freshest. With salmon, ask if it is farmed or wild. The flavour of wild is far better, if you can stand the price.

With fish freshness is everything. Get close to them and sniff – fresh fish smell of nothing but crisp saltiness (and fresh water fish are odourless). Look at the eyes, and get the fishmonger to turn the fish over and open its gills – the flaps behind the eyes. Inside the gills should be a rich pinky-red. The eyes should be bright and domed, the skin should have a smooth sheen to it. After a couple of days out of the water the eyes begin to go dull and hollow, the inside of the gills goes browner and the skin also loses its sheen and becomes slimy. As one of the best fish buyers in Billingsgate fish market summed it up, 'You buy by the eye. There's fish what looks dead and there's fish what looks alive.'

★ If you find yourself looking for white fish which will make a basic dish like fish pie, take a look at hake; it's an undervalued fish with a good flavour and big bones, it can be used in a lot of dishes which call for the more expensive cod.

Buying Shellfish

Molluscs (mussels, clams and so on) must be alive – which means they are either waving their little valves at you, as they do in the markets of Italy (where even the sea life waves its arms about), or they should be keeping the stiff upper lip which distinguishes the British mollusc and be tightly shut – if you tap them, they should clamp themselves too tight to open.

Seasons for Fish and Shellfish

R - rare and probably expensive
* available
** plentiful, prices may drop
W - wild salmon available

Shellfish and Molluscs

	J	F	M	A	M	J	J	A	S	O	N	D
Clams	*	*	*	*					*	*	*	*
Cockles	*	*	*	*	**	**	*	*	*	*	*	*
Crab (whole)				*	**	**	**	**	*			
Crawfish					R	R	R	R	R	R		
Crayfish					*	*	*	*	*	*	*	
Dublin Bay prawns	*	*	*	*	*	*	*	*	**	**	**	*
Lobster	*	*	*	*	*	**	**	**	*	*	*	*
Mussels	**	*	*		R	R	R		*	**	**	**
Oysters (native)	**	*	*	*					**	**	**	**
Oysters (Pacific)	*	*	*	*	*	*	*	*	*	*	*	*
Prawns	*	*	*	*	*	**	**	**	**	*	*	*
Scallops	R	R	*	**	**	*	*	*	*	*	R	R
Shrimp	*	*	*	*	*	**	**	**	**	*	*	*
Whelks	*	*	*	*	*	*	*	*	*	*	**	**
Winkles	*	*	*	*					*	*	*	*
Octopus	*	*	*						*	*	*	*
Squid (calamari)					*	*	*	*	*	**		

White Fish – flat

	J	F	M	A	M	J	J	A	S	O	N	D
Brill	*	*				*	*	*	*	*	*	*
Dab	*	*	*	*	*				*	*	*	
Flounder			*	*	*		*	*	*	*		
Halibut	*	*	*			*	*	*	*	*		
Megrim	*	*	*			*	*	*	*	*		*
Monkfish (anglerfish)	*	*	*		*	*	*	*	*	*	*	*
Plaice	*	*			*	*	*	*	*	*		
Skate	*	*			*	*	*	*	*	*		
Sole – Dover	*	*			*	*	*	*	*	*		
Sole – lemon	*	*			*	*	*	*	*	*		
Turbot	*	*		*	*	*	*	*	*	*		
Witch	*	*				*	*	*	*	*		*

White Fish – round

	J	F	M	A	M	J	J	A	S	O	N	D
Bass	*	*	*					*	*	*	*	*
Cod	*	*					*	*	*	*	*	
Coley	*	*					*	*	*	*	*	
Conger eel			*	*	*	*	*	*	*	*		
Haddock	*	*	*			*	*	*	*	*	*	
Hake	*	*	*			*	*	*	*			
Huss	*	*	*		*	*	*	*	*	*		
John Dory	*	*	*	*	*		*	*	*	*		
Ling	*	*	*	*			*	*	*			*
Mullet – grey	*	*						*	*	*	*	*
Mullet – red				*	*	*	*	*				
Pollack				*	*	*	*	*				
Sea Bream	*	*				*	*	*	*	*	*	
Whiting	*	*				*	*	*	*	*	*	

Oily Fish

	J	F	M	A	M	J	J	A	S	O	N	D
Herring					*	*	*	*	*	*	*	*
Mackerel	*	*	*	*	*	*	*	*	*	*	*	*
Salmon	*	*	*	*	*	*W	*W	**W	**W	*W	*	*
Sprat	*	*	*						*	*	*	*

Shellfish, such as crab, should be odourless, and a crab will often have frothy, brownish-white bits still clinging to the shell from the cooking – though some fishmongers brush these off, because the public dislikes them. A freshly cooked lobster should have a certain spring to its tail, so uncurl it. If it has lost its elasticity it is over a day old.

When buying a crab or lobster always pick it up and feel the weight for the size. Good ones feel heavy for their size, light ones may have starved too long as they waited to be sold, or may have just shed their shells and acquired larger ones. On crabs, look at the width of the tail (which is tucked under the shell); females have broader tails, and are less good value as the claws are also smaller.

Cleaning Fish

Fish are much easier and more pleasant to gut than animals, and even a slightly squeamish cook should be able to manage it. But first have a very sharp knife. Insert the point of the knife in the hole at the base of the belly near the tail. Then cut it open, like slitting an envelope – and with as much care not to slit the contents. Tip the insides out, and use a spoon to scrape away any that remain, including any blood that clings inside, as it will spoil the fish if left in. Rinse the fish well inside and out and remove the head, unless it is needed. Then slide your knife point along the lie of the bones holding the fins in place, cut the flesh away to either side. Tug the fins off firmly, pulling towards the head, and their 'root' bones should come away too.

Cooking Fish

Poached or steamed fish used to be invalid food – and fish got a bad name as a result – but poaching is the basic method of cooking fish and the preliminary to a lot of excellent dishes. A typical poaching liquid (court bouillon) would be 2 l (4 pt) of water with 12 peppercorns, ¼ pt of wine or cider vinegar, 2 onions and 2 carrots. Boil this court bouillon up for an hour and strain it.

You don't need a fish kettle to poach fish. Simply take a large piece of muslin – or any perfectly clean white cotton fabric. (If it is old linen, boil it several times, throwing the water away each time, to get rid of any left-over soap.) Place the fish on your fabric and tie the ends together above the head and the tail. (To stop the fish buckling in the middle as you lift it out, place a couple of long metal skewers or long bamboo chopsticks between the fish and the cloth, if you have them.)

Bring the liquid just to simmering point, then lower the fish into the pan. It is important that the water never boils. High temperatures can spoil the texture of fish and boiling may break up the flesh. When the fish is cooked you just lift the knots with a fork and (wearing thick rubber gloves) take hold of as much of the edges of the fabric as you can, so the fish is supported along its whole length as you lift it out, on its little sling.

Time it from the moment the water returns to simmering point – at which it should barely tremble. Fish is cooked when the flesh turns white (in the case of white fish), opaque and firm.

Fillets	6-12 mins depending on thickness
Steaks	10-20 mins depending on thickness
Whole small fish	4-6 mins a pound
Large whole fish	3½ - 5 mins a pound

Fish can also be cooked in the poaching liquid in the oven at gas no 4 or 180°C (350°F). The times are much the same.

> When cooking large fish you can't simply multiply the number of minutes per pound by the weight of the fish, and say 5 minutes per pound means a 10-pound fish takes 50 minutes. The shape of a fish and the nature of its flesh mean that *the larger the fish, the less time it needs per pound*. A 10-pound fish takes 30 minutes not 50 minutes.

Baking Fish in Foil

Baking in foil is one of the best ways of cooking fish, as all its delicate flavour is parcelled up. It also means that your pans don't limit the size of fish you can cook. Simply oil the foil to stop it sticking to the skin, place the fish on it – with any delicious flavourings and seasonings you wish – and make a tightly closed parcel of it. How long it will take to cook depends on the thickness of the fish as well as the total weight. But on average you need about 8 minutes per 500 g (1 lb) at gas no 4 or 180°C (350°F), plus 5 to 10 minutes. But bear in mind the rule on cooking large fish given above. For serving cold it is often best to let it cool in its wrapping.

Grilling Fish

The smell of fish tends to cling to a grill; a sheet of foil over the grid – with the edges turned up to stop the juices running off – prevents that. For grilling, fish should be de-scaled (below) and dried well, and thick skin should be slashed in places. Flat fish need 2 to 6 minutes a side; round fish and steaks take 4 to 7 minutes a side. But steaks tend to become dry and are much better baked in foil.

De-scaling a Fish

Fish can have the scales removed if they are large and would feel unpleasant in the mouth in a dish in which the skin is eaten. Just hold the fish firmly by the tail (dipping your fingers in salt gives you a better grip) and run the back of a knife firmly up the fish *from tail to head* until the scales come off. Then rinse well and dry.

Keeping Fish and Shellfish

Spanking fresh, fish is firm and delicious; as time passes the flavour fades and the flesh gradually becomes soggy and woolly. So, though fish will usually keep for 2 days in a refrigerator without going bad, at below 50 °C it may be little pleasure to eat at the end of that time. The only exceptions are plaice, skate and lemon sole which develop a better flavour by their third day out of the sea – but remember they may have had 3 days out before you

Addresses and suggestions for further reading are at the ends of chapters.

buy them. All fish keep best on an open plate in the refrigerator.

If you have to keep white fish a day longer than you should, sprinkle salt all over it, but rinse this off before cooking. If fish is a touch older than it should be, but still safe to eat, it can be redeemed by firmly rinsing any slime off the skin under a cold tap and then wiping with equal parts vinegar and water – then cook it at once. But this should only be done if fish is *just beginning* to age – and never with any shellfish.

Shellfish are even more fragile than other fish. Mussels, clams and similar molluscs should be eaten the day you buy them. Prawns, lobsters and other crustaceans should be eaten in 1 to 2 days. But you can never tell how fresh they are when you buy them. So if they even begin to smell other than sweet and fresh throw them away.

It is no coincidence that the fish which are smoked are the oily ones which generally keep least well when fresh. Even when smoked they should be eaten within 3 days, and though they will freeze, they need to be eaten quickly as they rapidly go rancid. Rancid smoked salmon is vile beyond belief and a dreadful waste.

Skinning and Filleting Fish

Skinning and Filleting Whole Flat Fish
Sole is sometimes half skinned, removing only the dark side. So start there. For Dover sole cut a crosswise slit in the skin near the tail. Wiggle your fingers inside to loosen the skin from the flesh as much as possible. Then hold it with a cloth or dip both thumbs and forefingers in salt. Hold the tail firmly with one hand and rip the skin from tail to head with the other. Do the same on the other side. For plaice and lemon sole you reverse this and start at the head end and peel the skin off diagonally downwards, but you need to both cut and pull or flesh may come off with the skin.

Flat fish make four fillets. Lie the fish flat and cut through the flesh down the length of the spine. Hold it flat and cut the flesh carefully off the bones, working from the slit out to the edge, until one fillet is free. Repeat for the other three fillets. If you need to skin fillets, proceed as for skinning round fish – below.

Skinning and Filleting Round Fish
With round fish the jobs are done in reverse order,

and you get two fillets per fish. Slice through the skin down the back from head to tail. Starting at the head end slide the blade close to the bones and cut the flesh carefully from them, working down to the tail. Free the fillet from the head and the tail. Repeat on the other side.

There are two schools of thought on skinning fillets; one says you lay the fish skin-side down, the other advocates skin-side up. Try it both ways and see which feels right for you. Either way the tail is towards you. I favour skin-side down, so place the skin-side on a board. With a very sharp knife cut the flesh from the skin at the tail end. Then hold the skin firmly between salted fingers and angle the blade of the knife into the gap between skin and flesh and half cut, half push the flesh from the skin, being very careful not to cut through thin skins like haddock.

Filleting Herrings
Slice through the flesh near the tail and head, at each side. Run your thumb firmly all along the spine, to loosen it from the flesh, with as many bones as possible.

Skinning eel
Raw eel is the very devil to skin. If you can possibly get it done for you, do so. If you have to do it, cut the skin right round the neck, and make a slit down the whole length. Hang it on a butcher's hook (if you have one) or get someone to hold the head *very* firmly; hold the edge of the skin with a cloth and yank the skin sharply off with all your might.

Fish with Special Needs

Crabs and Lobsters
Most crabs and lobsters are sold ready boiled, but if you acquire a live one it should be alive until the moment of cooking. It will live out of water for about 24 hours if it is kept moist. Cover it completely in a damp cloth or – better still – place it on damp sawdust and sprinkle damp sawdust all over without pressing it down. Putting ice with these creatures damps down their nervous system and makes them sluggish and easier to handle. But once a crab grabs you it will not let go unless

you sever its limb. A medium-sized crab serves 2-3, a lobster 2.

Cooking Crabs and Lobsters

There is no easy answer to which cooking method is least cruel. None of these creatures has a brain as we have. A crab has two nervous centres and a lobster has thirteen. So far there is no conclusive research to show how much they feel hurt, or whether one method is more or less hurtful than another: even the RSPCA doesn't know. The Universities Federation for Animal Welfare has looked into the matter, and recommends stabbing both a crab's nervous centres – as illustrated – just before cooking. However, they concede that not everyone can bring themselves to do that and there is no way of getting at the thirteen nerve centres of a lobster. In this case they say that plunging the lobster into boiling liquid, and holding it under, seems to be the least cruel.

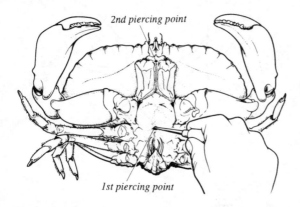

2nd piercing point

1st piercing point

To stab a crab lie it flat on its back, and thrust a strong skewer straight down into the hole which lies near the centre of the body. Stab it in and out, at slightly different angles, until the legs relax and stop moving. Next, pierce the other nerve centre by inserting the skewer below the mouth parts, as illustrated.

For once, kindness chimes with gastronomy, for chefs say that plunging the creatures into court bouillon also produces the best flavour. So plunge it in, turn down the heat, and cook it gently for 10-15 minutes per 450g (1lb). You may need to reduce the number of minutes per pound as you do in fish. One expert recommends 8 minutes a pound after the first pound.

Once cooked, both crabs and lobsters should be removed from the liquid and put in a cool place to chill, but they should not be icy cold on serving, as this kills their flavour.

Preparing a Cooked Crab

To open a crab, anyone who is not a judo black belt should put on an oven mit. Stand the crab on its flatter edge and give a swift karate chop, with the mittened hand, on the upper edge. This breaks the upper part from the lower. You can then lift the front and open it

up like a book. Clinging round the body there are grey fern-like structures called 'dead men's fingers' which should all be discarded – but they are nothing to be frightened of, despite the name. Also remove the tiny grey bag of the stomach, just behind the mouth. All the rest can be eaten. Serve it with good brown bread, mayonnaise, lemon wedges and a crisp salad. Few meals are nicer than one spent slowly picking the succulent flesh from a good crab, and savouring it morsel by morsel, as you can never do when it is dressed.

The small legs of a crab are best broken with nutcrackers; the claws need to be put in a plastic bag and hit gently with a hammer. Without the bag the pieces tend to ricochet about the room.

If you want to dress a crab, simply scoop the brown part out of the upper part of the shell and mash it with seasoning. Then pick every morsel of white from the body and legs – there is a great deal in the body if you cut it open. Rinse and dry the shell, and break off any surplus rim. Then combine both types of meat elegantly in the half shell and garnish it.

Preparing a Cooked Lobster

Split the lobster down its length, for serving, and remove the bag in the head and the intestine – which is a thin charcoal-grey line running the length of the tail. The greenish substance near the top is the liver and perfectly edible. Once cleaned, lobster can be served plain or briefly reheated with a sauce, but brevity is important or it becomes rubbery.

Crawfish (langouste) and Crayfish (écrevisse)

The situation on crayfish and crawfish is confusing. In Britain a crayfish is a fresh-water lobster, complete with claws. A crawfish is a clawless lobster which lives in the sea. However, in some other parts of the world they call the fresh-water ones 'crawfish', and the salt-water ones 'rock lobster'.

Crayfish are unusual among crustaceans in needing to be thoroughly washed and gutted before cooking. To gut them you twist the central section of the tail and pull, and the long tube of intestine should come away. It runs down the middle of the underside of the tail, and needs to be cut out if it doesn't come away as it can make the fish bitter. Crayfish take 10 to 15 minutes per pound to cook in court bouillon as for lobster (see above).

Crawfish is cooked exactly like lobster, except that the shell is opened up on the underside, so the meat can be removed, sliced and put back in the trough created by the back.

Eel

Smoked eel is served skinned and filleted like smoked trout. Serve fresh eel according to the recipe.

Haddock

The best smoked haddock is pale creamy Finnan haddock, which should be plump and moist. There are also delicious little Arbroath smokies which are younger haddock heavily smoked to an almost brown tone. The worst haddock is the bright-yellow-dyed variety, and

Addresses and suggestions for further reading are at the ends of chapters.

watch out for fish which looks like haddock but isn't: 'smoked fillets' may be cod or haddock, and 'golden cutlets' may be whiting.

Smoked haddock can be over-salty. To cure this either bake it in water with a tablespoon of vinegar per pint (for inferior haddock), or (for good haddock) cook it in milk.

Herrings by Other Names

Bloaters are herrings which have been left whole, cured and smoked, with their guts in to give them a gamey flavour. Remove the guts before grilling. Like smoked mackerel, they keep badly.

Kippers are herrings which have been gutted, salted and cold smoked. The best kippers are undyed and the flesh is a soft creamy colour from natural smoking. These taste infinitely superior to the rest, which have been dyed a very nasty shade of yellow. Look for a plump oiliness to the flesh and a good smoky smell. If they are very salty poach them in milk, though they are usually grilled and only take 4 to 5 minutes to cook.

The most labour-saving and least smelly way to cook kippers is the traditional method of jugging. Cut off the heads and tuck them, on end, into a tall jug. Pour in boiling water right to the top and leave them for 6 to 7 minutes. Remove them and pat them dry before serving.

Buckling are herrings which have been hot smoked and, to my mind, are far more delicate and delicious than any other smoked herring. They are eaten cold, with sour cream and dill pickles, either whole or skinned and filleted – which is very easy to do. They also make a very good pâté.

Sprats are smoked baby relatives of herrings.

Mussels, Clams and Cockles

In Portugal you can see men standing by the hour up to their knees in the sea patiently pumping a flat-bottomed cockle net rhythmically to and fro in the sand to acquire these elusive molluscs. In Britain, though cockle gathering used to be much practised on certain parts of the coast, such diligence in search of food is a lost art, and the cry of 'cockles and mussels alive, alive 'o' has long since ceased to echo in London's streets. Fortunately, mussels and clams have not yet vanished from the scene. They must be absolutely fresh when you buy them. Then you can clean them and plump them up, if you wish, by putting them in water for a day *or* a night (not longer) with 2 cupfuls of porridge oats to each gallon of water.

To prepare them for cooking you rinse them well, swirling them around in several changes of water until no sand comes out. Then beard them. This is just a matter of scrubbing them clean, and pulling off any straggly bits visible on the outside of the shell. You may have to scrape the shell with a tough little knife to clean them, if washing and pulling aren't enough. As you do this check them over. It is only safe to cook and eat them if they are alive until you cook them. So discard any which:

- have cracked or chipped shells
- are open and fail to close in a minute or two after being tapped with the knife
- are closed and will let you easily open them with your fingers
- are unusually heavy – they may be full of sand, which will ruin your meal.

Cook them within the hour, or you will have to check for dead ones all over again. You need only heat them with a cup of white wine, shaking the pan with the lid on over fierce heat for about 5 minutes, until they open. But you can cook them with chopped onion and parsley, and add cream to the sauce if you wish.

> All shellfish of this type are filter feeders, which means that if they are in water contaminated by sewage or chemicals the contaminants will stay in their bodies. It is therefore unwise to gather mussels yourself unless it is in an area where there is no possible risk of contamination.

Oysters

Don't worry about there being an R in the month before you eat an oyster. The prohibition wasn't because it was bad for *you*, but because it was bad for the oysters. There are two types of oyster. The native ones spawn in British waters and may not be taken during the summer months when they are spawning. The smaller Pacific oysters are farmed in British waters but, though they will grow here, they wisely deem our chilly waters too spartan for their offspring and refuse to breed. So they have no closed season and can be bought all year.

Prawns and Shrimps

In Britain shrimps are often called prawns. To explain the difference: Dublin Bay prawns (also known as Scampi or Norwegian lobster) have a fairly tough shell and a pair of claws, like miniature lobster claws. Shrimps are thinner shelled, have no claws and come in three sizes. There are the tiny brown shrimps, which are so delicious with brown bread and butter, the slightly larger pink shrimp and the fleshy deep water shrimp, which is most often called a prawn.

If you are tempted to go prawning take a big fabric bag in which you can keep the prawns with plenty of seaweed: they will die in plastic from lack of air. Prawns have to be kept moist or they die. A dead or dying prawn is no joking matter because chemical changes take place in a slowly dying prawn which make it poisonous.

Cook your prawns as soon as you get them home. But first throw away any that don't look lively, or are beginning to look cloudy and pale pink – these are dead or dying. Live prawns are almost translucent. Have ready a pan of well-salted rapidly boiling water, with a lid, and prepare to put the lid on. Throw in the prawns and cover instantly – or they may jump out. Let the water return to the boil. When it has boiled for about 30 seconds and all the prawns have risen to the top, and are pink, remove the pan from the fire, drain the prawns and let them cool. Sprinkle them with salt to improve their looks and taste. This brief cooking should produce the best prawns you have ever eaten.

The timing above is for prawns which are about 8 to 10 cm (3 to 4 in) long and about the size of a finger or thumb. Shrimps are cooked in the same way, but will be ready even sooner.

Recipes often fail to specify whether they mean raw or cooked prawns or shrimps. The difference is important; their flesh goes rubbery and tasteless with overcooking. If any recipe suggests cooking prawns, as opposed to warming them through, you can assume they are meant to be raw. So you may need to adapt the recipe and just throw in cooked ones to warm near the end. It won't taste as good as using raw ones, but it is better than eating rubber.

Salmon

If you intend to cut a salmon into steaks, first arm yourself with a very sharp knife and a good knife sharpener. Nothing blunts a knife like fish skin and it is essential to keep the blade perfectly sharp or you will be pressing at the flesh and making it pulpy.

Nothing short of a guillotine will cut through the bones in a salmon's back, so the thickness of your slices is set by the length of the backbones. If necessary, feel with a sterilized hat pin to gauge the length of the bones. They are almost the same length from head to tail so, once you have the measure of them, it's no trouble at all.

Slicing a side of smoked salmon is a much slower job than it might seem. Give yourself plenty of time; it is not a job to leave until just before guests arrive. First, feel over the surface and meticulously remove every fine bone with tweezers. For elegance if the salmon has a seam of dark meat down the centre it is removed with a V-shaped cut before you start slicing. It is perfectly good to eat – though stronger and oilier in flavour than the rest of the flesh. Then take a thin-bladed, *very* sharp knife and start slicing towards the tail, cutting along the surface and making each slice as thin as paper. But don't worry if you can't match a master chef: it will taste no worse.

Scallops

A scallop is one shellfish which doesn't have to be alive until you cook it. Even so they are freshest and best if they are opened as you buy them and haven't sat around ready opened. If you buy them closed, slip a knife blade through any cranny between the two shells and run it round the edge. Only then try to prise the shell open. Slice the flesh carefully from the shell. Keep the nice circular eye of flesh, and the half crescent of orange and beige coral and discard all the thin slithery bits. Rinse the shell and the scallop briefly under a tap and it is ready to cook. If you wish you can also use the point of a knife to slit open the dark vein of intestine that runs through the coral and rinse it clean.

In a pan they need only the briefest of cooking (3 to 5 minutes at low to moderate heat) and the simplest of

presentation to bring out their delicate flavour. Scallops are cooked the moment the flesh becomes white and firm, and they should be served immediately. Overcooking or waiting spoils their flavour and texture. Bake them gently in a fairly low oven on their curved shells (fishmongers will give these to you if you ask) with a rub of butter, milk (or cream), seasoning and a scrap of parsley and garlic. No fuss, no washing up, and perfection.

Skate

The wings are the only edible part of skate, and their skin is covered in an almost gluey substance which must be scrubbed off with plenty of cold water. Skate is then poached in court bouillon (page 48) and skinned before serving.

Squid

To prepare a squid, cut open the body sac and remove the transparent 'bone' and any slithery bits – leaving only the flesh. Also peel off any loose skin from the outside. It is then usually cut in rings or slices. It can be battered and deep fried as they do in Spain and Greece, or cooked in white wine and tomatoes as a sauce for pasta.

Trout

Trout needs no attention – just grilling or frying – and can be wrapped in cleaned leek leaves to keep it moist during cooking.

Smoked Trout

Smoked trout is often served lamentably dry and fishmongers sometimes suggest this is in the nature of smoked trout. It isn't. It should be beautifully plump and moist. Serve it as it is, or filleted, with brown bread and a good horseradish sauce.

FOOD HYGIENE

From some television advertisements you'd think germs behaved like some demon army, scurrying everywhere and leaping at us and our families from all directions, hell-bent on spreading death and disease. They don't. Germs are lazy things and usually let us do their dirty work for them.

Of course, they can be carried on droplets in the air – a sneeze sprays them for a truly astonishing distance. But most germs don't walk if they can ride, so they let us kindly carry them to where they'd like to be. And most of us all too often do so.

The Bacteria in Food Poisoning

Whatever may be said to the contrary, most diarrhoea is caused by bacteria. Of course a little bit of dirt never did anyone any harm; but the important word is – *little*: a small contamination with bacteria doesn't stay small. In the right conditions food poisoning bacteria divide to produce double their number every 20 to 30 minutes. So 1 cell becomes 2 million in 7 hours, and 7,000 million in 12 hours – and some can multiply much faster. One cell would do you no harm – but a few million can. Thousands of people in Britain go down with food poisoning every year. Most get over it, but it can kill – especially the young and the old.

Food poisoning is like burglary – it needs opportunity and it needs time. The bacteria are there, in small numbers, in the environment most of the time – up our noses, in excreta, in our pets, and particularly in the raw meat we buy. To cause poisoning they need both food to multiply on and enough time, at the right temperature, to do so. Bacteria multiply well on: meat, poultry, fish, shellfish, milk products, eggs, rice, anything made with any of these.

Not Giving Bacteria an Opportunity
Food poisoning is a rapidly growing problem yet the rules for preventing bacteria getting on to the food are simple:

1 Hands should be washed before handling food if you have been:

- using the lavatory
- touching sites of infection, like spots, cuts etc
- using a handkerchief (or nose picking)
- touching pets
- handling other raw meat or fish
- doing dirty cleaning jobs which get bacteria on to the hands.

2 *Don't* let raw meat or fish:

- drip on to other food in the refrigerator
- touch other food in the refrigerator
- touch kitchen equipment (knives, boards etc) later used for cooked foods, without washing them in between.

3 Prevent flies, cockroaches or other pests and even pets contaminating food – by keeping it covered.

Not Giving Bacteria Time
However clean we are, some food will always come into our homes with food poisoning bacteria on it. Salmonella, in particular, are in many animal foodstuffs, and production line gutting means that they are often transferred out of the guts on to the flesh of poultry and meat. So it can be safer to avoid buying ham and other cooked meats, from a butcher – unless the shop is set up so the cooked meat is well away from the raw meat, and has different staff and different equipment.

As bacteria on food need both time to breed and the right temperature to breed at, the biggest single preventer of food poisoning is the refrigerator (see temperature chart opposite). To give bacteria the least chance:

- cool food as rapidly as possible (but don't put it in the refrigerator while hot or it will warm up the other food)
- put cooked food in the refrigerator as soon as it is cool: don't wait for it to get cold
- when cooked food isn't being actively used refrigerate it *all* the time; don't let it sit in the warm ready for the next person to take some
- if food is being kept warm do so at temperatures above those at which bacteria will multiply

- don't keep warming food up and cooling it down: if you make a big stew, heat what you need for each meal and keep the rest fridge cold or, better still, frozen
- if possible thaw frozen meat and poultry in the refrigerator or microwave, not by leaving them for hours in a warm kitchen
- remember neither refrigeration nor freezing kill bacteria; cold may just stop them multiplying, but each time the food is brought into the warm they start to multiply once more.

Be extra careful with poultry and with rolled joints, especially large ones. Rolling the outside to the middle carries bacteria from the outer part of the meat into the centre where they are unlikely to get enough heat to kill them, and where conditions are perfect for one major food poisoning organism (clostridium perfringens, see table on page 55) to grow. Both poultry and rolled joints must be fully thawed before cooking: unthawed areas may not get hot enough in cooking to kill food poisoning bacteria. And some bacteria only die at exceedingly high temperatures. Cooking is no substitute for hygiene.

How To Tell If Food Is Unsafe
It would be helpful if one could tell at a glance whether food was safe to eat. You can't always do so. The appearance of food is no sure guide to whether it is safe. Food can carry enough food poisoning bacteria to make you seriously ill while looking and smelling fresh and lovely. And raw meat can be smelly, and even taste unpleasant when cooked, without containing organisms which will do you harm. Though food can, of course, be both off and poisonous. Knowing you treated it correctly is the best guide.

★ It is a myth that highly spiced food, such as curry, can't carry food poisoning. Some spices are anti-bacterial, but food poisoning bacteria have been found living in tins of curry powder.

Some food poisoning bacteria can have a bacterial version of an afterlife. So when the main part of a bacterium dies it leaves the essence of itself behind in a minute spore which has extraordinary powers of survival, withstanding quite extreme levels of heat, cold and dehydration. Then, when conditions are more congenial, the bacterium is reincarnated from its spore. So you can kill the active part of every single bacterium in a piece of food only to have it become dangerous all over again when the bacteria are reborn from the spores, and multiply. Luckily, not all bacteria make spores, and even spores can be killed by certain temperatures.

★ Raw pet food often carries food poisoning bacteria: it should be well cooked before storing in your refrigerator or freezer.

The Temperatures Food-Poisoning Bacteria Like

Food poisoning bacteria vary in the temperatures they prefer, and in the temperatures needed to kill them. On the whole, they stay on the surface of solid meat, but they will penetrate cracks, such as the slight gap between two sections of muscle. So, for safety, the *centre* of the food must reach the required temperature and stay at it for at least 20 minutes. However, for the *food* to reach that temperature the oven must be far hotter.

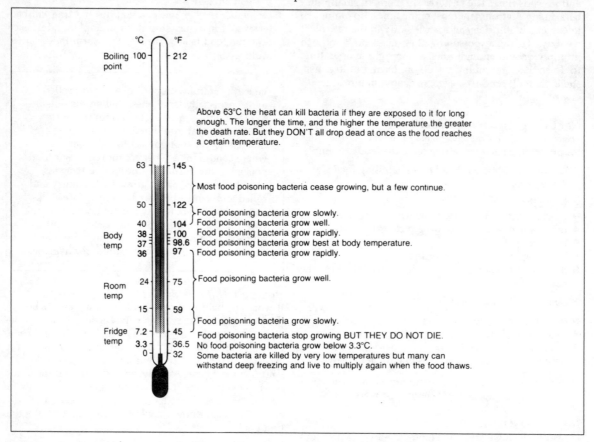

Other Hazards in Food Here & Abroad

Ciguatera

Ciguatera causes weakness and loss of sensation and can lead to paralysis and death. It is generally caused by eating large fish in the Pacific and Caribbean, and one theory is that a creature which produces a substance poisonous to man is eaten by small fish. Then lots of small fish containing it are eaten by middle-sized fish, and lots of middle-sized fish are then eaten by the big fish and the big fish is then very poisonous to us.

Diseases Carried by Food

Typhoid, paratyphoid, cholera and related infections can pass from person to person, so they are not strictly speaking food poisoning, but they also pass from human and animal (especially rodent) excreta into water. From there they can contaminate shellfish, food washed in contaminated water, ice made with it, and also cows (and their milk) if streams are contaminated. In less developed countries there is a danger that any food, or ice, may carry these infections.

Milk (and milk products) from cows and goats, which has not been sterilized or pasteurized, can contain the organisms which cause brucellosis (undulant fever). This is a serious disease which can make someone ill for months and even years. It has almost been stamped out in Britain, but overseas it is always wisest to boil untreated milk. Herds which are 'tuberculin tested' can still carry brucellosis and, even in Britain, there are several hundred cases a year. (Incidentally, it gets its name from a doctor called Bruce who first identified it.)

Moulds

There are at least 150 moulds which can produce substances which are harmful to men or to animals (mycotoxins). The best-known ones grow on bruised apples, peanuts and peanut butter and may cause cancer. Most peanut butter doesn't go mouldy but, if any does, throw it *all* away. The same applies to sauces, such as saté sauce, in which peanuts are an ingredient and to mouldy apples, apple puddings or apple juice.

The full range of moulds which can be harmful is still not known and it will be some while before we have any

Addresses and suggestions for further reading are at the ends of chapters.

Types of Food Poisoning

In Britain 70 per cent of those known to have had food poisoning can blame salmonella: not too surprising since there are over 2,000 types of salmonella. Next comes clostridium perfringens, then staphylococcus aureus and bacillus cereus. All the others are rare here.

	Bacillus cereus	Clostridium perfringens	Salmonella	Staphylococcus aureus
Source	Widely found in nature, especially on rice and other cereals. Not always killed in cooking. The bacteria multiply in rice kept for reheating. The most likely cause of food poisoning after a Chinese take-away.	Human and animal excreta, raw meat, fish, poultry, insects, dehydrated food. Typically causes illness when food has been cooked and left to cool too long in a warm room, then eaten cold or inadequately reheated.	In animals' guts – are transferred to the flesh when excreta spilled in slaughter. Poultry most likely carriers. Raw pet food and pets may be carriers, but tinned pet food should be safe. Also in human excreta and water or raw foods, polluted with sewage.	Mainly the skin and the nose, of carriers, also in boils, styes, spots, cuts and burns. It can be carried deep in the pores, so does not wash off easily. Most likely to contaminate cold meat, poultry and custards. Also comes in untreated milk from cows and goats.
Special characteristics	Multiply in moist conditions, with or without air, creating poisons in food. Prefer temperatures of 28°-35°C (82°-95°F) (more usual in a hot commercial kitchen than a home). Produces spores which can survive cooking.	Very hardy – spores can survive dehydration and boiling. Grow without air. Ideal temperatures 43°-47°C (109°-117°F), but up to 50°C (122°F), so multiply during long slow cooling and can release poison in the gut.	Can grow with or without air, and cause an infection.	Multiplies with or without air, forming a poison in the food as it does so.
Occurrence		Common in Britain and in many countries	Common worldwide.	Common in Britain and in many countries
Incubation	1-16 hours according to type.	8-22 hours	Usually 12-24 hours, 6-36 possible	2-6 hours
Symptoms	Violent vomiting and diarrhoea, stomach cramp, collapse; or just pain and diarrhoea.	Stomach pains, massive diarrhoea, nausea but seldom vomiting or fever.	Fever headache, aching limbs, diarrhoea and some vomiting. It can kill babies, the old, and the weak.	Severe vomiting, stomach cramps, diarrhoea, and possibly collapse, but rarely fatal.
Length of Illness	12-24 hours	24-48 hours	1-7 days	6-24 hours
Removing the Danger	Difficult: two different types of poison can be produced; one causes vomiting, the other diarrhoea. Former still active after 1½ hrs at 121°C (250°F).	Some forms are rapidly killed by cooking; but spores may not be killed by hours of boiling. To kill them needs temperatures of *over* 100°C (212°F) – only achieved in a pressure cooker.	Killed by cooking the food to a temperature above 55°C (131°F) for 20 minutes.	Killed quite easily by temperatures above 55°C (131°F). But the poison they create is only destroyed by temperatures *above* boiling point for 30 minutes — which requires a pressure cooker.

clear picture of which moulds are harmful to man and which aren't. Excellent as organically grown food may be in other ways, it is worth remembering that, as it has not been treated with fungicide, it needs more careful storage if moulds are not to be a problem.

The standard advice is that if jam becomes mouldy you can remove the mould, plus half an inch of jam under it, and eat the rest. But any jam which is liable to go mouldy is best kept in a refrigerator and eaten before mould appears.

Mould is so much part of the nature of cheese that it is reasonable to assume that if some cheese like cheddar goes mouldy it is safe to cut off the mould and eat the rest. But only time, and more research, will tell whether this is correct.

Shellfish

Mussels, and similar shellfish, can be poisoned when they consume large quantities of plankton, popularly known as the Red Tide, which contain a poison. These plankton occur mainly off the east coast of America and Canada, but they are also found off parts of Scotland and Yorkshire. Eating such mussels causes weakness and vomiting and can be fatal.

★ Certain combinations of food can give some people symptoms very similar to food poisoning. Combining spirits and shellfish is a common one.

Travellers' Food Poisoning

Reading the preceding pages should alert travellers to the major hazards. The risk depends entirely on the country, but it is easy to get mild food poisoning, when travelling, simply because each bacterium has numerous slightly different versions. So though you may be immune to your local variety of a bacterium, like escherichia coli, a new version can trigger diarrhoea. On top of that, less developed countries may combine unhygienic practices with unpurified water and inadequate refrigeration to create quite serious hazards. However, in most places which seem unhygienic the worst can be avoided with simple precautions.

● Stick to *freshly* cooked food – not cold food or dishes which may have been rewarmed.
● Keep to bottled drinks, even for teeth cleaning (preferably bottled in a hygienic country), or use water sterilizing tablets such as Boots' Sterotabs.
● Take no ice.
● Peel all fruit.
● Don't eat shellfish.
● Be wary of milk and milk products; they may be unpasteurized and carry TB or undulant fever.
● Avoid salads, unless you are sure the hygiene is good and the water they are washed in is clean.
● Avoid undercooked meat and fish.

Obviously, clean restaurants are better than dirty ones. But in countries where food hygiene isn't really understood, and cleanliness may not extend to the kitchen, it can sometimes be safer to eat from a stall, where you can see the raw food being cooked in front of you, than in a large hotel where the food may pass through more (potentially contaminated) hands and sit around for longer in the warm.

FROZEN FOOD, FREEZING AND FRIDGES

How long food will keep in a fridge or a freezer depends on the temperature you run it at. Food safety experts say a fridge should be run at – 0°C to – 4°C, and that freezers should be kept at – 18°C to – 23°C.

Defrosting

Freezers need to be defrosted when the layer of ice inside is about 1 cm (½ in) thick. You can scrape most of it off with a plastic spatula with the freezer filled and running. But every few months turn it off, remove the

food and thaw the freezer. You can speed up the job by standing bowls of hot water in it – though *not* on any working parts. In the meantime, keep the food in a refrigerator, or in the big insulated sacks from freezer food shops, and cover them well with newspaper and other insulation to keep out warm air. Run the freezer for about half an hour before replacing the food. Whatever the method, choose a cool day.

Freezing Fresh Food

Containers and Wrappings for Freezing

There are three types of food spoilage which can be prevented or slowed down by the right packing:

● loss of moisture
● oxidation from the effects of oxygen in the air (see page 57).
● picking up odours (and flavours) from other food.

So the best packing is a strong one which holds in moisture and keeps out air, and the air must be pressed out of containers.

The more closely containers can be packed together in a freezer, the better. So my favourites are the brick-shaped cartons used for fruit juice and milk. Put a freezer bag inside, pour in food such as soups or stews, tie up the bag, and freeze. The carton excludes more air than a bag alone.

Foil contains smell well and is specially recommended for fish and cheese, but the standard kitchen type is thinner than is ideal, and very easily pierced. For long storage you need heavy duty foil of around 0.03 mm, but you'll have a job finding it. It's far easier to wrap food in foil and put it inside a plastic bag for extra protection. Any acid in food eats into aluminium – which means it's probably getting into the food itself, so put a plastic film under.

★ Glass containers are risky, unless the glass is designed for freezers.

★ Lined tins such as coffee tins with air-tight plastic lids are good – if you doubt the lining, put a plastic bag inside. Nothing which could rust should be near food.

★ Baking tins can be frozen with pastry in them – but some tins may rust, so line them.

★ Freezer bags closed with a clothes peg are easiest for stiff hands to undo.

Labelling Frozen Food

The cheapest label is a piece of masking tape on which you write with a marker pen. The vital information is the type of food, the date and the quantity (e.g. 2 pork loin chops 5.6.93). Once frozen, it can be hard to see what's what, even in a clear plastic bag.

Packing Food for Freezing

I learnt the hard way that it was far better to divide food into portions for one or two – which allows one to thaw as many as one needs. Any items which may need to be removed individually should have two pieces of greaseproof paper between each one. Then you can slide a

---

Addresses and suggestions for further reading are at the ends of chapters.

knife between the two layers of paper to separate them and speed thawing.

Food expands as it freezes, so allow headroom in containers or they will crack or push off their lids. This doesn't apply to bags – so press as much air as possible out of them. Air is the great damager of frozen food, so pack food to make the air spaces between loose food as small as possible.

Freezing Techniques

Freezing techniques are designed to help the food keep its shape and minimize the ill effects of freezing. Which you use depends on the type of food but food for freezing should be in prime condition.

1 Berries keep their shape best if rinsed clean, spread on a baking sheet and frozen, then packed in containers. Plums can be rinsed, stoned, packed and frozen.

2 Fruit which would go brown if sliced and frozen (e.g. apples, pears, sliced peaches) can be blanched (see page 97) for 1 to 2 minutes in water or steam, chilled and packed.

★ Some people suggest freezing raw fruit in loose sugar or in a sugar syrup. As sugar draws the juices out of fruit this is just what you *don't* want. If fruit won't freeze well by methods 1 or 2 cook it before freezing instead.

3 I am told that fruit which needs blanching will also keep well after dipping in solutions of ascorbic acid (vitamin C) or lemon juice. I have never bothered with this – but if you want to try it dip the fruit in a solution of 1,000 mg per 250 ml (½ pt) water, pack and freeze immediately. Alternatively, use the juice of a lemon in 500 ml (½ pt water.)

4 Vegetables need to be prepared and blanched in water or steam (see page 97), or cooked in some other way. Blanching stops the action of enzymes which, even at very low temperatures, slowly make them taste 'off'. For easy access to loose vegetables treat them like berries above. If you are only going to keep a vegetable for a week or two you can use method 1. But don't risk this with cabbages, sprouts or broccoli or they will stink.

5 Meat simply needs to be bagged, or wrapped, chilled and frozen. It keeps best if excess fat is trimmed off.

6 Fish can be treated like meat but is best in cling film and then foil. If a fish is *very* special it may be worth using an ice glaze. For this you freeze it unwrapped then dip it in iced water, so the water freezes on it in a thin coat and freeze again. Repeat this 2 to 3 times until the ice coat is 3 mm (⅛ in) thick. Wrap it carefully in foil without cracking the glaze.

Putting Food to Freeze

Slow freezing and unstable freezer temperatures both badly affect the look and texture of frozen food: large ice crystals form inside the food and break down its texture. So ideally food should be frozen at – 21° to – 23°C (– 5° to – 10°F). The other rules for freezing food from fresh are as follows.

● Only one tenth of a freezer's space should be used for freezing food from fresh in any day.
● Set the freezer to 'fast freeze' an hour or two ahead. If you only have a thermostat a good temperature is between – 21° and – 23°C (– 5° and – 10°F). Keep it on fast freeze for about 18 hours if you have put several items in to freeze.
● Chill the food in the refrigerator before putting it in the freezer.
● Freeze food in the coldest part of the freezer: a fast freeze compartment, the bottom parts or close to walls.
● Don't put food you are freezing next to already frozen food, or it will increase spoilage.

Ill Effects of Freezing

Freezer burn: This leaves food looking much paler and means that water has left the surface of the food, making it tough and dry, and probably rancid. It is most likely to happen if there is a hole in the container and high protein foods such as meat, poultry and shellfish, are the most vulnerable.

Reduced setting: If frozen fruit is used in jam making it will set less well than fresh fruit because freezing affects the pectin. So extra pectin must be added.

Oxidation: interaction with air can turn fats rancid. Other food discolours or loses fat-soluble vitamins. Oily fish and pork are especially vulnerable.

Keeping Times

On the storage of food which you buy frozen there is only one thing to say – *follow the manufacturer's instructions.*

If food is stored at the standard freezer temperature (page 58) it will be safe to eat however long you keep it, *but* it will only be *enjoyable* for a relatively limited time. This is because chemical alterations slowly occur which affect food's colour, texture and flavour. On top of that, the action of freezing affects the structure of food, and fluctuations in freezer temperature every time you open the door aggravate this. So the longer food is kept, the less delectable it becomes.

Different experts give different storage lives for food. The truth is that storage life is never certain. It couldn't be, because it depends on so many unpredictable factors, like how often you open your freezer and whether it's in a warm or a cold place. The following are maximum storage times within which, on average, food should be reasonably pleasant to eat. Try to eat it before the lower figure – if there are two – by the upper one it may only be much less of a pleasure. The times are for raw food in a domestic freezer at about – 18°C.

★ Freeze egg whites in an ice cube tray for easy access.

★ If you add 2 teaspoonfuls of gelatine to each 500 ml (1 pt) of cooled fruit mixture, when making sorbets, the sorbet will hold its iciness for longer when you serve it.

Keeping Times for Food in a Domestic Freezer at About −18°C

Food	Months	Comments
Bacon joints and rashers not vacuum packed	1	
Bacon rashers vacuum packed	6	
Bacon joint vacuum packed	3	
Beef	12	
Bread	3-6	The richer doughs keep least.
Cakes	3-9	The less fat, the longer the keeping time. Fast freeze decorated cakes unwrapped, and wrap when the icing is hard.
Casseroles	3-4	Cooked and containing meat or poultry.
Cheese (hard)	6-9	Tends to go crumbly, best grated.
Chicken	9-12	Fatty birds keep the shorter time. Giblets only keep 3 months.
Cooked sliced meat	2-3 wks	It becomes very dry on long keeping and must be well packed.
Cream, whipped	2-6	Separates unless whipped. Both whipping cream and double cream at over 40% butter fat will usually freeze. Either keeps best with a little sugar in.
Duck	3	
Egg, whole or yolks – beaten whites	6 / 12	Add a good pinch of *either* salt or sugar per whole egg, less for a yolk. Whites need nothing added.
Fish: shellfish / white fish / oily fish	1-3 / 6 / 3	Try to eat it well before this.
Fruit: in sugar or syrup	9-12	Usually holds its flavour well, but the texture of soft fruit with thin skins spoils easily. Berries (e.g. currants) with firm skins freeze best and may keep even longer.
plain / juice / sorbet	9 / 4-6 / 1-2	
Game	4-6+	
Goose	4-6	
Hare	6-8	Salt the blood lightly and store separately for jugged hare.
Ice cream	1-2	The foam structure begins to break down after that.
Lamb	9-10	
Mince	2-3	
Offal	2	
Pancakes	4-6	Home-made layered with greaseproof.
Pastry	6	Flaky pastry even improves with freezing. Choux pastry should be cooked first.

Addresses and suggestions for further reading are at the ends of chapters.

Food	Months	Comments
Pâté	1	
Pies	3-4	Cooked pies containing meat or fruit.
Pork	9	
Potato (chips)	4-6	
(crisps)	3	Store in a box to prevent breakage.
Sandwiches	1	
Sausages	3	Sage tend to keep their flavour longest.
Spices in food	3-4	After that some alter their flavour.
Turkey	9	As chicken.
Veal	9	
Vegetables	6-12	If blanched.
Venison	6-8	
Yeast pastry	3-6	If cooked.
Yeast – fresh	3	Freeze well wrapped and pre-cut into 25g (1 oz) pieces.

Nutrition and Frozen Food

Vitamin C starts being lost from the moment vegetables are picked. But it is lost fastest under warm conditions (in 5 days peas lose a third of it). So fresh vegetables, which have spent time in the shop, often have less vitamin C than those which have been picked and frozen. But vitamin C continues to be lost while they are frozen. However, the lower the temperature and the shorter the time they are kept, the less will be lost.

Organizing Frozen Food

It is all too easy to keep using the food nearest you in the freezer (often the newest) only to find, months later, that the food at the back is past eating. There are two good ways to keep track of things. One is an exercise book divided into sections (say – starters, meat, fish, vegetables, fruit and puddings, other), and cross off as you use food. Another method is always to write two labels – one for the food and one for the door or lid of the freezer (work down or across the door to indicate newness). You then remove a label from the door as you remove the food (masking tape removes easily, other labels may not). This looks perfectly awful, but I found my children managed to remove labels, whereas a list in a book was totally ignored after the first week.

Power Failure and Doors Ajar

Don't think all your food has spoiled if there's a power cut. *Keep the freezer door shut;* then none of the cold is lost. If the power cut is in cold weather the temperature in a

freezer will hardly change in several hours, and the food will be fine for a while.

1 If the food is icy in the centre and only thawed at the edge you can refreeze it, but when you thaw it next time remember its life will be shorter.
2 If it is fully thawed but cold you can refreeze bread, raw pastry, fruit and cakes. Raw meat and fish can be cooked immediately and refrozen. Other food will be as it would be after a similar time in a larder.
3 If the food is warm it will have been thawed a good while and it is safest to destroy all precooked dishes, meat, fish and vegetables. But fruit may be edible and can possibly be refrozen after cooking. Bread and cakes may also be refrozen if they look and smell all right – unless they have cream in.

★ Most freezer centres can tell you how to take out insurance against accidents which ruin frozen food.

★ As a precaution, keep a bag of ice cubes in the top of your freezer. Then if there is a cut you can look at the ice cubes afterwards. The amount they have melted will show you how much your food must have thawed, and help you decide what must be done. This is also useful if your family tends to leave the door ajar.

Refreezing Thawed Food

People say you can't refreeze thawed food. You can. Manufacturers put 'never freeze once thawed' on packets for two reasons. First, thawing and refreezing causes more damage to the texture of food than freezing once and they don't want their product looking tacky. Second, every time food thaws it reaches temperatures at which harmful bacteria can multiply *if they are in the food* (they may not be). So the more thaws it undergoes, the greater the risk.

Safety depends on what happens to food when it's *out* of the freezer. If you observe the rules of hygiene (page 52) and make pâté, freeze it immediately, thaw it, put it in sandwiches and freeze them immediately, you will have safe sandwiches when you thaw them. *But if you* let the pâté sit about going bad, or infect it with food poisoning bacteria and then leave it in the warm freezing won't kill the bugs for you. The double thawing will mean two periods in the warm when the bacteria can breed. So if your family gets the trots once you buy a freezer don't blame the freezer, improve your hygiene.

Thawing

The worst effects of thawing are from 'drip' – the loss of liquid from the food because cells have been damaged by freezing, which makes meat seem tough and soft fruits soggy. So, ideally, food should be cooked as soon as it is thawed. The rule is the faster it was frozen, the faster it should thaw.

Will it Freeze Well?

Don't be misled into thinking you can only freeze special freezer recipes. Most food freezes well. The following foods *don't*.

Aspic loses its texture.
Apples cannot be frozen whole and raw.
Bananas go black – but are still fine for banana bread.
Bread dough is hard to freeze well in a domestic freezer.
Celery loses its crunch but all right for cooking.
Cream cheese: the fat separates from the water.
Cloves tend to become stronger with freezing.
Cornflour tends to separate, leaving the liquid thin again.
Custard and custard-style puddings tend to separate (cooked quiche).
Eggs: boiled, poached and fried eggs lose their texture. Freeze raw eggs separately.
Garlic: this can make food taste 'off' after freezing.
Gelatine takes on a nasty texture, but it isn't noticeable in mousses and other mixtures into which air is beaten.
Icing: boiled sugar types become sticky.
Jelly loses its jel.
Mayonnaise separates.
Melon can't be frozen whole, and pieces go soggy.
Meringue weeps.
Milk: the fat separates from the water unless homogenized but you can still cook with it. (Don't freeze in a glass bottle.)
Pears vary in their reaction to freezing, test your variety.
Potatoes: boiled ones may go watery.
Salad vegetables: lettuce, cucumber, radishes, endive, chicory all go inedibly soggy.
Tomatoes go soggy but are great for sauces.
Vanilla: if synthetic, becomes overpowering. Pod vanilla is fine.
Yoghurt separates on thawing unless highly sweetened. Even sweet ones need beating afterwards.

Using Frozen Food Compartments

Frozen food compartments are not the same as freezers. Only those which bear the symbol ★ ★★★ can freeze food from fresh. The others should only be used for keeping pre-frozen food because they are not as powerful as a freezer. How long any such compartment will keep frozen food depends on its star rating.

★ – 6°C (21°F)   keeps frozen food 1 week
★★ – 12°C (10°F)   keeps frozen food 1 month
★★★ – 18°C (0°F)   keeps frozen food 3 months (if the food will keep that long)

> Most freezers are also designed to run at – 18°C (0°F). They can keep food for far longer than frozen food compartments because the small size of the compartments means that putting unfrozen food into them raises the temperature far more than it would in a big freezer. The constant opening of a fridge door also causes variations in temperature which spoil frozen food more quickly.

FRUIT AND NUTS

Nowadays you can buy most fruit at almost any time. As each one goes out of season in one country it comes into season in another, and we import it. But those which are grown in Britain do have peak times when they are considerably cheaper, and even some imported fruit is more plentiful at one time than another. Fresh nuts, such as cob nuts or wet walnuts are the most strictly seasonal of all, only appearing for a couple of weeks each autumn. In their shells nuts may keep for months but become ever drier with age. So store them away from heat. But not in a musty cellar or near other smells or the nuts will taste like the smell. If they do dry out, soaking and cooking them after shelling is another way to put them to use. Though you will need to remove the skins (see Blanching, page 97)

Shelled nuts are a convenience food in every sense but will go rancid if kept for too long in the warm. If a big bag tempts you, keep it in the freezer. You might also try treating nuts like a vegetable – as they do in India and the Middle East. For example, peanuts, cashews and almonds can all be added to a casserole or stir fry, giving extra flavour, plus a soft crunch and extra protein, or soaked overnight in water and then cooked in a sauce.

With the current emphasis on avoiding sweets and saturated fats, dried fruit and nuts are due to play a larger part in our diets. Once children are old enough not to choke on them, dried fruit can be far better for them than sweets. For fruit provides real goodness, from vitamins, minerals and roughage, which sweets don't. However, most extra moist dried fruit carries an extra load of chemicals to prevent mould. And other dried fruit is often dusted with sulphur dioxide to stop it browning or to lighten its colour. As sulphur can affect some people it is wise to pick sulphur-free fruit for children. Sulphur is rarely used on prunes, figs or raisins (except bleached 'golden' raisins). Some shops also sell un-sulphured apricots but they may look much browner and less appetizing than those with sulphur.

Apples

A far wider range of apples can be found through farm shops and Pick Your Own places than you can buy in shops. When picking apples cup them underneath, lift and twist slightly. If they are ready for picking they should come free. Place them gently in a basket; if they are banged and bruised there will be no keeping them.

As each apple has distinct characteristics, noticing how each type of apple behaves, and choosing the right one for the job, rather than always using some all-purpose cooking apple, makes it very much easier to get good results. The beloved British Bramley, for example, is perfect for baked apples or apple snow, but its tendency to break up makes it a poor apple for tarts or blackberry and apple. Yet the French Golden Delicious, so dreary as eaters, really are delicious cooked in tarts, and keep their shape perfectly.

When eating apples it is worth exploring their affinity with cheese. Not for nothing are the apple growing areas of Britain close to some of the best cheese making ones. For almost every British cheese there is an apple which suits it to perfection – Cox's with Cheddar, and Red Worcesters with Double Gloucester are only two of the lovely combinations.

Apricots

There is a luscious and exotic air to ripe apricots. They not only make beautiful puddings and pastries but their pervasive sweet-sour flavour goes excellently with duck, pork or lamb. Choose those which are firm and glowing and deepest in colour to eat raw. If you cook them the flavour is greatly improved by using vanilla sugar or even a little pure vanilla essence in the cooking water. But keep the water to a minimum or the final dish will be too watery. They poach beautifully in a low oven, but tend to go brown if microwaved too slowly.

I was first persuaded to buy the dull-looking little brown dried Hunza apricots by a man running a fruit stall on a station platform in south Wales. They are a real find, with a beautiful flavour that more than makes up for their lack of looks. But pick them over before soaking, discarding those with holes as they may be inhabited. Soak and cook them without adding sugar or they will be too sweet. Ordinary dried apricots are perfect if simply soaked for 2 to 3 days with no cooking.

Asian Pears

Delicious, though pricey, these combine the shape and crunch of an apple with the colour, skin and juiciness of a pear and have a flavour between the two. Treat them like an apple or pear.

Babaco

Mid-green, turning golden yellow as they ripen, babacos are rather like marrows, but pointed at one end and with flat sides, like a pencil. They also have a marrow-like skin and a thick layer of flesh around a central hollow. The juicy flesh has a soft, almost scented flavour. Discard the woolly centre and eat it with the skin on or pare it off, thinly. Although refreshing chilled it's best offset by other flavours in a fruit salad – and quickly bulks one out.

Bananas

Bananas should never be put in a refrigerator as the cold blackens them. However, if they do become black for any reason they are still perfectly good to eat. But if you find them unappealing you can peel and freeze them as they are, for use in milk shakes or banana bread – which is one of the best of tea breads. Bananas are also delicious grilled or barbecued in their skins (discarding the skins after cooking), or peeled and baked with butter, brown sugar and a hint of rum.

West Indian recipes often call for plantain. This is a variety of banana that does not become sweet even when ripe, but sweet bananas can be cooked like plantain when they are green.

Blackberries

Blackberries are rich in names, being called brambles, brumbleberries, brumble-kites and even 'lawyers'. They are at their best early in the season when the tip blackberry in each spray ripens, those that come later are fine for jam but never have the full rich flavour of the master berry. This is perhaps why old wives spun the tale that it is unlucky to eat them after Michaelmas – 29 September – 'when the devil tramples on them'. Try soaking fat sweet ones in whisky for a night and eating them with cream. They freeze excellently.

Blueberries and Bilberries (whortleberry, blayberry)

Up to twice the size of a currant, blueberries are the big American brothers of our currant-sized European bilberries (by any name) but both have the colour and bloom of a black grape. When ripe they can be rinsed and eaten and have a distinctive but subtle flavour, and soft 'redcurrant' type flesh. In the Auvergne in France they use them in delicious tarts, in the USA in muffins and pancakes. Needing only a quick rinse before using, they are good as a garnish, or in fruit salads, or as jam. Unfortunately, hard sour unripe blueberries look just like ripe ones. So buy carefully. Those from America store a day or so in the fridge, but the thinner-skinned European ones spoil quickly.

Cherries

Cherries have so brief a season that they need to be used to the full. When buying always ask to taste – looks can be deceptive. But if they are sour, and you have a yen for cherries, make a pie with them, you may accidentally have bought one of the sour cherries, such as morellos, which are sold only for cooking, or as a dried fruit.

Cherries go mouldy fast, especially after rinsing. Store them in the refrigerator and rinse them only when you need them. To stone cherries for a tart scald a hairpin and poke the U of it into the stem end and hook the stone out; or use an olive stoner to push them out.

Chestnuts

Shelling Nuts
Don't believe those who say you should boil chestnuts before shelling them – it's a quick route to broken nails and a frayed temper. Instead cut a slit across the bump from side to side and pop them in a hottish oven until the slit just widens into a smile. Remove a few at a time and, while still very hot, hold them with a cloth and press the corners of the slit together. If the nuts are firm and fresh the shell should crack off most of the nuts easily and the rest can be dislodged with a knife end. Once shelled, you can boil them for stuffing or cakes.

★ Microwaving is even better than a normal oven. A few at a time, they need about 40 seconds on 700 watts.

★ Brazil nuts are far easier to shell when well chilled after several hours in the freezer.

Citron
Like enormous green lemons these are too sour to eat, but make the most delectable candied-peel of all.

Coconuts
Coconuts need to be bought just as carefully as fruit. Shake a coconut before you buy it. It should have liquid inside and three dry eyes. To open it use a hammer and strong skewer to make holes in two eyes, and pour out the milk – surely one of the most perfect drinks in nature. Then crack the nut open with a hammer. The flesh will freeze but, being fatty, not for long. If you find a green coconut try it. The soft jelly-like flesh is wonderful. For cooking, many Asian shops sell tins of coconut milk or blocks of creamed coconut which replace their fresh alter egos very well.

Crab Apples
If you have acquired a garden with a crab apple tree, and are wondering whether you can make crab apple jelly, the answer is: you can. Kew Botanical Gardens tells me that all types of crab apple are safe to eat – but some are very much better than others.

Cranberries
The secret of a good cranberry sauce is to use just a few spoonfuls of liquid and only add the sugar after the berries have cooked to tenderness. Adding it sooner toughens their skins. When adding the sugar do so little by little, tasting as you go – curiously there comes a point when more sugar increases rather than reduces their bitterness.

Currants
Currants store best rinsed, stripped from their stalks and sprinkled with caster sugar. Like this, they keep for several days in a refrigerator and the sugar draws out enough juice to bathe them, without bleeding the firmness from them. Once the juice runs they are perfect just as they are – with thick cream or stew them gently. To strip them quickly pull the stalk between the prongs of a fork.

Custard Apple (Soursop, Cherimoya, Annona)
This is really a whole family of very similar apple-sized fruit, some round, some pear shaped, with greenish rough or indented skin. Though rather fragile the custard apple's bumpy green and cream skin, petched with brown when ripe, would suit a dinosaur. But inside a delicious, soft, slightly acid pulp surrounds dark seeds. You just halve the fruit and eat it with a spoon, discarding the seeds.

Damsons
Damsons are a hedgerow fruit like a tiny black plum, but sometimes sold in the shops. The flesh is thin on a large stone but they make a delicious jam. But see box, below.

Dates
Worldwide there are scores of different dates, each differing in succulence and sweetness. More fresh dates are being imported. Try them if you can. But unless you like a little extra protein with your fruit it is wisest to cut open fresh dates before eating as they can be inhabited. If you chill them in the freezer, and bring them to the table very cold, it stops their sweetness being cloying. Dried dates cut most easily if you dip the knife in hot water between slices. So, indeed, does all candied and crystallized fruit.

Durian
Durians look like monstrous horse chestnuts and have a smell so overwhelming that, in the East, where they grow, it fills whole streets and causes the fruit to be banned from most hotels. You are unlikely to come across one in Britain but may be tempted to taste one abroad. Be careful: one of the oddities of this smelliest of all fruit is that it interacts with alcohol. To drink alcohol and eat durians in quick succession – or together – can make you seriously ill. To eat one you split it open and scoop out the pulpy white flesh which lurks in pockets. Whether you will find it heaven or hell is a matter of taste, but indifference is impossible.

Elderberries
In late summer the glistening flat heads of these tiny black berries hang in hedgerows all over Britain. They can be added to fruit salads, put in tarts or pancakes or cooked, sieved and made into a sauce. But see box below.

WARNING: Hedgerow fuit, such as blackberries, damsons and elderberries, should only be picked if you are *sure* no chemical sprays have been used nearby. And only if there is no risk of picking a poisonous berry by mistake: deadly nightshade also has glossy black berries.

Addresses and suggestions for further reading are at the ends of chapters.

Figs

There is a world of difference between the soft sensuously-ripe figs one can buy in hot countries and most of their tight-lipped sisters sold in Britain. But look for ones which are well rounded and give when gently pressed. Rinse them well and place them in the sun or a warm room, for they are not at their best chilled. Eat them just as they are, all but the stalk, or slice and serve them with cream delicately flavoured with Pernod – a strangely good combination.

Guavas

Fresh guavas seem related to their tinned selves only in scent. They need to be bought carefully for the guava is unusual among fruit in giving off a strong odour long before it is ripe. And an unripe guava is a rocky and disappointing affair. Only buy ones which 'give' slightly as you press them. Either pare off the skin and slice them, or cut them in half and scoop out the flesh. You can also halve them, scoop out the seeds (eating them some other way) and fill the hollow with other fruit and perhaps whipped cream.

Gooseberries

Gooseberries only store for a day or two, even in the refrigerator. To prepare them simply rinse them and use a sharp knife to snick off the parts which stick out at either end.

Whether gooseberries should be eaten raw or cooked depends more on ripeness than on type. Those which are plump and soft when pressed can be eaten raw. Those which are hard can be stewed with sugar for puddings or used in savoury sauces. But they are at their best cooked with elderflower.

If a recipe calls for puréed gooseberries do not liquidize them, the pips will create nasty wood chips; either mash them for a rough purée or rub them (tediously) through a sieve.

Grapefruit

One shouldn't have to do battle to extract the segments from a half of grapefruit at table. To avoid this run a sharp knife round the grapefruit just inside the outer skin of the segments. Then slip the knife down between the skin and the flesh to each side of every division and quickly cut them apart. Each half segment can then be eaten whole and skinless.

Grapes

There is no easy way to peel grapes; just pick ripe ones, but the seed can be hooked out with the scalded bend of a hairpin or kirby-grip.

Kiwanos (horned melon, jelly melon, horned cucumber)

These make a better decoration than a delicacy. Shaped like pear-sized golden rugger balls, with small horns all over them, they seem to promise exotic delights. Sadly, the brilliant green jelly within tastes like a dull cucumber mated with a dull melon.

Kiwi (Cape gooseberry)

One of the endearing things about the kiwi, apart from its prettiness when sliced, is that even when fully ripe it keeps for weeks in a refrigerator. If you find good ones at the right price, buy them for when you may need them. Store unripe fruit at room temperature until it ripens and has a little give when pressed. You can eat the skin, but the texture detracts from the fruit and it is easy to pull off those which are very ripe. It is a shame we don't have as charming a name for them as the French do, for in France they call them *souris vegetals* – vegetable mice. Use them raw in fruit salads, simply with one other fruit or as a garnish.

Kumquats and Limequats

The size of two fat olives, and looking like tiny oranges, ripe kumquats can be eaten skin and all, like a plum. They taste not unlike a tangerine and poached in syrup they are a wonderful addition to a compote or the basis for my favourite sauce for duck – although they are not, strictly speaking, a member of the orange family at all. The limequat is a cross between a lime and a kumquat and too sour to eat raw but makes a good garnis and can be cooked like a kumquat.

Lemons and Limes

The less air that circulates round a lemon, once cut, the better it keeps. To keep it longest, sit the cut side on a plate and put a glass over it. If you are using a lemon for juice it is useful to remove the zest, with a grater, zester or potato peeler, and freeze it for use later in cakes, apple pies, with stewed prunes, or for garnishing – according to how you removed it.

★ To get the most juice from these fruit warm them – in hot water, or a microwave.

★ Keep the squeezed halves of lemons in the refrigerator and stick your fingertips in them to remove smells from the skin.

Loganberries (boysenberries, dewberries, youngberries)

Loganberries (named after the US Judge Logan in whose garden they were found) are the grandparents of this complex family and are a cross between raspberries and wild blackberries. The rest result from further crosses. You can treat them all like blackberries or raspberries but they may be better stewed than raw.

Lychees

Lychees are one of the most delicious of fruit. Simply peel off the thin, pinky-brown leathery skin (the pinker the better) and eat the fragrant white flesh, discarding the stone. They need no addition, no elaboration, but are great in fruit salad or with strawberries. But damaged fruit has an acid tang.

Mangoes

When ripe, mangoes are golden or rosy, just soft to touch, and with a delicate perfume. If ripe keep them in a refrigerator, but unripe mangoes will ripen wrapped in paper in a warm kitchen, though they sometimes develop brown spots before they are fully ripe – and must be eaten at once for they will only spoil.

If a mango is really fresh and ripe you can slice round the middle, twist the two halves in opposite directions so that they separate from the stone. In Britain they seldom do. So the easiest way to serve this luscious fruit is to stand it on end and slice through the fruit at either side of the stone, to remove two shallow cups of flesh. Then cut across these in each direction, without going through the skin. They can now be pushed up, under the centre to open out the little cubes for eating with a spoon and fork. If you want to eat them less elegantly do it in the bath, for the juice runs everywhere.

Mangosteen

To enjoy a mangosteen: cut open the tomato-sized purplish-black leathery skin and inner pith. Then spoon up the fragrant and delicious white segments, discarding the stones.

Medlars

Medlars can't be bought, but you may come across a medlar tree. If you do, their curious feature is that they need to be picked and kept some weeks until they are bletted (soft). Then eat the brown mush with cream and sugar. I am told it is wonderful, but have never had the good fortune to find a medlar in fruit.

Melons

People say you should feel the end of a melon to see if it is ripe. This only works if everyone else hasn't been feeling it too – even the hardest melon softens if enough thumbs press it. So smell is a better guide. A distinct sweetness should waft from both the round and the rugger ball types – though it is weaker from the latter. In most round varieties there should also be a ring of cracking round the base of the stalk. These signs don't hold true for water melons, which remain odourless and rocky, so choosing them is pure guesswork. Having cut into a melon keep it very closely covered or it will lend its flavour unpleasantly to other foods near it.

Mulberries

Mulberries are lovely fruit. For picking them wear clothes which can stay stained – for it seems impossible to pick them from the beautiful spreading mulberry tree without others falling on you, and the stains may well be permanent. Serve the mulberries heaped on their own leaves (which are so loved by silk worms) with sugar and cream, or use them in summer pudding.

Nectarines

Nectarines offer everything a peach offers but without the nuisance of a furry skin. They taste similar, can be treated in the same way and ripen well in a warm room, but then go brown fast unless refrigerated.

Oranges

Oranges need no explanation, but people are sometimes puzzled about preparing them for salad. You do it like this. Slice the top from the orange with a sharp knife, cutting both pith and skin from the top segments. Then cut round in a spiral, removing both pith and skin, to leave a juicy outside. After that you can either slice it thinly into rounds or create skinless segments. For segments you run your knife down between a dividing skin and the flesh, repeat on the other side of the segment and free it. Continue round the orange until all the segments are freed. Prepared ahead of time and sprinkled with sugar they create their own juice. Grapefruit can be cut in the same way.

To make marmalade you need the sour Seville oranges. Some recipes combine them with eating oranges or other citrus fruit but eating oranges alone produce a flabby-flavoured marmalade which is no delight.

Papaya (paw-paw)

The papaya must surely be one of the ugliest trees in existence, with its solitary, almost leafless, stem and clusters of pendulous ripening fruit looking like so many green bottoms, but the fruit is delicious. In Britain they are seldom sold fully ripe, so keep them in a warm place until they turn golden and yield slightly when pressed. But if any soft patches appear the whole fruit must be eaten at once or it will quickly spoil. If the fruit is still unripe you can peel, dice and cook it briefly in a sugar and water syrup. Ripe papayas are best sliced open, like an avocado, and their glistening black seeds removed, before the flesh is eaten as it is, with lemon or lime juice sprinkled over. Papaya is a natural meat tenderizer.

Passion Fruit

Passion fruit look like shrivelled plums with particularly leathery skins. Cut them open and you find a cluster of seeds coated in delicate bitter-sweet pulp. Eat this as it is or fold it into cream for a delicate and unusual fool.

Peaches

A ripe peach is firm, but not hard under pressure. However, even ripe peaches can be unexpectedly tasteless if they have travelled badly. If you find you buy such fruit they can be salvaged if you peel and steep them in white wine and sugar. To peel, drop them in boiling hot water for a minute or two and then into cold water. The skin then slips off easily. To slice them make a series of cuts right through to the stone and the segments will fall off, if the peach is ripe.

Pears

Homer wrote of pears being one of the gifts of the gods and were it not for their habit of ripening rapidly, from perfect to soft and woolly, they would indeed be an ideal fruit. Keep bought pears in a refrigerator, bringing them into the warm a few at a time as you want them. Eat them with the softer cheeses, like Stilton and Brie, which are discordant with apples. Only the early varieties of pears ripen well on the tree. Pick the others as soon as they begin to soften round the stem. Keep them, well spaced, in a cool place until ripe. They freeze badly.

Pepino

Shaped like a monster plum, with a purple-streaked creamy skin these have an inviting sweet-sour flavour. Peel off the bitter skin and poach the sliced or diced flesh in sugar and water then eat it cold.

Pineapple

To check whether a pineapple is ripe try tugging out one of the leaves in its tuft. From a ripe pineapple they will come out easily.

The least wasteful way to remove the eyes is that practised by the thrifty Chinese on the street stalls of Penang. They carve diagonal Vs round the fruit, neatly removing the diagonally placed eyes. Then slice off the other skin more thinly. But it takes a sharp knife to do this. I find the flesh then tastes better cut thinly, as they do in parts of Africa, rather than in the doorstep slices we are used to.

Like paw-paw, pineapple contains an enzyme which breaks down protein. Unfortunately, this isn't as useful as it sounds because instead of making meat tender it makes it lose its texture. This enzyme also destroys gelatine. So, if you want to use pineapple in a dish with gelatine, boil the pineapple first to kill the enzyme or it will prevent the gelatine from setting.

Pitahaya

Looking rather like crimson kohl-rabi, when cut open pitahayas also have an astonishing purpley-pink inside, dotted with small black seeds. There is also a brilliant yellow variety. Either way, spoon up the flesh and you may find the colour is the most exciting thing about it, but a little sugar and lemon juice helps.

Plums, Greengages and Damsons

When cooking plums first slit them open, down their length, and check inside. They are more prone to caterpillars than most fruit and this is better discovered before cooking. Slitting also enables you – if you feel diligent – to remove and crack open the stones to add the kernels to the cooking fruit. Tedious though this operation is it lends a certain excellence to the final flavour, especially of damson cheese, though it is a job only a true gourmet undertakes.

Most plums freeze well, but remove the stones first or they may give an overwhelming flavour of almond during long storage, and cook them from frozen to prevent the fruit going brown.

It is hard to think of the sweet and delicately flavoured greengage as a plum, but plum it is. Which means it is just as easy to grow, making a small compact tree almost any garden could accommodate. It is a shame few gardens have one: few things are more delightful than freshly picked ripe greengages for breakfast. And, although you can stew greengages or make jam from them, they are so excellent fresh that such efforts are only worthwhile if there's a glut.

Pomegranates

Eaten by themselves pomegranates can be disappointing, but the shiny garnet seeds of pomegranate are one of the prettiest and easiest garnishes. If you simply pick a hole in the leathery skin, fish the seeds out as you need them, and cover the fruit with cling film a good pomegranate keeps several weeks in a refrigerator.

Prickly Pear

These are the golden, pink-tinged, fruit of a cactus. They can either be sliced open and the soft inner flesh scooped out, or you can peel off the skin and pith. To do either you need gloves, for fine hairs dotted on it penetrate the skin invisibly and are devils to remove.

Quinces

Quinces are one of the great fruit surprises, rocky and tasteless when raw but giving a beautiful flavour when cooked. First wash off the down which covers them. Then prepare them as directed in the recipe.

Quinces are so rare it is worth practising a little parsimony. If you have to peel and core them, keep the peel and core and boil them up. You can use the quince-flavoured liquid they yield for stewing apples. If you make quince jelly the quince has such strength of flavour that you can use equal amounts of apples and quinces (or even slightly more apples) and still have a jelly tasting purely of quince. This also improves the set. The purée which remains can make beautiful apple and quince snow, or fool, if you sieve it to remove the pips. Deep freeze it, if you can, to give the autumnal delights of quince at intervals through the winter.

★ Leave quinces about the house. The scent is delicious and, pear-like though they look, they have none of the pear's weakness of heart and will not go woolly.

Rambutan

In Malaysia rambutan stalls are vivid with the rose-pink and golden bunches. Fresh from the trees, their horse chestnut prickles erect, they look very different from the sad brown offerings which reach our supermarkets. But the taste, so close to that of lychees but somehow lacking their almost perfumed delicacy, is not so altered. They should simply be peeled and eaten.

Rhubarb

I am told that in forcing houses rhubarb can grow 5 cm (2 in) a day, and you can hear it growing. Poached in syrup thickened with potato flour, this uninviting stalk can be remarkably good, and rhubarb upside-down cake, made with the young rhubarb, is a good alternative to apple – if you add enough extra sugar.

Boiled up, the leaves and off-cuts produce an acid water that will clean aluminium and brass – which is why rhubarb should never be cooked in an aluminium pan (see page 66).

Sharon Fruit (persimmons, kaki)

A Sharon fruit looks like an orange tomato whose calyx has delusions of grandeur. It can be eaten when firm but, for the full flavour, ripen it in a warm room until almost squishy to touch, then slice off the top and eat the soft flesh with a spoon. It was from the rarer persimmon that Sharons were bred. Taste only their squishy perfection: they are inedibly sour until then.

Sloes

Traditionally, sloes were gathered after the first frost which softened them. Sloe gin was then made by simply washing the sloes, pricking them well, packing them in jars and pouring gin over to cover them. Like that they produce a very dry sloe-flavoured spirit, but about 350g (12 oz) sugar is usually added, with the sloes, for 1l (2pt) gin. But oversweetness is a common fault in sloe gin so it may be wise to reduce the amount you put in at first and add more later if you wish. Damson gin can be made the same way. With both sloes and damsons you first copy nature's frost with a day or two in the freezer to soften them.

> WARNING: People have been seriously ill through mistaking poisonous berries for sloes. Only go sloe picking if you know your sloes.

Star Fruit (carambola)

The five deeply ridged sides of the pale greeny yellow carambola give it its common name of star fruit. But, confusingly, there are two members of the family – both called star fruit – one more sour than the other. The one usually seen in British supermarkets is the sweeter one, correctly called carambola. Though refreshing in a very hot climate, and pretty when sliced into stars, it tastes like a disappointing apple. It can be eaten raw or poached in syrup like any other fruit.

Strawberries, Raspberries

Soft fruit needs careful buying – look at the bottoms of the punnets as well as the tops. Staining speaks of crushed and useless fruit.

Soft fruit, like strawberries and raspberries, lasts best if it is left unwashed with stalks on, and spread out in a very cool place (preferably the refrigerator) so the air can get all round each berry, or use a dry colander instead. Once sugar is put on these fruits it draws the juice out of them and they gradually become flabby.

Tamarillos (tree tomatoes)

Looking like plum tomatoes, this South American fruit has a strong sweet-sour flavour which is an acquired taste. Cut tamarillos in half and scoop out the soft parts to eat raw, or cook them to a purée.

Cooking Fruit

Fruit is very easy to cook but a few small points make a difference.

● It should be cut with stainless steel (ordinary steel can taint it), which is why some very old books refer to cutting it with a silver knife.

● Apples, pears and peaches must immediately be dropped into water containing lemon juice to stop them turning brown with the air.

● If you are preparing soft fruits and want a rich syrup you can draw out the juices by sprinkling the fruit with caster sugar. This dissolves better than granulated and so it suits fruit which will be briefly cooked or not cooked at all.

● For stewing, most fruit needs rather less water than would cover it and it should be cooked very gently. Often the best way is to poach the fruit in a low oven rather than on the top of a stove, as there is less risk of rushing it to ruin.

● Fruit should not be cooked in aluminium. The acid in it dissolves some of the aluminium into the fruit.

Preserving Fruit and Vegetables

Freezers have almost done away with the need to put fruit and vegetables by for the winter in bottles and jars. But even if a modern housewife has no need to bottle fruit, home-made pickles are infinitely superior to most one can buy. Making them is a soothing occupation for an autumn Sunday, and spiced pears or – better still – peaches can give a lift to a slice of cold ham or poultry which nothing else can quite achieve. And, tucking produce into boxes hardly compares to the pleasure of contemplating a row of gleaming jars, their contents softly glowing through the glass.

Bottling

Bottled fruit does not go bad for two reasons:

● all bacteria in the bottles, fruit and the water round them, have been destroyed by heat

● air has been shut out so no new bacteria can enter.

In addition, the acid in the fruit helps them to keep. Vegetables lack that acid and are more likely to go off – which can be dangerous. For that reason, the only exception is really a fruit – the tomato.

For bottling anything which needs to be sterilized you must have jars with rubber rings which will seal the air out, and it is best to have fresh rings every year. The steps are these:

1 Check the jars for chips on the rim.
2 Wash the jars well, rinse and leave wet.
3 Put the rubber seals to soak in warm water.
4 If you want to use syrup, sweeten water to your taste – there is no set amount – heating it gently until the sugar is dissolved. Boil for 2 minutes, skim off any froth, and leave to cool.
5 Choose unblemished fruit which is just ripe.
6 Prepare the fruit as you would for stewing.
7 Put a heap of fruit on your scales and note the weight.
8 Pack the fruit carefully into the jars, without bruising.
9 Note the weight of fruit you put into each jar.
10 Leave the top 1 cm (½ in) empty.

Addresses and suggestions for further reading are at the ends of chapters.

11 Fill to just over the fruit with syrup or water – noting how much liquid went into a jar.

12 Let the bubbles come out, helping them by tapping the base of the jar on a folded cloth.

13 Dip the rubber rings in boiling water, and place them on the jars.

14 Put the lids on. Those which screw on *must* be released a quarter turn before heating *or the bottles may burst*.

15 Sterilize by one of the methods below.

★ When bottling soft fruit which packs closely together it is best to add the syrup in stages, as you pack the jar, or there may be air bubbles which can't escape.

Hot Water Bath Sterilizing 1

There are numerous ways of sterilizing but this method is one of the most reliable. However, you do need a pan deep enough for the water to come right over the bottles, and a thermometer which will register 86°C (212°F).

Place something in the base of the pan to stop the jars resting on it. (Crumpled wire netting will do.) Put the jars in the pan. Cover them with cold water and take 1 hour to bring it up to 55°C (130°F). Then heat to the temperature given in the chart on the right and hold the water at that temperature for the recommended time. ★★ Lift the jars out on to a room-temperature surface – on a chilly surface they may crack. Tighten screw caps immediately. Leave undisturbed for a day and check the seal after 48 hours by removing the screw cap or clip and lifting the jar *slightly* by the sealed lid. If any are not sealed check the rim and underside of the ring for the reason, resterilize.

★ If you have no thermometer bring the pan to simmering over 1½ hours. Keep at simmering point for 6 to 15 minutes for soft fruit, 20 minutes for firm fruit, and 30 minutes for tomatoes.

★ When storing screw-top jars unscrew them, dry inside the screw threads, wipe a touch of oil round, then replace without over-tightening. Then they won't rust solid over the winter.

Quick Hot Water Bath Sterilizing 2

Pack fruit into *warm* jars, pour hot liquid over the fruit, put the jars in hot water and heat to simmering (87°C, 190°F) in 25 to 30 minutes and hold at simmering point for the time the fruit needs (see above). Then remove and treat as for 1. The fruit won't look so good by this method but it will taste fine.

Oven Method

There are several oven methods. A simple one is to fill the jars as above but only to within 2.5 cm (1 in) of the top. Leave any screw covers off. Stand them in the centre of the oven on a baking sheet which is covered with a piece of cardboard, leaving a 5 cm (2 in) space between the bottles. Set the oven to gas no 2, 150°C (300°F) and cook for the time given below. Remove and treat as for the water method above from ★★.

Bottling Cooking Times

	Water 1	Water 2	Oven
Apple slices Gooseberries Rhubarb Soft fruit	165°F for 10 min	2 min	1-4 lb 30-40 min 5-10 lb 45-60 min
Stone fruit Citrus fruits	180°F for 15 min	10 min	1-4 lb 40-50 min 5-10 lb 55-70 min
Pineapple	180°F for 15 min	20 min	1-4 lb 50-60 min 5-10 lb 65-80 min
Pears	190°F for 30 min	40 min	1-4 lb 60-70 min 5-10 lb 75-90 min
Tomatoes	190°F for 40 min	50 min	1-4 lb 70-80 min 5-10 lb 85-100 min

1 The weights given for each oven time are for the total weight of fruit in the oven, regardless of jar size.

2 More than 11 oz of fruit in a jar, or less than 5 fl oz of liquid, demand slightly longer at the final temperature.

★ Bottled pears tend to go brown, and tomatoes may be more usefully bottled once skinned and chopped. Sterilize them as for whole tomatoes.

★ Having used up fruit from a bottle with clips, don't put the clips back on the bottle or they may lose their spring.

Candying

Any spare orange, lemon or grapefruit peel can be converted into candied peel, including those from mandarin oranges. I find my candied peel does not look quite as smart and dry as the bought sort, nor does it keep so long, but the flavour is very good.

Wash the outside of the skins well and cut out any dye stamps. Put it in a pan with cold water to cover, bring to the boil and drain. Do this at least once more. Cover with fresh water and simmer until really tender (the sugar you add later will tend to toughen them). Drain well.

For 6 average oranges put 350 g (12 oz) of granulated sugar in a pan, with 175 ml (6 fl oz) of water, and 1½ tablespoons of golden syrup. Heat gently until the sugar dissolves, then add the peel and simmer until it is clear and the syrup almost absorbed. Drain on a wire rack. Then set the peel to dry on greaseproof paper in a warm place, like an airing cupboard. Cut it in pieces with sharp scissors some way through the drying process. Once dry, shake it in a bag with caster sugar before storing in a tightly closed jar.

Crystallizing

Crystallizing is almost a lost art but in *Elinor Fettiplace's Receipt Book* – a book of recipes dating from 1604 edited and put in context by Hilary Spurling – I found this:

to drie Apricocks, Peaches, Pippins or Pearplums

Take your apricocks or pearplums, & let them boile one walmes in as much clarified sugar as will cover them, so them lie infused in an earthen pan three dayes, then take out your fruits, & let boile your syrupe againe, when you have thus used them three times then put half a pound of drie sugar into your syrupe, & so let it boile till it come to a verie thick syrup, wherein let your fruits boile leysurelie 3 or 4 walmes, then take them foorth of the syrup, then plant them on a lettice of rods or wyer, & so put them into yor stewe, & every second day turne them & when they bee through dry you may box them & keep them all the yeare; before you set them to drying you must wash them in a little warm water, when they are half drie you must dust a little sugar upon them throw a fine Lawne.

Hilary Spurling says you put the fruit in the pan with sugar to cover them and dissolve it *very* slowly, only bringing it to the boil when fully dissolved, then remove the pan from the heat. The fruit can then sit in its pan for the 3 days. The instruction to 'take out your fruits' meant to put both them and their syrup in a pan which would allow boiling. So you can ignore that – unless you did put them in an earthenware bowl. They are then brought to the boil and allowed to cool on 3 consecutive days. A missing instruction is that the fruit should then be taken out of the syrup before the final sugar is added. In boiling it down, be careful not to take it to caramel. Stop if it hints at turning colour and put back the fruit. Hilary Spurling says the '3 or 4 walmes' mean bring it to the boil three or four times and that a stewe was a drying stove – use a plate warmer or airing cupboard instead. It is a recipe I have yet to try, but it has the touches which suggest it would work well.

Drying

Drying is a more hit-and-miss business than any other process. I suggest you try with a single apple, and find where in your house is dry enough, and then try with more. The late varieties tend to dry best.

Peel and core an apple and slice it in rings. Blanch the rings in a colander over boiling water, with a lid on, for 5 minutes. Thread on a clean (undyed) string or a bamboo pole in a dry place, spacing the rings so air gets between them. Or you can try them in the oven on a rack. You need a temperature of about 50°C (120°F) to start with, but this can be raised to 65°C (140°F) after an hour or so. Pears can be dried in the same way.

Frosting Fruit

This is a wonderfully easy way to produce a table decoration. Wash the fruit and dry it well. Beat up 1 egg white with 2 tablespoons of water and brush the mixture all over the fruit. Roll the fruit over a plate of caster sugar, and set it on a rack to dry.

Glazing Fruit

This is the way to produce those grapes coated in a crunchy sugar coating which are served among petit fours. Heat 500 g (1 lb) of sugar very gently with 125 ml (¼ pt) of water in a large pan. When the sugar has totally dissolved boil rapidly *without stirring* until a little dropped into cold water makes a crisp droplet. Let it

cool slightly then dip your fruit (grapes, cherries) and put them to cool on waxed paper. To make toffee apples you just cook the sugar until golden brown.

Pickling and Spicing

- If you want a vegetable pickle to stay crisp – as for pickled onions or cabbage – let the vinegar get cold before you pour it over.
- If a recipe calls for spiced vinegar you can make it by allowing 2 to 3 oz of pickling spice (Boots often sells it when supermarkets don't) to each litre (2 pt) vinegar. Heat the vinegar with the spice in until almost bubbling. Turn it off *before* it bubbles and leave it to stand for 2 hours before straining.

Making Jams and Jellies

If you haven't got preserving sugar you can make jam with granulated, preserving sugar just gives a greater clarity. You can make jam with any fruit, and even with some vegetables: marrow jam flavoured with lemon, pineapple or ginger is delicious – and cheap.

Jar Preparation

Wash the jars scrupulously clean before starting to make the jam. Drain but don't dry them. Then, without touching the inside, put them in a cold oven and turn it on to about gas no 2 or 150°C (300°F). Do this just as you start to cook the jam and leave them in for the time it takes to cook. Remove, holding them by the outside and fill while still fairly hot.

★ An old trick for reducing the amount of froth produced as the fruit boils is to wipe the preserving pan round with a butter paper before putting in the fruit. And buttering the base makes the jam less likely to stick.

★ Your jam will have a brighter colour if the sugar is heated in the oven before it is added to the fruit.

Jelly Bag

A jelly bag is a bag of thick cloth which is traditionally used for straining jellies of any kind. But several layers

---

Addresses and suggestions for further reading are at the ends of chapters.

of muslin or a piece of well-boiled sheeting (to get the residue of detergent out), tied to the legs of an upturned chair, work just as well as pricey bags.

Graining/crystallization

To avoid crystals let the sugar melt *totally* on a low heat before attempting to boil it, and once it is at around 118°-121°C (245°-250°F) stir to the bare minimum needed to stop it catching on the bottom. Adding a little liquid glucose or cream of tartar mixed with a touch of water also helps to prevent it from forming crystals.

Setting

To set well jams and jellies need to be made from fruit with a fairly high acid content and enough pectin, as acidity helps pectin to gel. Fruits vary with the season but some, such as strawberries, never have much pectin while others, like blackberries and blackcurrants, set beautifully. If you doubt the setting ability of your fruit you can test it after stewing, by putting a teaspoonful of the juice from the stewed fruit in a glass and adding 3 teaspoons of methylated spirits. When stirred gently it should clot. If it doesn't you may need to add pectin.

For poor setters, buy a pectin additive such as Certo or use Tate and Lyle's special preserving sugar called 'Sugar with Pectin' – but if you increase the pectin for fruits which gel well anyway you get a very solid jam which shrinks in the jar. Alternatively, put the sugar over the fruit overnight to draw out the juices; you can then cook most fruit with no added water. This produces a full-flavoured preserve with so little liquid to gel that you don't need a firm jelly-like result.

For a good set, jam must boil hard, and it will rise up the pan – only half fill the pan. If you are interrupted when jam is half boiled, turn it off or it may burn when you are not watching. Afterwards bring it back to the boil slowly and just continue boiling – it should be none the worse. But only cook for just long enough to get a good set – over-boiling will break down the set and darken the jam.

The setting point of jam can be found by putting a spoonful on a plate in the refrigerator. At setting point it will wrinkle slightly as you draw a finger through it, when cold, and the drop on your finger will not drip off.

Potting up

Let the jam stand until it forms a slight skin, then stir, before potting up. Cover at once with waxed paper circles, but leave until cold before covering with cellophane. Moisten the cellophane on the outside before covering the pot.

Storing Fruit – Long Term

Ripe fruit gives off a gas which speeds the ripening of other fruit near it. So if you wish to ripen some unripe fruit put it in a paper bag with a piece of ripe fruit and close the bag. To keep fruit do the reverse, removing any that become ripe, so they don't hurry on the rest.

One needs to know one's fruit: most apples store well, but not all; some pears store well, many do not.

For storing, hard fruit must have its stalk on and be perfect. If it isn't, it will spoil quickly. Pears must be picked before they are ripe, but apples can be allowed to ripen on the tree. If you have a choice of which fruit to store, small apples have smaller cells and this makes them store better.

Both pears and apples should be stored, spaced out in a cool airy place, away from strong smells. If there is a chance of them getting dusty, wrap them in newspaper. Check them regularly to remove any that are ripening or going bad. With pears this is more a matter of smell, as they ripen from the inside out.

GAME AND POULTRY

Hanging Game

In some of the houses I remember from my childhood there were chilly larders with thick walls and flagstone floors, through whose zinc-meshed air vents the sun never shone. In some, tall pine cupboards mesh-panelled against flies, covered whole walls. Few homes today are so well equipped for hanging game and, if you find yourself with birds to hang, careful thought should be given to where to hang them. They need a very cool place with plenty of air and – and here's the catch – absolutely no flies. Contrary to what many people think, feathers are not a protection against flies. Few culinary experiences are nastier than starting to pluck a bird and discovering it heaving with maggots. So great care has to be taken in the early part of the season.

Hanging birds and beasts for the right length of time makes an enormous difference to the flavour. It isn't just a matter of giving a bird the 'gameyness' one associates with pheasant. The hanging time is needed so that enzymes in the flesh can work on it, softening it and enriching the taste. Tradition has it that, among game birds, swimmers (e.g. wild duck) are hung by their feet and flyers are hung by their necks. Don't ask me why – but that is how it is usually done.

Unless you are an old hand who can tell by the feel of the air how a bird is doing you should check them daily, as the hanging times vary greatly with the weather. Thundery weather can turn a bird rapidly, even if the temperature isn't high, and birds hung in warm muggy weather need much shorter hanging than they would if it was cool and crisp and game tastes best when it matures slowly at a very low temperature.

★ The standard way of freshening up game which has become a bit too whiffy – but is still safe to eat – is to wipe it with equal parts of vinegar and water.

Feathered Game

Grouse

Check if a bird is young with the bursa test (see page 71). Old birds may be shedding a toe nail or have a line across the nail where one has been shed.

Freshly shot grouse are sometimes eaten at once – to launch the shooting season; after that they are generally

Game Seasons

The times of year at which each type of game may be killed in Britain are strictly controlled.

S = shooting forbidden on Sundays in Great Britain
X = shooting forbidden on Christmas Day in Great Britain
SS = shooting forbidden on Sunday in Scotland and some other UK areas
XS = shooting forbidden on Christmas Day in Scotland and some other UK areas

Blackgame	S X	20 Aug-10 Dec
Capercaillie	SS XS	1 Oct-31 Jan
Duck – Wild	SS XS	1 Sept-20 Feb (below spring high tide mark) 1 Sept-31 Jan (elsewhere)
Geese – Wild	SS XS	as duck
Grouse	S X	12 Aug-10 Dec
Guinea Fowl		Late spring to early summer
Hares	S X	11 Dec (Scotland 1 July)-31 March – on moorlands, elsewhere no closed season
Partridge	S X	1 Sept-1 Feb
Pheasant	S X	1 Oct-1 Feb
Plovers – Golden		1 Sept-31 Jan
Ptarmigan	S X	12 Aug-10 Dec (Scotland only)
Rabbits		No closed season
Snipe	SS XS	12 Aug-31 Jan
Woodcock	SS XS	1 Oct-31 Jan (England and Wales) 1 Sept-31 Jan (Scotland)

Deer		England and Wales	Scotland
Red	Male	1 May-31 July	21 Oct-30 June
	Female	1 March-31 Oct	16 Feb-20 Oct
Fallow	Male	1 May-31 July	1 May-31 July
	Female	1 March-31 Oct	16 Feb-20 Oct
Roe	Male	1 Nov-31 March	21 Oct-31 March
	Female	1 March-31 Oct	1 April-20 Oct

The dates were kindly provided by **The Game Conservancy**.

hung for 2 to 10 days, according to the weather. When ready they smell slightly 'high' but not unpleasantly so.

Partridge
If you have a choice, go for partridge with yellow or greyish legs. These are the native grey partridge and considered superior in flavour to the red-legged kind which are comparative newcomers – only having been introduced under Charles II.

Use the bursa test on page 71 to check the age and look at the legs: the legs of yellow-legged partridge are only yellow in their youth. Also look at the long feathers in the wing: in a young bird they open in a V at the ends; in an older bird they end tidily.

Early in the season partridge need only be hung for 3 to 5 days; later on old birds can be hung for as long as 7 to 10 days. This is another bird which some people like very gamey. A friend of mine has an aged aunt who even insists they aren't fit to eat until the heads fall off. However, for most people's palates they should not have more than a hint of a gamey smell.

Pheasant
Hang pheasants in feather by the neck for 3 to 10 days – and preferably singly, not in pairs, so the air can reach all sides. Country lore has it that a pheasant should be hung until the tail feathers drop out. But, for most people's taste, 7 days is the average hanging time. Use the bursa test on page 71 to check the age and cook it within 2 days of plucking.

As Dorothy Hartley rightly says: 'There is as much difference between pheasant well hung and cooked as game and the same bird cooked fresh, as there is between two different breeds of bird. One is game; the other practically brown chicken.'

Pigeon
Pigeons are best from May to October and should be plucked, drawn and eaten soon after killing. They are tasty but tend to be dry. So, except when very young, they are much better as a pot roast than as a roast. As there is little meat on the legs it is thrifty to serve only the breast and keep the carcass for making soup – for pigeon soup is excellent.

Quail
Quail can be hung for 3 to 4 days. Beloved by Italians, these birds were hugely popular in Victorian England but have become something of a curiosity today, though they make very good eating.

Snipe
Snipe are only hung for 3 to 4 days and then plucked, and possibly gutted – though they can be cooked ungutted, like woodcock.

Wild Duck
The ducks which are most likely to arrive in a kitchen are teal, mallard and widgeon. You should be able to tell them by weight, if nothing else. Teal are the smallest, weighing only 300 to 370 g (11 to 13 oz), widgeon weigh

700 to 900 g (1½ to 2 lb), while mallard weigh 1 to 1.3 kg (2½ to 2¾ lb). One of the curiosities of teal is that, by a quite remarkable piece of casuistry, they are classified as fish by the French Catholic Church, and may be eaten as such during Lent.

Young ducks have soft webbing which you can tear easily. Whatever the age, they only need to hang for 1 to 3 days, and when the weather is warm it may be best to gut them first. In cleaning them, make sure you remove the oil gland near their vent – with which they keep their feathers waterproof; leaving it in makes the flesh taste of turpentine.

Wild duck also have a bad reputation for tasting fishy. If you suspect this may be the case, Julia Drysdale says you should put an onion and a potato in the body cavity and place the bird in 0.5 cm (¼ in) boiling water and bake at gas no 4 or 180°C (350°F) for 10 minutes basting frequently. Then drain, throw away the onion and potato and cook as normal. These ducks are not fatty like most farm ducks and they need to be cooked like other game birds to keep them moist when cooking.

Wild Goose
On a young goose the markings are softer and less distinct than on an older bird and until November the tips of young tail feathers are separated into a V quite different from the normal closed feathers of older birds. Whatever their age, they need to hang for up to 3 weeks. They can only be roasted when young and the method for ordinary geese on page 76 should be followed – but wild geese are less fatty and need to be totally enclosed in foil before cooking to keep them moist.

Woodcock
Woodcock are diminutive birds eaten in a distinctly curious manner, which some rave about, but which is hard to stomach. They are plucked, but not gutted; and cooked and eaten, head, entrails and all. They are hung by the feet for 3 to 14 days (some like them almost decomposed) and are said to be ready when a droplet of blood forms on the beak. Traditionally they are roasted sitting on a slice of toast which catches their juices, with bacon covering them.

The Bursa Test
According to the Game Conservancy, this is a good test for judging the age of the major game birds once they are dead. When young they have a short cul-de-sac passage, called the bursa, between their vent (anus) and tail. As the birds age the bursa shortens and may vanish. So you can check the age of a bird by how far you can push the end of a matchstick into the bursa. The distances for young birds are these: grouse 1 cm (½ in); partridge 1 cm (½ in); pheasant 2.5 cm (1 in).

Plucking Game and Poultry
Any bird is most easily plucked when just killed and still warm, but if a bird has to be hung this is impossible. In that case you can dip it for 30 seconds (not more) into boiling water. But only dip it in water if you are going to cook it as soon as it is plucked, or the warmth may

make it go bad. To pluck it, just grab small feathers in handfuls, and large ones individually, and tug in the direction in which they lie. Go gently if game is very high or you will remove lumps of flesh. It is tedious, tough on the hands and takes far longer than you might expect, but it is very easy. Singe any remaining fluff with a candle.

Once plucked, game should usually be cooked the same day, but birds vary in their keeping time in a refrigerator, according to how high they already are. But they freeze well.

Drawing Game and Poultry
The only tricky part about drawing a bird is that you have to be very careful not to break the gall bladder. The yellow bile is very bitter and will spoil the bird, so go gently.

1 Slit the skin on the underside of the neck.
2 Cut the neck off very close to the body but leave the neck skin to leave a flap hanging from the body.
3 Remove the crop and the windpipe from the neck end.
4 Insert two fingers and gently loosen the contents of the body cavity.
5 Cut a slit crosswise between the tail stump and the vent (anus).
6 Insert two fingers through the hole and loosen the body contents.
7 Hold the bird firmly at the head end while drawing out the gizzard and intestines the other end.
8 Then carefully remove the heart and liver with the gall bladder attached.
9 Cut the gall bladder from the liver without breaking it, and split and clean the gizzard, stripping off all yellow parts.
10 Wash or wipe out the bird and set aside the giblets – heart, liver, neck (without head) and cleaned gizzard.

Cooking Game Birds
The best way to cook any game bird depends entirely on its age; old birds always need long slow cooking with lots of fat and moisture or they are tough and dry. If you have some old game and don't know how to cook it any good recipe for *coq au vin* will make a passable dish.

In autumn young birds are those which hatched the previous spring. But birds age fast, and one of the best game cooks I know reckons that past Christmas even these are getting on the old side. So she roasts young birds until Christmas, and casseroles all birds after that. Below are simply the key times and temperatures for roasting – from which you can probably deduce casserole times if you wish to be inventive.

The basic method for roasting all game is to put butter inside and out, season it and cover it with strips of fatty bacon or with thin slices of pork fat (if you don't like the bacon flavour). It also helps to moisten game birds by putting a peeled apple or sliced orange in the body cavity. Despite all this, they should then be basted *very* frequently during cooking. A more labour-saving method is to prepare them as above and just tuck the birds – singly or in groups – into roasting bags or in well-closed foil parcels. Then they baste themselves. An old version of this was to wrap game birds in vine leaves. Whatever the method, heat the oven first and lie the birds on their breasts – turning them to the other side at half time. Then the best meat is also the juiciest. Turn them right side up when nearly done and open the bag or foil if you wish them to brown.

Game	Time to Cook the Bird	Oven Settings to Roast Gas/Electric	Servings per Bird
Blackgame	casserole		3
Capercaillie	casserole		1-2
Grouse	25-40 mins	5, 190°C (375°F)	1-2
Partridge *or*	20 mins 20-25 mins	7, 220°C (425°F) 5, 190°C (375°F)	1-2
Pheasant	45-60 mins	5, 190°C (375°F)	3-4
Pigeon	20-30 mins	6, 200°C (400°F)	1
Ptarmigan	casserole		1
Quail	15 mins	5, 190°C (375°F)	1
Snipe	10 mins	7, 220°C (425°F)	1
Wild Duck: Mallard	30-35 mins	6-7, 200°-220°C (400°-425°F)	2-3
Teal	15-20 mins	6-7, 200°-220°C (400°-425°F)	1-2
Widgeon	20-25 mins	6-7, 200°-220°C (400°-425°F)	1-2
Woodcock	10-15 mins 20-30 mins	7, 220°C (425°F) bloody 5, 190°C (375°F) medium	1

Carving Game Birds

Game birds, large enough to be carved, are carved like chicken (page 75), except that the smaller breasts can be served whole, and they may be the only part of the bird worth eating. In this case, it is prudent to keep the rest of the carcass for soup.

★ An excellent and classic addition to game soup is dry sherry in which a few chillies have steeped. A cleaned-out Worcester Sauce bottle is the best container as the dropper top lets you administer it in moderate amounts.

Furred Game

Hare

Hares are at their best from September to February and at that time a young hare has small sharp white teeth, while in an older one the teeth are large and yellow. Some people paunch the hare the instant it is killed, as the guts come away most easily then. Others gut it after hanging. It is hung, head down, in fur, for 5 to 10 days (5 often being long enough), with a bowl containing a teaspoon of vinegar under to catch the blood – the vinegar keeps the blood from congealing. A good Jack (male) hare will serve 6 to 8 people.

Skinning and Gutting Hare and Rabbit

Tie the back legs together and hang the hare up with a bowl underneath. Cut round the legs, and slit the skin down their length, then pull it off down the body, like removing a dress. Cut the feet off at the first leg joint, and remove the head. Slit the animal down the stomach (without letting the knife pierce the contents) and carefully remove the insides, letting the bowl catch the blood. After gutting, remove the thin blueish membrane which coats the body and wipe it with a cloth damped in vinegar and water – but don't wash it. (In theory, washing is supposed to take the flavour away, but I know those who do wash hares with no ill effect.) Rabbits are skinned in the same way but you need not catch the blood. Cut away any pulpy areas where a bad shot has bruised the flesh.

Roasting

Only a young hare is suitable for roasting and even then it should first be marinaded in red wine, seasoning and herbs for 24 hours. It may also be more interesting only to roast the saddle, and casserole the legs or use them in some other dish.

If you need to divide a hare up treat it much like a chicken (page 75).

Roast a saddle for 35 minutes at gas no 6 or 200°C (400°F) covered with bacon fat and baste it often. Roast a whole hare in the same way for 45 to 50 minutes.

Rabbit

Rabbits are best from October to February. They should be gutted as soon as they are killed, and are best when hung for only 24 hours in a cool place then skinned like a hare (above). A young animal will have sharp teeth and claws, and ears which are easily torn. A whole rabbit serves 4 to 6 people; a saddle serves 2.

Trussing and Jointing

Pull all four legs towards the middle and tie them with white cotton string. Traditionally, a skewer is pushed through the head and into the back so the head is upright – but few people would welcome this sight today, and the head is best removed. Joint it like a chicken (see page 75).

Cooking

Rabbit tends to be dry and it is usually better in a casserole than roasted. If you wish to roast it, a thrifty and practical old way to remedy its dryness is to thread fatty left-over bacon rinds through the back to both moisten it and improve the flavour. * Otherwise, truss, spread with butter, season and cover with bacon slices before roasting. Best of all, marinade it overnight in red wine with a touch of oil, onion, garlic and bay leaf. Then proceed as from *, basting with marinade. Test if it is cooked, as for chicken (page 74); it should not be pink. An average rabbit takes 1 hour at gas no 6 or 200°C (400°F).

Venison

It is said that venison gave us the phrase to 'eat humble pie' for the 'umbles' of venison are (or were) pieces of offal such as sweetbreads, and 'stones', liver and so on. These are said to have been given to the people who sat at the bottom of the table, while those at the head of the table ate the flesh. It benefits from marinading for 24 hours in red wine with some onion, carrot, juniper berries, bouquet garni and just a *hint* of *wine* vinegar.

> He did give us the meanest dinner of beef shoulders and umbles of venison.
>
> Samuel Pepys

Venison is increasingly sold in supermarkets, such as Safeway, and comes in three forms; smoked, joints or sausages. It is a delicious, full-flavoured, meat well worth trying in any form. If you can't buy it locally, **The British Deer Farmers' Association** (page 123) has a list of companies which supply it by post.

If freshly shot it needs to be skinned, gutted and hung for 7 to 10 days after shooting or it will be tough. In preparing the meat, check for any flesh which is pulpy and bruised and cut it out. It is butchered like beef and the best part is the haunch, which can be roasted, as can the shoulder. If the meat is likely to be tender, steaks can be cut from the leg and chops from the neck, while the other cuts make excellent casseroles or pot roasts.

Venison lacks fat, so it really needs to be larded (page 101) with pork fat. But if you lack a larding needle just stick a slim-bladed knife well into the flesh and then push a strip of fat down the hole with the point, at intervals all over the meat.

In addition to larding it needs to be well covered with fatty bacon. Then roast at gas no 5 or 190°C (375°F) for 15 minutes per lb (450 g), or for 20 minutes per lb if under 4 lb (1.8 kg). Baste it constantly.

Venison should be rather underdone when you take it from the oven. As it tends to hold the heat and continue cooking for some while longer it can easily become overdone and leathery. It needs a rich gravy and a sweet-sour fruity flavour, such as red currant jelly, to go with it.

Smoked venison has an intense flavour, so benefits from being served with softer flavours as part of a mixed *hors d'œuvre*. It dries fast. So keep it well covered until needed. Or dress it with a little good olive oil, ground black pepper, and a hint of lemon juice.

Poultry

Chicken and Turkey

One used to test the youth of a fresh chicken by feeling whether the tip of its breast bone was bendy like the end of one's nose. Now you'd be hard put to it to find an old bird if you wanted one. On a fresh chicken look for eyes which are clear not sunken, and flesh that is fresh. Most birds have white skin, but maize-fed birds are sunflower yellow, and the new *poulets noirs* have curious black legs. But be very dubious if anyone says they are offering you a capon. A capon was a cock neutered with a hormone pellet or knife. This pellet is now illegal and there must be few farmers who trouble to castrate their cocks.

Check any frozen bird over, looking for pale dry-looking patches (freezer burn, showing it may be rancid) or signs of bruising. Then check the label. If it says polyphosphates anywhere they have been added to make the flesh soak up water, and who wants to buy water at the price of meat?

- Poussin are 4-5 week-old chickens, double poussin are 6 weeks old. They used to be a luxury. Now they are inexpensive and, at under 2 lbs in weight, ideal for 1-2 people. Salt, pepper and lemon juice are all the preparation they need, they can then be grilled, barbecued, roasted or – ideal – cooked in a roasting bag or foil. Or use any chicken recipe. A British firm, which *doesn't* use battery methods, now supplies most British supermarkets. So they solve a moral dilemma (see **Poussin Information Service**, page 124). However, I don't recommend those coated with dried herbs. Such preparation raises the price while lowering the flavour: dried thyme doesn't suit them.
- Broilers are fairly young birds weighing about 1.35 kg (3 lb).
- Roasting chickens are at their best when 1.8 to 2.25 kg (4 to 5 lb) and have more flavour than the younger birds.
- Boiling fowl are older larger birds weighing upwards of 2.7 kg (6 lb), but with lots of flavour.

Free Range Rules

EC rules now allow three types of living conditions to be called 'free range'.

1 **Free Range** with up to 13 birds per square metre of floor, free access to an open-air area half the time, a diet of 70 per cent cereals and a life-span of over 55 days.
2 **Traditional Free Range** with 12 birds per square metre of floor, day-time access to open air from 6 weeks old, more outdoor space, and a life-span of over 80 days.
3 **Free Range Total Freedom** must have conditions as good as 2 above, but also be free to range without fences.

I find it hard to decide whether the best full-sized chicken is free-range one or a maize-fed chicken. The free range win on moral grounds. But maize-fed chickens have an excellent flavour and an almost melting texture which is most appealing. And good British ones now rival the French imports and don't live in batteries, although they may not classify as free range. Failing either of these, the best flavour is found in chill-fresh free-range chickens. Happily, good supermarkets now stock all of these. And they are great time-savers, as they need no dressing up with sauces – unless it pleases you.

Keeping

It is best to cook fresh or thawed poultry within 24 hours of buying, even if it is kept in a refrigerator. But if it has travelled around in a warm car, or the weather is thundery, it could go off before that. Under the wings is usually the first place to go – so check for any change of colour or smell. If it is close wrapped in plastic open it slightly to let the bird breathe. Removing the giblets from the inside and inserting a peeled onion also makes it keep better. Do NOT let uncooked poultry touch or drip onto other food – see page 53.

Thawing

Because of the risks of food poisoning and because they go bad easily it is best to thaw frozen birds in the refrigerator. This takes a very long time with a large bird, so if you do thaw a bird in a room cook it immediately after; don't let it hang around.

Thawing Times For Poultry

Weight	Room temperature 16°C (65°F)	Refrigerator 5°C (40°F)
2 lb (900 g)	8 hrs	28 hrs
3 lb (1.35 kg)	9 hrs	32 hrs
4 lb (1.80 kg)	10 hrs	38 hrs
5 lb (2.25 kg)	12 hrs	44 hrs
6 lb (2.70 kg)	14 hrs	50 hrs
7 lb (3.15 kg)	16 hrs	56 hrs
9 lb (4.23 kg)	19 hrs	65 hrs
12 lb (5.40 kg)	22 hrs	70 hrs
15 lb (6.75 kg)	24 hrs	75 hrs
18 lb (8.10 kg)	27 hrs	80 hrs
22 lb (9.90 kg)	36 hrs	96 hrs

I am indebted to the British Chicken Information Service for the thawing times for the lighter birds and to the Turkey Information Service for other times.

Take any giblets (neck, liver and gizzard in a bag) out of the body as soon as you can. Poultry *must* be fully thawed before it is cooked.

Roasting Preparation

Remove giblets if they are inside the bird. Pre-heat the oven. Rinse the bird inside and out under a tap. Dry the skin well with kitchen paper (*do not use a tea towel or other kitchen cloth* – unless you want food poisoning).

★ Spread the outside well with butter and put a lump inside (unless you are stuffing it). Dust with pepper and salt, inside and out. Half a lemon inside is also good.

Many birds are sold with the giblets (neck, heart, liver and gizzard) tucked into the body in a bag. The liver can be diced, seasoned and lightly fried and eaten on toast, or garnishing a salad or omelette. The rest can be simmered, with water to cover them, and a carrot, bay leaf and onion with its skin on, while the bird roasts. The strained liquid can then be used in making the gravy.

Stuffing

The food safety pundits now say it is best not to stuff a bird in its body cavity, but only under the flap of skin at the neck. This is because of the risk of an inexperienced cook failing to allow for the extra time which a stuffing needs and serving undercooked stuffing which has been contaminated with salmonella from the chicken. If you do stuff a bird remember you *can't* assume the stuffing is cooked just because the meat on the thickest part of the thigh is done.

Roasting Chicken and Turkey

Chicken and turkey go dry very easily, so roast them in a roasting bag, or totally wrapped in foil, with the ends of the foil rolled to close it well. Place the bird on its breast – switching to the other side at half time. Near the end, right it and remove the paper so the breast will brown. If you have neither foil nor a bag, cover it with discarded butter papers and baste it every 15 to 20 minutes.

Roast chickens and *very small* turkeys for 20 minutes per lb (450 g) at gas no 5 or 190°C (375°F), plus perhaps 20 minutes extra, depending on the size of the bird and whether the oven is up to temperature. Roast a turkey of 8 lb or more for 18 minutes per lb (450 g) at gas no 3 or 160°C (325°F). The not-so-great British tradition of Christmas turkey spoiling – having dried it all day at gas no 1/4 or 110°C (225°F) – should long since have been abandoned.

Weigh any bird when oven ready – and count the stuffing as part of its weight when calculating the cooking time. *Never go by the timing alone; always test that a bird is cooked.* To test for this push a skewer deep into the thigh. If clear juice runs out when you remove it the bird is cooked. If it is at all pink it isn't. Never eat undercooked poultry. See also Stuffing, above.

Boiling a Chicken

Put a large pan of water to boil. Prepare as for roasting (above) to ★. Place in boiling water just to cover, with a washed carrot, 3 sprigs of parsley, a whole onion and a bay leaf (and possibly lemon zest or garlic). When it returns to boiling reduce the heat so the water hardly bubbles. An average modern bird takes 1 1/4 to 1 1/2 hours; a tough old hen will take longer. Test as for roast chicken. If you are not serving the bird at once let it cool in the liquor. The liquid can be used for sauces and soups, and the fat you skim from its surface when cold is excellent for frying.

Trussing a Chicken

Professional methods of trussing need a trussing needle – and who has one? Tie the ends of the drumsticks together with a figure of eight in white cotton string and use string or small skewers to fix each wing to the body. You remove the string before the bird goes to the table, so use any method that *works*; elegance is icing on the cake.

Addresses and suggestions for further reading are at the ends of chapters.

Jointing a Chicken

Pull the 'knee' above the drumstick away from the body. Cut through the skin linking limb to breast. Pull the knee towards the table until the 'hip' joint shows. Cut *between* the two bones. Cut an arc through the breast, close to the rib bones, and down towards where the wing must, logically, join the body, pull the meat away and sever the joint as above. Use kitchen scissors to cut through the lower ribs, to remove the breast. The breast can be split in half along the bone, if you wish, and the thigh separated from the drumstick. There is a lot of good meat on the lower ribs and base of the carcass which are left behind and these can be cooked as for boiled chicken to make soup.

Carving a Chicken or Duck

Poultry should be served so that each person has some white (breast) meat and some brown (leg, thigh and wing) meat. So, unless you are pre-carving the whole bird, alternate your cuts. Remove the leg and thigh as for jointing (above). The drumstick may be separated from the thigh afterwards by cutting through the joint. Then pull the wing away from the body in the same way and slice through the joint attaching it to the body. Now, slice the breast downwards in fairly thin slices, parallel to the breast bone, sliding the blade down the ribs in slices thin enough to be elegant but not so thin they fall apart.

Carving a Turkey

The limbs of most turkeys are too big, and often too sinewy, to serve whole. So you simply slice meat off the drumstick and thigh, and off the breast, to give portions of both types of meat. The drumstick meat is the driest, so slice the meat on the thigh first. Keep the slices fairly thin and cut through the skin joining thigh to breast to give a larger breast area to carve.

Duck

Contrary to popular belief, most ducks are now Pekin duck hybrids – not Aylesbury ducks – and they are really ducklings of about 49 days old, as mature ducks can be very tough.

If choosing a duck in feather check the bill and feet; young ducks have a pliable bill and feet with soft webbing which is easily torn. A freshly killed duck, in feather, should hang for 24 to 36 hours.

Ducks have big heavy bones and a shallow breast, so a 4-lb duck will only give 2 good servings, though you could stretch it round 4 in the family, with plenty of vegetables. For the rest:

2-2 ¼ kg (4½-5 lb) serves 3-4
2½-2 ¾ kg (5½-6 lb) serves 4-5
3 kg + (6½ lb +) serves 5-6

Trussing and Jointing

Truss a duck like a chicken. If you need to joint a duck the breast is so small that it is best to cut it down through the breast bone and then simply split each half into two through the breast.

Roasting a Duck

There are all kinds of stories about how to get crisp duck; one friend of mine singes her ducks with a blow lamp to help the fat on its way and another goes over it with a hair dryer. Ingenious though such methods are, the secret of cooking duck with crisp skin outside and succulent flesh inside is simply as follows – but it works best with gas:

- Preheat the oven to gas no 7 or 220°C (425°F) while you prepare a duck as for chicken (page 74) to ★, making sure the skin is really dry.
- Prick the skin *well* with a fork all over, so its fat can run out, but don't pierce the meat. To get deliciously crisp skin sprinkle it well with salt (preferably Maldon Sea Salt), adding pepper to flavour. Preheat the oven.
- Place it on a grid over the roasting tin – to keep it right out of its fat. Put it into the middle of the oven, uncovered at gas no 7 or 220°C (425°F) for 15 minutes, then cook at gas no 4 or 180°C (350°F).

Allow a total of 20 to 25 minutes per lb (450 g). *Do not* baste it while cooking, but prick it from time to time as it cooks to help the fat run out. Keep the fat which runs out; it is excellent for frying potatoes.

Timing is always variable. So, don't be a slave to the clock. Check the bird (see Chicken, page 74) ahead of time and serve it when it seems ready (see Carving, above).

Goose

A goose is a lovely bird and rightly lorded over the Christmas table until it was ousted by the fleshier charms of the turkey. Charles Dickens must have thought the same, for only an enthusiast could write, as he did in *A Christmas Carol*:

There was never such a goose. Bob said he didn't believe there was such a goose ever cooked. Its tenderness and flavour, size and cheapness, were the themes of universal admiration . . . everyone had had enough, and the youngest Cratchits in particular were steeped in sage and onion to the eyebrows!

Geese are bigger than ducks and slightly less fatty, but the same cooking methods apply, with or without the traditional sage and onion stuffing, but allow 13 to 15 minutes per pound (450 g). Like ducks, geese have heavy bones and a 12-lb goose only serves 8 to 10 people. If a goose has very little fat – as a wild goose may – baste it regularly during cooking and even cook it breast down or cover the breast loosely with foil. Carve like a turkey.

Before boiling up the giblets set aside the liver, to make liver pâté and afterwards be sure to keep the fat from the goose. Like duck fat, it is excellent for frying.

Guinea Fowl
Guinea fowl taste half way between a chicken and a pheasant, but cook them as pheasant – page 72.

GRAINS

Couscous

Couscous is the staple starch of Morocco, Algeria and Tunisia, is very easy to cook and can replace rice as a side dish. It is a type of semolina made from wheat grain milled into miniature cubes. Traditionally it is steamed slowly over water or broth. Having eaten it all over Morocco I find the following, far simpler, method which I devised gives an almost identical result. Pop it in a pot, add a lump of butter or a spoonful of oil, pour on enough boiling, slightly salted, water to *just* cover it, stir, and put a cloth over. Every minute or so I stir again and add a very little water if it looks as if it will absorb more. It is ready when it is just soft and the grains light and separate, not wet or gluey. The whole process takes about 5 minutes.

Flours

Probably no food has such an ancient history of snobbery as flour. Even in ancient Greece the nobility had white bread, while the plebeians ate brown. This was still going strong in Chaucer's time: the prioress ate white bread while the poor widow had to make do with brown and it remained a poor relation until the 1970s. But, there may have been more than snobbery in it.

Brown v White
Wheat grains aren't uniform. There is a small germ (the embryo of a new plant) which is rich in fat, protein and certain B vitamins. Then there is a big fibrous area (the bulk of flour) surrounded by a thin layer of protein, and a tough coating (the bran). These different areas react to grinding in different ways. When wheat is milled for white flour the coarser particles – the bran and wheatgerm – may be left behind and only the finer whiter areas made into flour.

The oils in wheatgerm mean that flour containing it will go rancid quite quickly. But once the germ has been extracted, flour will keep very much better. So the big white-brown divide was probably between the rich who ate white (and therefore unrancid) bread, and the poor who had to stomach a bit of rancidity near the end of the season. Of course, the millers have had a vested interest in pushing white flour, which would give them two spin-off products – bran and wheatgerm – to sell separately.

Wholemeal flour is the whole grain in flour. This gives it three times the fibre of white flour, but in most modern grinding, the speed of the rollers generates enough heat to kill some of the enzymes and vitamins. To have all the enzymes and vitamins you normally have to buy stoneground flour, though some millers – such as Jordans – produce the same effect by setting metal rollers to slow grind.

> Nowadays the enzymes which caused wholemeal flour to turn rancid more quickly can be made inactive. So most wholemeal flour now has a good shelf life.

Nutrition
Nutritionally you *can't* simply say – brown bread and brown flour = good; white bread and white flour = bad. Some brown bread and flour isn't really brown at all. It is white flour tinted brown by adding caramel – not a good additive. And, by law, calcium carbonate (chalk to you and me) *must* be added to all bread and flour except wholemeal, self-raising and wheat-malt.

So, if you want to avoid such additives you have to buy **100 per cent** wholemeal or **100 per cent** wheatmeal – as there would be little point in adding caramel to 100 per cent wholemeal bread and flour. However, that doesn't mean it is always additive-free. Preservatives are permitted, and used.

We should perhaps be grateful at the relative purity of our bread: in the mid-eighteenth century a tract was published entitled '*Poison detected, or Frightful Truths . . . a treatise on bread and the abuses practised in making that food*' and a hundred years later the first edition of *Enquire Within* said:

> *Bread and flour are adulterated with flour of inferior grain, Indian corn flour, potato flour, pea and bean flour, bone dust [!] &c. None of these are positively injurious. But they are also adulterated with plaster of Paris, chalk, alum, &c, and these are highly prejudicial to health, especially when taken continuously.*

Strong and Weak Flour
So far as performance is concerned, the big divide is between the grains which behave like chewing gum and

---

Addresses and suggestions for further reading are at the ends of chapters.

the grains which behave like bubble gum. Certain kinds, notably Canadian wheat, contain a substance called gluten in a form which is very elastic. When it is stretched and puffed up by yeast, it holds the air bubbles, as bubble-gum does, and produces the lightest bread. Other forms of wheat and other grains either have no gluten at all or have a form which behaves like chewing gum – stretching perfectly, but not being able to hold a bubble for the life of it.

For reasons best known to history, wheat flour made from the bubble-gum type is called strong, and the chewing-gum kind is called weak. Obviously strong flour is ideal wherever you want air to be held, while weak flour is ideal for flat crisp textures like biscuits.

Arrowroot
Arrowroot is very fine flour which, for some curious reason, you can often buy at chemists. Yet no less a gourmet than Escoffier admired its cooking qualities and wrote: 'It is . . . infinitely probable that before long starch, fecula or arrowroot obtained in a state of absolute purity will replace flour in the roux.' It is invaluable for thickening clear sauces or glazing tarts, as it thickens quickly to a clear jelly with no floury taste. Like cornflour, it needs to be mixed with a little water and then added to the other ingredients and cooked, while stirring.

Barley
This is a low gluten flour which has a pleasantly earthy taste, but makes a rather grey dry bread when used alone. It is best as a small proportion of the flour in yeast bread, as a minor ingredient in soda bread or as rolled whole barley in wholemeal bread or muesli.

Buckwheat (saracen corn, sarrazin)
This gluten-free flour is one of the biggest things Russia and America have in common: being as popular in American pancakes as in Russian blinis. But its lack of gluten means it is not a flour for bread making.

Bulgar Wheat (bulgur, burghul, cracked wheat)
These names are used for wheat which has been broken and processed so that it cooks quickly. It is used in Middle Eastern dishes but can also be used as a substitute for rice in some dishes.

Cornflour (cornstarch, maizena)
This is a very fine flour made from maize, which must be mixed with water before being added to other ingredients. It thickens rapidly, to a slightly cloudy, jelly-like consistency. It must not be overcooked or, by some disconcerting alchemy, it becomes thin again – a trick it repeats if frozen.

Durum Flour
Durum wheat is a very hard Italian wheat, with plenty of gluten, which gives firmness to dried pasta. Good pasta should say semolino (or semola) di grano duro or just grano duro on the packet, to show it uses this wheat. The term semolino (semolina) shows that the wheat was coarsely ground, but any wheat can be coarsely ground to make semolina.

> Durum flour takes longer to digest than other flour, so pasta releases its energy slowly – which is why it is often eaten the night before a sporting event.

Gram Flour
Gram flour made from chickpeas is sold in most Indian groceries and used in both sweet and savoury dishes.

Maize Flour (cornmeal, masa harina, polenta)
Maize flour is a rich yellow flour, and usually has a much coarser feel than most other flours. It is unique among the grains in being rich in vitamin A and it is used all over the world – in American spoonbreads or cornmeal muffins, in Mexican tortillas, in the heavy porridge-like mixtures which are staple in much of Africa and in a more sophisticated form in Italian polenta. What it lacks in lightness it makes up for in taste and nutrition and it deserves to be more used.

Oatmeal
Dr Johnson's Dictionary defines oats as, 'A grain, which in England is generally given to horses, but in Scotland supports the people.' The Scots get it right. Oats have the highest fat, protein and calcium content of all the cereals, and the most thiamin. Oatcakes and porridge are decidedly good for you, and oatmeal can be stirred into stews at the start of the cooking time to slowly thicken them.

Potato Flour (fécule de pommes de terre)
Potato flour behaves very like cornflour and is treated in the same way. It is excellent for thickening soups, and in Denmark they use it to thicken the juice of stewed fruit to give it a delectable gelatinous consistency which is most successful with rhubarb.

Rice Flour
This is a very fine flour which can be used to thicken sauces or to dust over bread to remove surplus moisture. It is not the same as ground rice, which is far coarser. Elizabeth David, in her bread maker's bible English Bread and Yeast Cookery, says it is particularly good for drying the surface of rich and sticky bread doughs.

Rye
This is the cereal on which the fungus ergot can grow, and rye bread got a bad reputation because of the ergot poisoning it caused. But this is not a problem with commercial rye flour today. Rye has quite a high gluten content, but it's a gluten of inferior elasticity. It is rich in fibre and vitamin B and though it makes a heavy dense bread the flavour is deliciously nutty.

Wheat Flours

Plain Flour

This is what is meant when a recipe says 'flour'. It is a fine flour milled at a low extraction rate, but with the vitamins thiamin and niacin added, plus iron and calcium. Being an all-purpose flour, it is normally a blend of strong and weak grains.

Self-raising Flour

This is plain flour with raising agents (mono-calcium phosphate and bicarbonate of soda) added to make it rise. It is excellent in scones and certain cakes. You can also get self-raising flour made from grains chosen specially for making cakes.

★ A proportion of self-raising flour in shortcrust pastry makes it lighter and more crumbly.

Strong Flour

This wheat flour is explained on page 76. It is essential for yeast cooking and is also good in other situations where air is held, such as puff pastry, and choux pastry.

Wholemeal or Wholewheat

As the main use is for bread, this flour normally has a high proportion of strong Canadian wheat in it. But the very properties which make this flour excellent for bread make it dreadful for pastry, cakes and biscuits. To be 'short' and crumbly is quite against its nature.

> This is by no means the full range of flour; there is also sweet potato flour, chestnut flour, water chestnut flour, banana flour, cassava flour (tapioca), almond flour, green bean flour and several others. But these are used mainly in the Far East and are not easily found in most parts of Britain.

Bread Making

> *Give me for a beautiful sight, a neat and smart woman, heating her oven and setting her bread! And if the bustle does make the sign of labour glisten on her brow, where is the man that would not kiss that off, rather than lick the plaster cheek of a duchess.*
>
> William Cobbett in *Cottage Economy*

Bread making is not the great hurdle most people suppose, though I reckon one batch always has to go to the devil before one gets the hang of it – my first effort broke a steel knife. Once you master it, the pleasure of this gentle art is enormous.

Yeast

Recipes may be written for fresh or dried yeast – 28 g (1 oz) dried yeast equals 56 g (2 oz) fresh yeast.

Mix yeast with water at 37°-42°C (98°-108°F) – it needs that temperature to get it going. If you lack a thermometer the water should feel neither hot nor cold to your finger. Mix water slowly into fresh yeast. For dried yeast reverse that – always add dried yeast to water *not* vice versa and stir *fast* as you do so, or it will clump. Dried yeast needs to work until frothy on top before being added to flour, but fresh yeast can be added immediately it dissolves – unless the recipe says otherwise. A pinch (*not* more) of sugar helps dried yeast to work, but too much checks it and fresh yeast does best without it. Salt holds yeast back, and vitamin C makes it work faster. So salty dough takes longer to prove, and if you want to hurry dough along dissolve 25 mg of vitamin C for every ounce (28 g) of yeast. But with dough, the more haste the less taste. 1 oz (28 g) will raise 3½ lb (1½ kg) flour.

Don't believe that the slightest draught will kill yeast. It prefers an even temperature and multiplies fastest in gentle warmth but, once it is mixed with the dough and has started to rise, you can leave it overnight in the refrigerator, and bake fresh rolls in the morning – if you are up to it at that time.

Kneading and Proving

To **knead** you press dough firmly away from you with your knuckles, then fold in back into a lump, and repeat this again and again until the dough is supple and springs slowly back if you press a dent in it. Rub your hands over with a butter paper before you start and it won't stick to them.

Leaving dough to **prove** means standing it in gentle warmth, but *not* in direct heat, until it has doubled in size. The ideal temperature is 18°-21°C (65°-70°F); if you feel comfortably warm in your shirt sleeves so will the dough. Keep it well covered during proving or the top will dry into a crust. Cling film over the bowl is ideal as you can have the pleasure of watching it rising

Knocking back is pushing or punching risen dough so that it returns to about the size before rising – surely the most disappointing moment in baking.

★ To tell if a loaf is cooked through knock on its base: if it sounds hollow it's done. If it has cooked in a tin remove it while hot (or it will go soggy) and place it on its side across the top of the tin to cool. If you want a soft crust, wrap it in a clean tea towel first.

Noodles

In the Far East noodles of every size and shape can be found tucked into soups, salads and stir-fries. More and more are now appearing in British shops. Like pasta, dried noodles keep for a year or so in a dry place. Fresh or cooked noodles keep several days in the fridge but lose their texture if frozen. Both kinds cook best in plenty of salted water. The timing depends on their thickness, and can range from a couple of minutes to several times that. But some are pre-cooked and cook very fast indeed. So it pays to check the wrapper. Cellophane noodles are a special case and need to be soaked in cold water for about 20 minutes before use and then absorb a lot of liquid in cooking. If improvising a recipe allow about 3-4 oz (100 g) of noodles per person.

Addresses and suggestions for further reading are at the ends of chapters.

Pasta

Somehow, since the Sunday supplements discovered pasta-making machines, the idea has grown up that fresh pasta is the 'best' and that dried pasta is a second-rate substitute. This is totally untrue. The Italian pasta cooking tradition is that dried pasta is correct for some dishes and fresh pasta for others. Also the shape must be right for a particular sauce, and this really does make far more difference than you might imagine.

A good pasta should have a distinctive flavour and there is a great deal of difference between the best dried pasta and the worst. Among the brands most highly regarded in Italy are Agnesi, Barilla, Ponte and Spigadoro, and my personal favourite is de Cecco.

The names of the shapes can be confusing. If you see two different names on what seem like identical pastas worry not. The Italians have never liked conformity and each region, and manufacturer, may have a different name for exactly the same shape and although the right shape does make a difference to the finished dish, it need only be approximately right.

Some brands of lasagne claim to need no precooking. Use them if you wish, but please don't call the dish you make lasagne. It is no more lasagne than a pancake is an omelette. It is some other dish with certain ingredients in common.

When buying fresh pasta ask about the proportion of eggs to flour and whether fresh eggs or dried ones are used. A good recipe should be similar to the one below, or see my book on page 125.

★ If you are making cannelloni buy big sheets of lasagne, cook them, cut each in half and roll the flat sheets round the filling. This is far easier than shoving stuffing down a tube.

Amounts

In Italy they allow 100-125 g (3½-4½ oz) dry pasta per person, according to their appetite. Fresh pasta is heavier, so you need 125-140 g (4½-5 oz) on average and more for a hearty eater. With stuffed pasta the numbers you need varies greatly with their size. Perhaps 20 tiny tortellini in a bowl of broth, 35-40 when served with a sauce, and 17-20 average-sized ravioli, agnolotti, or tortelloni in sauce. But it also depends on whether the pasta is a main dish or a first course. So it may be easiest to get the shop to weigh what *looks* right for one helping, then multiply up.

Cooking Pasta

The second great misunderstanding is the belief that pasta should be a soggy mess which sticks to the wall when thrown at it. To an Italian this is sacrilege.

Cooking pasta perfectly is very easy. Have a very large saucepan – for this you need at least 1 l (2 pt) of water *per helping of pasta* – and add 1 to 2 teaspoons of salt. Have the water boiling rapidly, drop in the pasta (but not lasagne, see below) and stir once to separate it. Let it cook at a rolling boil, giving a quick stir very occasionally. Putting 1 teaspoon of oil in the water before you add the pasta (fresh or dried) helps to keep it separate.

Lasagne has a great tendency to stick together. Slide it into the water one sheet at a time and don't cook too many at once. When it is cooked it is best to lift it out on a large perforated spoon and lay it flat immediately on clean tea-towels. If you have to tip it into a colander run cold water over it instantly so it is cool enough for you to pick up and separate at once.

A very fine fresh pasta may be cooked in 1 minute; an average spaghetti usually takes about 7 minutes; a big rustic pasta may take over 15 minutes. The only way to know when it is done is to take a piece out and bite into it. Dried pasta should be just *slightly* firm in the centre but not crunchy. This is what the Italians call *al dente*, literally 'to the tooth'. Fresh pasta will have lost the taste of uncooked flour and have a cooked look right through. Then drain it *immediately* and combine it with the sauce before it has time to stick together.

Reheating Pasta

Pasta doesn't reheat (or freeze) well. But if you have pasta left over with no sauce on you can microwave it or put it in a pan, pour boiling water over and leave it for just long enough to absorb the heat without overcooking. If it already has a sauce it can be *briefly* heated in the sauce, but some sauces – especially those with cream in – will turn oily and unpleasant.

Making Fresh Pasta

Making fresh pasta is one of the easiest and most soothing forms of cooking. All kinds of combinations of flour are used for different regional pastas, but what you need for most pasta is just plain flour. The proportions are 1 large egg for each 100 g (3½ oz) of flour and a pinch of salt. Work them into the flour with a fork or your fingertips (or whizz the whole lot in a blender as for pastry). Occasionally you may need to add a drop of water to get the right consistency. It should be soft and pliable but neither moist nor crumbly. Knead for 15 minutes, then put it under an upturned bowl to rest for 30 minutes.

For hand rolling you just roll as for pastry, turning the pasta constantly. For a machine start with the rollers at their widest spacing and keep re-rolling and folding the strip of pasta and passing it through again until it is perfectly thin and easy to handle (it may break up in the first few passes, but just repeat the process until it becomes more elastic).

Once the pasta is thin enough it can be cut to shape by hand or put through cutting blades on the machine. The essential point is not to have it too wet or it will stick to itself as you cut it.

If you ever feel daunted by cooking or eating pasta bear in mind the slogan on an advertisement in Italy for a brand of pasta from Naples, which boasts that it had the first pasta factory. It was addressed to other Italians and read:

> Think twice before laughing at the way foreigners eat pasta. Every Neapolitan may smile at the way you eat it.

Rice

Rice is the staple food in some of the world's most primitive kitchens, yet it has somehow become surrounded with mystery and labelled 'difficult to cook'. In fact, it's as easy to cook as a frozen pea, and almost as instant and there are all sorts of delightful variations to be tried, from the beautiful saffron rice of the Spanish paella to rice delicately cooked in coconut milk, which Malaysians eat for breakfast with a quite remarkable combination of chillies, 'whitebait' and peanuts.

Amounts
One cup of rice bulks up to 3 cups when cooked – or to 4 cups if it's easy-cook rice. Allow about 25 to 50 g (1 to 2 oz) per person, depending on how it is being used. It only has 31 calories an ounce.

Preparation
Round rice for puddings isn't washed, but the big question with long grain rice is to wash or not to wash. The answer depends on the type, brand and method of cooking. A lot of the free starch is removed in washing, so it is less likely to stick together or stick to the bottom of the pan. However, some of the vitamins in the rice go down the plug-hole too.

With most Basmati you have to get the bits of straw and stones out. But 'easy-cook' or American long grain cooks very well without washing if you use the draining method.

To wash it, swirl the rice around in a large pan of water, picking out any impurities as you do so. Use several changes of water until it looks clear. Then let the rice soak for about 15 minutes if you can (brown rice is greatly improved by soaking and is better with twice as long). Drain it well.

Cooking Long Grain Rice
The cooking time depends both on its variety and on the method of cooking. Rice is cooked when the centre is no longer hard, but it should be slightly firm and retain its shape. Don't let the publicity blurb about 'fluffy rice' mislead you. Rice *isn't* fluffy: it's light and separate.

No one method is 'right': using lots of water is quickest and virtually foolproof, but the absorption method gives you a better flavour. I shall start with the easy one.

★ If you plan to fry rice later let it be a little undercooked.

Surplus Water Method
For this method you only need to wash the rice if it has debris. You take at least 500 ml (1 pt) of water for every 50 g (2 oz) rice (5 mugs water to 1 mug rice). Bring the water to the boil, add about 1/3 teaspoon of salt per pint, throw in the rice, give it one stir to separate it and let it boil almost unstirred for about 15-20 minutes – but start testing at 12 minutes (see above). Drain the water, and serve.

If you can't serve it at once, leave it in the colander. If it clumps or goes cold just pour some very hot water through it, separating it as you do so. Drain and serve.

Absorption Method
For this method most brands of rice must be washed (see above). To cook it, you need 1½-2 cups of water for every cup of rice – 2-2½ cups of water for easy-cook long grain rice.

The usual method is to bring the water to the boil with a little salt, add the rice and a tablespoon of oil, stir, put the lid on tightly and simmer gently – without removing the lid – until the rice is cooked. For ordinary long grain this will be about 15 minutes. In theory, this produces perfect rice. In practice, there is a fine line between just cooked and just burnt. In some countries they make a virtue of necessity and regard the bits which are stuck together and browned on to the pan as great delicacies. Inventive, but not accurate.

● If it boils dry before it is cooked add *boiling* water, lightly fork it apart and continue cooking.
● If it is cooked before the water is absorbed you just drain it.
● If it is cooked and too damp but not drainable this can be cured with a *short* time uncovered in a warm oven – or a *brief* microwave. Watch it and fork it over if necessary or the top grains will be too dry.

A method needing less clairvoyance is to use the same amount of rice, boiling water and oil, cover closely and put it in the oven at gas no 4 or 180°C (350°F). It takes longer like this (how long depends on the rice, but a rice which cooks in 15 minutes on top of the stove could take 20 or more in the oven), however it is more likely to be perfect.

The advantage of the absorption method is that you can give the rice more flavour by using stock instead of water, or by frying onions, garlic and spices in oil, then adding the boiling water and rice – which is the ideal way to cook Basmati rice to go with Indian dishes.

Types of Rice
There are some 2,500 different kinds of rice. We are lucky if we can find half a dozen of them, but using the right type of rice for a recipe makes a difference.

The big divide is between **long grain** rice and **round** rice. Long grain rice is hard, stays separate more easily and suits savoury dishes. Round rice includes round pudding rice, Japanese glutinous rice and the Italian Arborio rice which is essential for risotto.

Brown rice has lost none of its vitamins and minerals, and tastes rather nuttier and more interesting. It normally needs very gentle cooking for about 40 minutes, but some brands take much less.

Wild rice is a brown rice which was found growing wild near the Great Lakes in North America. It is very long and thin, full flavoured and a good deal more chewy than other rice. Allow quite a bit more per person, as it does not bulk up very much.

White rice has been processed to remove the outer layers and with them much of the goodness. Just how much is lost is shown by the fact that in Asian countries beri-beri, which is caused by a lack of one of the B vitamins, only became a major problem after efficient rice milling was introduced. As we get plenty of vitamin B from other sources nobody should suppose white rice is bad for them. It isn't. But, if you feel strongly about the

Addresses and suggestions for further reading are at the ends of chapters.

loss of vitamins, buy brown or go for easy-cook rice which has retained more of its vitamins (see below).

Long Grain Cookability
Long grain rice divides into three types – pre-cooked, easy-cook, and rice which makes no claims at all.

Pre-cooked rice has been cooked and dried; all it needs is enough cooking to put the water back into it. This makes it the rice equivalent of instant coffee – with much the same pros and cons.

Easy-cook rice is also sold as 'par-boiled', 'pre-fluffed', 'non-stick' or 'boil in the bag'. Usually the rice has been steamed and partly cooked under pressure before being milled. This allows the goodness, which is normally isolated in the outer layer, to seep into the body of the grain. So less is lost in milling. Surprisingly, most easy-cook rice takes longer to cook than ordinary rice.

Untreated rice ranges from the cheapest and most basic rices to Basmati rice, from India and Pakistan, which has a fine flavour and a premium price.

★ Italians store truffles in rice, so the scent of the truffle permeates the grains. That way they have two truffle meals: the truffle and the truffle-flavoured rice.

EDIBLE FLOWERS

One of the easiest ways to make a dish look attractive is to add flowers to it and some supermarkets, such as Sainsbury, now sell flowers for garnishing. However, if you plan to pick your own be careful: some flowers are poisonous, others taste vile or may carry insecticide.

As nothing should go on a plate which cannot safely be eaten it is wisest only to use flowers you know are safe. If free of insecticide, these include the flowers of herbs which have edible leaves. They also include rose petals, pansies, violas and violets, nasturtiums, hollyhocks, primroses, scented jasmine, and the petals of pot marigolds (*calendula*).

Besides being decorative they can also be cooked with sugar and water to make a syrup which can be used in cakes, sorbets, and ice creams. A syrup made with elderflowers (*sambucus*) for example, tastes rather like muscatel grapes and combines exquisitely with gooseberries in fool, and with some other summer fruits. If you can find elderflowers which have definitely *not* been sprayed with pesticides or herbicides pick whole heads. (They keep for 24 hours in a closed plastic bag.) Simmer the flower heads, petal side down, in a light sugar and water syrup. When the liquid tastes deliciously of the flowers strain it and add it to your fruit.

HERBS, SPICES AND FLAVOURINGS

There is no easier way to make simple food delicious than by using fresh herbs. As M.F.K. Fisher wrote (in *How to Cook a Wolf*): 'The possibilities of their flavours, blended or alone, are limitless: the basils, the marjorams, thyme, the sages, mint, anise . . . what delights they conjure if you want them to!'

The same is true of spices, and their use is not limited to the exotic. Ground cumin sprinkled into home-made hamburgers, juniper berries tucked into pork chops or chillies added to basic pasta sauces (as they do in Southern Italy) bring verve to food which might otherwise be dull.

Buried deep in culinary history there is also the almost forgotten art of using herbs so that they not only delight the palate but also benefit the body. And scientists are discovering that their benefits are not old wives' tales.

It used to be thought that meat was more digestible if it was accompanied by tracklements – sauces and relishes based on the types of plants which grew where the animal had grazed. A charming idea, and certainly many herbs are markedly digestive and often included in food which is liable to cause wind. Others such as thyme, marjoram and chillies are preservatives, containing substances which kill bacteria, and food which contains them keeps better – as does food which contains alcohol.

Fresh v Dried

Though there are exceptions, like bay and rosemary, most dried herbs are not just ghosts of their fresh selves but desiccated and unpalatable corpses. Dried herbs can be used in a bouquet garni and other cooking, but as a garnish they do only harm. If you can't find fresh herbs for a garnish, they are best left out.

Obtaining Herbs and Spices

More and more shops sell fresh herbs but nicer still is to grow your own. If you have a garden you can tuck them into any border and many deserve a place on looks alone: few small shrubs are more attractive than variegated sage, and golden marjoram is the perfect ground cover, dense but not invasive. You can even grow many of them on city window sills.

When buying dried herbs and spices avoid the dusty packets of ill-frequented stores and buy them from shops where they sell quickly, for they lose flavour with age. The small resealable tins of the Rajah brand, widely sold in Indian shops are good as are Sharwoods which also makes a remarkably good range of chutneys.

Storing Herbs and Spices

For winter, fresh herbs can be spread out on a tray, frozen and packed in plastic bags. They will be too soft for garnishing, but impart a wonderfully fresh flavour.

Chopped basil can also be kept in olive oil, but it must be below the surface as any which meets the air will go mouldy. To keep mint for mint sauce the easiest way is to chop it finely and then push it well down in a small container of golden syrup. Then you can simply take a little out and heat it with vinegar to taste and your sauce is made.

Those herbs which dry well should be stored in dark

glass jars in a cool place, for the flavour lies in their volatile oils, which are harmed by light. Spices are equally vulnerable to heat and light.

Popular Herbs and Spices

In naming the following herbs and spices I have given the English name first, plus the botanical name and the French name, where appropriate. Finally, as ethnic food shops are the best source of many herbs and spices, I have given some names in Hindi.

Allspice *(Pimenata officinalis; poivron de Jamaïque; kabab chini)*
This dried berry is a distinct spice quite different from 'mixed spice', which is a mixture of spices. Looking like an outsized peppercorn, it tastes like a combination of cloves and cinnamon. Use a clean pepper mill to grind it lightly over meat before grilling, or add it to traditional fruitcakes and buns.

Angelica *(Archangelia officinalis; angélique)*
The soft, almost scented flavour of candied angelica is lovely in cakes and subtly delicious in cream cheese desserts. It's a ridiculous price, so it is well worth growing your own if you fancy the job of candying it. It makes a handsome addition to any garden, and seeds freely when happy.

Asafoetida *(stinking gum)*
This remarkably smelly gum comes from a type of fennel and is used sparingly in Asian cooking. It is sold as a block or as grainy brown powder. Keep it in a tightly closed jar.

Balm *(Melissa officinalis; mélisse)*
Balm is an easy-going perennial with a lemony flavour. Three hundred years ago it was described as *'a sovereign remedy for the brain . . . chasing away melancholy'.* A few sprigs infused in boiling water make a soothing, and calming tea. Some leaves placed in the bottom of a sponge cake tin give a hint of lemon to the cake.

Basil (Sweet Basil) *(Ocimum basilicum; basilic; tulsi)*
To the Romans this was the herb of fertility, and in the Middle Ages they said it would only flourish if tended by a beautiful woman. Certainly this family of herbs seems to capture the essence of summer. Dry basil is a pale shadow of the original, so this is one for a warm window ledge, where it happily doubles as a fly deterrent, and lasts well into the autumn. Its great partner is the tomato, whether in sauces or salads.

Bay Leaves *(Laurus nobilis; laurier; tej patta)*
Bay leaves are equally good fresh or dried, and their main use is in *bouquet garni.* A branch from a tree will dry in any warm room.

Borage *(Borago officinalis)*
A curious herb this, with tiny brilliant blue flowers and leaves so hairy that they feel rough in the mouth. With the aroma of cucumber, it is a traditional ingredient in Pimms, and can also be used to flavour soups and the flowers and leaves are lovely in salads.

Bouquet Garni *('or faggot of herbs')*
This is a sprig of thyme and several sprigs of parsley plus a bay leaf, tied together with white cotton (so you can remove them easily later) and used to flavour stews, casseroles and certain sauces. In some parts of France garlic is added, and in others orange peel.

Camomile *(Anthemis nobilis)*
Camomile makes a fragrant and soothing tea which has long been used as a tranquillizer and a treatment for insomnia, especially in children. Close-planted, it makes a dense carpet of glaucous foliage topped with attractive daisy-like flowers. It is the fresh or dried flower heads which are used to make the tea.

Capers *(Capparis spinosa; câpre)*
Capers are the pickled buds of the caper plant which grows in the southern Mediterranean. They are particularly good at cutting the richness of other ingredients and are essential in steak tartar, and *salade Niçoise,* and add a very special pungency to a number of sauces.

Caraway *(Carum carvi; carvi)*
These sickle-shaped seeds, with their aniseedy flavour, were the feature of Edwardian 'seedy cake'. That treat seems long lost but they are still popular in Central Europe for flavouring sauerkraut, dill pickles and certain cheeses, but use them sparingly for aniseed is a pervasive flavour.

Cardamom *(Elettaria cardamomum; illaichi)*
These aromatic little black seeds in their papery, three-sided cases are used mainly in Eastern dishes, but they were also very popular in ancient Rome. Their soft, almost scented flavour enhances rice, lentils and many other dishes. Cook them in or out of their lightly crushed seed cases, which should be a smoky green or a natural straw colour (or occasionally black), not bleached an unnatural off-white. The seeds can be crushed or ground in a pestle, but they need to be used that day as the flavour quickly fades.

Chewed and swallowed, the seeds are an antidote to the smell of garlic on the breath, and they are said to cure nausea.

Cayenne Pepper
Cayenne is a fiery red pepper, used mainly as a garnish, made from a blend of ground capsicums. It can, for example, be sprinkled on a prawn cocktail to give it a little zip.

Celery Seeds
You can harvest these tiny seeds just by letting a celery plant run to seed. They can be used to give a hint of celery to casseroles when celery sticks are not to hand, and on top of cheese before it is toasted or in cheese straws.

Chervil *(Anthriscus cerefolium; cerfeuil)*
Old recipes often suggest garnishing with 'chopped parsley or chervil', so it must have been a common herb at one time. It seems a curious alternative to parsley as its aniseed flavour is very different. But, its feathery leaves and frothy white flowers make it a charming decoration to cold food.

Chillies *(Capsicum annuum; hari mirch – green, lal mirch – red)*
Chillies are one of the very ancient flavourings, cultivated in Mexico for 9,000 years. There they eat 126 different varieties, and the market stalls are stacked high with their shining shapes in scarlet, orange, green and deepest rust, each for a different purpose. Even those on

Addresses and suggestions for further reading are at the ends of chapters.

sale here vary greatly in their flavour and fierceness, so it is always worth – cautiously – tasting each chilli before adding it to food. Red are not necessarily fiercer than green, but as a rule the smaller, the hotter. Bland flesh may conceal powerful little seeds, so the seeds are often discarded. But, whatever the variety, try to get them fresh or dried; most pickled chillies in jars have an unpleasant, metallic taste. South American jalapeño chillies are an exception. Fat, fleshy and green, they look as innocent as pimentos, but their fire is daunting and there are some excellent tinned brands.

Wear rubber gloves when handling chillies, lest you accidentally rub your eye with a fiery finger.

Chives (*Allium schoenoprasum; ciboulette, civette* or *cives*)
This tiny member of the onion family, with its long cylindrical leaves, is an easily grown pot herb. Both the leaves and flowers give a delicate onion flavour to salads or vegetables which they garnish.

Cinnamon (*Cinnamomum zeylanicum* or *loureirii; canelle; dalchini* and *cassia*)
Cinnamon was one of the most popular spices of the Middle Ages. Strictly speaking, it is the bark of the Sri Lankan cinnamon tree, but cassia bark from India is so similar that it too is sold as cinnamon. Powdered cinnamon makes a delicious addition to apple dishes and certain cakes, and can add a certain warmth to meat dishes. But the little sticks of rolled up bark are best in recipes, such as mulled wine, which have liquid to draw the flavour from them.

Cloves (*Eugenia aromatica; clous de girofle; lavang*)
In the West Indies you can see little bushes smothered with the rosy-pink clove buds, like icing rosettes, waiting to be picked and dried. It seems strange that such delicate blooms should have such a pungent aroma, but whether in bread sauce, mulled wine or apple pie, cloves are to be used sparingly and extracted before the dish is eaten, or they will overwhelm it. Which is why in savoury dishes like bread sauce they are stuck into an onion which can be easily lifted out.

They are also one of the oldest dental pain killers. Many dentists still put a dab of clove oil on a cavity they have drilled deeply, to desensitize the nerve, and clove oil placed on an aching tooth is often more effective than aspirin. Failing that chew cloves with the teeth which hurt, until you can get to a dentist.

Coriander (*Coriandrum sativum; coriandre; dhania patta* or *kotmil, dhania* – coriander seeds)
Coriander leaves, sometimes called Chinese parsley, are a herb, while the dried seeds are one of the oldest known spices, used by the Egyptians as long ago as 5000 BC. The flavour of the leaves and seeds is so different that one cannot be substituted for the other.

The fresh fan-shaped leaves of fresh coriander are one of the most pungent and versatile herbs. Try a touch in a green salad, or add a few to a fresh tomato sauce just before serving. Buy it in bunches from Greek and Indian shops and keep it in the refrigerator in a plastic bag, or standing in an inch of water. You can grow it from seed if you have a sunny border.

The seeds have a warm, totally different flavour, with a slight hint of orange, which goes particularly well with lamb and is a vital part of many curries. They can be dry-roasted over gentle heat in a heavy pan, to bring out the flavour and ground in a coffee grinder. But once ground, they lose their flavour quite quickly. So if you buy ready-ground seeds get small amounts, keep them tightly closed and fry them lightly to bring out the flavour before mixing with other ingredients.

Cumin (*Cuminum cyminium; graines de cumin; jeera* or *zeera*)
Cumin is one of the key spices in the combination which the British think of as curry. The little crescent-shaped seeds are best when newly roasted for 2 to 3 minutes in a heavy pan over a moderate flame until the spicy aroma rises, then crushed in a pestle and mortar. Powdered cumin quickly loses its flavour and must be kept in an airtight container. Like many of the 'curry' spices, it needs to be lightly fried until its spicy aroma tickles your nostrils. It's a flavour to give spice, but not hotness, to a whole range of food, from meat balls to plain yoghurt.

Curry Leaves (*curry patta* or *meetha neem*)
Curry leaves look like small bay leaves and give a distinctive curry flavour which is delicious in many Eastern dishes, especially lentils. They dry badly, losing their lovely aroma, but freeze well.

Curry Powder/Curry Paste
These are mixtures of ground spices largely created for the convenience of the British. They are *not* the basis of what Indians think of as curry, but rather the spice equivalent of chips with everything. True Indian curries are made by selecting varying proportions of the individual spices needed for that particular dish. All the same, the blend of flavours is useful in certain British dishes.

To develop its full flavour curry powder needs to be fried for a few minutes in oil or fat. So, when flavouring cold foods, such as mayonnaise, it is very much better to use curry paste.

Dill (*Anethum graveolens; anet(h)*)
This pretty feathery annual is much more than an ingredient in dill pickles – good though these are. Most of all it has a special affinity with potatoes. New potatoes or even a plain potato salad can be lifted out of the ordinary by a good sprinkling of freshly chopped dill or, better still, dill and sour cream. It also goes beautifully with fish, either as a garnish or as an ingredient in marinades and sauces. But its flavour fades dreadfully with drying.

Fennel (*Foeniculum vulgare; fenouil*)
Fennel is not one plant but a small family. You pass the flat yellow heads and feathery leaves of wild fennel in waysides all over the Mediterranean. There is also a delicate mountain fennel, whose tender shoots flavour Italian sauces, plus various types of the bulbous vegetable variety.

Fennel is also used against flatulence (which is why Italians eat wedges of the bulbous vegetable variety after meals). Equally, fennel water, made by steeping the seeds in boiling water (then cooling it), is an excellent remedy for wind in babies. Indians also dry roast them for a few minutes in a heavy pan over moderate heat and offer them in little bowls to be chewed at the end of meals as a mouth cleanser and digestive combined.

Fenugreek (Trigonella foenum-graecum; methi ke dane or *methre)*

Fenugreek is best known as a sprouting seed, but if you have seeds which are past their fertility period their distinctive, slightly bitter 'curry' flavour makes a pleasant addition to aubergine dishes, if they are used sparingly. Indian cooking also uses fenugreek leaves.

'Fines Herbes'

This French term is correctly used to describe a mixture of fresh chopped parsley, chervil, chives and tarragon used to flavour omelettes and grilled fish. But parsley, thyme, marjoram and chives, are an equally good combination for an omelette and these herbs are easier to acquire. Only in stuffing can dried herbs be substituted for fresh *fines herbes*.

Five Spice Powder (chinese five spice powder)

This is a subtle oriental blend of spices such as anise, cloves and fennel seed. When improvising, try a little in stir fries.

Galangal (galingale, laos)

This member of the ginger family was used in medieval European cooking but its use died out. Now it is found in Thai and Indonesian dishes. It tastes distinctly different from ginger but can be stored in the same way.

Garam Masala

Indian recipes quite often call for this ingredient. It is a mixture of spices, and there is no one recipe for the combination.

Garlic (Allium sativum; ail)

Garlic may be almost as health-giving as the old wives' tales claimed it to be. It seems to be strongly anti-bacterial and to thin the substances in saturated fats which can silt up the bloodstream. Its intensity of flavour varies with the variety, the vast cloves of elephant garlic being the mildest. You can also buy smoked garlic which is delicious chopped into salads. When cooking any garlic beware of burning it. Blackened garlic is acrid and spoils a dish.

Ginger (Zingiber officinale; gingembre; adrak or *soanth)*

There is a world of difference between the flavour of fresh ginger root and that of the dried powder. A whole rhizome keeps several weeks in the refrigerator, or you can deep freeze it. Since the sixth century BC the Chinese have prized it as a medicine as well as a flavouring, and the ginger tea which the Chinese drink after rich meals is an excellent digestive. They have long used ginger to prevent or relieve nausea, and in the West Indies it is used to treat morning sickness. It certainly works on some types of nausea: in recent scientific tests in America ginger proved to be as effective as any of the motion sickness tablets, but, without the sleepiness which some of them induce. The easiest way to take it is as crystallized ginger or ginger in heavy syrup.

Horseradish (Armoracia rusticana; raifort)

The twisted, dock-like leaves of horseradish can be found growing wild all over Britain. But in the garden it is monstrously invasive and hard to get rid of once established. Plant it in a sunken bucket and wear rubber gloves to peel and grate the fiery root. It can then be used to garnish steak or to make horseradish sauce by mixing 25 g (1 oz) of grated horseradish with 600 ml (1 pt) of whipped seasoned cream, and perhaps a hint of wine vinegar.

Juniper Berries (Juniperus communis; genièvre)

The colour of grapes and size of a blackcurrant, the pungent berries of the juniper tree are used mainly in marinades for game, and in the making of gin. They are also a good flavouring for pork.

Lemon Grass (Cymbopogon citratus; sereh)

Looking like a coarse grass with a slightly bulbous base, this is the ingredient which gives many Thai dishes a delicate and delicious flavour, which is like lemon but not lemon. If you can't buy it fresh, 2 to 3 tablespoons of dried lemon grass are the equivalent of one stalk, but it is best to soak it in a little liquid for an hour or so before use. If you buy the powder form use it very sparingly as it is highly concentrated. An Indonesian friend tells me it makes an unusual house plant, from which you can pick stems as you need them.

Lemon Zest and Juice

Lemon zest is the yellow part of lemon peel, without the bitter white pulp underneath. Use a lemon zester, or a fine potato peeler, or a grater, to remove it. It's also useful to take the zest from lemons before squeezing them and keep it to hand in a tiny box in the freezer.

It usually makes a big difference if you use freshly squeezed juice: bottled juice has the sourness without the fullness of flavour. But it is perfectly good to use in acidulating water.

Lovage (Ligusticum scoticum)

This attractive perennial was once thought to be an aphrodisiac, hence its name. It's a minor herb which can be used in salads, but its flavour is particularly good with eggs.

Mace (macis)

You find this neglected spice ground or in delicate dried tendrils around the shell of a whole nutmeg. Just as tarragon enhances the flavour of chicken, so mace has the ability to make beef more beefy, and improves beef casseroles.

Marjoram (Marjorana hortensis; marjolaine)

There is a good deal of confusion between marjoram and oregano and some people use the words interchangeably. But, in fact, they are two distinct plants with similar flavours. *Origanum vulgare* is the wild origanum which features in Greek cooking and grows in many parts of the Mediterranean. Either plant is useful in casseroles and in salads.

Mint (mentha; menthe)

Nobody needs to be told about mint cooked with new potatoes or with peas, but it is also very good in a whole range of cold soups, in varied Middle Eastern meat dishes, and chopped into yoghurt for eating with curry. A wide range of mints can be grown by anyone who has the space for this pushy herb. Mint tea is both refreshing and very digestive, and a sprig or two of ordinary mint in a pot of china tea makes an excellent cold tea for hot weather.

Mustard (rai or *sarson; moutarde)*

Since it takes moisture to bring out the pungency in mustard seeds, it gets its name from the must (fermented grape juice) with which the seeds were originally moistened. (See **Fox's** unusual mustards, page 123)

In Indian cooking both brown and black mustard seeds are used, the black being the stronger. The Indians treat both types of seeds in two completely different ways. Either they quickly cook the little seeds in oil to flavour the oil with a subtle sweetness quite different from the usual heat of mustard; or they crush them with a little liquid in a pestle or a coffee grinder to bring out the hotness. Buy mustard seeds in small quantities, as they go bitter if stored too long.

Nasturtium (tropaeolum)
I cannot agree with those who say pickled nasturtium seeds are a good substitute for capers: the flavour is completely different. However, the flowers, seeds and leaves all add an attractive peppery taste to salads. And nothing can convert a simple green salad into a party dish as swiftly as a scattering of these beautiful scarlet and orange blooms – but add them after the dressing.

Nutmeg (Myristica fragrans; noix de muscade)
Nutmeg is the nut-sized seed of a tropical evergreen tree. It is usually linked with cakes and puddings, but its delicate aroma has far wider uses. It is excellent with potatoes and with spinach, and makes a great difference to white sauce for lasagne and cannelloni. As it swiftly loses its flavour once ground, try to buy it whole, preferably in the hard seed case, keep it in a tightly closed jar, and grate it on a very fine grater when needed.

Orange Flower Water
Part flavour, part perfume, this is distilled from orange blossom petals and lends a delightful nuance to all kinds of summer fruits, and also to yoghurt.

Oregano See Marjoram.

Paprika
A mild, almost sweet, red powder made from ground capsicum, which is used in Central European cooking.

Parsley (carum; persil commun or persil frisé)
Parsley is becoming increasingly expensive. To make the most of it keep the stalks and freeze them for use when casseroles require a *bouquet garni;* they have just as much flavour as the leaves. And, if you have a freezer, freeze bags of finely chopped parsley when it's cheapest. It lacks the crispness of fresh parsley but has all the colour and flavour – which dried parsley does not.

Persillade is a mixture of finely chopped parsley and garlic used in French cooking.

Pepper (Piper nigrum; poivre)
Far and away the world's most popular spice, pepper is the fruit of a tropical vine which is treated in different ways according to whether white, green or black pepper is required. Whole pepper keeps its flavour well in a closed container but once ground it fades quite quickly. Keeping a few whole peppercorns with it counteracts this slightly, but freshly ground pepper is so good that it is well worth investing in a pepper grinder.

Pink peppercorns aren't peppercorns, they are the processed berries of a relative of poison ivy. They are slightly toxic if eaten in quantity.

Poppy Seeds (Papaver somniferum; graines de pavot)
Poppy seeds have a delicate, almost insipid taste, but are the basis of some excellent Central European cakes. In the north east of Italy, which was once part of the Austro-Hungarian Empire, they eat them with sugar and unsalted butter on home-made fettuccine – rather delicious. Keep them tightly closed in the dark lest they go rancid.

Rocket (arugula; roquette)
Perhaps this is really a vegetable not a herb. But, being a lovely addition to salads, rather than a total vegetable it seems to fit here. Although highly priced, you can grow it in any sunny patch.

Rosemary (Rosmarinus officinalis; romarin)
Rosemary dries well but, with its grey-green leaves and soft-blue flowers, it's a lovely shrub to have in a garden, though not completely hardy in the north. It is always associated with roast lamb, but I like it almost better with pork. It is best removed before serving as its spiky leaves feel unpleasant in the mouth.

Rosewater
This is a popular flavouring in the Middle East. It is distilled from rose petals, and there are some delicious desserts which can be made with it. Buy it from a chemist but be sure to ask for *culinary* rosewater, and keep it refrigerated.

Saffron (Crocus sativus; safran)
Saffron is the world's most expensive spice for it takes 13,000 of the yellow stigmas of the saffron crocus to make an ounce of saffron and every one of them has to be hand-picked. But half a dozen threads is all a dish needs. Dry roast them first by shaking them over heat in a tiny pan until they darken to reddish brown, and crush them slightly in a pestle. Then steep them for several hours in a few tablespoons of milk, or of the warm liquid from the dish you are cooking, until the colour runs, before adding this to your dish. Being very expensive, saffron substitutes and adulterated saffron are common, so it is safer to buy the threads, sometimes called 'leaf saffron', than powdered saffron.

Sage (Salvia officinalis; sauge)
Dried sage has a musty, almost unpleasant, taste but fry a few fresh leaves in the pan with liver to give it a subtle overtone, or tuck them under roasting pork – don't use too much or it can overwhelm the dish. Being powerfully digestive and antiseptic, it lends its benefits to any rich meat – pork, goose, turkey or offal. And if food tends to 'repeat', eating a sage leaf sandwich will often cure the problem.

Savory (Satureia montana and S. hortensis; sariette)
Both the summer and winter varieties of savory are useful in cooking. Both are easily grown and have a special affinity with broad beans – for which they are also companion plants to ward off greenfly.

Sesame Seeds (til or gingelly)
These tiny seeds are best known for their presence on top of hamburger buns, where they give their deliciously nutty flavour to the bland dough. But they are rich in calcium and lend themselves to use in both sweet and savoury dishes, and are at their best lightly fried or toasted. But, beware, they turn colour very fast and burn easily. They also tend to jump as they heat, so you may need an anti-splash cover. The flavour of sesame oil is

also an excellent addition to many foods and the perfect oil for carrot salad.

Shallots (*Allium ascalonicum; éschalote*)

Smaller, and perhaps more subtle, than their relatives the onions, shallots (scallions) emulsify more easily and are therefore the basis of a number of French onion sauces. Being smaller than onions, they are also useful whenever a small quantity of onion is needed..

Sorrel (*Rumex acetosa; oseille*)

The acid, highly piquant leaves of both wild and garden sorrel appear in omelettes, salads and soups in various regions of France, but its culinary high-point is an excellent sorrel sauce used to accompany fish, such as shad, in the Loire area. Hardy and very easy to grow, it is well worth experimenting with if acid tastes appeal to you, and tradition has it that it helps rid the body of poisons like alcohol.

Soy Sauce

Soya beans produce a whole range of dark-brown sauces which are used in the Far East, and each region has its own style. They range from the sweet types, favoured in Indonesia, to the dry, salty, Japanese varieties, and anyone interested in Far Eastern cooking will enjoy experimenting with them.

Tamarind (*Tamarindus indica*)

Tamarind is the bean-like seed pod of the tamarind tree. It has a most distinctive acid taste which is used in certain Indian and Far Eastern dishes. The paste is sold in packets and keeps well in the refrigerator, though one uses such small quantities that it is more practical to store it in the freezer. When you need tamarind pulp just break a piece off, soak it in a little water for a few hours and sieve the resulting pulp, adding more warm water until you have got the most from your lump. Keep it away from aluminium, copper and brass. The acid in tamarind can dissolve the surface of all these metals into your food.

Tarragon (*Artemesia dracunculus; estragon*)

Tarragon is the classic French herb for using with chicken, and it has a remarkable ability to enhance its flavour. This ability is doubly welcome when dealing with tasteless battery birds. Put a sprig or two, with a lump of butter, inside the chicken and baste it with the juices during cooking to get the fullest flavour. Or cook a sprig with any consommé or aspic destined for a chicken dish.

Thyme (*thymus; thym, faringoule* – wild Provençal thyme)

Thyme is a key ingredient in *bouquet garni,* and good in omelettes, and lemon thyme is lovely in veal stuffing. But dried thyme has an unpleasant, musty taste unless it is cooked for a long time, so it is not for garnishing or for briefly cooked food.

It also has a long history as a medicine. Its essential oil, thymol, is antiseptic and has been shown to fight salmonella and staphylococcus bacteria, and extracts of thyme are still used in certain gargles and mouthwashes.

Turmeric (*Circuma longa; haldi*)

We may think of this powder, made from a ground dried root, as an Eastern spice, but it's also the distinctive yellow spice in piccalilly. It has a soft, almost scented flavour, but it is a spice to use cautiously as too much can give a bitter undertone. It also becomes bitter if kept too long, so it is best bought from Indian shops which have a rapid turnover. Some recipes requiring saffron suggest using turmeric instead. The colour may be the same, but this is a recipe for disaster: the flavour is utterly different.

Vanilla (*Vanilla plonifolia; gousses de vanille*)

There is a world of difference between the flavour you get from a vanilla pod, which is the seed pod of a climbing orchid, and from vanilla essence. Put 2 or 3 vanilla pods in a large jar of caster sugar. It will give a delicious flavour when sprinkled over peaches, or used in cakes or stewing apricots. This way pods last for years. Where recipes require you to cook milk or cream with a vanilla pod you can rinse the pod in water afterwards and re-use it. Vanilla is the second most expensive flavouring, so such thrift is not just penny-pinching. When buying vanilla essence, check that it is pure vanilla essence not mere vanilla flavouring.

MEAT

Since the scare of mad cow disease the need for organic meat has become a big issue. But, as I write, there are no EC standards for it. So terms like 'organic', 'real', 'conservation grade', are all used. Such meat may be purer, more drug free, or from happier beasts but, without regulation, who knows? Where quality is concerned the length and conditions of hanging also matter. So ask what any claims mean, before you buy. Some butchers may, for example, meet standards set by an organization like the Soil Assocation.

Supermarkets also have a huge influence over how food is produced. So the more we ask for truly organic meat the more they will press farmers to produce it. Meanwhile, an association of independent butchers called the Q Guild claims to set high standards of quality, often buying direct from farms. Their meat has done well in taste tests (page 124). Or mail order companies (page 123) will supply 'organic' meat – at a price.

Increasingly, most butchers have resorted to convenience foods to tempt their customers. But every bit of creating, trimming and boning costs us money. For example, one meat industry journal told butchers that, although the profit on a whole turkey was only £5 to £6, the same bird sold in portions would give a profit of £15 to £16. That extra profit is our loss – it isn't hard to portion a turkey.

'We help you add value' proclaims the advertisement of one manufacturer of butchers' mixes for sausages and so on – a phrase which means the very opposite of what it says. For 'added value' is marketing jargon for cheaply altering a product to make it more attractive, so the producer can charge a far higher price. So the consumer gets *less* value.

With poor value may come more additives: most mixes contain them. By law any additives butchers use should be declared close to the place where the food is displayed – but have *you* ever seen a list of additives by a tray of sausages or faggots?

Buying Meat

Meat is muscle and its tenderness varies according to how much work the particular muscle has done. The less work, the more tender it will be. So veal is far more tender than beef, and lamb more tender than mutton. On beef the fillet, which lies under the rib bones and does virtually nothing, is the prized cut, while the neck, which held up a heavy head, is only fit for the stew pot.

All meat should look fresh and firm, not flabby, dry or discoloured, and should smell perfectly sweet and fresh. But it doesn't have to be bright red. Meat changes colour slightly in contact with air and perfectly fresh meat can go a deeper red. Dryness or a sweaty surface – not its colour – spell age.

Bulk Buying
In deciding whether you will save money by buying part of a carcass for freezing remember to re-calculate the quoted price to allow for wastage in bones, connective tissue and excess fat. The exact wastage will depend on the breed of animal and its weight, but of the following cuts the usable weight is typically:

beef hindquarter   67 per cent   side of pork   97 per cent
beef forequarter   70 per cent   side of lamb   92 per cent

This means that if you buy a 135 lb forequarter at £1 a pound, you will in reality pay £1.43 per pound for the cuts which are usable. Quite a difference.

It can be simplest to ask the butcher for a price based on the usable weight you will get from a carcass (even though you pay for the lot). Unless you say you don't want it the butcher should give you everything – bone, waste fat and all. If you want to use bones for stock ask the butcher to saw the shin bones into short cookable lengths. And don't forget about *marrow bone* (the soft centre of the bone) on toast – with plenty of pepper and a hint of sea salt. It's such a delicacy that Queen Victoria is said to have eaten it every day. The marrow bone ends are traditionally spread with a flour and water paste (to stop the centre running out) before being wrapped in muslin and boiled in water for about 2 hours.

To render spare fat into dripping simmer it for 2 to 3 hours in a pan of water. Let it cool in the water. When solid, lift it out, melt it down and pour it into containers for storage.

Fat v Lean
Given a choice between two steaks, one marbled with fine lines of fat and the other an unbroken lean, most shoppers buy the lean one. They are not getting the best buy. Fat in meat melts and runs between the fibres of the meat separating, softening and making it far more tender, as well as adding flavour. So often the most tender beef has a tiny marbling of fat through it, and although spare rib pork chops look less elegant than loin chops they can make far better eating. Meat which lacks this needs a good layer of fat over the outside and

should be basted constantly in roasting. The demand for meat with little or no fat has produced meat with less taste and tenderness. Yet the cholesterol risk in meat fat is slight compared to that in coconut products, as the table on page 623 shows.

Frozen Meat
To cook evenly, frozen joints should be totally thawed before cooking, especially if it is a rolled joint. It is also best thawed in the refrigerator. Chops and steaks can be cooked from frozen if you wish.

	Fridge thawed	Room thawed
Joint 3lb + (1.5 kg+)	4-7 hrs per lb (500 g)	2-3 hrs per lb (500 g)
Joint under 3 lb (−1.5 kg)	3-4 hrs per lb (500 g)	1-2 hrs per lb (500 g)

Raw Meat Storage
When you get meat home remove it from any plastic bag, handle it as little as possible – and only with freshly washed hands – and put it in the coldest part of the refrigerator where it won't drip on to other food. It is less likely to go dry if you cover it, but it won't keep better.

- Joints of beef, veal, lamb and mutton should keep 3 to 5 days.
- Joints of pork should keep 2 to 4 days.
- Mince, of any kind, keeps only 1 day.

★ To keep the surface of meat sweet if you can't cook it immediately coat the outside thickly with finely ground pepper. The pepper can be washed off before cooking. But don't try to keep meat longer than the recommended time.

Cooking Meat

Braising and Pot Roasting
The best way to deal with tougher joints of meat is to braise them. This is a delicious combination of roasting and stewing. The meat is browned all over in a little dripping or oil, then rests on a bed of diced vegetables, such as onions and carrots, in a pan with a tightly fitting lid, with just enough liquid (usually stock or wine) to stop it burning. It is then cooked gently on a burner or in the oven. Pot roasting is essentially the same but you add no liquid.

At gas no 4 or 180°C (350°F) allow the following number of minutes per pound, plus one extra pound 'for the pot': lamb 25 minutes, pork 30 minutes, beef 30 to 40 minutes.

These times assume the meat is tough and needs to be tenderized in the steam, so it will be served well done. If tender meat is cooked like this the time can be shortened.

Grilling and Frying
The exact timing will depend on the thickness of the meat and the fierceness of the heat, and the distance from the grill – (when grilling), so the following is only

a rough guide. The pan or grill needs to be very hot before you start.

A 1 in (2.5 cm) thick, rare steak needs 2½-3 minutes per side, a ¾ in (2 cm) thick well-done pork chop needs 4½-5½ minutes per side.

Roasting

The logic of meat cooking is obvious if you look at two extremes. To dry meat – to make African biltong, for example – you expose it to a very low temperature for a very long time. But if you want steak to be well done on the outside but very juicy and underdone in the centre you do the reverse, giving it fierce heat for a very short time.

With most roast meat you want something between those two. So moderate heat makes sense. At the same time you have to consider the size of the joint or bird. Heat takes time to get to the centre, and if large joints are cooked in too hot an oven the outside is overdone before the inside is ready.

Pre-heat the oven. Dust the joint with pepper. Whether you add salt or not is debatable. Salt draws out the blood, but if you add it just before cooking and start with the heat high, I doubt if it has time to do so – and it does improve the flavour of the outer slices.

Pork and lamb are improved if you make small holes deep into the meat, with a skewer or the point of a knife, and insert tiny pieces from a peeled clove of garlic. Both are also good with a sprig of rosemary under them in the roasting pan – either as well as the garlic or instead.

Pork with rind on needs to have this slashed at 1 cm (½ in) intervals with a very sharp blade in two directions – to form diamonds. To get crisp crackling brush pork skin with olive oil and stand it on a grid over the baking tin, so the crackling doesn't get moist in the meat juices. *Do not baste* – moisture and fat each make crackling leathery.

Traditionally, meat is roasted uncovered, with a little dripping in the container if it lacks fat, and basted regularly while cooking. But for meat, such as veal, which is inclined to go dry a roasting bag can save a lot of basting. The dripping doesn't have to be the same as the meat. Beef dripping, which many butchers sell, will baste all meat if you have no matching dripping. Failing that, use butter or put slices of fatty bacon over the top, if the flavour will suit the meat.

★ If you put two unskinned onions, with just their roots cut off, to cook in the roasting pan with the joint they give off dark brown juices which brown the gravy naturally.

Roasting Beef or Veal

Sear at gas no 7, 220°C (425°F) for 20 minutes. Then cook for 15 minutes per lb (550 g) at gas no 5, 190°C (375°F); 20 minutes for pink or 25 minutes for well done. However, joints under 3 lb (1½ kg) need about 5 minutes less per lb. Those over 10 lb (5 kg) need about 3 minutes less per lb.

Add 4 to 5 minutes a pound for lamb and 5 to 7 minutes for pork. Using a roasting bag extends the time. However, bones can affect the cooking time; so can the shape of the joint and whether you are cooking at peak time. So timing alone won't work – you must check the meat (see below). Pork must be well done (unlikely though it is with modern meat inspection, pork can carry tapeworms).

Roasting with Microwaves

Microwaves are not ideal for roasting meat. As microwaves can only penetrate a limited depth, you will get uneven cooking if the shape isn't uniform. However, the speed of cooking is appealing, and shoulders of lamb – being shallow and naturally tender – cook very well. Choose rounds of meat not more than 12 cm (5 in) across and turn all meat over at half time. Since meat is easily spoiled by the wrong timing I strongly recommend you to go by the handbook for your particular microwave, which will be right for its wattage. But the following is a rough guide.

First cover all projections and very thin areas with smooth foil – without it touching the sides of the oven. The approximate times per lb (550 g) using a 600-700 watt oven are these:

On Medium	On High
10½-12½ mins	5½-6½ mins rare
13-15 mins	7-8 mins pink
15-17 mins	8-9 mins well done

Cover the meat completely with foil, shiny side in, and stand for 15 minutes.

Testing that Meat is Cooked

You can test any meat by thrusting the skewer into the deepest part. On pork look for clear juice, with no blood in it. With other meat look for the degree of bloodiness – you may like it very bloody, or you may want to have it so well done no red blood oozes out at all.

Gravy

Gravy making is fast becoming a lost art, yet it is very easy. Tip all the fat and juices from the roasting pan into a jug (preferably a pyrex one). The fat will rise to the top. Spoon 2 to 3 tablespoons of fat into the roasting pan, let it warm on a burner and vigorously stir in enough flour to make a thick creamy mixture. Cook, stirring constantly, until it turns golden brown. *Immediately* pour in a cup of liquid, stirring fast with a loop whisk (or a wooden spoon). The best liquid is stock; failing that use a Knorr or Sainsbury's bouillon cube (the quality makes a lot of difference). Keep adding liquid little by little. If you have to use a spoon add the liquid very slowly, mixing well to avoid lumps. If you have a loop whisk you can be quite slap happy. Don't get it too thin before adding the meat juices. These should now have sunk to the bottom of the jug, so gently pour the fat into a bowl and add the juices and a little of the fat to the gravy. Darken with gravy browning if the gravy is too pale.

Keep the dripping for roasting potatoes or Yorkshire pudding, or basting other meat. Once it sets you may find some meat juices underneath which are delicious as they are, or can be frozen to add to the next gravy or sauce.

Addresses and suggestions for further reading are at the ends of chapters.

Carving

Meat carves best if you leave it for 15 minutes to settle, after removing it from the oven. This conveniently gives you time to make the gravy. Cover it with foil to keep it warm, and allow for the fact that it may continue cooking slightly as it sits. Meat for eating cold will be best if none is cut until it *is* cold: cutting into it when hot lets it bleed and makes it less moist.

The first (1856) *Enquire Within* had these words of wisdom:

> *Carving knives should be put in edge before the dinner commences, for nothing irritates a good carver, or perplexes a bad one, more than a knife which refuses to perform its office; and there is nothing more annoying to the company than to see the carving knife dancing to and fro over the steel, while the dinner is getting cold and their appetites are being exhausted by delay.*

Carving Beef

Beef is carved *across* its grain, and rounds of beef should be cut in the thinnest possible slices. This isn't meanness – though the joint does serve more; it is because it tastes better. The round should be stood on end and cut across the top with a *very* sharp thin-bladed knife. If you cut it on its side, like a loaf of bread, it is harder to cut it thinly and you tend to press the juices out of it. For safety, use a fork with a knife guard.

Carve sirloin on the bone down towards the bones and then release the slices by running the knife round close to the bone. You can't cut quite as thinly as on a round of beef, but the slices shouldn't be hunky – despite the lumps served at many carveries. The undercut or fillet (the smaller of the two eyes of meat beside the bone) is an exception: it is carved into slightly thicker slices along its grain.

Carving Lamb

Lamb is the easiest meat to carve as it is served in fairly thick slices. The bone is off centre in the leg, so prod with a fork to find which side is fleshiest. Place the meat so the fleshy part is farthest from you, and tilt the joint, with the fork, so this section is slightly away from the plate. Make several slices across the leg, into the middle of this area, cutting right down to the bone. The slices should be about ¼ inch thick and slightly slimmer at the bottom. Every few slices turn the knife sideways at the bottom of a cut so it severs them from the bone.

The bones in a **shoulder** form a Z, and one arm of the Z is the shoulder blade, which has a raised section down

its centre. You need to know where these bones lie before you can start cutting. So poke with your fork. Try to cut the largest slices the bones allow, angling them across the grain of the meat wherever possible.

A **crown of lamb, rack of lamb,** and **best end of neck** are cut between the long bones to divide them into cutlets. The bones slope diagonally, so feel carefully for the spaces. A saddle of lamb is cut in long – fairly thin – slices, along the spine. So, carve with the grain of the meat, not across it.

Carving Pork

A leg of pork is carved like a leg of lamb but slightly thinner, and a loin is carved like a sirloin. But a hand of pork is a curious cut which is hard to carve elegantly; prod well with a fork, decide where the bones lie and cut into the fleshiest parts first, cutting across the grain. When joints are boned and rolled carve like a loaf of bread – but thinner. Pork is carved less thickly than lamb but not as thinly as beef.

Types of Meat

Beef

> *Beef is good meate for an Englyssheman so be the beest yonge . . . Olde beef and cowe flesshe doth ingender melancholye humoures [yet] if it be moderately powdeyd and the grose blode by salte be exhawtyd it doth make an Englyssheman strong.*

> *Anonymous,* 14th century

Although the good cuts of beef are always more expensive than stewing cuts, the prices vary according to the demand. In many areas the better cuts – mainly hindquarter meat – are most expensive in summer when families are barbecueing steaks in the garden and roasting joints for cold cuts, and tourists are eating steak *ad nauseam*. To balance this the price of unwanted forequarter meat goes down in summer and this is the cheap time to buy it for freezing. The reverse is true in winter when the demand for casseroles and stew pushes up the price of the cheaper forequarter cuts, and demand for the expensive ones eases. So autumn and winter is the time when the prices of the better cuts of beef are most likely to fall.

For the best flavour and tenderness beef must be hung properly so the natural enzymes can work on it, and even with modern methods it needs two weeks. Not all butchers allow this. But some supermarkets now offer well hung, full flavoured, meat, such as Safeway's Heritage range. Talk to your butcher about how long his meat is hung. The more customers ask for properly hung meat, the more likely we are to get it.

Beef fat should be creamy in colour. If beef is very cheap check the fat. Very yellow fat is probably from cows not bullocks. It will taste much the same but usually be older, harder-worked and tougher. Though despised in the south, cow meat has always been used more in the north and can be a good buy for a long slow casserole. If your butcher doesn't have it look in areas where ethnic food is sold.

CUTS OF BEEF		
Leg or shin Hough/ Skink £	The lower part of a back leg tends to be called leg. while the same part of the foreleg is shin. It can include the shin bone for flavour and marrow bone when stewing.	Stewing potted beef
Silverside ££	A hard-worked leg muscle which is made into salt beef and tied in long rolls. Needs much basting if roasted.	For boiled beef/ pot roasting/ stewing
Toprump/ Thick flank/ Fleshy end ££	Coarser textured than topside. With more fat, but tender.	Pot roast braise
Topside ££	The top part of the leg where it joins the buttock. Tender, fine textured, full flavoured. Excellent for rare roast beef.	Roast
Rump steak/ Pin bone/ Pope's eye/ Hip bone £££	Fine grained tender meat with a layer of fat.	Grill/fry
Sirloin £££	Very tender fine grained meat with a very good flavour. Best cooked on the bone. But often boned and rolled, or sliced as steak. The home of entrecôte and T-bone steaks. A prime cut. Buy the thick end if you want the undercut (fillet) included.	Roast joint/ grill/fry steak
Fillet ££££	A long tender muscle running along the back *under* the bones. From it come medallions, tournedos and chateaubriand steaks.	Grill/fry
Baron ££££	This is the sirloin, on the bone, at both sides of the back – very expensive but good eating.	Roast
Hind quarter flank £	This is usually minced.	Any mince dish
Wing rib ££	Boned and rolled. Good meat from near the sirloin.	Roast/pot roast
Fore rib ££	Lying near the sirloin and almost as good but without the undercut. Best on the bone but can be boned and rolled.	Roast/pot roast
Middle rib/ Top rib £	Boned and rolled.	Braise/stew
Chuck £	Lean but tough, and often used for butcher's steak and kidney pie mix. A good cut for a long slow casserole.	Stew/braise
Clod Boasum/ Sloat/Lyre/ Gullet/Vein £	A very rough tough cut, mingling meat and fat. Often minced. Distinguished only in its names.	Stew
Sticking Neck £	Very tough meat which needs very long slow cooking.	Stew
Brisket ££	Boned and rolled, a joint with a horseshoe of lean and a core and rim of fat – much roasted in mass catering. Good but watch for gristle in the centre. Often salted.	Pot roast
Flat rib £	Mingled fat and lean.	Stew
Skirt ££	There are two kinds of skirt: goose skirt and feather skirt. One comes from the diaphragm, the other from near the belly. Both are thin and very lean, but only tender when rare. Excellent for steak tartare and Chinese beef dishes.	Steak tartare or stir fry

£-££££ shows the relative prices.

Cuts of Beef

The trouble with defining beef cuts is that the carcass can be divided in various ways according to the cuts which are needed. For example, a sirloin can be sold on the bone as a big carvery joint, be cut into T-bone steaks, or be boned and rolled into a traditional round of beef. This last leaves the meat from under its main bone free to be sold as fillet steak. So two cuts may well come from the same piece of meat butchered in different ways. To complicate matters still further, most cuts have different names in different parts of Britain.

Anyone who has become used to eating only the roasting and grilling cuts of beef, and is only acquainted with canteen stews of faded rubbery meat floating in tasteless gravy should have some pleasant surprises if they try some of the cheaper cuts in good recipes. With slow cookers they are very little trouble.

Goat and Kid

In some countries goat is a luxury meat. Similar to lamb in flavour, but less fatty, it has great potential. So some goat breeders are now promoting it and calling young goat 'capra' to avoid using the word 'kid'. Goat is still hard to find in butchers, but the body on page 123 can tell you who sells it.

Different breeds of goat fatten at very different rates, so the size of a joint isn't a good guide to age. But kid is usually 6-16 weeks old and a paler pink than adult meat. Either can be butchered and cooked like lamb or veal. If it is very fatless, marinade the meat overnight in oil, salt, pepper and herbs or spices before cooking. Failing that brush it well with good cooking oil, or butter. Either way, baste it (page 96) to stop it becoming dry. The offal can be treated like lamb offal and tastes similar.

Ham, Gammon and Bacon

Beef may have been the food of old England, but for most people it was the accommodating pig that provided the most meals. It would eat scraps, live in any yard and – best of all – its flesh lent itself to salting. To 'bring home the bacon' was to do well enough to feed your family. Their bacon would have been rather different from ours, and at one time each area had its own 'cure' using dry salt, brine, saltpetre, sugar, treacle and juniper berries in varying amounts before hanging the hams in wide farmhouse chimneys or special smoke-houses.

Names and Their Meaning

Most bacon is **'Wiltshire cured'**. Whole sides of pig are injected with a solution of pickling salts, then left to soak in salt water for 2 to 4 days before being hung up to mature for a week. At the end of the week it can be sold. This is 'green', 'pale' or 'plain' bacon and has pale rind and deep pink flesh. If it is to be sold as smoked bacon it is then hung over smouldering wood sawdust. The flavour will depend on the type of sawdust. Oak gives

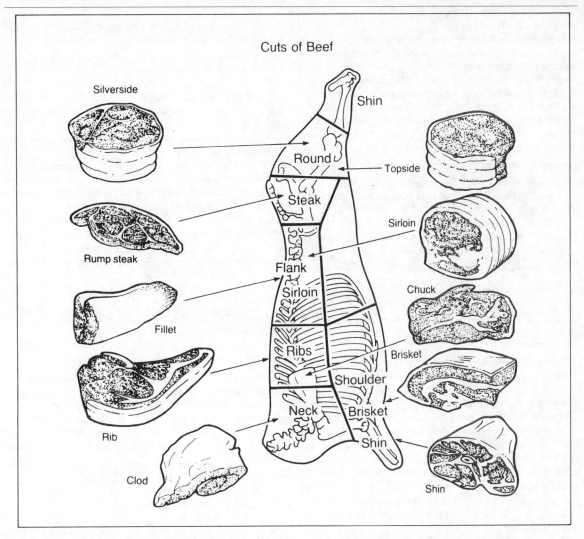

Cuts of Beef

Silverside
Shin
Round
Topside
Steak
Sirloin
Rump steak
Flank
Sirloin
Chuck
Fillet
Ribs
Brisket
Shoulder
Neck
Brisket
Rib
Shin
Clod
Shin

one of the best flavours, and is part of the secret of York ham. Legend has it that the original hams were smoked in the sawdust from York Minster. Sadly, bacon is not normally sold by its cure or its type of wood smoke. A pity, for there is a world of difference between the mass produced wet cured bacon often sold, and the best dry cured bacon.

Among other ways of treating bacon one of the most distinctive is the **Ayrshire** method used in Scotland. For this the side is skinned, boned and rolled before being brined.

Sweetcure, mild cure or tender cure bacon has not been laid down for salting. Instead a curing solution, which includes sugar as well as salt and spices, has simply been injected into the flesh over 2 to 3 days.

Gammon is a leg of pig, cured as for smoked bacon. When cooked and cold it is called ham. Other parts of the pig cured in the same way can also be sold as joints, but they are called joints of bacon, not gammon. There are also hams, such as Bradenham ham and York ham, which have been specially cured, smoked and cooked to give them a distinctive flavour.

TYPES OF BACON

Prime back	sold as rashers or boneless chops	£££
Prime collar	a good braising joint	£££
Prime forehock	not as elegant as gammon, but it tastes the same: can be divided into slipper (top) and butt (bottom)	££
Slipper	another slipper can come from inside the back leg	££
Prime streaky	as bacon rashers, or as a casserole joint	£
Middle-cut or through-cut	rashers or joint to stuff and braise	££
Corner of gammon	a thrifty boiling or braising joint	££
Middle gammon	the best joint or steaks	££££
Gammon hock/knuckle	a cheap, but bony gammon joint	£
Long back	frying rashers	£££

Water in Cured Meat

Some bacon has been reported as having as much as 16 per cent added water and not all the water has to be declared on the packet. If moisture comes out of your bacon when you fry it, or it spits a lot, it has more water in it than it needs for the curing process. If you see a white froth, polyphosphates have been used to make the bacon hold that water. There is only one solution: stop buying it. There are few things as powerful as a purse which doesn't open for bad goods.

> A monastery at Dunmow used to give a flitch (side) of bacon to any couple who could swear that they had not quarrelled for a year and a day and that neither of them had wished they were not married. In the 500 years from 1244 to 1772 only eight couples won it.

★ Gammon steaks can be too salty for pleasure. Soak them for a few hours in cold water to cure this.

★ Before cooking bacon or gammon rashers either cut off the rind or snip it at points with scissors, so it won't make the rasher curl up in the heat.

★ For easily chopped bacon, freeze slices in a block. Then slice through them with a very sharp knife.

Cooking Gammon for Ham

Gammon varies in its saltiness; if you find some you like, and cook it perfectly, note its details so you can buy the same next time, or it will remain hit and miss. Ask if it is salty when you buy it. If it is, soak it overnight in cold water – most gammon needs this even if it's not especially salty, but you can always check – if the shop-keeper *really* knows. If it is likely to be *very* salty bring it to the boil in plain water, throw this away and continue as below.

Drain and place in cold water with 12 peppercorns, a sliced carrot and a bay leaf. Ideally, you should also add a handful of clean hay to sweeten the meat. A romantic idea but, hay being hard to come by in cities, a table-spoonful or so of dark brown sugar (for a large ham) does the job just as well. Bring to the boil and then simmer it gently until the skin will peel off easily when you lift a corner – about 15 to 25 minutes per pound (500 g) from when it boils. The larger the gammon, the less time it takes per pound. For eating cold and plain remove the skin and leave it to cool in its juice. Better still, glaze and bake it.

For baked ham, stop cooking 30 minutes before the end, and then bake it for about 30 minutes at gas no 6, or 200°C (400°F). It will also bake very well next day provided it cools in its liquor.

To prepare a boiled ham for baking remove the skin and slash the fat in two directions to make diamonds. It is traditional to stick it with cloves and coat it with moist brown sugar and a hint of mustard. I find it is even more delicious coated with dark marmalade, but honey is an-other possibility, and ginger addicts may like to try ginger marmalade. To keep it moist put 2 to 3 soup ladles of cider, or its cooking liquid, in the dish.

★ Any coating for baked ham stays on best if you sprinkle the fat lightly with flour before coating it.

Braised and Casseroled Bacon

Bacon can also be braised. In this case cider is a good liquid to use. Cook it at gas no 4 or 180°C (350°F) for 20 minutes to the pound (500 g), but be sure it is well soaked, to remove the surplus salt.

Off-cuts and off ends of bacon which are going cheaply should not be despised. There are good casseroles to be made from them. Simmered with plenty of onions, garlic and lentils, and served with a tasty mustard, they can be most cheering on a cold day. Soak them (see above) to remove the excess salt, before use.

★ Don't throw away ham water. If it is not too sweet it is the best possible liquid for cooking lentils, beans or dried peas, especially as the basis for soups.

Lamb

Never you mind about the piece of needlework, the tam-bouring and the maps of the world made by her needle. Get to see her at work on a mutton chop . . . William Cobbett, Advice to a Young Man Getting Married

Lamb prices go up and down with the season, usually being cheapest in late summer, when spring lambs are ready for market, and most expensive in April and May. But this varies with the region and the type of lamb being sold. We know far less about lamb now than we used to. At one time even thieves chose care-fully.

The mountain sheep are sweeter,
But the valley sheep are fatter,
We therefore deemed it meeter,
To carry off the latter.

Thomas Love Peacock

To realize how recently such knowledge has been lost one only has to read *Food in England* by Dorothy Hartley, which – though published in 1954 – implored readers to cook different breeds of sheep differently, and be-moaned the recent loss of lambs' tails for making lambs' tail pies.

Today when cross breeds dominate the industry, we are deemed skilled if we can tell British from New Zea-land. And mutton is almost impossible to find. Though I am very much with the author of the 1858 edition of *Enquire Within* who wrote:

If you wish mutton tendere it must be hung as long as it will keep; then a good eight-tooth [i.e. 4-year-old] mutton is as good eating as venison.

Lamb should have white fat and be fine grained and a firm pinkish brown, but it darkens in colour as the sea-son progresses. It should have been hung for about 3 to 4 days, but hanging is not as critical with lamb as with beef or mutton. Being young all lamb is tender enough to roast or grill, but the nature of some cuts may dictate other treatment.

Addresses and suggestions for further reading are at the ends of chapters.

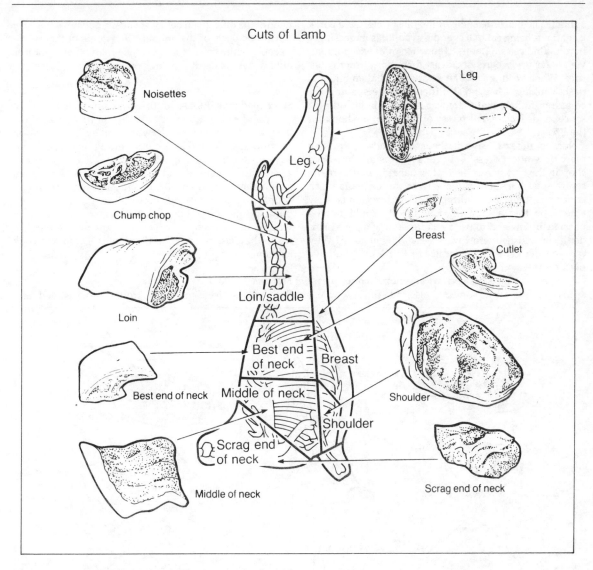

Cuts of Lamb

The naming of joints is regional. These are only the most common names.

Pork

Look at Pork. There's a subject! If you want a subject, look at Pork!

Charles Dickens, *Great Expectations*

The gusto of Dickens's tone makes me almost want to rush out and buy some. Whether that would be a good idea would depend on the weather. Pork goes bad faster than other meat, especially when it's thundery. This applies especially to brawn which, in muggy weather, can go very nasty very fast.

Pork is, therefore, a very seasonal meat little eaten in June, July and August. So that is when prices drop and you can get good value for a freezer. Its peak prices are November, December and January. The meat should be pale pink and smooth, and the fat firm and white. Whatever the weather play safe: cook it within 24 hours of buying and eat it in 2 days.

Veal

Veal is beef killed when very young – usually only 13 to 20 weeks, but the age varies from country to country. For Bobby veal the animal is only a week old. At one time air was blown into the meat, but this no longer happens. The meat should be pale pink and is almost fatless, and all cuts are so tender that only the shape determines the way it is cooked. Lacking fat it dries out easily, so it is best to cook it in a roasting bag. It can be almost too delicate a flavour unless enhanced with herbs or other flavourings, such as mushrooms.

Cuts of Veal

Being small, veal animals are cut up more like a sheep than like an ox.

Offal

Offal is the term used for all the bits and pieces of the

animal. They include some of the most delectable parts, but offal is being eaten less and less and it is increasingly hard to find certain items. Even when offal was popular, we ate far fewer parts of a beast than many other countries. When writing *Pasta for Pleasure* on Italian regional pasta cooking, I had great difficulty in persuading my co-author in Italy that there was no point in including a sauce made from small pieces of intestine in a book for the British.

Nor do Italians leave it there. The most surprising piece of window dressing I ever saw was in a butcher's shop in the backstreets of Naples: hanging plumb in the centre – with evident pride – were the genitalia of an enormous bull. And Elizabeth David recounts how when she told a French cook that it would not be possible in England to use a recipe needing a pig's bladder the astonished retort was, 'What do you mean? Why can you not get a pig's bladder in England? You have pigs, do you not?'

One person's lines between what is normal or unpleasant seem illogical to someone else, but those who eat

none of the offal given below are missing some of the most nutritious parts of the animal – and some of the easiest to cook. Some offal is more fragile than others, but it is always best to eat it the day you buy it.

Brains
Since mad cow disease hit Britain brains have become a rarity and eating calves or ox brains may be risky. However, if you are cooking elsewhere, calves' have the best flavour. They should look glossy and a greyish-pink and have no smell. You need about 500 g (1 lb) for 4 people. They *must* be cooked and eaten the day you buy them. Pull the membranes off the outside and soak them for a couple of hours in cold water. Then blanch them by plunging them into boiling salted water with a dash of vinegar, and turning down the heat the instant they are in, so they *just* simmer for 15 minutes. Drain and cook as the recipe suggests.

Feet and Trotters
Both calves' feet and pigs' trotters are cleaned and

Cuts of Pork

Fillet half leg

Knuckle

Knuckle

Chump chop

Fillet half leg

Belly

Fore loin

Hind loin

Belly

Fillet

Blade

Loin chop

Blade bone

Spare ribs

Hand

The naming of joints is regional. These are only the most common names.

Addresses and suggestions for further reading are at the ends of chapters.

scalded for sale. They have no real meat on them but they are useful for boiling with other ingredients to make a broth which will set to a firm gel.

Wash them well and remove any hairs. Soak in cold salted water for at least an hour, changing the water several times. Bring them to the boil in a saucepan of cold water, drain and wash again (often the butcher will have got them to this stage). Cook by simmering in liquid with other meat (to lend gel to the cold juice) or simply with an onion, carrot, stick of celery, peppercorns and a little lemon peel, salting lightly – the broth will be concentrated later and too much salt will ruin it. It may be 2 hours before the meat is tender. Once cooked, it may, for example, be served cold with a vinaigrette or deep fried.

Head

A much despised joint nowadays, but those on slim budgets could consider it. A pig's head can make an excellent dish of pork brawn. The lower jaw is sometimes sold separately as pork jowl. Being a mixture of fat and lean, it can be substituted for belly of pork in some recipes. Both calves' and pigs' heads can be treated just like feet above.

Pigs' cheeks are sometimes boiled, coated in breadcrumbs and sold as Bath chaps. They are hard to find, and rather fatty, but cheap and tasty.

Heart

Heart is a delicious meat. Lambs' or calves' hearts are the best, as ox heart tends to be tough. Recipes often make a palaver of preparing and cooking them. There is no need. Simply rinse them out under a cold tap, season, place in a small dish with a lid and bake, just like that, at gas no 5 or 190°C (375°F) for about 40 minutes. By that time they will be cooked but pink. Don't over-cook them or they become tough. They can be eaten just as they are, cutting off the rubbery and fatty top part: very plain but very tasty. Hearts are also good stuffed or as part of the meat in kebabs.

Ox heart needs to be diced and given long slow cooking. Any good recipe for a rich beef stew can be used, and the same timing. Trim out all rubbery ends of blood vessels, as you chop it.

Kidney

Lambs' kidneys can be bought nude or neatly encased in firm white fat. The fat is useful: if they are grilled with it on, it keeps the outside perfectly moist. Veal and ox kidney comes with a section of fat, and a few blood vessels on the inside, and these need to be removed.

Kidneys have three stages of tenderness: if you cook them until they *just* lose their pinkness they are deliciously tender with a good texture; cook them a little more and they become rubbery, and if you then cook them a long while they become tender again. In the last stage of tenderness, the texture is more grainy and the flesh less succulent. This is the stage to which they are usually cooked, but it seems a pity. If you try the short-cook method, cut the kidney really thinly; then the outside won't turn rubbery before the inside is cooked.

★ Soaking ox or veal kidney in salt water or milk for a few hours improves the flavour.

Liver

As I write, liver may be unsafe for the pregnant or very young. See In Health, page 604.

Calves', lambs' and pigs' livers are priced in that order, and that is also the order of their quality. Liver has the same three stages of tenderness as kidney. It either needs to be cooked very fast or have long slow cooking in a casserole – a good use of pigs' liver as the other ingredients can mask its rather coarse flavour.

Liver is often breadcrumbed, but it is unnecessary work. Persuade your butcher to cut lambs' (or calves') liver almost paper thin (only easy if the liver is chilled to firmness and he will cut it *much* thicker unless you insist). Season it. No more than wipe the bottom of a thick pan with oil, get it hot, put in the liver and when it has hardly had time to kiss the pan turn it over. If you have it thin enough it should be cooked through in no more time. (If it is thin enough it needs under 30 seconds a side.) Serve it *immediately* with lemon juice sprinkled over it and a scattering of parsley. Nothing could be quicker or easier, and it could revise your view on this highly nutritious meat.

★ To soften the flavour of pigs' liver soak it in salted water, in the refrigerator, for an hour or two.

Ox Tail

An ox tail has small nuggets of meat, cased in deep yellow fat, surrounding the tail bone. The meat has a distinctive flavour, but any oxtail dish needs to be cooked a day ahead. Then you can chill it and remove the fat once it hardens as it is excessively fatty.

Sweetbreads

These are the thymus and pancreas glands of a calf, ox or lamb. They look unappealing but their delicate flavour is very special. They must be blanched before cooking. First put them in a bowl of cold water under a trickling tap, so the water is changed constantly. Leave for 2 to 3 hours. Cover the sweetbreads with cold water, salt lightly, bring them very slowly to the boil and simmer for 6 minutes. Drain and wash them in cold water. Pull away any rubbery bits of casing which will come off. Pat dry on kitchen paper. Cook them as you wish, but lambs' sweetbreads simply need to be fried in butter until golden and served with lemon juice, and larger sweetbreads can be sliced and fried – they are particularly good when egg-and-breadcrumbed.

Tongue

Ox and lambs' tongues are sold both fresh and salted, and ox tongue is occasionally smoked. Salted or smoked tongues have the best flavour.

- Soak lambs' tongues for 1 to 2 hours if unsalted, 2 to 4 hours if salted.
- Soak ox tongues for 3 hours if unsalted, 8 to 12 hours if salted or smoked.

Having drained the tongue, place it in cold water, bring

it to the boil and then simmer for half an hour. Drain it again before putting it in cold water and adding 6 peppercorns and a bayleaf (salt too if the meat is not salted or smoked). Bring to the boil, turn down and simmer until a blunt knife easily pierces the tongue tip (lamb 1 to 1½ hours, ox 3 to 4 hours). It is easiest to remove the skin while it is still quite hot, simply pulling it off with your fingers. Find any small bones and pull them out. Tongue can then be carved across in slices and eaten hot with a piquant sauce to cut its richness. Or it can be pressed and eaten cold. For pressed tongue you simply curl it round in a circular container, pour in some good jellied stock (its own may be too salty), put a plate on top and press with at least 3½ kg (7 lb).

Tripe

This is the stomach lining of an ox. The first stomach is known as blanket, the second as honeycomb, the third as thick seam. Their textures are different but they all taste the same. They are opened, cleaned and scalded before sale. The length of the scalding affects the cooking time, so ask the butcher to advise you. Allow 4 to 6 oz per person. Some recipes call for 'cooked' tripe, simmer them in salted milk and water for about 1 to 1½ hours (unless your butcher has suggested otherwise).

METHODS AND PROBLEMS

Cooking Methods and Terms

Acidulate(d)

To acidulate is to add acid, as when you add lemon juice or vinegar to water into which you will put fruit or vegetables. The acid stops the oxygen turning the cut surfaces brown. Ideally, use lemon for fruit and vinegar for vegetables.

Agitate

To agitate a pan you shake it gently to and fro. The idea is to prevent fragile food from sticking, without stirring or turning.

Arroser

This either means to sprinkle with liquid or to baste.

Aspic

This is clarified stock or cooking juices from meat or fish, which will set into a firm jelly when cold. Well-cooked meat with a high proportion of gristle (e.g. shin) sets easily; fish stock may need a little gelatine added. Adding white wine to either improves the flavour. If you are only using a small quantity there are passable packet versions, such as Knorr.

Coating food in aspic is tricky as it tends to slide off. To prevent this chill the food and stand the aspic in a bowl over ice until nearly setting. When applied to the

chilled food it should set beautifully. To coat a mould with aspic chill it, and tip the cold aspic around in it.

Au Gratin/Gratin

When food is *au gratin* it is coated with a sauce, sprinkled with breadcrumbs – and/or cheese, and browned under a hot grill or in the oven.

Bain-marie

This is the technique to use when you want to keep a sauce warm, or cook something very gently, without direct heat – as you do when thickening sauces with egg. A *bain-marie* is any container half full of water, in which you sit the pan or dish containing the food that is being cooked. In the oven the water is simply round the sides of the inner container. But on top of the stove the water must always be underneath.

Baking Blind

Baking blind means you cook a pastry case before you fill it. It's best to refrigerate the pastry-lined tin for 30 minutes or so before baking, if you can. Then tuck greaseproof paper into it, pressing the paper into the sides, and three-quarters fill it with dried beans to keep it from rising. When cooking it, remove the beans and paper 5 minutes before the end of the cooking time and, if the filling may make the pastry soggy, brush the inside with beaten egg to seal it. Then finish baking.

Bard

This is to tie slices of fatty bacon over the breast of game or poultry to stop it drying out in cooking. It is usually removed near the end to let the breasts brown.

Baste

Basting is spooning over the food some of the fat or liquid in which it is cooking. This prevents it becoming dry, and regular basting makes a great difference to joints, chicken and roast potatoes.

Batter

Batter is the basis of many dishes – pancakes, Yorkshire pudding, toad in the hole, drop scones, fish and chips, and fritters. Pat food dry before battering it or the batter may slide off it.

The most basic batter is: 1-2 eggs, 100 g (4 oz) sifted flour, about ¼ l (½ pt) milk, and a tablespoonful of melted butter. The flour is flavoured with a little sugar or seasoning (according to its destination), the eggs stirred in and milk then stirred in *very* gradually until it is a thick cream which coats a spoon. Finally, the cool butter is mixed in and the mixture beaten with a whisk, more liquid being added if necessary. It must then rest for ½ hour to 4 hours so the starch can swell and the mixture lighten.

The liquid can be water and milk, beer, lemonade or even wine – beer and lemonade giving a lighter mixture. Some batters also use a little yeast, and others have a beaten egg folded in at the last minute to give lightness. You can use oil instead of butter – for greater crispness.

Addresses and suggestions for further reading are at the ends of chapters.

Blanch/Blanchir

If you are blanching large quantities by the first method you really need a basket to hold the food so you can lift it quickly out and still have the boiling water for the next batch.

a The most usual form is to throw the prepared food very briefly into boiling water, then drain it and plunge it into cold water. This is the method when preparing vegetables for freezing. The vital point is to have a lot of water – at least 4 l (7 pt) – to 500 g (1 lb) vegetables. Then the coldness of the vegetables doesn't lower the water temperature too much, and it rapidly returns to the boil. Have the burner on high and time the blanching from the moment the water returns to the boil – for freezing usually for 2-4 minutes.

Lift the food out and run it immediately under a cold tap. Instantly place in a big bowl of iced water to chill. When cold drain immediately and put to dry on kitchen paper over newspaper.

b Put food into cold water, bringing it just to the boil before draining. This draws out excess salt or blood from foods such as bacon or brains.

Steam blanching can be used to blanch foods before freezing when they are fragile. Simply place the food in a *thin* layer in a steamer or metal colander over rapidly boiling water and put a lid on. Time the blanching from the moment you put the lid on and allow half as much time again as for blanching in water. After blanching treat as for method **a**.

To blanch nuts put them in a bowl of boiling hot water until the skins are loose enough to pull off. Remove a few at a time. This method suits almonds, pistachios and walnuts. But to skin hazelnuts lightly grill them until the flaky skin will shake off in a paper bag.

Blend

Originally, this simply meant to mix ingredients together. Sometimes it now means to mix in an electric blender. But do beware of over-using the blender. The slippery softness of a slice of peach or the resilient starchy stickiness of a chunk of parsnip are far more delectable than a totally smooth peach or parsnip purée could ever be.

Boil

Boiling is the fiercest way to cook in water, and to be at boiling point (212°F 100°C) water must bubble and give off steam. A rolling boil is when it bubbles very fast. Some food is put into cold water and brought to boil (often to draw out the flavour); other food is put into the water when boiling. Assume the latter if the recipe gives no clue.

Bouillon

Bouillon is unclarified stock or broth from meat, fish or vegetables. If you have none, Knorr cubes can be substituted in some recipes – but only when the bouillon is not a central feature of the dish.

Browning

Browning food usually involves cooking it over a fairly brisk heat in a little fat, turning until it is brown all over. Whether you need a pale golden brown or a richer tone depends on the flavour you want; the darker the colour, the stronger the flavour; but too dark and the flavour is spoilt. You can also set food under a grill to brown or even in a hot oven.

Cake Making

Weighing Sticky Ingredients

The easy way to weigh sticky ingredients like treacle is to put the container on the scales, note what the total weight is and then remove spoonfuls, into your mixing bowl, until the scales have gone *down* by the amount you need.

Butter

If a cooking book tells you to butter a cake tin rub a used butter paper round it, for you only need a thin film. Better still, for most cakes, is to run a lard paper round, as lard is far less likely to burn.

Creaming

This is beating something – usually butter – until it is like thick lightly whipped cream. The aim is both to soften it and to incorporate air which will lighten the cake. It's easy with a mixer, but if you have to do it by hand, warm the bowl and put it in the sink (so it isn't too high) and grate the fat into it first. However, as I pointed out in my book *Supertips 2* no less a cook than Eliza Acton wrote: 'For all large and rich cakes the directions are to beat the butter to a cream: but we find that they are quite as light when it is cut small and gently melted with just so much heat as will dissolve it . . . It must on no account be *hot* when added to the other ingredients.' I totally agree. But you *do* need to cream when making cakes where there is no raising agent and a spongy texture is needed.

Once you have added the flour mix well but don't beat – beating at this stage makes a cake heavy.

Lining Tins

Time spent lining a cake tin with greaseproof paper is

well spent – it's a shame for a good cake to be broken in being levered from the tin. But if a cake will be even partly microwaved have no paper sticking up outside or it may catch fire.

Meringues are a special case. They must be put on vegetable parchment if they are not to stick. If you have none, oil greaseproof paper *very* well.

★ If you want the mixture to come easily off the spoon or spatula, and not leave a cook's treat sticking to it at the end, rub vegetable oil on the spoon first. (This works best on plastic.)

★ If you want a flat top spread the mixture so it dips in the middle.

Timing
Books seldom say whether the timing given for a cake is for a conventional tin or an aluminium one. Aluminium tins cook cakes a good deal faster. So when using one check the cake periodically to see if it's ready.

Peeking
Peeking in the later stages won't ruin the cake provided you avoid great whooshes of cold air entering. So open the door slowly, look quickly and close it *very* gently.

Testing that a Cake is Done
To test if a cake is cooked push a clean skewer deep into the centre. If it comes out clean (bar a cooked crumb or so) it is done. If there is even a hint of gunge on it the cake needs more time.

After Baking
For most cakes run a knife round inside the tin to loosen it as soon as it leaves the oven. Place a wire rack over the cake and turn the two upside down, so the cake comes out on to the rack. Then leave it on the rack to cool before filling or icing. However, Swiss rolls roll best while still warm, so turn them on to a sheet of greaseproof and fill with jam when not hot and roll immediately. If you want to fill one with cream just roll it up, rolling the paper in too, while hot. Then unroll it carefully and fill with cream when cool enough.

Fragile Cakes
Once baked leave a fragile cake – with a small proportion of flour – to cool and firm before removing it from the tin. Roll a roulade when cool but not cold. A light roulade will almost certainly crack – don't worry, the bursting look of it is part of the appeal.

Caramel/Caramelize
Caramel is sugar which has been cooked in a heavy pan over a gentle heat, with or without a hint of water, until it is a good brown. Browning starts at about 154°C (310°F) and darkens as the temperature rises. The strength of flavour increases as it darkens, and becomes unpleasant when too dark. Poured on to an oiled tin the caramel sets to a brittle toffee which can be broken into fine splinters which are delicious decora-

tion on cakes and puddings – but keep them dry and airtight.

Chocolate
How easy chocolate is to use depends on the amount of cocoa solids and cocoa butter it contains. Top quality chefs' chocolate, often called couverture, usually contains no other fats and a high proportion of solids. Giving a big flavour and a glossy finish. Bakers' chocolate has a high proportion of both but has some other fat and is sweeter. Ordinary plain chocolate contains far less of both. Couverture and bakers' chocolate can be bought by post (page 123).

If couverture is being used for coating anything it should be tempered first. This means you melt it, in a bowl over hot water, to 45°C (113°F) – or just fully melted. Then work it with a spatula on a flat surface or with a spoon in a bowl until it ceases to look streaky and has cooled to 28°C (82°F) – or will set very quickly on a knife tip. If it solidifies, reheat and try again. Otherwise keep it warm and use it immediately.

Don't be surprised if ordinary chocolate doesn't always melt in quite the way you'd expect. Even the makers couldn't give me any foolproof rules as it is altered by how it has been stored by the shop. Use plain, never milk chocolate; put it on a plate over hot *not* boiling water; don't stir it until completely melted and then use it at once. Or microwave on low until melting and glossy.

Chopping
Chopping may not seem worth mentioning; everyone knows how to chop. But if you haven't come across it, the swiftest way to chop an onion is to stand it on its root, cut a series of slices *almost* to the bottom in one direction, turn it and cut another set of slices across them. Then you turn it on its side and slice it, and it is chopped. You can space your slices so as to chop it coarsely or into minute pieces, and the chopping is perfectly even. Almost all other vegetables can be done on the same principle.

To chop parsley place it on a board, hold the tip of a sharp knife still (watching for your fingers) and lever the blade quickly up and down over the parsley with the other hand. Repeat, cutting the other way.

Clarifying Butter
This is butter which has been heated until foaming, then skimmed or strained through a coffee filter, to remove the milk particles which make it look cloudy and burn easily.

Clarifying Fat
Clarifying fat is just getting rid of the impurities by heating it and simmering it a while with about half as much water. Then pour it into a tall container to cool and when the fat sets lift it out (and scrape the underside if necessary) leaving the debris in the water. This is the method for cleaning dripping – if you need to.

Clarifying Stock or Broth
Broth is clarified by heating it with egg whites (first whipped until frothy but not stiff), with their shells added and preferably a small amount of minced beef and a little wine. Whip the mixture as it heats to boiling. Once it rises to the top of the pan remove it from the heat. Once it subsides, put it over low heat for 10 to 60 minutes without disturbing the crust which will form. It then needs to be strained slowly through a muslin or other fine cloth. Let the egg crust lie in the cloth so it acts as a second filter, and strain the broth through it several times if necessary.

For 1½ l (3 pt) broth you need about 2 egg whites, and 350 g (¾ lb) minced beef. The beef helps both the flavour and the clarification, but it can be left out if the broth already has a good flavour, in which case cook the broth for a shorter time.

Clotted Cream
Clotted cream is just thick cream which has been skimmed from the top of milk after it has been heated to boiling point and then left to stand in a wide pan. Anyone can make it – you don't have to leave it to the Cornish – but you can't make it with skimmed or homogenized milk. The richer the milk, the better.

Coulis
Strictly, this is the concentrated liquid, normally from meat or fish, obtained by long slow cooking.

Croquettes
Croquettes are cork-shaped mixtures of minced or puréed food, dipped in beaten egg, then in breadcrumbs, and deep fried.

Court Bouillon
A *court bouillon* is the liquid in which fish is cooked, and usually contains vinegar, onion, carrot and seasoning.

Croûtons
Croûtons are tiny cubes of bread, deep-fried until golden. They are mainly used to garnish soups, and add style and texture.

Dariole
A small, sometimes decorative, mould used for setting rice salads, jellies or creams.

Deglaze/Déglacer
With this technique you first cook some food in a pan – say meat browned in butter – and (usually) remove it. Then pour in some liquid, such as a little wine, and heat it while you scrape up the tasty morsels and juices which have browned on to the bottom of the pan. This makes the basis for a sauce.

Devil
Food which is devilled has been coated or marinaded in a mixture of fiery ingredients – mustard, Worcestershire sauce, chillies or any combination of hot spices which take your fancy. After that it is usually grilled or fried.

Dropping Consistency
A mixture that will drop easily from a spoon which is lightly shaken, but neither trickles off nor hangs on.

Duxelle
This is a purée of very finely chopped mushrooms, cooked in a nut of butter, with a little chopped shallot, until they are cooked but not too moist. The mixture can then be used for stuffing meat, or as a basis for sauces, and it freezes well until you need it. A great way to use up stalks – for, if you really love food, life's *not* too short to stuff a mushroom.

Flame/Flamber
This is to pour spirits – often brandy – on to a dish, let it warm, then set light to it. This burns off most of the alcohol as well as looking spectacular. But, spirits won't burn when cold: so, for example, Christmas pudding must be on a warm dish and the brandy warmed first.

Fold
Folding is a method of mixing two different ingredients or mixtures together without vigorous stirring. It must be very gentle, so as not to remove the air which has just been beaten into one of them. It is most easily done with a flexible plastic spatula, but a spoon will do. Slide the spatula down to the bottom of the bowl. Now make a C-shaped movement – starting at the bottom. Go across the bottom, then up, turning your wrist over at the top

as you lift. This takes the mixture from the bottom and deposits it on top. Turn the bowl a fraction and repeat. Keep going until the mixture is *just* combined.

Fool

A fool is a fruit purée into which has been folded about half its own volume of thickly whipped cream. Mash the fruit rather than liquidize it, so an occasional fruity nugget will land on the taste buds. Puréed it is too bland and uniform, and to purée gooseberries or raspberries is sheer disaster as the seeds become wood chips. Provided it is not over-sweetened, the acidity of the fruit makes it a beautiful (and easy) ending to a meal.

Frying

General Rules

Frying is cooking in fat on top of a stove, and the type, quantity and heat of the fat makes a big difference to the end result. Two rules hold good for all frying:

● The hotter the fat, the less it is absorbed into the food so the less greasy the food is.
● The hotter the fat, the faster the food cooks.

Each fat has a different temperature above which it cannot be heated without burning and giving an unpleasant flavour. In unclarified butter, for example, this happens at only 121°C (250°F), whereas lard reaches 205°C (400°F) before burning. The best fats for deep frying are those which reach high temperatures without burning.

Shallow Frying

For shallow frying use only just enough fat to stop the food sticking to the pan, then the food won't be greasy.

Stir Fry

This is shallow frying, often in a wok, over brisk heat while constantly turning the food over to prevent browning.

Deep Frying

● Use a heavy pan containing a wire frying basket.
● Have the food at room temperature so it won't cool the fat too much.
● Use a fat/oil which can reach the necessary temperature without burning or catching fire.
● Have enough fat to cover the food completely.
● Gently bring the fat/oil to about 182°C (360°F) – or slightly above before putting in the food. To test the temperature drop in a cube of bread. The oil should fizz hard and the bread bounce back to the surface and brown in about a minute.
● Adjust the temperature to the needs of the food. Raw food, which needs longer cooking, should fry at about the temperature given above. For cooked food, which only needs to brown on the outside and heat through, the temperature can be enough to brown the bread (as above) in under a minute – nearer 205°C (400°F).
● You don't need to use a thermometer, but if you want to use one make sure it can handle the temperature and preheat it in hot water, then dry it before putting it in the fat – or it could be dangerous.
● Don't let *any* water or other liquid get in the fat or it will spit dangerously. So dry the food first.
● Don't add too much food at once or the temperature will drop and the food cook badly.
● Breadcrumbed food fries best after a spell in the refrigerator, as the crumbs cling better.
● The frying basket should not be used for battered food as the batter will cling to it.
● If the fat seethes up DO NOT move the pan. Just lift the basket to remove the food.
● Drain the cooked food on kitchen roll over thick newspaper.
● Once cool, the fat should be strained through muslin to remove particles.
● If deep fat takes on the taste of food which has been cooked in it – such as fish – this can be removed by frying some raw potato in it.
● The smoking point – which comes before burning – is around 191°C (375°F) for animal fats and 232°C (450°F) for vegetable fats.

> WARNING At very high temperatures fat or oil will catch fire by itself. It must not be allowed to overheat and needs *constant* attention. NEVER move a pan of hot fat. *If fat catches fire DO NOT put water on it or move it. Cover it as closely as possible with a lid or thick cloth.*

Fumet

A *fumet* is the concentrated liquid in which fish (or

Addresses and suggestions for further reading are at the ends of chapters.

occasionally meat) has been cooked, or which has run from it during cooking.

Glaze
Glazing is coating food with a shiny finish. Like a tie on a man, it makes it look much smarter. On fruit tarts this is done with melted jam (especially apricot), on cold meat with jellied meat juices, on pastry with beaten whole egg, yolk or white, according to what is to hand. Bread and buns can have all kinds of glazes and the glaze can alter the crust: melted butter (soft crust), milk or water (crisp crust), sugar and water (or milk) syrup (soft sticky crust), egg and/or cream for a dark crust.

Grill
Grilling is cooking food rapidly under strong heat, without fat or liquid – though it can first be brushed with butter or oil, if you wish. Slow grilling will dry the food out, so preheat the grill. Americans call this broiling, as we used to in other centuries.

Icing
For smooth icing always sieve icing sugar before use.

Butter Icing
Adding one egg yolk makes it far more luscious – though softer. Add the yolk before the sugar. (Basic butter icing is just creamed butter into which is beaten twice its weight in icing sugar, then flavouring added – 75 g (3 oz) butter to 150 g (6 oz) sugar are the standard weights for an average cake.)

Fondant/Fondant Icing
This is just sugar and water boiled to 114° to 116°C (238° to 240°F), beaten with a wooden spoon until it becomes white, then kneaded on a board. It can be used to make sweets or thinned a little with sugar syrup – sugar cooked to a thin syrup with a touch of water – for icing a cake. Either way, it can be flavoured, for example with lemon juice.

Glacé Icing
This is simply sifted icing sugar worked with a little water and flavouring to the right thickness. I always like the look of it running down the sides of a cake, it has a certain generosity about it. But if you dislike trickles wrap a band of greaseproof paper tightly round the cake, so it stands slightly above the top, before you ice it. Then peel it off after the icing is set.

Royal Icing
To prevent royal icing being so rock-like that granny will break her dentures add a teaspoonful of glycerine (from a chemist but perfectly safe to eat) for each 450 g (1 lb) of icing sugar. To stop it being sickly sweet add the same amount of lemon juice.

To fill an icing bag easily, drop the end in a clean jam jar, and fold the top out over the edge of the jar.

Infuse
Infusing is letting a flavouring stand in hot liquid, or be gently heated with it, until the liquid takes it on.

Julienne Strips
Cutting vegetables into *julienne* strips means cutting them to the size and shape of a matchstick – not as slow as it sounds if you cut thin slices one way, stack them, and cut equally thin slices across the other.

The quick way to make *julienne* strips of orange or lemon zest is to use a lemon zester – a cheap and invaluable tool.

Jus/Jus de viande
The natural juices which run from meat in its cooking and set into a delicious jelly when cold.

Knock up
You knock up flaky pastry by making tiny cuts horizontally along its raw edge with a sharp knife, so that the layers separate more easily in cooking.

Larding
To lard meat you use a special larding needle to thread thin strips of fat through it, to give it flavour and moisture when cooking. This is done when meat lacks its own fat and pork fat is generally used.

Leavening or Raising
Any ingredient which will make others rise in cooking is leavening – yeast, baking powder, bicarbonate of soda, egg and so on.

Bicarbonate of soda and baking powder both foam when mixed with any acid, so using sour milk, lemon juice or even a touch of vinegar in any recipe which contains them produces a lighter result.

Baking powder tends to leave a dry after-taste in the mouth and, although it is often recommended in scones, I find a much better result is obtained by just mixing self-raising flour with sour milk and sugar. And bicarbonate and sour milk can be used in most cakes which use both baking powder and a liquid.

Macédoine
This is a mixture of vegetables, diced small, or occasionally a mixed fruit salad, perhaps of dried fruit.

Macerate
To soak food in a liquid, usually alcohol of some kind.

Marinade
To marinate meat or fish is to leave it for a number of hours in a combination of liquid and seasonings, to improve the flavour and/or tenderize it. The marinade is often wine of some sort.

Most recipes for marinades only use a small quantity of liquid, which may not cover the meat, so it needs to be turned over at half time. The easy way is to put the whole lot in a plastic bag. Then, to turn the food, you just turn the bag over.

Medallions
Small rounds of meat or vegetables.

Oiling a Mould

This is simply brushing a tasteless oil over the inside of a container, with a pastry brush, so that it will later be easy to turn food out. Get into all the nooks and crannies of shaped moulds, that is where food may stick. Then leave the mould upside down, on paper, to drain.

Papillote

A *papillote* is a paper casing folded round food so that the flavour is contained during cooking. Use grease-proof paper or foil.

Parboil

To part-boil or half cook by boiling.

Paupiette

A paupiette is a very thin slice of meat, or fish, which is then covered with a stuffing, rolled into a log, and tied for cooking.

Poach

This is to cook food in an open pan of liquid which is at slightly below simmering point i.e. 77° to 82°C (170° to 180°F). Most poaching is done on a burner, but it can be done in the oven, and confusingly the *bain-marie* technique (see page 96) of cooking may be called poaching. For poached eggs see page 46.

Purée

Puréed food has been sieved, mashed or liquidized. Whether you remove all the lumps or leave a rougher texture depends on what you want to do with it.

Reduce

Contrary to what you might suppose, reducing liquid doesn't mean chucking half down the sink. Instead you boil it rapidly so it evaporates and the flavour is concentrated. This will intensify the saltiness, so go gently before reducing.

Rest or Relax

This is the process of leaving batters, for pancakes or Yorkshire pudding, to stand for half an hour or so while the starch grains swell before cooking, so you get lighter results. It is also to put pastry in a cool place for an hour or two to let the gluten in the flour contract after the mixing and handling, so it is less likely to shrink in baking.

Rub

Rubbing in fat is a matter of literally rubbing the fat and flour lightly between the tips of your fingers to a crumb-like mixture. Lightness of touch is essential or the mixture will become hot and heavy. For good results freeze the fat, and grate it into refrigerated flour on a coarse grater. This keeps the mixture cool and makes rubbing in very easy.

Sauce Making

Béchamel/White Sauce

A *béchamel* is white sauce, made of flour, butter and milk, in which the milk is first flavoured by heating it with carrot, celery and an onion stuck with a clove. Start it with a *roux* (see below). The secret is to add the liquid gradually while stirring hard with a loop whisk – in that way you won't get lumps.

Beurre Manié/Kneaded Butter

This is equal weights of flour and butter worked together into a paste. Small balls of it can be dropped into casseroles to thicken the liquid, but there must be sufficient cooking time afterwards to remove the taste of raw flour. It can be kept ready for use in the refrigerator. But, though it's considered fearfully expert, I am no great fan. Lacking the prior cooking of a *roux*, the flour takes an interminable time to lose its uncooked taste. Being impatient, I prefer to make a quick *roux* and stir that in (see below).

Alternatively, thickening with a little cornflour, potato flour (*fécule*) or arrowroot, mixed with a spoonful or two of water gives a more translucent look to the liquid, which can be even better – though classically incorrect for some sauces, and not right for some dishes, such as soups. The advantage of potato flour or arrowroot is that these root flours never give the raw taste of uncooked cereal flours. Whatever you use, stir well as you add it to the hot liquid – using a loop whisk to avoid lumps – and simmer gently until thick. These flours thicken quickly, so you can add a little until the sauce is perfect.

Cream-thickened Sauces

To use cream there must only be a small quantity of other liquid, such as a little juice and fat from frying the meat and a little wine, which has been used to deglaze the pan. Into this you stir double cream, which should really be at room temperature (the acid in the wine is then less likely to curdle it). Cook it gently, stirring continuously, and it will slowly thicken. It's beautifully easy so long as the pan is wide. If you bottle a lot of cream up in a narrow pan you can wait till kingdom come before it thickens. And single cream won't thicken at all.

Egg-thickened Sauces

Sauce *béarnaise* is the classic among egg-thickened sauces, and egg thickening is, admittedly, tricky if it is not to end up scrambled. The essential ingredient is patience. Any sauce thickened with egg yolks must be cooked in a *bain-marie* (page 96), and the water underneath must not boil. The sauce then thickens very slowly, and you must stir it all the time. When thick it will be tepid, not hot. That is how it should be.

French Dressing

Whatever bastardized mixtures restaurants produce under this name, the correct and invariable ingredients are salt, pepper, olive oil and either wine vinegar or lemon juice. Sugar, mustard, garlic and other herbs can all be added – if you wish – but they are not fundamental. The proportions are about 1 part vinegar to 3 to 4 parts oil, and the ingredients are stirred together or put in a screw-top jar and shaken. It must be re-stirred just before pouring, as it separates rapidly.

Addresses and suggestions for further reading are at the ends of chapters.

It will only be as good as your ingredients – there is a world of difference between the result you get with sea salt, freshly ground black pepper, full-flavoured olive oil and good vinegar, and the sad affair concocted with table salt, packet pepper, malt vinegar and a tasteless cooking oil.

Roux
To make a *roux* you melt butter, stir in flour and cook it gently stirring constantly until white and frothy. This is the basis for sauces, such as white sauce, for thick soups and for the basic mixture in soufflés.

Brown Roux
For a brown *roux* dripping often replaces butter, and the fat and flour are cooked together until they are light brown before any liquid is added. This gives a brown sauce, and is a way to make brown gravy without using gravy browning. Finish as for *Béchamel*.

Vinaigrette Sauce
This is really French dressing (see above) with finely chopped onion and other flavourings, such as gherkins, parsley or capers, added to it to suit the food it dresses. In *haute cuisine* the different combinations of ingredients each form a sauce with its own special name.

Sauter/Sautéing
Sauter is French for to jump, so the food is jumped in the pan. This means it is cooked quite rapidly in a little hot butter or other fat while you shake or turn it so it cooks evenly.

Scald
Scald has two meanings: to heat milk to the point where it begins to bubble and rise, and to pour boiling water over something.

Season
This is to add salt and pepper to a dish until it tastes right. Cooked food should be tasted to check how much to add, but most raw meat should not be eaten, so seasoning it is guesswork.

Simmer
Liquid cooked on top of a stove is simmering when it shudders gently with only the occasional bubble at 85°-93°C (185°-200°F). If it bubbles all over it is boiling.

Skinning/Peeling
If you drop thin-skinned fruit such as ripe tomatoes and peaches into a bowl of boiling hot water for a minute or so, then run them under cold water the skins come off easily. You can also freeze whole tomatoes for sauces and, when you need them, run them under a hot tap, when rock solid, and the skin will peel off easily.

Aubergines and Pimentos
To skin aubergines and pimentos you need to grill them all over, until black, and then pull off the skin, rinsing the charred fragments from pimentos under a cold tap.

Nuts
Almonds, walnuts, pecans and pistachio nuts can be skinned after blanching (page 97), but add a pinch of bicarbonate of soda to make pistachios greener. Hazelnuts need to be grilled lightly; the skins will then shake off in a paper bag.

Fish – see page 49

Rabbit or Hare – see page 72.

Tongue and Gammon – see page 95.

Slake
To mix cornflour, arrowroot or similar substances to a thin paste with a little cold liquid. Use just enough liquid to give the thickness of thick pouring cream.

Steam
There are two ways of cooking food in steam:

1 Place it in a steamer (or any other heatproof container with holes which allows the steam through) over boiling water until cooked – a metal colander will stand in for a proper steamer. This suits vegetables, fish and so on.
2 Put the food in a heatproof basin, cover it well, place it in boiling water to within 4 cm (1½ in) of the rim and boil with the lid on the pan. The method for steamed puddings.

If long cooking is involved, by either method, top up with boiling water from time to time – adding cold water would alter the cooking time and maybe crack the basin. When covering puddings which will rise, make a pleat in the centre of the paper or foil to allow for expansion. If fragile food will need to be turned out of its mould after steaming, leave it to stand for a few minutes after removing it from the steamer.

Stewing
Stewing is really simmering at its gentlest: the liquid should hardly tremble. It is ideal for food, such as fruit, which would break up with rapid cooking. Normally, this is done on top of the stove, but on gas it can be hard to get the heat low enough. In this case, use a heat-reducing mat under the pan, or put the food in a covered dish in a low oven instead.

Sweat
This is the process of cooking vegetables very slowly, in butter or oil, to draw out moisture and soften them.

Sweet Making
The **crack** stage in boiling sugar is when it will form a brittle strand, when dropped into cold water, which cracks. This happens at around 154°C (310°F).
  Hard ball is the stage when boiled sugar mixtures form a hard ball when dropped in cold water. This happens at about 121°-124°C (250°-255°F).
  Soft ball is the stage in boiling at which sugar, or mixtures used in sweet making, can be made into a soft

ball with the fingers, after being dropped into a bowl of cold water – about 115°C (240°F).

When boiled rapidly sugar mixtures reach a point when they will pull into a fine **thread.** Short threads are about 1 cm (½ in) long, and long threads 5 cm (2 in) – give or take a bit.

Tenderize

Tenderizing is making meat more tender, and there are two methods. You can beat it into submission with a meat hammer or use pineapple (page 65).

Problems with Food

Bean Sprouts Going Soggy

Unlikely though it sounds, bean sprouts need to be stored under water. Put them in a large jar of water, keep it covered, and change the water every 2 days. But once they have gone soggy they are past rescue.

Biscuits Misshapen

If a recipe tells you to cut out biscuits and put them on a baking tray it is almost impossible to make them perfectly round. Instead, roll the biscuit mixture out on the *back* of the baking sheet, cut the biscuits out and peel away the surplus mixture from around them. Bake them where they are.

Bread

If you want a thawed, or less than fresh, loaf to taste like new just pass it *rapidly* under a cold tap – top and bottom – and place it in an oven at gas no 2 to 3 or 150° to 165°C (300° to 325°F) for about 20 minutes. You can use the same method for rolls and croissants, but they will be ready in as little as 3 to 5 minutes To refresh bread in slices microwave 10-20 seconds.

Bread not Rising

The yeast could be dead. When baking, check this by mixing the yeast with a little warm water and a hint of sugar and leaving it in a warm place. If it doesn't froth (called spongeing) in 15 minutes the yeast is dead and there is no point in mixing it with the flour. If the yeast has sponged, the bread will rise – in its own time – unless you have done something very odd.

Burnt Stews or Vegetables

Tip the food out into a clean pan *without* scraping the burnt bits in with it. Check whether it tastes of burning. With vegetables, cut the burnt side off and taste the remainder. Serve whatever tastes normal. If a casserole still tastes of burning you may be able to mask the taste by adding some fried cumin powder or other spice – but do choose flavours which go with the dish or it will only taste worse.

Burnt Roast Meat

Put a clean damp cloth on the burnt part for a minute or two. You should then be able to scrape it off.

Butter Desalting

If you need unsalted butter, and have none, cut butter into small pieces, pour boiling water over it and put the mixture to chill. The salt will be washed away in the water and the butter will solidify free from salt.

Butter Clarifying

The virtue of clarified butter is that it can be taken to quite a high temperature without burning, whereas ordinary butter burns easily. If you need clarified butter in a hurry your nearest Indian shop probably sells it as ghee (make sure it is butter not vegetable ghee) or, for most recipes, equal parts butter and vegetable oil is a very good substitute.

Cakes

Burnt or Dry

Cut off the burnt outside. Sprinkle on some suitable alcohol – sherry, brandy (or even fruit juice if you're teetotal) – to reduce the dryness. If it is very dry pierce skewer holes to help the moisture down. Ice completely, or ice in thin layers as for unrisen cake.

Cherries Sinking to the Bottom

Whole glacé cherries look wonderful when a cake is cut, but they do have a tendency to drop to the bottom of the cake. Tossing them in flour before you add them to the mixture, or washing the syrup off them, helps to stop this.

Dry

If an un-iced sponge type cake has been around a little too long and become rather dry you can revive it for family consumption by steaming it briefly in a colander over boiling water – but don't let water actually touch it. Microwaving for 10-20 seconds does the same.

Rising Poorly

There are several possible causes:

● you opened the oven door in the early stages
● you may have over-beaten it after adding flour
● the cake tin was the wrong size
● you didn't sift the flour
● it was a bad recipe anyway.

You may be able to salvage it by slicing it into several layers linked by a good icing.

Stuck in the Tin

When a cake is stuck, run a sharp knife right around the edge of the tin to loosen the sides and then stand the hot tin on a folded wet cloth for a few minutes. It may then come out quite easily. If that fails, just prise it out and glue the broken bits together with icing.

Next time line the tin with greaseproof paper and it won't happen. To do that draw round the base of the tin on the paper and cut it out. Cut a strip slightly higher than the sides, fold up the bottom 1.5 cm (½ in) and then unfold and slash it. Put the strip in first with the fold at the bottom, and the circle on top.

Addresses and suggestions for further reading are at the ends of chapters.

When Short of Eggs
If you are an egg short and the cake recipe uses a raising agent or self-raising flour you can substitute a tablespoon of vinegar for one of the eggs with no harm.

Icing Sliding Off
Icing is less likely to slide off if you either stick it on with a thin layer of jam (under marzipan and royal icing) or sprinkle a *minute* amount of flour on the cake first – use cornflour, potato flour (*fécule*) or arrowroot, so it won't taste floury.

Cheese Fondue Curdling
If a cheese fondue suddenly curdles, you can rescue it by mixing 2 or so tespoonfuls of potato flour with a very little white wine (or water) and stirring this into it with a loop whisk, over the heat, until the mixture comes together.

Chocolate Going Grainy on Melting
Chocolate is naturally unpredictable (see page 98), but you may also have over-stirred it. You can smoothe it by stirring in a hint of boiling water – if you want it to stay liquid – or a little butter if you want it to set later.

Choux Pastry Heavy
Choux pastry goes heavy if you don't pierce it straight after cooking to let the steam out.

Coffee Tasting Bitter
Coffee is far less likely to go bitter if you wait a few moments after the water has boiled and pour it on when off the boil.

Coffee Grounds Floating in the Jug
If you are making coffee by the simple expedient of pouring boiling water on to coffee grounds in a jug, the easy way to get the grounds to sink is to drop a spoonful of cold water into the jug. But only do this after the coffee has brewed for a few minutes.

Cream Going Grainy on Beating
This can't be rescued. To prevent it next time, have the cream refrigerator-cold and don't beat for so long.

Cream Sauce not Thickening
Pour the sauce into a *very* wide pan and continue heating – if the cream is double it will thicken. Or add a *little* cornflour or arrowroot mixed with a touch of milk and stir hard.

Custard Baking with Bubbles in
Custard will almost always go bubbly if you cook it too fast. Very slow cooking is needed. It also helps to prevent bubbles if you bring the milk to the boil, let it cool, then mix in the eggs and bake it standing in a tin of water – use gas no 1 or 140°C (275°F). Use 2 eggs to ½ l (1 pint).

Custard Curdling
If real egg custard – made in a double boiler – starts to curdle you can rescue it if you act fast. Either tip it into a bowl and beat hard with a whisk, or whizz it in a food processor, or put it in a clean jar or bottle and shake like mad. Speed is vital; if it goes too far nothing can be done.

Fat on the Surface of Food
The best way to remove fat is to chill the food and lift the fat off when it hardens. But when in a hurry mop it off with kitchen roll.

Fat Spitting
Fat spits when it reacts with water. If shallow frying, sprinkle in a little flour to absorb the moisture. If deep frying turn off the heat and cover – spitting can start a fire. Food should be dry before going into deep fat.

Fruit and Vegetables
Going Brown when Cut
A lot of white-fleshed fruit and vegetables go brown when cut because enzymes and other substances in them react with the air. To prevent it have a bowl of water with a squeeze of lemon juice in and drop them in as you slice them. The acid slows down the action of the enzyme. You can then drain and dry them for cooking. But the brown doesn't do you any harm.

Fizzy Fruit Salad
When fruit salad goes fizzy it is spontaneously fermenting and trying to make itself into alcohol. It feels oddly prickly on the tongue but is perfectly edible.

Hollandaise Separating
To make Hollandaise successfully all the ingredients should be at room temperature when you start, the sauce should be in the top of a double saucepan, and even the water underneath should only be *just* simmering. It should thicken *very* slowly. If it suddenly thickens it may be about to curdle. Remove it from the heat and stir in a teaspoon of cold water to cool it down.

If it separates *slightly* remove it from the heat, put a fresh yolk into a pan over slightly lower heat and very gradually work in the curdled sauce. But if it forms grains, it is past rescue.

Jelly or Aspic Stuck
Run the very tip of a knife all round the upper edge of the mould. Run the plate on to which you are turning it out under a tap and shake off the surplus water, but leave it damp. Have a basin of hot water and dip the mould in the hot water almost up to the rim, for just a *moment*. Put the plate *over* the mould and hold the two together as you turn the mould over. The layer of water should allow you to slide the jelly or aspic on the plate if it doesn't land in the centre.

Lettuce Limp
Lettuce can be crisped up by simply leaving it in cold water, but it crisps fastest if you put a peeled potato or two in the water with it. Curiously, a lump of coal is another aid.

Mayonnaise Separating

Remove the mayonnaise from the blender or bowl. Put in a fresh yolk and *very gradually* mix the curdled mayonnaise into it, as if starting again. It probably happened because you added the oil too fast; next time go more slowly. It is also easier to make mayonnaise if you have two egg yolks, not one, and if there is some mustard in the mixture. Mustard is a natural emulsifier and makes food hang together.

Marmalade Cloudy

Marmalade is much clearer if you add a dessertspoonful of glycerine for every 4 kg (8 lb) of jam half way through cooking.

Meringues Stuck to the Tin

Once stuck, there is no way to remove them without breaking – though heating the tin over a gas flame or candle and removing them instantly may sometimes help. Next time put them on vegetable parchment and they shouldn't stick at all. Failing that, oil greaseproof paper *very* well first.

Mince Rubbery

Mince tends to go rubbery if you add salt before it is cooked. Very long slow cooking may soften it – if you have made enough to warrant it. This doesn't apply to hamburgers and other dishes in which mince is cooked as a block of meat.

Pasta Stuck Together

Treat like rice. But if flat pieces are stuck they may be inseparable – it depends whether they stuck at the start of cooking or only later. Next time use *much* more water – pasta should be cooked in a very big pan not crammed together in a small one.

Pastry too Heavy

The main causes of heavy pastry are over-mixing, over-handling, hot hands, too much water and adding too much flour during rolling. But, there are some people who can't make pastry however closely they stick to the rules – I'm one. You may be too.

Pastry Shrinking

Pastry stretches in the making and needs at least 10 minutes in the refrigerator to 'relax' before use. Cover it with cling film while it does so or it will dry out. Some people stretch pastry more than others. If you do, then roll out the pastry and line your tin with it and cut off the surplus, leaving a large extra rim, and only trim it to size after it has shrunk in the cool.

Potatoes Going Brown or Black

Peeled raw potatoes rapidly go brown because air reacts with certain chemicals in them. So drop them in a bowl of water as you peel them. If you are leaving them for any time put lemon juice or vinegar in the water – but leaving potatoes in water reduces their vitamins.

Potatoes go black or grey when cooked if they have a

lot of iron in. To stop (or reduce) this reaction just add vinegar or lemon juice to the cooking water.

Salad Soggy

Any dressing put on lettuce will rapidly turn it soggy. Once this happens there is no redeeming it. The French trick for avoiding the problem is to put the dressing in the bottom of the salad bowl, then cross the salad servers over it and rest the salad on top. The salad is then tossed in the dressing just before serving.

Salty Stew

If a soup or casserole tastes too salty put a large peeled potato in it, cut in chunks, and cook it for about 10 minutes. Remove it and taste. There is a limit to how much salt it can absorb but it should cure mild over-salting.

Sauce-Béarnaise Curdling

If a béarnaise sauce separates, but isn't too far gone, it can be saved by adding a teaspoonful of lukewarm water for every 2 egg yolks and by beating furiously until it comes together. If it has become much too hot it will be past saving.

Sauce Having Lumps

Beat hard with a loop whisk or an egg beater – best of all, liquidize in a blender. The lumps probably happened because you added the liquid too fast, if you are adding liquid to a roux you need to go slowly at first. If you are adding cornflour and water (or any similar thickener) to thicken liquid, it too has to be added slowly while beating hard to prevent lumps. The lumps may be because it cooled and formed a skin.

Sauce Having a Skin

The lumps created by skin on sauces and custards can be removed by beating very hard with a loop whisk or whizzing them in a food processor. To stop skin forming next time spoon a thin layer of whatever liquid you are using in the sauce on to the surface before you let it stand. Alternatively, if it suits the sauce – let tiny pieces of butter melt on the surface. You can also keep sauces hot and skin-free by simply putting them in a thermos – useful when entertaining.

Soufflés not Rising

There is no rescue. It probably happened because the eggs were over- or under-beaten or folded in with a heavy hand, or because you looked to see how it was doing and let in cold air. Next time beat the whites until you can create a peak which just flops its tip over. Fold in and rub the inside of the soufflé dish with butter, so the mixture won't stick before it has risen, and only look when there are five minutes to go.

Tarts Stuck

If a jammy filling trickles over and sticks tarts to the tin, hold the tin over a flame to melt the stickiness and flip them out while still hot.

Addresses and suggestions for further reading are at the ends of chapters.

Tinned Meat Stuck in the Tin

Easy – open the other end and push it out. You can also open the wrong side of some sardine cans if the key breaks.

Toast Burnt

Remove the crusts. Slice through between the two toasted layers (to create two thinner slices) and toast the cut side of whichever half isn't burnt. The result is a slice of melba toast.

Yorkshire Pudding Heavy

The secret of light Yorkshire pudding is to leave the mixture to stand for an hour, and to have the fat in the baking tin *very* hot when you pour it in.

PULSES

Those who share my love of unusual information may enjoy knowing that the legume family, with its host of peas and beans, is the third largest flowering plant family, after orchids and daisies. In fact, they were considered so important in ancient Rome that they had the singular honour of giving their names to four of Rome's most distinguished families – Cicero getting his family name from the chick pea (then known as *cicer arietinum*). Italians often get it right where food is concerned.

The legume family is endlessly adaptable, cropping up in delicious dishes the world over: in hearty minestrones in northern Italy, smooth chick pea pastes in Greece and Arabia, cassoulets in France, refried red beans in Mexico and spicy dals in India. Yet in Britain we exalt only the pea – and the frozen pea at that – and let the other lovely possibilities pass us by. This is a pity because, besides tasting good, this family is rich in protein and in most B vitamins, and low in fat.

I am indebted to Harold McGee for the following figures comparing the food values of meat and pulses.

COMPARING PERCENTAGE FOOD VALUES

	Water	Protein	Carbohydrate	Fat
Mung bean	11	24	60	1
Soya bean	10	37	34	18
Lentil	11	25	60	1
Chick peas	11	21	61	5
Pea	12	24	60	1
Beef	60	18	-	22
Pork	42	12	-	45
Lamb	56	16	-	28

Since the type of protein is important it doesn't follow that pulses are *better for you* than meat but the poor children who once sang the skipping rhyme:

> Pease porridge hot
> Pease porridge cold
> Pease porridge in the pot
> Nine days old

weren't eating so badly after all, and pulses could cut any family budget.

Dried Peas, Beans and Lentils

Cleaning

Twigs and stones often appear in packets of beans and lentils. So put them in plenty of water in a big metal pan and swirl them round with your hand; twiggy bits will float to the surface and stones clink against the metal. Change the water until it stops looking dusty, picking out the stones on draining. But don't expect the water from washing split lentils to come clear; they always release a milky starch.

Soaking

Leave the beans or lentils to soak overnight in plenty of cold water. The little red lentils are an exception. Unless they are very old and tough, they can be cooked after soaking for as little as half an hour.

If you are short of time put the beans in cold water, bring them to the boil for a couple of minutes and let them soak in it for at least an hour. How well they respond to this shock treatment will depend on their age.

Cooking Dried Peas and Beans

Beans and lentils are peasant food, and wonderfully easy to cook. Pulses cook in their own time, and it's no good trying to be precise and modern with them. The timing varies with their age. The older they are, the longer they take to cook. So prepare them a day ahead. I have known very fresh mung beans become perfectly tender in just over 15 minutes, but old or large beans can take almost 2 hours, and very ancient chick peas can be boiled for an entire day without softening at all. Whatever their vagaries on first cooking, once cooked they reheat excellently and freeze well.

Dried Peas, Beans and Lentils – in Rough Order of Size

Name	Description	Cooking Time (approx)
Butter beans/ Lima beans	flattish, white and as large as two thumb nails	45+ mins
Black beans	similar to red kidney beans but bigger and black-skinned	35+ mins
Borlotti beans	pinkish cream with a marbling of wine, shaped like kidney beans	50+ mins
Pinto beans	very similar to borlotti but wider in proportion to their length than most	1+ hrs
Red kidney beans	a distinctive wine-red oblong bean	50+ mins
Cannellini beans	white twins to the red kidney bean	55+ mins
Dried peas	round and an unmistakably smoky green	40+ mins

Name	Description	Cooking Time (approx)
Flageolet beans	a soft smoky green but long and narrow	50+ mins
Chick peas/ 'garbanzos'	quite unlike other pulses, with a distinct growing point even when dry	1+ hrs
Black-eyed beans	small and creamy white with a distinct black eye at one side	30+ mins
Haricot beans	creamy white, very chubby and only a little longer than their width	1+ hrs
Soya beans	very like haricot beans but yellower and rounder	3+ hrs
Field beans	almost round and a pinkish brown	25+ mins
Ful medames beans	almost identical to field beans but browner	50+ mins
Split peas	round and yellow, like half a ball	25+ mins
Chana dal	almost the same as split peas but a little smaller: they are interchangeable if need be, but the flavours are not identical	20+ mins
Adzuki beans	very small beans, with almost square corners, like little pillows the colour of milky chocolate	25+ mins
Mung beans	distinctive tiny olive green beans	15+ mins
Moong dal	skinned and split mung beans used in Indian recipes	15+ mins
Brown/Conti- nental lentils	little discs a dull greeny brown	25+ mins
Red split lentils	shiny and skinless little half discs in melon yellow, called Masoor dal in Indian recipes	15+ mins

★ If you have to cook any of this family in a hurry putting a pinch of bicarbonate of soda in the water greatly reduces the cooking time – but you do lose some vitamins. McGee suggests 1/8 of a teaspoon of bicarb per cup of beans – but there is no need to be very exact.

★ Acid toughens the skins of beans by preventing the cell structure from being broken down by heat. This makes the beans remain hard no matter how long you cook them. The degree to which this happens varies with the acidity of the liquid, but if you want to mix them with an acid sauce – such as the tomato in chilli con carne – cook them in water first, and drain and add them to the tomato base when tender.

Beans and Wind

Scientists have identified, and given a cumbersome name to, the substance which they think is responsible for beans' legendary ability to cause wind. *Why* it causes wind is still mysterious. However, they do confirm that, as cooks have always known, some beans are more windy than others.

To reduce the wind-making tendencies of dried beans, put them in fresh cold water and bring it to the boil. Let it boil hard for 15 minutes, then throw away the water and start again from cold. Let the beans simmer in this second water until cooked. The less water they are cooked in the less food value is lost and the faster they cook. But, as they absorb water, they are more likely to dry out and burn while your back is turned – especially lentils.

> WARNING Red kidney and lima (butter) beans can contain substances which are poisonous. Red kidney beans are neutralized by boiling the beans *hard* for at least 10 minutes *with the lid off the pan*. After this treatment they are perfectly safe, and the rest of the cooking can be fast or slow. People have been ill after eating red beans which have been cooked slowly – even though the beans were completely cooked. Lima beans possess a different type of poison. Expert opinion seems divided as to whether it is driven off by cooking, but the American and European varieties, sold to Britain, have been bred to restrict the substance to a level so low it is no longer a hazard. However, there have been cases of poisoning in the tropics where other varieties are grown and neither bean should be sprouted.

To know when any of this family are cooked simply taste them. For some recipes, you must cook them until almost mushy; for others – such as baked beans – you need them firm and whole. Suit the cooking to the dish, but don't expect soya beans to go soft and floury like other beans; they have an almost waxy texture which never changes.

Sprouting Beans

The best beans for sprouting are mung beans. Freshly sprouted they taste 100 per cent tastier and crunchier than those bought from a shop. You need no special equipment but whatever you use must be *perfectly* clean. Having sprouted seeds successfully once, either scald the container or clean it with Milton, as bacteria can build up which rot the sprouts.

They grow to 6 times their volume, so only start with a tablespoon or two: when crowded they won't grow. Cover the beans with cold water and leave them overnight. Next morning, drain, rinse and put them in a large container. Stretch some very clean cotton across the top of the container and put in a warm dark place – such as an airing cupboard. Then, every few hours, pour water in through the cloth, and drain it without disturbing the beans. They mustn't dry out. Eat them when nicely sprouted.

Addresses and suggestions for further reading are at the ends of chapters.

I find beans are temperamental, sometimes sprouting perfectly and sometimes being a complete flop. It may well depend on the age of the beans. Buying them from seedsmen is more reliable, but also more expensive. However, seedsmen such as Thompson and Morgan do offer other seeds such as alfalfa and fenugreek, which give variety to salads.

★ A good container for sprouting beans is a large plastic sweet jar – free from sweet shops. If you pierce a few small holes in the bottom, with a hot skewer, water will wash through the beans without them being tipped up and disturbed.

QUANTITIES AND TEMPERATURES

Amounts of Food per Person

Judging exactly how much food to cook is a tricky business. Some people have far larger appetites than others, there is also the question of how many courses the meal has and what else you are serving at any course. To decide what works for your family and friends, I suggest you note what amounts are eaten at each party or dinner party – and by how many people. But if you are cooking for a large number you can't simply multiply one portion by the number of people.

Prue Leith shows it exactly when she gives these amounts. Biscuits 3 each for 10 people; 2 each for 30 people; 1 each for over 30 people.

Small roasting joints tend to shrink dramatically and serve fewer than their weight suggests. Also meat which is well done shrinks far more than meat that is underdone. Unskilled carvers, with blunt knives, who hack off chunks of meat instead of nice slices make a joint go nowhere. A large loaf usually has 18 slices if thinly cut. 8 oz softened butter will spread about 60 slices of bread.

Comparative Oven Temperatures

The container the food is in makes a difference. For example, thick iron and earthenware casseroles heat slowly, so the food takes longer to cook than it would in some other containers. This means oven temperatures are really only guidelines for working out how to get the best results in your particular situation, and deviation from them is not the heresy it may seem.

Variations Within an Oven
Gas ovens vary considerably in their behaviour even if they are the same size. At any temperature setting a gas oven normally has different heat zones within it. Recipes assume food is in the middle.

- The top of the oven will be higher than the setting.
- The middle of the oven will be at the temperature the oven is set for.
- The bottom of the oven will be cooler than the setting.

The difference in temperature is considerable. This means that by placing each dish on the shelf where it will get the temperature it needs, you can cook an entire meal in the oven at once, thus saving a great deal of time and fuel. The disadvantage is that if you want to cook a large quantity of small cakes, you can't fill the whole oven with them and expect them all to cook in the same time and come out equally well.

Some cooking books say which shelf any dish should be put on. Shelves are always counted from the top, so shelf 1 is the highest. The following table shows the variations in an average gas oven.

This table shows the difference between the oven setting and the actual temperature on each shelf.

Setting	E	1	2	3	4	5	6	7	8	9
Shelf 1	1½	2	3	4½	5½	6½	8	9	9	9+
Shelf 2	1	1½	2½	4	5	6	7	8	9+	9+
Shelf 3	E	1	2	3	4	5	6	7	8	9
Shelf 4	E	E/1	1	2	3	4	5	5½	6	7
Shelf 5	– E	E	E	E/1	1½	2	2½	3½	4½	5
Floor	– E	– E	E	E	E/1	1	1½	2½	3	4

E stands for Gas ¼-½.

Temperature Variation in Electric Ovens
In electric ovens with fans – the middle and upper end of the electric market – there is no difference in temperature between the top and the bottom of the oven. In a standard, non-fan-assisted oven, with side panels, the top is usually a few degrees hotter than the bottom, but it's not usually enough to make much difference to how food cooks. So you can't cook a wide range of foods at a single oven setting the way you can with gas, but if you are cooking a lot of small cakes you can be sure they will all cook correctly whatever shelf they are on.

Comparative Oven Temperatures

Description	Gas	Fahrenheit	Centigrade	Solid Fuel	Convection
very cool	¼	150°-225°	70°-110°	very slow	cooks at the
very cool	½	225°-250°	110°-120°	slow	same centigrade
cool	1	275°	140°		temperature as
cool	2	300°	150°	warm	a normal electric
moderate	3	325°	160°-170°	moderate	oven but it may
moderate	4	350°	180°		take a touch
fairly hot	5	375°	190°	fairly hot	longer
fairly hot	6	400°	200°	hot	
hot	7	425°	220°		
very hot	8	450°	230°	very hot	
very hot	9	475°-550°	240°-290°		

Weighing and Measuring

People are sometimes worried by rough quantities such as a 'nut of butter'. They wonder exactly how big a pinch or a handful should be. But if a good recipe uses these terms it does so because precision really doesn't matter. A 'nut' means a lump about the size of a walnut, a 'pinch' is the amount you can pinch up between thumb and forefinger and if your 'handful' is bigger than the next person's the food will still taste good. Few recipes require total accuracy.

Measuring without Scales

Those who don't have scales can improvise. But the weights will only be *very* approximate; a great deal depends on how level your 'level' is and how large your spoon. So don't use this form of measuring where precision is needed.

	Level tablespoons per 25 g, 1 oz	Weight per ½ pt measuring jug
Breadcrumbs – fresh	5	75 g (3 oz)
– dried	3	175 g (6 oz)
Cheese – grated fairly dry	4	110 g (4 oz)
Cornflour	3	175 g (6 oz)
Custard powder	3	175 g (6 oz)
Currants	3	110 g (4 oz)
Butter, margarine, lard	2	225 g (8 oz)
Flour – unsieved	3	175 g (6 oz)
Oats – rolled	4	110 g (4 oz)
Sugar – caster, Demerara, brown, granulated	2	225 g (8 oz)
– icing	2½	175 g (6 oz)
Sultanas, raisins	2	200 g (7 oz)
Syrup or treacle	1	400 g (14 oz)

Those who lack a measuring jug could substitute a mug. Most mugs take slightly over ½ pt.

For other quantities use a fraction of the packet.

Metric and Imperial Weights

10 g	½ oz
25 g	1 oz
50 g	2 oz
75 g	3 oz
110 g	4 oz
150 g	5 oz
175 g	6 oz
200 g	7 oz
225 g	8 oz
250 g	9 oz
275 g	10 oz
300 g	11 oz
350 g	12 oz
375 g	13 oz
400 g	14 oz
425 g	15 oz
450 g	1 lb
700 g	1 lb 8 oz

Liquid Measures

2 fl oz	55 ml	
5 fl oz	150 ml	(¼ pt)
10 fl oz	275 ml	(½ pt)
15 fl oz	425 ml	(¾ pt)
20 fl oz	570 ml	(1 pt)
35 fl oz	1 litre	(1¾ pt)

Converting American Measurements

Perhaps because of their wagon-train past, Americans like measuring with spoons and cups rather than scales. This can be disconcerting if you bring home an American cook book. What is more there aren't any standard conversion tables, because it all depends what you are measuring. An ounce of feathers may weigh the same as an ounce of lead, but a cup of rice crispies does not weigh the same as a cup of butter. The following table is not exact, but a working guideline, as no two cooks seem to agree remotely on the conversions. An American cup is similar to a British cup but not quite identical. It probably doesn't make much odds; you can just go ahead and use a teacup – filling it to the brim.

Addresses and suggestions for further reading are at the ends of chapters.

	US cups	g	oz
Flour	1	140	5
Caster or granulated sugar	1	225	8
Moist brown or Demerara sugar	1	170	6
Butter	1	225	8
Raisins or sultanas	1	200	7
Currants	1	140	5
Treacle or syrup	1	340	12
Rice – uncooked	1	200	7

Another difference between British and American measuring is that if a British recipe says 1 tablespoon it means one *rounded* tablespoon. If an American recipe says 1 tablespoon it means one *level* tablespoon.

- American fluid ounces are the same size as ours.
- American pints only = 16 fl oz; British pints = 20 fl oz.
- 3 teaspoons to an American tablespoon.
- 4 teaspoons to a British tablespoon.
- American spoonfuls are flat, British are rounded.
- 1 US pack of dry yeast = 7 g (¼ oz).
- 1 US packet of fresh yeast = 20 g (⅔ oz).
- 1 US packet of gelatine = 5 g (¼ oz).

Gelatine Measuring

All sachets of gelatine sold in Britain are the same weight. But if you have gelatine in other forms the equivalent measures are these:

6 leaves of gelatine, each 15 x 10 cm (6 x 4 in) = ⅖ oz powdered gelatine = 1 sachet = 3 slightly rounded teaspoons

Each of those amounts will set one pint of liquid and, according to the manufacturers, it doesn't matter whether it is thin liquid like fruit juice, or a thicker one like a mousse mixture.

SPECIAL COOKING METHODS

Microwave Cooking

I used to scorn microwave ovens. It was sheer prejudice: having tested them for a magazine article I'm totally converted. They reduce cooking to a fraction of the time. They also make it possible to thaw rapidly small items straight from the deep freeze. So the contents of a freezer suddenly become accessible without forethought. On top of that, they save fuel and washing up, allow you to cook vegetables without losing goodness into the water and enable dieters and those cutting down on fat to use fatless cooking.

Explaining Microwaves

Microwaves are much easier to use successfully when you know what is going on. This is very simple. Instead of heat flowing all round the food, as it does in other cooking, microwaves behave more like a beam of light. Like light, they travel in a straight line – hence the need for a turntable which presents every side of the food to their beam. They are beamed into the cooker in such a way that they hit the metal-lined walls and are bounced back at the food on the turntable, as light might bounce off a mirror. Even this doesn't give a very wide scatter, so some microwaves have rotating metal paddles, off which the beam will bounce in several different directions – like the light off a mirror ball in a discotheque.

Also like light, they can pass through some substances (e.g. glass), penetrate others slightly (e.g. food) and are reflected off others (e.g. metal). Microwaves aren't hot but they *are* energetic. So when they penetrate food they vibrate its molecules *billions* of times a second. It is the friction of the molecules rubbing against each other, as they vibrate, that creates the heat which does the cooking. It's like a dense crowd of people in which one shove gets everyone moving.

Transferring their energy to the food uses microwaves up, just as a light bulb uses up electricity. So they are not stored in the food – any more than light is stored in a room after you turn off the switch. In fact, they are high-frequency waves closer to radio waves than to the hazards of X-rays (see Facts and Figures).

Key Facts when Using Microwaves

Follow the maker's instructions regarding ventilation space at the top or side.

You don't have to use any special recipe to cook with microwaves but you do need to shorten the times greatly, and arrange the food slightly differently. The best course is to find a similar microwave recipe, allow for any difference in quantities, then set the timer for slightly less. If the food isn't done by the end you can always give it a few more minutes. Whatever you do, *experiment*. You won't go far wrong if you keep to the following rules.

1 **Microwaves can only go 2.5 to 5 cm (1 to 2 in) into food**. Thicker food only cooks because the heat created by the microwaves is conducted to the centre – as it would be in normal cooking – which considerably increases the cooking time. So:
   a cook food in a layer no more than 2.5 cm (1 in) thick – e.g. peas should not be heaped up
   b turn items like baked potatoes over at half time
   c stir foods such as sauces at intervals during cooking, bringing the edge to the middle
   d with larger amounts of food move sides to middle at half time – if possible
   e for large single items don't just multiply up the time needed for a small item, allow a good deal more and turn them several times
   f use round containers where possible as food cooks more evenly
   g try to space items so that all sides can be reached by the microwaves, e.g. place cup cakes in a ring, use ring moulds which allow the microwaves to get at food from the middle as well as the sides –

or stand a glass in the middle of the dish and put the food around it.

2 Microwaves cannot pass through metal; they bounce off it, and small quantities of metal can cause sparks which could damage the oven. This means:

a you *can't* cook food in metal cake tins or pans as the waves just won't reach it (or will reach the top but not the sides – disaster to a cake)

b you *can't* cook food in containers made of metal but enamelled on the outside – e.g. casseroles

c you *can't* use containers with metal parts any-where – rims, handles, or even as part of a pattern (patterns cause arcing – i.e. sparks)

d you *can't* close oven bags with metal ties as these can cause sparks.

e you *can* use foil to protect small areas, like the ends of drumsticks which, being thin, would otherwise cook much faster than the rest. Use smooth foil, in small pieces, dull side out – and it must be 2.5 cm (1 in) away from the sides of the oven as the food goes round.

f if the oven has a metal trivet it shouldn't be used when just microwaving, but it *can* be used when cooking with microwaves and convection at the same time.

> WARNING Metal used incorrectly in a micro-wave oven may cause sparks which can dam-age the cooker. If you see sparks, turn the oven off *at once* and remove whatever metal is caus-ing them. Even gilt decoration can do it.

3 These can be used for cooking because microwaves pass through them:

a **glass** – provided it can stand the heat of the food (remember liquids may reach boiling point) but *not* leaded glass, cut glass or other high quality glass as it may be damaged

b **china** – if it can stand the heat and has no gilding on it (see **2c**)

c **pottery** – but heavy earthenware slows down the cooking

d **plastic** – provided it can stand heat – yoghurt pots etcetera won't but some heavier containers will, so will roasting bags and cling film.

e **paper** – but only for very brief cooking or heat-ing or it may catch fire, and not if wax- or plastic-coated.

Test the vessel by putting a cup of water in it and microwaving for 1 to 2 minutes. If the container gets hot and the water doesn't, don't use it.

4 Microwaves heat different types of food at different speeds:

a The fattier a food, the faster it cooks so:
– cheese, cream, rich fish and shellfish overcook easily
– cream sauces tend to separate on reheating in a microwave

– the fatty yolk of an egg cooks before the white.

b Sugar cooks very fast so:
– sugary toppings may be done before the food they top
– the inside of jam tarts turns to caramel before the pastry is done (nasty)
– larger tarts will be dangerously hot inside when straight from the oven

c Food which is moist cooks more slowly than dry food.

d Open textured food, such as bread, cooks faster than dense food like meat.

Don'ts for Microwaves

- Don't cook an egg in its shell – it may explode from the steam.
- Don't heat alcohol, oil or melted fat which is not mixed into the food, they could overheat and catch fire.
- Don't try to cook bread, pizzas, batters, roast pota-toes, small tarts, meringues or soufflés.
- Don't expect food to brown – it usually won't.
- Don't expect it to make reheated food crisp – a microwaved slice of bread is moist and delicious, a microwaved croissant is as depressing as a soft watch.
- Don't try to use a normal thermometer in a micro-wave.
- Don't add salt to meat, fish or vegetables until they are cooked as it can make them dry if added earlier.
- Don't try to cook a cake in a container more than 20 cm (8 in) across: the middle may remain soggy – unless it's a ring mould.
- Don't use as much fat as usual. Less fat is absorbed in microwave cooking. (Great for slimmers.)

Do's for Microwaves

- Cover foods which may spit with kitchen roll.
- Cut the amount of liquid you use, by a third or a half as it won't evaporate away. Vegetables will cook in a tablespoonful or so.
- Cut food into even-sized pieces.
- Keep in the moisture by covering food with cling film – but allow a space for steam to escape.
- If heating whole foods with skins (e.g. tomatoes or apples) pierce the skins with a fork to let steam escape.
- Place pastry or bread on kitchen paper when reheat-ing so the bottom won't become soggy.
- Use roasting bags for poultry and joints of meat, as it prevents spattering. But close them with string, and pierce them to allow the steam out.
- Remember that things cook faster at the edges so place portions of meat or fish with the thickest part to the outer edge.
- Reheat at the level to suit the food.
- Cook pastry cases blind; then fill them.
- Put a dish of water in the microwave when heating tiny quantities to stop it arcing (sparking).
- Stand cakes on a cooking rack at least 3 cm (1¼ in)

Addresses and suggestions for further reading are at the ends of chapters.

off the oven base to ensure the underside is fully cooked.

- Remember that the food goes on cooking for a little after the oven switches off.

Safety with a Microwave

Microwaves may only be sold in Britain if they meet a set standard. All the authorities agree that microwaves made to that standard are safe – there is no risk of radiation or anything else. But before buying a cooker check that it does carry an approval label, and follow the safety rules when using it.

- Never operate one which has a fault in its door.
- Never try to repair a microwave yourself.
- Keep a dish of water in the bottom when not in use, in case it is accidentally switched on.
- Keep the seal round the door perfectly clean and in good condition.
- Don't worry about opening the door during a cycle – the microwaves will automatically switch off.

Timing Food in a Microwave

The correct timing depends on the power of your microwave. Some ready-made food carries a microwave code mark on the packing, from A to E. If so, see if your microwave also has a code letter – the latest ones do. If it does, use the timing given for your microwave's code letter. Otherwise use the timing for its level of power.

Most fresh foods can be cooked very quickly on high. But eggs, cheese, shellfish and fish, and meats which are tough, need longer cooking, and a medium or low setting is best.

The more you put in the oven, the longer the food will take to cook. This isn't simply a matter of a big cake taking longer than a small one (it would in any oven), but of four small *individual* items – say four chicken drumsticks, nicely spaced – taking longer than one cooked on its own. This means that you can never predict exact times for anything cooked by a microwave unless you follow a recipe and use exactly those quantities. But everything cooks so fast that if you have to put anything back to cook for longer it seldom takes more than a minute or two. Generally speaking, if you double the quantity you must add a third to a half to the cooking time. If you reduce the quantities by half reduce the cooking time by rather more than half.

When the microwaves are turned off cooking doesn't stop immediately. The molecules in the food keep on bouncing. This is why recipes often allow a standing period after the oven is turned off. During this, cover the food with foil to keep in the heat.

Wattages

The wattage of a microwave is whatever it gives out at its highest setting. At lower settings the wattage is lower. Unfortunately, microwaves haven't been standardized but the vast majority are 650 to 700 watts and most microwave recipes are written for them. If you need to adjust timings for less than 650 watts the rules are these:

Time at 650 watts	Equivalent time at 500 watts
10 seconds	13 seconds
15 seconds	20 seconds
30 seconds	40 seconds
45 seconds	1 minute

For larger amounts, needing longer cooking, you can work the timing out by the following rule. For each minute of cooking time at 650 –

> add 10 to 15 seconds for a 600 watt oven
> add 15 to 20 seconds for a 500 watt oven
> add 20 to 25 seconds for a 400 watt oven

Hints and Tips

★ Citrus fruits yield more juice if microwaved on full power for a few seconds.

★ To melt gelatine stir it into the water and give it 2 minutes on defrost.

★ To soften butter for cake making 'defrost' for 30 to 40 seconds.

★ When baking cakes use a soufflé dish instead of a cake tin – but line it so you can remove the cake easily.

★ Although food doesn't brown, you can make it look less ghostly by brushing it with paprika, or soya sauce or (if the flavour works) brown sugar and Worcestershire sauce before you cook it. Better still finish it under a grill.

★ If you have to cook food in a square container shield the corners with foil to stop them overcooking.

Pressure Cooking

The principle of a pressure cooker is that when water reaches boiling point in an ordinary pan it lets off steam and that stops the water getting any hotter. A pressure cooker holds the steam in and allows the water to reach a higher temperature – so cooking the food faster.

It is most useful for foods which take a long time to cook – dried beans, bottling fruit, Christmas puddings and certain casseroles.

The precise instructions for each cooker *must* be followed but these points apply to all brands.

- Pressure cookers should only be used with the recommended amount of liquid in. There will usually be a set minimum and maximum.
- It is dangerous to try to remove the lid before the pressure has dropped. Check the indicator and do not open it until it shows it is safe.
- Foods should not be cooked in pressure cookers which might rise up and block the vents.
- In working out the pressure cooking time for a normal recipe you can calculate that it will take about one-third of the time of ordinary cooking.

★ When steaming puddings add lemon juice or vinegar to the water to reduce the discoloration of the pan.

★ After use wash and dry it well and leave with the lid upside down so air can get in. If you leave it closed it may smell musty when you next open it.

Haybox Cooking

Haybox cooking is an ancient way of cooking by simply

holding the heat in a pot after taking it from the fire. Take a strong wooden box like a tea chest and line it with about 25 layers of newspaper. Cover this with brown paper and fix it in place. Put a thick layer of unchopped hay in the bottom of the box and place on it the casserole you will want to use. Check there will be space round it for a thick lining of hay. Make a bag which will exactly fit the top of the box, and fill it with hay to make a cushion and sew up the opening. Cook the food in the pan, on a normal stove and, when it is at the stage where you would normally simmer it bring it to the boil. Then, *without* opening the lid, put it in the hay box and pack hay tightly round it. Cover it with a sheet of newspaper – to keep the hay off the lid – and cover it with the hay cushion and more newspaper to keep in as much heat as possible. Put a lid on the box and leave it.

How long the food needs to stay in the box is a matter of your convenience, unless it is likely to spoil with overcooking. Some foods will be ready to eat; others will need to be finished on top of the stove.

It is a useful way of cooking some foods which would otherwise consume a lot of time and fuel, such as vegetable soups (allow 3 hours) or stewed fruit (allow 2 to 3 hours), but it is not advisable for meat or fish as the temperature could drop to a point which would allow food poisoning bacteria to multiply.

Vacuum Flask Cooking

A wide-necked vacuum flask can be used to cook any kind of dried fruit. Simply put the fruit in, pour on boiling water and close. By next day the fruit should be cooked or almost so – saving both fuel and trouble.

★ Put cling film round cork tops to vacuum flasks or they take up the smell of the food.

★ When vacuums are empty, lumps of sugar inside stop them smelling stale.

STORAGE TIMES

No matter how tightly sealed anything seems, it probably isn't totally impervious to air – unless it's a tin or a sealed glass jar. Even plastic fizzy drink bottles aren't airtight – only they do the reverse and allow a minute amount of gas to escape *out* through the plastic itself. So everything will spoil with time.

There are two issues here – how long the food lasts at its best and how quickly it goes bad. The times given below are for using the food at its best, unless otherwise stated. After that food may become unpleasant and lose food value but, in many cases, it will do you no harm.

General Store Cupboard Foods

If food is sold well packed in sealed bags or packets leave it like that. Don't transfer any foods to a home container until you are ready to use them, as it will shorten their shelf life. Once opened, all dried foods are easily contaminated by mice and attacked by biscuit beetles, so then they are best kept in jars. Failing more decorative containers, most sweet shops throw away large plastic sweet jars which will hold bulky dry goods like cereals. But check the plastic hasn't cracked, as they can be brittle.

The counsel of perfection (and thrift) is to date all goods, with a marker pen, as you put them in a store cupboard and put them at the back of the shelf, moving older food to the front. The following times are for a cool, dry kitchen cupboard, unless otherwise stated.

★ When camping, or if the fridge fails, stand a milk bottle in an inch of water and put a cloth over the bottle with its bottom edge in the water. The evaporating water will cool the bottle. You can also use this on a doorstep if you have a friendly milkman and are out when he delivers.

Keeping Times for Store Cupboard Foods

Food	Time	Comments
Biscuits – cream-filled	3 mths unopened 1 wk opened	Store in a tightly closed jar or metal box once opened.
Biscuits – plain or crispbread	5 mths unopened 10 days opened	Store in a tightly closed jar or metal box once opened. Will stay crisp longer if sugar lumps are put with them.
Bouillon cubes	9 mths	
Coffee – ground – beans	18 mths in a sealed pack 1 wk opened 9 mths in a sealed pack 1 wk opened	For longer keeping once opened roll up the top, close tightly with a bulldog clip and freeze.
coffee – instant	12-18 mths unopened 4 wks opened	Avoid leaving lid off, as the flavour 'dies'.
Dried beans and lentils	9 mths	Will last for years but become harder to cook.
Dried fruit or crystallized fruit (except prunes)	9 mths unopened 6 mths opened	May become drier, with sugar crystals on the outside, but still usable unless mouldy. Soak very dry ones in water to restore juiciness.
Fizzy drinks	9-12 mths unopened 1 day reclosed	These times are for those in plastic bottles.

Addresses and suggestions for further reading are at the ends of chapters.

Food	Time	Comments
Flour – plain	13 mths	Most flour usable longer. Flour will sweat if closed in a plastic bag. Use a container which keeps mice and biscuit beetles out, yet lets air in.
Flour – self-raising	10 mths	As plain flour
Flour – wholemeal (rye, wheat, barley, buckwheat)	3-6 mths	Some stoneground or cool-ground flour keeps the shorter time.
Jam and honey	Indefinitely unopened but best within 18 mths. Use as soon as possible once opened.	Pure fruit jams need cool and are best in the fridge.
Muesli and rolled grains	5-6 mths	May have additives which allow longer keeping.
Nuts – shelled	4+ mths	Nuts can go rancid. Best in the freezer.
Oats – rolled, porridge, or oatmeal	9-12 mths	This assumes the oats have been heat-treated, as most modern oats have been, to stop the enzymes turning them rancid.
Oil	3-12 mths	Oils go rancid with heat and light, best stored in a cool dark place. Use walnut in 3 mths, olive will keep a year.
Pasta (dry), rice, custard powder	9 mths	Pasta and rice usable longer but may need more cooking.
Pastes and spreads	3-6 mths unopened. Once opened refrigerate and use rapidly.	Go bad more easily than many foods. Don't store longer, eat rapidly once opened.
Peanut butter	1 yr unopened	See page 54.
Prunes	2-12 mths	Modern prunes don't keep well. For long storage freeze them. Cook in tea with lemon zest.
Sugar	18 mths at best	To stop moist brown sugar going solid, put a piece of bread with it and keep well closed.
Tea	18 mths unopened. Use within weeks once opened.	Best kept airtight as it takes up the taste of other foods.
Yeast – dried	6 mths	Keep tin well closed.

Tinned Food

The keeping time of tinned food is often misunderstood. If a tin is perfectly sealed and there is no rust on it then the contents will be safe to eat for far longer than the number of years given below. But the acids in food gradually eat into the lining of tins and the food acquires a metallic taste. British tins are now all steel, lined with tin, with no lead in the seam, so this may do you no harm. But lead-seamed tins from abroad may not be so harmless. Acid food in poor tins has a relatively short life. One of the problems is that you seldom know when it was packed. Heinz tins are an exception. Look at the top row of the numbers stamped in the end. The first three figures tell you which day of the year (out of 365) it was packed, and the last figure is the last figure of the year. So 0028 would be 2 January 1988, and 3658 would be 31 December 1988.

Once a tin is opened, tip the contents into some other container. Aided by air, the food will interact with the lining quite quickly.

WARNING Tinned food only keeps because the air has been kept out. Once air gets in it is just as likely to go bad as any other food. BEWARE of all the following:

- tins with dents – especially dents on the seam
- those which have signs of rust on the outside
- any even slightly domed at the end (these are already going bad)
- any which smell odd.

Keeping Times of Tinned Food in an Average Kitchen Cupboard

Food	Time	Comments
Most tinned food	2 yrs	In perfect conditions in a British climate. In hot damp climates tins rust rapidly.
Prunes, rhubarb	1 yr	The high acid content makes them a special case.
New potatoes, most fruit	18 mths	Fruit in its own juice keeps as long as fruit in sugar syrup.
Milky foods	12-18 mths	Milk may go thick and caramelize. It should be safe if it tastes normal.
Solid meat e.g corned beef, fish in oil	5 yrs	WARNING Tins of pasteurized meat weighing over 1 kg (2 lb) only keep for 9 months and should be kept chilled.

Keeping Times for Fresh Food

The keeping time of fresh food is far more variable than the times for dried foods. For meat, fish and poultry, see index.

Bacon – slices or joints vacuum packed	15 days in fridge	They may not have a packing date but you may be able to judge how fast they are moving in the shop.
Bacon – slices or joints not vacuum packed	10 days in fridge	Bacon also freezes well. Cut whole packs crosswise, when frozen, to make chopped bacon – but have a sharp knife.
Butter	8 wks (from packing) in fridge	Butter has no packing date, but a good shop shouldn't keep it long so it should keep several weeks.
Cake	3 days-1 yr+ in cake tin in a kitchen cupboard	Each type has its own time limit: fatless sponges become dull in a day or two, while rich fruit cakes are excellent after a year. Keep longer with a slice of bread or a chunk of apple.
Cheese – goat	1-2 days at their best in a cool place	Wrap in foil and put in vegetable drawer of refrigerator.
Cheese – hard or hardish blue	3 wks in vacuum pack; 1-3 wks opened in cool place or a fridge vegetable drawer	Keep in foil, in a tin, in a cool place. Put at room temperature for 1 hr before eating – but cheese will spoil if repeatedly warmed and cooled. For cooking, grate and freeze.
Cheese – soft curd style	4-7 days ideally chilled at 1-5°C	Grows mould very easily. Ricotta is extra fragile.
Cheese – soft ripened (e.g. Brie)	2-3 days in a cool place	Wrap in foil and put in a cool place. Will ripen in cool but not in fridge. If it must go in a refrigerator, use the vegetable drawer. Put at room temperature for 1 hour before serving to restore softness.
Cheese – mozzarella	about 6 days in a fridge	For eating raw, keep in water. For cooking it can be frozen.
Eggs – natural	Several wks below 10°C (50°F)	Eggs are coated with a natural preservative, only broken down by water – so do not wash before storage. Store pointed end down.
Eggs – lard-coated	2-4 wks if room temperature, 4-6 mths in a cold place	To keep eggs longer rub lard all over the shell to hold moisture and carbon dioxide in the shell.
Ham and similar cold meats	Sliced – 2 days in fridge	Home-cooked ham joints keep longer.
Macaroons	A wk in cupboard	Put a slice of bread in the tin to keep their soft centre.

Addresses and suggestions for further reading are at the ends of chapters.

Food	Time	Comments
Mayonnaise – fresh	Several days in fridge	To stop home-made going oily: when you finish making it, beat in 2 tbsps hot water for every 3 egg yolks.
Milk	Varies with the weather; 2-3 days average in fridge	Must be tightly closed or it will pick up smells from other food and taste odd. A metal top pressed open with a thumb is replaceable.
Olives	9 mths in fridge	Cover unstuffed olives in olive oil in a clean jar. Any keep 6 mths in a freezer and can be sliced from frozen for a garnish.
Pasta – freshly made	24 hrs in fridge	If it is really freshly made – and not fresh chilled – it can go mouldy very quickly.
Pâté	3 days in fridge	If pâté has been out of the fridge much eat that day.
Yeast – fresh	2 wks in fridge	In a screw-top jam jar, or wrapped in plastic film.

VEGETABLES

The three big issues in vegetables are novelty, flavour and organic production. The range of vegetables on supermarket shelves constantly expands. I only have space to cover the major ones, but the *Book of Food* mentioned on page 125 also covers exotics.

EC rules now say that if 'organically grown' – or any similar tag – is used, produce must meet set standards and producers must be approved by a certification body, such as the Soil Association. Even organic methods won't give flavour to a poor variety. So big supermarket chains like Sainsbury and Safeway are, at last, beginning to encourage producers to grow for flavour as well as looks. They will only keep doing so if we keep pressing for more taste – and buy the results.

Although water is mainly used as the cooking medium, most vegetables are better cooked with a minimum of water, as in a microwave, and are excellent cut up small and stir fried in the Chinese way, or emerge beautifully from long slow cooking in oil in the Mediterranean style.

Variety in vegetables is not just a matter of how they are cooked; how they are prepared also makes a great difference. It was a cook in France who first taught me that a finely sliced Salade Niçoise, in which one can have all the flavours mingled evenly in one mouthful, is quite unlike a coarsely chopped one. There is a place for coarse chopping, but if you are interested in what texture does to flavour try taking a lettuce and some French dressing. Tear part of the lettuce coarsely, slice another part in half-inch slices and chop the last section in shreds thinner than a matchstick. Dress them and eat them separately and you will have three different salads from the identical ingredients. And the flavour of every vegetable we cook is equally affected by its preparation.

The timings in this section are intended to be guidelines. They cannot, alas, be gospel because a lot will depend on the variety of the particular vegetable, how old it is, how large you cut it, how much water you use, or how you space it on the dish for microwaving. Often vegetables are cooked for *far* too long. This wastes both energy and their vitamins. For the most goodness and best flavour cook all vegetables until only *just* tender when poked with a fork.

The lid must be left off the pan when members of the cabbage family are cooked. It may seem logical to keep lids on to shut smells in, but that isn't what happens. The smell from the cabbage family is produced by acids which they release, and when the lid is on these smelly acids become more and more concentrated each time they condense on to the lid and drop back into the water – and the smell becomes equally concentrated. But if you leave the lid off the smell wafts away in its weakest form. The other big smell causer is simply overcooking them. This family need very brief cooking indeed.

A useful trick when cooking many vegetables is to drop them in boiling water and cook them fast until three-quarters done, then drain them and chill them *rapidly* with cold water. After that they can wait until you need them – later that day – and be simply tossed in butter for long enough to heat them. This gives a brilliant green to most green vegetables, and is a boon if guests are coming.

★ With keeping, some of the natural sweetness of a tomato vanishes. To restore it add a pinch of sugar to tomato sauces and other dishes made with chopped tomato.

★ If you have a surplus of green tomatoes when the season ends, those which are sound, and have a stalk attached, will sit happily on a warm window ledge and ripen, to provide deliciously fresh tomatoes in the winter months.

Potatoes

Potatoes are a very underestimated food. In 1860 William Cobbett, the author of *Cottage Economy*, was instructing gardeners that there is 'an infinite variety of *sorts*'; and suggested using Lancashire methods as 'potatoes are grown to perfection by the Lancashire people' – which is still true.

There are still a wide variety of sorts, and old varieties, like Pink Fur Apple, a little knobbly potato excellent for salads. The names must, by law, be written on their bags. It's worth asking what you are buying, as potatoes differ just as much in their cooking qualities as apples do. To try making a salad with floury potatoes or mashing waxy ones is asking for disappointment. And for chips you need a potato like Maris Piper, with just the right sugar content. But how well a potato performs will depend on growing conditions and how it is cooked. Even the waxiest potato will break up in a very dry year or with overcooking.

The best uses for the major potatoes are: Home Guard/Portland Javelin – boiled, salad; Desirée/Maris Piper – all bar salad; Cara – boiled, baked, chips; Pentland Crown/King Edward – baked, roast; Ulster Sceptre – boiled, chips, salad; Wilja – boiled.

The vitamins and minerals in the potatoes boil out into water, but there is a limit to how much that water can absorb. So cook them in water which only just covers them. Better still – steam, bake or microwave them. If you have potato water use it for gravy or as the liquid in soup.

● The most nourishing part of the potato is just under the skin, and the skin itself is splendid roughage. To save work *and* be healthier leave potato skins on and just scrub them well. Even chips can be made with the skins on.

● New potatoes cook best when put into boiling water, but maincrop potatoes cook more evenly if put into cold water and brought to the boil – unfortunately, this destroys more vitamins than putting them into boiling water, so you have to choose between texture and food value.

● Always store potatoes in the cool and the dark.

● When potatoes go green, that area tastes unpleasant and contains a poison called solanine. Cut out all the green parts – the rest of the potato will be safe to eat, though I wouldn't give it to a child. (If you've just eaten a green potato don't worry: it isn't a strong poison, just one we are better off without.) Sprouting potatoes are also poisonous once the sprouts are growing but the budlike beginnings should do no harm.

● Don't worry if a potato or a potato crisp has a pinkish-purple patch on it. This is just a natural vegetable colour similar to that in red cabbage.

The Basics of Vegetable Cookery

Key
Months in heavy type show the peak season when prices are normally lowest.
Microwave times are for an oven of about 650 watts set at 'high', and for 450 g (1 lb) unless otherwise stated.
To 'top and tail' a vegetable is to cut off just enough to remove the stalk and any spiky or hard bit at the other end.
N/A = Does not apply.

Best Season	Buying	Preparation	Basic cooking method	Microwave	Comments
Artichoke – Jerusalem **January**	They should be plump and not too knobbly.	Peel thinly, dropping into acidulated water. Leave whole or cut in halves or quarters.	Boil/steam 15-40 mins. Purée for soup. Serve with sauce, but not plain.	10-12 mins	Stain hands – wear gloves. Delicious puréed as cream soup with nutmeg and milk.
Artichokes – Leaf/Globe **July**	Choose them fat and fleshy with no browning of the 'leaves'.	There's no need to mutilate the lovely double-pointed leaves by cutting. Invert in salted water for a while to remove wildlife. De-stem.	Cook in boiling salted water for 25-50 mins. Drain when an outside leaf pulls away easily and its fleshy base is tender.	Put 2 artichokes in 2 tbsp salted water. Cover, cook 5½-8½ mins. Stand 3-5 mins.	Serve hot with Hollandaise sauce, or butter melted with black pepper and a dash of vinegar. Or cold with vinaigrette.
Asparagus **May, June**	The best is plump but not woody; the very fine sprue is cheap and tasty, but inelegant.	Pare off any woody outside near the base. Trim the bottoms, rinse off any dirt.	Tie in portions with white string. Wrap foil round tips of bundles. Boil, lying down, 10-40 mins according to size and age.	450 g (1 lb) in 2 tbsp water. Cover and cook for 5½-6 mins. Stand for 3 mins.	The foil round the tips allows you to cook them on their sides without the tips breaking.
Aubergine **All year**	One of the few vegetables in which bruises do not taint the other flesh.	Slice 0.5 cm (¼-½ in) thick, sprinkle with salt, leave in a colander to drain 1 hr.	Pat dry, dip in egg beaten with a little milk. Then in flour. Deep fry until golden.	Only with other vegetables.	Combine best with other vegetables, but are very good fried like this.

Addresses and suggestions for further reading are at the ends of chapters.

Best Season	Buying	Preparation	Basic cooking method	Microwave	Comments
Avocado Pears **All year**	They should be just yielding to the touch, not soft or brown.	Only cut open within an hour of eating or the air browns them and the flavour spoils.	Eaten raw all year.	N/A	Covering with cling film makes cut ones keep their colour longer. Rubbing the cut surface with lemon juice stops browning, but alters the taste.
Beans – Broad June	The smaller, the tastier. Pods should be plump.	If only little-finger-thickness or smaller, cut in lengths like French beans; if big, shell.	Boil 5-10 mins according to age. Cook young ones simply in butter.	4 tbsp water 5-10 minutes. Stand 3 mins.	Try white sauce with chopped parsley on boiled ones. In old age remove their little coats. Cooking with the herb savory adds flavour.
Beans – French **All year**	They should be very slim and snap crisply if fresh.	Top, tail and string if necessary; leave whole or cut in short lengths.	Drop into boiling salted water 6-8 mins or steam; they should be slightly firm to bite into.	450 g (1 lb) in 4 tbsp water 7 mins. Stand for 5 mins.	Dress with melted butter or garlic butter, &/or toasted almonds.
Beans – String **Late summer**	Buy only when slim and tender. They must snap easily, and have no fibrous layer.	Top, tail, string and slice finely on a diagonal.	Boil in salted water until *just* tender, 4-10 mins.	450 g (1 lb) in 4 tbsp water. Cover and cook for 6-8 mins. Stand for 3 mins.	When young they need nothing but a hint of butter; when fibrous not worth eating.
Beetroot All year	If raw, check that the roots aren't broken and there is 5 cm (2 in) of stalk on still. Small are best	Rinse gently.	Put them in plenty of boiling water with 1 tbsp salt for 1 kg (2 lb) beetroot, simmer 1-2 hrs. Or bake in a low oven 2-4 hrs.	450 g (1 lb) in 6 tbsp water. Cover and cook for 23-25 mins. Add more water if needed.	They are cooked when the skin comes off easily. Baking gives better flavour. Small beet very good with white sauce. Eat in 2 days once cooked.
Broccoli May	The flowers must not be yellowy and the leaves should be perky.	Strip the woody skin off thick stems. Wash.	Stand in boiling salted water until the stems are almost done. Then lie them on their sides till done, 8-12 mins. Or slice stems and divide heads and stir fry.	450 g (1 lb) in 3 tbsp water (florets to the centre). Cover and cook for 5-7 mins. Stand 3 mins.	Stores badly. Cook within 1 day unless close wrapped. *Do not put the lid on when cooking or it will smell.*
Brussels Sprouts **November,** **December, January**	Check they have no flies or mould, or yellowing.	Cut a fraction from the base; remove bad leaves. Cut an X in the base.	Drop into boiling salted water and boil 5-10 mins until *just* tender.	450 g (1 lb) in 2 tbsp water. Cover and cook 7-9 mins. Stand 3 mins.	*Do not put a lid on the pan or they will smell.*
Cabbage – Green **or White All year**	Check open cabbages for flies and other nasties.	Cut out the hard core and slice as you wish. Rinse in salted water.	As sprouts but briefer, or stir fry 6-10 mins.	1 medium, sliced cabbage in 1-2 tbsp water. Cover, cook 8-13 mins. Stand 3 mins.	Cook with *no lid on the pan,,* and keep it crisp. Finely shredded, it may only take 3 mins.

Cauliflower is nothing but cabbage with a college education. Mark Twain

Best Season	Buying	Preparation	Basic cooking method	Microwave	Comments
Cabbage – Red **All year**	It should be shiny and crisp-looking.	As white cabbage, above.	It can be boiled, as white cabbage and then tossed in butter with a little fresh root ginger, but is usually given long slow cooking with vinegar and spices.	As white cabbage.	Though seldom used as a salad it is just as good as white cabbage and much more decorative.
Carrots **June, July**	Many slim carrots taste like soap; small rougher-looking ones are often excellent. Taste before you buy: they should be sweet and full of flavour.	Very young carrots just need a scrub, top and tail. Older ones need scraping and slicing.	Drop into boiling water with a pinch of sugar for 6-10 mins. Or cook slices very slowly in butter, with a tbsp of liquid.	450 g (1 lb) in 2 tbsp water, and a pinch sugar. Cover and cook 6-7 mins if sliced, 7-8 mins if small, whole. Stand 3 mins.	Young carrots are sold in March, April and May. Dress with butter and chopped parsley. If big and woody only fit for slow casserole.
Cauliflower **September**	A fresh cauliflower has a crunch in its eye.	Soak in cold salted water. Cut off the base and leaves; divide into even florets unless you need it whole.	Drop into boiling salted water and boil for 10-15 mins or steam, or boil 4 mins, drain, stir fry 3 mins with coriander or chillies.	450 g (1 lb) in florets, in 2 tbsp water. Cover and cook 7-12 mins.	Whiten with a little lemon juice in the water. To cook whole and perfect wrap in muslin so you can lift it out. Good with cheese sauce. *Put no lid on the pan* or it smells.
Celeriac **January, February**	Choose ones which are firm, plump and not too dirty.	Peel with a potato peeler. Put in acidulated water immediately.	Dice, boil until tender and purée with potatoes. Or shred, blanch and mix with mustardy mayonnaise or cut and cook as chips.	Diced as carrots.	Lemon juice in the water when cooking keeps it white. At its best in a salad.
Celery **All year**	The tastiest celery has some earth still on. Failing that, look for crispness and whiteness.	Wash, remove brown areas and slice in 1.5 cm (½ in) slices for boiling or halve lengthwise for braising.	Boil in salted water 10-15 mins, or braise 1½ hrs, onion, carrot, and a little bacon moistened with stock.	450 g (1 lb) in 3 tbsp water. Cover and cook 7-10 mins sliced or 12-15 mins halved.	Boiled celery is best smothered in cheese sauce.
Chicory (Belgian Endive – the cigar-shaped vegetable) **Not June or July**	Those which are green may be bitter.	Wipe dust off with a cloth; don't wash. Remove any brown parts.	Boil till done. Better baked in a covered dish with butter at gas no 3 or 160°C (325°F) about 60-75 mins.	450 g (1 lb) sliced with 1 oz butter. Cover and cook 7-12 mins. Stand 5 mins. Stir once while cooking.	Very good with cheese sauce. Sliced finely in salads, it goes well with orange. Slice with a stainless steel knife; other steel gives it a metallic taste.
Courgettes **July, August, September**	The slimmer, the better – within reason.	Rub any dirt off under a tap. Top and tail; slice like bread.	Drop in plenty of boiling water. Drain as soon as the water returns to the boil, toss in butter, or sweat in butter, or stir fry.	They tend to taste bitter when micro-waved.	Have a natural affinity with tomatoes and garlic. Very good finely sliced in salads.

Addresses and suggestions for further reading are at the ends of chapters.

Best Season	Buying	Preparation	Basic cooking method	Microwave	Comments
Fennel **Summer**	Look for compact fat ones, not those which are long.	Rinse, remove any brown parts and quarter.	Boil in salted water 10-15 mins. Or bake with butter in foil parcels 20 mins at gas no 6 or 200°C (400°F).	2 heads, halved lengthwise, in 4 tablespoons of water or broth. Cover and cook 15-18 mins.	Best with a cheese sauce. Also a lovely salad vegetable.
Kohl Rabi **November to April**	Best very small – larger than a tennis ball they are tough.	Cut off stalks and root. Drop in boiling water, bring back to boil and cook 2 mins. Transfer to cold water and peel. Dice in 5 mm (½ in) cubes.	Boil in salted water 4 mins, or steam 7 mins.	As carrots.	It goes well with cheese and with ginger.
Leeks **January, February**	Slim leeks have the best flavour.	Cut off the root, trim off the dark green and brown parts in layers. Slit half-way down or slice in 2.5 cm (1 in) lengths. Soak them in water, stirring and changing the water till no more grit.	Drop into boiling salted water, 7-10 mins until just tender, not sloppy. Or stew whole very slowly in oil with seasonings.	450 g (1 lb) sliced in 4 tbsp water or 25 g (1 oz) butter. Cover and cook 6-10 mins. Stand 2 mins.	They need a cheese sauce or melted butter with a dash of boiled vinegar and black pepper.
Mange-touts **May, June**	They should be crisp and very small, with no bulging peas.	Top, tail (and string if necessary).	Drop in boiling salted water. Cook 1-3 mins.	Rinse, cook covered in film for 1 min.	Must be quite crisp. Dress with butter.
Marrow **Late summer**	The younger, the better; a fingernail should scratch the skin easily when young.	Cut off stalk and rough end. Peel very thinly. Halve, scoop out the seeds, cut in 2.5 cm (1 in) slices.	Drop into boiling salted water and drain when just *beginning* to look translucent. Or steam. Time varies with age.	1 medium-sized in chunks with 25 g (1 oz) butter. Cover and cook 6-7 mins. Stand 5 mins. Cover young halves, cook 8-10 mins. Stand 5 mins.	When very young drain and serve with butter and black pepper; when older with white, or cheese, sauce.
Mushrooms **All year**	The tighter the better, unless you want big flat ones for frying.	Rinse off any dirt. Don't peel unless from a field. Slice or leave whole.	Toss in butter with a hint of salt for 5 mins. Add a touch of garlic or white wine or herbs if you like.	225 g (8 oz) whole in 25 g (1 oz) butter. Cover, cook 2-3 mins. Stand 2-3 mins.	If sliced mushrooms in advance lemon juice squeezed on will keep them white.
Onions **All year**	Avoid any that are sprouting or have a musty smell.	Cut off the root.	Bank in a moderate oven 1-1½ hrs according to size. Or steam 30-40 mins.	4 medium-sized, dotted with 25 g (1 oz) butter. Cover and cook 9-12 mins. Stand 5 mins. Turn at half time.	Best with white sauce.

Best Season	Buying	Preparation	Basic cooking method	Microwave	Comments
Parsnips **September, to April**	Small ones are most tender.	Top and tail, and remove any bad or woody parts. Peel thinly. Quarter length-wise or cut in chunks.	Boil in salted water for 20-30 mins or roast with a joint, like potatoes – but watch them: they can cook fast.	450 g (1 lb) quartered in 6 tbsp water and a nut of butter. Cover and cook 8-16 mins. Stand 3 mins.	If boiled mash with plenty of butter and cream, seasoning well. If roasted take them out when nicely golden and return to the pan when the meat is almost done.
Peas **All year**	Only worth shelling peas if they are young and the pods fairly slim and very green.	Shell, removing any with maggots.	Drop into boiling salted water with a pinch of sugar, add 2-4 nicer pods, to improve the flavour. Boil 5-15 mins according to age.	450 g (1 lb) in 1-2 tbsp water and a pinch of sugar. Cover, cook 6-8 mins. Stand 3 mins.	Even better stewed in butter with chopped lettuce (dark outer leaves are fine) and a hint of onion.
Pimentos **All year**	Avoid any with soggy bits or mould: it can taint the whole vegetable.	If you have to clean them don't wash until the last minute as water makes some go bitter.	Grill until the skin is black; peel off under a cold tap. Remove the stalk and seeds. Also stuffed, unpeeled	2 whole stuffed. Cover and cook 6-7 mins. Stand 5 mins.	Grilled peppers excellent tossed in oil and garlic or cold with French dressing.
Potatoes **All year**	Look for unblemished ones of a suitable variety (page 117-118).	Only peel if you intend to mash them. Otherwise scrub well.	Boiling in salted water takes 15-30 mins according to size. Jacket potatoes take 1-1½ hrs at gas no 7 or 220°C (425°F). For roasting boil for 5 mins first. Drain, then cook with the joint, basting with hot fat	Two 175 g (6 oz) in jackets. Pierce, cook 6-9 mins. Stand 5 mins. 450 g (1 lb) peeled, quartered in 7 tbsp water. Cover, cook 7-10 mins. Stand 5 mins. New, in roasting bag with 25 g (1 oz) butter, 5-6 mins. Stand 3 mins.	New in May-July.
Pumpkin **September to November**		Remove the skin, seeds and woolly centre. Dice.	Steam 30 mins or roast in butter and lemon juice for about 1 hr.	Diced with 1 tbsp water 4-6 mins, stand 5 mins.	It makes a beautiful basis for soup, but turns sour quickly.
Salsify **May**		Top and tail, scrub well.	Boil in salted water about 30 mins. Drain and peel. Cut in lengths and toss in cream and Parmesan or dress with vinaigrette when cold.		
Spinach **March to July**	Spinach should be lively and squeak as the leaves are pressed into a bag.	Swirl in plenty of cold water to rinse off the dirt. Discard yellow leaves or parts of leaves. Tear out any large ribs.	Put in a large pan, add a little salt and put the lid on. Cook gently with no extra water until tender.	450 g (1 lb) with no added water. Cover and cook 6-8 mins. Stand 3 mins.	Place in colander and cut slightly to release its excess water. Toss it in a pan with butter or cream and a hint of pepper and nutmeg.

Addresses and suggestions for further reading are at the ends of chapters.

Best Season	Buying	Preparation	Basic cooking method	Microwave	Comments
Swedes (those with yellow flesh) **January**	Let them not be too big or they become woody.	Peel and dice.	Boil in salted water for about 20 mins, until tender. Drain and mash well, with butter over a low flame so they dry in the mashing. Season.	As parsnips but beware: microwaved flavour is *very* strong.	An underrated vegetable – except by the Irish.
Sweetcorn **July to October**	Pull back the silk and check the grains are small, plump and pale yellow.	Strip the green husk and silk. Cut off the stalk and point.	Drop into boiling *unsalted* water – salt toughens the grains. Cook for 5-6 mins, or more if old.	2 ears in 4 tbsp water. Cover and cook 5 mins. Stand 5 mins.	Drain, serve and let each person roll them in butter, salt and pepper, before chewing the grains from the cob. Cooking a few of the surrounding 'leaves' improves flavour.
Sweet Potatoes **August**	Buy whole, unbroken ones.	Wash them gently.	Boil whole in salted water, or peel and roast like potatoes, or bake at gas no 5, 190°C (375°F) for about 45 mins – until soft when poked with a skewer.	450 g (1 lb) whole baked. Pierce and cook 5-6 mins.	If plain boiled, serve with butter; if roasted, sprinkle a little brown sugar on.
Turnips **April to June**	They should be very small – large ones have a woody underskin.	Peel, dice.	Boil in salted water 6-20 mins according to age; toss in butter and herbs.	450 g (1 lb) diced in 2 tbsp water. Cover and cook 6-15 mins.	A young turnip is delicate and delicious; an old one coarse and best reserved for stew in very small amounts.

USEFUL ADDRESSES AND BOOKS

Mail Order

B.R. Matthews & Sons, 12 Gypsy Hill, London SE10 1NN Tel: 081 670 0788, sells by mail chefs' chocolate (couverture), bakers' chocolate and equipment for using it. Catalogue. (P.98)

British Deer Farmers' Association, Holly Lodge, Spencer's Lane, Berkswell, Nr Coventry, CV7 7BZ Tel: 0203 465957, sells an inexpensive paperback on cooking venison and has a free guide (send A3 sae) to suppliers, including mail order. (P.73)

Fox's Spices, Masons Road, Stratford on Avon, Warwicks CV37 9NF Tel: 0789 266420, offers spices, including hard-to-find items like vanilla pods plus their own unusual blends of mustard. (P.85)

Heal Farm, Kings Nympton, Umberleigh, Devon EX37 9TB Tel: 0769 572077, supplies by post *very* high-quality meat, reared without hormones or antibiotics, and properly hung. It is not cheap. (P.86)

Rodda's Clotted Cream, The Creamery, Scorrier, Redruth, Cornwall, TR16 5BU Tel: 0209 820526, sell real Cornish clotted cream by post. (P.45)

Food Sources & Information

Berrydales, Berrydale House, 5 Lawn Road, London NW3 2XS Tel: 071 722 2866, makes a range of foods for those with allergies, plus recipes avoiding lactose, gluten and/or eggs (sae for recipes or list of outlets).

Books for Cooks, 4 Blenheim Crescent, London W11 1NN, has an astonishing range of cooking books, including many on special diets, and will mail them worldwide.

British Goat Society, 34-36 Fore Street, Bovey Tracey, Newton Abbott, Devon TQ13 9AD Tel: 0626 833168, can tell you where to find goat's-milk products and direct you to goat-breed societies which can help you obtain goat meat. It also has a leaflet on allergy to cow's milk, and will advise on goat keeping. (P.90)

British Goose Producers Association, High Holborn House, 52-54 High Holborn, London WC1V 6SX Tel: 071 242 4683. (P.76)

The British Nutrition Foundation, 52-54 High Holborn London WC1V 6RQ Tel: 071 235 4904, publishes a series of inexpensive leaflets on various aspects of diet. The foundation is funded by the food industry, but its sponsors have competing interests.

The British Trout Farm Association, 10 Barley Mow Passage, London W4 4PH Tel: 081 994 6477, can tell you about trout farms which sell to the public. (P.52)

British Turkey Federation Ltd, High Holborn House, 52-54 High Holborn, London WC1V 6SX Tel: 071 242 4683. (P.73)

British Turkey, British Chicken, British Poussin, British Egg and Frozen Food Information Services Ltd are all at Bury House, 126-8 Cromwell Road, London SW7 4ET Tel: 071 244 7701 (turkeys); 071 373 7757 (chickens); 071 244 7359 (poussins); 071 370 7411 (eggs); 071 373 7500 (frozen food).

Dried Fruit Information Service, 3 Friars Lane, Richmond Surrey TW9 1NL Tel: 081 940 4144, has information on storage, nutrition and recipes. (P.68)

Duck Information Service, Thames View House, 6 St Peters Road, Twickenham, Middx TW1 1QX Tel: 081 892 2720. (P.75)

The Farm Shop and Pick Your Own Association Ltd, which has leaflets on farm shops and pick-your-own, and the **Farming Information Centre**, which can tell you about farms which can be visited. (P.61)

Farmhouse Cheesemakers Ltd, 13 Union Street, Wells, Somerset BA5 2PU Tel: 0749 670994, has a list of makers of farmhouse cheese, some of which have farm shops. (P.43)

Flour Advisory Bureau, 21 Arlington Street, London SW1A 1RN Tel: 071 493 2521. (P.76)

Food Additives Campaign Team, Science Policy Research Unit, Mantell Buildings, Sussex University, Brighton BN1 9RF Tel: 0273 686758, has the lowdown on additives. (P.40)

The Food Commission, 3rd Floor, 5-11 Worship Street, London EC2A 2BH Tel: 071 253 9513, is a watchdog on consumer interests and an information source. Hard-hitting reports on issues like irradiation and diet for the under-5s.

The Game Conservancy, Fordingbridge, Hants SP6 1EF Tel: 0425 52381, kindly provided the permitted dates for shooting on P.70.

The Meat and Livestock Commission, Snowdon Drive, Winterhill, Milton Keynes. Tel: 0908 677577, will answer queries on meat. It can also give you the name of your nearest Q Guild Butcher. (P.86)

National Dairy Council, 5 John Prince's Street, London W1M 0AP Tel: 071 499 7822, has leaflets. (P.43)

The National Eczema Society (see In Sickness)

mentions the makers of additive-free food in its magazine. (P.42)

National Farmers Union, 22 Long Acre, London WC2E 9LY Tel: 071 235 5077.

Potato Marketing Board, Broad Field House, 4 Between Towns Road, Cowley, Oxford OX4 3NA Tel: 0865 714455, has a consumer advice service. (P.117)

The Soil Association and British Organic Farmers, 86 Colston Street, Bristol B1 5BB Tel: 0272 299666. This is the major body granting organic status to farms of all kinds – not just fruit and vegetable growers. It sells leaflets and a book on sources of organic food. British Organic Farmers runs farm walks. (P.117)

Specialist Cheese Makers Association, c/o The Milk Marketing Board, P.O. Box 256A, Thames Ditton, Surrey KT7 0HR Tel: 081 398 4101, has information on British farm cheeses, and a booklet of major retailers and cheese farms you can visit and buy from. (P.43)

Supermarket Advice Services. The big supermarket chains have customer advice services, with experts who will advise on cooking, food storage, and diet. Your nearest branch will tell you where to ring or write.

Tate and Lyle, Enterprise House, 45 Homesdale Road, Bromley, Kent BR2 9TE Tel: 081 464 6556, has advice on using sugar. (P.103)

The Vegan Society, 7 Battle Road, St Leonards-on-Sea, E. Sussex TN37 7AA Tel: 0424 427393, M£M, M, B, L.

The Vegetarian Society of the United Kingdom Ltd, Parkdale, Dunham Road, Altrincham, Cheshire WA14 4QC Tel: 061 928 0793 – RC, M£L, M, B, HC. *Handbook of Wholefood* lists suppliers of organic foods. (P.117)

WI Markets all over Britain sell high-quality home-grown and home-made food. Your local WI group should have the details or contact The Markets Department, National Federation of Women's Institutes, 104 New King's Road, London SW6 4LY Tel: 071 371 9300.

Women's Farming Union, Crundalls, Matfield, Tonbridge, Kent TN12 7EA Tel: 0892 722803, has information leaflets on farm shops, and pick-your-own. See also next section.

Useful Books
Complete Book of Chocolate, Good Housekeeping – tells you everything you want to know about using chocolate, complete with recipes your figure may regret.

Delia Smith's Cookery Course, BBC Publications, 3 vols, Paperback.

Jane Grigson's Fruit Book, Penguin.

Jane Grigson's Vegetable Book, Penguin.

Leith's Cookery Course, Fontana, 3 vols, Paperback.

Your Greatest Guide to Calories, Slimming Magazine – on manufactured food.

Andronet, *Guide du Fromage*, Aidan Ellis.

Betty C. Hobbs and Diane Roberts, *Food Poisoning*

and Food Hygiene, Edward Arnold – a standard work on the topic yet remarkably readable.

Claire Ferguson, *Gourmet Vegetarian Microwave Cookery*, Gruff Street Publishers.

Drew Smith and David Mabey, *The Good Food Directory*, Consumers Association/Hodder and Stoughton – lists shops selling good quality foodstuffs.

Elizabeth David, *English Bread and Yeast Cookery*, Allen Lane.

Felicity Lawrence, ed., *Additives – Your Complete Survival Guide*, Century.

Frances Bissell, *Book of Food*, Sainsbury – tells you about every imaginable food ingredient.

Geoffrey Cannon and Caroline Walker, *The Food Scandal*, Century.

Good Housekeeping (Ebury Press) do an excellent range of microwave cooking books.

Henrietta Green, *Food Lovers Guide to Britain*, BBC Books – gives the details of the best speciality producers and sellers of British food.

J. Muus and Preben Dahlstrom, *Collins Guide to Sea fishes of Britain and North Western Europe* and *Collins Guide to Freshwater Fishes of Britain and Europe*, Collins.

John Tovey, *Feast of Vegetables*, Century.

Julia Drysdale, *Classic Game Cookery*, Papermac.

Leslie Johns and Violet Stevenson, *Complete Book of Fruit*, Angus and Robertson.

Maurice Hanssen, *E for Additives*, Thorsons.

Moyra Bremner and Liz Filippini, *Pasta for Pleasure*, Fontana – gives regional pasta dishes from the whole of Italy.

P. Rance, *The Great British Cheese Book*, Papermac.

For delicious recipes go to any book by Elizabeth David or Jane Grigson.

The magazine *The Grocer* publishes a list of cash and carry outlets. Some require evidence of a business need – e.g. that you run a shop or guesthouse.

'Manual of Nutrition', HMSO. (P.630)

See also **Health Education Authority** leaflets. (P.640)

Drink

Aperitifs and Friends • Wines from Australia to Spain

This chapter can only dip a toe into the vast sea of information which exists on drink of all kinds, and especially on wine. One of the great difficulties of writing about the major wine producing nations is to strike a balance between them. Even the most expert tasters are by no means unanimous in their judgements as to which are the most important wine-producing countries, let alone on which ones make the best wine. So, in picking the countries to cover, and the space to give them, I have been guided by what you will be most likely to find in the major supermarkets and shops.

Equally, drink is a complex and fascinating area and I can only cover a small fraction of the available facts on any country or drink. So I have tried to combine the key information you might need when buying, with some of the background details which I myself find irresistible. For, most of all, I hope this chapter will awaken your curiosity, and prompt you to browse more widely, both within some of the bottles and within some of the pages of the books I suggest at the end of the chapter.

APERITIFS AND FRIENDS

Aquavit

Aquavit or schnapps is found (with varied spellings) throughout northern Europe. The basis can be potatoes or grain, flavoured with caraway seeds, herbs or citrus peel. Like vodka, it should be served freezer-cold, not just fridge-cold, in very small glasses and is the ideal accompaniment to rich fish like herring, served as a first course or canapé.

Brandy and Armagnac

Any spirit made from distilling fermented grapes can be called brandy. Unfortunately, it's not easy to tell from the label whether a bottle will be good, bad or indifferent. For example, Italian and Spanish labels award more stars the *lower* the quality; Greek brandy may need 5 stars to be drinkable, and the French allow stars to be used any way a maker pleases. For quality, Cognac is safest; for flaming the Christmas pudding you can get by with the Greek fire water Metaxa.

The finest Cognac comes from the chalky soil around the sleepy town of Cognac, at the centre of the area of France confusingly called Grande Champagne.

Much of its quality comes from selective double distillation. It is then aged in Limousin oak, sugar or caramel added as necessary, and carefully blended to create the style of the particular 'house'.

Grades of Cognac & Armagnac

3 Star	at least 3+ years in wood
VSOP (Very Special Old Pale) or VO	4+ years in wood
Extra, Napoleon, XO Réserve, Vielle	5+ years in wood
Hors d'age	25 years or more in casks

Armagnac comes from Gascony, home of Dumas' musketeer d'Artagnan. For Armagnac, wine is distilled and then aged in casks made from local oak so sappy it can scarcely be sawn. Like Cognac, it only matures in the wood not the bottle. Really old Armagnac is a beautiful spirit with a full but delicate bouquet. Store it upright, at about 12°C so the alcohol does not attack the cork.

★ If you want to check the quality of a Cognac or Armagnac rub a little between the palm of your hands (clean and free from soap or scents) and smell it. The warmth of the skin brings out all the qualities the tongue would find if you drank it.

Serving Brandy

The big balloon-shaped glasses are said to have come about because that shape can be knocked on its side without spilling. And such glasses should never be filled so high that the glass cannot lie on its side.

Connoisseurs, however, say that the vast balloons allow the aroma to get lost and recommend small balloons. Any adequate glass with an in-curving rim which will allow you to savour the bouquet is ideal, and a good brandy is to be taken very slowly.

Marc

Marc is made from the debris left after grapes have been pressed for wine. It is a very strong colourless spirit, with more fire than flavour. You'd probably be more grateful for being brought it by a St Bernard than for being offered it after dinner. It goes by national names: *grappa* in Italy, *pisco* in Peru, and so on.

Calvados

Calvados, the distilled cider of Normandy, has such a reputation as a digestive that the term *'trou Normand'* is applied to it, to show that even if you were full it would make a hole in your stomach ready for the next course.

Addresses and suggestions for further reading are at the ends of chapters.

After being distilled twice over, it is aged in oak for up to 25 years. This creates a beautiful dry drink with a lovely appley scent which is most welcome after a heavy meal, whether or not it makes a hole.

Gin

Gin! Gin a drop of Gin!
When, darkly, Adversity's days set in,
And friends and peers
Of earlier years
Prove warm without, but cold within.
                    Thomas Hood, 1799-1845

By the end of the seventeenth century gin had become such a 'comforter' that in some areas there were gin factories at the end of every street and alcoholism was so rife that gin production was banned for 30 years.

Thomas Carlyle called it *'Liquid madness sold at tenpence the quartern'* and a music hall song early this century contained the surprising line 'too many double gins give ladies double chins'. Gin as we know it today seems to have been first made by Franciscus de la Boë , a professor of medicine at the University of Leyden in the seventeenth century, from rye spirit distilled with juniper berries, the name gin being an abbreviation of the Dutch name for juniper berries – *jiniverbes*.

Gin is now made from grains and redistilled with juniper and other herbal flavourings such as coriander seeds or orange peel.

London gin dates back to the eighteenth century, when the ban on gin was lifted and distilleries set up over the artesian wells in Clerkenwell and Goswell, Gordon's Gin being the first of these companies.

London Gin is the classic gin, Plymouth gin is perhaps a touch more highly flavoured and the gin from Holland has a most distinct flavour which may well be more like the first gin ever made.

Pink Gin

Pink gin is a controversial mixture. One classic method is to put several dashes of bitters in a glass, swirl them round, discard the surplus and add a measure of gin and iced water to taste.

Driver's Pink Gin

Driver's is a teetotal 'pink gin' of bitters, ice and slimline tonic. Being dry, it is one of the few drinks that is easy to stick to until the drive home.

> *Gin is adulterated with water, sugar, cayenne, Cassia, cinnamon, grains of paradise, sulphuric acid[!], coriander seeds, angelica root, calken root, almond cake, orris root, cardamom seeds, orange peel, and grey and white salts, and is 'fined' by alum and salt of tartar. The best way is to purchase the unsweetened gin, for the sweetening is employed to disguise the flavour of the various adulterations.*
> *Enquire Within, 1856*

Liqueurs

Liqueurs are among the few things in life which have not yet been confined within international definitions and restrictions. There is no official description of what is and is not a liqueur. The French call sherry a liqueur wine; we wouldn't, and *vive la différence*. We all know what we mean even if the officials don't.

Liqueurs may only be occasional delights, but they are exceedingly old ones. As long ago as 800 BC Egyptian masons carved pictures of stills into their bas-reliefs, and many of today's liqueurs stem from the praiseworthy efforts of monks in earlier centuries to make their herbal remedies more acceptable. Indeed, at Chartreuse, high in the mountains of the Haute Savoie, they still use a secret recipe to produce a medicine linked to the liqueur. (Much sought after for sick horses and – having tasted it – I am happy for the horses to have it.) But it was not for their medicinal properties that liqueurs became all the rage in the *belle époque*, and the 1960s.

Most liqueurs are spirit infused with flavouring and sweetened. In Holland – probably the greatest liqueur drinking country in Europe – they serve liqueurs in the early evening in V shaped glasses like miniature cocktail glasses. But many say the ideal glass is a small balloon shape which will hold the bouquet or 'nose' as the trade like to call it. Whatever the glass, most liqueurs are drunk after meals, improve with chilling and keep through many pourings.

Many liqueurs are very good in coffee, topped with cream which has been poured on to the back of a spoon held close to the surface of the liquid, so it floats on the top. Among the best combinations are Gaelic Coffee (Irish whiskey), Prince Charles (Drambuie), Monks' (Bénédictine), Calypso (Tia Maria), French (Cognac).

Madeira

As fewer and fewer meals are now lingered over, fortified wines have faded into the background. It is a pity. For we are missing something by ignoring them.

Madeira originated in rough wine which this lush little island, off the coast of Africa, sold as ballast for sailing ships. Wine spirit was added to stop it fermenting and British sailors found the hot trip to the colonies and back, in the ship's hold, transformed the ugly duckling into a swan. So, some enterprising merchants developed ways to store the wine so it 'cooked' to deliciousness in the island's heat without sending it to sea, and Madeira was born.

Buying Madeira

Madeira can be made from four different grapes. Each gives its name to a different style of Madeira. In increasing sweetness these are:

Sercial: light, clean, deep golden and excellent as an aperitif, or with game broth or consommé,
Verdelho: pale amber, with a soft, almost nutty, flavour, good before or after meals,
Bual: a medium sweet, tawny-brown, complex, dessert wine,
Malmsey: a luscious, honeyed, dessert wine, fruitier than Bual.

Few Madeiras are now given vintage years. Instead they

are made by the solera system. This involves a sequence of barrels each containing Madeira older than the next. Wine is drawn off for bottling from the oldest, and the barrel replenished from the next oldest, which is replenished from its neighbour, and so on. By a minor miracle of wine making, when young wine is mixed with old it quickly grows up and takes on the maturity of the older wine. So, the date on a solera bottle is the date of the barrel from which the wine was drawn (i.e. the oldest).

Storing and Serving

Madeira is probably the world's most indestructible wine. It can last 100 years in bottle, needs no special storage and will keep for months when opened.

As aperitifs, Sercial and Verdelho are best chilled for an hour or two in the refrigerator, but Bual, Malmsey and Verdelho are better after dinner at room temperature. Serve it in relatively small quantities in in-curving wine glasses, perhaps with Madeira cake if you are serving it after dinner.

Marsala

I was compiling my book *Pasta for Pleasure*, when a Sicilian restaurateur was horrified to find that I didn't already know and love Marsala. He insisted I must taste bottle after bottle and, though some say it's an acquired taste, I found it a taste remarkably easy to acquire.

In fact, it was the British passion for port, sherry and Madeira which, in 1760, persuaded John Woodhouse, a shipper from Liverpool, to look for a wine to rival them. He found it at the western tip of Sicily: a distinctive dry light wine which is highly alcoholic.

Woodhouse adapted it to British palates, adding *vino cotto* – wine 'cooked' to give it a bitter-sweet flavour, and brandy to stabilize it. It was an immediate success and Admiral Nelson proclaimed it 'fit for a Lord' and bought it for his ships.

By the end of the nineteenth century Marsala was so fashionable that Sicily was exporting 4 million litres a year. But, sadly, in this century many people have linked the name with travesties, flavoured with eggs. Like Falstaff, serious wine drinkers can do without '*pullet-sperm*' in their brewage. And, fortunately, those beverages may no longer be labelled Marsala. So it is time Marsala was restored to its rightful place as one of the most interesting, and certainly the most versatile, fortified wines.

Types of Marsala

In a country like Italy which has had more governments since the war than there have been years you can't expect wine labelling to be simple – and it isn't The following categories have to meet different legal requirements, and some say that *vergine* is better than *superiore*, which is better than '*fine*'. But try them and see. The best tend to come from companies which have not been absorbed into larger enterprises.

Marsala Vergine is gold or light amber and always dry. It is an excellent aperitif but also very good with clear soups, and partners certain cheeses beautifully. *Vergine Soleras* is at least 5 years old, but *Stravecchio* or *Riserva* must be over 10.

Marsala Superiore must be 2 years old, *Riserva* 4 years. It can be *secco* (dry), *semisecco* (medium dry), or *dolce* (sweet). *Superiore* is a sociable drink to serve with a rich dessert, or sip happily for hours as you linger over coffee, nuts or *petit fours*, or simply sit by the fire. And if the pleasure tempts you to a glass too many, I'm told it is kind to the head next morning.

Marsala Fine is over 1 year old. It is often darkened with *vino cotto* and is usually sweet rather than dry. *Fine* isn't fine Marsala, but it makes an inexpensive and cheering tipple.

Its fall from grace has left Marsala free from the snobbery which surrounds most other wines. This includes the correct temperature. Serve it as you like – though chilling often brings out the excellence of the best and mutes the alcohol in the less good, making it appear better balanced than it really is.

Port

Wars, trade treaties and market forces seldom combine to create something great: port is the striking exception. Hostilities between Britain and France meant French wine was banned. Happily, in 1703, a treaty with Portugal made Portuguese wine the obvious substitute. But one was so rough that a jingle of the time ran:

Mark how it smells. Methinks, a real pain
Is by its colour thrown on my brain
I've tasted it – 'tis spiritless and flat . . .
But fetch us a pint of any sort,
Navarre, Galicia, anything but Port.

The inspired solution was to add wine spirit, stopping fermentation of the base wine at a point which left it sweet and full bodied. It was a huge success.

The right to make port was given solely to the Douro region, making it one of the world's oldest designated wine areas. And a flourishing port trade was operated by the British families whose names still appear on bottles.

Over 5 main varieties of grapes combine to give port its character and depth of colour, and fermentation is stopped by adding 1 part of wine spirit for every 4 of port. This holds the sweetness in the wine. It is then aged either in wooden casks or in the bottle. Wood ages it faster but the result is less fine than bottle ageing. So the best wines of the best years make vintage port, which is mainly bottle aged.

Buying Port

Although other countries make port-like wine, under EC law only that of Portugal's Douro can call itself port. That apart, port labelling is a mess. It is perfectly legal to sell a stripling like 3-year-old port as 'Vintage Character' because no set age is established in law. And elegant names, like 'Superior' or 'Special' are given to liquids which aren't.

Addresses and suggestions for further reading are at the ends of chapters.

Types of Port

Experts divide wood-aged port from bottle-aged. But I shall stick my neck out and list them all in rough order of quality – although the quality from two different makers will vary.

Ruby is an unsophisticated blend of wines cask-aged for 3 years, then bottled.

Tawny (not Old Tawny) is made like ruby but from wine which makes it lighter, browner and nuttier.

White is made from white grapes, and is a dry aperitif similar to sherry.

Late Bottle Vintage (**LBV**) is from a single vineyard in a non-vintage year, and is cask-aged for 4-6 years, to mature it fast.

Vintage Character is several good ports blended after 4-5 years in cask and is sometimes better than LBV.

Crusted is several vintages blended, then cask-aged for 3-4 years. It then ages in bottle, ideally for 5-10 years, throwing down a crust.

Old Tawnies are blended high-quality wines, wood-aged to an amber, with a delicate nutty flavour, then sold ready to drink, at 10-40 years old.

Quinta do (or **de**) indicates fine wine from one vineyard (*quinta* means farm) which would be made into vintage port in a vintage year. Though usually sold ready to drink, it will mature for up to 15 years in bottle.

> In books one sometimes finds references to a pipe of port. Those who order one must be prodigious drinkers for a pipe contains 534 litres which is about 56 dozen bottles.

Vintage Port is only made in years when the weather is ideal and the grapes produce excellent wine: strong, rich and very dark. Each shipper may declare his own vintage years. It is bottled and sold after 2-3 years in wood and needs 14-30 years to bottle age. At its best a very great wine. It requires a proper cellar and the same conditions as red wine (page 133), and must be kept on its side with the label uppermost, as a crust of sediment forms on the underside. It therefore needs decanting (page 134), buy it a day or so ahead and let it stand, so the sediment which was shaken up in travelling can fall to the bottom.

Most of the port we see is made by British-owned companies. But non-British port houses, such as Krohn or Calem, tend to make part of a vintage year into **Colheita port**. This is aged in wood for 7-40 years, with delicious results. It is worth seeking. In fact, it is worth trying Portuguese brands of port of any quality. The style is different from that of the British port houses, and you may prefer it.

Storing and Serving Port

Vintage port, Crusted port and Single Quinta port are all aged in the bottle. So either buy them at maturity or keep them in a cellar until that age – they will spoil if kept at the wrong temperature.

Other ports don't need keeping, although LBV will

Vintage Years

Nobody can be sure how good a vintage year will be until the port is mature nor when this will be. For a truly great year it will mature far more slowly than a very good one. And the more slowly the port reaches its peak, the longer its mature life will be. However, some houses make lighter ports which mature faster. A large number of shippers declared these vintage years. Fast maturing port may be ready sooner and its prime of life will end sooner.

Vintage	Comments	When to drink
1945	superb, still going strong	until 2000
1947	now past its best	no more
1950	well past its best	no more
1955	past its best	no more
1960	good but now getting past its best	asap
1963	One of the very great classic ports	until 2000+
1966	underrated year, good value	until 1997
1970	big year; underrated	until 2000+
1975	fine year in some houses, especially Fonseca	asap
1977	one of the great years	2000++++
1980	much underrated, too soon to predict its life span	1995+
1983	too soon for predictions but don't drink before	1998/2003??
1985	seems likely to live longer than 1983	2000++

improve a little. They can be stored for several years at moderate temperatures without spoiling.

Once a bottle of port has been opened its life span depends entirely on its type. Port which has been wood-aged will keep happily for a month if it is tightly corked. All bottle-matured port should be drunk the day it is opened.

Port is a mellow contemplative wine to sip slowly, after the main eating is over, accompanied by the gentle cracking of nuts. No need to wait for Christmas.

Traditionally, it is served at cool room temperature, but chilling is essential for white port, and does great things for a fine old tawny. It is often served in small glasses. But port aficionados say that, to appreciate the bouquet, port must be served in in-curving red wine glasses, filled only a quarter or a third full.

Rum

Nobody knows how rum got its name but there are some colourful possibilities, such as the shortening of rumbustion, meaning a big noise. Originally it came from the West Indies, made from the sweet, slightly cloudy liquid which comes from crushed sugar cane. By the eighteenth century it was the standard drink of the British navy, and gave the language the useful term 'groggy'; too full of rum to be good for much. It was adding lime juice to the rum ration which kept sailors free of scurvy and gave them the nickname 'limeys', and it was also the standard 'anaesthetic'. It varies in colour and flavour according to its origin, is usually 70 per cent proof, and must, by law, be 2 years old. All rums combine well with fruit juice for a long drink, and dark rums are good in coffee and for cooking.

Sake

Sake should be kept in a cool place and drunk fairly soon, as it loses its quality with keeping. The Japanese make it from rice which has been fermented and then matured in wood. Colourless and very faintly sweet, it is served warm in tiny cups and is usually only 12 to 16 per cent alcohol by volume. To warm it, stand the bottle in a jug of hot water just before serving.

Sherry

> *The next that stood up*
> *With a countenance merry*
> *Was a pert sort of wine*
> *Which the moderns call sherry.*
>
> *Bacchanalian Sessions,* 1693

Hugh Johnson has rightly described a fine sherry as 'an expression of wine and wood as vivid and beautiful as any in the world', and a good sherry is an elegant drink, to be chosen and drunk with care. It takes its name from Jerez in the sunbaked chalky southern tip of Spain where the vines grow low against the ground to evade the wind from Africa. Originally, sherry was just one of the heavy, sweet Mediterranean wines. It was called 'sack' in Shakespeare's day, probably from the Spanish *sacar* – to draw out – rather than from *seco* (dry) for sack was always sweet.

> *A good sherris-sack hath a two-fold operation in it. It ascends me into the brain; dries me there all the foolish and dull and crudy vapours which environ it; makes it apprehensive, quick, forgetive, full of nimble, fiery and delectable shapes; which, deliver'd o'er to the voice, the tongue, which is the birth, becomes excellent wit.*
>
> *Sir John Falstaff,* King Henry IV, Part II,
> *William Shakespeare*

Despite occasional upheavals between England and Spain, it has managed to keep its popularity through 300 years. Pepys fortified himself with it before a tricky speech, Victorians considered it the 'genteel' drink to offer to visitors. And it became drier and more sophisticated as the public demanded.

By law, only sherry made in the Jerez area can now use the name 'sherry'. So we don't come across bogus sherry such as Charles Dickens described:

> *Cloudy fluid served up by shabby waiters in vinegar cruets to disconsolate bachelors at second-rate restaurants and miscalled sherry.*

Sherry Making

The fermentation and creation of sherry is still one of the most unpredictable processes in the wine industry. The liquor is aged in oak barrels and one of the fascinating features of sherry is that there is a rare yeast in the air of Jerez which gives sherries their particular flavour by consuming the sugars in the wine and dramatically altering its chemical composition.

The capricious little yeast does as it pleases, growing a thick white coating (called *flor*) on the surface of some barrels and leaving others alone – nobody knows why. And it cannot be made to grow where it doesn't choose to: which is why no two butts of sherry taste quite the same. Its extent makes a sherry *fino, amontillado* or *oloroso*. But adding brandy can stop the *flor* growing. And blending, and solera ageing (page 128) can create sherries which are consistent.

All sherry is dry, adding sweet grape juices makes it medium dry, medium sweet or sweet. But even dry sherry may be slightly sweetened for the British market.

Fino is the most elegant of sherries, created by a thick coating of *flor*. It does not improve with storage, is dry, light and delicate and can be drunk young. A good example would be the Gonzalez Byass Tio Pepe.

Amontillado is barrel-aged 8 years, but the *flor* dies after 2-3 years (or is killed by brandy). Good ones combines dryness with richness of flavour.

> In Spain the word *amontillado* means 'a sherry in the style of the Montilla district'. Among commercial sherries in Britain it is often used simply to indicate *sweetness* and any medium sweet sherry may be called '*amontillado*', although *amontillado* can be dry.

Oloroso means 'fragrant', it grows no *flor*. They are softer, darker, and in a way, fruitier for that, though dryness varies. Fine olorosos vary greatly with age, and deserve far wider use, after meals. For a *fine old oloroso*, such as Mathusalem, drunk with nuts or cheese can be a superb end to a dinner.

Cream, Milk, Golden, Full and Amoroso are commercial terms for commerical *oloroso* sherries sweetened, and often darkened, for the British market.

Manzanilla is from the area of Sanlucar de Barremeda. Its special flavour is said to come from the sea, but it could be due to the unusual strength of the *flor* of the region. Plain manzanilla is *fina*: dry and aromatic. Manzanilla *pasada* is long aged and deep amber but crisp and dry.

Serving Sherry

Fine dry sherry is harmed by air. Ideally serve it lightly chilled and finish it that day. Serve medium sherry chilled or at cool room temperature, decanting it if you wish. Rich dark sherries can be re-corked and kept several weeks.

Addresses and suggestions for further reading are at the ends of chapters.

Tequila, Mezcal and Pulque

These three drinks are made in Mexico. Tequila is made from the heart of the agave – which has a rosette of leaves similar to a yucca. Sauza is the best-known brand. When new, tequila is as clear as water but the best are matured in oak and take on a pale golden tinge. If you see a Sauza marked *Hornitos* try it neat for a taste as pure and clean as any drink you will find. But don't suck a segment of lime and take salt before swigging your tequila. Good theatre, but it never seems to improve the taste, and at 40° proof it is a drink to sip rather than swig.

Pulque is the fermented sap of the agave, and is not a spirit. Mezcal *is* made from cactus. It is a rough thing but much used to tease tourists, for, by tradition, it has a fat caterpillar soaking in the bottom of the bottle. Mexicans insist on calling it a worm – but it is clearly a caterpillar and certain caterpillars are a great delicacy in Mexico.

Vermouth

Vermouth is a mixture of wine and herbs strengthened with pure alcohol, and named from the German *wermut* – for the herb wormwood (*Artemisia absinthia*). It is still made in the foothills of the Alps, which have provided the flowers and herbs for it since the eighteenth century. The infusions are blended, chilled to precipitate any impurities, and then pasteurized and aged.

People often make too much of nuances in drinks but with vermouth the reverse has happened. It attracts about as much connoisseurship as orange squash. Different vermouths do, however, taste very different.

All vermouths can be served with ice and a twist of lemon peel, or can be lengthened with soda, and the dry white is the essential side-kick in a dry martini – though my mother, who was young in the days when martinis were too, insists on using half dry white, half sweet white, plus the usual proportion of gin, to make the most dashing martini I know.

Unopened vermouth will keep for years, once opened it will only keep for months.

Whisky, Whiskey and Bourbon

It's a pity we never think of this complex, intriguing spirit by its original name. *Uisge beatha* (water of life) was the romantic Gaelic name for it, so whisky became.

Making Whisky

Traditionally, malt whisky is made by soaking barley in water for about 48 hours, then spreading it out, in a golden carpet, on concrete floors in a warm place to germinate and produce enzymes. This 'malting' changes starch into sugar, which ferments to make alcohol. Nowadays most malting is done in drums, and the barley dried in kilns traditionally fired by burning peat, which gives the 'peat reek', the distinctive peaty flavour. Whether a distillery uses only peat and for how long it dries the grain can greatly alter the final liquor. The malted barley, plus a certain amount of unmalted cereals, is then crushed with water, fermented and twice distilled, then put into casks for 3-15 years.

Types of Scotch Whisky

Only whisky made in Scotland, to approved methods, may be called Scotch whisky, and the big divide in Scottish whisky is between blended whisky and single malts.

Blended whisky can be a mixture of numerous whiskies from different distilleries. It relies on a blender sniffing a sample of single malt or grain whisky in a tulip-shaped glass and telling, by nose alone, what it will bring to the blend.

A single malt is what whisky drinking is really about. Made from malted barley distilled in a single distillery, single malts are individualists with great variations in flavour and personality. There are regional characters too. Highland malts made north of Dundee tend to be light but full flavoured. The Mull of Kintyre's whiskies have a strongly smoky flavour. While Islay whiskies can be pungent, almost oily, and are often added to blends for extra depth. They are sold at 8-60 years old, the biggest ones needing most age.

Well-known single malts include Glenlivet, Glenmorangie, Glenfiddich and Talisker. However, one has the curious name of 'Sheepdip' – and rumour has it that it was named so that vets who needed a warming nip while lambing, could get the invoice past the revenue as a business expense. But the Gloucestershire firm at whose behest it was created dispute this.

Irish Whiskey

Irish whiskey uses the same process as Scotch with a few variations, and is distilled in sherry casks for at least 5 years – 12 years for a high quality blend.

Canadian and American Whisk(e)y

Wherever the Scots and Irish emigrated, whisky began to be made. By convention Scotch and Canadian whisky is spelt without an 'e', Irish and American whiskey with an 'e'. Canadian whisky is often called 'rye', although the main grain used to make it is maize with only a certain amount of wheat and rye, and it is aged in oak for at least 3 years.

American bourbon is made from 51 per cent maize grain and matured for 2 years in charred oak barrels which impart a distinctive taste. It can be more aggressive than Scotch. 'Straight Bourbon' is unblended; all other bourbon is blended. There is also a 'Rye Whiskey' which must be 51 per cent rye. Then at the bottom of the market is 'Corn Whiskey', not to be recommended.

Serving Whisky

Mixers can be added to blended whiskies – not single malts. Whether you drink a single malt neat or add ice or water is entirely a matter of taste.

WINES

For centuries wine making gently evolved. In the last thirty years change has become jet-propelled: new wine countries have been created, semi-dormant ones re-awakened, and established ones shaken up. At the same time the demand for wine has become so great that the major off-licence chains and major supermarkets, such as Waitrose, Safeway, Tesco and Sainsbury, go to great lengths to find good wine at good prices world-wide and offer wines from more countries than ever before. And an increasing number of wine shops specialize in particular countries and sell by post (pages 153-154).

Wine has become an international industry with an extraordinary degree of cross-fertilization. Thirty years ago new-world wine makers learned their skills in Europe. But their approach has been so innovative – and so successful commercially – that there is now a world exchange of information, with old wine countries learn-ing from new ones as much as vice versa. Increasingly, long established European wine houses – notably the big champagne houses – are buying vineyards in the new world, so they can join the competition, if not beat it.

The new techniques which have been developed don't turn every red Bordeaux into a Château Lafite but they do allow wine makers to get better results from their grapes, reduce some of the ill effects of weather, and make good, drinkable, wine in areas which once made mere plonk. They also enable wine to mellow faster, so it can be drunk without long years in store.

At the same time, the huge success of fresh, fruity, Australian and Californian wines made with these tech-niques has revolutionized the approach to wine making world-wide. The great names in wine still need the long bottle-age which used to be the mark of most good wine. But the trend, in middle-range and inexpensive bottles, is towards wine which matures fast and can be drunk young. Even the tradition-loving French are now changing the style of some of their wines and using new techniques to make better Vin de Pays.

The success of new-world varietal wines, made from named grape varieties, has also influenced old-world wine producers and they are increasingly naming their grapes – if only on a back label – so making it easier for us to know what to expect from a bottle. Although, ironically, the old world is coming up with single grape wines just as the new world is learning to make increas-ingly good blends. The result of all this is that it is now easier to find a drinkable bottle, at a reasonable price, than it has ever been.

There are, however, two downsides. First is what I would call the Marks and Spencerization of wine. For, while standards are getting more and more reliable, a certain sameness is creeping in, as almost every country in the world comes up with wine made from popular grapes, like Cabernet Sauvignon and Chardonnay, rather than from less commercial regional grapes. So, countries like Spain, Portugal and Italy, which still use their traditional grapes, deserve our support.

The second is that the EC wine rules (right), which idiotically allot quality grades to whole regions, rather than just to wine makers, and restrict what the wine maker may do and what labels can say, do more to prevent innovation and clear labelling than they do to ensure quality. Yet even imported wines must, to some extent, conform to them. So there is a danger of these ill-conceived rules spreading – unless consumers object.

Choosing Wine

The simple way to choose good wine is to have a good wine merchant or follow the columns of reliable wine writers. Sadly, there is no way you can totally predict quality from a label but you can look for pointers to what may be a good bottle. There are some factors:

- the grape variety, or varieties
- the age of the vines (old are often best)
- the soil the vines are grown in
- the weather that year, in that area
- the method of making (who made it)
- how old the wine is

An ordinary vineyard can lie next door to a great one, and be almost the same on the first four factors above. So knowing where the great wines are grown can be a good start to finding a less famous neighbour which may have a lot going for it at a lower price.

Once you know the flavours of each grape, you can, to some extent, predict the flavour of wine, though not its quality. Next, discover how the same grape tastes differ-ent when grown in different climates or soils, or when used in different ways, and the wines begin to fall neatly into place.

Another factor which needs to be considered is whether the wine is aged in wood, and if so, whether small or large barrels. Wood ageing gives a distinct fla-vour to wine, and small barrels, often called *barriques* give a more intense woodiness. Compare a wood-aged Chardonnay with one which is not wood-aged, to taste what wood does. On page 154 I suggest a book which is an ideal guide to all these factors.

The quality labelling used throughout the EC is less help than it should be but does give you some guidance. Each country has roughly the same grades, but uses dif-ferent letters to denote them, as the table below shows.

EC Quality Labelling

Spain/ Portugal	France	Germany	Italy		
Vino de Mesa	Vin de Table	Deutscher Tafelwein	Vino de Mesa	T A B L E	W I N E
Vino de Terra	Vin de Pays	Landwein	Vini Tipici		
Denomina-cion de Origen (DO)	Vin Délimité de Qualité Superieur (VDQS)	Qualitat-swein bestimmte Anbaugebi-ete (QbA)	Denomina-zione de Origine Controllata (DOC)	Q U A L I T Y	
Denomina-cion de Origen Calificada	Appéllation d'Origin Contrôlée (AOC)	Qualitat-swein mit Pradikat	Denomina-zione de Origine Controllata		W I N E

Some of the Major Grapes Used in Making Wine

There are thousands of different wine-making grapes. Those below are only some of the most widely grown. And many of the world's greatest wines use a blend of several grapes. However, wine made almost entirely from one grape, and sold as such, is referred to as a 'varietal wine'.

Key ♥ red ♥ white ♈ rosé

Vine	Quality & Style	Keeping Potential
Cabernet Sauvignon	A great claret (Bordeaux) grape. Big, almost muscular flavour, high in tannin. So immature Cabernet Sauvignon is mouth-puckering stuff, often softened by blending with Merlot.	Usually long. It takes time for the tannin to reduce and reveal the rich dry flavours beneath.
Chardonnay	The great grape of white Burgundies (Chablis, Macon etc) and an important element in champagne. Crisp, dry style, wood ageing adds roundness.	Often oak matured. Can be long-lived and take a while to mature.
Chenin Blanc	The main Loire grape, making soft rich wines such as Vouvray, also used for Anjou whites.	Can be good.
Gamay or	The grape behind Beaujolais. Light fruity, undemanding. Also used in Touraine (Loire).	Months to a few years.
Gewürztraminer	Distinctive strong muscat bouquet, and spicy flavour, such as those of Alsace.	A few years
Grenache or	The main grape of Rioja. Also important in Midi and Rhône Valley. Makes a strong, highly perfumed red, & very good rosé.	Variable, can be very long.
Merlot	Often combines with Cabernet Sauvignon in claret, and in wine of the Médoc. Full, generous and soft without flabbiness. Typical Merlot wines are St Émilion and Pomerol.	Yes, but needs less than Cabernet Sauvignon.
Müller-Thurgau	A Riesling-Sylvaner cross. Light, flowery white wine, low in acid, with a slight muscat flavour. Often rather average, but can be excellent in sweet wines. The main grape of Germany.	Usually needs to be drunk young.
Pinot Noir or	The grape of the great Burgundies and used for much champagne. At best subtle and full of nuances, not always fruity but with sweet overtones. Often difficult outside France. Often given local names e.g. Pinot Nero (Italy), Spätburgunder (Germany)	Varies greatly with the year and location.
Riesling (pronounced Rees-ling)	The classic of Germany and Alsace. An unmistakable perfume, like early summer; flowery, delicate and fresh. Can make subtle wine, with a beautiful balance between sweetness and acidity, but can be very heavy and over sweet	Spends little time in cask but often repays bottle age.
Sauvignon Blanc Also called Fumé Blanc or Blanc Fumé	Makes Loire wines like Pouilly Fumé, and Sancerre. Also in some white Bordeaux. Often described as like 'cat's pee on a gooseberry bush'. Highly acid, strong grassy/green in aroma, almost smoky flavour. Very variable, from delicious to thin.	May keep well but often to be drunk young.
Sémillon	The great feature of this grape is that it gets botrytis (see page 135). 'Rotting' grapes are hand selected for the great Sauternes of Bordeaux and other 'noble rot' dessert wines. Superb deep intense flavour.	Very long, from a good year.
Sylvaner	Rather bland with little acid. Essentially for fresh dry table wine. Grown more for quantity than quality.	Best drunk young.
Syrah or Shiraz,	The major black grape of the Rhône. Big dark wines with distinct cigar box bouquet, such as the French Hermitage.	Long.

Unfortunately, names aren't used universally. The Germans call Pinot Noir 'Blauburgunder'. Australians call Chenin Blanc 'Sémillon', and call Sémillon 'Hunter River Riesling'. They also call Syrah 'Hermitage' whereas South Africans use 'Hermitage' for Cinsault – and every new country has examples of this.

The grades ensure that the wine is made from grapes specified for its type of wine, grown in a set region, and so on. All useful stuff but each country interprets the rules a little differently, and though they look equivalent on paper, the grades on page 132 should really be divided by a wiggly line. So that French Vin de Table is usually a blend, and can even use wine from other countries. Whereas Vin de Pays must come from a single, named, region of France, and say *Vin de Pays*. Once a grape type is named at least 85 per cent of the wine must be from that grape.

Sometimes, in France, my mnemonic for the French categories VDQS and AOC (see page 141) – Very Drinkable Quaffing Stuff and Any Old Château – are all too true. The vital thing to look for on French wine is that the words Appéllation Contrôlée flank the words denoting the **maker** not the area.

Containers can be deceptive. On the whole, wine boxes, tetrapaks, tettrabriks and screw caps are signs of low quality wines. But some of the better wine boxes contain perfectly good quaffing wines. And some bottlers put identical wine into both screw-top and corked bottles and sell them at different prices to different markets.

Bordeaux   Burgundy   Alsace

Champagne   Rhine/Mosel   Bocksbeutel

Storing Wines

Wine is not like a tin of soup: it is a living thing which will alter according to how it is treated. Keep it in the cool and dark away from strong smells, vibrations (e.g., trains) and with the air neither too dry nor too moist. The ideal temperature is about 10°-14°C (50°-56°F), but for short term storage 5°-15°C (40°-60°F) if it doesn't chop and change. So a partitioned cardboard wine box on its side in a cool place is far better than a smart rack hung high on a kitchen wall.

Any wine bottle with a cork needs to be stored on its side. The wine then keeps the cork moist and expanded and no air gets in to spoil the wine. It also means that the cork is easier to remove: it is said to take four times the pull to remove a dry cork.

★ Get wine bargains by buying the dozen – almost all wine shops give a discount that way.

Length of Life

Wines vary enormously in their length of life. Some are at their best when very young and rapidly go over the hill, becoming flat and dull. Others taste utterly foul for years but, with time, develop a fullness and beauty of flavour which only an expert could have guessed from their early showing.

The longer a wine takes to mature, the longer it usually stays at its peak. Big beautiful Sauternes may take 10 to 15 years to peak but may drink well for as long again; one of the greatest Italian reds can take 50 years to mature; new Beaujolais can be over the hill in 3 months. But, broadly speaking, the better the year, the bigger the wine, and the longer it takes to mature – if it's capable of doing so. However, now that much wine is being made for earlier drinking, old rules about how long to keep each type of wine don't always apply. So buy from a good supplier and ask advice when you buy.

Serving Wine – Letting it Breathe

Most red wine needs to be opened 1-2 hours before drinking, to 'breathe'. But taste it and judge what it needs. The right amount of oxygen brings a red wine to its peak; too much makes it die a little. If you need to knock the corners off a poor wine quickly pour it into a jug and leave a large surface exposed to the air. Then return it to the bottle for serving. But this is not a trick to try on precious wine or if you hope to keep half for the next meal.

The bigger a wine, the longer the breathing time it needs. Most of the big Italian reds need 2 to 3 hours and some Portuguese reds may even benefit from being opened the day before. Also, new wine-making techniques mean that, if you *want* to spread your drinking, many fruity new-world wines keep perfectly well for a day with the cork in – or even a little longer. However, a very old and delicate wine may need to be served the instant it is opened: air takes it over the top.

Serving Wine – Ideal Temperatures

The temperature for wine is a matter of personal preference but, in general, the more full-bodied the red wine the closer to room temperature it should be and the sweeter a wine the more you chill it. Once opened, set red wine in a warm (not hot) room to warm gently. But don't expose it to sudden heat. It will change – for the worse.

Overchilling white wine simply kills it. Indeed, some people would say that the temperatures I have given for champagne and white wine (page 134) are too low and spoil the flavour. It is a matter of taste.

But chilling champagne is not *just* a matter of flavour. Only when it is well chilled is it possible to open

Addresses and suggestions for further reading are at the ends of chapters.

champagne without it frothing out. Gas expands as it warms; when warm the pressure of the gas in a champagne bottle is the same as in the tyre of a double decker bus.

Very big tannic reds	18°C (65°F) 2-12 hrs
Fairly heavy reds	16°C (60°F) 1-2 hrs
Rosé's, light reds, new Beaujolais	Refrigerate 10°-13°C (50°-55°F)
Dry sherry, tequila, Marsala Vergine, rum, & dry whites	10°C (50°F) 1 hr
Sparkling wines and champagne	7°C (45°F) 2 hrs
Sweet dessert wines, old tawny port	6°C (42°F) 2+ hrs
Vodka	very cold – 2 hrs in a *freezer*

Decanting

Decanting has three uses. It looks attractive. It lets you conceal a cheap bottle from snobbish friends, and it allows you to separate a fine bottle of wine from its sediment. Fine mature wines, like vintage port or a 20-year-old claret, need to be decanted, but with great care. This is how the head of Dow's Port advised me to do it.

- Fill the decanter to the brim with water (not hot water, it may crack) to get rid of any old stale smells.
- Tip out the water and shake out any drops.
- Rinse the decanter out with some inferior port/wine to get rid of the water (if you aren't a port shipper you may want to skip this and just let the decanter drain upside down in an airing cupboard).
- Drape a clean piece of butter muslin, moistened and wrung out (he uses cheap port to moisten it), inside a clean (odourless) funnel in the neck of the decanter.
- Set a lamp at the level at which you will be pouring the bottle so the light will shine through it.
- Pour the bottle very gently through the muslin, stopping before any deposit is in danger of coming out. This usually means leaving the last 1½ inches of a vintage port.

Choosing Glasses

Only a tulip shape does justice to wine: its in-curved shape holds the bouquet and, as smelling is a large part of tasting, this really does make a difference. For sparkling wines and champagne the tall slim tulips also hold the fizz; whereas the dish-shaped champagne glasses allow the bubbles to vanish faster. The larger the space for the air the better, so big is best for all wines. The varying sizes of wine glasses (page 4) are a matter of etiquette not winesmanship.

General Information

How Much Wine to Serve

A wine glass should not be more than half full – a third if the glass is large. Then its bouquet is held in the glass.

a half bottle yields: 3 glasses of 125 ml (4.5 fl oz) each
75 cl (1½ pt) yields: 6 glasses of 125 ml (4.5 fl oz) each
a litre bottle yields: 8 glasses of 125 ml (4.5 fl oz) each

The amount drunk *per person* increases with the number of people at table – as there are more hands to start the wine circulating. For 4 people you need 2 to 3 bottles. With 5 people allow 4 bottles, and after 6 reckon a bottle a head, for safety. But if half the people are staying 'dry' to drive home the whole picture alters.

Magnum = 2 bottles
Double Magnum – Bordeaux = 4 bottles
Jeroboam – Champagne = 4 bottles
Rehoboam = 5 bottles
Methuselah or Imperial = 8 bottles
Salamanazar = 12 bottles
Balthazar = 16 bottles
Nebuchadnezzar = 20 bottles

Wine Problems

Corked wine isn't a few bits of cork in the glass. A corked wine betrays itself by a smell, reminiscent of a swimming bath – though fainter. If wine has this smell recork it and return it.

A badly made wine can also give off a musty smell. But occasionally, the pocket of air at the top of a good wine turns nasty. If this has happened the smell will vanish when the bottle has been open a while.

Sometimes a cork will have tiny white crystals on the bottom. These are called tartar, and are harmless. They are formed by the mineral salts which the vine drew from the ground and are most likely to be found if the grapes were left long enough on the vine to become deeply sweet.

Wine with Food

People tend to talk as if there were hard and fast rules as to which wines go with which foods: there aren't. The rule of thumb is white wine with white flesh (whether fish or fowl), red wine with red flesh (meat or game). But don't worry a jot if your preferences are different. What follows are only guidelines, and sauces are every bit as important as the main ingredient. The wine which goes with white fish with a cream sauce won't suit cod with a powerful sauce of tomatoes and coriander. So go by the dominant flavour not the main ingredient.

Asparagus and artichokes make wine taste metallic. May be best without wine but try sherry or Muscadet.

Beef or lamb (roasted): good red Bordeaux, Rioja or new-world Cabernet Sauvignon (but mint sauce kills them).

Beef casseroles: the bigger the dish, the bigger the wine. Provençal stews with bags of flavour need a hearty Portuguese, Australian, or Italian red.

Cheese: people disagree more over this than over any other area of wine and food. Whatever you serve, someone will probably love it and someone loathe it. On the whole, the very rich fatty cheeses are best with white wine, and it can be surprising what they go with. A wine merchant insisted I try Roquefort with a Sémillon. I was sure a powerful blue cheese and a sweet muscaty wine would be disastrous. I was wrong. Port is the classic with Stilton. In fact, the common factor for wines with cheese is not colour but fruitiness and power.

Chinese food: Hong Kong is one of the world's biggest importers of Cognac because the Chinese drink cognac with their food. The Japanese, rice wine, *sake* also goes well.

Curry: some curries may be improved by wine: I have yet to find them. Nor do curries enhance wine.

Fish (white) and shellfish: most fish needs a clean fairly dry white with a bit of body to it.

Fish (oily): smoked fish needs an assertive white and one based on Sauvignon Blanc can be good and Tornes Esmeralda did well in tasting. Another solution is to drink a very dry *fino* sherry.

Game: Hugh Johnson puts it perfectly when he says: 'Drink (very) good red Bordeaux with unhung game, (very) good red Burgundy with any game which has been hung.

Game soup and other broths: sherry or dry Marsala, or Madeira, and put some in the soup too. Even a simple turkey broth is very good like that. An old colonial tip is to put medium dry sherry in a rinsed-out Worcestershire sauce bottle with several dried red chillies. The chilli-flavoured sherry can then be shaken into broths.

Liver or kidney: fruity reds – Burgundy or new world.

Meat pâté or terrine: some like a full-bodied red with a bit of tannin to cut through the richness, others a sweetish white. But one of the traditions of gastronomy is the serving of Sauternes with *pâté de foie gras*.

Oysters: Champagne is classic, Chablis good.

Pasta: suit the wine to the sauce but drink Italian wines with genuine Italian recipes. They marry perfectly.

Pork: either a big Chardonnay or an Alsace or Rhine wine. Light wines taste watery and acid when faced with its richness.

Poultry: with roast duck, or duck in a heavy sauce, a fruity Burgundy or full-bodied white, with a light chicken dish an elegant white would be better. Duck and goose are rather good with a well-balanced Alsace or Loire Savennières as these cut through their richness.

Puddings are a problem. Fruit salad may not go with any wine. Fruit tarts are better with Calvados than wine. While chocolate kills almost any wine. And anyone who has a liqueur to serve might end the meal on a chocolate pudding and serve the two together. The really easy puddings to match are the soft creamy ones, which can be drunk with a dessert wine; sickeningly rich but heaven.

Salad: vinegar ruins the taste of wine, a French dressing made with lemon juice is better.

Vegetables and vegetable soups: Carrots and wine usually fight; tomatoes need big gutsy reds without too much breeding; cabbage is easy going, but potatoes go with everything.

Wine Terminology

The wine terms covered here are those most commonly used. Others are defined in the text.

Blending: mixing two or more wines together

Botrytis cinerea: (noble rot or *pourriture noble*) is a mould which penetrates the skin of ripe grapes and sucks the moisture from them, so the flavour and sweetness become wonderfully concentrated.

Brut: driest standard grade of champagne or MC.

Chaptalization: adding sugar to aid fermentation. Done in bad years when the grapes hadn't had enough sun to develop their sweetness, or simply to push up the alcohol level.

Climat: used in Burgundy for a particular vineyard.

Clos: at one time this was a vineyard enclosed by a wall, but it is now used for any wine estate.

Crémant: usually a wine with less fizz than is usual for champagne, but more than simply *pétillant*.

Cru Classé: literally 'classed growth'. In 1855 wines in the Bordeaux region were grouped according to *price*, into 1st, 2nd and 3rd class. These classifications remain and others, such as *cru bourgoise* have been added. Not all wines show their class on the label: Château Lafite doesn't, Château Latour does and they are both *Premier Cru*. And the price of a wine in 1855 doesn't always denote its quality today, some '2nd and 3rd class' wines then could be first rate now.

Fermentation: yeasts converting the sugar in basic fruit mush or juice into alcohol.

Secondary fermentation (malo-lactic fermentation): the stage when malic acid is converted into lactic acid and carbon dioxide – which makes the wine less acid.

Fortified wine: any wine to which strong alcohol was added to stop fermentation.

Méthode Champenoise (MC): wine made by the same method as champagne – EC law says only if such wine comes from the Champagne region of France may it be called 'Champagne'. And if the method isn't just right a wine can't even call itself *méthode champenoise*'.

Must: the juice extracted by pressing grapes.

Oxidation: for good or ill – the effect of air on wine.

Pétillant: a faint hint of fizz which tingles in the mouth.

Racking: the process of moving wine from vat to vat leaving behind any deposits.

Tannin: a natural substance, drawn from the pips and stalks of grapes during pressing. It helps wine to keep well and tannic wines age longest.

Terroir: an area within a vineyard which has particular characteristics affecting grapes grown within it.

Tête de Cuvée: the wine came from the best vat.

Ullage: oddly this means either the air space between wine and cork, in a bottle, or the practice of topping up wine in a barrel to stop air getting at it.

Vinification: turning grape juice into wine.

Vin ordinaire: a cheap wine of no known origin.

Vintage: this has two meanings. It is either the annual harvest; or it can mean 'of a very special harvest'.

Addresses and suggestions for further reading are at the ends of chapters.

American Wine

You Americans have the loveliest wines in the world, you know, but you don't realize it. You call them 'domestic' and that's enough to start trouble anywhere.

H. G. Wells

That quote from an American publicity hand-out fails to say whether H. G. Wells himself was speaking or whether he put those words into the mouth of a flatterer. They are not lovelier than those of France. However, there is far, far more to American wine than a Paul Masson carafe.

Wine making in America has a surprisingly long history, dating back to the early need for sacramental wine, but the big explosion has been in the last twenty years. Today its wine making is among the most sophisticated in the world and America is planning for expansion. Approved Viticultural Areas (AVAs), similar to the AOCs of France, have been named all over America, but the main regions which export to Britain are California, Oregon and Washington State. All three make very good wine but America's costs are high. It may compete with Australia and New Zealand on quality but rarely on price. However, some American wineries are trying to compete on price as well, and succeeding, so it is well worth watching out for good buys.

California Wine

Californian wine won European prizes in the nineteenth century. Today it is California's gold. The soil offers a cross section of the best wine-growing soils of Europe. So they have planted the great European grapes and used modern technology and diligent research into traditional methods to produce some wines of very high quality – and it is constantly improving.

However, even using the classic grapes there is a distinct fruity, up-front, Californian style.

Reading California Labels

You can expect the maker's name, the region and the grape on most bottles.

If a particular grape is named on a bottle of American wine you know that 75 per cent of the wine is made from it. But some of the best wine is being made with blends of several grapes which complement each other. As Americans tend to plaster the back label with everything except the brand of the corking machine you can get any other information you need from there.

Choosing California Wine

California is such a vast state, with so many regions and wine makers that the safest route to a good California wine is probably to go for a respected wine maker. There are a great number to choose from. Among them Stag's Leap, Heitz and Grgich Hills are noted for Cabernet Sauvignon, Firestone excels at Chardonnay, as does Saintsbury; Mondavi, Freemark and Inglenook make too many good varietals to name and Wente offers some good value for money. However, though you may like, or dislike, a particular style it is hard to find a really badly made wine from America. So you are pretty safe whatever you buy.

It is difficult to predict the keeping qualities of California wines, twenty years of wine making is too short a time in which to discover how the best wines mature. But most of the whites are ready after 1 to 3 years.

The Pacific North West

Oregon first found international fame at a Pinot Noir tasting in Paris in 1979. Rare in offering conditions which suit that difficult grape, Oregon's Willamette Valley is being called the Burgundy of America. The top wine makers are still emerging but Tualtin and Knudsen Erath are noteworthy and The Eyrie is highly regarded. In addition, distinguished wine makers from France and Australia have set up vineyards here. The region makes excellent Chardonnays, lighter than those of California. So I suspect this state could make a bid to become America's champagne bowl. I have yet to drink an American champagne to match Australia's Croser – but Brian Croser is among those who have bought land here. So watch this space.

The grape plantings of **Washington State** are second only to California and have some very good wine makers. Among the top wineries are Chateau Ste Michelle, noted for its Fumé Blanc but also making some classy Cabernet Sauvignon and Merlot. Look out too for Fumé Blanc from Staton Hills or Hogue Cellars and for Hogue's Chardonnay. Among dessert wines Kiona makes a Late Harvest Riesling of charm. All the wineries are still experimenting to see which grapes make the most successful wines and opinions are divided as to whether the dice will fall red or white side up, for virtually every grape succeeds except Pinot Noir.

Atlantic North West

This area runs from New York State west to Chicago and has as many wine makers as the Pacific North West. But it has traditionally grown French-American hybrids little known elsewhere. Only recently has it moved into names which we would recognize in Britain. Which may explain why so little is exported to us that it isn't yet worth covering it in detail.

Argentinian Wine

Amazingly, Argentina is the world's fifth largest wine producer. But, at present, it majors in quantity rather than quality. Price for price I don't find it competes with Australia, New Zealand or Chile. However, it is a country to watch. Its home market isn't strong, it needs exports and it has its eyes on Chile's growing success. So there is now a switch towards better quality wines from the major international grape varieties. It may not be long before we see foreign companies buying into here, and really good wine from varietals, such as Cabernet Sauvignons and Chardonnays coming out.

For the moment some of the most reliable names to look for on labels are probably Trapiche, San Telmo, and Proviar – which belongs to the French Champagne house Moët Chandon.

Australian Wine

That bottles bearing the names like Seaview, or with a label so nautical that it shouts yo-ho-ho and a bottle of rum, ever left the shelves is a credit to the open-mindedness of the public. But they did. And rightly so. Australia is an inspired rebel. Its genius has been to use European grapes and techniques as a springboard, not as a template. Its wine makers have tried to retain as much fruit as possible. More than any other country, Australia created the market for fresh, young, fruity, approachable wines. In the mid-80s their verve made up for their lack of elegance. The low-price, high-impact wines still offer value for money but a new restraint and sophistication has emerged. There is still room for greater length and complexity in most Australian wines, and they still major in wine made from a single grape variety, not a subtle blend, but that makes drinking them a great way to learn to understand wine. And the quality is improving and blends are increasingly being made. Already a few Australian wines can compete with some of the best in Europe and many are remarkable value for money.

Buying Australian Wine

You can't organize Australia neatly into regions, as you can France, and say one region makes big reds, another light whites and so on. Each winery is likely to grow several different types of grape and will often make two whites and two reds in very varied styles. And many producers buy in their grapes from growers who may be quite distant. So the grape type and maker's name are the best clue to the style and quality of a wine.

Labelling

Australian labels are easy to read. Look for the year, the grape and the maker. There may also be marketing names like 'Chairman's Selection'. Blends must list the grapes in descending order of importance, non-blends must have 80 per cent of the named grape and/or region. There may also be a useful back label with a thumb-nail description of the wine.

Laying Down Australian Wines

Although usually drinkable when young, some deserve to be laid down. Much depends on the year and the quality, but most Sémillons are better for 2 to 3 years in the bottle and some repay 15 or so. The very best reds, epitomized by the Grange Hermitage from Penfolds, also mature beautifully over as long as 30 years. But even quality wines tend to be shorter lived than French equivalents.

The problem is finding a good Australian wine at the right age. As one wine merchant put it, 'There's a lot of infanticide where Australian wine is concerned.'

Picking a Good Year

In Australia most wines are made everywhere, and the weather may vary between areas, so it's more difficult to pick the best years for wine than it is in France. This means that you really do need a wine merchant who keeps tabs on the quality of the different vineyards.

Who Makes What Where

Australian wine being relatively new, and lacking very obvious regional styles, it can be hard to know what to buy. So here is a quick guide to names worth looking for. It doesn't, of course, mean that only these names are worth drinking. Nor does it mean that wine by these names will always be good but it should stack the odds in favour of the bottle being enjoyable. Where a producer excels at particular types these are mentioned.

SOUTH AUSTRALIA		
Area	Some Top Producers	Wines of Note
Adelaide Hills	Petuluma	Chardonnay *Méthode Champenoise* Botrytis Riesling
Pathaway/ Keppoch	Lindeman's Hardys Sepelts	
Coonawarra famed for its Cabernet Sauvignon	Mildara Lindemans Wynns Redmans Brand's Laira Rouge Homme	Cab. Sauv. Cab. Sauv./Shiraz Cab. Sauv. Shiraz
McLaren Vale	Hardy Château Reynella Geoff Merrill Andrew Garrett	Sémillon/Pinot Blanc Sémillon/Cab. Sauv.
Barossa Valley The best of this area age well.	Orlando Seppelts Penfolds Wolf Blass Hill Smith Yalumba Peter Lehman	Grange Hermitage

---

Addresses and suggestions for further reading are at the ends of chapters.

NEW SOUTH WALES

Area	Some Top Producers	Wines of Note
Hunter Valley	Robson	Chardonnay Sémillon
	Lake's Folly	Chardonnay
	Tyrells	Sémillon and Pinot Noir
	Rosemount	Chardonnay
	Lindeman's	
	McWilliams	
	Hungerford Hill	
	Wyndham Estate	
	Petersons	Chardonnay, Sémillon, Shiraz
	Rothbury	Chardonnay, Sémillon, Shiraz
Mudgee Very good wine but little in UK	Huntington Estate	
	Montrose	Chardonnay Shiraz Sauvignon Blanc
Riverina	De Bortoli	Botrytis Sémillon

TASMANIA

Piper's River	Piper's Brook	Chardonnay Pinot Noir
	Heemskirk	Chardonnay
	Moorilla Estate	

VICTORIA

Great Western	Best's	
Milawa	Brown Brothers	
Echuca	Tisdall	Chardonnay
Avoca	Taltarni	Shiraz and Cab. Sauvignon
Yarra Valley	Yarra Yering Yarraburn	Cab. Sauv., Shiraz
Central Goulburn Valley	Chateau Tahbilk	Marsanne
Rutherglen	Bailey's Campbells Stanton and Killeen Morris	All make liqueur muscat

WESTERN AUSTRALIA

Margaret River	Vasse Felix	Cab. Sauvignon
	Moss Wood	Chardonnay Cab. Sauvignon Sémillon
	Cape Mentelle	Cab. Sauvignon Sémillon
	Cullens	Chardonnay Cabernet/Merlot
	Leeuwin's – winery of high prestige	Chardonnay Cab. Sauvignon
Swan Valley	Houghton	Chardonnay Cab. Sauvignon
Often late released ready for drinking.	Evans and Tate	

Austrian Wine

Oddly, though German wine sells well in Britain, Austrian wine is hardly sold at all. A pity, for it makes good-quality wine, very similar to Germany's. The vast majority is white, ranging from dry elegant Pinot Blanc to richly honeyed dessert wines. It also makes a surprising amount of red wine, and is now experimenting with international red grape varieties. It is also trying to offer better value for money and compete directly with Germany.

Austria's Grapes

Its grapes are both international and national. It claims to make the world's best Riesling – though Germany would disagree. From the local Gruner Veltliner it produces both table wine and most distinctive, almost peppery, fine wines the best of which need 3-8 years in bottle. Sauvignon Blanc is used, under the name Muskat Silvaner, to make very elegant dry wine – though some styles are too acid for most British palates. And, predictably, Gewürztraminer, known here as Traminer or Rote Traminer, produces its usual appealing range, from dry to sweet, excelling as Trockenberenauslese. Austria also makes fine sweet, but lemony, muscat-style dessert wines with the Muskat grape. Like Germany it also makes champagne style *sekt* and is beginning to make some exceptional wine with the grape Scheurebe. On top of those, it is beginning to get results with Chardonnay, known as Morillon, and with Pinot Noir (Blauburgunder) and Cabernet Sauvignon.

Traditionally Austrians have aged wine in barrels so old that no flavour is imparted to the wine. But, to woo the export market, top companies are now experimenting with oakier wines, and with new wine-making methods.

Finding Your Way Around

Austria uses the same vocabulary as Germany (see page 145). It is also standardizing to EC quality grades and only *Qualitätswein* (quality wine) is allowed to be exported to Britian. At the same time it is trying to make its labels less Germanic, easier to understand, and often featuring the grape variety. This is very necessary, for its wine regions are an infuriating set of divisions and sub-divisions with unmemorable names. However, some names worth looking out for are these:

Neusiedlersee: its climate uniquely favours botrytis, so it is famous for fine dessert Trockenberenauslese and wonderfully rich Eiswein. It is also at the forefront of experiments with new grapes and new styles, in both red and white wine,

Klosterneuberg: both a village and Austria's most famous wine school, noted for well-made wine,

Sudsteiermark: noted for fine Chardonnay and Gewürztraminer. Village names to look for are Leibnitz and Arnfels.

Weinviertel: the main area for sparkling whites, but also makes good value, light drinkable reds and whites. The output of Lenz Moser includes some notable reds.

Wien (Vienna): not a great area but some interesting red from Breyer.

Good vintages: '61, '68, '69, '71, '73, '76, '77, '79, '81, '85, '86, '87, '88, '89, '90.

Bulgarian Wine

Since the mid-1980s Bulgarian wine, notably Cabernet Sauvignon, has been immensely popular in Britain. It used to be state controlled, heavily subsidized, and imported by a single organization bent on maintaining standards. All that is no longer true, and individual vineyards have yet to make their mark. But the labelling remains a useful guide and the best are great value for money.

Understanding Bulgarian Labels

The labelling is usually very clear, giving region, grape and quality. Broadly the quality levels are these:

- Mehana (bistro): very basic wines using any grapes they can get,
- Country Wine: blends of named grapes from named regions, without vintage,
- DGO wines: give the region and the town or village,
- DGO Reserve: DGO wines from selected grapes and oak-aged for a set time,
- DGO Controliran: obey strict rules on area, grape variety, making and ageing.

What to Buy

Happily, the prices are still remarkably low. But I have the impression that the quality range is widening – downwards. However, often two wines with a £2 flavour gap have only a 50p price gap, so buying quality isn't punishing. The choice is between major international grapes and a number of traditional grapes. Some of the latter are worth trying, for example Melnick or Gamza Reserve or Controliran, or Mavrud – a famous grape of the Asenovgrad region – which improves with 10-15 years in bottle.

Among international grapes Cabernet Sauvignon and Merlot are winners, although Reserve Cabernet varies with the region. The most full-bodied comes from the south, and Oriachovitza's seems to me superior to that from the more northerly Suhindol where the vines get less sun. Oriachovitza also produces Controliran Merlot.

I am told the Khan Krum region makes the best Reserve Chardonnays, that Burgas Country wines are good value and that drinkable champagne-style wine is coming. The Chardonnays are fresh, clean and unsubtle. The Burgas and champagne I have yet to taste.

Having bought it, drink it. Only exceptions like Mavrud improve with bottle age, although Reserve and Controliran wines will keep 2-3 years if they must.

Chilean Wine

Chile has recently emerged as a great source of well-made wines at reasonable prices, and they are now stocked by discerning chains, such as Waitrose and Safeway, as well as by specialist suppliers. It has both an ideal climate and a surprising asset. Most of the popular international grape varieties, Cabernet Sauvignon, Chardonnay and so on, were introduced there almost 150 years ago. This was before the vines became infected with the phylloxera, which still bedevils wine production throughout most other wine countries.

Largely thanks to the work of distinguished foreign wine makers, such as Miguel Torres, who have bought land here, it is now exploiting these assets by using the most modern techniques for wine making. There has been enormous investment and that is expected to show results by 1996. But already Chile produces some very good, full-bodied reds – mainly Cabernet Sauvignon, and clean, well-balanced Chardonnays and Sauvignon Blancs. The styles used to be French but the trend is towards the new-world style with up-front fruit.

Chile has some way to go before it offers the range and interest of Australia or New Zealand. But already the quality and reasonable prices of these wines show Chile's enormous potential and we can expect great developments. At present the wine is slightly uneven, and there is no established system of quality labelling, any grand words on the label are the maker's own, so it helps to pick a good name. You shouldn't go far wrong with: any wine from Torres; Calinterra's Chardonnay; Santa Rita's range of big Cabernet Sauvignons; Viña Carmen; Viña San Pedro whose reds are particularly good; Cousino Macul; widely considered one of the best wineries; or Montes Alpha which produces very up-market Cabernet indeed.

English and Welsh Wine

If you are wondering why I don't entitle this British Wine, it's because that term is reserved for wine made in Britain from imported grape juice: English and Welsh wine is made from home-grown grapes.

The Romans made wine here but modern wine making really dates from the 1960s. It has come on astonishingly since then. There are around 450 separate estates and their wine is winning prizes internationally, and appearing on more and more off-licence and supermarket shelves (notably Waitrose). The majority are white or rosé but they cover a surprising range of styles, from the steely Germanic to the most luscious dessert wines. That variety means there are no regional patterns.

Buying English Wine

At present, the EVA symbol of the **English Vineyards Association** is the only quality indication being used. However, as I write, words denoting levels of quality are still being agreed with the EC. Although crazy EC rules may prevent the labels from carrying other quality indications if wine from hybrid vines has been used – even if the hybrids make better wine.

Most of the wines name the grapes which have been used but the great variation in British weather can make choosing a good year slightly tricky. I suggest you either get advice from your local shop or contact the English Vineyards Association (page 153) for its leaflet on vineyards open to the public and go to tastings. They tend to be clustered so you could visit several in a day.

Addresses and suggestions for further reading are at the ends of chapters.

There are some supermarkets now selling English wine and vineyards which are predictably good – although British weather can create big differences between years. Among the most interesting winemakers are:

Bibbenden: producer of the prize-winning Ortega and others,

Carr Taylor: stylish *méthode champenoise* and various table wines,

Chiddingstone: its carefully oaked blends have been served by the Queen,

Chiltern Valley: outstanding wines, include luscious Noble Bacchus dessert wine,

Lamberhurst: a competition winner with Huxelreber and Schönburger,

Pulham (Magdelen label): a prize-winning estate making good Chardonnay,

Three Choirs: a prize-winner making a wide range.

French Wine

Whatever competition she may face on value for money among the cheaper wines, France is still the home of some of the greatest – perhaps *the* greatest – wines in the world. Trying to write about French wine is like trying to describe the ceiling of the Sistine Chapel – which angel does one start with? For angels there are among the wines of France. Archangels even – remarkable thought-provoking mouthfuls which linger on the memory months and even years later.

As truly great wines come my way only slightly more often than archangels I find it impossible to write about French wine without a tinge of annoyance. Not because of my lack of good fortune in this matter, but because the labelling of French wine does little to enable us to find good wine at moderate prices, for the system is chaotic. Some wine regions, like Champagne, make just one kind of wine, others have numerous sub-regions, each singing their own song. There is no copyright on château names. So any wine maker can use a château name on his wine (but see below).

Some names, such as Graves are a region and a style of wine, some, like Aligoté, a grape and a style of wine, and Bordeaux reds are called claret but there is neither an area nor a grape of that name. However, things *are* improving. The sales of new-world wines which name the grape varieties are encouraging the French to follow suit. It's a start.

Wine Labelling
Naturally, French wine fits into the EC grades on page 132, but they aren't the clear guide to relative quality which you might expect. Unfortunately, the AOC and VDQS categories have such rigid rules on which grapes can be used in which areas that it prevents innovation. So some new, innovative, wines are now sold as plain *Vin de Pays* – however good they are. Conversely, AOC status can be given to a whole region, like Bordeaux, to a sub-region, like Pomerol, or to a particular wine maker, or wine. However, the words *'Appéllation'* and *'Contrôlée'* must go on either side of the château name, area or region which has AOC status. So *'Appéllation*

Château La Ronde *Contrôlée'* indicates fine wine from an AOC château, but 'Château La Ronde *Appéllation* Bordeaux *Contrôlée'* could be poor wine made within the fine-wine region of Bordeaux. And those naming sub-regions fall between the two. However, the following marks do denote long-established excellence – although they may not be a perfect guide to relative quality today.

For Bordeaux	For Burgundy
Premier Grand Cru Classé	*Grand Cru*
Grand Cru Classé	*Premier Cru + village name*
Grand Cru	*Deuxième Cru*
Cru Bourgeois	*Appéllation Village*

French Wine Regions
The only easy way to understand what the different regions produce is to look at the great wines of each. For that also shows the types of wines which most producers will be aiming for at any price point.

Alsace
Having belonged to both France and Germany, its wines are un-French, and its labels usefully feature the grape varieties. It excels with Gewürztraminer and its distinctive, full-bodied, whites are excellent with rich food. Among its great delights are the *vendange tardives*: late-picked, intense white wines, if well made sweet but clean; and its *selection de grains nobles*: botrytized, and very sweet yet elegant. Not cheap but a treat. Two very different makers to look for are Leon Beyer and Paul Blanck.

Example of a French wine label

① CHATEAU DES TOURS ②

1970

MONTAGNE-S²-ÉMILION ③
④ Appellation Montagne-S²-Émilion Contrôlée

LOUIS YERLÈS, PROPRIÉTAIRE ⑤
A MONTAGNE (GIRONDE) ⑥
⑦

① The grower's château or vineyard.
② Bottled within the château.
③ The sub-region, of the St Émilion area, from which it comes.
④ Shows the area is AC.
⑤ The name of the château owner.
⑥ The French 'county' of origin.
⑦ The village within the Montagne AC wine area.
⑧ Made in France.

Bordeaux

Bordeaux is the greatest wine making area of France: home of some of its greatest names in wine: the clarets, Château Lafite, Châteaux Latour and Mouton-Rothschild. A third of France's AOC wines (page 141) originate here and many are *Premier Grand Cru Classé* or *Grand Cru Classé*. However, the term *'Grand Vin de Bordeaux'* (great wine of Bordeaux) is misleadingly allowed on any Bordeaux.

The great reds of the region are usually a blend of Merlot, Cabernet Sauvignon and Cabernet Franc, but different areas and makers favour different balances of the three. Pauillacs tend to major on Cabernet Sauvignon, but Pomerols often bring Cabernet Franc and Merlot to the fore. The great white dessert Sauternes and Barsacs are made from botrytized Sémillon often blended with Sauvignon Blanc.

The Major Areas of Bordeaux

Don't look for the word Bordeaux on labels. Look instead for the area, and the maker – usually a Château. But, even from this great area, don't expect every bottle to be fine, or even good. You get what you pay for – and the best are dear.

Médoc, Haute Médoc and **Graves** run down the south bank of the Gironde embracing some of the greatest château wines of France (such as velvety Margaux) and noted ones like St Julien and Pauillac. They all produce delicate, elegant reds which age beautifully and Graves also produces very fine white wine. Tucked into Graves, like the stone in a peach, are **Sauternes** and **Barsac**, areas famous for sweet, clean, deeply fragrant white wines, such as Château Yquem. At their best, exquisite and perhaps the world's greatest white wines. The best wine of all these areas needs time to mature and can be laid down for many years.

Entre-Deux-Mers produces attractive light, lunchtime whites from Sauvignon grapes.

St Emilion's most famous château is Cheval Blanc, and the area's superb red wines are sometimes called 'the Burgundy of Bordeaux', though they have a un-Burgundian softness. Adjacent is Pomerol, another area of velvety reds, home of Château Petrus, perhaps the world's most expensive wine.

Burgundy

If Bordeaux is the King of France's wine regions, Burgundy is the Queen. Its varied areas are strung out down the Sâone, like misshapen pearls. Its main grapes are Pinot Noir, Chardonnay, Aligoté and Gamay, often blended with a host of others. Most famous of all are its big highly complex reds, but you also find delicate, elegant, white Chablis and rich, oaky, whites like Pouilly-Fuissé, and dry, nutty Mersault. Plus a great deal of table wine.

Burgundian Labels

- *Grand Cru* wines give only the name of the vineyard (e.g. Montrachet).
- *Premier Cru* wines show the name of the parish and of the *cru* (e.g. Nuits-Saint-Georges-Les-Porets).

- *Village* wines show just the parish (e.g. Nuits-Saint-Georges).
- At the bottom are those which only own up to the region and simply say Bourgogne.

Below *cru* level this makes it hard to know what you are buying. For the *'village'* name can be owned by dozens of adjacent producers – some making nectar, others cat's pee. Even great wine names, like Gevrey-Chambertin, belong to numerous producers. So you just have to trust your supplier. (See also AOC, page 141 and above).

The Areas of Burgundy

Chablis is known for dry elegant whites most associated with Chardonnay grapes. At its best, often far more complex than new-world Chardonnay but quality and price are particularly closely linked: cheap Chablis is unlikely to be good.

Côte de Nuits is said to be the world's greatest area for wine from Pinot Noir grapes. These are usually blended with other grapes to make gorgeous reds such as Nuits-Saint-Georges and Gevrey-Chambertin – favourite of Napoleon. Some of the small vineyards also make very good wine at reasonable prices.

Côte de Beaune produces big beautiful white wines, such as Montrachet and Meursault; reds such as Volnay, Beaune and Pommard, which are lighter and mature faster than the reds of the Côte de Nuits.

Côte Chalonnaise has increasingly good reds very similar to its neighbour Côte de Beaune.

Mâcon is a great Chardonnay region, the most famous wine being Pouilly-Fuissé. There are also fruity easy-going reds made with Gamay and Pinot Noir, sold as Passtoutgrains. Mâcon *villages* are always dry, fruity and white, and best drunk young. On labels the name of

Vintage Chart of the French Wine Regions

★★★★ Exceptional Vintages: 1921, 1928, 1929 ★★★★

VINTAGE	Red Bordeaux	White Bordeaux	Red Burgundy	White Burgundy	Côtes du Rhône	Alsace	Pouilly s/Loire Sancerre	Anjou Touraine	Beaujolais
1945	★★★★	★★★★	★★★		★★★				
1947	★★★★	★★★	★★★		★★★★			★★★★	
1949	★★★★	★★★	★★★★		★★★			★★★	
1955	★★★	★★★	★★★	★★	★★★			★★★	
1959	★★	★★★	★★★★	★★	★★	★★★★		★★★★	
1961	★★★★	★★★★	★★★★	★★★	★★★	★★★		★★	
1962	★★★	★★★	★★	★★	★★	★		★★	
1964	★★	★	★★★	★★	★★	★★			
1966	★★★	★★	★★★	★★	★★★	★★★			
1967	★★	★★★★	★★	★★	★★★	★★★			
1969	★	★	★★★	★★★	★★	★★		★★	
1970	★★★★	★★	★★	★★★★	★★★★	★★		★★★	
1971	★★★	★★	★★★	★★★	★★	★★★★		★★	
1973	★★	★★	★	★★★		★★★		★	
1974	★	★★	★★	★★		★		★	
1975	★★★★	★★★	★	★★	★★★	★★		★★	
1976	★★★	★★★	★★★	★★★	★★★	★★★★		★★	
1977	★	★	★	★★		★		★	
1978	★★★	★★	★★★★	★★★	★★★★	★		★★★	
1979	★★★	★★	★★	★★★★	★★★	★★★	★★	★★	★
1980	★	★	★★	★★	★★	★	★★	★	★
1981	★★★	★★	★	★★	★★	★★★	★	★★	★★
1982	★★★★	★★	★★	★★★	★	★★	★★★	★★★	★★
1983	★★	★★	★★	★★★	★★	★★★★	★★★	★★	★★★★
1984	★	★	★	★					
1985	★★★	★★	★★★★	★★★	★★★★	★★★★			★★★
1986	★★★★	★★	★★	★★★	★★	★	★★★		
1987	★	★★	★★	★★		★	★★		
1988	★★★	★★	★★★★	★★★	★★★	★★★★	★★★	★★	★
1989	★★★★	★★	★★★	★★★★	★★	★★★★	★★★★	★★★	★★★
1990	★★★	★★	★★★★	★★★	★★★	★★★★	★★★	★★	★★★
1991	★	★★	★★	★★	★	★★	★★★	★	★★★★
1992	[HIGH VOLUME, QUALITY INCONSISTENT]								

Average & Medium vintage	Good vintage	Great vintage	Exceptional vintage
★	★★	★★★	★★★★

These appreciations are based on averages, the exception proves the rule the village is added to the name of the region e.g. Mâcon-Vire.

Beaujolais

Here Gamay is the main grape. It gives a light, pleasant wine, drinkable before its secondary fermentation. However the year's new wine can only be sold as Beaujolais *nouveau* or *primeur* between the third Thursday in November and 14 December. Drink it immediately, only very good years mature in bottle. Beaujolais has numerous villages of AOC status making quality wines. But its best wines are the *cru Beaujolais* such as Fleurie, Morgon, Julienas, and Moulin-à-Vent.

Champagne

Only wine from grapes grown and processed by a set method, within the area of France called Champagne, can bear the name champagne. Wine made *anywhere* else, by that method, is called *méthode champenoise*. Areas within Champagne have *Grand cru* (No 1) or *Premier Cru* (No 2) status, and the top champagnes of individual makers may be called *cuvée prestige*. *Extra Brut* is very dry and crémant has less fizz.

Unlike most French wine the best non-vintage (NV) champagne is a blend of dozens of base wines. These use both Chardonnay and two black grapes, Pinot Noir and Pinot Meunier – pressed so no colour is drawn from the skins. This is why champagne purely from Chardonnay is called 'Blanc de Blancs' – white (wine) of white (grapes). Vintage champagne uses superior base wine, and is aged longer. The best value is found in less-known names or supermarket own brands – which can be big names in disguise. The best champagne has an almost bready smell when you first drink it.

Côtes du Rhône

The northern sections of the Rhône valley is famous for Hermitage – a big, dark, spicy, wonderfully complex red wine. It is typical of wine from the Syrah grape, the pride of this area. The southern Rhône grows an astounding range of grapes, dominated by Grenache. Its most famous wine is Chateauneuf-du-Pape, a blend of 13 grape varieties – in varying amounts according to the maker. This is also the home of good affordable reds such as Cairanne or Gigondas and of popular dessert wines such as Beaumes de Venise.

The Loire and Anjou-Saumur

The winding valley of the Loire is one of the coolest regions. Ripening less deeply, the grapes, which are mainly white, keep a certain acidity which gives Loire wines a lightness of touch. Chenin Blanc is the main grape, producing wine of surprising diversity, from the elegant, full, dryness of Savennières, through frivolous, flowery, fizzy Vouvray blends, to richly honey dessert wines Bonnezeaux and Coteaux du Layon – which deserve to be better known. But, at the river's mouth you find Muscadet, clean, light, good with fish and usually affordable – the best being *sur lie*. Lower down you find Anjou Rosé, then the sophisticated whites of Sancerre and Pouilly Fumé. And amid all these lie the light reds

of Chinon and Bourgueil, best served chilled. When buying wines of this area remember the structure of the industry is similar to Burgundy, and read the small print. Look too for Vin de Pays using non-regional grapes, like Chardonnay.

Jura and Savoie

This region features both light-hearted fizzy wines and intense, sweet, *vins jaunes* which mature under *flor*, like sherry. The latter need great age and are priced accordingly.

Languedoc Roussillon

In quality Languedoc Roussillon used to be wine-box, not bottle, country. Now new techniques are being used to make better wine and old established AOC producers, like Fitou, are polishing their spurs. It is making good value *vin de pays* and has appealing crémant and dessert wines, notably its Vins doux Naturels.

Provence

Provence has always been a source of bistro wines but its quality is rising rapidly, especially in Bandol and its reds are to be watched.

South West France

The lack of name tells you this region between Bordeaux and the Pyrénnees is a neglected area. It has always produced good wine, such as the big reds of Cahors and the fine, sweet whites of Monbazillac, but its general lack of renown gives scope for change. Here the French are trying to beat the new world at its own game, applying modern techniques to the long-established vineyards. It could offer bargains. Look out for its *vin de pays*.

German Wine

It is a shame that people's first contact with German wine is so often with a bland, inoffensive, blended wine marketed by a big brand name. German wine reaches perfection in luscious Rieslings of exquisite fragrance, full of nuances. There are also complex wines from slatey soils, steely, elegant and sophisticated. However, we expect wine to be for drinking at meals, whereas often German wines are at their best alone.

German wine makers dogged by bad weather, go to extraordinary lengths to get the best from their unpredictable raw material, sometimes treating each batch of grapes differently. And though Germany is noted for sweet wines it is also a country of businessmen. The world wants crisp, fruity, dry wines, so it is now making them. What Germany does it does thoroughly. Its forte is reliability. Even when it makes low-priced own brands for supermarkets they are usually very drinkable, if unsophisticated.

The most exciting development is that young wine makers, such as Rainer Lingenfelder, are challenging tradition and using modern techniques on Pinot Noir (called Spätburgunder here) and maturing it in wood to make remarkably stylish red wine. And also using less well-known grapes such as Scheurebe, to produce

Addresses and suggestions for further reading are at the ends of chapters.

prize-winning white wines which range from dry, beautifully structured Kabinett and Spätlese to wonderfully honeyed Auslese (see terms below).

For the most part, however, the differences between Germany's regions are nothing like as distinct as those in France, nor is the range of wines, or styles, a fraction as great. And, oddly, though they also meet the EC grading criteria (page 132) German wine grades rest on the sugar content of the grape juice. The cheapest *Tafelwein* has a minimum of 5 per cent, whereas *Prädikat* wine goes up to 21.5 per cent. And makers are allowed to add sugar to all but *Prädikat* wines.

Labelling Terms

In addition to meeting the EC rules, wine which is *Qualitätswein mit Prädikat* may also give one of the following classifications showing its style and sweetness. The minimum alcohol given is the pre-fermentation potential.

Kabinett: grapes harvested at the normal time, minimum alchohol 8-6% – elegant and mature.

Spätlese: grapes harvested at least 7 days later, minimum alcohol 10% – dry to full and rich.

Auslese: very ripe grapes carefully selected and separately pressed, minimum alcohol 11.1% – usually medium sweet to very rich.

Beerenauslese: selected overripe grapes affected by botrytis (noble rot), minimum alchohol 15.3% – an intense honeyed, fruity wine with a distinct nose and taste.

Eiswein: grapes of Beerenauslese age and quality which have frozen on the vine and are hand-picked and pressed while still frozen, minimum alcohol 15.3% – extraordinary fruitiness and concentration.

Trockenbeerenauslese: selected grapes left to shrivel on the vines, minimum alcohol 21.5% – great concentration and style.

German wine is, all too often, given the name of its village or locality. This is meaningless, as several producers of varied skills may all make wine of that name. So, the name of the maker is much more important than the grape correctness and all the other bureaucratic details the EC categories (page 132) ensure. All the information you need is usually on the label. However, the following is a translation of the major terms.

Anbaugebiete: region
Aus eigenem Lesegut: from the producer's estates
Bereich: district
Diabetikerwein: diabetic wine (max 4 g. unfermented sugar per l.)
Edelfäule: botrytis (noble rot)
Eigene Abfüllung: estate bottled
Einzellagen vineyard
Erzeugerabfüllung: estate bottled
Grosslage: group of vineyards
Halbtrocken: semi-dry
Herb: dry, sparkling, i.e., Brut
Perlwein: carbonated wine
Rotwein: red wine
Schaumwein: sparkling wine

Schillerwein: rosé from mixed red and white grapes
Seewein: lake wine
Sekt: sparkling wine (with quality controls)
Trocken: dry
Weinkellerei: winery
Weissherbst: rosé wine from red grapes
Weisswein: white wine
Winzergenossenschaft: cooperative

German Vines and Vintage Years

Although Germany does make red wine almost all the exported wine is white. Riesling still holds the crown, but Müller-Thurgau is more prolific. The other main vines are Sylvaner, Kerner, Gewürztraminer, Rulander (Pinot Gris), Scheurebe and Morio-Muskat (a very flowery muscaty wine). In most areas the following years have been the best: '76, '83, '85, '88, '89, '90.

Germany's Main Wine Regions

Germany is divided into 11 wine-producing regions, or *Anbaugebiete*, whose names are on most labels. All of them are clustered along the banks of the Mosel and Rhine rivers and their tributaries.

Baden produces vast amounts of very ordinary wine. But it also has excellent carafe Riesling, called *Mauerwein* and some famous wine houses which produce fine Riesling, Traminer and Rulander wines.

The wine of **Franconia** is known for distinctive flagon-shaped bottles. It is often fuller bodied than other German wine and a touch flintier – and often pricier.

Mosel-Saar-Ruwer is a mass of small vineyards dominated by Riesling grapes. They draw a certain flintiness from the slatey soil, especially in the Saar area. This gives the wine a clean clear finish. The wines have high natural acidity but are fresh, light and well balanced. These wines can be Riesling at its best. However, the Saar area is cold and the quality of wines here varies immensely from year to year. In a warm year the wine is superb, in a cold one it can be undrinkable.

Nahe is blessed in its soil and its climate and its wine reflects this. Riesling is its greatest grape but it is also producing some very good Scheurebe. Its wine often has particularly good balance, fragrance and delicacy

Rheingau is the *crème de la crème* of areas, and its major growers include a prince and a bevy of lesser nobles. Hochheim district gave its name to hock. Riesling vines excel, producing wines of great elegance, but at the extreme west Pinot Noir grapes are used to make that rare thing – an interesting German red wine – Assmannshausen.

Rheinhessen is the home of most Liebfraumilch. But bottles carrying the *grosslage* Rehbach, are worth looking out for.

The **Rheinpfalz** (or Palatinate) was an important wine area in Charlemagne's time. Wines by producers like Bürklin-Wolf, can be excellent, but much of its output is simply table wine.

'Summer Champagne'

In 1856, when the first edition of *Enquire Within* was printed, it was fashionable to dilute German wines with mixers and the author gave this recipe for 'Summer Champagne':

> To four parts seltzer water add one of Moselle wine (or hock), and put a teaspoonful of powdered sugar into a wineglass of this mixture; an ebullition takes place and you have a sort of champagne which is more wholesome in hot weather than the genuine wine known by that name.

Seltzer water was a naturally sparkling mineral water from Weisbaden in Germany. Any of today's fizzy waters would probably stand proxy, but I wonder whether the recipe is not a trifle heavy with the water.

Greek Wine

It's easy to dismiss Greece as merely the home of the throat-scorching brandy Metaxa, and wine tasting like pine bark. But maybe we shouldn't scoff at a country which was enjoying wine when we were barbarians.

Greece is now bringing her wine making up to date and grouping her wines into the EC classes (page 132). Blessed with 300 native, and highly regional, grape varieties, she is wisely according them status and perhaps has the potential to offer alternatives to the world glut of Chardonnays and Cabernets.

Whether she will produce serious wine remains to be seen. But major wineries like Boutari and Achaia Claus make some unexpectedly palatable bottles. Try Achaia's Mavrodaphne of Patras, an intriguing rich dessert red, or the raisiny Muscat also from Achaia, or the Samos 'Vin Muscat' or almost any of the Boutari range. And you could do a lot worse than make a brandy and soda

with a Cambas V.S.O.P. What's more, as Greek wine has no reputation, if a shop risks stocking it, it may well be because it offers good value for money.

Hungarian Wine

Hungary's wine making dates from the tenth century and now it no longer has to pander to Soviet pockets – and palates – it is changing its wine to woo more discerning countries, and offering good value for money. It also has some great traditional wine.

New-world wine makers have introduced modern methods. Vineyards have been planted with grapes such as Chardonnay, Merlot and Sauvignon Blanc. And easy-to-understand, Australian-style labels have been adopted. Most of the wine is white or rosé, clean, light, well made and at reasonable prices. *Some* of the country wine, made with traditional grapes, can be early summer in a glass, and the sparkling wine is getting praise.

Traditional Hungarian wines are also well worth looking for despite their tongue-twister labels naming national grapes and regions. Don't be put off: the wine is far easier on the tongue, and watch for these regions:

Mátraalja, Hungary's main region for quality white wines such as the greenish-yellow honeyed elegance of Debröi hárslevelü.

Skekszard produces some of the best reds, notably from the Kadarka grape, although Bull's Blood, Hungary's best known red comes from Eger.

Balaton and **Badacsonyi** are neighbours on the hills flanking Lake Balaton. The Balaton wines tend to be drier. Both produce full, stylish, richly fragrant wines with real Hungarian character, both from Hungarian grapes, such as Kéknyélü and Furmint (the grape of Tokaj) and from Riesling.

Tokajhegyalia is the home of Tokaj (pronounced tokeye) one of the world's most distinctive wines. Made from botrytized grapes (called *aszu* there) and oak-aged, it has a beautiful flowers-and-honey scent, remarkable balance of sweetness and acidity and ages wonderfully. As the word 'Tokaj' can be on the label of any wine from the region, look for the word *aszu*, plus *puttonyos* and a number, 2–6, showing how many grape-pickers' baskets (*puttonyos*) of *aszu* grapes went into the barrel. The more it took the more intense the flavour of the wine and *aszu essencia*, with no basket number, is the most concentrated of all.

Italian Wine

Italian wine is like the Italians: individualistic, assertive and unpredictable. One of the best minor wines I have ever drunk was one I tasted when, after many flight delays, I tumbled exhausted into a Sicilian café. With typical Italian generosity the owner, hearing that I was writing about Italian food, gave me a bottle of his best wine – an astonishing brew, the colour of dilute redcurrant juice. Maybe it was the jet lag that made it taste ambrosial, or maybe it was one of the small unsung miracles of Sicily. I shall never know, for I was certain that I would never forget its name as long as I lived – but I did. I mention it only because it is typical that his best wine should have cut clean across all my preconceptions as to how wine should be. That is true of all Italian wine. It is disastrous to take to it the expectations created by French wine or to drink it with most French food. It is totally distinctive.

It has had time to gain its individuality: six centuries before Christ the Etruscans were making wine there and worshipped a wine god – called Fufluns. And Pliny said that 154 BC was the year in which Italy became the greatest wine growing country in the world. It took two Italian professors 5 substantial volumes to describe the main grape varieties of Italy – compare this with the eight major vines used in Germany. A three-volume encyclopaedia of Italian vines lists 3,811.

All that suggests immense potential. With major exceptions, it is a potential still largely unfulfilled. For Italy's vast range of vines and extraordinary diversity of wines also makes her one of the most uneven wine making countries of the world. Having long produced wine in quantity, rather than quality, some regions have been slow to adopt modern standards and techniques. But there have been big changes.

In trying to modernize, some producers have, alas, joined the Cabernet Sauvignon/Chardonnay bandwagon, making perfectly acceptable varietals. However, Australia often does them better and Italy's real potential lies in her traditional wines. Here standards are rising. Some producers making renowned world-class wines and classics, like Chianti, are more consistent than they were. At the same time, Italy's passionate individuality has led to the production of charming, highly original, wines which can be found nowhere else – such as her light, sparkling reds.

If, bored with the plethora of Chardonnays and Cabernet Sauvignons, you want a full-bodied, concentrated red wine without lots of up-front fruit, or a deliciously fragrant white which tickles the palate in new places, look to Italy. But to buy well you either need a good book, like those on page 154, or a good retailer. As I write, this is more likely to be a specialist shop than a supermarket.

Labelling and Quality 'Controls'
Unfortunately, the Italians applied EC standards and labelling (page 132) in such a way that the letters and words which should show a wine's quality are virtually meaningless. For although a DOC or DOCG may limit the grapes which can be used in a wine, it can cover a vast area, or a single vineyard, and embrace hundreds of producers. DOCG Chianti, for example, is any wine made with certain (quite variable) combinations of grapes, grown within several thousand vineyards, in 7 different areas of Tuscany, all with different microclimates and soils, and made by many hundreds of wine makers – of varied ability. So, some makers of excellent wine just don't feel the letters are worth the hassle. Others make very good wines using combinations of grapes which the bureaucrats never listed as permissible for DOC wines. So, some wines bearing only *vino da tavola* on the label can be better than DOC wines. Since DOC and DOCG rules fail to control the quality in a particular

bottle, some producers have set their own standards, and established quality control boards which let producers put VIDE on wine which, *in a particular year*, reaches their standards. So VIDE is something to watch for.

With or without the letters, Italy offers some wines which are world class, and others which are simply enchanting. Michelangelo said of one Umbrian wine that it 'kisses, licks, bites, thrusts, and stings'. One never knows whether the next Italian bottle will be such a seductress.

Example of an Italian wine label

① GAUDIO AMILCARE

② VENDEMMIA 1980

③ GRIGNOLINO
DEL MONFERRATO CASALESE ④
⑤ denominazione di origine controllata
imbottigliato nella zona di produzione da ⑥
⑦ GAUDIO AMILCARE
BRICCO MONDALINO - VIGNALE MONFERRATO (AL) Italia ⑧
0.75 lt e ⑩   R I N 29 AL   ⑨ 11,5% Vol.

① Producer.
② The year of harvesting.
③ Type of wine.
④ Area of production.
⑤ From a DOC region.
⑥ Bottled where it was produced.
⑦ Name of the bottler.
⑧ Where it was bottled.
⑨ Alcohol content.
⑩ Quantity in the bottle.

Words Used on Italian Wine Labels

abboccato	a sweet rather mild wine
amabile	medium sweet
annata	year of the vintage
asciutto	dry
bianco	white
cannellino	sweet or medium sweet
cantina (cantine)	wine cellar or winery
classico	shows wine was made at the heart of the production zone
co-operativa vinicola	wine co-operative
dolce	sweet
fattoria	wine growing estate
imbottigliato all'origine or messo in bottiglia nel origine or dell produttore all origine	estate bottled

imbottigliato nella zona di produzione	bottled in the production zone (but not estate bottled)
infiascato in zona d'origine	put in flasks where it was grown
infiascato (or imbottigliato) nello stabilimento	put in flasks (or bottles) on the producer's premises
invecchiamento	ageing
liquoroso	a dessert wine fortified with alcohol
passito	wine from dried and semi-dried grapes
pastoso	medium sweet/mellow
profumato	heavily aromatic
rosso	red
secco	dry
semi-secco	medium dry
uva	grape
vendemmia	year of vintage
vino frizzante	slightly sparkling
vino liquoroso	sweet wine with 16-20 per cent alcohol
vino rosato	rosé
vino santo	an amber wine from grapes slightly dried between harvesting and pressing
vino spumante	sparkling
vino vecchio	wine aged 1-2 years beyond the legal minimum for its type (but younger than one marked *riserva*)
viticoltore	wine grower
vitigno	grape variety

> The terms *vecchio, stravecchio, riserva* and *riserva speciale* mean that the wine has been aged in barrel or bottle for a set time, which varies according to its type.

Choosing Italian Wine

Whatever else it may say on a label, there are only three facts of constant value. The style of wine – Chianti, Barolo or whatever – the year, and the name of the maker. Most of the best wines use local grapes, so knowing the main world grapes won't usually help.

When drinking in Italy, I find it pays to express a deep interest in local wine. It is a fiercely regional country and they then recommend something good, instead of a duff product from another region. In Britain the easiest route to buying well is to pick the style of wine, then buy from a good supplier. Or use the books on page 154 which give the names of good producers of each style of wine and the best years for each. Both Anderson and Ashley are good on this.

The Main Wines of Italy

Piedmont produces two of Italy's greatest wines: Barolo and Barbera. Barolo is known as the 'King of wines and Barbera. Barolo is known as the 'King of wines and wine of Kings'. Made from Nebbiolo grapes it is, at its best, a big, subtle, austere, fruity, complex red with great finesse. However, it needs 5-25 years in bottle and varies enormously between vintages and makers, ranging from the sublime to the undrinkable.

Barbaresco is sometimes called the Queen of Italy's wines. Though also from Nebbiolo grapes, and wood aged, it is softer, easier drinking and needs only 5-20 years in bottle. Piedmont's Asti Spumante couldn't be more different. A flowery white fizzer, from Muscat grapes, it has as much class as a cancan dancer. But it's delightful if well made and drunk in a year. Better still is charming Moscato d'Asti, from Fontanafredda – perfect with strawberries.

Tuscany's lovely hilly landscape, which formed the backdrop to so many Renaissance paintings, produces three of Italy's major wines: Chianti, Brunello di Montalcino and Vino Nobile de Montalcino. All are distinguished reds, when well made, but they need age and, though standards have improved, they are still unpredictable, so it's vital to choose a good maker.

Emilia-Romagna's Lambrusco is both a grape and a family of wines, and unusual in being red and slightly fizzy – though white and rosé versions have now been produced. Classically it is dry, for export it's usually sweetish. Rarely more than a picnic wine, at best.

One of the gems of the region round **Venice** is Recioto della Valpolicella Amarone. At its best a unique, complex, fruity, sweet-dry wine to end a meal with. Not to be confused with the, much cheaper, standard Valpolicella, which is often mere plonk, nor with Recioto di Soave, a charming golden, soft, rich, apricot and honey, dessert wine. However, the region's very different Soave Classico, by makers such as Anselmi, is a white wine few could dislike – or get too excited about. But without youth Soave has nothing.

That is also true of **Latium's** Frascati. Few believe me when I say that, from a good producer, it is a perfect summer lunch drink: round, light, full of flavour. Too often it's water pale, flat and dull.

In addition to these names, don't forget that in any village there could be some unsung gem.

Keeping Italian Wines

Almost all Italian white wines need to be drunk within 1 to 2 years, the exceptions are the very sweet dessert wines, some of which will keep as long as 20 years. The reds are a different story and the rule is simple: the bigger the wine, and the more tannin when young, the longer it will need in bottle. Just how long that is varies with the wine and its year. Ask your supplier.

New Zealand Wine

Although The Mission vineyard was established back in 1851, wine making in a big way only began in the early 1970s. So in the 1980s New Zealand's wine was an adolescent showing promise. It has now come of age: regional styles are emerging and it offers some extremely good wines. There is very good Sauvignon Blanc and Chardonnay, with other whites competing, and some exceptional Cabernet and Merlot, including some interesting blends. Yet her wine makers are still experimenting. So, just now, the Chardonnays tend to be lighter and less oaked than they were, and the reds slightly less meaty – which I rather regret. However, she is beginning to produce some interesting sparklers and, as European champagne houses are buying vineyards here, we can expect more and better.

However, it is only *just* of age. Its promise is such that big developments are still to come, as new wine regions are planted, new wine styles and blends developed and existing vines gain character with age. Unfortunately, seeing the success of wine makers, some farmers who used to supply them are having wine made in their own names in anonymous wine factories – producing wine which offers no hint of the pleasures of vineyard wines.

Choosing New Zealand Wine

The labels are easy to understand. They normally give the grape, the estate which made it and the region. When bringing wines into Britain, New Zealand obeys EC rules on naming grape varieties. The easiest way to buy is to decide the type of wine you want, pick a grape variety, then go for a company that uses it well. So here are the main grapes and some companies to look for. Those in italics are notable, brackets show the particular one to look for.

Sauvignon Blanc or **Fumé Blanc**: *Cloudy Bay*, Delegat's, Esk Valley, Hunters, Collard, Mission, Giesen, *Montana*, Moreton Estate, Nobilo's, Villa Maria, Coopers Creek, Hunter's, Vidal (Private Bin)

Chardonnay: *Babich (Irongate)*, Cloudy Bay, Cooks, Coopers Creek (Swamp Road), Delegat's, Hunter's, Martinborough, Matua Valley, Moreton Estate (Black Label), Nobilo's (Dixon Vineyard), *Vidal (Reserve)*, Villa Maria (Reserve), Redwood Valley, Neudorf

Cabernet Sauvignon: Brookfields, Cooks, Delegat's, Matua Valley, Montana (Wairau Valley), Vidal (Reserve), Villa Maria (Reserve)

Pinot Noir: *Ata Rangi, Martinborough*, Palliser, Rippon, St Helena, Waipara Springs

Riesling: Collard, Martinborough, Montana, *Ngatawara (Late Harvested)*, Redwood Valley (Late harvested or Dry)

Among New Zealand's excellent blends you might try the Cabernet-Merlots of Brookfields, Cloudy Bay Collard (Rothesay), *Kumeu River*, Matawhero, Stoney Ridge, Goldwater Estate, Nesbit, *Te Mata (Coleraine)* or Ata Rangi's (Celebre), which also contains Shiraz. Interesting white blends using **Semillon, Sauvignon Blanc** and **Chardonnay** are made by Corbans, The Mission, Babich, Montana, and Corbans (Stoneleigh). Watch too for muscat liqueur dessert wines.

Vintage Years

The major vineyards are in pockets down the length of New Zealand, with different latitudes giving different weather conditions, so a good year in one area may be poor in another. But in general the best years are as follows. Those which were only good for reds or for

whites have an r or w beside them: '81r, '82r, '83-'85, '86, '87r, '88, '89, '90r, '91w, '92w.

Portuguese Wine

Apart from port, Portugal isn't a country for great wines but it does have the sort of wines which most of us can both enjoy and afford. The best known are, of course, Mateus rosé which hasn't looked back since Sachaverell Sitwell publicized it in the *Sunday Times* in 1951 – and *vinho verde* – one of the lightest, freshest wines for a hot day. However, the great undervalued wines of Portugal are her full-bodied reds, good partners for steak and joints, and very much to the British taste drunk at the right age.

Happily, although EC subsidies have prompted the grubbing out of poor-quality vines, and some Cabernet Sauvignon and Merlot have crept in, most producers are keeping to traditional grapes. Since joining the EC, however, wine makers have been changing their style. Using more stainless steel, newer oak and modern processes they are moving away from the traditional, highly tannic, long-keeping wines in favour of fruity approachable wines for swifter drinking. But you can still buy the older style of wine which is often better half a day after opening, when the air has softened it. Either way, Portuguese wine is still relatively undiscovered and can offer good value for money. (For Port see page 128.)

Labelling Portuguese Wine

Portugal has designated wine regions (demarcada) and uses EC quality grades (page 132). On some wines you may also see the words *Garrafeira* or *Reserva*. *Reserva* may only be used for an outstanding year. But *Garrafeira* must also spend a set time in wood casks. So some wine makers make their best wine *Garrafeira*, others prefer it to be *Reserva*. And either can be a blend from several regions or vineyards, for the Portuguese blend much of their best wine.

The Regions

Alentejo is not yet demarcada but likely to be. Its red wines are generally considered better than its whites and tend to be big plummy wines, quite high in alcohol. The cooperatives Borba, Redondo, Vidigueira and Reguengos are all said to produce good wine.

Algarve is better known for its tourism than for its wine – and rightly so (**Carcavelos** too).

Bairrada is a prime area and is dominated by the Baga grape which produces big fruity red wines which one nineteenth-century wine writer said was a 'match for three men – one to drink it and the other two to support him afterwards'. The region also makes heavy, spicy whites, sparkling whites and marc (brandy). Both red and white are oak-aged, and the reds usually mature well in bottle. Reliable producers include São João and the giant Sogrape.

Bucelas is a tiny area and only one firm makes wine here – Caves Velhas. The wine is a light white.

Colares is an extraordinary area, so sandy that vines are planted in exceedingly deep trenches. It is noted for its red wines which age to a deep richness, which makes them ideal with game, but has disappointing whites.

Dão is one of the biggest wine regions with few *quintas* or single estates. Cooperatives dominate but the wine is very consistent. If you like one bottle you will probably like the next from a different firm. But usually, Dão reds are far better than whites, with a smoothness which comes from slow fermentation.

Ribatejo is not a demarcated area but worth looking out for. It is the home of some of Portugal's best *garrafeira* wines. Among the producers to look for are Carvalho, Ribeiro of Ferreira and Caves Velhas.

Setúbal is the home of Moscatel de Setúbal, rated one of the world's best dessert wines it is fortified and needs long ageing to reach its prime. The 20-year-old is the one to buy. This area is also the home of good basic reds and of a few wines of *garrafeira* quality.

Vinho Verde is both a region and a style of wine which is made there. It is a most confusing name for one of Portugal's most distinctive wines. Literally, it means 'green wine', but green not in colour but in the sense of youthfulness, for, contrary to popular belief, *vinho verde* can be either red or white but is dry, light and delicate with a faint natural fizz. Go for a bottle with Quinta, Solar or Palacio on the label, such as Quinta de Avaleda, it is likely to be more fragrant than that from a large cooperative.

If you wonder where Mateus rosé is made, it originally came from Vila Real but is now made in several other regions. So it has no real location.

Words which Appear on Labels

adamado	sweet
adega	cellar
aguardente	brandy
branco	white
bruto	brut (dry)
carvalho	oak
casa, solar, palacio	house/palace (used for wine from one estate)
casta predominante	Major grape used is . . .
clarete	rosé
colheita	vintage
doce	sweet
espumante	sparkling
engarrafado	bottled at
generoso	very alcoholic, often sweet
licoroso	fortified
maduro	matured
quinta	farm or estate
sêco	dry
tinto	red
vinho	wine
vinho de mesa	table wine, possibly blended
vinho de mesa regional	table wine with 85% of grapes from a defined area

Keeping Portuguese Wine

The rules on keeping Portuguese wine are changing as the wines change. However, the wine with the briefest life is *vinho verde*, which must be drunk before the next harvest. And most Portuguese white wine is best drunk within 1 to 2 years, bar the white wine from Colares which usually needs 4 to 5 years. Most Portuguese red wine needs several years to age, and Bairrada and Dão will often need 10 years in cellar while some Colares red may even reach its peak after 20 years.

Vintages

If a year is good in one part of Portugal it is usually good in most. The very best years have been: '66, '70, '75, '80, '83, '85, '87, '89, '90, 92.

South African Wine

South Africa is rapidly becoming one of the world's most interesting wine areas – and its sales are rocketing. It has an ideal climate for vines and wine has been made here for three hundred years, but only since opportunities for export opened up has the promise of its grapes really begun to be developed. It is in an ideal situation: its wine has the benefit of old vines but it is still learning new techniques.

It has taken an interesting route: sending its sons to France and Germany to learn traditional methods, and to Australia and California to learn the latest techniques. So some wineries produce elegant classic styles, others favour easy, approachable, quaffs. But, whatever the style, a lot of money and effort is going into it. South Africa has some of the most sophisticated wineries in the world and in the past ten years its wines have got better and better and are now winning international prizes. More importantly, competitive prices and consistently good quality are earning it a growing place on both supermarket and specialist shelves.

Most of the wineries are in the southern tip, fanning out from Cape Town. But there are also vineyards farther inland along the valleys of the Rivers Orange and Overberg.

In addition to classic reds, such as Merlot, it grows Pinotage, a hybrid of Pinot Noir and Cinsault (Cinsault is called Hermitage there) which makes reds of increasing charm and class. The distinctive white is the Steen, a relative of the Loire's Chenin Blanc which produces every style of wine, from dry sparklers to sweet, still desserts. There are also two Rieslings: Cape Riesling (Crouchen Blanc) which gives a dry, grassy wine which can age badly, and Rhine Riesling (Weisser Riesling) which is the classic flowery variety.

Vintages

The weather is nothing like as variable as that in Europe, but it does vary – and the wine with it. So it takes an insider to know which years are best. Take the advice of *Platter's Guide* (page 154) or a good wine merchant.

Most of the white wine is made to be drunk young. So only the most complex whites grow old with grace. But many of the reds have the structure and tannin which

---

Addresses and suggestions for further reading are at the ends of chapters.

will allow them to age for up to 15 years, and a few of them positively need bottle age.

The Wine Makers

Wine making is divided between **estates** which make wine from grapes plus bought in grapes (and wine), and **cooperatives** which process grapes from all their members. However, cooperative is not a dirty word. By far the largest is KVW which makes only for export and, as an ambassador for South African wine, makes a number of very good wines at appealing prices. Other good co-ops are Simonsvlei and Vredendal. Among the estates and producer-growers the following have made exceptional wines, and many of them have good lower priced wines too.

Boschendale: some of SAs best *méthode champenoise*, plus an interesting range, especially the Chardonnay.
Buitenverwachting: an organic winery making very good Merlot and whites.
Danny de Wet: noted for Chardonnay.
Hamilton Russell: fine Pinot Noir (needing age) and other very attractive wine.
Kanonkop: excellent reds, notably Pinotage.
Klein Constantia: a prize-winner, fine reds, elegant whites and fine dessert wines.
Meerlust: exceptionally good reds especially blends like Rubicon.
Nederburg: a very good range, with fine botrytis wines.
Rustenberg: a very old estate with fine reds.
Simonsig: fine Cabernet and Chardonnay plus a wide and reliable range.
Van Loveren: a wide range of medium priced wines.

There are also a number of makers which excel at dessert wines from Muscat d'Alexandrie, Rieslings, Chenin Blanc and blends of these. The wines range from clean, elegant and flowery to opulent but rarely are they dull.

Understanding South African Labels

The labels used to have a red, blue and green certification seal, nicknamed the 'bus ticket'. The seal is now black and white and still tells you the grapes are what they say they are. The labels also tell you the year, the region and the estate. You may also find the following terms:

Edel laat-oes	noble late harvest
Edelkeur	botrytized grapes
Gebottel in	bottled in
Geproduser	produced
Geweek an gemaak op	grown and made in
Jerepigo	a sweet liqueur wine
Kooperatiewe (also with other spellings)	cooperative
Landgoedwyn	estate wine
Laat-oos	late harvest
Oesjaar	vintage
semi soet	semi sweet
spesiale laat-oes	late harvest usually with some botrytized grapes
stein	a semi-sweet style

Spanish Wine

Occasionally one encounters a wine which has the velvety smoothness of brushing a pansy against one's cheek. One such was a Rioja bought for me in New York years ago by an Englishman who had lived long in Spain and knew what to look for. It is one of the qualities of a fine wine to linger long in the memory.

I mention that wine simply to show that not all the best Riojas (pronounced Ree-oka) are kept in Spain. So far as most people are concerned Rioja *is* Spanish wine, but there is far more to Spanish wine than Rioja. For example, Spain has always made cava, its equivalent to champagne. Recently this has been the biggest growth area in Spanish wines, and the standard has shot up. Indeed, Spain's quality and range is increasing steadily. For in every type of wine Spain is experimenting with the latest techniques, while having the advantage of long-established vines.

Recently there has been a revolution in Spain's white wines. Stainless steel has replaced the traditional wooden casks, to produce a new style of wine. The wineries of Rioja, Navarra La Mancha and Penedés are leading the way in this. In the hands of the better makers this has produced whites with a new delicacy and freshness, but some are thin and lacking in appeal. Mistakes are inevitable, but Spain is increasingly producing well-made wine at affordable prices – including some country wines which are remarkable value. However, as yet, it has only a handful of wines with strong individual identities. So one must often buy by the region and/or the maker.

Words which Appear on Labels

año	year
blanco	white
bodega	cellar/winery
cepa	wine or grape variety
clarete	a light red wine
cosecha	vintage
criado y embotellado por . . .	grown and bottled by . . .
crianza	see under Rioja
dulce	sweet
elaborado y anejado por . . .	made and aged by . . .
embotellado de origen	estate bottled
engarrafado de origen	estate bottled
espumoso	sparkling
rosado	rosé
seco	dry
tinto	red
vendimia	harvest
vina or *viñedo*	vineyard
vino de cosecho propria	made by the proprietor
vino de mesa	table wine

Spain now uses the same wine grades as other EC countries and is trying to see that they ensure standards of real quality. It also has its own DE classification which falls roughly between a *Vino de la Terra* and a *DO* (page 132).

Wine Regions of Spain

Rioja

Among regional wines Rioja undoubtedly has the strongest identity and most immediate appeal. However, it is both a style of wine and a large region and is made by scores of different producers from a variable blend of up to 7 grapes, in which Temperanillo and Garnacha usually major. So it is important to pick a good producer. Rioja can range from a very enjoyable everyday wine to a very fine wine indeed.

Traditionally red Rioja gets its seductive hint of vanilla from fermentation in small oak casks of 225 litres or less, called barriques. But some makers are unwisely dropping this. To buy true Rioja with cask-age, see what it says on the back label or buy one marked **Gran Reserva, Reserva, Vino di Crianza** or **Con Crianza**. Of these **Gran Reserva** will have had the longest time in cask and should also be from an exceptional year.

However, **Sin Crianza** Rioja has no wood age and is seldom fine when it's white.

Catalonia – Penedés and Carra

The vineyard owner Miguel Torres almost single-handedly brought wine making here into the twentieth century, introducing new techniques and blending traditional Spanish grapes with international ones. Torres wines, from the Penedés region, range from very good whites to excellent reds such as Gran Coronas Reserva Black Label. Yet they are so reasonably priced for their quality that it is easy to underestimate them. Even his inexpensive Viña Esmeralda is well made and combines with a wider range of food than almost any white I know, being particularly good with difficult dishes such as smoked salmon.

This area is also famed for its cavas. Freixenet is the best known but not necessarily the best. More highly esteemed is Juvé y Camps and several others are also impressive.

Ribera del Duero

This is a promising area. The home of Vega Sicilia, a very big, traditional, red which needs long wood age, and is Spain's most expensive wine. It now makes other interesting reds and good rosé and its wines may rival Rioja in time. It already has some most appealing wines, such as Yllera. Like a number of wines from this area, its quality is way above its official class and shows just how unhelpful the EC denominations are.

Rueda

An up and coming area for fresh, fruity whites. These are often blends of local grapes and Sauvignon Blanc, sometimes with a little oak ageing.

Navarra

Navarra, which nestles close to Rioja, used to produce the favourite wine of Catherine the Great of Russia. Today it seems to be producing the favourite Spanish wine of my local wine merchant. These are not the big reds of old, but fresh cold fermented whites, and fruity

rosés which appeal to the British palate. Chivité and Ochoe are good *bodegas* to look out for.

The Best Years

Those underlined are outstanding (r or w mean red or white only).

Penedés '67, '70, '73 '74, '78, '80r, '81, '82, '84w, '86, '88, '89, '90

Rioja '70, '81, '82, '85, '87, '89, '90

Navarra '78, '81, '82, '83, '85, '86, '87, '88, '89, '90

Ribera del Duero '76, '79, '80, 81, '82, '83, '85, '86, '87, '88, '89, '90

Wine Elsewhere

Wine seems to be one of the flavours for which man longs, and wherever he has a little leisure he tries to make it – though not always from grapes. You can find rice wine in China and papaya wine in Kenya, and interesting, and even excellent, grape wines can be found in unlikely places. Who would expect war-torn Lebanon to produce a wine as delectable as Château Musar? Or that Turkey, Switzerland and Canada would be entering the wine race? As yet their wines enter few of our shops, and until they are widely sold I must leave them out. The books on page 154, especially the big atlases, cover countries which this chapter cannot match.

Home-made Wine

Some may feel that mention of home-made wine has no place here. I disagree. Nobody pretends that apple crumble is *haute cuisine* but very good it is, and life would be the poorer without such pleasures. The same holds true of home-made wine.

Having fond memories of childhood sips of rhubarb champagne, I had intended to include a list of organizations to join if you wanted to find out about making home-made wine. Alas, I can find none, but page 154 has some books which could set you on the road. I list them in order of sophistication, starting with those most suited to a beginner. Being lured by the romantic nostalgia of wine making, I have a soft spot for a charming

Addresses and suggestions for further reading are at the ends of chapters.

little book by Molly Harris of 'The Archers'. Called *A Drop o' Wine*, it makes wine making sound as easy as it truly is.

A Few Tips

★ One thing which books never seem to tell you is that new corks will only go into a wine bottle if they have been well soaked in hot water first. Put them to soak in a jug, then you can keep them below the surface of the water by putting a cup in the top.

★ If you don't have a cellar where corks can blow off in safety, as the wine continues its fermentation, buy a demijohn with an airlock.

★ Two tips which Molly Harris gives are that you can make perfectly good wine with dried yeast, and that if a wine comes out too dry you can put it right by adding ½ fluid ounce of glycerine to each pint of wine.

★ When wine is being made it needs to be in about the same temperature that you would like to work in – the mid-sixties Fahrenheit - but not in full sun or it will fade.

★ To decant wine, or indeed beer, from a large container into bottles you will need a length of plastic tubing. To transfer the liquid out you simply put one end of the tube in the liquid – being careful not to let it go down into any sediment at the bottom. Then suck the liquid up the tube (not hygienic, but traditional and effective). Pop your thumb quickly over the end, so the liquid is held in the tube, and put it into a bottle which is standing lower than your main container. Spills always happen, so it's useful to stand the bottle in a bowl. It also helps if you can have the whole of the container higher than the bottle.

★ Keep metal away from wine – plastic and glass are better. Keep flies away too, especially the tiny fruit flies which like nothing better.

★ Wine making equipment *must* be well sterilized, each time, before use with camden tablets (from chemists).

You don't have to scour the country for the basics for wine making. Most of what you need can be found at the larger branches of Boots, and Self-Sufficiency and Smallholding Supplies (see under Mail Order in Domestic Matters) has most of the others by mail order.

Beer and Ginger Beer

Wine is by no means the only drink you can make at home. The 1856 edition of *Enquire Within* was rich in recipes for home-made drinks; among them the recipe for ginger beer, which I include because one never can find a recipe when in the mood to make it. The quantities are large but can easily be halved or quartered.

> *White sugar, twenty pounds; lemon or lime juice, eighteen (fluid) ounces; honey, one pound; bruised ginger, twenty two ounces; water, eighteen gallons. Boil the ginger in three gallons of water for half an hour, then add the sugar, the juice, and the honey, with the remainder of the water, and strain through a cloth. When cold add the white of one egg, and half an ounce of essence of lemon; after standing four days, bottle.*

Beer can also be made at home but to be sure of really fine beer I suggest you contact the **Campaign for Real Ale** which can tell you where to find it.

USEFUL ADDRESSES AND BOOKS

Beer

Campaign for Real Ale, 34 Alma Road, St Albans, Herts AL1 3BW Tel: 0727 867201, will tell you where to find the best hop. M£L, G, A, L. (Above)

Sources of Information on Wine

German Wine Information Service, 262a Fulham Road, London SW10 9EL Tel: 071 376 3329, has information, a video, and can suggest speakers. (P.144)

Wine Institute of California, 19-25 Argyll Street, London W1V 1AA Tel: 071 287 3132. (P.136)

Wines of South Africa, 260a Fulham Road, London SW10 9EL Tel: 071 351 4500. (P.150)

Wine and Spirit Education Trust, Five Kings House, 1 Queen Street Place, London EC4R 1QS.

Wine & Food from France, Nuffield House, 41-46 Piccadilly, London W1V 9AJ Tel: 071 439 8371. (P.141)

Italian Wine Centre, 37 Sackville Street, London W1X 2DR Tel: 071 439 2991, offers wine information. (P.146)

English Vineyards Association, 38 West Park, London SE9 4RH Tel: 081 857 0452, has a leaflet on vineyards to visit – sae needed. (P.140)

Portuguese Government Trade Office, 22-25 Sackville Street, London, W1X 1DE Tel: 071 494 1517. (P.149)

Wines from Spain and Sherry Institute of Spain, 66 Chiltern Street, London W1M 1PR Tel: 071 486 0101. (P.151)

Austrian Wine Information Service, 120 Wilton Road, London SW1V 1JZ Tel: 071 828 7029. (P.139)

Wine experts will often give talks and tutored tastings to groups. Any of the wine information services may know of experts who can be booked, and some of the companies belonging to **AITO** (page 697) run courses in the countries themselves.

Sources of Wine

Stevens Garnier, 3-5 Hythe Bridge Street, Oxford, OX1 2EW Tel: 0865 791313, retails direct and by mail, and also wholesales, wines of Portugal, Chile, Argentina, Australia and Canada.

Cape Province Wines, 1 The Broadway, Kingston Road, Staines, Middx TW18 1AT Tel: 0784 451860, sells numerous South African wines by mail. (P.150)

Bibendum, 113 Regents Park Road, London, NW1 3UR Tel: 071 722 5577, has a wide range of well-chosen, competitively priced growers' wines from all over the world. Only sells 12 bottles at a time but they needn't all be the same. Also has a list of fine and rare wines. Free delivery within the M25 and in much of the Midlands and North of England.

Bordeaux Direct, New Aquitaine House, Paddock Road, Reading, Berks RG4 0JY Tel: 0734 481711, is a wine club. There is no commitment to buy. (P.142)

Christopher's, 19 Charlotte Street, London W1P 1HB Tel: 071 636 4020, sells American wine by post or shop. (P136)

Margaret Harvey Fine Wines of New Zealand, P.O. Box 476, London NW5 2NZ Tel: 071 482 0093, will advise and supply mixed cases by mail. (P.148)

Thomas Peatling, 63A Clerkenwell Road, London EC1M 5NP Tel: 071 250 1522, offers a wide Australian range, also by mail. (P.138)

The Wine Society, Gunnels Wood Road, Stevenage, Herts SG1 2BG Tel: 0438 741177, requires membership but there is no obligation to buy.

Useful Books on Wine

Hugh Johnson, *Wine*, Emblem.

Hugh Johnson, *World Atlas of Wine*, Mitchell Beazley.

Jancis Robinson's lighthearted book *Mastergran*, Pan, is an ideal introduction to the art of comparing and understanding wine.

Jancis Robinson, *Vines, Grapes and Wines*, Mitchell Beazley.

Tom Stevenson, *Sotheby's World Wine Encyclopaedia*, Dorling Kindersley.

Bob Thompson, *Webster's Wine Tours: California, Oregon and Washington*, Simon and Schuster.

Halliday's *Australian Wine Guide*, Angus Robertson – an exhaustive valley-by-valley briefing.

James Halliday, *The Australian Wine Compendium*, Angus Robertson.

Thomas K. Hardy, *Pictorial Atlas of Australian Wine*, Grape Vision.

Don Philpott, *The Guide to the Vineyards of Britain*, Morland Publishing.

Graham Chidgey, *The Wines of Burgundy*, Century.

Rosemary George, *French Country Wines*, Faber.

Hugh Johnson, *The Wine Atlas of France: A Traveller's Guide to the Vineyards*, Mitchell Beazley.

James Long, *Cognac and Other Brandies*, Century.

The Macdonald Guide to French Wines.

Pamela Vandyke Price, *Champagne*, Century.

Pamela Vandyke Price, *The Wines of Bordeaux*, Century.

Steven Spurrier, *Écoles du Vin*, Century.

Hugh Johnson, *Atlas of German Wines*, Mitchell Beazley.

Ian Jamieson, *German Wines*, Faber.

Ian Jamieson, *The Wines of Germany*, Mitchell Beazley.

Burton Anderson, *Guide to the Wines of Italy*, Mitchell Beazley, a useful paperback.

Burton Anderson, *Vino*, Papermac – an authoritative tome on Italian wine, good background reading, not a buyer's guide.

Maureen Ashley, *Italian Wine*, Sainsbury's – very readable, and all the vital facts, including the best years and makers to buy, invaluable.

Nicholas Belfrage, *Life Beyond Lambrusco*, Sidgwick and Jackson.

Ben Hawkins, *Rich Rare and Red*, International Wine and Food Society on port.

Jan Read, *The Wines of Portugal*, Faber and Faber.

Jan Read, *The Wines of Spain*, Faber and Faber.

Jan Read, *Wines of Rioja*, Sotheby publication.

Julian Jeffs, *Sherry*, Faber and Faber.

John Platter's South African Wine Guide is *the* book on SA wine: a most invaluable and readable handbook when buying. Imported and sold by mail by Clarion International Vintners, Unit 8, Old Wharf, Dymock Road, Ledbury, Herefordshire HR8 2DS Tel: 0531 5060.

Useful Books on Wine Making

C. J. Berry, *First Steps in Wine Making*, Argus Books.

Bryan Acton, *Recipes for Prize Winning Wines*, Argus Books.

Bryan Acton and Peter Duncan, *Making Wines Like Those You Buy*, Argus Books.

Bryan Acton and Peter Duncan, *Progressive Wine Making*, Argus Books.

Domestic Matters

General Cleaning • Specific Cleaning • Employing Help • Clothing and Shoe Care • Equipping a Home • Laundry, Stains and All That • Mail Order • Pests

GENERAL CLEANING

I shall never forget a friend of mine returning aghast from a stint as an au pair in Germany and recounting how she had been made to scrub the trunks of the trees nearest the house. In contrast, when Katherine White-horn wrote an article about how to be a bit of a slut, and sweep the dirt under the carpet, she was showered with letters from women who felt they could now own up to being less than perfect housewives. However, sluttish-ness is no modern development. This piece of advice appeared in the 1856 edition of *Enquire Within*.

> *Never put away plates, knives and forks, &c. uncleaned, or sad inconvenience will arise when the articles are wanted.*

Most of us are far too busy to keep a house *perfectly* clean – unless we employ someone else to do it. Between slobbishness and tree scrubbing there is a happy medium. But the art is keeping everything at the level with which *you* feel comfortable, not trying to conform to some mythical norm of what a good housewife or house-husband would do.

The essence of cutting down work is to know exactly what to use for what. So I have tried to deal with every type of surface that you might possibly want to clean and give the fastest and safest way to clean each. In choosing the methods and products to use on fine surfaces I have been advised by those working in museum conservation departments. However, if a valuable object may need special treatment, any museum with fine objects and furniture will advise you.

Choosing Cleaning Products

You will find very few brand names here. This is either because there is very little to choose between one brand and another or because there are good reasons for not recommending one.

I have a private passion for science and technology, which makes me a natural audience for the latest miracle product. Yet I keep coming back to so-called 'old-fashioned' basics because they get faster and better results. I realize that it is hard not to have a sneaking worry that one is somehow doing second best. This isn't surprising. Multi-billion pound industries have spent fortunes making us feel like that. But if you feel guilty using basics remember it's big brother from the chemical industries whispering in your ear, not common sense.

> Used correctly, basics like paraffin, ammonia, white spirit, acetone and turpentine are often better than many branded products. But such chemicals should not be breathed in, and some people can develop an allergic reaction to some of them. This reaction may not occur at first, but acute sensitivity can develop after repeated exposures. So rubber gloves should always be worn when handling these – or other – house-hold chemicals and the windows should be open.

If you prefer branded products, such as spray-on cleaners, Friends of the Earth (see Free Time) has a list of those which won't harm the environment or the ozone layer. It would make a big difference if all of us bought 'green' products whenever possible, and recycled our waste. And it can cost less than using harmful products.

The greatest time saver is to make more use of the cheapest and, arguably, the most powerful and versatile chemical we have in the home – H_2O – water. Experts in the top public health laboratory in Britain say water is better than most disinfectants at removing harmful bacteria from surfaces. What's more, leaving water to work away quietly will halve the general cleaning. So, fill dirty pans with water the instant you empty them, leave little pools of water (or wet sponge cloths) on top of awkward marks and stains – on cookers, work surfaces and floors, and soak clothes which need to be washed.

> I do *not*, of course, suggest that you soak clothes which should not be soaked (page 51 onwards), or use water where it could cause damage or an electrical hazard.

The other great saver is to stop using all the products you don't need to use. Every new product not only costs money but also time, when you fetch it from the cupboard.

Basic Equipment

While far too much is often spent on cleaning products, far too little tends to be spent on basic equipment for cleaning jobs. Half the homes in Britain are probably washing up with one washing-up implement, be it brush or cloth. Cleaning is done so often that whoever does it deserves the best equipment the household can afford.

The minimum kit for washing up is a washing-up brush, a looped scourer (for egg and substances which clog other scourers) and an abrasive nylon pad. A bottle brush is a good idea too. There should also be an old abrasive pad for cleaning surfaces like the stove, and perhaps soap-filled pads for bringing up metal or getting stubborn stains off pyrex. In any kitchen there should also be *two* wiping down cloths – one for the kitchen surfaces and the sink, and another for the floor. A cloth which has been used for wiping the floor should *never* be used on anything to do with food preparation or washing up. To put it frankly we all walk on pavements which animals have used as lavatories. We walk traces of that on to our floors. To wipe the floor with a cloth and then wipe the kitchen surface is to transfer such substances to our food. Not a pretty thought.

When it comes to ordinary household cleaning there is an equal need for good equipment. Not only is a vacuum cleaner essential but it is almost as necessary to have a small hand-vacuum, such as a Dustbuster or one like a plastic can on wheels with a long trunk, such as that made by Rowenta, which will clean stairs easily and get up on to curtain tops or into corners. Besides an ordinary duster, a long-handled furry or feathery duster saves a lot of stretching and bending, and instead of cleaning basins with soft cloths, which make hard work of it, use one of the nylon abrasive pads sold for saucepans (but don't use the abrasive side on taps). And keep old toothbrushes for getting into all the awkward places.

With the right equipment and the right products cleaning takes very little time: with the wrong ones it can be a great waste of time.

Disinfecting and Sterilizing

We are bombarded by advertisements which tell us that product X or Y kills germs. That is only part of the story.

Sterilization kills all known germs (viruses, bacteria). For true sterilization you need to heat something to 121°C (249.8°F) for at least 15 minutes with enough liquid to create steam: just possible in some pressure cookers. (Dry heat sterilization in an oven needs 160°C (320°F) for 45 minutes.) The only other method practical for the home is burning – you needn't worry that it will release germs into the air: the particles will be sterile.

Any disinfectant only kills a certain *range* of germs and under certain conditions, and it won't usually kill the spores (see page 53). Bleaches, for example, kill a wide range; phenolics (Dettol, Izal and so on) vary in their effectiveness with the particular formulation and pine disinfectants tend to be fairly limited.

Contrary to what advertisements would have us believe, the *most* effective way to disinfect anything is simply to use water. Germs wash off. What's more, spores, which are not killed by chemicals, are removed by thorough cleaning with hot water. Use a good detergent on most surfaces, and washing soda (with rubber gloves on) where there is grease. The only place in most homes that needs regular disinfectant is the lavatory – as you can't wash it with hot water.

SPECIFIC CLEANING

The counsel of perfection is to clean almost everything every day, and clean one room very thoroughly every week. It makes for a marvellously clean house and a dreadfully dull life. The counsel of sanity and efficiency is to clean certain key areas, like the kitchen and basins, every day and then do all the others in rotation according to where you live, how much the rooms are used and how clean you like things to be.

Acrylic – see Baths, page 157.

Adhesives

To peel off a self-adhesive label put a piece of foil over it, iron it lightly with a hot iron and peel it off while still warm. The same method works for sellotape. If the label is on the outside of a plastic container just fill the container with the hottest water it can stand, wait for the heat to act on the glue, and peel the label off. If a residue of glue is left it can usually be removed with methylated spirits. But beware of using this on some fabrics or on wallpaper (see A Roof Over Your Head).

When young, Blu-tack will roll off most surfaces if gently rubbed, but it gets cantankerous in its old age and refuses to budge. At this stage if you roll the tacky side of masking tape over it, it will usually come away. But on wallpaper the masking tape may take the paper with it.

Alabaster

Alabaster is often mistaken for marble. In fact, it is far more fragile and dissolves in water. It is not porous like marble, but it is far softer. Use a perfectly clean dry duster, or if moisture is essential, a rag *just* moistened with a *very little* white spirit.

Armour and Arms

Both armour and all kinds of armaments which are purely for display, need to be cared for as to their metal, with moving parts oiled with a fine oil such as WD40. Keep them in rooms which are free from damp.

Bakelite and Celluloid

If you live in an old house with bakelite light switches the best cleaner is Duraglit metal polish wadding. This is just as effective on celluloid. Remove every trace with a soft cloth.

Baking Tins

If baking tins become encrusted with burnt-on food you can soften the whole crust to a removable state by boiling the tins in a pan with a good handful of washing soda. The worse the dirt, the longer the boil; leave very dirty ones in the pan to soak overnight after boiling. But don't use soda in or on an aluminium pan as it will pit it.

Baths

On acrylic baths use a gentle cream cleaner. It is also sheer masochism to use an abrasive cleaner even on an enamel bath. Once you remove the glassy surface with the abrasive the bath becomes twice as hard to keep clean. Instead install a big bath-cleaning brush and a bottle of thickish washing-up liquid in the bathroom. This means each person in the family can put a little washing-up liquid on the bristles, scrub round the tide mark and splash the soap off with the remaining water before it runs out. So that's *one* job the 'houseperson' doesn't have to do.

To clean an already grimy enamel bath, paraffin can make short work of both tide-marks and limescale. It also does a good job on taps. But it leaves a dreadful smell which needs thorough rinsing. (See also pages 215-216.)

To treat an even greasier enamel bath fill it with hot water and add several cupfuls of washing soda. Swish it around to dissolve it and leave it overnight. Next morning brush it out with a stiff bath brush.

Stains on a Bath

Bath enamel, unlike cooker enamel, can be damaged by acids. However, sometimes only acid will remove a stain. I find acid products to remove bath stains work no better than home remedies. Either way, work swiftly and realize you take a risk.

The brownish crusty deposit which forms if hard water lies round a plug hole, comes off with hot vinegar and salt. Apply it with an old toothbrush, leave it to work until you can scrape it off with the end of the toothbrush handle. Don't use metal or you will scratch the bath. Bad stains may need several doses. This mixture can also be used to remove water deposits from shower coils.

Rust marks can usually be bleached out with a mixture of salt and lemon juice or lemon juice and borax. Leave the paste in little heaps over the stain and keep remoistening with lemon juice for a day or two or rub rust stains on white baths with a little hydrogen peroxide. Or use Jenolite instead.

Blinds

Festooned blinds need to be regularly vacuumed with a trunk-style vacuum cleaner. When spring cleaning they need to be dry-cleaned or washed – according to the fabric.

Roller blinds which can't be washed can be cleaned by rolling a ball of dough across them which you have made from flour and water. It needs to have the texture of pastry, so it leaves no trace behind.

To clean Venetian blinds run an L, made from a crust of new bread, along each slat, replacing it when it becomes too dusty. Alternatively, wear a pair of old cotton gloves, moisten them and run the slats between your fingers.

Bolts

Give unused bolts a slide each time you clean whatever they are on. Once a year they also benefit from some graphite or a drop of penetrating oil (watch that it doesn't drip on to pale wood, fabrics or carpets). Apply this to French windows at the end of summer; then they won't be immovable by spring.

Books

Both heat and moisture are enemies of books and friends of the moulds and insects which can destroy them. The ideal temperature is about 15°C (60°F) with low humidity and a good circulation of air. Store them with their spines outwards, unless they are too big to put on any shelf, in which case they are best lying flat. If they need protection use acid-free board (see page 215).

To dust books, brush the pages clean with a dry shaving brush, or run a vacuum nozzle over, while holding them closed. But be careful with nozzles near good books; it is easy to scratch and damage them.

For fine leather bindings I was given this recipe by one of Britain's top book restorers. Take equal quantities of *pure* lanolin (from a chemist) and neatsfoot oil (from a saddler) and mix them together over warm water until they form a smooth cream. Apply this once a year to leather bindings, with a clean soft cloth, rubbing it gently in and polishing it off. The mixture can be used over the gilding and is just as good for leather desk tops as for books.

If you spill water on a book you can usually stop the paper distorting by patting it dry immediately and drying it at once with a hair dryer.

Brass and Copper

Brass and copper need different types of cleaning and different degrees of shine according to where they are. Modern brass of no value can be cleaned with any brass polish, but Solvol Autosol – a chrome cleaner from auto-accessory shops – is recommended by some conservationists, and cleans my brass faster than any other brass cleaner.

If brass knobs and handles on valueless objects, such as modern front doors, need a thorough polish, make a cardboard shield with a hole cut out to the exact shape of the metal and slip it over to protect the paint. There is also a strong argument for saving all this work and lacquering them (see page 158).

Brass on Fine Furniture

Where brass is on furniture don't attempt to bring it up to a fine shine with metal polish. To do so is to risk permanent damage to the wood, and antique furniture with brass ornamentation is not meant to look as shiny as a row of horse brasses. A regular rub with a clean fabric duster or polishing glove is all the care it needs. If handles are deeply dirty they can be removed and cleaned before being carefully replaced in exactly the same positions. Label each one as you remove it (marked 'top left' etc.).

Lightly tarnished brass and copper can be cleaned with Goddard's Long-term Silver Cloth, but keep a separate cloth for each metal, and a third for silver.

If inlay is deeply tarnished it can be cleaned with infinite care by rubbing with powdered charcoal, or fine oil and whiting (see page 215), on the end of a cotton bud or 0000 wire wool (000 is too coarse and will scratch the surface). Take care the wood is not rubbed at all, and be constantly aware of the danger of removing, or blunting the definition of fine patterning in the metal. Tarnish is infinitely preferable – and diminishes the value of an antique far less. Once a shine is achieved you can polish both the wood and the metal with Renaissance Wax (see page 215), a special polish developed for museums which will retain the shine.

Verdigris

Verdigris is a greenish deposit on brass or copper. A wipe with neat ammonia will remove it instantly. Rinse the ammonia off afterwards and dry the metal.

Very Tarnished Brass and Copper

If brass or copper, of no value, is tarnished to almost black wipe it over with hot vinegar and salt (the proportions don't much matter). This will lift deep tarnish with amazing speed, but wipe it off before it dries on the metal, or you will put petrol-blue stains into the brass which are very hard to remove.

The other danger with salt and vinegar is of causing 'bronze disease' in which the metal weakens so badly that it can even fall apart. It is rare but can be triggered by any chloride – such as salt or washing soda. So this is not a treatment to use on the family heirlooms.

Another treatment for deeply tarnished brass and copper, which can even be used when rust has set in, is a solution of citric, tartaric or oxalic acid. The amount you need to use depends on the state of the metal. Start with about 15 g (½ oz) in ½ l (1 pt) water, and use hot water if you want to boost the effect, as all acids are more active when hot. Simply swab the solution on to the metal (out of doors or with floors well protected) – without getting it on yourself or near children and pets. Then leave it for a little while to eat off the tarnish, and rinse it off. If the strength is right it will reveal yellow metal and even remove ancient rust. From there, polishing is a relatively easy job.

Lacquered Brass

Acrylic lacquer can cut down on cleaning but it's important to choose one which both goes on easily and stays on well, but comes off easily once the first breaks in its surface appear. One of Britain's top experts on metal conservation recommends Ercalene (see page 215). Most lacquers will come off with either acetone or methylated spirit. But these will damage polished furniture, so brass handles must be removed before you strip them.

Bronze

Bronze needs the utmost care. It has recently been realized that water can harm bronze and there is the additional risk that chlorides in many cleaning fluids can trigger bronze disease (see Brass). It can also be damaged by numerous other substances and it should not be washed, polished or cleaned with spirits.

Polishing is especially harmful because it removes the patination which is an essential part of its character. Just brush it clean *very* occasionally with a very clean soft brush, and carefully use a cotton bud to remove the dirt from the crevices.

Brushes

Hairbrushes

It's amazing how often people forget to wash their hairbrushes. Most just need soap on a nailbrush, but real bristle hairbrushes need more care. Put a teaspoon of washing soda and a few drops of ammonia in a basin of warm water and tap the bristles gently in this, *without* getting the roots of them wet. Rinse in the same way, and dry, bristle down, away from direct heat. **G. B. Kent** (page 215) will rebristle old-fashioned brushes.

Shoe Brushes

The clogged polish will float off shoe brushes if you just stand the tips of the bristles in white spirit. Pat the brush up and down in the spirit, then stand it on thick newspaper to drain before rinsing the spirit out in water and washing-up liquid – without getting the wood wet or the bristles will loosen.

Cane, Bamboo, Rush and Coconut Matting

These are all easily discoloured by soap. Instead, they should be scrubbed with strongly salted water then with clear water. However, with coconut matting there is a slight risk of a tide mark. So do a test patch first where it won't show and let it dry totally.

If they have become greasy add a few drops of ammonia to the water. If yellow scrub it with a solution of ½ teaspoon oxalic acid in 500 ml (1 pt) water and let it dry naturally. But keep the acid off your skin and away from pets and children. If any marks remain try removing them with methylated spirit.

Chair seats in cane or rush which have sagged should be washed equally on both sides, so that they tighten up evenly.

The experts in the National Trust find that rush matting lasts longest if it is kept moist. This means that on wood floors in dry houses it needs to be watered several times a week.

Addresses and suggestions for further reading are at the ends of chapters.

Carpets

Some shops try to talk customers into having a new carpet sprayed with a stain blocker. But experts say stain blockers work best when they are built into the carpet. And that you may get patchy results if they are used later.

The biggest danger to carpets is grit, which can cut into the pile. So any carpet should be vacuumed regularly. An upright cleaner, can be used for velvet piles, but use a plain suction cleaner for loop or shag piles (brushing damages the surface). And the best suction cleaners now have enough power to work well on velvet pile too.

To remove the dust left round the edge of a room by most upright vacuum cleaners use a small battery-operated cleaner like the Dustbuster, which is also invaluable for stairs, crumbs and cars. Failing that, use a trunk-style vacuum or put on a pair of old rubber gloves (of the soft rubbery sort) and brush with your fingers. This is less tiring than using a hand brush and raises less dust. Rake very long piles with a pile rake.

Stair carpets easily wear through on the edge of each step. To avoid this, move the carpet a few inches up or down each year – or even every 6 months, if it's well trodden. Loose carpets in rooms can also be turned round so the wear is distributed more evenly.

★ Rub a burn instantly with a cut potato to minimize the damage. The only way to remove the brown mark is careful clipping with nail scissors.

★ Dents in carpets will usually vanish overnight if you leave an ice cube on them, but wool responds much better than man-made fibres.

Static in Carpets
Any carpet with a high proportion of man-made fibre is liable to get a build-up of static from the friction of feet; and static attracts dust. To cut this down spray the carpet with an anti-static spray (see page 215 or use about 4 to 6 tablespoons of water with 1 tablespoon of fabric softener in a plant sprayer. Fabric softeners vary in strength.

You can also use a clean duster wrung out in this mixture for dusting acrylic and perspex, which also have static problems.

Soot
Carpets should be *very* well covered before a chimney is swept, but if soot does fall on a carpet immediately sprinkle it thickly with salt and leave it for half an hour before you vacuum it up.

Sweeping Carpets
When sweeping a carpet the dust flies up and lands straight back again. To stop this sprinkle the carpet with slightly damp salt or tea leaves – but if these are too damp they could leave tea stains.

Washing
The **British Carpet Manufacturers' Association** (page 215) recommends using a shampoo meeting the British Standard and carrying a BS number, but says there aren't many which do.

I find a shampoo called 1001 removes spots beautifully. But I can't guarantee its safety or effectiveness on all carpets. Some tool hire companies hire out machines which spray shampoo into the carpet and suck the water and dirt back out again. Some are astonishingly effective and easy to use, and save a great deal of time.

> WARNING Whatever the shampoo, all carpets must be treated with a minimum of liquid. Foam-backed carpets may rot if they get too wet and other kinds may shrink dramatically.

Carpet dyes are very prone to misbehaving. So always test any shampoo or stain remover on an off-cut or on a patch of carpet which won't show, and let it dry thoroughly before using it where it would matter. Never use soap, ammonia or bleach. If you use a dry-cleaner-style spot remover, let it dry *totally* before using carpet shampoo, and vice versa.

With any shampoo only use lukewarm water and the recommended amount: extra will just leave a deposit in the carpet to attract dirt. Apply it with a soft-bristled brush – stiff bristles rough up the pile – spreading on the *foam* rather than saturating the pile, and ending with strokes which leave the pile in the right direction. Do not walk on the carpet while it is wet or put furniture on it. It is at its most fragile then and furniture may have hidden metal under the feet which would leave rust stains. If it *has* to stand on it put a small piece of strong plastic under to prevent this – but weight on damp carpets will leave a bad dent. (See also page 162.)

Chamois Leather

A chamois leather needs to be washed with pure soap, as detergent would remove the natural oils and harden it. Rinse it clean and squeeze the water out without wringing. Hang it to dry away from sunlight or direct heat, and wiggle it gently from time to time as it dries, stretching it slightly in each direction, so it becomes soft and pliable, otherwise it will dry stiff as a board. But don't overdo the pulling or it will tear.

Never be tempted to store a chamois in a plastic bag as it will quickly become slimy and useless.

China and Porcelain

The cleaning of ordinary household china is covered under washing up (page 171), but with old china and porcelain ornaments it is always wisest to assume they are very vulnerable. Never rub at stains with anything hard – not even bristles on a brush – or use strong chemicals. And to dust intricate china wear clean cotton gloves and, holding it firmly in its place dust it with the gloved fingers.

When it needs spring cleaning be very careful. Some ceramics, such as biscuit ware, are totally unglazed. This means they should only be wiped and may need expert cleaning if the dirt is ingrained. Gilt should also be wiped very carefully, *not* washed, as the gilding may come off.

For glazed china which is very greasy some experts recommend washing with Synperonic N first (see page 216) and, if this fails, wiping it with a mixture of equal amounts of white spirit and water with a teaspoon of Fairy Liquid per pint.

It is perfectly safe to hang china, with the hangers which have sprung holders, provided the hanger is the correct size and that plates with cracks are not hung, lest the pressure break them completely. A small square of chamois leather should be put under the clips, to prevent damage to the rims. Pieces of chamois can also be put under the feet of china and porcelain which might scratch a polished surface. Unlike felt, chamois won't leak dye if it becomes damp.

Chrome

Most of the floor and wall cleaners have some ammonia in and this cleans chrome excellently. On stubborn marks use a little neat household ammonia on a damp cloth – but don't breathe it in and do have the windows open wide. If you lack ammonia and the taps are marked, try paraffin or toothpaste. For an extra shine use Solvol Autosol, rub it off with a clean cloth and finish with a chamois leather.

Water with a dash of ammonia is good for removing traffic film from chrome on cars, but don't splash it on to the paint. It shouldn't do any harm, but who knows what they will put into paint next? Or use Solvol Autosol.

Cigarette Ash

It was in a little bar in Assisi, just near the tomb of St Francis, that I discovered how to clean ashtrays. The barmaid used a dry pastry brush to remove every trace of ash. Unless some cigarette has left a tarry patch a dry brush is far more effective than washing and doesn't release the smell the way water does. (You do not, of course, use the brush for pastry.)

Clocks

Old clocks should be kept away from extremes of heat or humidity and guarded from dust. You can't stop daily dust falling on them but you can encase them in protective plastic before doing any dust-raising job in their vicinity.

If it stops, a clock of any real age needs a clock repairer used to old clocks. Any museum specializing in fine furniture should be able to give you the name of someone suitable, or contact the Victoria and Albert Museum in London.

Cloisonné

If you use either water or metal polish on cloisonné there is a danger that the moisture will get down the cracks and lift off the delicate enamel. The only possible cleaner

for it is a silver polishing cloth, but be extremely careful that the cloth doesn't catch on any corner of metal and pull it out of place.

Computers

The greatest enemy of a computer is any kind of liquid spilt over the keyboard, as it will trickle down into the works. Dust and static electricity are also bad. So the doors of the disk drive need to be kept closed and if there is a man-made fibre carpet in the room which might generate static electricity the carpet should be regularly sprayed with anti-static spray.

The best cleaner for the screen is anti-static spray and a soft cloth. Any good liquid cleaner can be used on the plastic casing of the various parts of the computer – provided a dust-free cloth is used and absolutely no moisture is allowed into any cracks.

Dust under the keys could, eventually, stop them working and a small tool for removing the keys is sold by some computer shops. But first unplug the computer and make a plan of the keyboard. Each key has a spring and if this is sticking remove and clean it, or put in a new one from the manufacturer.

> Computers vary: *before cleaning a keyboard like this ask the makers whether it could do any damage to their machine.*

Cooker Cleaning

Burners
If the area round burners has burnt-on food cover the areas with a cloth wet with detergent and leave it an hour. It will then be much easier to clean.

Glass Doors
Washing-up liquid is all you need to remove minor splashes on the glass doors of ovens. But if the dirt is tougher paint stripper which contains methylene chloride is rather effective. But wear rubber gloves and keep it away from pets and children, and all other kitchen surfaces. Rinse it off well, too.

Ovens
The easy way to clean an oven is to wipe it out every time it is used. But few of us manage such perfection. Proprietary oven cleaners are usually more expensive than caustic soda, even when it is their only ingredient. So one may as well use caustic soda and save money. Treat it with *great care* as it can damage other finishes in your kitchen and do serious injury especially to eyes. *Store it well out of reach of children:* they could make the fatal mistake of thinking it was sugar.

Put 1 tablespoon of caustic soda into 500 ml (1 pt) of hot water in a plastic bucket or large pyrex container. *Put the soda into the water, NOT the water onto the soda.* Wearing thick rubber gloves, swab the whole inside of the oven with this mixture. If there is a risk of any dripping on to the floor cover it with plastic before you

Addresses and suggestions for further reading are at the ends of chapters.

start work and keep children and pets away. Leave it until a test patch wipes clean with a plastic saucepan scourer. Time is the vital element; only with a filthy oven will you need a stronger solution of caustic.

When the caustic has softened the dirt, wipe it off with a plastic scourer and *rinse the inside well*. You don't want a residue of caustic dripping into your food. Finally, wipe the inside of the oven over with 1 tablespoon of bicarbonate of soda in ¼ l (½ pt) of water. This makes the oven easier to clean next time.

★ If you have a drop-down oven door avoid having to turn upside-down by checking the roof with an old mirror.

★ Soaking oven shelves overnight in water with washing-up liquid and a good dash of bleach makes them far easier to clean.

★ If something spills over in the oven, or on top, sprinkle salt thickly over it, then it won't burn on so easily. This is more effective with some food than others, but always worth a try.

Drains

It pays to treat drains well: cleaning them when they clog up isn't a pleasant job. So, nothing solid should ever be put down any ordinary drain. That includes not only vegetable rubbish and tea leaves but also liquid fat which will harden in the pipe.

From time to time, pour some neat, or slightly diluted, bleach down the plug holes of basins and sinks and leave for about 3 minutes before rinsing well. This will clean off grease and old scum. Or half fill with very hot water, add a handful of washing soda and when it has dissolved let the water out. With metal sinks you can be even more drastic and use soda and boiling water. (*Don't do this if the drain might be blocked by ice or the pipe may burst.*)

Drains Outside
If an outdoor drain becomes blocked you may need to use the solution of caustic soda used for stripping wood (see A Roof Over Your Head). If that fails you either have something nasty blocking it or you may have tree roots growing into it.

Either needs professional attention. Look in the Yellow Pages under Plumbers and Drains, and in Thompsons under Drain Clearance. Dyno-Rod can be found in most areas of Britain. They cover all types of problem.

★ The easiest way to clean waste disposal units is to drop in a lot of ice cubes, and switch on. The cubes will scrape off any deposit as they go round.

★ To clean heavy iron outdoor drain covers put them on the edge of a bonfire for just long enough to remove the slime and debris.

★ If you have a drain on to which a washing machine regularly disgorges fluff and fabric you can keep it clean by just attaching the foot of an old pair of nylons to the bottom of the pipe. *But* do remove the stocking and throw it away at *very* regular intervals. If the water can't get out because the stocking is full the washing machine will either break or overflow all over your home.

Dustbins and Kitchen Bins

The quickest way to clean metal (*not plastic*) bins is to place lightly crumpled newspaper in and (at a safe distance from anything which might catch fire) put a match to it. Plastic dustbins and waste bins should be cleaned with a solution of water and bleach – at the strength recommended on the bottle. Keep a pair of rubber gloves just for this job.

It was an American friend who had trouble with marauding racoons, who taught me that to keep animals out of bins you just need to sprinkle a little ammonia inside the lid. Even racoons beat watery-eyed retreat.

Duvets, Continental Quilts and Sleeping Bags

Duvets, and their relations, need regular shaking and airing, so the sweat they absorb can dry out. (We all sweat a surprising amount in the night.) Wash or dry clean those filled with man-made fibres according to the maker's instructions. Those filled with down and/or feathers are trickier. Not all dry cleaners do a good job. So, for years, I have washed duvets and pillows in hand-hot water, in a bath, using Persil. Then spin the water out and hang them to dry, shaking them regularly to separate the clumps of down and feather as they dry. I find it works well. But, be warned, I cannot guarantee it will work, and if the maker doesn't say the item is washable, you wash it at your own risk. And make sure all holes are mended first. The filling will float out through even the tiniest one.

Enamel

The enamel used on enamel boxes should never be washed, as the water may get into minute cracks and lift off the top layers. Just wipe it with a dry cloth. See also Cloisonné, page 160.

Finger-marks

Remove finger-marks from gloss paint by using a little white spirit on kitchen roll – but be careful with old or unusual paint as white spirit may soften it.

Fires

Cast Iron – see Stoves and Grates

Tiles
It was a housewife in Cheshire who wrote to tell me that her mother had always cleaned glazed tiles around the fire with soapy water and wood ash. It works beautifully and almost instantly removes burnt-on dirt which soap and water alone won't touch. But it must be wood ash: coal ash could scratch the glaze.

Floor Mops

You wouldn't think that anything would want to eat a floor mop, but some bacteria like nothing better. That's why sponge mops tend to go squishy and fall apart long before they are worn away. To stop this you need to rinse the mop after use in a phenolic household disinfectant such as Dettol or Boots Pine Disinfectant. But don't try to kill the bacteria with bleach or chlorine, as these will damage the sponge.

Floors

Dents
Dents in any kind of floor are just dirt cups so fill them in. First, scrape every bit of dirt and grime out of the dent. Then drip candlewax into the dent – you can use children's wax crayons to colour the wax to the right shade. (Just warm the wax and a piece of crayon together in the bottom of a washed-out tin over some hot water.) Having dripped the wax into the hole quickly wipe and scrape off any excess while still warm. Finally smooth it perfectly with wire wool. This can easily last for several years.

Polishing Wood Floors
Whether wood floors need polishing very much depends on their type. Plain boards which have been stripped may be much better sealed with a strong polyurethane sealer. Equally, some very old floors which have never enjoyed a high polish hardly need one. When floors do need polish it can be kept to a minimum if you wipe them over with a wool cloth impregnated with equal parts of malt vinegar and paraffin. This removes dust and leaves a shine with a minimum of work. Then, floor polish only needs to be used two or three times a year.

Sealed Floors
Floors such as cork and wood sealed with a strong polyurethane sealant only need sweeping, but extra stubborn dirt can be washed off. As the seal is shiny there seems little point in making work by polishing them.

> *HOW TO REMOVE STAINS FROM FLOORS. – For removing spots of grease from floorboards, take equal parts of Fuller's Earth and perlash, a quarter of a pound of each, and boil in a quart of soft water; and, while hot, lay it on the greased parts, allowing it to remain on them for ten to twelve hours; after which it may be scoured off with sand and water.*
>
> *Enquire Within,* 1856

Stone
Porous stone should never be washed with soap as it will absorb it and gradually become slippery and dangerous when damp. Instead, use water containing a little ammonia or washing soda.

If grease has left an immovable mark cover the patch with a paste made of Fuller's Earth (from a chemist) or Sepialite (see page 215) and oil of eucalyptus. Cover it with pierced cling film and let it stay there until the top cracks, then pull it off. Some of the oil should have been absorbed by the mixture, but it may take several applications to clean it entirely and not all grease marks can be fully removed.

Sweeping Floors
The old practice of throwing used tea leaves on floors before sweeping has fallen into disuse. But it is worth remembering if you are moving home and have a floor to clean before carpeting. Failing tea leaves, even grass clippings will keep the dust down to a less choking level.

Tiled Floors
If builders have failed to clean off all the cement scum after fixing you can remove it with Quarry Cement Remover. Many builders' merchants and tile shops sell it, but you can also get it from a company called **Dennis Ruabon** (page 215). Otherwise, a sweep and wipe over with a mop (with a touch of washing-up liquid for glazed tiles or, for quarry tiles, Quarry Clean – also from tile shops), is all the care they need. Traditionally, when quarry tiles are new, linseed oil is wiped over them and left to sink in – try it on a spare tile and see if you like the effect. I don't.

Vinyl Floors
Strong alkali will gradually draw the plasticizer from vinyl and make it shrink and crack, and some proprietary floor cleaners are alkaline enough to cause long-term damage. Manufacturers of vinyl floorings recommend using a little neutral washing-up liquid and a touch of vinegar instead. But do avoid being generous – a soapy coating will make it dangerous when wet.

Vinyl is just as vulnerable to chemicals such as bleach, hair dye, paint thinners, fabric dyes, photographic chemicals, nail varnish and varnish removers. All will either stain or dissolve it. There is no cure for such marks, but surface marks, such as those produced by black rubber heels, can be removed with a fine metal scouring pad, sold for saucepans.

Vinyl doesn't really need any polish and, if you like the look of polish, go gently. Even with only two coats a year the edges will become yellower than the middle. When you can't bear this, remove it with $1/2$ cup of ammonia in 4 l (1 gallon) of cold water plus a dash of washing-up liquid. Wipe it on to the floor. Leave it for 5 minutes to bite into the polish, then remove it with a cloth and a looped nylon saucepan scourer. The alkali of ammonia could damage the vinyl so rinse it afterwards with a cup of vinegar in 4 l (1 gallon) water.

Flower Vases
Flower vases quickly build up tide marks. If they don't come off with water and detergent fill the vase with water, add a good dash of bleach and leave it for a while. The dirt should simply vanish. Rinse well afterwards.

> Bleach could harm old or fragile containers and should not be used on them.

Freezers and Refrigerators

Both refrigerators and freezers can build up a mingled smell which is as unattractive as that muddy brown paint one produced as a child by mixing every colour together. To remove it: first wash the plastic with warm water, then go over it with a cloth wrung out in a strong solution of bicarbonate of soda and water.

To keep the smell down put some lumps of charcoal at the back of a shelf, changing them every few months.

Fungus and Mould

If fungus grows on walls or window frames where moisture collects it will wash off. There are fungicides which you can buy to stop it returning, but a solution of bleach and water will deter it as well as anything. But do wear rubber gloves and do a test patch to see that the bleach doesn't cause the paint to fade.

If a bread bin or crock grows mould, or the bread goes mouldy quickly when stored in it, wash it out well, then wipe it all over inside with neat vinegar.

Gilt

Gilt on a deeply carved mirror seems so gloriously substantial that it is hard to realize that the layer of gold is so thin that if you held the gold leaf edgewise it would be invisible. This means it is very easily removed by cleaning. To make matters worse, there are two types of gilding – water-based and oil-based – and only the very expert can tell which is which. This means that, as one museum conservator put it, 'I cannot warn people too strongly against even attempting to clean gilding themselves.' Even dusting very old gilding can dislodge loose areas.

Nor can you assume that your local gilder is necessarily the person to go to if an antique gilt frame needs repairs.

Gilders fall into two camps: those who restore the old and add a minimum of new gilt – which keeps the value of the piece – and those who save themselves time by just putting new gilding over everything – which can halve the value of the object. (See also **Liberon Waxes**, page 215.)

Those warnings do not, of course, apply to modern gilding on plain picture frames, which stand up to dusting, and even to a damp cloth, without a murmur. But a more elaborate frame may be real gilt however modern it is, so age isn't always the guide.

Glass and Crystal

Crystal chandeliers are made so they can be taken down in sections for cleaning – which is a long job. So one chandelier owner devised the following method.

Instead of taking the chandelier down, put on clean cotton gloves, stand on a tall ladder with a bucket of water containing a dash of washing-up liquid (though Synperonic N, page 216, is even better) and a dash of vinegar and wet your gloves with the solution. Hold each section of chandelier firmly in place with one hand while you run the finger of the other hand over it to clean it. Obviously, it takes a good deal of dexterity to do this without falling off the ladder or accidentally unhooking and dropping a section of the chandelier.

Decanters and Fine Glass

Glass is not a single substance. Its composition varies with the period and the maker, so it is never safe to assume that a treatment which works for one piece will work for another.

The first step in the care of decanters is not to leave small dregs of alcohol lurking in the bottom or they will dry to a nasty stain. Relatively new alcohol stains can often be removed by soaking them in neat malt vinegar. Older stains are very hard to remove, and can be impossible. *Do not, under any circumstances*, use a denture cleaning tablet. Such tablets may clean some glass, but they are capable of etching other glass to a cloudiness which is far worse than any stain in the base could possibly be.

If vinegar fails to remove a stain try tearing newspaper into *tiny* pieces and dropping it into a decanter filled with water, and leaving it overnight. This sometimes does the trick. Then rinse it out and dry it carefully. Failing that, some museum experts claim that potato peelings may do the trick.

Glass can also be clouded by the fluorine in water if a decanter is washed and the stopper put in before it is totally dry. The fluorine then condenses on to the inside of the glass and etches it. The cloudiness can only be removed by using formidable acids to eat away the inner layer of glass. Some of the top makers of cut glass will do this job – especially if they made the decanter.

The best place to dry a decanter is upside-down in an airing cupboard – quite a few have slats spaced widely enough for the neck to slip down between them. But be *very* careful or you might find that the neck is knocked off.

★ The only way to undo glass which has stuck is to use the fact that glass expands when it heats. If two glasses are stuck one inside another fill the inner one with iced water. Then stand the outer one in warm water and gradually increase the heat of the water until the inner one can be lifted out.

A Stuck Stopper

If a ground glass stopper has become stuck, put a little penetrating oil round the neck and give it a few hours to seep in. If the stopper can't then be removed you need to heat the neck of the vessel while keeping the stopper cool. Running warm water over the neck, or wrapping a warm towel round it may work – but heating thick glass too suddenly may crack it. So move gently from warm to hot. If the stopper still won't come out, try tapping the stopper all round, gently, with a wooden spoon. Vibrating the glass like that usually works – though if you do it too hard it will chip.

Windows and Mirrors

You can clean sheet glass with a host of substances, but quite the worst is the thick type of cleaner which leaves a deposit around the edge. One of the fastest ways to clean slightly dirty glass is simply to rub it over with a damp newspaper and dry it with a dry one. The printing ink does great things for the glass – if not for your hands.

If glass is really dirty wash it with water in which there is some ammonia (use rubber gloves) to cut the grease of the atmosphere, or just use a little washing-up liquid. Rinse it clean with water containing either vinegar or methylated spirits. To give it an extra good shine polish it dry with a chamois leather. Mirrors, and pictures with gilded frames, need a little care (see Gilt).

★ If the glass is marked with hair spray remove it with methylated spirits.

Pictures

The glass on most pictures can be cleaned like a window. But there is an exception where chalk and pastel drawings are concerned. Rubbing the glass can set up an electrical charge which will draw the tiny particles of loose pastel off the paper and on to the glass, clouding it and spoiling the drawing. Just give glass over pastels a slow gentle wipe.

Graffiti

If vandals draw or paint on your property, and wire wool fails to remove it, your local council may have a graffiti-removal squad which will remove it for you – free or for a fee. Or they may be able to advise you on how to do it yourself. Alternatively, high-pressure water jets, from tool-hire shops, may work on brick or wood, and there are special chemicals for the job which your council should tell you how to find. Using anti-graffiti paint on the area the vandals spray will make cleaning much easier in future. Page 270 has a supplier.

Iron

Obviously water and iron make poor bedfellows. But once rust does set in it can be removed with citric acid. An alternative cleaner is paraffin and 000 wire wool. Whatever you use bear in mind that iron can be fractured quite easily.

Ivory

The great thing with ivory is to curb one's enthusiasm. It should age to a gentle cream. Trying to keep it looking like new will only damage it. All over it there are hairline cracks into which water can seep – so washing it can have disastrous results in the long term. Blow the dust off it, and when it really *has* to be cleaned use a little methylated spirits on a cotton bud. Using a duster on carved ivory risks catching and breaking it on a loose thread, and the methylated spirits should be colourless as there is a slight risk of the colour staining the ivory. If you are cleaning piano keys be very sparing, any excess may soften the glue which sticks them on. To clean an ivory comb use methylated spirits on dental floss.

Horn and antlers, whether on knife handles or on trophies, should be treated like ivory.

> BEWARE Some books suggest using bleach, lemon juice or peroxide to clean ivory. Any one of these may seem to do no harm, but they burn ivory and, in time, it will become powdery and dull.

Jade

Jade is an easy-going substance. Treat it like glass but avoid using anything which might scratch it, as the surface is quite soft.

Jewellery – General Points

It is easy to clean most jewellery at home but it takes a little care and you need to consider both the type of setting and the gems which may be set in it. Anything you wear often may need cleaning every week, but once a month is often enough.

Check old jewellery to see whether it is closed in behind the stones. If it is, *don't* wash it. At one time, foil was used to back stones with this type of setting, and if the foil is washed it can permanently discolour and ruin the piece. All you can do to clean this type of setting is give it a rub with a clean chamois leather or Goddard's Long Term Silver Cloth.

Pearls, ivory and certain types of inset in jewellery need special treatment – see below before you start cleaning.

For open settings the basic method is to have washing-up liquid and warm (not hot) water in a bowl (not a wash basin – any stones which come loose will go down the plug hole). Put the jewellery in and leave it a little, then brush it clean with a soft bristle toothbrush. If settings have become clogged with soap pick out the soap carefully with a toothpick. (You may find that methylated spirits help remove the soap more easily.)

Rinse the jewellery very well and dry it with a hairdryer or fan heater set to cool. Strain the washing-up liquid through a very fine nylon sieve and check whether any stones have fallen into it. If they have it is a very good thing; any stone which falls out with this gentle treatment would soon have been lost in the street.

Fragile Stones

The fragile stones you are most likely to find in jewellery are opals, turquoise, pearls, coral, jet, amber and emeralds. Pearls and emeralds are special cases (see below); all the others can be washed with soap and water, but not subjected to anything stronger.

Acrylic Jewellery

Acrylics aren't as tough as their modernity might make you suppose. Treat them like fragile stones.

Emeralds

Emeralds look as hard as diamonds but they are more prone to flaws than other precious stones. To disguise these flaws some countries soak their emeralds in a fine green oil which seeps into the cracks and conceals them perfectly – so perfectly that even an expert can't always tell a flawed stone from a perfect one without testing it. The danger is that if you soak an emerald in washing-up liquid – or, indeed, wear it for washing up – you may draw out the oil and reveal a hidden flaw. So leave cleaning to the professionals.

Gold and Platinum

Gold or platinum is often much dirtier than it looks. If you have anything which is plain gold – with nothing set in it – try dropping it in methylated spirits for 3 minutes – not longer. Then remove it, brush any loose dirt off with a soft bristle toothbrush and rinse it. It should look entirely different.

IMPORTANT: Read Jewellery – General Points before using these methods.

Opals

Opals are a curious combination of silica and water and will craze and lose their colour if they get too dry. So they must be kept well away from heat, and are best left uncleaned or wiped with a piece of silk. If they become dull and scratched they can be repolished professionally.

Pearls

Tradition has it that pearls lose their lustre if they aren't worn at fairly regular intervals. But they are also extremely vulnerable to acids of all kinds, including the acid in some people's skin; these will eat into them and dull them. Wipe them with a piece of silk after you take them off, to avoid the risk of skin acids staying on them and never apply perfume and hair lacquer after you put them on.

Silver

Professionals often clean silver jewellery with silver dip – if it has nothing set in it – the advantage being that no polish lodges in the cracks. But a jewellery designer I know prefers to use a soft toothbrush and toothpaste. It works extremely well and is always to hand. See also page 168.

Kettles

A kettle which is encrusted with hard water deposits uses up more fuel than a clean one. Furring can be kept to a minimum by putting a seashell inside to attract the scale. But to remove scale which has formed, less than half fill the kettle with equal parts of vinegar and water, and bring it to the boil. The mixture will rise up dramatically as it heats, so *don't overfill it*, and be ready to turn it off the instant it looks as if it might overflow. Leave it to work on the scale before rinsing it out. Do this regularly so there is never a heavy deposit to remove. Once the inside is very coated it will take a lot of applications to remove all of it. (There are also branded products to descale kettles, but they aren't cheap.)

Kitchen Ranges

An old cast iron kitchen range which is the one surface on which you can use quite a stiff wire brush, and don't have to use the finest wire wool. For cleaning liquids avoid water (see Iron, page 164) *totally* and stick to paraffin or methylated spirits. There are no secrets to bringing a range back to life – it is sheer hard work. But they can look wonderful when finished.

Lacquer

Lacquer ranges from the sublime to the shoddy. Fine antique lacquer is so fragile that even white flour can scratch it, and a drop of water can eat into its surface. Clean it as little as possible and then only with an immaculately clean silk cloth. However much care you take, the surface may become tacky with age. There is no way to prevent or reverse this.

Cheap modern lacquer is scarcely related and you can clean it with a damp cloth, but avoid cleaners which might scratch it.

Lampshades

Hard lampshades of glass, plastic or other substances should be cleaned according to what they are made of – bearing in mind that water should not be used unless the shade is removed from the electrical fitting. Glass shades need ammonia in the water if they are very dirty.

A fabric shade can be washed *if* the trimmings have been attached with waterproof glue and the fabric is washable. First vacuum or brush off any loose dust, then dip it in pure soap dissolved in lukewarm water. Hold it upright or – if it must lie on its side – move it from side to side. On its side the weight of even a little water may make it stretch or tear.

If a fabric shade isn't washable you may wish to risk using a spray-on dry-cleaner if it is too dirty to use without it.

Lavatories

Urine Stains

The most effective lavatory cleaner is often bleach. It kills germs, and gets rid of the yellow deposits some cleaners allow to build up. But most bleach isn't good for the environment, so, unless you use non-chlorine bleach, keep its use to a minimum. Bleach needs time to work, so pour it in and brush it round before going to bed. (If you have young children who might go to the loo alone at night, do it in the morning while they can be kept elsewhere.) For a neglected loo repeated bleaching may be the only answer. Use the thick bleaches, well up under the rim, or the urine smell will stay.

Hard Water Stains

In hard-water areas use a cleaner that says it treats lime scale. Or use the vinegar treatment given for baths on page 157. If that fails to shift them paint on a solution of 1 teaspoonful of oxalic acid in half a cup of hot water and leave it to work. Wearing rubber gloves, scrape it with a hard plastic edge, and repeat. Not a nice job, but then a stained loo isn't lovely either.

Marble

Marble may look as strong as a rock, but in fact it's rather fragile. *The cleaning of valuable marble should be left to a conservator* and it should simply be dusted with a *perfectly* clean duster.

Marble's complex structure of crystals can be broken down internally by a hard knock, and even using water on it can draw out iron in its composition and slowly cause rust stains. Research, with electron microscopes, suggests that water may also encourage the growth of bacteria which slowly discolour it. Of course, people do have marble floors which are washed, but they are most common in dry countries, such as Greece, where moisture seldom lingers. And, as the staining is very gradual, it has only recently been realized that water is responsible for the long-term discoloration.

Marble is also vulnerable to spirits and to acids. A scent bottle or drink will eat into marble and leave a mark as rough as sandpaper. To polish this back to smoothness is a very long job, using wet and dry paper and may be best left to an expert.

If mundane marble is so dirty that you have to use some sort of moisture then white spirit is less harmful than water. If it needs even more thorough cleaning one expert in marble conservation recommends Solvol Autosol, obtainable in car accessory shops. You rub it on in small areas with a small, clean rag and remove any residue with white spirit.

Companies which lay marble floors can now seal them with clear lacquer. But I have yet to find a DIY lacquer which is recommended for marble. So, to prevent stains getting into marble so easily wipe on a fine wax such as Renaissance Wax (from **Liberon Waxes**). Immediately wipe off any residue and polish it up. Finally sprinkle it with *pure* talc (from a pharmacist; not any old talc which could have additions which would harm the marble) and brush off the surplus.

★ Marble will draw moisture out of cement, and with it chemicals from the cement which can ruin it. Cement should never be used in installing marble. It is equally vulnerable to stains from metal pins used to hold it in place. The only metal which is totally safe is stainless steel – and then only certain types. Before installing marble take advice from a knowledgeable museum conservator.

Stains on Marble

Don't try to remove stains from any marble you value – any stain removal can spoil its surface.

If you spill ink on ordinary marble immediately cover it liberally with salt. This should absorb the ink. Then brush it off, or vacuum it up. Sour milk left on the stain may bleach it out over several days, and much will depend on the type of ink. Treat it afterwards with Sepialite (from **A. J. Lopez**), as below.

Brown and grey iron stains can often be bleached out with repeated applications of salt and lemon juice. Finally, draw the salt and lemon out of the marble by covering the area with a thick layer of Sepialite mixed to a stiff paste with water. Leave it until the surface is cracking then pull it off.

For felt-pen marks apply a paste of Sepialite mixed with colourless methylated spirits. Cover this mud pack with cling film with holes pierced in it – to slow down the evaporation rate – and peel it off as above. It will usually take several applications to remove a stain.

Red wine, tea and coffee will all come out with repeated applications of hydrogen peroxide – applied with a paint brush so it only covers the stain. Don't use bleach.

Mattresses

A new sprung mattress needs special care in the early weeks to make the springs and fillings bed down evenly. For the first two months it should be turned over one week and rotated head to the foot the next. In that way all the springs will settle evenly.

Any mattress needs daily airing. Throw the covers off the end on to a chair, so the moisture of the night can blow away. Every few months, vacuum the mattress with a nozzle for fine fabrics, or brush it clean.

Mattress covers are stained by water. Even a leaky hot water bottle can leave a stain which looks like something much nastier. So it is always advisable to put a plastic sheet on any bed occupied by a young child lest it spill something in it.

If a mattress does get wet immediately turn it on its side, so the wet doesn't drip through and rust the springs, and mop the wet up rapidly. Sponge the area with a clean cloth, or use a suitable dry-cleaner if it is a dry stain (see Stains). Leave it on its side until it is totally dry.

Foam Mattresses

Foam mattresses must have a ventilated base or condensation will collect on the underside and the mattress may rot.

Futons

Instead of being left flat a futon should be loosely rolled up each day, so the air can circulate and the moisture dry out. If you spill something on a futon mop the liquid up at once and wipe it with a damp cloth. If necessary, apply a suitable remedy then leave it to dry.

Microwave Ovens

The insides of microwave ovens need to be cleaned regularly as you can't bring them up to scratch with caustic in the way you can an oven with an enamel interior. See stainless steel page 169.

The base of the oven and particularly the mechanism for turning the food need to be kept spotlessly clean, so it can turn easily: microwave motors burn out surprisingly easily if a strain is put on them. It is also important to keep the seal round the door clean so it closes properly; use the same cleaner as for the stainless steel.

Oil Lamps

Only a smoke-coated chimney can mar the soft beauty of the light from an oil lamp, but luckily the chimney is easily cleaned. For reasons which are unexplained, washing a chimney makes it more liable to crack. Wipe it out with newspaper instead: the printing ink helps to remove the soot.

The wick should be soaked in vinegar when new and left to dry, then it will be less liable to smoke, and trim it straight across at each lighting.

Ormolu

True ormolu is brass, or bronze, coated with gold, but some ormolu is gold over zinc, and what seems to be ormolu can sometimes be lacquered brass. Neither should be washed or rubbed hard. Dust it lightly with a soft brush: any polishing may remove the surface metal and ruin it. This means that china and glass with ormolu mounts cannot be washed. Instead, wipe them clean without letting water touch the gold.

Addresses and suggestions for further reading are at the ends of chapters.

Paintings and Pictures

There is only one rule: *don't* clean anything unless it is so dreadful there isn't a hope of it having any value. Scarcely a year passes without someone finding that some neglected drawing or painting is a lost masterpiece.

If an oil painting really is totally valueless you can try cleaning it by wiping the surface gently with a clean rag dipped in dilute household ammonia. If it has any value ask a professional museum restorer to advise you.

Any pictures which are on paper are at risk from damp, insects and too much light. They should be kept away from extremes of all kinds and insects must be dealt with rapidly.

Paths

When green algae form on paths they can be cleaned off by rinsing the area with a fairly strong solution of bleach, such as 1 part bleach to 6 parts water, or with a special product such as ICI's Moss Gun. Leave the chemical on for an hour or two while keeping children and pets inside. Then remove the algae with a very strong jet of water (bounce-off may bleach your clothes). If necessary, scrub the stones with a stiff brush to get the green right off. I find bleach best but the snag is anything you have growing beside the path may die. However, the Moss Gun is also for moss in lawns so if you have stones inset into grass it can be used there without damage to the grass.

Pewter

Sharing, as it does, the colour of silver, it is tempting to expect pewter to have at least some of its sheen. But it is a mixture of tin and other metals and shines with difficulty. Just make the most of its soft sheen by keeping it dust-free and rubbing it occasionally with Goddard's Silver Cloth. Work *round* the circle of a goblet or tankard to produce the best effect. For display you can keep its sheen by polishing it with Renaissance Wax (from **Liberon Waxes**). But, if the surface of any valuable pewter becomes powdery and white consult a conservator at once. It may have pewter disease and need special treatment.

Don't rub it on the inside: pewter absorbs smells, so polishes can make it impossible to drink from. That would be a shame, for pewter holds the cold. So if you wish to drink cool wine in a hot garden chill a pewter mug in the refrigerator with the wine: a tradition begun by the ancient Romans who also used cool pewter goblets when they slaked their thirst under the sun.

But rinse wine, and any other drink out of pewter as soon as possible because it is very vulnerable to acid. Oak contains very strong tannic acid which it releases into the air and tankards which have stood too long on oak have been known to lose their bases and pewter must not be kept in an oak drawer or cupboard.

> Those who feel tempted to polish vigorously should bear in mind that the difference in value between a piece of pewter with its touch marks in perfect condition and one with them rubbed off can be thousands of pounds.

Plastic Laminates

The laminated surfaces in kitchens need more care than they appear to. To chop food directly on them, or scour them with an abrasive cleaner is to convert an easy-care surface into one which won't look good whatever you do. Stick to thin liquid cleaners, use a chopping board and don't put a very hot pan on the surface or there may be a permanent scorch mark.

Laminates are also stained by clothes' dyes and the colourings on some food labels. Some come out if you leave a pool of washing soda and water over the place for a few hours; others vanish under a pool of lemon juice – but a few shift for neither.

Porcelain Washbasin

The fastest way to clean a basin is to use a cleaner, with no foaming agent, and a saucepan scourer which has sponge on one side and a rough surface on the other.

Rust stains can be removed from porcelain washbasins by leaving a paste of cream of tartar and water to work on them. See also China and Porcelain, page 159.

Pillows

Pillows need daily plumping up by shaking them vigorously and pushing the sides towards the middle several times. This separates the filling and disperses the moisture which has gone into the pillow during the night and keeps them fluffy. (For washing see Duvets, page 161.)

Record Player Heads

Dirt on a stylus distorts the sound. The professional way to clean it is to use equal parts of distilled water and isopropyl alcohol (from a chemist). Put this on a fine brush and brush the stylus with it, very lightly, from *the back towards the front* – any other direction may bend the stylus.

> Treat isopropyl alcohol with great care. It can etch a mark into anything.

Records

Almost every method of cleaning can result in a badly damaged record – and that includes some methods I have heard advocated on the radio. They should *never* be washed – invisible traces of dye can run into the tracks and distort the sound. Nor should they be wiped – this forces dirt off the tops of the tracks and deep into them.

According to scientists in the record industry, the safest way by far is to use an anti-static gun sold by top record shops. Quite a long way behind, is an anti-static cloth. But *don't* wipe the record with it – that just pushes the dirt into the delicate grooves. Instead, rotate the record on a turntable while holding the cloth so it only *just* touches the surface.

If you don't have an anti-static cloth put a clean fine cotton handkerchief in a box with some wet tissues – but not touching them. The moisture will slowly evaporate out of the tissues and condense on to the handkerchief. You can then use it like the anti-static cloth, but the effects won't last so long. A dry anti-static cloth can be moistened in the same way.

No amount of cleaning will do much for a neglected record, so hold records only by the edges, put them away immediately after use, and – most important of all – when putting them away, or taking them out, open the sides of the sleeve so the record doesn't rub against the paper. It is the friction of going in and out of the sleeve which creates most of the static which draws dust on to a record.

Warped Records
If a record warps slightly put it between two perfectly clean sheets of glass in a warm airing cupboard. If the warping isn't too severe the warmth and the slight pressure will flatten it out.

Rugs and Mats

The first essential with mats and rugs is that they don't present a hazard. Rugs on top of carpets can be kept close to the carpet by putting the hook side of a piece of stick-on velcro under each corner. The hooks then mesh into the carpet and hold it firmly. Mats on polished surfaces should lie on a non-slip underlay.

Shaking rugs damages their edges, but most rugs can be vacuum-cleaned, provided the strength of the suction is suited to their age and fragility. An ordinary hard-wearing rug will benefit from an extra thorough clean on some days: vacuum three times – front, back, front. Strong rugs also benefit from being placed face down on dry grass (not newly cut) – or ideally snow – and beaten.

Most mats and rugs can be spot-cleaned and shampooed like carpets (see page 159) but fine rugs normally need to be dry-cleaned (see page 215) so ask about this when buying. Oriental rugs should only be cleaned after expert advice as their dyes are unpredictable.

Modern rag-rugs can sometimes be washed. But there is always a risk that even if the rag part washes beautifully the strings on which it is woven may shrink. *Only* wash a rug if you are prepared to take the consequences if it goes wrong. Beat and/or vacuum the rug very well to get it as clean as possible – grit could damage your bath. Dissolve some pure soapflakes in a pint of hot water in a bath. Half fill the bath with cold water and immerse the rug. Leave for several hours or overnight. Then press the water through until a lot of dirt has come out. Drain and rinse in cold water again and again until it is entirely clear. (Very dirty rugs may need two soapy soaks to reach this stage). Press out as much water as you can. Lift it carefully, supporting it well, and spread or hang it to dry in a clean place outside, away from direct sunlight.

Fur rugs are cleaned like fur (see page 176).

Silver and Silver Plate

There is absolutely no need to acquire a glow of sweat and virtue rubbing away to bring silver to a shine. It can be cleaned with silver dip. This acts on the oxides which are tarnishing the silver, whereas polishing rubs away a little of the silver itself. So dipping is the method silver experts prefer.

But silver dip is only for solid silver, not plate, and don't dip items into it if they have non-silver decoration like ebony or ivory knobs.

To make your own put a plate-sized sheet of aluminium kitchen foil in a saucepan with water and a handful of washing soda. Heat this up and drop the silver in for a minute or two – until the tarnish and stains are just off (don't leave it for a long time). Remove and rinse it and rub with a long-term silver cloth to put a sheen on it.

If the silver cloth is not enough, the fastest effective polish is a mixture of whiting (see below) and methylated spirits. Use it just as you would any other metal polish. If you lack methylated spirits mix the whiting with water and a few drops of ammonia. Rinse the silver afterwards and dry it carefully.

> Whiting is a fine white powder sold in old-fashioned hardware stores, but more easily found in the south of England than in the north. It is made by **Blanchard's** (page 215).

How far you should go in the matter of removing tarnish is a matter of dispute. Some museums leave old silver looking as if it was made yesterday. It seems a pity. A hint of tarnish in the crevices brings out the design. However, intricate silver is best cleaned with a soft brush to prevent the polish lodging in it.

Black stains on Silver
Black stains caused by acid should be rubbed with salt and lemon juice. Stains made by salt come off most easily if rubbed with the whiting mixture plus salt. If that sounds like the mythology of the 'hair of the dog' just try for yourself. But do rinse both off afterwards and watch out for scratching with the salt – it is a remedy of last resort. Another curious interaction is that if an egg spoon becomes darkened by egg, dipping it in the water in which an egg has cooked will clean it.

★ If you want to make your own polishing cloth mix 4 teaspoons of whiting with 2 tablespoons of household ammonia and 3 cups of water. Soak a piece of towelling in this, wring it out, let it half dry and store it in a plastic bag.

Storing Silver
Silver has several enemies: rubber, salt, ink, acid, air and light. Exclude all of them and silver will keep its shine

for a remarkably long time. You can buy Tarnprufe bags (see page 216), made of a fabric which is impregnated with a substance which will prevent stored silver from tarnishing. These are very much better than storing silver in plastic bags. For, although plastic keeps out the air there is a risk of tarnish from air already in the bag.

Having polished silver, put on cotton gloves and rub it once more to remove any traces of finger acids. Wrap each piece well in special dark, *acid-free* tissue paper (page 215). (Don't wrap it in baize. Baize gives off hydrogen sulphide which tarnishes silver, as do many of the linings of presentation boxes. And *don't* use rubber bands. The chemicals released by rubber can penetrate the paper and eat into the silver, leaving marks which can never be removed.) Either wrap all the tissue-covered pieces up together in more tissue, or put them in Tarnprufe bags.

If silver is on display in a cabinet its tarnishing can be reduced by putting a Carosil capsule (page 216) in the cabinet. These are used by some museums, but are only effective if the cabinet is kept closed.

Silver Plate

Silver plate is a thin layer of silver on base metal, such as copper. It is far more fragile than solid silver because the layer can be rubbed off. Polish it no more than is really necessary.

A product, called the Silver Solution (page 216), puts a thin layer of silver on to silver plate which clings by a chemical interaction. It can be used on worn cutlery and seems too good to be true. The snag is the silver wears off more quickly than it would if it had been electroplated. This means you have to keep using it again and again which is far from cheap.

> The Silver Solution makes the buying of plate far more risky, as a piece may look perfect, yet simply have the thin layer of silver provided by this solution. So beware.

Silver Gilt

This is a thin layer of gold over silver. It needs no polishing, just washing when dirty, and it should be treated gently, not rubbed.

Slate

Marks on slate hearth stones and floors usually come off with 000 wire wool. To polish and protect slate, use a *light* coat of linseed oil.

Stainless Steel

The smooth sheen of stainless steel is easily damaged by even a nylon scouring pad, let alone anything more abrasive. It must only be cleaned with a cloth dipped in a thin liquid cleaner, such as Sainsbury's All-Purpose Liquid Cleaner or in water with a dash of ammonia. I find these more effective and less expensive than products made for stainless steel.

Steel

Antique steel needs to be checked carefully before you start to clean it: engraving or gilding could be ruined by the wrong treatment. If anything intricate is found check the best mode of cleaning with a museum conservator. For ordinary steel, which just needs a slight clean, use Solvol Autosol chrome cleaner (from car accessory shops) which is mildly abrasive and effective.

Steel rusts easily, but the rust comes off with paraffin. If necessary, put small objects in a bath of paraffin for 24 hours, or lay a rag soaked in it overnight on a larger surface. But it can't remove the pitting which rust causes.

To bring up a shine on steel, use 000 or 0000 steel wool (coarser will scratch it) lubricated with paraffin or turpentine. To produce a smooth sheen work to and fro in straight lines always in the same direction, *not* round and round. A light coating of paraffin or WD-40 will then help to keep it shiny. For knives, see page 171.

Steps

If steps *have* to be scrubbed despite the cold, put salt or methylated spirits in the water, then it won't freeze into lethal ice before it dries. Use a tablespoon of either for each 500 ml (1 pt) of water.

Stoves and Grates

Cast iron isn't as tough as you'd suppose and shutting a door or lid too hard can fracture it. Water is another risk, as it is liable to trickle through the design and rust the inside where there is no enamel. It is far better to clean enamelled cast iron with a cloth moistened in white spirit (when the fire is *out*) or with 000 wire wool if it becomes grimy. But don't touch the panes with this.

To get the black lead finish on old-fashioned stoves and grates you need a product called Zebrite. Thin it to a cream with white spirit, then paint it on with a cheap paint brush – when the stove is *out* – and leave it for 24 hours to dry. Then buff it up with a soft shoe brush kept specially. A messy job, but thank goodness we don't have to make our own.

> *Blacking is now always made with ivory black, treacle, linseed or sweet oil, and oil of vitriol. The proportions vary ... as paste or liquid blacking is required ...*
> Enquire Within, 1856

Tortoiseshell

Tortoiseshell is easily clouded by water or sunlight. If it becomes clouded it can be reburnished professionally. And one of my *Supertips* readers wrote to tell me that she has restored tortoiseshell by rubbing in a product called Vitapointe, sold for dry hair. Hair and tortoiseshell are very similar substances so this isn't too surprising. In fact, they are so alike that customs men test for real tortoiseshell by scraping off a fraction and burning it: if it smells like burning hair it's the real thing. What can't be predicted is whether Vitapointe could make clouding worse in the long run.

Upholstery

The fabrics on chairs and sofas vary in the type of care they need, which makes some far better suited to a family than others. Before you buy ask the retailer what care is necessary. If he doesn't know ask him to find out – and if he won't you should go elsewhere. Having obtained instructions on how to clean any cloth, follow them exactly.

Cotton and Wool Upholstery
Regular vacuuming, to remove the surface dirt, is basic, and many can be cleaned with either a dry-foam upholstery shampoo or with a dry-cleaner aerosol. Whatever the fabric, don't think that the zips on cushion covers are there so you can take them off and wash them.

★ If you lack a vacuum cleaner for upholstery, put a damp sheet over it and beat it. The sheet should catch the flying dust.

Dralon Upholstery
If you fit arm covers over upholstery make sure they are lined with calico. If Dralon rubs on Dralon, the pile underneath may be damaged by the friction.

Vacuum working against the pile one way, and return the opposite way. If you spill anything mop it up with a clean, white cloth as soon as possible. You may then be able to remove any stain by wiping it gently with lukewarm water and an appropriate amount of 1001 dry-foam upholstery cleaner. First, test on some part that won't show, that this has no effect on the colour. (You could have bought a Dralon look-alike which might react to it. If it seems alright work very gently without getting the upholstery too wet or rubbing the pile too hard.

Leather Upholstery
Leather has several different finishes and the correct treatment depends entirely on the particular finish. Suede is easily recognized. An aniline finish looks and feels as soft as skin, with no real shine on it. Both these are easily damaged by every kind of stain because they have no coating to seal them. It may be possible to protect them by using one of the leather sprays designed to prevent dirt penetrating shoes. But check with the manufacturer of the furniture. Once stains have formed they need expert treatment unless you want to risk trying some of the methods given for leather clothes (see page 176).

Pigmented leather feels firmer and has a shine to it, but there is an intermediate finish called semi-aniline. To test which you have, moisten a white tissue and press it against some hidden part of the leather – but not a seam. If it produces a dark patch the finish is semi-aniline and needs careful handling, like aniline.

Pigmented leather is quite tough, but it can still be stained by grease, so keep anything oily well away from it. Dust it regularly and if it looks dirty wipe it over with a cloth wrung out in warm water and pure soap (not detergent). The cloth must not be wet or water may trickle through a seam and get on to the back of the leather, which will shrink and distort. In a centrally-heated home pigmented leather needs to be treated 3 times a year with Connolly's Hide Food or with the mixture given for books on page 157.

Loose Covers
Whether loose covers should be washed or dry-cleaned will depend on the fabric (see Washing Problems, page 190), but only wash them if you are *sure* they are both washable *and* preshrunk, and even then put the covers back on the chairs while still quite damp and let them dry like that. Then they will stretch to size. You may be able to iron them while still on the chairs (if it is tough, old-fashioned upholstery) or you may have to take them off.

Tapestry and Embroidery
These should be treated very gently and not cleaned with water, upholstery shampoo or dry-cleaning aerosols. Plain tapestry (needlepoint) can *only* be vacuum-cleaned each week, very gently, with a nozzle vacuum attachment *without rubbing at the surface* to keep the dust from sinking in. Embroidery which is fixed in position (as in chair seats) may be more fragile and can only be vacuumed if it is sturdy and has no beads or other ornaments which could be pulled off. Otherwise you may just have to go over it very gently with a baby's hairbrush.

If needlepoint or woven tapestry (or embroidery of any age or value) needs more thorough cleaning only a few highly specialized cleaners know how to do so without damage. The **Royal School of Needlework** (page 215) will clean and repair needlepoint and embroidery, and woven tapestry can be cleaned by **Pilgrim Payne and Co Ltd** (page 215). Removing tapestry from chair seats is a tricky job which should be done by an expert upholsterer or by the School of Needlework itself.

Vinyl and Plastic Upholstery
Leather-look plastic and vinyl dislike fierce heat, so keep them a respectable distance from both fires and radiators. Detergent, polish or spirit cleaner make the plastic go hard and crack. Instead, wipe with warm water and pure soap, and rinse it off afterwards. There is also a product called 'Son of a Gun', made by STP for simulated leather vinyl car seats. On car seats it does a remarkable job and it could be worth asking the maker of any vinyl-covered suite whether it could be used on it.

Vacuum Flasks

Vacuum flasks can be cleared of smells with the bicarbonate of soda mixture given on page 163. Smells can also be removed by leaving a crushed egg-shell in water in the flask overnight.

Wall Cleaning

Distemper and Whitewash
Both distemper and whitewash are impossible to clean. The only solution is to repaint.

Vacuum fabric-covered or wallpapered surfaces with a battery-operated vacuum cleaner or trunk extension, or tie a clean towel around a broom and brush the walls with this: arm-aching but effective.

One of the best substances for removing small marks from wallpaper is a piece of fresh bread. It is damp enough to ease marks off, and soft enough not to rub the surface as much as a rubber. When I was on BBC Television, I discovered it was even used by the BBC design department.

Some marks will come off with a soft eraser, but you have to be very careful not to leave a pale patch. So, work from the centre, feathering the edge with small outward strokes.

Grease is almost impossible to remove, but putting blotting paper over the stain and ironing it may reduce it. You can also try spray-on-dry-cleaner – but do a test patch somewhere it won't show.

Grubby patches, such as those around light switches, on a non-washable wallpaper, can sometimes be cleaned by a gentle rub with a cloth moistened with ammonia. But ammonia could affect the dyes in the paper, so do a test patch – where it won't show. And don't rub so hard you destroy the surface of the paper.

Tiles

Glazed wall tiles can be washed with a foam-free floor and wall cleaner or with a paint cleaning mixture. If grouting has gone grey you may be able to improve it with a little bleach (wear rubber gloves). But see A Roof Over Your Head.

Vinyl Papers

Vinyl papers can usually be wiped with any detergent, but don't get the seams wet and wipe the paper over afterwards with vinegar and water.

Washing Paint

Walls must be washed from the bottom upwards. If a trickle of water runs down over a dirty lower section it leaves a line which you may never be able to remove.

There is no point in using fancy products for cleaning paint. Almost all of them contain foaming agents, so you use one bucket of water to wash the wall and three to rinse the suds off – which is crazy. It is far easier to use a basic mixture such as ½ cup ammonia, ¼ cup vinegar, and ¼ cup washing soda. Another version is ½ cup vinegar, 1 cup ammonia, ¼ cup washing soda. Either goes in a gallon of water. Both mixtures are powerful cleaners, which should only be used wearing rubber gloves and with the windows open, as ammonia is not good to inhale. But both mixtures will cut through dirt on walls with ease. And you can use small quantities of them to keep walls routinely clean.

Washing up

Washing up is a rare skill. The skilled washer-upper makes sure everything is washed in order of cleanliness – greasiest last. They also wash everything – except cutlery – one at a time to avoid bangs and chips.

By the old kitchen rules, glass comes first, followed by cutlery, china, dishes and pans. They are rinsed in hot water containing a good dash of vinegar to remove the soap.

If the handles of good knives don't have visible pins to hold them on keep both the handle and the junction out of the water. Until quite recently, the handles of good knives were stuck on with a glue which comes unstuck in hot water and, though they won't fall out in an instant, the glue will swell and the handle will gradually push away from the cushion of the blade which it rests against, and become loose.

★ If raw egg, blood or flour are washed with hot water the heat cooks them on to the surface and makes them harder to remove. All three should be rinsed off under a cold tap, then washed in hot water afterwards.

★ Cutlery dries with spots on if it is left lying on a draining board, but put it on end in any container and it may dry spotless.

Glass

As vinegar counteracts the alkali in washing-up liquid, a dash in the rinsing water will give glass a better shine.

When washing fine glass make sure any central tap is turned out of the way and put a folded tea towel or a pad of foam rubber in the bottom of the basin. Then an accidental knock won't cause a chip. Avoid having the water too hot, otherwise immersing a thick piece of glass may lead it to expand at different rates in different parts, and cause it to crack. Wash one piece at a time, never leaving anything soaking in the water – lest someone else 'helpfully' drops something in.

Gilding is damaged by strong cleaners, so it is best to wash gilded glass in pure soap.

Glass should be dried in the opposite way to everything else: you hold the cloth still and turn the glass against it. That way, you don't risk wringing a glass off its stem.

Stainless Steel

Stainless steel which is regularly washed in a machine tends to develop a murky coating. Drop it in soapy water with a couple of tablespoons of bleach per pint of water. Leave it to soak until the coating brushes off easily. Then brush it clean and rinse it well. Wear rubber gloves and keep the bleach off everything around – including your stainless steel sink. Paradoxically, some sinks react badly to it.

Steel Knives

Steel knives, which aren't stainless, need to be hand-washed and dried straight after use or they become rusted and pitted. If that has already happened use a butler's trick: put some scouring powder on the end of a moist cork and rub this hard up and down the blade and the stains will vanish.

Tea Stains

China which is stained with tea can be cleaned effortlessly by soaking them for a few hours in water and washing soda. The stains then wash off. Or use salt, or bicarbonate of soda instead – though they are slightly less effective. Gilding can be damaged by any of them, so gilded china must not be soaked. It can be carefully rubbed with salt to remove stains from the places where there is no gilding.

Washing up Bad Food

If food in a container has clearly gone bad or may have food poisoning bacteria in it throw the food away (preferably straight in the dustbin or down the lavatory). Wash it very thoroughly *after* all the other items, rinse it in the hottest possible water and leave it to dry in the air. *Don't dry it up.* Then soak the washing-up brush or cloth in bleach for a while. If it is a pan of food, you can be doubly careful by boiling water in it with the lid on for half an hour, then washing it.

Drying-up cloths can transfer bacteria from one surface to another. So virtue and laziness always go hand in hand: the most hygienic method is to rinse everything in hot water and let it dry in the air, without drying it up.

Wooden Boards and Bowls

Wash wood up immediately after use – it is easily damaged by soaking and if food is allowed to dry only a soak will remove it. If flour has been used rinse the board in *cold* water or the flour will cook on to the surface. Salad bowls don't even need washing; simply wipe the inside out with kitchen paper. That way the dressing oils the wood.

Aluminium Pans

Don't fill a very hot pan with cold water – the base of aluminium is likely to distort.

Aluminium will dissolve in acid. This means traces of aluminium end up in any acid food you cook in them (see Food), but if you want to clean a blackened pan boil up a few rhubarb leaves, then let the acid liquid stand in the pan until the metal gleams. Then wash it very well, for rhubarb leaves are poisonous. If you don't have a vegetable garden substitute 1 teaspoon of cream of tartar for each ½ l (1 pt) water. For really shiny pans use a soap-filled metal pad.

Burnt Pans

There is no need to chuck out burnt saucepans or throw away hours of your life scouring them. All you need is salt, and patience.

Put in enough water to cover the burnt area, add a handful or so of salt (the amount really depends on the size of the problem) and boil it up for a while. Then leave it overnight. If it isn't soft enough to scrape off with the plastic end of a washing-up brush add more salt and boil it up again. With severely burnt pans you may need to repeat the whole process on an underlayer which the salt couldn't reach.

When deposits are burnt on to the outside of a pan you can boil them up in a larger pan, but clean small areas with neat salt on a damp cloth.

Enamel Pans

Enamel will crack with sudden changes of temperature and will also stain if strongly coloured food is left in it.

To remove – or reduce – such stains fill the pan with water and boil it up with a handful of washing soda.

Frying Pans

A heavy iron frying pan should be 'seasoned' when you first have it, then food will be less likely to stick to it. To do this you cover the bottom with salt and rub it in to the metal, then heat it thoroughly. Repeat this twice, then wipe it clean without washing it.

Cleaning frying pans is a waste of time. Food is far less likely to stick if you avoid scouring them. So simply pour the surplus fat into some newspaper or into a container for the birds (it may block the drain if you tip it down the sink), then brush out all the debris and remaining fat under a hot tap immediately after use, without resorting to soap.

★ Milk is less likely to stick if you rinse the pan with water first. Then fill it with hot water the moment you empty it, to make it easy to clean. Do the same for any pan which has had egg in it.

Non-stick Pans

To scour non-stick pans is to remove the surface and throw away your money. Filling them with hot water immediately after use stops the food sticking and removes the need for rough treatment. Then just wash them with soap and water. Unless the manufacturer advises otherwise cover any stain with water and add two tablespoons bicarbonate of soda and 125 ml (¼ pt) vinegar for each 250 ml (½ pt) water. Boil this up for 15 minutes and the stain should have vanished or be ready to wipe off. If it hasn't, try again. Rinse the pan well, and rub in a drop of cooking oil.

Smells Which Won't Go

Occasionally a pan seems to hold the smell of food most unpleasantly. To clear this fill the pan with water, add a good dash of vinegar and boil it up. The smell will disappear.

Fill smelly plastic containers with water, add 2-3 teaspoonfuls bicarbonate of soda for every 500 ml (½ pt) water and leave this overnight. The smell should go completely. If it doesn't, repeat using more bicarbonate.

Woks

Woks can be washed in the normal way, but after drying them do as the Chinese do. Put a drop of oil in, heat it and rub it well all over the inside with a piece of paper. This prevents the surface rusting.

Washing-up Machines

Although all the following are kitchen or tableware, they cannot be put in a washing-up machine without damage or serious risk of damage:

- wood items other than wooden spoons
- good-quality glass and lead crystal
- very thick glass
- china with gilding
- bone-handled or old knives.

Addresses and suggestions for further reading are at the ends of chapters.

If any glass is repeatedly washed in washing-up machines it may develop cloudy patches. This is called etching and according to Lever Brothers there is no known cure.

Smelly Washing-up Machines

Washing-up machines should be run regularly on a hot wash, with detergent, *when empty* to prevent a smell developing that will get into the washing up in an aging machine. There are special products to remove the smell but you must also clean the machine out thoroughly, removing any debris caught in traps and filters.

Waste Bins and Baskets

In an ideal world, people would only put paper in wastepaper baskets, but families are seldom like that. Put an unwanted plastic carrier bag across the bottom of every bin and basket. Clean bins out according to what they are made of.

Wood Furniture

Wood furniture divides into three groups: oiled wood, modern varnished wood, and old furniture finished with wax or French polish.

Carved Wood

In Yorkshire they have the charming tradition of using a whole duck's wing, with its sweeping fan of feathers, to dust tricky surfaces. Less elegantly, you can use a decorator's dusting brush.

Oiled Wood

Tropical hardwoods, such as teak and afromosia, have a very high resin content and oiling is all they need, or like. You can buy oils sold as 'teak oil' or you can use boiled linseed oil, which is cheaper and smells just the same. Just put a little on a ball of cotton wool, wrap a rag around it and rub. You want a thin layer going right into the wood. If it is left on the surface it will interact with the air and form a hard sticky layer which is very nasty.

Varnished Wood

Modern varnished wood can be wiped with a damp cloth and have the occasional lick of polish if old age has dulled its shine. It needs no more than that. If stains start showing in the wood, the varnish has flaws which are allowing liquid to seep through. The only solution then is to remove the varnish. Most have no solvents and have to be sanded off, but check with the maker.

Polished Wood

Caring for polished wood is a lot easier than most people imagine. The main essential is never to let anything hot or wet stand on the surface, and never to write on it with a biro without several layers of padding.

Goodness knows what puritan mythology put the word out that wood had to be constantly polished and 'fed', but it simply isn't true.

It is impossible to feed wood. All polish does is make it look nice and stop moisture getting out. But enough is enough, and extra polish is as unnecessary as wearing two mackintoshes. Wood, which already has a polish, need only be polished twice a year. The rest of the time just rub it over with a clean duster. Or give it a quick sheen with the magic vinegar and paraffin cloth recommended for floors (page 162). If a cotton velveteen duster is used the surface is far less likely to develop an unwanted bloom, but you don't have to work as hard as the Victorian ethics of the first *Enquire Within* suggested.

> *The cleaning of furniture forms an important part of the domestic economy, not only in regard to neatness, but also in point of expense. The readiest mode indeed consists in good manual rubbing, or the essence of elbows, as it is whimsically termed . . .*
>
> Enquire Within, 1856

Since polish hardly ever needs to be used there is no need for 'time-saving' aerosols. In fact, there is every reason to avoid them. In *Supertips* I warned against their use, but the conservator of the National Trust puts it even more strongly. 'The surface can acquire a slight milky look. No remedy has yet been found. It is IM-POSSIBLE [her capitals] to remove this aesthetically objectionable film without first stripping and then resurfacing the object.'

There is another aspect. When we look at anything we really see the light reflected from it. No two surfaces absorb and reflect the light in quite the same way, and part of the beauty of old furniture is the special way in which old wax polish reflects the light. To varnish it, or to use a different type of polish, is to alter this subtle quality for the worse.

For good furniture Antiquewax is a perfectly good polish, or the recipe used at one of the top museums has the advantage of being more resistant to finger marks than most polishes. Take 2 parts beeswax, to 4 parts paraffin wax, and 4 parts carnuba. (A hardware shop should have beeswax; a pharmacy the other two.) Melt these in a basin over hot water (*not over a flame as they are inflammable.*) Stir them together and stir in about four times their combined volume of *real* turpentine to make a cream. Apply it *very* sparingly (a common fault is too much polish and too little elbow grease) and leave it to dry for several hours before polishing. Treat carved wood like shoes and use a brush to apply the polish and another to remove it. This stops the polish clinging in the dips.

Cleansing

If furniture has a bloom on it, like a grape, it means the atmosphere has left its mark. Wipe it over with a cloth wrung out in warm water and a very good dash of vinegar, drying as you go.

Reviving

Some furniture either cannot or should not be revived – notably old oak and very early furniture and anything with inlays. However, when plain old mahogany furniture, finished with shellac or French polish, has dirty patches where finger dirt has built up it can be vastly improved with reviver. This is a recipe used by restorers and little known to anyone outside the business. Take 2 parts pure turpentine, 2 parts methylated spirits, 2 parts malt vinegar and 1 part raw linseed oil. Put them all in a bottle and shake well as you use it, for it separates easily.

Put some on a ball of cotton wool and test it on a small area which won't be noticed. If the surface of the wood is French polish or shellac a shine will begin to show through. If you work right through the dirt and fail to reveal a shine the surface is wax. It is far safer to give wax to a professional to clean as inexperienced cleaning could cause dirt to enter the wood itself. A third possibility is that it will have no impact at all. If so, you probably have a case of oxidized linseed oil – and that is a suitable case for experts as it is incredibly tough.

On French polish do realize that all DIY treatments carry a risk, and that furniture of any real value is best left to experts. Work very carefully, doing a small area at a time, and never leave drops of the mixture to eat into the surface. Keep changing your cotton wool, or you will just shift the dirt from place to place. From time to time look at the whole object. No old furniture should look like new, keep the differences between the edges and the flats of the wood which speak of its use. It is far better to do too little than too much. The patina of years cannot be replaced, but you can always do more tomorrow.

Damaged French Polish

If French polish on a valueless piece of furniture is badly marked the best course may be to remove it. But it is important for a good piece to have its original finish.

French polish can be totally removed with methylated spirits. You need to work carefully, constantly taking fresh pieces of rag so you don't rub it into the grain.

The ability of meths to 'melt' French polish also means it can sometimes be used to blend out a scratch. This is delicate and tricky and should *not* be attempted on furniture you value. You slightly moisten a very small ball of cotton wool with methylated spirits, wrap a piece of clean cotton rag around it and rub it across the scratch extremely carefully so as to blend it into the rest of the polish. Work very smoothly across the surface; pressure will imprint the weave of the rag on the polish.

Water Marks on French Polish

Miracles seldom happen, but the ash and oil treatment for the white marks on French polish is as close as you are likely to get. On dark wood simply mix cigarette or cigar ash with a little vegetable oil and rub it firmly in until the mark vanishes. If the mark doesn't go it isn't French polish. There is no way you can remove stains from polyurethane coatings.

If the water mark is on French polish on a pale wood rub with an oily Brazil or metal polish wadding – but there is a risk with any proprietary product that the formula will be changed and damage a surface it isn't designed for.

> Some people claim that oil and salt is the mixture to use, but this may scratch the polish. Ash is easily obtained from any pub.

Marquetry

Marquetry is one of the most vulnerable forms of decoration. The thin sections of wood are stuck on to a much thicker base; so heat and moisture can produce different changes in the two and make layers lift off. Furniture with marquetry needs to be positioned very carefully, so it isn't near a fire or radiator. It should also be kept away from windows, as some of the colours may fade very quickly in bright light.

Avoid polishing marquetry, and never use reviver or any other oily substance on it. Instead, dust it with a very soft brush – a duster could catch a corner which had risen slightly.

Oak

If light oak gets very dirty scrub it using a teaspoonful of ammonia in 1 l (2 pts) of water. Wipe off the wet, leave it to dry totally, then sprinkle it with French chalk from hardware shops or **Liberon Waxes Ltd** – and dust off any excess.

Dark oak is usually very old and its original finish may well contribute to its value. Before allowing any would-be restorer to strip it down and resurface it, talk to the Victoria and Albert Museum conservators. Some restorers have very little knowledge about *when* they should renovate.

Pine

Pine is porous and soaks up stains like blotting paper. The only way to avoid this altogether is to seal the surface with polyurethane. But there is no pretending that the surface really suits the character of pine unless it is modern. It may be better to leave an old table bare and just scrub it and bleach off any stains with lemon juice.

A pure wax polish really looks best on pine furniture, of any age. But one has to expect every last drop of water to mark it. Once a polish is achieved it needs no more polishing than other wood (see above) and a wipe with a cloth moistened with white spirit removes water marks from the wax as well as anything.

Positioning Furniture

The two enemies of wood are sunlight and dryness. Central heating is a modern invention which antiques were not designed to withstand. Use humidifiers in every room or have plenty of plants around (though *not* on the antiques) so their earth gives off moisture or tuck saucers of water out of sight in odd places.

Sunlight will bleach dark wood. If a piece is near sunlight do make sure that nothing ever stands on it for very long or you will be left with a dark mark where that section of wood wasn't bleached by the sun. Pages 217-218 have sources of help and advice on caring for precious things, plus companies which sell the products you need.

Addresses and suggestions for further reading are at the ends of chapters.

EMPLOYING HELP

If you are in a hurry to find help of any kind, the agencies listed on page 214 can help you find the sort of person you want quickly. Some specialize in temporary help in emergencies. Some cover straight domestic work, others cover nursing and there are some who can provide people for jobs like animal or house sitting, or accompanying children to stations. Agency charges and terms vary considerably and one way to by-pass an agency fee on a nanny is to get one through a training college (see page 214) – most of which make no charge. The snag is that the nanny may only be available at the end of the summer term.

The classic route to help in the home is an advertisement in the magazine *The Lady*. It appears weekly on Thursdays and an advertisement must be handed in 8 days in advance. Through it you can find anyone from a cleaner to a butler trained in martial arts. Another route is via an agency. I have given some on page 214 but check agency terms before using one. They can charge high fees.

If you are not in a hurry, you may find it cheapest to use local advertisements. Make your advertisement reasonably precise. It is far better to have 2 applicants who are right for the job than 10 who aren't, so give the key details. Vague wording like 'Help needed with two lovely children in Hampshire' could get you Mary Poppins or Dracula. And, having asked for 2 references, follow them up – there is no guarantee the references aren't invented.

> There is not anything to be gained in economy by having very young and inexperienced servants at low wages; they break, waste, and destroy more than an equivalent for higher wages . . .
>
> *Enquire Within*, 1856

Agreeing Job Details

Before you take anyone on, come to a firm agreement about pay, hours, conditions, and give them a written list of exactly what you expect them to do. If you don't see eye to eye, drop them then and there. Taking on someone who has any doubts about their role, or whom you have any doubts about, creates more problems than it solves. Having agreed the work before they start, arrange that you will discuss it again at the end of the first week. That way you both have a forum for change.

★ If someone will be looking after an elderly person – who may have certain things they do and do not like to be helped with – list what those things are in some detail. This cuts down the friction which easily happens with the elderly.

The following information provides broad guidelines, but it is not hard and fast.

Au Pair and Au Pair Plus

An au pair is 17 years old or more, is usually from abroad, and lives as part of a family. She is *not* a domestic servant, but she should be prepared to share the household jobs with her hostess, and help look after the children, for about 5 hours a day. The pay and conditions are set by the Department of Employment, and adjusted with the cost of living, so they need to be checked with the DoE. But, as I write, an au pair should have her own room and full board, and she must have 5 consecutive hours' free time a day, 3-4 free evenings, and 1 free day. As an au pair plus a girl is paid slightly more and works about 6 hours a day for 6 days a week. Au pairs may not be capable of coping with children alone.

Mother's Help

Mother's helps and nannies have traditionally lived in, but more and more live out and fit into the schedule of a working mother.

A mother's help can cope with the children alone, if necessary, and does light housework. However, she is not qualified to care for a very young baby. She normally works 5 full days, plus some baby-sitting, and has 2 free days a week.

Nanny, Nursery Teacher or Governess

A nanny should be qualified or experienced and able to take total charge of children. She does everything a mother would do when on duty, but does no housework except that involved in caring for the children. A nursery teacher or governess cares for children from the age of 2 upwards and whereas, in theory, a nanny is mainly concerned with the children's physical needs, this role involves more emphasis on manners and mental stimulation. She normally has 1-2 free days a week.

Housekeeper, Domestic or Maid

A maid or domestic may do all the household cleaning, cooking, washing and ironing, with 1-2 free days a week. A housekeeper is expected to do those jobs, or supervise others in doing them, and to run the household, with 1 or 2 free days a week. None of these is expected to look after children as well.

Butler

Butlers can be obtained to cover a lunch or a dinner as well as for full-time work. You are unlikely to find one for less than a five-figure salary, full-time. Butlers do no heavy cleaning or child care but they do an enormous range of other jobs, from serving food to looking after their master's clothes. Hours tend to be flexible and open to negotiation but they usually have 1½ days off a week.

CLOTHING CARE

Removing every speck of dust and fluff from clothing makes an enormous difference. If a clothes brush fails, wrap sticking plaster or sellotape round your hand several times – sticky side out – and run this over the garment. It will often pick up fine hairs brushes leave behind. Running wetted hands over a garment can also be effective.

★ If a garment doesn't have a button where you need it or one falls off at the last minute, a small piece of double-sided sticky tape does duty. But don't use it on delicate fabrics, velvet or corduroy.

Feathers

If large feathers need to be cleaned they should be wiped gently with a clean soft brush dipped in white spirit, and allowed to dry in the air. Small feathers, such as you find in a feather boa, can be dipped into pure soap and water and well rinsed, then fluffed up gently with a hair drier.

Fur Care

This is not the place to go into the rights and wrongs of wearing fur. There are furs in lots of cupboards whose original four-legged owners are long past being able to wear them. And, in my view, it is adding insult to injury for those coats not even to be decently cared for.

Wet is the big enemy of fur – especially modern fur, which is thinner skinned than the old kind. Once wet gets through to the leather backing it can stiffen and wrinkle it. A wet fur should be shaken dry as soon as possible and hung in an airy place *away from heat*. A doorway in a centrally heated house is ideal.

The less fur has to be cleaned the better. So, if possible wear a scarf at the neck to keep make-up off it. If you do get make-up on it very gently work Fullers Earth – for brown fur, or magnesium carbonate – for white (both from a chemist) through it with your fingers. Once it is worked in, leave it for not less than 30 minutes and then shake it out. (The old-fashioned method was to work in warm bran and this is still fine for a thick old fur. These methods can also be used for greasy stains. Any other spots and marks can often be removed by gently wiping – in the direction of the fur – with a damp cloth. But it mustn't be wet.

Unless you wear it constantly a fur should only need professional cleaning every 2 to 3 years.

Fur coats can become sadly bare at the edges while the main part is still perfectly good. A good furrier can usually put this right quite inexpensively. Furriers often advertise in the glossy magazines. Get comparative prices: some companies quote three times as much as others and look at their workmanship. There could be a reason for a low price.

Putting furs into cold storage obviously keeps pests off but it is expensive. However, fur cannot be kept in plastic or it gradually dries out, changes colour and splits. To protect it against moths make a cotton bag rather longer and wider than the garment. Put the closed end of the bag at the bottom and bind the open end *tightly* round the neck of a coat hanger. Moths won't go through cotton to get to the fur. The snag is that woolly bears will (see page 208). So you may have to choose between the damage done by keeping fur in plastic and the damage these creatures will do. Keep the coat in a busy cupboard – insects prefer quiet – and inspect the coat each month. Look for any little twist in the fur – it means a moth has made a nest for its young who will soon come out to dine.

Glove Care

In gloveless days the niceties of glove buying tend to be forgotten. A perfectly fitting kid glove should feel too tight when you put it on, and you should need to ease each finger down over yours by gently stroking it with finger and thumb from tip to base.

You are less likely to tear the seams of new gloves if you take my grandmother's tip and put them in a warm place before wearing.

You can get some of the dirt off pale gloves by rubbing them with a pale India rubber, and wearing the gloves and rubbing your hands through warm flour will also remove some of the dirt. Dark suede which has flattened can also be restored with one of the rubbers made for rubbing suede – but go very lightly.

I never feel a washed glove looks quite as good as it should, but you can buy glove shampoos for certain brands of gloves. Leave doeskin gloves unrinsed, as the soap helps to keep them supple and press all gloves dry between towels and dry away from heat.

The 1856 edition had the following instructions for washing kid gloves, and if you have no glove shampoo they are as good as any.

> *Have ready a little new milk in one saucer, and a piece of brows soap in another, and a clean cloth or towel folded three or four times. On the cloth, spread out the glove smooth and neat. Take a piece of flannel, dip it in the milk, then rub off a good quantity of the soap to the wetted flannel and commence to rub the glove downwards towards the left hand. Continue this process until the glove, if white, looks a dingy yellow, though clean; if coloured, till it looks dark and spoiled. Lay it to dry; and old gloves will soon look nearly new. They will be soft, glossy, smooth, shapy and elastic.*

You can substitute any pure soap for 'brows soap', whatever it was and, whatever the method, gloves should be wriggled at regular intervals as they dry, or they will not dry soft at all.

Hats

Grease on the fabric band inside a hat comes off easily with a drop of hair shampoo on a soft brush. Wipe the shampoo off with a damp cloth afterwards. Or use a spray-on dry-cleaner – but keep it off the parts that show. Greasy leather bands can be cleaned with saddle soap – it won't get the grease out but it will let you wash off any surface grime.

Felt and velour hats need to be brushed, with the nap, with a soft brush, and if they get out of shape hold them in some steam, press them to shape again and let them cool, supported by crumpled paper if necessary.

Pale straw hats can usually be brushed clean. But a real straw hat, such as a boater, can be scrubbed with a little lemon juice and left in the sun if it becomes dingy.

Leather Garments

The labels on leather can be deceptive. Leather garments sometimes say they are 'washable' when they are merely spongeable. However, some suede is genuinely washable – if you follow the maker's instructions perfectly.

Addresses and suggestions for further reading are at the ends of chapters.

Some shiny leather responds well to saddle soap or being wiped with milk – do a test patch where it won't show.

Any leather with a shine usually resists stains extremely well – but wipe off grease or oil fast as it could be absorbed and mark it. Other marks usually come off with a lightly damped cloth. The real danger is from scratches, so avoid excited pets.

Suede or leather with a dull sheen will be very vulnerable to stains unless you treat it with a spray-on protection and leather protector, but it is best to ask the makers of the garment whether such a spray can safely be used on their particular leather.

If suede starts to become flat rub it with another piece of suede of the same colour. The special rubbers sold for cleaning suede are also useful but use them gently and be very chary of rubbing suede with metal suede brushes. They tend to rough up the surface and produce what the trade calls 'feathering', i.e. loose floppy bits which make the suede look decidedly tatty.

Leather needs expert dry-cleaning and even then it changes colour. So any set must be cleaned together – whether all the parts need cleaning or not.

Baggy Leather

Baggy leather isn't as easily cured as baggy cloth. So hitch up skirts and trouser knees and avoid over-bagging them. However, a *little* steam can somewhat reduce the bagginess of leather – but do check with the maker before you try it as it could be very harmful to certain leathers.

Don't hold leather close to a strong jet of steam from a kettle spout; just let it be in the clouds of steam above. Then lie the garment flat and smooth it gently to shape with your hands. Some experts go so far as to iron the leather but amateurs could wreak havoc on the skins, so I don't recommend it.

★ Some people suggest putting leather in the freezer to remove bags. *Don't*. Certain finishes will be permanently destroyed by very low temperatures.

Handbags

Handbags need to be treated like leather garments, except that you can occasionally give them a very sparing shine with a colourless shoe polish. But do rub it off very well, or it will transfer grease to your clothes.

It really isn't practical to dye large leather items, but handbags and shoes are perfectly possible. There are two kinds of dye – the kind which sinks in and the kind which you paint on to the surface. Of the two, the first looks far better and stands up to bending and rubbing, so it can be used on soft leather handbags as well as on shoes. Alas, the good range of colours is in the paint kind. But you will get the best result if you paint the dye on, in several thin layers, with a soft artist's brush.

★ Acetone or white spirit will condition shoes ready for most dyes.

Storing Garments

If garments are going to be put away for any length of time – even from spring to autumn – clean them first.

Everyone sweats more than they think and perspiration left in a fabric will create permanent stains unless it is removed while still reasonably fresh.

This even applies to a wedding dress which has been worn only once. After all wedding dresses tend to be worn at long intervals – to say the least of it. After it has been cleaned store it in a large box lined with acid free tissue paper (storing fabric in plastic bags for any length of time will cause white to yellow). Keep it in a cool dry atmosphere.

If you are storing any other clothes for more than a few weeks it is also wise to prepare for the worst. You may think you haven't got moths or woolly bears but you can't be sure they won't fly in through the next open window. So if anything is being stored it should be protected against them – see Pests.

★ It is thrifty to mark the back of any pair of tights before putting them on; then all the snags made by the backs of the heels stay on one side and the other side remains respectable.

★ Putting washed tights or stockings in a bag in the fridge and freezing them before removing and drying, does seem to give them more strength to stand up to the snags of life.

★ If a ladder begins to run the best way to stop it is with nail varnish. The second best is with the soft side of a cake of soap.

★ When I was in my teens tights hadn't been invented and the popular joke was that a girl always carried an aspirin and could use it for one of three things – to cure a headache, to hold between the knees (as an infallible contraceptive) or to put in suspenders when the 'button' went. It still works for suspenders and headaches, and most restaurants keep some.

★ If a zip becomes stiff, and isn't clogged with its two great enemies – salt and loose threads – it probably needs lubrication. Run a 2B lead pencil up and down the teeth several times, then raise and lower it, until it runs easily. Better still, use the powdered graphite sold for locks – being careful not to mark pale fabrics.

SHOES

Buying Children's Shoes

Children's shoes can be one of a parent's worst headaches. Children want to look good from a remarkably early age and it can be almost impossible to find shoes which are good for the feet and fashionable. There may be a straight choice: either the child suffers from less stylish shoes for a few years or from bad feet for many years. And the choice is the parent's, not the child's – for the parent is paying. I know they kick up a dreadful fuss, but it is not a fashion decision – it is a medical decision.

While a child's feet are growing the bones are still soft and can be damaged by the wrong shoes, even if they don't hurt. A child's feet must be carefully measured in both length and width before shoes are bought. (Clarks, Start-rite and K Shoes all make children's shoes sized in both directions). On average, children's feet grow a whole size every 6 to 12 months, so new shoes need to be 16 mm ($^2/_3$ in) too long to allow for growth. Because they need this extra room, children will slip forward in their shoes unless there is support over the instep.

The backs of the shoes should fit lightly but firmly, without cutting into the ankle bones, and the right toe room is as important as the right length. Shoes which press down on the toes or draw them together will, in time, cause corns and distortion. The line down the inner side of the foot needs to be almost straight and the leather of the toe shouldn't touch the child's toes underneath. High heels are also damaging. They throw the weight on to the ball of the foot and can permanently damage a child's feet. Tight stockings can be as harmful as tight shoes. Avoid stretch socks if possible or else buy stretch socks a size larger than the makers specify. On non-stretch socks a foot which will comfortably go right round the knuckles of someone's clenched fist should fit their feet.

The barefoot children of the Victorian poor have made people link bare feet with poverty. But, in fact, a child who goes barefoot wherever it is safe and warm enough will grow up with healthier feet than one who is always shod. After all, feet were not designed to wear shoes. On uncarpeted floors bare feet are much safer than socks, which could slip on polish.

The **Children's Foot Health Register** is a register of the shops throughout Britain which have staff trained to fit children's shoes, offer children's shoes in four widths and in both half and whole sizes. The list is free with an sae to the **British Retail Consortium** (page 218).

Buying Adult Shoes

The **Society of Chiropodists** (page 640) has useful leaflets on the foot-care aspects of buying shoes, plus the addresses of chiropodists – if the advice comes too late. If, however, you have problem feet, there are a number of organizations which can help you. The **British Footwear Manufacturers' Association** (page 218) has an inexpensive leaflet on obtaining footwear for special needs. And the **Disabled Living Foundation** (page 591) gives advice and has the addresses of those supplying unusual sizes as special shoes for certain disabilities. Or **Solemates** (page 218) runs an unusual service for people who have two feet of different sizes, or only one foot – but *do* send a sae.

Complaints about footwear should first go to the shop, then the local Trading Standards Officer, and if that fails to the **British Retail Consortium** (see page 218). But they can only deal with complaints about members of their federation.

Shoe Care

Aniline Leather Shoes

If a shoe isn't suede but isn't very shiny ask whether it is aniline leather. This easily absorbs dirt. So ask the shop whether the shoes can be sprayed with a leather protector to keep out dirt and wet. Even so, treat them carefully. If aniline leather does get muddy, wipe it with a cloth barely damped with cold water. Allow the leather to dry and clean it with a recommended cream.

Fabric Shoes

Shoes made of fabric and rubber are sometimes so well bonded together that they will stand up to a spin in the washing machine – but they might fall apart.

If fabric shoes get muddy, let the mud dry before trying to remove it. Then brush it off with a clothes brush. There are shampoos designed for fabric shoes but they sometimes lighten the colour. So it's best to test their effect on the tongue, if the shoe has one. White canvas shoes can be cleaned with whitener. For dyeing fabric shoes check with Dylon, page 188.

Leather Shoes

Leather shoes should be polished regularly and kept with shoe trees in, so folds don't form too deeply.

If mud gets on to leather shoes let it dry, then brush it off carefully with a stiff brush and gently sponge off any that remains using as little water as possible. Let them dry completely before polishing with a matching polish designed for the purpose. The easy way to make sure you don't apply too much polish is to use one soft brush for both putting it on and taking it off.

Plastic, Patent and Wet-look Shoes

Patent, plastic and other wet-look shoes should be sponged clean and wiped dry. To give patent a good shine rub it with a little vaseline, or milk or even face cream. Genuine patent leather easily creases and may crack when worn if it is not properly stored. Patent shoes need shoe trees (or a wedge of paper in the toe and a springy stick to keep the shape) and vaseline over the surface, to keep them flexible.

Suede and Nubuck Shoes

Spray suede and nubuck shoes with a protective spray when brand new. It makes these leathers look good for very much longer. Dirt is best brushed off with a stiff *bristle* brush – those metal brushes sold for suede risk making the nap too rough and causing the long straggly bits. But if suede gets shiny it is sometimes possible to remove the shine by gently using a metal brush or a little fine sandpaper *very* carefully.

> Leather shoes which pinch can be stretched by applying a branded leather stretcher to the inside. It also helps to rub the tight place with the end of a broom handle on the inside when the leather is warm.

EQUIPPING A HOME

Auctions

Anyone furnishing a home with limited funds should consider buying at auctions. They offer great bargains and great fun. It's a myth that if you so much as scratch your nose the auctioneer will think you have put in a bid for thousands. The truth is that you may have trouble catching the auctioneer's eye if you aren't a face they are used to.

The catalogue of any good auction house will have a page giving all the rules and conditions, and it is advisable to read this before you buy or sell through them.

In some salerooms prices fluctuate with the season, dropping in January and in mid-summer. They may also vary with what is being sold where. Very large pieces of furniture sell badly in cities, but better in the country, for example. Despite the eagle eyes of dealers, there are good things to be had – not so much antiques as comfortable chairs that someone else was tired of, or perfectly good curtains that didn't fit new windows, good linen sold after a death and so on. However: the law is far less strict about auctions than about other types of sale (see under Law). For this reason they can be a very bad source of electrical goods.

Buying at Auctions

Every auction has a viewing day when you can wander round at leisure, poke and prod the goods judiciously, check that there really is pine under the ghastly paint and look for stains on the beds. The catalogue lets you see how the object has been described and what its lot number is. A 'lot' can be a single object, a set of objects which go together or a random collection of junk.

Porters are great sources of help and information and will say what they think a lot will go for. A porter will also bid for you if you ask him to, but you must tell him the maximum you are prepared to bid, and ask him not to bid above that sum. Allow for the fact that if he gets the item you will be expected to tip him suitably, and you will pay a 'buyer's premium' on top of the bid price, of about 10 per cent. This applies whether you bid or a porter bids.

If you want to bid yourself, you can ask what time the lot is likely to come up. Get there earlier in case the sale goes faster than they thought. To bid, simply make a clear movement with your hand or catalogue so the auctioneer can see it. He will look at you as he accepts your bid, then turn to look for a higher bidder. You can bid again whenever you want.

If you find you have accidentally bid for something you didn't intend to, tell the auctioneer *at once* – then they can usually put the item back into the sale. If you have bought something you will be asked for your name and address and often a deposit while the auction continues. At the end of the sale you pay for the item. You then arrange to remove it within a reasonable time. If it's a house sale this is usually within 24 hours.

Selling by Auction

If you want to sell anything in an auction, ring a sale room that sells similar items and ask if they might be able to sell yours. If there are a lot of items the auctioneer may visit and decide. The auctioneer will usually expect you to get the goods to the auction, but some companies will arrange free collection; others collect and charge for it. The goods are then likely to be put into a sale within 2 to 3 weeks. You can choose whether you give the auctioneer a 'reserve price' below which the goods may not be sold, or whether they simply go to the highest bidder, however low the best bid. The auctioneer takes a percentage of the selling price. It can be as much as 17 per cent, and is unlikely to be below 10 per cent. Usually, the less valuable items attract the higher percentage.

There are no rules as to what happens if an item is unsold, but the policy of some auction houses is that if there was no reserve or a reserve recommended by the auctioneer there is no charge and the owner can take them away or put them in the next auction. But if the seller puts a reserve on which is higher than the house recommends and the goods aren't sold there is usually what they call a 'buying-in fee'. This fee should be discussed when you set the reserve on your goods.

★ It is illegal to sell secondhand furniture which uses the old, highly inflammable, foam rubber which was put into furniture before 1989.

Finding an auction

Most auction houses publish an auction calendar but the main source of information is the *Antiques Trade Gazette*. *Antique Collector* also gives regular information on the better auctions and house sales and the *Daily Telegraph* lists auctions in its Monday editions; *The Times* lists them on Tuesdays, and the *Independent* may have them on Fridays. Auctions should also be listed in your local papers.

Complaining about Goods

If something you have bought isn't good enough (see under Law) your first step is to complain to the head of the company which sold you the item, The Office of Fair Trading (see below) suggests you stop using the goods and complain immediately.

- If you write keep a copy of the letter.
- Get proof of posting.
- Do not send receipts or guarantees, only photocopies.
- If you ring keep a note of the name of the person you speak to.
- Have your facts clear before you ring.
- Note what you say and what they say.
- Note the date and time of your call.

The shop ought to collect the faulty goods but you may do better to take them back and see the manager. If they really are faulty he or she should refund your money or replace them. If this doesn't happen, see Law.

Help and Information on Complaints

Reading the pages on consumer law will give you a good idea of what your entitlements are. The useful leaflet 'A Trader's Guide' from the **Department of Trade** (page 694), telling traders just how they must treat customers who have a complaint, is a good-eye opener for customers too. On top of that, the **Office of Fair Trading (OFT)** (page 692) has clear, readable leaflets on every aspect of consumer rights and special versions for Scotland and Northern Ireland. However, the OFT cannot deal with complaints.

A complaint always leads to one of the three Cs – compensation, compromise, or a claim in the courts. If you want to avoid the courts then one possible route to compensation may be to get the company's trade association to insist that it sticks to a professional code of practice. The OFT has leaflets on these which the local Citizens' Advice Bureau should have – and is itself another source of advice as are Law Centres.

If you think the law has been broken the Trading Standards Officer may be able to take up the case. Infuriatingly, the section of a local council which houses this useful person has no unified name across the country. If you tell the council switchboard the kind of help you are looking for, you should be given the right people. Or the OFT has a list.

If a trader has broken the criminal law on trading, the officials may take the matter up directly. If it is a breach of civil law they can advise you on your rights, and perhaps draft letters or put you in touch with relevant trade associations. They may even act as middle men and help you and a trader to agree a solution. However, if you buy something from a company in a different borough you must contact the seller's local Trading Standards Officer, not your own. The exception is when the work was done in the buyer's area – as with installing double glazing.

The **Consumers' Association** has a Personal Service (page 496) to which you can subscribe separately from the *Which* magazine. The association will advise subscribers on their rights, help them take action, and take up complaints with retailers and manufacturers if necessary. It will also help with taking a case through the county court.

Disposing of What You Don't Need

Under a public health act local authorities are obliged to remove 'household refuse' from your home. But they generally interpret this to mean the daily rubbish. If objects are too big to go in a dustbin, the refuse department will normally collect them – but at a price. Ask for an estimate (some charge nothing for a single item) or take them to the council tip yourself; dumping them is usually free. And **Friends of the Earth** (see page 692) can tell you about guides to disposing of many items so you help rather than harm the environment. If you need to dispose of rubble and wood, skips can be hired through companies in the Yellow Pages. The company then removes the rubbish with the skip. But a local refurbishing scheme may need furniture. Your local **Council of Voluntary Service** should put you in touch, or send a sae to **Community Furniture Network** (page 214).

Disposing of Throw-Aways via Charities
A directory called 'Waste Not' can be bought from the **Charities Aid Foundation** (page 214). It tells you the throw-aways collected by most major charities – from postage stamps to furniture – and where you should take or send them. It also gives addresses of organizations which can tell you how to recycle anything from cans to sump oil. The directory isn't expensive and its

price helps charity, your local library should have it – or get it if you ask.

Car Boot Sales
Car boot sales are advertised in the local papers and usually anyone who has something to sell can take it along in his or her car, pay the entrance and parking fee and sell. There are rumours that the law on this may be tightened up. So ring the organizer's number when you see a sale advertised and see what the rules are.

Recyclable Waste
Councils are increasingly providing skips for such items as bottles, paper or cans which can be recycled. Any efficient council should be able to help the environment this way and save money on the council tax, so it pays to press your council to do this. Friends of the Earth have information on the facilities in every area.

Doorstep Selling

If someone arrives at your home, or rings suggesting he or she should visit, the key question is 'what do you get from letting people come in and talk which you wouldn't get any other way?' The answer is usually *nothing* – if so, don't let them in. It is all too easy for people to pose as members of legitimate companies and enter your home under false pretences. So the rules for protecting yourself are these.

● Before letting people in check that they have documents which show they do represent a legitimate company.
● Be suspicious if they talk about benefits for your children – they are just playing on your love to make cash for themselves.
● Don't believe those who say you have been chosen for a prize. If it involves you paying a penny, it's just a con.
● Never let anyone 'advise you on security'. The police will do this for free and *they* aren't casing your home.
● Don't believe any sob stories, or any claims to special expertise.
● If you haven't already looked at, *and priced,* similar items in the open market, don't buy. Ask the seller to go away and say you will ring him.
● If anyone wants payment in advance, don't buy.
● Don't trust offers of special terms or discounts unless they are made in writing – and don't believe those who say they will send them in writing.
● Wait until you are absolutely sure of the identity of the company and the salesperson before signing anything.
● Check that the product carries a guarantee.

Remember home selling both in person and on the telephone is so successful because we are all used to being polite to people in our own homes. So it is far easier for sales people to talk us into something we don't want than it would be if we were in a shop. Sales teams are trained to play on this fact. However, **The Direct Selling Association** (page 215) sets standards of conduct for those who sell in this way and deals with complaints.

Addresses and suggestions for further reading are at the ends of chapters.

And, by law, you may change your mind about any purchase you agree to away from the seller's premises. But you only have a few days in which to cancel. So check your rights *quickly* with your trading standards officer.

Equipping a Kitchen

Gadgets are fun, but if you want to cook well – with reasonable speed and efficiency – it is essential to have the right tools, and that starts with a good knife and the most versatile pan you can find. Below I cover the basics without which it is hard to cook well unless you are one of those people who can cook good food on an open fire with a few sticks and a knife. And if you care about cooking, or just want things easy, check out the shops and mail-order lists (page 217) which supply chefs. High-tech materials are now solving a whole range of cooking problems.

General Equipment

Balloon whisk: a loop whisk (balloon whisk) is the secret of smooth sauces and gravies (see Food). A medium size in stainless steel is most versatile. If you don't have a blender or your gadgets go wrong this whisk will also stand in for beating eggs, and making cakes or mayonnaise.

Chopping block: hygiene experts say wood, being porous, allows bacteria from contaminated food – such as raw chicken – to be passed to cooked food – such as ham. So, instead of wood, they recommend polyurethane or plastic-laminated blocks. To me there is something comforting about the sound and feel of knife on wood. If you feel the same and can run to two boards, I suggest a polyurethane one for raw meat and a good wooden block for everything else. Avoid chopping boards with seams. Once wet the wood will swell, stretching the grooves, and that loosens the joints so they fall apart.

Colander: choose one with holes which rice won't dive through, and large enough to sit over a saucepan and double as a steamer. Avoid plastic.

Electric kettle: jug-shaped kettles use the least energy and cordless ones with a soft rubber grip handle which separate automatically from the base are safest.

Grater: the classic is 4-sided stainless steel.

Jug: an accurately marked pint-sized measuring jug. Pyrex are the most useful as you can also stand them in boiling water to heat, or cook in them in a microwave.

Kitchen scissors: the best can be bought with left-handed grips as well as right ones. Wilkinsons make a very simple sharpener for theirs – a boon as kitchen scissors blunt easily.

Knives: a good knife – which will last almost a lifetime – costs less than a tank of petrol and makes cooking a great deal faster and more efficient. But a blunt knife or a poor blade can double the time for any job. Nowadays you no longer need to buy expensive chef's knifes. The knife I have from the moderately priced 'Professional' range of Kitchen Devils is better than its Sabatier equivalent. Whatever the brand, look for a firm blade with no sideways bend to it – which is really sharp and can be sharpened. It should feel comfortably heavy and well balanced in your hand. The minimum number is two: a small sharp one for dealing with fruit and small vegetables, a larger one for meat and larger vegetables. But the more sophisticated your cooking is, the more knives you need.

★ Have a small stainless knife for fruit. An ordinary steel knife can react with the acid in fruit and give it a sharply metallic flavour – which is why old cookery books say fruit must be cut with a silver knife.

Lemon zester: takes strips of zest off in seconds for cooking or garnishing (a nice optional extra).

Palette knife: if you are icing cakes with smooth icing this is essential and there is a world of difference between using a cheap stiff one and using an expensive flexible one.

A knife is only as good as the sharpness of its blade. So, unless your knives are self-sharpening, a steel is essential. Using one is very easy if you use the method which has been in my family for generations. It isn't conventional, but it works, and you won't cut yourself.

Hold the knife and the steel so they form an X almost parallel to the floor, with the blade on top with its hilt close to the steel. The blade shouldn't lie flat against the steel but be at a *very slight* angle to it. (If you think about the shape of the edge that you want to put on the blade the correct angle will be obvious.) Now, hold your left hand still and move your right to the right – and very *slightly* away from you. Keep the blade and steel lightly but firmly in contact as the length of the blade slides up the steel. Repeat this with the blade under the steel.

The blade will need to caress the steel 5 or 6 times but don't over-sharpen – once the edge is good, stop. It takes a little practise but even doing it slowly and hesitantly will improve the edge, provided you have the angle of the blade right.

Potato peeler: the kind which twirls on its handle removes the thinnest layer, and leaves the most goodness, as the minerals and vitamins are concentrated under the surface of many vegetables.

Spatulas: a wooden one is invaluable for scrambled eggs and sautéeing, a plastic one for scraping out bowls fast. Don't get rubber: it softens in contact with garlic.

Water purifying jug: is needed if you live in an area in which the water tastes of chemicals. But the first essential is surely to be able to have a decent cup of tea or coffee, and this is impossible with chemical flavoured water. You don't need an elaborate or expensive version: the very simple Crystal jug does the trick. But the filter *must* be changed after the correct period or bacteria could build up, making the water less healthy than it should be.

Pans

The pans you need are decided by the kind of food you cook. So, before buying, think how you would like to cook – then buy what suits you. Below are some points to think about. They aren't the last word but they may give you something to disagree with.

It is easy to get trapped into the 'three bears' concept of saucepans. But though a small, a medium and a large pan may sound sensible it often isn't. Big ones give you a choice of how much food you will cook; small ones limit you. The large base also makes better use of the heat from your burner, and saves fuel. The basic minimum is probably one small one which pours well – for sauces, scrambled egg, and heating milk – say 750 ml (1½ pt) – plus two or three large ones for vegetables. It has not been proved that aluminium has ill effects on the brain but, as long as the slightest question mark hangs over this, I cannot advise anyone to buy aluminium. Lightweight enamel is often cheap and practical but it chips easily. Glass pans cook well, are easier to keep clean than stainless steel and let you see at a glance if the water is getting low. However, stainless steel cooks more evenly, and will respond faster when you raise or lower the heat. But, whatever the material of the pans, if you ever cook pasta, buy one *really* big pan. Pasta cooks best in lots of water and you can always use a big pan for small quantities. But you can't do the reverse, so it pays to go for generous sizes.

On a budget that stretched to luxuries I would also have a little electric pan called Le Saucier, which thermostatically controls the heat of the pan and stirs it at the same time – the nearest thing to having a spare pair of hands that I have yet found.

Pans v Casseroles

Before opting for too many conventional saucepans stop and think about the type of food you like cooking. If you are short of space or money it may be better to buy casseroles, in glass for thrift or in heavy enamelled cast iron for looks, instead of saucepans. It is perfectly reasonable to heat a portion of frozen peas in the bottom of a casserole, but you can't bring a saucepan to the table with a stew in it. Very wide, relatively shallow casseroles are more useful than tall narrow ones.

Frying Pans

The best frying pans have heavy bases. The cast iron ones don't look glamorous but are hard to beat. Don't even consider a frying pan with a base of less than 23 cm (9 in): bacon won't lie flat in it. Good frying pans get better and better with use, provided you only rinse them – see page 172.

A useful second frying pan is a proper copper omelette pan with a tin lining. It really is easier to make a good omelette in this. The ideal size is 24 cm (9½ in) across the top.

Deep Frying

More fires are started in homes because of chip pans than from any other single cause. Therefore the only type to have with safety is an electric one which keeps the heat below danger level and has a locking lid. When there is a good filter this also makes frying almost odourless. They aren't cheap – but neither is having your home gutted by fire.

Microwave Pans

A microwave doesn't need special pans. You can cook in pyrex or in any china or pottery which will take the heat of the food. In practice, not everyone has suitable containers of the right size with no metal on them. If you have to buy for a microwave useful items are classic white soufflé dishes – which are multi-purpose and can now be bought with glass lids for microwave cooking; and a pyrex ring mould – which heats food evenly and will also cook cakes.

Slow Cooker

Anyone who likes casserole cooking and has to be away from the home much should consider getting a slow cooker. They are exceedingly cheap to run and allow you to prepare a casserole at breakfast time and come home in the evening to find it ready. The largest size takes a good-sized chicken.

Mixers and Food Processors

Food processors and mixers aren't totally interchangeable. For kneading bread, or mixing large quantities of Christmas pudding or terrine a big mixer, like a Kenwood, is almost essential. For chopping meat and other food very finely, liquidizing soups, or shredding, grating or slicing vegetables, food processors have the edge. Unless you will only be cooking for two, buy the biggest processor you can afford. The containers can't be filled with liquid, so to liquidize several servings of soup you must do batch after batch if you have a small one – which is tedious and time-wasting.

Choosing a Freezer

There are only two golden rules:

1 All freezers take more than you'd think from looking at them.
2 Once you start using one you will fill it however big it is. Choose the biggest you can afford, and fit in to the space available. Think carefully about where you put it. Freezers must have air space around them, and the cooler the air, the less the temperature changes when you open the door, and the lower the running cost.

For efficiency there is nothing to choose between upright and chest freezers, but an upright with drawers is by far the most convenient, as one hunk of food never blocks another. Whatever the type, make sure it has a 'fast freeze' control if you want to freeze food from fresh, or

---

Addresses and suggestions for further reading are at the ends of chapters.

you won't get good results. The value of automatic de-frosting is more dubious. It is pleasant to be spared the chore of scraping off ice and emptying a freezer. The snag is that the temperature is likely to alter at each defrost, which isn't good (see freezing under Food).

Buying a Microwave

All microwaves look small and cook more than you'd think, but there is one severe limitation: many have a turntable which ensures even cooking, but it does mean that the corners are dead space and you can cook rather less at a time than if the food was still. Therefore, unless you will only use it for one or two people, buy the biggest you can afford.

A few foods, such as bread or meringues, don't cook well by microwaves alone. So the most useful ovens are those which combine both microwave and convection. Convection cooks the food with hot air, at the same temperatures as any electric oven, and produces much the same results. So the combination ovens allow you to cook food quite normally but cut the cooking time by zapping it with the occasional burst of microwaves. Many companies now offer microwaves which have other forms of heat and, even, a grill. The great weakness of a microwave is that it doesn't brown. One solution is to buy a microwave incorporated into a conventional oven.

Microwaves will go on improving for some while yet. So it will pay to look at as many models as possible before buying. Whatever the extras, the basic points you need to check when buying are as follows:

- Does it meet government standards on heating food to the safe temperature?
- Wattage – see A Roof Over Your Head.
- The range of settings – 5 is ideal.
- What is the maximum number of minutes it can be set for? It is annoying to have only short periods on an oven which includes convection.
- What is the minimum time for which it can be set, and does it increase in convenient steps?
- Does it tell you when it stops? A tone which tells you is very useful, but hear it before you buy – some are ear-splitting.
- If it combines convection what temperature steps can it be set at?
- How easy is it to work? Some have such sophisticated controls that it is hard to remember the sequence you need.
- Do they have a helpline on which you can phone a domestic scientist if you are having problems?

This last point is important. Cooking with microwaves is easy, but anyone can take a few days to adjust and some instruction books are none too clear. So it is useful to have someone to call. Several microwave manufacturers have phone helplines, cookery demonstrations and a magazine. Some also have a video you can borrow. These are facilities it is worth asking about before you buy.

FURNISHINGS

Furniture and Fittings

If you are furnishing a home, carry with you small samples of the carpet and curtain material, paint or whatever else you have already chosen whenever you go shopping. You may find the very thing you think you need to complete the room just when you haven't got them with you to check the colour.

Before you buy anything check it carefully for size, comfort, wearability and any other features which matter – *never* assume the maker must have got it right.

If you have a dispute with a retailer and cannot resolve it you can go to the **British Shops and Stores Association** (page 214). It is a trade association for shops other than food shops and operates a code of practice for its members. It uses **Qualitas** (page 215) for adjudications related to furniture.

Qualitas was set up to maintain standards in furnishings and flooring. Its members are both manufacturers and retailers (including some mail-order companies) and they must keep its code of practice. Its adjudication is binding on its members but not on any member of the public, so you can still take the matter to court. It will also advise you on dealing with non-members.

If you are paying for anything you have an absolute right to make sure it is what you want and has been properly made – in fact it would be crazy not to. It isn't rude to check goods carefully – the shop buyers (if they know their job) do it to the makers, and you can do it to the shops. But it has to be done politely and without damaging the goods.

If you find any faults, change it for another sample or make – and check that one as carefully – *or* ask for a reduction. Shops are often glad to get rid of items which might otherwise linger until the sale, and you may get a bargain – provided the fault is one you can remedy. Remember shops bargain down the price with their suppliers, so there is no reason why you shouldn't do the same to them. I have obtained reductions in the snootiest shops – and they didn't even seem surprised. But, of course, if you do get a reduction you may not be able to change the goods if any other faults develop.

Beds

As we spend a third of our lives in bed, bed buying deserves a bit of thought. Try them out (shops expect this and there should be protectors to stop your feet dirtying the covers). Don't just lie neatly on your back – beds which feel perfectly comfortable like that may seem rock-like on your side. Try every position – within reason. And if you are buying a double bed see it isn't so soft that you roll together.

Alas, this isn't a guarantee against it forming a valley. One way round it is to buy the type of twin beds which clip and zip together to make a double. Identical beds are often made with different firmness of mattress. So you can have a firm mattress for him and a soft one for her – or vice versa – if you wish.

Somehow word has got around that it is a good idea for everyone to have a 'hard' bed, sometimes called an 'orthopaedic' bed. This is a misunderstanding. The bedding industry insists there is no such thing as an orthopaedic bed. It is just a misleading name for a hard bed, and hard beds *aren't* necessarily good for you. What is needed is a bed which, when lying on your side, will let the shoulders and hips sink in far enough for the other areas of the body to be well supported with the spine in a straightish line. Only then is strain avoided at every point. So what most spines need is not a hard bed but a supportive bed. This is not to say that a hard bed may not relieve pain from certain conditions, but we don't all walk with crutches just because they help those with broken legs. And you can *get* backache from sleeping on a bed which is too hard.

Bed Sizes
Small single 90 cm × 190 cm (3 ft × 6 ft 3 in)
Standard single 100 cm × 200 cm (3 ft 3 in × 6 ft 6 in)
Small Double 135 cm × 190 cm (4 ft 6 in × 6 ft 3 in)
Standard Double 150 cm × 200 cm (5 ft × 6 ft 6 in)
Queen 165 cm × 200 cm (5 ft 6 in × 6 ft 6 in)
King 180 cm × 200 cm (6 ft × 6 ft 6 in)
Super King 215 cm × 215 cm (7 ft × 7 ft)

Though the sizes are standard the names aren't: So buy by size not by name. You can have a bed made, for a price, to any size you wish.

Mattresses – Foam
The options for mattresses are foam or springs. Foam is non-allergenic; usually lighter than springs (useful if you need to move the bed much); doesn't usually need turning (useful for the elderly); and won't absorb general dampness in the way other mattresses will – good in weekend cottages, and caravans. The best foam mattresses have layers of different densities but it can be difficult to judge the quality of a foam mattress. The unpredictability can make springs a better buy.

Mattresses – Sprung
There are two aspects to the comfort of a mattress – the outer layers and the springs inside. For outer layers fleece wool and dacron, or white cotton felt, are expensive but good insulation while hair is expensive but greatly increases the comfort. Recycled fibres and coir fibre or thin foam are less good. Pocketed springs with separate coils, each in its own cover, stand up best to the stress of two sleepers in a bed and sag least but comfort will also depend on the number of springs and the thickness of their wire.

Children don't need expensive beds but they do need ones with mattresses which will support them properly – not old sagging ones. And it is dangerous to put them into bunk beds until they are old enough to be sensible – that is *at least* 5 years old.

Alternatives to a Normal Bed
BEDS FOR THE POOR – Beech-tree leaves are recommended for beds for filling the beds of poor persons. They should be gathered on a dry day in the autumn and perfectly dried. It is said they smell grateful, and will not harbour vermin. They are also very springy.
Enquire Within, 1856

Nowadays people may not be that spartan, but they are often tempted to make their own boarded bed. Before doing so why not consider buying a futon? Futons are Japanese mattresses made entirely of layers of blown cotton (or wool and cotton). They suit those with certain allergies, are remarkably comfortable to sleep on (especially the type with wool in) and actually *like* to be rolled up during the day, which makes them ideal for children's rooms. There is nothing wrong with sleeping on the floor in a well-heated vermin-free house, and it is time it lost its bad name.

Or you can make a bed area on top of a structure of drawers, shelves, record space – or whatever suits you. Companies selling futons are easy to find in the phone book as their name usually starts with the word 'futon'.

Bedding
The average person releases ½ pint of sweat during the night and this can either linger in the air round the body or be absorbed by the bedding and evaporate into the air on the other side. Since natural fibres absorb more moisture they are better to sleep in than man-made ones.

BED CLOTHES – The perfection of dress, for day or night, where warmth is the purpose, is that which confines around the body sufficient of its own warmth, while it allows escape to the exhalations of the skin. Where the body is allowed to bathe protractedly in its own vapours we must expect an unhealthy effect upon the skin. Where there is too little ventilation escape, insensible perspiration is checked, and something analogous to a fever supervenes; foul tongue, ill taste, and lack of morning appetite betray the evil.
Enquire Within, 1856

Blankets and Underblankets
Pure wool blankets are warmer and last longer than any other, but those with mixed wool and acrylic have the advantage of being moth-proof. Avoid rayon and cotton mixtures if you can. Their artificially-created fluff weakens and rubs off in washing.

Any bed is much warmer with a blanket under the bottom sheet, but the underblankets which make a really big difference are the new ones which look like sheepskin. Two good ones are Woolrest (which refunds your money if you don't sleep better) and Brinkhaus. They are a luxury, but ideal for someone who needs extra warmth and might forget to turn off an electric blanket.

Duvets
A good duvet should last 20 to 25 years, and you need it to be at least 45 cm (18 in) wider than the bed, but at least 250 cm (100 in) wide for one adult, 295 cm (118 in) for two people, whatever the width of the bed.

Duvets work like double glazing. We each generate about 100 watts of heat an hour and the air trapped in the filling makes a barrier between the warmth of the body and the air outside. The usual rule is that 4.5 tog is a very lightweight duvet, 9.0 tog is a medium weight and 13.5 tog is extra warm. On the whole, you get what you pay for and it is only worth going for a cheap filling if that is all you can afford, or you know children will ruin it so soon it needs to be disposable.

The various qualities of down and feather fillings can be confusing, but they go like this:

- goose/duck down with feathers – need only have 51 per cent down
- 'pure' white goose/duck down, piroshka or eider down – BSI set minimum down content of 85 per cent.

The piroshka down is from live free-range geese and so is the eider down. The eider duck uses its down to line its nests, and the down is gathered from these when the birds leave them. So no harm comes to the birds from either of these.

For those who are allergic to feathers, but dislike duvets of man-made fibre, there are duvets filled with silk or cashmere from **Brinkhaus** (page 214), at a price.

In man-made fibres there have also been big improvements. The closest to down, in my view, is Quallofil.

Pillows

The fillings of pillows are almost identical to those of duvets in range and quality. Goose feathers are stronger than duck feathers and keep their bounce longer, ordinary feather pillows are usually poultry feathers which are naturally straight and have to be curled to give them bounce – which means they uncurl in time and give a flat heavy pillow.

Carpets

Most carpets are blends of different types of fibre. Those which flatten easily are the ones most likely to develop curious shading where two sections flatten in opposite directions so beware when buying. Shops will often fit for free. If not, the **National Institute of Carpet Fitters** (page 215) has a list of fitters. It will also help with complaints.

Fibres used in Carpets

Acrylic fibre looks like wool but has far less bounce and gets grubby more easily, but some liquid stains come off easily.

Nylon is mixed with other fibres to lengthen their life. But it flattens and soils more easily than wool. It also collects static and an anti-static spray may be needed (page 216).

Polyester is strong but lacks bounce and only takes light use.

Polypropylene flattens easily and is usually used in looped piles.

Rayon is a cheap fibre which flattens and gets grubby easily.

Wool is the best fibre. It keeps its bounce, and doesn't attract dirt. A high-quality blend is 80 per cent wool, 20 per cent nylon; it gives the bounce of wool with the strength of nylon.

Look for the Carpet Manufacturer's Associations Carpet Performance Rating on carpets. Choose the higher grades, of the six, for areas which get a lot of wear and only use the lighter ones in rooms such as bedrooms.

Checking a Carpet

Carpets need very thorough checking if they are to give you decent wear.

- Check what it is made from – if you find the wool-mark, it means the carpet must have 915 grams of wool per square metre and a decent depth of pile.
- Bend it backwards and see how close together the tufts are. The closer the tufts, the longer it is likely to last.
- Look to see if the colour goes right down the length of the tufts. Printed-on patterns may wear off.
- If there is a foam or fabric backing try to peel it off. You shouldn't be able to without considerable difficulty.
- Try tugging and twisting some tufts. If they come out they will do the same in use.

★ It can be less wasteful to buy one width than another, so calculate the quantities in more than one width. The standard widths are 3 ft, 12 ft and 4 m.

Inbuilt protective coatings such as Scotchguard, which are sometimes on the carpet (or fabric) when you buy it, can make a dramatic difference to the ease with which a carpet can be kept clean and stain-free.

British and Foreign Quality Labels

The British Standards Institution (BSI) is an independent organization under Royal Charter. Its expert committees set the standards which products should meet for reliability or safety. Only in matters of safety are manufacturers *compelled* to meet the BSI standards. For a manufacturer to put a BS number on a product which does not meet the BS standard is a breach of the Trades Descriptions Act. However, BSI numbers do sometimes appear on goods which have not been BSI tested. For example: BS 1970 – with no accompanying BSI label simply shows that the manufacturers *think* their hot water bottle conforms to the standard set for hot water bottles.

When a manufacturer applies for a BSI label for a particular product, both it and the production methods are tested by the BSI. Only if both pass the tests – and continue to pass the BSI's spot checks – may it carry the BSI mark. Foreign manufacturers can also obtain and use BS numbers, if their company and products reach the required standards.

The kitemark shows the product meets the general standards – including safety standards – set by the BSI, and that production meets the BSI's standards of reliability.

This is the Safety Mark indicating that the goods have reached a safety standard. It may or may not have reached other standards. So this mark is increasingly being replaced by the more comprehensive kitemark.

If a shopper finds faults in a product bearing the kite-mark or safety mark and is not able to sort the matter out with the retailer or the manufacturer the BSI Certification and Assessment Department will take up the complaint and test the item to see whether or not it does meet the set standard.

If a product carries one of the two marks above the BSI will investigate any complaint about the product.

If a product carries a label saying CE is does not mean that any safety standard has been passed, it merely means the product has reached certain minimum legal standards set by the EC.

Ecolabelling

Ecolabels are awarded to products which do least harm – or most good – to the environoment, when compared with other products in their category. The comparison looks at factors like energy use in its making, what it is made from, what its effects are in use and how 'green' its disposal can be. An Ecolabelling Board in each country will be arranging for products to be assessed but, as yet, it is only a voluntary scheme – if products don't want to be tested they won't have to be. On the other hand maybe, before long, lack of a label will tell us that the manufacturer *doesn't* care about the environment and should be avoided.

Electrical Safety

Labelling

The **British Electrotechnical Approvals Board (BEAB),** is the independent organization supervising the safety testing of most types of electrical appliances destined for British homes. Products which reach the established European standard, when tested in Britain or another EC country, are awarded a BEAB certificate and carry the label shown below.

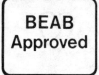

If you have trouble with a BEAB Approved appliance the BEAB will investigate your complaint and, if it is a British product, it may withdraw the manufacturer's licence. If it was made in another EC country it will contact whichever authority gave its approval.

With electrical goods there are very big differences in the way seemingly identical machines perform and last. *Which* magazine is essential reading to get value for money and is in public libraries.

There are advantages in buying from a shop which is a member of the **Radio, Electrical and Television Retailers' Association (RETRA)**. A single code of practice for electrical goods has been agreed between RETRA and AMDEA (**Association of Manufacturers of Domestic Electrical Applicances**). Under this code:

- if you order goods and pay a deposit you will be given a refund if they aren't delivered on time
- if during the guarantee period the retailer is unable to repair it within 15 days you will either be lent another until yours is ready or the guarantee will be extended by the amount of time you are without your equipment
- if you move to another area your retailer will try to arrange for another RETRA member to take over the servicing arrangements under the guarantee
- you should be offered a service call within 3 working days and told if a minimum charge will be made
- you should be advised of minimum charges for repairs and if possible given the cost of the work needed
- most repairs should be guaranteed for 12 months (3 on some smaller items).

RETRA also deals with complaints against members but it does not have an arbitration scheme. Instead, complaints can be put to a conciliation panel.

> Seemingly identical machines can perform very differently. *Which* magazine (on subscription or in public libraries) gives the facts which let you get value for money. It is well worth reading it before buying any major electrical appliance.

Fabrics for Furnishing

Fabric looks so simple it hardly seems worth checking for faults: it is. Go over it carefully then ask about its washability and whether it has been treated in any way – e.g. against spills. Check that it is suited to the job you want it to do. Material not designed for curtaining may fade quickly in the light. Finally, get them to write down how much shrinkage you should expect. Keep that statement in case the shrinkage is worse but, if in doubt, have material laundered before it's made up.

Children's Toys and Safety Equipment

The British Standards Institution has set safety standards for toys and children's goods which are designed to protect children from a wide range of dangers. Those goods which meet the safety standards will carry a BSI number and/or label (see above). If you only buy goods which carry a BSI label it will ensure the cot doesn't have bars so wide the baby's head will get stuck, that the harness really will stop it falling from the pram and that the materials being used won't poison a child – as some old-fashioned materials used to.

Each year new products come on the market to make life safer for children. But most home safety depends not on how many gadgets you have but on how careful you are about doing basic things safely. This quiz will give an idea how safe a child is in your home.

1 Is your medicine cupboard lockable or too high up for a child to reach even on a chair?
2 Do you dispose of medicine in the dustbin?
3 Do you keep all chemicals in their original containers, and where children cannot get to them?
4 Do you turn saucepan handles back, out of reach of children always, sometimes or never?
5 Do you ever put hot drinks in places where children could reach them?
6 Are any sharp tools or knives in places where children could get them?
7 Are there bars or anti-thief locks on upstairs windows to stop them being opened by children?
8 Would you put a gate at the top of the stairs to prevent toddlers from falling down?
9 Are matches and lighters kept where children could reach them?
10 Do your electric plugs have 'sleeves' on all but the tips of plugs?

Score 1 for each yes to questions 1, 3, 7, 8, 10; and 1 for no to 2, 4, 5, 6, 9. For question 4 score 2 for always; 1 for sometimes. Congratulations if you scored 11; 7 to 11 you are being reasonably careful; under 7 and it's time to think about being more careful.

Those who teach their children 'family' safety rules, like 'don't go to such a cupboard, it has poisons in', tend to forget that visiting children haven't learnt the same rules. Large numbers of children are injured, and even killed, in other people's homes. It may be easier to warn children against hazards but it is safer to remove the hazards – then nobody's children get hurt. But teach them safety as well: other people may not be so thoughtful. Children may even come to grief visiting grandparents, who have long ago forgotten that bleach or weedkiller in a lemonade bottle can be dangerous.

★ If you keep used plastic bags, tie a knot in the top of each so children aren't tempted to put them over their heads.

★ Don't give pillows to babies. They don't need them and they could be smothered by one.

★ Kiddi-proof, Boots and Mothercare sell plug covers which will prevent toddlers pushing hairpins into sockets or plugging appliances into them.

★ Children underfoot in a kitchen can be a danger. If a kitchen is small enough for children to be a hazard, have a gate on the kitchen door. Then children can see in but not come in. Children who grow up with this arrangement accept it happily.

The **Royal Society for the Prevention of Accidents**, produces a booklet on children and safety. Another by the **Child Accident Prevention Trust**, called 'Keep Them Safe', gives details of equipment for child safety. The **Department of Trade and Industry** (see Organizations) has leaflets on general safety in the home.

DRY CLEANING

Cleaners need to be chosen very carefully, as certain fabrics need chemicals which only a few cleaners use. The trouble is that there are more dry cleaners than there are fully trained and experienced staff to run them. So, taking clothes or furnishings to the cleaners is no guarantee that they won't be harmed.

Some protection is given by using a member of the **Textile Services Association,** (page 216). Its code of practice covers laundry, cleaning – but not launderettes or coin-operated cleaning machines. Members must pay compensation if the TSA's conciliation service says so, and its members don't limit their legal liability to negligence or restrict compensation to some multiple of the cost of cleaning – which is a common ploy with non-members. But if something does go wrong, and the cleaner doesn't give you satisfaction, the TSA runs a conciliation service, and members must pay compensation fast if the decision is against them. Failing that, you have a right to pursue your claim through the small claims court.

The TSA also runs a **Dry Cleaning Information Bureau** covering both dyeing and dry cleaning with its members' services listed on computer. So it can help you find a suitable dry cleaner.

If you have something fragile it is worth telling the dry cleaner that it *is* special (they may send it to head office) or paying for a special dry cleaner. If you can't find a suitable dry cleaner locally **Pilgrim Payne and Co Ltd** and **Jeeves of Belgravia** (addresses on pages 215-216) will accept cleaning by post from all over Britain,

Coin-operated Cleaning
Before using a coin-operated dry cleaning machine check the care label inside each garment carefully (see page 189-190). Some of them mean that clothes can only be cleaned in special solvents, which are not likely to be used in such machines.

If you have problems, and the launderette is not being reasonable, write to the **National Association of the Launderette Industry** (page 218) with the details. They will encourage the launderette to sort it out and, if that fails, the conciliation committee will look into it.

DYEING AND COLOURING

You can now dye most fabrics and use a whole range of techniques – hot, cold and washing machine – and combine dyeing with painting the fabric. It's a marvellous way to convert old summer clothes to new but you can't:

- dye acrylics
- dye wool or silk in a washing machine
- cover patterns with dye
- cover stains and marks with dye (but you can cover them with fabric paint)
- dye anything a really perfect black
- remove the colour from polyesters before dyeing them
- dye drip-dry fabrics
- dye waterproof fabrics.

The colour mixing in dyeing is just the same as in painting. If you have a yellow T-shirt and dye it blue it will come out green; dye it red and it will come out orange.

How to Dye Successfully
- Weigh the garment while dry and note the weight.
- Remove all dirt and stains before dyeing.
- Choose the right dye for the type of fabric you are dyeing.
- As the existing colour will combine with any dye you start by removing the colour – unless the colour combination will produce what you want. A Dylon product removes the colours from most fabrics which aren't fast dyed (but don't use it on polyesters).
- Use exactly the recommended amount of dye, water and fixing medium for the *dry* weight of the fabric.
- Have the dyeing vessel large enough for the fabric to be moved about in it, or the dye won't get to the folds.
- Make sure the water is the correct temperature for the type of dye you are using.
- Have enough water to cover the fabric totally.
- When dyeing two items which need to match, but can't be dyed together, you must make sure that there is no variation anywhere in the process. All quantities must be precisely measured and exactly the same amount of time taken for each stage.

> After most dyes a washing machine has to be cleaned out with the longest hottest wash, plus bleach and soap powder. So don't dye in a washing machine unless you are prepared to do this.

★ Adding some very dark blue dye to black dye gives a darker result.

★ If you have a problem, Dylon (page 216) has a helpline and leaflets.

LAUNDRY

Whatever the instructions, it is far better to wash or dry clean clothes and other items gently before they get really dirty, rather than leave them until they need a good seeing-to. The more gently any item can be treated, the less it wears the fabric. If you are unsure how to clean any fabric, the **Home Laundry Consultative Council**, or **Lever Brothers** consumer advice service, will advise on

how to wash fabrics of all kinds, while the **Fabric Care Research Association** advises on dry cleaning (addresses page 216).

> This section covers the washing and ironing of most fabrics which are encountered. However, nothing written here is intended to overrule any instructions which are supplied by the manufacturers of garments or furnishings. My information is for times when no label has been used. Any instructions on labels should always be followed to the letter – if they aren't you will have no come-back if the garment or furnishings shrink, run or are otherwise spoilt.

International Textile Care Labelling Code (ITCL)
More and more fabrics now carry the international textile labelling code, which is as follows.

 Shows it must not be washed – this *doesn't* mean it can be dry cleaned.

 Shows hand washing is needed.

 Shows it can be machine washed at the programme which uses the temperature given.

 A line below the picture shows that a programme for synthetics should be used.

 Two lines below mean wash on a wool programme.

 Shows that chlorine bleach can be used.

 Shows chlorine bleach cannot be used.

 This means it can be ironed, one dot means use a cool iron (120°C), two dots means a warm iron (160°C), three dots a hot iron (210°C).

Addresses and suggestions for further reading are at the ends of chapters.

Do *not* iron – the fabric would be harmed.

 Can be dry cleaned in all solvents.

 Dry clean in perchloroethylene, or white spirit. But use a process for delicate items when this symbol has a line under it.

 Dry-clean with care, not in a coin-operated machine. This is found on velvet, acrylics and some woollens.

 This used to mean clean with special care in white spirit or solvent 113, but 113 is bad for the ozone layer and is no longer used. As I write no substitute exists.

 Do not dry clean.

 Improved by tumble drying.

 Do not tumble dry.

How Hot Do They Mean?
Here is how to judge whether you are providing the right temperature for a fabric when you hand-wash it:

100°C	boiling – as if straight from a kettle
95°C	just off boiling
60°C	hotter than hands can bear
50°C	as hot as hands can stand
40°C	comfortably warm
30°C	cooler than the hands

Ironing

There are only 4 things to remember when ironing:

- have the iron as hot as the fabric will stand – and no hotter
- keep the iron moving all the time – or the fabric will scorch
- have the fabric evenly damp all over – spray it if necessary
- order your ironing so a part you have done is never creased in smoothing another part.

On the matter of dampness there really is no substitute for taking off the line when it is just right and ironing it then and there. At the right degree of dampness any fabric irons twice as well in half the time.

The most bizarre information on 'ironing' clothes that I have ever found is this entry in the first edition of *Enquire Within*.

> SOAP MAY BE DISUSED, or nearly so, in the getting up of muslins and chintzes, which should always be treated agreeably to the oriental manner; that is, to wash them in plain water, and then boil them in congee or rice water: after which they ought not to be submitted to the operation of the smoothing iron, but rubbed smooth with a polished stone.

Ironing Pleats
If you simply iron knife pleats you will find that the underfold of the pleat imprints a line on the upper surface which spoils it. To avoid this have a piece of plain white card and slip it into the underside of the pleat, covering the underfold. Then when you iron you have a flat surface to press on.

Order of Ironing
On some garments the order in which they should be ironed is obvious, but blouses and shirts often seem to puzzle people. The best system I know is this: **Collar** – ironing from the points towards the centre, **Shoulder** and **yoke, cuffs, sleeves** (ironed flat, except on a woman's shirt which would be spoilt), **back, fronts** then button up alternate buttons, fold and re-press the upper part of the **front**.

★ If fabric is too dry a plant sprayer moistens it fastest.

★ The best way to damp over-dried fabric is to splash it with warm water, roll it up tightly and leave it for a few hours.

★ If the thermostat on an iron isn't working test it as irons were always tested before thermostats were invented: spit on it. You can tell by the fizz whether it is cool, medium or hot.

> Why is the flat iron hotter, if the saliva runs along it, than if it adheres till it is evaporated? Because, when the saliva runs along the iron, the heat is sufficient to convert the bottom of the drop to vapour . . .
> *Enquire Within*, 1856

Pressing
Pressing is to a garment what a face lift is to a star – it takes the years off. The first essential is an immaculately clean white cloth – such as a piece of old cotton sheeting. Putting the cloth between the iron and the garment avoids making shiny iron marks.

Mild pressing can simply be done by using a steam iron to iron through this dry cloth. That may be enough for very light fabrics. For heavyweight, wet the cloth under a tap, wring it dry and place it on the garment where you wish to press it (unless the fabric is averse to water). Iron the cloth slowly with a fairly hot iron.

Pressing to Remove Bagginess
If you want to press bagginess out, lay the baggy area out flat (open trouser legs out sideways not front to

back). Then work from the outer edge of the bagginess towards the centre pressing it repeatedly through a damp cloth until it flattens. Then remove the cloth and place a sheet of clean brown paper on the garment. Iron the paper thoroughly all over and it will absorb the moisture from the cloth and make it hold the pressing better. Make the baggy bit the last part of the garment which you press. Then let it lie in place until cool.

Pressing in Pleats or Creases

If you need to put in a perfect pleat or crease deal with any bagginess first, then fold the fabric *exactly* on the crease line (see above, Ironing Pleats). Press with the damp cloth method and, as you remove the cloth, replace it with the 'banger' described in Crafts. Let the fabric cool, then move to the next section of the crease.

Starching

The modern spray-on starches are slower than traditional starch and the floor ends up like a skating rink. The best way to starch anything is to use a powder starch, which you mix with either hot or cold water as a final rinse. Nothing could be simpler.

The strength recommended on the packet usually produces a pleasant crispness. However, to make the front of a dress shirt really stiff make a solution 3 to 4 times stronger. I find the best way to starch a dress shirt with a stiff front is to dip the whole thing in starch at normal strength, spin it dry, then use a clean pastry brush to brush the extra strong starch very well on to both sides of the cuffs, and front. The detached collar can then be dipped in what remains. If it still feels too soft when it begins to dry, yet more can be brushed on. Iron the stiffened areas while still quite damp. At this stage the starch will try to stick to the iron, so use a hot iron and work swiftly, starting on the inside.

Stiffening Lace

Lace is seldom stiffened nowadays, but stiff lace may return to fashion. The Edwardian way to stiffen it was to pour 250 ml (½ pt) of boiling water on to 30 g (1 oz) of gum arabic, stir until the gum dissolved and dip the lace in this *once it was cool*. The strength was varied to suit the lace and it was finally ironed under white tissue paper.

Washing Problems

The first job with washing is always stain removal (pages 199 to 205). If you wait until afterwards you may well find the washing process has set the stain so you will never be able to remove it.

After stain removal comes soaking. Almost any washing, bar wool and fine fabrics, is the cleaner for a soak in ordinary washing powder in a bucket of water overnight.

Hand-washing is simply a matter of squeezing soapy water (see the individual fabrics for temperatures) through the material until all the dirt seems to be out, rubbing it against itself where necessary to get the dirt to shift (if the material will take rubbing.) The vital final stage is to get the soap out by squeezing the garment in basin after basin of water until the water remains perfectly clear on the last rinse.

Faded Garments

When garments fade there are three possible causes: the dye has run, the garments have spent too long in the sun (on the line or on the wearer), or there is a build-up of soap which is masking the colour. This last can be helped by putting a dash of white vinegar in the final rinsing water, as it helps to get rid of the soap. Fading received more hazardous treatment in the past.

> BLACK REVIVER FOR BLACK CLOTH – *Bruised galls one pound, logwood two pounds, green vitriol half a pound, water five quarts. Boil for two hours, and strain.*
>
> Enquire Within, 1856

Fabrics which Run

You can reduce the chances of a fabric running by soaking it in a solution of salt and water. Use a tablespoon of salt to 500 ml (1 pt) of water. It may not make it totally fast but it should improve things.

Fragile Fabrics and Lace Curtains

Fragile fabrics are usually best left unwashed or handed to professionals, but if you find you need to wash something fragile this is the method used by many museums. It can very well be applied to lace curtains which may have been weakened by sunlight to a point where they cannot support the weight of water.

Fold the material carefully into a manageable rectangle or square. Then tack all the layers together with big loose tacking stitches. Soak it overnight – if it will take soaking – in warm soapy water; using pure soap not detergent. Drain and press the water out of it flat against the bottom of a basin. Put it in fresh warm soapy water and press the water very gently through it, then drain and rinse it in the same way until the water is clear. If the fabric is lace put a couple of tablespoons of salt in the final rinsing water to give it a little crispness. Dry it flat, on towels, in the shade.

Very Dirty Garments

If you have trouble with greasy overalls (for heavy motor oil see page 202) or white shirts or sheets which teenagers have forgotten to change, soak them overnight in a bucket of hot water to which you have added half a cup of ammonia. (Mix the water and ammonia before soaking the garments). Ammonia will fade coloureds, so this is a method for non-synthetic whites only.

Limited patches of dirt, like a dirty line around a collar, can be spot-treated by rubbing on a block of Fairy soap before washing, and if necessary going over it with a nail brush.

★ To hang a garment on a hanger on a washing line use two hangers, with the hooks facing opposite ways. Then it won't blow off.

★ If you put too much soap in and a washing machine overflows with suds, pour in vinegar or fabric softener.

Addresses and suggestions for further reading are at the ends of chapters.

Washing Individual Fabrics

Acetate

Acetate is a cellulose fibre and must be handled gently when wet. Wash it by hand in cool water or on ITCL programmes 6 or 8; avoid wringing it, and don't give it more than a brief spin. Iron it with a warm iron while still damp.

Acrylics, Modacrylics and Orlon

Acrylics have a nasty tendency to crease and go flat and saggy. They need the greatest care to prolong their decent life. You *can* wash them at ITCL 6, but they last longest if washed and rinsed by hand in cool to warm water, without rubbing or even very hard squeezing. To reduce the static use fabric softener in the last rinse. Give them a *very* short spin, and put acrylic pullovers flat on a towel to dry or they will stretch dreadfully. Ironing over patterns will flatten them, but iron stocking-stitch lightly through a damp cloth and leave the garment in place on the ironing board until it cools.

Antique Fabrics

Antique textiles present a whole range of problems which need to be seen before the best treatment can be recommended. Most museums which contain furnishings have a textile expert who will advise you. However tempted you may be, *don't* try to clean antique fabric without taking advice. Even an antique fabric which looks quite sturdy may fall to pieces the moment you wet it or crush it during washing or dry-cleaning.

Blankets

Blankets should be treated according to what they are made from. Spin them well and hang them *over*, not from, a washing line.

Brocade

Brocade used once to be silk, by definition, but it's now made in a wide range of fabrics; cotton, viscose, polyester, acetate and a variety of blends. Treat it according to the fibre from which it is made – some will need dry-cleaning. Don't iron it too heavily, and allow for the fact that it frays easily. Velvet brocade is a luxury cloth and needs to be dry-cleaned by a cleaner who knows his stuff.

Broderie Anglaise

As broderie Anglaise is pierced and embroidered white cotton, or poly-cotton, treat it like these fabrics, unless it is used to trim more fragile fabric. But don't put it in a washing machine with garments which have exposed hooks and eyes which can catch and tear it, or let the tip of the iron catch in a hole. If necessary, iron through white tissue paper.

Buckram

As buckram is made for stiffening it is heavily dosed with size. If it is washed this comes out and it becomes a very sad affair. Dry-clean only. Press with a hot iron – if necessary – through a dry cloth.

Bunting

Nowadays bunting is usually cotton, but old bunting was often wool. In either case, the fabric frays easily and the colours are likely to run. Woollen bunting needs to be hand washed as wool. Cotton bunting can be washed by hand or in a machine, as cotton – bearing in mind the risk of colours running. Iron accordingly.

Cambric

Cambric was once the great fabric for cotton petticoats. It's a cotton like that used for handkerchiefs – in fact, some handkerchiefs are cambric. It takes a hot cotton wash and can be starched successfully. Iron with a hot iron while rather damp.

Candlewick

I'm told that candlewick takes its name from the fact that originally the wicks of candles really were used to decorate the cotton. Today the fluffy nap is either pure cotton or – more often – cotton and some synthetic fibre.

It really needs tumble-drying to refluff it – unless it has a foam-rubber back, as some bath mats have. If it can't be tumble-dried shake it well before hanging it out and try to choose a windy day, so the wind tumbles it into softness. Using a fabric softener when washing it also helps. Candlewick fades easily, but dyes just as easily – especially in a machine.

Canvas or duck

Canvas can normally be washed in a machine like cotton, but it is so stiff it needs a machine to itself. It is usually more practical to scrub it with block soap and a stiff brush, then dowse it well with water to get all the soap out. Watch out for decorations, like leather buckles on canvas handbags, which may react badly to water.

Cashmere

You'd think any wool from a mountain goat would be hard-wearing, but cashmere is far more fragile than lambswool. Some experts say it should be dry cleaned, but I have found that after being dry cleaned several times cashmere loses its bounce and starts to bag like an old acrylic, whereas with careful hand-washing it seems to stay perfect for years. Treat it as wool (page 196), being exceedingly careful and avoid pressing it or do it very lightly.

It easily forms little balls on its surface. Good haberdashery departments sell a small device for removing these and it keeps cashmere and angora looking new far longer.

Cheesecloth

Cheesecloth is cotton and takes a hot wash – although it may shrink. It is naturally a crinkled fabric and isn't usually intended to be smooth, so it is usually best to tug it flat in all directions when wet and leave it unironed.

Chiffon

Silk chiffon needs dry cleaning and so do most synthetics, but nylon chiffon may be washable. Avoid pressing

---

IMPORTANT: Read note on page 188 before washing or soaking fabrics.

it if you can; hanging creased chiffon up in a steamy room will often smooth it instead. However, if you have to press it, do so very lightly with a cool dry iron. Heavy ironing will over-flatten it and take away its character.

Chintz

Chintz is really any flowery cotton furnishing fabric, but glazed chintz is a finely woven flowery fabric with a shiny surface. It may have been sized to stiffen it slightly or glazed with a resin. It is best to ask the manufacturer whether it can be washed or must be dry cleaned and how careful any cleaning must be. It is often inclined to shrink and washing can make it loose its crispness and deprives a glazed chintz of its sheen. Modern washable chintz simply needs a hot iron when rather damp. Chintz which needs careful dry cleaning can be sent to **Cadogan Co** (page 215) which specializes in such fabrics and will restore tired chintz.

Ciré

The ciré seen most often today is nylon ciré, used for thin showerproof rainclothes. Ciré means 'waxed' in French and, as it's a treated fabric, you need to avoid removing the dressing. So sponge it instead of washing it, let it drip dry and only use a cool iron through a dry pressing cloth.

Corduroy

Corduroy is usually pure cotton but its colour is very inclined to run and its nap easily picks up fluff from anything else in the machine. Check the pockets carefully – a tissue handkerchief washed with corduroy can be disastrous. And turn the garment inside out so the nap won't pick up the fluff which may be in the machine. Wash it on ITCL 2 or 5 according to the depth of colour, or by hand. Iron it on the wrong side, with a fairly hot iron, while still damp.

Cotton

Cotton can be washed at a wide range of temperatures, and some white cotton will even stand boiling – but it needs hot water to get out the soap, and some dark shades run easily. Use ITCL 1, 2 or 5 (page 189) or wash it by hand. The exceptions are good clothes which always look better for hand washing and may have interlinings which make dry cleaning essential. Cotton calico shrinks considerably.

Most cotton can be starched (see page 190) and pure cotton is far easier to iron than the fabrics from man-made fibres. But you must iron it when damp.

Madras cotton needs to be washed entirely alone as the dye usually bleeds massively. Spin it dry and hang it out at once or the dye will transfer in patches all over the garment.

★ If someone has a cold, soak their cotton handkerchiefs overnight in a solution of salt water – 1 tablespoon to a 500 ml (1 pt) of water. This removes the catarrh.

★ Cotton viscose is often used instead of pure cotton jersey, see viscose (page 196).

Crêpe de Chine

Crêpe de Chine was originally a Chinese silk with a crêpe texture. Some polyesters now imitate this so well it is extremely hard to tell the difference. But, if the label is no guide, 'dishpan' hands can be: any pure silk fabric will always catch slightly on hands if they are even a little rough; polyester will slide smoothly over them.

Crêpe de Chine in man-made fibres is handled as for the fibre. The safest bet with silk crêpe de Chine is to have it dry-cleaned, as the colours run easily and it can be hard to iron it so it looks perfectly smooth without flattening the texture of the crêpe and making it look a little tired. However, some people do wash it successfully (see page 196) and crêpe de Chine underwear obviously has to be washed. But this is not something to try, with top garments, unless you are prepared to risk spoiling them. Use a warm iron when slightly – and evenly – damp.

Cretonne

This hard-wearing cotton fabric washes well, and takes starch (though it seldom needs it). Use a hot wash and hot iron while damp (see page 189).

Curtains

The washability of curtains depends on their fabric and on their lining and interlining. Most interlinings and many fabrics are not washable so should be dry cleaned. Cotton curtains with cotton linings can usually be washed, but check with the manufacturer. They will almost certainly be less robust than they seem. Sunlight and chemicals in the air eat into curtains – especially the linings – and a curtain can go into a washing machine, looking normal, and come out as strips of rag having fallen apart at every fold. Unless you are *certain* that the fabric hasn't been weakened in this way it is far better to wash curtains by hand.

If there is any risk that the curtains will shrink – and there usually is – undo the hems of the main fabric before washing.

Start by soaking washable curtains overnight in plenty of cold water in the bath (having first removed all curtain hooks). Drain and rinse. Press all the water out, then run a bath of hand-hot water and a good detergent. Let them soak in this for an hour and then squeeze the water through them without twisting or pulling, until all the dirt is loose. Drain and rinse until no more soap or dirt comes out. (Really dirty curtains may need two washes with soap). Press the water out and leave them sitting in the bath a while for more to drain down. Press again (so as not to handle them with too much weight of water in). Spin dry in a machine. Carefully open them out and hang them *over*, not from, a washing line, so the line runs across their width. Iron with a hot iron while rather damp, working up and down the curtain to minimize shrinkage – and hang before they are fully dry, closing them across the window so the air can get to them.

Damask

The damask you are most likely to find in the home is in the form of double damask dinner napkins. Old damask will be cotton or linen, and take a high-temperature wash and a hot iron. If you want beautifully crisp damask, iron it when thoroughly damp. If ironed when too dry it will be limp and miserable no matter what you do. Unlike linen, overdried damask will iron well after being damped, tightly rolled and left a while. Iron it on the right side to give it a sheen. Modern damask may be part viscose and need less heat (see Viscose, page 196).

Denim

Treat denim as cotton but expect shrinkage, unless it is pre-shrunk, and keep it away from other items until very well faded, as it runs repeatedly. Iron when rather damp.

Dralon

Dralon is washable at a low temperature but if it is attached to chairs see page 215.

Duvets

Duvets in man-made fibres can be washed in a large washing machine but use only one third the usual amount of soap powder and wash at 40°C. Then give it 4 to 5 rinses, before spinning it for not more than 30 seconds at a time – if necessary keep switching the machine off. Man-made fibre duvets can then be tumbled dry in warm – not hot – air, until the cover feels dry. Then give it 24 hours' airing to let it dry completely. For feather duvets, see Pillows.

Embroidery

Embroidery needs care, as you have to consider both the background cloth and the threads used on it. Any embroidery on canvas should be dry-cleaned, so should embroidery on silk, and old embroidery needs expert attention. The **Royal School of Needlework** (page 215) will advise over the phone on the cleaning of embroidery, tapestry and beadwork, and also runs a cleaning service. The items can be taken in or sent by registered post. There is no standard price but they will send an estimate.

White cotton or linen embroidered with *white cotton* thread can be washed in fairly hot water, without rubbing. Stains can be soaked out in bleach – at the dilution recommended on the bottle – provided the fabric is not very old or delicate. Whether you can machine-wash stronger items depends on the nature of the stitches – most stitches are vulnerable to being pushed out of place in the rough and tumble of a machine, but the type with a cut-out design edged with buttonhole stitch usually survives it well. Only you can judge.

Coloured embroidery may run. First take a very damp piece of fabric (white silk lining material is ideal), place it over each of the colours in turn and iron it. If even one colour bleeds on to the silk the item must be dry cleaned. If none of the colours run you should be able to hand-wash it. Use pure soap flakes and cool water at about 30°C (86°F). The less it is handled the better, so soak it first for an hour or two. Then squeeze the soapy water through the material, by pressing it with

a clean sponge, disturbing the sewing as little as possible. *Never* rub. Rinse in water of the same temperature using several changes until it is completely clear. Let all the water run out, gently pressing the embroidery against the bottom of the sink. Spread it out on a towel to dry, out of direct sunlight. Iron it while still rather damp.

To iron embroidery which has a raised pattern, pad the board with two layers of blanket, and cover it with a sheet. Then iron the embroidery face down. If the embroidery has a pierced design use a pressing cloth lest the iron rip it.

Fringes on an embroidered shawl are the very devil if they are washed loose, and the tangle they get into can be indescribable. Before washing, tie the threads together in small bundles with white thread or plait small groups and tie the ends. Press the soapy water carefully through each group or they will be less clean then the rest. Before drying the shawl, unplait them and lay them out smoothly.

Felt and Baize

Felt and baize cannot be washed as they may shrink seriously. Dry clean both.

Flame-retardant Fabrics

These are usually fabrics treated with a flame-retardant finish, so it is extra important to follow the washing instructions *exactly* or the finish could be removed.

Flannel

Flannel used to be only a high-quality wool fabric but today it is often partly man-made, and may be totally man-made for school uniform. Strictly speaking, man-made flannels are treated as for the fabric and wool flannel is dry cleaned. However, if a son of mine had white wool cricket flannels I would wash them very carefully (see page 190), but if the care instructions don't say they can be washed you will have no come-back if they shrink.

Georgette

Georgette is dry cleaned or washed and ironed according to its fibre. Check the care label. If you decide to wash silk georgette – which is really a job for an expert – you may have problems; it crinkles up and has to be carefully ironed while quite wet and pulled to shape.

Lace

Blond lace can be revived by breathing upon it, and shaking and flapping it.

Enquire Within, 1856

Would that it were that easy. Lace ranges from robust modern lace in synthetic fibres to fragile old lace which needs special treament. Very old and fragile lace is best taken to the **Royal School of Needlework** (page 215). Robust modern lace can be washed or dry cleaned according to what it is made from. Slightly older lace deserves gentle treatment. Use pure soap, *not* detergent, and with very fine lace use distilled water at every stage.

IMPORTANT: Read note on page 188 before washing or soaking fabrics.

Let it soak for ten minutes in the warm soapy water before washing. The washing method then varies with the strength of the lace. A piece which won't tangle and is not strong enough for handling can be put in a large jar (even a big plastic sweet jar from a sweet shop) with the soapy water and shaken vigorously. A larger piece which is not too fragile can be put in a pillow case. You then squeeze the suds through the pillow case without handling the lace. More fragile lace, or any which would tangle, is better pinned out on a polythene-covered board, and covered with a layer of net. Then gently brush suds through it with a soft brush and rinse it by pouring water over it.

After rinsing old lace, pat it gently dry with a towel and put it in shape to dry flat. To get it perfectly to shape you may need to pin it out on a softboard covered with polythene. Use *stainless steel* pins and put them between the threads *not* into them. Finally, it should be ironed with a warm iron through white tissue paper – so the point of the iron cannot catch and tear the lace. For lace curtains see Net, opposite.

Today we might not go along with simmering a lace veil, but in other respects these instructions from the 1856 *Enquire Within* can hardly be bettered.

> *TO WASH A WHITE LACE VEIL. – Put the veil in a strong lather of white soap and very clear water, and let it simmer slowly for a quarter of an hour. Take it out and squeeze it well, but be sure not to rub it. Rinse in two cold waters with a drop of liquid blue in the last. Have ready some very clear weak gum arabic water, or some thin starch, or rice water. Pass the veil through it, and clear it by clapping. Then stretch it out even, and pin it to dry on a linen cloth, making the edge as straight as possible, and opening out all the scallops, and fastening each with pins. When dry, lay a piece of muslin smoothly over it, and iron it on the wrong side.*

Linen

Linen is very easy so long as you pander to its needs. It likes a hot wash (barring deep shades) and a very hot iron. But to iron up well it must be very much wetter than cotton need be – not dripping but very damp. Then it comes up beautifully without effort. If you let it get too dry before ironing it, it is the very devil and responds neither to damping nor to steam irons. Re-wet totally and re-dry to the right point. The ironed surface tends to shine, so iron it on the wrong side if you don't want this.

Be careful: there are also linen-look fabrics which are cotton and polyester, which need lower temperatures of both water and iron.

Loose Covers

The fact that a cover is loose does not mean the makers intend you to remove it for washing. Most loose covers shrink dreadfully when washed and must be dry-cleaned. If you are putting new loose covers on a chair wash the material before the covers are made up. Then you have guarded against the worst of the shrinking. Even so, when you wash the covers after use avoid very

hot water and put the covers back on the chairs while they are still rather damp. In that way they won't end up smaller than the chairs. You can run an iron over them both before you put them on the chairs and when in place – if whatever is underneath will take the heat.

Milium

Milium is a trade name for an aluminium coating sometimes found on the linings of coats and curtains. If you are making up curtains with it place the metallic side to the inside. It can usually be treated like cotton, but check the maker's instructions.

Net and Tulle

If the washing instructions say nothing to the contrary one would expect net to be washable. It can be made of all kinds of fibres. Cotton net may go sad if not ironed while still quite damp, and is best starched. Nylon net keeps its spring well if washed in cool water. But I did discover that to help the tutus of the ballerinas in Covent Garden stand out perfectly the wardrobe mistresses run a circle of crinoline wire through a net casing on one of the middle layers about half way from the body.

Net Curtains

The secret of keeping terylene net curtains white is simply to wash them often. Ingrained yellowing is hard to remove but Dylon's product for whitening curtains does make a difference. They are best washed by hand using soap powder or detergent and warm – not hot – water. Give them an overnight soak in a warm soapy solution. Rinse until the water is totally clear and then hang them to drip dry *without* spinning or wringing. Re-hang while still damp but, if necessary, iron them lengthwise with a cool iron first. Nylon net is treated in the same way (see nylon, below).

Nylon or Polyamide

Nylon absorbs dye very easily but loses it easily too. Beware of washing dark colours with light. White nylon can be washed at ITCL 3, but coloured nylon at 4, or hand-wash in medium hot water and give cool rinses. Using fabric conditioner in the final rinse will reduce static. Avoid wringing or over-spinning and drip-dry if possible. Iron with a very cool iron as it melts easily. Grey nylon can be whitened with Dylon's curtain whitener (see page 216).

Organza

Silk organza can be washed as silk, unless the label says dry clean only. Polyester organza must be dry cleaned, and viscose organza can be gently hand-washed in warm water, and ironed with a warm iron when slightly damp.

Permanent Pleating

Permanent pleating is usually heat set in a man-made fibre. So heat can unset it. Stick to low temperatures, wash it by hand and drip dry.

Pillows and Duvets

Using an underslip or pillow protector keeps a pillow

Addresses and suggestions for further reading are at the ends of chapters.

cleaner much longer. When it does get dirty there are several options. Down and/or feather pillows and duvets can be dry cleaned, but unless they are done by a company which removes the filling and cleans the cover and filling separately (an expensive process) the cover may not look very clean. Alternatively, they can be washed but this is very much at your own risk, as makers don't recommend it. I do, however, find it is very successful. One risk with washing is that some pillow ticking – especially on cheap pillows – is treated on the inside to stop the feathers coming through. After washing, the feathers may come through more easily.

To wash a pillow soak it overnight in a bath of lukewarm soapy water (pure soap not detergent). Wash it in the same way next day, putting a few drops of ammonia in the water, and rinse it in the same temperature until the water runs clear. Spin dry with a series of brief spins and then either tumble it dry – by itself so there is plenty of space – at a low temperature or peg it to the bottom of a wire coathanger and hang it to dry in a warm place. The secret of getting it to come up well is to plump it up as often as possible.

Pillows with synthetic fillings are washed as duvets, but until quite recently they came up incurably lumpy. Mercifully, the better modern fillings such as Quallofil seem to have got over that fault.

Polyester, Polyamid or Polyester and Cotton
Have you ever wondered why polyester or poly-cotton sheets, which are so beautifully crease-free at first, gradually need more and more ironing to be presentable? The answer is that they are finished with a resin which makes them resist creases, but this resin very slowly washes out. The other reason is that at a temperature of about 70°/80° C the molecules of polyester mysteriously change their structure and acquire the ability to 'remember' the shape they were in at that temperature. So, if they are scrunched up in a washing machine at the time they will ever afterwards try to return to those creases. For polyester the rules are:

- wash and rinse it at 60°C or less
- don't wash dark and light colours together or they may run
- a full or partial tumble-dry fluffs it up and cuts down creasing, but it should not be overdried and should be removed from the dryer the instant it finishes or it will crease in the folds it ends in.

Poplin
Poplin is washed according to the fibre and is usually cotton or poly-cotton. Proofed poplin may not be washable – check the instructions.

Quilting
Quilting ranges from the most robust nylon quilted dressing gown to heirloom bed quilts. Handle ordinary quilting according to the fibre.

Bed quilts need to be dry-cleaned, by a skilled cleaner, or washed with great care, according to the fabric. The problem is to get one clean without disturbing the layers. So if it is washed it must be done gently by hand in a bath. On old and valuable quilting take advice from a museum textile department.

Sailcloth
Sailcloth is usually cotton or polyester and cotton. Treat it accordingly, but strong colours may run.

Satin
The care of satin depends both on the fibre it is made from and on the quality of the cloth. Satin in man-made fibres usually washes beautifully. Silk satin underwear can often be washed as silk (below) but a satin used for top garments will usually need to be dry cleaned.

Seersucker
Wash seersucker according to the fibre, but drip dry and do not iron or the bubbles will flatten out.

Silk
Silk varies hugely in its washability, but it always needs careful handling. It is usually best to dry clean the following types: silk taffeta, chiffon, brocade, georgette and organza (but see also by name above); also printed scarves and ties. And, whether it says so or not, silk which rustles must never be washed as washing will remove the metallic dressing which gives it the stiffness.

Some silks which appear to wash beautifully are tricky to iron well. Some silks are even difficult to dry clean and need very skilled handling. If any silk looks out of the ordinary it is worth using a specialist cleaner.

Silk takes up dye easily but releases it just as gladly. So it is always risky to wash patterns, and each item should be washed alone. To test if the dye will run wet a corner which won't show, place it on a piece of white fabric or kitchen roll and iron it with a warm iron. If no dye comes off it shouldn't run in washing. Wash silk by hand, not in a machine, using very cool water and pure soap, squeezing the liquid through it. It must never be rubbed, scrubbed, bleached or boiled, and can take only very brief soaking. Nor should you rub on block soap to treat a dirty area: it may develop a pale patch at that point.

Rinse it very well at the same temperature, and put ½ cup of white vinegar for every 4 l (1 gallon) of water in the final rinse. It gives silk the feel which old-timers in the cleaning trade charmingly call 'scroop' – a certain crispness. Then roll it in a towel and press out the moisture. Hang it to dry away from heat or direct sunlight. Tumble-drying is not good for it.

Silk needs skilful ironing if it is not to look shabby. It must be evenly damp all over. Garments never dry evenly so let it dry then put it in a plastic bag with a few tablespoons of water, close the bag and leave it for a few hours to moisten evenly. But don't leave it longer and keep it in a cool place (like the fridge) or mildew could set in and this is virtually impossible to remove. Iron it on the wrong side with a warm iron while still decidedly damp.

This method of washing and ironing will suit most silk

IMPORTANT: Read note on page 188 before washing or soaking fabrics.

underwear, some slub silk, and some crêpe de Chine. Slubbed and ribbed silks need a damp pressing cloth over them or they may be roughed up. Shantung is an exception: it must be ironed when dry and damp ironing can mark it.

> White crêpe de Chine, which has been frequently dry-cleaned, may become too yellow to wear long before it is out of fashion – let alone worn out. At this stage to risk washing it is no loss but you can't use bleach on silk and I was hesitant to use any strong chemical. However, having tested Dylon's Super White on just such a shirt I found that, though it didn't bring it up like new (it never claimed to), it did restore enough whiteness to make the shirt wearable again. It claims to work on any silk, and on wool and nylon.

Terylene
A polyester fibre, see Polyester.

Ticking
Ticking is closely woven cotton made to keep feathers in pillows. Wash it as cotton and iron when damp. The traditional way to make it more feather-proof still works: you rub the inside well with beeswax (from good hardware stores or by mail from **Liberon Waxes Ltd**.

Ties
Ties look harmless enough but any tie cut on the bias (with the threads not running straight up and down the tie) will usually twist irreversibly when wet, and the interlining is prone to shrinking. Leave ties to professionals if you possibly can. If you really can't do that tack all the layers together before you even try any extensive spot cleaning.

Tricel and Triacetates
Tricel and the triacetates are made from acetate fibres which wash well and won't shrink or stretch. But they are best hand-washed in warm water without wringing and should be left to drip dry. Iron them with a warm iron. Tricel velour is an exception and can have a brief spin.

Velvet, Velour and Velveteen
Velvet is very variable; most good-quality velvet can only be dry-cleaned, but versions such as jersey velvets in man-made fibres wash well. Follow the care label religiously. This is not a fabric to gamble with.

Velveteen normally washes like corduroy, but check the care label.

Viscose
Viscose is made of cellulose from wood pulp and waste cotton, which makes it sound tough, but it isn't, and needs tender treatment. Whether on its own or in a blend, hand-wash in water hot enough to have your hands in comfortably, drip dry (or spin *very* briefly) and use a warm iron.

Viyella
This is traditionally a combination of lambswool and cotton and needs to be treated like wool. There is also pure wool viyella and pure cotton viyella – the latter being more robust.

Waterproofed or Waxed Fabrics
To keep waterproofed or waxed fabrics clean you *must* follow the maker's instructions. Fabrics which have lost their waterproofing – or which need waterproofing – can sometimes be waterproofed at home. **Nikwax** (page 216) sells by mail order waterproofers for just about everything: nylon, polycotton, cotton, quilting and even leather and tents. If, however, a Barbour needs reproofing it may be safest to send it back to **Barbour** (page 216) or use the product the company sells for the job. It comes with instructions. Meanwhile, keep a Barbour clean by wiping it with plain cold water.

Wool and Angora
Wool has three enemies: heat, rubbing and water. All woven wool is normally dry-cleaned, but most knitted wool can be either dry-cleaned or washed – unless the care label says otherwise.

Knitted garments are almost always better washed by hand than in a machine, though blankets can usually be washed safely in a machine with a wool programme.

The secret of keeping wool soft is to use water which is almost cold – for both washing and rinsing – and handle it gently without rubbing. So dissolve the soap thoroughly in 1 part (1 pt, 1 l or whatever) of hot water, then add 3 parts (3 pt, 3 l etc) of cold water. Let a single woollen item soak for 10 minutes in this and then wash it by gently pressing against the bottom of the basin, lifting *slightly* and pressing it down again. Rub spots gently with a cake of Fairy soap and press this extra soap through the wool with the finger tips. But never rub wool or it will mat and felt.

When the dirt has come out, drain the basin and press the surplus water from the garment before lifting it out (lifting very wet wool stretches it). Rinse in several changes of water, *the same temperature as before*, until no more soap comes out and the water is quite clear. Some people like to use a fabric softener for wool. Alternatively, 1 to 2 teaspoons of glycerine in about a litre of cool water makes a softening final rinse without the synthetic smell.

Press out as much water as you can and then spin the water out with a fast spin in a machine, one garment at a time, before lying it out flat on a clean towel to dry. Heavy jumpers should always be dried lying flat like this, or they will stretch out of shape. But a lightweight garment can be hung on an inflatable hanger after a thorough spin. If you have no inflatable hanger simply thread the legs of a pair of tights down each armhole, pull the body of the tights through the neck and peg

---

Addresses and suggestions for further reading are at the ends of chapters.

both this and the two feet, to the line. This avoids the marks which are made if you peg the wool itself to the line. (Incidentally, men can pop a drip-dry shirt inside the pullover and peg it in the same way.)

Whatever the method, wool must be kept out of the sun and away from heat until dry – a tumble dry is disastrous.

If you can't spin wool, lie it out flat on a towel and then roll the towel up like a Swiss roll. If two people take either end of the towel and twist in opposite directions the water can be wrung out without any harm to the wool. Or, if you're alone, walk on the towel.

The less knitting is ironed the better. But it seldom needs it if it has been laid out flat. If it does, use a cool iron on the wrong side, through a slightly damp cloth.

> I started by saying that woven wool should only be dry cleaned. However, my artist son sometimes covers his clothes with so much paint and charcoal that I am loath to present them to a dry cleaner. I wash his heavy pure wool tweed trousers in totally cold water and pure soap, spin them dry, hang them in the shade and press them carefully. They look like new. I *don't* recommend washing woven wool; it could well ruin it, but if a garment which has no interlining is past cleaning by any other method it could be worth a try, *if you don't mind the risk*. But do stick to cold water and pure soap.

SKIN CURING

It has always seemed to me a great shame that the beautiful fur of the rabbits which hang outside butcher's shops should be thrown away. It seems almost insulting to waste. With that in mind, and memories of a muff of rabbit skin which I had when very young, I have tried to cure skins, but it has never worked well. So, as I feel the old skills should be cherished, I turned, for this book, to the **Women's Institute** – always an excellent source of practical information. What follows are methods recommended by a member.

The methods can be used for rabbit, goat and lamb skins, and were given to the WI member by one Miss Mendel, who described them as 'trusted and tried methods' and said the dry method was the easiest. They also carry a note that: 'It must be borne in mind that this is a craft requiring practice and care, and sufficient time devoted daily to the instructions given below. Otherwise, failure must inevitably follow.' The best skins for curing are from rabbits of 6 to 8 months old, and that the skins of those under 4 months, or 'summer skins' are not very suitable. (Alum is sold by chemists.)

Skin Dressing – Dry Method
Skin the animals (not more than 24 hours after killing for a tame rabbit), and remove the inner skin from the pelt as soon as possible. Pin the skin out on a large board with drawing pins, in a good shape, with the fur underneath. Rub well in 2 teaspoons of salt and 2 teaspoons of alum mixed together. Remove it from the board and fold it in quarters, fur side out. Leave for 3 days, then wipe and scrape it well on the inside. Hang it on a line, fur side out, so it dries slowly. For 3 weeks or more scrape, pull, stretch and rub it daily, treating it as if you were washing it, to keep it soft. Also brush the fur. If you can rub some oatmeal in during this process it helps to absorb moisture and whiten the skin, or rub it with pumice. At the end of 3 to 4 weeks it should be cured and soft.

The vital point is that the skin must not be allowed to become hard. Once hard, it is very difficult to get it soft again. The skin side can be rubbed to and fro over a chair back to soften it.

> The recipe says only a small quantity of salt and alum is needed and gives that amount, which is very much less than in the next recipe. Perhaps the amount depends on the size of the skin. I would suspect that if too little is used to treat the whole skin, parts will become rotten, but I may be wrong. I would also suggest leaving it in the coolest place possible, well protected from flies – though the recipe does not say so. And the line must be somewhere cool and shady.

Wet Curing for Skins
Put 2 lb of bran in 1 gallon of water. Fold the skin, fur side in, and immerse it in the water for 1 ½ to 2 days in summer, 3 in winter. Hang it over a line, fur side out, for about an hour to dry. Take it down and rub in 57 g (2 oz) of alum, and 85 to 113 g (3 to 4 oz) of salt for small skins, making sure it goes right to the edges. Fold in quarters, fur side out, and leave to pickle for 1 day (see note above). Check it and rub in more salt and alum if needed, fold and leave for 1 more day. Scrape out all inner skin. Hang it on a line, fur side out. Let it hang for 2 to 3 weeks daily, stretching and rubbing it as for the dry method above. Brush the fur clean.

Skin Curing Especially for Lamb Skins
Remove any loose fat and skin from the skin. Place in cold soft water for 24 hours, changing the water very frequently. Drain the skin and put it on a board, fur side down. Rub in a dressing made of 1 large tablespoon of salt, 45g (1½ oz) of alum boiled together for 3 minutes in a pint of water, and used while still warm. (Don't let the dressing get on the fur.) Fold the skin in half and leave flat for 24 hours. Repeat the dressing and folding and leave 24 hours more. Hang the skin over a line to dry *very* slowly; as it dries it must be repeatedly pulled, rubbed and stretched, as for the dry method above, until soft. Put the skin fur side up and wash the fur well with

warm soapy water *without getting the soapy water on the skin*. When totally dry rub the skin down with pumice or glasspaper.

STAIN REMOVAL

Stain removal is one of the trickiest of subjects to explain because so much depends not only on what you do but on how and when you do it. The same method used by two different people on the same stain can produce two quite different results simply because one person was too rough or too impatient. Fabrics can also be unpredictable: I rubbed a little pure soap on a tiny grease spot on a pale-grey pure cotton jumpsuit. It should have been the ideal treatment but the material was so poor that the dye faded instantly from the area, making a brand-new garment unwearable. So, it's impossible for me to guarantee that any of the following methods are safe, and it's important to read my warnings before attempting to remove a stain.

Of course, when fabrics respond badly to methods which should normally be perfectly safe you can claim against the makers, but it's a hassle to *prove* that you didn't do the wrong thing and money hardly makes up for the loss of a garment you enjoy wearing.

> The great thing is that once you get used to removing stains you begin to know automatically which type of substance will do the trick on other surfaces. Often it is a matter of alkalis acting against acids and so on and it helps if you look for these relationships. You don't need even 'O' level chemistry to do this, just be prepared to observe and experiment. After a while you may find that, like me, you almost delight in seeing a stain for the sheer satisfaction you will get in beating it.

Rules of Stain Removal
Rule 1: *Act at once.* Forget anything your mother told you about saying 'Don't worry, it doesn't matter a bit', and letting a stain sit there. People feel far less embarrassed at having spilt something if they can see it removed before it creates a permanent mark. So get the surplus substance off the surface immediately.

- Scoop up solids with an implement which lifts them out of the fabric without scraping at it.
- Mop up liquids instantly – with a clean light-coloured cloth. (Beware of dyed paper napkins: they will shed dye.)
- Put a clean cloth under the stain, and press between the top and bottom cloths.
- Either get the stained item to a suitable dry-cleaner before the stain dries, keeping it in a plastic bag *en route* with cloths to stop the stain touching other areas, or treat it yourself – *first reading the warning and rules below.*

> Do not attempt to remove stains from the following fabrics. They are too delicate to clean at home: silk chiffon, most brocade, watered silk, any silk with a rustle to it, silk jersey and velvet or lurex (unless marked as washable).
>   Silk often has fragile dyes which may become blotchy with stain treatment. Carpet dyes are also fragile and may fade.

Rule 2: *Always test any method of stain removal on a patch which won't show or on a spare piece of fabric or carpet unless you are* **sure** *the fabric can take it.*

Rule 3: *Suit the treatment to the surface the mark is on.* Treat wool like wool, acetate like acetate and so on, wherever you find it.

Rule 4: *Bear in mind the structure of the item.* You can't push stains through a carpet or upholstery in the way you can through loose cloth, and you must be *very* careful not to over-wet the surface or you may damage any carpet backing, padding or even interlining in a garment. Expect all underlayers to be more fragile and more likely to shrink than any surface fabric. Keep mopping up the liquid with clean white tissues between applications.

Rule 5: *Almost all surfaces are fragile.* You can damage the individual threads with rubbing and create a permanent mark even though the stain itself is removed. Go gently: dabbing not rubbing. A professional technique for stain removal is called '**tamping**' which is tapping the cleaning solution patiently through the cloth, again and again, with the tips of the fingers, or a clean cloth. It looks as if it is having no effect, but little by little it is.

Rule 6: *Start at the edge of the stain and work towards the middle,* so you go from clean to dirty, not vice versa. And, if possible, work from the back of the fabric to push the stain out the way it came. Wherever possible have a thick cloth under the stain and keep moving it as it absorbs it.

Rule 7: *Give any remedy time to work.* Gentleness and infinite patience are vital. Many good methods take a day or more to work.

Rule 8: The distinction between fabrics which are washable and those which 'dry-clean only' isn't very helpful. Most dry-cleanable fabrics can be moistened with *very cool* water, without harm – think what the rain would do if this wasn't so. This means cold and lukewarm water can be used in stain removal on some 'dry-clean only' fabrics. How risky it is will depend on the particular fabric so do a test on a patch which won't show. (See also the warning above.) Upholstery is an exception – nobody expects it to get rained on, so any water may damage it.

Addresses and suggestions for further reading are at the ends of chapters.

Rule 9: *Don't switch from method to method without giving any single one a decent try.* And never switch from a water-based to a spirit-based method – or vice versa – without letting the fabric dry *totally* or you may cause shrinking and felting. This means you can't dry-clean a garment until it is totally dry after stain removal. Nor should you wash it while a spirit-based cleaner is still moist.

Rule 10: *Don't use any cleansing substances, or methods without realizing – and accepting – their limitations and dangers (see above and below).*

When you try to remove a stain yourself rather than use a professional dry-cleaner, you risk damaging the item in question. It is very easy to misjudge the make-up of a fabric and use the wrong method on it, or to be slightly rougher than you intended to be and damage the surface. The following methods are tried and tested by me, and work well, or are recommended by top authorities, but please realize *there is no guarantee they will not do damage in your particular case.* Do *not* attempt it unless you accept the risk involved. Remember if you take a tricky stain to an expert and there is a disaster you can usually claim against the firm. If you cause the disaster you have no claim on anyone.

Acetone
Acetone should be avoided. It will melt fabric containing cellulose acetate; so it harms Tricel, Dicel and all their relatives. Beware too: some fabric has just the occasional acetate thread supplying a particular colour or texture. Instead of acetone, use amyl acetate (from chemists) which removes the same stains without this risk – but it may make some dyes bleed.

Ammonia
Household ammonia will bleach certain dyes and must *never* be used on fabrics containing wool. Use from a few drops to a teaspoonful in 250 ml (½ pt) of water. Only increase the strength if a tough stain will budge no other way, and you are prepared to risk damage to the fabric. If a stain won't move with 1 part ammonia to 3 parts water, ammonia probably isn't the answer. Avoid breathing its fumes, have the windows open when using it, and wear rubber gloves.

DANGER: Nothing which has ammonia on it should be bleached, or vice versa, without thoroughly removing whichever chemical was used first.

Bleach
Bleach can only be used with total safety on white cotton and linen, or on pale-cream-tones of those fabrics – if you don't mind making them lighter. Even then it must

not be used on crease-resistant, drip-dry, piqué or embossed fabrics. It will fade coloured cottons and actively damage silk, wool and man-made fibres (unless they say they can be bleached). Never let undiluted bleach touch fabric or it may burn a hole in it. Mix the water and bleach, stir well, and then submerge the fabric. Move the fabric in the bleach so it is evenly exposed. Soak no longer than is necessary.

Hydrogen Peroxide
Hydrogen peroxide is a mild bleaching agent sold by chemists in various strengths. Buy '20 volumes', and use 1 part of this to 6 parts water. Do not use it on flame-resistant fabrics or on nylon. But, unlike bleach, it can be used on wool and silk.

Methylated and other Spirits
Methylated spirits, lighter fuel, petrol and any other spirits are all used neat, but they can make some dyes go blotchy and create a permanent mark at the rim of the spirit. In the dry-cleaning trade they call this a 'sweal' – see feathering, below. They will also damage fabrics such as those which are rubberized or made of cellulose acetate – see acetone, above. Only use when unavoidable, and then do a test patch first where it won't show.

NEVER USE A SPIRIT OR BRANDED CLEANER WHILE SMOKING OR IN A ROOM WITH ANY FLAME BURNING – EVEN A PILOT LIGHT.

Proprietary Cleaners
Branded dry-cleaning fluids, such as Beaucaire and Dab-it-off, should only be used on fabrics recommended by the instructions. Even then there may be a risk of a 'sweal' (see methylated spirits above). You can lessen the risk of this by 'feathering'. This is making little strokes out from the centre so you don't leave a neat ring.

Pure Soap
Pure soap is a product which *says* it is pure soap. This usually means a block soap made for washing clothes, or pure soap flakes (trickier to use), or a pure soap liquid or powder made for washing wool. You can't assume that bath soap doesn't contain some substance which is bad for dyes.

Vinegar
Stick to white vinegar or you may get brown staining. But do not use it on any acetate or triacetate fabrics.

When All Else Fails
If a stain is resolute, and the fabric won't be damaged by boiling water, stretch the material *tightly* over a heat-proof jug or bowl, with an elastic band, placing the stain in the middle. Pour boiling water from a height on to, and through, the stain until it vanishes. It may help to have some pure soap on the stain before pouring on the water or to rub on some powdered borax. Several kettles of water may be needed.

WARNING: Read pages 198-199 before trying to remove any stain

WARNING: Any remedy in this chart could damage some fabrics

Adhesive	While Still Wet	Once It Has Dried
Araldite/Epoxy Resin	Very tough to remove. Scoop off surface adhesive before it can dry. Apply Arco Cupran (page 216), or cellulose thinners.	Either of the instant remedies can also be tried on dry resin – give them time to work or use commercial paint stripper.
Evostik Resin W	Easily removed when wet; far harder when dry. Scoop off surplus and sponge off with a clean wet cloth. Make sure it is out of the fabric as well as off.	Try leaving water to soak into it (e.g. a moist sponge on top of the mark). Try to tamp it off once it softens.
Evostik Impact II	Apply Evostik cleaner (if you keep it). Try paint stripper, or white spirit mixed with washing-up liquid.	Extremely hard to get off once dry. Try Evostik cleaner, but it may fail. (see 'wet' remedies, left).
Supaglue	Put anything it gets on to in water for a long time – including skin.	It's a forlorn hope but try soaking in water.
Tile on Wood (Polycell)	Get it off fast – using water.	Amyl acetate.
Tile Grout (Polycell)	Water.	Hydrochloric acid (e.g. some patio cleaners) but use with great caution and expect damage to fabrics.
General Purpose Filler (Polycell)	Water.	Water.
Frame Sealant (Acrylic), Silicone Bath Sealant, Ready-mixed Filler, Coloured Tile Grout (Polycell)	Water.	Paintbrush cleaner.
Unibond, Copydex	Water.	Dry-cleaning fluid such as Beaucaire or Dab-it-off.
Polystyrene Coving Adhesive, Unistik Contact Adhesive, Unilast Gap Filling Adhesive	Water.	Trichlorethylene or amyl acetate (or acetone, but see page 199).
Woodworking Adhesive, Waterproof Fix n'Grout	Water.	Paintbrush cleaner or possibly white spirit.
Waterproof Woodworking Adhesive, Fire Cement (Polycell)	Water.	There is no solvent for it.
Cork Tile Adhesive, Multipurpose Flooring Adhesive	Water.	White spirit.
Cerafix PVA Adhesive	Water.	Amyl acetate or acetone (see page 199).
Waterproof Tile Adhesive	Water.	Amyl acetate or possibly white spirit.
Bitumen and Bitumen Gutter Sealant	White spirit.	White spirit.
Prit, Gloy, Copydex Child's Play, Solvite	Water.	Water.

If you use any water-based method of stain removal, finish by tamping clean water through the area and repeatedly mopping it dry, to remove all trace of the ammonia, borax or whatever else was used. Finally press the area dry with clean cloths.

Basic Stain Removing Kit

If you keep the following in the house you will be able to cope with most stains: glycerine, oil of eucalyptus, borax powder, pure soap, 1001 carpet shampoo, white vinegar, household ammonia, white spirit, Fuller's Earth and possibly an enzyme washing powder. As you can see, the ingredients are very cheap and will keep indefinitely. If you prefer to use a branded product, Beckman's

Addresses and suggestions for further reading are at the ends of chapters.

Stain Devils have come out best in some tests though I have not found them totally successful myself. As with any stain remover, it depends how swiftly you act. Once a stain has thoroughly dried, or been unsuccessfully washed, even the best stain removal methods may fail. But it is always worth a try.

★ Enzyme detergents break down protein. So don't use them on fabrics made of protein, such as silk or wool.

★ Any stain can be removed more easily when softened. Old stains which are to be treated with a water-based treatment can be softened by rubbing in glycerine and leaving it for an hour or two.

Adhesives
With adhesives you don't have a lot of choice: if a glue needs strong chemicals to remove it you either use them, and risk spoiling certain fabrics, or decide to live with a glue stain. There simply aren't safe alternatives.

Many glue manufacturers will supply a solvent for their adhesive – if one exists – but the following immediate remedies were suggested by the glue manufacturers themselves. In all cases, work the suggested solvent into the glue, and let it have time to take effect. Then try to mop the stain off with a clean cloth. Follow the rules for stains (page 198-199).

Ballpoints and Biros
The chemistry of inks varies with the maker, so results are unpredictable. Red ink is always extra hard to remove and may be impossible (see page 203). The following methods may shift blue or black marks.

● Tamping pure soap and lukewarm water through the stain again and again with a clean cloth underneath.
● Spray on hair lacquer then press out the stain and the lacquer with a clean cloth. (This can work marvellously on light nylon).
● Tamp with methylated spirits. If the stain is on plastic you can wipe it off with this, but a little of the plastic will come off too – so go gently. The same applies to shiny leather but the dye may be affected.
● Tamp with hot or sour milk, or soak washable items in it.

Beer
Beer leaves a brown mark, which can be hard to remove, if allowed to dry. Having mopped it up, sponge with lukewarm water, or with 1 part white vinegar to 5 parts water (not on acetate or triacetate). Lacking this, clean it off with soda water. Wash, or soak, washable fabrics before they dry out, and use carpet shampoo on carpets. On acetate and triacetate use 1½ teaspoons of borax in 250 ml (½ pt) lukewarm water.

Dried stains may be treated with methylated spirits or the branded spot remover K2r.

Beetroot
Having mopped up all liquid, tamp with lukewarm water containing 1½ teaspoons of borax per 250 ml (½ pt) of water. If necessary add a few drops of ammonia.

Some people swear by gin or vodka on beetroot. I have yet to try it, but I do cherish the tip which I was sent by the mother of a 3-year-old. He rubbed ripe pear on a beetroot stain and so enabled her to wash it out with remarkable ease – a method I have tested with equal success.

Bird Droppings
Scoop up the dropping and sponge off any stain with pure soap and water, the borax solution given under Beetroot, or a carpet or upholstery shampoo, such as 1001. If the laundry on the line was dive-bombed, relaundering should do the trick, using an enzyme powder if necessary. But if the bird has been eating berries the stain bleach may need peroxide, or see 'When all else fails'(page 199).

Blood
Beware of heat: even hot water sets the protein in blood and the stain may then be impossible to remove.

Having mopped up all the surplus, treat bloodstains with cold salty water while still wet. Soakable fabrics can be left to soak. Tamp others repeatedly – if necessary using a little pure soap too. Once the stain has almost gone wash carpets with carpet shampoo and cold water. Wet stains should come out quite easily, but once blood dries it is tough to remove. Soak in an enzyme washing powder and cold water or apply cold water and ammonia but wash the stain out with cold water before laundering. Remove any soap or ammonia with clean cold water.

Chewing gum
Don't dab at it – the gum will be pressed in. Remove any large lumps – unless on a corduroy or velvet pile which will come off with it. Then use a spray-on hardener sold by G.E.Holloway and Son (page 216) as directed and break it off in flakes. Failing that, put the fabric in a plastic bag in a freezer. When hard pick off the brittle gum, wiggling the fabric to get it out of the weave. When every trace is removed wash or dry clean. If breaking hardened chewing gum threatens to take the pile off velvet or corduroy hold the back of the fabric over a steaming kettle spout (beware of burning yourself) and see if picking the chewing gum off when very soft is any better. You may then be able to freeze it again and remove the last traces safely.

Chocolate or Cocoa
Scoop up as much as possible with a spoon, or mop up the liquid. Then work glycerine into the stain and tamp it with lukewarm water and pure soap. Remove the soap by tamping with clear lukewarm water. The borax solution for beetroot is another method.

Coffee
Get coffee out while wet: it is difficult to remove once dry. Having mopped it up, tamp glycerine into it. Give this a few minutes to work then tamp it out with lukewarm water and pure soap. On suitable fabrics use a teaspoon white vinegar to ¼ 1 (½ pt) water.

WARNING: Read pages 198-199 before trying to remove any stain.

Cosmetics

Cosmetic stains can often be lifted off the surface of leather by dabbing it *lightly* with the sticky side of sticky tape. But be careful not to pull off the leather's surface. They wash out of fabrics.

Creosote

This is a nasty one. Take 'dry-clean only' fabrics to an expert. On washable fabrics you may be able to remove the stain by soaking it in glycerine, then tamping with soap – or by applying oil of eucalyptus.

Curry

There are usually two main elements to a curry stain: fat and turmeric. Turmeric gives the yellow colour and is the harder to remove. Applying glycerine at once may stop the stain setting. Then rinse washable fabrics in lukewarm water. On dry-clean only fabrics tamp the stain with the borax solution given for beetroot. On carpet sponge on the borax mixture and leave it for 15 minutes, then sponge the mixture out and shampoo as usual. It may be necessary to apply hydrogen peroxide or bleach – if it will take them.

Dyes

Since I wrote *Supertips* a lot of people have written asking how to remove the dye from garments which they have put into a washing machine with something which has run. Washing the item without letting it dry first helps, but to remove all the dye you have to resort to bleach – if it was a white fabric which will take it – or to a dye-run remover, such as that sold by Dylon and by Beckman. This will also remove the original colour of the garment. You then have to dye it back. Alas, there is no product clever enough to remove selectively the dye you don't want and to leave the original one.

Splashes of dye can be treated with methylated spirits or with ammonia and water.

Egg

If fabric can take it, the best treatment for egg stains is the old-fashioned mixture of lukewarm water and a few drops of household ammonia or a solution of enzyme detergent. A safer mixture is 250 ml (½ pt) water with 1½ teaspoons powdered borax tamped through the stain.

Excreta (human or animal)

How badly this stains will depend greatly on the diet of the depositor, so what will remove a stain on one occasion may fail on another.

Scoop it out of the fabric, or carpet – a paint scraper is ideal for this. Get as much as possible out by wiping very thoroughly with tissues. But be careful not to rub so hard you break up the texture of the carpet or fabric. Shampoo a carpet immediately with a carpet shampoo such as 1001 – doing a test patch first if you haven't used it on the carpet before. Put suitable fabrics to soak in enzyme detergent and lukewarm water. Tamp the stain out of 'dry-clean only' fabrics with lukewarm water and pure soap.

There are now products which claim to use harmless bacteria to 'eat' the stains and smells from such accidents, and so remove them. 'Odour Eliminator' seems to do the job. Some pet shops stock these products, or contact the manufacturers, the **Veterinary Drug Co** (page 216) for stockists.

Fats and oils

When fats and oils are really thick soap simply can't penetrate them, so first you need to thin them down with a finer oil. The best is oil of eucalyptus (from chemists). Dab off as much oil as possible – without smearing it – with a clean tissue. Then tamp with oil of eucalyptus on a clean cloth until the oil begins to shift. It can then be washed out, tamped out with water and soap, or removed with a dry cleaning fluid, according to the fabric.

If you have no eucalyptus oil and do have a dry-cleaning fluid, or even lighter fluid, these may loosen the grease or oil – or may even remove the stain entirely. But they are more likely to affect the dye. In the last resort, heavy oil and grease can be thinned by working in poultry dripping before washing.

If colourless fats or oils have stained leather or upholstery warm some Fuller's Earth (from a chemist) or potato flour, put a heap of it over the mark and cover immediately with foil and a cloth to keep the warmth in. Leave it for 24 hours. If the stain has lessened try repeated applications of fresh powder. There are also branded grease removers for leather; fabric upholstery may respond to a cleaner like K2r and so may some wallcoverings.

Fruit and Fruit Juice

Mop up as much as possible with a white cloth or tissue, or pour over dry starch and let it absorb as much of the stain as possible, then brush it off. Press glycerine into the stain to stop it setting. Then press tepid water and borax or pure soap through the stain until it vanishes. Once it is allowed to dry it will be far harder to remove. But in this case apply glycerine, leave it an hour and then tamp as above.

Stubborn stains may need to be bleached out or removed with hydrogen peroxide, or with lemon juice and salt as for rust. If that fails try 'When all else fails' (page 199) applying borax before pouring on the water, or use dye remover (above).

Grass stains

Grass stains are among those deceptively simple stains that can frustrate the best of efforts. Nothing is guaranteed to remove them but the following remedies are the most likely to be successful. A soak in mild bleach (as directed on the bottle). Tamping with glycerine, leaving a few hours, then tamping with pure soap and lukewarm water; or tamping with methylated spirits or with the ammonia solution.

Hair Lacquer

Hair lacquer should really be applied before dressing as it stains some fabrics. Remove the marks by tamping

Addresses and suggestions for further reading are at the ends of chapters.

with 1½ teaspoons of powdered borax in 250 ml (½ pt) of lukewarm water.

Ice Cream
Ice cream should sponge off but treat chocolate ice cream as for chocolate, and real fruit ices as for fruit.

Ink
Serious staining, such as a pen leak in a jacket pocket, is best taken to a professional cleaner – see also **Parker Pens** (page 216).

However, it is fascinating to drop an inky handkerchief or shirt into a pan of hot milk and watch the blue ink flow out of the fabric and into the milk. This can be tried with any black or blue non-permanent ink and fabrics which can't be soaked in milk can be tamped with it. If milk fails some inks will come out with salt and lemon juice, others with ammonia and water. Yet others will need alternate tamping with ammonia and pure soap. If these methods fail you may find that tamping with methylated spirits works. It will be more effective if heated over a bowl of hot water (without a flame). But some brands won't come out totally.

Red ink is an eosin dye which is almost impossible to remove except by using methylated spirits or a product such as the dye remover given for felt-pen ink (below).

Ink on Carpets
Instantly put salt liberally on top. Salt absorbs liquid and will draw the ink out of the fibres. Once the salt has absorbed the free liquid, vacuum or sweep it off very carefully without spreading the stain. Then treat it with hot or sour milk to loosen the ink. Finally, shampoo with carpet shampoo or the milk will smell.

Ink on Leather
Ink on leather may come out if dabbed immediately with milk, but it may take a lot of dabbing and there is a risk of the milk leaving a grease mark in some types of leather.

Felt-pen Ink
Felt-pen inks vary enormously. Some will come off if treated like blue ink. Red felt pen can react like red ink, and permanent markers may need drastic treatment which is likely to remove the dye. The two possibilities are to tamp it with petrol (which may make the dye run), or to rub in a product called ReDuRan designed to remove industrial dyes from the hands (see page 216). The latter will remove both the felt pen and the dye of the fabric – but you could wash the whole garment, get rid of any remaining dye with Dylon's dye remover and re-dye it. And the **Parker Pen Company** (page 216) has solvents which remove its inks.

Iodine
Mop up the stain, and tamp immediately with pure soap and the water and ammonia mixture.

Jam, Ketchup and Similar Substances
The problem with these substances is that you may be dealing with a natural fruit colour or a food dye or both. If marks don't wipe off with lukewarm water, try tamping with the borax solution for beetroot, or with methylated spirits. Or soak washable fabrics in the borax solution.

Lipstick
Place a pad of tissues or towelling under the stain. Dab with oil of eucalyptus. Let this soak into the stain. Blot off the lipstick and repeat. If necessary, leave the oil in overnight then blot up all loose lipstick and tamp with pure soap and water as hot as the fabric will stand – or on 'dry-clean only' fabrics omit the soap and water and dry-clean afterwards. The effectiveness of the treatment varies with the make, but the eucalyptus may totally remove the stain.

White cotton handkerchiefs with lipstick on will boil or bleach clean. Occasionally eucalyptus fails, in which case try glycerine or surgical spirit – though the latter may shift dye.

Mascara
Waterproof mascara stains should be tamped with oil of eucalyptus then with soap and lukewarm water. Other mascara stains can have soap and water straight away. If these fail, tamp with ammonia.

Mildew or Mould
Mildew on fabrics is decidedly to be avoided as it is one of the hardest stains to remove. The most reliable method is still that recommended in the *Enquire Within* of 1856.

> Take soap, and rub it well [into the stain]; then scrape some fine chalk [white blackboard], and rub it also on the linen. Lay it on the grass. As it dries, wet it a little, and it will come out in twice doing.

The author was an optimist, give it 2 days of soap, chalk and sunlight before you try the alternative – which is to tamp it with 10 per cent hydrogen peroxide – which may harm delicate fabrics.

Mud
The secret with mud is never to try to remove it until *totally* dry. Then brush it off. Working on it while wet just pushes it into the fabric.

Nail Varnish
Nail varnish remover may contain acetone (see page 199).

Paints and Lacquers
Artists' paints should come off using the same methods as for household paints but Winsor and Newton make Win-sol, a paint remover for their paints (from art shops).

Water-based paints can be washed off with water and pure soap if you catch them while wet. Wet oil-based paints and lacquers come off quite easily with white spirit, turpentine or paraffin and on the whole these do not shift dyes – though check all the same. Then remove all trace of these substances.

Once paint or lacquer has dried you have a far tougher job on your hands – and there is always a risk that any substance which shifts dry paint will also shift the dye of whatever you are cleaning. Oil-based paints and lacquers will come off quite miraculously with a hand cleaner called Cupran. Amyl acetate will shift cellulose paints, and tamping with equal amounts of ammonia and turpentine mixed together will sometimes shift other paints, so will paintbrush cleaner/ restorer.

Perfume

If perfume stains it is because the alcohol in it has affected the dye of the fabric. This cannot be cured.

Perspiration

Perspiration varies with the body's health; sometimes being acid, sometimes alkaline. This makes removing perspiration stains a matter of trial and error. Tamp acid stains with ammonia, alkaline stains with lemon juice. But go carefully lest these shift the dyes and don't be surprised if the stain won't budge. Perspiration can damage dye and nothing can reverse that.

Plasticine

Remove as much as possible, with your fingernails. Either use hot water and soap or a branded spirit stain remover to dissolve the deposit – according to the fabric.

Printing Ink

A friend of mine in Fleet Street rang me in despair one day asking how she could remove printing ink from a favourite summer skirt. The answer was a solvent such as Dab-it-off. But put a thick pad of clean tissue underneath and work very carefully as such a dark stain is easily spread and very easily leaves a sweal so it needs careful feathering, and immediate dry-cleaning once the stain is out.

Rust

The ease with which rust stains come out of light cotton or linen makes them almost a pleasure. Simply put the fabric in the sun (first catch your sun) and sprinkle a good heap of salt on the rust mark. Then pour over enough lemon juice to moisten both salt and fabric. Leave it in the sun, moistening it with more lemon until the rust mark vanishes. It may take a few hours or a couple of days, depending on the mark. But you don't need to *do* anything except moisten and wait. I have used this successfully on pale-cream pure silk – but with anything other than white cotton or linen there is a risk that the lemon will leave a stain or bleach the dye.

N.B. This method of removing rust works just as well for rust marks on wood. And it will work without the sunlight, though more slowly.

Scorch Marks

How a scorch mark should be treated depends entirely on what it is on. On man-made fabrics a scorch is normally a lost cause, as some of the fibres melt. On cotton or linen a surface scorch may simply wash out, may respond to tamping with hydrogen peroxide, or may fade if rubbed with lemon juice and left in the sun. On wool you may be able to brush off the burnt fibres. On delicate fabrics try applying a paste of water and magnesium carbonate (from a chemist) and leaving this until totally dry, then brushing it off.

Scorch marks are also a prime target for folk remedies. Among the oddest are Brown Windsor soup, and the following curious mixture: 60 g (2 oz) of Fuller's Earth, 250 ml (½ pt) vinegar, 2 to 3 chopped onions boiled together, applied when cold, and brushed off when dry. And my very early edition of Mrs Beeton has that same recipe plus ½ oz soap and 1 oz dried fowl's dung. So if all sane remedies fail you may like to try these. Some people still swear by them.

Shoe Polish

Tamp repeatedly with white spirit, blotting up the liquid and colour as it loosens. Remove the white spirit with pure soap and water or 1001 Carpet Shampoo if necessary.

Tar

Tar comes off quite easily with eucalyptus oil (this can be used safely on people and animals). Put a good pad of tissue under the fabric and dab with white tissues well saturated with the eucalyptus oil, throwing each tissue away when it has traces of tar on it. Continue until no more tar sits on the surface. To get the last traces out of the fibres tamp pure soap and water through until it comes clean.

In the absence of eucalyptus, petrol and lighter fuel will both remove tar – more hazardously.

Tea

If a tea stain has glycerine rubbed into it the moment it is spilt it should be very easy to remove by tamping with pure soap and lukewarm water. If a stain has dried, leave glycerine to soak in for several hours before trying to remove the stain. Tamp with the borax solution for beetroot. Lemon juice or acetic acid will also remove tea stains but these risk creating a new stain in some fabrics.

Tipp-Ex

I tracked down the cure for liquid tipp-ex at the request of a friend who tipped a bottle down a navy blue dress. Instantly scrape off as much as possible – without pressing it into the fabric or damaging the threads. Tamp the remainder with white spirit, with a cloth underneath, until it has all been removed.

Urine

If a puppy, kitten or child puddles on a carpet mop it up *instantly* and squirt the patch well with soda water. Remop, repeat and re-mop. If the puddle is caught before it dries and enough soda is used as an antidote there should be no stain. Failing soda, use Perrier or any mineral water.

Vaseline
Don't let vaseline encounter heat before you try to remove it: it can fix the stain for ever. Vaseline can be tamped out with turpentine before you wash or clean the fabric.

Wax from Candles
Leave wax well alone until hard. If it is in carpet, remove as much as you can with your nails. If possible chill the wax in a freezer, then break it off in pieces. (Wiggle the fabric to get the particles to fall from the weave.) If it is in carpet, remove as much as you can with your nails. Then place the fabric between two sheets of absorbent paper and iron with a hot iron (moving the paper) to remove as much wax as possible. But keep moving the paper so the wax is absorbed by a clean section, and be careful not to let a fragile fabric or carpet overheat. Wash in the hottest water suitable for the fabric, or dry-clean. (If necessary, apply paraffin, to thin the wax, before washing.)

Wine
The great thing about a red wine stain is that nature has provided the natural antidote: white wine. Unlikely as it may sound, the best way to prevent red wine staining is to pour white wine over it before it has time to dry. Just mop up the surplus red wine (making sure you don't in your haste do as I once did and grab a brilliant red paper napkin with loose dye). Then pour enough white wine over the stain to wet the stain nicely. Mop that up and you may well find the stain has almost gone. If it hasn't, keep washable fabrics moist until you can put them in to soak. If you have no white wine, mineral water will sometimes do the trick, and so may tap water but less surely.

Old red wine stains can be soaked with white wine before washing, or you can rub glycerine into the stain and leave it for several hours before washing. If that fails the only solution may be to tamp the stain with equal parts of water and hydrogen peroxide.

White wine simply leaves a sticky stain which will wash or dry-clean out without trouble.

> Despite what is often said, red wine should *never* be doused with salt. On some fabrics this may prevent a stain but on others it will set it permanently – this isn't a good risk to take.

MAIL ORDER

Mail order is covered by at least three different acts, but these only say how things *ought* to be, and give you rights in court when things go wrong. They don't *stop* things going wrong and, at best, getting redress is time-consuming.

Every year companies simply vanish with the customers' money, or supply goods far inferior to those promised. Order only from well-established companies, with a good reputation, or from those covered by one of the consumer protection schemes. On the other hand, good companies do save you the hassles, and travel costs, of conventional shopping and sometimes offer savings. They also enable you to support charities or buy things which you can't find locally. On pages 217-218 I have given some mail order companies which help to fund charities, plus the addresses for the main mail order catalogues. Then, in the address lists throughout this book, you will find companies which sell unusual goods which may be difficult to get any other way, or sell a particularly good selection of goods which may be hard to find if you live far from a major city. However, I have not tested them all and they carry no 'Moyra Bremner warranty of good trading'.

The safest companies are often those belonging to one of the mail order trade associations, which have codes of practice to which members must conform, and will arbitrate if you are dissatisfied. Members' catalogues must carry a statement that they conform to this code. Even then, keep an exact record of all the details you would need to supply if you had to make a complaint (see page 206).

Mail Order Trade Associations

As I write there are discussions on laws to regulate postal selling throughout Europe. Meanwhile, if you buy by mail from abroad the law of the selling country normally applies. If you want to know what rules apply within the EC the **Consumers in the European Community Group** may be able to advise you. This organization both provides information and is a pressure group putting to the EC the views of British consumers and professional organizations. Within Britain, your main protection comes from the trade associations. The **Direct Marketing Association** (page 217) is the trade association for the direct marketing industry. Its members include companies selling products such as books and records, by mail order, charities with mail-order lists and also those who sell lists of addresses for such companies to use. A copy of its full code of practice can be seen at CABx and Trading Standards Offices, or the Association will send you free notes on the code. If you cannot resolve a problem with a member company the Association has an arm which claims to be independent and will investigate any complaint and recommend redress.

The **Mail Order Trader's Association** (page 217) covers the major catalogues. Its code of practice includes the following.

- The catalogue must give a clear statement of prices, credit terms, and conditions of trade.
- You have a right to cancel any order up to the moment it is despatched.

WARNING: Read pages 198-199 before trying to remove any stain

- If you return goods within the set time limit your money must be promptly refunded in full, provided you have taken 'reasonable care' of them. Get proof of posting.
- Money must be promptly refunded on goods returned because they are unsatisfactory.
- A conciliation and low-cost arbitration service to help you sort out disputes with its members.

The **National Newspapers Mail Order Protection Scheme Ltd (MOPS)** (page 217) was created to protect you if you buy through an advertisement in a national newspaper asking for 'cash with order'. It has a central fund to repay those who lose their money through advertised goods failing to be delivered when an advertiser ceases to trade. However, an awful lot of advertisements in the national press are not covered as it only covers advertisements accepted for the MOPS scheme. Those it does cover must carry the MOPS symbol. So do look for it in press press advertisements. And if you often buy from advertisements get the leaflet spelling out all the MOPS rules from the address on page 217.

Under MOPS *you must claim within 3 months of the advertisement appearing*. Write to the advertising manager of the paper which carried the advertisement, sending details of the advertisement, plus the date of your order, evidence of payment and the correspondence about the order. They do not accept photocopies. But keep photocopies in case the originals get lost in the post, and ask the post office for proof of posting (free).

Magazines, periodicals and regional and local newspapers are not covered by that scheme. The **Periodical Publishers Association** (page 217) covers most magazines and periodicals, and **The Newspaper Society** (page 217) covers most regional and local papers. These two bodies run voluntary mail-order protection schemes. Under these, members refund all, or part of, the money you paid in advance, if the company which advertised the goods has gone bust. However, the publications don't *have* to belong to these schemes. And, as with MOPS, you must apply for the money within 3 months of the advertisement appearing.

Neither these schemes nor those of MOPS apply to classified ads, nor to inserts, nor to goods bought from a catalogue – even if the catalogue was advertised in the publication. If you get no joy from the publication itself you can ask these organizations to take the matter up.

Obtaining or Cancelling Mail Order Catalogues

You have the right to prevent your name being put on mailing lists. The organization which can prevent it is **The Mailing Preference Service** (**MPS**) (page 217). It is a free service run by the direct mail industry and it works in two ways. If you *dislike* unsolicited mail you can get MPS to delete your name from the mailing lists of all their members and MPS can also prevent companies from mailing you when they use public lists – such as the phone book. But if you *like* such mail you can ask MPS to put your name on their members' lists. However, you can't say you want to be on some lists but not on others.

Terms and Conditions

The code of practice of the Advertising Standards Authority covers all printed advertisements. This means the advertisement should be truthful (Note: *should* is not the same as *is*) and that, if money is paid in advance, it should be refunded in full (not as a credit note) if the goods are not delivered within a set time (usually 28 days) or if they are returned undamaged within 7 days.

Payment

The terms of payment vary greatly and need to be looked at very carefully. The golden rule is, if a company doesn't lay out its payment terms so you can understand them, don't buy from it. See also Credit, under Law.

Complaints about Mail Order

Any complaint could end up going to court, *so if you have to make any complaint keep copies of every letter from or to you, and make notes on every phone call – with the date.*

If goods don't reach you within 28 days, you should complain to the company. With this, or any other complaint, write to the department first and if that fails write to the Managing Director.

The next two steps are interchangeable. You could either write to the appropriate trade association or you have a choice of public bodies to turn to – a Citizens Advice Bureau, a Consumer Advice Centre or the local Trading Standards Officer or you can take advice from a local law centre or legal aid solicitor on whether you would be likely to win in court. Such claims can be taken to the small claims court without much cost, but it is always worth getting advice before embarking.

If you sent money in advance for something advertised in the press and never received it because the company went bust, you may be able to get your money back under the MOPS scheme (opposite) by contacting its secretariat. But not all such advertisements are covered by the 'Readers' Protection Scheme'. For example, classified advertisements aren't covered, nor are those for which you didn't send money in advance.

Whoever you complain to will need to know:

- your name and address
- the date of the order
- how much you paid
- the trader's name and address
- the address the goods should have gone to
- the full details of the goods ordered
- what form the payment took – e.g. cheque
- whether you have a receipt or acknowledgement of the order.

PESTS

Ask someone if they ever have pests in their garden and they will cheerfully admit to greenfly, blackfly and goodness knows what else. Ask them about house pests and they will probably change the subject. House pests are seen as a sign of dirt and bad housekeeping, and it is rather shameful to admit to them. It is time this myth was exploded. Pests may well come into any house because they sense there are delicious things to eat there, or be brought in on something you buy – that is no reflection on anyone. Cleanliness has nothing to do with their *arrival*, only with how long you let them *stay*. Not letting them stay is what this section is all about.

The first edition of *Enquire Within* instructed readers to exterminate beetles with the deadly delicacy of red lead mixed with sugar and flour, to kill cockroaches with oatmeal and plaster of Paris (which presumably constipated them to death) and to deal death to ants by putting quicklime into their nests. In comparison with that today's insecticides seem positively benign.

Suitable products and the companies which make them are listed on page 218.

Controlling Pests outside Britain

Most of what follows concerns pests within Britain. When travelling overseas it is worth remembering that creatures which do not carry disease in Britain can do so in many hotter climates. So *far* more care should be taken to avoid insect bites. Carry with you an effective, broad-spectrum, insect killer or repellent (see page 218), and in certain areas use a product like Deet to keep pests away (from **MASTA**).

Using Professional Pest Control Companies

If you have pests in the house which could be a health hazard your local council has a duty to do something about them. Contact the local Environmental Health Officer and see if the pest comes within the council's guidelines.

If it doesn't you may need to call in a pest control company. They use chemicals which are not available to the general public. The trouble is you have no way of telling what they are using. This means that only reputable companies should be used. Most reputable companies belong to the **British Pest Control Association** (page 218) and it will provide a list of them, if you send a sae. It also sells an A to Z of household pests which includes some of the rarer ones. Its members keep to a code of practice set up between the government and the association.

DIY Pest Control

Insects often lay their eggs in deep cracks – out of reach of the chemicals used by pest control companies. How soon these eggs hatch will vary with the temperature, but they can often hatch after the effectiveness of the pest control treatment has worn off – though this obviously depends on the life of the spray. This means that most insects will need more than one treatment to eradicate them.

All insect sizes given below are for adults.

Ants (*garden ants 3 to 5 mm*)
Ants don't deserve to be thought of as pests. They may be unwelcome visitors, but in Britain the major ant is the black garden ant and, as one expert put it, 'They are cleanly little things which keep their houses tidy, follow each other along clean paths, and don't feed on anything dirty.'

The only ants likely to be a health hazard are the minute pharaoh's ants. They like moisture and are not choosy where they find it. In hospitals they have been found on anything damp, however nasty. They can make several inaccessible nests in a house and may need professional clearance, but some councils will deal with them (see opposite).

In the tropics ants can present a different hazard entirely. A phalanx of soldier ants is a formidable, and almost unstoppable, army, which will even kill pets and babies in their path. For this reason alone, a crying baby should get prompt attention in such countries.

Black garden ants home in on the smell of sweetness. So, the best course is simply to keep all sweet foods in closed jars, and put some strong-smelling substance – like a little ammonia on cotton wool – at their entry hole to put them off. As they only wander into houses on a seasonal basis, this is often enough. But if you *must* kill them there are two approaches. Either you kill the workers who have come to scavenge or you destroy the nest. There are plenty of ant sprays and powders (see page 218) to kill ants which invade. To destroy the nest you can resort to old-fashioned methods and either pour boiling water on it or spread sugar and borax powder (from a chemist) where the ants walk, or use a branded product based on borax. The workers then take the borax back and feed it to those in the nest, and so poison them. Then they have no young to scavenge for.

Bats
Bats are not pests at all. In Britain they are timid harmless creatures which are protected by law and should be cherished as the friends they are. The stories about them getting in hair are totally unfounded; and they help us by keeping down midges and night-flying garden pests. They are also quite enchanting.

Bed Bugs (*round, mahogany-coloured 6 mm long*)
Bed bugs are about the size of a ladybird but flatter – hence the nickname 'mahogany flats' – though, as they can drink five times their weight in blood, they aren't flat all the time. They lurk in the cracks in a bed, and in the wall around it and in folds in the mattress. As they feed on human blood a bed makes a perfect dinner table – though you occasionally find them in padded chairs. They don't transmit infection, but they do leave very itchy bites. (A flea bite has a red spot at the centre and a halo of paler red, whereas a bed bug bite leaves a hard white swelling.)

Fortunately, insecticides have made bed bugs extremely rare in Britain, but if you do find any the council should fumigate. If you are travelling rough, and might meet them, carry an insect spray (see below). Spray it into any cracks and folds or, as they only come out at night, keep the room dark for a while, then hunt them with a flashlight. If you lack a spray, leaving the light on all night will reduce their activity.

Use an aerosol against beetles based on permethrin (page 218) which is approved for use in the kitchen and let the bed dry totally before sleeping on it. (If you can check that the product will be safe to sleep on, it is wisest to do so.) In the old days methods were more deadly:

AN EFFECTUAL LIME FOR THE DESTRUCTION OF BUGS. – Two ounces of red arsenic, a quarter of a pound of white soap, half an ounce of camphor dissolved in a teaspoon of spirits rectified, made into a paste of the consistency of cream: place this mixture in the openings and cracks of the bedstead

Enquire Within, 1856

Bees
Bees are, of course, friends not foes. If you need to get one out of the house, empty a match box, half open it and slip it over the bee. Then close it gently, you can then release the bee outside.

Biscuit Beetles *('drug store beetle', Stegobium paniceum, red-brown, smoothly oblong, 2.0-3.5 mm long)*
This beetle looks very like a furniture beetle and has a remarkable ability to bore holes, and endure a quite extraordinary diet. It has a special liking for red pepper, and in chemists' shops used to live in poisons like strychnine and belladonna. In the absence of such deadly delicacies, it will take up residence in almost any kind of dried vegetable – flour, bread, cereal and packet soups are favourites – and it will eat through containers to get to them. It will also bore through books – even going from end to end of a shelf and eating through lead and tinfoil if they get in the way. These beetles will also walk round the screw threads of screw-on lids, if there is room, so about the only sure way to exclude them is to put foodstuffs in glass jars with ground glass lids which fit exactly.

Unpleasant as they are, these creatures aren't dirty and are no danger to health. If dry food contains them you can bake it in a closed container for 1 to 1½ hours at gas no 4, 100°C (200°F). This will kill the beetles, their eggs and grubs and you can then eat the food – if you want to.

To get rid of them either heat treat all dry food, as above, or throw it away. *Remove all food from the food cupboards*, and use a pirimiphos-methyl- or permethrin-based insecticide which is approved for use near food (see page 218) spraying especially in cracks. Place some appealing bait – like a biscuit – on each shelf, to encourage the insects to walk across the sprayed area to get to it (having told the household not to eat the biscuits). Leave the food off the shelves until you have removed the insecticide (see page 213). There may be unhatched eggs in cracks, but how often you need to repeat is unpredictable, as hatching times depend on tempera-

ture. The total life cycle is 7 months and the creatures move about both in the early stages as grubs and as mature beetles.

A very similar beetle, called the cigarette beetle, gets into coriander and caraway seeds – and tobacco. Use the same treatment.

Carpet Beetles or Hide Beetles *(Dermestidae usually 2-4 mm but up to 12 mm)*
The larvae of carpet beetles (commonly known as woolly bears) do millions of pounds' worth of damage in Britain every year and can also be a health hazard. They can carry human parasites, and even carry anthrax. There are some 50 types with slightly varied food preferences, one kind enjoying the larder, another preferring the wardrobe, but they all live on dry animal proteins – wool, leather, fur, dried meat and fish. The most voracious kind (Anthrenus) will even eat cotton and synthetic fibres if protein is on them – as in a food stain. These creatures leave neat round or oval holes which are well spaced. They can also eat into wood, and there is one record of a wooden ship sinking because these creatures peppered it with holes, having been attracted by its cargo of dead penguins.

They may be brought into houses in birds' nests, fly in through a window, or walk down water pipes from the loft. The larvae look like tiny furry caterpillars, similar in size to the adult beetle.

It is the larvae which do the damage not the beetles, but if you see either I cannot counsel you too strongly to take immediate action. A female lays about 100 eggs at a time, and in a warm house there is no closed season on egg laying. How fast they hatch will vary with the temperature; at 17-23°C (60°-70°F) it could take several months, and the cycle can extend to years if it is very cool. So, since eggs hidden in crevices may not be killed by spraying, it could take monthly treatments to get rid of them.

This is not a pest for which you can call in the council, but private pest control companies will spray against it. A good spray leaves a film which will kill any carpet beetle or woolly bear which crosses it for some while to come – but ask for how long any treatment will be effective. You may also want to take action yourself, and there is quite a lot you can do.

- The beetles are likely to lurk in cracks such as between the skirting and a fitted carpet. Thorough vacuum cleaning will remove some of them, but the eggs are cemented in place.
- Dry-cleaning kills beetles, eggs and larvae.
- Temperatures *below* –18°C kill beetles, eggs and larvae (most domestic freezers run at around –18°C and go below this when on fast freeze – but check your instruction book).
- Powder insect killers for beetles can be used between skirtings and fitted carpets, or in cracks in floorboards (see page 213).
- Insecticide aerosol sprays against beetles can be used on surfaces and to get into cracks in wood in cupboards and drawers (page 213).

Addresses and suggestions for further reading are at the ends of chapters.

- Liquid pesticide sprays for household beetles can be used (page 213).
- Borax powder, from chemists, kills the beetles.
- Washing (see page 159) kills them.
- They often get into houses via birds' nests in lofts or dead vermin there, so use a permethrin smoke generator in lofts if you can. (If I were moving home, I would use one in every room before I moved in, to reduce the chance of pests being left by the previous occupants. Insect powder between the floor boards is an additional safeguard – especially if put there just before laying the carpet, so it has no time to degrade in the sunlight.)

Obviously, the action you take will depend on what you are trying to treat. Putting tiny things in plastic bags in the freezer is the best option for things which won't dry-clean well (such as real fur toys or padded hangers). Leave them at fast for 24 hours but don't overfill or the temperature won't go low enough.

Borax down right round the edge of the carpet, or in other likely places is one of the oldest, cheapest and possibly one of the safest insecticides, but it is not as quick or as effective as modern ones.

All fabrics which could be eaten by them should be washed, dry-cleaned or deep chilled, and then kept in tightly closed plastic bags until *at least* a year has passed with no sign of them. But don't think you can starve them out – they can live without food for 10 months.

Cockroaches (1-4.5 cm long – in Britain)
If you have a nose for such things you can detect cockroaches just by sniffing. They have a characteristic odour which also taints the food they crawl over. In Britain we have the black Oriental variety, the smaller German type, and the big (rare) American ones. All three emerge by night, and are easily distinguished from other beetles by their long, waving feelers.

They seek warmth and moisture, and often live in sewers, drainpipes and round lavatories, carrying disease-causing bacteria in their gut and on their feet – causing food poisoning.

They breed abundantly and the time to get rid of them is when you see *one*. However, they are not easy to get rid of as they may keep re-emerging from drains and also take up to 4 months to hatch. So repeated spraying is needed to kill new generations. Use one of the sprays for cockroaches on page 218. In confined places where the powder would not be disturbed, the old-fashioned method is to sprinkle borax round the cracks where cockroaches might appear. A cup of borax in 4 litres (1 gallon) of water can also be used to wash the floor. But it should not be used if pets and children will crawl on the floor. As cockroaches need to be eradicated with all speed there is an argument for using both old and new methods.

Fleas
There are two aspects to the behaviour of fleas: where they feed and where they breed. Most fleas will travel and feed on several different types of animal, but will only breed on one or two.

The human flea will live and feed on animals like dogs, cats and some wild animals, but it only *breeds* on people or pigs. Man can also be bitten by fleas from cats, dogs, hens, pigeons and certain rats – each of which have their own type of flea but these fleas won't *breed* on man. Cat and dog fleas won't live for long if they have only people to feed on – although it may be unpleasant while they are making up their minds.

It is easier to keep fleas down if one knows how they live. Any time a cat or dog goes out and about it is likely to pick up fleas. These rapidly breed in the fur and little pearly white eggs are deposited everywhere it goes. These hatch into tiny grubs which eat the droppings from adult fleas. Then comes a chrysalis stage, in which they can sleep for months but hatch into fleas the instant they sense the warmth and vibration of a mammal nearby. This is why you can get bitten looking over empty houses.

Obviously it is better for animals not to have fleas but you could wear yourself to a frazzle trying to keep animals totally free of them. So some moderation is needed. However, the risk of worms needs to be remembered. Cat and dog tapeworm eggs are eaten by flea larvae and are then present in the adult flea. In grooming itself an animal can eat the flea and so get tapeworms. A child at the crawling stage can get tapeworms too, as the larvae can easily be on its hands. But the only disease carried by fleas is plague – and there are very few places where that is a problem.

Fleas don't like dryness so they are less of a nuisance when central heating is on. But the biggest enemy of fleas is the vacuum cleaner. Regular vacuuming of all the places where flea eggs, grubs and excreta could lurk will normally stop them becoming a problem. But if you move into a house which has had animals you can expect it to have fleas looking for a host, and dinner will be on you. If you simply suspect there may be fleas you could use a smoke generator in each room or use one of the insect sprays (see page 218), but if you *know* it is infested you can call in the council.

Flies (Blowflies, 8-12 mm)
The really nasty flies are the blowfly family: bluebottles, greenbottles and the grey flesh fly are the main ones in Britain, and are easily recognized by their brightly coloured metallic bodies. They are among nature's refuse collectors, being attracted by dead flesh, excreta, garbage and pus. So they are usually swarming with bacteria (on average 27,000 germs per fly). It is the smell of meat or fish which attracts them into houses and they will immediately land on food to lay eggs and feed. They then spit on it and suck it up when the spit has predigested it. In addition they leave constant droppings and these habits make them a common cause of food poisoning. Kill any blowfly you see – a rolled-up newspaper is as good as a fly spray. More importantly, keep meat and fish covered all the time and if you see a blowfly land on it immediately slice off that surface and throw it away. If meat is found with blowfly eggs on, it has clearly been heavily contaminated and the whole thing

is best thrown away. The eggs are oblong and white and easily seen.

Keep dustbin lids tightly closed, so they have nowhere to breed near you, and if necessary spray the insides of dustbins, or bags, with a fly killer.

Fruit Flies (3-4 mm)
These are tiny flies which are drawn to rotting fruit or any kind of fermentation. Tradition has it that if they fall into wine they turn it to vinegar overnight. My experience confirms this, but an expert on the subject insists that it is the other way about: they are drawn to vinegar, and I must have been drinking dreadful wine. Either way, keep vinegar, wine and pickles covered if these tiny creatures are about. They do no harm apart from falling in.

Horseflies (clegs, breeze flies, greenheads, deer flies, 6-10 mm)
Horseflies are similar in size to a bluebottle, with iridescent eyes, and are rather good-looking – for flies. However, they are particularly to be avoided because the females feed on people and their bites can leave very painful swellings. They can home in on their victim at the remarkable speed of 31 mph – so swat quickly. They breed in damp and marshy areas, and are only occasional visitors to houses.

Houseflies (grey 5-7 mm)
Houseflies are a drab grey and like decaying vegetable matter. However, they can still carry disease – especially in hot climates. A fly spray will work against both these and blowflies, and there is a block which gives off fly-killing vapour (page 211). But prevention is best and since flies home in on food through its smell, the old-fashioned system of having strong-smelling plants on the window ledge also makes good sense.

Hornets
Hornets are like super-wasps with super-stings – so they are definitely to be avoided. They live in hollow trees but one may stray into a house. Kill it with fly spray – or open the windows and wait for it to go.

Lice
It is said that after St Thomas à Becket died his body was seen to 'boil' with the seething mass of lice which left his body as it cooled. The body louse has probably died out in Britain, but two others remain: the head louse and the pubic louse (crabs). The head louse varies in colour from dirty white to greyish black as, rather cleverly, it adapts to the colour of hair it is on. Head lice are only found on the head, but pubic lice can also infest other hairy parts, and even the eyebrows and eyelashes.

Head lice don't restrict themselves to dirty people or dirty hair. Anyone can get them, and school epidemics are common, probably because children put their heads together and tumble about. Crab lice can be caught in sexual intercourse, or possibly from shared towels, bedding and lavatories.

In theory, all lice can transmit infections like typhus and trench fever. In practice, the body louse is the one which does so. This is worth remembering when travelling in the tropics. Even in Britain, lice leave nasty itchy bites which may lead to other problems like impetigo. So they need prompt treatment.

Any chemist will sell you an anti-louse preparation, but they are meant to be used as directed by a doctor. A good shampoo lotion will kill both the eggs and the adults. But the little white egg cases (nits) may still be left sticking to the hair. You can remove them with a very fine-toothed metal comb.

Anything which might carry lice – bedding, towels, hats and so on must also be thoroughly cleaned or washed. Hats can be sprayed with an insect spray containing permethrin (see page 218); once the creatures are dead, expose the inside to the sun for a few days to neutralize the chemical.

Mice (Mus musculus, body 79 mm, tail 78 mm)
If you have mice the first thing you may notice is droppings: oblong pellets like plump tea leaves. These are dirty enough, but the really nasty thing about mice is that they have no sphincter on their bladder, so as they run across your food and china they leave a steady trickle of urine, which you don't see. And both rats and mice can carry a family of diseases called leptospiroses. The best known of these is Weils disease which is a serious and sometimes fatal illness. The main victims of these diseases are those whose work takes them into sewers, ditches, and so on. But they are not the only people who catch them.

Mice can also do a great deal of damage. Their teeth never stop growing, so to keep them short a mouse has to spend much of its life gnawing. In the process it could gnaw an electric wire and cause it to spark and start a fire. So mice within the walls can be dangerous.

As they are nervous creatures, and keep to the edges of rooms, traps or other mouse killers should be put round the skirtings, having left unbaited nibbles in the same places on previous days – this also applies to rats. The main mouse killer used to be warfarin, but many mice are resistant to this. One effective alternative is made by Sorex (see page 218) and, among other ingredients, contains enough vitamin D to disrupt their metabolism. However, this doesn't mean it is harmless to pets and children – use it only as instructed and *clear it up before they enter the room.*

Instead of making the bait inconspicuous, as modern manufacturers do, the 1856 *Enquire Within* recipe included phosphorus and said:

> *Small portions of this mixture may be placed near rat holes and, being luminous in the dark, it attracts them, is eaten greedily and is certainly fatal.*

Mites (disc-shaped, pale and 0.2-2 mm long)
The main mite to infest man is known as the itch mite, or scabies mite, which burrows into the skin. Most of the burrows are on the hands and wrists, so they are easily seen. These mites are the cause of scabies. They are caught by close contact with someone who has them, but

Addresses and suggestions for further reading are at the ends of chapters.

are unlikely to be detected until 3 to 4 weeks later – when the itching begins. Several creams kill the mites and severe and unusual itching should be taken to a doctor in case this is the cause.

Other mites occur in food, especially cereals, and look like mobile white insect eggs. The best prevention is to keep all foods based on cereals in a dry place, as they need humidity to thrive. You could kill them in the food by baking (see biscuit beetles, page 208) but it will taste of mites, so it is better to throw it away. If you feel they are in the cupboard itself, remove the food and treat with a spray based on pirimiphos-methyl (see page 218).

Mosquitoes *(under 1 cm)*

In hot climates mosquitoes carry diseases like malaria and yellow fever and the parasitic worm which causes elephantiasis. The type that spreads malaria is Anopheline which sticks its bottom up when resting; the yellow fever type sits level. We do have Anophelines in Britain but, they only carry malaria if there are people they can get it from. Mosquitoes need water for their larvae to breed, so get rid of standing water (even rainwater in an empty can will breed them) or put a little fine machine oil on the water to block the tiny tubes which the larvae thrust up through the water to breathe. Adults can be killed with a fly spray, but swatting is all that is usually needed.

Moths

There are five slim, white- or brown-winged moths, all with a wing span of 12 to 22 mm, which can wreak havoc in fabrics. They lay their tiny white eggs on any suitable surface, and it is the emerging larvae which eat fur, wool and feathers – and especially favour areas stained with sweat or urine. They also thrive in opened bags of blood fish and bone fertilizer, or in flour or grain. In the house they leave a trail of ragged interlinked holes and partly eaten fibres.

Traditionally drawers were made with cedar bottoms, as moths and other insects were thought to be discouraged by the smell of cedar. Herbs or moth balls were put between clothes for the same reason.

> *When linen is well dried and laid by for use, nothing more is necessary than to secure it from damp and insects; the latter may be agreeably performed by a judicious mixture of aromatic shrubs and flowers, cut up and sewed up in silken bags, to be interspersed among the drawers and shelves. These ingredients may consist of lavender, thyme, roses, cedar shavings, powdered sassafras, cassia lignea, &c. into which a few drops of otto of roses, or other strong scented perfume have been thrown.*
>
> Enquire Within, 1856

Scientists don't agree on whether female moths are put off by strong smells but if you put anything which is free from moths in a tightly closed plastic bag it is safe, and paper is just as effective – provided it has no holes in it. So blankets can be stored in several layers of newspaper, firmly sealed at all joins with sticky tape. There are

mothproofing sprays but any gaps in the mothproofing will be vulnerable.

If you find moth eggs or grubs wash or dry-clean the item – if it isn't past use. Treatment as for carpet beetles (page 208) but any likely fabric which is being stored over winter, or for longer, needs protection.

> Although extreme cold will kill moth eggs and grubs – the temperatures used in most fur stores only keep them dormant. So eggs laid the previous season will hatch when you bring the furs home. (See page 176.)

Rats *(Rattus norvegicus, body 230 mm long, tail 200 mm)*

Rats carry harmful bacteria and distribute them through their urine and droppings, and through their fleas. They can also bite and, having the same teeth problems as mice, do considerable damage to almost anything they can get their teeth into. In Britain the most common rat is the brown rat. It is more aggressive than the black ships' rat, and the female will even take on a man in defence of young. Though rats are resistant to it in some areas, warfarin is still the recommended poison. If rats seem resistant consult the Environmental Health Officer about another rodenticide. DO NOT LEAVE ANY RODENT KILLER WHERE PETS OR CHILDREN COULD GET AT IT.

Red Spider Mite

These are tiny scarlet garden mites which sometimes hibernate in the house. They do no harm but stain the walls if you squash them. Use fly killer.

Silverfish *(silver, carrot-shaped, 12 mm)*

Not only are silverfish *not* a health hazard but, in the opinion of one expert on insects, they make excellent pets. They will be very happy in a jam jar and fed on flour. They are, he says, 'to be pitied and loved' because they are as old as the dinosaurs but failed to evolve very far. So they get stranded in dry slippery places, like wash basins, because their feet have just never learnt to cope with shiny surfaces.

They like damp nooks and crannies close to kitchens, coming out at night to feed on starch. They are not a health hazard, but it is unpleasant to have insect life in food. They also eat the starch from old wallpaper pastes, and from bookbindings – which makes them an expensive pest in libraries of old books – and may sometimes eat fabrics.

Keep all starchy foods in jars and boxes, and make the area as warm and dry as possible. They do not survive for long in such conditions. Traps can be set for them by putting down small jars, containing a little flour, with rough-surfaced adhesive tape over the outside. They will then be able to climb in, but their inadequate feet will prevent them from climbing out. If you must kill them use one of the insecticides for crawling insects on page 218.

If you are trying to keep rats out bear their quite remarkable athleticism in mind. According to Norman Hickin, in his book *Pest Animals in Buildings* (published by George Godwin) rats of one kind or another can achieve the following feats:

- enter an opening larger than 1.25 cm square
- climb vertical and horizontal wires and cables
- climb vertical pipes 4 to 10 cm in diameter
- climb the outside of pipes up to 7.5 cm in diameter
- crawl along any pipe or conduit
- jump vertically 1 m from a flat surface
- jump horizontally 1.2 m on a flat surface
- jump horizontally 2.4 m from a height of 4.5 m
- drop 15 m without being killed or seriously injured
- burrow vertically into earth to 1.25 m deep
- climb ordinary brickwork to the first floor
- climb vines, shrubs, trees, telephone wires and power lines
- swim 0.8 km in open water against a substantial current
- dive through plumbing traps
- gnaw through lead or aluminium sheeting, and cinder blocks.

It makes you wonder why nobody organizes a rat pentathlon.

Spiders

Goodness knows how the dislike of spiders started but it is quite unnecessary. They may not be exactly pretty, but I doubt if they like the look of us much either – and British ones never attack us, unprovoked, as we attack them. In Britain we should regard them as friendly fly-catchers and let them be. (Incidentally, they aren't insects – insects have six legs, spiders have eight.)

In hot climates, spiders should be given a wide berth; some have venom 15 times as potent as rattlesnake venom. (But, as they inject you with very much less, you are far less likely to die of a spider bite than of a rattlesnake bite.) They tend to hide in heaps of timber, in clothing left hanging in sheds and so on, so avoiding them only needs sensible precautions.

Ticks

Both people and pets can pick ticks up on walks. A tick must never be simply pulled off, as it will leave its mouth parts behind to create a nasty sore. Instead, cover the body with cotton wool soaked in ether or chloroform or smear the body with paraffin or vaseline. After a while it will loosen its grip and can be removed.

Prevention is much better than removal, as ticks occasionally carry disease. And even in parts of Europe, they carry diseases which can be fatal. When walking in a potential tick area (especially central Europe) tuck trousers into socks, and wear long sleeves and a wide-brimmed hat. If there is a major risk from them use a repellent like Deet (from MASTA, page 592) on clothing.

Wasps *(usually 1-1.5 cm)*

Wasps are scavengers, and none too fussy where they walk so they should be kept off food. Don't try to shoo them off: flailing arms may provoke them to sting. Trap them in a jam jar with sweet water or beer in the bottom. Cover the top with paper and push holes in it with a pencil, so they can go in easily but not out.

Some councils will deal with wasps' nests, some won't. Wasps take a fresh nest every year, and do no harm to a building. I had one in the roof above my bed one year and the wasps vanished peaceably at the end of the season. However, if the nest is a nuisance, and has only one entrance, you could either block it with Polyfilla or spray with fly spray designed for wasps. Take care, a spray not designed for wasps may provoke them to sting and if you block, or spray into, one hole when they can get out of another they may well leave the nest and attack.

There is often confusion between wasps and hoverflies. Hoverflies are gentle harmless creatures which should never be killed as they feed on aphids. Being totally unable to defend themselves, they are camouflaged to look like wasps. To tell which is which look at the shape of the tail end: a wasp is pointed, a hoverfly is round. Also look at their flight: hoverflies hover like helicopters; wasps don't.

Woodlice *(grey with segmented armour, 5-20 mm long)*

Being related to crabs and lobsters, woodlice like it moist and are a warning that somewhere is damper than it should be. They do no harm at all.

Woodworms *(wood-boring beetles, usually 2-3 mm long)*

Woodworms aren't worms at all: they are beetles. They fly into houses in the late summer and take up residence in any wood they can find. The most common type makes a neat hole about the size of a pin head. You will often find these holes on old furniture. Look for signs of fine dust on or near the mouth of a hole. If you see it, the beetles are very much alive; if all the holes look old and dark, and there is no dust, they may all be dead.

Prevention is much better than cure. New timber going into a house should be painted or sprayed with any good woodworm killer. Furniture should be treated with a branded woodworm killer made for furniture. But check that it is not hazardous (**London Hazard Centre**, page 218) and that it is appropriate (some cannot be used on polished surfaces) and be very thorough. Exposed rafters can be treated with a permethrin smoke generator (page 218).

Death-watch beetles live in the heart of hardwood timber, but come out on fine days; they look like an ordinary woodworm but are 7 to 8 mm long and get

Addresses and suggestions for further reading are at the ends of chapters.

their name from an eerie series of clicks they emit to attract a mate.

Choosing Pesticides

Today's insecticides are not as poisonous as the old ones and some – not yet on the retail market – should be totally harmless to man. However, it is still the opinion of one of the authorities in the field that 'all conventional pesticides are potentially toxic.' One reason for this is that the safety of any chemical can depend on what it is mixed with. Something which isn't normally absorbed by the skin might be absorbed if put with a particular propellant. And a minor ingredient could produce a reaction while the main ingredient produced none. This means we have to choose insecticides carefully and use them sensibly – not simply assume that if they are on sale to the public they must be safe whatever we do.

Certain chemicals turn up in product after product. One such is permethrin (and related substances ending in 'thrin'). Permethrin is a synthetic relative of the long-established insecticide pyrethrum, which comes from a plant in the chrysanthemum family. Both kill the vast majority of insects as soon as they touch them. The World Health Organization's reports suggest that they are remarkably safe for man. They are also odourless and will not give a flavour to food, whereas organophosphates like pirimiphos-methyl may do. However, there have been some allergic reactions by those with asthma. So it might be wiser for asthmatics to keep out of a room in which these are being used.

How to Use Insecticides (or pesticides)

Don't be tempted to use garden sprays in the home. In 1985 a law made it illegal to use pesticides other than as directed on the container – which means it is illegal to use garden chemicals on house pests. The law also made it necessary for all household pesticides, and their instructions, to be approved by the government.

Unfortunately, few directions give much guidance on the situations you meet in the home. Before spraying insecticide I want to know how soon I can safely put the bag of flour back on the shelf, or whether a baby or a pet can safely play on a sprayed carpet the same day. I have yet to find a container which gives any guidance on such things.

What's more, when I tried to find someone in the ministry who knew the answers I was told that manufacturers are not asked about situations like that. Nor did the manufacturers have more detailed answers.

If you want to use insecticides safely work out exactly where and how you would like to use them and write to the makers and ask some very detailed questions. If enough people ask how soon the baby may crawl on the carpet, they may realize there are real problems and print some informative leaflets to go with their products.

Some pesticide strips are made to be hung in a kitchen and some sprays say they are safe near food and people. But unless you have other advice from the manufacturer – via the container or a letter – the following minimum precautions will do no harm.

- Read the instructions and follow them precisely.
- Always keep pets and young children away when using pesticides and keep them off the surfaces for *at least* 24 hours.
- Wear rubber gloves when using a pesticide and a face mask so you don't breathe it in.
- Don't use insecticides on or near food unless the makers say it is safe.
- Before spraying any fabric, carpet or other fragile surface (e.g. polished wood) try a test patch somewhere which won't show if the chemicals cause staining and leave it for 24 hours.
- When the insecticide has done its job wash down the surface with plenty of water (wearing rubber gloves) before putting food on it.
- Don't smoke or have naked flames when spraying. Some of the propellants can catch fire.
- Never transfer insecticide into any other container or leave it where children could get at it.
- Throw left-over insecticide down an outside drain.
- Clean out containers very thoroughly if they have been used for mixing insecticides

As the sixteenth-century poet Thomas Tusser wrote in his *Hundreth Good Pointes of Husbandrie*:

> Take heede how thou laiest the bane for the rates,
> Lest thou poison thy servant, thyself and thy brats.

Both water and sunlight break down many household insecticides and make them harmless. So if you want an insecticide to keep on working, shut out the light. Washing down kitchen shelves that have been sprayed will usually make them safe to put food on – once they are dry.

★ A neat way to de-bug a single item is to spray the inside of a plastic bag, let it dry, then put the item into it, close the top and leave it for a day or two. The creatures walk on to the plastic and die. A black bin liner is best as most household nasties move about most in the dark.

★ All insects – fleas, lice and so on – are killed by being soaked for a short while in water at over 60°C. As that is the temperature for minimum-iron fabrics in most washing machines it is easy to de-bug anything which is washable.

> Most insecticides are in spray cans. There seems no point in getting rid of bugs while ripping up the ozone layer. If you want to avoid this check the cans against the ozone safety list published by **Friends of the Earth** (see under Free Time).
> On many pesticides you will see Gamma-HCH as one of the ingredients. This is a technical name: it is better known as lindane, the chemical which kills bats, and is to be avoided.

More information

British Pest Control Association (page 218) is the professional body of companies making pest killers and carrying out pest control. It has a list of members and they keep to a code of practice. If you need someone to do pest control it will give you the names of companies in your area and answer queries. It also sells a good booklet on pest control. For an unbiased view contact the **London Hazard Centre** (page 218) which has information on chemical dangers. It also sells a useful book called *Toxic Treatments: wood preservative hazards at work and in the home* plus a leaflet on remedial measures called *After the Sprayer.*

USEFUL ADDRESSES AND BOOKS

Employing Help

The following organizations serve all parts of Great Britain unless otherwise stated.

Babysitters Unlimited Tel: 081 892 8888 provides experienced or qualified babysitters plus party helpers and Cordon Bleu cooks. London only. (P.175)

Bligh, 25 High Holborn, London WC1V 8QA Tel: 071 405 7061, specializes in Australian and New Zealand nannies and mother's helps, plus some companions to the elderly. (P.175)

British Nursing Association, 82 Great North Road, Hatfield, Herts AL9 5BL Tel: 07072 63544, provides both nurses and professional carers. (P.175)

Care Alternatives, 206 Worple Road, London SW20 8PN Tel: 081 946 8202, provides unqualified staff or nurses to look after the elderly or disabled by day or night. (P.175)

Childminders, 9 Paddington Street, London W1M 3LA Tel: 071 935 2049/9763, London and the wider home counties, a babysitting service, using experienced sitters. Also supplies ironers and domestic help. (P.175)

Consultus, 17 London Road, Tonbridge, Kent TN10 3AB Tel: 0732 355231, supplies nurses, midwives, maternity nannies, nannies, mother's helps, cook housekeepers, companion housekeepers, proxy mothers to cope with families, and helpers for the elderly. (P.175)

Country Cousins and Emergency Mothers, 10A Market Square, Horsham, West Sussex RH12 1EU Tel: 0403 210415, specializes in short-term help in emergencies. Helpers live in as part of the family and will stand in if a mother is ill, or if an elderly or handicapped person needs care. They also live in with pets while owners are away and escort people to airports, trains, etc. Salaries similar to a housekeeper's. (P.175)

Homesitters Ltd, Buckland Wharf, Buckland, Aylesbury, Bucks HP22 5LQ Tel: 0296 630730, supply responsible retired people to house sit, and care for the pets, while owners are away. (P.175)

Kensington Nannies, 49-53 Kensington High Street, London W8 5ED Tel: 071 937 2333, for qualified nannies. (P.175)

The Lady, 40 Bedford Street, London WC2E 9ER Tel: 071 379 4717. (P.175)

The **Nanny Service**, 9 Paddington Street, London W1M 3LA Tel: 071 935 6976/3515, supplies mother's helps, daily and live-in nannies, and temporary nannies, also maternity nannies. (P.175)

Occasional and Permanent Nannies, 2 Cromwell Place SW7 2JE Tel: 071 225 1555 (24 hours answerphone) supplies nannies, mother's helps, maternity nurses, here and overseas. (P.175)

Universal Aunts, P.O. Box 304, London SW4 0NN Tel: 071 738 8937, supplies a multitude of personal services. In addition to temporary and permanent staff and helpers of every kind, they have people who will house sit, pet sit, dog walk, shop, cook, take people sightseeing, meet people from stations and airports, and even queue for visas, mend your clothes or witness your marriage. (P.175)

Ivor Spencer School of Butlers, 12 Little Bornes, London SE21 8SE Tel: 081 670 8424, supplies part-time and full-time butlers in Britain and overseas and toast-masters for events. (P.175)

Training Colleges for Nannies

Chiltern Nursery Training College, 16 Peppard Road, Caversham, Reading, Berks RG4 8JZ Tel: 0734 471847. (P.175)

Princess Christian College, 26 Wilbraham Road, Fallowfield, Manchester M14 6JX Tel: 061 224 4560. (P.175)

Equipping a Home

The Association of Manufacturers of Domestic Electrical Appliances (AMDEA), Leicester House, 8 Leicester Street, London WC2H 7BN Tel: 071 437 0678. (P.186).

Brinkhaus, Unit A, Bowers Mill, Branch Road, Barkisland, Halifax, W. Yorks HX4 0AD Tel: 0422 310206, makes duvets with fillings of wool, cashmere, silk or camel hair. They also make wool-filled pillows. (P.185)

British Electrotechnical Approvals Board (BEAB), Mark House, The Green, 9/11 Queen's Road, Hersham, Walton-on-Thames, Surrey KT12 5RN Tel: 0932 244401. (P.186)

British Shops and Stores Association, 37 Cheval Place, London SW7 1EU Tel: 071 225 3635. (P.183)

British Standards Institution, Certification and Assessment Department, P.O. Box 375, Milton Keynes MK14 6LL Tel: 0908 220908. (P.185)

Charities Aid Foundation, 48 Pembury Road, Tonbridge TN9 2JD Tel: 0732 771333. (P.180)

Child Accident Prevention Trust, 18-20 Farringdon Lane, London EC1R 3AU Tel: 071 608 3828, produces leaflets on child safety. (P.187)

Community Furniture Network, Highbank, Halton Street, Hyde, Cheshire SK14 2NY. (P.180)

The Crafts Council, 44 Pentonville Road, London N1 9BY Tel: 071 278 7700, has a register of craftsmen all over GB. Its slide library, showing who makes what, is open to the public (but ring and check the hours). It also gives start-up grants to craftsmen and women, on merit.

The Design Centre, 28 Haymarket, London SW1Y 4SU Tel: 071 839 8000 has new design ideas.

The Direct Selling Association, 29 Floral Street, London WC2E 9DP Tel: 071 497 1234, operates a code of practice and will help you to resolve complaints. (P.180)

The Home and Contract Furnishing Textile Association, Reedham House, 31 King Street West, Manchester M3 2PF Tel: 061 832 8684, will supply leaflets on the care of furnishing fabrics. However, they no longer offer arbitration if you are dissatisfied.

Lighting Association, Bryn, Bishop's Castle, Shropshire SY9 5LE Tel: 0588 640658. If you can't find a particular light fitting in the shops, send them an accurate description or a photograph and they will usually be able to put you in touch with the manufacturers.

The National Bedding Federation Ltd, 251 Brompton Road, London SW3 2EZ Tel: 071 589 4888, has leaflets on beds but does not deal with bedding. (P.183)

The National Institute of Carpet Fitters, Wira House, West Park Ring Road, Leeds LS16 6QL Tel: 0532 743721, will give you the name of a fitter in your county who meets certain standards, and if you have a complaint the Institute will refer it to the British Carpet Technical Centre. (P.185)

Qualitas, 30 Harcourt Terrace, London W1H 2AA Tel: 071 706 2458, offers dissatisfied customers independent adjudication – for a fee. (P.183)

The Radio, Electrical and Television Retailers' Association (RETRA), Retra House, St John's Terrace, 1 Ampthill Street, Bedford MK42 9EY Tel: 0234 269110. (P.186)

Royal Society for the Prevention of Accidents (ROSPA), Cannon House, The Priory, Queensway, Birmingham B4 6BS Tel: 021 200 2461, produces a booklet on children and safety. L, B, F. (P.187)

Useful Book
Deyan Sudjic, *The Lighting Book*, Mitchell Beazley – a useful guide to what you can do with lighting.

Cleaning and Conservation

Atlantis Paper, 146 Brick Lane, London E1 6RU Tel: 071 377 8855, claims to be the UK's largest art shop. It also stocks conservation materials such as acid-free papers and boards. Open 7 days a week, plus mail order. (P.157)

Blanchard, Martin & Simmonds Ltd, 237 Walworth Road, London SE17, makes whiting and can tell you of stockists. (P.158)

The British Bathroom Council, Federation House, Station Road, Stoke on Trent ST4 2RT Tel: 0782 747074, has a leaflet on cleaning bathroom fittings. It can also give you the names of companies making fittings of all kinds. (P.157)

The British Carpet Manufacturers' Association, Royalty House, 72 Dean Street, London W1V 5HB Tel: 071 734 9853, publishes leaflets on carpet care. (P.159)

Cadogan Company, Cadogan House, 95 Scrubs Lane, London NW10 6QU Tel: 081 960 8020, specializes in cleaning furnishings and carpets and will accept them by post. But get a quote, specialist cleaning is seldom cheap. (P.192)

W. Canning Materials Co Ltd, P.O. Box 288, Great Hampton Street, Birmingham B18 6AS Tel: 021 236 8621, makes and will supply the brass lacquer Ercalene. **H. S. Walsh and Sons**, 12-16 Clerkenwell Road, London EC1M 5PL Tel: 071 253 3186, is a London stockist of Canning's Products. (P.158)

The Carpet Cleaners Association, 126 New Walk, De Montfort Street, Leics LE1 7JA Tel: 0533 554352, will supply a list of members in your county. They must have taken courses in cleaning carpets and upholstery and in spot removal. The Association will take up complaints. (P.159)

Connolly Brothers, Wandle Bank, London SW19 1DW Tel: 081 542 5251, restores leather upholstery. (P.170)

Dennis Ruabon, Hafod Tileries, Ruabon, Wrexham, Clwyd, North Wales LL1G 6ET Tel: 0978 843484. (P.162)

G. B. Kent and Son PLC, London Road, Apsley, Hemel Hempstead, Herts HP3 9SA, Tel: 0442 232623, rebristles period hairbrushes. (P.158)

Liberon Waxes Ltd, Mountfield Industrial Estate, Learoyd Road, New Romney, Kent TN28 8XV Tel: 06796 7555, sells, by mail, a good range of products for finishing wood and restoring furniture and fine objects, including gilt waxes which can be shaped to repair chipped gilt mouldings. (P.163)

A.J. Lopez, King's Cross Goods Yard, York Way, London N1 0AT Tel: 071 278 7589. Will sell Sepialight by mail. (P.166)

Meech Static Eliminators, 140-144 Clapham Manor Street, London SW4 6DA Tel: 071 622 4555, makes anti-static sprays. (P.159)

The Museums and Galleries Commission Conservation Unit, 16 Queen Anne's Gate, London SW1H 9AA Tel: 071 233 3683, has a list of conservators who will restore items of value.

Picreator Enterprises Ltd, 44 Park View Gardens, London NW4 2PN Tel: 081 202 8972 sells unusual cleaning materials and substances used in conservation, by mail order only; these include Renaissance Wax and also Volpex, a special liquid soap which can be used in varying dilutions to clean almost anything from a feather to a stone statue. (P.158)

Pilgrim Payne & Co Ltd, 290-294 Latimer Road, London W10 6QU Tel: 081 960 5656, specializes in drycleaning furnishings, including woven tapestry and fine carpets. Runs a delivery postal service. (P.170)

Royal School of Needlework, Apartment 12a, Hampton Court Palace, East Molesey, Surrey KT8 9AU Tel: 081 943 1432, will clean and repair needlepoint and other embroidery. Ring for an appointment – security at Hampton Court prevents the admission of unexpected visitors. (P.193)

Sheffco Ltd, 50-52 Chancery Lane, London WC2A 1HL Tel: 071 405 8868, for stockists of the Silver or Gold Solution. (P.169)

Stuart Stevenson, 68 Clerkenwell Road, London EC1M 5QA Tel: 071 253 1693, sells materials for conservation, such as glues for ceramics and Synperonic N, by mail order. (P.160)

The Tarnprufe Co. Ltd, 68 Nether Edge Road, Sheffield S7 1RX Tel: 0742 553652, makes Tarnprufe bags, cutlery rolls for storing silver without tarnishing, Carosil capsules and silver cleaning mitts. At branches of John Lewis and good silversmiths. (P.169)

The Victoria and Albert Museum, Cromwell Road, London SW7 2RL. Tel: 071 589 6371 can put people in touch with conservators around Britain. Its experts will also advise on conservation. Speak to the appropriate department *before* taking objects to them.

The Vitreous Enamel Development Council Charnwood, Frenze Road, Diss, Norfolk IP22 3PB Tel: 0379 650340, tests cleaning materials for vitreous enamel and suitable cleaners usually carry its mark. (P.157)

Useful Book

Hermione Sandwith and Sheila Stanton, *The National Trust Manual of Housekeeping*, Penguin – gives ideal temperatures and humidity for most types of fine objects.

Laundry, Stains and Dry Cleaning

ARCO, P.O. Box 21, Waverley Street, Hull HU1 2SJ Tel: 0482 27678, sells ReDuRan and Cupran and will supply by mail on request. Their industrial hand cleansers also remove stains from the skin. (P.203)

J. Barbour & Sons, Simonside, South Shields, Tyne and Wear NE34 9PD Tel: 091 455 4444, supplies tins of water proofer to rewax Barbours, or will clean and rewax them for you. (P.196)

Dylon International Ltd, Worsley Bridge Road, Lower Sydenham, London SE26 5HD, consumer helpline 081 650 4801, L. (P.188)

The Fabric Care Research Association Ltd (FCRA), Forest House Laboratories, Knaresborough Road, Harrogate, N. Yorks HG2 7LZ Tel: 0423 885977, can advise you on dry cleaning. (P.187)

G.E. Holloway and Son (Engineers) Ltd, 12 Carlisle Road, Colindale, London NW9 0HL Tel: 081 200 0066, make a chewing gum remover. (P.201)

The Home Laundry Consultative Council, 7 Swallow Place, London W1R 7AA Tel: 071 408 0020, has advice on laundering. (P.188)

Jeeves of Belgravia, 8-10 Pont Street, London SW1X 9EL Tel: 071 235 1101, operates a world-wide postal service. You would not expect this service to be cheap – nor is it. And check on insurance in transit. (P.187)

Lever Brothers Ltd, Consumer Advice Service, Lever House, 3 St James's Road, Kingston upon Thames, Surrey AKT1 2BA Tel: 081 541 8200 will deal with your queries about washing. (P.188)

National Association of the Launderette Industry, South Lodge, 79 Glen Eyre Road, Southampton SO2 3NN Tel: 0703 766328, has a conciliation committee which investigates complaints. (P.187)

Nikwax, Durgates Industrial Estate, Wadhurst, East Sussex Tel: 0892 783855, sells waterproofers for most materials, from nylon to quilting or leather. Plus products for washing down-filled or waterproofed or waxed materials, and for rewaxing waxed clothes. (P.196)

Parker Pen Co Ltd, Service Department, P.O. Box 6, Newhaven, Sussex BN9 0AX Tel: 0273 513233, has solvents for its inks, and information. (P.203)

Tech-spray, Unit 8, Acorn Business Park, Grove Park Court, Skipton Road, Harrogate, N. Yorks, HG1 4DP Tel: 0423 520699, makes anti-static sprays and can supply the names of stockists. (P.185)

Textile Services Association (TSA) and **Dry Cleaning Information Bureau**, 7 Churchill Court, 58 Station Road, North Harrow, Middx HA2 7SA Tel: 081 863 7755, Advice line: 081 863 8658 has a database of dry cleaners and helps with complaints. (P.187)

Veterinary Drug Co, Common Road, Dunnington, York YO1 5RU Tel: 0904 488444. (P.202)

Learning About Fine Things

Membership of the **National Trust** gives free entry to all NT houses, and there are numerous events (address p.378).

Antique Collectors' Club, 5 Church Street, Woodbridge, Suffolk IP12 1DS Tel: 0394 385501 – M£M, vgM, NG, B, auctions listed in magazine, worldwide.

Georgian Group, 37 Spital Square, London E1 6DY Tel: 071 377 1722, for lovers of Georgian architecture and decorative arts. M£M, A, G, weekends, courses, private views.

National Association of Decorative and Fine Arts Societies (NADFAS), 8A Lower Grosvenor Place, London SW1V 0EN Tel: 071 233 5433 – M£M, M, NG, A, vis., Lect., H, Disc. Also young NADFAS for age 8+.

National Heritage: The Museums Action Movement, 9A North Street, London SW4 0HN Tel: 071 720 6789 – M£M, M, museum handbook, private views.

National Trust, see p.378.

Old Water-colour Society's Club, Bankside Gallery, 48 Hopton Street, London SE1 9JH Tel: 071 928 7521 – M£M, M, A, Disc, sae.

The Thirties Society, 58 Crescent Lane, SW4 9PU Tel: 071 738 8480 – campaigns for the preservation of the best post-1918 architecture and design. M£L-M, M, A, T, sae.

Victorian Society, 1 Priory Gardens, London W4 1TT Tel: 071 994 1019 – M£L-M, G, A, preservation society.

Useful Books

The British Art and Antiques Directory, Ebury Press, lists antique dealers, specialist societies and courses on all aspects of fine arts.

HMSO Books, P.O. Box 276, London SW8 5DT Tel: 071 873 0011, not the sexiest of publishers but they publish beautifully illustrated art books often based on museum collections, as well as the Ordnance Survey maps and official documents.

Mail Order

Mail Order Trade Associations

The **Direct Marketing Association (UK) Limited**, Haymarket House, 1 Oxendon Street, London SW1Y 4EE Tel: 071 321 2525, covers companies selling books, etc. by mail order. (P.205)

The Mailing Preference Service (MPS), Freepost 22, London W1E 7EZ, but do not phone. (P.206)

The **Mail Order Traders' Association**, 100 Old Hall Street, Liverpool L3 9TD Tel: 051 227 4181, covers the major catalogues and has a code of practice. (P.205)

The **National Newspapers Mail Order Protection Scheme Ltd (MOPS)**, 16 Tooks Court, London EC4A 1LB Tel: 071 405 6806, covers certain advertisements in the national press. (P.206)

The Newspaper Society, Bloomsbury Square, 74-77 Great Russell Street, London WC1B 3DO Tel: 071 636 7014. (P.206)

Periodical Publishers Association Ltd, Imperial House, 15-19 Kingsway, London WC2B 6UN Tel: 071 379 6268. (P.206)

Useful Books

The Good Book Guide, 24 Seward Street, London EC1V 3GB Tel: 071 490 0900, day or night, is a world-wide mail order business offering any book in print – including paperbacks. You don't have to join to buy from them but if you want you can subscribe to their magazine which reviews some 3,000 of the latest books each year, and this also gives you preferential rates. There is also a children's list.

Household

Anything Lefthanded Ltd, 57 Brewer Street, London W1R 3FB Tel: 071 437 3910, sells kitchen and other equipment for the left-handed. Send three 2nd class stamps for the catalogue. There is also a shop at this address. (P.181)

Continental Chef's Supplies, Unit 11, South Hetton Industrial Estate, South Hetton, Co. Durham DH6 2UE Tel: 091 526 4107, has very good professional cooking equipment. (P.181)

Cookware Francais, 5 Priory Close, Bishop's Waltham, Southampton, Hants SO3 1AP Tel: 0489 896887, has the professional cooking equipment one can seldom find, including excellent baking and pastry moulds and some high-tech aids, such as the amazing Silpat non-stick baking mats, used by chefs – no more stuck meringues. (P.181)

David Mellor, 4 Sloane Square, London SW1W 8EE Tel: 071 730 4259, has a good range of stylish high-quality kitchen equipment. (P.181)

Divertimenti, 45-47 Wigmore Street, London W1H 9LE Tel: 071 935 0689, has a very good range of kitchen equipment. (P.181)

Fast Feathers, 36a Canaan Lane, off Morningside Road, Edinburgh EH10 4SU Tel: 031 447 9044, sells feather cushions, pillows etc. and also makes to order, converts eiderdowns into duvets, and renovates duvets. You can also buy their cambric cases to fill yourself. (P.185)

Lakeland Plastics, Alexandra Buildings, Windermere, Cumbria LA23 1BQ Tel: 05394 88100, (CC) – sells plastic bags, containers, clingfilm, microwave cookware, freezer items, kitchenware and seasonal gifts.

Laura Ashley Ltd, Mail Order Customer Services, P.O. Box 19, Newtown, Powys, Wales SY16 1DZ Tel: 0686 622116, (CC Amex, Access, Visa) – sells the company's range of furnishings, furnishing fabrics and papers. You can order made-to-measure curtains, and any item can be sent as a gift. Catalogue charged for.

Siesta Cork Tile Co, 21 Tait Road, off Gloucester Road, Croydon, Surrey CRO 2DP. Tel: 081 683 4055.

Small Holding Supplies, Pikes Farmhouse, East Pennard, Shepton Mallet, Somerset BA4 6RR Tel: 0749 72127, sell everything for the smallholder and backyard farmer.

For companies supplying fabrics, chair covers, etc., See Crafts (P.414-415).

Mail Order Catalogues

Empire Stores, 18 Canal Road, Bradford, W. Yorks BD99 4XB Tel: 0274 729544), has household and garden goods, men, women's and children's clothes including fashionable items. (P.205)

Freemans, 139 Clapham Road, London SW9 0HR Tel: 071 735 7644, has household, electrical and garden equipment, plus clothes for men, women and children – including some young and trendy items. (P.205)

Grattan PLC, Anchor House, Ingleby Road, Bradford, W Yorks BD99 2XG Tel: 0800 333444, offers a wide range of household, linens, electrical, casual clothes for adults and children. After sales service. 7 days a week local telephone order lines. (P.205)

J. D. Williams & Co Ltd, 53 Dale Street, Manchester M60 6ED Tel: 061 236 9911 for orders; 061 236 4488 for service, sells some men's wear and household goods but mainly clothes and shoes for women. Emphasis on large sizes, up to 30, and wide shoe fittings. (P.205)

John Moores, Kershaw Avenue, Crosby, Liverpool L70 1AH Tel: 051 928 6611, sells furniture, electrical goods, toys, bed linen, men's and women's clothing for the younger age group. (P.205)

Marshall Ward, Home Shopping Department, Devonshire Street North, Manchester M60 6EL Tel: 061 273 7171, offers quite stylish clothing for adults and tots to teens, electrical, furniture, carpets, linens, kitchen equipment and toys. (CC) (P.205)

Mail Order for Charity

★★ Those carrying this mark do a Christmas catalogue, possibly with cards.

Camphill Products, Botton Village, Danby, Whitby, N. Yorks YO21 2NJ Tel: 0287 660871, is a charity for the handicapped which offers handsome engraved glass, pottery, wooden toys, etc.

Charity Christmas Card Council, 221 St John Street, London EC1V 4LY Tel: 071 242 0546, can give you the addresses of charities selling Christmas cards.

National Trust sells mainly gifts, clothes and stationery.

Oxfam Trading, Murdock Road, Bicester, Oxon OX6 7RF ★★ Tel: 0869 245011, 9 am-5 pm weekdays, sells mainly clothing, household, gifts and stationery.

Save the Children, SCF Trading Department, 17 Grove Lane, London SE5 8RD Tel: 071 703 5400 ★★ mainly gifts.

Web Ivory Ltd, Queensbridge Works, Queen Street, Burton-on-Trent, DE14 3LP Tel: 0283 66311, has information on most charities that do mail order, whether for Christmas or other times and actually handles the mail-order side of many charities, such as the NSPCC and the RSPB, so it could be a short cut to catalogues.

Pest Control

I make no claim to be an expert on insecticides. The following list is of some of the companies and their products recommended by those who should know.

British Pest Control Association, 3 St James Court, Friargate, Derby DE1 1ZU Tel: 0332 294288. (P.209)

The **London Hazard Centre**, Headland House, 308 Gray's Inn Road, London WC1X 8DS Tel: 071 837 5605, will advise you on the hazards of individual chemicals and products – even if you're not a Londoner. (P.212)

ICI Garden Products, (which also covers household products), Fernhurst, Haslemere, Surrey GU7 3JE Tel: 0428 645454, makes Waspend – an aerosol based on pirimiphos-methyl (an organophosphate) for use against flying and crawling insects. It also makes Ant Killer Dust, also based on pirimiphos-methyl. It will also kill other insects which crawl over it.

PBI, Britannica House, Waltham Cross, Herts EN8 7DY Tel: 0992 23691, makes Kybosh, a permethrin-based aerosol against most flying and crawling insects. And a permethrin-based powder for killing ants. But if other insects walk across it, they too will die. (P.208)

Rentokil Group PLC, East Grinstead, West Sussex RH19 2JY Tel: 0342 833022 has a wide range of chemicals for insect control and good information leaflets.

Sara Lee Household and Personal Care Ltd, 225 Bath Road, Slough, Berkshire SL1 4AU Tel: 0753 52397, makes Coopers Mothproofer and Coopers Ant and Crawling Insect Spray.

Sorex Ltd, St Michael's Industrial Estate, Hale Road, Widnes, Cheshire WA8 8TJ Tel: 051 420 7151, makes Sorexa CD – a mouse killer, which kills mice which resist Warfarin. (P.210)

Synchemicals Ltd, Owen Street, Coalville, Leics LE67 3DE Tel: 0530 510060, make Nippon Liquid Ant Killer, based on borax, and Nippon Ant Powder – based on permethrin, is also authorized for use on most house pests and suitable for large areas.

Shoes and Shoe Care

British Footwear Manufacturers Federation, 72 Dean Street, London W1V 5HB Tel: 071 437 5573. (P.178)

British Retail Consortium, Bedford House, 69-79 Fulham High Street, London SW6 3JW Tel: 071 371 5185. (P.178)

The **Shoe and Allied Trades Research Association (SATRA)**, SATRA House, Rockingham Road, Kettering, Northants NN16 9JH Tel: 0536 400000, produces leaflets on shoe care. (P.178)

The **Society of Master Shoe Repairers**, St Crispin's House, 21 Station Road, Besborough, Northants NN14 2SA Tel: 0536 760374, will tell you where to find a skilled repairer. (P.178)

Solemates, 46 Gordon Road, London E4 6BU. (P.178)

A Roof Over Your Head

**Buying and Selling • Building and Maintenance •
Moving Home • DIY • Painting and Papering**

BUILDING AND MAINTENANCE

Building, alterations and decorations cover an immense range of work; from getting a painter to repaint your front door, to building a whole house. The aim of this section is to show how you could use the different professions which are involved, what you can expect and how you can get the best possible job for your money.

Architects and Their Role

Whether a building job needs an architect depends on the work to be done and the other skills available in your area. There are firms which specialize in certain jobs – loft conversions or conservatories, say – whose package deal may work well if you don't have special needs. (But compare several companies.) Some builders do a very good job without an architect, though their design skills are likely to be limited and if you have strong ideas about design, a surveyor may prove to be what you need (see pages 268-269). But an architect may provide imaginative solutions and save worry – if not money.

Building a house, or buying one and having alterations done to it, is one of the few areas in which something is purpose-made to your needs. So be very clear about what these are. Suppose you want an extension – one storey or two? Using measures for energy saving or not? And so on. Only when you know exactly what you want will you be able to find the best person to create it for you.

Finding an Architect

The easy way to find an architect is to approach one of the architects' organizations, listed on pages 268-269. If you take pot-luck through Yellow Pages check his qualifications and make sure you use a 'chartered architect'. Only someone who is properly qualified and a member of the **Royal Institute of British Architects (RIBA)** (page 269) can use the title *'chartered* architect'. But someone *with no qualifications at all* can now use other titles such as 'architect' or 'architectural consultant'. So some who call themselves architects or architectural consultants are fully qualified but some aren't.

The RIBA recommends that, before choosing an architect, you visit several, ask about fees, look at photo-graphs of previous work, note some addresses and ask for names and addresses of former clients as references. Then speak to some former clients.

Paying an Architect

The first consultation is usually free. Any work he does thereafter may need to be paid for – whether or not you decide to use him – even preliminary sketches.

Fees are usually a percentage of the total cost of the project, and payable in stages. There are no set fee levels; it is entirely negotiable between you and the architect. Get a note of what he will charge, and what he will do for it, in writing. Check also what extras are outside the fee. For a start, VAT is extra.

A leaflet from the RIBA explains all the details. But remember: each time you change your mind while work is in progress you pay for the privilege and if you cut the building cost by doing some yourself the architect's fee may still be based on what a builder would have charged.

The Responsibilities of an Architect

1 Drawing up a preliminary design for the client to approve.
2 Designing a scheme to the client's budget.
3 Submitting the design for planning approval.
4 Drawing up the specifications to meet regulations and putting them before the authorities.
5 Advising on grants towards the cost.
6 Assisting in finding a suitable builder.
7 Architects do not supervise building sites daily but they should make regular checks. And your instructions to the builder should be given through the architect.

Using an Architect – Caveat Emptor

When using a professional we usually think we are paying them high fees to take the load off our backs and do the thinking for us. The truth is even the best architect (or doctor or lawyer) has his/her mind ninetenths occupied with the needs of other clients. You are the only one able to give undivided attention to yours.

Don't be carried away by pretty plans; try to imagine it all in three dimensions. One major architectural firm managed to design a large NHS hospital without lavatories. So take nothing for granted.

The codes of conduct of some professional associations are more concerned with preventing architects from poaching each other's clients than with ensuring client satisfaction. And the arbitration only covers a narrow band of complaints and may also be limited to written evidence only. So if things go badly wrong you may need to take the matter to court. Both the **Royal Institute of British Architects** (page 269) and its Scottish brother have good leaflets which may help.

Builders and Decorators

The building and decorating business is full of cowboys just itching to take you for a ride. You can only protect yourself by using firms with a good reputation locally or ones which are members of established trade associations. This won't guarantee that you are totally satisfied but at least – in most cases – they won't *intend* to do a bad job. And if they do, you may be protected by an established system of compensation. Whatever the job, avoid using anyone who comes uninvited to your door or rings up offering services. On the whole, a good firm doesn't need to. Page 269 lists several organizations such as the **Building Employers Confederation (BEC)** or the **Federation of Master Builders**, which you can use to avoid the cowboy companies. But even their members may have no training or qualification, and the organization may have little clout if things go wrong. For example, if one of its members does unsatisfactory work, you can complain to BEC. However, BEC cannot *insist* that a member satisfies a client, although it will advise a member to do so. So it is safest to use a firm whose work you have seen.

Estimates, Quotations and Contracts
If the job is simple enough to need no drawings or survey, you can approach contractors direct. But don't approach anyone until you really do know what you want. The charges may be different if you so much as change the brand of paint, let alone if you swop from paint to paper or want a wall in a different place. Always ask a contractor if he will give a free quotation and specification. And ask for references and find out his qualifications.

Any contractor will normally give you an estimate of what the job will cost. But this is just a guess and is *not binding. Always* get a *written* quotation (some firms call them estimates, but once in writing they are legally quotations) pricing all the work item by item. It should also show whether VAT will or will not be added. Compare several before deciding which firm to use.

Having chosen a firm, tell them that you are interested in them doing the work, subject to you approving the contract. They should then send you a written contract clearly showing what work is to be done for what price. For example if a room is to be painted it should mention washing down or burning off old paint. *Nothing* that you would like to have done should be left out. It should also show:

- whether materials are included in the total price (they may not be)
- whether any sub-contractors will be used
- who will be liable if there are problems
- the completion date
- what cancellation rights you have – if any.

Check the small print in any contract carefully before signing; that's usually where the sting is. You may want to insert a clause that the quoted price may not be exceeded without your agreement. And you can ask for a penalty clause by which they lose money if the job isn't completed on time; the builder may or may not agree. The changes should be written into a new contract and sent to you. If you don't like the contract you can say so and find another firm – provided you have done nothing which committed you in law. If you want to accept the contract do so in writing, and refer to it by date – then you have proof of which version you accepted.

> Part of the value of using advisers like surveyors or architects is that they are used to dealing with such contracts and know what should and should not be agreed.

Grants and Permissions
A good builder should be able to tell you what permissions are needed for the work you propose. Don't be tempted to build without permission. If the council discovers unauthorized building it has a right to make you take it down at your expense. And when you sell your home the buyer's solicitors will have to check on whether the proper permissions were obtained.

Organizing the Work
- Ask which work has to be done first – so you can clear the rooms concerned.
- Find out how they plan to dispose of rubbish – so the method suits you as well as them.
- Agree details like lavatory and coffee-making facilities for the men.
- If constant radio music is your idea of hell discuss whether men can be sent who can work without it.
- If you don't want anyone to smoke, get them to agree to this.

These details can create problems if they aren't sorted out at the start.

Inspecting the Work
If you have used a surveyor or architect you should inspect the work when it is finished. Go over it with a fine tooth comb *alone*. Don't just look at things, try using them – flush the loo, check that the immersion heater heats, check the workmanship everywhere, and so on. Make a note of every single problem. Then go over it again with a representative of the building firm, and ask for them to be put right. If you are asked to sign a 'satisfaction note' and you haven't yet done this check,

or are in any doubt about any aspect of the work, it is best not to sign it.

If you think that materials used for you were incorrect and need to prove it, the **Building Research Establishment** page 269 will carry out tests, for a fee.

Payment

In principle, payment should only be made for work which has been done, and done properly. But contracts can be structured so payments are in stages, or a firm may need a small sum on deposit if something has to be purpose-made. This should *never* be large or be given to a firm you don't know and you should always get a written receipt on paper *printed* with the company's name and address.

Never pay the final bill until a week or so *after* all the work is done. It sometimes takes a few days for faults and omissions to show up, and during that time do try out everything they have installed – even if you don't *need* to use it.

Timing

Even if your contract doesn't give a completion date, firms have a legal obligation to complete a job in a reasonable time. If they don't, you should write giving a date by which they must finish and saying you will cancel the job if this is not kept to.

Surveyors

If you are about to do any major alterations or extensions a surveyor can be the ideal middle option, provided you don't need the creativity of an architect. Use a fully qualified one with the letters FRICS or ARICS. A surveyor can do most of the practical tasks an architect would do (page 219). Discuss precisely what you would and would not like him or her to do and find out the costs.

The Royal Institution of Chartered Surveyors (RICS) (page 269) sells a booklet on the conditions of engagement for building surveying services which explains in detail what you can expect.

For jobs like valuations and surveys the charge is normally a flat fee. But if a surveyor takes charge of building work for you, the fee will be a percentage of the cost of the job, and 10 to 15 per cent is usual.

Different surveyors specialize in different fields, and it is essential to choose someone who is experienced in your type of job. The RICS will give you the names of surveyors in your area. The rules about choosing an architect apply here too (page 219) and, as always, personal recommendation is the best route.

Problems and Complaints

The RICS has a strict code of conduct and a scheme for the protection of the client's money in the event of a surveyor being dishonest.

If you have any complaint about a chartered surveyor, or about a firm in which at least one partner is a chartered surveyor (as in some estate agents), send the full details to the Professional Practice Department of the RICS. The Institution will investigate and the surveyor can be reprimanded or expelled from membership. It will not, however, deal with cases which need to go to law.

Damp

The key point about damp is that there is always a reason for it, and it should be cured quickly before it causes rot. The most likely causes are:

- lack of a damp course in an old house
- a faulty damp course
- soil or debris building up above the damp-course (it should be 15 cm (6 in) below the damp course
- a fault in the roofing
- loose flashing round a chimney or on a flat roof
- a blocked gutter making excessive water pour over brickwork
- building mortar and other debris that dropped into the cavity wall and now form a bridge by which water can travel to the inner wall
- a leaking downpipe or gutter
- blocked airbricks, so normal damp doesn't evaporate
- cracked brickwork or failing mortar
- condensation.

The first step is to find the cause and do something about it. Built-up soil can be removed, blocked drains and airbricks cleared. If gutters and drains are blocked you may be able to unblock them yourself; sometimes the block is at the bottom of the downpipe.

A leaking gutter or downpipe can be mended with a gutter and drain sealant which can now be squeezed straight from an applicator into the problem area.

If damp comes in through gaps round windows or doors these can easily be filled by injecting a polyurethane foam filler (sold in canisters) and a mastic used to seal on the outside and protect the polyurethane from weather.

Condensation is a special problem. The cure for condensation in general is better insulation (see page 224), more warmth and more ventilation. However, selective insulation can increase the problem. For example, windows may suffer greatly if the walls of a house have been insulated but there is no double glazing. The only solution here is to double glaze (see page 225).

Abundant moisture on the windows doesn't, however, prove the house has rising damp or anything worrying like that. It forms because the moisture given off by human bodies (several pints a day) and by cooking or paraffin heaters will land on any cold surface, and the glass is the only cold surface around.

Dampcourses

Serious problems like a faulty dampcourse or roof are best treated swiftly by professionals. Anyone can spot a crooked wall, but how many of us can tell a proper chemical dampcourse from a botched job? This makes the installation of dampcourses (along with wood preservation) a prime area for the operations of rip-off merchants. Official estimates are that about £150 million a year is spent on these two treatments and less than half that money is paid to those actually qualified to do the work. A list of contractors qualified to install dampcourses can be obtained from the **British Wood Preserving and Damp Proofing Association** (page 269) which has replaced the old Chemical Dampcourse Association. Members of the association must use trained staff to carry out surveys, and give reports which are honest and free from exaggeration. However, they no longer have to use products approved by the Association, nor need they carry insurance. Some may, however, offer a guarantee protection scheme, through the **Guarantee Protection Trust** (page 269). It could be useful as this is an industry where companies come and go. Not all the Association's members use the trust, so ask when choosing a contractor and get several estimates.

Electricity

Dating Your Wiring

Most houses built or rewired after the early '60s have ring circuits. On this all the sockets are 13 amp and the plugs match them. The older radial system had a range of plugs supplying 15 amp, 5 and, occasionally, 2 amps, often with round pins. If you have any sockets other than those which take big flat-sided pins you don't have a ring circuit, and your wiring is probably more than 30 years old and needs replacing. (Though the reverse isn't always true; having new sockets doesn't always mean the wiring behind them has been renewed, so do check.)

Electricity companies will test the wiring of a home and report on what faults need to be put right. They charge according to the size of the property. **The Institution of Electrical Engineers** (page 272) recommends that wiring should be checked every 5 years, and the insulation on wires is not expected to last more than 20 to 25 years and can perish sooner.

Appliances and Sockets

It is very important that the total wattage of the appliances isn't greater than the plug can safely carry. Check the wattage on the back of appliances before putting them on an adaptor. A socket of:

15 amps can safely carry 3,000 watts in total
13 amps can safely carry 3,000 watts in total
5 amps can safely carry 300 watts in total
2 amps can safely carry 60 watts in total

The big gap between the capacity of 5 and 13 amp sockets may look odd, but the fittings for the lower amps are made differently. So they are far more likely to overheat and cause a fire at high wattages.

Electrical Installations

The trouble with electricity is that its hazards are hidden. Some 3,000 fires a year are caused by faulty wiring, yet anyone can call themselves an electrician and put your life at risk. Use a fully qualified electrician. The **National Inspection Council for Electrical Installations (NICEI)** (page 272) has a list of properly qualified contractors which is in public libraries. All NICEI electricians have been approved by the council, are regularly inspected, and should display the NICEI sign. That means they come within the council's complaints and guarantee scheme, and other electrical bodies given on page 272 also set standards for work.

Electric Gadgets

Anyone setting up home should really look round some of the major exhibitions and see what technology is on offer. Failing that, the Design Centre Index or the Lighting Association may help you find products of a particular type. Here are just a few of the things to look out for.

- Plug-in lighting sockets for ceilings and walls which allow you to remove the fittings. (They have a lock so they won't fall.)
- Brand new neat 2-pin plugs for appliances which use very little electricity – e.g. turntable, tape deck, amplifier. The pins plug into a small adaptor.
- Remote controls which plug into a ring main to allow you to turn on appliances in other rooms.
- Timer devices of all kinds.
- Thermostats which can run each radiator or fire at a different temperature.
- Dimmers which are part of table lamps; others which attach to the cord of a lamp or are on remote control.
- Light sensitive mechanisms which will draw curtains and switch on lights.
- Remote control light switches.

★ If you decide to install a new boiler control be systematic. There will be getting on for 20 wires inside. Unless you label each wire *as you take it out of the old mechanism* the chances of placing it correctly in the new one won't be good.

How Much Electricity We Use

If you've ever wondered about the cost of running a light bulb or electric appliance the calculation is very simple. A unit is simply 1 kilowatt of electricity being used for 1 hour (kWh). The power of any piece of electrical equipment is given on it in either watts (W) or kilowatts (kW). So the calculation is this:

1 kilowatt plate warmer x 1 hour of use = 1 unit used
2 kilowatt fire x 1 hour of use = 2 units

1 kilowatt is just a way of saying 1,000 watts, so: 100 watt bulb x 10 hours of use = 100 x 10 watt hrs = 1,000 watt hrs = 1 kilowatt = 1 unit used. Equally: 10 bulbs of 100 watts x 1 hour = 10 x 100 x 1 watt hrs = 1,000 watt hrs = 1 kilowatt = 1 unit used. Or: 8 bulbs of 60 watts x 2 hours = 8 x 60 x 2 = 960 watt hrs = almost 1 unit used.

Once you know how many units an appliance uses you just multiply that by the cost per unit and you have the cost of running it for that length of time. So, if electricity costs 5.5 pence a unit, then running a 1 kilowatt fire for 1 hour would cost 5.5 pence, but running it for 3 hours would cost 5.5 pence x 3 = 16.5 pence.

Fires can use a lot in a quarter. For example, a single 2kW fire used for 5 hours an evening during the winter months would use 1,800 units of electricity – costing over £100 – against roughly £18 worth for a colour TV.

Wattages vary from one manufacturer to another, but those given below are the average wattages and consumption.

WARNING: Electricity can kill. Always turn off at the mains before doing any electrical work.

Electrical Consumption

Appliance	Wattage	Use	Units
Cooker	12,000	average wk's family meals	17
Coffee percolator	750	75 cups	1
Dishwasher	3,000	a full load – cold fill	2
Drill	250-500	2-4 hrs	1
Electric ⎱ over blanket ⎰ under	150-350 60-120	1 week 1 week	2-3 1
Extractor fan	75	13 hrs	1
Food mixer	120-700	4-25 hrs	3
Freezer	300	1 day	1-2
Hair dryer	350-800	3 hrs	1
Heated rollers	500	20 heat-ups	1
Heaters – convector – fan – oil-filled radiator – radiant bars – storage	 1,000-2,500 2,000-3,000 500-2,500 500-3,000 2,000-3,000	 2 hrs 30 mins 2 hrs' warmth 20 mins a wk	 2-5 1 1 1 approx 45-75
Iron	1,250	2 hrs	1
Kettle	2,000 – 3,000	12 pts – boiling	1
Lawn mower	250 upwards	3 hrs	1
Microwave oven	600	8 chicken pieces	1
Plate warmer	1,000	1 hr	1
Radio	5 up	200 hrs	1
Refrigerator	100	1-1½ days	1
Slow cooker	80-170	8 hrs	1-2
Spin dryer	300	5 weeks	1
Tape recorder	25-75	24 hrs	1
Television	80 B & W 100 colour	6-9 hrs	1
Toaster	1,050-1,360	70 slices	1
Tumble dryer	2,500	4 kg (9lb)	2½
Vacuum cleaner	500	2 hrs	1
Washing machine	2,500	weekly wash for four	5
Waste disposal unit	250	50 lb waste	1

Meter Reading and Paying for Electricity – see Organizations, page 679

Energy Saving and Insulation

A lot can be done to reduce heat loss and cut fuel bills. But before you start any insulation work, find out about the availability of grants. There is usually a government scheme to help those with special needs or low incomes. The schemes vary from year to year, but you are unlikely to get a grant if you do the work before you apply for it. General renovation grants, for those on low incomes whose houses are below the official standard, come under the **Department of the Environment**. But insulation grants can come under several government departments, so ask the public-information units of **Environment, Energy** and **Social Security** (pages 693-694). Also ask your local authority, the bodies on page 271, and any charities linked to your situation.

It also pays to take a look at the facts about what will and will not save you money. There are actually two aspects to energy saving – the need to save world energy resources, and the need to save money on your own energy bill. So far as the first is concerned, any measures which save energy are good news. But to save money you need to save more on energy than the installation costs in the first place – and that means spending wisely.

Since April 1990 the building regulations have required all new buildings (including all but the tiniest extension) to reach a new, high standard of insulation. But high standards are worthwhile anywhere.

● The best value for money is a 10 cm (4 in) jacket for a hot water cylinder. It should pay for itself inside a year. But a new tank should have a factory fitted one already. If you already have a jacket on the tank put the new one under. Two insulations are better than one.

● Inexpensive draught strips are also a good investment and easy to apply yourself. Draughts can account for 15 per cent of your heat loss. But have enough ventilation in any room where there is a fire which is not electric; all flames need air.

● The next best value is to insulate your loft with at least 150 mm (6 in) insulation. Any new buildings, including extensions above a certain size, must have this thickness, by law. Up to 25 per cent of your heat may go out through your roof, so this should save you at least £50 a year on your heating bill. This means that if you install it yourself – which is very easily done – you should be saving money within 2 years. (But wear a face mask and gloves when installing insulation; it is better not to breathe it in.) And if your current insulation is 30 mm (1¼ in) or less you may be able to get a local authority grant to help you increase this (but check *before* you do the work).

● If you insulate your loft it is *vital* to insulate your pipes as well, as they will no longer be kept warm by the rooms below. Also insulate the lid and sides of any water tanks – but NOT under them. There are DIY kits for these jobs.

● Cavity wall insulation is the next best value. About 40 per cent of British houses have cavity walls and a lot of heat can be saved. It needs professional installation but it should pay for itself in 5 years – or even less on a detached house in an exposed position. But see page 221 on condensation.

● Double glazing is the *least* cost effective form of insulation (unless you do a nifty DIY job). In one Consumers' Association report on double glazing they found that double glazing costing £1,250 would save £22 to £25 a year in heating bills. So if fuel costs were static it would be about 50 years before the windows began to pay for themselves. Of course, fuel costs aren't static, but nor does double glazing last forever. That doesn't mean double glazing is always a waste of money. At DIY prices the same windows could have been double glazed for £250. So, allowing for a rise in fuel costs, the windows would be earning their keep in about 7 years. It also reduces condensation on the glass. And it may reduce the risk of burglary. But remember a window a burglar can't break is also one you can't break in a fire. On factory-sealed units look for the kitemark. If you haven't got double glazing, put a lining and interlining on your curtains – it makes a real difference.

Insulation

If you use contractors discuss any estimates in detail and make sure they plan to insulate to the thickness you want. To insulate cavity walls you need permission from the council. The main danger of cavity wall insulation is that when not done correctly the insulation can act as a bridge for damp. Any contractor should hold an Agrément Board Certificate which shows that his work and materials meet certain technical standards or have British Standards Institution (BSI) registration which allows those they approve to use a BS or BSE number on their letterhead if they meet the standards of the BSI code of practice.

Another way of insulating walls is to put some type of cladding on them. This is not a cheap process. So it is really only suitable for adding to a home if existing cladding needs to be renewed anyway.

> As I write, the **Energy Efficiency Office** is giving a big discount to those who replace their old, energy-guzzling boiler with a new condensing boiler. This isn't a means-tested scheme but nobody knows how long this scheme will last.

If your income is very low you may be able to get help with insulation costs. The **Winter Warmth freephone line** (page 271) advises on grants and on energy saving. However, the names of the organizations, the rules on how low someone's income must be, or what benefits they must be on to qualify, vary with the mood and the colour of the government. As I write, the scheme is cash-limited: so apply early or the kitty may be empty. Also, even non-earners can't get a 100 per cent grant. But, you can get a grant for DIY insulation *provided you agree it with the authorities first*.

In this chapter's address list I have given the organizations current as I write. However, the schemes set up by the Department of the Environment tend to change. So if you have a problem getting help or advice contact the Department's information service or its leaflet office or a CAB. The elderly are especially at risk from cold, and **Help the Aged** and **Age Concern** (page 324) can advise them.

Fire

In 1988 regulations made it illegal for the trade to sell new furniture containing unmodified foam in the upholstery. But, given enough time, modified foam still burns and gives off poisonous fumes. And unmodified foam, in old or second-hand furniture, can fill a room with deadly fumes in under 2 minutes. So you and your family are safer with chairs with old-fashioned fillings. The Department of Trade and Industry has leaflets explaining the labels found on upholstery.

Fire is one of the most preventable accidents. There are general hazards which are easily avoided and, on top of that, each room has its own special hazards. How does your home score for fire risks?

Fire Safety in the Home

Some of the most important safety precautions are the easiest.

- Have enough ventilation for boilers and open fires to burn safely. Too little air could mean a build-up of poisonous gas, or the gas going out and leaking dangerously.
- Shut all doors at night so that if a fire starts it will spread more slowly.
- Have gas and electrical appliances serviced regularly and stop using anything if you even suspect it isn't in perfect working order.
- Fit smoke detectors to BS specifications.

If a chip pan catches fire:

- DON'T try to move it.
- DON'T put water on it – it will make this type of fire much worse.
- Put a lid on it fast to smother the flames.
- No lid? – Smother the flames by dropping a thick damp cloth over.
- Leave the pan 30 minutes before touching it.

If a chimney catches fire:

- Throw water on the fire in the hearth. The steam from that should rise up the chimney and put the fire out.
- Phone the fire brigade – even if you think the fire is out. It may not be.

> FIRE SPREADS IN SECONDS – only try to put it out if it's very small. Otherwise LEAVE THE ROOM FAST and shut the door.
> FORGET VALUABLES.
> GET EVERYONE OUT OF THE HOUSE FAST. DIAL 999

In the *very* early stages use a home fire extinguisher, throw water on – except on a chip pan – or smother the flames with anything which shuts out air. Once

---

Addresses and suggestions for further reading are at the ends of chapters.

furnishings are well ablaze the fumes could make you unable to get away. Just shut the door on the room and get out *fast*. YOU MAY HAVE ONLY 2 MINUTES BEFORE THE FLASHPOINT when the whole room is full of flames and it spreads to other rooms.

Paraffin Heaters

- Paraffin heaters need plenty of air but should never stand in a draught or where they could be easily knocked over. Nor should they be near curtains or furniture.
- Keep the wick trimmed and having filled the stove wipe off all surplus fuel with lavatory paper and throw the paper down the lavatory.
- If possible, store paraffin in a cool place away from the house – such as a shed.

Paraffin heaters are now designed so that they will put themselves out if they are knocked over. To be safe they should carry a BS number. They should be checked regularly by any shop which carries a Paraffin Heating Advisory Council sticker.

Glass and Glazing

Double glazing is an area in which companies tend to spring up looking for quick profits. Membership of the **Glass and Glazing Federation** (page 269) is no guarantee of expertise but it may protect your money.

Double Glazing

Before embarking on double glazing check how much (or little) energy it will save (see page 223). It isn't necessarily the best way to spend your money, but read the GGF leaflets.

How well it retains heat or shuts out noise depends on the type of glass, and the width of the gap between the two panes. Effectiveness increases with the gap. The GGF has produced the following table.

Heat Loss in U Values			
	Exposure to Wind		
	Sheltered	*Normal*	*Exposed*
Single Glazing	5.0	5.6	6.7
Double Glazing			
5 mm airspace	3.3	3.6	4.0
6 mm airspace	3.2	3.4	3.8
8 mm airspace	3.1	3.3	3.7
9 mm airspace	3.0	3.2	3.5
12 mm airspace	2.8	3.0	3.3
20 mm airspace or more	2.8	2.9	3.2

A gap of 20 mm (¾ in) gives about as much heat insulation as you will get, but sealed units, with an air space of only 6 mm (¼ in), which it may be possible to install

yourself may well be the best value. For good noise insulation you need 100 mm (4 in) or more.

Double Glazing – Safeguards

In double glazing there are highly trained salesmen who telephone uninvited and ask to come and tell you about their product. The wise answer is 'no'. This isn't usually the best way to buy. You need to shop around and compare prices and styles. If you let them talk to you, check your rights (see Law) before you sign anything. And it might be best not to sign at all if the company isn't a GGF member. Their representatives must carry a GGF card and the GGF code says you can change your mind within seven days of signing, with no penalty.

Safety

A building regulation says that glass in vulnerable areas must either be unbreakable or break safely. Three kinds of glazing meet the standard:

1 toughened glass
2 laminated glass
3 polycarbonate.

Use these wherever there is low level glass, or a glass section to a door, and in wet areas, such as round a shower. A GGF leaflet gives the thicknesses and types of glass which can safely be used.

Heating and Plumbing

Anyone can call himself a plumber, so when having heating or ventilation installed, or plumbing done, there are benefits in using a member of one of the trade associations on page 271. They don't all provide the same protection for the client. So check what safeguards a particular association offers under its code.

Members are sometimes covered by a guarantee under which if they cease to trade or work is unsatisfactory, and complaints to the company prove fruitless, the association will take up the complaint and the problem may be put right by another member, free of charge. The work of any job a member does is guaranteed for 12 months.

Before Using a Contractor

Before you even see a contractor, look into the pros and cons of gas, oil, electricity or solid fuel, and if possible read up the latest developments in the field and talk to the advice organizations for each fuel. Things change rapidly and the perfect solution could be something you have never considered.

Even when using members of an association, always get at least 3 estimates. In an emergency ask about the call-out rate, the hourly rate and other charges. These can vary hugely.

Getting estimates from 3 firms lets you pick their brains. But before a contractor can advise you or give you an estimate you must agree:

- the rooms and areas to be heated
- the temperature they need to be heated to
- the number of air changes assumed for each room or area

- the type of house insulation to be used and whether the contractor will be involved in this or not.

Regulations

Water by-laws vary from area to area and may cover details such as the size of cistern you can have or the design of your water system. If you have done alterations to plumbing in a house in one area and then move it is not safe to assume that the same rules will apply. However, one rule is general: any water leaks on your property are your problem; any leaks on public property are the water company's job.

Using a Central Heating Contractor

All those agreed facts should be restated in the central heating quotation the contractor gives. It should also show his terms of trading, conditions of payment and guarantees, plus the following information – which looks complex, but is just basic, logical and essential.

Heat generator – fuel type, heat output, make, type, location.

Fuel storage – capacity, site.

Pump – type, location, how it can be isolated for maintenance.

Controls – on the main generator, room controls, hot tank controls, control of hot water temperature.

Hot water tank – size, type, insulation, material, location, whether gravity fed or pumped, immersion heater back-up type and rating etc.

Heating elements – (radiators) make and type, number, position in each room, responsibility for painting.

Towel rail(s) – size, type, make.

Linen cupboard – method of heating if not from the hot tank.

Cold water tanks – location, connection to mains, size, overflow arrangements, insulation, means of isolation.

Pipework – size of pipework, materials, position whether on surface or concealed, position of stopcocks and valves, type, thickness and extent of insulation.

Electric wiring – description, position, whether on surface or concealed.

Building work – who does what in relation to: accommodation and ventilation for the heat generator, adaptation of existing chimneys or construction of new, provision of storage for fuel, lifting and replacing floor coverings, disposal of rubbish and rubble.

Check all these points are as you want them and ask about anything you don't understand. Misunderstandings can be expensive.

> Make sure any plumber shows you where stopcocks are (if you don't already know). And check that he leaves them in a state which allows *you* to turn them in an emergency – most plumbers don't allow for smaller biceps.

★ If you simply want to refurbish a tired-looking bath – or make it match a new basin, there are companies, like **Renubath** (page 268) which do this.

Gas

The great thing that gas has in its favour as a fuel is immediacy. Whether it's for a boiler, a sitting-room fire or a burner on a stove, there is no time lag while the element warms up. Its other asset is price, although those who have to rely on bottled gas may find it expensive. Even so, in some situations, the new free-standing, high-efficiency gas fires which run on Calor Gas could be a boon.

Gas showrooms now try to show more appliances working, and should be able to tell you where you can see any appliance, as computer links are being installed. Many gas boards have 'Home Service Advisers' who will visit customers in their homes and specialize in helping families with budgeting problems, and in advising the elderly and handicapped about adaptors which may make gas appliances easier to use.

Balanced Flues

The balanced flue allows gas to be used in rooms which don't have a chimney. The air the boiler needs to burn safely is drawn through a pipe in an outside wall and the fumes are released through a parallel pipe into a 3-inch flue which goes up the outside wall. Appliances with this system are often called' room sealed'.

Gas Central Heating

The days of vast gas boilers are long gone. They can be hung on walls, tucked into cupboards or even put at the back of a fire, with a gas fire in front of them. And, like fires, they no longer need the chimney or large flue they used to require. The one essential is that they have enough air to burn safely. One of the most interesting developments is the condensing boiler which allows you to heat water almost instantly when you need it – and can give considerable savings. Gas is probably the cheapest fuel for central heating.

Gas Fires and Room Heaters

You can buy gas room heaters as radiators, as conventional gas fires and in the form of imitation solid fuel, and they no longer have to have a chimney behind them. The efficiency varies – ask about the cost of any heater in relation to its heat output.

Anyone wanting the homeliness of an open fire without the work of tending one might consider one of the gas fires which imitate coal or logs. I'm not crazy about fakes, but if any fakes work these do. Some of the early fires were very inefficient as heaters, giving out only 12 per cent of the gas as heat. That has changed: the gas board now has a selection of these fires which are 45 per cent efficient and the newest Glow-worm Derwent is 90 per cent efficient. That is even better than the usual radiant gas fires which are only about 70 per cent efficient.

Gas Stoves

It is much easier to cook well on gas than any other fuel, as you can turn the heat up or down or right off with no need to think ahead. This makes it ideal for both burners and grills. As oven heat, it has advantages and disadvantages

Addresses and suggestions for further reading are at the ends of chapters.

Installing Gas

Gas isn't available everywhere, but if you live within 25 yards of a suitable gas main British Gas must normally supply you. If you live farther from a main than that they can choose whether they supply you or not. If you decide to be connected up for gas the first 30 feet of pipe in a public highway are laid free, and so are the first 10 metres of pipe not in a public highway. Any other pipework is charged for according to how far it has to go and how easy it is to lay.

Gas fittings without a built-in flue must have enough air to let them burn – or they could go out and the gas leak could be dangerous. This means that if you are having a gas fire fitted in an existing fireplace the chimney should be swept first, and the flue checked.

Domestic gas appliances may only be installed by 'a competent person' who is a member of the **Confederation for the Registration of Gas Installers (CORGI)** (page 271). However, there are mutterings in the trade that the assessment of competence is not strict enough. So some old hands say it is safer to use a fitter who is registered with British Gas, as its fitters must be both qualified *and* insured.

Safety with Gas

The first *Enquire Within* had little to say about safety, but there was the occasional useful warning such as: *Do not tamper with gunpowder by candlelight*.

None of us would be so crazy – even were we in the habit of keeping gunpowder around – but gas is a far more dangerous substance than people often realize. If it collects in any quantity the smallest spark can set it alight and a quantity of gas catching fire creates an horrific explosion.

If you smell gas:

1 DON'T LIGHT ANY KIND OF FLAME and DON'T SWITCH ON THE LIGHT – switching on a light causes a small spark in the switch which could set the gas on fire.
2 Open windows and doors to let the gas out.
3 Turn off any appliance which has accidentally been left on. If it is a minor leak and that solves the problem leave it at that. Otherwise:

- Turn the gas off at the meter. There should be a large handle on the pipe – swing it down so it runs parallel to the floor.
- Call the gas board immediately – they run a 24-hour emergency service.
- If you cannot turn the gas off and there is a very strong smell, or the smell continues to be very strong even after turning it off, get yourself and others out of the building *fast* and call the police.

If you think a gas appliance isn't working properly STOP USING IT IMMEDIATELY and call a qualified fitter through your gas showroom or CORGI. But don't wait for gas fittings to go wrong. For safety:

- gas appliances must be serviced regularly
- chimneys and flues must be checked and kept in good condition

- gas appliances must have enough air in the room to burn safely
- don't use a second-hand gas appliance without having it checked by someone from the gas board. Half the accidents from faulty appliances are caused by second hand ones.

See also Gas (page 678)

Oil as Fuel

Compared to gas, oil is relatively little used as a fuel (apart from in rural areas) but anyone who needs information on it, or on boilers which use it, can contact **OFTEC (Oil Firing Technical Association for the Petroleum Industry)** (page 271).

Solid Fuel

Solid fuel has more scope than appears at first sight. There are now solid fuel boilers which look like sitting room fires but double as a boiler, heating hot water and radiators in other rooms. And if you already have a central heating system an open fire which also heats water can be linked into the system to provide more options and less dependence on a single fuel.

Looking After Solid Fuel Appliances

The snag is that solid fuel appliances need looking after and flues must be kept clear, and brushed out every month. If there is a throatplate at the top of the firebox it must be taken out and cleaned once a month too. One of the most important jobs is to make sure that the flue or chimney is swept at least once a year. And, of course, an open fire has to be emptied and relaid each day – although this isn't true of stoves.

★ Having riddled a stove to get the ash into the ash pan, give it time to settle. Carry the ash drawer with a damp cloth draped over. Then it won't float all over the room.

Safety with Solid Fuel

★ Fires have a silent and invisible risk: carbon monoxide poisoning. All fires with flames use up oxygen as they burn and give off carbon monoxide. If there is too little fresh air in the room the carbon monoxide can build up to dangerous levels. Each year 200 people in Britain die from this. If you feel sleepy in a room with a fire, carbon monoxide could be the reason. Let air in and have your appliance and the ventilation to it checked by experts.

- All open fires (and radiant heaters) should have a fireguard and if there are young children around this guard should be fixed so they can't move it.
- By law if a child under the age of 12 (7 in Scotland) is allowed into a room with an unguarded fire, and is badly burnt, the person responsible can be prosecuted.
- To burn properly – and safely – fires also need a certain amount of air. A room should not be too

draught free. If you have double glazing air vents may be needed.

One piece of advice in the 1856 *Enquire Within* is just as good today as the day it was written.

> *Another consideration as far as economy is concerned is . . . to buy at the proper season; for there is with every article a cheap season and a dear one; and with none more so than with coals: insomuch that the master of a family who fills his coal cellar in the middle of summer, rather than the beginning of winter, will find it filled at less expense than it would otherwise cost him; and will be enabled to see December's snows falling without feeling his enjoyment of his fireside lessened by the consideration that the cheerful blaze is supplied at twice the rate that it need have done had he exercised more foresight.*

The difference in rate is less than double, but summer coal is certainly cheaper. (See also pages 684 and 685.)

Wood

In a stove, where sparks are contained, the type of wood is less important than in an open fire, where certain wood, such as poplar and sweet chestnut, can be a real danger. But the amount of heat a wood gives out and the speed at which it burns varies considerably from wood to wood.

When I was compiling *Supertips to Make Life Easy* I was sent a traditional country rhyme appraising the burning qualities of different wood. On checking it with experts on timber, I found it was totally correct. Ash is the best wood for burning, beech and oak are good but the derided poplar, for example, gives out little more than half the heat of the same weight of oak.

Kitchens

If you own a home, improving its kitchen really does make it more saleable. The choice in fitted kitchens gets wider every year, and the number of companies offering to install them increases equally. However, it is one thing to sell a set of units, and another to have the skilled men to install it perfectly. Before buying, ask for the names of previous customers and talk to them, and see the kitchens if they'll let you.

There is far more on offer than the average fitted kitchen company suggests. German companies, especially Leicht, have been coming up with some brilliant ways to make the most of space. They are great sources of ideas and a few of these kitchens simply stand against the walls – so you could take it with you when you go. (A point to ask about when buying a house. Imagine buying a house for its kitchen and finding it had vanished.)

If you are budgeting look at kitchens sold by DIY chains, some are now surprisingly good. Or, if you enquire carefully in specialist shops you will find that a few of the more stylish kitchens at the more expensive end of the market are suitable for DIY fitting (though nobody rushes to tell you this). You might find that fitting them yourself would cost no more than having a far less interesting kitchen installed professionally.

> Before buying any system measure and check whether the cupboard in which you plan to put plates will take a full-width plate, and that the drawers are deep enough to take a decent spatula. More than one company has made fittings too small for such things.

Roofing

Roofs and roof spaces really ought to be checked from time to time. You don't have to be a professional to see if a timber is sagging, to smell rot or to notice an attack of woodworm.

★ If you have climbing plants make sure no tendrils go near the roof. The most delicate-looking shoot can lift a roof tile with its little finger. Window cleaners will often chop off invasive bits which are too high to be reached without a long ladder.

Flat Roofs

In theory, flat roofs can be made as weatherproof as any other roof. In practice, the layers of bitumen-covered felt, which cover flat roofs, all too easily leak in time, and the flashing which links the roof to any adjoining wall may let trickles of water through when the wind blows under it.

In particular, over kitchens and bathrooms, the heat and condensation may make the roof surface distort and leak. Condensation can also cause the timbers of the roof to rot, and this risk increases if the roof is insulated from underneath. The only safe way to insulate is to place insulation over the bitumen, which isn't always satisfactory. So heat loss is another disadvantage.

However, if you do buy a house with a flat-roofed extension, or build one, don't dream of making a terrace out of it without checking it has the right timbers – or it won't take the weight.

Roof Repairs

Unless you have a great deal of skill and a head for heights, roofing repairs are usually best left to professionals, such as members of the **National Federation of Roofing Contractors** (page 269). Standards for roofing are laid down jointly by the BSI and the Federation.

Security

Over 150,000 homes and 40,000 cars in England and Wales are broken into every week. Most of the thieves aren't skilled criminals but simply dishonest people (or young people) making the most of an opportunity. The first step to crime prevention is blocking the opportunity. You don't need sophisticated burglar alarms to do that, just a few basics – strong locks, spy holes, light in the right places and a bit of thought.

Burglar Detection

Burglar detectors are becoming more sophisticated all the time, and anyone buying a new house should look into the possibilities early on. For example, you can buy

Addresses and suggestions for further reading are at the ends of chapters.

a computerized system which controls the central heating, fire warnings and burglar alarms or wire-free alarm systems which can be switched on from a control pad. At the other end of the scale, you can buy small devices which will howl if their beam is interrupted, and lights which switch on if anyone passes them. New products in this field are coming on the market all the time. Check with some specialist suppliers before you decide what to have.

A burglar alarm which meets the British Standard for burglar alarms may bring down your insurance premium. Unfortunately, many of the alarms which you can fit yourself don't meet this standard. That doesn't mean they are no good. Some could be very useful as a deterrent. There are lights for using on back paths and dark doorways which automatically switch on when the daylight falls below a certain level, and switch off again when it increases.

And, for your personal safety, there are now lights on remote control systems which you can switch on from your car, and garage doors can be opened in the same way.

If you need a security alarm it is safest to use a firm which belongs to the **National Supervisory Council for Intruder Alarms** (page 271) which insists on strict checks on employees' life honesty.

Marking Your Belongings

Marking your belongings can make them not worth stealing. It can also increase the chance of you getting them back if they are stolen. Mark them in an area which cannot be removed or erased. The police recommend marking with your postcode plus house number. But they warn that expert advice should be sought on marking antiques and items of much value.

- An ultraviolet pen can write on surfaces like silver – but the burglar won't see the marks. However, it wears off and needs renewing every 6 months. (Ask the crime prevention officer at your police station where you can buy these pens.)
- Some surfaces can be safely scratched with a sharp-pointed tool or nail – obviously not for anything of value.
- A fine drill can be used to engrave the marks.

Precautions against Burglary

No time is too brief for a burglar. Always lock up completely even if you think you'll only be gone a minute, and don't leave downstairs doors or windows open while hoovering or watching television upstairs. Every police area has a crime prevention officer who will advise – free of charge – on your particular security needs. Major lock and security companies will too.

- Fit security deadlocks on all doors (see Locks, page 243) – many other locks are very pickable. To be safe a front door must have a lock which can be deadlocked when you leave so that only a key will open it. Then nobody can break a pane of glass and undo it. It should carry the number BS 3621. This only

applies to locks with a large number of key variations, so someone else's key is unlikely to open your lock.

> For locks of this type new keys are often supplied only by the manufacturer and only then if the request comes with the owner's signature. If you buy a house, find out if this applies and get a letter from the previous owner telling the lock company that you are the new owner, and send this with your signature. When you do this, ask how many keys have been issued for the lock. Then check if you have them all. If you haven't it would be wise to change the lock at once.

- Fit locks which stop the windows opening wide enough to admit a burglar. This isn't hard to do yourself and gives a great sense of security. Get expert advice on how narrow an opening to leave. I once saw a fireman, in full gear, go through a fanlight I'd have thought too small for a child.
- Fit a chain or similar device so no stranger can push in if you open the door.
- Fit mortice security bolts on vulnerable doors inside and out, and use them when away from home.
- Fit a peephole in doors so you can see who is outside.
- Install lights over porches and back paths which automatically switch on.
- When out at night have lights on timer switches so they occasionally go on and off.
- If your drainpipes are climbable, paint them with anti-climb paint which stays sticky. But only do so from 2 metres above the ground and have a notice warning people, or your window cleaner could have a claim for spoilt clothes (page 270 has manufacturers).
- When ordering new keys by post get them sent to a friend at another address – then, if they are lost, nobody identifies them with your home.
- If you have an answering machine leave a message on it suggesting you are busy and not able to take the call, not that you are out.

Safes

Before installing a safe, talk to your insurance company. There are likely to be rules as to which safes will allow a reduced premium. The main types are free standing, under-floor and wall-fitted. Some of the under-floor safes would be quite easy to fit yourself, and there are concealed safes which look like part of ordinary household fittings.

Thatch

If you have trouble finding a thatcher or need a surveyor who knows about thatch, the **Thatching Advisory Service** (page 269) can help. It claims to be the UK's biggest thatching company and even runs a 24-hour emergency service.

Timber Treatment

The problem which is most likely to need treatment is dry rot. The fungus causing it is *Serpula lacrymans*. The name comes from the little droplets of water, like tears, which you may see near the fungus. You too may weep at the amount of demolition which treating this fungus may take, but at least you can save yourself the tears which might follow from using an unqualified contractor to treat it. You can recognize the mould-like fungus very easily as it drapes itself in soft cloud-like formations across the wood it destroys.

As timber treatment is a field which is full of unqualified operators, use members of the **British Wood Preserving and Damp-Proofing Association** (page 269).

> WARNING: It is illegal to kill or injure a wild bat, but some timber treatments can be fatal to them. If you find bats where you wish to treat timber, contact the Nature Conservancy Council (see Free Time).

CHANGING PLACES

Buying a Home

The only really easy home purchase is when a leaseholder or a tenant uses a statutory right to buy it. Council tenants and leaseholders of most houses have, for some time, had a right to buy the freehold. The Leasehold Enfranchisement Act has extended that right to other houses and to many leasehold flats. However, the lease must have been for 21 years, or more, *when it was signed*, and a set proportion of the tenants in a block must want to buy their flats. With this type of purchase there are strict rules on the sale price which the **Department of the Environment** can tell you. There are also moves to make ordinary home buying easier. The trend is towards large companies bringing all the facilities under one umbrella.

Some building firms provide a house, carpets and fitments. This may make house buying a lot easier, but nobody should be deceived into thinking these extras are free, and if you want to move soon after buying you may not get as much as you paid for the house as all those goods will then be second-hand.

Companies offering an all-in package are likely to be members of the **National House Building Council (NHBC)** (page 269). And, if you are wanting a mortgage on a new house the lender may well want to know whether it was built by a NHBC member, and there could be problems if it wasn't. The NHBC also sells publications on topics such as disputes over defects.

Estate Agents

Anyone can set up as an estate agent. They can be totally untrained and do what they like within the law. So, as house buying involves large sums of money, it's wise to check that any estate agent you use belongs to one of the professional bodies or is covered by the Estate Agents' Ombudsman scheme. The **Federation of Independent Estate Agents** covers many of the smaller independent firms. The **National Association of Estate Agents** draws members from individuals, from independent firms and from the corporate estate agencies belonging to the big financial organizations. And the Ombudsman scheme was set up by, and is funded by, the major agencies – but his judgements are independent. Happily, it is now illegal for an estate agent, or anyone acting in a similar role, to describe key features of a property incorrectly, such as the size of rooms. However, the law does not apply to misdescriptions by the owner.

Normally, finding a property is a matter of getting your name on the books of as many likely estate agents as possible. Try to find one person in any office who has a real interest in finding you precisely what you want.

A quick way to get to know the market is through Homelink: you brief a Homelink member of the National Association of Estate Agents, or the head office (page 268) with the details of what you are looking for, and where. Then they arrange for a Homelink member in that area to send you details of properties.

Surveys

Before buying a house which is not brand new it is usually worth getting an independent survey. This will tell you what defects you will need to remedy if you buy. The normal procedure is a written report. But those on a tight budget can ask the surveyor whether he can reduce the fee if he just tells you on the phone. If you make accurate notes that may be enough. Or a member of the **ISVA** (page 268) will do a standard valuation and report, for a lower charge than a full structural survey.

Those on an even tighter budget can adopt another strategy. Many firms which do work on woodworm and rot, or deal with damp courses, will check a house for these faults – which are some of the most expensive to put right – and give a free estimate of the cost, if they find them. This is not as good as a full survey and it won't tell you whether the roof needs tiling or the bricks pointing. But it is better than no survey at all.

If a mortgage is being taken out, the bank or building society will need a survey too to make sure the property is sound. The buyer pays for this but some mortgage lenders will use a buyer's survey – provided the choice of surveyor is agreed first – and others will let the buyer see *their* survey. But, be warned, a mortgage survey is not as detailed as a full structural survey.

The **Council of Mortgage Lenders** (see Money) has a very useful free leaflet on house purchase if you send an A5 sae. Alternatively, you can buy a kit and build your own timber-frame house or buy one ready made. The **Timber and Brick Information Council** (page 269) has information on both these options.

Conveyancing

Legal checks are needed to convey the property from one owner to another (see Law).

Addresses and suggestions for further reading are at the ends of chapters.

Land Registry – see Law and the Legal System page 453

> BE WARNED: Buying property abroad can be very risky, especially timeshares. The law in other countries may offer you no protection from sharks and many people have lost their money. Before you sign anything, or part with money, read the booklet on timesharing free from the Consumer Affairs Division of the **Department of Trade and Industry** (page 694). It also covers the latest UK laws on timesharing.

Selling a Home

Who Sells What for What

Estate agents are mainly working for the sellers of the property, and advise them on the price to ask. Nobody has to take that advice, and it is also up to the owner to decide which items will be left in the house as fixtures and fittings.

Estate agents vary greatly in their efficiency. Before putting a property into the hands of one, make out you want to buy a property and see how well they perform. They should also belong to a professional body (below), so that your money is safeguarded.

The estate agent who succeeds in selling the property takes a percentage of the price as commission. There is some variation from region to region and company to company, but the main possibilities are these:

Sole agency	Only one agent is instructed, but the seller can still sell the property privately. May be the lowest commission.
Sole selling rights	One agent has exclusive rights to sell. So if the seller sells it privately the agent still gets the commission.
Multiple agency	Several agents are asked to sell the property and whoever succeeds gets the commission. This may bring more buyers but the commission may be higher.
Joint agents	Two or more agents co-operate. The commission is usually more than for sole agency, but less than for multiple agency
Sub-agents	The main agent allows a sub-agent to offer it too and they agree to share the original commission.

Estate Agents – Complaints

Estate agents must act within the law (see Law, page 452). They are also governed by the code of conduct of their professional association – if they belong to one.

If the estate agency concerned does not satisfy you, when you complain, take the matter up with the local Trading Standards Officer or the professional body to which the agency or individual belongs. Or, corporate estate agents, owned by big financial bodies, can be reported to the Estate Agent's Ombudsman. The main professional bodies are the **National Association of Estate Agents** and the **Federation of Independent Estate Agents** (page 268).

Selling by Auction

For an auction to be effective the property has to be advertised and the cost of this is borne by the seller. One key advantage is that purchase by auction is binding. There is none of the delay and uncertainty connected with other forms of sale. Read the ISVA leaflet – see page 268.

Points to Remember when Selling a Home

- Don't allow in callers off the street, they could be burglars – or worse.
- If you are alone in the house, ask the estate agent to send a representative with would-be buyers.
- Make the place look, and feel, good.
- All light fittings must work.
- Cupboards must be tidy enough to look spacious if opened (a pre-move clear-out may do the trick)
- A well-kept garden (try to sell at its best or have photos of it in full bloom)
- Make the place look attractive with pot plants and flowers.
- If any room has dreadful decorations (as teenagers' may) painting it white could pay off handsomely.
- Make it smell good.

Finally, remember that a cross or distracted viewer is unlikely to buy – and radio, television, music, children and pets all constitute a distraction. Turn them off, or corral them as best you can.

Letting Property

If the mortgage has not been paid off you will need permission, to let, from the mortgage company. And do get legal advice on the type of tenancy to offer. It makes a big difference to how easily you can get back the use of the property if you need it (see Law). You also need to make an inventory of the entire contents, and prepare a suitable tenancy agreement.

Never be tempted to make an informal arrangement to let to someone. Friends may be totally trustworthy, but a son, lover or relative might move in with them and then decide to stand on their 'rights', and if there was nothing to show they didn't have those rights you would be stuck with the undesirable relative.

If you find a tenant yourself, ask for references and take them up. An estate agent will do most of the work for you – for a commission. But, if they will be collecting the rent, make sure they are a member of a professional association and that a bonding certificate protects both the tenant's deposit and the rent.

Renting Property

Before renting property, check the terms of the tenancy carefully. Better still, get a lawyer to check them. A few of the possibilities are in Law. Also see what outgoings there will be and check with the rent control office to see whether a fair rent has ever been set for the property, and whether the rent being asked is the same – or at least in proportion, if it was some time ago. Then, get an inventory of everything in the place and check that everything the landlord says is there *is* there. If it isn't, say so at once.

Council Accommodation

The housing departments of local councils have a certain amount of freedom as to the policies they adopt. You normally have to go to the housing department and apply for a house, and are usually expected to have lived in the area for anything from a week to 5 years depending on the authority.

Some councils *must* put you on the list if you fit the terms of those who are allowed to have council houses. Other councils may refuse to have someone on the list, if they wish. How soon you will get a home will partly depend on your place in the queue and partly on how you score. For example, you might get points for each child, more for a child with a handicap, and so on.

Buying a Council House

Under the 'Right to Buy' scheme a tenant can buy the council house he or she is living in. There is a large discount on the price depending on how long you have lived there, or have been a tenant in any other property in this scheme, such as those belonging to:

- District Councils
- London Borough Councils
- new town development corporations
- non-charitable housing associations

★ The **Citizens' Advice Bureau** should have the facts on other tenancies which would count in your favour.

To buy you must have lived in such a property for at least 2 years and the discount rises in stages, with each year after that to a set maximum. For those who can't quite afford a normal mortgage there are Rent to Mortgage Schemes which ensure that the mortgage payments are no bigger than the rent was. A good option as the price and terms of the sale don't rise while you save up to buy.

Tenants of charitable housing associations aren't entitled to buy but they may be able to get help with buying a house or flat on the open market or offer a partial sale.

Those who want to buy should ask their landlord for a 'Right to Buy Claim Form' (RTB1) and hand it in personally – and get a receipt – or use recorded delivery. It is important to have that date because it sets in train a legal timetable in which the landlord has to make certain responses within a certain time. And if he or she fails to do so it is very much in the tenant's favour.

The steps in purchase are clearly laid out in the DoE booklet.

Buying a Council House You Don't Live In

A few councils are operating schemes in which they sell empty council houses to first time home buyers who live in the borough but *aren't* living in accommodation which entitles them to buy. These properties are sold to those thought to be in greatest need.

Moving From Council Accommodation

One of the more astonishing aspects of bureaucracy is that council tenants must get permission from the council before they can so much as swap houses with another council tenant. But they do now have a right to exchange their home with another council tenant, in their own area or in a different part of the country. And they can search for someone to swap with by using Home Swap (below). However, someone who is *waiting* to get council housing has no right to transfer his or her position in the queue to a waiting list in a different area – even if the other area is the only place where there is a job. If any council allows that, it is doing you a favour.

Home Swap (as H.O.M.E.S. below) is a government-backed system for helping people to move if they live in council, or housing association property. To use it, complete one of the forms provided by your local authority and send it to the address given on the form, so your details can be circulated. Also go to the housing department each month and look to see if a likely swap is on the list. If you spot one, write direct to the people concerned. If both you and they favour a swap you must then get written permission to move, from the department from which you rent the accommodation. As bureaucratic wheels grind slowly, it can take a month or two.

Housing Associations

Housing associations form a middle way between private rented property and council housing. Some are totally independent, some are linked to organizations such as MENCAP; and others are essentially cooperatives in which people convert property for their own use. What they all have in common is the fact that they are non-profit making, so rents are relatively low.

Your local CAB should be able to tell you what associations there are in your area. Failing that, H.O.M.E.S. or SHAC (page 270) may be able to help you.

Moving Home

There are those who say the only advice on moving is a four-letter word: don't. But, both professional removers and those who have been much-moved seem to agree that the following points are the ones to remember if you want to emerge victorious.

Moving Everything Yourself

The cheapest option is obviously to move everything yourself. Some car hire companies (in Yellow Pages) not only hire out vans, but also the tea chests and other equipment. But check your insurance – it could prove very expensive in the long run if anything is damaged.

★ To move a long case clock the golden rule is 'weights, pendulum, pendulum, weights'. Which means that to avoid damage, you first remove the weights, then the pendulum – and put them back in reverse order.

Addresses and suggestions for further reading are at the ends of chapters.

Using Removal Firms

Removals firms range from vague hippies with vans and free time, to experts bulging with bladder wrap and a fixed determination to take over totally. The more valuable the goods and the farther you are going, the more expert the removers need to be. Asking an inexperienced firm to negotiate your goods through the complexities of shipping and foreign customs is likely to be more trouble than it's worth.

- The best remover is one recommended by at least one friend who has done a similar move. Or if you have valuables to move, local antique dealers often know the good firms. Failing that, or for overseas moves, use a remover who is a member of **The British Association of Removers (BAR)** (page 269). If the remover goes bust while your goods are in transit another member finishes the job without extra charge.
- To move you abroad make sure they will give a door-to-door service. Some only do door-to-port – which can leave your goods standing in some dock.
- Get at least 3 estimates.
- Before getting estimates, list *everything* you want them to move – including the garden tubs, and the things in the loft. Also list everything you *don't* want them to move (whatever you will move yourself, or you've agreed to leave as fixtures and fittings). Then give each firm the same *written* list – if you rely on telling them, it's odds on you'll vary it, so the estimates won't compare.
- Indicate which items will need special treatment; most removals men can't tell Ming from Marks & Spencer's. (But bear in mind the risk of burglary if you do this with a fly-by-night firm.)
- If you are wondering about moving some of it yourself, or packing some things but letting them move them, make out two different lists. Then ask each firm for comparative estimates. But choose the items carefully: insurance won't usually cover anything not packed by the removers.
- Don't be tempted to get a lower estimate by 'forgetting' to tell the companies awkward facts about the new address. It's far better to tell them the worst – whether it's parking problems or low doorways. If you don't they have a right to breach the estimate and charge you more – and by then it's too late to negotiate.

Insurance While Moving

If you have a household policy your valuables are usually only insured while in that house. And you can't assume that your goods are automatically covered in transit by the removals firm. Many are only insured for a few pounds *per cubic foot* of space taken up by the goods – regardless of their value.

1 You can extend your household policy but this risks a loading on your policy, in future, if there is damage.
2 You can ask the removers to get insurance quotes, giving them an overall valuation plus a note of items of special value. They usually charge for this, but the charge may be hidden in the premium they quote.

Make sure the insurance covers any time in store or in customs; this may not be automatically included. And check the terms. Confidence in cover for £100,000 could be a touch misplaced if you can only claim up to £200 for *any one item*.

Whom to Notify of Your Move

The following need to be notified before the minimum times given here.

Accounts: in all shops with which you have an account – late payment could cost you interest.

Bank: all banks you have dealings with.

Car registration: write to the **Driver Vehicle Licensing Agency** (see page 445) giving details of your car and registration.

Council tax: departments of both areas.

Credit cards: as accounts above.

Dentist you don't need to deregister.

DSS National Insurance: write to DSS Newcastle Central Records Office (page 693) giving your full name, date of birth and national insurance number.

DSS benefits: tell your present office and ask them to notify your new office.

Doctor: deregister if you are moving out of the area.

Electricity company: at least 3 days before, and ask for a reading on the day, and *sign on with the company for your new home*. The electricity will be disconnected, if nobody has signed on as a new user.

Football pools: inform your collector or notify them on the coupon.

Gas company: at least 3 to 4 days' notice that you want the meter read on the day of the move, and notify the gas company at your new address of the day you are taking over. Ask for a reading that day there too.

Hire purchase: notify every company.

Hospital or clinic: if receiving treatment.

Income tax: the address on your tax forms.

Insurance: house, contents, car and yourselves, at least 7 days before or you may not be insured.

Mail: arrange for mail to be forwarded. There is a sliding scale of charges according to how long you wish it to continue. But one fee covers everyone in the family – if the surname is the same.

Mail order: any company you use.

Pensions: ask the Post Office.

Personal giro: ask the Post Office.

Professional advisors: accountants, lawyers, stockbrokers.

Schools: as soon as possible.

Standing orders: tell any companies you pay.

Stocks and shares: write to the company registrar of all companies in which you hold shares.

Subscriptions: to magazines, clubs etc.

Telephone: give a week's notice to each end and arrange for the bills to change names on the correct day, and for your new phone to be connected.

Traders: cancel milk, papers, etc.

TV licence: ask at the Post Office.

VAT office: if you pay VAT.

Water company: at each end.

Preparing for the Move

You can never do too much too soon. All the little jobs

take far longer than might be thought. Throw away everything you don't need to take. Drain the lawn mower, and so on. Also:

- Eat the freezer down – completely, if you can. It is a myth that it should be moved when full: it is not designed to carry the weight. If you leave a small amount pack it round with crumpled newspaper to keep in the cold and mop up the drips. If a freezer has to be stored, prop the door slightly open, as mould will flourish inside if it is not running.
- Find out from the vendors of your new home exactly where everything is – fuse box, water heating, stop cocks. You'll never need a hot bath more than on the day you move.
- Agree whether they will leave essentials like light bulbs.
- Make an exact plan of your new home on graph paper and cut out outlines of the furniture. Then you can tell if something won't fit.
- Allocate each room a letter of the alphabet, and put a matching letter on to every item for each room. Either go ahead and label the doors accordingly or give the removals men a floor plan.
- If goods will be going into store put 'Keep Forward' notices on everything you will need earliest.
- Check the instruction books of appliances. Some need to be secured with special braces and you may need to obtain them.
- If you can leave children and pets elsewhere on moving day do so. Moving can be murder – you don't want to commit it too. If you have to move with children in tow it helps to lay in a treat for each child. You won't have time to give them attention, and there is nothing like lack of attention to bring out the worst in a child. So fool them. Pre-record a story on tape for young ones, buy a book or absorbing toy for older ones, and some treat foods so they don't feel left out. Get the television out of the old house last and into the new one first, with a good video or two at the ready – if possible.
- Prepare a separate box with everything for the moving day (loo paper, washing bag, towel, passports, dog food, etc – if they apply) plus tea, coffee, an electric kettle, sugar, UHT milk, plenty of mugs – removals men work best on a constant stream of praise and refreshments. Label this box 'NOT TO BE REMOVED' – and take it with you.

On the Day

The removers should pack everything – unless you arranged otherwise – then unpack it and put it in place. Check it for damage before they leave and show any damage to the foreman immediately – you have very little come-back otherwise.

★ Before moving out, check the meters and make a note of the reading, just in case the company's don't get to them.

DIY

This section covers the basics of do-it-yourself which the average person can easily tackle. It also deals with repairs which any home is likely to need. In the course of this I have tucked in as many tips and short cuts as I possibly could. For it's often the little details that make the difference to doing a job well and easily.

But first, a word of caution. In Great Britain 3 million people a year seek medical aid after accidents in the home, and many die from their injuries. Many more are hurt but deal with it themselves. Women are the most vulnerable, perhaps because they spend more time in the home. The most common cause of accidental death is someone over the age of 75 falling; fire comes second. But they aren't the only people who get injured. Two prime causes of accidents to active adults are:

- failing to use a circuit breaker on jobs which could damage an electric flex
- chemicals catching fire on their own when overheated. These include petrol, oil, paraffin, certain polishes, adhesives and aerosols. Keep such items away from direct heat or sunlight.

Abrasive Papers

People talk about sanding a surface but, strictly speaking, there is no such thing as sandpaper. The real situation is this.

- The sandy-looking paper most of us call sandpaper is 'glasspaper'. It's for smoothing wood, and the grades range from extremely coarse to very fine.
- The black paper, often called 'wet and dry', is coated with silicone carbide. This can be used dry or slightly damped. It is particularly used for smoothing down metal and paint – such as in car body repairs. It leaves a sludgy mess behind which you need to wipe off. There are also sponges coated in silicone carbide which are ideal for shaped surfaces and very good for giving a key to paint.
- Emery paper is also black but is very tough and only used for smoothing metal. Great for rust removal.
- The grey-green flour papers are the finest papers of all. They are used in jewellery making.
- For belt sanders there are cloth-backed abrasives in two weights. X weight, in grades 24-320, is the heavier and stronger; J weight, in grades 60-400, is more flexible.

Sanding Techniques

The trick is to use finer and finer papers until you have a perfect surface. With a piece of planed wood, for example, you might start with a 50 or 60 glasspaper. Then move to an 80, then a 120 before painting. But if you were going to varnish or polish the wood you would go on to use finer papers still.

> It is never wise to breathe in the particles created by sanding, and a mask should be worn. After using a chemical stripper, the wood dust will have the chemicals in it and very shiny or very old paint may well contain lead.
>
> It is also advisable to wear goggles. A sander can always dislodge a loose fragment and send it flying into an eye.

Addresses and suggestions for further reading are at the ends of chapters.

If you have to sand by hand wrap the paper round a cork block (DIY shops sell them). This makes sure that a large surface is in contact with whatever you are sanding and the cork has enough give not to press the debris from the paper into the surface below it. A wooden block does just that and may create scratches on the very surface you are trying to smooth. **UGW** (page 270) can tell you where to find unusual grades of abrasive papers.

When choosing an electric sander the same rule applies and the softer the pressure, the smoother the finish you can get, but the more slowly it will work.

★ To unclog a piece of sandpaper put the back of it against the edge of a table and drag the paper to and fro across it – to open the grain.

Bath Gap Sealant

Sealing the gap between wall and bath, with one of the silicone rubber sealants, is one of those jobs which look so easy it is tempting to try to do it in an odd moment. Don't. The filler sets very rapidly and you must get the whole job done at once. It also takes considerable care to get a perfect result. First clean the area, scraping out any old filler thoroughly.

Rub the area well with methylated spirits: any traces of soap will stop the filler sticking properly. Then run masking tape along the bath and the wall where you want the edges of the filler to come (unwanted sealant is much harder to remove than you might think). And, if the gap is very big, stuff it with a twist of paper. Or, use an expanding polyurethane filler foam to fill it below the bath level.

Choose a time when you won't be interrupted and have some cling film and some washing-up liquid to hand. If you are interrupted put cling film tightly over the sealant. It hardens by absorbing moisture from the air, so shutting out the air keeps it soft for longer.

Starting at a corner, push, rather than pull, the sealant, evenly in a continuous bead. *The instant* it is all the way round, smooth it to shape with a finger dipped in washing-up liquid (which acts as a smoothing fluid and stops it sticking to your finger), and remove the masking tape *at once*.

> There is a limit to how wide a gap these sealants will fill. Very wide gaps are better covered by a special plastic sealing strip, shaped rather like the curved cornice between a wall and a ceiling. You stick this on with a special waterproof adhesive. Cut the corners at a 45 degree angle (see page 265), butt them perfectly together, and fuse them with a special adhesive, so no water can get through.

Carpet Laying

Provided you can cover the area without having to make seams, carpet laying is rather easy. Standard widths are 3.66 m (12 ft), 4 m (13 ft) and 4.57 m (15 ft). Very little carpet is now made in the old 91 cm (36 in) and 69 cm (27 in) widths, so seams are seldom used.

Tools
To lay a carpet you need:

- Stanley knife
- kneekicker – hireable
- hammer
- staple gun (optional)
- bolster (a tool) – for grip strips only – hireable
- hacksaw – for grip strips only
- gripper strips – if being used
- nails
- double-sided tape – for foam-backed only
- metal strip or carpet to protect it at doorways
- 2.5 cm (1 in) carpet tacks – if tacking it down.

★ Carpet should not be laid over plastic/vinyl tiles. They gather condensation and the carpet will eventually become mouldy and smelly.

Preparing the Floor
The first essential is to have a flat surface to put the carpet on. Concrete must be given a smooth surface as for tiles (page 241). If the surface is already smooth but dusty you can either use the levelling compound to stop the dust or go over the concrete with Unibond. Floorboards must be made level (page 241) or covered with hardboard as for tiling (page 241).

An amazing amount of dirt and cold comes up through gaps in floorboards, so it's a good idea to fill any big gaps between them. If the gaps are extremely wide you may find soaking twists of brown paper in wallpaper glue and laying them into the gaps is easiest. If you are going to sand the floor you can leave the filler a little proud and sand it smooth.

Under the Underlay
Put a layer of thin cardboard called 'felt paper' on the floor before putting down a foam-backed carpet or rubber underlay. It provides another layer of insulation and means there is no risk of the carpet or underlay sticking to the floor – a nuisance if you want to replace the carpet or take it with you when you move.

Planning the Fixing
Foam-backed carpet can be stuck down with double-sided tape. For non-foam-backed carpet you can turn the edge under and hammer in tacks at intervals. This is cheap and very easy. Or you can fit gripper strips which are thin lengths of wood with nails all tilting at an angle towards the wall. The carpet is then hooked over the nails and held down by them. This sounds easy but, in my experience, is far harder than using tacks.

Seaming
Sewing a seam is tougher on the hands than you'd think possible. Luckily, one seldom needs to do it unless mov-

ing a carpet from one room into another and needing to patch odd corners.

Use a curved needle and linen thread, and wear tough leather gloves with a thimble inside. The technique is then to put the two edges right side to right side and oversew them together. Check the tension of your stitches to see they will hold the two edges firmly, but still allow the carpet to open flat.

There are tapes which can be used to hold carpet together, or you can use a strip of hessian and a PVA glue. Many people find these perfectly good, but I personally feel that the only tape which makes a totally satisfactory seam is the one professionals heat weld to the carpet.

Underlay

Foam-backed carpet needs no underlay; all other carpets do. Rubber underlay is considerably better than felt. If you can't afford it you might consider contacting a company that does contract flooring and see if you can buy their offcuts when they do a big job. Good quality rubber underlay can be pieced together like a jigsaw with adhesive carpet tape on the fabric side, and is none the worse for it.

Carpet Repairs

If a carpet has a stain which can't be removed, or a burn, a neat patch may be less noticeable. Unless the carpet has a pattern in it that you want to follow, mark a neat square exactly on the grain of the carpet. Stick a skewer in the centre of this and hold it up off the underlay as you cut an X in the centre of this so you can get your hand in. Hold the carpet up firmly and cut the square out neatly with a Stanley knife. Place the piece on top of an offcut of carpet, match any pattern exactly and cut out the new piece. Push a circle of strong fabric through the hole and smooth it out under it. Apply carpet adhesive to either the carpet or the fabric – whichever is easier. Press the carpet on to it. Put adhesive on the patch and press it into place.

★ It's a good idea to keep any decent-sized pieces of waste carpet. If you stain the carpet in the room you can test stain removal methods on them. You can also use them to patch the carpet if necessary. And if there is an area which gets a tremendous amount of wear or dirt, putting a section of the same carpet down as a mat is far less intrusive than a mat of a totally different sort. If you want to do this, coat the back with PVA adhesive to stop the edges fraying.

Carpet Tiles

Carpet tiles are laid on a plain smooth surface just like vinyl tiles (page 241), and the planning and laying are organized in the same way. They usually have the non-slip direction of each tile shown on the back. If so they should be laid so the arrow alternately points forwards and sideways. This stops them gradually creeping if the wear is more in one direction than another.

Rugs

If the rugs are on top of a carpet, you can stop them curling up by putting self-adhesive velcro on the corners of the underside – using the hooked half of the velcro.

The best way to stop a rug sliding is to put a rubber underlay under it, or you can buy anti-slip strips to put on the back of rugs. Alternatively, use the foam type of stick-on draught excluder or – on a rug of no value – coat the back with a PVA adhesive (letting it dry very well before putting the rug on the floor). If the corners turn up on a hard floor use a double-sided tape at each corner.

China Repairs

Broken china and glass can easily be repaired with epoxy resin such as Araldite. The snag is that the resin turns yellow, so no amount of care can stop a yellow line showing on glass. For earthenware which is not going to be used and washed up – such as a display plate – it is better to use Durafix or Evostick Resin W. Araldite can run into the body of the earthenware and create a stain.

When using Araldite the greatest possible care must be taken to leave no glue on the surface, and to prevent it getting on gilding or lustreware.

For a really good result have everything to hand before starting. First try matching the pieces together to see how they fit. Make sure that the surfaces are totally free from grease by wiping them with acetone, or methylated spirits. Let this dry. Then piece the object together using the sharpened end of a matchstick to apply no more glue than will *just* cover the surfaces. But if some does ooze, carefully wipe it off with a little methylated spirits while it is wet, without pushing the pieces out of true.

If a small piece is missing it can be rebuilt by mixing a little kaolin powder (from a chemist) into the Araldite or adding a suitable powdered clay to the glue for pottery or earthenware. This can even be tinted to match with ground artists' pigments, but these are expensive. Powder colour will work at first but the colour will slowly change with time.

The firmest way to hold the pieces in place is with gummed brown paper tape: it tightens as it dries, and by moistening it you can take it off without tugging at the break.

While it dries the object must be very well supported. Use anything which works – such as plasticine or clay. You can stand a plate on its edge in a biscuit box of moist sand – with the mended section uppermost. Cups and bowls are usually best resting on their rims.

When the glue is firm but not totally hard, wet and remove the tape, pare off any surplus glue with a razor blade, and wipe it clean with methylated spirits or acetone, *without* letting any run into the joint.

There are, of course, special china mending cements. The ceramics conservation unit of a major museum recommends HXTAL NYL-1 or Ciba Geigy's VPXW from **Stuart Stevenson** (page 268). If you want advice on mending fine china or other objects invisibly, the restoration departments of museums are usually extremely helpful. The 1856 *Enquire Within* was not:

> *The white of an egg, well beaten with quicklime, and a small quantity of very old cheese, forms an excellent substitute*

Addresses and suggestions for further reading are at the ends of chapters.

for cement, when wanted in a hurry, either for broken china or old ornamental glassware.

Door Problems

Door Trimming

If a door has to be shortened to fit over new flooring take it off its hinges. Turn it upside down, rest it on the flooring, upright against the frame, and mark the amount it stands above the lintel. Most people then mark a line so the door will be about 0.5 cm (¼ in) shorter, to allow for the fact that the weight of the door will have pressed a carpet down. But on a hard floor where draughts are a problem you may want simply to cut to the door side of the line.

If you have any doubt about your ability to keep the saw totally vertical – so both sides of the door are cut to the same amount – clamp a length of thick wood along the line on the upper side of the door. Then keep your saw against it. For tips when sawing (especially veneer) see page 265.

If you miscalculate and a door is too long, an electric sander is the best solution. Failing that, hang the door, put a sheet of sandpaper under the point which is too long and swing the door to and fro over it while standing on the ends of the sandpaper. Gradually raise the sandpaper by putting newspaper underneath. Not quick, but at least it has a better chance of hitting the spot than hand sanding with the door off.

Squeaking Hinges

Most squeaking hinges can be cured by applying powdered graphite (from locksmiths), penetrating oil or thick washing-up liquid. Suit the lubricant to the type of door. (Graphite is also a safe cure for squeaking piano pedals.)

Sticking Doors

Doors will stick when they expand in wet weather or when coats of paint build up and enlarge them. But first check the hinges, a loose screw can let the door lean away from the lintel and stick on the other side. If excess paint has built up the paint will usually be scratched where the door scrapes. The place can then be sanded down, to allow room for fresh coats of paint.

Sliding Doors which Fall Out

If a hardboard sliding door falls out it is usually because the lower edge has worn down and allowed the door to drop low enough to fall out of the upper rail. The solution is to glue used matchsticks at intervals along the bottom of the door with wood glue. I have sliding doors which have run perfectly on them for 6 years, so it's not just a temporary solution.

Drawers which Stick

A drawer which sticks can usually be cured by rubbing a candle or a cake of soap underneath its runners. If this doesn't cure the problem the wood may have swollen at the sides and this area needs sanding down until the drawer enters cleanly.

Electrical Appliances

On the whole, electric appliances are best left to experts. However, the law of nuisance dictates that they only break down when you have the greatest possible need for them. And if, for example, the video fails on Christmas Eve you may be less worried by the gamble of damaging it than by the prospect of the entire family fighting over which film to watch.

Improving Radio and Television Reception

The insides of radios and televisions are not designed for DIY and it is safest to leave them alone. However, if reception is poor there may be quite a bit you can do without touching the inside.

The Department of Trade and Industry (see Organizations) has a booklet 'How to Improve Television and Radio Reception' and the BBC produces a leaflet on how to get the best out of stereo radio.

> If you have pets which sit on the television, or if you ever put anything on it, or above it, which might shed leaves, petals or fluff (especially a Christmas tree), the debris which gets down through the little slits could well cause reception problems. It could also cause a fire. The television should be cleaned out regularly by a professional and nothing which sheds should sit on it.

Refrigerator Door Seals

If the seal ceases to work on a freezer or refrigerator it is usually extremely easy to replace it yourself. Most seals are held in place with a few cross head screws and the manufacturer's service centre should be able to tell you whether there are any snags and be able to post you a new seal if there aren't.

> WARNING: Any DIY on an electric appliance is risky. You might accidentally cause expensive damage, and its guarantee may cease to be valid. Only attempt repairs if these are risks you are prepared to take.

Tape Recorder Troubles

Three faults commonly afflict tape recorders: crackle on the tape, unclear recording and play back, and the tape getting tangled in the machine. Crackle could be a duff, or ancient, tape or a loose microphone lead at the time of recording. You can test this by making a recording and wiggling the lead. A new cable, or a professional repair, should cure it.

Fuzzy sound is likely to be caused by dirty heads. Clean the heads with head cleaner or methylated spirits on a clean lint-free rag, *without* letting any meths get on other parts of the machine.

BEFORE WORKING ON THE INSIDE OF A TAPE RECORDER UNPLUG IT FROM THE ELECTRICITY SUPPLY.

If a tape gets wound into the works of a machine the chances are that it's a 120-minute tape. These tapes are much thinner than the others, as so much more has to be packed into the cassette, and they tend to cause this problem. (This makes them a bad buy.) Their thinness also means that if they do get tangled you have to be very careful or bits will break off and stay in the machine. Instead of tugging hard at the tape, work in light jerks teasing and wiggling it into unwinding without breaking. Often it helps to use tweezers.

Video Failure

BEFORE YOU DO ANYTHING UNPLUG BOTH MAINS AND VIDEO LEADS INCLUDING THE CONNECTION VIA THE TELEVISION.

If playing back a video gives a very poor picture or nothing but white crackle on the screen the head may need cleaning.

If you have the type of video in which a section rises up to take the tape, remove the cover to this small section (it's usually held on with a couple of screws). If the video isn't of this design, you may need to remove the whole top. The head is a metal disk with a rim the depth of a video tape. Rub the edge of this head with a freshly laundered handkerchief, slightly dampened with methylated spirits until it looks spotless, without touching that part with your fingers – finger oils could make the picture worse. Even if the rim doesn't look dirty give this treatment a try. Dirt which is invisible to the naked eye can make a difference. But *don't* be tempted to rub it with anything rougher than the cloth. A scratched head would be a useless head. Then replace the cover and try it.

> It is important to use a clean cloth, *not* tissue or cotton wool because if tiny fragments came off and got stuck in the machine they could do damage.

Washing Machine Troubles

There are few things more annoying than a washing machine failing with a full load locked inside it. But the solution could be quite simple. Many modern washing machines have a kind of mechanical 'appendix' for catching things which shouldn't have been in the machine in the first place. When this catches something the machine may automatically switch off, fail to empty, overflow or whatever its whim is. This appendix is usually in the front of the very bottom of the machine, often behind a slim panel which can be opened, provided you have absolutely no fingernails or don't mind losing those you do have.

First check your instruction book carefully to see if your machine has such a device. If it has, there should be instructions on exactly how to get at it and free the offending object. The machine will then work again.

If the machine has simply gone off, check the fuse in the plug and the fuse on the fuse board before calling out the repair company.

Washing-Up Machine Troubles

If a dishwasher ceases to wash well there may be trouble with its rotary arms. A common problem is something caught under them so they can't rotate on the central pillar. Try wiggling them. They may come free. If that isn't the problem they may be dirty inside or the holes may be blocked. If not, you need to remove them. The instruction book may tell you how. If it doesn't, only you can tell whether you want to take the risks involved in working on the machine without the maker's blessing.

If you want to go ahead, there is often a screw top to the pillar which unscrews in the reverse direction to a normal screw. Or there may be a metal clip which is sometimes very hard indeed to replace.

If water leaks from under a dishwasher or washing machine it is always worth pulling it out and checking the hose. Often it is only held on with a screw-up ring and a new hose can easily be put on. With call-out charges as high as they are, this is money well saved.

Electrical Work

Extending a Flex

The best way to make a flex longer is to remove it entirely and fit a new flex the right length. But if you need to make a temporary extension, the only safe way to do it is with a flex connector. This has metal connectors, into which you screw the flexes, within a plastic container which insulates them. The important point when wiring it is that the blue wire must lead directly to the blue wire and the brown wire lead directly to the brown one. You should also use the same type of flex at both sides of the junction.

> TO JOIN FLEXES WITHOUT USING A PROPER FLEX CONNECTOR IS TO INVITE A FIRE. To put the joined flexes under a rug or mat is doubly dangerous.

Fuses

There are fuses inside square-pinned plugs and on the fuse board of the house. If a single electric appliance fails the first thing to check is whether the plug has fused. This is just a matter of unscrewing the central screw in the plug to open it, prising out the oblong fuse and replacing it with another.

Use the fuse recommended by the maker of the appliance. Failing that, there is no danger in using 13 amp fuses for everything, and you can certainly do so if you want to. *But* the whole role of a fuse is to act as a buffer when things aren't quite right. If you have a 5 amp stereo, and put a 13 amp fuse in its plug it will work perfectly – but if there is a power surge (which can happen) the 13 amp fuse fails to block it and the stereo could be damaged. But a 5 amp fuse would break, cutting off the electricity and the stereo would be safe. So using the right fuse for the appliance can be a useful protection.

WARNING: Electricity can kill. Always turn supply off at the mains before doing any electrical work.

The Electricity Council says that the easy rule is to use a 3 amp fuse for all appliances below 700 watts – the wattage is given on the back of any appliance. However, some appliances, such as televisions, create a brief power surge as they are switched on and a low amp fuse may fail rapidly. For them a 13 amp is more practical.

> Electric blankets *must* be fitted with the fuse recommended by the manufacturer (usually 3 amp) *not* with a 13 amp fuse.

★ If you replace a fuse and the appliance still doesn't work check the fuse by putting it in the plug for a light and seeing if the light works with it in. Fuses can be duff.

Fuses on the Consumer Unit (Fuseboard)
If several lights or sockets cease to work a main fuse has probably gone. The solution will be found on the main fuseboard, which is usually near the meter and probably in the garage, or a cupboard of some sort. There are three types of fuseboard:

- circuit breakers with either buttons or switches
- cartridge fuses – for which you need cartridges of the right amps
- fuses taking fuse wire – for which you need the correct fuse wire.

Circuit Breakers
The trend is towards circuit breakers. The great thing about them is that to restore the electricity you simply TURN OFF THE FUSEBOARD, press the button which has snapped out, or switch a switch from off to on, CLOSE THE COVER and SWITCH THE BOARD ON again. (For safety it is important to stick to this order.) If it immediately switches off again there is an electrical fault which must be put right.

In addition to the ordinary circuit breakers, some homes now have what are called RCDs (residual current devices). These switch off the current the instant there is an imbalance between the live and neutral wires anywhere on the circuit. This could save your life. So, if a house is being rewired it will be safer if you ask for a circuit-breaker-style of board with an RCD. But get expert advice on its fitting.

> If you don't have this type of board use a plug-in circuit breaker for all outdoor jobs and any which could cut a flex.

Repairing Cartridge Fuses and Wired Fuses
FIRST SWITCH THE FUSEBOARD OFF. Some boards seem to have several switches, on and around them. Switch them *all* to off and you won't go wrong.

The fuses need to be pulled out of the board to check them, and they can be devils to get out. They may be colour-coded which should give you a clue which to look at.

5 amp – white – will be for lighting circuits
15 amp – blue – will be for an immersion heater
30 amp – red – will be for the ring circuit of the main sockets and cooker or shower
45 amp – green – will be for the cooker or high-powered shower

Cartridges are easy to replace but when these blow they don't show it – and it takes a special meter or continuity tester to check them. To find the culprit try a new cartridge in each fuse in turn, switching the board back on and checking whether things are working again after each one. Start with the fuses with the most likely amp. To replace the fuse you simply unscrew the fuse carrier, fit the new fuse and screw it up again firmly. DON'T FORGET TO CLOSE ANY COVER BEFORE SWITCHING ON AND TO SWITCH OFF THE FUSEBOARD AFTER EACH CHECK.

On the oldest kind of fuse a wire runs either across the top, or through a little ceramic channel down the centre and is held by a screw at either end. Look for a fuse in which this wire is broken. Then unscrew one screw to release the old wire. Wind a new wire of the CORRECT AMP (the amps are marked on the cards of wire and on the back of the fuses or on the board) round the screw and screw it in. Thread the wire from one screw to the other, wind it round the second screw and screw it in firmly – without making the wire too taut. Replace the fuse. CLOSE THE COVER TO THE BOARD BEFORE SWITCHING ON.

> NEVER mend a fuse with anything other than wire of the right ampage. Using heavier wire allows the cables in the house to overheat. More than one family has been burnt to death that way.
>
> A blown fuse can be a warning. If a fuse blows again the moment you mend it there is a serious fault. Try to remember which appliance you switched on just before it blew the first time. Unplug it and see if this solves the problem. Even if the fuse doesn't blow immediately it's a good idea to find out why it blew. Are you running too many appliances off a single socket and overloading it? Is the wiring in a plug or fitting causing a spark? Fires are caused that way. If any fuse blows twice in a short period call an electrician: it is cheaper than a burnt out home.

★ Many fuseboards, infuriatingly, give no indication of which fuse belongs to which part of the circuit. Having found the culprit write a label saying which lights or points that one belongs to and stick it on the fuse box above that fuse.

Flexes and Cables
Unless you are a competent electrician it is safest to leave the hidden cables alone and confine yourself to the flexes and fittings which show on the room-side of the wall.

All flexes look much the same and it's tempting to

WARNING: Electricity can kill. Always turn supply off at the mains before doing any electrical work.

think that the small differences don't matter much. They do. It can be dangerous to use the wrong flex for the job.

Choosing the Right Insulation on a Flex

The safety of a flex depends on its being insulated correctly for the job. If a flex will be taking a lot of wear it is safer to use a heavier flex than the appliance demands. The main types of insulation are these:

Parallel twin PVC	clocks
Light duty PVC	televisions, food mixers, table lamps, hairdryers, refrigerators
Light duty PVC (85°C)	hanging lights
Ordinary duty PVC	washing machines, tumble dryers, kettles, slow cookers
Rubber (60°C)	plate warmers or electric frying pans etc
Rubber with braid outside	irons, toasters, some room heaters
High temperature rubber 80°C	immersion heaters, storage heaters

> If an appliance has had a 3-core flex the replacement flex *must* also be 3-core. 2-core flexes should only be used when the makers say they are correct.

★ A 0.5^2 mm flex for a hanging light will hold up to 2 kg (4lb 6oz).

Rule 1	**Rule 2**
You can safely put a 3-pin plug on a flex which has only 2 wires.	It is *not* safe to put a 2-pin plug on a flex with 3 wires.

Wiring a Plug

Plugs are extremely easy to wire provided you do it *exactly* like this. The instructions are for a standard 13 amp plug. But the basic method and position of the wires is just the same for any 3-pin plug. But do bear the following rules in mind.

Colours of Wires and What They Mean

	Live	Neutral	Earth
EC and modern British appliances	brown	light blue	green and yellow
Major cables and old British appliances	red	black	green
Appliances in America	any colour	white or grey	green

Cable Grip

The correct wiring is shown in the illustration. The easy way to remember which wire goes where was taught me years ago by an electrician. With the flex towards you brown and red – which both have the letter R in – go to the Right. Blue and black – which both have the letter L in go to the Left. And green for grass grows up. Alas, it doesn't work for American colours.

If there is no green or green/yellow wire just put the other wires in their correct places and make sure the empty screw for the earth wire is screwed in firmly so it won't fall out, or it could fuse the plug.

To wire a plug you need a screwdriver and something to strip the wires. Wire strippers are easiest, but nail scissors or a sharp blade will do, if used carefully.

1 Undo the large screw in the centre which holds it together, and remove the back.
2 Undo the two screws which hold the small bar at the bottom in place. Sometimes there is a V-shape in plastic instead.
3 Tuck the flex under the bar and decide how much of its outer coating you must cut off (if it isn't already stripped) to let the inner wires reach the 3 contact points with ½ cm to spare. Remember the outer coat of the flex *must* be under the bar, so the flex can be held firmly in place.
4 Cut back the flex coating to the point you have marked, without cutting into the coating of the inner wires.
5 Cut the core wires so they are ½ cm longer than they need to be to reach their contact point and strip about 1.2 cm (½ in) of coating off the end of each. Then twist the little wires inside neatly together.
6a If the wires are to be inserted into holes in the pins fold the bare section neatly in half and squeeze it to a compact end – this holds firmly. Loosen the screws in the pins, and insert the wires, placing the colours exactly as illustrated. (You may have to take the fuse out to get at one. Just push it out of its clip with a screwdriver.) Tighten the screws to hold each wire firmly.
6b On some plugs the wire is put between two brass discs held down with a screw. For this type don't fold the ends but coil each into a little circle, so the screw will go through the centre with the discs holding it down firmly all round.

WARNING: Electricity can kill. Always turn supply off at the mains before doing any electrical work.

Finally, when the wires are in place, screw the grip firmly down over the flex. Check that the fuse is correct. Then screw the back on.

Flooring

Floor Tiles
The following method is for laying cork or vinyl tiles. For ceramic tiles see page 263.

Preparing a Wood Floor
To lay cork or vinyl tiles you need a perfectly flat surface so lay sheets of hardboard on to the boards and then lay the tiles on top. Tiles shouldn't be laid on new boards as there will be movement while they settle down. Old boards need to be made flat by knocking down any protruding nails and sanding down any edges that stand up, or they may buckle strangely as the weather changes. To condition hardboard brush the rough side over with about $\frac{1}{2}$ l (1 pt) water for every 4 sq m (approx 4 sq yds) and leave it for about 5 days in the room where it will be used.

When you have done this nail the board to the floor, rough side up, cutting it carefully to shape (see ★) with a fine saw to fit exactly round obstacles like radiator pipes. (If it only fits roughly the tiles have no support at the gaps and may break off with wear, leaving an ugly hole and a dirt trap.) Nail the boards down firmly but not too hard or they will be pulled down into dips as they warp with age.

> If you are laying very thin vinyl tiles it may be better to put the hardboard smooth side up or the roughness will eventually show through the tiles.

★ To cut hardboard to shape easily cut a pattern of the floor in newspaper, lay this on the board, mark round it and cut the hardboard to shape.

Preparing a Concrete Floor
Few concrete floors are perfectly flat: the answer is to cover the floor with a self-levelling compound, but this is one thing I haven't tried myself. You mix it according to directions, pour it on the floor, let it find its own level and spread it gently with a plasterer's trowel so it covers the entire area. Then let it set and dry completely (usually 24 hours).

Marking the Tile Positions
Mark the mid-point on each wall, at skirting level. Stretch cotton twine from side to side of the room between each pair of marks, and nail it into the floor or skirting base at the mid-points on the wall. Check with the corner of a newspaper that the strings cross at a perfect right angle (square corner). If necessary, adjust them until they do. Rub chalk along the underside of each string, lift and ping the string against the floor to leave a straight chalk mark.

Place a row of glueless tiles from the string to the wall. If a gap of less than 6 cm ($2\frac{1}{2}$ in) is left you will have a fiddly border of small pieces at both sides of the room. Adjust the position of the string and place a line of loose tiles right across the room and check you haven't created an annoying border on the other side of the room either. Repeat in the other direction.

Laying the Tiles
Start tiling from where the strings cross. If the tiles aren't ready-glued spread the recommended adhesive for the tiles evenly over about a square metre (yard) of floor. Put the first tile in place, with its two sides exactly against the angles of the chalk line. Butt the next one *exactly* against it, with no gap at all, and one edge against the line – lowering it into place on the glue, not sliding it. Repeat, working away from the centre in each direction.

The easy way to cut part tiles for the edge is to place a tile *exactly* on top of the last whole tile. Put another tile partly on top of it but with its edge resting against the skirting. Hold the stack firmly and mark the line of the edge of the top tile on the one under it. Cut the tile along the line with a Stanley knife (it helps to have a block of wood to cut on). Then glue it in place against the wall.

When tiles have to be fitted round awkward shapes either use a profile gauge (from an ironmonger) or fit the corner of a newspaper in the angle formed by the laid tiles and slash and cut it until it is exactly the shape the tile needs to be. Place this on the tile, mark the outline, and cut it out. For safety put an X on the upper side of the paper to avoid turning it over by accident.

Finishing Off
Vinyl tiles need no sealant, and most cork tiles are sold with a polyurethane coating. However, those that have no coating need to be sealed. First, let the adhesive dry thoroughly. Then make any edges and corners totally flat with fine glasspaper. Wipe the floor over with white spirit to remove the dust. Apply 3 coats of polyurethane varnish, according to instructions.

Replacing Damaged Tiles
The golden rule when replacing tiles is *never* to lever a tile out by the edge. As most tiles are stuck down with either a bitumen or rubber solution there's a good chance that heat will soften the glue. So put a piece of kitchen foil over the tile and iron it with a hot iron, *giving plenty of time for the heat to penetrate.* While it's still hot stick something sharp into the middle of the tile, and see if you can lever it up by the centre. Normally a tile will come out quite easily. If it won't come up remove it with a hammer and chisel. Work from the centre out to the edges, being careful not to damage the surface under the tile. Make the surface smooth and clean. Spread glue on a replacement tile, and press it into place. Varnish when dry, if necessary.

Hardwood Flooring

The square sections of hardwood which imitate parquet are usually called wood mosaic panelling and are made in 46 cm (18 in) squares. They are laid very much like vinyl tiles (page 241). Use graph paper to work out exactly how you will place them for minimum wastage. But do buy enough, on another batch the wood could look slightly different.

The floor surface needs exactly the same preparation, and marking up as for vinyl tiles. But the wood squares are much harder to cut than the vinyl, so position the strings so that on two sides of the room the sections come exactly to the edge, leaving a 12 mm (½ in) expansion gap at each edge to allow the wood to move. So cut yourself a strip of wood 12 mm (½ in) thick, and place this against the wall when fixing the squares nearest the edge.

Use a fairly fine toothed tenon saw (page 265) to cut the wood and a bitumen adhesive to stick it down. If you mark it with bitumen remove it *at once* with white spirit.

The small gap all round the room is then filled with a strip of cork. The doorway needs to be finished with a threshold strip of matching wood, which can be shaped to come level with the flooring in the next room. Before the bitumen is completely dry, check the floor for any edges that stand up. Place a wood block over them and hammer it to press them down. Let the flooring dry completely. If necessary, sand any corners or edges that aren't perfectly smooth. Remove the dust, wipe down with white spirit and varnish with a polyurethane varnish made for floors.

There's no need to rip off an existing skirting. You can buy lengths of small in-curving beading – rather like a plain ceiling cornice – which can be put up against the skirting on top of the edge of the parquet to hide any small gaps. It's a good idea to prime and undercoat this before fixing it. And if the wood is unvarnished give it all its coats of polyurethane varnish before you fix this beading.

Sheet Flooring

Buying

Most sheet flooring today is vinyl and the choice is between the flat and the cushioned kinds, but there are no standard widths for either. The cushioned kind is softer to walk on but it will become dented if you put heavy furniture on it – such as a kitchen table. It also has a fairly short life. Flat hard vinyl lasts longer.

Sheet flooring will wear quickly if the floor under it is uneven. So prepare the floor as for laying floor tiles (page 241). Then, if the flooring is to be loose laid, cover the floor with felt paper, leaving a bare margin.

Meanwhile leave the flooring in a warm room to relax – cold sheet flooring may crack as you unroll it. Plan how to lay the flooring to avoid the seams being at the door or anywhere else which gets a lot of wear. You also need to avoid having a narrow strip of flooring which will lie badly. (A sketch of the room to scale, on graph paper, can help.)

Laying Sheet Flooring

A lot of the vinyl flooring now on the market is designed to be laid loose and stay flat. This makes it very easy to lay. Check the measurements of the room in several places – few rooms are perfectly even. Take the longest measurement and cut the flooring 10 cm (4 in) longer. If you are laying more than one sheet make sure you cut the lengths so any pattern will match.

Lay the flooring in place, with one edge nicely against the wall or fittings. Lay the next length overlapping. Vinyl is inclined to shrink slightly, and linoleum stretches. So leave it just like that for a few weeks – you can walk on it meanwhile.

When it's ready to trim start by getting rid of the overlap. The pattern may be one which needs to match exactly, in which case it is best to seam it edge to edge and cut the excess off at the outside of the room. Other patterns will only match if you overlap and cut them.

To cut an overlap, line up the two layers so the pattern will match at the seam if you cut through both layers. Hold it firmly in position with plenty of masking tape. Double check that the pattern hasn't shifted out of true and that the flooring still reaches the edges of the room. Try to choose a cutting line where the design will hide the seam. Then cut through both layers with a Stanley knife against a long steel rule.

Having cut the seam, use one side of strong double-sided tape, or whatever tape the manufacturer recommends, underneath to hold the two sections together. Fix it to one half, then place the other carefully on top, making sure the seam is closed tightly.

Next, trim off the surplus at the edges. If the flooring is flexible you can simply press it into the angle of the wall with a metal rule and cut along it with a knife. Where it has to go round bends cut lots of slashes from the edge of the flooring down towards the floor. This allows it to take on the shape – but be careful not to cut too far. If the flooring is harder have a ready-made newspaper pattern of the room to place on top of it and cut round.

Start by cutting the flooring to length or width – whichever has the least complicated outline – measuring and cutting carefully and allowing a little extra on the second edge. Then trim off the excess – when you are sure it really isn't needed. For this, hump the flooring up in the middle of the room. Finally, use a tube of seam sealant to close seam entirely and make sure there is no trap for dirt or water.

Most flooring will lie perfectly smooth and unmoving, but it is even better to fix it under the edges with double-sided tape, and sheet flooring which needs to be stuck down can now be fixed with the recommended adhesive.

★ Keep off-cuts in case you need them for repairs or to test stain removal methods.

Repairs to Soft Vinyl Flooring

Scratches, dents and cigarette burns are the most common damage. On soft flooring there is nothing you can do about any of them. The best repair is to cut out a

---

Addresses and suggestions for further reading are at the ends of chapters.

section of floor along any strong lines in the pattern – very easy with a tiled pattern. Cut a matching section from your offcuts and stick it in place with flooring tape on the back, then seal it with seam sealant.

Repairs to Hard Vinyl Flooring

Major damage to a harder sheet flooring can be repaired in the same way, but it may not hold so well, and on a plain floor the repair may show more than the mark.

Burns can be made less noticeable by rubbing them with fine wire wool until the brown section vanishes – though this leaves a dip.

Scratches which show up pale against darker plastic can be toned down with shoe polish, but a better method can be to melt a candle and children's wax crayons together to get the right colour, then drip this into the dip and smooth it off. Make the dent spotlessly clean and, having dropped in the wax, smooth it with a finger while still hot and use a blade or wire wool to make it perfectly level. Wax fillings I inserted are still invisible after five years of heavy wear.

Glass Buying

The cheapest place to buy glass is usually a specialist glass merchant (listed under Glazier in the Yellow Pages). The standard sizes are 3 mm, 4 mm, 5 mm, 6 mm and 10 mm. On small windows 4 mm is enough but if the panes are large or very exposed 6 mm or even 10 mm would be better. And glass which is low or where someone might easily break it should be safety glass.

Any glass merchant will cut glass to size for you, but you can cut it in just the same way as a glazed tile (page 263), and if a small amount has to be removed from an edge it can be broken off with pliers after the glass has been scored.

Lavatories – see Plumbing page 259

Locks

Maintenance

The best substance for keeping locks, bolts and everything else of that sort running smoothly is an annual dose of powdered graphite from a locksmith. This may well loosen a jammed lock.

Oil should not be used on locks because it attracts and holds dust, and this will jam the lock. However, it is sometimes impossible to get the graphite into a lock – for example, if a car door is jammed. In this case use penetrating oil which is graphite suspended in fine oil. It does, however, carry the same risk of dust collection as any other oil.

Changing a Rim Lock

If you have a rim (surface mounted) lock it is very easy to change it yourself. The vital thing is to remove the lock and take it to the shop with you. Then you can be certain the new lock will fit in the same holes. The other important point is that many of these locks have a connecting bar which has to be cut to length for the thickness of each door. This is the only part of installing a new lock which needs a special tool. But, if you have the old lock with you to show the correct length, ask the shop to do this for you.

To remove the lock simply unscrew every screw you can see and remove them all. Sometimes they may be very long and act almost like bolts within the lock, so they may take a little pulling out. Putting in the new lock is simply a matter of screwing them in again. However, the connecting bar often has to be set at a particular angle if the lock has a deadlock system. So check the instructions on this.

★ Don't throw the old lock away, put it in a bag with all its keys. Next time you lose your key and feel a burglar could use it you simply put the original lock back again – and so on, *ad nauseam*.

Nails and Nailing

There is a lot more to nails than appears at first sight. The range of shapes and sizes is extraordinary and using the right one for the job can make it far easier to get good results.

Pick a hammer with the right weight of head for the job – and for you. The heavier the nail, and the tougher the surface, the heavier the head. Strictly speaking, different shapes of hammer are meant for different jobs, getting the weight right matters more than the shape. On wood use the finest nails which will hold it, and place oval ones so the oval runs the length of the grain, to avoid splitting.

When joining two pieces of wood together the nail needs to be 3 to 4 times as long as the depth of the upper wood. There is always a risk of splitting the grain if nailing near the end of a plank or if two nails are placed in a line along the same grain. If necessary, near the end of a piece of wood, drill a hole, slightly smaller than the nail, before driving it in.

Nailing down into the end grain of wood is largely a waste of time. If a proper joint can't be made use plenty of good wood glue (the end grain also absorbs glue) and then use fine joinery nails to hold the glued sections firmly in place.

★ To insert a short nail without hammering your fingers hold it with tweezers or put Blu-tack, putty, clay or chewing gum round it.

★ To avoid denting the wood if you miss, push the nail through a piece of cardboard (corrugated is good). Tear it off before the final – careful – blow.

Removing Nails

You can remove a nail with the split end of a claw hammer, or with pincers, and tacks can be lifted with a tack lifter (a V-shaped notch sometimes found at the end of other tools). The most powerful of these is the hammer but the pincers are far better for getting a grip on a tricky nail. Both are used with a rolling movement, not by pulling upwards. To protect the surface from denting by either tool, slip a wallpaper scraper under them before levering.

PAINTING AND PAPERING

Painting

With painting, as with anything else, the right tool for the job makes a great difference.

- Rollers are fastest but bad for gloss. They don't leave as smooth a surface as pads or brushes, and foam rollers tend to spray paint around but are good on textured surfaces: the deeper the pattern, the deeper should be the pile of the roller.
- A large paint pad covers the area rather faster than a brush and leaves a better surface than most rollers.
- A 10 cm (4 in) brush is slowest but easiest to clean, and produces the most reliable finish. You will probably need one to get into awkward corners anyway.
- Spray guns can be hired. They are very quick in a bare room and good for awkward shapes like louvred doors but they can clog and splutter, inject the skin with paint dangerously, and the fiddle of thinning the paint and cleaning the spray eats into the time you save.
- It takes skill to get a good result. And, unless you have a very large area to cover in an empty house it is hardly worth using one, but wear a face mask and have plenty of fresh air in the room, if you do.

★ Tie a piece of string across the paint tin from handle to handle. Then you can wipe off surplus paint without getting the rim clogged up.

Awkward Places
- A very small radiator roller is the easiest way to paint the wall behind the radiator.
- A roller with an extension handle is the easiest way to cope with a ceiling which is out of reach.
- A large paint pad firmly anchored to a broom handle will paint high walls you can't otherwise reach; it will also get into corners where the roller can't go.
- With care you can use the long-handled radiator brush to do the angle between ceiling and wall which rollers and pads can't handle.

Skirtings
The important tool here is called George. This is a useful curved piece of metal with which you can shield the flooring while painting the very bottom of the skirting.

★ Choose professional quality paint brushes with split ends to the bristles; they produce a smoother finish.

Cleaning Brushes, Rollers and Pads
Brushes used with water-based paints should be washed *immediately* after use – the paint can dry rapidly. *Don't* leave them in deep water, or when the wood dries the bristles will be loose and shed all over your paint.

After being used for oil-based paints, brushes need cleaning in white spirit, turpentine or turpentine substitute, paraffin or brush cleaner. Once clean a brush should be washed in soapy water, rinsed well and dried. Then it should be left to dry completely with a piece of paper wrapped round the bristles and held with a rubber band to hold the bristles in line.

If a brush becomes hard the commercial brush restorers will do a very good job of cleaning it if you give them time.

★ To avoid bristles becoming bent through brushes standing on them drill a hole through the wide part of the brush handle when you buy it. You can then stick a skewer through the hole and hang the brush in the jar.

★ If you don't want to clean brushes used for oil-based paints because you'll use them next day, put a few drops of white spirit in a polythene bag, pop the brushes in and close the bag tightly round the handle.

Rollers hold a lot of paint, so roll as much as possible out on newspaper. Dismantle the roller and remove the sleeve, wash out water-based paints as for a brush. Oil-based paints are most easily cleaned out in a strong polythene bag with some white spirit. In case it dries stiff, put the cleaned sleeve back on and let it dry on the roller.

Paint pads can be cleaned like brushes but don't leave them soaking in spirit; if you do they may fall off their handles.

> Many of the chemicals used in DIY, such as white spirit and methylated spirits, can set up severe allergic skin reactions in some people. It is not unusual for someone to use these chemicals for years without trouble and then become sensitive to them. Unfortunately, the skin trouble may persist for a long time and even be permanent. Wear protective gloves when using any solvents and have plenty of fresh air so the fumes are not breathed in.

Getting Ready to Decorate

Cracks
Despite the phrase about papering over the cracks, they need to be filled in and sanded smooth for both paint and paper.

Brush and scrape the loose particles from any cracks. If they are wide, undercut them slightly, so they will hold the filler. Most cracks indoors can be filled with an ordinary filler. But outdoor cracks need an exterior filler, and very fine cracks need the very fine ready mixed filler. Until you have used it you may not believe how perfectly a hairline crack can be filled. It saves a lot of sanding later if you wipe the surplus off with a damp cloth or tissue, or the end of a damp paint brush, while it is still wet. When it's really dry, sand the surface perfectly smooth.

If the wall has moved and created a slight 'step' use an electric sander to remove the step and make the surface level. This creates an immense amount of dust and protective covers are needed over everything.

Paint Types

Primers

Primers provide a buffer between a bare surface and the covering paint. Most surfaces can be treated with an All-Purpose or Universal Primer, but some need special primers (pages 246-249).

Surfaces which have been painted before don't need primer – unless patches are bare. If it is suitable, use a quick drying acrylic primer, then you can do the next coat the same day. But when any primer is dry, rub it lightly with fine abrasive paper and wipe the dust off with white spirit.

Undercoats

The undercoat both blots out the colour underneath and provides a base for the topcoat. If an unusual primer has been needed, or you will be using a liquid (as opposed to non-drip) gloss or an eggshell finish on wood, an undercoat is a good idea. But it's often quicker just to apply the topcoat until the effect you want is achieved. If you do use an undercoat, put oil-based undercoat with oil-based topcoat, water-based under water-based – but it doesn't have to be the same brand.

Topcoats

There are now so many names like vinyl, acrylic and silthane it's hard to tell what paints are suitable for what. But the situation is simpler than it seems. The big divide in paints is between those which are oil-based and those which are water-based. Don't mix the two. If you want to know whether a paint is one or the other look at the instructions. If you can thin it with white spirit it is oil-based, if you thin it with water it is water-based.

Gloss Paint and Satin or Eggshell Finish

The range of these paints has grown. You can now buy both oil-based and water-based versions for almost all purposes. Use water-based ones if you can, they are kinder to you and the world. But check that the brand you pick will do the job. Some brands are more versatile than others. And use a suitable primer.

Gloss paints are intended for use on wood and metal but can be used on other surfaces. Liquid gloss and non-drip gloss are both made for indoor use. The non-drip is easier to use. There are also special gloss paints for surfaces like stone or exteriors.

Emulsion Paint

Emulsion is always water-based. Modern emulsions are usually vinyl-based and, unlike the old-time emulsions, wash well. The important difference between them is usually the degree of sheen. None of these paints has the really matt finish of distemper and old emulsions, but aim for the paint with the least sheen. Plaster is seldom dead flat and the more sheen a paint has, the more every bump and line shows.

★ Paints vary enormously in density and sometimes a brand which seems expensive will cover in 1 or 2 coats what a cheaper brand will cover in 2 or 3.

WARNING: Teething toddlers bite anything hard they can lay their jaws on. Before painting anything which might be bitten by a toddler make sure the paint is not toxic. A primer containing lead must NEVER be used for anything a child might bite as lead can poison children. By law, any primer containing lead must say so on the tin, so if it doesn't say that, your primer will be all right. Most ordinary paint shouldn't be harmful to children, but it might be wise to check with the maker. There are also special nursery paints on the market.

Special Paints

There are special paints available which it may be worth knowing about. The major paint manufacturers are listed on pages 270-271 and will tell you whether they make a certain paint, and give the nearest stockist.

Microporous Paint or Varnish

The idea of microporous paint is to allow wood which has not fully dried out to lose its moisture through pores in the paint instead of lifting the paint off. This may make the finish last longer on new wood but there is no advantage to using this over old paints.

Rust Repellent Paint

Iron drainpipes sometimes stain the walls of houses and spoil the effect of a pale paint finish. This paint is devised to stop rust stains forming.

Textured Surfaces

Before applying a textured surface, think twice. You can conceal an uneven wall just as well with a textured paper and the paper is far easier to remove when you tire of it.

If you still want a texture the best option is to go for one which can be removed on a backing paper. Brolac's Tartaruga, for example, has a special backing paper which allows it to be peeled from the wall with the upper layer of paper. Or line the walls with lining paper before putting up the textured surface.

Water Repellent Paint

This is a clear liquid which can be applied to exterior bricks to stop them absorbing moisture. It can also be used on stone, plaster and other surfaces.

Stripping Paint

There are four ways to strip paint and varnish – sanding, caustic soda, proprietary strippers, and heat. For removing French polish see page 247, and varnishes on metal may come off with acetone – but always do a test patch first in a place where it won't show if the chemical and metal interact badly.

Burning

Burning is often the fastest and cleanest method of removing old paint. Modern electric heat guns are exceedingly easy to use, and work excellently. Make sure you have somewhere safe to put it when very hot. On the floor it is all too easy to put a hand or foot on it – very nasty indeed. And check that there is nothing which might catch fire in the area. The heat gun is far less likely to scorch wood than a flame, especially if you keep it moving, but it can crack glass if pointed at it.

Have plenty of air in the room, as the paint may give off harmful fumes. Start at the bottom of the paint so the heat rises to the rest of it. Play the heat gun over the paint until it can easily be scraped off with a suitable scraper, such as a combination shave hook which is especially good for moulding, or a stripping knife. Be careful not to make gouges in the wood as you scrape.

Caustic Soda
This is the cheapest way of removing paint. You need an area out of doors and a water supply.

Safety
Before using caustic soda get into old clothing and put on wellingtons, thick rubber gloves and goggles. Caustic burns slowly. If you have a hole in the rubber gloves you may find a neat patch of skin has been eaten away. It is therefore extremely dangerous to eyes. Keep pets and children indoors.

> If caustic does splash on to skin wash it off with plenty of water AT ONCE.

Mixing Caustic
Have a plastic (not metal) bucket of water (it is made more powerful by hot water) and add a few tablespoons of caustic soda to 2 gallons of water, then stir with a stick. The strength you need depends on the paint. Apply a little, leave it for 10 minutes and if the paint isn't reacting add a little more caustic to the water and test it again.

> WARNING: NEVER *put water on to soda*. It can cause a violent reaction in which the soda erupts like a volcano giving off very strong fumes which are dangerous to breathe, and possibly splashing into your face.

Using Caustic Soda
- Brush the liquid on with an old plastic washing-up brush or something similar. (It will melt the bristles of a paintbrush.)
- Leave the chemical to work until the paint looks very soft and puckered; don't rush it – washing it off before it has time to penetrate makes extra work.
- Remove the paint with water, either using a jet of water from a hose or a brush and bucket of water.
- You may need to repeat this several times. Be careful not to roughen the surface of the wood when getting off the last fragments of paint.

- Go over the bare wood with water containing a good tablespoon of vinegar per pint. This neutralizes the caustic.

You can also make a plastic bath of caustic and dip small items in it. But this can dissolve the glue at joints and it may not be easy to put them together again. Caustic may also cause colour changes in wood, and very strong caustic can cause small black spots.

Proprietary Strippers
There are several brands of stripper which can be used. Nitromors even makes one for polyurethane varnish – which has always been the hardest surface of all to remove – but I have yet to test it. Some strippers come in paste form, some as liquids. Before buying one for indoors, check how the stripper needs to be removed. Some have to be washed off with a lot of water, others only need to be wiped off with spirit.

Give the chemical plenty of time to penetrate deep into the paint before you try to remove it. It should scrape off as in burning, using the same tools. For intricate moulding or carving, a friend of mine gets excellent results by applying a paste stripper, wrapping it in cling film or plastic and leaving it overnight. The wrapping stops the paste drying out, so it goes on working for hours. In the morning the paint peels out of the tricky bits in nice chunks.

> WARNING: Keep these strippers off the skin and out of the way of pets and children. Work with the windows well open as the fumes may make you feel ill.

Removing Gesso
Gesso, the white chalky substance which was used as a basis for finishes earlier this century, is especially hard to get off. Getting water into it is the secret, and wrap it in wet newspaper and keep wetting the paper for hours so the gesso gradually becomes sodden.

Preparing Varied Surfaces for Painting or Papering

Aluminium
Rub aluminium down with a fine wet and dry but use white spirit instead of water. Wipe clean with white spirit. Then prime with a Metal Primer containing zinc chromate.

Anaglypta and Supaglypta
Anaglypta and supaglypta need no preparation before emulsion, but the first coat is usually thinned – check with the paint or paper manufacturer. Before an oil-based paint, whether eggshell or gloss, these papers need a coat of acrylic primer/undercoat. All this applies whether the pattern is in paper or blown vinyl. A sheepskin roller is often best.

Addresses and suggestions for further reading are at the ends of chapters.

Bare Wood

Before painting or varnishing, wood which isn't perfectly smooth must be sanded down (see page 266). Make sure all dust is removed with white spirit. If screws or nails show on the surface place another nail on top and hit it lightly. Failing that, the heads need to be coated to prevent them rusting. A dab of metal primer and a touch of gloss, when that dries, is ideal. (In an emergency you can even use clear nail varnish, but sand it afterwards to give it a key.)

Go over all knots with Knotting, using 2 coats on very resinous wood to stop the resin coming through.

Prime with an Aluminium Wood Primer (especially on resinous woods) or All Purpose Primer, using 2 coats on the endgrain, as this is far more absorbent. *After* the first priming, fill cracks and dips with an all purpose filler. Or use extra fine, ready mixed filler on very fine cracks. Sand the filler smooth when dry and prime.

> Some woods are not ideal for painting. Teak has natural oils which make it retain paint and varnish poorly. On oak it will begin to crack and flake far sooner than on other woods. For exterior sills it is simpler just to oil them occasionally with linseed oil. Columbian pine exudes resin from its entire surface, not just from knots. It is best left unpainted, but if you must paint use aluminium primer first.

Brick, Concrete, Stone, etc

First treat any sign of mould or lichen so it isn't spread to other areas (see Mould, page 248). Remove and replace loose mortar or cladding and fill all cracks. Brush down and remove all signs of dust or loose particles. If there is a chalky or dusty surface use a sealer. Get advice (see pages 270-271) as it needs to be thinned to suit the surface trouble.

Cane and Wicker

Clean old cane by scrubbing with sugar soap. Dry it out *completely*. Apply an All-Purpose Primer, thinning it enough to avoid clogging up the weave. Then use a gloss or eggshell paint or a spray paint (see **Plastikote**, page 270).

Chalky and Powdery Surfaces

For distemper and whitewash see below. Other chalky surfaces can be treated with a stabilizing solution, which penetrates the surface and binds it in place. Use the same treatment before papering. Manders, Sandtex and Crown all make one.

Creosote

If wood has been treated with creosote the creosote will stain the paint. But the older the creosote is, the fewer the problems. Smooth the wood (see page 266). Then apply 2 coats of aluminium primer. If the top coat can be dark it obviously reduces the chances of stains being too unsightly.

Damp Walls

Neither paper nor paint will cling to a damp surface. Once the damp has been cured you can prevent any stains showing through your new paint by first applying a damp resisting composition.

If it is impossible to cure the damp it may be necessary to put up an inner wall on battens, with room for air to circulate behind it. If the problem is condensation a layer of sheet polystyrene on the walls usually prevents this. Let the polystyrene dry for several days before crosslining (pages 254-255), and then either paint or paper on top of that. But see page 249.

Distemper and Whitewash

Distemper is an old-fashioned finish which produces a creamy paste if you rub it with a damp cloth. Before painting or papering you must get rid of it. It may wash off, but it is often on lining paper. If so, strip the paper. If you scrub it off and get back to bare plaster, give it time to dry. Then paint it over with a stabilizing solution which will bind the powdery remains together. Treat whitewash the same.

Emulsion Paint

Before painting or papering, emulsion paint must have any rough or flaking areas sanded down to a smooth firm surface. Ideally, it should be rubbed lightly with wet and dry paper to give a 'key' and washed down with Sugar Soap. The sponge pads with a sanding surface are ideal as they let you wash and sand in one; all you need do then is rinse. Take extra care with the washing anywhere that there might be grease on the walls, as paint will not hold over grease, and start at the bottom. For cracks see page 244.

French Polish

The French polish must be totally removed or it will dissolve into the paint. A paint stripper will do this. So will methylated spirits. The latter is the best method to use if, instead of painting, you want to bring the wood to a natural shine with wax.

Galvanized Metal

New galvanized metal resists paint and it will flake off. The traditional way of making it possible to paint galvanized metal is to let it weather for 6 months to 1 year, but experts recommend using one of the following methods to give it a surface which will take paint.

1 Go over it with white spirit and 00 wire wool, then paint it with a primer containing calcium plumbate (this contains lead, so beware).

2 Treat it with Mordant Solution (from builders' merchants supplying the trade), use white spirit to degrease any areas which don't go black. Then prime with an all-purpose primer.

Gloss Paint

If the surface is good, just rub it down lightly with a fine wet and dry paper (about 320) to give a 'key', and wash it with Sugar Soap. But any paint which is loose or raised should be rubbed down until the surface is smooth, then finished off with fine wet and dry.

If much paint is loose or flaking it will need to be stripped (see pages 245-246). Rub down all bumps and 'steps' to give a smooth surface. Rub any rust back to bright metal with wire wool or abrasive paper, and prime with an anti-rust primer. You can now get water-based gloss and it is kinder to you and to the environment (see also page 245). Before papering gloss paint give it a key, then wash it to remove any gritty bits and cross-line (pages 254-255) before putting up the main paper.

> Remember: if the undersurface is rough you can never get a smooth topcoat. Paint *won't* smooth out the dips; it will sink into them.

Gutters and Drainpipes

All types need to be thoroughly cleaned of dirt and debris and, if possible, flushed out with water. But don't use anything abrasive on asbestos. Check that there are no leaks at the seams, and repair as necessary. Treat as for the material they are made from. There is a special anti-climb paint for drainpipes (see Security, page 229).

Hessian

Hessian must usually be completely removed – treat it like wallpaper, but try to get at one corner so it can pull off in sheets. Then wash the wall down well to remove all traces of fabric.

Before painting over hessian remove all dust. Cover it with a thin coat of cold water size (similar to wallpaper paste). This may stop the paint filling up the weave.

Iron

Iron needs great care. If there is a solid coating of paint don't tamper with it. Just rub it with sandpaper, wash it down and paint it. If there are flaws or rust, rub it back to good paint, or to bright metal. Wipe clean with spirit and prime within an hour with an All-Purpose Primer or an anti-rust primer based on zinc phosphate, if there is no rust yet, or one based on zinc chromate if there has been rust.

If the outside has been painted with bitumen it needs a good coating of Aluminium Primer to act as a barrier between the bitumen and the topcoat. Then use any oil-based paint. However, the primer won't prevent the paint cracking as the bitumen moves. To avoid cracking you can use a paint like Berger's Weathercoat No 1 (not 2 or 3), although the colour range is limited.

Lincrusta

Lincrusta is made with linseed oil. First, get rid of surface grease by wiping it down with white spirit. You can then apply an oil-based paint or an All-Purpose Primer. If you want to use emulsion paint apply an oil-based undercoat first. (See also page 245).

Linoleum

Most paint isn't good at standing the wear and tear of feet, but if you move into a place with old linoleum it will take paint well. The lack of wear in the paint won't matter if you just use it round the edges. Remove any wax or polish with white spirit and a rough nylon scouring pad. Scrub with detergent and then use 2 coats of an all-purpose primer, then an undercoat to suit your top-coat.

Masonry Paint

The first job is to sand off all loose, bubbling or flaking paint, rubbing smooth. On a powdery surface a stabilizing solution must be used.

Mould or Lichen

If there is mould or lichen, treating it must be the first job, or surface preparation may just spread it. Apply a fungicidal liquid according to instructions while wearing gloves and goggles, and keeping it off other skin surfaces. Leave it for the recommended time (usually 24 hours) and then scrub off. (Paper must be stripped afterwards.) If the growth is severe 2 treatments may be needed. When dry, the surface can be made good and papered or painted with mould resistant paint. It is also possible to wash the surface with 1 part of household bleach to 5 parts of water. Leave this for 48 hours and then rinse it off.

Nicotine Stained Paint

Nicotine has remarkable powers of penetration, and the yellowing will slowly seep through and stain new paint and even pale-coloured paper. To stop this, wash the surface *very* well with Sugar Soap, and rinse thoroughly. Apply an aluminium primer or alkali-resisting primer – which should be in shops supplying the trade. Undercoat twice, then paint with your topcoat.

Plasterboard

Before papering, plasterboard must be painted with a primer, so you will be able to strip the paper without the water damaging its surface. It should then be cross-lined. Apply a primer sealer before oil-based paints, but emulsion can be applied direct.

Plaster

New plasters vary greatly in their drying times – some can take a year. Ask the plasterer how long it will be before you can paper over it. If you paper too soon the moisture in the plaster will make it stick badly. Fully dry plaster only needs a layer of wallpaper paste to stop it absorbing the paste from the back of the paper.

Before painting, fill any holes or cracks, rub down, dust off the surface. Emulsion paint can be applied directly to the plaster, with the first coat thinned according to instructions. For the first year it should not be painted with an oil-based paint. Instead, use a cheap contract emulsion from a builder's merchant, such as Covermatt. The cheaper emulsions are porous enough to let the moisture come out of the wall.

Addresses and suggestions for further reading are at the ends of chapters.

Plastic (PVC)

Stiff plastic of the type used in window frames and drainpipes can easily be painted. Wash with detergent to remove any surface grease. Rub lightly with a *fine* abrasive paper to give a key and paint with gloss paint (but check with the maker of any water-based gloss).

Polystyrene

Polystyrene can have paper applied directly to it with wallpaper paste, but not with any solvent based glue. Before painting, wash it with hot water and washing-up liquid. When totally dry paint it with any emulsion.

> Oil-based paints are bad for you and for the environment and are tougher on brushes. There are now water-based paints for almost all purposes, including gloss painting, and they have the advantage of yellowing less. So it's wisest to use them. But do check that the brand you pick will do the job you have to do, and use a primer to suit them. Oil based-paints must *not* be used on polystyrene as it increases the danger in a fire.

Putty

Pick out and replace any old or cracked putty or water will seep under your new paintwork. Apply an all-purpose primer.

Radiators

Rub any rust spots back to bright metal with wet and dry paper or wire wool and coat it with Universal Primer. Or simply wipe a new, ready-primed radiator with white spirit to remove any grease, apply an undercoat made for gloss or eggshell paint and give this a 'key' with wet and dry paper when totally hard. If you are painting them white, use a water-based gloss as it won't go yellow as oil paint does. It also comes in colours. But make sure the brand *can* be used on radiators. Some brands can't. And use a water-based primer.

Textured Surfaces

Before papering, textured surfaces have to be stripped. A few are applied to double-backing paper and the top layer will peel off. Others are on lining paper – which means a tough paper-stripping job. Those put straight on to the plaster or paint may respond to steam stripping or paint stripper. If you know the make of the finish, write to the manufacturer and ask how best to remove it. Before painting, clean it as best you can, then use a primer sealer.

Tiles

Polished quarry tiles won't take paint well. If tiles have no wax on, wash them clean with Sugar Soap. Allow them to dry completely – the joints take longest – and apply a primer sealer (2 coats on the joints improves the finish) before painting.

Woodstains

There is always a danger that woodstain may seep through. Contact the advisory service of the company which made the stain or the paint you plan to use.

Problems with Paint

Crazing is likely to happen if a coat of paint isn't totally dry before the next one is applied. Surface crazing can be rubbed down and repainted. Deep crazing needs complete stripping.

Gloss paint goes **dull** if it gets damp before it has time to dry. Repaint in better weather.

Efflorescence is an almost frothy white deposit which comes out from under the paint and pushes it off the wall in crumbly pieces. Don't wash the area. Putting water on the plaster will only increase the problem. Instead sand down and leave it bare until the salts have stopped appearing, wiping the area with equal parts of vinegar and water. When the salts no longer appear, sand off any remaining crystals, prime and repaint.

Flaking and blistering happen when one coat of paint isn't sticking to another, because gloss paint has not been rubbed down well enough or because of moisture or grease between coats. Sand down to a firm surface, wipe with white spirit and repaint.

Trouble-Free Painting

- Before painting with gloss, wipe the surfaces down with white spirit.
- Don't wear any clothing which has fluff, or it will fly on to the paint.
- Stir all paints – except jelly paints – well before use.
- Flick the dust from new brushes before using them and break them in on undercoats.
- Before using a paint pad, brush it hard with a stiff brush and wash it in soapy water, with a nail brush to get rid of surplus fluff.
- To save time cleaning up afterwards put the roller tray in a bin liner bag and close it at one end loosely enough for the bag to dip down into the tray. Fill the tray with paint on top of the bag.
- Paints give off fumes which are bad for you. *Always* work with the windows open. Better still, use the new water-based paints.
- Never try to paint when moisture will land on the surface soon after. So don't paint outside late into the day when dew is about to start or steam up the kitchen just after decorating. In time it will flake off.
- Don't paint when a surface is hot.
- Put an open paper bag by the telephone, then you can stick a painty hand in before picking it up.
- Stretch a section of old tights firmly across a large jar or clean empty tin, with a rubber band and pour the paint through the tights.
- Fix a section from a pair of tights across the top of the paint can so it dangles in. Pressing your brush down against the nylon will force the paint up through it.

★ When painting a ceiling cut a small slit in an old sponge, and stick the handle of the paintbrush through the slit. The run-back is absorbed by the sponge and doesn't proceed down your hand and arm.

★ Wear an old hat when painting a ceiling – one always puts one's head against the ceiling sooner or later.

★ If you wear spectacles put a smooth layer of cling film over them before painting ceilings. Then splashes won't get on the lenses.

Method of Working

If a whole room is being painted the basic order is ceiling, walls, gloss paint on doors, windows and so on. You start high and work down and start near the light and work away from it.

- Brush up and down, then across a square and finish by going up and down. Keep the edges of each new square thin.
- With a roller you need to have the paint in a roller tray and apply in a big W-shape, then roll crosswise, then up and down.

All the final strokes should be in the same direction. And work so that you are never going over the edge of another patch after it has begun to dry. This means working up and down a long wall, not along it, and the same with a ceiling – and working fast in hot weather.

Panelled Doors

No two experts agree on the 'correct' order in which to paint the sections of a panelled door. Having a system, and working fast enough to prevent any paint drying before you go over it from another direction, are all that matters. Remove door handles and anything else on the door before you start. But make sure one handle is left in the room lest the door slams.

Pipes

Hold a sheet of cardboard between the wall and a pipe when painting it. Be extra careful if painting near brick as the paint will never come off. Outside a house paint the pipes first with exterior gloss paint, let them dry totally, wrap polythene round them and paint the walls.

Radiators

There are very small rollers, on long handles, for getting behind radiators. These are by far the easiest way to paint the wall there.

Windows

★ Windows easily get paint flecks on them. Protect them – just before you get to them – by placing a sheet of wet newspaper flat against the glass. It clings perfectly.

★ Textured glass which may get splashed can either have newspaper held over it with masking tape or be brushed with slightly diluted washing-up liquid.

★ If you want to cut down the time the windows must be open you can make paint dry more rapidly by adding Liquid Dryer to it. This is a product only sold in shops for professional decorators and is used very sparingly; 1 teaspoon well stirred into a litre of paint is enough.

If you have a steady hand and patience it is less work to use a proper cutting-in brush to paint a window frame near the glass than to apply masking tape.

If you apply masking tape, place it exactly where the edge of the paint should be, and remove it while the paint is wet or the paint may peel off with it. Avoid using other tape – it won't come off the glass easily – and don't use masking tape on a window in full sun on a hot day: it seems to fuse itself to the window.

Include any edges which will show from whichever side you are working (inside or outside) when the window is open. Over putty go $1/16$ in on to the glass to stop moisture running behind it. Windows need to be painted early in the day and left open to dry for as long as possible. Long after paint is dry to the touch it will stick to another layer of paint.

Marks and Stains

★ If you splash paint on to carpet or furnishing clean it off *that instant*. Water-based paint will come off with water. Oil-based paint needs white spirit – but first *always* test a little of the spirit on a patch of carpet, or fabric, which won't show if a mark is made.

★ If splashes of emulsion paint get on to gloss, a little methylated spirits will sometimes take them off.

On Stopping

★ When you finish with paint clean the rim of the tin with a cloth dipped in white spirit, put the lid on firmly and store upside down – then the skin forms on the bottom, not the top.

★ Paint the lid of any tin of paint with its contents before storing it. Then you know exactly what shade is inside.

★ The easiest way to store a small quantity of left-over paint is to pour it into a jam jar. Make sure the screw ring has no paint on it, close and store upside down.

★ If you want to leave brushes uncleaned overnight you can drop them in enough water just to cover the painty section. Both oil-based and emulsion paints stay flexible under water.

★ One of the neatest ways to clean a brush with spirit is to put a little spirit in the corner of a strong plastic bag. Then pop the brush in. It uses far less spirit and you can rub it into the bristles with your fingers through the bag, without getting your hands dirty.

One way of getting rid of the smell of paint is to put dishes of sliced onion round the room. But don't eat the onion.

Special Effects and Decorative Finishes

If you are tired of the look of a room, but the paint is in perfectly good condition, you can simply clean the walls impeccably and change the whole effect by adding a decorative finish. You can also use sponging and ragging to conceal any unevenness in a wall or simply use the matt emulsion glaze to give shiny emulsion the really matt look which is such a deliciously subdued foil to certain styles of furniture.

Using any of the following techniques is enormously satisfying but it does take practice to achieve really expert results. Try a technique on a loo wall before embarking on the sitting room.

Important Basics

- Cracks must be perfectly filled. Even use very fine filler to close the hairline crack between two sections of wallpaper or lining paper.
- The basic paint on the wall must be as perfect as if you planned to do no more painting.
- Start work with plenty of hours ahead. Leaving a wall half done can create an edge of hard colour which will spoil the effect.
- Assemble everything you need before you put a drop of paint on the walls.
- Work quickly. The edge of the previous bit of painting must always be wet when you join on the next section: work up and down a wall not along it. For broken finishes like ragging, avoid laying on the sections in a neat band. Instead, have bulges and indentations.
- For techniques where flat paint is applied and then broken up while wet, work with someone else if you can. It reduces the risk of a line where paint has dried before you could get to it.
- The paint drying too quickly will be your biggest problem. Turn off the heating, avoid working in very hot weather, and don't use a fast drying paint.
- It is easiest to get a professional result if you choose shades which are fairly close in tone: say, a cream base coat, with soft apricots, or even close tones of two different colours such as blues and greens. But the stronger your colours, the more perfect your work needs to be.
- Be sure to mix enough for the whole room. It will be almost impossible to match it exactly on a second mixing.
- The linseed oil in glaze makes it increasingly yellow as it dries. So, pale blues can turn greeny, pale pink goes orange. Follow the instructions on the tin very carefully and use as little glaze as possible when working with colours which might be spoilt by yellowing.
- When using paint and glaze add the glaze to the paint, *not* vice versa. Like any rule, this one can be broken. If you want glowing transparent autumn tones – apricot, orange or brown – you can achieve this by mixing a little artist's oil paint, of the shade you want, into the glaze.
- If you have put a delicate decorative finish on woodwork and want to make it stand up to wear, coat it with several coats of polyurethane varnish, just as if it were wood. But you may have to varnish all the woodwork to match.

★ There is no problem about painting over either the oil paint glaze or the emulsion glaze when you want to redecorate the room.

The First Stage

The room must have been painted with at least two coats of the base colour in either emulsion paint or an eggshell. You can use either oil- or water-based paints, but don't put new coats of one on top of the other. Although new water-based gloss and eggshell can go over oil-based paint which has been up a few years.

All the finishes here need to be thinned. Oil-based paint must be thinned with white spirit, water-based emulsion with water. Add the liquid slowly, mixing well between each addition.

A slightly see-through effect is needed for all of them, but a colour wash will use the thinnest paint and paint for dragging will usually be the least thinned. The trick is to make it thin enough but not so thin it trickles down the wall. For the best effect, oil-based paint should be made more manageable by adding Radcliffe's Oil Scumble Glaze.

★ Radcliffe also makes an emulsion with a high sheen, with moderate sheen or very matt which can be used to protect your finished walls and make them wipeable, without changing the colour.

Colour Washing

Colour washing can be done with either water-based emulsion paint, or with an oil-based eggshell finish, or by adding colour and white spirit to Radcliffe's Scumble. It is a deliberately patchy effect with brushstrokes in paint thinned until semi-transparent.

First, see the Basics above, and complete the First Stage, having the paint very thin. For an average room use a 100 mm (4 in) brush, but in a tiny loo you might prefer a narrower one. Start at the top in a corner and have only a little paint on the brush, to avoid runs. Brush quickly and roughly, using short individual strokes going every way so some cross and reinforce the colour, and others don't quite cover the base coat. Let this dry totally. You can leave it at that or end with a coat of special emulsion glaze.

Ragging

There are two completely different methods of using rags to create a finish: ragging on, and ragging off. Ragging off is often called rag rolling.

Ragging on is the simpler of the two, and it is easiest to get a really good effect if you use two different tones on top of your base colour. You use crumpled plain cotton fabric or plastic to print its pattern on the wall. But have plenty of it, as you need a new cloth whenever the one you are working with is too soggy and a change of weave or weight will show.

Read the Basics above, then complete the First Stage. Crumple a rag or the crackly type of thin plastic carrier bag up into a loose shape, dip it lightly in the paint, take the excess off on the side of the paint tray then dab away. Keep your arm loose and constantly alter the angle you dab at. Otherwise the rag will produce a dreary set of identical marks like a set of cat's paws walking up the wall.

When this coat has totally dried you can go over it with another tone, or emulsion glaze as for colour washing (see above). If the effect is too heavy you can also fade the colour slightly by going over it with a coat of the base paint diluted until it is thin and milky.

An oil-based paint is best for **ragging off** (rag rolling) and you can use all kinds of rags. Some people prefer chamois leather, and you can even get a very crisp effect with a crumpled plastic bag.

Read the Basics (page 251) and complete the First Stage. Then, working systematically from one of the corners, paint a patch of wall with the diluted paint and immediately roll a crumpled rag across it – so it lifts the wet paint off in uneven patches. Leave about 30 cms (12 ins) from the edge unragged (you do that bit when you roll the next patch) to give a smooth join. Keep repeating this on neighbouring patches of wall, so the ragging covers the entire surface. Constantly open and re-crumple the rag, and discard it when it ceases to pick up paint well. When this coat has totally dried a second decorative colour can be applied in the same way. The rags can be washed out in white spirit and re-used, and if you use a chamois it is constantly rinsed in spirit as you work.

Sponging

Sponging is one of the easiest methods to use successfully, especially if you use two shades rather than one. You need a big natural sea sponge with a fairly open texture. Read the Basics on page 251 and complete the First Stage. Have your colour in a paint tray. Dip the sponge *lightly* in it, dab any excess off on a piece of newspaper. Dab the wall lightly at fairly close intervals to produce speckled clouds. Keep turning the sponge so the outline isn't always the same in any one direction, and don't press too hard or you will have a big splodge. When dry, go over the same area with a darker or lighter shade. If some areas become too heavy the base coat can be sponged on to correct the weight of colour.

Stencilling

Stencils are a very effective way to make a wall look unusual and several companies now sell stencils (see page 270). First paint the wall. Let it get very dry indeed – to stencil sooner is to court disaster. (Or thoroughly clean your existing walls.) Spray the back of the stencil with a light coat of the spray mount used for mounting photographs. Let this dry. Coat it again. When it is dry it will have a tacky surface which will hold the stencil against the wall but allow you to remove it easily. A heavy stencil may need a few pieces of masking tape too, but beware of pulling the paint off.

★ Before you try stencilling the walls, experiment on some large sheets of paper until you get just the effect you want.

Use a spirit level and plumb line to place the stencil perfectly on the level or upright. Press it against the wall and stencil carefully. Use subtle colour combinations rather than sharp contrasts, in oil-based paint, emulsion paint (matchpots provide small quantities) or even artists' acrylics, with a small piece of fine-textured synthetic sponge, or a stubby stencil brush.

A lot of professionals use car spray paint for soft effects. An even better option may be the new range of **Plastikote** (page 270) silk finish polyurethane spray paints in DIY shops. Before spraying, mask the wall with newspaper and the room needs to be *very well ventilated*. You should also wear a proper protective mask, and car spray should not be used by someone who could be pregnant.

★ When spraying, you can get colour variations either by having several stencils and opening up different sections of the pattern on each, or by closing sections of the pattern with pieces of paper or masking tape.

★ To mitre the corners of borders, use a set square to draw a faint pencil line at 45° from the wall. Lightly place a piece of wide masking tape so it masks the wall on one side of the line. Stencil up to and just over it, and remove the tape. Let the stencilling dry totally, then put the masking tape to mask the stencil side of the line and stencil in the joining section. The pencil line will rub out when the paint is dry.

If the final effect looks a little sharp and hard you can soften it by thinning the paint you used for the walls until it is very milky and put a very light wash of this over the top.

> The stencils used for walls can just as easily be used for fabric, so walls and curtains or cushions can have the same motif. **The Stencil Store** (page 270) sells paint for fabric stencilling. Tips for using stencils on fabrics are:
>
> ★ Only use cotton.
>
> ★ Wash and iron the fabric first.
>
> ★ Stencil a piece of paper and try positioning it on the fabric to find the best spacing for the design. Then use tailor's chalk to mark out all the positions for the edges of the stencils over the whole of the fabric.
>
> ★ Attach the material firmly to a board with drawing pins before you attempt to stencil.

Sources of unusual products or useful information and advice on all aspects of painting and on decorative finishes are on pages 270-271.

Papering and Wallcovering

When I first started to paper walls there was little choice. Now there is an enormous range, and Crown has even given dreary old anaglypta a new look by creating anaglypta Victorian and Edwardian cameo friezes, art nouveau dados and even one paper which looks like Renaissance Spanish leather. These could be a boon to anyone trying to restore a period house on a budget.

Even now the selection of papers in vinyl and washable finishes is nothing like as good as the range in those which are not washable. An almost forgotten solution is a product called Gard. This is a milky fluid which can be painted on to any ordinary paper. It dries to a clear washable finish and lasts remarkably well.

Wallpaper: to Strip or Not to Strip

If a wall is papered you can often paint over it very well,

Applying Wallcoverings

The maker's instructions should always be followed. My suggestions are only for when wallcoverings lack them.

Wallcovering	Method	Comments on Hanging
Anaglypta and Supaglypta	Use all-purpose or heavy-duty paste but with a fungicide if the paper is vinyl. Don't roll the seams and be careful not to stretch or flatten.	Vastly improved of late. Can be painted with emulsion, even when in blown vinyl.
Flock	Use fungicidal paste and keep it off the surface at all costs.	Take care not to flatten when smoothing, and don't roll the seams flat; press with the brush.
Foil paper	Use fungicidal ready-mixed paste.	Easy but the shine highlights bumps in the wall. May lift at seams in steamy rooms.
Grasscloth, Silk, Woolstrand	Use ready-mixed adhesive. Silk often put up head to tail.	Fragile but easy on a flat surface. Very tricky at overlaps and round obstructions. Needs skill.
Hessian: paper-backed	Use ready-mixed adhesive.	Easy to apply, but paste needs soaking in for a while.
Hessian: not paper backed	Use heavy duty or ready-mixed adhesive.	Easy but needs meticulous care, see page 257
Lincrusta	Crown Lincrusta Glue, ready-mixed or all-purpose adhesive.	Cross-lining first is essential, using all-purpose adhesive. It is not overlapped at angles. Fill gaps with putty.
Ordinary wallpapers	Use any wallpaper paste.	Handprinted papers may not be colour-fast; check before putting up.
Vinyl	Use heavy-duty paste with a fungicide. On overlaps glue with Vinyl Overlap or Copydex.	Usually very easy to hang. Use a sponge to smooth the self-glued kind.
Washable papers	Polycell Plus suits most, but suit the glue to the weight of the paper. Make sure edges and corners are well stuck down or they curl off.	These are papers with a film of plastic. They can be wiped but not scrubbed.
Woodchip	Hang with ready-mixed heavy-duty paste.	Hard to cut at the top and bottom, and tears easily. Don't paint until the glue is thoroughly dry, 1-2 days

especially if the faint seam lines are filled with extra fine filler. The exceptions to this are flock papers, the shiny types of vinyl and washable papers. (The soft blown vinyls used in anaglyptas are a different matter.) The paint may go on perfectly well but it may not last. The other snag is that some ordinary papers bleed if you paint over them. Test these with both water and spirit, for colourfastness.

If you are going to paper the wall, the counsel of perfection is to strip off all the old paper and get back to a clean bare wall. But, in some houses paper has been laid layer upon layer over the years until now they seem almost held up by these papiermâché walls. However, if you do paper over, your paper will only be as firm as the weakest underlayer. The other disadvantage is that you will have to manipulate the placing of your seams so none of them come exactly over any previous ones. Tricky if you are centring the paper over the fireplace and the last person did too.

★ On vinyl-coated paper get your nail under *just* the vinyl coating and carefully tear it away. If it comes off smoothly –

leaving the backing paper in good condition, and well stuck to the wall, the manufacturers say you can treat this as lining paper and put your new paper over it. But not all professional decorators are happy about using it as lining, especially if the top paper is heavy.

How to Strip Wallpaper

For large areas it's well worth hiring a steam stripper (below). There is a certain childish pleasure in ripping great strips off a wall, but it palls quite quickly and, when doing it by hand, you are left tearing and scraping long after it has ceased to amuse.

> If there is any mould on wallpaper it should be treated (page 248) before you start stripping, otherwise the washing will just spread the spores even further.

If you haven't dealt with any vinyl coating (see the tip above) do so. Other papers need to be thoroughly scratched. Buy or hire a tool called a perforator for doing this, or slash them with an old Stanley knife blade or scratch it with several metal skewers held with their ends level.

> Once paper starts falling it is very easy for the perforator or Stanley knife to become hidden – but they could cause a very nasty accident if stepped on. It is best to clear the floor *totally* before starting to strip, and *put any dangerous tools in a safe place.* Then protect every inch of floor and furniture: stripped paper is very messy.

A **steam stripper** can be dangerous. People have been seriously burnt from using them incorrectly. Make sure that the machine is supplied with full instructions on basic use and safety precautions *which are legible* – not covered with other people's wallpaper. Avoid directing the steam plate at your skin, especially when stripping a ceiling, but you can also get burnt by a whoosh of steam shooting out if you open the tank while it's very hot or pour water on to hot elements when it has boiled dry. So the basic precautions are these:

- Stand it on a level surface.
- Don't fill the tank too full.
- Don't allow the hose to get a kink in it, or pressure could build up.
- Check the water level every 30 minutes – having first turned the tank off and given it time to cool.
- NEVER open the tank when it is fully hot.
- If you accidentally let the tank boil dry, let it cool before adding water.

The right-handed will find the fastest method is to start at a bottom-right-hand corner. Then you can scrape off the paper with a wallpaper scraper in your right hand as you move the steamer to the left with you left hand.

> WARNING: Stop stripping if you see unpainted plasterboard under the paper. Water or steam is likely to damage it. On plasterboards you can only paper over the paper. And don't steam where there could be cracks, or you may damage the plaster.

For **hand stripping** sponge the paper over to make it thoroughly wet. Adding products such as Polypeel or washing-up liquid helps the water to seep in, and the hotter, the better, but Liquid Polypeel will work with cold water. Wear rubber gloves with these products.

Wet the paper thoroughly, and go and have a cup of something while the liquid works. There is no point in scraping away until it has. Once soggy, start scraping at it with a wallpaper scraper and keep sponging as you go. Trickling water down behind loose paper speeds things up.

Finally give the wall a good wash to remove all the bits

and pieces and leave it clean and smooth. If the surface under the paper is firm it is ready to be painted. If not treat it appropriately.

Essential Tools
Papering takes more equipment than painting, but it lasts for years.

- Paper hanging brush.
- Large scissors (wallpaper will blunt dressmaking scissors dreadfully).
- Paste brush.
- Long metal ruler – a metre is good.
- Coiled steel measure for measuring walls and paper.
- Plumb line – a penknife on string isn't bad.
- Large table – you can buy a fold-up papering table.
- Seam roller.
- White loo paper to remove surplus glue.
- Bucket for wallpaper paste.

Ladders, pasting tables, scaffolding for stairwells and so on can be hired.

Paperhanging brush

Plumb line and bob

Bucket   Paste brush

Scissors   Trimming knife   Seam roller

★ When hanging any paper on fairly new plaster use a ready-mixed adhesive. It is less likely to rewet the plaster and therefore sticks better.

Using Lining Paper
In theory, all walls are best cross-lined (see page 255), before you hang paper, and a wall in bad condition should be lined before painting with one called finished extra white. The benefits of lining paper are these:

- It helps to conceal any unevenness in the surface (use the heaviest weight).
- It stops the main paper shrinking or stretching over any unevenness.
- It makes the top paper less likely to bubble or develop glue marks.
- It lessens the risk of shrinkage and joint gaps.
- You can use special pitch-coated lining paper on surfaces inclined to be damp.

Addresses and suggestions for further reading are at the ends of chapters.

Metric Wallpaper Calculator

Wall height from skirting in metres	Measurement round room in metres (including doors & windows)													Number of rolls needed
	10	11	12	13	14	15	16	17	18	19	20	21	22	
2.0-2.2 m	5	5	5	6	6	7	7	7	8	8	9	9	10	
2.2-2.4 m	5	5	6	6	7	7	8	8	9	9	10	10	10	
2.4-2.6 m	5	6	6	7	7	8	8	9	9	10	10	11	11	
2.6-2.8 m	6	6	7	7	8	8	9	9	10	11	11	12	12	
2.8-3.0 m	6	7	7	8	8	9	9	10	11	11	12	12	13	
3.0-3.2 m	6	7	8	8	9	10	10	11	11	12	13	13	14	
3.2-3.4 m	7	7	8	9	9	10	11	11	12	13	13	14	15	

- 'Cotton' lining paper can be used to cover wood and conceal serious problems – but it's expensive.

In practice, on a sound emulsioned wall a paper will often go up perfectly without any lining. So lining can be a lot of work for very little benefit. However, not lining is taking a gamble.

Under paint, lining paper runs from floor to ceiling. But, if you will be wallpapering over, it runs the other way – from wall to wall. This is called cross-lining. Use the same glue that you will use for the paper or heavy paper may pull the lining off. Let it dry completely before papering over.

Buying Wallpaper

Wallpaper widths are not totally standardized, but most paper is 52 cm (21 in) wide and the roll is 10.05 m (33 ft). Mercifully, very few papers are untrimmed now. Untrimmed paper needs a special trimming machine to trim it correctly and this will mean using a professional decorator with the machine and the expertise. When buying any paper certain points are worth checking.

- Is the paper the usual width and length? Those based on fabrics are often in fabric widths.
- Are the edges ready trimmed or will it need trimming?
- Do all the roll numbers match? On different print runs the colours may vary.
- Will the shop take back any unopened rolls if you overbuy? Many will.
- What is the depth of the pattern repeat? When calculating the number of rolls needed you will need to allow for the wastage this causes on every length.

Although it's almost impossible to calculate the exact amount of paper needed, the chart above* gives you the rough calculation. To be safe add the depth of the pattern repeat to the height of the wall you will cover, use that as the height of the wall when reading the chart and allow for error.

* I am indebted to Laura Ashley Plc for this chart.

Hanging Wallpaper or Lining Paper

Papering can only be done after all the paintwork (doors, windows, ceiling, etc) has had its last coat of paint and is thoroughly dry.

If you are papering the ceiling, start there (page 257) but don't paper a ceiling unless it will really pay dividends: it's tricky and exhausting. For walls one traditional place to start is beside the main window, or the central strip over the fireplace. But I suggest unpractised paperers start wherever is least noticeable – then the less perfect parts won't catch the eye.

Choosing the Paste

Choose a paste suited to the type of wallpaper. Follow the wallpaper manufacturer's instructions on wallpaper paste or see page 253. If a vinyl paper comes ready-pasted there is no need for any other glue.

★ To avoid having a nasty bucket to clean out afterwards put a bin liner in the bucket and fix firmly with masking tape.

★ Tie a string across the bucket tightly from handle to handle, so you can wipe the brush against it.

Preparing the Paper

Check your rolls so you can see how patterns will match, and that there is no colour variation in plain ones. If there is a large pattern decide where you want to place it in relation to features in the room. A big pattern should always be centred over a fireplace, its height will dictate the positioning of all the other lengths. If so, measure and cut that length of paper and (if you aren't starting papering at that point) match the patterns of all other pieces to this before cutting. The fabric cutting rule of 'measure twice, cut once' applies here too.

Each drop needs to be the length of the wall plus 10 cm (4 in); always cut the strip of paper before pasting, so you can match the patterns before you cut.

Marking a Guide Line

Door edges and windows are seldom as upright as they look. So, hold the top of a weighted string against the top of the wall where you want your first seam to come. Let it hang freely. When it hangs unmoving, get someone to hold it firmly at exactly that point while you draw a line beside the string.

Gluing

Papers vary in how they need to be treated. Ready-pasted paper is put in a trough of water for a set time. This works best if you roll the paper up, leave it in the water until half-time and then roll it the other way (in the water) – otherwise there are often dry patches. Read the instructions carefully. Ready-pasted sounds like an easy option but you are handling messier wetter paper than in any other method.

Where there are no instructions, you can assume you are meant to do the following. Spread out the paper so the edge just sticks out beyond the edge of the table. Paste that side and the centre thoroughly (make sure there are no lumps of badly dissolved glue). Shift it so the other edge sticks out beyond the table and paste that section. Quickly fold it in loose Z-shaped folds.

Support it well as you take it to the wall. Put the top edge above the top of the wall by about 5 cm (2 in), with it exactly beside the upright line. Use the paper hanging brush to smooth the paper on to the wall upwards and downwards, unfolding the lower layers once the top is in place. Work carefully away from a single point or you will trap air in pockets.

Smooth quickly and lightly: if the brush is used heavily it will stretch the damp paper – especially on a paper with a raised pattern.

If you like a slippy surface to work against, or the wall is lined, put a coat of size or thinned wallpaper paste over each section of wall before hanging the paper.

Trimming the Top and Bottom

Once a length is in place use the brush edge to push it right into the angle of the top of the wall. Fold the surplus down, making sure the fold is *exactly* at the top of the wall. Pull the top of the paper away from the wall and cut off the surplus – cutting not on the fold but immediately above it gives the best fit. Brush it back into place and repeat at the bottom.

Repeat, making sure the seam is perfectly edge to edge, without the slightest gap, and matching the pattern at the seams *exactly*. Roll each seam flat with the seam roller unless the paper has a raised pattern. Wipe off any excess paste gently with clean white loo roll but don't rub hard: the surface can be surprisingly fragile.

To reduce the risk of tears in the paper, when cutting to shape or width, measure and draw the cutting lines on the paper when dry, apply the glue, and cut when the stiffness goes.

Papering Corners and Bends

At corners measure the distance from the edge of the previous length of paper to the corner, at the top, bottom and middle. Cut to the *greatest* width plus 4 cm (1½ in) for going into a corner, or plus 8 cm (3 in) for going around one – trim it once in place so only 2.5 cm (1 in) is left.

Brush the paper right up to the corner, then hold it firmly while you push it into or around it with the brush. For the next length mark an upright line, as before, a suitable distance from the corner and position the paper against it. (Keep any pattern motif at the right level.) Brush it into place on the wall and over the underlap (using special glue for vinyl) and trim off the surplus overlap, from this top layer, in other places.

> Professional paperhangers often place a strip of wood *firmly* down the corner and tear the surplus top paper off with a quick *downward* movement. Done correctly, this leaves a softer edge than cutting and the overlap becomes invisible when dry. Of course, it only works with paper.

If a bubble of air under the paper won't smooth down, pierce it with a hypodermic needle, where it won't show, and suck the air out, smoothing it with the brush as you do so. If you discover a bubble after the paper has dried inject a little thin glue under the paper.

Papering Round Doors

Measure up and cut an upside-down L-shaped paper to hang, which overlaps the frame by 4 cm (1½ in) (if there is that much spare) at the top and side. Proceed as for a corner, cutting a diagonal to the angle of the door frame. Crease and cut off the surplus where it meets the upright door frame. Then smooth the section above the door into place and do the same at ceiling and skirting.

Papering Round Windows

You hang paper round windows with projecting frames as you would round doors. Those inset deep into the wall – with a reveal – need other treatment. The conventional method is to paste a section of paper over the centre of the top of the window, bending it round the angle and into the upper part of the reveal. Paper the two small sections of the upper part of the reveal which are usually to either side of it, then the sides of the reveal, and then paper the wall to each side matching the paper to the central strip.

Papering Round Radiators

Getting round the brackets which hold radiators on the wall is done by measuring carefully from the edge of the last paper to the bracket and making a slit up the paper from the bottom to the point which will touch the top of the bracket. You may also need to cut a hole out of the paper to fit round the bracket. Then brush both halves into place – one of the little rollers sold for applying paint behind radiators is ideal.

If a radiator is hot the lower paper rapidly dries. Turn off the radiator long before you reach that point in the room.

Papering Round Switches and Sockets
Turn the electricity off at the mains, remove the front plate and paper just under its edges, with a hole carefully cut in the centre. But foil papers must not go under the plate lest they conduct electricity.

Papering Round Light Fittings
For lights it is best to switch off at the mains and remove them. Make an X in the paper and push the wires through, then trim off surplus paper which will come under the fixing (keep foil *well* clear of electric wires). Immovable ceiling roses are treated like light switches.

If you find a section of papering hard to do quickly, *don't* leave the under layers folded up against each other. Once they begin to dry together you can say good-bye to that length of paper. Unfold them and let them hang. If paper starts to stick to the wall at the wrong point you can usually pull it off without damage – especially if you sized the wall first.

Papering a Ceiling
Unless a room is remarkably low you will need two stepladders and a plank running between them. You also need a third stepladder (preferably with a platform top) or spring-loaded pole with a papering platform (which can be hired).

Ceilings are normally papered with the paper running *across* the ceiling as you look at the main window. But paper across the shortest distance: vast lengths of gluey paper can have a life of their own.

Establish a line to start from by measuring back from the wall a paper's width minus 2.5 cm (1 in), at intervals across the ceiling. Draw a straight guide line joining the marks. Measure, paste and fold the paper as for a wall (pages 255-256) adding the same allowance to the length. Push it well into the angles. If the walls are not to be papered, fold and trim the surplus as for the bottom of walls. Otherwise, simply trim the ends to run 2.5 cm down the walls and cut a slash in the corner so it can overlap neatly.

Papering Stairwells
The secret of papering a stairwell is to have a really secure working platform. Do size the wall, this buys you extra time in which to manipulate the extra long paper.

Preparing Friezes
Friezes can make a tremendous difference to a simple paper. If a room is too high you can improve its proportions by taking the wallpaper only up to where the picture rail would be. But do use a spirit level to mark the line for the frieze.

You can also take friezes down the wall in stripes or all round the edge of the paper like braid. When joining two sections of frieze, match the patterns exactly. Use special adhesive over vinyl.

> Keep your offcuts of wallpaper. If a stain is made on the paper, which can't be removed, or a child scribbles on it, you can sometimes cover a mark completely.
>
> If you put an ordinary paper over a greasy patch on the old wallpaper the grease is likely to betray you by working its way through to the front of the new paper. To stop this put a coat of paint over the grease spots. In a kitchen you probably won't be able to find all the small spots, so stripping really is necessary.

Fabric Wallcoverings

Hessian and Felt – on Backing
Paper-backed hessian is usually 52 cm (20½ in) wide, felt is 79 cm (31 in) wide and there is less wastage than with paper as you can buy it by the metre or in very long rolls. Backed fabric can be treated like unbacked hessian (see below). The only difference is that some is put up edge to edge, not overlapped.

Felt can be very heavy. Put it on a cardboard roll (fabric shops and carpet shops throw them away). The ends of the roll can then rest on a pair of flat-top steps.

With any fabric keep the glue off the front or remove it the instant any gets on.

Decorative Felt – Unbacked
Decorative felt is made in a marvellous range of colours and produces the slightly muted acoustics that one associates with very expensively furnished rooms. It is, however, exceedingly wide – 183 cm (6 ft) – and heavy, which makes it hard to handle. Put it on a roll and treat it like the paper-backed version above. It helps to have someone to turn the roll while you glue it down as it can be unwieldy.

Apply a coat of size to the wall, and let this dry. Then put heavy-duty ready-mixed adhesive (the less spare moisture there is, the better) on the wall, and roll the felt against it, with a paint roller, through a piece of polythene. Otherwise, treat it like hessian (immediately below).

Furnishing Hessian

Ordinary furnishing hessian is remarkably easy to put on walls. It is very inexpensive and usually sold in several weights. The width can be 91.5 cm (36 in), 102 cm (40 in), 114 cm (45 in), 137 cm (54 in) or 183 cm (72 in), but the plain corn-coloured shades tend to be in the wider widths and the best colours in the narrow ones. It is a fraction of the price of the backed kind (see page 257) but won't totally conceal the colour of the wall behind, so either use lining paper or first paint the wall.

- Iron the lengths of fabric before you put them up. Pressing them against the wall *won't* remove the creases.
- Apply the paste to the wall.
- Use a paint roller to press the fabric in place.
- Take care to keep the weave on the straight.
- Overlap the seams by 2.5 cm (1 in).
- Leave all surplus at the top, bottom and round fittings and also the seam overlap – *untrimmed* until the hessian is *totally* dry – in case it shrinks.

Once dry trim off the surplus at the top and bottom with a sharp blade cut through the mid-point of the seam overlap from top to bottom. *Very carefully* pull off the surplus (if threads aren't properly cut it will cause fraying, so be ready with nail scissors). Put glue under the two edges and use a seam roller to press the edges perfectly flat. (Have plenty of spare blades to hand: cutting against the wall blunts them very quickly.)

You could apply any fabric which was heavy enough not to let the glue come through and would stand up to being slashed at the overlap. But man-made fabrics' behaviour will be unpredictable. **Russell and Chapple** (page 270) sell a suitable range of hessian and **Muraspec** (page 270) sells felt in a terrific range of colours plus other unusual fabrics.

Plumbing

Air Locks

If some of the radiators in a central heating system are cold while the rest are hot, there is probably an air lock. Air locks can also cause a hammering sound in the pipes when a tap is turned on; or the water may come out in fits and spluttering starts.

Curing Cold Radiators

Place a washing-up bowl or bucket under the end which has a small square socket. Insert a radiator key into the socket and turn it very carefully until you can *just* hear a hissing sound or a drip of water comes out. *Stop the instant* either of these happens and let all the air come out until seeping water follows it. Let the water drip a little, until you are sure no air comes with it, and then screw the valve in tightly again. If more than one radiator is cold you may need to do this to each. Do this with someone else around. The thread to these valves is very short and it's extremely easy to turn it one turn too many

and have it shoot out under the pressure. The scene as one tries to stem the spurting water with one finger while desperately stretching for the out-of-reach valve with the other hand is worthy of farce, but it's far from funny when it happens.

Alterations to Plumbing

Alterations to a plumbing system, other than replacements and repairs, are controlled by law. Each water authority has its own bylaws covering things like stop cocks and tank sizes. There are also building regulations which must be complied with. If you break any of these regulations you could be prosecuted, fined heavily and held liable for any damage which results – and water in the wrong place can do an awful lot of damage. So check the bylaws.

Frozen Pipes

Pipes in a loft must be properly insulated to avoid freezing (page 224), but they can freeze elsewhere in the system if taps are left dripping in icy weather. So make sure the washers are working before the winter comes and, when conditions are bad, keep the plugs in all the basins, then if someone does leave a tap dripping it won't spell disaster.

The best way to avoid freezing is to keep the house at least one degree above freezing. If you are away it is usually cheaper to run the heating at this minimal level than to pay for the damage from burst pipes. NEVER PUT UNATTENDED HEATERS IN THE LOFT TO KEEP THE PIPES WARM.

Dealing with Frozen Pipes

The first sign of a frozen pipe is usually that a tap won't run. If any part of the *hot* water system is frozen there is a risk of explosion if the boiler is left on: so TURN IT OFF. Check first in the loft: the insulation may have fallen off a pipe making it easy to spot a culprit. Look carefully: if there is no sign of a crack thaw it *gently* with a hot water bottle draped over it, a towel wrung in very hot water, or a hairdryer, starting at the end closest to its outflow. NEVER USE A BLOWTORCH. Have a bucket ready, and know just where your stopvalves are – you could be wrong about that crack. If there is even a slight chance that pipes feeding the hot water system could be frozen call a plumber. Plumbers are cheaper than explosions.

Frozen outflow pipes are harder to get at. If there is no access pouring hot water down may clear them, but you may need to do this repeatedly, draining the water through the trap under the basin after each attempt.

Dealing with a Burst Pipe

1 Wrap the pipe tightly with something waterproof and put a bucket underneath.
2 Turn off the boiler.
3 Turn off the appropriate stopvalve – or all stopvalves.
4 Flush the lavatories to drain the system rapidly.
5 Also run the *cold* taps – saving the water in buckets, basins and saucepans. You may need to wash, cook, and use the lavatory before the pipes are repaired.

Addresses and suggestions for further reading are at the ends of chapters.

6 *Don't* turn on the hot taps or the water cylinder may collapse if part of the hot water system is frozen.

7 Switch off the immersion heater.

8 Call a good plumber or use a pipe repair kit.

How Plumbing Works

Every building is slightly different but the fundamentals of plumbing are always the same. It is worth locating and labelling each stopvalve some wet Sunday. Then you can act faster in an emergency – and, if disaster strikes while you are out, whoever is home has a sporting chance of dealing with it. BEFORE DRAINING DOWN ANY SYSTEM REMEMBER TO TURN OFF THE BOILER.

- In the pavement, garden or forecourt there will be an external stopvalve which belongs to the water authority. Turning this clockwise cuts off the water to the entire building.
- Hidden inside the house (e.g. the cellar, or under the stairs) there will be another stopvalve. Sometimes this turns off all the cold water, sometimes only the kitchen tap – in which case, the other cold taps must be fed from a storage tank near the roof and there should be another stopvalve on a pipe coming down from it (try the airing cupboard).
- If you turn off all these stopvalves and run all the water out through the taps you will drain most of the system – and modern plumbing systems usually include drain cocks, near the stopvalves, from which you can drain any remaining water. There will also be drain cocks on the boiler and the hot water tank.

Jammed Stopvalves

If a stopvalve jams try grasping it with the longest handled pliers or wrench you can find, and then turning – the extra leverage the long handle gives may do the trick. Applying penetrating oil may also help.

Knocking in the Water System

Air which causes knocking in the pipes needs to be forced out. The standard way to do this is to take a short length of garden hose pipe and 2 Jubilee clips (screw tight rings). Fix one end of the hose to the cold tap in the kitchen (or any other tap fed directly from the mains) and another to the hot, turn on whichever tap in the house seems closest to the knocking, then turn on both the taps linked by the hose. This should force the air out of the system.

Lavatory Blockage

A blocked lavatory can often be cured by using a sink plunger as in sinks (see page 260). Another method which may work is to take a bucket of water and pour it from as great a height as you can manage. But watch out – if this fails to shift the blockage the water may overflow on to the floor. If you think the blockage may be just round the bend, there is a bendy drain clearer you can thrust through it. Failing that a distasteful option is to bale the loo out and (in rubber gloves) try to reach it – a piece of thick wire bent to a hook can help, but go

carefully or you scratch the glaze of the lavatory. If all these fail, it's a job for a professional.

Lavatory Cistern Problems

Overfilling

If a lavatory cistern overfills, lift the top off the cistern and check inside. The ballcock which should float on the water and shut the water valve may have sprung a hole and taken in water, so it no longer floats. Flush the loo and keep the bar in the cistern held up to stop water entering. Unscrew it from the end of the bar and empty it. Dry the ball and mend the hole with a suitable waterproof glue before replacing.

The other possible cause is that water deposits have built up round the hinge where the bar moves up and down. Scrape off the deposits with a screwdriver or use a bath or kettle scale remover (first checking that none of the components of the cistern are substances on which that chemical shouldn't be used).

Occasionally, the trouble may be that the washer in the cistern needs replacing. As there are numerous different designs it's a job for a plumber. But you can watch what he does and do it yourself next time – on some cisterns it's a simple job.

Poor Flushing

Loos flush badly when the plunger action, which connects to the handle lever, isn't dead above it. If a flushing is poor, open the top of the cistern and look at the bar which connects to the handle. A chain or rod will be hanging from it. If it can be moved, move it until the rod or chain hangs straight down from it – *not* at an angle. Then tighten the nut on the bolt holding it in place. Occasionally, in modern plastic cisterns, the whole mechanism inside tilts over. Shoring it up with strong wire will keep it running if you don't mind a Heath Robinson interior to your cistern. If, however, the plunger has stopped working it is often easy to replace the mechanism oneself. Flush the water out, wire up the ballcock to stop more water entering. Then *carefully* undo the retaining bolts and washers and remove the plunger unit from the cistern. Take it to a plumber's merchant for an exact match and fit the replacement.

Plumbing Maintenance

- Never empty fat, tea leaves and vegetable scraps down a sink. In time they will form a solid block which is very tough to shift.
- Replace the washers on taps, and on ballvalves in cisterns, as soon as they start to drip – one drip a second can waste 400 gallons a year. Because of this some water authorities offer a free re-washering service. Check with the phone number on your water rates.
- Turn each household stopcock briefly off and on once a year. If they aren't turned regularly they may become immovable.
- Turn radiator valves once or twice a year to stop them locking.
- Having turned a radiator full on, turn it back a half turn – then the valve won't stick to the top and lock it at 'full on'.
- Have the boiler serviced regularly.
- Check the water tank annually for corrosion – brown or white patches – and call a plumber if you spot any.
- Clean out the gutters at least once a year and check that the down pipes are working.

Sinks and Basins Which Won't Drain

The best time to deal with a blocked sink is when the water starts draining slowly, not when it blocks totally. It is often possible to clear the pipe just by using a sink plunger (a stick with an inverted rubber cup on the end). As water is going out, put the plunger over the outlet and use it to 'stamp' on it repeatedly. If you lack a sink plunger, a rubber ball which will squish down and cover the whole outlet will do, or even a dense sponge.

If that doesn't work, the trap under the basin needs to be cleared. The trap is a U-bend, or other shape, between the pipe leading down from the basin and the pipe leading into the waste system. It should be attached to these pipes by large nuts. Put a bucket underneath then use a long-handled wrench to unscrew both nuts. Wiggle the trap part until it parts company with the pipes, and clean it out with a hook of wire and by flushing water through. Brush the screw threads to get any dirt and deposit off and then oil them with penetrating oil before screwing the trap back on. Be *very* careful not to cross thread the nuts. It is easily done.

Tap Troubles

If a tap drips the washer usually needs changing. Taps basically divide into those which can be changed without turning off the water supply and those which can't. If you are having any building done it's a good idea to ask the plumber to show you how the washer should be replaced on the taps you have chosen and ask him to tell you the size of washer needed for each tap. Then write to the manufacturers of the tap and ask to buy some suitable washers. At present all new taps have to be sold with washers which meet water company standards for safety. But, amazingly, washers bought loose do not have to meet these standards and some are not as safe as they should be.

Leaking Spindles

If a tap oozes water round its middle, or at the top, it has a leaking spindle. You don't have to turn the water off. Just get at the tap mechanism – as for ordinary washers below. The nut at the very top of the tap mechanism is the gland nut: tighten it. If this fails to cure the leak, undo the nut and replace the gland packing. On old taps this may be string covered in vaseline – so you can just make that. Newer ones will need an O-ring or a washer. Then screw it up again.

Replacing Mixer Tap Washers

The washers on mixer taps are usually in the domed ring which sits at the base of the central tap section. Just undo this – it may be held by a small screw – and replace them. There is no need to turn off the water.

Replacing Ordinary Washers

Turn off the supply at the stopcock. Turn the tap full on. As taps come in various designs you need to adapt what follows to suit the tap you have. If there is a big knob to turn the tap on there may be a screw to undo in the top; then you can remove it. Others come off if you continue to turn them after the tap is full on. Round the middle of a conventional tap – or of what is revealed when you remove a knob – there should be a large nut. Use an adjustable wrench to undo this – protecting any chrome by wrapping a cloth round it first. If it is stiff you may need to hold the rest of the tap with another wrench so as not to strain the pipework. Lift off the tap mechanism and the washer is at the base. Replace it, undoing any nut which holds it. Wipe down any screw threads, smear them lightly with oil or vaseline to make them easy to undo next time, and reassemble – keeping the tap full on. Turn the water on again and only turn the tap off when it has come through.

Replacing Supatap Washers

Supataps don't need to have the water turned off. The tap mechanism hangs from the end of a curved pipe which rises from the basin or sink. For these you just turn the tap on slightly, then use a spanner to undo the nut which is above the body of the tap. Turn the tap until it comes free. Then press the end of the tap on a flat surface and the inside should pop up. Lever out the washer which is shaped like an outsized drawing pin. Replace it with a new one the same size. Put the tap back by reversing the procedure. If this doesn't cure the leak, the anti-splash device which holds the washer may need replacing. This you can do in the same way.

Shower Hose Replacement

Provided a shower is turned off its hose can simply be undone at the nuts at either end and replaced at will.

Addresses and suggestions for further reading are at the ends of chapters.

Repointing

Repointing neatly is a touch harder than it looks, but Polycell now makes a pointing mix to which you just add water, which at least spares you the worst of the mixing – although it is not an economical option for large areas. Try pointing, at first, where it won't show. You will need a small diamond-shaped pointing trowel, and a hawk to carry the mortar on. You can make a hawk by screwing a bit of broom handle on to the centre of a piece of plywood or hardboard.

Scrape the loose pointing *very thoroughly* with a hooked piece of metal, and if necessary use a masonry chisel. Then brush out the dips very well.

If you need to make your own pointing mix 1 part of lime, 1 part of cement with 6 parts of builder's sand – tell the merchant what it's for so they give you the right kind. The amounts are by volume not weight. Mortar dries fast: don't mix more than you can use in half an hour. The trick is to add just the right amount of water. If there is too much it trickles down the wall and leaves marks which are extremely hard (or impossible) to remove. Add the water a little at a time, mixing very well. It should be wet enough not to crumble and dry enough not to slide off the trowel or trickle if the trowel is tilted.

Standing to the left of the area (if you are right-handed), press the mortar carefully into the dips; keep it off the bricks as much as possible, and trim off any excess with the tip of the trowel. Work a neat square about a metre each way. If the first mortar is becoming hard you can use an old brush to brush any surplus off the surface. Look to see what shape the other mortar is. Smooth to shape carefully with whatever will give the shape you want.

★ If you find that the mortar has stained the bricks you may be able to get the stains off by rubbing them with another piece of brick.

Screwing

Screwing is such a simple job that it's easy to suppose anything goes provided the screw looks long enough to hold the two parts together. This isn't quite the case. Having the right screw for the job and using it in the right way matters.

Buying Screws
The right screw has to be chosen for its thickness (gauge), its length, what it is made of, its head type, thread type and coating. This is the order in which the description of screws appears in catalogues.

★ If you have screws and need to check their gauge, measure across the screw head in sixteenths of an inch, double the number and subtract 2. That is the gauge number.

Situations Needing Special Screws
Several materials react chemically if a steel screw is in them. Oak, for example, contains a lot of tannic acid. This may have made it the perfect wood for galleons but it reacts with the ordinary steel used for most screws, and creates blue stains in the wood. Afromosia and idigbo will also be stained by steel. So only brass or stainless steel screws can safely be used in these woods.

Brass isn't strong enough to screw into hardwoods without breaking. First screw in a twin steel screw, then replace it with the brass one. On metal there can also be interactions, particularly between steel and aluminium alloy – which will rapidly corrode and become hard to move. The rule is to choose a screw in the metal you are working on.

★ In a damp atmosphere ordinary steel will rust. If you will ever want to remove the screws, use aluminium alloy, brass or stainless steel instead.

Inserting a Screw in Wood
Ideally, a screw should be inserted into a hole drilled to take it. If you lack a drill, a bradawl is a lot better than nothing. It's a cheap tool because it's simply a shank with a tapered screw thread at the tip and a crossbar handle, like a basic corkscrew, and it's made in several sizes. You screw it into the place where the screw should go to start the hole.

When joining two pieces of wood together you need to drill two different widths of hole. In the upper section of wood drill a 'clearance hole' the same width as the screw. In the lower section, where you want the screw threads to bite, drill a 'pilot' hole smaller than the screw. How much smaller depends on the wood. On hardwood it should only be a little smaller, on softwood it should be quite a bit smaller.

★ For a screw with a countersunk head also drill an inverted cone to let it sink into the wood.

★ When drilling a series of holes mark the correct depth on the bit with a band of masking tape above that point.

★ To mark two pieces of wood at exactly the same point for drilling and screwing find the correct position on one. Make a small hole with a bradawl. Rest a ball bearing or gravel chip on this dip. Place the other wood in position on top. Protect the wood with a wallpaper scraper and strike a firm hammer blow on top. A matching dent will appear on the underside.

★ To cure a loose screw remove it, insert a Rawlplug and replace it. Otherwise, matches or other slivers of wood can be glued into the hole and left to dry, then the screw re-placed. Place them so the pressure will be against the long grain of the wood, not pushing the grain apart or the wood may split.

★ If you don't have a Twinfast screw and need to screw into chipboard you can use any screw without risk of the chipboard crumbling if you drill a hole slightly larger than the screw, and glue in a wood fibre Rawlplug. When it has set, the screw will hold perfectly.

★ It is impossible to screw up into hardboard. Always organize things so you can screw down through hardboard into a thicker base.

★ Ratchet screwdrivers work best if treated with powdered graphite (from a locksmith), not with oil.

★ All screws go in more easily if the tip is rubbed in beeswax polish. They will also be easier to remove.

Inserting Screws in Walls

Making the Hole

In theory, you can make the hole by hammering a Rawl-tool in as you turn it, or with a hand operated bit and brace. But a Rawltool will only work on certain types of wall and, as tools are so easy to hire or borrow, it seems masochistic to do it with anything but an electric drill. And some surfaces can only be drilled this way. Use a masonry bit and, if possible, have a drill which will go to a lower speed for working on hard surfaces. As you work, keep withdrawing the drill to pull out the debris, and have a newspaper under to catch it.

> WARNING: When you drill into a wall it is always possible that an electric wire may be hidden in the plaster. There are little battery-operated gadgets which light up if you run them over a wall which has a wire in it. If possible, use one to check the place where you plan to drill. Failing that, protect yourself by wearing rubber gloves and rubber-soled shoes as you drill.

Securing the Screw

Screws only fix into walls if they have something to bite into, such as a Rawlplug or filler compound. Both fibre plugs and plastic ones work well, filler is more of a nuisance. There is also a greater risk that the moisture in it will make the screw rust immovably.

Choose the plug to suit the screw. In some brands of plug one size covers several gauges of screw; in others the sizes must match. Moulded wallplugs with ridges on the outside are less likely to break the screw or crack the wall than smooth-sided extruded plugs.

The hole you drill should be the same size as the plug you plan to use. If the hole is the right size the plug should push home with a few taps of a hammer, but it must not be loose.

★ If you plan to screw the screw right in, so the smooth part of the shank will enter the plug, use a size larger plug and suit the hole to this. Otherwise the wall may crack.

★ If a Rawlplug is too long for the screw cut off the inner end before inserting it.

Screwing into Cavities

If you want to fix something on a thin wall with a cavity behind it is not impossible. There are some splendid devices, such as cavity toggles, for doing just that.

The big question is how much weight the wall will stand. Before hanging anything of any weight on a thin surface check what it is made of. Then ask the manager of a timber yard to advise you on the load it can carry.

Screw Removal

If a screw is firmly stuck, there are several ways of tackling it. A power drill with a screwdriver attachment is the easiest. Failing that, put a strong screwdriver in place on the screw, tilt it at a slight angle and give it a few sharp blows with a hammer to shift the screw in the direction in which it should turn. If this fails try some blows straight down to shift it in its bed.

If you happen to have an open fire an old-fashioned but effective trick is to hold the tip of a red hot poker against the end of the screw and make it very hot. This makes it expand and when it cools down it should be looser in its bed. If all else fails, the head of the screw can be drilled off.

Squeaking Stairs and Boards

If a stair creaks the quick and easy way to repair it is to put an L-shaped bracket underneath to support it.

Squeaking floor boards are usually cured by puffing French chalk between two boards which are creaking against each other, or by nailing the loose board down.

Tiling

Ceramic Wall Tiles

Buying

The standard sizes of factory-made British tiles are 150 x 150 mm (6 x 6 in) and 115 x 115 mm (4½ x 4½ in) and they usually have little knobbly bits at the edges called spacer lugs. There are also imported tiles in all shapes and sizes.

Beware: standard factory-made British tiles are easy to cut to shape: not so some Continental hand-made tiles. They often look marvellous but use other clays which may refuse to break neatly where they are cut. Some may need an expensive, and potentially dangerous, rotating cutter to go through them: expect a lot of hassles and wastage.

★ The smaller tiles are slightly thinner. Some people think this makes them easier to cut. In fact, the reverse is true. It is far easier to cut the heavier tiles without breaking them in places where you don't want them to break.

What You Need

cement spreading knife or **trowel**	**battens**
	masonry pins
notched cement spreader	**grouting**
	pincers
spirit level	**carborundum stone**

tiles – including some with curved edges to use at the top and or sides.

tile cement – waterproof if the tiles will be in a wet atmosphere, like a small bathroom, otherwise ordinary tile cement is fine.

tile cutter (one of the simplest and most effective is the Cintride tungsten-tipped tile cutter)

★ Check that all the tiles come from the same batch or there could be large colour variations.

★ Even if all the tiles are from the same batch there may be small variations in colour. To avoid these showing start by mixing up all your tiles, both within a single box and between boxes. Small variations from one tile to the next won't show but a block of tiles a shade lighter than the next would.

Addresses and suggestions for further reading are at the ends of chapters.

Stage 1

- Use a spirit level to find the lowest point on the floor (or bath or whatever the tiles are above).
- Mark a point exactly one tile's width above this.
- Using a spirit level, draw a line, from that point, round the area to be tiled and *perfectly on the level*.
- Use masonry pins to fix battens in place with their top edge *exactly* on the line.

Stage 2

There are two rules for how to position the tiles; sometimes they work hand in hand; sometimes they fight. Only you can see which is the most important in a particular room.

- The central tiles should be at the mid-point of the wall.
- There should never be an awkward break in the pattern or a cut tile at a point which will hit the eye as you enter the room.

Bearing these rules in mind, use a plumb line to mark a vertical line where the edge of the last whole tiles will come at one side and fix an upright batten with its edge at the line.

Stage 3

Spread tile adhesive to cover 1 m (1 yd) square in the area close to the two battens. Scrape a notched spreader firmly across the adhesive, pressing it against the wall, to leave a series of even ridges. Line up a tile carefully against the two battens and press it firmly in place. Line up another tile carefully beside it and press it firmly in place. Continue this process until the entire square of cement has been covered.

★ If the tiles have no lugs provide a space between the tiles by putting two matchsticks sticking out between them, and do this between each pair of tiles.

★ If you want to include heavy items like soap dishes scrape off the cement where they should be, put an ordinary tile lightly in place with a couple of pieces of tape going behind it and sticking out above and below. Then, when all the tiles are *totally* dry and solid, pull out the spacer tile by the tapes, spread cement on the back of the soap dish, scrape it into ridges as on the wall, and press it into place. Then secure the tile with masking tape to the firm tiles to either side of it. Only grout when this fitting is dry.

Stage 4

To cut a tile to size:

- measure the exact size it needs to be, top and bottom
- mark this on the glazed side and, using a straight edge, run a tile cutter firmly down the glazed surface on this line
- place the cutting line exactly resting along the length of a pencil
- snap the tile by pressing on its raised ends.

On L-shaped cuts pincers can be used to nibble off the tile in sections after marking and scoring. If you have to cut a U shape to go round a small pipe you can mark the curve with the tile cutter, then drill a series of holes, within that curve, with a masonry drill. These should allow you to break off the small sections neatly.

Rough edges can be smoothed with coarse glass paper or a pumice or carborundum stone.

★ To drill a hole in a glazed surface, without the drill sliding, make a small mark on the glaze with the tip of the tile cutter. If you have the wrong sort of cutter for that, put a piece of sticky tape or elastoplast over the spot instead. Once the tip of the bit is in, make a wall of plasticine or Blu-tack round the hole and put a little paraffin inside this to oil the bit as it sinks in.

Stage 5

Remove the battens and fit the lowest row of tiles, cutting or filing them to size as necessary.

Stage 6

Leave the tiles to dry for 24 hours, then fill in the gaps between the tiles with grouting. Press it well into the gaps and smooth the surface with the round end of a stick. Wipe the grout off the surface while still moist.

★ At one time all grouting was white. Now you can buy it in all kinds of colours. As white grouting always greys with age it makes more sense to choose a colour if it suits your tiles.

Old grouting can become dingy and dull. Scrub it clean with detergent, then paint it over with a product such as Versa Tile. The white version will bring old grouting up to white; the coloured versions can be used to create a checked effect. If you use such a product, put plenty of newspaper down underneath. The process involves washing off the surplus and it sticks to everything it falls on to.

Ceramic Floor Tiles

The method for ceramic floor tiles is almost the same as for walls but bear in mind the following.

- You need to start with a perfectly flat floor. This is easiest to create with hardboard nailed on top of a smooth wood floor (see page 241).
- The adhesive needs to keep a little give in it.
- Put battens on the floor, along one end and up one side to form a *perfect right angle*.
- The thickness of the tiles can make them hard to break.

Replacing Broken Tiles

Damaged ceramic tiles are very easy to replace: you simply break them up with a hammer. The pieces will fly dangerously so wear glasses or goggles, and be doubly safe by fixing a sheet of strong plastic across the top with masking tape. Once a tile is broken it can be levered free. Then sand down or chip off the remains of adhesive, or the new tiles will stick out.

Cork Tiles

Cork tiles are easy to fix on a wall. Draw an upper guideline with the help of a spirit level and fix them to the wall with a heavy duty wallpaper adhesive. There is no need to use contact adhesive – as some books suggest – and it makes it hard to remove them without damaging the wall. They can be cut using a steel rule and a Stanley knife.

Mirror and Metal Tiles

Mirror tiles are attached with adhesive foam pads. If the wall isn't smooth, you can get the tiles to the same level by stacking the pads one on top of the other. They are cut by scoring down the line with a glass cutter and pressing as for ceramic tiles (page 263).

The soft metal of metal tiles can often be cut to size with kitchen scissors.

Polystyrene Tiles and Sheet Polystyrene

Polystyrene tiles are often used to conceal a poor surface. Some fire authorities are not keen on their use. They are now made with a flame-retardant material, but even flame-retardant is not the same as flame proof. They should be reserved for rooms with radiators rather than fires, or stoves.

Polystyrene tiles are centred on the ceiling as for floor tiles, and fixed it with heavy duty wallpaper adhesive over the entire back of the tile – you'll find the ready-mixed form is strongest. Work away from the points where the lines cross, butting the tiles carefully against each other.

Polystyrene sheeting is sometimes recommended to reduce condensation in a room, as it provides a warm surface which the moisture won't settle on. It is put up just like wallpaper, but without pressing.

★ Some fire authorities feel polystyrene ceiling tiles are so dangerous they will not allow them in offices – yet we can still buy them for our homes. The danger is that, if flames reach polystyrene and it catches fire, flaming droplets will fall over other parts of the room, spreading the fire rapidly and giving off poisonous fumes. There are now polystyrene tiles available which have been treated to make them less of a fire hazard, but the fire brigade say even treated tiles are not entirely free from risks.

Tools

FAMILY TOOL CHESTS – Much inconvenience, and considerable expense might be saved, if it was the general custom to keep in every house certain tools for the purpose of performing at home what are called small jobs, instead of always being obliged to send for a mechanic and pay him for executing little things that, in most cases, could be sufficiently well done by a man or boy belonging to the family, provided the proper instruments were to hand.

Enquire Within, 1856

Obviously, the tools you need vary with what you want to do. Whatever you buy, it is worth choosing a really good quality. A good tool will last a lifetime. A poor one will disappoint you from the first day. A bad workman doesn't blame his tools: he buys bad ones.

Electric Drills

An electric drill is vital if you plan to do anything which needs you to put screws into anything harder than softwood. Which type of drill you should choose depends on how much you will use it and what you will use it

for. The key points to look out for when buying a drill are simple.

- A hammer action is really a must for concrete or masonry.
- The lower the speed a drill will run at, the thicker the bit it will take. So at high speeds the outer edge of large bits would go so fast they would overheat.
- If you think you will ever want to use the drill as a power screwdriver (useful for those without muscular arms), it must be able to drop down to very low speeds. But a drill loses power unless it has 'torque' control too. So look for those two features together. And – a point it's easy to forget – if you might want to use it for taking screws *out* it must be able to go in reverse.

Bits and When to Use Them

To get good results it is vital to have the right bit for the right job. For large holes in wood there are big flat bits but for most holes in wood there is a conventional bit with a twist designed to cut a clean hole and shunt the debris out at the same time.

A masonry bit has a flat carbide section at the tip. This helps the drill's hammer action bite into hard surfaces. Metal needs a completely different sort of strength and the whole bit must be made of high speed steel (HSS). Many metal bits are chrome vanadium instead of HSS. They may be a bad buy as the metal loses its edge fast and could distort in use. HSS, on the other hand, can – at a pinch – be used as an all-purpose bit. For glass or tiles you need a tile bit with an end like a small trowel.

Hammers

Choose a small to medium claw hammer with a hickory handle. The claw is useful for taking out nails, and the hickory handle is the best wood for any hammer. Hickory has long fibres so it can take the vibration of the hammer without risk of the head coming loose, and it feels less jarring to use.

Saws

'Trim the plastic to length with a tenon saw', the double glazing instruction says blithely. Most of the time one can work out what is meant by a term because only a tool of a certain kind could possibly do the job. That is not so when it comes to saws. There is nothing in the look of a saw that gets up and shouts at you that it's a tenon saw rather than a hacksaw. So here is a brief run-down on saws, for those who are not yet on first-name terms with them.

Buying

Saws vary greatly in quality: one in tempered steel is a 'hardpoint saw', meaning it should keep its sharpness.

The blades of panel and tenon saws are graded by the number of points they have to the inch (they have defied metrication). A saw with 10 points to the inch is called a ten-point saw. Panel saws range from 7 to 10 points to the inch, tenon saws from 10 to 13. The fewer teeth there are to the inch, the faster it will probably cut, but the more roughly it will do so.

Addresses and suggestions for further reading are at the ends of chapters.

Care

Saws should be hung up somewhere dry and after use a saw should be wiped clean and given a light coat of any machine oil, but this is best wiped off before use on wood or it will make oil marks.

Hacksaws: are rather what they sound like: general purpose saws for hacking through metal. So a hacksaw is a plumber's saw. The blade can be changed. Suit the size of the teeth to the thickness of the metal: the thicker the metal, the coarser the teeth. But don't use fine teeth on very soft metal or it will stick in them.

A panel saw or handsaw is the classic wood saw with the large blade. It is made to cut through planks of timber up to 2.5 cm (1 in) thick. But it can easily handle jobs like cutting the bottom off a door. It's a thoroughly useful saw.

A tenon saw is made for finer jobs on wood, such as cutting joints. The strut of metal along its upper edge prevents it bending and makes exact cutting possible. A useful size is a 30 cm (12 in) with 12 points to the inch.

Coping saws are made to cut shapes in wood, such as a U-shape round a radiator pipe in a floor board. The thin blade is detachable, so you can cut a hole in the middle of a piece of wood by drilling a hole and threading the blade up through it before attaching the blade to the saw. Confusingly, there are also coping saws made for metal, which look almost identical. The difference is that the blade of the wood saw can be turned at an angle – which often makes it far less awkward to cut a curve. If you are buying a coping saw make sure you get the right one.

A fretsaw is part of the same family as a coping saw, but the blade can only handle relatively light jobs.

A padsaw is essentially a long thin knife with a saw edge where the blade should be. It's a weak saw of last resort, but the only one which can saw a keyhole – after you've drilled the main hole, of course.

★ Having marked a line to cut along, cut just to the unwanted side of it. Cutting *on* the line will leave the wood a blade's width too short.

★ To saw easily only press on the saw stroke *away* from you and try to saw with a steady rhythm.

★ To make a panel saw slip better rub the blade with a candle.

★ To stop wood gripping the saw, and making it hard to move, put a wedge of wood in the saw cut to open it up.

★ If it's hard to saw a straight line clamp on a batten with its edge on the line you want to saw and keep the side of the blade against it.

★ To stop thin ply whipping about when you saw, clamp battens to it.

★ If you have to saw across the grain of a veneer – as when shortening a veneered door – it's easy to avoid the jagged tears in the veneer which sawing can cause. Just score through the cutting line on both sides of the door, very deeply with a Stanley knife, before sawing.

★ You can buy a block of wood, called a mitre box, which has slots at 45°. To cut wood to this angle you just clamp it in the box and slip your blade into the slot and saw. You will then cut a precise angle with ease.

Screwdrivers

Three screwdrivers are vital: a small electrical screwdriver, a medium sized screwdriver for X-head screws and a decent sized ordinary screwdriver – about 6 mm across the tip and 26 cm long, with a wide 'cabinet' handle which makes it easier to tackle tough screws.

Shavehook

A combination shavehook is ideal. The varied shapes of its sides fit most situations.

Sharpening Tools

Tools which need to keep an edge, such as chisels, should be sharpened on an oiled carborundum, and (ideally) finished on an oiled arkansas stone. There is, however, an art to making a blade really sharp on a stone which takes a little practice. A chisel, for example, needs to be rubbed to and fro while held at an absolutely steady angle of 30 degrees to the carborundum. If you are doing a lot of woodwork and don't find this easy you can buy a honing guide to keep it at this angle. Sharpening is an art which is well worth practising, as sending tools off for sharpening is a time-consuming business.

The secret of keeping the carborundum and stone in good condition is to lubricate them, with the cabinet maker's mixture of neatsfoot oil and paraffin in equal parts, for other oils clog up the stone and make the particles of steel stick to it. If, however, you have either a stone or carborundum which has already been spoilt by such oils it can easily be restored by simply putting it on a sheet of blotting paper in an oven which has just been turned off. If this doesn't put it in good heart it needs regrinding. You can regrind it by simply putting some silver sand and water on a sheet of glass and rubbing the carborundum on this until the surface is restored. (Neatsfoot oil is sold by shops selling horsey sundries.)

If you lack a carborundum, any nice piece of sandstone will sharpen a steel knife, and in some parts gravestones were often used for the purpose.

★ To see at a glance which screws and nails you have, put each kind in a different screw-top jar.

★ To store the jars neatly make a hole in the centre of each lid and use a screw to fix each lid to the underside of a shelf.

★ If tools have to be stored unused for a while give the blades a smear of 3 in 1 oil to keep off rust. If you have no oil, vaseline is better than nothing. The exception to this is a ratchet screwdriver which should be treated with graphite not with oil.

★ To be safe the distance from wall base to ladder should be not less than 1/4 the height of the ladder. On soft ground there should be a plank under it.

★ If you want to make life easy for yourself buy tools, such as spanners and wrenches, with the longest handles you can find. The laws of physics dictate that the longer the handle, the less effort it takes to lever with them.

★ Smooth the path of a metal plane by rubbing a candle on the underside. On an old wooden one use linseed oil.

Wood

The trend recently has been towards leaving wood unpainted. In response, wood finishes have greatly improved. You can now buy polyurethane varnishes without the glaring plastic shine of the old ones. There are also microporous varnishes which allow the wood to dry out through invisible holes in their surface, and non-drip varnishes which help you make a smooth job of it. Many also claim to stretch with the wood instead of cracking.

For rough wood there are now wood preservatives which act as a base coat and save the need for creosote, and Timbercolours which will stain garden sheds or fences to shades which blend with the garden. The stains for indoors include translucent colours as well as wood shades. There are also new products which claim to arrest rot and firm up wood which is going soft.

Buying Timber
The most important point about buying timber is to buy from a timber yard, *not* a general DIY shop – unless it is really well-stocked. A good timber yard will offer a bigger and better selection and instead of having to buy ready-cut wood to the size the makers decided, you can buy ready-cut wood to the exact size you need. If you have no good timber yard near you, **Fitchett & Woolla-cott** (page 270) supplies good planed timber anywhere in Great Britain. In pine it is well worth buying the joinery quality, ordinary white pine is extremely soft, and good for very little.

Man-made Boards
Among the man-made boards the newest and best is called MDF. This is essentially a wood pulp bonded with glue under pressure. It looks uninviting and sounds worse, but it is extremely strong and will take screws like wood if it is correctly drilled. A friend of mine who is a first class cabinet maker says it will even make dovetail joints.

Chipboard is light, cheap but it breaks easily if asked to carry a load with too little support, won't take screws well and tends to crumble at the edges.

Blockboard is very different and made of long chunks of wood sandwiched between two layers of veneer. The best type is called lammin board. Blockboard's great fault is that the chunks aren't always bang up against each other and if you cut it down a gap you can be left with a useless edge of two pieces of veneer with no filling. However, if you are making book shelves to rest on wall brackets, it's cheap, strong and the veneered sandwich can be matched with a stick-on veneer edging strip. So you can make a strong set of shelves, which don't have to be painted, for far less than the price of a set of flimsy ready-made shelves from a DIY shop. A timber yard will cut boards to the size you need.

Polyurethane Varnishes
If a plain pine table needs a coat of varnish to protect it from the assaults of family life polyurethane is ideal. It is also the one to choose if the varnish rubs off a modern piece of furniture, or a decoratively painted piece of furniture needs a protective coat.

But if the furniture has any antique value at all polyurethane should *never* be used. To put a modern finish on an old piece is to ruin its value. There are also practical considerations that should make you pause.

Applying Varnish
Varnish is no different from applying paint except that, being transparent, it is less forgiving. The wood must be prepared in just the same way but the surface sanded even more finely (down to a 150 paper). For outside it is wise to start with a wood primer which doubles as a preservative. Do include the parts which don't show – like under the legs of garden tables and chairs, which is where moisture is most easily sucked up.

The varnish is then put on just like paint but it is even more important that the surface is *perfectly* dust free, and to get a good finish you must work in a warm place. Give it even more time to dry than the makers suggest, so you have a really hard finish and rub down lightly with very fine wet and dry paper (about 180). This is vital as the first coat of varnish brings up little 'hairs' on the wood which will forever spoil the finish if not removed. But don't rub hard. For a really perfect finish give it a light rub down after each coat with an even finer wet and dry – say 220 down to 320.

> The success of any wood coating depends partly on the wood it covers. Oak, for example, has very strong tannins and any varnish applied to it is unlikely to last more than 2 years – if that. It is very much better to leave oak bare and rub in linseed oil. Some of the very resinous woods such as teak, afromosia or Canadian pine can also present problems and lift the varnish. Afromosia, teak, mahogany, rosewood and iroka can all be given linseed oil instead of a varnish and several sparing coats of this will gradually build up quite a good shine as the linseed oil oxidizes and becomes hard and shiny. Use 1 part linseed oil and 1 part turpentine mixed together. But be careful not to leave trickles as they will be hard to remove.

Rot in Wood
The most damaging fungus is **dry rot**. Despite its name, dry rot starts when spores from the air germinate on damp wood. The spores will germinate anywhere which is dark, has still air, timber with 20 per cent moisture and a temperature of about 20°C (68°F). Unfortunately, if the other conditions exist the fungus can even attract moisture to the wood to give it the damp it needs.

Dry rot needs drastic – and usually professional – treatment the instant it is found, as it spreads fast.

Addresses and suggestions for further reading are at the ends of chapters.

Timbers must be cut back to 60 cm beyond the last point of rot. Plaster that has fungus on has to be removed, and all surfaces in the area have to be treated with a fungicide.

Wet rot is really any rot other than dry rot and the essential difference is that wet rot can only live if the wood is naturally wet. When you take away the source of moisture it dies. The treatment for wet rot is to remove the rotten wood and stop the source of moisture.

Rot Prevention

Prevention is a matter of treating all timbers with a combined fungicide and insecticide which will stop the rot growing on it. These should be applied after wood is cut to shape, so all cut surfaces are covered. Immersing the wood is often the easiest method. However, many of the chemicals used for such treatments can be dangerous if you breathe them in or get them on your skin. Wear clothing and rubber gloves which stop the chemicals touching you. Also use a good face mask when spraying, and have as much air going through the area as possible.

Even with treated timber you should guard against conditions which encourage rot. Damp should not be allowed to enter and leaking roofs, gutters, poor damp-courses and so on should be put right.

Wood Furniture Repairing

When repairing furniture it is vital to suit the treatment to the age of the furniture. Totally permanent glues like Araldite, which cannot be undone, should never be used on wood furniture. But modern wood glues, which are very strong and easy to use, are fine for gluing most modern furniture. However, they should not be used for repairing old furniture; the old glues which are on the furniture could react with the PVA wood glue and make a very unsatisfactory join. Also, if one part of a piece of furniture comes loose the chances are other parts will follow suit. Eventually, the best repair may be for an expert to undo all the joints, clean them and re-build the whole piece. If one section has been repaired with a modern style of glue it would make this difficult or impossible.

For old furniture buy an animal glue such as Pearl Glue or Comet Glue. Good DIY shops sell them or you can get them by mail order from shops which supply furniture restorers. But Comet smells particularly foul.

Pearl Glue comes as little brown granules and needs to be heated over simmering water. Only heat very small quantities, as melted glue will go bad if stored for long.

The effectiveness of any furniture mending depends on the two surfaces being held really tightly together until the glue is dry. If the inner tube and string clamping suggested below won't suit what you have to mend it is well worth buying a G-clamp.

Broken Legs and Struts

When wooden chair legs, struts and table rails break they normally do so at a long sloping angle. The repair is simply a matter of applying a good wood adhesive, placing the two sections exactly together and clamping them tightly with a G-clamp.

If the angle is short, the repair won't be strong enough and the strongest method is to drill a hole down the centre of each piece (like coring an apple) and glue in a strong piece of dowelling linking the two. This can only be done if you have drilling equipment which will let you line up both sections at exactly the same angle to the drill.

Loose Crossbars

The crossbars which hold the legs of old chairs together often come loose. To fix them scrape the old glue out of the hole and off the end of the bar. Check how well the two sections now fit. If the fit is loose you will need to slide a sliver of matching wood into the hole where it won't show. The piece from one of the rolls of self-adhesive veneer for edging shelves is often ideal. But it must be placed against the long grain of the hole, so there is no risk of the extra pressure splitting the wood. Apply a good wood glue and insert the crossbar. Use an inner tube 'clamp' to hold the legs together. Failing that, wet some cotton string, and wind it as tightly as possible between the legs, padding them where it might cut in, for cotton twine tightens as it dries. It can be drawn tighter still by inserting a stick and twisting it, then propping the stick so it can't untwist.

★ A free and effective way to clamp many types of repair is to have wide rings cut from a section of inner tube. Any tyre company will give away inner tubes in a whole range of sizes and you just cut them with a sharp blade and wash them in detergent. But do be careful where you put the clamp. In the wrong place it will open the break, not hold it tight.

Uneven Legs

If any piece of furniture has one leg slightly shorter than another make a paste with a little sawdust and a good glue. Put a thick sheet of paper on a hard floor and have the furniture by it. Put a little heap of the paste on the bottom of the uneven leg and press it down on to the paper until the legs are all perfectly even. Trim off any paste that shows, let it dry, then tear the paper off.

Veneer

Veneer has a tendency to lift as the wood under it swells and shrinks with the weather. If a corner comes up it should be stuck down with all speed or it will soon be broken off in dusting. It is usually a job best left to a professional: the wrong glue could disrupt the other veneer around it.

However, if you are prepared to risk the damage you could do if you get it wrong, it may be possible to stick it down with one of the mild glues given on page 200. But this can only be done if the veneer still fits in the space it has risen from, and any glue which gets on to the surface of the furniture must be wiped off immediately with a moist rag. A piece of thin paper should then be placed over the veneer and a book or two placed on top to hold it down as it dries.

Weak Corner Joints

The angles round the frame of a chair seat, or of a table, often become loose with age. If there is a plain right angle inside each corner it can be strengthened by gluing in a block in the shape of a right-angled triangle from which the apex has been trimmed. On modern chairs of no value you can simply use a purpose-made metal L.

General Tips

★ To keep air out of a quick dry paint, while you have a cup of tea, cover the tin with cling film – it's quicker than hammering on a lid.

★ New bricks will age fastest and blend with an existing house if you brush them with milk.

★ Sashcords on windows run more smoothly if you rub soap on the part which passes over the wheel.

★ When filling cracks in walls have a wet paintbrush to hand. Having smoothed the filler, brush it with the paintbrush. It will have a smoother finish and need less sanding.

★ To make polystyrene accept paint more easily brush it over with wallpaper paste and let this dry.

★ If you are using more than one tin of paint there is no guarantee the shades are identical – especially if the paint has been made with one of the new mix-in-the-shop colours. Before painting tip all your paint into a bucket, stir well and return it to the tins. Then all the wall will match.

★ To plaster a dusty wall after alterations, or apply new pointing to an area where it hasn't held well, brush the surface with a PVA adhesive like Evo-bond. When this dries, it sticks the dust to the wall and gives the plaster or rendering something to grip onto. Check the dilution with the makers.

★ Never lean a ladder against a gutter. Some gutters collapse from rust, others from lack of natural strength.

★ If rendering on walls has large flaws, all loose and flaking material must be brushed out and the gap filled with a mixture of 1 part of masonry cement to 5 parts of soft sand. Use two coats, and smooth the last coat level with the old rendering.

USEFUL ADDRESSES AND BOOKS

General

British Association of Removers (BAR), 3 Churchill Court, 58 Station Road, North Harrow, Middx HA2 7SA Tel: 081 861 3331, can give you the names of removers who are expert an anything, from moving goods to Australia to cosseting family heirlooms. (P.233)

British Standards Institution Enquiry Service, Linford Wood, Milton Keynes MK14 6LE Tel: 0908 226888, will tell you the standard (BS or BSEN) number for any product.

The Design Centre Index should be able to give you the names of manufacturers of products of different types. The **Lighting Association** (page 272) may also be able to help you.

Pickford Removals Ltd, Marketing Department, 492 Great Cambridge Road, Enfield, Middx EN1 3SA Tel: 081 367 0045, have free leaflets on most aspects of moving. (P.233)

Renubath, 248 Lillie Road, London SW6 7QA Tel: 071 381 8337, is one of the most established companies refurbishing and resurfacing baths. It will also chemically clean and polish old baths and loos and mend chips in acrylic baths. (P.226)

Stuart Stevenson, 68 Clerkenwell Road, London WC1M 5QA Tel: 071 253 1693, sells gilding and art materials and adhesives for China restoration – shop and mail order. (P.236)

Useful Books

Dennis Young, *Repairing and Restoring Antiques*, Peerage Books, covers antiques and fine objects of all kinds, not just wood furniture.

Householders' Action Guide, Consumers' Association.

Judith Larney, *Restoring Ceramics*, Barrie & Jenkins.

Judith and Martin Miller, *Period Details*, Mitchell Beazley, shows exactly which doors, cornices and so

on, should be in houses of different periods, and also has a directory of useful specialist firms.

Nigel Williams, *Porcelain Repair and Restoration*, Colonnade/British Museum Publications.

Architects, Auctioneers, Estate Agents and Surveyors

The Architectural Association, 34-36 Bedford Square, London WC1B 3ES Tel: 071 636 0974, is both a school for architects and an association. However, being a *member* of this association does *not* indicate that someone is a qualified architect. (P.219)

Federation of Independent Estate Agents, The Courtyard, 4 Alexandra Road, Clevedon, Avon BS21 7QE Tel: 0275 343560, will only accept members who have a track record, and has a code of practice which enables complaints to be handled through an arbitration scheme agreed with the Chartered Institute of Arbitrators. (P.230)

The Incorporated Society of Valuers and Auctioneers (ISVA), 3 Cadogan Gate, London SW1X 0AS Tel: 071 235 2282, is a society for qualified estate agents, surveyors, property valuers and property auctioneers. Its members must conform to a professional code of conduct. (P.230)

National Association of Estate Agents (NAEA), Arbon House, 21 Jury Street, Warwick CV34 4EH Tel: 0926 496800, has a code of practice and will advise on aspects of sale or letting. (P.230)

Ombudsman for Corporate Estate Agents, Suite 3, Old Library Chamber, Chipper Lane, Salisbury, Wilts SP1 1YQ Tel: 0722 333306. (P.230)

The Royal Incorporation of Architects in Scotland (RIAS), 15 Rutland Square, Edinburgh EH1 2BE Tel: 031 229 7205, publishes a directory of architectural practices detailing their specialities. It also has advice leaflets and an advisory service. (P.220)

The Royal Institute of British Architects (RIBA), 66 Portland Place, London W1N 4AD Tel: 071 580 5533, has an advisory service and free list of architects suitable for a particular project; vg L, Rg. (P.219)

The Royal Institute of Chartered Surveyors (RICS), 12 Great George Street, Parliament Square, London SW1P 3AD Tel: 071 222 7000, has leaflets on every conceivable topic related to property. (P.221)

Building: Trades and Information

The Building Centre, 26 Store Street, London WC1E 7BT Tel: 071 637 1022, has a permanent exhibition of building items and an information service (9.30 to 5.15 on weekdays and 10 to 1.00 on Saturdays). If you want to know who makes a particular building product ring the enquiry service.

The Building Conservation Trust, Apartment 39, Hampton Court Palace, East Molesey, Surrey KT8 9BS Tel 081 943 2277, has a permanent exhibition showing how different types of fault need to be repaired in houses of all periods. (Open 9.30 to 5.00 Monday to Friday. Last admissions 4.15.) The Trust will also suggest people who can advise and help with particular problems.

Building Employers Confederation (BEC), 82 New Cavendish Street, London W1M 8AD Tel: 071 580 5588, is the largest association of its kind. Its members are vetted by local committees, and must have been trading for a reasonable time and keep to a voluntary code of conduct. (P.220)

British Wood Preserving and Damp-Proofing Association, Building No. 6, The Office Village, 4 Romford Road, Stratford, London E15 4EA Tel: 081 519 2588. Members have to reach a set standard, their work is subject to spot checks, and the association will look into complaints against members and try to resolve the problems (P.230). However, any firm can go out of business and the 20- to 30-year guarantees then become worthless. To avoid this, you can pay a small one-off fee to the **Guarantee Protection Trust**. (P.222)

Building Research Establishment, Buckhall's Lane, Garston, Watford WD2 7JR Tel: 0923 894040. (P.221)

Federation of Master Builders, 14-15 Great James Street, London WC1N 3DP Tel: 071 242 7583, has a National Register of Warranted Builders. To be on the register a builder need not have any qualifications or reach any set standards, they simply need to have two references and to have been in business for a year. Their warranty scheme is very similar to that offered by BEC (above). (P.220)

Glass and Glazing Federation (GGF), 44-48 Borough High Street, London SE1 1XB Tel: 071 403 7177. To join, a company must have traded for two years. No qualifications are needed, but members must conform to the Federation's code of practice as well as the British Standards and Technical Trade Standards. Membership is no guarantee of expertise. However, the GGF also provides a fund which safe-

guards the client's deposit – up to a certain level – if a member goes out of business before the job is finished. (P.225)

Guarantee Protection Trust, P.O. Box 77, 27 London Road, High Wycombe, Bucks HP11 1BW Tel: 0494 447049. For a small one-off fee, your guarantee from a GPT member's wood preserving or damp proofing will be insured for 20 years. And if the original firm goes out of business any remedial work will be done by another firm. (P.222)

Interior Decorators' and Designers' Association, Crest House, 102-104 Church Road, Teddington, Middlesex TW11 8PY Tel: 081 977 1105, has a list of interior designers.

National Federation of Painting and Decorating Contractors (see **BEC**, opposite).

National Federation of Roofing Contractors, 24 Weymouth Street, London W1N 3FA Tel: 071 436 0387, will supply a list of experienced contractors. They will also give technical advice on roofing, and will arbitrate on disputes between one of their contractors and a member of the public. Its members offer a guarantee scheme if the client pays a small extra percentage on the bill. (P.228)

National House Building Council (NHBC), Buildmark House, Chiltern Avenue, Amersham, Bucks HP6 5AP Tel: 0494 434477 or 5 Manor Place, Edinburgh EH3 7DH. The telephone hotline (031 226 7115) also has a list of developers building sheltered accommodation and old people's housing. The NHBC sets standards for new buildings built by members and gives a 10-year warranty on them. (P.230)

Period Brick and Tile Co, Clawddnewydd, Nr Ruthin, Clwyd LLI5 2NB Tel: 08245 285, supplies bricks and tiles to match old buildings. Delivery is wide.

Scottish Building Employers Federation, 13 Woodside Crescent, Glasgow G3 7UP Tel: 041 332 7144, is a professional trade association with a code of conduct and a disputes procedure if things go wrong. (P.220)

The Society for the Protection of Ancient Buildings, 37 Spital Square, London E1 6DY Tel: 071 377 1644, will advise on all problems affecting very old buildings.

Thatching Advisory Service Ltd, Rose Tree Farm, 29 Nine Mile Ride, Finchampstead, Nr Wokingham, Berks RG11 4QD Tel: 0734 734203, claims to be Britain's biggest thatching company, with franchises everywhere. (P.229)

Timber and Brick Information Council, Gable House, 40 High Street, Rickmansworth, Herts WD3 1ES Tel: 0923 778136, has information on timber-frame houses, and on who to buy them from, and sells paperbacks on DIY in timber and brick houses and on related topics. (P.230)

Timber Research and Development Association (TRADA), Stocking Lane, Hughenden Valley, High Wycombe, Bucks HP14 4ND Tel: 0494 563091, provides lists of those making timber-frame housing, and some thought-provoking leaflets on the structure and problems of timber-frame housing. (P.219)

Useful Book
Murray Armour, *Building Your Own Home*, Orion, tells you how to build a home from foundations to chimney.

DIY

Black and Decker, Westpoint, The Grove, Slough, Berks SL1 1QQ Tel: 0753 511234, information and service centre.

Fitchett & Woollacott, Willow Road, Lenton Lane, Nottingham NG7 2PR Tel 0602 700691, supplies good planed timber. (P.266)

Laura Ashley, does a range of stencils. (P.254)

Liberty, Home Ideas Department, Regent Street, London W1R 6AH Tel: 071 734 1234, has stencils. (P.252)

Lyn Le Grice, The Stenciled House, 53 Chapel Street, Penzance, Cornwall TR18 4AF Tel: 0736 64193, sells a chaming range of stencils by mail order, send A4 sae for catalogue. (P.252)

Martek Ltd, P.O. Box 20, Redruth, Cornwall TR15 2UF Tel: 0209 219911, makes bit sharpeners which claim to be able to sharpen even HSS bits. The bit manufacturers are less convinced, and I have yet to try it.

Muraspec Ltd, 79-89 Pentonville Road, London N1 9LW Tel: 071 278 0161, sells wall felt by the yard plus hessian, suede and metallized PVC. Branches in other major cities. (P.258)

Ploton Ltd, 273 Archway Road, London N6 5AA Tel: 081 348 0315, sells the special materials for decorative finishes and for gilding. It also sells artists materials (mail order in Britain and overseas) but beware: it is only open 8.15-3.15 Monday to Friday.

Polycell Products Ltd, Consumer Services, Broadwater Road, Welwyn Garden City, Herts AL7 3AZ Tel: 0707 328131.

Russell and Chapple, 23 Monmouth Street, London WC2H 9DD Tel: 071 836 7521. (P.258)

The Stencil Store, 91-93 Lower Sloane Street, London SW1W 8DA Tel: 071 730 0728, is a shop with a big range of stencils, plus all the materials for using them (mail order in Britain and overseas). Inexpensive and tempting catalogue from P.O. Box 30, Rickmansworth, Herts WD3 5LG Tel: 0923 285588. (P.252)

UGW Ltd, Sales Department, Doxcy Road, Stafford ST16 1EA Tel: 0785 223281, will tell you the nearest stockist of any abrasive paper you can't find. (P.235)

Useful Books
Alex Davidson, *Interior Affairs: the Decorative Arts in a Paintbrush*, Ward Lock.
Jocasta Innes, *Paint Magic*, Windward/Berger.
Lyn Le Grice, *Art of Stencilling*, Viking.

Finding or Selling a Home

H.O.M.E.S., 26 Chapter Street, London SWIP 4ND Tel: 071 233 7077, has lists of housing associations all over Britain, and runs a scheme to help people in council or housing association properties to swap with those in other areas. Directories on housing for the elderly and those with special needs should be in a public library. (P.232)

Housing Corporation, 149 Tottenham Court Road, London W1P 0BN Tel: 071 387 9466. (P.232)

SHAC (The London Housing Aid Centre), Kingsbourne House, 229-231 High Holborn, London WC1V 7DA Tel: 071 404 7447, offers advice and help with any type of housing problem. (P.232)

Useful Books
Housing Year Book, Longman – lists all local authority planning departments, statutory and voluntary housing associations, aid and advice centres.
Marion Cutting, *A Housing Rights Handbook*, Penguin.

Paint

Crown Berger Paints Advice Centre, Hollins Road, Darwen, Lancs BB3 0BG Tel: 0254 704951 (for information and stockists) or Freephone 6067 (for advice). Also covers Brolac paints.

Dacrylate Paints Ltd, Lime Street, Kirkby-in-Ashfield, Nottingham NG17 8AL Tel: 0623 753845, makes an anti-climb paint for drainpipes, and an anti-graffiti paint, and can tell you how to get them. (P.249)

Dulux, Wrexham Road, Slough SL2 5DS Tel: 0753 550555.

Eurochem Manufacturing Ltd, Eldon Close, Crick Motorway Estate, Crick NN6 7UD Tel: 0788 823986, makes an anti-climb paint. (P.249)

International Paint, Customer Services, 24-30 Canute Road, Southampton SO9 3AS Tel: 0703 226722.

Manders Paints Ltd, P.O. Box 9, Old Heath Road, Heath Town, Wolverhampton WV1 2XG Tel: 0902 871028.

The Paintmakers Association of Great Britain Ltd, 93 Albert Embankment, London SE1 7TY Tel: 071 582 1185, will give you the details of companies making paints which cope with special problems.

Paper and Paints, 4 Park Walk, London SW10 0AD Tel: 071 352 8626, are colour specialists. The excellent range includes period shades for historic houses. They will also mix paint to match fabric or paper, and sell tools and glazes for decorative finishes.

Plastikote, London Road Industrial Estate, Sawston, Cambridge CB2 4TR Tel: 0223 836400, makes a very good range of environmentally friendly spray paints for stencilling, radiators and so on. (P.247)

Sandtex, Akzo Coatings (Decorative Department), 135 Milton Park, Abingdon, Oxford OX14 4SB Tel: 0235 862226.

Technical Paint Services (Uxbridge) Ltd, The Paint

Centre, Horton Bridge Road, West Drayton, Middx UB7 8JR Tel: 0895 446232 will supply many paints which are hard to find elsewhere, such as rubberized floor paint, swimming-pool, luminous or flame-retardant paint. Plus special undercoats for problem surfaces and equipment for decorative finishes. All by mail or rail, with some paint shades to special order.

Plumbing, Heating and Energy Efficiency

British Board of Agrément, P.O. Box 195, Bucknalls Lane, Garston, Watford, Herts WD2 7NG Tel: 0923 670844, has lists of approved installers of insulation, including those doing such things as roofing and chimney lining. (P.224)

Confederation for the Registration of Gas Installers (CORGI), 4 Elm Wood, Chineham Business Park, Crockford Lane, Basingstoke, Hants RG24 0WG Tel: 0256 707060, registers gas installers, but doesn't arbitrate in disputes, and its fitters don't have to be insured against any damage they cause. And there are doubts about its standards. (P.227.)

Draught Proofing Advisory Association Ltd; External Wall Insulation Association; National Association of Loft Insulation Contractors; and **National Cavity Insulation Association** are all at P.O. Box 12, Haslemere, Surrey GU27 3AH Tel: 0428 654011. They will supply the names of contractors, and the latter has a customer protection plan. (P.224)

Energy Action Grants Agency, Eldon Court 2nd Floor, Eldon Square, Newcastle-on-Tyne NE1 7HA Freephone: 0800 181 667, has free leaflets on energy saving, and administers the Home Energy Efficiency Scheme (HEES) which gives grants to those on certain benefits so they can have better insulation. The **Energy Efficiency Office** and **Winter Warmth Line** can advise you. (P.224)

Energy Efficiency Office, 1 Palace Street, London SW1 Tel: 071 238 3000, has information. (P.224)

Energy Saving Trust, 11-12 Buckingham Gate, London SW1E 6LB Tel: 071 828 1346, runs a new-boilers-for-old scheme.

The Heating and Ventilating Contractors' Association, ESCA House, 34 Palace Court, London W2 4JG Tel: 071 229 5543, or **Home Heating Linkline** 0345 581158 (charged at local call rates) will provide the names of members. They must have traded for two years. Branches in Edinburgh and Belfast. Inf. Ad.

Home Energy Efficiency Scheme (HEES), P.O. Box 1NG, Newcastle-on-Tyne NE9 1NG, gives grants, to those on low incomes, for certain types of insulation. (P.224)

The Institute of Plumbing, 64 Station Lane, Hornchurch, Essex RM12 6NB Tel: 0708 472791, is for individual plumbers. The membership must 'satisfy the Institute regarding their workmanship'. The Institute's directory is in public libraries.

The National Association of Plumbing, Heating and Mechanical Services Contractors, 14-15 Ensign Business Centre, Westwood Way, Coventry CV4 8JA Tel: 0203 470626, insists members must show technical competence. Code of practice, warranty scheme, and gives details of members.

Neighbourhood Energy Action, St. Andrew's House, 90-92 Pilgrim Street, Newcastle-on-Tyne NE1 6SG Tel: 091 261 5677, has details of local action groups which, using a grant, insulate the homes of those unable to do it because of income, age or illness. (P.224)

OFTEC (Oil Firing Technical Association for the Petroleum Industry), Century House, 100 High Street, Banstead, Surrey SM7 2NN Tel: 0737 373311, provides information on all aspects of oil-fired heating. (P.227)

The Scottish and Northern Ireland Plumbing Employers Federation, 2 Walker Street, Edinburgh EH3 7LB Tel: 031 225 2255, covers plumbing and domestic central heating, has a code of practice and will arbitrate. It also offers warranty and insurance schemes.

The Solid Fuel Advisory Service, Hobart House, Grosvenor Place, London SW1X 7AE Tel: 071 235 2020, sponsors Real Fire Heating Shops all over Britain where real fires are displayed. And its service includes a free home visit to discuss your needs. It will also advise on maintenance. The **National Fireplace Council**, at the same address, publishes a catalogue of fire places by a large range of manufacturers. (P.227)

Winter Warmth Line, Freephone 0800 289404, from October to March can tell you about grants, and help you solve winter-warmth problems. (P.224)

Useful Book
Energy Savings With Home Improvements, Consumers' Association.

Security

Master Locksmiths Association, Units 4 and 5, Woodford Halse Business Park, Woodford Halse, Daventry, Northants NN11 6PZ Tel: 0327 62255, will supply the names of locksmiths. Its members must be properly qualified and abide by a code of ethics. If a member's work is not satisfactory the association will take it up. (P.228)

The National Supervisory Council for Intruder Alarms, Queensgate House, 14 Cookham Road, Maidenhead, Berks SL6 8AJ Tel: 0628 37512. This regulatory body vets those who install electronic security devices of all kinds. The firms it recognizes must have traded for two years and be run by people with experience in the business. The firms must also conform to a code of practice. Under this code, they must take a 20-year history of their employees to, as far as possible, ensure their honesty. The Council will give you the names of members in your area. (P.229)

Things Electrical

Members of **The Electrical Contractors' Association**, ESCA House, 34 Palace Court, Bayswater, London W2 4HY Tel: 071 229 1266, must have traded for 3 years and have other credentials. If a member fails to complete a proper job it will be completed by another member, at no cost. (P.222)

The Electrical Contractors' Association of Scotland, Bush House, Bush Estate, Edinburgh EH26 0SB Tel: 031 445 5577, sets a code of practice for its members and operates a complaints procedure. (P.222)

The Institution of Electrical Engineers (IEE), Savoy Place, London WC2R 0BL Tel: 071 240 1871, publishes the IEE wiring regulations for electrical installations. (P.222)

The Lighting Association, Stafford Park 7, Telford, Shropshire TF3 3BD Tel: 0952 290905, will supply a list of companies which specialize in lighting of particular kinds.

National Inspection Council for Electrical Installation (NICEI) Vintage House, 37 Albert Embarkment, London SE1 7UJ Tel: 071 582 7746, is concerned with consumer safety and professional standards. (P.224)

The Family

Family Matters • Education and Home • Education: Sixteen to Ninety • Retirement and After

Of all the subjects in this book none is bigger, or perhaps more important, than coping with a family. It is a topic which is impossible to cover in anything like the detail it deserves in less than a whole book. In the first section, on child-rearing, for example, it has only been possible to cover a few of the key problems which worry parents. In isolation what I say may seem fragmentary or superficial. I would rather risk that than have a reader with a crying baby find nothing to help them. But, being trained in teaching and psychology, and a parent of long standing, I am powerfully aware that neat solutions and easy answers are not part of the currency of child-rearing. Each child is different and can only be raised in the context of its own particular character and needs. No solution works for every child, nor would it be right to apply it to every one. All I can do is offer suggestions and leave you to judge whether they seem worth a try.

The middle section of this chapter covers education, training and careers. While I was revising it the government was still tweaking its changes to the education system. For a curious feature of the last Education Act is that it gives the government a remarkable amount of leeway to make future changes without putting them before Parliament. This being so, parents may need to keep tabs on the latest ones via the education press.

Tucked into adult education you will find pointers to pursuing hobbies and interests at any age. And among the addresses at the end are a selection of major clubs and organizations which can be joined by adults or children either for companionship or to pursue some hobby or sport.

The third section of this chapter covers the less shifting sands of coping with retirement, housing in later life and the incapacities of old age.

FAMILY MATTERS

Adoption

Adopting a child is a big step, and there can be problems that are hard to envisage. So, before adopting, it may be wise to learn more about its joys and pitfalls by talking to organizations like the **Parent to Parent Information on Adoption Service (PPIAS)** and the **Post Adoption Centre** (page 317). All local authorities deal with adopters in their area. The book *Adopting a Child* by the **British Agencies for Adoption and Fostering (BAAF)** (page 317) lists all voluntary and state agencies offering babies and/or children, and libraries should have the *Social Services Yearbook* which lists approved adoption societies. Having found which agencies would suit you, *don't ring*, write to each giving all the details about yourself (and your partner) – including your racial group and religion – and saying whether you want a newborn baby or will accept one slightly older.

There are very few normal, healthy British babies available and some agencies have so many parents already waiting that they even close their lists. Most agencies expect adopters of healthy babies to be:

- married for over 3 years – but not for more than 10
- healthy but unable to have a child
- over 21 (by law) but in their 20s or 30s
- of the same race as the baby.
- Some agencies may have religious requirements.

> The Natural Parents Support Group will help those whose child has been adopted. The National Organization for Adoptees and their Parents helps those groups.

Adopting an older child, a family of children, or a baby or child with a problem, is a totally different situation. Agencies are mainly concerned to find the right placing for a child with a particular problem. So those who wouldn't stand a chance of adopting a healthy baby may be welcome to adopt a child who needs special care or is older. Apply to your Social Services Department and to any other agencies near you in the BAAF book (page 317).

You can also widen your choice by using the exchange service of BAAF which puts would-be adopters in touch with suitable children all over the country. It sells a tabloid newspaper several times a year called *Be My Parent* which gives details and photographs of children needing parents. If you don't want to buy it, a reference library should have it. See also page 317.

The Cost of Adopting
It is illegal for an agency to charge for offering a child for adoption. To formalize the adoption you shouldn't need a solicitor, so it will cost very little. And, if you are adopting a child with special needs, the agency usually pays this. Once the child is yours it becomes a drain on

your income, just like any child, but children with special needs may be eligible for a special allowance. See also Law page 478.

Fostering

If you might want to become foster parents, the **National Foster Care Association** (page 317) will put you in touch with other foster parents who can tell you more about fostering. It really means looking after a child as if it was your own for a limited period of time.

Most of the children put out for fostering are older children with problems. Moreover, those who do the best job are those who, instead of capturing the child's love for themselves, really try to keep the links with its natural family going as the Children Act requires. It takes immense generosity of spirit to do that.

If you want to foster talk to BAAF (page 317), to your local authority and to children's homes like Barnardos. Foster parents should be able to obtain money to cover the cost of caring for the child.

Birth of a Brother or Sister

Think for a moment how you would feel if your husband or wife left home one day saying he or she would come back soon, stayed away for several days and came back unexpectedly in the arms of a lover. That is roughly what a young child experiences when a mother goes off to hospital and returns with a new baby. The child first feels deserted and then is faced with a rival. It's amazing more toddlers don't turn to infanticide. But, being upset, they are often demanding just when their mother has quite enough on her hands with the demands of the baby.

- Tell the child/children about the coming baby but don't make too much of it being someone to play with. Newborn babies are poor playthings and you don't want to add disillusionment to the other feelings.
- Before you go away, record bedtime stories, and chat, on tape so your child can still hear you talking to it.
- Try to ring home at least once a day and talk to the child. If it is old enough to find presents, have little presents hidden round the house and each day give it the clue to finding one. They can be tiny – they are just to show you thought about it.
- Don't return home carrying the baby. Let your partner carry the baby, so you can hug the child.
- Don't buy a present for the child to give to the baby, buy a present for the baby to give the child. Don't leave the child out when people bring a present for the new baby.
- Once you are home don't let the baby overwhelm any special time you used to have with the other child. Try to give it some time with all your attention each day – maybe just before bed when your partner can deal with the baby if it cries.
- Don't let the child hear you saying adoring things about the baby which might put it in the shade.

- Let the child play a part in caring for the baby and *praise* what it does.
- Don't let any change in an older child's routines – such as weaning from a bottle, toilet training or moving to a big bed – happen as the new baby arrives.

Child Battering

Few parents can swear that never for a moment have they wanted to hit one of their children exceedingly hard or post a screaming baby out of a window. Those that have been spared these feelings may well have been spared the circumstances which can make a parent that desperate. In most parents such feelings are fleeting moments which are instantly controlled. To have these emotions from time to time is not unnatural; to give in to them is. And it is just as dangerous to attack a child with cruel and violent words as with fists.

Where to Get Help

If you feel that you may batter your children, or have already done so, you need to talk to someone about it. Don't be so ashamed of the feelings that you can't ask for help. Talking about them will make you far less likely to do whatever you fear you may do.

If there is no one to talk to among your friends and family, phone one of the organizations which help. **Parents Anonymous** (page 319) has a helpline for all child-related problems and will help and advise parents who feel they may attack their children physically, sexually or verbally. The Samaritans (in your phone book) will also help you; so will the NSPCC (page 319) and Parentline (page 317).

You don't *have* to give your name and address – even if they ask it – so you can talk without the risk of your children being put into care.

You can also ring these lines if someone in the household is already battering a child. The people on any of these lines can tell you how to get help, or you can go to your doctor.

Child Development

One of the burdens of parenthood is that it is almost impossible to avoid comparing your child with the next one and wondering whether its behaviour and achievements are normal or advanced for its age. This means that parents are very quick to spot that a child isn't developing quite normally and a mother shouldn't be afraid to take a child to the doctor if she feels something is wrong, but if nothing is found amiss, don't worry yourself sick about the oddness or slowness of your child. Keep on doing all the things which give the child a chance to learn and develop and remember that children aren't standardized products, each has its own pace for everything it does and that it is the pace which is right for it. One friend of mine has a daughter who refused to crawl or stand until over 2. This odd behaviour remained a mystery but she grew up not only physically normal but extremely brainy.

Addresses and suggestions for further reading are at the ends of chapters.

Having watched my own children and a multitude of their friends from nappies to employment, I have to tell you that:

- There are no 'normal' children – every child is different.
- Slowness and even failure at any stage are no indication that a child won't do brilliantly as an adult, nor, alas, do the swift walkers and primary school stars always go on to great things.

However, since parents *will* make comparisons, here are some guidelines as to what that totally mythical animal, the normal, child, may do.

1 month:	grasp a finger tightly
6 weeks:	smile back at you, gurgle
2 months:	a baby lying on her tummy can lift her head
3-4 months:	reach out and touch an object, roll around but not over, can stop her head lolling about
5-6 months:	begin to make sounds like Da-da or Ma-ma (but they have no meaning)
6-7 months:	briefly sit unsupported
8 months:	sit securely without support
7-9 months:	slide across shiny floors on her tummy
9-10 months:	master crawling, pull herself to standing by holding on to the furniture, say a real word – and mean it
10-12 months:	clap hands, begin to help to undress herself
13-15 months:	stand without holding on, systematically bang a drum
15-18 months:	begin to stand up from sitting, start walking – unsteadily, put big bricks on top of each other, play will be more deliberate
20-24 months:	slide downstairs feet first on her tummy (if taught to – safer than trying to walk)
2-3 years:	go up and down stairs, begin to draw (not just scribble), undo screw tops, and turn door handles, jump up and down, kick a ball (roughly), thread large beads on a shoelace, undo large buttons, manage some dressing and undressing
3 years plus:	manage buckles on shoes, cut with scissors

From this point a child learns to do such a multitude of things that it is impossible to list them.

★ If your home is warm there is no need for a tiny child to wear shoes. Bare feet are much less likely to slip when learning to walk.

★ If a child is ill he or she may slide back a few stages but will soon catch up when well again.

Do keep a diary on your child if you possibly can. One of my biggest regrets is that I failed to keep up the one I started on my children. Early motherhood is so engulfing that one feels one will never forget the day they . . . but one does, totally. And the children forget too. It is a great loss. One of the loveliest things one can have is such a diary and – to judge from my children's response to my fragment – it is something the children will find fascinating too.

Crying

Anyone with a crying baby has all my sympathy: few things are more exhausting. If it's your first child you may be wondering what you are doing wrong. The chances are the answer is 'nothing'. Some babies cry and some don't. So if you are sure a baby isn't hungry, wet, dirty, sore (nappy rash is very nasty) or windy, and hasn't got a nappy pin sticking into it, the physical problems are probably solved. That doesn't mean a crying baby is being naughty. It should *not* be left to cry to expand its lungs; that is an old wives tale with *no* truth in it.

We all have times of feeling downright lonely and miserable, so there seems no reason why babies can't too. Think of the cosy, unvarying security the baby knew in the womb, lulled by the beating of its mother's heart. Then compare it with the world full of quietness and sudden strange sounds, cold air and new sensations which a baby has to adjust to. It isn't really surprising if a baby feels a bit lost and miserable, is it? And *it's important that the baby is quickly comforted and reassured.*

Predictably the things which soothe a crying baby are those which restore some of the sensations it had in the womb: rocking, being held close and warm, rhythmical sounds, the smell of its mother's body. When I was in Africa, where black mothers carry their children constantly on their backs, I never heard a child cry and one solution is to wear a harness which lets it ride on your back. Tiring, but probably less so than for ever picking it up to comfort it. (See also page 283.) But if a baby cries more than normal, talk to your doctor or health visitor. Meanwhile, ring BM Crysis (page 317) if you need support.

Crying and Anger in Older Children

The British often react as if crying was a bad thing. It can be, but it needn't be. One of the important roles of a parent is to help a child to accept and understand its own emotions, and feeling sad is one of them. If a child wants to blub over a minor hurt it does no harm at all to give it quick sympathy and then distract its attention and encourage it to be braver. But children do experience real grief and loss – even if it is only the death of a much-loved pet – and at these times a good parent will help a child release the pain inside it and let it cry. It is heartbreaking to hear a child weeping, but adults have to be strong enough to bear that and not say 'don't cry' and not try to distract it until they feel the *child itself* is beginning to be ready to end its tears. Meanwhile, they should just give quiet comfort and support, and expect the grief to come back from time to time.

Exactly the same thing applies to anger. Not all the emotions a child feels are good or comfortable. It may be desperately jealous of its brothers and sisters and have moments of hating its parents. These feelings can only be handled well if they are acknowledged and perhaps talked about. Yet so often parents force a child to fake emotions, saying to one who has not yet got over a row, 'Come and kiss Mummy then', which rides rough-shod over the child's real feelings. It's far better to say gently, 'You're still angry with me, aren't you? Do you want to talk about it or would you like to be by yourself for a while?' That shows that the child's anger is accepted and understood (children can be very frightened of their own feelings) and that the parent will let the child decide how to handle it in its own time. The parent also needs to give children opportunities, to discuss ugly feelings once the worst is over. This helps a child understand itself and other people.

Death in the Family

People are sometimes embarrassed about telling a child about death. But it is important that a child grows up feeling at ease with the world, and everything in the natural world is born, grows and dies. If a child can see the loss of a human loved one in the context of the whole order of nature, death will seem less alarming. This is something which can be touched on lightly when dead-heading flowers or going for a walk in autumn. Children find patterns comforting and the patterns of nature can be a useful anchor.

If someone known to a child dies it may have more impact on the child than you'd expect. Young children go through a stage when they feel the world revolves around them. At this stage a child feels all powerful and can easily believe that the bad thoughts it had about the person concerned – which may easily have included wishing they'd go away for ever – caused the death. Similar feelings can afflict an older child if it has been brought up with religious views which suggest it can do harm by having bad thoughts.

So give any child a good reason for a death that is totally unconnected with the child. For example, you could say that Granny was old and very tired so she asked God to be very kind and take her to heaven to rest and God took her there. That way death isn't expressed as something nasty which has been done to Granny by a bad child, or anything else, but as a positive release.

If a child finds it hard to get over a death or wets its bed for a long time after it or has real problems of any other kind, it is worth bearing in mind that it may be blaming itself and feeling dreadfully guilty. If so it may need professional help to get over these wrong ideas.

It can be very hard to tell a child that someone is dying but children should not be lied to. If you pretend to a child that someone who is dying is just going away for a little while, they will never feel safe when people go away because they will have learnt that those who 'go away' don't come back. It is far better for them to be told the truth about one death than imagine a score of deaths whenever those they love go away.

When there is a death in the family it can sometimes be easier to talk to a professional comforter by ringing the Samaritans or some other helpline, than to express grief to friends and family. Whatever means you choose, it is important not to hold grief in.

Organizations such as SANDS and FSID (page 642) offer much to those who have lost a baby. Also charities related to conditions which can be fatal (see pages 587-590) often have support groups for families both during the time leading up to a death and after it. In addition, on page 318 I give organizations which support the bereaved emotionally and perhaps also in the practical problems which come with any death.

Discipline

The first thing to sort out where discipline is concerned is whether or not a child is really being naughty. A friend of mine found her 4-year-old twin grandchildren busily covering her newly painted white front door with a thick layer of mud. Being a forbearing woman she held her fire and asked them what they were doing, and they solemnly replied that they had almost finished painting it. The distinction between paint and mud isn't as clear to a 4-year-old as it is to us.

Misunderstandings like that happen with children all the time and if they aren't to feel the adult world is most unfair, it pays to stop and wonder – and ask – *why* a child is doing what it is doing. Experienced parents don't need to, they can see at a glance whether the 4-year-old poking hairpins in the electric socket is trying to learn about sockets or planning to wire up the baby. The look on the face becomes unmistakable.

When a child is very young it can't tell you why it does what it does. The only solution is to get into the habit of trying to see things from the child's viewpoint. That doesn't mean being a martyr to your child but, once you understand the reasons for a child's behaviour, it is a lot less annoying. If you know that a child pouring water out of the bath on to the floor is discovering that water falls (for all it knows it might fly) you can talk about the matter, explain firmly that the bathroom floor isn't the place for this experiment, and provide a suitable alternative. That way you are spared the mess and the child goes on learning. But if you just get angry and say it is naughty, you are teaching it that learning about the world is a bad thing to do. A tiny child who learns that cannot be expected to do well in school, can it? At the same time children feel more secure and more loved if they have a framework of sensible rules and parents who won't let them do anything they like. Children even appreciate the rules which they kick against and protest at, as it lets them know where they stand. Some modern parents prefer to be a 'friend' to their child and avoid setting rules; this can be very cosy and is great for the parent's delusions of youth but it can leave a child confused. Children can find their own friends; finding parents is much harder.

Punishment or Reward?
Studies which have been done with animals show that all animals learn better when they are rewarded for doing the right thing than when punished for doing the wrong one. Human animals are no exception.

Many parents think of punishment as smacks and rewards as treats. In fact it is the parent's love, attention and approval which is the greatest reward a child can have, and the withdrawal of attention and approval is the greatest punishment.

Yet one of the greatest – and most natural – pitfalls of parenthood is to ignore a child who is quietly doing something good and give it attention the moment it is bad. Thus neatly teaching it that it gets the reward of your attention for bad behaviour, but not when it's good. It's wise to revise this. The other great reward is getting its own way. The key to stopping a child behaving badly is to make it very unsatisfying and unrewarding for the child. This takes almost superhuman strength, but it is possible. Just. Most of the time.

Every battle lost prolongs the war, so the sooner a child knows it can't get away with murder, the better life will be for all of you, however, a fine line must be drawn. Despite the fact that even a delinquent toddler can reduce an adult to a gibbering wreck, children don't feel powerful. A balance has to be struck: guidelines must be tight enough to maintain order and make a child secure but not so tight, and so inflexible, that the child feels it has no hand in its own destiny. Parents who say no and change it to yes when a child screams and frets are just letting it down, but ones who can *never* be persuaded to change no to yes when presented with a *reasonable* argument (as opposed to an aggressive one) just make a child feel helpless, and that can make it very hard for it to succeed at other things.

> No relative should ever withdraw love or threaten to withdraw love as a punishment. Nothing a child does deserves such cruelty.

- Have clear rules, but not too many of them.
- Try to notice when a child is behaving well and give it attention and praise (just saying it is good or clever, plus a smile, hug or kiss is often enough).
- If a child is naughty punish it immediately (delayed punishment confuses a young child as it can't work out what it is being punished for). Usually all you need do is say it is being naughty, get cross and then put a distance between you and it. If you are giving it attention, and it behaves badly, leave the room saying you don't like being with it when it behaves like that. If the child wasn't getting attention, give it even less by banishing it to its room, or putting it there. Ignore it for a while, then say it can only come out if it behaves. If it doesn't behave, put it straight back and ignore it for longer. If it comes out sooner and says it's sorry and shows it intends to be good, accept it.
- If a child is being bad and you tell it to stop and it doesn't, make a firm threat, such as 'If you do that again we will go home' (assuming it is enjoying being where it is). There is an age – usually between 2 and 4 years old – when children are determined to find out where the lines are drawn and have to test such situations. If you want peace from then on you *have* to do what you have said you will do (so if it misbehaves at the zoo, do avoid saying that if it does that again you will throw it to the lions). Carry out your threat even if it spoils the day for everyone (you should have thought of that before).
- Don't let yourself be worn down by repeated grizzling. If you've said it can't have a second ice cream, stick to it, or you will just train it to grizzle – which will be a rod for your own back. If it goes on, put space between you and the child – if it's safe to do so.
- Sometimes a child is just generally vile without doing anything you can easily punish, or you may be somewhere which means punishment can't be given – like out to tea with friends. In this case a severe telling-off once you get the child alone may be enough, but if the behaviour was bad enough to warrant actual punishment, stop the child having some treat – saying it is because he or she misbehaved badly. A very young child will need to miss the treat almost at once or it won't seem fair (no bedtime story, no ice cream for supper or whatever); a child of 8 plus can, if need be, understand a punishment several days later. So you can let the rest of the family stay up to watch a special programme but not the naughty one.

Obedience
You can use a child's imagination – which is very powerful – to foster obedience. One of the most useful tricks I ever learnt for bringing up very young children was counting to 5. You tell a child to do something and if it doesn't you say – in a voice which suggests trouble may be on the way – 'I'll give you until I count 5'. You then start counting slowly, out loud – rather as if pretending to be a giant. Most children will do nothing for 1, 2 and 3, so start moving towards them in a giant-like manner (it needs to be half in play, half serious). By 4 most children will rush in giggling alarm to do what they've been told to do. A child of spirit or at a very rebellious stage will stay put. Give it space to be defiant, by saying 'four and a quarter, four and a half, four and threequarters' in a voice which gets more and more mock threatening. Most children will comply *just* before 5. The great thing about the method is that it allows a rebellious

child to rebel harmlessly by not going until the last moment, and allows you to get obedience without anger or punishments. But children do grow out of it. If a child won't budge by 5, grab it and carry it off to do what it ought to, inflicting some harmless 'punishment' like tickling it or holding it upside down – and don't try it again, the child is too old for the method.

To Smack or Not to Smack

Smacking does great things for parents: it releases all the pent-up emotion that an exasperating child can rouse in the adult breast. Unfortunately it does very little for the child and can do real harm. It should be avoided if possible and kept to the very minimum if it can't be avoided. However, there may be a case for using it if your child does something very bad when it is impossible to use any other serious punishment. For example if it puts its life in danger by running across a road you might grab it and give one quick smack immediately, on its bottom, through clothes. The very fact that you *don't* normally smack your child will make it realize that this is something you feel very strongly about. You will also need to explain *why* you feel so strongly.

Divorce

Parents thinking of divorce sometimes wonder whether they should hang on until a child reaches a certain age before they break up the marriage. Children need both parents (or whoever else they have learned to love) at every age, so there is no good time for dividing a child from one of them. There may, however, be especially bad times. Some psychologists would say that one of these is in the pre-school period, between about 18 months and 5 years. This is because children have a self-centred view of the world and haven't yet realized that other people have their own lives which are quite unconnected to them (the child). As they think the whole world revolves around them they also tend to think they *cause* much of it to happen.

This means that if a parent leaves a child of this age it may believe that the parent has gone away because it is a bad or unlovable child. If a child gets this idea it can be a dreadful burden to it and lead to very severe depression and all sorts of behaviour problems. At this age telling it something different doesn't help much as it can't yet grasp the complexities of relationships and the feelings of early childhood bite deep, so even learning the truth later in life doesn't always lift the sense of unworthiness and guilt.

Effects of Not Seeing Parents

It is not unusual for lawyers and well-meaning friends to suggest that the parent with whom the children aren't living should make a 'clean break' and stop seeing the children. The idea is that this will allow them to make a new start with some step-parent and save pain on both sides.

There are some parents who are so violent or corrupt that their children may be harmed by them. But in normal circumstances all the evidence suggests that not seeing a parent is very bad for the children. If children learn that when they loved and trusted their father or mother, he or she was capable of deserting them *totally*, they are not going to find it easy to love and trust again. Indeed it could make it hard for them to trust a member of the opposite sex in marriage either.

However hard it may be for the adults, the children should see as much of the distant parent as possible and that parent should make it very clear that he or she still loves them and misses them, and takes a real interest in them. This shouldn't just be a matter of the statutory weekend outing but also of the occasional phone calls and doing things with the children which they specially enjoy – whether it's kicking a football with them or going to the seaside. It should also mean taking an interest in the things they do, and turning up to sports days and school plays. It doesn't mean giving the children expensive presents or letting them get away with murder so as to gain favour – which is trying to bribe and corrupt them and is quite unworthy of any decent parent.

If this is to work, the partner who is looking after the children needs to be very careful not to criticize the other parent to the children. This is a huge temptation, but one consolation is that if the other parent really is a ****** he or she will soon reveal it, and the children won't need any telling. And if he or she isn't as bad as you think, but just failed you, you will have avoided having your children think badly of you for slagging off someone they love. So you gain either way.

The National Children's Bureau (page 317) has a booklist on children and divorce, and it is important that parents try to see the break-up from a child's point of view as well as from their own.

> Just how important both parents are to a child was shown by a study done by psychologists in Cambridge in which they showed that children aged 5-9, whose fathers were simply away from home more than usual because of their work, were less obedient and more likely to be unpopular at school and to have temper tantrums.

Disabilities

Those who find that their child or baby has a mental or physical disability often feel terribly alone. But disabilities, of some kind, are sadly common and it can help greatly to get advice and information from those who understand the disability. There is a special organization for almost every problem and some of them have local groups through which parents can support and help each other. At the end of this chapter and on pages 590-592 I have given some of the major ones; the rest can be found in the directories I mention on page 341. Many have excellent books and leaflets.

Addresses and suggestions for further reading are at the ends of chapters.

The Law and Disabilities

In general the law which applies to the average citizen also applies to those with disabilities. But within many acts of Parliament there are special clauses relating to them – for example, clauses concerning their employment. **MENCAP** (page 320) publishes a complete list of relevant acts, grouped according to which aspect of life they affect.

When They Grow up

Though parents may want to care for their handicapped children for as long as possible, they have no legal obligation to house and care for any child after the age of 18. From then on the social services have a duty to provide accommodation and care. Many parents feel guilty about asking for this, which is a pity. Of course, those with disabilities should have every possible loving care: every human being has an equal right to live – as opposed to exist. But caring for a child with a severe disability can deprive the rest of the family of their rights to love and care, and make it impossible for the parents to have a marriage which offers any real fulfilment. So in every decision about care, it is not the disabled person's needs alone which have to be considered. For the sake of the rest of the family, there can sometimes be a strong argument for residential care. Moreover, adults with disabilities often want independence and adult relationships which they cannot have at home.

Leaving home may mean adults with mental handicaps are put in a mental handicap hospital. However, their needs are beginning to be understood and there are some excellent units with special housing, and even facilities for married couples. Meanwhile the gap is filled by voluntary organizations. Organizations for physical disabilities often run training courses, or can advise on where to find them. Others, like the **Camphill Village Trust**, run communities and training centres for those with mental handicaps. And MENCAP, for example, runs family-sized homes for the mentally handicapped. It also manages inherited money for them, and parents can contribute a specific sum to MENCAP which will ensure that, after their death, their handicapped child will be regularly visited by a voluntary helper who will take a personal interest in his or her welfare.

Helping at Home

There are all kinds of practical reasons why children should help in the home but the most important one is probably that they need to learn the trade-off between rights and responsibilities. As they get older they gain more freedoms and privileges; helping is the flip side.

The best time to teach children to help in the home is when they are under 5. At that age everything is a game and an achievement. A child will *love* making wet patterns on a kitchen floor with a mop and will easily learn how to do it quite thoroughly, or be fascinated watching the bubbles go down the basin after helping you clean it out. And a simple skill like brushing dust into a dustpan properly helps it to co-ordinate. Skills learnt at this age will stay for life – even if they lie dormant a while.

> DANGEROUS CLEANING FLUIDS SHOULD NOT BE USED WHILE YOUNG CHILDREN ARE HELPING. If they see you using them they may, one day, try to use them alone.

As a child gets older it can begin to take responsibility for certain jobs. For example, a 4-year-old can easily lay the table for tea. By starting with a job like this, the consequence of not doing it follows naturally without nagging or punishment: until the table is laid the child can't have tea. Extra jobs can be added as a child gets older and they should – as far as possible – be linked to the child's needs, for example:

- from 5 a child can feed its own pet – if reminded – unless it's a horse
- from 6 a child can make a bed with a duvet
- from 7 a child can put its dirty clothes in a laundry box, put away clean clothes and clean its shoes
- an 8-year-old can easily make a proper bed
- a 9-year-old can dust and vacuum its own room at least once a week
- a 10-year-old can help dry up
- a 12-year-old – of either sex – can sew on its own buttons
- a 12-year-old can hand wash its own smalls or special jumpers
- a 13-year-old can do most basic mending, if taught
- a 14-year-old – of either sex – can iron some of its own clothes. Unless it genuinely has something important to do – like work, not play – any child over 10 can also help clean up and wash up any meal it eats.

I don't suggest that children should come home from a long day in school and wade through homework only to be faced with a heap of washing and ironing. But they should learn to do the small quick jobs themselves and not expect a hard-pressed parent to do them, and during the holidays they can easily do rather more, though grade the amount of work to the age.

Of course, children will try to foist the whole lot on to their parents – especially in adolescence. But the secret of getting kids to help is never to do the jobs they leave undone. If you have said 3 teenagers should clear Sunday lunch and wash up and find they don't do it, make it clear that no other meals will be served until they do clear it. If they should have ironed something and didn't, let it stay unironed. Sooner or later they will need that garment to go out in. They may decide to go out in it unironed, and you will wince at what people will think. Just grit your teeth, sooner or later your scruffy son in the shaming unironed shirt will meet a girl he wants to impress and ironing skills will suddenly emerge.

To some people all this will seem old-fashioned, but it has benefits for the child as much as the parent. Children who clean their own rooms have more privacy than those who don't and when they leave their home they have at their fingertips all the skills they need to look after themselves. This is no small advantage. However, it does assume that the parents are hard working too. You can scarcely expect a child to do its own cleaning while its parents lead the life of Riley.

Children and Safety – see page 186

Putting Toys Away

Putting toys away is the first job children do. It can be one of the games you play with a child – while they are very young putting bricks into a bag is as much fun as taking them out. Of course, parents have to do the lion's share in the early years, but if children always help tidy up, protests are far less likely. And when a child fails to put away something *it was well able to*, just remove it from the toy stock. When the child next wants it you say it can't have it because it didn't put it away. The child will be very cross and you can then say it can have it to play with if it puts it away this time. If the child agrees, it gets it. It then needs to be reminded to put it away and if it fails a second time it should be without it for several days and be told why. But do be reasonable in *how* you expect things to be put away. Demands for excessive order can be counter-productive.

★ Children seldom do one jigsaw at a time. To make putting away easy, allot a different letter of the alphabet to each puzzle and put it on the back of every single piece, plus the number of pieces in a puzzle – so if puzzle A has 36 pieces A36 is written on every piece. Then you just count all the As into the same bag.

★ Most jigsaw puzzle boxes break – keep puzzles in the plastic nets fruit is sold in.

★ Make it easy for children to put toys away: have big containers to put things in. Plastic bowls and baskets can stack in a corner, big 'shoe' bags will hang from hooks under a bookshelf, plastic sweet jars can stand on the floor or have their lids screwed to the underside of a shelf.

Illness

A child can become ill either for physical reasons or for mental ones and if worried or upset may very easily make itself vomit: I was so miserable at boarding school that I often used to throw up on the last day of the holidays. I wasn't putting it on; my body was simply reacting to my desire to stay at home. Lots of children do that.

When a child becomes ill for mental reasons, what it needs most is love and attention, so this is no time for brushing it off with a few brisk words about it being all in the mind. At the same time it is not a good idea for a child to learn that it can evade life for very long by being ill. So the best approach is to give plenty of love and attention while making it clear that there is a definite limit to how long it can last.

When a child is ill with some infection it is likely to be bored, fretful and return to more babyish ways and need more 'mothering' than it does usually. You can more or less judge how fast a child is recovering by how good it is. A very sick child is usually very good, and the better it gets the more restive it becomes. When it ceases to be listless give it plenty of things to do. Televisions, radios and tape recorders can be a boon but don't forget some old-fashioned play things too. There is nothing quite like a stiff dough of 2 parts flour to 1 part salt and a little water, which a child can pinch and punch and generally vent its frustration upon.

Illness in Hospital

Illness is stressful for everyone, and for a young child hospital doubles the distress. It is taken into a strange place, and surrounded by people it doesn't know, who wear peculiar clothes and do things which are often unpleasant and sometimes painful. What's more a child under 5 has no real concept of time and, if its mother leaves, it may feel deserted for ever. The distress this can cause should not be underestimated. Children should only be admitted to hospital if they cannot be properly nursed at home, and in hospital they need a parent with them as much as possible.

Since 1961 Action for Sick Children (page 316), which I helped to found, has, with the aid of enlightened members of the medical profession, campaigned for parents to be allowed to stay all day and all night with children. This is now official NHS policy, and parents have a right to ask for this, and to use every persuasion to obtain it. It is also important that children are nursed in children's wards, not with adults, and that they have an opportunity to play. That said, parents have a duty to help, not hinder, the staff.

If hospital staff don't understand children's emotional needs they may say that parents should not visit as 'it upsets the child'. This is frankly poppycock. Children don't cry because their parents *come* but because they *go*. And it's a strong argument for them staying all the time, not for their staying away. But if they do have to go – and those with several children may have to – then at least the child knows that they cared enough to come and has been able to express its sense of loss by crying when they leave. This is far better for a child than sitting alone feeling deserted and rejected with no outlet for this sense of loss. Evidence shows that the unvisited young child, who gives no trouble and stays dry-eyed, takes longer to recover from illness, is often deeply depressed and has severe behaviour problems on leaving hospital. Whereas those who have their parents with them recover quickly and have few problems afterwards.

If parents cannot stay with a young child in hospital they should not be surprised if it is difficult for a while when it returns home. Some children cling, or wet their bed, or suck their thumb, as they did in babyhood. Others appear to be saying 'you rejected me and now I'm going to reject you' and go for aggression and disobedience. This calls for a delicate balance between rejecting it still further, and letting it get away with too much. Give it lots of love and attention, plus harmless things to get aggressive with – hammering toys, drums, finger paints – and a chance to talk about being in hospital and say it was cross and hurt. And, when you feel exasperated, think how you might feel towards your husband if he walked out on you – the child is feeling much the same.

There are enormous problems for parents who have several children if one of them is in hospital, and it can be very difficult for a mother to know where to give her time. She should talk to the doctors about this. Some hospitals have play groups which the other children might be able to attend while she was visiting the sick child. She may also be able to leave tape recordings of bedtime stories, so even when she has to leave, the sick child doesn't feel totally deserted.

Sex and Children

It might be convenient if children were, as the Victorians believed them to be, innocent about sex until adolescence stirred. They aren't. A child's body is its first plaything and it will naturally explore its whole body, not leave patches untouched. If you see your child 'playing with itself' don't be shocked or cross. It is totally normal, and does no harm, and you should not make it feel that there is something bad about touching those parts of itself. The Almighty didn't make dirty bits and to suggest to a child that some parts of its body are worse than others may make it harder for it to be a responsive sexual partner when adult. But a child does have to learn that there are some things it doesn't do *in public*; picking its nose and handling its private parts are two of them and they should both be treated in the same, matter-of-fact, way.

Exploring other Children

Children are curious about everything and other children's anatomy is no exception. It is a good idea to explain to a toddler that boys and girls are made differently, as soon as it has had any chance to see the opposite sex. Some children who aren't told get quite worried and think a girl has had a penis chopped off (and worry about losing theirs) and a little girl I knew scratched herself raw trying to find one, believing it was hiding. Children can be told that little girls have a secret place in their tummies, like their mother has, which means they will be able to carry a baby in there. Then they know that each sex has something special. The more matter of fact a parent can be about such things, the less likely a child is to spend much time taking down the knickers of other children, but the more secretive or shocked you are, the more it will be fascinated and curious. Most children do go through a brief phase of this but calling them to food will usually distract them from the game.

The Facts of Life

The time to tell children the facts of life is when they ask, and this is not a question to brush aside. If you ask them question to find out what they want to know and tell them simply and honestly, it is very easy to explain. Don't worry about them being too young; they will forget anything they can't understand, and ask more questions as they get older. But if they haven't asked by 6 or 7 it is time to manoeuvre an opportunity. You could, for example, ask if they have ever wondered how they were made, and whether they would like to know. If you don't tell them they will be told in the playground and it is much better for them to get the basics from you, not learn a lot of nonsense. The very young child only needs the basic anatomical facts but, even at this age, it can be put in the context of love and caring. Then as they get older they can be told a little more, to suit their curiosity and age and parents can talk about the morality of sexual behaviour and about contraception. A child should have clear guidelines as to what is, and is not, acceptable behaviour long before it will be tempted to experiment sexually – by 12 in many children. And girls should know about periods before they happen – which can be as young as 10 years old (see also below).

Homosexuality

Adolescents usually get crushes on members of their own sex. Whether it's a teacher a pop star or a sports star this is very normal and should be accepted without comment or teasing. It is also quite normal for a child to get emotionally attached to a friend of their own sex. In some children this remains an unfulfilled love which never has any physical expression beyond holding hands; in others there may be a certain amount of homosexual activity. This can be very hard for parents to take and the big worry is that the child is going to be homosexual for life. And even a deeply liberal parent may worry about AIDS or regret the possible loss of grandchildren which that would entail.

However, loving one's own sex is a normal stage in adolescence, which affects most children. Even if a child has indulged in full homosexual behaviour it does not mean that he or she is 'a homosexual' and the child should *not* identify itself as one. In some people attraction to the opposite sex doesn't develop until the 20s, so even if homosexual behaviour extends into the student years the die is not cast. But it would be wise to talk seriously to a boy about the risks of AIDS. It can be pointed out that as heterosexual love can include saying 'no', homosexual love can too.

The big danger comes if parents accuse a child of being a homosexual, or it feels ashamed and cut off from friends who are less drawn to their own sex. This can mean that he or she feels cut off from the opposite sex and it may then be impossible to build that type of relationship, if and when it is wanted. If a child never grows out of loving his or her own sex the parents have no choice but to go on loving the child and to accept its sexual choice, however hard this may be.

Sexual Abuse of Children

The sexual abuse of a child is any sexual activity which abuses the trust a child places in adults. It is not only *what* is done but the *spirit* in which it is done which matters.

Since the huge publicity about fathers abusing their children, some parents have become nervous about perfectly normal activities like fathers bathing their daughters or romping around tickling them, or about kissing and hugging. These are an important part of showing love and there is no need to worry. But if, while playing quite normally with children, a parent or *any* adult finds that they (the adult) are getting any kind of sexual stimulation out of it *that is the moment to stop*. Those games should *not* be repeated and nor should any others which have a similar effect.

It is all too easy to move from the seemingly innocent to the not so innocent. What's more, children are very quick to sense an adult's mood. We all know that even a very young child knows a loving hug from a phoney hug, and it is just as quick to spot the sexual hug and feel alarmed by it. It may not be able to say *what* is wrong but it will know that *something* is. And it will know this long before an adult has behaved in a way which is actually assault – and be upset.

How Do You Tell if a Child is Being Abused?

If a child is sexually abused it is likely to show in its behaviour. It may not be easy to pin down the difference between a child who is disturbed because of sexual abuse and one who is upset in some other way, but these are some of the signs to look for.

The abuse will probably be a terrible secret which it can tell nobody. Carrying such a secret can be a barrier to friendships and to reasonable responses to adults (it, quite rightly, thinks adults don't understand how it feels, and loses trust and respect for them). So it may seem in some way cut off from all those around it.

It may behave in sexual ways which are quite odd for its age – either directly or in play with dolls, or in what it draws – or may masturbate openly, or be sexually aggressive.

There may be almost any kind of behaviour problem: bedwetting, nightmares, loss of appetite, unexplained pains, depression or learning problems – though all these could have other causes.

A child may be 'good' but seem watchful and uneasy in the presence of a particular adult, or of adults in general, when it wasn't like that before.

Preventing Sexual Abuse

It is important for parents to trust a child's dislikes. If a child says he or she doesn't like some adult babysitting, or putting them to bed or bathing them, the child may have a very good reason which it simply can't explain. If a child *is* just fussing it does no harm to indulge them. If it has sensed something is amiss, distress has been avoided. That doesn't, of course, mean that any adult a child takes a dislike to should be suspected of sexual abuse – he or she may just have cold hands or bad breath.

There are now campaigns which help to train children not to talk to strangers and to say no to those who tell them lies about taking them to Mummy. However, the sad truth is that children are far more at risk from someone they know than from strangers. It may be the milkman, the postman, a lodger or one of their own family. And it isn't restricted to those who lack the education or intelligence to understand the damage they may be doing. But you can make them less likely to suffer an attack.

- Tell them they must never go off with any stranger and arrange a code word with them, so that if you are

ever unable to fetch them the person you send will say that special word. It needs to be one they won't forget – like the name of their favourite doll – and only you and the child should know the code.
- Don't let young children be out by themselves.
- Don't let young children use public lavatories alone.
- Don't let anyone babysit or take care of a child without checking them out carefully.
- If children are old enough to come home alone from school or to go to the shops alone, arrange a safe route and explain why it is important to stick to it.
- Tell children that if *any* adult hurts them or tries to do anything which they dislike or find frightening, they should forget normal rules and scream, bite, scratch and defend themselves in every way possible.

You can do all this without talking about sex or alarming a child. All it needs to know is that some adults get bad feelings which make them hurt children, even though they are kind at other times, and that children have a right to defend themselves, *whatever the adult says*. Kidscape advises on this.

Traditional stories can be a help. It was my own daughter who pointed out to me that Little Red Riding Hood was a marvellous story for teaching a child that people aren't always quite what they seem and that if any kind and familiar person suddenly begins to behave in big, bad ways, which are not like their normal selves, a child should keep very calm and be very sensible and get away fast to its mother. The great thing about using a story like this is that it allows you to distinguish between the kind normal person who is usually in evidence, and the bad one who emerges when the adult gets in the grip of a perverted sexual drive.

What to Do if a Child Talks About It

It is seldom easy for a child to talk about anything which is deeply upsetting and, if a child even begins to say something which suggests it has had a bad experience – of any kind – the most important thing an adult can do is simply *listen*. It needs to feel that it has the adult's attention and that *nothing* will interrupt. If its first attempts to talk are brushed aside because you need to make a meal, watch TV, or leave the house, it may not get up the courage to speak again. If necessary miss the train to work, and burn the dinner.

Whatever the child tells you, keep calm and let it feel you can cope and will support it. Children very seldom lie about these things, so *believe it* and gently encourage it to tell you more. A child who has been abused may well feel very guilty and needs to be reassured that it is not to blame for what has happened. It will also need to get the burden off its chest, so don't say anything which suggests it should not talk about what has happened. Sometimes the incident may be distressing but relatively minor, but if something illegal has happened you should ring one of the organizations given on pages 318-319 and discuss the best course to follow.

The important thing is to protect the child and prevent it ever happening again but, however horrifying the

Addresses and suggestions for further reading are at the ends of chapters.

situation may be, don't forget that a child is quite capable of divided feelings. It may love a particular adult when that adult is being normal and be terrified and repulsed by them when sex overwhelms them. What the child may want, therefore is to get rid of the 'bad' part of the adult but keep the 'good' part. So getting a close relative, especially a father, sent to prison may not always be in the best interests of the child, and may leave it with a burden of guilt which it will find hard to handle. In a situation like this the child's needs must come first and it should not be separated from a non-molesting parent. The **National Children's Homes** (page 319) runs treatment centres, around Britain, at which abused children and their families can receive counselling. You can ask your GP or Social Services to try to get a child this outpatient counselling On pages 318-319 you will find other organizations which help abused children, parents and adult survivors.

Remembering Abuse Years Later
None of us remembers every hour of our life. And the brain is especially good at half forgetting painful experiences. The desperate grief at lost love or the death of a loved one also fade from memory eventually – even though it seems unthinkable at the time. This forgetting is the brain's way of keeping us sane. For fully to remember every grief, every pain, we experience would surely drive us mad. The brain can go farther, totally blocking experiences too terrifying to handle. People may forget, for example, the moments immediately before a horrific car crash.

A young child's smallness in comparison with an adult makes even a relatively mild sexual assault terrifying. So such an event may be blocked from conscious memory for years, only to suddenly flood back in adulthood, when something associated with the event triggers recall. However, both the victim and his or her family may want to believe the memory is false. This is natural: nobody likes taking skeletons out of cupboards. But if such memories surface, complete with the feelings from that time, they have as much right to be believed as any other long-forgotten memory which surfaces. To suggest that someone has invented a memory, simply because they did not – consciously – have it yesterday, risks making them a victim a second time and can prevent vital healing.

Sleep

The Sleep a Child Needs
There is no set amount of sleep a child must have at a certain age, but most tiny babies sleep most of the time. Then the morning and afternoon periods shorten little by little, and after a while the morning sleep can be dropped.

How early children should go to bed is a tricky issue. Children need quite a lot of sleep if they aren't to be irritable and difficult – and parents need a decent break in the evenings if they aren't to be the same.

Television and working mothers have pushed back the hours and people now spend more time enjoying their children than they used to.

But you can have enough of even a very good thing and parents with a sense of self-preservation set bedtimes so that they get enough time to rest and enjoy each other. You can put tinies to bed at 6 to 6.30 and have any child under 10 in bed by 8 at the latest with a clear conscience – if it suits your family. If you stagger the bedtimes, letting them go to bed 15 minutes later each birthday, you have a structure which will allow you to give each child some undivided attention at bedtime. If children are difficult, lack of sleep may well be the cause, so try putting them to bed earlier.

Some experts say that for children to feel secure and sleep well they need to sleep in only one place. For some children this may be true, but it is convenient if children grow up knowing that they can sleep safely anywhere. Until they were well into primary school I used to take mine out with me, and they would sleep on any spare bed anywhere and stay nine-tenths asleep when I carried them in their sleeping bags to the car and back into their own beds. Most children will adapt to almost anything if you start it young enough.

Getting Children to Bed
If children are told to stop playing a good game or watching the television in order to go to bed you make bed the thing which takes them away from the fun. (The same happens if bed is used as a punishment.) If children are enjoying themselves, make them stop a little before bed and tidy up. Then bedtime is the nice time they escape to from boring tidying.

If a tiny child refuses to go up to bed, turn off the lights in all the other rooms, but leave a light on in its room. Children, like moths, head for the light. (But don't do this unless it's safe.)

Helping Babies and Children Sleep
There are many ways you can stack the odds in favour of a child going to bed when you want it to and either sleeping or staying quiet. There will be times when some – or even all – of them won't work. But they are always a step in the right direction and the secret is to find a method and stick to it.

> To reduce the risk of cot death very young babies should lie on their back or side to sleep. But not always on the same side. Also they should not be too hot. About 18°C (65°F) with light clothes under cosy bedding is recommended.

★ 2-3 is the worst age for sleep problems – try to survive until a child is 4 or more.

A baby or toddler can sleep anywhere and it maybe less stressful to have a baby asleep in a crib under the table or beside your bed, than screaming in its own room. Some babies seem to need to be slowly weaned from constant human company (which they had in the womb) just as they need to be slowly weaned from the breast or

bottle, in which case gradually have it sleep a little farther from you as the weeks and months pass.

- Small babies often sleep better to gentle sounds. Research suggests that the tapes of human heartbeat
help; so does quiet gentle music of almost any kind.
- Babies may sleep better if quite firmly wrapped in a
shawl.
- Small babies will fall asleep when rocked.
- If you find a baby is having trouble getting to sleep
in the evening, wake it earlier from the afternoon
sleep. (However, it is very restful for mothers if some
afternoon nap is kept up for a good number of years.
If the routine is never broken a child will sleep or play
quietly for an hour each day, giving its mother a much
needed break. A child who rests in the afternoon is
usually calmer and easier to get to bed in the evening
too.)
- Be reasonable, don't expect a child to lie quietly with
nothing to do. Give babies interesting (and safe) dangles above their heads so they can pat them and make
them move, but nothing which it can throw out of the
cot or it may scream until you pick the missing object
up. Give toddlers safe and comforting toys in their
bed, and let older children have things they can safely
and quietly play with in their room.

That said, everything a parent does has to be suited to
the age and development of the child. A baby who cries
for food is doing what it has to do and should not be left
to cry, nor should any tiny baby be left to cry even if there
is no obvious reason for the crying (page 275). Equally
a slightly older child may be genuinely frightened or wake
from a nightmare and need swift attention and a good
deal of comforting. So may a sick child or a child when
there has been some sadness or upheaval in the family.

If a child hears you going to a new baby in the night it
may – quite reasonably – fear that you love the baby
most and need to be given extra love and reassurance.

There is a world of difference between these reasons
and the crying of a child who wants attention and holds
a family to ransom with its screams. If you stop to think
you will know whether your child really needs your love
and attention or is being a tyrant. It is the child who is
just trying it on who must not be rewarded. But if you
expect the child to control itself, you need self-control
too. You can't get a child up from its bed to play because
you came home late, or allow it down so you can show
it off to visitors, and then expect it to sleep the next night
when you want it to.

- At any age a child sleeps best in the dark (unless it
wants a little light), in a bed which is warm (a hot
water bottle sees to this but only use water at bath-
water temperature, from the tap – a bottle filled from
a boiling kettle can burst and scald a child).
- If you find a child gets your attention by climbing (or
falling) out of a cot, put the mattress in a play pen and
put it to sleep there. Then it can't hurt itself and has
more room to play.
- Make bedtime a cosy, comforting ritual in which the
child calms down and gets more attention than usual.

Bath and play with it, put it to bed and read it a story
or sing it nursery rhymes. (Children are often soothed
to sleep by having their forehead stroked or their face
or head very lightly tickled.)
- If a child cries go to it at once and and find out what
is the matter and try to sort it out with the child in its
bed (not picked up – unless it clearly needs comforting) – or at least in its room. Bringing the child to join
the rest of the household is a reward to avoid if you
can.
- Some children sleep best with a nightlight and many
need the door ajar so they don't feel alone. There is
no need to be quiet: normal noise makes a child feel
safe.

One school of thought says that if a child wakes at night
a loving parent will sacrifice his or her sleep to care for
it and if this means you are dropping with exhaustion
that is the price of parenthood. Others – of whom I'm
one – say that the most important thing a parent can do
for its child is survive with reasonable sanity. Excessive
loss of sleep, combined with a tired and naughty child,
can drive the gentlest to the brink of child battering.

There is good evidence that most children wake from
time to time at night. Some wake and go quietly to sleep
again, others wake and cause mayhem. I believe that
many of the latter do so because they have learnt that
bad behaviour brings rewards. Suppose you woke in the
night and experimentally started yelling, and people
you loved rushed in with glasses of wine and plates of
food and hugged and kissed you or got you up and took
you to a party. Might you not be tempted to do it again
next time you woke?

> Very restless handicapped children may need a
> sedative to sleep, but it is not wise to give any
> child a sedative without consulting a doctor.

If a child wakes and cries at night, most psychologists
say *don't* take it into your bed. A parent's bed is quite
the nicest place for a child to be so if you do that you
have given it the best possible *reward* for crying – it can
cause awful problems. Children in bed have been known
to wreck their parents' sex life, and a single mother is
setting the scene for bitter rivalry between the child and
any man she ever shares a bed with. This does not, of
course, mean that it *always* causes problems or that
a child can't have a cuddle in bed sometimes. And
sometimes a child will go to sleep happily alone in its
parent's bed and can be carried to its own bed when they
turn in.

When a child reaches the age when it comes down for
drinks it may be genuinely thirsty. Let the child have an
unrewarding drink – plain room temperature water and
if it's hungry give it a plain slice of brown bread – no
butter, no jam, no nothing. If it protests, say it can't have
anything else as it would be bad for its teeth – which is
perfectly true. Then take the child *straight* back in bed.
The next night put a mug of water and some bread in its

room. You may then find it will call or come down on a new pretext. Then you know it is attention seeking. If it has a good reason for needing more attention, give it. If it doesn't, explain that enough is enough.

> There are hyperactive children who seem to need so much activity that they simply can't handle being alone, and they may also be crying babies in the first 4 months. Part of the trouble seems to be that in the first year or two of childhood their desire to *do* things far exceeds their ability to play constructively. My first child was like that and I know how hard it is to handle. There is no choice but to give such children attention until they reach the age when they can occupy themselves. Often they are very intelligent and, with a bit of encouragement, can learn to read at a remarkably early age and then spend hours with books. Meanwhile I suggest you cling onto the thought that Mrs Mozart had a tough time too: you could have a genius on your hands.

Once you know a toddler is just trying it on, firmness is the only answer. Make sure it has plenty to play with safely in its room. Then put it firmly back and tell the child it *must* stay there but can sit and play quietly on its bed if it isn't sleepy. This is when a battle of wills starts. If it tries to leave its room, pick it up and put it into bed that *instant* (don't tell it to go – carry it). If it screams or throws a tantrum, tell it very firmly to stop – then leave. Let it cry for several minutes – by the clock – then go in and coolly calm it down. If necessary pick it up for long enough for the tears to ebb, then put it to bed saying it is being very silly and that it doesn't matter how much it cries, it must still stay in its room. Then put it in bed and leave. If it cries again repeat the treatment, leaving it to cry for rather longer each time. Sooner or later the child will realize that if it cries nothing nice happens – and peace will reign, provided you never waver. But you *must* pretend to be *very* cool and calm during all this. The message the child has to get is that you are a rock. You love it and can be counted on to be there if it is genuinely upset, but if it is trying to push you around you can't be moved. (See Discipline.) This method can be used for children who won't settle at night, for those who wake during the night and for those who insist that if they wake early the rest of the house must too. But it is only for the child who *wants* attention, not for the one who *needs* it.

Step-Parenting

One of the great, hoped for, consequences of divorce is a second marriage. But unless you divorce in the first dew of youth you are likely to find that almost all your potential partners are divorced too – so a posse of children may be part of the package. There has been a tendency to think that, provided neither side takes exception to the other, step-parenting is much like any other kind of parenting. The experience of more and more couples shows this simply isn't so; in fact, in the words of one experienced counsellor to step-parents, 'the emotional minefield is quite terrifying'. Some people say that is why one in every two second marriages breaks up, and it can certainly be a contributory factor.

- The step-parent may have to handle huge pressures from ex-husbands and ex-wives – this can happen even if the step-parent played no part in the break-up, and is even more likely if they *were* the cause. It is a very restrained ex-partner who manages to never say a word against someone they feel is the cuckoo in the nest.
- The step-parent who has his or her own children has to struggle to treat both step and natural children equally, *and* not let any joint new arrival be unduly favoured as the non-problematic child of the family.
- The step-parent who has no children can easily feel that the stroppiness which afflicts most adolescents is hostility towards him or her as step-parent. They then meet imagined hostility with actual hostility and before they know what's happening it's practically pistols at dawn.
- Most girls instinctively flirt outrageously with their fathers, and have another phase of playing up to them sexually in adolescence. The child is just practising for adulthood, just as it practising bouncing a ball, and means nothing by it but it can sorely try the patience of a mother (and tempt some blood fathers). When the 'father' has only been acquired by marriage, the situation is potential dynamite. It takes a lot of maturity for the adults to defuse it.
- When children are being brought up by two sets of parents, there are bound to be conflicts of standards, to which there are no easy answers.
- A couple may have conflicting expectations of their roles. For example, a mother who has been worn down by trying to discipline sons of her own, may suddenly expect her new husband to lay down the law. While he, not yet having gained their affections, may – quite reasonably – be wanting to tread a little gently for a while. She feels unsupported (and lacks one of the key things she looked for in marriage), he feels bullied when she nags him about it and suddenly romance seems out of the window and the children seem to have pushed it out. So both parents are fed up with them. The children then feel that the marriage has made their parent less loving and then they *really* start to raise mayhem.
- Step-parents often feel they ought to love their step-children. It would, of course, be lovely if this emotion could flow sweetly over them with the confetti. It doesn't. Nor is there any reason why it should. Actively disliking a prospective partner's children has always seemed to me a good reason for not marrying a man, or woman. But to expect more than a glow of goodwill in the early stages is not common sense. With gentleness, honesty and goodwill, love will have a chance of growing, but those who feel they have to fake love, or expect to *be loved* immediately,

may make the real thing impossible. Children detect the phoney and they don't trust it.

Being a Step-Child

About a million British children have step-parents and it's every bit as hard for them as for their parents – and probably harder. The adults have at least chosen the situation, the children have had it thrust upon them. Even if they have managed to go through infancy without hearing a single story about a wicked step-mother, the idea of being landed with a new relative isn't necessarily pleasant. Why should a child even like, let alone love, someone just because one of their parents does?

Nor does liking the step-parent always smooth the path. Relationships are complicated and children often look for people to blame when things go wrong in their lives. If they blame their mother for the fact that their father left (and they may well do so, whether she was much to blame or not) they may well find it much easier to take their anger out on her new partner (whom they aren't afraid of losing) than on her. So behaviour may not be what it seems.

All children go through periods of depression and misery in adolescence – it's the hormones moaning – and they usually think their family are being lousy to them. A child with a step-family isn't necessarily any more miserable than any other, but he or she has to hand a ready-made fantasy that everything would be different if only their real mother or father was there. And in a job lot comes resentment against the step-parent who is wrongly seen as being the cause of their adolescent dumps. Then the step-parent, who may be doing his or her very best to be tolerant of a less than easy child, feels wrongly disliked and a vicious circle of genuine resentment is started.

All that is before you even consider what the arrival of a new baby may mean to the other children in the family. For children aren't slow to realize that a child which belongs to both parents may have an edge in the popularity stakes. The trouble is that mother nature got it wrong when she programmed children's behaviour. When a child feels unsure that it is loved you might expect it to behave in ways which are extra lovable – like a cat does. Instead it is usually naughtier, noisier, and less appreciative and affectionate. It may also wet its bed, and even steal. Understandably, parents and step-parents may react to the bad behaviour rather than to what is causing it and so the child feels even less loved.

The Solutions

The examples I have given are only a random selection of the friction points which can arise in step-families. Every family is different but there is one thing families with problems all share: you can't solve them unless you are prepared to remove the layers of misunderstanding by talking about them. It isn't always easy to start doing this within the family itself. So some people may find it is easiest to talk to a counsellor at the **National Stepfamily Association** (page 318). This organization for step-parents offers confidential telephone counselling and other help. There are also some useful books on the topic.

Toilet Training

It used to be thought that you could train a child to be clean and dry well before it was 18 months old. Science has shown that what really happened was the *child* trained the *mother* to put it on the pot at the times when it was most likely to perform anyway – such as just after a meal. But believe me, it isn't worth making the big issue of toilet training which used to be fashionable, all it does is make work for the mother and upset the child.

The truth is that no child begins to have control if its bowel and bladder until it is at least 18 months old and the sensation of being about to go, and the act of going, don't get clearly linked in a child's mind until around 2 years old. By all means pop a baby on the pot after meals if you want to avoid the occasional dirty nappy, but don't leave it there for long and don't expect it to become the slightest bit trained. The easy way to start bowel training is just to put a child on the pot for a minute or two – not longer – after every meal from the age of 18 months or 2 years old. Don't tell it what to do, just let it sit a little while. Usually nothing will happen. No matter, it has got used to the pot – so far so good. But one day, on the laws of chance its bowels will move as it sits there. This is the moment to make the child feel it is the cat's pyjamas. Praise it warmly and say it is a big boy like daddy or a big girl like mummy and give it a big kiss. There's nothing a child likes as much as pleasing.

Don't expect it to repeat the miracle, but try to notice how long after a meal it usually 'goes' and time the pot sitting to around that time, giving more praise each time. Once the idea is established you can suggest a child tells you when it wants to go – and praise its success.

Staying dry comes harder and later because the sensation isn't so strong. Start training when your child can stay dry for a couple of hours during the day and obviously knows when he or she is going. That may be any time between 2 and 3 years old.

If you leave rubber pants off, a child may well be more likely to notice wetness – especially if you open a door or window and let in a gust of cold air. If it remarks on being wet, change it and tell it how you are making it comfy in a 'nice dry nappy or pants' – but *don't* reverse this and say wet or dirty nappies are bad. Comfort is the issue, not virtue or cleanliness. Once a child dislikes being wet you can offer it a pot as a way of solving the problem. If a child does manage to tell you it wants to go, it will only know at the very last minute. Act swiftly, but if it sits down too late don't be cross, *sympathize* and say it will work better next time. You, the pot and the child all need to be on the same side. It's not a question of you imposing cleanliness on an unwilling child, but if a child does go in the pot praise it warmly.

★ Don't expect a child to be dry or clean at night until it is well established by day.

★ Never get cross with a toddler for accidentally failing to get to a pot in time. Even once it is trained it can easily be so absorbed in what it is doing that it simply doesn't notice it needs to go. Clearing up after it may be a darned nuisance but it wasn't naughty.

★ Don't worry about the age at which a child is trained, choose a time when the child is ready and it suits you. If it's a bother to get it out of thick winter clothes, wait until early summer and train it when it can be out of doors in pants without plastic.

★ Don't let speed of potty training become a race between you and the next mother. However much others boast, they are only showing that they care more about using a child to boost their own ego than about letting it mature in its own time – and *that* isn't much of an achievement.

★ If a child seems frightened of a pot and doesn't want to sit on it, sit on it yourself (fully dressed) to do something nice like read a story or play with the child. Once you've done this a few times, sit on the floor to read the story with the pot beside you and suggest it as a good seat for the child to get close. Once it's used to sitting on it fully dressed, go on from there.

★ Don't be surprised if a child who is ill or upset wets or dirties its pants or its bed. We all know that in the heat of battle grown men can lose control – why should we expect more of a toddler when it finds life hard? Put a rubber sheet on any bed a child occupies until it is well past the years of risk. Long after they stop wetting they smuggle drinks to bed and spill them, so it's all to the good.

Bed Wetting

Any child may wet its bed occasionally until about 6 years old. It may dream it is on the lavatory and go in good faith, or it may have had too much to drink before bed and been too heavily asleep to wake. But a child who is never dry at night, even by late toddlerdom, may need help. Talk to your doctor or contact the Enuresis Resource and Information Centre.

There are also children who become dry and then suddenly start bed wetting and keep doing it night in, night out. It creates a mountain of washing which can be very hard to tolerate and may go on for years. There is a wide gulf between doctors and psychologists as to why this type of bed wetting happens. The truth is nobody really knows. However, it often follows a deeply upsetting experience – such as someone in the family dying, or the parents divorcing – and psychologists say it is a substitute for weeping. Such children need counselling or therapy. Failing that there is only one certain cure: time. The time may seem endless, but no bed wetter ever reached 21 still wetting the bed. It has to stop. Meanwhile the child needs to feel well loved and supported.

★ Don't worry about the child lying in the urine. It isn't pleasant, but if you go in and change the sheets when you go to bed you make twice as much washing and double the chances that you will feel overwhelmed and angry. It is far more important for you to keep calm than for the child to keep dry.

EDUCATION AND HOME

Child Care while Mothers are Away or Working

The 1989 Children Act put an obligation on local authorities to inspect, as well as register, play groups and day-care centres for the under-5s and in the long run these may become more evenly spread and better organized. Meanwhile, the desperate shortage of such child-care facilities makes it very hard for mothers, and single fathers, who go out to work. **The Day Care Trust, Working for Childcare** and the **Working Mothers Association** (page 319) are campaigning to change this. These organizations try to help mothers cope with the practical problems they face when working and bringing up a family while unable to pay an au pair or other help (see page 214).

Childminding

More children go to childminders than to any other form of care while parents are at work. Children over 5 can be looked after by anyone the parent chooses, but, by law, anyone who looks after a child under 5 in their own home (as opposed to the child's home), for cash or kind, must be approved by the local authority and properly registered. Some childminders are excellent but don't be too impressed by registration. Some minders do attend courses but they do not have to be trained *in any way* and there are no national guidelines on standards. A minder is simply visited by the social services department to see if she seems suited to looking after children and that her house is clean, and the house may be checked by the fire brigade. She also has to sign a declaration that she is in good health and that neither she nor any member of her family has been convicted of an offence against a child or had one taken into care.

If you want to find a childminder you can ring the local social services and ask whoever is responsible for childminders to let you have a list of those in your area. This may well be more depressing than cheering: in some areas there are several hundred childminders and most of them have no vacancies. So it could take an awful lot of calls to find a place.

You may well find it better to contact the **National Childminding Association** (page 319) which campaigns for proper recognition and standards of childminding and is in touch with local groups of childminders who tend to know who has vacancies and who hasn't. So it could be a route to committed childminders who have learnt about what a growing child needs.

In most areas minders are registered to look after 3-4 children under 5, including their own. But they may also look after over-5s out of school. There are no set hours or rates, although the NCMA does issue guidelines.

The fees normally cover everything the child eats or uses (paint, paper) while there. And before taking on a minder you need to agree not just fees and hours but the sort of food she will give, how she would punish the child, and her approach to things like play, toilet training, bad language and masturbation. If her views on these things run opposite to yours you could have a very confused child. You also need to agree what will happen if she or the child is ill – minders don't normally look after sick children. Having agreed the details, put as much as possible in writing and both sign it. Those who cannot afford the full amount may be able to get the social services to pay part.

Children will settle most easily if they visit the minder with their mother several times before being fully left. At these times, they can get used to their mother leaving them alone with the minder for gradually increased periods, starting with only a few minutes out of the room, and a good minder should encourage this. When a child is left it is essential to give the minder the following information:

- parents' address and phone numbers at home and work,
- address and phone number of another person to contact in emergency,
- the name and address of the child's doctor,
- details of the child's age, immunizations, allergies, etc.

Nursery Care

There is absolutely no obligation of local government to provide any kind of schooling or care for the under-5s – unless they have special needs which cannot be met at home. However, some boroughs do have nursery schools or day nurseries. Responsibility for them may be split between the education department and social services. So, if you want to know about everything on offer for under-5s in your area, contact both and ask for the 'under 5 unit' – if an authority has one it is your best source of information There is also a Nursery Schools Information Service.

Day nurseries are run by nursery nurses and operate from 8.30 to 6.30 on weekdays. So they will cover the hours when you might be at work.

Nursery schools or **nursery classes** attached to a school are run by trained nursery teachers – so they are likely to give a child more stimulation – but most only open from 9.00 to 3.30, and they keep to term times and normally take children from age 3 upwards. To get a child into one you put its name down at birth.

Private nurseries and **nursery schools** can employ more or less whomever they like but they usually run only during term time and often take children in the morning *or* the afternoon.

Pre-school play groups are set up by mothers for mothers. Any group of mothers can set one up, and employ staff they choose, provided the premises are approved by the local authority. The Pre-School Playgroups Associations (page 319) have the details on them; however, the groups usually meet only 2 or 3 times a week. They are a good way to get a break, but they don't meet the full needs of the working mother.

Choosing a School for the Under-5s

Check any school or nursery to which you plan to send your child. The key points to look for are much the same as in a primary school (see page 297), but there should be more messy play with water, paints and plasticine.

Workplace Nurseries

In many ways the ideal solution is a workplace nursery as the children spend the minimum of time away from you and you are spared extra travel time and hassles.

Such nurseries are gradually increasing, in both colleges and companies, but are still thin on the ground. If you want advice on how one can be set up, the following organizations can help: the Working Mothers Association, the PPA, your trade union, Working for Childcare.

Older Children Outside School Times

There is a serious problem over the care of school age children after school and during the holidays. If you have turned to this page wondering at what age you can safely allow a child to come home from school to an empty house, I have to disappoint you. There are ages below which the law would frown on a child being alone, but there is no school age at which anyone can say that a child can be *safely* left alone, day after day, in the late afternoon and through the holidays.

Children can be divided into two age groups: those too young to be left to take themselves home and cope alone, and those who are old enough to get up to no end of mischief if they have too little supervision. Children who have long unsupervised gaps between the end of school and a parent's return have the freedom to sniff glue, take drugs, make love while under age and commit crimes.

Obviously some children in their teens are well able to cope alone for an hour or two after school and can be counted on to behave well. But it is never safe to assume that *every* child can be left alone like that. Even within a single family one child may be quite safe alone and another may not. Bear in mind how a child would cope if something went wrong. Suppose that in making tea they burnt themselves – could they handle it? And, safety and delinquency aside, many children need the support of coming home to an adult if they are to cope with the stresses of school.

One solution is the **Kids Clubs Network** (page 319), a charity which helps in setting up schemes, of all kinds, to look after children after school. It can put you in touch with existing schemes or help you to set one up. The local authority should also have information on centres to which children can go after school.

In some areas there are clubs and other voluntary organizations for children to go to between school and the end of the adult working day. But in most places there is a yawning gap between the care that is needed for children out of school, and what is available, and it will be some while before parents who are school governors hold enough sway to make schools provide the facilities which are needed after school hours. Meanwhile, it may be necessary for them to go to relatives or to a childminder for far longer than you might imagine – until you think about what they could get up to alone.

Teaching in the Early Years

A child learns more between birth and 5 than at any other time in its life – and its parents are the main teachers, even when they don't realize it. People often forget just how much a child needs to learn. Stop and think for a moment about what the world must be like

Addresses and suggestions for further reading are at the ends of chapters.

to a new baby who doesn't yet know up from down, hard from soft, and has no idea why it is lying on a blanket one minute, in water the next. Somehow its immature brain has to make order out of the extraordinary chaos that must seem to surround it.

Teaching it about the world starts the moment you first hold it and it learns the feel of your body. From then on it needs lots of varied experiences to help it sort the world out. There's proof that the children most likely to do well in school are those who were given lots of stimulation in early childhood. You may not be able to make your child a genius, but what you teach it from birth to 5 can make the difference between it being a success or a failure for the rest of its life.

Talk to it from the very first so it learns language – but use normal English, there's no point in giving it the extra work of learning both gee-gee and horse. Whether in pram or crib it needs something to focus its eyes on and things to touch so it can learn to co-ordinate hand and eye to touch them. Give it something which will swing if it touches it or make a noise, but make sure everything it is given is safe for it to chew. Babies are also learning what is edible.

It would take pages to explain all the things you can do to help a baby and toddler learn, but knowing what to do is half instinct, half imagination. If you try to see the world from the child's point of view and realize all the things which are new and strange, and all the skills it doesn't have, you will soon work out what a child needs. The great thing is to remember that a child is learning from each thing it does. To a child *all* play is learning. Once you see how hard it works at it and how quickly it will latch on to each new experience, being a parent becomes much more interesting. To us a child with a rattle is just a child making a noise. To a baby it is a discovery at least as important as learning to drive is to an adult. It learns that such a sound exists and – far more important – it learns that it has the power to make sounds with something other than its own voice.

A young child doesn't need expensive toys. A wooden spoon tied to the side of a cot, and a row of empty, brightly painted, cotton reels hanging above it, which swing when touched, give it just as much to learn from as anything you can buy. (But keep them out of chewing distance.) Pictures from magazines can decorate its wall and give it new shapes to look at. As it gets older, saucepans and wooden spoons make great (if ear-splitting) drums, water and sand teach it vital lessons about the amount which a container will hold – which is important in mathematics. Newspaper is just as good for early attempts at painting as any art paper.

In all this don't expect a child to stay clean, tidy and quiet. To think that a 'good' child is one who is like that is to misunderstand childhood. A child who is really developing its brain regards every day as a series of experiments and experiments are messy. Half the art of parenthood is setting up situations where the mess can be limited to places where you don't object to it. The other half is learning to answer questions. Children have an uncanny knack of asking questions at quite the worst moments, but however many they ask, or however odd they may seem, no parent should ever get cross with a child for asking. To do that is to tell the child to stop thinking – and a quick route to a child who won't learn in school either. If you don't know the answer say so, and perhaps try to find it out together (see also page 291).

Preparing a Child for School

Imagine how you would feel if your nearest and dearest got you up early one morning, put you into big and unfamiliar clothes, then took you by a strange route to a vast building full of scores of others much larger than you and making a lot of noise – and then walked out on you. I, for one, would find it alarming – wouldn't you? Yet that is what an unprepared child experiences when going to primary school for the first time. And it doesn't help that the child probably can't tell the time, so its mother saying she will be back at 3 o'clock won't mean very much. It doesn't have to be like that.

- It will be much easier for a child if it has been to some kind of playgroup, can cope with other children and knows that if its mother goes she also comes back.
- Dress the child in the new uniform around the home from time to time, so it feels as if it belongs, and try to give it enough wear to make the fastenings easy for the child to undo alone, or it may be defeated and wet itself, which is a horrid humiliation.
- Good primary schools often let children visit the school with their parents before they are due to start. If the school doesn't normally do this you could offer to help in a class for a day while bringing the child with you. (Don't worry that you don't know anything about teaching, extra hands are always useful.)
- Take your child to functions like sports days or nativity plays. Then talk afterwards about how it will be able to be an angel or run races when it's at a big school.
- Try to teach your child to read its own name before it goes to school, then it will easily find its own peg and find other possessions in school. If it can't manage this, sew something distinctive, like a coloured ribbon, inside its coat and use a biro to draw a picture inside the top of each wellington. Then it will be able to find its own clothes.
- If you are allowed to stay with your child on the first day or two of school do so. If you aren't, know this beforehand and explain to the child that you will have to leave but that you will be back in the afternoon, and plan with it a special celebration tea for the end of the first day so it has something to look forward to.

> Whatever you do, all the new experiences of school are demanding and a child may be very tired for the first few weeks. It's a good idea to avoid doing too much after school and to cherish it a little. Put it to bed rather earlier than usual, giving it extra attention at bedtime, until this phase passes.

Teaching at Home

There are three aspects to teaching at home during the school years: teaching a child totally at home because you have an objection to schooling, teaching a child at home because illness or absence abroad makes it impossible to attend school, and simply boosting what is done in school by doing a certain amount yourself. The reasons, and the age of the child, will affect what you teach, but there are certain principles which apply to all teaching whatever the age of the child. Those I briefly cover below.

Should Parents Teach their Children?

Many teachers lack confidence and feel threatened by the thought of children being taught by their parents. After all, if any old parent can teach, what price the teacher's training and experience? This is very understandable, but it is not only a good idea for parents to teach their children, it is essential. And I speak as a teacher.

The best and easiest time for anyone – child or adult – to learn anything is when they feel like doing it. Yet teachers simply aren't there in the vital early years and even the best teacher with the smallest class cannot notice and stimulate the special interests of every schoolchild every day. And with children there is more to learning at the right moment than just pleasure. They are marvellous learning machines and a confident child keeps pushing back the frontiers of his or her achievements, step by step, always progressing to the next thing which can *just* be managed. You can see them doing it physically: walking along the tops of walls as soon as they are footsure on level ground. They also do it mentally, unerringly choosing the next activity they are ready to master. If we can follow a child's leads and teach it what it wants to know it learns quickly and easily. It doesn't matter a jot whether the activity is officially 'right' for its age, what a child *wants* to learn *is* right for that child. If it points to words at 1 year old, and asks what they are, it wants to read – so teach it. And if stacking bricks is its great delight, give it bricks to stack. The child is the best judge of what it needs to do.

This doesn't mean that if you are educating your child at home you sit there waiting for it to take an interest in nuclear physics. Adults have to try out topics and ideas and see which ones children latch on to. Only if you play them music will you discover whether they enjoy it. However, if you are educating a child entirely at home, and nothing excites it, some basic teaching will do no harm at all if it's done the right way.

The Basics of Teaching a Child

If you start to teach your child anything – reading, games, music or mathematics – there is one basic rule which always applies, whatever the age or ability of the child. The child must enjoy it and get satisfaction from it. Many adults use teaching children as an excuse to show the children how big and clever they – the adults – are. Thus making the child feel small and unable to do things. To teach you must leave your own ego behind. All teaching must be designed to make the *child* feel big and clever and it should feel more confident and more successful with each new thing it learns or tries to do. So play down your own prowess, make some mistakes yourself, and laugh about them – so failure isn't a bogey man.

At the same time keep the child's risks of failure to a minimum. This means that each new task should always be just a little step up from what it has already mastered, so it is within its ability. If it can read 10 words give it those 10 to read, then add 1 more. When it can read 11 words, add 1 again. Don't try to rush it by leaping from 10 to 15 in a burst of parental pride – unless the child shows you that it wants to learn faster. This doesn't mean the child has no challenges, it means they are always the right size for it. Only a bad rider tries to take a young horse over hard jumps before it has mastered basic ones, and we should use horse sense with children.

> It is because teachers now believe in keeping failure to a minimum that you may see that some mistakes in your child's homework are not corrected. If a child makes a lot of mistakes and every single mistake is pointed out it is very discouraging. So good teachers often correct only the mistakes a child can learn from – at that moment.

If you watch children you will see they will learn to bounce a ball, and for a few days they bounce it everywhere, revelling in this achievement. Then suddenly they begin throwing it against the wall and catching it. They've learnt, they've practised and they've moved on. Copy this pattern and make the practice a pleasure. All kinds of learning games can be invented to do this. But watch the child. Stop just *before* the child has had enough, so it is hungry for more next time.

If you want to teach any creature to do something you link learning with reward. To a child learning is itself rewarding (unless it's taught badly), but it is doubly so if an adult (especially one it loves) praises its achievement. Children grow intellectually on a diet of praise and encouragement the way a plant grows on fertilizer. Whether you are teaching it to do up its own shoes or read, give it plenty of love and praise whenever it even *begins* to get something right, and largely ignore mistakes – except where a slight explanation is essential (to help them, not to satisfy the parent's ego). Don't be afraid that praising a child for getting things a little bit right will take away its incentive to do even better. Children, like adults, can take praise till it's coming out of their ears and still be glad of more. When did *you* ever find that you were praised so much that you gave up trying? Nor will it get big-headed, it's the child who doesn't really feel good enough who is most likely to boast.

Addresses and suggestions for further reading are at the ends of chapters.

The Pitfalls of Home Teaching

The most common pitfall is that parents naturally want their child to succeed, and even shine. The temptation is to push the child, forcing it to work when it should be playing, getting impatient when it makes mistakes and so on. This is not only nasty for the child but a bad way to get results. The parent who makes learning unpleasant is actually teaching their child *not* to learn. And so is the parent who *always* has to know best, and win at every game, and who chooses to lecture rather than discuss. It is also worth remembering that each child has its own sequence and its own pace. You can never expect it even to follow the pattern of its brothers or sisters.

If you are teaching a child something and ever feel impatience or anger rising, *stop teaching that instant* and leave it a day. Once a child links learning with your anger, it will switch off its brain faster than you'd think possible. There are only three reasons why young children fail and make mistakes – the adult has given it an unsuitable task, the adult has gone on for too long, or the adult has taught it in the wrong way. In all three cases the child deserves no anger.

All that may seem very soft. It isn't, it's plain time and motion study. The only quick way to teach anyone anything is to use their eagerness and fuel it with satisfaction.

The second pitfall is the one of trying to channel children into one's own interests. Every child differs, but inside each is the ability to be deeply interested in something, and one of a parent's greatest roles is to introduce each child to the widest possible range of experiences and when it shows an interest in one, feed that interest.

The final pitfall which teachers, rightly, fear is that of parents imposing on children outdated and damaging methods which will make them thoroughly confused. Reading and mathematics are the two subjects most vulnerable to this. It is pointless for parents to use methods which conflict with those used in school even if they think that modern methods are daft. It is easy enough to ask a child to show you how its teacher does a certain type of sum or gets it to read words, or go and ask the teacher. Any parent who makes it very clear that they ask in a spirit of co-operation, so that they can help their child by the 'right' method, should find teachers only too happy to explain. On page 320 I list some books and organizations which may also be of use to parents.

Teaching a Child to Read

The moment you first sit a child on your lap and show it the pages of a book you are starting to teach it to read. Even if the book only has pictures it is learning that books have interesting things in them. That's important, so a child should be shown picture books from a few weeks old, and read stories as soon as it will begin to understand them. And children who learn rhymes learn to read faster.

When you show them pictures avoid the temptation to name letters of the alphabet. Learning the alphabet does more harm than good. When we read we use the *sound* of the letters, not the names (you only need the alphabet to look things up in dictionaries and telephone directories). But if you've already taught your child the alphabet don't worry, it will get over it.

There are all kinds of reading systems and they all work. If a child is under school age the method which is least likely to clash with anything a child later learns in school is simply to teach it to recognize whole words. Children do this very easily. You show it the word cat and you say cat quite normally, not c-a- t. Teach it with ordinary letters, e.g. cat, *not* capitals, and the younger the child the larger you should write them. With a preschool child a couple of inches high is ideal. Put each word on paper and make the first words it learns ones which are important to it – its own name, mummy, daddy, its pet or whatever. When it can recognize a lot of nouns you can start adding other words like is, and, here, and build them into sentences. With an older child modify this to its interests, and if it prefers to read from a book let it do so.

At any age it doesn't matter if the word is quite long, children recognize a house just as easily as a table and, with the whole word method of teaching reading, size makes no more difference to words than it does to objects. They can be written large on sheets of paper and a good game to play is to put 2 or more words down (according to the stage the child is at) and ask it to find a particular word and pick it up. You can then praise each word it picks up correctly, and make much of counting how many it got. This game can be used for quite advanced readers using quite a lot of words and 'racing' them to find one – the child must win most of the time.

★ I have found that when reading is done by recognizing a word and picking it up, rather than saying it, any child can do it – even an autistic child or one with a speech problem.

Once a child can read a few words on paper you can pick out those same words in the books you read to it, and let it read the words it knows – or make a book with a story about itself. Before long it is reading whole pages. This means that if a child is a slow reader you can read books to it which are right for its age – and let it read the words it knows from them – rather than condemning it to the humiliation of books which are too young for it. Once a child can read quite well you can, for example, point out the way words like sand, hand, land all have 'and' in, and you and the child can start looking for patterns and playing with letters and building words with them – spelling is born.

Even if you have time for nothing else, do get your child to read to you a little, once it starts learning at school, and praise its efforts. Research shows children learn far better if they have this encouragement.

Teaching a Child Maths

The first blessing a parent can bestow on its child's mathematical ability is never to let it hear you say you hated maths or were bad at it. Then it won't expect it to be a bogey.

Children have all kinds of things to learn before they can do sums. They have to learn the language of maths. We take the words for granted but a child has to learn what numbers are and what things like roundness are. It's so easy to play counting games with a toddler's fingers and toes and to say 'look at that big *round* ball', or that *square* red brick – not just a big ball or red brick. It also needs to learn about more and less. In the bath it can have plastic containers of different sizes and pour water from one to another. Gradually it will grasp the fact that what fits in one won't always fit in another. When it has a slice of bread you can say you will cut it in half or in quarters and do so. Later on it can do the cutting. Take it shopping and let it hear you using money and later help to get coins from your purse. And, when a child starts to add up, you can change the rules of dominoes: instead of matching 2 to 2 and 4 to 4, match the dots so they add up to 10.

All those things sound very simple – but they are the basic mathematics it will use all its life, and the child who learns such things has a great foundation for maths in school.

> Modern maths teaching in schools can look like nothing but play. There is method in this. The new maths teaching lets children learn about real situations and then transfers this learning to numbers on paper. It is no good chanting the times table before you have grasped that 'three twos are six' actually means that if you have 3 bags of apples, with 2 in each bag, you have 6 apples.

Transferring to Middle or Secondary School

Transfer to a new school is both exciting and stressful for most children, much as taking a new job is for an adult. Adults usually get some immediate benefits out of the stressful experience, such as better pay. It is no bad thing to blunt the edge of the child's change-over in a similar way, with a pocket money raise the first week and by giving a deliberately celebratory air to shopping for school equipment. But beware of buying your child anything which is outstandingly good quality. It may make it harder for your child to lend to others.

Parents also need to express confidence in the new school, even if it wasn't their first choice, but they shouldn't tell false tales of how much fun it will be. It could make the child feel they are deeply out of touch.

As when starting primary school the child is likely to be far more tired than usual for a few weeks, which could mean that instead of flopping it will be tetchy and obnoxious. There may also be difficulties in settling down to the business of homework. It will help if a routine is established from early on.

> Children usually have exaggerated ideas of how much grown-ups – especially parents – know and understand. This can lead them to think a grown-up must *know* about an unfair (or perverted) teacher or about bullying in the school. It's a good idea to explain to a child, from primary school onwards, that you aren't able to tell what happens in the school and that you want them to tell you if they are ever upset or worried about anything.

Bypassing Schooling

By British law a child must be educated, but education is not defined as schooling. All the relevant Education Acts say that parents have a duty to see that a child is educated according to its needs and that Education Authorities must as far as possible see to it that children are educated in accordance with their parents' wishes. The parents' rights are also enshrined in the United Nations Declaration of Human Rights which says:

- everyone has the right to education,
- education shall be directed to the full development of the human personality,
- parents shall have a right to choose the kind of education that shall be given to their children.

Equally, the European Convention for the Protection of Human Rights and Fundamental Freedoms says: '. . . the state shall respect the right of parents to ensure such education and teaching is in conformity with their own religious and philosophical convictions.'

At the same time parents can be taken to court, and a child put in care, if an LEA believes the education they give is not adequate. So parents who intend to educate their children themselves would be well advised to talk to others who have tried it and know what the authorities accept or quarrel with. **Education Otherwise** (page 320) can advise you and put you in touch with other parents, and WES (below) has useful home tuition courses.

Home Education Overseas

Parents who have to go abroad for their work may find themselves needing to keep their children abreast of British education so that they can return to it – if only with the right examinations to get into further education. The major organization which provides parents with what they need to achieve this is the **Worldwide Education Service (WES)** (page 320). It is an arm of the Parents Educational Union which has several schools around Britain, and its Home School service provides an education programme by which a parent can teach a child at home with the postal guidance of a WES tutor, who is a qualified and experienced teacher. Its courses include a nursery education course for 3-5-year-olds, designed for parents or nursery teachers, and a course for 5-13-year-olds, plus single subject courses for children who are attending a local school abroad which lacks certain vital subjects.

Addresses and suggestions for further reading are at the ends of chapters.

The courses show a parent how to teach a child, as well as offering a course of what to teach it, and provide assessment and references which can be offered to future schools. Older children need to use one of the open learning schemes leading to exams (see page 309).

The State Schooling System

Describing the British education system is a bit like shaking hands with an octopus: there is no obvious point at which to start. Nor does it make it any easier that it is currently undergoing such a shake-up that this particular octopus keeps waving its tentacles about just when you try to grasp one. What follows is the state of play as I write. Before taking any major educational step, it would be wise to double-check that nothing important has changed since this was written. What is certain is that the Parents' Charter gives state school parents a right to more information, about the system and about their child's progress, than they have ever had. So it is well worth getting the Department for Education (DFE) leaflet explaining the Charter in detail (page 321). The DFE is also planning to have a range of freephone information lines.

> What follows concerns England and Wales. Please assume that all references to the DFE include the Education Department of the Welsh Office. Scotland, however, may be different and, where possible, I have tried to show this.

Types of State Schools
State schooling divides up a child's school life in various ways. Some LEAs use one, some another, and some authorities seem to dislike the term 'middle school' and have two stages of primary school or two stages of secondary school. Many have several different systems operating at once. These are some of the options:

5 to 7, 8 or 9 – infant or first school,
5 to 11 – primary school,
8 to 11 – junior school,
8 to 12 or 9 to 13 – middle school,
11 to 18 – chosen by selection – grammar school,
11 to 18 – *not* chosen by selection – comprehensive,
16 to 18 – VI form or tertiary college.

City Technology Colleges
These will normally cater for 11 to 18 year olds, across the full range of ability in their area, and are state schools registered as independent schools – yet charge no fees. Pupils follow the National Curriculum but there is emphasis on science, technology and maths and a broad range of enrichment activities. So pupils may work a longer day, and the terms may have a different pattern from those of other state schools. In selecting pupils, they may give preference to the technically inclined.

Grant-Maintained Schools
These are state schools that have chosen to opt out of LEA control and come directly under central government (see page 294). A grant-maintained school is then run by its board and with a freedom similar to that enjoyed by independent schools, except that it is directly under the DFE

Voluntary Schools
About 1 in 3 of the state schools in England and Wales are voluntary schools. Most of them are Church of England and Roman Catholic schools, but there are 3 types of voluntary school. In all of them religious instruction is in the hands of the voluntary body. They are funded partly by the LEA and partly by the voluntary body.

Many are **aided schools** in which a voluntary organization (e.g. a church) appoints most of the governors (who in turn appoint the teachers), and pays for external repairs and extensions. The LEA pays for all the running costs, from salaries to internal repairs.

In **controlled schools** the building was originally set up by a voluntary body but the LEA pays all the costs, and fewer of the governors are appointed by the voluntary organization. And, in practice, the governors have considerable say over the appointment of teachers.

Special agreement schools are ones in which an LEA agrees to contribute to the building of a voluntary school, but most of the governors are from the voluntary body. See also Assisted Places at Independent Schools, page 299.

State Education in Scotland
In education, as in most things, Scotland is a law unto itself. The normal pattern is for children to attend coeducational primary schools from the age of 5 until 12. Denominational schools (mainly Roman Catholic) are a major feature of the system. Scotland is also one area where village schools still remain. After 12, state schools are comprehensive, even though some still call themselves grammar schools, and take a child through the next 6 years. At the primary stage teachers have been free to teach whatever curriculum they like but schools are guided in the secondary curriculum by the Consultative Committee on the Curriculum.

The LEA sets a catchment area for each primary school and children have been expected to attend the school in their area, and all move on to a single secondary school. But now parents can ask for their child to go to another school, even in some other LEA, and the LEA must agree unless there is good reason not to. If an LEA refuses, the parents can appeal to an independent committee and from there to the sheriff.

The assisted places scheme (see page 299) operates in Scotland as it does in England. The rules on special education are also the same as for England. For information on parental choice and assisted places in Scotland, write to the **Scottish Education Department** (page 694).

Authority and Where it Lies
The school system is supervised by the Department for Education (DFE). The other bodies involved in education are the education departments of the local authorities (LEAs), the churches and other voluntary bodies who have schools within the state sector, the

sponsors of city technology colleges, the governing bodies and the teachers. One of the key issues at present is how much control and influence should rest with the DFE (and the Education Department of the Scottish Office) and how much with the other educational bodies. Neither the 1944 Education Act, which is still the foundation of the system, nor the Act which followed it gave the DFE much power. It controlled the educational building programme, could accept or reject LEA plans for school reorganization and decide disputes between parents and local authorities, but until recently did not administer or play any part in what was taught. This has changed and is still changing. The 1988 Education Act established a national curriculum and a system of assessment and, by setting detailed rules on specific subjects, put the DFE firmly in the driving seat. At the same time, creating grant-maintained schools, funded by government not by the LEAs, and giving all schools the right to decide how to spend their budgets has weakened the LEAs. Just how much these measures will really put power into the hands of parents, as the government promises, remains to be seen.

Curriculum

A new national curriculum has been set by the government, via the Schools Curriculum and Assessment Authority (SCAA). It applies to all children in state education, including those with special needs. The core subjects are English, maths and science. The foundation subjects are technology/design, history, geometry, music, art and PE, plus a foreign language. Programmes of study are published for the core and foundation subjects, plus targets that children should achieve in each subject by certain ages. And the new system broadly lays down the way children must be taught. For example, in language teaching there is more emphasis on spoken languages. SCAA has been told to make sure that all external exams, such as GCSE, set a consistent standard.

To keep children – and teachers – on target, the SCAA is setting tests in core subjects at various ages, plus arranging assessment in the foundation subjects by teachers. The aim is to ensure that children learn basic skills, such as reading, spelling, and maths. As I write, the details of testing are undecided; however, most children will, at 16, be expected to take GCSE in English, maths and science. Those who cannot reach that standard will be assessed by teachers. Their results will then be entered on the National Record of Achievement, which every school leaver will now be given.

The overall results for each school will be published by the DFE. If you want to see them, ask your LEA. The results obtained by individual children will not be made public but will be sent to their parents as part of the annual report on each child which every school is now legally obliged to send to parents. As I write, nobody knows what will happen when the tests show that a child is lagging behind, although high achievers may be able to move up faster.

Other Government Departments Involved in Education

The Department of Employment is playing an ever-growing role in courses for those over 16 and its local Training and Enterprise Councils (TECs) now fund and give information on such courses. So government is also involved in what is happening to the older age groups without being restricted by the DFE-LEA relationship.

At the other end of the age range social service departments, which come under the Department of Social Security, provide day-nurseries and certain educational facilities for the mentally handicapped.

Finally the Department of Industry has been involved in the introduction of computers in schools, and provides training at Information Technology Centres, and industry itself is now being brought in to sponsor City Technology Colleges. So the whole framework of education is changing.

Local Education Authorities

Almost all the education authorities of England and Wales are simply branches of local councils. Each is run by a Director of Education or Chief Education Officer and an education department. The elected councillors of the county or metropolitan councils influence decisions via an Education Committee. But only half the members of the Education Committee need be elected councillors, and it includes members co-opted for their expertise. The 1944 Education Act made LEAs responsible for the moral, spiritual, mental and physical development of their communities by ensuring that 'efficient education . . . shall be available to meet the needs of the population in their area'. The 1992 Education Act emphasized the same values and established the concept of Education Associations responsible for restoring good education to schools which are failing. The Parents' Charter gave parents a right to know how their child's results compare with those of others of the same age. Also how their child's school compares with other schools.

Compulsory Schooling

An LEA must educate a child, or ensure that it is educated, from the beginning of the term which follows his or her 5th birthday and a pupil must stay at school until the end of the spring term if their 16th birthday is between 1 September and 31 January, or until the Friday before the last Monday in May if their birthday is in the rest of the year. Between 16 and 19 schooling is optional but if a pupil wants more education the LEA has a duty to provide it.

Funding of State Schools

State schools are mainly funded by the government. Grant-maintained schools are totally government funded, via the Funding Agency for schools and can spend the money as they wish. And Voluntary Schools have certain outgoings paid by the voluntary body which established them – usually a church. Colleges are directly financed by central government with extra money from the industry. Other schools get money from both the goverment and the local authority via LEAs.

★ The 1988 Education Act enables both these and ordinary LEA schools to charge parents for certain aspects of education which used to be free, such as music lessons and some out-of-school activities.

Addresses and suggestions for further reading are at the ends of chapters.

LEAs' Duty on Meals
An LEA may provide meals for all children in school, and/or milk at break in primary schools, but it has no duty to do so and may charge what it wishes. The only exception, at the time of writing, is that it must make 'appropriate provision' for free meals for the children of those on certain state benefits.

LEAs' Duty on Transport
LEAs must provide free transport to and from school where they think it necessary. In practice this means they normally provide it if the child is at its nearest state (or voluntary) school and lives more than walking distance away. However, 'walking distance' is 2 miles for those under 8, and 3 miles for those over 8.

You will notice that this means that if parents choose a school which is not the one nearest to them, this could leave them with the travel costs. In practice LEAs vary considerably in how generous they are; some charge pupils for riding on a school bus if they don't have an automatic right to be on it.

The Role of School Governors
The 1986 Act gave school governors more control over the way money is spent. Each school has a budget from the LEA and it is up to the governors to decide the staffing levels and spending priorities, although in practice they may often be guided by the head teacher, who handles the budget on a day-to-day basis. With the head, governors and the LEA also have a new obligation to ensure:

- the balanced presentation of opposing political views when political issues arise in the classroom
- that any sex education should encourage moral values and that the school's policy on sex education is made available to parents.

The governors of GMSs and CTCs have similar overall responsibilities, although a CTC sponsor may allocate funds to particular projects.

Governors' Duty to Report to Parents
The Act says that the governors are answerable to the parents and must submit an annual report to them each year containing the following:

- the names of governors and who appointed them,
- the name and address of the chairman and clerk,
- a summary of what the governing body has done that year,
- a financial statement by the LEA,
- details of how the governors spent any money allocated by the LEA,
- details of any gifts to the school,
- details of outside exam results (secondary schools),
- describe what has been done to improve the school's links with the community,
- give details of the policy on sex education,
- details of the annual general meeting (AGM).

An AGM must be held within 2 weeks of issuing the report. The meeting is open to all parents of children registered at the school, plus the head, the governors and anyone the governors wish to invite. The meeting gives the parents a chance to discuss how the governors, head and financing body have acted during the past year, and it can pass resolutions, but only if the number of parents present is equal to 20 per cent of the pupils on the school roll. The governors *must* consider these resolutions and pass resolutions related to them.

The exact working will take some time to shake out, but already there is more emphasis on explaining things to parents. However, parents are also being called on to do more for the school in terms of fund raising.

The Authority of Parent Governors
The 1986 Education Act made big changes in the role that parents can play in the state education system. Before the Act a school of 300-599 pupils, for example, would have 26 school governors, half of them appointed by the local authority and likely to toe the party line. Today that school would have only about 16 governors and a significant number would be parents.

Parent governors are elected for a four-year term by a secret ballot in which all parents can vote. Governors must produce an annual report and hold an annual meeting for parents. Since 1989 all Scottish schools have had a school board consisting of elected parent and teacher representatives and co-opted members of the local community. The head teacher is not a member but acts as an adviser. The boards do not have such wide powers as English and Welsh boards of governors and act more as a forum for parental views but they may see, and query, education budgets.

Learning to Govern
Under the 1986 Act, all local authorities must run free training courses to help governors understand what is expected of them. The National Association of Governors and Managers runs training courses and the Open University (page 309) has a course called 'Governing Schools' which is designed to help school governors understand their role and the system within which they have to work. It could be of interest to any parent now that there is more interaction between parents and governors. The **Advisory Centre for Education (ACE)** (page 321) has a briefing on how to be a school governor.

Any parent who is well-informed on changes in education is obviously in a stronger position when discussing what should happen in a school. The education sections of the *Guardian* and the *Independent* are worth reading, and *The Times* has a weekly *Times Educational Supplement* – sold separately from the paper.

Under the Act schools may decide to opt out of their local education authority and become grant-maintained, taking their funds not from the local authority but from central government. And if enough parents want a school to opt out, the governors *must* consent to it.

The Authority of Teachers
Schools have the right to make rules on behaviour and school dress and to impose sanctions to enforce them and must provide parents with details of a school's code

of conduct and sanctions. Parents do not have the right to ignore them; if they want rules changed they must approach the head teacher or school governors.

Supporting Teachers

Teaching large groups of children is a conjuring trick which depends on the children not seeing too clearly how easily they could topple the whole set-up. If parents want their children to learn anything it is vital that the children behave in a disciplined way – and they won't if they feel the teachers don't have the backing of parents. So, *for the child's sake*, parents must seem to back the school whenever possible.

However, teachers aren't saints: sometimes they behave badly and make the wrong decisions. A parent who supports teachers even when they are clearly behaving stupidly or being seriously unfair looks to a child like someone who is on the side of authority and not of what is right – and that is not a position a child respects. So, support has to be tempered with a little caution. If a teacher behaves badly a parent may be able to sort it out by talking to the teacher (if it's appropriate) or help the child understand that the teacher may have a good reason for a wrong action.

Punishments

The usual range of punishments which a school may give include such things as not taking part in activities which are specially enjoyed, doing extra work, or staying in when others play. There may also be a Pupil Referral Unit to which children are sent if they upset their normal class. By law such units should offer effective education, not simply keep pupils out of trouble.

No matter how difficult a child is, corporal punishment is now illegal. So banning a child from school (exclusion) has become the final punishment. The 1986 Education Act set out the step-by-step procedure which has to be followed if a child is excluded. And exclusion covers any situation in which a child is told to stay away from school, whatever the school or LEA calls it.

There are 3 kinds of exclusion: **fixed** exclusion usually only covers a few days, so **indefinite** exclusion is more serious, and **permanent** exclusion the worst of all. Under the 1986 Act if there is a fixed exclusion:

- a parent must be told immediately,
- the LEA and governors *only* need to be told if a child is excluded for a total of more than 5 days in any term, or will miss a public examination.

If the exclusion is indefinite or permanent:

- the parents must be told immediately *and* given the reasons for it,
- the LEA and governors must always be told

The same rules apply to grant-maintained schools except that no LEA would be involved.

What a Parent Can Do

The steps a parent can take are quite complicated and the Advisory Centre for Education (page 321) has a detailed briefing on them. But the basics are as follows:

- ask the head to tell you why the child was excluded and what type of exclusion it is (it's best to ask in writing but a phone call is better than nothing),
- ask to see the head and discuss it. It may help to take someone with you. If the school has been unreasonable try to take a parent governor,
- if that fails write and tell the Chief Education Officer that you want to appeal against the suspension.

In all this, make sure you keep copies of any letters you write and replies you get.

An independent panel may hear your appeal and the reasons given by the governors. Normally no written evidence is used on either side, but you should plan what to say and it would be good to have all the letters with you. The independent appeal panel can reject an appeal, but if they approve it the head must either take the child on a date set by the panel, or permanently exclude the child. If the head opts for permanent exclusion the ball lands back in the LEA court: it must place the child in another school or provide it with home tuition. In some areas LEAs tend to forget this and leave a child out of school for long periods. They are breaking the law and you should remind them of that.

Anyone who feels the appeals procedure wasn't properly run can complain to the Local Ombudsman through a local councillor, and may even complain to the Secretary of State – though this is not likely to get results. In general, the more a parent is interested in a child's school, and takes part in its activities, the better it is for the child. On page 321 I list some of the organizations that can help parents understand the system.

Choosing a State School

Since the 1980 Education Act, parents have had the right to choose the state school their child goes to. At the primary level there are only LEA schools and voluntary maintained schools, but from 11 onwards there are also grant-maintained schools and city technology colleges (CTCs) in some areas. These follow the national curriculum, like other schools, but CTCs also emphasize skills in technology. The former will take children from any distance away. However, a CTC will only take those living within a geographical region set by its governors and must, by law, select children across the full range of ability – including those with special needs. Its intake must also reflect the ethnic make-up of its area.

If you, as a parent, contact a CTC or a grant-maintained school, it must provide the same information on itself that an LEA school has to give (see below). But if you want to know more about these types of establishment in general, contact the **Grant-Maintained Schools Foundation**, and the **City Technology Colleges Trust**.

An LEA must send your child to the school you choose, if it can. This includes not only ordinary state schools but also voluntary maintained schools (see page 293). Parents can even apply for a school in a neighbouring authority, or for a place in a state boarding school.

To give parents a foundation for their choice of school, each LEA must provide the following information free of charge:

Addresses and suggestions for further reading are at the ends of chapters.

- the LEA policy on primary and secondary education and a list of the schools,
- the LEA policy on admission and appeals,
- the arrangements for school meals, transport, uniform and maintenance grants,
- the policy on school transfer,
- the policies for children with special needs,
- how they identify children with special needs,
- the policy on entry for public examinations.

The following information must be sent free of charge by the school itself in a prospectus:

- the curriculum and subject choices,
- the details of how the school is organized,
- its policy on discipline and pastoral care,
- its policy on school uniform and its cost,
- the main activities outside the school curriculum,
- its policy on public examinations,
- the most recent examination results,
- any possible reorganization plans.

The Parents' Charter says you should also be able to see the results achieved by pupils in the National Curriculum tests, at each age level, and in GCSEs and certain other major examinations. Once you know which schools you are interested in you can ask the head teachers whether you can see round each. This is not a privilege. It is something you have a right to do – at the school's convenience.

How to Check Out a School

In any school, if the teachers assign a child or two to show you round it is a very good sign. It shows the school has nothing to hide and is prepared for you to quiz the children. Do so: children will tell you far more than teachers.

Don't just wander round looking; take time to sit and listen quietly. Ask the head if you may sit in on some classes – and pick different age groups and subjects. If you find the teachers boring your child may too.

Try to talk to other parents. The gaggle found outside most schools at the end of each school day will be more than willing to talk about their children's education.

If you can see into the playground, stand outside and watch at break-time. You will soon see whether children play happily, or gang up on the weaker children, and you may be able to tell whether they get up to other mischief.

In primary schools look for:

- children who seem to be enjoying themselves without excessive noise,
- lots of evidence of creative activities – models, paintings,
- children responding willingly to the teacher,
- a library with books children would *want* to read,
- equipment they can climb and play on outside.

Ask:

- how mathematics, reading and writing are taught,

- whether you may stay and help in the class if your child needs you in the first few days,
- if they have family grouping,
- do children keep one teacher as they go up the school or do they get a new teacher as they move up a form (the latter means that if they don't get on with one teacher they have a chance with another),
- what facilities there are for science and music,
- about the policy if a child develops learning difficulties,
- what the arrangements are for school meals,
- about the qualifications and experience of the teachers,
- the policies on any issues you care about – sex, religion, etc.,
- about the policy on homework,
- about the parent-teacher (home and school) association,
- what equipment they have for teaching children to use computers or foreign languages.

Listen to *how* the head replies as well as to what is actually said. Do you have the impression that he or she really wants you to know and likes parents being involved? Or are you just a necessary evil?

It's politic to write and thank the head of any school you have visited, and say how much you enjoyed the visit. You can also tell the head of the school you have chosen that you hope he will be able to accept your child (he or she may have no say – but who can tell). To the other heads include a let-out clause – unconnected with how the school is run – such as you are not sure how easy it would be for your child to get to school by public transport. You could find your child is allocated to one of these schools instead of to your first choice and there's no point starting your relationship with the head as one of the parents who rejected the school.

In secondary schools ask:

- about the range of subjects which can be taken at GCSE and at AS and A level,
- how flexible they can be over odd combinations of subjects at GCSE or AS or A level,
- whether any tutor is assigned to keep a particular eye on a pupil's welfare throughout the years in school,
- about the number and qualifications of teachers in key subjects, especially mathematics and science,
- about the policy on remedial teaching,
- about the policy on homework,
- about the policy on discipline and how much the children help to run the school,
- what punishments are given (having first read what they put in writing),
- about the policy on foreign languages – which do they offer and what methods and equipment do they use,

- what facilities they have for practical subjects like design and technology,
- what facilities are there for computer studies and what are the qualifications of the teacher,
- what part music, drama, art and sport play in the life of the school and also whether practical subjects like cooking and child care are open to all pupils – and both sexes – or only to girls or those who aren't academic. A good school should find time for all these *and* get good exam results. It is illegal to exclude one sex from any subject.

The information the school puts out should show you how well pupils have done in public exams. Your LEA should be able to give you DFE tables showing how the schools within it compare. Ask the school or LEA about any facts which aren't clear.

Absorb the atmosphere of the place: is there a feeling of reasonable order or do classrooms feel as if they could erupt at any minute? Are the children polite and confident, or over-polite and nervous, or sloppy and rude? Do the teachers seem to care or is there a feeling that they are time-serving?

Getting a Place at the School You Want

Parents have a legal right to be given a place for their child in their first choice of school, unless it is full of children with a stronger claim. However, LEAs and school governing bodies, vary in what priority they give to which criteria. Some give high priority to the children who live nearest, most give them to the brothers and sisters of these already at the school, others to those in greatest need, and so on. Voluntary schools (see page 293) don't have to follow their LEAs' rules and may give priority to those belonging to the church which founded them – which may look like racial discrimination, even though it isn't. And grammar schools will make passing an 11+ test a condition for entry. All criteria must be published in good time and be clear and easy to understand. Parents also have a right to be given a realistic idea of their child's chances of getting into a particular school.

Most LEAs expect applications for places to be in by the end of January for the following September, but this varies and the education department concerned will tell you how to apply. There is nothing to stop you putting your child down several years before – if the school will let you – and, if a school is very popular, this can sometimes increase a child's chances of getting in, provided he or she meets the set rules for admission. Even so, if you are asked to give a second and third choice, do so. It won't reduce the chances of getting a place in the first-choice school, and if that is full your child may go to your second choice.

All that advice also applies if you wish your child to attend a grant-maintained school (GMS) or city technology college (CTC). However, a grant-maintained grammar school may expect entrants to pass an 11+ exam. And, as a CTC has to accept children across the whole spread of ability, including the less able, a test of ability may be used to select children. CTCs also look for parents who are firmly behind the CTC concept.

If you want your child to go to a GMS or a CTC you should apply *both* to that school *and* to LEA schools – in case your child isn't accepted by the GMS or CTC. On the LEA application you may give first, second and third choices of LEA schools, just as you can if you have also applied to an independent school, and you need not reveal that you have also applied elsewhere.

If Your Child is Refused

The number of places in a school is decided by the DFE, based on the space available. And schools must fill every space – if there are enough applicants – the LEA cannot, by law, distribute children around to even up the numbers.

If your child is refused by a CTC or grant-maintained school there is no formal appeals procedure but you can write to the governing body. For an LEA school there is a set appeals procedure before an independent committee. It is explained in documents which you should ask the LEA to send to you. Unless you appeal, you have no legal right to see any reports from previous schools which may have caused your child to be rejected. But you must act fast because there may be a time limit of as little as 14 days. Appeals must be in writing and you should give your reasons for wanting the school of your choice. You can:

- say why you don't like the school which has been allocated
- say why you aren't convinced by the reasons given for refusing a place
- add anything else which helps your case.

You will then be sent a note of the date of the appeal hearing. You can ask for a different date, if you have a good reason for this. But tell them at once. The other side has to reveal all relevant documents 7 days before the hearing, including any reports on your child which may influence the decision. You then need to prepare what you will say. Find out all you can about the admission arrangements in the area and the school they want to send your child to, and be sure to take with you your original letter and notes of everything you want to say, and any evidence you need. Unfortunately, now that popular schools will be filled to capacity the chance of being able to squeeze your child in on appeal are bound to be slimmer. But it is still worth a try.

> Once a child is attending the disliked school the LEA has a case for saying that it obviously *can* get there and has settled in. So, in practice, parents who keep their child out of school while fighting this battle are more likely to win. However, they must – by law – see that the child is being educated in a suitable manner at home. If they fail to do that the child could be taken into care and sent to school.

If the committee rules in your favour the school *must* take your child. If it rules against you, and you are not satisfied with the procedure, you can complain to the Local Government Ombudsman (page 694). As I write the Ombudsman doesn't cover special agreement and grant-maintained schools, but there are plans to change this.

In theory, if your appeal is turned down you can appeal to the Secretary of State for Education at the DFE (see Organizations) setting out your case clearly and concisely. Those in Scotland write to the Secretary of State at the Scottish Office, those in Wales to the Secretary of State for Wales at the Welsh Office. In practice, you haven't much chance of getting the decision reversed, but if the procedure was unfair in any way get your local councillor to complain to the local ombudsman. (The ACE booklet *School Choice Appeals* gives some useful advice on preparing an appeal and explains the rules – so you can tell if they were broken.)

Assisted Places at Independent Schools
The 1980 Education Act encourages fee-paying schools to take a proportion of children from families who cannot afford fees. The parents then pay according to their income and the difference is paid by the DFE. The schools select the pupils for assisted places, usually at 11 or 13, although many of them are for the A-level years. Parents must apply to the school for a place and the child must take the entrance examination in the usual way (see Independent Schools, below). There are also some music and ballet schools, which take children with special talent, under this scheme.

Your local LEA will hold a list of all independent schools in your area, as well as state schools. Or you can get advice and information from organizations like **Gabbitas, Truman and Thring** or **ISIS** (page 320). However, the scheme has its limitations. A child can only benefit from it if it has, at some time, attended state school for at least two years. The state contribution then covers tuition and expenses such as travel and uniform on a sliding scale linked to family income, but not boarding costs. But some schools don't ask for boarding fees (or full boarding fees) from these pupils. The DFE's Assisted Places Team (page 320) or the Scottish or Welsh Education Offices can give you the details.

Gifted Children
Only the least sensitive would deny that a severely handicapped child needs special help. Sadly the severely gifted child is less fortunate. Few people realize that the child who thinks in ways which nobody around can understand, and has interests the rest of the class can't share, can be just as miserably isolated as a child with crippled legs. So the isolation and frustration of gifted children is hardly given a thought, and to suggest that there should be special teachers to meet the needs of such children seems like indecently heaping educational riches upon those already rich.

Psychologists estimate that one child in every hundred has exceptional gifts. For some this is remarkable intelligence, which may show in early talking and reading, for others it may be a talent for music or mathematics which will develop later. But a gift can be a very mixed blessing. Only the most understanding parents and teachers find the energy to meet the child's endless quest for new information. It is hard for a child to have 10 sums returned covered with corrections, but it is at least as discouraging when a child who has eagerly completed the entire book in an evening is rounded on by a teacher irritated at having a whole term's homework schedule destroyed at a stroke. Yet this does happen. Worst of all, the interests of gifted children seldom match their age, so they become the odd ones out, and may be ridiculed for their strange hobbies and use of long words. So, partly out of a need to conform, partly out of frustration, many drop out and become unhappy misfits and even delinquents.

Any parent whose once quick and responsive child becomes difficult and starts getting bad results at school, should wonder whether the child may be gifted. Parents shouldn't judge the child by themselves: most of the best minds in history didn't have very exceptional parents. Nor should they expect them to seem like geniuses. Albert Einstein and other geniuses have been considered 'slow' in class. And some brilliant children are classified as subnormal because they think in ways others don't, can even think up such complex answers to intelligence tests that they get them wrong. So an average child may get higher marks than a brilliant one.

In Russia and China such children are given every encouragement in special schools. Here in Britain schools have a legal obligation to provide each child with education to suit its ability. But though some local authorities do try to provide for the very able, most pretend they do not exist.

As long as the state fails to fulfil its obligation to educate these children according to their needs, the best option for some may be a scholarship, or assisted place, into the private sector – though only the very best schools will offer what they need, and they will still be in a tiny minority. The **Gifted Children's Information Centre** and the **National Association for Gifted Children** (page 320) will advise parents on how to stimulate, support and educate such children from infancy to university.

Independent Schools

The term independent school covers those, for children of all ages, which are not state run. They range from well known public schools – which are, of course, private – to private nursery schools. Your LEA has a list of independent schools in your area and you can get advice and information on them from **Gabbitas, Truman and Thring Education Trust** or the **Independent Schools Information Service (ISIS)**.

What Does Private Education Offer
The state *v.* private schools argument is complex. I have taught in both sectors and the overwhelming advantage which the private sector offers is simply – variety.

If state schools were as quirky as private schools, and parents could choose a school with marvellous music for a musical child, and one with great rowing for a rower, and so on, the private sector might well be struggling. While sending a child to a state school may mean having the authorities place it in a school which will make it a square peg in a round hole, parents may feel that the state isn't the ideal option for certain children. And if the DFE uses the new curriculum to put a strait jacket on teachers in the state sector this may increasingly be so.

Parents tend to think that what their child needs is a 'good school' and the suggestions on choosing a state school (page 296) apply just as much to the private sector, but it isn't as simple as that. Independent schools vary greatly in what they offer and in how they handle the children. Some put huge emphasis on academic achievement, others on sport, others on the arts. Some expect uniform of almost military neatness, others use home clothes and are extremely relaxed about tidiness. Yet all of these extremes could be very good schools – though a child who might thrive in one could be a miserable failure in another. What is needed is a school which suits a particular child, which will foster his or her strengths and help overcome any weaknesses. This sounds extremely obvious but it's amazing how many parents focus all their attention on the qualities of the school and none on the qualities of the child, or assume that because a school was good for them it has to be good for their son. If in doubt it can be worth using an educational psychologist to assess a child's potential before deciding on schools. Sometimes children who fail to shine in junior school can be very able indeed.

Nursery Schools and Kindergartens – see page 288.

Preparatory Schools
These schools usually take children from 7, 8 or 9 to 11 or 13. Most belong to the Incorporated Association of Preparatory Schools (IAPS). To join this association a school must be inspected and approved so it is some guarantee of quality. The classes tend to average 10-12 pupils, and each school usually takes 80-150 pupils in all, either for boarding or day school, or a mixture of both. Their aim is mainly to prepare children to enter public schools through passing the Common Entrance examination, which may require subjects which can't normally be obtained at that age in a state junior school. However, even when they are the junior half of a public school, attending one may not guarantee a child a place in the senior school – or even give it a better chance of getting in, though it may do. It can be just as effective – and far more convenient – to have a child at a prep school nearer home. Because good prep schools are the easiest route to the public schools, the best are overwhelmed with applications and it is wise to get a child's name down soon after birth.

Senior Schools
Senior schools range from excellent top-flight public schools – for which the term independent is increasingly used – down to establishments which are, quite simply, a racket. Nobody should be deluded into thinking that all private schools are necessarily better than all state schools. Some are undoubtedly better than many state schools, but they are not better than all of them. Many private schools are, in fact, a good deal worse than many

state schools and may lack facilities which are basic in the state sector.

Unless you plan to send a child to a school which is so well known and respected that its standards are beyond question, consult an impartial organization like Gabbitas, Truman and Thring or ISIS (page 320) over the choice of school. If you don't you could be paying through the nose for very little.

To get into an independent school your child must usually be able to pass an entrance examination and you must be able to pay the fees. The exams for the best schools are very tough indeed but most give scholarships for academic ability or for skill in certain subjects like music, and these reduce or kill the fees altogether for those able to win them. There may also be scholarships for those in special categories such as the children of clergymen. But to get a scholarship you usually need to apply for it. The *Independent Schools Year Book* notes scholarships and assisted places beside each school, and Gabbitas, Truman and Thring's book *Which School* also has information on these. The other possibility is an assisted place – page 299.

Boarding Schools
In the private sector you can find boarding places for children as young as 5, but the normal age to start boarding prep school is 7. Although public schools are known for being boarding schools there is no need to start that young, some pupils don't board until 13, and others go through the whole of their private education as day pupils.

There are fierce arguments for and against boarding education, and the issue is too big to cover here. But, there is no evidence whatever that sending a child to boarding school when young helps it to stand on its own feet – in fact rather the reverse. Second, parents should not underestimate the difficulty of keeping close to children, and having a real influence on their development, once they go to boarding school. Some do manage to stay close but when you only see your child for a quarter of the year you are bound to have less chance to maintain links than if your child comes home each day. So it takes more effort on both sides.

Senior Schools – How to Get In
The majority of senior schools are single sex and boarding, with day and co-educational schools a small minority, but more and more boys' schools admit girls to study A levels. Although entrance is by a competitive examination, and possibly an interview, many schools will only allow a certain number of children to sit the examination and may close their books several years before. So, for safety, applications to day schools – for which demand far exceeds supply – should be made by the time a child is 5, and for boarding schools at least 3 years before the exam.

Entry to girls' schools is usually by a Common Entrance examination at 11. Some boys' schools also have entry at 11, usually through their own examination, but for the majority entry is via Common Entrance at 13 – a standardized exam with the pass mark varying from school to school. For a child from a state school there may be practical problems. Common Entrance has compulsory papers in English, Maths, French, History, Geography, Scripture and Science, at a very high standard for the age of the children. Children who have not been to a preparatory school may not have covered the syllabus. This can be remedied with good coaching, but it may take at least a year. However, some very good schools take a broader view and base entry on a school report and personal interview.

Specialist Schools
Within the independent sector there are schools which are totally unlike the rest – music schools, stage schools and so on. Others, such as the Steiner schools, are unusual in their total attitude to education. Steiner schools take children from 4½ to 18½ and offer an education which is decidedly alternative. At some Steiner schools parents make contributions, instead of paying set fees, and the emphasis is on the whole person and the creative, spiritual and emotional life of the child as much as its intellectual development – children may need to move to take GCSE and A-level examinations. Quite separately there are special Steiner schools for the maladjusted and handicapped.

Special Needs

Dyslexia and other Reading Problems
There used to be a bad joke that if poor children couldn't read they were stupid and if rich ones couldn't read they 'had dyslexia'. That isn't the case. Any child who finds reading and writing much harder than other subjects may be dyslexic. But caught reasonably early no reading problem need be a permanent handicap to an able child. Even dyslexics can get degrees in subjects that need a lot of reading and writing. **The British Dyslexia Association (BDA)** has advice and help (page 319). So does the **Gifted Children's Information Centre** (page 320), as many gifted children are dyslexic.

Defining Dyslexia
Dyslexia simply means 'difficulty with words' but experts apply it to a particular type of reading difficulty and suspect that there may be a physical problem in the brain which scrambles certain messages. This may be inherited or, for example, be caused by lack of oxygen to the brain during birth. Whatever the cause a dyslexic child's ability in reading and writing isn't what you'd expect for its intelligence.

To diagnose dyslexia takes professional testing, but if your child is over 8 and more than one of the following applies you ought to have tests done soon. Don't wait and hope he or she will 'grow out of it'. Does he/she:

- find reading much harder than other subjects?
- find writing much harder than other subjects (except reading)?
- manage to do some hard things in maths but get muddled on basics?
- manage to write b for d, or 29 for 92 or confuse dab with bad?

- have trouble telling left from right, yet manage things which are much harder?
- sometimes write words with letters jumbled?
- have a bad sense of direction?
- have more trouble tying shoe laces and ties than is usual for his or her age?

You can ask the school to arrange for the local educational psychologist to do tests or you can contact the organization on page 319 and see a psychologist privately. If dyslexia is officially diagnosed it usually means that extra time is allowed for taking public examinations – and a dyslexic may well need this.

There are also children who don't show the classic muddle of dyslexia but do find reading and writing far harder than they should, given their intelligence. In my experience these children sometimes have quite big emotional problems too. But the cause can just as easily be practical problems like temporary deafness caused by ear infections or a family upset or spell in hospital just when it should have got to grips with reading. So dyslexia is by no means the only reason why a normal child may be a slow reader.

What to Do if a Child has Reading Problems
If a child is diagnosed as having dyslexia it has a 'specific learning difficulty' under the Education Act and the school should provide remedial teaching. There are also private classes in some areas which the BDA (page 319) should be able to put you in touch with, but if a child isn't attending such a class parents can do a lot to help any slow reader.

In helping a child with reading problems you need to realize that it has two difficulties: the actual learning difficulty, and the sense of frustration and failure at finding it lacks basic skills which children who are no brighter have mastered. The longer this has gone on, the more the child will have grown to hate and fear the tasks which humiliate it – namely reading and writing. So the first block to overcome is usually a refusal to risk the humiliation of failing, by trying. This means it *must* start with reading it can succeed with quite easily.

Parents who are tolerant can help a child to overcome these feelings (though probably not if the causes are emotional). Those who have to see their children achieve may need to avoid trying to help; the child will feel their annoyance when it fails – even if they keep their mouth shut – and this will humiliate the child still further.

Those who feel they could help their children can try the methods I have given for teaching a child to read on page 291. They are the ones I devised when I specialized in teaching reading. I found they also worked with slow and dyslexic readers. Those who consult experts may find they are given different advice and should then follow it: it is important to follow *one* system. However, I am alarmed to find some experts say words should be broken down as much as possible when teaching dyslexics. In my experience dyslexics can learn to recognize *whole* words quite easily but when words are broken down the end may be scrambled with the beginning. This matches their behaviour in everyday life. Even the most dyslexic never confuse a chair with a table, but ask them to sit on the left arm of a chair and they may well sit on the right.

So for the sake of dyslexic children, I'm going to stick my neck out and suggest you should be very cautious about breaking down words, and get any expert who suggests it to give you some very good reasons for it.

★ Some children who write b for d and so on get them right when typing. Typing also allows their work to look much more grown up. This gives them a great feeling of achievement and also makes it easier for teachers to mark the *content* of their writing. As children like reading their own work it also gives them practice at reading print. So a typewriter – or a computer with a printer – can be a big boost.

★ If possible get a teach-yourself typing course and encourage the child to learn to touch type – then it will make fewer mistakes, work faster, and have a skill other children don't have – another confidence booster.

★ Computer games where the child has to make something move around the screen are valuable for smoothing out its left/right confusion.

★ Computer games which ask the child to type in words are a good incentive to reading and writing.

★ If a child can't read well it will never want to do so unless it learns to enjoy books. So it is doubly important that it is often read to and that the books are ones which *really* interest and excite it. Don't worry about whether they are literature or not. But don't just read to the dyslexic child while the others read to themselves or it will just feel humiliated. Make reading an activity which is part of family closeness and love.

An adult who thinks they may be dyslexic can ask to be tested by the psychology service of the Manpower Services Commission, and may be able to attend a dyslexia clinic. Or testing can be arranged through the British Dyslexia Association.

Children with Disabilities and Special Needs

Children who have mental or physical difficulties or special problems are now called 'children with special educational needs'. The 1944 Education Act rule that children must be educated according to their needs and abilities applies as much to them as to any others. And LEAs have a legal duty to ensure this happens. Government policy is that as far as possible children with special needs should be educated in ordinary schools if it is 'reasonably practicable', and follow the National Curriculum as far as they are able.

★ The LEA must also say what non-educational provision your child needs and arrange for the District Health Authority to provide it.

Assessment of Problems

If a child under 2 has problems talk to your GP or clinic. If *you* want an assessment made of its mental or physical abilities the authorities have a duty to give one, but if anyone suggests your child should be assessed you can refuse. If a problem is found you should be able to get special equipment under the health service and special toys from toy libraries.

If a child aged 2 or more seems to have a problem it should really be assessed at least a year before starting school at 5. LEAs have a duty to provide assessment. This gives time to sort out the best possible schooling. The rules are these:

● if parents want an assessment it cannot, unreasonably, be refused
● the authorities have a duty to identify children who will need special schooling and at this age parents must allow assessment (or appeal against it)
● parents must be told their child will be assessed and have 29 days in which to write asking that no assessment be made, giving their reasons
● when a child is assessed they have a right to be there and to give evidence of its abilities and problems
● if the LEA refuses an assessment or decides the child has no special needs the parents may appeal to the Secretary of State for Education in writing
● if the LEA decides a child does have special needs it must send the parents a draft statement of the professional advice it was given
● a parent who disagrees with an assessment has 15 days to say so and ask to see an official
● a parent who still objects to what has been issued must be told to appeal and where and how to appeal to the Appeals Tribunal
● only if your child has serious problems will the LEA write a Statement of Special Educational Needs
● if the appeal is dismissed a parent can appeal to the Secretary of State for Education
● all children classed as having special needs must be re-assessed at between 12½ and 14½.

How Long Does Assessment Take?

The time an educational assessment takes varies with the problem, but a child may need to see as many as 6 different people at different times and this can take months. If you ask, the LEA *must* tell you who suggested the child should be assessed and who will do the assessing – and how – and show you all reports which have been made on your child. You also have a right to know about any case conferences on your child and can ask to be invited to them.

The LEA must also give full details of their policy on educating children with special needs and on any schools to which they might send your child. And there should be a special advisor for parents to talk to.

Where Will a Child be Educated?

In its Statement the LEA must detail your child's special needs, and the education it recommends, and name a suitable school. And having said what *should* happen the LEA must, by law, see it *does* happen (unless parents object) even if that means giving extra money to the school to make it possible. Parents of a child with special needs have just the same right to choose a school as they would for any other child. They can appeal against the decision in the same way as against any other school choice (page 298). But there is seldom a choice between different schools catering for a particular problem.

What Education is Best for a Child?
If you have a child with special needs and are wondering whether it would be better in an ordinary school or a special school, there is really no easy answer. So much depends on the disability, on the child, and on the facilities it will and won't have in either establishment. I suggest you contact any organizations for the condition from which your child suffers (see In Sickness) and talk to other parents in the local branch. They will know whether enough money has been spent on integrating the children into normal schools or whether the equipment will be much better at a special school. The **Centre for Studies on Integration in Education** (page 319) can advise parents of children with special needs on what is being done in different areas and on what they can do to try and get their children into a normal school.

The schooling provided locally by LEAs isn't, of course, the only option. There are a few boarding places in the state sector and you also have a right to educate a child with special needs at home (page 290), or find it a place in an approved independent school. If the LEA chooses such a placing – it must pay the fees.

A child will be assessed as needing special schooling mainly on the advice of an educational psychologist. If you feel your child has been incorrectly assessed, for example you think it is deaf but bright and the LEA has classed it as unintelligent, you need evidence on your side. It would help if you could get another educational psychologist to assess your child and present that independent view to the LEA or appeals board. Organizations catering for those with particular disabilities may be able to help you find a suitable psychologist. Most are listed elsewhere in this book, but if your child has a rare disorder, or you are confused about your rights, the **Voluntary Council for the Handicapped Child** will send you a complete list of such organizations – large sae. Or write, with a sae, or ring, the **Independent Panel of Special Education Experts** (P.319). It helps parents get a second opinion on a child's needs, advises on the legal issues and helps parents put their case to the authorities. **The Advisory Centre for Education** (page 321) may also be able to help you.

When You Move
If you leave the area in which a child has been assessed as having special needs it may take a little while for you to get information on how the new area educates children with such needs. So write and ask well in advance. The assessment can be transferred from one area to another, but if you don't want it transferred you can ask the new area for a fresh assessment. The new authority may still see all the old reports and may be influenced by them, but this does give you a chance to muster new evidence and argue your case again.

Speech Problems
The situation on speech therapy is complicated. Logically speech is part of education, and some LEAs *do* include it in their duties. But the law is unclear on who is really responsible for it so some authorities pass the buck to the Health Service which usually employs the therapists. The Health Service has no obligation to act fast since speech problems aren't fatal. There is, in addition, a national shortage of speech therapists. If your child has this problem you should ask for it to receive therapy and be prepared to lobby very hard until it gets it. The earlier it gets help the better. AFASIC (page 590) will help parents both to get their entitlements and to help a child with this problem. See also page 563.

Schools are no longer inspected by Her Majesty's Inspectors, nor are all inspectors experts in education. Instead the Education (Schools) Act 1992 set up an independent register of inspectors, drawn from many walks of life, which is regulated by the Office for Standards in Education (OFSTED). These inspectors also cover higher and further education.

EDUCATION: SIXTEEN TO NINETY

Career Advice and Exam Choice

The most important, though sometimes neglected, issue in deciding what to study and what qualifications to get after school is what career they will lead to. Ideally everyone would get independent career advice at 14, before deciding on GCSEs and other courses, for it is all too easy to close doors to a particular career by having the wrong combination of exam subjects to get the necessary degree or other training. So it is worth doing some career research before choosing exams, even though it may seem far too young to decide on a career.

At one time the education system offered neat, arbitrary divisions. There was a division between courses and exams done in school and those done as part of further or higher education after school. Exams were largely for the 'brainy'; university was for the very bright; professional qualifications were taken when young; and most of those who didn't go to college expected no paper qualification at all.

That is no longer so. There is a drive to ensure that all children show some proof of their ability, to give more recognition to skills learnt at work, and to make it easier for adults to train or retrain. Running parallel with GCSEs, A and AS Levels and conventional degrees, there are now vocational exams, notably NVQs (page 305), which extend from basic skill up to the equivalent of postgraduate work, thus spanning both Higher Education (HE) and Further Education (FE).

Moreover, now that former polytechnics are universities, it is likely that degrees will increasingly embrace practical, as well as academic, knowledge and skills. The growth of the Open University, in-work training schemes, modular courses and open learning have also made it easier to get new qualifications later in life. In fact, the pundits predict that most people will need to retrain for a different career at least once – and the more intelligent someone is the more often they will retrain. Thus the traditional route to a degree or professional qualification via A or AS Levels, a good university and the right training before the age of 25 is no longer the only one. However, it is still one of the easiest, so it pays to think ahead when choosing which exams or awards to take.

With GCSE (and Scottish Standard Grade) being a 2-year course, the time for a child to start thinking about what it wants to do after 16 is now pushed back to the early age of 13 or 14. The new, broader approach provided by AS-levels may smooth out some poor choices, but it may not cope with all of them.

Examinations

GCSE
GCSE (and Scottish Standard Grade) is structured to give every child some proof of their achievement at school. It is taken at around the age of 16 and the avowed aim is:

- to make pupils feel that their work in school is valued,
- to show what pupils *can* do, not what they can't
- to provide a unified system for every school,
- to have general criteria applying to all subjects,
- to foster practical skills and the application of both skill and knowledge to real-life situations.

At the end of a 2-year course the children take an examination which is marked by an outside examiner. In other ways it differs from the old GCE.

- Where all pupils can't do the same task, different exercises are set for groups of different ability. There are also 'differentiated' exam papers (see below).
- English language, for example, now includes practical materials like writing letters and instructions.
- There is an emphasis on talking and listening, in both English and foreign languages. To pass English, pupils must now reach a certain grade in spoken English as well as written English.
- In science the emphasis is on scientific methods, and the syllabus contains more practical work and less learning by rote. The application of science, and its impact on the environment, is also emphasized.
- Work done during the 2 years may be assessed by teachers and count towards exam marks. Special projects are usually assessed rather than the entire

body of work for the year. Independent assessors check that the marking doesn't vary from school to school.

Those who fail to reach the minimum standard for grade G are ungraded and won't get a certificate. Everyone else will.

The Scottish exams are not identical to those in England. The Standard Grade of the Scottish Certificate of Education has the same 7 levels of award as for GCSE (but numbered 1-7, not ordered alphabetically); 7 simply shows the course was completed. The Scottish Higher covers more subjects than A-level and is usually taken in one year. There is also a prestigious Certificate of Sixth Year Studies (CSYS) which can be taken by those who pass Higher in the first year and wish to stay on another year or be admitted to an English university. But for a Scottish university Higher alone is enough. If a candidate's results are far less good than would have been expected, an appeal can be made. In which case the papers will be re-marked and the pupil's usual school work looked at.

GCSE and Standard Grades Compared

GCSE			SCOTLAND Standard Grade	% (approx)
A		credit	1	100 - 77
B		credit	2	76 - 65
C		general	3	64 - 50
D		general	4	49 - 40
E		foundation	5	39 - 30
F		foundation	6	29 - 20
G		foundation	7	

Differentiated Papers
The idea behind differentiated papers is that there can, for example, be 4 papers, each slightly harder than the previous one. Each pupil would only take the 2 which suit his or her ability. Both the papers which are taken and the standard reached in them give the final mark. So, for example, those who take papers 1 and 2 can get grades G up to E – depending on how well they do them. Those who take 2 and 3 can get grades F up to C. But only those who take – and do well in – papers 3 and 4 can get grades A and B. Pupils are likely to be taught in separate groups or sets.

Addresses and suggestions for further reading are at the ends of chapters.

> The amount of work assessed varies from subject to subject, but children will always be told whether a piece of work is counting towards their exam or not.

Stepped Papers

Stepped papers assume that all the pupils may be in the same class and will sit the same papers. But within each paper there are different grades of question. It is like mental mountain climbing: everyone answers the questions on the lower slopes and they then climb to the upper slopes of the harder and harder questions according to their intellectual muscle.

How it is Administered

The examination is administered by four examining groups in England and one in Wales working to nationally agreed criteria and the Schools Curriculum and Assessment Authority, which is independent, will monitor examinations to maintain a uniform standard

> All pupils must be given a **Record of Achievement** when they leave school. This is a summary of what a pupil has achieved in all aspects of his or her school life, which can be shown to potential employers or training schemes.

CPVE (Certificate of Pre-vocational Education)

CPVE is a course which is designed to provide a bridge between school and work, or further training for work. It is for pupils of 16 plus who aren't able to take A or AS levels, and the course can be taken either in school or in various types of college. The standards for CPVE courses are set by the City & Guilds and the BTEC and its 10 subject areas range from social skills to science and information technology. However CPVE is being phased out by the end of 1994 in favour of NVQs and GNVQs.

A and AS Levels

Pupils usually take from 1 to 3 A level subjects, which they study in depth, over 2 years. But, the very able may be allowed to take more than 3 subjects and to take them in a year.

AS level is a parallel examination for those of the same age and ability. AS courses are designed to take about half as much work as an A level, but reach the same intellectual standard. The aim is for pupils to take 2 AS levels in place of one of their A levels. So they can study more subjects, and choose ones which complement or contrast with their A levels. For example, a scientist could do two sciences at A level, plus an AS foreign language and an AS in economics. The grades and standards for AS are exactly the same as for A level.

Universities, colleges and professional bodies usually accept 2 AS levels as equalling one A level (at the same grade) for entrance to DipHE and first degree courses;

so do UCAS and the Civil Service. However, there may be some variation as to *how many* A levels may be replaced by AS levels and universities may expect an A, rather than AS, level in the subject that someone is applying to read.

The A level marking system now uses Grade C to cover a wider range of marks, and grade N means someone has narrowly failed, but doesn't count as any grade of GCSE. Any mark below N is U, unclassified.

NVQs and GNVQs

The current emphasis on education as a preparation for work has led to two new ranges of vocational qualifications: National Vocational Qualifications (NVQs), or Scottish Vocational Qualifications (SVQs), and General National Vocational Qualifications (GNVQs), or General Scottish Vocational Qualifications (GSVQs). The aim is to provide a comprehensive framework of qualifications which can cover a wide range of skills, subjects and levels.

GNVQs (and **SNVQs**) are at 3 levels and are mainly for those at school or college, but can be taken at any age and by Open Learning as well as attending classes. Whereas NVQs focus on specific areas and careers, for example real life marketing skills, GNVQs give background knowledge which may be useful in a range of careers, for example business. Level 2 'Intermediate' GNVQs are meant to be similar to GCSEs in their level of difficulty. Level 3 'Advanced' GNVQs are meant to be like vocational A levels, may take 2 years to prepare for, and may be accepted as entrance qualifications for university. To get on a 'Foundation' Level 1 course, or even on a Level 2, you are unlikely to need any paper qualifications. But to get on a Level 3 course, you may need some GCSEs. However, FE colleges can give 'accreditation of prior learning', allowing those with the right work experience to be accepted on a course without the usual exams. Such work experience may also count as a credit towards part of the course itself, as may National Curriculum achievements.

NVQs (and **SVQs**) are for those in work and are assessments of real-life skills and practical knowledge. They have 5 levels with several separately assessed units, combining to give the NVQ at a particular level. The standard will range from basic skills at Level 1 to work of postgraduate standard at Level 5. Assessment may be by someone at work, or by a local Training and Enterprise Council (TEC), or Scottish LEC, as appropriate. There is no time limit on taking the different units; some can be completed in a few weeks, others might need 2 years' work. However, you needn't have succeeded in any other exam, test or assessment to take them.

You can even get tax relief towards NVQs and SVQs. The Inland Revenue (page 693) has a leaflet on tax relief for vocational training. To find out more about all these exams contact your LEA, TEC, LEC, or Jobcentre, or College of Further Education. Failing that contact the **National Council for Vocational Qualifications** (page 322).

National qualification framework

BTEC and SCOTVEC

BTEC and SCOTVEC exams and awards can be found in schools, further education colleges and other institutions and span both schooling and in-work training at different levels. Unlike GCSE and A levels, the subject areas all relate to work: for example, engineering, catering, finance and computing. The modular courses can be full or part-time and many professional bodies accept BTEC National Awards for entry to degree courses.

However, as I write BTEC is undergoing a revolution. It is government policy to have *one* main range of vocational qualifications. So, as GNVQ's (page 305) are phased in, the BTEC awards are being phased out and the council which administers them is adapting its courses to fit the needs of GNVQs and GSVQs. This is a gradual process, starting with those subjects and courses which were already most similar, and will take several years to complete. So, for a while, *at any level*, some subjects may lead to the old awards, others to the new ones. All the details have yet to be finalized, but the following pattern seems to be emerging:

● those successfully completing a short course, or individual unit of study, may get an NVQ, GNVQ or BTEC Certificate of Achievement
● those 16+, with or without an exam qualification, can study for a GNVQ Level 2 or BTEC First Certificate or Diploma
● those 16+ with GCSE Grade C or better, a BTEC First award, or an appropriate CPVE, will be able to study for GNVQ Level 3 or a BTEC National Certificate or Diploma
● those 18+ with appropriate A or AS levels, or GNVQ Level 3, or BTEC National award, will be able to study for GNVQ Level 4 or BTEC's Higher National awards
● those over 21 needing skill in particular subjects can opt for a BTEC Continuing Education Certificate or Diploma, and may get on the course through either work experience or paper qualifications.

SCOTVEC is involved in similar changes, with its Scottish National Certificates and Higher National Certificates and Diplomas, being offered at the same time as SVQs and GSVQs, but with possible switch-overs.

To find out what courses are available in any area contact BTEC or SCOTVEC, but applications for a place on a course should be made directly to the institution running it. Many are organized so that people can teach themselves in their free time. You register with an institution which runs that course, then have the support of tutors who assess your work and teach key classes.

City & Guilds and Pitman Awards

These cover exams and awards ranging from Certificates of Achievement, for courses in basic skills, to postgraduate qualifications. Most courses are linked to business but some cover general education, English as a foreign language and hobbies. They are structured to give experience in rising steps, and may last from a single term to several years. Like BTEC, this single organization will gradually be unifying its examinations with NVQs and GNVQs. But for the moment it offers City & Guilds, or Pitman, awards in some subjects and NVQs or GNVQs in others. Its exams are taken in both Scotland and England.

The City & Guilds of London Institute (page 322), which incorporates the Pitman Examination Institute, provides syllabuses and guidelines for City & Guilds and Pitman examination and certification throughout the British Isles. The courses are taught in schools, colleges of further education approved training centres, and adult institutes. There are no age limits for most courses. Although prior qualifications may be recommended, you apply to the school or college and entry is at its discretion. Courses usually start in September.

It is also possible to prepare for many City & Guilds exams at home, but entry to the examinations must be through the local examinations secretary at a centre where City & Guilds courses are taught, and the closing date for entry may be as much as 8 months before the exam. Information of the courses and awards are from the C & G address (page 322)

RSA Awards

The Royal Society of Arts Examinations Board sets and examines courses in single subjects, such as word-processing or book-keeping, for which it gives its own awards. It also runs examinations, at a series of levels, in foreign language skills in relation to business, and is an examining body for a range of NVQs and GNVQs. The RSA publishes a guide to its examinations and can tell you which educational bodies teach them – and therefore where to apply for a course.

Applying for Admission

If you know what you want to do, but have left school, your local TEC (or LEC in Scotland) can tell you how to apply for almost any course in your region – and any public reference library should have the TEC's or LEC's address. If you don't, or want to know how to find out about advanced courses or courses outside your locality page 310 on careers and the organizations on page 322 may be useful.

To get a place on most courses you apply direct to the institution which is running the course. In Scotland you

---

Addresses and suggestions for further reading are at the ends of chapters.

also apply direct to universities. In the rest of Britain (with some exceptions) to get into a university you should apply *at least a year before you want to start the course* as explained on page 308. However, gaps do occur at the last minute and it is always worth trying to get in, even at the start of term.

Degrees and Other Higher Examinations

In addition to the traditional degree courses offering 'learning for its own sake', there are more schemes than ever to help people train, retrain or extend their learning. The division between student and adult education has become almost non-existent as educational institutions have increasingly focused their courses towards the workplace, so that initial training and adult retraining are happening side by side.

The universities are developing new courses to update adult employees in skills needed in business and industry, and links are being formed between companies and universities which provide advanced courses in leading-edge technology.

At the same time the old rigidity of the British system is beginning to break down in favour of a modular system in which achievements on one course can be counted towards another, and people can move from one discipline, or one institution, to another without having to treat education like Monopoly and return to 'go'. See also Open Learning page 309.

There are more schemes than ever to help people train, retrain or extend their training. The local Jobcentres and the Area Division Offices of the Training Agency are the places to find out about aspects of funding which fall outside the usual provision of grants.

Credit Accumulation and Transfer Scheme (CATS)
The Credit Accumulation and Transfer Scheme (CATS) allows previous work experience or study to count towards a degree or award at a university or college: and therefore towards admission. So if you dropped out of a degree course after a year you may be able to gain exemption from part of a similar degree course. And someone may be able to put together a very personal degree using units from different courses. **ECCTIS 2000** publishes a directory of CATS schemes but it is still early days for this scheme and each institution has a slightly different approach.

Choosing a Course
One of the most surprising features of our education system is that every university is free to devise its own degree courses, set the standards for them and award the degrees. Despite the supervision of the Higher Education Quality Council, standards can therefore vary widely between one university and another – and between different subjects in a single university. However, a Charter for Higher and Further Education now sets standards which students have a right to expect, relating to information on choices and the performance of the college, and standards of administration and teaching.

At one time a central council validated the awards of polytechnics and colleges but polys, now that they are universities, have the same freedom as the older universities. So the council has been abolished and colleges are now validated by appropriate universities. On top of that there are numerous other examining bodies in Britain, each setting their own courses and giving different awards and qualifications, often linked to a particular trade, occupation or profession.

This means that for a degree or other exam to get you a good job it needs to be from an institution, or department, which is highly regarded *in that particular field*. A university can be the tops in Chinese, but have a computer department that is a joke in the industry. So candidates need to read all they can. University and college prospectuses and handbooks are free for the asking, and the students'. union may be able to sell you a handbook produced by the students – with insights lacking in more official publications. The books on page 322 offer unbiased information, and it is also worth sounding out anyone who might know anything useful. But make sure the information is up to date: a place that was good a generation ago may not be so today.

If you are aiming for a particular career (page 323), it is worth asking the professional body related to it, which degrees or awards, from which examining bodies, will give you the best chance of success in that field. Then you can apply first to that university or college, or find a suitable course through the examining body. You might also try the ECCTIS database or contact HEIS, or one of the other bodies on page 322.

This is also the time to learn what grants, scholarships or other money may be available. You can't assume that you will automatically get a grant for any course: the rules may not be what you or I would assume to be logical or fair. The Training, Enterprise and Education Directorate (TEED) should have information or the local Jobcentre, TEC or LEC should know about funding which lies outside the usual range of grants (see also page 534).

The JUPITER Consortium Ltd (page 321) was set up to provide industry with information on postgraduate courses in technology management at the leading edge of development, and to identify gaps in the system. It has compiled a unique guide to such courses and, though not set up to advise the public, will give information on what courses are available in this field and where they can be found.

Postgraduate business courses are offered in many universities. They embrace both specialized courses, in subjects such as marketing, and more general MBA courses. The Open Business School section of the Open University offers an MBA course, among its range of management courses. The **Association of Masters of Business Administration** (page 321) can send you a guide to MBA courses worldwide that meet its criteria; this guide also has useful information on the business school or departments which run them. (MBA courses which lack its blessing may be very good, but there is less guarantee of their standard.) For other business courses you can scour the handbooks and directories or try the **Association of Business Schools** (page 322), or the **Association of Management, Education and Training** (page 321).

Finding Postgraduate Courses

Most universities offer postgraduate courses. These are listed in the handbooks of the individual universities, or of their departments, in the ECCTIS database (page 322) and also in the major directories on university courses which I have listed on page 321. There are also specialist sources of information. For example, the professional body of any profession which requires postgraduate training can usually advise you on that training. There are also specialist bodies related to technology and business.

Getting Into College or University

The Art and Design Admissions Registry (page 322) covers BA Hons and BTEC HND courses in art and design. Application forms are available from early February and must normally be in by mid March.

Central Register and Clearing House (page 321) covers B.Ed degree and DipHE courses, while the Graduate Teacher Training Register, at the same address, covers the Post Graduate Certificate in Education. All forms and booklets are available from September the previous year.

The **Universities and Colleges Admissions Service (UCAS)** (page 321) processes applications for admission to full-time first degree courses at all the universities in Great Britain. That includes those universities which were once polytechnics, and also certain colleges and teacher training other than art and design. The following is only a rough guideline on possible procedure – it is essential to check the instructions in the UCAS handbook as the rules change remarkably often.

Even within one subject different universities vary considerably in what they offer and what they require from applicants. Before filling in an UCAS form read the handbooks of likely universities.

University Application Procedures

Application for university places should reach UCAS about a year before the applicant wants to go up to university – check the UCAS handbook for closing dates. The actual closing date is some while later. The UCAS form allows for several universities to be chosen, and different courses may be applied for at different universities. It is wise to apply for as many as the form allows.

> Oxford or Cambridge need applications direct to them and to UCAS. Their deadline is usually far earlier than the general UCAS date, so this should be checked in good time. It may be as early as March *the year before*.

A few people are offered unconditional places on the strength of their past results. If you accept one of these offers you are committed to that university.

Most will be offered places at some of the universities they have applied for, provided they obtain certain grades in the exams they are about to take. The grades required by these conditional offers will vary with the university but a candidate must reply, through UCAS, within a set time and is limited to one firm acceptance and one insurance acceptance. *Fill up every section of the UCAS form; blanks are counted as refusals.*

The August exam results are sent directly to UCAS by the boards, and from there to the universities. They then decide whether or not to confirm their conditional offers, and may confirm a place even when the set grades have not been reached.

Some people will be rejected by all their universities. In that case any candidate, or his school, can apply to another university – quoting his UCAS number and the clearing procedure given below. To know where there are vacancies and on which course, contact the organizations given in this chapter or check the serious press. In addition, *The Observer* has an information service.

Clearing

If an applicant receives no offer, UCAS will automatically suggest an application for a place through Clearing and send the necessary form. Anyone whose grades were too low for their conditional places to be confirmed is sent one. The system allows someone to be considered for *any* course for which they have appropriate qualifications, though their preferred universities and regions are taken into account. They must, however, apply for a clearing place *one university at a time*. Only if the first university refuses them, during Clearing can they apply to a second and so on.

Clearing shouldn't be seen as a dumping ground. Some very good universities are short of applicants for certain courses. However, some Clearing offers aren't made until the university term has almost started – so stay in Britain until term begins.

Scholarships and Awards

The scholarships offered by universities are given in their prospectuses and it is up to a candidate to apply to the universities for these. Industrial sponsorships may also be available and the UCAS handbook tells you how to apply for these.

University of Buckingham

The University of Buckingham is a university which is totally outside the system and is therefore fee-charging. Its degrees are awarded after 2 years of study. Students work 4 terms each academic year, which starts in January. There is no closing date.

It offers both undergraduate and postgraduate courses and the bias is towards those which have some links with business or industry: business administration, law, languages, economics, computer science, and biological science. An unusual feature is that all students who aren't fluent in two languages take a language as part of their course, whatever their main subject.

Apply through UCAS. Students are accepted on the basis of their potential as well as their achievements, and

---

Addresses and suggestions for further reading are at the ends of chapters.

mature students may be judged on their work achievements as well as on their academic qualifications. Students can obtain the usual LEA mandatory grant plus a grant towards one third of the cost of fees, and some bursaries are available from the university for those who need them.

General Private Sector Courses
Many subjects such as secretarial work, dance training, or beauty therapy are covered by colleges operating outside the state sector. The DFE no longer inspects and approves such courses, but an accreditation scheme is operated by the: **British Accreditation Council for Independent Further and Higher Education** (page 322), which can supply the names of approved colleges.

Women Returners
Women with children can have special problems in finding courses and jobs that they can combine with the demands of a family. The open learning schemes (below) can be ideal but some women may be desperate to get out of the home. Fortunately, colleges are becoming more aware of the needs of women, but they vary enormously. The **Women Returners Network** (page 322) is a charity advising women on how to return to work. It publishes a Directory of Education and Training for Women which includes courses with crêches, and gives useful contacts and addresses for more information. It runs conferences, has useful leaflets and will put women in touch with other organizations fostering women in the workplace. The Department of Employment also publishes a New Horizons leaflet that you can get from 'Inf 2' at the DFE (page 693).

Students with Disabilities
The Warnock Report described the provision for students with disabilities as 'confused, patchy, and inadequate', and recommended better, more co-ordinated, provision. However, the take-up on the courses which do exist is patchy, with some classes closing for lack of interest, while others in the same area are over-subscribed. Those looking for a course would do well to look at every possible option: a good deal is available but it takes a little finding. Many of the charities specializing in a particular disability have education advice services. There are also general sources of information. The Open University (page 323) has a special adviser for such students. The OU Students' Association also helps and it has a fund to provide such students with equipment they need for studying if they can't afford it. And the **National Bureau for Students with Disabilities**, and the **Scottish Centre for the Tuition of the Disabled** (page 320) have additional advice and information.

Overseas Courses
If you want to study abroad, especially within the EC, the **British Council** and the **Central Bureau for Educational Visits and Exchanges** (which have merged but retained their names, and are both reachable via the latter's address) are good starting points. The Bureau provides information, advice and help to those who want to work, study or travel abroad for educational reasons. It also runs exchanges for teachers, graduates and undergraduates who wish to extend their language skills and administers an EC-funded scheme in this area. There are also a growing number of books on this and information direct from embassies and the EC itself.

Open Learning and Distance Learning

Open learning covers all levels of education, from the most basic to postgraduate, and most forms of open learning are open to those who lack the qualifications to enter conventional courses. This is one of the exploding fields of education and can be found in several ways.

1 Some organizations, such as the Open University, exist purely for open learning. Others, such as London University, make it easy.
2 Some conventional examining bodies are now structuring their syllabuses and materials so that people can follow the courses without attending an educational institution. You can always ask.
3 More and more educational institutions are becoming aware that not everyone who wants to study can enrol as a full-time student. So they are letting people enrol, and use facilities like libraries and special tutorials, while doing most of the course at home. The best way to find this type is often to ask local educational institutions whether they would let you study that way.
4 Use one of the courses put out on radio or television.
5 Use a correspondence course, such as those run by The **National Extension College** (page 323). But stick to courses approved by the **Council for the Accreditation of Correspondence Colleges** (page 322) or you could waste your money. It will send you a list.

The BBC issues a publication on its educational programmes which you can get from BBC Education. Some local radio stations also have education programmes, so ask the station manager. For education programmes on independent radio or television write to the information officer of the company. Both the BBC and ITV publish rather good books, so it's worth asking for a publication list too.

Open University (OU)
Having pioneered the mass availability of open learning, the Open University has a substantial range of courses and study packs, and aims for both personal and professional development. In addition to degree and degree-level courses, there are postgraduate-level courses on such topics as manufacturing, or the industrial applications of computers, and short courses on parenting and planning for retirement.

Its Open Business School has the blessing of the British Institute of Management and has already been used by many of Britain's biggest companies. It offers short courses, lasting 12-30 weeks, which can be combined to give a certificate, diploma or MBA. The courses cover topics such as international marketing, women into management, accounting for managers, and starting your own business, and use multimedia techniques –

tapes, television, books, assignments and residential weekends – to create a training package which can be fitted into the day of those who work full-time.

No qualifications are needed to start most OU courses, but some other higher level study may count towards an OU qualification, and equally some OU credits are now accepted by other institutions. On some short courses, if you look at the material and realize you can't do it you can return it and have your money back provided you do so within a set time (check the brochure). So decide *fast*.

Fees range from a few pounds to several hundred pounds. There are regional offices in most county towns or contact the student enquiry office at **Open University**.

The Open College
The Open College has courses for those who want to improve their business or technical qualifications and gain qualifications such as GNVQs, GSVQs or those of BTEC, SCOTVEC or City & Guilds, or to credits towards them.

Courses use a combination of text, audio and video tapes and written tutorials using materials provided by the college. Students also have access to Open College centres, often within existing educational institutions, where they can join and get advice, information, tutorial support and practical training. But if you live somewhere remote, you can discuss your problems with a tutor on a telephone hotline instead of visiting a centre.

You can enrol at any time. The charges vary from quite a small sum to several hundred pounds but it may be possible to be funded by LEA grants, government training schemes, or an employer.

Open College of the Arts
The Open College of the Arts is affiliated to the Open University and offers serious and scholarly courses in subjects such as art, art history and music. These courses last from 1-5 years, use the same multi-media approach as the OU, and include both theory and practice.

Adult Education

Adult education is usually associated with evening classes in pottery or flower arranging. It does cover these, but it also covers every level up to higher degrees, and adult is usually defined as over 18. Make enquiries in midsummer with your education authority, or in Scotland contact the Scottish Community and Education Council, as many courses get booked up and only those who apply early on the first day get in.

There is also the **University of the Third Age (U3A)** (page 322). This is not a university but an organization of self-help groups for those over 50. It organizes classes all over Britain which cover every level of ability and interest and provide a chance for like minded people to meet.

There are also a wide range of residential courses. **NIACE** (page 321) produces a twice-yearly directory of short residential courses which are purely for interest and pleasure and not aimed at any qualification. Also an increasing number of travel companies offer painting holidays, wine appreciation holidays and so on (see **AITO** page 697).

Adult Literacy
Most public libraries have information on where to obtain help with basic skills in reading, mathematics and spoken English. Failing that, contact the **Adult Literacy and Basic Skills Unit** (page 321).

Workers' Educational Association (WEA)
The WEA is a voluntary movement to spread adult education and increase individual development. It is a democratic organization in which the members decide what they will learn and how they will learn it. Classes are taken by professional teachers and lecturers and cover topics like history, women's studies, arts, music, or social sciences. There is great emphasis on enjoyment and involvement.

The courses are usually 1½-2 hours a week for 10-24 weeks, and are funded by local and central government and, to a lesser extent, by fees. Many of the classes have child care facilities attached, so mothers of young children can attend. The address of the nearest WEA classes should be available from your local library, or from the head office (page 322).

Career Advice and Job Finding

The LEAs must provide a career advice and information service for all pupils in full-time education at every educational establishment (except a university). The careers officers are also meant to help pupils find a job.

There is a mass of free information available elsewhere on almost any career. Almost every professional body or trade association has a helpful booklet or leaflet. So do many less obvious organizations, for example, the Countryside Commission has a booklet on careers in conservation. These booklets are normally free and very informative, and usually detail the qualifications which are needed or the in-service training which is provided. The addresses of many such organizations are in this book. If they aren't your library will have a directory.

It is also possible to get training while in the armed forces or at work. The military recruiting offices and the **National Council of Industry Training Organizations** (page 322) can tell you what in-work training is available where, what qualifications can be obtained, and what exams – if any – you need to get on such training courses. In-work training can range from basic skills to high-flown qualifications.

Certain publishers have large ranges on career and educational opportunities and a good bookshop should be able to show you their booklists or give you their address, so you can get their list yourself. Among them are Kogan Page, Longman, Hobsons Press and Careers Consultants. This last covers topics like finding jobs overseas or running your own business. Local libraries should also have a good range of such books and reference librarians are usually good at finding the right ones to solve a particular problem.

Addresses and suggestions for further reading are at the ends of chapters.

On behalf of the Department of Employment, the **Career Occupational Information Centre (COIC)** sells a remarkably good range of publications, from those giving job information for teenagers to others with ideas on how an adult can retrain or a housewife take up a career. Many of them should be in a school careers library but to buy books write to the address on page 323. There are also COIC bookshops in many major towns and London boroughs – well worth a browse.

Another source of help is your local Training and Enterprise Council (TEC in England but LEC in Scotland). Your public library or Jobcentre should have the address (or contact the TEC Secretariat on page 322). These have details of youth training programmes, business start-up schemes, courses for those running small businesses, special programmes for the long-term unemployed, and so on.

Or your local Jobcentre or unemployment benefit office may help. These usually have advisory services that can tell you about local job opportunities and programmes. For example, they may be running work programmes which allow someone to do a job for a trial period of 3 weeks. The idea is that the employee can try out the job, and the employer try out the employee, without commitment on either side. They may also run Job Clubs, where those who have been unemployed for several months can get support and encouragement, plus help with job applications; and they may be able to refund the cost of going for job interviews in other areas.

Youth Training (YT)

These government-backed schemes are administered by TECs and designed to introduce school leavers to work and give them a basic training in the process. They are taken on as trainees by an employer, in a field they are interested in, and given in-service training with a guaranteed number of weeks, 'off-the-job' training as well, plus paid holidays. All 16-17 year olds have a right to 2 years of YT if they wish; those 18-19 are entitled to 1 year. As it is a training programme rather than employment the weekly money is not as high as the wage for a similar job. There is no guarantee of a job at the end but qualifications via NVQs (page 305) are designed to make job finding easier. The local careers office or TEC has the details.

Career Guidance

The careers advisory service for school leavers is run systematically by local education authorities, but there is no nationwide educational and careers advice service for adults. Instead there is piecemeal provision by assorted bodies and some areas are far better provided for than others. The **National Educational Guidance Initiative** has details of local educational guidance.

Sheer pressure of numbers means that it is impossible for the state advice services to assess someone's abilities and aptitudes in great depth, and a good private assessment may be worthwhile, if it can be afforded. Such assessments are not cheap, but can stop a square peg drifting into a round hole and being miserable – and unsuccessful – for ever more. The problem is in knowing how good an assessment centre is. Check several before booking and choose the one which offers the most.

Any worthwhile centre will give a battery of tests which will take at least a morning and a psychologist should spend a good while discussing the results with the client and pointing out the options they suggest. Most companies use standard psychological tests, so there is not likely to be much difference between them on that score. The important difference is the skill with which each psychologist relates the results to the client's personality and sums up their suitability for the jobs which their abilities would allow them to do. This is impossible to assess from outside, but you can ask whether they provide information on courses in the careers they suggest, and whether they also advise on finding a job in that field, making job applications and handling interviews.

The companies on pages 323 are a starting point for enquiries, but their presence here should not be taken as a sign of recommendation, as it has not been possible to vet them all. Unfortunately, most private career guidance centres are clustered in London and the rest of Britain is very ill served.

Setting up a Business

The government is keen to encourage small businesses. TECs have information on courses in business skills and Local Enterprise Agencies have free advice on grants, allowances and loans – and there is a surprising amount of money to be had. But the schemes keep changing, so ask the Department of Employment what else is on offer. For example, URBED runs training for the unemployed and The Prince's Youth Trust, which will assist those under 26. The local library or Jobcentre should have their addresses. The Industrial Society (page 698) and the Small Business Bureau (page 691), which embraces Women into Business, may also be helpful. Or the **Greater London Business Centre** (page 323) has a freephone line offering advice and information – and much of it applies to the whole country.

RETIREMENT AND AFTER

There are very few areas in which the elderly are different from anyone else, so most of their needs are dealt with in the rest of the book. However, they do suffer one special handicap: society's expectation that they will not just clock up birthdays but become fragile, slow-witted, stiff (in mind and body) and generally ill. This may be the case but, unless there is some specific mental or physical illness, it isn't a necessary part of old age. In the Far East you see elderly people sitting cross-legged on the ground. Yet all they did to achieve this suppleness was never *stop* sitting on the ground.

Essentially the secret of making the most of old age is simply to keep on doing whatever you did when young, and if possible do things you never did before. The route to making the best of being old starts at about forty, and think of old age as a time for winding up, not winding down. By then all your responsibilities should have shifted to other people's shoulders and instead of wrapping yourself in cotton wool you can really begin to live in a carefree way and do all the things you never had time for.

Giving up Work

To give up work suddenly after a lifetime structured by its routine can be a terrible shock. Nor is it just a matter of habit. If you have devoted yourself to your job you may have hung your whole identity on your role at work; you may *be* a bus driver, an accountant or whatever that role has been. To you this may be even more 'you' than your name or your role as husband, wife or parent. To cease to have that job can feel like ceasing to exist in the real world. This problem has to be tackled head on. The **Pre-Retirement Association** (page 324) in England and the **Pre-Retirement Council** in Scotland both run courses in preparing for retirement. So does the Open University. And your firm may be prepared to pay for all or part of these courses.

Moving from Work into Retirement
Good employers may now let people work a gradually decreasing number of days a week, so they can become used to the freedom. It is well worth enquiring about. Even if a company isn't doing it already the personnel officer might be persuaded to give it a try. Of course, the temptation may be to give the utmost to the job right to the end, working longer than ever – as if to prove that retirement isn't necessary whatever the rules say. The sad truth is that this is most unlikely to win the admiration and appreciation it deserves and may leave you doubly stranded on retirement day. Long before you retire, try to find new roles which you can enjoy and in which you can feel that you matter to other people and have something to contribute.

Fun in Old Age
Retirement is also the time to learn new skills and take up new interests. The adult institutes are already full of canny pensioners making use of the cheaper rates at which they can attend classes. In a few areas this is being taken one step further and adults are attending classes in ordinary schools. This provides an even larger range of classes, fills schools which have falling rolls, keeps teachers on their toes, and makes it far harder for the young to mess about or get violent in class. It seems such an excellent idea that I feel one really constructive thing pensioners could do is press to be allowed to study in schools.

Housing in Old Age

Away from it All?
People often dream of retiring to a place by the sea or in the country. There is something to be said for selling a family home which is too large, moving to a smaller place and using the difference in price to provide a better income. But research suggests that people should look around carefully before choosing a new area, and shouldn't wait until retirement before they move. Old age is a time when friends are needed – even if it's only to do the shopping when you have a cold. The elderly should also think very carefully about how near they should be to their nearest and dearest. There is no surer way to strain a relationship than by moving too close and no way to guarantee loneliness more than by moving so far it is an expedition for them to reach you.

Carrying on in Your Own Home
Wherever someone elderly lives, the ideal situation is for them to be able to stay in their own home until they die. Luckily technology is making this easier. There are now alarms which can be carried constantly which allow someone to get emergency help by telephone even if they have fallen and cannot reach the phone, and some will automatically call for help. This is likely to be an expanding field, so check with the **Disabled Living Foundation** to see what is available. And, **Anchor Housing** has a fact sheet on staying put.

Those who want to stay in their old home may be able to get grants to make it more suitable. If it's too big the best answer may be to convert part of it into accommodation which can be rented out. If it's the right size but difficult to get about in, aids can be added or rooms switched around to make it more suitable. Either way the timing of this needs careful thought. Once your income has dropped after retirement you may be able to get a grant for such work, even though you would not be eligible for a grant while working.

If it's a matter of making improvements **Age Concern** has a fact sheet on where the elderly can get financial help, and **Help the Aged** (page 324) has a leaflet on grants for insulating your home.

Housing and Widows
Not all widows are elderly, but the vast majority are and, at any age, the fear which many widows share is that if a home is rented or mortgaged in the husband's name they will have no right to live there once he is dead. This is not the case; a widow has a right to continue to live in what was her home. However, a widow may be faced with too much home and too little income or a widower find the family home too large to manage.

The worst time to make a decision to move is when suffering from the grief and shock of a bereavement. Once that is over there are plenty of solutions. If the home was rented a smaller home can be found, and some of the organizations on pages 324 can help. If it is owned, some of the options given above may apply, or selling it may provide enough spare capital to give a better income. Don't forget that if a house was bought from a council it may be possible to sell it back to the council, and continue to live in it paying a rent which is lower than the mortgage repayments – or the council may be able to help with mortgage repayments. These are only some of the possibilities, so talk to your local Citizens' Advice Bureau.

When Living Alone is Too Much
When living alone becomes too much, the first thought may be to look for an old people's home or a nursing

home. But it is no small thing to give up independence and the possessions of a lifetime and accept life among strangers. It is all too easy to be over-protective and rush an old person into a home when they seem frail and then discover this was only due to a temporary illness. It may well be better for someone to live 5 happy years wearing themselves out coping at home, than live 10 miserable ones mourning for their lost freedom. Even if they become quite infirm it may be possible for them to stay at home with the right help.

The National Health Service and Community Care Act 1990, which came into force in April 1993, changed the way in which care for the elderly or disabled is provided. Its aim is to:

- give more appropriate help to the elderly or disabled,
- make it easier for them to stay in their own homes,
- provide better support for carers,
- give those who need residential care more say in where they are placed (they can even ask to go to a home in another part of Britain which is closer to a relative or friend),
- provide a more effective complaints procedure.

The Social Services Department in each local authority must assess each person who needs care, of any kind, and define a package of care tailored to their personal needs. Then it should buy in that care, at the best possible price, from private, voluntary or state organizations.

In practice Social Services may lack the money and manpower to provide such a personal service, and it may prove hard to co-ordinate services drawn from numerous different bodies. However, both the elderly and their carers have a right to ask for what the Act says they should have and organizations like Age Concern and the Carers' National Association can advise you on what you can expect, and on how to get it. You could approach Social Services, but it may be better to talk to the GP, as the Act gives GPs a duty to spot when someone needs help and alert Social Services and she may have a leaflet on what is available in your area.

Local authorities vary hugely in how much assistance they will provide to help someone manage in their own home. Here are some of the services which should be available. If they are provided, even an elderly person with quite a severe disability may be able to have the pleasure of staying in their own home for longer.

- Meals on wheels.
- Visiting chiropody and/or physiotherapy.
- Bathing by a district nurse.
- Laundry service, including incontinence supplies.
- It may be possible to have a nurse get them up in the morning and put them to bed at night.
- Social Services will also install aids like handles by a bath, a raised lavatory or a second stair rail.
- If Social Services don't provide a home help it may be possible to get a supplementary pension to cover the cost of paying for help.

However, it has to be said that even under the most efficient local authorities, someone elderly may find themselves alone for too long at weekends. Some of the agencies which offer carers are on page 214 and local agencies are listed in Yellow Pages under 'Nurses'.

Leaving Home

Once someone elderly decides to leave their own home the possibilities are:

- more suitable ordinary accommodation – possibly from a housing association at low rent,
- a purpose-built house or flat with a warden on call nearby, is basic sheltered accommodation,
- a self-contained room in a private home for the elderly to which they take their own furniture,
- a room in a state-run home for the elderly,
- a room in a state or private nursing home or hospital,
- they can live with their family.

Low Rent Accommodation

Low rent accommodation only solves one problem, but it may be the most pressing one in early old age. The Pre-Retirement Association (page 324) has a list of housing associations which rent reasonably priced accommodation to the elderly, and local councils may be a source of other names. The **National Association of Almshouses** (page 324) has a list of all the organizations which administer almshouses. And professional bodies, trade associations, unions, livery companies and so on may offer low-cost accommodation to former members of their trade or profession and to their widows.

Sheltered Accommodation and Nursing Homes

Building sheltered housing for the elderly is a field which is still finding its feet, and those considering such accommodation may find it revealing to read a report on it by the **Centre for Policy on Ageing** .

Imperfect though some sheltered accommodation may be, it's much in demand and to get a place in a block of flats with a resident warden you may need to put your name down several years before. The same goes for rooms in sheltered homes for the elderly run by charities. Some of these will care for someone who becomes ill while a resident, but will not take on someone who is already infirm. So, you may need to get your foot in the door while still spry. If you once worked for a large organization, find out whether it has any links with sheltered accommodation. Quite a few large institutions help charitable organizations and in return recommend ex-employees for places.

State-run Sheltered Accommodation

Unfortunately state-run schemes are quite rare, and the standard option is what the officials call 'Part 3 Accommodation' in a local authority residential home, run much like a state hotel for the elderly. Usually the personal possessions which can be brought into these are very limited and many local authorities only accept those who already live in the area, so it can be difficult to move a relative closer to where you live.

Local authorities charge a set weekly fee and state benefits may help. The details are constantly changing but Age Concern (page 324) and Counsel and Care for the Elderly (page 324) have good information leaflets on everything you need to know and will also help and advise.

Where People Fall Between Two Stools
Unfortunately there's a crying lack of accommodation for those who can't quite manage alone but aren't ill. Even to get into Part 3 accommodation you have to pass a fitness test. The catch is that some elderly people fail this test but are not ill enough to be accepted by a state nursing home or hospital. So they are refused a place in a home *and* in a hospital.

The Caring Trap
Some people may want to have an elderly parent to live with them until they die, and take on the responsibility gladly. But nobody should take on an elderly relative believing it is just a step towards state care. Once an old person is living with you it is likely to be for the rest of their life.

If an old person can't manage alone it is far wiser for one of the family to go and live in with them, until the matter is sorted out. You have only to show that you *can* take them in for the council to rule that they don't need to look after the old person because you can. It doesn't matter that you are caring for them at the price of giving up work and squashing the children into one bedroom. Once a council has shifted the burden on to the family it tends to stay there.

Families have no legal obligation to house any relative over the age of 18, so if you refuse to look after an elderly relative the state *must* find a place for them – if necessary by assisting with the cost of care in the voluntary or private sector. It isn't easy or pleasant to take things that far but it may be the only way if you can't cope with caring for them.

Looking After Someone Elderly
There are undoubtedly some wonderful old people who need looking after having lost only their physical strength. Unfortunately, there are also many who through mental illness or deterioration are little more than a shadow of the person they once were. Those who care for them face a special problem of grief and alienation. They should not feel guilty if they find it hard to handle. To have someone you love look at you with eyes which no longer recognize you, or behave in ways of which their old self would have been ashamed, is a heartbreaking experience which is becoming familiar to more and more families as medicine swells the numbers living to a ripe old age.

Looking after an elderly person is at least as trying and tiring as looking after a small child. There is also the emotional upheaval of reversing the roles – having someone you once relied on relying on you. This can bring with it anger and guilt which is compounded by the fact that if someone becomes deaf you cannot talk to them without raising your voice, and may feel angry simply because you are shouting.

Boredom is a big problem for the immobile. Yet constant television can make people, of any age, tired and irritable. Many reference libraries have audio tapes,

including book readings. There are also talking book services (page 590) which will send tapes by post and the **British Jigsaw Puzzle Library** (page 324).

If an old person has ceased to enjoy life, the carer will sometimes resent the seemingly pointless burden of caring and wish the old person were dead. To feel this, even occasionally, about someone you love, or even about a helpless stranger, is not easy to handle – yet almost every carer feels it at some time. It may help to read how other people have experienced it (see books on page 324).

Coping With Caring
Any carer needs to get as much practical help as possible to lessen the burden and the **Carers' Association** advises on this. Some local authorities offer far more help than others, but it is worth trying any or all of the following:

- a good family doctor should be able to refer you to other help if you talk frankly – don't put a brave face on it and don't be fobbed off with pills
- some areas have an incontinence adviser – ask a GP
- the family doctor should be able to arrange for a district nurse to come and do the medical chores
- a community psychiatric nurse can help to nurse the mentally ill at home
- some health authorities will admit an old person to hospital while the carer has a holiday
- if an old person is leaving hospital, the hospital social worker should put you in touch with help
- some areas have day-care centres and the elderly are collected from home and returned
- residential homes may take the elderly for a couple of weeks to give the carer a break
- social services departments may arrange holidays for the old and infirm.

You may be able to get help from the voluntary services. Some social services departments have volunteer organizers who can put you in touch, or contact your Citizens' Advice Bureau.

Nursing Homes and Other Residential Care

When looking for a home or nursing home be wary: some agencies take fees from the nursing homes so they are not unbiased, and many do not inspect the homes they recommend. A better first source of information is the local social services department, or the health authority. These have departments which inspect and register residential homes and nursing homes, and you may be able to find out from them if any would particularly suit you or your relative's needs. If someone is being discharged from hospital, the hospital social worker may also be able to suggest somewhere suitable. Do inspect any accommodation, nursing or residential home before accepting a place – the quality varies from excellent to disgraceful and even places which are recommended may change hands. On page 324 I give some organizations which should be reliable.

One of the best sources of detailed information on private and voluntary residential and nursing homes for the elderly is the charity **Counsel and Care for the Elderly** which inspects every place it recommends and tries to match a person's individual needs to a home. Unfortunately this service *only covers Greater London*. However, it provides some grants to elderly people, of limited means, anywhere in Britain, and the advice service on problems related to old age is open to anyone.

The **Elderly Accommodation Council** can tell you where to find almost every type of accommodation for the elderly. It covers both private and voluntary bodies throughout Britain. Its list ranges from slightly sheltered housing to hospices for the terminally ill. You fill in a form and the computer prints out addresses which match your needs. There is a nominal fee for names and addresses but those who are hard up can get free information. However, the accommodation is not inspected. It can also tell you of charities that help the hard-up elderly to meet their accommodation costs.

Homes for the Elderly – What to Look For

A home should be a home in the best sense of the word. It should also be registered with the authorities and if the registration isn't displayed, ask to see it. It isn't easy to do a thorough assessment of a home in a brief visit. So the following list gives points to look for: they come from Age Concern and Counsel and Care for the Elderly, plus some of my own.

- Is the atmosphere attractive and welcoming?
- What are the other residents like? Would the person concerned get on with them?
- Do the residents have their own rooms or must they share?
- Can people bring personal belongings, like ornaments and small pieces of furniture?
- Do the bedrooms lock, and is there a place to lock away valuables?
- Is there a telephone the residents can use and does it take both outgoing and incoming calls?
- What level of care does the place offer – will they help with washing or dressing if necessary?
- What is the food like? Can residents make their own snacks or drinks? Do they provide for special diets?
- Is it warm enough?
- What is the daily routine? How rigid is it? And will it suit the person concerned?
- Can people go to their rooms whenever they wish?
- Are there free visiting hours and can the residents see their visitors in private?
- What activities go on there? Can the residents continue their hobbies?
- Are residents involved in the running of the home?
- Do residents keep their own GP?
- Is the home clean and safe? Look in the kitchen and the bathrooms.
- Are there aids in the bathroom and lavatory? Like a bell in case of trouble?
- How are medicines given and what records are kept?
- Under what circumstances would a resident be asked to leave?
- What are the fire drills and when was the last practice?
- Will a pet be accepted?

Mobility in Old Age

Car drivers should check the rules for holding a driving licence in old age and be careful not to drive when taking certain medicines.

Those who need a walking stick should have one the right length. The top needs to be about 8 cm (3 ins) up to the wrist when the arm is hanging straight down.

Wheelchairs for indoors, whether hand or electric powered, can be supplied free by the NHS provided a doctor recommends it. Electric wheelchairs for outside are not supplied by the NHS but, by law, can be driven on the pavement at up to 4 mph. Get their details from the **Disabled Living Foundation**, which also has them on view in London for those who book an appointment.

Personal vehicles are now made to carry the disabled or elderly short distances. They are usually electric and range from sturdy glorified tricycles to rather natty miniature cars which are so much fun that I long to possess one. They need to be bought privately and may all be driven on the pavement without a licence up to 4 mph. But larger vehicles like electrically assisted pedal-powered cycles and tricycles driven at up to 15 mph must go on the road, though they can be used without a licence or helmet. The Disabled Living Foundation has the details.

Safety and Old Age

Many old people are at special risk from their own forgetfulness, from being unsteady on their feet and from lack of money to have things seen to, and relatives need to think about their special needs.

- Is the wiring old and dangerous? (They may be unable to pay for renewal.)
- Are the stairs a hazard – torn carpet, poor lighting, weak banisters? Better no carpet than a broken leg.
- Is the kitchen arranged so that nothing heavy can fall from a height?
- Are the handles of kettles and pans able to be held safely by arthritic hands?
- Are rugs on non-slip backings?
- Are there trailing flexes that might not be seen?

Finally, is there a phone wherever they might need to call for help? If not, installing a phone line could be the best Christmas present they could have.

Warmth in Old Age

Cold is a special hazard for the old. It is not simply a matter of poverty. Any old person is at risk. With age, the ability to notice changes in temperature diminishes – just as eyesight and hearing diminish. So even those who can afford to heat their home properly may still die of hypothermia through just not noticing how cold the room has become. And once someone's temperature falls below a certain level he or she will simply fall into a deep and fatal sleep. For safety the elderly need heaters with timers and thermostats so they will automatically be kept warm enough. The elderly should aim for a room temperature of 21°C (70°F).

Keeping warm is also a matter of keeping in the warmth the body makes: lots of layers of warm loose clothing, which trap the air between them, are warmest, especially if at least the inner ones are wool. The old-fashioned idea of a shawl or rug is very cosy (especially with a hot water bottle under), but modern science can even go one better. Camping shops sell large thin sheets of foil-coated plastic, often called Space Blankets. They are for wrapping round mountaineers to help them survive cold, as the foil reflects back heat. They make Granny look a touch like a space man but are cheap and work wonders whenever you need to keep the cold out. More information from Help the Aged. See also Insulation (page 224).

USEFUL ADDRESSES AND BOOKS

Clubs, Hobbies and Activities for Parents or Children

Boys Brigade, 1 Galena Road, London W6 0LT Tel: 081 741 1721 – M£Var, Rg, G, ages 16-18, A.

Girl Guides Association, 17-19 Buckingham Palace Road, London SW1W 0PT Tel: 071 828 8317.

Girls Brigade, Foxhall Road, Didcot, Oxon OX11 7BQ Tel: 0235 510425.

Mensa Ltd, Freepost, Wolverhampton WV2 1BR Tel: 0902 772771, is a club for the bright.

The Mother's Union, The Mary Sumner House, 24 Tufton Street, London SW1P 3RB Tel: 071 222 5533/4/5, is a worldwide organization of clubs for Christian women (a few men now join). Emphasis on traditional Christian values, and on service. A, toddler groups, pram service, discussions, supportive holidays for parents under stress. Also runaway children can phone them and they will pass on the child's message to home.

National Alliance of Women's Organizations (NAWO), 279/281 Whitechapel Road, London E1 1BY Tel: 071 247 7052.

National Association of Boys' Clubs, 369 Kennington Lane, London SE11 5QY Tel: 071 793 7987, is for boys and young men (mainly 11-19). Clubs for almost every activity – sport, drama, etc. – and special projects relating to unemployment, drugs and other youth problems.

National Association of Women's Clubs, 5 Vernon Rise, King's Cross Road, London WC1X 9EP Tel: 071 837 1434/5/6, is an educational charity coordinating 620 affiliated women's clubs covering a wide range of activities.

National Federation of Gateway Clubs (see Gardening, p. 377), offers varied leisure activities for the mentally handicapped, helpers welcomed.

National Federation of Women's Institutes, 104 New Kings Road, London SW6 4LY Tel: 071 371 9300, is not the fuddy-duddy organization it sounds. It covers both town and country and provides every conceivable activity from jam and gym to political lobbying. Own adult education college. M£L, M, A, L, B, HC, HD, sae.

The National Union of Townswomen's Guilds, Chamber of Commerce House, 75 Harborne Road, Edgbaston, Birmingham B15 3DA Tel: 021 456 3435, is open to all women. It aims to improve life for women and broaden their education. Monthly meetings. Activities range from arts, crafts and sports to political debates and lobbying on international issues. RC, M£L, M, A, HD, T, HC, G.

The National Women's Register, 9 Bank Plain, Norwich NR2 4SL Tel: 0603 765392 – international, autonomous linked groups of 'lively minded women' meet to discuss topics other than house and home. M, L, RC, M£L.

Rotary International, Kinwarton Road, Alcester, Warwicks B49 6BP Tel: 0789 765411, links men (not women) in service and fellowship – but membership by invitation. M, G, RS.

The Scout Association, Baden-Powell House, 65 Queens Gate, London SW7 5JS Tel: 071 584 7030, is now for both sexes aged 6 onwards, no upper limit. A, Ins, HD, HC, B (addresses of local troups at libraries).

Sports Council and **British Sports Association** (see Free Time, p. 342).

United Kingdom Federation of Business and Professional Women, 23 Ansdell Street, London W8 5BA Tel: 081 938 1729, aims to help working women use their full potential in society. M£Var, M, Rg, G, Inf.

Women's Royal Voluntary Service, 234 Stockwell Road, London SW9 9SP Tel: 081 733 3388 – for both men and women who would like to use their free time to help others. Members do community work such as Meals an Wheels and toy libraries.

Youth Clubs UK, Keswick House, 30 Peacock Lane, Leics LE1 5NY Tel: 0533 629514 – numerous G, HD, social and other activities for both sexes 11-25. Scheme for the young unemployed.

Youth Hostels Association, Trevelyan House, 8 St Stephen's Hill, St Albans, Herts AL1 2DY Tel: 0727 44216, has adventure activities, good-value accommodation all over Britain and overseas. All ages. RC, M£L, Rg, G.

Family Matters

General Childcare and Parenthood

Action for Sick Children (formerly **NAWCH**), Argyle House, 29-31 Euston Road, London NW1 2SD Tel: 071 833 2041, advises on the needs and rights of children in hospital. Pressure group RC, M£L, ChS, F&F, M, L, B, G, HD, sae. (P.280)

BM Crysis, London WC1N 3XX Tel: 071 404 5011, provides support for the parents of crying babies. (P.275) See also the book below.

The Children's Society, Edward Rudolf House, Margery Street, London WC1X 0JL Tel: 071 837 4299, runs many projects to help families, including centres to help families stay together and sheltered accommodation for adolescents.

Church Army, Independent Road, Blackheath, London SE3 9LG Tel: 081 318 1226, is an evangelistic organization (C of E), offering counselling, advice and support on most human problems regardless of race or creed, RC, M, L, V, G, Rg, Res, A, HC, HD, sae.

Enuresis Resource and Information Centre (ERIC), 65 St Michael's Hill, Bristol BS2 8DZ Tel: 0272 264920, Ad, Inf, help, low priced L.

Exploring Parenthood, Latimer Education Centre, 194 Freston, Road, London W10 6TT Tel: 081 960 1678, has discussion groups where parents can exchange ideas with each other and with doctors, therapists and psychologists. National courses and workshops on topics like step-parenting or child development. Will also run workshops for groups of parents anywhere on a subject of their choice. M£M, RC.

Family Welfare Association, 501-505 Kingsland Road, London E8 4AU Tel: 071 254 6251/4, offers support on problems of any kind: bereavement, loneliness, unemployment, difficulties over housing or education, and accommodation for the elderly. It also makes grants to those in serious need. Useful book list.

Home Start, 2 Salisbury Road, Leicester LE1 7QR Tel: 0533 554988, uses volunteer visitors to support families with young children through difficulties and crises, and reduce the isolation of parents of young children. RC.

Meet-a-Mum Association 58 Malden Avenue, London SW25 4HS, offers support by mothers for mothers – including those with post-natal depression, one-to-one contacts and G, sae.

National Association of Nappy Services, 23 London Road, Loughton, Milton Keynes MK5 8AB Tel: 0908 666968, can tell you of local nappy-washing services.

The National Children's Bureau & Voluntary Council for Handicapped Children, 8 Wakeley Street, London EC1V 7QE Tel: 071 278 9441, is an information source with a library and excellent book lists on most of the topics which can affect a child. (P.278)

The National Toy Libraries Association, 68 Churchway, London NW1 1LT Tel: 071 387 9592, provides information and advice about the 1,400 toy libraries around Britain. Also some special advice on toys/aids for those with disabilities RC, M£L.

Parentline (formerly **OPUS**), Rayfa House, 57 Hart Road, Thundersley, Essex SS7 3PD Tel: 0268 757077 (24-hour helpline), is a network of self-help groups and of parents trained as counsellors. It offers support and advice on all aspects of parenting. (P.274)

Salvation Army Tracing Service for Missing Persons, Tel: 071 387 2772.

Shelter, 88 Old Street, London EC1V 9HU Tel: 071 253 0202, offers advice, support and housing for the homeless.

The Soldier's, Sailors' and Airmen's Families Association, 19 Queen Elizabeth Street, London SE1 2LP Tel: 071 403 8783, assists the families of those who are, or have been, in the forces with problems of any and every kind. RC.

Useful Books
Children in Hospital – an action guide for parents, NAWCH/Consumers' Association.

Dr Christopher Green, *Toddler Taming*, Century.

Dr Haim G. Ginott, *Between Parent and Child*, Staples Press.

James Robertson, *Young Children in Hospital*, Tavistock.

Dr Miriam Stoppard, *Baby Care Book*, Dorling Kindersley.

Sheila Kitzinger, *The Crying Baby*, Viking.

Adoption and Fostering

British Agencies for Adoption and Fostering (BAAF), 11 Southwark Street, London SE1 1RQ Tel: 071 407 8800. (P.273)

National Foster Care Association, Leonard House, 5 Marshalsea Road, London SE1 1EP Tel: 071 828 6266/7, has information on all aspects of fostering. RC, M£M, M, L, B. (P.274)

National Organization for Counselling Adoptees and Their Parents (NORCAP), 3 New High Street, Headington, Oxford OX3 7AJ Tel: 0865 750554, offers self-help counselling for adoptees over 18, adoptive parents and those who gave a child for adoption. Advises adoptees on tracing their original parents. Pressure group for computerized adoption register allowing birth/adoptive parent exchange of medical and other non-identifying information, RC, M£L, M, sae. (P.273)

Natural Parents Support Group, 3 Alder Grove, Normanton, W. Yorks WF6 1LF Tel: 0924 894076, is for those whose child was adopted by others.

Overseas Adoptions helpline Tel: 071 226 7666. (P.273)

Parent to Parent Information on Adoption Service (PPIAS), Lower Boddington, Daventry, Northants NN11 6YB Tel: 0327 60295, adoptive parents help and advise would-be adopters on where and how to find a child to adopt, based on shared experience. They also have information on adopting from overseas. Support group RC, Opt. M£L, S, M, L, B, G, sae. (P.273)

Parents for Children, 41 Southgate Road, London N1 3JP Tel: 071 359 7530, is a voluntary adoption agency which finds school-age children, usually those with problems or disabilities, adoptive parents living within 100 miles of London. (P.273)

The Post-Adoption Centre, 8 Torriano Mews, Torriano Avenue, London NW5 2RZ Tel: 071 284 0555 Thursday 5.30-7.30, other weekdays 10.30-1.30. It provides professional advice and counselling for adoptees, adoptive parents and those who give children for adoption. (P.273)

Stork, 9 Woodland Green, Upton St Leonards, Gloucestershire GL4 8BD, mutual support for parents who adopt from abroad, sae. (P.273)

Useful Books

A Guide for Parents with Children in Care, Parents' Aid, 66 Chippingfield, Harlow, Essex.

Hedi Argent, *Find me a Family*, Souvenir.

The Social Services Yearbook lists approved adoption societies.

Death in the Family

Cruse – Bereavement Care, 126 Sheen Road, Richmond, Surrey TW9 1UR Tel: 081 940 4818 (admin), 081 332 7227 (helpline), offers counselling, information, and contacts with others to those suffering from any bereavement. M£L, M, G, L, Ad, inf. (P.276)

The Compassionate Friends, 53 North Street, Bristol BS3 1EN Tel: 0272 665202 (admin), 0272 539639 (helpline), offers direct support, through its county secretaries, and creates parent-to-parent links for those who have lost a child of any age – even an adult child. Special groups for those whose child died from murder or suicide. M£L, after that, M, L, G, RC. (P.276)

The National Association of Widows (NAW), 54-57 Allison Street, Digbeth, Birmingham B5 5TH Tel: 021 643 8348, provides an advice service for widows and is also a self-help group. G, L, sae. (P.276)

War Widows Association of Great Britain, 17 The Earl's Croft, Coventry CV3 5ES Tel: 0203 503298 helps war widows and their families, champions their cause to government and keeps them in touch with new legislation, allowances and pension rights. It also may be able to help with accommodation. RC, M£L, M, L, RG, some A.

See also Depression. (pages 560, 589)

Separation, Divorce, Single Parents, Step-parents

Gingerbread, 35 Wellington Street, London WC2E 7BN Tel: 071 240 0953, for solo parents of both sexes. G, M, L, A – children welcome, mutual help, Ad and Inf on problems such as housing, benefits, law etc, pressure group, sae. (P.278)

National Council for One-Parent Families, 255 Kentish Town Road, London NW5 2LX Tel: 071 267 1361, can tell single parents (unmarried/divorced/bereaved) where to find support and advice. Plus leaflets and books on all aspects of single parenthood. Pressure group, RC, M£L-M, sae appreciated.

National Federation of Solo Clubs, Room 8, Ruskin Chambers, 191 Corporation Street, Birmingham Tel: 021 236 2879, clubs for the single, widowed, divorced or separated of both sexes aged 25-65. Aims: to relieve loneliness by social activities and group holidays at home and abroad, sae.

National Stepfamily Association, 72 Willesden Lane, London NW6 7TA Tel: 071 372 0844 (admin), 071 372 0846 (confidential telephone counselling),

also has local groups where step-parents can exchange problems and solutions, leaflets and courses on how to be a step-parent, and general help M£M, M, A, G, Ad. (P.286)

Relate – National Marriage Guidance Council, Herbert Gray College, Little Church Street, Rugby, Warwickshire CV21 3AP Tel: 07885 73241, offers counselling to couples, both married and unmarried, on difficulties in relationships. You pay what you can afford. Some centres offer sexual therapy. Listed in phone books as 'Marriage' or as 'Relate'.

Scottish Council for Single Parents, 13 Gayfield Square Edinburgh EM1 3NX Tel: 031 556 3899, advises single parents. L, Ad, G, RC.

Useful Books

Ann Mitchell and Christine Richard, *Children in the Middle*, booklet from the Stepfamily Association.

Ann Mitchell, *Coping with Separation and Divorce*, Chambers.

Brenda Maddox, *Step-Parenting*, Unwin.

Elizabeth Hodder, *The Step-Parent's Handbook*, Sphere.

Kathleen Cox and Martin Desforges, *Children & Divorce*, Sheffield Psychological Service, 9 Newbound Lane, Sheffield.

Maggie Drummond, *How to Survive as a Second Wife*, Robson.

The National Children's Bureau has a booklist on children and divorce.

Sexual, Verbal and Physical Abuse in Childhood

Child Abuse Survivor's Network, P.O. Box 7, W3 6XJ Tel: 081 743 7614 (admin), 081 992 5522 (help), helps those who were abused, mainly adults. (P.283)

Childline: free helpline for abused and unhappy children 0800 1111 or write to Childline Freepost 1111, London N1 0BR. (P.281)

Childwatch & The Kate Adams Crisis Centre Tel: 081 593 9428 offers telephone support and face-to-face counselling for adults and children who have been sexually abused. (P.281)

Crisis Line, Tel: 081 593 9428 – telephone support and face-to-face counselling for adults and children who have been sexually abused. (P.281)

Everyman Centre, 30a Brixton Road, London SW9 6BU Tel: 071 793 0155 (admin) or counselling line 071 793 0255, helps men who are worried by their violence. It will refer men from other areas to their nearest centre. (P.274)

In Support of Sexually Abused Children, P.O. Box 526, London NW6 1SU Tel: 081 202 3024, helps non-abusing parents of abused children. (P.281)

Kidscape, 152 Buckingham Palace Road, London SW1W 9TR Tel: 071 730 3300 advises parents worried about the risk of sexual abuse, and has free leaflets for parents and teachers on how to help children avoid sexual abuse. (P.281)

Mothers of Abused Children, 25 Wampool Street, Silloth, Cumbria CA5 4AA Tel: 0697 331432, offers telephone counselling and advice by volunteers. (P.281)

National Children's Homes, 85 Highbury Park, London N5 1UD Tel: 071 226 2033, counselling for abused children and their parents. (P.319)

National Society for the Prevention of Cruelty to Children (NSPCC), 67 Saffron Hill, London EC1N 8RS Tel: 071 242 1626, is on call 24 hours a day – see your phone book. Reports of child neglect, cruelty or abuse are totally confidential – names are not revealed. Children are not always taken from the family. There are also counselling for parents in distress, playgroups, day-care centres, grants for families in crisis, and support through family centres, plus referral to other supportive organizations. Pressure group on child cruelty issues. Parent Care Club for NSPCC supporters offers substantial discounts on children's goods by leading brands. RC, ChS, L, M. (P.274)

Parents Against Injustice (PAIN), 3 Riverside Business Park, Stanstead, Essex CM24 8PL Tel: 0279 647171, advises and supports parents and children when a child is mistakenly thought to have been at risk or abused. It can suggest solicitors.

Parents Anonymous, 13 Montpelier Rise, London NW11 9SS Tel: 071 263 8918, will help parents who feel they may attack their children physically, sexually or verbally. Also puts parents in touch with sources of help on any child-related problems, from a crying baby to a drug-taking teenager. (P.274)

The Samaritans (in your phone book) will also help you.

South London Women's Centre, 302-304 Barrington Road, London, SW9 7AA Tel: 071 274 7215, can put women in touch with survivors' groups for those abused in childhood. (P.283)

Women's Therapy Centre, 6 Manor Gardens, London N7 6LA Tel: 071 263 6200, can advise on sources of help nationwide.

Playgroup, Nursery School, Childcare

British Association for Early Childhood Education, 111 City View House, 463 Bethnal Green Road, London E2 9QH Tel: 071 739 7594, is a watchdog on areas of concern. RC, M£L, M, B, good booklets. (P.288)

The Day-Care Trust & Working For Children, Wesley House, 4 Wild Court, London WC2B 5AU Tel: 071 405 5617. (P.287)

Kids Clubs Network, 279-281 Whitechapel Road, London E1 1BY Tel: 071 247 3009. (P.288)

National Childminding Association, 8 Masons Hill, Bromley, Kent BR2 9EY Tel: 081 464 6164. (P.287)

Nursery Schools Information Service, Montessori Publishing, P.O. Box 5, Brecon, LD3 8YX Tel: 0874 638007, sells an information pack on nursery schools in each area of Britain. Phone for recorded details on obtaining it. (P.288)

The Pre-School Playgroups Association (PPA), 61/63 Kings Cross Road, London WC1X 9LL Tel: 071 833 0991, tries to help parents to understand children

and help them to develop. Links parents through playgroups, and parents and toddler groups, and a few groups for kids with disabilities. Good information on nursery care and parenting skills, RC, G, B, L, L, F, V, HD. (P.288)

Pre-School Playgroups Association: Scotland, 14 Elliot Place, Glasgow, G3 8E Tel: 041 221 4148. (P.288)

Pre-School Playgroups Association: Wales, 2A Chester Street, Wrexham, Clwyd LL13 8BD Tel: 0978 358195. (P.288)

Working for Childcare, (address as Working Mothers Association), advises companies and individuals on childcare in the workplace, training, conferences, RC M£L. (P.287)

Working Mothers Association, 77 Holloway Road, London N7 8JZ Tel: 071 700 5771, sells a *Working Mother's Handbook*, a women returners' pack, and an employer's guide to childcare. Its local groups have information on local childcare provision and provide links so mothers can pool problems and solutions, M£L, M, G, Ad, inf. (P.287)

Schooling

Disabilities and Learning Problems

AFASIC: Overcoming Speech Impairments, 347 Central Markets, Smithfield, London EC1A 9NH Tel: 071 236 3632, offers advice and inexpensive leaflets on educational rights and facilities for children with this problem. (P.303) See also stammering, p. 563.

British Dyslexia Association (BDA), 98 London Road, Reading, Berks RG1 5AU Tel: 0734 668271, provides referral to sources of help, information, advice, seminars, conferences, list of suitable schools/clinics. M£M, S, ChS, F&F, M, L, B, E, Rg, C, HC, HD, sae. (P.301)

Camphill Village Trust, Delrow College, Hilfield Lane, Aldenham, Watford, Herts WD2 8DJ Tel: 0923 856006, provides communities where those over 21 with mental disabilities live, work and gain training which may lead to outside employment. There is a long waiting list – apply early. The Trust also runs schools.

Centre for Studies on Integration in Education, 4th Floor, 415 Edgware Road, London NW2 6NB Tel: 081 452 8642, can advise on how to get their child into a normal school and on what is being done in different areas. (P.303)

Independent Panel of Special Education Experts, 12 Marsh Road, Tillingham, Essex CM0 7SZ Tel: 0621 779781 or 0628 478986, helps parents get a second opinion on a child's special needs, advises on legal issues and rights. (P.303)

National Association for Special Educational Needs, 2 Lichfield Road, Stafford ST17 4JX Tel: 0785 46872, is for teachers of those with learning difficulties but parents can buy its publications and some would be useful with any child.

National Autistic Society, 276 Willesden Lane, London NW2 5RB Tel: 081 451 1114, advises parents and runs local networks, schools and centres. M£L, MG, L, Adv, B. (P.302)

National Bureau for Students with Disabilities, 336 Brixton Road, London SW9 7AA Tel: 071 274 0565, gives advice and information, plus useful books and leaflets on courses, support services and educational options, most are free to handicapped students. RC, M£L, S, F&F, M, L, B, EI, Rg, C, HD, sae. (P.309)

National Educational Guidance Initiative, WHAFHE Headquarters, Bowling Green Terrace, Leeds LS11 9SX, has details of local educational guidance.

National Library for the Handicapped Child, Wellington House, Wellington Road, Wokingham, Berks RG11 2AG Tel: 0734 891101, helps and advises parents of children with disabilities who have problems with reading and communication. (P.301)

The Open University (page 323) has a special adviser.

Royal Society for Mentally Handicapped Children and Adults (MENCAP), 123 Golden Lane, London EC1Y 0RT Tel: 071 454 0454, has 500 affiliated local groups which provide practical help and advice. Many run pre-school playgroups, youth clubs, and holiday schemes. RC, M£M, S, ChS, F&F, M, L, B, V, F, E, G, H, Rg, Res, A, C, legal, Ins, HD.

Scottish Centre for the Tuition of the Disabled, Queen Margaret College, Clerwood Terrace, Edinburgh EH12 8TS Tel: 031 317 3439, arranges volunteer tutors for handicapped people in Scotland who need special help. (P.309)

See also Steiner Schools (page 321) and organizations for specific disabilities in In Sickness.

Education at Home

Education Otherwise, P.O. Box 120, Leamington Spa, Warwickshire, CV32 7ER Tel: 0926 886828, helps and advises those who want to educate their children themselves. Links to the US counterpart. RC, M£M, M, L, B. Guide to parents' rights. (P.292)

World-Wide Education Service (WES), 35 Belgrave Square, London SW1 8QB Tel: 071 235 2880, provides home-tuition courses for children being educated at home, while abroad or out of school. (P.292)

Useful Books
Any book by Michael Holt on maths teaching is worth reading.
Do You Panic About Maths?, Heineman Educational.
Dr Roger Morgan, *Helping Children Read*, Methuen.
Geraldine Taylor, *Be Your Child's Natural Teacher*, Penguin.
Glen Doman, *Teach Your Baby to Read*, Jonathan Cape.
Laurie Buxton, *Maths for Everyman*, aimed at parents who don't like maths and would like to help their children.

Gifted Children

Gifted Children's Information Centre, 21 Hampton Lane, Solihull, West Midlands B91 2QI Tel: 021 705 4547, is run by an educational psychologist who provides assessment and counselling (for a fee). It also publishes teaching packs and computer programs for gifted children, including those who are dyslexic or left-handed. vg B Inf. (P.299)

The National Association for Gifted Children (NAGC), Park Campus, Broughton Green Road, Northampton, NN2 7AL Tel: 0604 792300, is a pressure group. It also offers mutual support for parents and clubs where gifted children can get together. M£L-M, G, V, Ad, excellent list of books and leaflets, sae. (P.299)

The Advisory Centre for Education page 321 may also help.

Useful Books
U. Axline, *Dibs: In Search of Self*, Penguin – a real insight into the problems of being gifted.
Peter Congdon, *Helping Children of High Intelligence*.
R. Povey, *Educating the Gifted Child*, Harper & Row.
A. Stevens, *Clever Children in Comprehensive Schools*, Pelican.

Parent-Teacher & Home-School Links

Home and School Council, 40 Sunningdale Mount, Sheffield S11 7HA Tel: 0742 364181, publishes leaflets on fostering home and school links.

National Confederation of Parent Teacher Associations, 2 Ebbsteet Industrial Estate, Stonebridge Road, Gravesend, Kent DA11 9DZ Tel: 0474 560618, is a federation of parent-teacher associations (or Home-School Associations) all over Britain. Area officers have information on local issues and on education law. Publications on schooling and child-rearing.

Scottish Parent-Teacher Council, 30 Rutland Square, Edinburgh EH1 2EW Tel: 031 228 4726, encourages partnership between parents and teachers and publishes booklets and a newsletter.

Private and Public Schooling

Assisted Places Team, Mowden Hall, Darlington, Co. Durham DL3 9BG Tel: 0325 460155. (P.299)

C.E. Publishing Ltd, Ashley Lane, Lymington, Hants SO4 9YR, sells old Common Entrance papers. (P.300)

Gabbitas, Truman and Thring Education Trust, 6 Sackville Street, London W1X 2BR Tel: 071 734 0161, provides free information and advice on all types of education in the private sector, including tutorial colleges, schools for special problems or abilities, finishing schools abroad, and schools in GB where foreigners can learn English. It also recommends educational psychologists who will assess a child's ability and publishes a range of books including a guide to independent further education. (P.299)

Independent Schools Information Service (ISIS), 56 Buckingham Gate, London SW1E 6AG Tel: 071 630 8793, publishes a book on over 1,300 independent schools, and has information on school fees, insurance schemes, and how grandparents can help with fees and has a list of schools which offer assisted places. (P.299)

Steiner Schools Fellowship, Kidbrooke Park, Forest Row, East Sussex RH18 5JB Tel: 0342 822115, offer alternative education.

State Schooling
Advisory Centre for Education (ACE), 1B Aberdeen Studio, 22-24 Highbury Grove, London N5 2EA Tel: 071 354 8318, is a pressure group and information centre for state schooling and education. Free advice by letter and phone. Bulletin for members, briefs on what to do about exclusion, being a school governor, handbooks on key topics, plus Education A-Z on where to look up information on education. M£L, L. (P.295)

Campaign for the Advancement of State Education (CASE), 158 Durham Road, London SW20 0DG Tel: 081 947 5728, is what it says – a pressure group. M£L-M, M, L.

City Technology Colleges Trust, 15 Young Street, London W8 5EH Tel: 071 376 2511. (P.293)

Grant-Maintained Schools Foundation, 36 Great Smith Street, London SW1P 3BW Tel: 071 233 4666. (P.293)

The National Association of Governors and Managers (NAGM), 21 Bennetts Hill, Birmingham B2 5QP Tel: 021 643 5787, organizes good courses for governors and potential governors and sells leaflets on governorship and education. (P.295)

Useful Book
Felicity Taylor, *Choosing a School*, ACE (see above).

Degrees, Training and Qualifications

Degrees & Postgraduate Studies
Association of Management, Education and Training, Department of Business and Management, Stirling University, Stirling FK9 4LA Tel: 0786 50906. (P.308)

The Association of Masters of Business Administration, 15 Duncan Terrace, London N1 8BZ Tel: 071 837 3375, has information on MBA courses. (P.307)

Cambridge Inner Collegiate Applications Office, Kellet Lodge, Tennis Court Road, Cambridge CB2 1QJ Tel: 0223 33308, information on colleges and you either apply here or direct to the colleges between March and mid-October a year before. (P.308)

Central Register and Clearing House and Graduate Teacher Training Register, P.O. Box 239, Cheltenham, Gloucestershire, GL50 5SL (no phone calls). (P.308)

Committee of Vice-Chancellors and Principals, 29 Tavistock Square, London WC1H 9EZ Tel: 071 387 9231, has information on university courses. (P.307)

Department for Education, Publications Centre, P.O. Box 2193, London E12 EU Tel: 081 533 2000, publishes a brief guide to student grants.

JUPITER Consortium Ltd, 93 Hampton Road, Hampton Hill, Middx TW12 1JQ Tel: 081 977 9033, has information on postgraduate courses in high-tech. (P.307)

Oxford Colleges Admissions Office, Wellington Square, Oxford OX1 2JD Tel: 0865 270207, has information and forms and handles all applications between 1 September and mid-October the year before. (P.308)

Scottish Universities Council on Entrance, 12 The Links, St Andrews, Fife KY16, publishes an entrance guide. (P.308)

The University of Buckingham, Hunter Street, Buckingham MK18 1EG Tel: 0280 814080, is totally outside the system. (P.308)

Universities and Colleges Admissions Service (UCAS), P.O. Box 28, Cheltenham, Gloucestershire GL50 3SF Tel: 0242 222444, processes admission to almost all universities and many colleges. (P.321)

See also Higher and Further Education and Open Learning.

Useful Books
Brian Heap, *How to Choose Your Degree Course*, Careers Consultants.
How to Apply for Admission to a University, free from UCAS.
The Education Year Book, Longman.
The Student Book, Papermac.
Universities' and colleges' own prospectuses and handbooks – free from them.
University Entrance: The Official Guide in most libraries.
University Entrance 19.., *The Official Guide*, Sheed and Ward.

General Adult & Community Education
Adult Literacy and Basic Skills Unit (ALBSU), Kingsbourne House, 229-231 High Holborn, London WC1V 7DA Tel: 071 405 4017 or freephone 0800 700 987, directs people with reading problems to their nearest source of help. ALBSU may also be able to direct would-be helpers towards a suitable organization. (P.310)

Community Education Development Centre (CEDC), Lyng Hall, Blackberry Lane, Coventry CV2 3JS Tel: 0203 6383660, promotes community education and runs general courses. (P.310)

Education Service for Adults, 2nd Floor, Glendinning House, Murray Street, Belfast BT1 6DN Tel: 0232 244274. (P.310)

National Institute of Adult Continuing Education (NIACE) (England and Wales), 19b De Montfort Street, Leicester LE1 7GE Tel: 0533 551451, sells a useful paperback on residential short courses taken for interest, not qualifications. (P.310)

Scottish Community and Education Council, Rosebery House, Haymarket Terrace, Edinburgh EH12 5EZ Tel: 031 313 2488, is a quango concerned with community education – youth clubs, evening classes, and other communal activities – which will give information on this aspect of education, and also has some publications. (P.310)

Scottish Institute of Adult and Continuing Education, 30 Rutland Square, Edinburgh EH1 2BW Tel: 031 229 0331, publishes a handbook. (P.310)

University of the Third Age (U3A), 1 Stockwell Green, London SW9 9JFD Tel: 071 737 2541, has learning centres for the elderly all over Britain. (P.310)

Workers' Educational Association (WEA), 17 Victoria Park Square, London E2 9PE Tel: 081 983 1515. (P.310)

Higher & Further Education, Training & Qualifications

The Art and Design Admissions Registry, Pen House, 9 Broad Street, Hereford HR4 9AP Tel: 0432 266653, covers BA Hons and BTEC HND courses in art and design. (P.308)

Association of Business Schools, address as Higher Education Quality Council.

British Accreditation Council for Independent Further and Higher Education, Middlesex University, Bounds Green Road, London N11 2NQ Tel: 071 935 9947. (P.309)

Business and Technician Education Council (BTEC), Central House, Upper Woburn Place, London WC1H 0HH Tel: 071 413 8400, approves and awards BTEC qualifications. (P.306)

City & Guilds of London Institute, 46 Britannia Street, London WC1X 9RG Tel: 071 278 2468, provides syllabuses for City & Guilds and Pitman examinations and certificates throughout the British Isles. (P.306)

ECCTIS 2000 Ltd, Fulton House, Jessop Avenue, Cheltenham GL50 3SH Tel: 0242 518724, has a database on courses in further and higher education leading to qualifications. ECCTIS will answer personal queries, but computer links to Prestel in public libraries and local careers offices allow you to delve the database directly. It also has credit transfer information, but it won't answer open-ended questions about what you could do. (P.307)

The Henley Management College, Greenlands, Henley on Thames, Oxfordshire RG9 3AU Tel: 0491 571454, runs post-experience management courses including some which cater for open learning.

Higher Education Quality Council, 344-354 Gray's Inn Road, London WC1X 8BP Tel: 071 278 4411.

National Council for Industry Training Organizations, 10 Amos Road, Unit 10, Meadow Court, Sheffield S9 1BX Tel: 0742 619926. (P.310)

National Council for Vocational Qualifications, 222 Euston Road, London NW1 2BZ Tel: 071 387 9898. (P.305)

The Royal Society of Arts Examinations Board (RSA), Progress House, Westwood Way, Coventry, CV4 8HS Tel: 0203 470033, sets examinations and assessment schemes ranging from shorthand and typing to business studies. (P.306)

Scottish Examinations Board, Ironmills Road, Dalkeith, Edinburgh EH22 1LE Tel: 031 663 6601.

Scottish Vocational Educational Council (SCOTVEC), Hanover House, 24 Douglas Street, Glasgow G2 7NQ Tel: 041 242 2168. (P.306)

TEC Secretariat, Central England TEC, 7 The Oaks, Clewes Road, Redditch, B98 7ST Tel: 0527 550955. (P.305)

Training, Enterprise and Education Directorate, Moorfoot, Sheffield S1 4PQ Tel: 0742 753275, has information on schemes, grants and YT.

Women Returners Network, 8 John Adam Street, London WC2N 6EZ Tel: 071 839 8188. (P.309)

Useful Books

Andrew Paton and Martin Good, *Second Chances – The Annual Guide to Adult Education and Training Opportunities*, National Extension College.

British Qualifications, Kogan Page, lists all the different types of qualifications you can obtain in Britain.

Compendium of Advanced Courses in Higher and Further Education, from the LASER Advisory Council, Chenies House, 21 Bedford Square, London WC1B 3HH Tel: 071 637 3073.

David Dixon, *Higher Education – finding your way*, HMSO.

Higher Education in the United Kingdom, Longman, is updated annually. Lists all the places which offer diploma, foundation, degree and/or postgraduate courses in a subject, and the length of each course.

Higher Education Courses in Scotland, from Publications, P.O. Box 142, Holyrood Road, Edinburgh, EH8 8AH.

Making the Most of Higher Education, Consumers' Association and Hodder and Stoughton.

Scottish Handbook on Adult Education in Scotland, from SIACE.

Scottish Handbook of Adult and Continuing Education (public libraries).

Second Chance in Scotland: A Woman's Guide to Education and Training, edited by Lesley Hart, SIACE.

The Directory of Further Education, CRAC (vast, in libraries).

The Directory of Independent Training and Tutorial Organizations (DITTO), Elizabeth Summerson and Maureen Davies, Careers Consultants Ltd.

Open Learning & Correspondence Courses

The College of the Sea, The Marine Society, 202 Lambeth Road, London SE1 7JW Tel: 071 261 9535, offers a vast range of correspondence courses to those at sea. (P.309)

The Council for the Accreditation of Correspondence Colleges (CACC), 27 Marylebone Road, London NW1 5JS Tel: 071 935 5391, officially inspects such colleges. It is safest to use correspondence courses which are CACC approved. CACC has a brochure of such courses or if you are dissatisfied with a correspondence course, complain to CACC. (P.309)

London University, Senate House, Malet Street, London WC1E 7HU Tel: 071 636 8000, has a scheme for external degrees without attending a course. However, it offers only single degrees and diplomas identical to those taken by full-time students. Write to the Secretary for External Students.

National Extension College, 18 Brooklands Avenue, Cambridge CB2 2HN Tel: 0223 316644, courses range from hobbies, and how to study effectively or use a computer, through GCSE and A levels, to London University External Degree courses. (P.309)

The Open College, 781 Wilmslow Road, Didsbury, Greater Manchester, M20 8RW Tel: 081 434 0007, has courses towards business or technical qualifications. (P.310)

Open College of the Arts, Houndhill, Worsborough, Barnsley, S. Yorks, S70 6TU. (P.310)

Open University, P.O. Box 200, Milton Keynes, MK7 6YZ Tel: 0908 653231, has informative booklets on its courses. (P.309)

Scottish Council for Educational Technology, Dowanhill, 74 Victoria Crescent Road, Glasgow G12 9JN Tel: 041 334 9314, has information on open learning. (P.309)

Useful Book
Open Tech Directory, usually in Jobcentres and TECs.

Studying Abroad
British Council, address as below.
Central Bureau for Educational Visits and Exchanges, Seymour Mews House, Seymour Mews, London W1H 9PE Tel: 071 486 5101, provides informa-tion, advice, help and a list of courses for British people who want to study abroad and for foreign students who want to study in Britain.
Commission of the European Community (see Organizations, page 695).

Careers and Work

Careers
Career Analysts, Career House, 90 Gloucester Place, London W1H 4BL Tel: 071 935 5452, offers a thorough careers guidance service for all ages from mid-teens upwards. (P.310)

Career Counselling Services, 46 Ferry Road, London SW13 9PW Tel: 081 741 0335, uses a combination of tests, interviews and self-evaluation writing and drawing exercises. (P.310)

Career and Educational Counselling, Tavistock Centre, 120 Belsize Lane, London NW3 5BA Tel: 071 794 1309, is part of the Tavistock Institute of Medical Psychology. It offers career advice for all ages. (Also in Bristol and Cambridge). (P.310)

Career Occupational Information Centre (COIC), Sales Department, Room E414, Employment Department, Moorfoot, Sheffield S1 4PQ Tel: 0742 594565, sells good booklets giving information on finding a first job, retraining, and so on. Can retrain or help a housewife take up a career. Many of them should be in a school careers library. There are also COIC bookshops in many major towns and London boroughs – well worth a browse. (P.311)

Independent Assessment and Research Centre, 17 Portland Place, London W1N 3AF Tel: 071 935 2373, offers vocational guidance from teens to middle age, and guidance on children, aged 7-14, with educational problems. (P.310)

Vocational Guidance Centre, 34 Cromwell Road, Bramhall, Stockport, Cheshire SK7 1DA Tel: 061 439 5553, offers advice for all ages from mid-teens upwards. (P.310)

Useful Books
An A-Z of Careers and Jobs, Kogan Page.
Careers A-Z, Collins/Daily Telegraph.
Graduates and Jobs, HMSO assesses job prospects after different types of degree.
John Morrison, *A Positive Future*, Hutchinson.
Juri Gabriel, *Unqualified Success*, Puffin/Penguin.
Occupations 19.. (updated annually), Department of Employment.
Ruth Miller, *Equal Opportunities – a Career Guide*, Penguin.
The Job Book, edited by Denis Curtis, Hobsons.
Thelma Barber, *Careers and Jobs Without 'O' Levels*, Hobsons.
Which Subject? Which Career? by the Consumers' Association and Hobsons.

Finding Work
The Apex Trust Employment Resource Centre, 1-4 Brixton Hill Place, London SW2 1HJ Tel: 071 671 7633, is a charity which provides advice and training for those who face special problems in the job market – such as ex-offenders. (P.310)

Greater London Business Centre, freephone 0800 222 999, advises on setting up your own business. (P.311)

Industrial Society (see Organizations, page 698)

Jobhunter helpline 0800 884411 advises on looking for work. (P.310)

Network Scotland Ltd, 57 Ruthven Lane, Glasgow G12 9JQ Tel: 041 357 1774, offers advice and information on education and training opportunities throughout Scotland, in both the public and private sectors, including facilities for those with disabilities.

Small Business Bureau (see Organizations, page 698).

Vacation Work, 9 Park End Street, Oxford OX1 1HJ, produces guides to finding work world-wide, both during vacations and longer term.

Useful Books
Guy Dauncey, *The Unemployment Handbook*, National Extension College.
Nice Work If You can Get It, as above.
Second Chances from the COIC. (p. 299)

Retirement and Old Age

Caring for the Sick or Elderly
Carers' National Association, 20-25 Glasshouse Yard, London EC1A 4JS Tel: 071 490 8818 (admin), 071 490 8898 (helpline), is an invaluable source of

advice and support. RC, M£L, M, G, L, pressure group. (P.314)

Useful Books

Dr Brian Long, *Coping With Caring*, Mind publications (from MIND, see In Sickness).

Mace, Rabins and others, *The 36-Hour Day*, Age Concern/Hodder and Stoughton.

Jenny Pulling, *The Caring Trap*, Fontana, a carer's story.

Housing in Retirement & Old Age

Abbeyfield Society, 186-192 Darkes Lane, Potters Bar, Herts EN6 1AB Tel: 0707 44845, sets up houses all over Britain, run by resident housekeepers, in which elderly people live together, each with their own furnishings in their own room, and at reasonable rent, RC. (P.314)

Anchor Housing Association, Anchor House, 269a Banbury Road, Oxford OX2 7HU Tel: 0865 311511, provides sheltered housing for the elderly all over Britain. (P.314)

Centre for Policy on Ageing, 25-31 Ironmonger Row, London EC1V 3QP Tel: 071 253 1787, sells a range of publications on aspects of old age, including housing. (P.314)

Counsel and Care for the Elderly, Twyman House, 16 Benny Street, London NW1 9PG Tel: 071 485 1550 (admin), 071 485 1566 (advice), has information on residential homes. (P.313)

Elderly Accommodation Council, 46a Chiswick High Road, London W4 1SZ Tel: 081 995 8320/081 742 1182. (P.314)

Friends of the Elderly, 42 Ebury Street, London SW1W 0LZ Tel: 071 730 8263, has a long history of running homes for the elderly. (P.314)

Grace, 35 Walnut Tree Close, Guildford, Surrey GU1 4UL Tel: 0483 304354 or linkline at local rate 0345 023300, advises on private nursing and residential homes in southern England. Homes are regularly inspected. There is usually a fee for advice. (P.314)

National Association of Almshouses, Billingbear Lodge, Wokingham, Berks RG11 5RU Tel: 0344 52922, has a list of all the organizations which administer almshouses. (P.314)

Useful Books

Janice Casey, *Housing in Retirement*, Age Concern.

Moving Home in Retirement, by Shac/Anchor Housing Association 189a Old Brompton Road, London SW5 Tel: 071 373 7276.

Safety in Retirement, ROSPA (see p. 274).

Where to Live in Retirement, Consumers' Association.

Pre-Retirement Planning

DPS Consultants, Dodds Lane, 27 Preston Street, Faversham, Kent ME13 8PC Tel: 0795 531472, runs pre-retirement counselling courses for senior and middle management, usually paid for by an employer. (P.312)

Pre-Retirement Association, Nodus Centre, University Campus, Guildford GU2 5RX Tel: 0483 39323, offers advice on preparing for retirement. (P.312)

Scottish Pre-Retirement Council, 212 Bath Street, Glasgow G2 4HW Tel: 041 332 9427, runs courses on retirement. (P.312)

Useful Books

Henry Miller, *Countdown to Retirement*, Hutchinson Benham, gives food for thought.

The Open University (p. 309) has a course on preparing for retirement.

The Time of Your Life: A Handbook on Retirement, Help the Aged, Tel: 071 253 0253.

Retirement and Old Age: General

Age Concern – England, Astral House, 1268 London Road, London SW16 4ER Tel: 081 679 8000, exists to 'help elderly people by every possible means'. Local groups, listed as Age Concern in the phone book, offer help, advice and information, plus useful leaflets on benefits, medical services, residential care and so on. (P.313)

Age Concern – Northern Ireland, 3 Lower Crescent, Belfast BT7 1NR Tel: 0232 245729. (P.313)

Age Concern – Scotland, 54 Fountainbridge, Edinburgh EH3 9PT Tel: 031 228 5656. (P.313)

Age Concern – Wales, 4th Floor, 1 Cathedral Road, Cardiff CF1 9SD, Tel: 0222 371566. (P.313)

The British Jigsaw Puzzle Library, 8 Heath Terrace, Leamington Spa, Warwicks CV32 5LY Tel: 0926 311874, is a postal loan service (callers only by appointment) for jigsaws which suits the puzzles to the taste of the borrower. Membership 3 months, 6 months or 1 year, sae with enquiries. No children's puzzles. (P.314)

Help the Aged, 16-18 St. James's Walk, London EC1R 0BE Tel: 071 253 0253 or Freepost, London EC1B 1BD, has free advice and information leaflets. (P.312)

Free time

Active Games • Board Games • Cards • Party Games for All Ages • Joining a Club • Dating Agencies • Entertainment

ACTIVE GAMES

In this section you will find the basic rules of the sports and games you may suddenly want to play with family and friends. It is designed to fill the gap when you can only half remember how to play something, and no official rule book is to hand, or when you know how to play but can't recall the dimensions of the court or area of play – as can happen with croquet. Those who want to know the full rules for match play, or seriously take up any of these sports and games, should consult the official bodies. The **Sports Council** (page 342) has their addresses.

Boules (*petanque, 2-6 players*)

There are several versions of boules but, in Britain, petanque is probably the most popular – often with sets brought back from French holidays. A set comprises several metal balls (boules) somewhat larger than a tennis ball, and a very small ball called a cochonnet. You need a flat expanse of ground, and a boule is thrown underarm, with it under the hand as it comes forward. The aim is to get your boules as close as possible to the cochonnet – or knock the other team's boules away from it.

Two teams play against each other. With one or two in a team each player has 3 boules; with more each player has 2 boules. A coin is tossed to decide who throws the cochonnet. That person then draws a circle 36-50 cm (14-20 in) across, stands in it and throws the cochonnet 6-10 m (20-30 ft), and not nearer than 50 cm (1 ft 8 in) to an obstacle. Then a member of his team stands in the circle and throws a boule as close to the cochonnet as possible. Someone from the opposing team then throws from the circle, trying either to get his boule even closer or to knock the opponent's boule farther away. Once the first two boules are in place, whichever team has a boule *farthest* from the cochonnet continues to play until someone places one nearer or they run out of boules. Then the other team plays all its boules.

The British Petanque Association says 'the winning team gets as many points as it has boules better placed than the best of the losing team's'. So if team A has 3 boules nearer than the nearest one of team B, A gets three points. For the next game the circle is drawn where the cochonnet previously was, and the first team to total 13 points in a series of games wins.

Croquet (*2 or 4 players*)

Correctly played croquet is nothing like its P. G. Wodehouse image. Far from being a lackadaisical game for idlers, it is a game of strategy in which you try to get your own ball through a sequence of hoops, while shunting your opponent's balls into bad positions.

It is played on a lawn using 6 hoops, a central peg and wooden mallets, and 4 balls. Four players play as two teams, each person having one ball; blue and black opposing red and yellow. Two players use two balls each, blue and black versus red and yellow.

The aim is to get the ball through all 6 hoops, in the right order, twice over – once from each direction. Whoever does this first wins – no matter how many strokes it takes. Alternatively, a game can have a time limit and the winner be whoever scores the most points in that time. Score one for hitting a ball through a hoop, and one for hitting it against the peg at the end – so 13 points is the maximum for each ball in a round.

Toss to start; the winner either chooses to play first *or* picks the colour of ball(s) she will play. The first stroke at each ball is taken from one of the baulks (see diagram on page 326).

- To get all balls in play the sides play alternately, playing one ball at each turn.
- Each player keeps to her own ball(s).
- The sides play alternately.
- *Within* each team the players need not play alternately; whoever has a ball in the most advantageous position at any turn plays, even if it means one player, in a team, monopolizes the game for turn after turn.
- A basic turn is one stroke with one ball – but the exceptions are the very essence of the game, and a skilful player can extend a single turn to reach right to the final peg.

The exceptions are as follows.

1 If a ball goes through a hoop the player may play 1 more stroke.

2 If the ball hits one of the other three balls (a roquet)

centre
25.6 m
28 yds
35 yds
32 m

baulk line
1 yd in from
edge

Start

Direction of Play

the player may have 2 more strokes. These *must* be a croquet shot and a continuation stroke.

Croquet Shot After a Roquet
The player picks up her ball and puts it so that it touches the ball she roqueted. Then she strikes her ball so the other ball moves. Failure to make the other ball even wobble is a foul and the player's ball is replaced where it was before.

Having been roqueted, a ball cannot be roqueted again in that turn – unless the player's ball goes through a hoop first. Going through a hoop restores the right to roquet any of the three balls.

Continuation Stroke After a Roquet
This is an ordinary stroke, played with the ball just used in the croquet shot. If, during this shot, another ball is roqueted, or it goes through a hoop, the rules for these apply all over again.

Out of Bounds
If a ball goes over the boundary line a player places the ball a yard (about a mallet's length) in from the boundary, near where it went off, and continues.

Fouls
The striker must not:

- touch the head of her mallet with her hand
- kick or hit the mallet on to the ball
- rest herself or the mallet on anything while making a shot
- move a stationary ball, which is resting against a peg or hoop, by hitting the peg or hoop
- strike the ball with anything but the face of the mallet
- touch any ball which is in play with any part of her anatomy (except to put it in position)
- hit a ball, which is resting against a hoop or peg, towards that hoop or peg
- hit the ball twice in any ordinary shot.

A foul must be called before the next stroke is played. The penalty is the ending of the player's turn with no points scored.

Darts *(any number of players)*

There are various games which can be played with darts and a darts board. The standard game is this:

1 The board is hung so its centre is 5 ft 8 in (173 cm) from the floor.
2 The throwing line in international championships is 7 ft 9¼ in (237.5 cm) from the board, for both sexes. But many pubs have lines farther away from it, and the players agree on a line before play.
3 Play can be by individuals, pairs, or teams of any agreed number.
4 Either toss to start or throw and see who gets closest to the bullseye.
5 To start scoring a player must get his or her dart inside the outer rings – that dart is scored, but darts played prior to that dart have no score.
6 In team play scoring starts for the whole team when one team member gets a dart inside the outer rings.

The starting total is 301 or 501, or 1,001 – the players agree which to use. Scores are deducted from that total.

- A dart in the inner bull scores 50.
- A dart in the outer bull scores 25.
- Darts in the sectors score according to the sector.
- Darts in the outer double ring score double the score for that sector; in the inner double ring they score treble.
- Darts outside the outer double ring score nothing.

Traditionally, in pubs, if someone wants to join a game he offers to 'chalk' (write up the score) for the other players on the blackboard. He then plays the winner.

The winner is the first player to reach exactly zero. But zero may only be reached by throwing a double. So, if a throw would bring the score to one, or take it past zero, that throw is not scored, and the turn ends.

Eight Ball Pool *(2 players or 2 teams)*

Pool is played on a pocket billiards table, using a white cue ball and 15 other balls. The balls can be given numbers from 1 to 15. The key ball is black, which is number 8. There are also spot (or yellow) balls numbered 1 to 7, and striped (or red) balls numbered 9 to 15. It can be played by two players or two teams, and the order of play with each team doesn't vary.

Aim
The aim is to pocket the 8 ball first, having first pocketed all the balls of a particular group. This group is decided by the opening play. To start the balls are arranged in a triangle, as illustrated, with the 8 ball on the spot. You toss a coin to start. The winner decides who will make the first shot ('the break').

The Break
The first player plays the cue ball from anywhere within the 'D', aiming for any of the balls in the triangle. The aim is to pocket a ball, or make at least 2 balls hit a cushion (the padded sides of the table). If they fail to do this the game is restarted with the balls back in the

triangle. This time the other player (or team) begins and the previous team forfeits a turn – so their opponent has two consecutive turns.

If a ball is pocketed as the result of a break that type of ball (e.g. striped) becomes the type which the player or team must play for throughout the game, and the other side is automatically allotted the other type.

If a player pockets balls of both types, on the break, he/she can choose which to play for.

Bad Breaks
- If, in pocketing the first ball, the cue ball is also pocketed, or any other foul stroke is made, then the ball doesn't count in deciding which balls will be played for.
- If a player pockets the 8 ball on the break the game must be restarted by that player without any penalty – even if there was a foul.
- If no balls are pocketed on the break, but it is still a valid break, then turns alternate between players/teams until a ball is pocketed.

Play
The cue ball is always played from where it comes to rest. A player's turn continues until he fails to pocket a ball on any shot, or commits a foul. Once a player has pocketed all the balls of his group he can try to get the black into any pocket, and so win the game.

Fouls
The penalty for a foul is loss of the next turn, and on the first shot of the following turn the opponent can hit *any* ball on the table without a penalty. The fouls are:
- pocketing the cue ball
- hitting the opponent's balls before your own
- failing to hit any ball with the cue ball
- playing a jump shot (one ball leaping another)
- hitting the 8 ball with the first impact of the cue ball while your own balls are still on the table
- pocketing an opponent's ball
- striking the cue ball twice over in a shot
- not striking the cue ball with the tip of the cue
- balls landing off the table (these are respotted on the 8 ball spot or as close as possible without touching another ball on a direct line between the spot and the centre of the 'D'. But for this the cue ball is replayed from anywhere in the 'D'.)

- touching any ball (except to respot it or position the cue ball when required by a foul)
- not having at least one foot on the floor
- playing out of turn
- playing before the balls have come to rest
- letting the cue touch balls other than the cue ball.

Snookering
A player is snookered when his way is blocked, so he cannot play a legal shot. If this happens as the result of a foul shot then the usual foul shot clauses apply but also the cue ball can be played from the 'D'.

Loss of Game
A player loses the game if he or she:
- pockets the cue ball when potting the black
- pockets the 8 ball before pocketing all the balls in his/her group
- pockets the 8 ball in the same shot as another ball, except after a foul, when only the 8 ball and the other team's balls are on the table
- if he doesn't try to play some ball of his own group.

Snooker (2 players, 2 pairs or 2 teams)

Snooker is played on a standard billiards/snooker table, using 15 red balls, 6 coloured balls and 1 white cue ball.

Basics
1 Toss to start and set up all the red balls in a triangle, as shown in the diagram, and the coloured balls are set up on the spots marked on the table.
2 Pairs and teams play as for singles, with turns alternating between the sides.
3 Within each side they play in the same order throughout the game. *Throughout the game only the white cue ball can ever be struck by the cue.*
4 In any turn a player must first aim to hit a red ball – unless there are no red balls on the table.
5 If a player fails to pocket a ball at any stroke his or her turn ends.
6 Apart from the first break of the game, the cue ball is always played from wherever it came to rest in the previous player's turn. (The only exception to this is when the cue ball has been pocketed, in which case it is played from the semi-circle.)
7 Players must always have at least one foot on the floor (i.e. not lie on the table).

Play
1 The first player puts the white cue ball within the marked semi-circle, and plays it so it strikes any red.
2 If a red is pocketed the player continues his 'break' by attempting to pocket any non-red ball.
3 If a coloured ball is pocketed the player now tries to pocket a red. This sequence of red and coloured balls alternates as long as there are reds on the table.
4 If the cue ball comes to rest against a ball, which is *not* the next type to be played, the stroke must be played without even wobbling the ball that the cue ball

touches, otherwise a penalty score is awarded to the opponent as in penalty scoring.

5 If the cue ball comes to rest against the type which *is* due to be played the player may play a ball of either colour next, or even miss, with no penalty.

6 Red balls which are pocketed stay in the pockets.

7 Coloured balls which are pocketed are *immediately* put back on the spot they occupied at the start of the game (respotted) – even in the middle of a break.

8 The player who pockets the last red ball may then try to pocket *any* coloured ball, and this is respotted. After that the balls must be struck by the cue ball – and pocketed – strictly in the order of their value, starting with the lowest. At this stage, coloured balls are *not* respotted.

9 The winner is whoever has the highest score at the end of the game. If there is a tie the black is brought back into play and the first to score from it wins.

Setting up the balls for Snooker

Scoring

Each correctly pocketed ball is added to a player's score as follows:

red = 1   **brown** = 4   **pink** = 6
yellow = 2   **blue** = 5   **black** = 7
green = 3

Fouls and Penalty Scores

After any 'foul shot' a player loses his turn (keeping his score up to the shot before the foul) and a penalty score is awarded to his opponent. Fouls are as follows but the minimum penalty is 4:

● If a cue ball is pocketed 4 is added to the opponent's score.

● If the cue ball fails to hit a ball its value is the penalty.

● If the cue ball hits the wrong ball (e.g. red, when it should be coloured) the penalty is the value of the correct ball.

● If the wrong ball is pocketed the penalty is the value of whichever ball is higher (between correct and pocketed).

● Simultaneously hitting or pocketing 2 balls, other than 2 reds, the penalty is the value of whichever is higher.

● Pocketing 2 balls in one shot, the penalty is the value of the higher of the two.

● For pushing a ball, jumping it over another or playing it out of turn the penalty is the value of the ball hit.

● For forcing a ball off the table the penalty is the value of the 'on' ball or the ball which was hit, whichever is higher.

● For playing 2 successive reds the penalty is 7 points.

Respotting Balls

● An illegally pocketed coloured ball is respotted *immediately*, whatever the stage of the game.

● If a coloured ball can't be replaced on its spot, because another ball has rolled on to it, the coloured ball is put on the vacant spot with the highest score.

● If all the spots are covered the ball goes as close as possible to its spot (without touching another ball) and on the shortest direct (imaginary) line between its spot and the top cushion. The only exception to this is if there is no space between the covered spot and the top cushion in which case the ball must be placed in a direct line to the bottom cushion.

Snookering

A snooker is when a shot is blocked because a ball which must not be hit is directly between the cue ball and the ball to be hit next. However, the shot must be played, and the usual penalty is scored if the player misses or hits another ball first.

If that situation arises because the previous player fouled the above rule does not apply, and any ball on the table may be played. If this ball is pocketed it scores 1 – except if there are no reds on the table. In that case it takes the score of the ball which the 'snooker' prevented him from playing.

Table Tennis *(2 or 4 players)*

The standard ball is white or yellow and 38.2 mm (1½ in) in diameter. The racket can be any size, provided it is a single piece of wood, and covered with a sheet of rubber. To win a player, or pair, must score 21 points. But if the score reaches 20 all, winning then requires a 2-point lead. A match can be one game, the best of 3 or the best of 5.

To start toss a coin; the winner either decides who serves first *or* picks his/her end.

Serving

The server lightly tosses the ball, from waist level using a flat hand, and hits it so it bounces once on the serving side, and once on the opponent's side. At the moment of striking the ball, for service, the bat must be behind the end of the table.

Service changes to the other player or pair after every 5 points. But, once the score reaches 20 all, opponents serve alternately. In singles this is simple. In doubles there is a set order of service and of play.

● The server stands at the right of the table.

● The serve must travel diagonally across the table, starting by touching the right-hand section on the server's side.

● The sequence of service in doubles is:

A to T
T to B (A & B having swopped sides)
B to S (S & T having swopped sides)
S to A (A & B having swopped sides)

Play for Singles and Doubles

- On a return the ball must cross the net without bouncing on the returner's side.
- A return which touches the net or supports is still good if it lands on the opponent's side.
- The ball *must* bounce once after crossing the net.
- The ball may *only* bounce once before being returned.
- Players change ends after each game, and also when the score reaches 10 in the final game.

The sequence of play in doubles follows a strict order in which the players on each side take the returns alternately, as follows:

A serves to T; T returns service
B must take T's return; S must take B's return
A takes the return from S, and so on.

Points are scored when:

- an opponent fails to hit the ball
- an opponent breaks any of the rules of play
- an opponent strikes out of sequence in doubles play.

A let is a rally which doesn't result in points and the serve is retaken. This occurs when:

- the ball touches the net or supports during service, and still lands correctly
- a ball is served when the receiver isn't ready and has *not* attempted to hit the ball.

BOARD GAMES AND OTHERS

In this section you will find the rules for some of the most popular family games, from chess to tiddlywinks. Mah Jong and Go I have reluctantly had to omit as they are far too complex for a book of this sort. Games like Monopoly and Trivial Pursuit are also omitted because if you have the pieces you probably have the rules.

Backgammon *(2 players)*

This is an excellent game which can be played with or without a gambling element. It probably came to Europe from the Middle East, as a primitive board suggests it was played in Sumeria in 2600 BC. When it was introduced in the eleventh century it took both nobles and commoners by such storm that both Church and state tried to suppress it as an immoral time-waster. For centuries it remained immensely popular with the upper classes, and only the eighteenth-century craze for cards ousted it from fashion, upon which it became a favourite game with the clergy.

Before starting play, each player places her 15 pieces on the board as shown below. To start, each player throws one of the two dice. (It is customary to call the dice score at each throw.) The highest starts, using the two numbers just thrown. Thereafter they play alternately, throwing the two dice each time. The dice dictate the number of points the pieces may be moved. For example, throwing a 4 and 6 allows you to move one piece along 4 points then on 6 points (or vice versa), provided either the 4th or 6th points are free, or move one piece 4 points and another 6 points – moving in your own direction of play. If a double is thrown the potential moves are doubled. So double 3 allows you to move any variation of four 3s. You may not land on a point occupied by 2 or more of an opponent's pieces; but you may cross it at any stage of the journey.

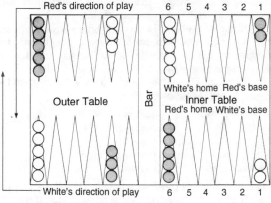

Direction of Play

A single piece on a point is a 'blot'. An opponent may land on it and place it on the central bar. It can only be brought into play by its owner throwing a number corresponding to a free point (i.e. an empty point or one with only one of the opponent's piece's, or any number of the player's own) in his base. So, tactics concentrate on 'making points' (placing 2 of one's pieces safely on the same point), and in trying to land on one's opponent's 'blots' and remove them from the board.

When you have all your pieces home you can 'bear off' pieces from the points the dice allow. So a 5 and 2 allow one piece to be removed from point number 5 and another from point number 2. Or moves to the value of 5 and 2 can be made, or one piece removed and another moved. If a 6 is thrown and there are no pieces on the 6 point a piece is removed from the next highest point – and so on.

The winner is whoever bears off all his pieces first. A hit is when the loser has also reached the bearing-off stage. A gammon is when all the loser's pieces are not yet home. A backgammon is when the loser still has a piece in her opponent's home table.

Gambling at Backgammon

The players first agree a stake, and place the doubling die on the bar, with 64 uppermost. If the loser has managed to bear off one or more stones she only pays the agreed stake. If the loser has all 15 men on the board she pays twice the stake. If she has any on the bar she pays three times the stake. If doubling has taken place the same rules apply but to the doubled stake.

If a player feels he is at an advantage he can double the basic stake. His opponent can either stop the game and pay the stake first agreed or agree to double and continue. The doubling die is then put on the bar with the 2 uppermost. The doubled player then has control of it so the other cannot double again. If he in turn feels lucky he can redouble – to 4 times the original stake. And his opponent has to pay up or agree – and so on.

Battleships *(2 players)*

As a child, I inherited an ancient board for battleships drawn out under a sheet of yellowed perspex. It looked as if it dated from the First World War and must have had very different connotations then.

Each player needs 2 sheets of ordinary squared paper and a pencil. On each paper draw a big 'board' ten squares by ten, and labelled A to J across and 1 to 10 down. Each player then labels one 'board' 'Enemy Fleet' and the other 'Home Fleet' and marks in his fleet on the home 'board' as follows:

The Fleet	Squares Filled
1 battleship	4 per ship
2 cruisers	3 per ship
3 destroyers	2 per ship
4 submarines	1 per ship

Take turns, to call out a square (e.g. D5). If your opponent has no vessel on the square he says 'no'; if there is a ship on the square he calls 'hit'. Tick X on your enemy fleet 'board' so you can see what is where. To sink a ship you must hit all of its squares, and each player must say when a ship is sunk. The winner is whoever sinks all the enemy ships first.

Chess *(2 players)*

Chess is said to have been invented by an Indian philosopher, in the sixth century AD and it reached Europe between 700 and 900, becoming an essential skill for travelling minstrels.

It is played on a board of 64 squares, using 16 pieces. One player takes 2 pieces, a white and a black piece,

The Pieces on a Chessboard

switches them around behind his back and holds his hands out. The other chooses, and accepts that colour. Have a white square at the lower right-hand corner of the board. White makes the first move.

The object of the game is to achieve a position from which the opponent's King could be captured. When someone sees that their next move will achieve this they must say 'check'. The opponent must protect the King, or it is 'checkmate' and the game is over. During play an opponent's piece may be taken off after a move which lands the capturing piece on the same square.

Each type of piece is allowed a different type of move, as follows. Only the Knight may hop over *all* other pieces. Obviously, the greater the scope for movement, the more powerful the piece: it is seldom worth sacrificing a powerful piece to capture a low one.

Piece	Moves	Takes
King	One square in any direction, including diagonally	As it moves
Queen	Any number of squares in any direction, including diagonally	As it moves
Rooks/ Castles	Any number of squares forward or backwards or at right angles	As it moves
Bishops	Any number of squares forward or backwards on a diagonal	As it moves
Knights	An L-shaped move, 2 squares one way and 1 to the side, travelling in any direction except diagonally. To do this they may hop over other pieces	As it moves
Pawns	Only move forward. Each may move 2 squares on its first move. Only 1 square otherwise	Takes on a diagonal

Three Special Exceptions
1 *En passant:* if in moving two squares forward, on its first move, a Pawn lands *beside* an opponent's Pawn it may be taken just as if it had only moved one square and landed diagonally to it. The winning Pawn is put on the square the victim would have occupied had it only moved one square.
2 If a Pawn reaches the opponent's back row it may be converted into *any* piece the player wishes.
3 Castling is a double move made in a single turn to safeguard a King. A Rook and a King must be in their starting positions with no pieces between them. The King moves 2 squares towards the Rook. The Rook moves to the square next to the King on the far side – jumping over the King to do so.

Chessboard Notation
In chess books each square is named after the column and row of the *colour which is playing*. So each square has two names, as in the example. The piece moving is named first, then the square of its own colour on which it moves. So P-QB3 means a pawn does the move shown. X means 'takes'.

Chess pieces are named after the Queen's or the King's

Addresses and suggestions for further reading are at the ends of chapters.

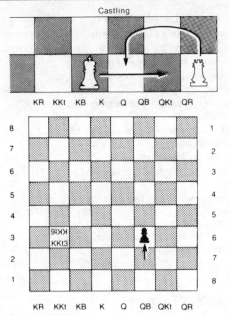

Castling

KR KKt KB K Q QB QKt QR

| | | | | | | | | |
8 | | | | | | | | | 1
7 | | | | | | | | | 2
6 | | | | | | | | | 3
5 | | | | | | | | | 4
4 | | | | | | | | | 5
3 | KKt6 KKt3 | | | | | | 6
2 | | | | | | | | | 7
1 | | | | | | | | | 8

KR KKt KB K Q QB QKt QR

side of the board. Pawns are named according to the piece they stand in front of.

Dice

Liar Dice *(4 or more players, gambling)*
This is one of several versions using 5 poker dice. Throw one dice each – highest starts. You also need to agree what stake will be lost for each call or challenge which proves false. *Throughout the game the dice throws are concealed from everyone except the person throwing.*

The first player throws all 5 dice, then calls their value – e.g. 'a pair of fours, a pair of aces, and a two'. The call can be true or any part of it can be a lie and all 5 dice are called at each call. The concealed throw is slid to the next player, clockwise, who may rethrow all or part of the throw keeping them all concealed. Whatever is thrown, the call *must* be higher than the previous call, and so on round the table. Each player may say the person before was lying, upon which the throw is revealed. If it was a lie the liar loses a chip to the challenger; if it was correct the reverse happens. Play starts again with all 5 being rethrown. The possible calls, in ascending order, are as follows:

● one pair
● two pairs
● three of a kind
● low straight – i.e. 1-2-3-4-5
● high straight – i.e. 2-3-4-5-6
● full house – i.e. three of a kind, and a pair
● four of a kind
● five of a kind

In all pairs and runs 6s would win over 5s, and so on. Aces are high. If you don't want to play for money let each person have three chips and, having lost all their chips, they are out. If you are playing for money, chips have an agreed value.

Poker Dice *(5 players or less,)*
Roll to decide who starts, as in liar dice. Each person has 2 throws per turn. On the second you can rethrow all 5 dice, or just some of them, or leave the first throw unchanged, and not throw a second time. A note is made of the throw thus achieved. The highest throw wins, using the rank order given in Liar Dice. Two equal throws are settled by a play-off.

Dominoes *(2 or more players)*

One type of domino set takes the numbers up to six, the other up to nine. The sixes version has 28 pieces, and the nines 55. The rules vary widely, so agree them before play starts. Here is one version.

Place the pieces face down and shuffle them. Take 5 pieces each (7 with few people and/or a large set). Stand them on edge, so the other players can't read them. Whoever has the highest double puts it down, then takes another piece. Each player plays one piece in turn and picks up a replacement. The pieces are played by placing a 4 dot against another 4 dot, and a 2 dot against a 2 dot – and so on anywhere on the table. All the pieces are placed end on except the doubles. Doubles go at right angles to the main line and can be added to at both ends and both sides. When someone cannot match any piece on the board either the turn is missed or the player must take a piece without playing – which makes the game more interesting.

Whoever gets rid of her pieces first wins. If pieces are left, but nobody can play, the winner is whoever has the lowest total of dots. In a series of games the winner of each game subtracts her dot total from the total for all the other players. This gives her score for the game. The first to total 100 is the overall winner.

Draughts *(chequers, 2 players)*

Draughts is played on a chequerboard, with 8 squares each way, and each player has 12 men. You can either win by capturing all your opponent's pieces or by surrounding them so they cannot move.

Place the board with the white square at the bottom right-hand corner. Decide who will play which colour as in chess (see page 330). The men are placed on the 12 dark squares nearest each player. Dark always starts play. The players make one move each, alternately.

1 A basic move is one square diagonally forwards.
2 To capture an opponent's piece it must be diagonally next to yours, with a space on the far side. You then jump it, taking the jumped man as you do so. You can use one move to take as many as are available in one journey, zigzagging if necessary.
3 A man that reaches the farthest row on the opponent's side becomes a King (a spare man being placed on top). It can then move diagonally forwards or backwards at will.

Play with any piece ends when a player removes his hand and a piece may not be touched if it is not going to be played.

If a man could have been taken, but wasn't, an

opponent should say so and the player replace the man he has moved and make the move that would take the other man. This stops a player avoiding taking an opponent if it will put his man in a vulnerable position. In tournaments this now replaces the 'huff' rule.

Nine Men's Morris (2 players)

A seemingly simple, but very intriguing, game which dates back to the Bronze Age. It can be marked out on earth or sand and played with stones.

Each player has 9 pegs. Each alternately puts one peg anywhere on the board until all 18 pegs are in place. After that, at each turn, a player can move one peg to the next hole along the lines on the board.

The aim is to get 3 pegs in a row along one of the lines on the board. This entitles a player to remove 1 of his opponent's men from anywhere on the board, except where it is part of a line of 3 – unless no other men are available. Once a player has only 3 men he may move to *any* empty hole on the board. The winner is whoever reduces an opponent to only 2 men, or makes him unable to move.

It is not usually permitted to break and re-form a line of 3 on successive moves, but some people allow this.

Roulette (any number of players)

Roulette is an eighteenth-century game, which had its heyday in the casinos of a hundred years ago. Players bet on a certain number or chance on the table. The croupier calls out 'Rien ne va plus', – no more play – to end the betting and the wheel is spun so a ball tumbles between red and black numbered pockets. When it stops the ball settles in a pocket – and those who bet on that number, colour or group win. The rest lose their money.

The numbers are dotted about and the European has 37 pockets, but the American 38 including a 00.

The board, on which bets are placed, has no effect on play and is simply designed to make it easy for the croupier to see who is betting what. The players put their chips (counters indicating their bet) on their chosen number(s) or colour. There are two designs – European and American. The options are almost the same, but the European version uses French terms. To place one's chips on each is to bet as follows:

How Bets can be Placed	Potential Win
Rouge (a red diamond) – red will win	even money
Noir (a black diamond) – black will win	even money
Pair – an even number will win	even money
Impair – an odd number will win	even money
Manque – a number 1-18 will win	even money
Passe – a number 19-36 will win	even money
En plein – stake on a single number	35-1
À cheval – stake on line between 2 numbers	17-1
Transversale pleine – on 3 numbers in a horizontal row	11-1
En carré – on 4 numbers in a square block	8-1
Transversale simple or sixaine – 6 numbers in 2 horizontal rows	5-1
Colonne – on a vertical column of 12 numbers	2-1
Colonne à cheval – on two adjacent columns	2-1 on, or 1-2
Douzaine – on 12 numbers, either 1-12, 13 24 or 25-36. Stake on first dozen, second dozen or third dozen	2-1
Douzaine à cheval – on two adjacent dozens	2-1 on, or 1-2

Solitaire (1 player)

Solitaire is said to have been created by a French nobleman, during his imprisonment, and makes a particularly good pastime for someone confined to bed, as it doesn't require the flat surface needed for patience.

With any game of solitaire you are trying to get all the men off the board except one, leaving that piece in a position which you decided at the start – such as the centre. There are various types of board, but the traditional one is octagonal with 37 holes in it. A move is always to jump another man and remove the jumped man from the board, and the standard lay-out is to fill all the holes except that in the centre.

Anyone who is bored with the basic form can try playing so as to leave a chosen pattern.

Spillikins (pick-a-sticks, jackstraws, 2-5 players)

You need a set of spillikins. These are fine straight sticks marked in different colours, with pointed ends. Draw lots for the order of play. The last player then holds the spillikins in a bundle with the points just touching the floor and lets them fall in all directions. The first player removes as many spillikins as he can, but the moment another player spots movement in a stick which an opponent is not trying to remove she calls out and the player's turn ends. This continues until all the sticks have been removed. The person with the most can be the winner or you can allot different scores to type colours before play starts.

A player may not attempt to move one spillikin, fail and try another, but may use a spillikin she has already drawn to help move another; in some versions she may only do this if the spillikin is a certain colour.

CARD GAMES

This is not the place for a treatise on card games for card addicts, such as bridge or canasta. They deserve books to themselves. It is just a selection of some of those games which are amusing enough to pass a wet afternoon, and can be learnt fast enough for beginners to enjoy them. For most card games there are no definitive rules, so these versions may not be your versions. They are fun for all that.

- A pack needs 52 cards covering 1-10, jack (knave), queen, king, ace, in each of four suits – hearts, clubs, diamonds and spades. The joker, if there is one, is removed unless otherwise stated.
- Any pack which is used must be well shuffled.
- Play always starts with the player on the dealer's left, unless otherwise stated.
- Numbered cards normally score their face value, and court cards score 10. Aces can be 1 or 10 according to the game – 'aces high' means they score 10.
- To 'cut' you each take a group of cards from the stack; the one at the bottom is yours. Highest wins.

Black Lady (*3-7 players, easy*)

This is a simple version of Black Maria. The aim is to get the *lowest* score in a series of games. Queen of spades = 30. Hearts score: ace = 11; jack, queen, king = 10. Other hearts have face value. No other cards score.

Cut to deal – highest deals (aces high). Deal the whole pack – if the number of players won't divide into 52 exactly remove some 2s before dealing.

Players look at their hands, choose 3 unwanted cards and pass all these at the same time, to the player on their left (queen of spades may not be passed). Then play starts.

The first player places any card face up in the centre. Each player in turn places on it one card of the same suit (the number sequence doesn't matter). Someone with no cards of that suit follows with a card of any suit.

At the end of the round, whoever placed the highest number of the opening suit takes that trick and places it on the table in front of them. They then place the first card for the next round – choosing any card they wish.

When all the cards have been played the score is totalled. All hearts in someone's hand or in their tricks are counted against them, as is the queen of spades. However, having *all* the hearts *and* the queen of spades is a grand slam: it scores zero – and 125 penalty points are given to each of the other players.

Cheat (*3 players upwards – very easy*)

The aim is to get rid of all your cards first. Ace is both high and low, so it can be followed by a king or a 2.

Deal the whole pack — add packs so everyone has 8 or more cards. The first player puts down 1, 2, 3 or 4 cards face down in the centre, calling what has been played (e.g. 'three 9s'). This call may be true, but it can be as false as the player wishes.

Each player in turn then plays 1, 2, 3 or 4 cards on top of the first ones, calling truthfully or untruthfully, but the call must always be the next number above or below the previous call (i.e. three 9s could be followed by 8s or 10s).

After a call anyone can say 'Cheat' and turn over the cards just called. Cheaters, who are found out, must take all the cards in the centre, but if the call was correct the challenger picks them up instead. This continues until someone has no cards left – and so wins.

Pelmanism (*2-6 players – a memory game*)

Cut to start – highest starts. Place a shuffled pack, face down, in rows, to form a rectangle. Each player in turn then turns up 2 cards, so everyone can see them. If they match (e.g. two black 6s, two red kings etc) the player takes them. If they do not they are turned face down again. This continues until all the cards have been removed, and whoever has the most pairs wins. In another version making a pair gives another turn.

Poker (*3/5-7, ideally 5-7 players – easy to play, hard to play well*)

There are numerous versions of poker. Anyone playing a serious game or for high stakes should read up on it in a book by a card expert: it is easy to lose a lot of money – especially if your companions play an unfamiliar version.

A chip value is agreed before the game starts and so is a maximum stake. The player on the dealer's left puts a chip on the table in front of her. This is the ante. (Hence the term 'to up the ante'.) The second player puts up chips – called a straddle. These, plus all the later stakes, form the 'pool'.

The dealer gives each player 5 cards, face down. Aces are high. Players decide whether their cards are good enough to play with – if not they can drop out. The third player 'speaks' first. She can drop out or put up a stake of twice the straddle (i.e. 4 chips). The other players in turn can throw in their hand, or stay in by putting up chips which either equal the stake of the previous player or double it. Those who put up the ante and straddle can throw in their hand (losing what they put up) or raise their stakes to the appropriate total. Stake raising round the table continues until nobody wishes to go further.

Those in the game can keep the 5 cards they have, or try to improve their hand by giving 1, 2, 3, 4 or 5 cards back to the dealer, who places them at the bottom of the pack before dealing replacements. (Changing 4 or 5 cards is slightly mad, but it is not against the rules.)

The betting then starts with the third player. In turn each player may throw in their cards (and lose their stake), say 'check' and remain in without increasing their stake, or raise their stake by any amount within the limit. When everyone is at 'check' all the players show their hands and the best hand takes all the stakes.

An alternative ending is that checks are not allowed. When two players remain either may raise her stake to equal that of another player and say 'see you'. Her opponent must then raise her stake, to avoid being seen, or show the hand. The higher hand wins.

The strength of the hands, in descending order, plus the odds against most being dealt in the initial hand, is as follows:

Royal straight flush – ace, king, queen, jack, 10 of one suit
Straight flush – king, queen, jack 10, 9, or any lower run of 5 in a suit (of two straight flushes the higher run wins) (64,973:1)
Fours – 4 cards the same – e.g. 4 fives (higher cards win) (4,164:1)
Full house – 3 cards the same, and 2 cards the same – e.g. 3 nines and 2 fives (of two full houses that with the higher 3 wins) (693:1)
Flush – 5 cards of the same suit – e.g. jack, 9,7,6,3 (of two flushes that with the highest card wins, if these are the same the second card decides it) (508:1)
Straight – 5 cards in number sequence, of varied suits – the highest first card wins, two equal cards split the pool (254:1)
Threes – 3 cards the same, plus 2 odd ones (46:1)
Two pairs – e.g. 2 kings, 2 sevens, plus an odd card – highest pair wins (20:1)
One pair – e.g. 2 jacks, plus 3 odd cards (15:11)
Highest card – 5 assorted cards – the highest card wins

Pontoon *(vingt-et-un, 3-7 players)*

The aim is a hand which makes 21, or just under. Ace = 1 or 11; court cards = 10; others at face value.

1 Whoever cuts the pack at the highest card becomes banker. He then deals one card to each person, himself included. Everyone puts up a stake (according to how good their hand looks). If the banker holds a good card (e.g. ace, court card, 10,2) he may want to tell everyone to double their stakes.
2 A second round is dealt, face down. Anyone who now holds a 'natural' – cards adding to 21 (i.e. ace plus court card or 10) – must reveal it. The banker then pays 3 times their stake and they will take the bank at the next game.
3 The banker offers another card — each player may:

● 'buy' a card (for not more than his original stake),
● 'twist' – have a card dealt face up,
● 'stand' – take no card, if his cards total 15 or more.

4 This proceeds until up to 5 cards each, but having twisted a player may buy no more cards. A player may not buy a fifth card if his hand totals 11 or under. If, at any point, someone's hand adds up to more than 21 they must say they are 'busted' and lose their stake.
5 The banker turns his cards face up and adds 1, 2 or 3 cards to it, in turn. At any point the banker can stop and say he will pay anyone with a higher hand – e.g. with a 6, 4 and 9 the call would be 'pay 20 and 21'. The players then reveal their hands. The pay-out is as follows:

● hands equal to the bank or lower lose their stake
● hands higher than the bank and under 21 are paid their stake

● hands of 21 are paid double their stake
● five cards totalling under 21 get double their stake
● a hand of three 7s gets triple its stake.

If the bank is 'busted' it pays out a stake to everyone still in. If the banker has 21 or 5 and under, he gets single stakes from anyone with the same and double stakes from everyone else.

★ If someone has a pair they may say 'split' and make two hands by placing a bet on the second hand equal to their first stake, and the banker deals a second card to each hand. The player then plays the two hands separately.

★ If there are several naturals the one to the dealer's left has priority. If the banker has a natural he shows it and each player pays him twice their original stake – except a player with a natural who only pays the original stake. The game ends there.

Racing Demon *(2-4 players, fast, competitive)*

Use old packs, one pack per person – they will swiftly get dog-eared. For scoring each must look different.

Each person deals 13 cards face up to their left, and places 4 cards face up in a row beside them. On the word 'Go' everyone starts to play, as if playing patience. The following moves are allowed.

● Turn over the cards in your hand in threes.
● Put aces in the centre.
● Build on anyone's aces in ascending order, (2,3,4 etc.) in suit, using cards from the pile of 13, from the row of 4 or from the remaining cards as you turn them over.
● build on your own row of 4 in descending order, alternating red and black, using cards from the 13, from other rows or from those you are turning over.

The first person to get rid of all the 13 cards in that pile wins and calls 'out' – and all play stops. Each person's score is the number of cards he or she has in the middle, minus the number left from their stack of 13.

Rummy *(2-6 players, very easy)*

Rummy has at least five variations. This is a basic version. Ace is 1, court cards 10. Others at face value.

Deal 10 cards for 2 players, 7 cards for 3-4, 6 cards for 5-6. The remaining cards are placed face down, with the top card face up beside them. Each player in turn picks up a card – from the face-up or face-down stack – and then discards one face-up.

The aim is to make sets of 3 or 4 cards (i.e. 10s or 3s or kings) or to make runs of 3 or more (i.e. 2,3,4,5 or Q,J,10,9,8 in the same suit. Both sets and runs are allowed in the same hand.

The first person to get all his cards into sets or runs says 'rummy' and shows the hand. (A card cannot appear in a set *and* a run.) The game then stops and any cards in the other players' hands which are not in a set are counted against them. The person with the lowest score, after an agreed number of games, wins.

The Shop Game *(4+; the more the better, 1-2 packs)*

Despite its title, this is not just for the very young – I learnt it from someone who played it as a rowing Blue. Each person is dealt an equal number of cards (any left over are set aside) and they are left face down in front of each player. Starting at the left of the dealer, each person in turn announces what shop they are (any shop they wish). They only say it once and nobody may name anyone's shop during the game.

Going round the table each player turns up one card from his hand. If there is already another card of that number/type on the table, of any suit, each owner must name a product sold in the other's shop. Whoever is slowest takes all the upturned cards in front of the other player and puts them at the bottom of his own hand. Once a product has been called it cannot be used again by any player. The first to get rid of all cards wins.

Whist – Knock Out *(2-6 players, very easy)*

The dealer cuts, and the card revealed is trumps. He then deals 7 cards to each player. The first player places a card in the centre. The next player follows with any card in the same suit, or trumps it with a card from the trump suit. (If they can do neither they discard a card on to the heap.) At the end of the round whoever placed the highest trump wins and takes that trick. If there are no trumps the highest card in the initial suit takes the trick. This continues until all hands are used up. Whoever has the most tricks wins that game; those with none are out.

Each successive game is played in the same way, but with one less card per person per game. At each game the winner of the previous game can choose trumps *after* having seen her hand. Anyone who fails to get a trick in one game becomes 'doggy' in the next and is dealt only one card. But 'doggies' may pass in any round and play nothing. If they again fail to get a trick they become 'blind doggy' and are not allowed to look at their one card before playing it. If they again fail to get a trick they are out. If a doggy or blind doggy gets a trick they get the same number of cards as the other players on the next round.

GAMES OF PATIENCE

Aces and Spaces *(1 pack)*

This sounds very simple, but it may surprise you.

Lay out 4 rows of 13 cards, face up, from left to right, to use the whole pack. Remove the aces and place one to the left of each of the four rows (position them to make it easier to get the patience out). You may now move any card into any space *provided* it is the same suit

as the card to the left of the space, and one higher than that card. Try to get each of the 4 suits, started by the aces, in correct order reading from left to right.

Demon *(1 pack)*

Place 13 cards in a stack to the left, all face down except the top card. And lay 4 cards face up in a row.

Place 1 card, face up, above the 4. This card decides what cards will be built on to get the patience out. If a 10 is placed there each of the other 10s will be placed beside it, as they show up, and each of these will be built on in suit in ascending order (i.e. 10, jack, queen, king, ace, 2, 3-9). The 4 cards face up at the start are built on in descending order (red, black, red, black) with cards from the pack, or with ones from the top of the 13 to the left, or by moving cards from one row to another. Any card may go into an empty space in this row. Turn up the remaining cards in threes. When a run through these produces no result place the top card to the bottom (this may be done only twice before being out) and run through again.

Klondike *(1 pack)*

This is one my daughter taught me. How hard it is depends on the number of cards you choose to turn over in the pack. One variation is that you go through once in threes, once in twos, once one at a time. Another to go through them only once — in ones.

Place 1 card face up to the left; put 6 cards face down in a row to its right. (Call them rows 1-7.) Place a card face up on row 2, and one face down on 3,4,5,6,7. Place a card face up on row 3, and one face down on 4,5,6,7. And so on until each row ends with one card face up.

Rules of Play

- You may move face-up cards from one row to another placing them on top of one another, in descending order (7,6,5, etc.), alternating red and black. But if a space opens you may only fill it with a king.
- Any ace which comes up immediately goes to a row above the seven. And aces are built on in ascending order (ace, 2, 3, 4) in suit.
- The cards remaining in the pack are turned over in threes, and the top card can be placed, as appropriate, on any row or ace pile. Once the top card of the three has been played the one beneath it may be played too – and so on.
- The patience is out when all the cards are stacked on the aces of their suit in correct order.

PARTY GAMES FOR ALL AGES

Games tend to evolve, gathering regional and family embellishments and alterations. So I don't pretend my versions are the 'right' ones (if such exist), and I apologize to anyone who is frustrated by failing to find their favourite game here. Use these versions as a starting point for your own additions. They range from the simplest games for toddlers, to those designed for teenage and adult parties with dancing. But there aren't really any neat divisions between children's games and adult ones. Barring the self-consciousness of adolescence, most games can be enjoyed by almost anyone, if the mood is right. I know of some middle-aged intellectuals who scored a hit by giving a birthday party for adults, complete with party tea, children's games and going-away presents. So, I've first given the lowest possible age for each game, but only set an upper limit when physical or emotional developments dictate a ceiling (Granny had better not play musical bumps). I have marked each game 'out', 'in', or even 'out/in' according to their potential.

Some 'outdoor games' can be played in a large (damage-proof) room; some 'indoor' ones, such as musical bumps, are rather better on grass. Games marked 'travel' can also be played in transit if those near you can stand it, though some games may need advance preparation like carrying paper and pencils.

The minimum number of players is given: + after means more can play; ++ means it would be *better* with more. How many more will vary with the room, the age (and unruliness) of the players. Most find 12 children at a time enough, unless they are very, very good.

Organizing Games at Children's Parties

Organizing games takes all one's attention, so have a helper to handle distractions – children bent on destruction, mothers who come early or leave late, or tinies with over-excited bladders. There is no faster recipe for chaos than leaving a group of children in mid-game while you escort one desperate infant to the loo.

The other factor to bear in mind is the order of the games. Children arrive noisy and energetic or shy and withdrawn. Either way, start with games that release both energy and inhibitions – preferably one which latecomers can join. They need to work off enough restlessness to sit still and eat. Those after tea should be calmer – some children throw up when over-excited. For your sanity, punctuate the proceedings with games which enforce silence – I recommend Beans and Straws and Kim's Game.

Treat it like a military operation. Everything you need for each game must be *totally* ready in advance, and to hand. And prepare the territory as if for an invasion – remove everything which might get damaged, lock every door they shouldn't enter and keep the keys.

The rules for some good games are given below but don't forget Chinese Whispers, I Spy, Pass the Parcel, Musical Bumps and Chairs, Shipwrecks, Treasure Hunts, Wellie Throwing and Egg and Spoon Races – none of which need rules from me.

Prizes at Children's Parties

If a prize is given for any game it is essential to give one for *every* game, or there are hard feelings. Ideally there should also be some team games in which the winning team each get a prize. That way every child should win something. Unfortunately, some mothers use the size of the prizes to compete with other mothers. This is cruel to the less well-off, and brings out the worst in children. One answer is to establish a truce between mothers by agreeing a no-prize rule, or a severe limit to the value. Failing that, hide wrapped prizes in an improvised bran tub of shredded newspaper in a big box. Let each child pick its own prize which you immediately put in a bag labelled with its name for it to take home. That rules out any comparison of prizes while the party is in progress.

Alphabet Game *(age 6+, nos 3+, in/out/travel)*

Decide on a topic – say food or pop singers' names. Then the first person says one beginning with A, the next person one beginning with B, and so on, in turn (e.g. apple, banana, custard, etc.). If you can't think of one you are out.

Apple Bobbing *(age 5+, nos 2+, in/out)*

Tie long strings firmly to the stalks of as many apples as there are players. Hang them, at mouth level, from a swing frame, doorway, or French window lintel. Each player stands in front of an apple and on the word 'Go' starts to eat their elusive apple – without touching it with their hands. The first to finish and hold it in the teeth wins. Or have clean buckets of water with apples in. (Leave the stalks in if you want to make it easier, remove them if you don't.) Part of the fun is watching, so have two 'sittings'.

Baby Face *(age 15+, nos 8++, in)*

Each guest gives you a photograph of themselves as a baby (name the backs instantly). Display each with a number, and keep a list of which is who. Everyone has to list the babies by name; whoever gets most right wins. In groups which don't know each other play Star Face, naming photos of well-known people.

Balloon Dancing *(age 10+, nos 10++, in)*

Disco dancing goes on while a balloon is patted from person to person without touching the ground. If the balloon hits the ground the person who lets it fall is out, or pays a forfeit.

In another version a balloon must be held between each couple while they dance. They are not allowed to touch each other (or the balloon) and must keep time to the music. Start with an easy tempo and make it progressively harder. Those who drop it are out, but it is hilarious to watch.

Beans and Straws *(age 3+, nos 2+, in)*

Give each player a drinking straw and an empty jam jar, and scatter small dried haricot beans, or split peas, on the floor. On 'Go' they collect beans by sucking them, one at a time, on to the end of the straw and dropping them into their jar. Touching them is not allowed. Whoever gets the most within a set time, wins.

Addresses and suggestions for further reading are at the ends of chapters.

Boom *(age 4+, nos 4+ in/out/travel)*

Count round the group *fast*, the first person saying 1, the second 2, and so on up & up. But whenever a number has a 4 in it (e.g. 4, 14, 24,) the person says 'boom' instead. Anyone who says the wrong number or fails to say 'boom' at the right time is out. You can replace any number with 'boom'. Try 1 as 'boom' for giggles with older children.

Botticelli *(age 14+, nos 6+, in/out/travel)*

A game for players of equal knowledge or some will feel put down.

One player 'becomes' a well-known person, and tells the rest his or her initials. Everyone else in turn asks a question designed to reveal who the person is being. If the initials were J.C. this might be 'Are you a famous actress?' The person being questioned isn't allowed to say 'no'. They have to think of an actress with those initials and their reply must be 'No, I am not Joan Collins' (or whoever). If they can't manage this the questioner gets a second turn in which he may ask a general question such as, 'Are you male or female? – yes or no answers to these are allowed. If the questioner thinks he knows who the person is he can ask directly, e.g. 'Are you Julius Caesar?' If right he now takes the celebrity seat, if wrong he misses a turn. An easier version is to use only one initial not two.

Charades *(age 10+, nos 8+, in)*

Two groups are formed. Each goes away and prepares to act out – with or without costumes – a long word or proverb, or the title of a book, film or play, for the other group to guess. First, the actors say whether they are doing a word, proverb or title – and whether of a book, film or play. The title is then acted out syllable by syllable, or word by word. Each scene *depicts* one syllable or word, and that syllable or word is also mentioned at least once. (If 'seasons' was in the title either the whole word could be acted or there could be one scene about the sea and another about sons.) Then, in the final scene the whole word, phrase or title is acted out and said at least once. The group which is guessing may try to guess the word or phrase at the end of each scene – and the charade ends if they guess the whole title. But no clues are given. At the end the group may confer before guessing the complete word or phrase – and in some families only a set number of guesses are allowed. Then this group acts their charade.

The Chocolate Game *(age 4+, nos 4+, in/out)*

Everyone sits on the floor in a circle. A plate is put in the centre with a large bar of chocolate, plus knife and fork. Also in the centre are a wellington boot, funny hat, pair of gloves (oversized for the players) and false nose. The players throw a dice in turn. Whoever throws a 6 must don the costume and eat as much chocolate as possible, *with the knife and fork*, while the others throw the dice. When a 6 is thrown that person stops eating and the thrower takes his place. This continues until the chocolate is eaten. (Have some spare chocolate for those who never got a turn in the middle.)

Consequences *(age 6+, nos 2++, in/out/travel)*

Each person has a pen and a very long, narrow piece of paper. A series of 'facts' will be written down and, after each, the papers folded, to conceal the writing, and passed on. Then at the end you all take it in turns to read out the paper you have. The order of what is written is this:

1 a man's name – famous or invented
2 a woman's name – famous or invented
3 the place where they met
4 what he said to her
5 what she said to him
6 what he gave her
7 what she gave him
8 what the consequences were
9 what the world said.

Dictionary Games *(age 7+, nos 6+, or 2, in/out/travel)*

One team looks up a difficult word in the dictionary and each of them gives a definition for it – only one of which is correct. The other team confers and guesses which is correct.

This can also be done in reverse, with one team picking a difficult word and the other team having to give the correct definition. Or one person reads out a definition and the others each write down the word they think it refers to. On holiday it can be played with two languages – providing painless learning.

Donkey *(age 3+, nos 4+, in/out)*

A large picture of a donkey (with no tail, but a dot where it ought to start) is displayed on a surface which will take drawing pins. Each player in turn is blindfolded and given a large fabric tail with a drawing pin through the upper end. She then tries to pin the tail on the right spot. The pin hole is marked with her initials and whoever gets closest to the tail dot wins.

Feeding Time *(age 6+, nos 4+, in/out)*

Pairs sit opposite each other cross-legged (on a washable floor or outside). One is given a *large* bib and has his hands tied behind his back. The other is blindfolded and has a spoon and some messy food (e.g. jelly or mousse) which, on 'Go', they must feed to their partner. The first couple to finish wins. The best part of this is watching, so do two 'sittings'. This is an end-of-party game. The mess is so memorable that my adult children still fondly recall the party for which I invented it.

Fish Blowing *(age 3+, nos 4+, or team, in)*

You need a shiny floor and identical fish outlines cut

from newspaper. The players stand behind a chalked line with a named fish in front of each, and there's another line chalked some way down the room. On 'Go' they blow their fish down the room. The first fish to cross the line wins.

For the team game half of each team stands behind each line. The first person in each team blows the fish until it crosses the opposite line, the next blows it back and so on, until the last player crosses the line.

The Game *(dumb crambo, age 10+, nos 10+, in/out)*

Two teams each make a list of song/book/film/play titles which they would like those in the other team to act. Each person in turn is given his title by the opposing team and then has to mime it for the rest of the team to guess. The whole title can be acted or the words or syllables acted in any order.

The actor is allowed to make the following signs to help his team understand. The team then call out what they think each sign means and the actor may nod or shake his head or repeat the sign if they are wrong.

- Put hands together, as if praying, and open like a book = book title.
- A dramatic gesture while opening mouth = song.
- Use two hands to outline the shape of a theatre curtain = play title.
- Hold one hand up to the eye, like a lens, and wind with the other = film title.
- Hold up spread fingers to show how many words there are in the title.
- Hold up fingers to show which word in the title they are about to act (e.g. 3 fingers is third word).
- Hold up fingers (as above), then place them on the forearm to show how many syllables the word has. Then place them on the forearm again to show which syllable of the word is to be acted (e.g. 2 fingers in the air, then 2 on the forearm, then 1 in the air and on the forearm says 'I'm going to act a 2 syllable word starting with the first syllable').
- Describing a circle with both hands means you will act the whole phrase. To act a word which *sounds like* one in the title, first tug your ear.

The team call out the word or syllable they think is being acted (or even the whole title) as soon as they have a clue and the actor can nod, shake or even make beckoning signs if they are getting close.

Some families set a time limit, and time each performance – the fastest team winning – but most just play it for the fun.

Grandmother's Footsteps *(age 4+, nos 5 +, in/out)*

The players gather at one end of a room with just enough space to move, all facing a 'Grandma' a little bit in front of them. 'Grandma' moves down the room, doing curious movements, which the others have to copy while trying to creep up on her. 'Grandma' can turn round at

any time and anyone seen moving is out. The first person to touch 'Grandma' is the winner. With young children, just creeping up is enough, and Grandma can stand in one place.

Hangman *(age 7+, nos 4+, in/out/travel)*

Each in turn says a letter of the alphabet, chosen so that it could make a word. Someone who says a letter which completes a word is out – even if a longer word would have been possible e.g. p,a,r, T (Y). The rest then start on a new word. At their turn anyone may challenge the previous player if they suspect him of saying letters which wouldn't make a word. If he can't name a real word he is out.

Islands *(age 4+, nos 10+, in/out)*

Small, well-spaced islands are marked on the floor with chalk, or created with objects. While the music plays everyone dances or bounces about. When it stops they must get on an island. Anyone at 'sea' is out. At each turn an island is rubbed out, or made smaller. The last person in wins. If you like you can operate an 'only one person per island' rule. (Beware of islands which might slip on a polished floor.)

Jigsaw Treasure Hunt *(age 4+, nos 1+, in/out)*

A picture is cut up (preferably after being pasted on thin cardboard) and the pieces hidden all round a room, or a garden. The players then have to look for the pieces and form them into a picture. A time limit can be set if you wish, or it can be played in teams and a different 'jigsaw' hidden for each team – each being numbered, or given a colour on the back, to avoid confusion.

Kim's Game *(memory game, age 5+, 2+, in)*

Between 10 and 25 small objects are placed on a tray – according to the ability of the players. The players each have a pencil and paper, and form a circle. The tray is put in the centre, and they have a minute (in silence) to look at it. Then it is removed while each person lists what they can remember. The best list wins.

Knees Tease *(mixed ages, nos 10++, in)*

The teenage or adult males go out of sight and bare their legs, then parade across a stage or doorway which has been curtained so only their lower legs and knees can be seen. The rest guess which legs belong to whom – either jointly or on paper.

Knees Up *(age 10/12+, nos 18++, in)*

Everyone dances, and when the music stops the girl has to sit on her partner's knees with her feet off the floor. Those with the girl's feet on the ground, or who fall over, are out. The last pair in is the winner.

Addresses and suggestions for further reading are at the ends of chapters.

Matchboxes *(age 4+, nos 8++, team, in/out)*

Each team leader is given the outer section of a matchbox. On 'Go' the team leader places the matchbox on his nose and, using the nose only, passes it to the next nose in the team and so on. The first team to get it to the back of their line wins. A dropped matchbox is picked up and replaced.

Variations: An orange is held between the chin and the collar bone, and passed – the Orange Game. A round balloon is passed with the knees – the Balloon Game.

Matchbox Treasure Hunt *(age 4+, nos 3+, out)*

Each player has a matchbox and has 2 minutes to put into it as many different types of things as they can find. The one with the greatest number wins.

Matching Pairs *(age 5+, nos 10++, in/out)*

This is a good ice-breaker at parties where people don't know each other. Make a list of pairs, chosen to suit the ability of the players (e.g. cup/saucer, bread/butter for young children; Michael/Jackson, Jason/Donovan for teens; Bonnie/Clyde, Laurel/Hardy for adults). Write cup (say) on one piece of paper, saucer on another, and so on. As each guest arrives you pin one of these on their back, without them seeing it, and tell them they have on their back half the name of a household object (or a film duo, pop star or whatever) and they must pair up with whoever has the other half. Anyone can ask any question they like but the only permitted answers are 'yes' or 'no'.

If you want this to lead to dancing, write the first half of each pair in black and the second in red. Then give blacks to males and reds to females. If you want it to lead to team games you can plot balanced teams by listing in advance who ends up red and who black. The pairs then split for the team games.

Murder *(age 8+, nos 6+, in)*

Take as many cards from the pack as there are players, making sure they include a jack and an ace. Each person draws one. Whoever gets the ace is the detective and the jack is the murderer. The detective goes away into a lighted room, with the door shut, while the lights are put out in the rest of the house (or just one room) and all the other players move about in the dark. The murderer chooses a victim and taps him three times on the shoulder. The victim must then count to 10, scream and fall to the ground, dead. When the victim screams the players must stop exactly where they are. And on hearing the scream the detective puts the lights on and goes round noting people's whereabouts. Then they sit down in the same room while the detective cross-questions them. Everyone must tell the truth except the murderer. When ready the detective may accuse someone of being the murderer. If the detective is wrong the murderer

goes free; if he or she is right the murderer must confess and pay a forfeit.

Two classic Victorian forfeits were 'Kneel to the wittiest, bow to the prettiest, and kiss the one you love best', or 'Laugh in one corner, cry in another, sing in another and dance in another. 'But it can be anything to amuse the group and tease the person paying it.

Noisy Animals *(age 4+, nos 8++, in)*

This game can be an end in itself or a way of setting up pairs for some other game. But you need a room in which nobody will knock anything over in the dark. List animals which make distinctive noises (e.g. pig, donkey), having half as many animals as there are players (if you run out just repeat some). Secretly allot each animal to two different players. Nobody must know what anyone else is. Switch off the lights and tell everyone they must make their animal's noise, and pair up with whoever else makes it. But they must go silent on finding their 'twin'. Switch on the lights when you can only hear two people. The last two noisy animals have to pay a forfeit when the lights go on.

Obstacle Race *(age 3+, nos 4+, out)*

This one needs play, not party clothes, and shoes should be removed first if there is water (most children won't unless you tell them to). An obstacle course is constructed from anything you can lay hands on – planks balanced on bricks, plastic garden cloches to wriggle under, boxes and barrels to crawl through, a paddling pool to splash through, and so on. The players have to negotiate the course in the shortest possible time. The fastest wins. You can also make them get from one obstacle to another in different ways. One can be run, another hopped, another skipped and so on. Or add a ball to kick or hit from A to B. One of the best parties I ever went to was costume obstacle croquet.

The Paper Game *(age 5+, nos 4+, in/out)*

There are two versions: one for younger children, another for disco and adult parties. Young children are each given a sheet of newspaper, and bounce around, to music, holding it. When the music stops they must fold it in half and stand on it. This keeps being repeated and those falling off are out. Adults have one sheet of newspaper per couple and they dance while the music is on, then fold it and stand on it. Either way, the last one(s) in win.

Question & Answers *(age 12+, nos 6++, in/travel)*

Everyone has a pencil and two pieces of paper. Each person in turn asks one question, to which everyone – including the questioner – must secretly write an answer. When everyone has had a turn, each person puts their name at the top of their paper. Then all the papers are handed to the organizer, who numbers them and reads out each list of answers in turn. Everyone then guesses, and writes down, who they think each list of answers belongs to. The organizer then says who each list really belonged to and the person who identified the most lists wins. This can only be played by people who know each other, and the idea is to ask questions with revealing answers. So it can be dynamite in the wrong hands. If there are delicate relationships, temperamental teenagers or dodgy marriages in the group, and/or people foolish enough to ask upsetting questions, it is best avoided.

Shopping *(age 3+, nos 2++, in/out/travel)*

The first person says, 'Aunt Julia went shopping and she bought a pound of apples' (or anything else). The next person repeats exactly what the previous person said and adds one thing to the shopping list. And so on, in turn, with people dropping out whenever they make a mistake in the list. Quarrelsome children may need an arbitrator who notes the purchases in order.

Simon Says *(age 3+, nos 3+, in/out)*

The players stand facing 'Simon'. 'Simon' calls out instructions which the players must *only* follow if the words 'Simon says' precede them. (e.g. Simon says, 'hands on head'. Simon says, 'left leg up'. 'Stand up'.) Anyone who stood up would have been out. Little children get muddled quite easily; older ones need the instructions to be very rapid. The last one in wins.

Singing Game *(age 7+, nos 3++, in/out/travel)*

You go through the alphabet, each person singing a song whose title or first line starts with that letter – or, at a pinch, any line starting with the right letter. So 'Roxanne' could be followed by 'She Loves Me' and so on, with those who can't think of a song dropping out.

Squeak Piggy Squeak *(age 7+, nos 6+, in)*

One person is chosen as piggy and stays alone, while the others go and dress up, disguising themselves with cushions, false beards, etc. Then they go into a room on all fours and the lights are put out. Enter piggy on all fours. Piggy tries to catch someone and guess who they are. He may feel them, and say 'Squeak Piggy Squeak' at which the caught person must squeak. If he can't guess them correctly, in one guess, they go free. If he is right they become piggy. Disguises are swopped, out of piggy's sight, before carrying on.

Team Drawing *(age 4+, nos 8++, in/out)*

Make a list of things which must be drawn – suited to the ages of the players, for example a cup is easy but 'happiness' is hard. The two teams are in different corners of the room with pencils and lots of sheets of paper. Each sends a player to the organizer, to get the name of something to draw. The player then draws it as fast and as accurately as he can and the rest of the team have to guess what it is. Once they guess correctly the next member of the team comes up. The first team to guess their whole list wins.

Team Tie Ups *(age 7+, nos 12++, in/out)*

Each team stands in a circle, and one person is given a long piece of string on the end of which is tied a spoon (at my daughter's college they used a kipper, but I don't recommend it). On 'Go' they thread the spoon *down* under their clothes, and pass it to the next person who threads it *up* under their clothes, and so on. The object is to get every member of the team linked and the two ends of string tied together in the least possible time. Some people play it by threading the spoon down, or up, the *next* person's clothes – but that is up to you.

Word Making *(age 7+, nos 2+, in/out/travel)*

A very useful game because it needs no preparation and produces silence. Choose any really long word, with a wide range of letters in, and ask them each to write down as many words as they can make from the letters in the word. The one with the longest correct list wins (exclude proper names if you wish).

JOINING A CLUB

If you want to *do something* it is very easy to find others to do it with. There's a club for everything from astronomy to bicycle polo; organizations for men, women, professionals, the brilliant, the less able, the widowed, those angry about some issue – and many more.

I couldn't possibly list them all, but some are in the address lists of other chapters. For example, general clubs for adults or children, such as the WI or Scouts, are in the Family chapter, garden societies in Gardening, pet clubs in Animals and so on. It was hard to place bodies like the Georgian Society. However, as going round old houses provides ideas for the home, they went in Domestic Matters.

Of course, you may want to become a supporter, helper or fund raiser for a voluntary organization, charity or pressure group. Many have local branches, and most have newsletters, so even the housebound are kept in touch. Once again, there are far too many for me to list them all, but some are in the chapters closely related to them. For example, pressure groups, such as Friends of the Earth, are in Organizations, while those related to specific problems are in chapters dealing with those topics.

The addresses are correct as I write. But many change

as new officials are appointed. In which case your local reference library may have an update slip in its *British Directory of Associations (BDA)* (see below).

Finding Those Not Listed Here

If you want to find a club or body which I haven't listed, the *British Directory of Associations (BDA)* is in most reference libraries. It lists almost every possible body in alphabetical order and indexes them by topic. And, if you phone, the librarian may be kind enough to check it for you. Women may find it even more useful to contact the **National Alliance of Women's Organizations (NAWO)** (page 692). It is both a pressure group on behalf of women and an umbrella for over 250 women's organizations, of every kind and size. It will gladly suggest ones to suit your interests.

In addition, the Sports Council (page 342) has a list of clubs for almost every sport known to man. And the **British Sports Association for the Disabled** (page 342) knows about opportunities for the disabled.

MUSIC, DRAMA AND ENTERTAINMENT

If you want funding for an arts event, approach one of the regional arts boards, which channel Arts Council funds locally. If you simply want to attend one they often have free information on arts events, and can tell you about 'friends of' schemes which enable you to support the arts locally and often gain entry to their private views at art galleries or get priority bookings for theatres and concerts. The **Arts Council** (page 692) can give you the details of the board you need. For information on less exalted entertainment, such as drag racing or karting, try the local paper or local reference library.

If you want to take part in something like a music festival, or find out what's on in an area you may be visiting, there are several routes to information. Tourist boards are mines of information on every kind of event from big arts festivals to quaint local rituals. You can find the details of regional tourist boards, and of those for Northern Ireland, Wales and Scotland, through your local Tourist Information Centre – under T in the phone book. Or, if you want to pick your festival and then pick your holiday, send the **British Arts Festival Association** (page 342) a sae for a free leaflet with the details of 25 major festivals. To see the full range of festivals or arts events browse through the publications *Arts Festivals In Britain and Ireland*, and *British Performing Arts Year Book*, both published annually by Rheingold, which your reference library should have.

SHAPE helps anyone with a disability enjoy the arts. It has a network of agencies providing information on such things as ease of access, aids for those with hearing problems and so on.

The best sources of information on amateur festivals are organizations such as the British Federation of Music Festivals, which are linked to the particular arts, whether music, poetry, or dance. The **British Arts Festivals Association** has the addresses.

Entertainment in London

The national press has the details of entertainment in London. Or the **Society of West End Theatres** will send out a free London theatre guide which gives facts about each theatre, including such things as their facilities for those with disabilities, and whether they give discounts to students or pensioners.

The best way to buy tickets is through the theatre. Even reputable agencies, like **Ticketmaster**, may charge a booking fee of 25 per cent, and less reputable ones may charge far more. Theatre box offices are open from about 10 am until the evening performance starts, and tickets paid for by credit card usually need to be collected a set time before the show.

Even if a show is officially booked up there is always a chance of getting tickets which have been returned. And cut-price tickets are sold, for the same day, in a booth in Leicester Square after 12 am for matinees and from 2.30 to 6.30 pm for evening performances. They are half-price plus a service charge, for cash only.

MARRIAGE AND DATING AGENCIES

If you are finding it hard to meet the right person of the opposite sex you aren't alone. Most people say there is less social life than there used to be and fewer opportunities for likely encounters. So more and more people are advertising or using dating agencies – and doing so has become more accepted. However, an expanding market has tempted new agencies to enter it and not all of them are good news. I have heard of some not vetting their clients properly, or taking people's money and introducing them to nobody. And of others which vanish with their money, either fraudulently or because the agency goes bust. So it is wise to check the background of any agency.

There are three professional bodies which agencies may belong to. These bodies will give you the address of their member agencies. They all have codes of conduct. But they aren't all equally strict. So some agencies accept clients without interviewing them. For example the code of the **Association of British Introduction Agencies** says that:

● members must give clients a realistic number of introductions
● all information from clients is strictly confidential
● the agency must state whether it limits membership to those who are unmarried and, where this limit applies, ask for a signed statement of freedom to marry.

The code of conduct of the **World Association of Introduction Agencies,** which will make international introductions as well as British ones, is similar. However, the **Society of Marriage Bureaux** (page 343) has a stricter code of conduct. It says:

- they will only accept clients who are genuinely free to marry.
- a client will only be accepted after an interview
- a client's name and address will not be given to anyone without their consent
- the client's descriptions will not be published in any media

If you don't find an agency through one of these professional bodies at least use one which has been recommended by a friend. Being ripped off could be a sad and expensive business.

Most agencies ask a set fee for a given number of introductions, or for a year, or both — often plus a lump sum, from each person, if a marriage results. But they vary considerably in the number of introductions, the types of people, the regions of Britain in which they have a good selection, and the thoroughness of the vetting. So check the details of several before you sign on with one. The professional organizations may be able to give you the addresses of marriage and dating agencies which serve your area.

The far cheaper route to a date is a 'lonely hearts column'. The oldest major one is probably that in the *New Statesman*. But more and more papers have them and the chances are that someone like you will read the same paper or magazine. But, if you answer advertisements or place one, you can't know whether the other people are single, and normal. They could be unbalanced or dangerous – or have jealous partners. So, if you advertise:

- use a box number and ask for a phone number and address in any replies
- talk to likely ones on the phone but don't give your number and, if you are in the phone book, use a false name (you don't want a disappointed nutter ringing you hourly if you won't see him/her
- trust your instinct – don't agree to meet anyone who seems odd
- agree to meet 'possibles' in *safe* public places where you can talk. Somewhere like a pizza parlour is better than a club or pub, and tell a good friend where you are meeting and the details of the other person
- find out as much as you can about them, including where they work and the address and work number. But don't tell them your address or phone number or let them take you home, or accept or reject them. Say you want to think about things and you'll contact them
- if you don't want to meet again send a note, with no phone number or address, saying so. It's cruel to leave them hoping
- if you want to meet again ring the work number, this ensures they are who they say they are, and the switchboard operator may even be able to tell you if the person is married. From then on, it's up to you.

If you answer an advertisement give just a work number, if you can, and no address. Either way, the sooner a woman takes a man home, or goes home with him, the sooner she takes a risk. It is far safer to get to know each other in public places first. I realize all this sounds over cautious. But protecting yourself is part of respecting yourself. And anyone who doesn't respect you for that is probably trouble.

USEFUL ADDRESSES AND BOOKS

Countryside

National Trust (P.378)

Useful Books
Anthony Chapman, *The Countryside and Wildlife for Disabled People*, from **RADAR** (see In Sickness).
Nigel Hildyard, *The Macmillan Guide to Britain's Nature Reserves*, Polity Press.

Entertainment

British Arts Festival Association, 23 Orchard Road, London N6 5TR. (P.341)
Shape Agencies, 1 Thorpe Close, London W10 5XL Tel: 081 960 9245. (P.341)
Society of West End Theatres, Bedford Chambers, Covent Garden Piazza, London WC2E 8HQ Tel: 071 836 0971. (P.341)
Ticketmaster, 071 379 4444 – 24-hour CC booking, some shows with no booking fee. (P.341)

Games and Sports

British Chess Federation, 9a Grand Parade, St Leonard's-on-Sea, East Sussex TN38 0DD Tel: 0424 44250 – players of all standards are welcome, though few have facilities for child players. (P.330)
British Sports Association for the Disabled, Hayward House, Barnard Crescent, Aylesbury, Bucks HP21 9PP Tel: 0296 27889, is the co-ordinating body for sport for those with physical limitations. RC. (P.341)
English Bridge Union, Broadfields, Bicester Road, Aylesbury, Bucks HP19 3BG Tel: 0296 394414.
Sports Council, Information Service, 16 Upper Woburn Place, London WC1H 0QP Tel: 071 388 1277 – open 9 am-5 pm (Mon-Fri). Information on the usual sports clubs, associations and residential and holiday courses. (P.325)
The National Backgammon Players Society, 27 Moorfield Road, Manchester M20 8UZ – M£H, age 18+, G, Competitions, also events for under 18s. (P.329)

Useful Books
Hubert Phillips, *The Pan Book of Card Games*, Pan.
John Pulman, *Tackle Snooker*, Stanley Paul.
Mollo and Gardener, *Bridge for Beginners*, Pan.

Official World Encyclopaedia of Sports and Games, Paddington Press.

Oswald Jacoby, *The Backgammon Book*.

Reginald Moore (ed), *Official Rules of Sports and Games*, Kaye & Ward.

R. C. Bell, *Discovering Old Board Games*, Shire.

Waddington's Illustrated Encyclopaedia of Board Games, Pan.

Skip Ferry, *Complete Book of Dice Games*, Hart (New York).

Marriage and Dating

Association of British Introduction Agencies (ABIA), 25 Abingdon Road, London W8 6AL Tel: 071 937 2800. (P.341)

The Society of Marriage Bureaux (SMB), 1 Mandeville Place, London W1M 5LB Tel: 071 935 3115. (P.342)

World Association of Introduction Agencies (WAIA), 108 Earls Court Road, London W8, Tel: 071 937 2912. (P.341)

Gardening

Planning a Garden • Visiting Gardens • Bulbs, Corms, Tubers and Rhizomes • Herbaceous Plants • Lawns • Pests and Diseases • Propagation • Pruning • Seeds • Soils and Fertilizers • Shrubs, Trees and Roses • Tools • Vegetables • Weed Control • Drying Flowers • Indoor Plants

This chapter is designed to offer a few solutions to the most common gardening problems. A wonderful range of plants is available to those who venture beyond the inadequate gardening sections of many DIY stores. So, wherever possible, I have suggested sources of plants, seeds, information and advice. The nurseries chosen either have an established reputation or a list of special interest. That they will live up to these is something I cannot guarantee.

PLANNING A GARDEN

It is very much the fashion to have clumps of shrubs, or independent shrubs, upon grass-plats: people must follow their own taste; but, in my opinion, nothing is so beautiful as a clear carpet of green, surrounded by shrubs and flowers, separated from it by walks of beautiful gravel.
William Cobbett, *The English Gardener*

Good gardens are about surprises. A garden you can see all in one glance may look beautiful but is no more interesting than a story to which you already know the ending. So even the smallest garden should be given at least one hidden corner which has to be discovered. And paradoxically, cutting off part of a garden from view makes it seem bigger, not smaller.

The British climate also needs to be considered. Most of the time we are looking out of the windows. So that should be the point from which the garden looks best – especially in winter. This means having some choice winter-flowering shrubs and early bulbs close enough to enjoy them.

Another secret is tailoring a garden to meet your circumstances. There are two sides to this. The first, and most neglected one, is fitting it to your lifestyle. If you are busiest in late March, beds full of roses, which need pruning at that time, will be either a burden or a disappointment. The lay-out of a garden can make a vast difference to the amount of time you need to spend on it.

Plants need to be spaced so they will have room to achieve the beauty of their form, but there is something gentle and restful about a garden in which the plants are allowed to touch and, so to speak, put their arms around each other.

At the same time a garden has to be practical. A garden of any size without space to burn rubbish or make compost is like a house without a bathroom and lavatory. But these necessities need to be incorporated so that they don't spoil the view, and so does any garden shed. If they are planned for from the start it is easy enough to tuck them behind a hedge or decorative trellis which adds to the design. See also Lawns, page 347.

Choosing Plants

The wrong way to buy plants is to walk round a garden centre, see a pretty flower and be seduced. The right plant should:

- like the soil
- like the amount of sun or shade you can offer
- like the amount of moisture, or lack of it
- be hardy enough for your garden
- look good with the plants around it
- provide flowers and foliage when your garden needs them
- fit into the space below ground as well as above it (see Law on tree roots).

> Quite a few plants can produce allergic reactions, mainly as very nasty rashes. If you have been gardening and develop an unexplained rash the following plants are the most common cause:
>
> | | |
> |---|---|
> | Bamboo | Euphorbia |
> | Marrow | Tomato |
> | Hyacinth | Cucumber |
> | Rue | Geranium |
> | Chrysanthemum | Primula |
> | Daffodil | Courgette |
> | Conifer | Hogweed |
> | Hellebore (Christmas Rose) | Rhus |
> | Runner bean | |

Tubs, Pots and Boxes

Plants will grow in almost anything provided it will hold soil and has drainage holes at the bottom to let out water. In Greece houses are often brilliant with flowers growing in old tin cans. Whether it's a window box or a tin can, place it where you intend it to stand. Put flower pots in saucers for better watering and raise other containers slightly on pieces of tile so water can run away. Put about 2.5 cm (1 in) of broken flower pots, old china, stones or bought coarse gravel in the bottom through which water will drain easily. Top with John Innes No 2 potting compost. Plant anything which will fit into the container when fully grown – an increasing number of shrubs and roses can. Water and fertilize regularly and protect them from frost by wrapping a plastic sack round with straw, hay, or even polystyrene granules between the sack and the tub.

> Few things are more cruel to a plant than to under-water it. Under-watering causes roots to grow towards the surface and so makes it harder for it to reach the moisture deep down in a dry season. A small shrub needs at least a gallon of water at a single watering in dry weather, and a large shrub needs as much as 4 gallons. Herbaceous plants need enough water to penetrate 30 cm (1 ft) into the ground. So douse areas thoroughly.

VISITING GARDENS

There is no better way to get inspiration than seeing what other people have achieved. At almost any time of the year you can visit the gardens open for charity or see the **Royal Horticultural Society** gardens at Wisley. There are also some fine gardens attached to major nurseries. You will find them listed on pages 377-379, and Tourist Boards often have information on gardens in their areas.

BULBS, CORMS, TUBERS AND RHIZOMES

Few plants give such good return on money, space and labour as bulbs. For a few pounds you can have splashes of colour all over an average garden, even in the bleak months of the year. There are tulips, frothy alliums, and elegant creamy galtonias for flower beds; early snowdrops, daffodils and nodding fritillaries to go in grass; the beauties of colchicums, bluebells and tiny cyclamen to clothe the bare patches under trees and shrubs. There are bulbs for every size of garden, from towering lilies for shrubberies to miniature bulbs for sink gardens. Once in, most *prefer to stay in* and pests and diseases are rare. Even hyacinths can be freed from their potted imprisonment to naturalize into glorious drifts in a southern garden.

> Throughout this section 'bulb' will usually include both bulbs and corms.

Look at some species varieties. For example, species crocuses offer a far softer range of colours than the gaudy basics, and species tulips will happily naturalize when others must be lifted or risk disease. Get a catalogue from a good bulb specialist, to see what varieties are available. They withstand postage well.

When buying bulbs, corms, tubers and rhizomes plumpness is a good sign. They should also have no sign of mould or disease. Choose lily bulbs which are small to medium-sized, as they establish better than larger ones.

Planting for Indoors

Plant bulbs in pots 2½-3 months before you want them to flower. Place stones over the holes of a largish flower pot, to allow good drainage. Make some John Innes No 1 potting compost thoroughly damp (if the container has no drainage holes use bulb fibre). Three-quarters fill the pot. Position the bulbs so the noses of large bulbs just rise from the compost, and smaller ones are just covered, and fill in firmly with compost or fibre.

Put them in a cool, dark place – under a black bin bag in the garage, say – for 2 months, out of reach of mice and rats. Keep them damp – but don't overwater. When 2.5 cm (1 in) of shoot is showing put them in a cool room until buds show – early warmth can make them budless.

Planting Outside

Dig the hole *at least* 3 times the total length of the bulb from top to bottom. To plant bulbs thickly, stagger them and plant some deeper. Deeper planting also lets you adjust their flowering time; if planting is too shallow bulbs may lack the water and food they need and fail to flower. However, irises with rhizomes must be planted so the upper surface is visible, for the sun must ripen them to produce the next year's blooms. Only the grandest, such as lilies, should hold court singly. To give a natural effect, throw bulbs and plant them where they fall. In tubs and window boxes use John Innes No 2 rather than soil. For planting times see the calendar, pages 368-371.

★ Colchicums are often called autumn crocuses. This confuses them with the crocuses which flower in autumn; a different family entirely. Count the stamens – crocuses have 3; colchicums have 6.

★ Plant colchicums where their coarse leaves, which come after the flowers, will be hidden.

A difficulty arises over cyclamen. Some say these fragile ballerinas like their tubers only *just* covered with soil; but a top supplier advises 5-10 cm (2-4 in) in very open soil with plenty of leaf-mould and light shade. Once planted, they resent disturbance.

★ If you can't decide which is the top of the cyclamen tuber and

Choosing Bulbs For The Garden

Planting times

a = autumn	g = when in leaf	N = November	
ea = early autumn	O = October	Mar = March	
sp = spring	S = September	M = May	
ls = late summer			

Soils

r = rich soil	a = any good garden soil
p = peaty	wd = well drained
nd = not dry	c = needs a cool position

Colours

r = red	p = pink	o = orange	b = blue	
w = white	c = cream	y = yellow	m = mauve	

Positions

s = likes sun　　　　S = full sun essential
ss = prefers semi-shade/either option tolerated

	Planting Time	Colour	Soil	Situation	Jan	Feb	Mar	Apr	May	Jun	Jul	Aug	Sept	Oct	Nov	Dec
Allium (ornamental onion)	a	pmy	r	S					×	×	×	×	×			
Anemone (wind flower)	a	rwbmp	c	s/ss		×	×	×	×							
Chinodoxa (glory of the snow)	a	b w	nd	s			×	×								
Colchicum (naked lady, meadow saffron)	s	pm	r wd	s	×	×							×	×		
Crocosmia (montbretia)	a	oy	wd	s						×	×	×				
Crocus	a	wymbc	a	s	×	×	×	×					×	×	×	
Cyclamen	g	pwm	pwd	ss	×	×	×			×	×	×		×	×	
Dahlia plants (dormant tubers)	M/J A/M	rpmyw	rwd	S							×	×	×			
Fritillary	S/O	m	rwd	ss				×	×							
Galanthus (snowdrop)	sp	w	a	ss		×	×									
Galtonia	a	w/c	a	s							×	×	×			
Gladioli	Mar-M	por	rwd	s						×	×	×				
Hyacinthoides (bluebells)	a	b	a	ss					×							
Hyacinthus (Roman hyacinth)	a/g	pwm	nd/wd	ss				×								
Iris	a	lybmw	rwd	S	×	×	×			×	×					
Leucojum (summer snowflake)	ea	w	rnd	ss					×	×						
Lilium (lily)	O/sp	pwoyr	wd	ss						×	×	×	×	×		
Muscari (grape hyacinth)	a	wb	a	s					×	×	×					
Narcissus (and daffodil)	S/O	yc	a	s		×	×	×	×							
Ornithogalum (star of Bethlehem)	a	w	a	s					×		×	×				
Scilla (squill)	a	b	a	s				×	×							
Tulips	O/N	proy	r	s		×	×	×	×							

× means a reasonably hardy variety of that bulb flowers in that month. But if you choose any *one* variety of a particular bulb it may only flower for one of the months given. Of course, hardiness depends on general conditions as well as temperature.

Addresses and suggestions for further reading are at the ends of chapters.

which the bottom (a common problem) plant it on its side – it will sort itself out.

Dahlia tubers should be planted about 10 cm (4 in) deep, but plants should be planted according to their soil level. Space all dahlias according to their final size – their width will be about a half to three-quarters of their height. Put a stake in the hole as you plant them – adding it later risks piercing a tuber – suiting the thickness to their final size. A large dahlia needs a really thick stake.

Feeding and Care

Bulbs prefer a rich well-drained soil and those which like semi-shade enjoy leaf-mould. If the drainage is poor, tuck a little sharp sand at the bottom of the hole before planting them. They can then be kept happy with a dressing of bone meal in autumn and dried blood in spring. They also need to be watered in the months after flowering, if these months are dry, and given a liquid feed high in potash. Daffodils look tidier if you break off the seed head but are best left to die down, with no tying or fuss. Grass should not be cut until the foliage of any bulbs in it yellows. If you remove green leaves bulbs can't store up the food for next year's flowers.

Pests and diseases are mercifully rare. The biggest problem is narcissus fly and this can be treated with a proprietary insecticide. Tulip fire is relatively rare and far less likely with bulbs which are deep planted. It can be treated with an anti-fungal powder.

Storing and Propagating

Most bulbs don't like being lifted and stored but, if you have to lift them, put them in a cool airy place and brush them clean when dry. Then store them in straw in a cool dry place.

Large-flowered gladioli won't stand frost. Lift and store them in the autumn, as above (small-flowered gladioli will naturalize happily, unless conditions are very cold). Conventional tulips need to be lifted, but species and hybrid tulips can be left to naturalize provided the plant is cut off at ground level and removed when it yellows. Otherwise, disease may develop.

When daffodils, alliums, crocuses and montbretia form large clumps dig them up, just as the leaves have died, and gently divide them. They can then be stored in a cool place or replanted immediately.

Irises with rhizomes should be lifted after flowering, when they become crowded. Cut the leaves in a neat fan 10-15 cm (4-6 in) long – remove dried-out rhizomes and replant the young ones facing towards the sun, with their roots firmly down under them, and the top of the rhizome exposed.

Lift dahlias as the first frost wilts them. Cut the stems to 10 cm (4 in). Leave them upside down for a few days in a cool, airy place, brush off the soil, dust with fungicide and store in a cool place in dry peat. (You may just get away with leaving them in the ground if you cover the ground with peat and heap bracken or straw over it. Keep this down, with angled sticks or bean net-

ting pegged over. Whether they then live or die will depend on the season, the coldness of your soil, and how far north you live.)

HERBACEOUS PLANTS (PERENNIALS)

Herbaceous plants are among the showiest in the garden, but they have the unfortunate habit of dying down each winter, leaving their site empty but for a few desolate stalks. A border mixing shrubs and herbaceous plants conceals this.

When they die in the centre dig the clump up in autumn or spring, split it in half, using two forks back-to-back if necessary. Remove dead and over-woody sections, split into manageable sections and replant. But some plants – generally those with fleshy roots, such as peonies – resent this disturbance.

Choosing Herbaceous Plants

The 20 plants on the following pages are among the easiest to grow and the least demanding, while being showy in either flower or foliage.

LAWNS

If you haven't got a lawn stop before you create one. In country gardens you can limit the lawn area with careful planning, and small town gardens may be far more manageable – and just as attractive – with good paving, bricks, tiles or even gravel. It costs more to lay these, but you don't have to buy a mower or edge trimmers and they will never need so much as a teaspoonful of fertilizer. If you *are* laying a lawn remember it will probably be the largest single thing in the garden. This visual domination means that its shape dictates what the whole garden will look like. A strip of straight-edged lawn creates a garden like a green railway line. Curve it and introduce hidden surprises and you can make a small garden seem big, and a big one charming. Make shapes with a long rope or hosepipe before deciding how the lawn should be.

Creating a Lawn

November to March is the best time to prepare for a lawn. Clear the ground, removing deep weeds and rubble. Dig it thoroughly, adding peat, compost or leaf-mould to improve it. Also add coarse sand if the ground is heavy: waterlogged ground encourages numerous lawn problems.

Level it carefully with a rake and the edge of a long plank, and roll it *lightly*. Then leave it for a month or, better still, all summer. If necessary, use a systemic weedkiller to eradicate problems, such as bindweed.

Choosing Herbaceous Plants

Plant	Appearance	Flowers	Support	Soil	Position	Height
Alchemilla mollis (Lady's mantle)	Neat pale-green leaves with frothy greeny flowers.	July	No	Dry or moist	Shade	45 cm (18 in)
Anemone japonica (Japanese anemone)	Rose-coloured anemone flowers on tall stems.	Aug/Sept	No	Any humus	Sun or shade	45-80 cm (18 in - 3 ft)
Aster varieties (Michaelmas daisy)	Clusters of delicate daisy flowers in pinks and mauves – new varieties are bigger and better	Sept/Oct	Maybe	Any	Sun	25-90 cm (10 in - 3 ft)
Campanula persicifolia (Persian campanula)	Delicate papery bells in white or mauve on firm stems	May/July	No	Moist	Sun	90 cm (3 ft)
Chrysanthemum indicum varieties	The florist's-style chrysanthemum in singles and doubles in every shade.	Sept/Oct	Maybe	Rich loam	Sun	60-90 cm (2 - 3 ft)
Chrysanthemum maximum (Shasta daisy)	Clumps of neat dark foliage throwing up numerous big white daisies with yellow bosses.	July/Aug	No	Loam	Sun	50-80 cm (18 in - 2½ ft)
Dianthus varieties (Garden pinks)	Like small carnations on fine stems with heady scents above grey-green foliage.	June on	No	Well-drained loam	Sun	15 cm (6 in)
Gaillardia (Blanket flower)	Bold daisy-like flowers.	July-Sept	Yes	Light well drained	Sun	60 cm (2 ft)
Gypsophila	Clouds of tiny white flowers on grey-green stems.	Aug/Sept	Yes	Any deep	Sun	1 m (1 yd)
Hellenium	Daisy-like flowers in yellow or bronze.	July-Sept	Maybe	Any	Sun	80 cm (3 ft)
Helleborus varieties (Christmas rose)	White and greenish white anemone-shaped flowers borne in the worst weather.	Jan-April	No	Prefer rich moist loam	Shade or semi-shade	30-60 cm (1 - 2 ft)
Hemerocallis varieties (Day lily)	Clusters of big satiny trumpet-shaped flowers above strap like leaves, in yellows, reds and oranges.	July-Sept	No	Any	Sun or semi-shade	60-80 cm (2 - 3 ft)
Hosta varieties	Handsome spade-shaped glaucous leaves with delicate understated mauve flowers.	July/Aug	No	Moist	Shade or semi-shade	45-75 cm (18 in to 2 ft 6 in)
Iris germanica (Bearded iris)	Sculptural fans of flat leaves above which rise big beautiful flowers in every possible colour.	June	No	Any well drained	Sun	75-100 cm (2½ - 3 ft)
Lupinus polyphyllus (Russell hybrid lupins)	Tall spikes for numerous pea-type flowers in almost every colour. Eye-catching.	June	Maybe	Light loamy	Sun	60-80 cm (2 - 3 ft)

Addresses and suggestions for further reading are at the ends of chapters.

Choosing Herbaceous Plants

Plant	Appearance	Flowers	Support	Soil	Position	Height
Papaver orientalis (Oriental poppy)	Dramatic silken poppies in scarlet, salmons and pinks with silky black stamens.	June	Yes	Dry light	Sun	75 c (2 ft 6 in)
Peony officinalis	Big silky cabbagy flowers in ruby, pink or white varieties.	June	Yes	Rich	Sun or semi-shade	46-76 cm (1½ - 2½ ft)
Phlox paniculata (Garden phlox)	Flat panicles of satiny flowers in pinks, reds and mauves and white.	July – early Sept	No	Well-drained loam	Sun or semi-shade	80 cm (2 ft 8 in)
Pyrethrum	Bold daisy-shaped flowers in pinks and crimsons.	May/June	Yes	Loam	Sun	60 cm (2 ft)
Sedum spectabilis (Ice plant)	Fleshy glaucous leaves and flat wine red heads of tiny flowers massed together.	Aug/Sept	No	Any	Semi-shade	20 cm (8 in)

Seeding a Lawn

The grass family is enormous and the best of the new grass mixtures give strength and limited growth and a compact look. But many grasses professional lawnsmen use are not sold to the general public. Instead, outdated grass seed is often offered. Even well-known companies sell mixtures based on coarse agricultural ryegrasses which, in the opinion of one turf expert, are not suitable 'even for low quality football pitches'.

The best lawn grasses are only sold in large quantities. But gardening clubs and those prepared to buy 25 kg or more might find it useful to obtain the inexpensive leaflet 'Turfgrass Seed' from the **Sports Turf Research Institute** (page 377). It lists grasses used by professionals and analyses each for shortness of growth, summer greenness and compactness – plus seed merchants who may sell them. A lawn needs a combination of grasses. For a family lawn which will withstand reasonable wear but look fine-leaved and uniform a good mixture is:

50 per cent turf-type (not agricultural) perennial ryegrass
20 per cent smooth-stalked meadow grass
20-25 per cent red fescue
5-10 per cent bent

If you pick varieties in the 'Turfgrass Seed' leaflet which score As or Bs for low growth and compactness (density), you should be able to create an impressive lawn which needs a minimum of maintenance. The fescues, which score A on growth, only grow 12.5-15.5 cm (5-6 inches) in a full season. Or pick varieties recommended by a *Gardening Which* trial.

Grass seeds like warm ground. So, sow from late August through September, or April-May, according to the weather, when the soil is damp, not wet. First rake in 60 g (2 oz) of Growmore per sq m (sq yd), or an autumn lawn food, even if it's spring. Then sow evenly, allowing 40-50 g (1½-2 oz) of seed per sq m (sq yd).

★ Just weigh it out once, put it in an old yoghurt carton and mark the level on the carton for future batches. Sow half across the square and the other up and down it.

★ If you are vague about the size of a square metre (or like to be exact) make a yard wide 'railway line' with two long strings and place yard-marker sticks across.

Rake the seed in *lightly*, water regularly and don't walk on it. With this much seed bird theft should be no disaster, but re-sow bare patches after 8 weeks. When the grass is 5 cm (2 in) high, roll it *lightly* (e.g. pull a mower over it without mowing) and mow *very* lightly next day. Keep *just* trimming the tops until it's established, but don't use it for 3 months, and go easy for a year. Don't use weedkiller until it's grown up.

Creating a Lawn with Turf

Turf creates a lawn faster, but the grass is less. Check it carefully before you buy. The best time to lay is October or November – though you can still lay until February. Place a plank against the lawn edge. Stand on the plank and lay the turfs against it, butt them closely together. Place the plank on the turfs – your weight will firm them. Lay against the previous row – but stagger the joins, like bricks – and cut turfs to shape with a half-moon lawn edger. Water it, and leave it unmown and unwalked on for 4-6 weeks. Then treat it very gently for several months, never letting it dry out.

Lawn Care and Maintenance

Mow grass, if it's growing, when it needs it. If the weather is very mild there's no point in letting the grass get long just because it's December. Mow to a shorter length for well-fed luxury lawns made from fine grasses. Most family lawns will be better if mown to a longer length.

Have the blade set high for the first mow or two, and leave *short* clippings on the lawn; they keep it healthier. Long clippings, however, must be removed as they kill the grass.

Feeding

Each mowing takes goodness away from the grass. So, unless the lawn gets something back, it will slowly decline. In the spring and early summer it needs nitrogen. In tests by the Consumers' Association, home-made lawn sand, Growmore or sulphate of ammonia all compared well with branded lawn foods costing more. There are several recipes for lawn sand, but theirs was 1 part ferrous sulphate : 3 parts ammonium sulphate : 20 parts sharp sand, applied at 140 g per sq m (4 oz a sq yd). For Growmore and sulphate of ammonia use about a handful to the sq yd. All three need only be applied in spring and perhaps again in summer. The ferrous sulphate in the lawn sand will also deter moss.

Lawns also need humus and, as they like acid, a scattering of fine peat in autumn is good. (If the soil is clay use 2 parts peat:1 sharp sand.) Apply enough to cover well without stifling the grass. This isn't essential, but you get a better lawn. Add potash too if you can.

Problems in Lawns

Bare Patches
Prick the earth all over with a fork. Sift on a thin layer of good soil. Water it, and sow and treat it like a new lawn.

Brown Patches
Brown patches can be caused by urine from bitches, vixens, spilt oil or petrol, leatherjackets (daddy-long-legs' larvae) eating the roots, and certain diseases. Spike the area well to improve the drainage and discourage leatherjackets, and – if the patches are persistent – water with Benylate against diseases, or apply an insecticide to kill the leatherjackets.

★ To catch leatherjackets water the grass in the evening, and cover it with a plastic or a tarpaulin. Next morning the leatherjackets should be on the surface ready to be removed.

Bumps and Troughs
It is easier to fill in dips than remove bumps. So start by sifting soil into any dips, so it almost covers the tips of mown grass. When it grows through sift on some more, and repeat until the hollow is level.

For bumps, make shaped slits straddling the bump. Cut away under the grass roots, roll it back, level the soil, roll back the turf, firm and water it.

Disease
Treat red thread, which causes pinkish patches, with sulphate of ammonia. Fusarium, a disease causing yellowy brown patches on lawns, can be treated with Benylate.

Fairy Ring
This is a ring of fungus which releases nitrogen, and makes the grass a deeper green, but will kill it in time. Use a fungicide.

Generally Poor Condition
A lawn which is well past its best can be renovated. In late summer rake it very well, removing moss and matted grass. Fertilize as page 349. In September sow with a fine turf-type ryegrass at 20-25 g (1 oz) to the sq m (yd). If you can't get a top professional seed go for Hunter – a variety which is available to gardeners. If

necessary you can mow over it with a rotary mower (until it reaches blade height), but not with a hover. Next spring mow it in gently, setting the blades high at first.

★ For moles there is no sure cure, except enlisting a mole catcher, or a rodent officer from the local council. It is variously claimed that garlic, mothballs and slices of lemon down their holes, or *Euphorbia lathyrus* planted at intervals, deter them.

Moss
Moss is worst in shade or when drainage is poor. To keep it at bay rake the grass regularly, spiking it to let the air in, and feeding it well. There are also moss-killing granules and sprays which will kill moss for a season. But unless you get rid of the cause it will come back.

Weeds
Weeds should be little trouble if a lawn is mown regularly. If you use a lawn weedkiller apply it immediately after mowing, and at the next mowing leave the box off so the clippings lie on the lawn. They should *not* be composted. Mowings after that can usually be composted, unless the manufacturers say otherwise, but cannot be used as a mulch.

Slime
This is found when the ground is waterlogged and compacted, especially under trees, and is a coating of algae. Unless the cause is cured it will keep returning. Improve the drainage by major spiking; scatter coarse sand or fine gravel on the area and brush it into the holes; cover it with peat and sand and re-sow.

Lawn Watering

Lawns should not be watered every day – even in a drought – it encourages a shallow root system. Instead, water more thoroughly less often. A lawn needs about an inch of rainfall a week. Put an empty jam jar within the spray area and move the hose when the jam jar holds an inch.

Lawn Mowers

There is no one mower which has all the answers. If you must have stripes rotary mowers do the best job. But the fast, efficient, petrol-driven ones are heavy to turn, and the starter cord is often an invitation to back trouble. The electric ones are slower and have all the hassles of the electric flex, without the ease of movement you have with a hover. To make up for this, some, such as the Qualcast Concorde range, have a lawn-raking attachment which makes very short work of one of the worst jobs in the garden.

If you simply want an easy life a hover, *with* a box which collects the grass, has the edge. It will cut a swathe through long grass and nose neatly under the unstaked shrubs which tumble across its path. It also feels effortless. The disadvantages are that the sward never has quite that brushed-velvet finish, there is no weight to roll out bumps and you have to contend with the cable.

Whichever you buy, do get a machine that is large

enough. There is no point in marching 30 times the length of your lawn if you can cut it in 20 with a wider blade.

★ The cable from electric lawnmowers is easier to control if you put it over your shoulder. But it is wise to use a circuit-breaker.

Lawnmower Care

Clean a lawnmower well at the end of the season and send it to be sharpened, and overhauled if it needs it. If it doesn't come back with oiled blades use an old-fashioned cotton-headed dish mop to apply oil – then your fingers won't get cut. Cover the engine with a large paper sack to keep out dust and leaves. But turn the motor over every few weeks in winter, then it will be easy to start in spring.

PESTS AND DISEASES

Skill with these has two aspects – reducing the vulnerability of the plants, and attacking the pests and diseases before they get a hold. One of the more unlikely methods of doing this was put forward in the first edition of *Enquire Within*: to get rid of grubs in fruit trees and bushes it advised that a fire should be built in the orchard:

> *so that the smoke may blow among the trees, you will destroy thousands; for the grubs have such an objection to smoke that very little makes them roll themselves up and fall off.*

Reducing Vulnerability

● Good feeding and watering make strong healthy plants more able to withstand attacks of any kind.
● Choose varieties which resist disease.
● Burn any dead material so it won't harbour trouble.
● Encourage the natural parasites of potential pests.
● Grow companion plants (see page 353).

Snails are particularly fond of bran; if a little is spread upon the ground, and covered with cabbage-leaves or tiles, they will congregate under them in great numbers, and by examining them every morning, and destroying them, their numbers will be materially decreased.

Enquire Within, 1856

Nipping Trouble in the Bud

● Check plants regularly and pick off any diseased leaves, or remove the first signs of caterpillars by hand.
● At the first sign of trouble introduce any biological controls which are available.

Or

● Decide at the start of the season that you will use chemicals and plan your spraying programme before trouble starts. Many pests have life cycles in which it is essential to catch them at a particular stage if they are to be killed. Whitefly, for example, has 5 stages and is only vulnerable to pesticides in 3 of them. By hitting pests at a vulnerable stage you can often stop trouble quickly using a minimum application. But if you let a pest get established, you may need to spray again and again to get results.
● Most diseases are fungal. There is usually a three-way choice; cross your fingers and hope it won't spread, destroy the plant or spray.

Before resorting to sprays read what Dr Stefan Buczacki (page 377) has to say about using garden sprays for particular problems. Some are very good, but he is decidedly pessimistic about the effectiveness of chemicals on certain problems – you could just be using up your leisure for very small returns.

Treating Pests and Diseases

Problem	Natural Method	Chemical Method
Aphids	Introduce or encourage ladybirds and hoverflies. Hoverflies like bell- and daisy-shaped flowers and adore buckwheat. One hoverfly larva will eat 1,000.	Spray with pirimicarb (Rapid) (designed not to harm bees, ladybirds or lacewings).
Blackspot	Buy resistant rose varieties. Remove and burn affected leaves. Hard prune the following year to remove infected wood.	Spray with 'Roseclear' (designed not to harm bees, ladybirds or lacewings).
Canker on fruit trees	Cut out infected area or cut off the branch and burn it. Use a wound seal on the cut.	Spray new trees with benomyl, but established canker may resist it. If so, burn the tree.
Carrot root flies	Delay sowing until May to miss one generation of flies. Sow very thinly (thinning attracts them). If you must thin, remove thinnings and water to damp the smell. Have a string soaked in creosote (but not dripping) stretched above the row. Plant onions next to carrots and pull thin carrots. In winter clear the ground totally and put mothballs down.	Not well controlled by chemicals, but apply bromophos or diazinon granules to seed drill, then in August/September drench the soil in a solution of trichlorpon.
Caterpillars	Pick them off by hand on sight, and crush all eggs. Most effective when done early.	Spray with an insecticide such as HCH or permethrin (Picket).

Treating Pests and Diseases

Problem	Natural Method	Chemical Method
Clubroot	Apply lime before planting and improve soil texture: it is worst on poorly drained acid soils. Use a long rotation and burn affected plants immediately. Scrub tools with hot soapy water.	There is no known cure for this. Dipping plants in a clubroot dip before planting may help.
Codlin moth	Use the pheromone trap 'Trappit' (page 379) to catch the males from mid-May, so they fail to mate. Encourage tits: they eat the caterpillars.	Spray with permethrin (Picket) or fenitrothion about mid-June, after blossoming and again 3 weeks later – *before* damage is seen.
Earwigs	Stuff straw into flowerpots and upturn them on sticks. Burn the contents each morning.	Treat plant with malathion or HCH.
Eelworm	Burn all infected plants – bulbs, fruit, onions, phlox, etc. Keep those plants off the soil for 3 years.	None.
Fireblight	This disease is subject to statutory control; it is widespread south of a line from Preston to Hull. But you need not destroy the plants, and only nurseries need notify the Ministry of Agriculture. It is caused by a bacterium. Prune out and burn infected branches to below the staining. Treat the cut with a bacterial paste and sterilize tools afterwards.	There is no chemical treatment.
Leaf miner	Remove and burn affected leaves. Get rid of groundsel and sowthistle, which may harbour the pest.	Spray with Lindex or Symbol 2.
Mildew	Remove affected leaves and burn them.	Spray with buppirimate and triforine (Nimrod I) or propiconazole (Tumbleblite).
Onion root fly	Plant carrots by them – the scent of carrots masks the onion scent. The pupae overwinter in the soil. Dig well in autumn.	HCH helps but can contaminate the onions. Apply bromophos, diazinon or chlorpyrifos granules before sowing.
Silverleaf (a silvery sheen to leaves of plum trees with a mauve fungus on dead branches)	Wood must be sawn off by mid-summer and burnt. Sometimes the problem clears itself up. If not, dig up the tree and burn it with as much root as possible. Treat as fireblight.	There is no chemical solution to silverleaf.
Wilt in seedlings (the lower stem blackens and they bend)	Start with clean compost and a clean greenhouse or propagator and you shouldn't get it.	Drench the soil with Cheshunt Compound or a fungicide containing benlate or mankozeb at the first sign of trouble
Woolly aphid	A natural parasite of woolly aphids called *Aphelinus mali* is now established in southern England. Avoid using chemicals if it may be present. Prune out severely infected wood. Grease bands can be applied in September and left until spring.	Systemic insecticides like dimethoate or formothion or contact insecticides like malathion or HCH.
Mealy bugs	Introduce the Australian ladybird *Cryptolaemus montrouzeri* which eats these and scale insects. Or swab off with cotton wool and methylated spirits.	Their coating resists contact insecticide. Use a systemic such as formothion.
Red spider	Introduce a mite called *Phytoseiulus* which eats them.	If you spray; change the chemical regularly as they rapidly become immune.
Scale insects	Swab off with meths on cotton wool.	Easily killed with a contact insecticide in the early crawling stage. Once attached use a systemic such as formothion.
Slugs	Create slug pubs by sinking yoghurt cartons or saucers filled with beer slops (free from pubs) at intervals in the soil; or put bran under cabbage leaves and seek and destroy those that collect each morning.	Slug pellets – there is also a slug and snail powder which claims to be totally harmless to birds.
Whitefly	Introduce the chalcid wasp (*Encarsia formosa*) which eats them. Grow some nasturtiums nearby to keep whitefly or greenfly off tomatoes.	Spray with permethrin every 7 to 14 days.

★ Some insecticides are formulated to be harmless to bees. If using any others don't spray until evening, then the bees will out of harm's way.

Addresses and suggestions for further reading are at the ends of chapters.

Pest predators only control pests once they have bred and built up numbers. Not all domestic greenhouses have the right conditions for this, and they may walk out through the ventilation without doing their job. **Natural Pest Control** (see page 379) sells them, but check if they suit your situation.

Companion Plants

It has long been thought that some plants protect others from pests and diseases. The scientific evidence for this is, on the whole, lacking. But it's hard to believe that anything would be passed down for centuries if it had no truth in it. Some traditional pairings are:

- sage to keep away cabbage whites
- savory to keep blackfly off broad beans
- cabbage near celery to ward off leaf miner
- French marigold near cabbage to ward off cabbage whites
- nasturtiums with tomatoes against whitefly and greenfly
- garlic with roses against whitefly and greenfly.

★ Bird damage to fruit can be prevented by throwing an old net curtain over any small bush. Birds get entangled in cotton but not in curtains.

★ If mice are prone to pinch the pea seeds or crocus corms tuck holly leaves round these as you plant them. Mice hate pricked noses. A less charming method is to taint the seeds by rinsing them in a weak solution of paraffin.

Biological controls are nothing new. In ancient times the Chinese fostered the ants which ate destructive insects, and even built bamboo bridges so the ants could cross from one tree to the next.

PROPAGATION

Most plants will root if you pick the right part of their anatomy. They usually root best by the type of tissue which makes up the biggest portion of their structure. So trees root from hardwood cuttings, plants with big tap roots do best from root cuttings, and fleshy leaved houseplants root best from leaf cuttings, Whatever the cutting, take plenty as some always fail.

To a professional gardener the divisions between stem cuttings, green-wood cuttings, softwood cuttings and semi-ripe cuttings are subtle and important, but the method is broadly as follows.

Shoot Cuttings

- Take 8-10 cm (3-4 in) shoots.
- Remove all but the top 2-3 leaves, and shorten to just below a leaf joint.

- Dip shy rooters in hormone rooting powder.
- Push them into pencil holes in a moist mixture of equal parts sand and peat.
- Stand the pot in a plastic bag, with sticks to keep the bag off the leaves. Close and place on a north- or east-facing window ledge.
- Wipe out excess condensation.
- Repot individually and harden off when roots form.

Geraniums are an exception. Leave the bag off and don't water: they like it dry. Harder wood and cuttings in a greenhouse or frame can also do without the bag.

Hardwood Cuttings

In winter take newly ripened wood from a shrub or tree, cut to 13-25 cm (5-10 in) lengths, cutting the tops at an angle and the bottoms straight across. Dig a trench in some fertile soil, insert the cuttings a hand's span apart so only the top 2-3 buds show. Fill in the soil and firm it. Water for 9 months and then transplant.

Root Cuttings

These are just 5 cm (2 in) lengths of thick root which are placed in compost and allowed to sprout. Lie them on their sides and *don't* use rooting powder on them – you need shoots not roots. Try this with oriental poppies, acanthus and phlox.

★ When carrying cuttings from other gardens blow up a plastic bag, like a balloon and tie the neck tightly: the moist air will cushion the cuttings against knocks.

★ The purpose of plants is reproduction. If we frustrate by dead-heading many will flower week after week in their attempts to produce seeds. With others dead-heading produces more next year. So it pays dividends.

★ If you have a hanging basket which is too high to water easily, just lob ice cubes in. If you include fertilizer in the ice cubes put that ice tray in a labelled plastic bag – fertilized gin and tonic is no joke.

To find fertilizers and grow bags based on organic materials contact the **Henry Doubleday Research Association** (page 377).

Layering

Find a young, flexible, fast growing shoot near the ground – on the sunny side of the shrub. Prepare the ground under it with slow release fertilizer, such as bonemeal, adding sharp sand and organic matter to give a potting compost texture. Dig a short trench some 15 cm (6 in) deep, as shown.

Make a slash on the underside from just below a leaf node, up towards the tip to the centre of the stem. Insert a used matchstick into the slit and brush on hormone rooting powder, for hardwood cuttings. Remove leaves below soil level and peg it down with strong bent wire.

Cover and firm well in. In about 18 months the plant should be ready. Cut it carefully from its parent a few weeks before potting it up and only lift it if the roots seem well established.

John Innes Potting Compost

Even the best soil isn't ideal for growing seedlings and potting up, so a special mixture is usually recommended, the most popular being John Innes No 1 or 2. Although John Innes compost is available commercially, anyone can make it themselves if they can buy the basic ingredients. The recipe was devised at the John Innes Research Institute and made freely available as a contribution to the war effort in the Second World War. The basic mixture is:

3 parts granulated peat (e.g. sphagnum moss peat)
7 parts loose medium loam (stacked a year and sterilized if possible)
2 parts coarse lime-free sand.
    The fertilizer used with this is made by mixing:
2 parts hoof and horn meal
2 parts by weight superphosphate of lime
1 part by weight sulphate of potash.

> The measuring container will be far larger for the basic mixture than for the fertilizer.

John Innes No 1: mix 110 g (4 oz) of the fertilizer mixture to 8 gallons of the basic mixture. This is used for potting delicate plants. Also add 20 g (¾ oz) of ground chalk or limestone to each 8 gallons unless you will be planting lime hating plants.
John Innes No 2: add 8 oz of the fertilizer, and limestone as above. This is used for most plants.
John Innes No 3: a rich mixture using 12 oz of fertilizer and is for well-established plants.

PRUNING

Pruning depends on:

● the type of plant
● its particular variety within that family
● the conditions in your area
● how long the plant has been established.

Why Prune?

The main reasons for pruning are:

● The leading bud in a shoot is always dominant and will take the lion's share of the food available to that twig or branch, leaving side shoots to get the leftovers. Only by removing the leader can you stimulate side shoots. As many plants flower or fruit on new wood, this gives twice the crop.
● To stay healthy some plants need to throw up new shoots from the base. They will only do this if others are cut out from the base – or fairly near it.
● Vigorous plants grow so thickly that branches may die back if the plant isn't given air. Pruning gives it air without spoiling the shape – nature may not be so careful.
● Leaving dead or unduly old wood on a plant fosters pests and diseases.
● Shortening stems reduces the risk of the wind rocking the plants and loosening the roots.
● Pruning newly planted shrubs almost immediately often helps them to establish. (With container grown plants only prune in the correct pruning season.)
● Some shrubs and trees just need to be kept to a good shape or prevented from getting out of hand.

How to Prune

If disease and die-back are to be avoided the first essential is to have really sharp secateurs and (if needed) a sharp saw which won't bruise the stem, drag at the bark or leave rough pieces standing up.

● Pruning cuts must be *just* above a growing point (bud or eye) and must slope away from it.
● On woody branches the buds may not show. So, cut dead wood back to a healthy branch at a neat angle.
● Cuts which are more than 1 cm (½ in) across must be painted with a 'wound paint' to fight possible infection.
● To decide where to cut, look at the shape of the whole plant.

How Much to Prune

Evergreens seldom need pruning. With deciduous shrubs, the amount of pruning needed varies greatly according to the individual plant. Buddleias, for example, need to be cut right back to within a few inches of the growing point of the branch. This looks like a massacre, but by July the long arching branches will have returned, whereas unpruned it will become a straggly mess. Most shrubs need less draconian measures. When in doubt remove one third of the oldest growth to ground level on shrubs and climbers over 3 years old. But it is far better to find out their exact needs; even roses don't conform to the rules you might expect. Pruning stimulates growth, so the more vigorous the rose the less harshly you prune.

The importance of meeting each plant's needs holds good not just between families – shrub roses needing less pruning than bush roses – but also between individual varieties. For, like people, even roses within a single family have their own strengths and weaknesses to be considered before you cut. Learning to understand their personalities can be one of the most satisfying aspects of gardening. Anne Countess of Rosse, who created Nymans and Birr Castle, attributes her success to 'love ... of plants and motherly understanding of their whims'.

When to Prune

To know when to prune you have to know the habits of the plant in question. The nursery you bought it from should be happy to advise you. However, trees and shrubs can broadly be divided into two groups: **those which flower or fruit on last year's wood** you prune soon after flowering, to give it a full year to grow those flower buds; **those which flower or fruit on this year's wood** you have to prune a little earlier the same year – or prune so late the previous year that no growth will occur after pruning.

Fruit Pruning

Fruit pruning varies greatly with the type of fruit. However, for most fruit, pruning is light for the first year, then in the following years a third to a half of the length of the main shoots is removed. When trained on walls many types of fruit benefit from having unsuitable side shoots removed between July and September.

Rose Pruning

This subject needs the details found in Christopher Brickell's book, *Pruning* (page 377). What follows is simply an outline. On all roses:

- Cut dead or diseased wood away to where the stem looks healthy.

Too   Wrong   Jagged   Correct
close   angle   cut   cut

- Cut to an eye which points outwards in a suitable direction. Cut immediately above the eye at 45°.
- On types which develop mildew or blackspot cut out enough wood to let the light get to all the leaves when they develop.

- Halve the length of any blind shoots – those which have no bud at the end when others are flowering.
- Dead-head to the first outward pointing leaf below any divisions for the flowers.
- Most roses are grafted on to the roots of wild roses. Any shoots thrown out from *below* the rootstock (the point from which the main shoots spring) are suckers of the wild rose type (the leaves have more sections). Remove them on sight, or they will take nourishment from the main shoots. If you cut them they will produce *two* suckers for every one. Instead, dig back to where they come from and tear them roughly off.
- Burn the prunings immediately or they can harbour disease.

Floribundas
The first spring cut all stems back to 15-23 cm (6-9 in) from the ground. When spring pruning in following years:

- cut new shoots by only a third
- cut year-old wood 15-23 cm (6-9 in) long
- cut older wood 10-15 cm (4-6 in) long
- completely remove stems crowding the centre.

Pruning a Floribunda Rose

Hybrid Teas
Cut back in March to about 15 cm (6 in) the first year. In other years cut vigorous stems to 23 cm (9 in), the rest

Pruning a Hybrid Tea Rose

to 15 cm (6 in) and cut out branches which crowd the centre.

Climbers and Ramblers

Climbers and ramblers fall into several groups and the pruning needs more detail than there is space for here, but Chistopher Brickell's book *Pruning* (page 377) gives it all. Dead-head by cutting back the flowering shoot to 3-4 eyes.

> When planting new roses cut the first few inches from the stems and trim off any bruised or broken roots before planting.

Species and Shrub Roses

Hybrid musks, rugosas, gallicas, moss and damask roses, China roses and Bourbons are not pruned for the first year but need some pruning in February or March after that, and some also need summer pruning. This is usually light but varies considerably with the type.

SEEDS

Preparation for Sowing Outside

- Dig over the area and remove weeds.
- Rake the soil until fine, but not dusty, removing debris.
- Tread firm and rake in phosphate fertilizer.
- Draw lines to mark where the seeds go.
- Draw drills (minute trenches) in the soil with a stick if the seeds will be sown in lines.
- Sow thinly (1-2 cm, ¼-½ in, apart is ideal).

★ Mix very fine seeds with fine sand to make it easier not to sow too thickly.

★ To get seeds off to a moist start, mix them into some wallpaper paste. Put it in a plastic bag, cut a very small corner off the bag and squeeze the seeds and paste out along a row as if icing a cake.

Golden Rules for Success

- Sow seeds when the temperature will never be above or below the levels they need for germination (page 357).
- On average sow them not more than 1-2 times their own depth – unless otherwise instructed on the packet.
- Keep them watered but not sodden.
- Thin out seedlings at 1 in high or if they have 2 true leaves.

★ Mark out the edge of each flower you are seeding, with a channel filled with sand then you can see which seeds are where.

Seed Sowing Inside

- Fill a seed tray with *moist* seed compost – garden soil

contains weeds and bacteria (but if you want to use it you will get better results with 1 part of peat : 1 part of sharp sand : 6 parts of soil.

- Don't sprinkle fine seeds too closely, and place pea or similar seeds 2.5 cm (1 in) apart.
- Cover the tray with glass or cling film, then with paper to block the light and place in a warm position.
- When the first shoots appear remove the paper and place the tray in full light.
- When the shoots become tiny plants remove the glass or film.
- When just large enough to handle, transfer to another seed tray a couple of inches apart.
- Plant them out when well established and the weather is warm enough.

★ The trays can be anything with drainage. If you have nowhere to plant seeds inside, big polystyrene boxes discarded by fish markets can be used as a cold frame outside.

★ Try sowing seeds in compost in a half-round gutter in a greenhouse or propagator. For transplanting you just remove the gutter end and slide the seedlings off with the minimum of disturbance.

★ Store seeds in a concertina file. If each section is allotted a month, or half month, you can allocate each packet to the month for sowing. For succession sowing move it on through the file after each sowing.

Problem Seeds

Certain seeds will only grow successfully when given special treatment. Those which will not transplant usually say so on the packet. If seeds need to be pre-chilled sow them in small trays or pots and put them in the salad section of a domestic refrigerator (about 1°C, 33°F) for 3-5 weeks. If you haven't got room for that pop the sealed packet in there for the 3-5 weeks before sowing.

For marrow and courgette seeds and others of this family counteract the strait-jacket of their tough little coating by making a small nick in the edge and soaking them in lukewarm water for an hour or so.

Parsley is a slow germinator, but is improved by a soak in hot water a few hours before sowing. The old saying is that whoever can make parsley grow wears the trousers in the household.

Flower Seeds – Shelf Life and Germination

I am indebted to the seedsmen Thompson & Morgan for the following tables. These show their research findings on the conditions needed for successfully growing the most popular flowers and vegetables from seed. Storage times are, of course, for quality seeds, packed in foil and kept in a cool even temperature. Seeds in an open packet may keep less well, but they are usually best in a screw-top jar in a cool dark place.

Addresses and suggestions for further reading are at the ends of chapters.

Flower Seeds – Shelf Life and Germination

Flower	Storage Time in Years	Ideal Germination Conditions °C	°F	Factors Affecting Germination	Days till Germination	When to Sow
Ageratum	2	21°-24°	(70°-75°)	Needs light	10-14	Sp
Alyssum	3	18°-24°	(65°-75°)	Needs light	7-14	LW/ESp
Antirrhinum	2	18°-24°	(65°-75°)	Needs light	10-21	Sp
Aster	2	18°-21°	(65°-70°)	Pre-chill perennial asters for 2 weeks	10-21	Sp
Begonia	nil	21°-27°	(70°-80°)	Don't cover with soil; put plastic over seed box	15-60	LW/Sp
Cactus	nil	24°-27°	(75°-80°)	Sow uncovered in furrows in box	5-180	Green
Calceolaria	nil	15°	(59°)	Above this temperature less germination	14-21	Green
Coleus	2	18°-24°	(65°-75°)	Indoors only in good light	10-20	LW/Sp
Cyclamen	1	13°-16°	(55°-60°)	Above this temperature germination may stop	30-60	LW/Sp or LS/A
Dahlia	nil	18°-21°	(65°-70°)	Keep compost moist	5-20	Sp
Delphinium	nil	10°-13°	(50°-55°)	Less germination above this temperature	14-28	LW/Sp
Dianthus	2	18°-25°	(65°-77°)		14-21	LW/Sp or LS/A
Geranium	1	22°-24°	(72°-75°)		3-21	LW/Sp
Gloxinia	nil	18°-24°	(65°-75°)	Don't cover seed; keep moist; put plastic over box	15-30	Green
Impatiens	2	21°-24°	(70°-75°)	Needs high humidity	21-30	Sp
Marigold	3	21°-24°	(70°-75°)		5-14	Sp
Nicotiana	2	21°-24°	(70°-75°)		10-20	Sp
Pansy	1	18°-24°	(65°-75°)	Pre-chill for 2 weeks	14-21	LW/Sp or LS/A
Petunia	1	18°-25°	(65°-77°)	Germinates best at the higher temperature	10-21	Sp
Primula – indoors	nil	13°-16°	(55°-60°)	Higher temperatures reduce germination	20-25	Green
Salvia	1	18°-27°	(65°-80°)	Pre-chill 3 weeks	10-14	LW/ESp
Sweet peas	2	13°-16°	(55°-60°)	File or soak seeds	10-20	LW/ESp
Wallflower	3	18°-24°	(65°-75°)		10-14	LSp/ES
Zinnia	1	21°-27°	(70°-80°)	Sow in individual pots	10-24	Sp

ESp = Early Spring   S = Summer   A = Autumn
Sp = Spring   LS = Late Summer   LW = Late Winter
Pre-chill – see page 356   Green = sow in a greenhouse

Vegetable Seeds – Shelf Life and Germination

Vegetable	Storage Time in Years	Ideal Germination Conditions °C °F	Factors Affecting Germination
Artichoke	1	13°-18° (55°-65°)	
Beans – French	1	24°-27° (75°-80°)	Won't germinate below 51°F
Beans – broad	1	21°-24° (70°-75°)	Germination from 41° to 90°F
Beans – runner	1	24°-27° (75°-80°)	Won't germinate below 51°F
Beetroot	4	open ground	Germination from 45° to 80°F
Broccoli	3	21°-24° (70°-75°)	Germination from 41°-90°F
Brussels sprouts	3	21°-24° (70°-75°)	Germination from 41°-90°F
Carrots	3	open ground	Germination from 45°-80°F
Cabbage	3	21°-24° (70°-75°)	Germination from 41°-90°F
Cauliflowers	3	21°-24° (70°-75°)	Germination from 41°-90°F
Celery	4-5	10°-18° (50°-65°)	Only those temperatures work
Celeriac	4-5	10°-18° (50°-65°)	Only those temperatures work
Chard	4	open ground	Germinates from 45°-80°F
Chicory	3	open ground	
Chinese greens	3	21°-24° (70°-75°)	
Corn salad	2	open ground	
Courgettes	4	24°-27° (75°-80°)	Won't germinate below 56°F
Cucumbers	4	24°-27° (75°-80°)	Won't germinate below 56°F
Curly endive	3	open ground	
Gourds	4	24°-27° (75°-80°)	Won't germinate below 56°F
Kale	3	21°-24° (70°-75°)	Germination from 41°-90°F
Leeks	1-3	21°-24° (70°-75°)	Germination from 45°-75°F
Lettuce	3	open ground	
– butterhead			Won't germinate above 77°F
– crisphead			Won't germinate above 85°F
Marrows	5	21°-24° (75°-80°)	Won't germinate below 56°F
Mange-touts	1	open ground	Germination from 41°-90°F
Melons	4	21°-27° (75°-80°)	Won't germinate below 56°F
Onions	1-3	21°-24° (70°-75°)	Germination from 45°-75°F
Parsnips	nil	open ground	Germination from 45°-80°F
Parsley	1	open ground	
Peas	1	open ground	Germination from 41°-90°F
Pimentos	1	21°-27° (75°-80°)	Only above 60°F
Radishes	4	open ground	Germination from 41°-90°F
Spinach	1	open ground	
Spinach beet	4	open ground	Germination from 45°-80°F
Sweetcorn	1	21°-27° (75°-80°)	Only above 51°F
Tomatoes	4	21°-24° (70°-75°)	Only above 51°F
Turnips	1	open ground	Germination from 41°-90°F

Those marked 'open ground' must be planted directly into their final site when the temperature is right for germination. The rest can, in theory, be started in a greenhouse or out of doors, but the temperature needed for germination may make an outdoor site unsuitable at some times of the year – or, indeed, at all.

Addresses and suggestions for further reading are at the ends of chapters.

SOILS AND FERTILIZERS

There are three important qualities to soil:

- the size of the particles
- the extent to which it is acid or alkaline
- its richness in a whole range of plant foods

The ideal soil is a loam with a good balance of clay, sand and humus (organic matter). Put a few spoonfuls of your soil in a tall glass container, add water, shake it well and wait to see what layers it settles in. Humus will largely float and provides many plant foods. Sand will go to the bottom and clay will sit on the sand. Sand has large particles; clay very fine ones. But the extent to which the clay sticks together into 'crumbs' varies according to whether it is acid or alkaline. How well it 'crumbs' dictates how fast water drains away. This, in turn, makes it a cold or warm soil.

All those factors determine the kinds of plants which will do well. To try and make a plant which likes warm well-drained soil thrive on clay is like trying to make an alligator thrive in the Arctic.

Acid v Alkaline

Soils range from the very alkaline soils on chalk and limestone, to very acid peaty soils – though not all peat is acid. Most plants grow less well in acid soils because vital foods are locked up by the acid. There are simple kits to test what you have. They give a pH value between 0 and 14. Where soil is concerned a pH below 6 is acid, 6-7 is neutral and above 7 is alkaline. Soil testing is interesting but looking at neighbouring gardens and seeing what thrives will tell you as much.

When soil is too acid the usual cure is hydrated lime, but it is almost impossible to increase the acidity of alkaline soil. The amount of lime you need to apply depends on the type of particles as well as on the degree of acidity. Clay needs considerably more liming than acid sandy soil. But go carefully; too much lime will stop plants growing just as effectively as too much acid, and some vegetables take exception to it.

Topsoil v Subsoil

Topsoil is the fertile layer of soil into which humus has decomposed over the centuries. Deeper down is a less fertile layer but builders sometimes take – and sell – the topsoil. If you need to buy in topsoil remember a cubic metre weighs about 1 tonne. You will need a layer at least 30 cm (1 ft) deep. So 1 tonne will cover an area 3 x 3 m.

Fertilizers, Conditioners and Mulches

Different chemicals have quite specific effects on plants, and these dictate when to use them. But a balance between the chemicals may be needed before plants can use them properly.

Nitrogen boosts plant growth and leaves. So use it during the growing period – especially in spring – and on leaf vegetables. Not at flowering time. Lack of it produces stunted plants with pale or bluish leaves.

Potassium stimulates the production of flowers and fruit, so use it when those are being made – usually summer and early autumn. Lack of potash produces potatoes which cook badly and have black patches, and can give a burnt look to fruit tree leaves.

Phosphates increase root development and maturity – use when planting, on root vegetables, and generally.

Calcium is needed to make cell walls.

Soil Types

Type	Particles	Effect	Fertility	Action
Clay (heavy)	Very fine, particles stick together.	Holds water and is slow to warm in spring. Hard to dig.	Usually good.	Add lime in autumn to bind the particles. Add compost, manure, leaf-mould and sharp sand.
Loamy	Fine and coarse mixed.	Half way between clay and sand – the excellent middle way.	Usually good.	Just because it's good don't neglect it. Every soil needs compost or manure.
Chalk	Fine.	Alkaline, but the soil is sticky and unpleasant to handle. Plants yellow from lime-induced chlorosis.	Usually poor.	Needs very large amounts of humus to reduce both alkalinity and stickiness.
Peat	Fine to medium.	Often acid, and water-logged, but plenty of humus.	Fair, but too acid for many plants.	Add lime to reduce acidity if it is acid.
Sand (light)	Very coarse, open soil.	Water drains very fast, but it warms quickly in spring. Easy to dig.	Poor. Plant food quickly washed from the soil.	Often needs lime against acidity. Add compost, manure or leaf-mould to hold moisture.

Hungry plants may need some 'fast food', for example, liquid tomato fertilizer will bring on most flowers and fruit rapidly. Branded fertilizers always give plant foods in a set order, e.g. 1:2:3 means 1 part nitrogen:2 parts phosphates:3 parts potassium (or 1N:2P:3K). Fertilizers should be dug or watered in.

All soil needs to have organic matter added to it to keep the texture healthy and open. In nature what came out of the ground is returned to it. Our tidy gardens deprive the soil of its natural roughage and we need to make good the loss. Earthworms play a vital part in keeping the soil open, and save us digging, but they need humus to live and work for us. The more compost you add, the happier the earthworms are and the more there are to do your digging.

Applying organic matter as a mulch saves even more work: it keeps down weeds and holds in moisture; as the worms will gradually drag it underground it also adds humus to the soil. Hoe, water and apply a layer several inches thick in April or May and don't disturb it during the growing season.

Wood ash is a useful source of potash though short-lived. Use a good handful of bonfire remains per sq m (sq yd) at any time.

Composted bark and wood chips can be spread as a mulch an inch or so thick under shrubs and trees. They look good and work very well. But they have no food value and bacteria will take nitrogen away from the plants to break them down. So nitrogen fertilizer *must* be used on the bed before they are applied first.

Blood, fish and bone meal is an invaluable general fertilizer combining all the main plant foods. Use a handful or two per square metre a week before sowing or planting and again during the growing season.

Bone meal is high in phosphates with some nitrogen. It releases these very slowly.

Compost contains all the foods plants need and can be dug in or used as a mulch. It also improves the texture of all soils. Compost making is really very easy. Any container with strong sides which allows in air will do – tough Netlon made into a square with four stakes for example – and you can compost anything except:

- food which attracts rats or flies.
- matter which decays very slowly, such as paper
- branches, twigs and very woody stems
- diseased matter
- invasive weeds such as bind-weed or couch grass: they may not be killed.

Vegetable matter rots because of bacteria which are in the soil on your weeds anyway – but add some earth if the heap is mainly mowings. These bacteria need moisture – so moisten it if you add dry matter. And those which produce compost with a nice earthy texture need air. (Without it other bacteria take over producing a stinking sludge.) Given these conditions, any heap of garden refuse would rot in time. But to speed up the process use sulphate of ammonia activator, like Garotta, on every hands' depth of debris. The traditional additive was slops, for urine is an excellent activator, so if you do run out of chemicals . . .

The heap can be any size but cover it with dark plastic, or an old carpet weighted with bricks, to keep in the heat. Start a new heap each year, or when the bin is full, leaving the other until it almost resembles soil before spreading it.

Alternatively, you can now get a plastic compost bin with insulated sides and top. By keeping the heat in, this rots vegetable matter down very much faster, which can be convenient in a small garden. It is called the Hotte-Rotter (page 379). As with all composting, it works best if the matter put into it is moist and cut into small pieces, and a bit of sweetness seems to help: so add kitchen peelings if you can.

Leaves can be included or make a heap of their own, or just put them in vegetable nets or well-perforated refuse sacks, with some activator, and let them rot by themselves. They can be dug in or used as a mulch before other compost is ready.

Dried blood is high in nitrogen and also contains potassium, sodium, calcium and phosphate compounds, and releases these quickly into the ground. Use about 50 g (2 oz) to the square metre (sq yd).

Fish manure is now hard to find but is an excellent general fertilizer. Use 100 g (4 oz) a square metre (sq yd).

Green manure is a term used for plants grown on bare ground and then dug in. Apart from leguminous plants, which fix (store) nitrogen from the air, they contain nothing which wasn't in the soil they grew on, but they do improve the texture and they allow fertilizers which might have been washed from light soil to be retained for future plants. The best green fertilizer is probably comfrey.

Growmore is a general inorganic fertilizer containing all 3 plant foods.

Hair, feathers and hoof and horn meal all contain nitrogen which they release very slowly. They can be dug in or added to a compost heap.

Horse and other manure is a mixture of animal waste and whatever was used as litter. The litter is the snag. Bacteria need nitrogen to break down substances like straw, and especially wood shavings. Until these have

Addresses and suggestions for further reading are at the ends of chapters.

been broken down, putting manure on a bed will *take vital nitrogen away* from the plants, not add any. Unless you have room for a manure heap, only buy manure when well rotted. Use a barrowload of horse manure to about 12 sq m (12 sq yd) either dug in or as a mulch. Other animal and bird manures usually contain less litter but some are very strong. Apply them when well decomposed, and in lower concentrations.

Lime reduces the acidity of soil; it also provides calcium. It binds clay into clumps. Add it in autumn, not in spring, and if clay is very acid use gypsum in preference to lime.

Seaweed conditioners do break down clay – but they don't work miracles.

Seaweed manure is very valuable, though low in phosphates. Use a barrow load for 10 sq m (10 sq yd) and add bone meal to make up the phosphates.

Sedge peat is especially useful for improving the texture of soils, helping it to hold moisture without becoming heavy, and is slightly acid. Applied as a 2.5-5 cm (1-2 in) mulch on shrub borders; it also combats weeds.

Spent hops improve soil texture and add nitrogen. Use a bucketful to a square metre (sq yd).

Spent mushroom compost is an excellent mulch which helps the soil hold water and improves its texture.

Sulphate of ammonia is high in nitrogen and a dusting round plants will boost them in the early spring. But using it in the compost heap and then spreading the compost is even better.

Sulphate of potash is alkaline and rich in potash. Apply 100 g (4 oz) per square metre (sq yd).

SHRUBS, TREES AND ROSES

Shrubs and small trees are too often the also-rans of a garden, yet they deserve the place of honour. Nothing, except bulbs, outshines them in a labour-saving contest. Many of the most beautiful need no pruning, tying or tending. Though they may each play prima donna in their flowering time, they are also the back-drop against which the rest of the garden is acted out, and for a garden to look good through the dog days of winter there should be a *far* higher proportion of evergreens than are usually planted.

It takes time for shrubs and trees to grow into these roles. Most good catalogues give the final height and width of each shrub but, if they only give the height, a rough guide is that most shrubs are slightly wider than their height, and most trees narrower. It is all too easy to over-buy and plant shrubs according to their initial size, rather than the final size. This means none will develop their proper form and some will eventually have to be removed, which is a wasteful exercise. And shrubs, like people, are only easy-going when they are happy.

For mail order choose a reputable nursery but when picking them yourself look for:

- a strong straight trunk on trees
- even growth in all directions
- branches which are free from disease or wounds
- a well-developed root system – if you can see it
- maturity – mature shrubs establish better than young fleshy ones.

Buying Climbers

With climbing plants bear in mind which way the wall faces. Most have distinct preferences and good garden catalogues list climbers according to which aspect they prefer. The range of possible plants, for any wall, is a lot wider than the prevalence of climbing roses would suggest and it's well worth looking at some of the lesser known options. The ground must be deeply fertilized, as it may be hard to get at again, especially if it is set in paving.

Buying Roses

In the 1970s if you wanted a sturdy, heavily scented rose you had to turn to old varieties. That is no longer true. Nurseries like **Le Grice** (page 379) have now bred sturdy, disease-resistant roses with the heavy scents. There are also new ground-cover roses and low growing roses for small areas. The range of possibilities has never been so wide. Don't buy from the meagre range in many garden centres until you have looked at some good catalogues (page 379).

If you are searching for a particular rose you loved and lost, the **Rose Growers Association** (page 379) has a pamphlet to help you find it.

Planting Trees, Shrubs and Roses

For the best time to plant see the Gardening Year, pages 368-371. Planting at the right time is essential for bare-rooted plants, and an advantage even for container grown ones. If you plant shrubs and trees in a dry spell it will take a *lot* of watering to make them thrive.

Dig the ground thoroughly, if possible a month before planting. Water container-grown plants regularly while they wait to be planted and an hour before planting. If they have arrived bare-rooted and you can't plant them immediately, because of cold or wet, heel them in. For this put the roots of bare-rooted trees in a trench, with them lying on the ground, cover the roots with earth and tread it firmly.

To give the plant a good chance you need a hole which is deep enough to repeat the old soil level, with the roots comfortably spread out to their tips.

A small tree	needs a hole	50cm (18in) deep
A tree 2.8m (9ft) high	needs a hole	1m (3ft) wide
Taller trees	need a hole	1.4m (4ft 6in) wide
Shrubs 50cm (18in) high	need a hole	60cm (2ft) wide

Mix half the soil with an equal amount of peat or compost, plus 2-3 handfuls of bonemeal per barrowload or use one of the planting mediums, such as Fisons Greenleaf, which retain the moisture in the soil and make it easier for shrubs to establish. These can replace the soil and peat mixture or simply be used close to the

Trees and Shrubs Through the Year

E = evergreen   ★ indicates that no pruning is needed

Name	Description
Amelanchier	A compact fast tree covered with a froth of white blossom in spring, with brilliant scarlet leaves in autumn, plus tiny crimson berries if soil and weather suit it. Grows almost anywhere.
Azalea – many varieties E★	The dwarf evergreens of this family are ideal for the front of any moist lime free border. Providing a brilliant display when in flower and a nice cushion of evergreen leaves afterwards.
Buddleia 'Lochinch'	Not the prettiest shrub but graceful, undemanding and beloved by butterflies. Prefers slightly dry soil and sun. Fast growing. Cut right back in March.
Camellia japonica varieties E★	Camellias, with their glossy leaves and rosette-like flowers are so lovely they look difficult to grow. In peaty soil and semi-shade nothing is easier. But the flowers go brown if early sun strikes them. Not totally hardy so best on a sheltered wall.
Chamaecyparis Lawsoniana varieties E★	These conifers are indispensable in any garden. They offer a wide range of colours, from the golden yellow of *lutea* to the blue green of *Ellwoodii*, and their conical shape gives height to any bed they are used in.
Choisya ternata E★	This Mexican Orange Blossom produces masses of sweet scented flowers and attractive foliage in any good soil, though it prefers sun. Remove dead wood after March flowering.
Cytisus scoparius varieties ★	The most upright of the garden brooms. A spectacular smother of pea-like flowers. Long green stems all winter. Likes any not too wet soil, and sun or semi-shade.
Euonymus 'Emerald Gaiety' E★	Very easy going shrub with silver and green glossy variegated leaves. Will thrive in any soil and in tubs. There is golden variegated form too.
Forsythia varieties	Too common to need recommending, but nothing else provides quite so much colour in early spring. Grows almost anywhere. Prune overcrowding straight after flowering.
Genista lydia ★	This has the same flowers as a broom but it makes a low mound of glowing gold, in light soil and sun. Totally trouble free.
Hydrangea paniculata 'Grandiflora'	The hardiest of all hydrangeas and very striking with huge conical heads on elegant arching stems. Cut last year's growth by half each spring.
Magnolia loebneri 'Leonard Messell'	A magnolia with a cluster of deep pink star-like flowers. Likes a warm well-drained peaty soil. Hardy and trouble free.

Addresses and suggestions for further reading are at the ends of chapters.

Trees and Shrubs Through the Year

Flowering colours	Jan	Feb	Mar	Apr	May	Jun	Jul	Aug	Sept	Oct	Nov	Dec	Size
white				×									6 m x 5 m
red yellow white pink				×	×	×							1m up × 1m
blue							×	×					2 m x 1.8 m
white pink red		×	×	×									1.5 m x 1.5 m
													1.2 m up × 50 cm up
white			×						×				1.8 m x 2 m
gold lemon cream ruby red					×	×							1.5 m x 1.5 m
													60 cm × 80 cm
yellow		×	×										2 m x 2.4 m
gold					×	×							60 cm x 80 cm
creamy white fade to pink							×	×					2 m x 1.8 m
pink				×									3 m x 1.8 m

Trees and Shrubs Through the Year

E = evergreen	★ indicates that no pruning is needed

Name	Description
Mahonia aquifolium 'Charity'　E★	One of the most handsome evergreens. An imposing plant, with toothed leaves and sprays of lily-of-the-valley-scented flowers. Dislikes waterlogged soil and prefers semi-shade. If leggy prune after flowering.
Malus (crab apple) 'John Downie'	An attractive tree with spring blossom and scarlet orange fruit which make excellent jelly. A good combination of fruit and beauty.
Osmanthus delavayi　E★	A plant to grow for its scent, though the handsome dark green leaves are a good foil for other flowers too. Any sunny well drained soil.
Philadelphus varieties (often wrongly called *Syringa*)	Free-flowering, heavily scented shrubs which are trouble free in any well drained soil, in sun or semi-shade. Thin out old wood after flowering, if crowded. Charming flowers.
Pieris 'Forest Flame'　E★	Eye-catching shrubs for lime free soil, with rosettes of new leaves a clear red and panicles of waxy flowers. Choose a sheltered semi-shade position with moist soil – cold wind scorches new growth.
Prunus (Flowering Almonds Cherries and Plums) most varieties	No other flowering tree matches the profusion of prunus blossom in spring – with cherries especially. They like sun and some are small enough for town gardens. *Subhirtella autumnalis rosea* is a good one for winter blooms.
Pyrus salicifolia 'Pendula'	A charming weeping tree with slim silver-grey leaves but inconspicuous flowers. Trouble free and unfussy, its colour, size, and shape make it a good foil for other plants, in a small garden.
Rhododendron yakusimanum hybrids　E★	If the soil is lime free and moist this king of shrubs flourishes untended. When happy some grow to vast size, but these are dwarf hybrids to suit an average garden, in beds or in tubs. Flowering depends on having enough water the year before and on dead-heading before seeds form.
Rhus cotinus 'Royal Red'	A beautiful foliage plant with striking wine-red leaves from spring to autumn, but it must be pruned to 2-3 'eyes' in March to get the best effect. Easily grown in sunny well-drained soil.
Rosa Hybrid Musk	It was a Frenchman in 1904 who created the first of these delightful, underused shrub roses. They form hedges or dense tumbling mounds which are smothered in heavily scented densely petalled blooms in May and June, and will flower on until September if dead-headed. But they flower in such profusion that this dead-heading is lengthy. Buff Beauty excels in scent, colour and form.
Rosa bourboniana	The Bourbon roses of the last century may have been ousted from most gardens by the hybrid tea, but not deservedly. Large, almost cabbagy, fragrant blooms and an easy going habit which needs no pruning, except removing dead wood makes them an excellent buy.
Senecio greyi　E★	A mound of attractive grey-green foliage, invaluable in vases, and daisy-shaped flowers make this New Zealand shrub invaluable. Not *very* hardy nor very tolerant of wind. If straggly in old age prune after flowering.
Viburnum tomentosum 'Mariesii'	This is, admittedly, too wide for many gardens. But when the full length of its tiered branches carries its flat white heads of florets, the cascade effect is so ravishing it cannot be excluded from this list. Unfussy as to soil or site. Or for winter flowers there is Bondnantese Dawn. A quite different type of viburnum but just as valuable.

Trees and Shrubs Through the Year

Flowering colours	Jan	Feb	Mar	Apr	May	Jun	Jul	Aug	Sept	Oct	Nov	Dec	Size
lemon	×	×											1.8 m x 1.5 m
pink & white				×	×								5 m
white				×									1 m x 1 m
white						×	×						1.8 m x 1.5 m
white pale-pink cream				×	×	×							1.8 m x 1.5 m
pink white				×	×	×		also Autumn					3 m up x 3 m up
													3m x 2.5 m
white pink red apricot mauve yellow					×	×							1 m x 1 m
													1.8 x 1.8 m
white pink apricot yellow red					×								1.2 m x 1.5 m
pink white crimson						×	×						1.5 m x 1.5 m
yellow						×	×						1.2 m x 1.5 m
white					×	×							2.1 m x 3 m up

roots. Having made the hole, work half a bucket of manure or compost into the next 25 cm (9 in) of soil.

Stand the plant in the hole and check that its soil surface line will be just below soil level. Lift trees and shrubs by their root ball, then their roots won't be torn. If it is bare-rooted check that the main root goes straight down, and the roots can fan out. Deepen or fill as necessary. Recheck the depth, and hammer in a sturdy stake about 12 cm (5 in) from the trunk of anything with a tall main trunk. Place it on the side from which the wind mainly blows (look at trees nearby to find this) and hammer it well in before planting the tree.

Some plants hate lime and love acid. The most common lime haters are: azaleas, rhododendrons, lupins, magnolias, camellias, heathers, lithospermum, gentians, styrax. On soil which is not acid enough their health and happiness can be improved by putting peat into the planting hole and by regular applications of a plant food which contains sequestered iron.

In dry weather water the base of the hole well. Check a bare-rooted plant and cut off any broken or bruised sections of root. Spread bare roots out, or centre a root ball, in the hole and fill in gradually with the soil and peat and tread it gently in as you go, disturbing the pot shape of container grown plants as little as possible. Leave a slight dip on the surface, and water this unless the soil is wet.

Tie the tree to the stake with a plastic tree strap just below the branches.

★ When fences need to be treated to prevent them rotting use Cuprinol not creosote. Creosote can injure plant shoots for a long time after it is applied. Before erecting the fence, stand the bottoms of the supporting posts in a large can of waste sump oil (from a garage) for a few weeks to protect the wood against underground wet.

Good Shrubs

No boy will face a holly hedge of any degree of thickness.
William Cobbett, *The English Gardener*

The table on pages 362-365 gives 25 shrubs and trees which have a lot to offer almost any garden, yet demand a minimum of care and attention.

Most are hardy, but those living in the colder regions may not be able to grow all of them. Between them, they provide a range of flowers and foliage to give interest in every month of the year. But which will grow best will depend on your soil and your situation, or you may find you prefer a different member of a family to the one I have given. This is just a starting point for exploration.

Wall Supports

It pays to prepare a wall for a climber well before the plant needs the support. The cheapest supports are vine-eyes, screwed into drilled holes, with wires stretched between them. But for plants like clematis, attach Netlon to the vine-eyes. If inserting a lot of vine-eyes is a problem sink two long bamboo poles into the ground near the wall and only insert vine-eyes near their tops. Lash the tops to them with wire and tie the Netlon between them. A more attractive option is trellis, but the lack of air behind the climber will increase the risk of mildew.

TOOLS

If anybody will have a piece of cabbages, and will dig between the rows of one half of them twice during their growth, and let the other half have nothing but a flat-hoeing between, that person will find that the half which has been digged between will, when the crop is ripe, weigh nearly, if not quite, twice as much as the other half.
William Cobbett, *The English Gardener*

The essential tools are those given below, plus a trowel and lawn edging shears. To them you can add all kinds of extras – like rakes, cultivators, hedge trimmers and so forth – which your particular garden demands.

Good tools last for years; bad ones drive you mad for years. Handle each before you buy. Go through the movements you'd use and check that it suits *you* – and anyone who may use it. **Wolf Tools** (page 379) use a special system which allows a selection of heads (for hoes, cultivators, rakes, etcetera) to be clipped firmly on and off handles in a range of lengths. So nobody of any height needs to get backache from using the wrong length of handle and there are less handles cluttering up the garage or shed.

Grecian saw

Swoe

Secateurs

Long-handled secateurs

A **fork** and **spade** tend to be bought as a pair. But the spade has to be lifted with a weight of earth, whereas a fork does not. So it may be less back-breaking to have the spade slightly smaller.

Addresses and suggestions for further reading are at the ends of chapters.

There are three major types of **hoe**: the Dutch, the draw and Wilkinson's the Swoe. The easiest to use in a small garden are the Swoe and the Dutch hoe, with the former having a decided advantage round roses and shrubs.

If you buy a **rake** choose one with prongs which spring smartly back into place if you pull them back slightly. If they bend it will be useless in no time.

Every garden needs a **rubbish carrier**, but in small gardens it is most convenient to have a vast bag or a dumper sheet with handles. If you have to buy a barrow, the ball-wheel Ballbarrow is hard to beat. The same company makes a plastic **roller** which is weighted by putting water in, so you can adapt it to light or heavy rolling.

★ To save back strain: face your wheelbarrow in the direction you intend to go *before* you fill it, then you never turn it fully laden.

If you have any small branches or very thick rose or shrub stems to cut through, a curved-bladed **Grecian saw** is essential. The best I have used is by Wolf Tools (page 379) and can be attached to a short handle for using on roses or to a long one to reach up to branches.

Buy the very best **secateurs** you can afford: cutting plants with inefficient ones just causes them to die back. Those with curving blades are least likely to cause bruising.

If you have thick branches to cut buy long-handled secateurs too. The less strong you are, the longer the handles should be: by the rules of leverage the longer the handle, the less effort you have to put in. **Wilkinson Sword** (page 379) now make some at over 61 cm (2 ft) long and the extra inches do make a difference. Tree-lopping versions of such secateurs will even reach right up to small branches. Wilkinson Sword have an approved list of companies which sharpen them and run a postal sharpening service (see also **Fiskars**, page 379).

There are some very sophisticated bits of equipment among today's **watering kits**. They include meters which will turn a tap off once a set amount of water has been delivered, hoses which roll flat as tape for easy storage, hoses for laying round the garden to release a gentle trickle from end to end, and sprinklers which will spray a set pattern to match the shape of your flowerbed. The possibilities get better all the time.

Tools last best if scraped clean and wiped with an oily cloth after use, then hung up in a dry place.

VEGETABLES

It is most miserable taste, to seek to poke away the kitchen garden in order to get it out of sight. If well managed, nothing is more beautiful . . .

So wrote William Cobbett in *The English Gardener* in 1845. Not everyone would agree with him. But one way of bridging the gulf is to sow some of the more unusual and decorative vegetables in the borders with the other plants. Tall roses make no objection to being interplanted with dwarf French beans, the occasional courgette is rather attractive between shrubs and some of the smaller vegetables, like those below, can be tucked into any border.

New vegetables are coming on the market each year and some long-standing kinds are less cultivated than they deserve to be.

Corn salad: a favourite in other parts of Europe this produces small leaves with a most distinctive flavour late in the season. Easily grown in a mixed border.

Kohl-rabi: a tasty vegetable which is happy in poor dry soil where other vegetables may sulk.

Land cress: a splendid substitute for watercress which thrives in ordinary soil and grows like a weed.

Rocket: has slightly peppery leaves much loved by Italians. A delicious addition to salads which can be grown in any flower bed as you only pick a few leaves at a time.

Swiss chard: an easy form of spinach with a big central rib which can be cut out and cooked separately.

★ When growing sweetcorn plant it in blocks; it is wind pollinated and pollination may not be good in a single row.

Cloches and Cover-ups

Vegetables only grow when the day-time temperature is comfortable (comfortable for vegetables that is) – about 6°C (43°F). Only by keeping out the elements can a gardener buy extra time and raise crops which like it hotter than the average British summer. If you don't want to buy cloches make wire arches, covered with strong polythene, stretched tight and weighted. **Lakeland Plastics** (page 217) sell a kit by mail order. Make a ventilation hole at either end to suit the length of the tunnel.

★ When the weather is cold protect plants in the greenhouse by covering them with newspaper.

Winter Storage

Onions: can be stored in old nylon tights knotted to keep each onion separate and hung in a cool dry place. They will keep through the winter.

Marrows, pumpkins, vegetable spaghetti: can be hung in netting or spaced on shelves in a cool, dry place and will keep 2 to 4 months.

Potatoes: must be stored in the dark and cool – but not below 4°C (40°F) as frost changes their chemistry unpleasantly. A big paper sack from a frozen food wholesaler is ideal.

Carrots, swedes, turnips: can be left in the ground if it is covered with straw and polythene, but may be attacked by pests. They may be stored in a box of slightly moist sand in a cool place.

Beetroots: store in sand as above.

Brussels sprouts, cabbages, leeks: can be left growing until harvested.

★ An old trick for getting early crops is to tilt the bed against a wall at a 40° angle towards the sun. You remove the topsoil, create an angled bed with subsoil or rubble and cover with topsoil.

WEED CONTROL

The old saying that one year's seeding is seven years' weeding has been proved to be scientifically correct –

The Gardening Year

	BULBS, CORMS AND TUBERS	CLIMBERS	FRUIT	GREENHOUSE	HERBACEOUS PLANTS	LAWNS
JAN	Check pot grown bulbs. Bring indoors those ready to flower.	Prune wisteria.	Apply tar-oil emulsion to fruit trees to clean them of insect eggs and moss – on a dry day. Prune apples when the weather is frost free. Plant bare-rooted trees.	Clean out and disinfect. Plan spring sowing. Sow sweet peas and begonias.	Take root cuttings or hardwood cuttings as needed.	Sweep up leaves, cut and repair edges.
FEB	Plant alliums, anemones and tigridias. Also snowdrops in the green, or divide clumps. Bring pot-grown bulbs indoors if ready.	Cut Jackmanii clematis to 1 m (3 ft) near end of month. Thin weak wood in summer bloo-mers. Prune wisteria.	Prune fruit trees and feed with general fertilizer like Vitax Q4. Spray peaches, almonds and nectarines against peach leaf curl. Plant.	Sow summer bedding plants such as tobacco plants and lobelia near end of month. Sow tomatoes.	Divide and replant established clumps. Top dress with complete fertilizer.	Spike 5 cm (6 in) deep all over with a fork to let in air and improve drainage.
MAR	Feed with general fertilizer. Plant galtonia, and schizostylis, montbretia and gladioli. Enjoy the display and plan additions	Cut back Jackmanii clematis, as February, if not done.	Last chance to plant bare-rooted trees and bushes. Spray against apple and pear scabs as buds open.	Sow half-hardy annuals. Sow tomatoes here or on a window ledge. Pot on early sown tomatoes.	Plant from mid-month. Lift and divide establi-shed clumps.	Rake off leaves. Mow lightly to 3 cm (1¼ in) if growing. Apply moss-killer if it's needed. Roll.
APR	Plant dormant dahlia tubers 6 in deep in warm areas if mild. Plant freesias and gladioli. Dead-head narcissus and tulips. Leave foliage as it is.	Remove very old stems from roses.	Spray gooseberries and straw- berries every 2 weeks against mildew. Remove blossom from first-year trees to let them build their strength.	Sow tomatoes, marrow. Sow courgettes and sweetcorn from late in month.	Plant until mid-month. Put supports in place. Feed with blood, fish and bonemeal.	Mow weekly (1¼ in). Roll if bumpy. Prick and reseed bare patches. Feed.
MAY	Plant gladioli early, then crocosmia and agapanthus, also dahlia tubers. Lift tulips, if need be, after flowering.		Hang a pheromone trap in apple and pear trees to catch coddling moths before they lay eggs for maggots. Treat gooseberries with Benlate against mildew. Put fruit protection under strawberries.	Sow sweetcorn, pumpkin. Spray for pests if necessary. Root cuttings of herbaceous plants and shrubs.	Divide and replant clumps of primroses and polyanthus. Plant out. Stake tall plants.	Mow twice a week, to 1.5-2.5 cm (½-1 in) long. Fertilize or use combined weedkiller and fertilizer.
JUN	Move any that need to be moved. Keep gladioli well watered. Tie up dahlias as they grow.	Tie in new shoots.	Thin excess fruit from branches after June drop. Net soft fruit against birds. Spray gooseberries against mildew every 2 weeks. Root strawberry runners. Spray apples against red spider.	Shade the sunny side. Pot on as needed.	Take cuttings of phlox and dianthus. Move and divide bearded irises after flowering. Dead-head regularly.	Mow twice a week, to 1.5-2.5 cm (½-1 in) long. Water in dry weather.

Addresses and suggestions for further reading are at the ends of chapters.

The Gardening Year

ROSES	DECIDUOUS SHRUBS & TREES	EVERGREEN SHRUBS & TREES	SOWING FLOWERS OUTSIDE	VEGETABLES	SUNDRY
Find manure ready for mulching.	Plant if weather mild.	Choose sites to receive these later, possibly dig the holes – but cover to prevent waterlogging.		Set early potatoes to sprout. Plan the sowing for the year. Sow peas and early broad beans. Also shallots in the warm areas.	See to lawn mower. Fork empty beds. Tidy up. Shake snow off shrubs.
Plant. Prune hybrid teas, floribundas and standards and any others if newly planted – in warm areas.	Plant if weather is mild. Give slow-release fertilizer e.g. bonemeal. Prune forsythia after flowering. Take hard-wood cuttings.	Dress area with slow fertilizer as above. Take cuttings of conifers and place in cold frame.	Risk some perennials in a cold frame – say lupins and hollyhocks.	Cover ground with polythene or cloches to warm it. Sow Brussels sprouts, leeks, and lettuce under cloches at end of month in warm areas. Sow broad beans, plus possibly early carrots, cabbage and onion in warm areas.	Prepare wall supports for wall plants. Shake snow off shrubs.
Plant. Feed early with fertilizer such as Vitax Q4. Prune hybrid teas, floribundas and standards and any newly planted. Lightly prune shrub roses. Spray with fungicide.	Plant if weather is mild. Prune many summer flowering shrubs and feed with balanced slow release fertilizer.	Cut out any winter damage. Shake off snow before it breaks branches.	Sow hardy annuals, like sweet peas, from mid-month if weather good.	Put cloches over soil to warm it. Sow spinach, beet, radishes, spring onions, leeks, broad beans, Brussels sprouts, sweetcorn onions. Sow lettuce, and carrot under cloches – week 4. In the south plant asparagus.	
Spray every 2 weeks against blackspot and mildew. Mulch when warm enough with compost or manure. Prune hybrid teas and floribundas in cold areas.	Prune early spring flowerers. Mulch.	Good time for planting. Prune if needed, unless in flower. Mulch.	Sow annuals like sunflowers. Plant out violas, lobelia, alyssum if frost is over.	Sow radish, cauliflower and lettuce. Sow parsnips from late in month. Plant out courgettes under cloches. Plant out brassicas. If late, sow courgettes in window ledge and runner beans in pots. Transplant brassicas (cabbage family).	Hoe weeds down. Keep new planting well watered.
Spray against greenfly. Spray fortnightly against diseases. Mulch as April.	Prune winter damaged branches, and privet hedges. Dead-head winter flowering heathers and mulch with sedge peat.	Dead-head azaleas and rhododendrons. Prune winter-damaged branches.	Sow hollyhocks in position. Sow annuals. Sow biennials in boxes. Plant out half hardy bedding plants. Sow perennials.	Sow winter cabbages, from week 3. Sow Chinese cabbage and swedes week 4. Plant outdoor tomatoes. Sow French, runner beans and parsnips. Transplant brassicas large enough to handle. Thin as needed.	Water new plants. Mulch. Plant window boxes, hanging baskets and tubs.
Spray fortnightly against diseases. Feed with balanced fertilizer. Dead-head. Water if dry. Liquid feed.	Take cuttings of those which flower early. After flowering prune those which flower on year-old wood.	Dead-head azaleas and rhododendrons.	Sow calceolaria and cineraria, for pot plants next winter, in a cold frame.	Sow cauliflower, courgettes, marrows and chicory in weeks 1 and 2. Sow beetroot, French beans, kohl-rabi and early peas. Plant out courgettes, tomatoes, cabbages, sprouts. Spray blackfly. Thin seedlings.	Keep hanging baskets moist. Water garden when dry.

The Gardening Year

	BULBS, CORMS AND TUBERS	CLIMBERS	FRUIT	GREENHOUSE	HERBACEOUS PLANTS	LAWNS
JUL	Water dahlias and gladioli. Mulch dahlias with compost or manure and tie up. Plan bulb order for autumn planting.	Prune long new wisteria growths to 6-7 buds. Tie in new growths.	Prune currants after fruiting. Root strawberry runners.	Layer carnations. Root semi-hardwood and pelargonium cuttings. Sow biennials and perennials. Spray against whitefly.	Divide bearded irises, cutting leaves by half, replant. Dead-head.	Mow twice a week, to 1.5-2.5 cm ($^1/_2$-1 in) long. Possibly feed as in May. Water when dry.
AUG	Plant autumn crocuses, colchicums and Madonna lilies. Begin to plant narcissus (daffodils). Protect dahlias against earwigs.	Tie in new growths. Prune wisteria if not done. Prune rambling roses after flowering.	Layer blackberries. Spray gooseberries and strawberries against mildew. Summer prune as needed. Cut raspberry canes to ground level after fruiting. Plant new strawberry beds.	Fumigate at night against pests and diseases. Don't let dead leaves lie about. Sow cyclamen. Pot fuchsia cuttings.	Sow in seed beds for planting out next year. Dead-head. Spray against mildew Divide and replant irises as July.	Mow twice a week, to 1.5-2.5 cm ($^1/_2$-1 in) long. Use combined weedkiller and fertilizer if needed. Water when dry.
SEP	Plant spring bulbs and corms, hardy lilies and bulbous irises. Lift dahlia tubers once frosted. Disbud dahlias for larger blooms. Plant bulbs in pots for indoors.	Tie in new growths. Prune climbing and rambling roses.	Prune off surplus shoots on wall-trained trees and prune fan shapes from mid-month. Prune raspberries and gooseberries. Order fruit trees for autumn/winter planting. Fit grease bands in week 4 against winter moths.	Sow pansies, viola, godetia and clarkia. Remove shading from the glass by mid-month. Prick out earlier seedings in trays.	Dead-head. Plant early season flowers from mid-month. Divide and replant irises if not done. Position plants seeded in the spring.	Rake lawns to remove dead grass and moss. Spike to let air in. Mow to 2-3 cm ($^3/_4$-1$^1/_4$ in) once a week. Autumn feed and dress.
OCT	Plant tulips, winter aconite, anemones and spring bulbs not yet in. Plant narcissus in bowls for Christmas. Lift dahlias once frosted. Lift gladioli.	Tie in new growths.	Plant soft fruit canes and fruit trees. Spray apple trees against canker. Spray peaches, almonds and nectarines. Prune fan-trained forms. Order for winter planting. Cut out fruited raspberry canes, tie in new canes.	Pick the last tomatoes and cucumbers. Wash and disinfect throughout. Allow corms to die down, dry and store corms.	Plant until mid-month. Position plants seeded in the spring. Lift, divide and replant large clumps. Take cuttings of shrubby ones.	Rake off leaves. Mow to 2-3 cm ($^3/_4$-1$^1/_4$ in) once a week if mild. Autumn feed and possibly top dress if not done in September.
NOV	Plant tulips. Bring bulbs in pots into cool room in week 4. Lift dahlias. Feed with bonemeal.	Hard prune outdoor vines after leaf fall. Prune wisteria	Prune apples and pears after leaf fall. Apply insecticide against woolly aphis. Cut out canker on fruit trees. Plant new trees from now on.	Fumigate against pests and diseases.	Mulch well with manure. Cut back dead growth if you wish. Tuck dead leaves and slug pellets over tender subjects under twigs in week 4.	Rake off leaves. Mow if mild and grass still growing to 2-3 cm ($^3/_4$-1$^1/_4$ in).
DEC	Finish planting tulips.	Hard prune outdoor vines if not done. Prune wisteria. Plant. Protect tender ones with bracken or straw at roots.	Plant bare-rooted trees. Finish pruning – if frost-free.	Check and tend over-wintering plants.	Put slug pellets near hellebores. Tie the tops of kniphofias together to keep out wet.	Clear blown leaves

Addresses and suggestions for further reading are at the ends of chapters.

The Gardening Year

ROSES	DECIDUOUS SHRUBS & TREES	EVERGREEN SHRUBS & TREES	SOWING FLOWERS OUTSIDE	VEGETABLES	SUNDRY
Spray fortnightly against diseases. Liquid feed once if not in June. Water if dry. Dead-head.	Trim hedges. Lightly prune those which need post-flowering pruning. Trim broom. Feed with liquid general fertilizer.	Dead-head rhododendrons. Feed with a general fertilizer.	Transplant biennials.	Early on sow beetroot, calabrese, chicory, Chinese cabbage, winter radish, autumn spinach, spinach beet, kohl-rabi, lettuce. Liquid feed tomatoes.	Water when dry
Spray fortnightly against disease. Spray for aphids if necessary. Dead-head. Water if dry. Remove suckers.	Trim hedges. Take cuttings of elderly shrubs. Pot up. Place in greenhouse or on cool window ledge. Prune some early flowers.	Layer rhododendrons and azaleas to propagate.	Sow spring flowering annuals such as Iceland poppies and antirrhinum.	Sow spring cabbage, Brussels sprouts, kohl-rabi, winter radish, lettuce, endive, spinach, turnip. Cut back artichoke stems after heads have gone.	Water when dry.
Spray fortnightly against diseases. Dead-head. Remove suckers.	Plant container-grown plants. Order bare-rooted plants for planting in winter. Take semi-hardwood cuttings.	Good planting time. Take cuttings for cold frame.	Plant out polyanthus seedlings. Plant out biennials such as wallflowers in flowers' sites. Sow hardy annuals on site.	Sow winter lettuce under cloches. Plant out cabbages, spring greens and Savoys. Ripen off onions under cloches. Lift carrots in warm areas and store. Harvest and store most of your crops.	Keep weeds down. Tie plants against autumn winds. Rake up leaves.
Spray against diseases until mid-month. Prepare beds for planting. Remove suckers. Dead-head. Cut bushes to half in windy positions.	One of the best times for planting.	Good time for planting.		Plant out spring cabbages, cauliflowers and lettuces in a cold frame. Lift root vegetables. Sow corn salad, winter radish and spinach. Lift and store carrots in cold areas. Start winter digging.	Rake up leaves and store for leaf-mould.
Best time for planting if bare rooted. Plant from containers. Prune climbers which flower more than once. Prune tall bushes to reduce height by half in windy areas if not done.	Best time for planting. Prune beech and hornbeam hedges.	Plant heathers.	Plant out pansies, sweet Williams, and violets. Put cloches over autumn-sown hardy annuals.	Lime soil which grew brassicas. Plant garlic, Protect globe artichokes with bracken or straw. Protect lettuce with cloches. Sow early broad beans in warm areas. Prepare chicory for forcing.	Protect tubs with plastic wraps round straw, leaves or bracken.
Clear away dead leaves to reduce risk of mildew and blackspot next year. Disinfect soil with Jeyes fluid.	Remove snow from branches after heavy falls. Plant if weather good enough.	Remove snow from branches after heavy falls – especially from conifers. Plant if weather allows.	Plan planting for next year. Note the results from this year.	Protect globe artichokes as November.	Treat algae on paths and steps. Sweep up leaves. Order seeds and plants for spring.

and that's assuming you don't slack during the seven years. But though seeded weeds are the most numerous, they are by no means the worst.

New Gardens

Anyone with a brand new, uncultivated plot is well advised to spend the first year just getting rid of any serious weeds. Once you have plants in place it can be impossible to remove weeds which multiply with long underground roots. While the earth is bare you can repeatedly dig and remove the roots; or use a systemic weedkiller though the least decorative method is one of the most effective: cover the ground with black polythene, or an old carpet, for 6 spring or summer months. Ideal for those who have moved into a house with carpets they hate, though it may not endear you to the neighbours.

Seeded Weeds

To keep weeds to a minimum have well-fed healthy plants which are fairly close planted. Where there have to be spaces, such as around roses or shrubs, the ground can be mulched or use ground cover plants to fill in gaps.

For vegetables peg down sheets of black polythene, cut slits in it and plant the seedlings through the slits – or run strips of polythene between seeded rows. Make sure the ground was watered first and put down slug pellets before you lay the plastic or slugs will decimate the careful rows.

★ To avoid introducing new weeds let any container-grown plant stand for several weeks before planting and remove the weeds which emerge.

Troublesome Weeds

Regrettably, sometimes chemicals are the only answer. Some of the weeds listed here cannot be removed from among established plants in any other way.

★ Shepherd's purse, in particular, should be kept clear of vegetable patches as it belongs to the brassica family and can harbour clubroot.

Using Weedkillers

The great drive of the chemical companies is towards weedkillers which are highly selective and only kill particular types of plant. But the main types of weedkillers are these:

Contact weedkillers, such as paraquat, kill any foliage they touch.

Residual weedkillers contain chemicals which do not break down quickly, so they will stop weeds germinating. These are used on drives and stone paths. They can be selective or non-selective. Some non-selective forms, such as sodium chlorate, dissolve easily in water and leach both downwards and sideways through the soil, putting at risk plants growing nearby – and their effects last for 6 months. Such chemicals are to be avoided unless there is no alternative.

Dandelions Dock Sorrel	These can be dug out, but may re-grow if any of the tap root is left. Use a systemic weedkiller based on glyphosate (Tumbleweed).
Bindweed, Couch grass, Creeping thistle, Ground elder, Horsetail, Stinging nettles	Hand weeding these creeping roots is depressingly like pruning: remove one shoot and you get two. Repeated digging on bare ground may remove them. Otherwise a systemic weedkiller is the answer. Use glyphosate (Tumbleweed) or Fisons' Killer for problem weeds. Apply these when there are several leaves showing but the top growth isn't enormous, and repeat the application at least once a week for 3 weeks. It works slowly. It also needs 6 hours without rain, after you apply it, as it is absorbed slowly.
Oxalis	This leaves little bulbils which sprout fresh plants. A systemic weedkiller may be the only way to get rid of it.
Creeping buttercup, Brambles	Both these send out runners which root avidly, and only relentless digging will get rid of them. Otherwise buttercups may need glyphosate and brambles a brushwood killer.

Systemic (translocated) weedkillers are put on the foliage of deep-rooted weeds, and sink into the plant, and travel through the whole system. But it may take several applications to make a tough weed die. Both selective and non-selective ones exist.

★ Never increase the dose of a weedkiller to make it work faster. The doses are scientific; if you add more or less you will make it work **less** well.

★ If you need a funnel for weedkiller cut the top from a plastic squash bottle, just below the 'shoulders', for one you can use and throw away.

DRYING FLOWERS

There is something very satisfying about preserving some of the blooms of summer against the bleak days of winter. A great mystery is sometimes made out of the business of drying flowers, but very few demand special techniques, and some, like teasels and honesty, even dry themselves in the flower bed if you are prepared to leave them there – a policy for which tits reward you with a fine display of acrobatics as they rootle out the seeds from the teasel heads.

Below are the main methods, and some of the plants you can use them on. But experiment: sometimes two different methods bring out totally different colours in the same plant.

The flowers or leaves must be picked when *dry* and in *perfect* condition, and usually *just* before they are fully open.

Cool Air Drying

Tie the stems firmly in small bunches and hang them in a cool, dark, airy place. This is the method to use for any plant with seeds which might ripen and burst from their anchors if in the warm. If plants don't lend themselves to bunching fill a big container with perfectly dry sand and stick the stems in this. But don't use this for heads which may droop as they dry.

Hot Air Drying

For hot air drying hang bunches in a hot dry place, such as an airing cupboard, or above a boiler (but not if they could cause a fire hazard). This removes the moisture before a flower has time to fade. So it keeps the colours of flowers far better than using cool air.

Preserving in Glycerine

For this method pick twigs in summer when they have lost their youthful tenderness but are still perfect, with the sap rising in them. They will fail to take up the glycerine properly later in the season.

You need 1 part glycerine (from a pharmacy) to 2 parts hot water. Mix the water and glycerine and put the mixture in a tall narrow container which will allow the liquid to come 10-13 cm (4-5 in) up the woody stem. Put the stems into this mixture and leave this somewhere dry and not too light. When any sweatiness appears on the surface they are ready; hang them up in a paper bag to await use.

Preserving in Borax

Drying flowers in borax is an excellent way of preserving flowers. Some do go brown, but others stay astonishingly true to their summer colours.

Put an inch of household borax (from a pharmacy) in a box, place the flowers on it, sift over more borax to cover the petals in a deep layer, then put the box in a warm airing cupboard. The best way to immerse the flowers in the borax varies with the shape of the flower.

Daisy shapes can be stood on their faces with only a relatively short stem left, while delphiniums need to lie on their sides. Some may even prefer to be hung so they dangle in it.

Leave the flowers in the borax for 10 days, until the petals are dry enough to have a slight rustle. Support them underneath as you lift them very carefully from the borax. Use an artist's brush to brush off the borax. Then store them carefully in a cardboard box out of reach of dust. (Borax is a fairly mild chemical but, as always, keep it away from children and pets and wash after using it.)

Pressing

For pressing flowers and leaves all you need is a big book or a well-trodden rug on a dry floor. The rug method is ideal for ferns and larger flowers. Put newspaper under the rug, spread the ferns on it, put more newspaper on top, and cover it with the rug until the leaves are dry and pressed. For flowers use clean paper lest they take up the newsprint.

Book pressing is ideal for small flowers like pansies. Put them between paper in the pages of a big book, and weight it with more books.

Both methods are lovely for children. There is the fascination of flowers almost miraculously preserving their colour and it takes only a touch of glue for even the least artistic to produce an attractive picture.

Special Exceptions

Bulrushes easily burst into fluffy seeds. To prevent this, spray them very well, with a strong-hold hair spray, hang them in a cool place, until totally dried. Use this for any seed head which may not hold.

Iris foetidissima needs a different cosmetic treatment: use a dab of clear nail varnish to glue on its brilliant orange berries just as they show.

Physalis (Chinese lantern) need to be picked before they seem ready. That is just when the *first* lantern turns orange. They will all gain brilliant colour as they dry.

For **honesty** wait until it is fully dry, then rub each disc-shaped seed case to remove the dull outer coating and reveal the silvery disc within.

Plants to choose

Cool Air Drying	Warm Air Drying
Acanthus	Clarkia
Achillea	Delphinium
Acrolinium	Eryngium
Alchemilla	Gypsophila
Allium	Sedum
Anaphalis	
Artichokes (globe)	**Borax Preserving**
Cow parsley	Cornflower – blue
Fennel	forms
Golden rod	Dahlia
Grasses and	Delphinium – the
rushes	best method
Gypsophila	Montbretia
Delphinium	Parsley
Eryngium	Rue
Helichrysum	
Honesty	**Glycerine**
Hydrangeas	Beech
Nigella seed heads	Box
Poppies – seed	Camellia
heads	Eucalyptus
Physalis	Fatsia
Rhodanthe	Ferns (variable)
Rushes	Garrya
Sedum	Love lies bleeding
Many seed heads	Mahonia
Stachys	Nigella
Statice	
Teasels	

Arranging

Push large stems into dry sand, which weights the container as well as supporting the flowers. For lighter sprays in cottage-style arrangements simply make a lattice of sellotape across the vase. Formal arrangements need the support of *brown* oasis held in position with wire or by a pin holder.

Wiring Flowers

Florist's wire can replace the stem. Good garden centres and flower shops sell it; so do flower arranging societies.

For flowers such as helichrysum a gauge such as 210 mm works well. The wire can either be pushed up through a hollow stem, or it can be pushed down through the flower – won't show. The trick is to bend the very tip of the wire into a tiny hook, so that when you pull it down to hide it, it will not pull out completely.

INDOOR PLANTS

Being drawn from different climates all over the world, houseplants demonstrate even more vividly than garden plants the huge diversity of plant preferences. Among them are plants which love heat, hate heat, want jungle conditions, prefer a desert and abhor the light. To get the best from them mimic the conditions they originally came from. So, for example, you can grow heat-loving garden plants, such as geraniums, very successfully in a conservatory, but to put a shade-loving houseplant there would condemn it to death. Not all houses have the conditions to suit all houseplants, so it's wise to check the growing details before buying. Those which like full sun should also thrive in a conservatory. But for a good range of conservatory plants you need a specialist nursery, like Read's or Sunbeam (page 378). They can advise you best on what will suit your needs. Describing individual plant needs is outside the scope of this book. What follows are general points which houseplants have in common and the information needed to choose one to suit your situation.

Cleaning Indoor Plants

If dirt and dust accumulate it stops them breathing through their leaf pores. So they need to be kept clean.

Cacti, hairy-leaved plants and succulents: brush the dust off with a soft paintbrush and give cacti a wash and brush-up with clean water and a shaving brush.

Large smooth-leaved plants: brush dust off gently with a brush or duster, wipe with damp tissue or a product made to clean and shine the leaves.

Small smooth-leaved plants: brush off dust as above, shower *gently* but thoroughly or wrap a plastic bag firmly over the soil and, holding this in place, swish the leaves in a bath or bucket of tepid water.

Botanical Name	Common Name
Agapanthus	Blue African Lily
Aucuba	Spotted Laurel
Bromeliads	Urn Plants
Calceolaria	Slipper Flower
Chlorophytum	Spider Plant
Dieffenbachia	Dumb Cane
Fatsia	Castor Oil Plant
Hedera	Ivy
Impatiens	Busy Lizzie
Iresine	Chicken Gizzard
Maranta leuconeura	Prayer Plant
Monstera deliciosa	Swiss Cheese Plant
Myrtus	Myrtle
Pachystachys	Lollipop Plant
Pelargoniums	Geraniums
Philodendron scandens	Sweetheart Plant
Philodendron hastatum	Elephant's Ear
Sansevieria	Mother-in-Law's Tongue
Santapaulia	African Violet
Solanum	Winter Cherry
Spathiphyllum	Peace Lily
Syngonium	Goose Foot Plant
Thunbergia	Black-Eyed Susan
Tolmiea	Piggyback Plant

Conditions for Houseplants

As houseplants are hijacked from their native environment, it is only thrifty to choose plants which can be happy in the positions we provide. There are plants for almost any environment – except sitting on a television or next to a gas stove. Televisions get hot and plants don't like having their roots cooked and gas creates fumes which certain plants cannot tolerate. But the position they like isn't always the one we might choose for them. Pricey azaleas, for example, are far better suited to a loo than a sitting room.

★ If you want to check the relative light at different points in your rooms set a manually operated camera for a very fast film and using its light meter, compare the f-stop setting you would need at different points in the room.

Feeding

Houseplants need more food during the growing period than during the dormant months – which are usually October to March.

Don't feed at all for 2-3 months after repotting. If you have used a potting compost there will be enough food in the soil. Whatever food you use, follow the maker's instructions exactly and, if the soil is dry, water first then apply the fertilizer. Overdosing a plant, or giving fertilizer on dry soil, can burn its roots.

★ For thrift use a general liquid fertilizer, such as Liquinure, *carefully* diluted to the right strength for a very small quantity.

Pests and Diseases

If pests strike, you can try getting rid of them by putting a plastic bag over the soil, to hold the plant in its pot, and swishing the leaves in cool soapy water (pure soap not detergent). See pages 351-352 for other natural methods.

There are good houseplant insecticides. Fisons now produce an aerosol spray which can be used on succulents – which many such can't. Take the plant out of doors to spray it, and only use sprays made for houseplants.

Addresses and suggestions for further reading are at the ends of chapters.

Ideal Conditions for Indoor Plants

Sunny window ledge or very close to a sunny window facing south	Very close to an east or west window	Bright light but no direct sun (e.g. a little way into the room)	A fair distance from a sunny window or in a dull room	Right away from a window but in daylight	
Pilea (win), Anthurium (win), Citrus Impatiens (win), Kalanchoe (win) Poinsettia (win)	Croton, Coleus, Dracaena Palm, Capsicum, Ferns (if under 23°C, 72°F), Dieffenbachia (win), Hypoestes, Hippeastrum Impatiens (win), Kalanchoe (sum), Iresine, Pelargonium, Pilea (win), Sansevieria ★, Saintpaulia, Spathiphyllum (win)	Anthurium (sum), Aphelandra, Bromeliads ★, Begonias, Caladium, Dieffenbachia (sum), Gloxinia, Impatiens (sum), Peperomia, Maranta (win), Poinsettia (sum), Pilea, Sansevieria ★, Schefflera, Scindapsus, Syngonium – variegated, Spathiphyllum (sum)	Cyperus, Fittonia, Maranta (sum), Monstera, Philodendron, Sansevieria ★, Schefflera, Syngonium – all green	Ficus elastica ★, Sansevieria ★	Average central heating but using humidifiers to keep the air moist in summer and winter
Cacti and succulents, Zebrina ★, Nerium	Chlorophytum ★, Ficus elastica, Decora ★, Zebrina ★				Rooms heated to over 15°C (60°F) all year & *dry*
Cacti and succulents ★, Beaucarnea	Asparagus ★, Chlorophytum ★, Calceolaria, Coleus, Celosia, Solanum, Yucca, Ficus (tree type) ★, Spathyphyllum (winter), Thunbergia	Azalea, Chlorophytum ★, Cyclamen, Hedera ★, Aucuba, Fatsia ★, Hydrangea, Primula, Vines, Ficus (tree type) ★, Spathyphyllum (summer)	Aspidistra ★, Fatshedera ★, Fatsia ★, Hedera helix ★, Helexine ★, Tolmiea	Aspidistra ★	Rooms usually at 10°-15°C (50°-60°F) and slightly cooler at night
Carex, Fatshedera (win) ★, Agapanthus	Carex, Fatshedera (win) ★, Cacti and succulents ★, Heliotropium, Myrtus	Acorus, Aspidistra ★, Aucuba, Carex, Fatshedera (sum) ★, Ophiopogon, Clivia, Saxifraga ★, Tolmiea	Aspidistra ★, Aucuba, Tolmiea	Aspidistra ★, Tolmiea	A very cool room, around 5°C (40°F) to 10°C (50°F) in winter

★ Means the plant is very easy to care for. NB. sum = summer; win = winter.

Potting Up

Repotting is only necessary when a plant outgrows its pot. If the roots are a closely felted mass on the surface it is pot bound. This doesn't always mean you should put it in a bigger pot. Some plants flower best that way. So check. To repot take a pot only one size up.

Watering

Most plants will accept water from above or below, but cyclamen, African violets and gloxinias object to the top of their compost being wet, so they must only be watered via the saucer. Either way, use room temperature water and check the saucer 30 minutes later and

Common Problems with Indoor Plants

Problem	Cause	Problem	Cause
Brown tips or edges to leaves	Dry air Bruising from handling	**Lower leaves drying and falling**	Lack of light or water More heat than it likes
Brown and yellow tips and edges	Any fault in culture can cause this; look for other symptoms	**Rotting stems**	Disease, fostered by more water than is needed – especially in winter
Curling leaves which fall	Less heat than it needs More water than it likes Draughts	**Rusty or reddish streaks on amaryllis**	A bulb mite – destroy the bulb
Dull, lifeless, faded leaves	More light than it likes Red spider mite Dirt on the leaves	**Slime on the pot**	Too much water is lingering
Flower buds falling	Drier air than it likes Less water than it needs Less light than it needs Shock/Insect damage	**Spots on the leaves** – dry light-brown – soft dark-brown – cream or white – like blisters	 Less water than it needs More water than it needs The water was too chilly for it Spraying leaves which dislike water on them Disease
Flowers wilting fast	Less water than it needs Less light than it needs Drier air than it likes More heat than it likes	**Variegated leaves turning plain green**	Less light than it needs
Flowers failing to be made	Less light than it needs Drier air than it likes More food than it needs Too much room in the pot	**White crust on the pot**	Hard water Overfeeding
Leaves falling off suddenly	Shock – quite common on being moved, also if moved from shade to sun Much less water than it needs	**Wilting leaves**	Too little water More sunlight than it likes More heat than it likes Drier air than it likes Pest damage Water not draining properly
Little or no growth – in winter – other times	Normal Less food than it needs Less light than it needs Less water than it needs.	**Yellow leaves** – which stay on – which fall	 Hard water when it dislikes it Calcium in the compost when it dislikes it Old age of leaf – quite normal More water than it likes Cold draughts

throw away any water which is lying there. Sitting in water can kill them.

Most plants like their soil to be *just* moist all the time. But azaleas, for example, like to be positively wet. Dunk them every day in a bucket up to their compost level, leave for an hour and drain. In contrast, Swiss cheese plants like to become rather dry between waterings. Check on each plant's special preferences.

There are several ways to keep plants happy while you are away on holiday. How long they last depends greatly on the weather and the type of plant. In summer move plants into a cool room, but if you are turning down the heating in winter find them a warmish one. In summer a bathroom is often ideal.

- Put plastic in the bath (to keep it clean), then a thick layer of wet newspapers or bath towels. Water the plants and stand them on the wet surface.
- Put a thick layer of peat in the bottom of a container much bigger than the plant pot. Stand the pot on the peat and fill round the sides with peat. Water so the peat is moist right through.
- Push a length of material into the hole on the base of a pot, as a wick. The pot then sits on the lid of a carton full of water and the wick goes through a hole in the lid and into the water.
- Stand a bucket of water higher than the plants. Tie pieces of string to the bucket handle so that one end goes to the bottom of the bucket and the other goes down to a pot plant.

Addresses and suggestions for further reading are at the ends of chapters.

USEFUL ADDRESSES AND BOOKS

General Organizations

The **Back Pain Association** has a leaflet for gardeners. (address on page 590)

Common Ground, 45 Shelton Street, London WC2H 9HI Tel: 071 379 3109, is dedicated to preserving the distinctiveness of Britain's regions – especially its flora.

Cottage Garden Society, 5 Nixon Close, Thornhill, Dewsbury, W. Yorks WF12 0JA Tel: 0924 468469, promotes cottage gardening, has a plant-finding service for members M£L, A, Ad.

The Garden Centre Association Ltd, 38 Carey Street, Reading, Berks RG1 7JS Tel: 0734 393900, tries to maintain standards in garden centres and has an inspection policy. Its members conform to a helpful code of practice and check the rules.

The Garden History Society, 5 The Knoll, Hereford HR1 1RU Tel: 0432 354479 – M£M, M, Lect, H, Visits. Pressure group for preservation of historic gardens.

Henry Doubleday Research Association, National Centre for Organic Gardening, Ryton Gardens, Ryton-on-Dunsmore, Coventry CV8 3LG Tel: 0203 303517, promotes and researches organic gardening. Provides mail order seeds, organic fertilizers and pesticides. M£L, M, Ad, Inf, B. (P.353)

Horticultural Therapy, Gould's Ground, Vallis Way, Frome, Somerset BA11 3DW Tel: 0373 64782, advises those whose age or disability makes gardening harder.

National Association of Allotment and Leisure Gardeners Ltd, Hunters Road, Corby, Northants NN17 1JE Tel: 0536 66576 – has some 1,500 societies around Britain. They also obtain bulk buys of seeds, chemicals and garden sundries which can considerably cut the cost of gardening. M£L, M, A, Disc, legal.

National Federation of Gateway Clubs, 117 Golden Lane, London EC1Y 0RT, advises on gardening for the disabled.

Royal Horticultural Society (RHS), 80 Vincent Square, London SW1P 2PE Tel: 071 834 4333 – Britain's premier gardening body. M£H, M, B, Ad, Lib, free entry to the gardens at Wisley and summer flower shows. (P.345)

The Soil Association, 86 Colston Street, Bristol BS1 5BB Tel: 0272 290661, is an international organization to promote organic market gardening and farming. It sets standards for commercial producers. Members can obtain a list of those members who produce organic food commercially, but it will advise smallholders and anyone can obtain the paperback they publish giving sources of organic produce. M£M, M, B.

Sports Turf Research Institute, Bingley, W. Yorks BD16 1AU Tel: 0274 565131, for advice on lawns. (P.349)

The Woodland Trust, Autumn Park, Dysart Road, Grantham, Lincolnshire NG31 6LL Tel: 0476 74297 – will plant trees to commemorate someone, and promotes the protection of woodland.

There are also numerous organizations devoted to individual flowers, from auriculas to irises. The **Royal Horticultural Society** has their details.

Useful Books

Tony Biggs, *Vegetables*, Mitchell Beazley.

Christopher Brickell (Director General of the RHS), *Pruning*, Mitchell Beazley. Few books manage to be totally clear and very comprehensive. This is both.

Christopher Brickell (ed), *The Royal Horticultural Society's Concise Encyclopaedia of Gardening Techniques*, Mitchell Beazley.

Philip McMillan Browse, *Plant Propagation*, Mitchell Beazley.

Dr Stefan Buczacki, *Gardeners' Questions Answered*, Collins.

Dr Stefan Buczacki and Keith Harris, *Collins Guide to Pests, Diseases and Disorders of Garden Plants*, Collins.

Beth Chatto, *The Damp Garden*, Dent.

Beth Chatto, *The Dry Garden*, Dent.

Brian Davis, *The Kingfisher Guide to Garden Plants*, Kingfisher.

The Good Gardener's Guide, Consumers' Association, lists good nurseries both by area and by speciality, with detailed information on what each offers, and says which have gardens to view. Invaluable to anyone planting up a garden.

Penelope Hobhouse, *Colour in Your Garden*, Collins.

Gertrude Jekyll, *Wood and Garden*, Papermac.

Christopher Lloyd, *The Well-Tempered Garden*, Penguin.

Christopher Lloyd, *The Well-Chosen Garden*, Hamish Hamilton.

Chris Philip and Tony Lord, *The Plant Finder*, Headman, tells you the nurseries which stock hard-to-find plants: invaluable.

Diana Saville, *The Illustrated Garden Planter*, Penguin, groups plants by their use.

Allen Sawyer, *The Plant Buyer's Directory*, Ebury Press, gives plants grouped by flowering season.

Alan Titchmarsh, *The Allotment Gardener's Handbook*, Penguin.

Bulbs and Friends

Avon Bulbs, Burnt House Farm Mid Lambrook, South Peverton, Somerset TA13 5HE Tel: 0460 42177, sells a wide range of bulbs. (P.345)

Walter Blom & Sons Ltd, Coombelands Nurseries, Thurleigh Road, Milton Ernest, Beds MK44 1RQ Tel: 0234 782424, sells a wide range of bulbous plants, particularly tulips. (P.345)

Broadleigh Gardens, Barr House, Bishops Hull, Taunton, Somerset TA4 1AE Tel: 0823 286231, sells many bulbous plants, foliage plants, Californian irises. (P.345)

Useful Books
Brian Matthew, *The Year Round Bulb Garden*, Souvenir Press.
Martin Rix, *Growing Bulbs*, Croom Helm.

Conservatory Plants

Read's Nurseries, Hales Hall, Loddon, Norfolk NR14 6QW Tel: 050846 395, specializes in plants for conservatories. (P.375)
Sunbeam Nurseries, Bristol Road, Frampton Cotterell, Avon BS17 2AU Tel: 0454 776926, majors in plants for conservatories. (P.375)

Useful Books
Kenneth A. Beckett, *Growing Under Glass*, Mitchell Beazley.
Kenneth A. Beckett, *The RHS Encyclopaedia of House-plants*, Century.
Dr D.G. Hessayon, *The House Plant Expert*, PBI.

Flowers and Flower Arranging

The best way to send flowers is to look in the Yellow Pages for a florist which says Interflora or Teleflower. There is little to choose between them: both have high service charges on top of the cost of the flowers themselves, and both will send flowers overseas as well as within Britain. If your Yellow Pages is mislaid, or you want to complain, the head offices are:
British Teleflower Service Ltd, Unit 35, Romsey Industrial Estate, Great Bridge Road, Romsey, Hants SO5 0HR Tel: 0794 511114, mainly handles complaints.
Interflora, Interflora House, Watergate, Sleaford, Lincs NG34 7TB Tel: 0529 304141, mainly handles complaints.
National Association of Flower Arranging Societies, 21 Denbigh Street, London SW1V 2HF Tel: 071 828 5145 – G, Rg, L, M, H.

Gardens to Visit

Cottage Garden Society and **Garden History Society**, see page 377.
National Gardens Scheme, Hatchlands Park, East Clandon, Guildford, Surrey GU4 7RT Tel: 0483 211535, lists numerous private and National Trust gardens, in England and Wales, which open for charity; guide published February. (P.345)
The National Trust, 36 Queen Anne's Gate, London SW1H 9AS Tel: 071 222 9251; Membership enquiries: P.O.Box 39, Bromley BR1 1NH Tel: 081 464 1111. In addition to having wonderful houses open to the public, the Trust also owns some of Britain's loveliest gardens. They not only have wonderful landscape gardens but also some specializing in particular aspects of gardening or particular flowers: such as the remarkable garden of old roses at Mottisfont. Members get in free, non-members pay. Open to the public as well as to members. The Trust also sells

some excellent gardening books and puts on events. RC, M£L-M,M. (P.345)
National Trust for Scotland, 5 Charlotte Square, Edinburgh EH2 4DU Tel: 031 226 5922, has some beautiful gardens and it will also plant a tree or shrub to commemorate someone. (P.345)
Royal Horticultural Society Garden, Wisley, Nr Woking, Surrey GU23 6QB Tel: 0483 224234, keeps Sundays for members only, but is open to everyone the rest of the week from 10.00 am to 4.30 pm in winter – or until later as days lengthen. And only closes on Christmas Day. (P.345)

Useful Book
Historic Houses, Castles and Gardens, Papermac.

Hardy Plants and Friends

Alpine Garden Society, The AGS Centre, Avonbank, Pershore, Worcs WR10 3JP Tel: 0386 554790.
Architectural Plants, Cooks Farm, Nuthurst, Horsham, West Sussex RH1 6LH Tel: 0403 891772, specializes in striking hardy exotics which give form to a garden.
Blooms of Bressingham, Bressingham Gardens, Diss, Norfolk IP22 2AB Tel: 037 988 464, sells a good range of herbaceous plants and also has a garden to view.
Beth Chatto Gardens, Elmstead Market, Colchester, Essex CO7 7DB Tel: 0206 822007, sells unusual herbaceous plants and a lovely garden to view.
Hardy Plant Society, Bank Cottage, Great Comberton, Nr Pershore, Worcs WR10 3DP (no phone).
Herb Society, P.O. Box 599, London SW11 4RW (no phone).
Kelway Nurseries, Barrymore, Langport, Somerset TA10 9EZ Tel: 0458 250521 – irises, peonies and daffodils are the specialities, but also sells other bulbs and border plants.
Scotts Nurseries (Merriott) Ltd, Merriott, Somerset TA16 5PL Tel: 0460 72306, sells herbaceous plants and an unusually large range of fruit.
Philip Tivey & Sons Nurseries, 28 Wanlip Road, Syston, Nr Leicester LE7 1PA Tel: 0533 692968, sells dahlias and chrysanthemums.
See also **Henry Doubleday Research Association** (page 377).

Useful Books
Margery Fish, *Ground Cover Plants*, Collingridge – a marvellous introduction to ground cover.
Christopher Lloyd, *Foliage Plants*, Penguin.

Mail Order Seedsmen

Chiltern Seeds, Bortree Stile, Ulverston, Cumbria LA12 7PB Tel: 0229 56946 (CC) – their selection includes many British wild flowers.
Thompson & Morgan, Poplar Lane, Ipswich, Suffolk IP8 0BA Tel: 0473 688821, (CC) – its large flower and vegetable catalogue includes many unusual seeds.

Unwins Seeds Ltd, Histon, Cambridge CB4 4ZZ Tel: 0945 588522 (CC).

Roses and Friends

David Austin Roses Ltd, Bowling Green Lane, Albrighton, Wolverhampton WV7 3HB Tel: 0902 373931, sells a wide range of roses, including many period roses. (P.361)

Peter Beales Roses, London Road, Attleborough, Norfolk NR17 1AY Tel: 0953 454707, sells a wide range of roses, including many period roses. (P.361)

British Rose Growers Association, c/o Cants of Colchester Ltd, 303 Mile End Road, Colchester, Essex CO4 5EA Tel: 0206 8440088, sells an inexpensive booklet called 'Find That Rose' listing over 2,000 roses and which nurseries sell them. (P.361)

R. Harkness & Co Ltd, The Rose Gardens, Hitchin, Herts SG4 0JT Tel: 0462 420402, is a rose specialist, and will export. (P.361)

E.B. Le Grice (Roses) Ltd, Norwich Road, North Walsham, Norfolk NR28 0DR Tel: 0692 402591, sells a good range of roses. (P.361)

Mattock's Roses Ltd, Nuneham Courtenay, Oxford OX44 9PY Tel: 086 738 265, sells a good range of roses. (P.361)

Notcutts Nurseries Ltd, Woodbridge, Suffolk IP12 4AF Tel: 0394 383600, sells a range of trees, shrubs and roses, and one of the most informative catalogues in the business. (P.361)

See also **Kelway Nurseries**. (P.378)

Shrubs, Trees, Fruit and Friends

National Fruit Centre, Brogdale Orchards, Brogdale, Faversham, Kent ME13 8XZ Tel: 0795 535286, encourages the planting of the best traditional British regional varieties. Open days, in season, for buying and tasting, instruction days, festivals. Sells unusual varieties. For list write with sae (don't phone).

J.O. Sherrard and Son Ltd, Wantage Road, Donninton, Newbury, Berks RG16 9BE Tel: 0635 41097, sells a large range of shrubs and trees. (P.363)

Steele and Brodie, The Beehive Works, Kilmany Road, Wormit, Newport-on-Tay, Fife DD6 8PG Tel: 0382 541728, stock the pheromone trap Trappit.

See also **Scotts Nurseries**. (P.378)

Useful Books
Brian Davis, *The Gardener's Illustrated Encyclopaedia of Trees and Shrubs*, Viking – all the facts a gardener really needs plus excellent photographs: invaluable.

Fred Roach, *Cultivate Fruits of Britain*, Basil Blackwell, a classic, and substantial survey of the whole field including many almost lost varieties.

Brian Vines, *Trees for Small Gardens*, Pelham.

The Apple Source Book, edited and published by Common Ground, 45 Shelton Street, London WC2H 9HJ, tells you which apples have been traditional in which regions and which nurseries supply them.

Orchards: A Guide to Local Conservation, edited and published by Common Ground.

Tools and Sundries

The British Agrochemicals Association, 4 Lincoln Court, Lincoln Road, Peterborough PE1 2RP Tel: 0733 349225, has a consumer information service with free and low-cost leaflets.

Fiskars UK Ltd, Customer Service Department, Brocastle Avenue, Bridgend, Mid Glamorgan, Wales CF31 3YN Tel: 0656 655595, will repair and sharpen Fiskars and Wilkinson Sword tools sent by post or tell you where to find a local sharpening service. (P.367)

Fisons PLC Horticulture Division, Paper Mill Lane, Bramford, Ipswich IP8 4BZ Tel: 0473 830492 – the consumer information service for both Fison and Murphy.

The HotteRotter, The Old Rectory, Bryn, Abergavenny, Gwent NP7 9AP Tel: 0873 840328. (P.360)

ICI Garden Products has a consumer information service with useful booklets. (See Pests, p.218)

John Innes Manufacturers' Association, Lonks View House, Harrogate, N. Yorks HG2 8HR, provides information on using John Innes Potting Composts.

Natural Pest Control Ltd, Yapton Road, Barnham, Bognor Regis, West Sussex PO22 0BQ Tel: 0243 553250, supplies predators to control insect pests. (P.353)

If you don't live in a nautical area rope can be hard to find but **W.R. Outhwaite and Son**, Town Foot, Hawes, N. Yorks DL8 3NT Tel: 0969 667487, sells ropes of every kind.

The Royal Horticultural Society has a list of companies supplying insect predators. (address P.377)

Wilkinson Sword, Brunel Road, London W3 7UH Tel: 081 749 1061. (P.367)

Wolf Tools, Alton Road, Ross-on-Wye, Herefordshire HR9 5NP Tel: 0989 767600, services and sharpens its own tools. (P.366)

See also **Henry Doubleday Research Association** and **National Association of Allotment and Leisure Gardeners** (P.377).

Useful Book
Guide to Gardening Without Chemicals, Consumers' Association.

Crafts

Basic Sewing • Crochet • Embroidery and Tapestry • Knitting • Knots • Patchwork • Soft Furnishing

BASIC SEWING

This section is designed to fill in some of the gaps left by patterns, and to explain the basic techniques and stitches, plus the key methods used in mending. There isn't space for a complete sewing course, only for the problems which occur most often.

Bias Strips

Making bias strips for binding or for enclosing piping cord takes a great deal more fabric that you might suppose. Buy generously, or use newspaper to work out the amount you need. Either:

● Take a square or rectangle of material and fold in a triangle as illustrated. Pin and cut along the fold. Sew the triangle to the other end.
● Draw lines, parallel to the angle you have cut, the width you need. Cut the strips out.
● Machine your bias strips as illustrated.

Or fold fabric selvedge to selvedge, and seam – so you have a tube. Cut round the tube at a precise diagonal (fold the fabric to mark this) until you have a long diagonal strip which can be cut to the width needed.

Button Sewing

Basic Buttons

I once had a friend whose husband's buttons never seemed to stay on for two days together: his wife sewed the buttons on without a shank. Unless you want to make a career of resewing buttons give each one a shank. When you draw the first thread through there should be about ½ cm of thread between the button and the fabric (*more* on a thick garment, like a coat). This starts the shank.

Hold the button between your first two fingers, *keeping the shank as long as before*. When you have done enough stitches to make the button secure, wind the thread several times round the shank, between the button and the garment, then finish the thread off with several small tight stitches into the back.

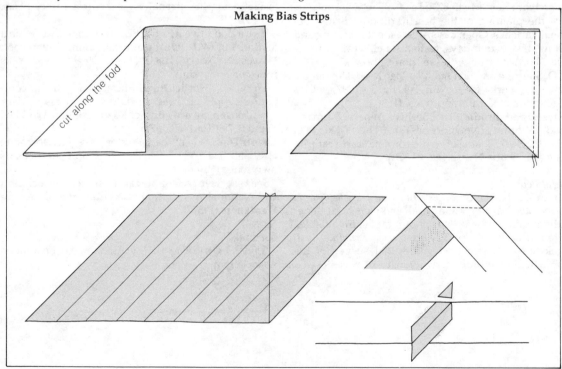

Making Bias Strips

cut along the fold

Addresses and suggestions for further reading are at the ends of chapters.

★ If a button has to take a lot of weight on a heavy coat, use a small flat button on the inside to take the strain. This is sewn on as you sew on the upper button, so the thread goes through its holes when it goes to the back of the fabric. It lies flat against the cloth with no shank.

★ An old tailoring trick is to have a block of beeswax, from a hardware store, and rub the thread across it. For a waxed thread will last far longer.

Buttons on Soft Fabrics

Soft fabrics, such as jersey which may be pulled by a button, can have a smaller reinforcing button put on the inside (as above). You can also support a button by putting a circle of leather cut from an old kid glove on the inside or face the button edge with tape or ribbon.

Buttons in Space

If you have to sew a button on a yawning gap in a child's shirt don't despair. Just sew it on to a length of matching strong tape. Then pin the tape on the inside of the hole, so the button goes through it, and hem in place.

Chiffon, Tulle, Net, Mohair

Fine fabrics need special handling.

- If transparent fabric needs an ordinary flat hem, allow twice the hem you think you need. With the turn-in the full depth of the hem, its edge comes on the fold and no line will show against the light. Chiffon, however, needs a rolled hem and tulle normally needs no hem at all.
- Cut these fabrics out with very sharp scissors or it will be tricky to get a straight line.
- You have to tack these materials as pins fall out. Have the fabric resting on a table to prevent it going out of shape.
- Sew with the finest needle you can and set a loose tension and small stitch, with a slight zigzag for machining chiffon and tulle, to allow for stretching.
- If fine fabrics won't slip through a machine use strips of tissue paper to give the seam body. Whether you need the paper on top, underneath or on both sides varies with the fabric. Afterwards tear off the paper. If you don't have tissue paper, newspaper will do the job – but newsprint may come off on the fabric.

★ On chiffon pin from the seam out towards the allowance: or pin holes may show in the body of the fabric.

Collars

For a collar to lie well the upper layer of fabric must be slightly larger than the lower one – it has to travel a little bit farther. There are two ways to ensure this.

- When pinning the upper layer (and its attached interfacing), match the true outer seam line of the underside with a line about 3 mm (1/8 in) closer to the edge on the upper fabric (tapering to nothing at each collar point).
- If a collar is to have a fold, fold it along the neck fold, tacking the raw edges together. If the collar is then sewn in place it should lie perfectly.

Darning

Darning is rather unfashionable. But there is something rather satisfying in keeping a beloved jumper going with a judicious darn or two.

★ Shrink darning yarn before use as it might shrink in the wash. Ten minutes in a steamer over boiling water should do the trick – but don't get it wet. Dry it thoroughly before using.

★ You can double the life of a jumper by sewing leather elbow patches on it while it's still fairly new (it is much harder to sew them on to the curve of an old and stretched sleeve). Good haberdashers sell ready-made leather patches which wash well and are ready perforated for sewing.

Dutch Darning

By far the best form of darning is Dutch darning, in which the darning thread follows the path of the knitting wool – as in Grafting page 399. It is very easy when the knitting is just thin. But for a hole you need to thread a knitting needle through each row from one side to the other, and sew over it, then sew the stitches into the row above. This is considerably trickier. Darn well into the area which is unthinned. Stop each row at a different point so that there is no hard edge and match the wool perfectly, then the repair will be almost invisible. But do use a round-ended needle.

★ The trick for threading a needle with darning wool is to fold the wool over the needle. Pinch it together firmly and slide it off the point of the needle, then push this flattened loop through the eye.

Standard Darning

Basic darning is only a little faster than Dutch darning and shows far more. Use a round-ended needle, which won't cut the threads, rather than a darning needle, and stretch the area over a darning mushroom. Take the thread to and fro across the gap using little running stitches at either side of the hole, and going well beyond the weak area. Keep the threads parallel and close together, and leave a little loop when you return, to allow for pull during wear. When the hole is filled go back *across* it in the same way, but run the needle over and under the threads it crosses – like weaving.

Elastic

The traditional way to **insert elastic** into, say, a pair of knickers is to stitch it to the eye of a bodkin and thread the bodkin through. But pinning on a safety-pin and threading it through is much quicker. To **replace elastic** just sew or pin the new elastic to one end of the old, then just pull out the old, pull in the new.

Feather Fillings

Feathers have an extraordinary capacity to work their way through fabric. Only very closely woven fabric, such as pillow ticking, will frustrate them. An extra precaution is to rub the inside of the fabric thoroughly with beeswax before stuffing it.

If you have to transfer feathers from one pillow to another be prepared for them to fly. One way to avoid this is to make matching openings in the two pillows, sew the two openings mouth to mouth and push the feathers through from one to the other. A faster way was devised by an ingenious manageress of a bookshop in the Midlands. She cleaned her vacuum cleaner, removed the bag from it, attached a pillow in its place and sucked the feathers out of the old container – with an extension nozzle – straight into the new one.

Hems

The techniques for finishing a hem vary according to the type and thickness of the fabric, and whether the hem is on a fairly straight line or round a curve. But before sewing, trim the hem allowance so that an even amount will be turned up all round.

★ Full skirts drop where they are on the bias. So hang them up for a few days, to drop, before the hem is put up.

Human anatomy is much less even than we might suppose. For the best hemline, wear the garment and the shoes you intend to wear with it, and get someone to mark an even distance up *from the floor* with tailor's chalk, and a long ruler.

Easing Fullness
If a skirt is full, extra fabric has to be eased in – binding should be attached first.

1 Run gathering threads round the upper edge of the hem. Draw them up so the turned-up edge fits perfectly. Pin it down. Tack it in position. Press the edge in place. This is a good method when there is only a little extra fullness to be lost, and on wool you may find that pressing makes the easing perfectly flat. The hem can then be herring boned (see right).
2 Pin up the hem, matching seams to seams and also matching the straight of the material (i.e. the vertical weave). Take lots of tiny 'darts' to ease in the fullness between the pinning. Pin, press, and sew them down.
3 A very slight amount of extra fabric can be disposed of by making your hem stitch a little to the right of where it would normally be. (The left for left-handers.)

Plain Hem

This is a hem for lightweight fabrics. Turn the hem up on the marked line and pin it in place. Trim it even if necessary. Turn the upper edge in less than 1 cm (½ in).

Then press and pin it all round, taking darts as shown above if needs be. Perfectionists tack the hem but, at a pinch, you can get away with pinning only – unless it's on a very full skirt or a very soft fabric. Try the garment on, check the hem and adjust if necessary. Hem stitch in place as shown.

Some people hem most comfortably with the lower edge of the hem towards them; others with the garment towards them. The stitch ends up the same, either way.

Bias-edged Hems
A bias-edged hem suits a fabric which would make a bulky line if it were turned in. Equally, if there isn't enough material to make a decent width of hem use wide bias binding. It should match as closely as possible.

Establish the depth of the hem and trim any unevenness. Open one folded edge of bias binding and pin it along the edge of the hem without stretching or puckering, and machine it along its fold line. Hem like a plain hem.

Herringboned Hem
Herringbone stitch is mainly used for stretch fabrics, as it stretches more than ordinary hemming. It is also good on trouser hems, and moderately thick fabrics which might create a ridge by other methods.

If the edge might fray oversew it. Otherwise pink it. Turn up the hem and pin leaving the upper edge flat, not turned under. Sew as illustrated, being careful not to pull the thread too tight or it will press the hem edge against the right side and form a ridge.

Addresses and suggestions for further reading are at the ends of chapters.

Blindstitched Hem

pinking

catch stitch

This is ideal for thick fabrics as the upper edge isn't pressed against the right side, so a ridge is avoided.

Finish the edge as for a herringboned hem (see illustration on page 382), but pin the hem in place 1 cm (½ in) down from its top edge. Tack if necessary. Fold back the fabric and sew as illustrated above, using catch stitch, being careful not to pull the thread too tight.

Rolled Hem

This is used on the edges of silk scarves and is used on chiffon and similar fabrics. Hold the fabric as illustrated for hem stitch and hem it finely, but just rolling the very edge under with your thumb and hemming it down. This is very tricky to do at first, but it gets easier.

Sometimes a tiny edge is turned in and machined down, then rolled by hand afterwards. Try both ways on scraps and see what suits you and your material.

Removing Hem Lines in Tough Fabrics

Margaret Thatcher says that the secret of being able to put hems up or down as fashion demands, is never to press a sharp edge in a hem. She has a point. But if a hem already has a sharp fold in tweed, undo the hem and open it out on an ironing board. Using a damp cloth, and an iron as hot as the fabric can stand, press the fold out as much as possible. Then place a thick piece of old-fashioned white cotton twine exactly along the foldline on the *right* side, and press with a damp cloth again. Remove the cloth and cover the area with the wooden 'banger' described on page 385. When the fabric is cool remove the wood and move on to the next section. The string should remove the dent. But if it doesn't, repeat the process. This time get someone to hold the string taut along the line while you hit it firmly into the line with the 'banger'.

★ To make a doubled thread less likely to twist into knots put a knot in each end separately.

Interfacing

Suit the weight to the fabric and the job in hand, and match the interlining to whether you will wash or dry clean the garment. The stick-on kinds can be useful for quickly made garments, like children's clothes, but the woven interlinings give a more professional finish.

On something like a cuff first attach the interlining to whichever side will be uppermost – then the interlining conceals the ridges created by the seam allowances.

Jersey

The ease with which jersey can be sewn varies with the fibre it is made of. Heavy jersey is easy; fine silk jersey is for the expert or the incautious.

● Use a ball-ended needle – pointed needles can cut the thread and make jersey ladder.
● Use a *very slight* zigzag stitch to give a little stretch to the seam. This prevents the thread breaking when the garment is worn.
● Very fine glove and lingerie jersey may need to be sewn with tissue paper, like chiffon (page 381).
● Hand oversew open seams.

★ Out of the packing it's hard to tell which needles are ball-ended and which aren't. For instant recognition put a dab of nail varnish near the top of all ball-ended ones.

Leather

When sewing leather there is no room for error. You can't pin it and you can't take stitches out without leaving a permanent line. The following instructions are for making soft leather garments. Heavy handbag and belt leather needs a heavy duty machine or hand sewing.

Patterns for Leather

As leather is limited in size you either have to choose a pattern with quite a few seams or be prepared to create seams where none exist. Plan extra seams carefully so they will match up front and back. As you can't unpick leather, the pattern needs to be carefully fitted and altered and if the leather is expensive, make the garment in calico first to make sure it fits perfectly.

Cutting Out Leather

First check the skin for flaws. If it has any, mark them exactly in chalk on the wrong side, so you can skirt round them. Place the pattern pieces on the leather so that any nap will run down the body on all the pieces. Stick them down with sellotape. Draw round the outline with school chalk – tailor's chalk contains grease and may mark leather. Make pencil holes at the marking points on the pattern and mark these points with chalk (or a biro works well on the wrong side). Cut out.

Sewing Leather

Those who can't sew a straight line should draw the seam lines with a ruler on the wrong side. Hold the sections together with paperclips, bulldog clips or sellotape bent over the seam allowance. But be sure to keep all these strictly to the seam allowance, to avoid marks.

To sew it, by hand or by machine, use a special three-sided leather needle – leather clings impossible to round needles. Choose the smallest one which will handle the thickness, and do a few samples to see what stitch length looks right.

Slit sewn darts open almost to the point, trim to look like seams and stick darts, hems and seams down with a touch of rubberized adhesive – unless the leather is fine enough for this to spoil its softness.

Machine Sewing

Ending Stitching

If it is left unfinished off machine stitching will undo just as much as hand sewing. When you come to the end of a dart, or any section which won't be reinforced with other stitching, sew the stitching back up for 1.5 cm (¾ in) to secure it.

Stitch Size

The size of stitch needs to be altered to suit each type of fabric. On the whole, thicker fabrics need longer stitches, but the texture also matters. So check the stitch on off-cuts of the same number of layers, then pull them open and see how it will look on seams.

Turning Corners

1 Stop just short of the corner.
2 Turn the large wheel, on the right of the machine, by hand, until the needle reaches the exact point you want. Then wind the needle *well into the fabric*. Lift the foot.
3 Turn the fabric until the foot is pointing down the next section. Bring the foot down and machine the next section.

Turning Points

Oddly, you will get a sharper effect by not sewing a point at all. Sew almost to the point. Turn the foot as above. Sew one or two stitches across the point – depending on the length of your stitches. Turn the corner again, and continue.

Exactly the same method is used when a neckline has a faced slash at the centre front.

★ The quick way to change from one sewing thread to another, on a machine, is to break the old thread near the reel, tie the new one to the broken end and pull the new thread through to the needle.

Marking Up Dressmaking

It saves a lot of time if all the markings are transferred to the fabric before the pattern is removed from it. This means you can match one section precisely to another with the minimum of fiddling about.

Where the pattern has a V notch, cut a V sticking out from the seam allowance.

Where there are holes or black dots the method of marking them needs to be chosen to suit the situation: there is no point in spending hours using method (1) on a child's cotton dress.

1 Have a long tacking cotton, on the double, and take a

stitch into each marking point, through the paper. In two layers of fabric you leave the ends *very* long. When you unpin the pattern you pull the two layers slightly apart and cut between them, leaving tags of cotton in both.

2 A soft lead pencil marks cottons beautifully and washes out if you aren't heavy-handed with it.
3 You can mark through the holes with tailor's chalk, but it tends to rub off, so sew up soon after.
4 A small spiked tracing wheel used with tailoring carbon paper gives a line of dots on basic cottons.

Matching Stripes *(and other patterns)*

Bold patterns or horizontal stripes or checks have to match at seams if the garment is to look good. This needs forethought when you cut the pieces out, and some careful pinning when you sew it. Buy enough material to shunt the pattern pieces about.

Cutting Out Stripes to Match

When you need patterns to match it is usually safest to cut each piece singly. With the fabric the wrong side up position and pin a pattern piece on to it. Mark on the paper the exact position of any major lines or patterns. Then mark the position of the pattern piece on the fabric with tailor's chalk. Then *turn the paper over* and place it for cutting the other half, using the marks you made on the paper to get a perfect match to stripes or patterns. When you have done this with all the pieces, and are sure that they will all fit on the fabric, cut the first piece of each pattern. Turn the uncut fabric over and place the paper patterns – with the fabric still attached – on the positions you chalked. Match the lines or patterns perfectly, pin in place and cut out.

Matching Stripes

Sometimes it is impossible to have stripes or a pattern meeting everywhere. So decide which part will most catch the eye and try to get the best match at that point. Then let the rest look after itself.

Sewing Patterns and Stripes

Books often insist that to get a perfect match you must tack your seams. This simply isn't true. Tacking is much looser than frequent pinning. You get the best match by

---

Addresses and suggestions for further reading are at the ends of chapters.

using long thin tailoring pins. Roughly pin your seam edge to edge. Then start at whatever point on the seam most catches the eye and exactly match the sections of fabric on the seam line, pinning so the pin is at right angles to the seam. Do this at small intervals all down the seam and machine it immediately. If you have used fine pins, the machine should go over them without breaking the needle.

Moygashel and Linen

These loosely woven fabrics have a dreadful tendency to fray. The only way to prevent this is to oversew the seams as soon as you cut out the pattern pieces. But first work out where you will need to trim them.

Patching Knees

When small boys are at that age when they are all knees and elbows abandon hope of them having decent trousers for everyday and patch them on the inside as soon as you buy them. They may look stiff in front but they will last twice as long without springing a hole. This is no situation for 'cordon bleu' sewing. An iron-on patch is the answer.

★ Once a knee is through you may find enough for a patch inside a pocket. You can then replace it with a different fabric or sew up the pocket.

Pattern Fitting

Check that a pattern fits before cutting it out. It allows you to take a pattern up somewhere above the bottom edge, make a tuck or insert a section (but remember to redraw the seam line so it looks right, a tuck may have produced a stepped effect). If you have to add or subtract from seams it is much better to adjust several slightly than make a big change on one.

Bear in mind that there must always be a few inches extra so the garment flows over the body instead of hugging it like a sausage skin. The standard amounts for a close-fitting style which will skim the body are:

skirt 7.5 cm (3 in) larger than your hip size
bust 10 cm (4 in) larger than your bust measurement
sleeve 5 cm (2 in) larger than your upper arm

For loose styles or sizes 102 cm (40 in) hip or over, the ease should be greater.

Some adjustments are very tricky. For example, adjusting for uneven or very sloping shoulders. If this is your problem, put in shoulder pads and adjust the thickness to make the shoulders balance.

Plastic and Plastic-Coated Fabric

PVC-coated cotton tends to stick to the machine foot. The solution is just to brush a little cooking oil down the seam line before sewing. But be sure to wash it off with soap as oil hardens some plastic.

Light plastic needs paper on the seam (page 389). Use a long stitch, as the plastic is weakened with every needle hole, and if it suits the situation, strengthen it by sewing in straight tape or seam binding.

Pressing

The most important way to make garments look less home-made is simply the old tailor's trick of pressing each seam as you go along (though not on velvet or other fabrics which cannot be ironed). Use a steam iron on lightweight fabrics. On most wool use a clean, very damp cloth between the iron and the fabric.

Wool fabrics tend to spring up even after pressing. Tailors cure this by using a 'banger' (also called a 'basher' or 'knocker') – a piece of wood about the size of a brick with a flat base. Tailors use a good bit of hardwood, but a chunk of smooth pine is fine. Rest this on the fabric, for a minute or two, immediately you remove the iron: the wood absorbs the steam and you get a perfectly flat result. If an area is obstinate – and the fabric can stand it – bang the seam into docility with it. But it won't cure excess thickness where surplus should have been trimmed off (page 388).

★ To make the two halves of press studs match perfectly sew the male one on first. Rub chalk on its 'nose'. Press this against the other section of fabric. Push a pin up through the chalk mark, sit the female half on the pin, and sew it in place.

Rouleau Ties *(shoestring straps)*

To make the very thin fabric cords used as shoestring straps, cut a strip of material, on the bias, twice the width you want the strap to be, plus a small seam allowance. Fold in half lengthwise, wrong side out, placing a length of twine inside sticking out at each end. Machine down the length, about half way between the fold and the edges. Then sew twice across one end across where the string sticks out. Pull the string and ease the rouleau down over it until it is right side out. Then cut the string off at the end where it is attached.

Seams

Open Seams (Plain Seam)
The basic seam is an open seam. For this you just put the two right sides together, edge to edge, machine down it and press it open. The classic seam width is 1.5 cm (⁵/₈ in). The edges are finished as follows:

Cutting with pinking shears if the fabric won't fray.

Oversewing, by a machine zig-zag or by hand. Hand oversewing is one of the best finishes of all.

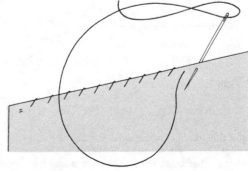

Hand Oversewing

Turning the edge in and machining it down. This suits very fine, firm fabrics like lawn.

Turning In

Using Bias Binding to Finish a Seam

Self-finishing by trimming one seam allowance short and folding the other round it and hemming it. For very fine and sheer fabrics.

Self-finishing

Curving Open Seams
When an open seam has to go round a curve, slits must be cut in the seam allowance which goes round the longer curve and V-shaped notches cut from the smaller.

Double Stitched Seam (Flat Seam)

Double Stitched Seam

1 Make this like an open seam.
2 Trim *one* seam allowance to 5 mm (³/₁₆ in).
3 Fold the other seam allowance over it and iron on the right side to get a sharp seam.

4 Fold in the edge of the longer allowance, tack down and machine down from the right side.

When this is used as a decorative seam (welt seam) start by making the open seam so it opens with the raw edges on the *right* side.

Simple Flat Seam
For interlinings just overlap the edges by 1.5 cm (⁵/₈ in) and machine down them.

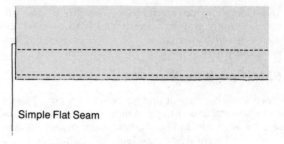

Simple Flat Seam

French Seam
This starts the opposite way to most seams. Pin the *wrong* sides together, and machine down only 1 cm (³/₈ in) from the edge. *Iron the seam open.* Fold along the seam line, *right* sides together. Pin together and machine along the main seam line (having first trimmed off any seam allowance which might stick out through the seam.)

★ This is good for sheer fabrics where a seam will show. Open seams can also be converted into a kind of French seam by folding the raw edges in towards each other and holding them together with a fine running stitch. This is the best way to finish armholes on transparent fabrics.

★ When the initial seam is made like an open seam, but not opened up, as at the edge of a cuff or collar, press *open* the seam as if it was going to be used as an open seam, *then* fold it to its final flat position.

Silk

Silk is easily spoilt by the wrong handling and frays very easily. So work as quickly as possible, and don't fuss over it too much.

● Use fine tailoring pins.
● Use a fine needle (e.g. a machine needle, such as number 70).
● Sew with silk thread, use silk lining material – such as jap silk, and for very fine silk follow the tips for fine fabrics (page 381).
● Finish off raw edges by hand.

Sleeve Insertion

An excellent method of inserting the head of a sleeve smoothly into an armhole is one I was taught to use when tailoring.

1 Turn the sleeve inside out and the 'bodice' right side out. Put the 'bodice' down the sleeve so that the two armholes match.
2 Pin the underarm seams and matching notches.

Addresses and suggestions for further reading are at the ends of chapters.

3 Pin round, with pins at right angles to the seam, easing the fullness over the top of the armhole and pinning at frequent intervals to distribute it evenly. Press on a small ironing board or tailor's ham if this is appropriate. Sew.

Having the sleeve as the top fabric when you machine also makes it easy to avoid sewing in little wrinkles. Distributing gathers evenly is also easier this way.

> With a bulky garment it may be impossible to put the top half down the sleeve. In that case, just turn the sleeve head back as illustrated. Then machine in two operations – sew the top with it turned back like that, then sew the bottom from the other side.

Turning a Sleeve Head Back

Stitches

Backstitch can replace machining – if you can sew straight enough (have a chalk or pencil line). Bring the needle up a stitch length ahead then down through the front of the previous stitch. And so on. The length of each stitch should mimic the size of a machine stitch.

Backstitch

Tacking (basting) is a long stitch used to hold a seam before it is machined. Chalk a line to sew along or stretch the thread ahead of you and hold it down with your thumb as a guideline. The stitches are each about 2 cm (½ to 1 in) long (see above right).

Tacking

Lock stitch is a *very* long, loose stitch used to hold the lining and interlining to a curtain so that they move as one. Only a thread of the main curtain material should be picked up.

Lockstitch

For *running stitch (gathering stitch)* make a series of stitches each a small fraction of a centimetre long. Do this several stitches at a time by just dipping the point of the needle in and out, until the needle-tip is full. As there is always a risk of a gathering thread breaking put two rows of running stitch very close together for gathering and pull both at once.

Divide the area to be gathered into halves, or quarters, or even eighths and sixteenths, if necessary, and mark the same fractions where the gathering will be attached. Then the points can be matched. When the gathering is the correct length put a pin in and wind the threads round it in a figure of 8 to hold them.

For *stab stitch* you bring the thread up to the right side then, *very* close to where it came out, stab the needle down and through to the back. The stitches at the back are slightly longer than those at the front. It *cannot* be

Stab Stitch

done as a single movement, and to do it well you need the shortest, finest needle which will hold your thread.

Tools

Machines
Modern computerized sewing machines can do wondrous things, but only the most dedicated seamstress will use a fraction of them. It should be easy to change the foot and the needle and it is useful if the base plate sticks out like an ironing board end, then you can curve an armhole around it. If a machine can do the following it will do most jobs:

- sew forwards and backwards with easy adjustment of stitch size
- do a basic zigzag stitch in varying stitch sizes
- do a zigzag created by lots of little stitches.

Needles for Sewing Machines
Using the right type of needle makes a difference.

Standard needle: Size 80 (11) for fine sewing. Size 90 (14) for medium weight fabrics. Size 100 (16) for heavy fabrics. Size 110 (18) for thick threads.

Ballpoints are for sewing jersey. Use size 70 (9) for very fine jersey, other sizes as standard. Ballpoints can also be Teflon-coated, to prevent the needle skipping on Lycra. Needles with names like 'Perfect Stitch' are specially ground to get better results on man-made fibres – but an ordinary ballpoint and a slight zigzag copes with most fabrics.

Spearpoint Needles are 3-sided for leather use: size 80 (11) for chamois, size 90 (14) for most clothing leather.

Denim Needles also sew canvas, heavy linen, twill, heavy plastics and imitation leather. Size 90 (14) light denim. Size 100 (16) denim. Size 110 (18) fur fabric or very heavy upholstery. Size 120 (19) canvas.

Needles for Hand Sewing
The most essential tool is a fine needle. Not even an archangel could sew a fine seam with the rapiers which people often use. Strictly speaking, different types of needles should be used for different jobs, but for most dressmaking you can get good results with a no 10 crewel. This is not really correct, but its long eye is easier to thread than a round-eyed needle like a between, it is flexible enough to do good hemming, and long enough to sew on buttons. Even so, a very short, fine between must be used for stitches like stab stitch.

However awkward it feels at first, anyone who intends to sew should learn to use a thimble. It makes sewing much faster and more accurate. It goes on the middle finger and should be metal, as plastic can crack.

Pins
Choose long fine tailoring pins in good steel.

Scissors
Sharp cutting-out scissors, with long blades, are essential for dressmaking. Left-handers who have trouble finding

them should write to Wilkinson Sword (page 379 or see page 217). This company also makes a remarkably effective and inexpensive device for sharpening scissors.

Threads
Use a thread which is the same fibre as whatever you are sewing – or as close as you can get. Man-made fibres are infuriating to thread through a needle. Mercerized cotton is the most pleasant thread for wool, cotton, and blends. For synthetics, and stretch fabrics where the strength of synthetic threads is an advantage, get a mixed thread combining a synthetic core with a cotton coating, such as Coats Duet or Sylko Supreme.

Thick button-hole threads are used for button-holes. The polyester version is widely available, the silk version isn't, but is much more pleasant to sew with.

★ If thread knots during hand sewing put the point of the needle through the loop and gently tug each end of the thread in turn. One of them will pull and allow the slip knot to undo.

★ If you have to use synthetic thread run it through a block of beeswax before sewing to stop it twisting.

★ To thread synthetic thread through a needle, have very sharp scissors and cut it at an angle. The same may work with cotton thread, but if it doesn't, wet it and bite it flat.

★ You can buy needle threaders to make it easier to thread machines; failing that, the finest fuse wire bent to a similar shape will do the job on some needles.

Trimming Bulk

Whenever seam allowances threaten to produce unsightly bulges they need to be trimmed so they lie flat – after you have checked that the sewing is correct, and the fit good. How close you cut must be varied with the type of fabric; those which fray easily need far bigger turnings. A balance has to be struck between leaving bulk and trimming off so much that the seam is weakened – judge each situation on its merits.

If you cut several layers as one there will be a nasty ridge when the area is pressed. To avoid this trim the seam allowances in a series of steps, with the allowance which will be closest to the surface of the finished garment the longest one.

On points the angle of cut should leave the angle of the seams smaller than the corner they have to fit into when it is turned right side out.

Whenever gathering has to be pressed flat, within a small space – such as a waistband – it should, ideally, be trimmed to flatten it.

Velvet, Velour, Velveteen and Corduroy

These vary enormously in handling. Ordinary cotton velveteen and corduroy can almost be treated like any other fabric, but high-pile velvet is probably the hardest of all fabrics to sew successfully at home and may be impossible to press. Beginners should avoid it and even the expert be wary. The only exception is certain furnishing velvet.

Pattern Choosing
It is hard to get a good finish on seams on velvet. So

choose a pattern which has no seams in places which catch the eye. For most velvet avoid patterns which need buttonholes: it may be impossible to make satisfactory ones.

Making Up
All these fabrics must be cut out so the nap runs the same way on all the pieces. This is normally up the body on clothes, but downwards on curtains – so it catches the dust less. But these rules aren't sacred; hold it up and choose the effect you prefer.

Corduroy can be sewn like any other fabric, but all the others in this family need more care. Tack and machine all seams *in the direction of the pile*, and don't have too tight a stitch, or they may pucker. If they still pucker put tissue paper *between* the two layers of fabric. If it still puckers hand sew every seam. Jersey velvet should be treated like jersey (page 383).

★ On velvet use stab stitch for inserting a zip.

Pressing
Some velvets mark permanently when pressed. Experiment on spare pieces of fabric to discover how far you can go – it varies considerably with the composition of the fabric. Try putting a spare piece face up, with the section you are ironing face down over it, so the pile is cushioned. If you can't press it properly at home a dry cleaner may be persuaded to do it for you.

Waistbands

Most patterns tell you to use fabric on both sides of a waistband. On fabric of any thickness sew a length of stiff Petersham ribbon to replace the inside section. This makes the band much less bulky.

★ Most fabrics have a right side and a wrong side. On plain fabrics where the two are similar check the selvedge. The wrong side usually has a less finished edge.

Zips

Basic Zip
- Sew up the seam to a point a fraction above where the base of the zip will come – stop and machine back for 2 cm.
- Tack the remainder of the seam together on the seam line, using rather short tacking stitches.
- Iron the seam open on the wrong side.
- Pin the zip so the top is just below the waistband or top of the opening with the teeth exactly behind the centre of the seam. Tack in place.
- Using a zip foot, machine, turning in the corners as on page 384.

★ For a couture finish sew the zip in by hand using stab stitch (see page 387).

Concealed Zip
For a lapped or concealed zip, sew the seam as above.

- Use chalk or tacking to mark the seam line up each side of the zip opening.

Concealed Zip

- Tack the other (rear) seam allowance so that the folded edge will lap under the other side, by about 3-4 mm, when the marked seam lines meet. Cut the seam allowance to let it lie flat. Press. ★
- Tack the zip as illustrated, and machine with a zip foot.
- Catch the front section so the seam lines meet. Then tack the zip where it lies against it. And sew in, using stab stitch, for the neatest finish of all.

> If machining, leave the ends long where the machining stops at the bottom. Thread the top thread on a needle and take it through to the back and finish it off. Finish off the back thread by hand too.

Replacing a Skirt Zip
To replace a zip in a skirt or dress unpick the stitches holding the zip in place. If unpicking part of the skirt band is too difficult, or you won't be able to resew it, cut the zip off flush with the waistband. (When you sew in the new zip you can't insert the tops tidily under the band. But you can turn them at right angles and sew them down.) Having removed the zip, pull out every scrap of thread from the old stitching. Then insert the zip as in method (1) or (2) above.

Inserting or Replacing a Trouser Zip
Sewing a zip in trousers looks very complicated. In fact, it is very easy if you take it step by step. The steps are the same as for a Concealed Zip up to the ★.

- Place the work face up and fold half the garment out of the way so you can tack the zip to the seam allowance on the undersection. Machine it in.
- Put the fly opening in place and lock stitch closed.
- Turn wrong side up and fold the undersection of the garment out of the way so you can tack and machine the free half of the zip to the underlap extension.
- Tack the zip guard (which stops the zip catching

where it hurts) and machine it to the underlap extension.

● Turn right side up and machine the curve of the fly.

Replacing a Trouser Zip

CROCHET

The basic operation in most crochet is pulling a loop of thread through a loop, or loops, already on the hook. A huge range of stitches can be produced but you really need a pattern. So what I have given here are the basics of how to start, plus the stitches which are used most often. When I refer to a certain number of 'loops on the hook', both completed loops and a wind of yarn round the hook count as 'loops'.

Basics

Unless crochet is being used to edge some existing work there are usually three steps to starting.

1 A chain is made to the length needed.

2 A foundation row is often used to give firmness.

3 The pattern rows. (In the first row the hook should pass under the top *two* threads of the foundation row, at each stitch, unless the pattern says otherwise).

Beginning

Have the hook in your right hand like a pen. Attach the yarn to the hook with a slip knot. Twist the yarn round the little finger of the left hand, so it emerges over the back of the finger, passes under the ring finger, and over the second and first finger. Hold the other end of thread, which trails from the loop, between the thumb and second finger of the left hand, and keep the yarn taut to the ball by lifting your first finger.

To make a loop you then sweep the hook under and round the yarn, moving towards you, and draw the yarn back through the loop made by the slip knot. The knack is to have the yarn comfortably firm, but not too tight, and to roll the hook towards you, as you draw the yarn through. (Left-handers reverse the use of the hands.)

For a Chain just keep pulling each loop through the one before until you have the right number. In counting stitches the loop on the hook is not included.

Turning Chains

A unique feature of crochet is that each row has a height which is not related to the thickness of the thread or the size of hook. So you can't simply stop at the end of a row and turn to go back. On all but the shallowest rows you need to add a few chain stitches at the end of each row, which are carried up the edge of the work. This 'turning chain' varies with the height of the stitch to be worked in the following row – which is why instructions often tell you to put the hook through the second, third or fourth stitch to start a row, and into every stitch after that. If you crochet stripes start working in the new colour at the *beginning* of the turning chain – or you will have the wrong colour running up the end of the next row.

Finishing the Work

Cut the thread a few inches away from the last loop. Slip the thread through the loop and draw it tight. Then darn the end of thread invisibly with a tapestry needle.

Crochet in mercerized cotton should be washed when it's finished and sewn up. Then block it to shape as for knitting and iron it through white tissue paper.

Increasing and Decreasing

In crochet the methods of increasing and decreasing vary according to the stitch you are doing, and a good pattern should give the details.

Joining Yarn

To join new yarn lie the remaining tail of old yarn along the top edge of the work, with the end of the new yarn beside it. Then, as each stitch is made, the two are bound in. If you change colour bind in the old colour only, then bind in the new colour on the return row.

Tension

You should work a pattern square to see if your tension

agrees with the pattern before starting the work. The size of the crochet hook can be adjusted up or down to alter the size of the work – just as in knitting.

Stitches

Slip stitch is a very flat stitch.

1 Make a chain of the required length (unless you have some other row to work from).
2 Slip the hook through the nearest stitch of the row you have made, and draw the yarn through both this stitch and the loop on the hook. Repeat into each stitch along the chain for the length needed.

Double crochet produces a strong close fabric.

Double Crochet

1 Make a chain of the required length.
2 Slip the hook through the chain, one stitch away, and draw a loop through (2 loops are on the hook).
3 Hook the yarn and draw it through both loops.
4 Repeat 2 and 3 into every loop in the chain.
5 Make a turning chain of 1 stitch at the end of the row.

Half Treble creates a slightly more open fabric.

1 Make a chain of the required length.
2 Twist the yarn once round the crochet hook.
3 Slip the hook through the chain, at the third stitch, and draw a loop through (3 loops are on the hook).
4 Wind the yarn round the hook and draw it through all the loops on the hook – to leave one loop on the hook.

5 Repeat steps 2, 3 and 4 into *each* chain.
6 Make a turning chain of 2 at the end of the row.

Half Treble Crochet

Treble follows steps 1, 2 and 3 as for a half treble but into the fourth stitch, then:

Treble Crochet

4 Wind the yarn around the hook and draw it through all but the last loop (2 loops on the hook).
5 Wind the yarn round the hook and draw it through both loops on the hook.
6 Repeat steps 2, 3, 4 and 5 into each chain.
7 Make a turning chain of 3 at the end of the row.

Sizes for Crochet Hooks

The sizing of crochet hooks grew up with the centuries, and the result is chaos. In Britain, they are now measured in millimetres. But crochet hooks tend to travel down the generations, so you may meet hooks using old sizing.

The old British sizing uses two different numbering systems – one for the larger hooks made of aluminium and plastic, and one for the smaller steel ones – and there is a confusing patch where they overlap in the middle. The American sizing uses the same principle but excels itself with two number series and one alphabet series – but they always do it bigger in the States.

The yarns given below will give a reasonably close piece of work, a larger hook creates a lacy effect.

	Mercerized cotton						Up to 4 ply wool or cotton		Double knitting cotton or wool		Chunky yarns								
No.	60	60	40/50	20	10	5													
mm	0.60	0.75	1.00	1.25	1.50	1.75	2.00	2.50	3.00	3.50	4.00	4.50	5.00	5.50	6.00	7.00	8.00	9.00	10.00
British	6	5	4	3	2½	2	1	2/0											
British							14	12	11	9	8	7	6	5	4	2	1/0	2/0	3/0
US								1	2	4	5	6	7	8	9	10½	12	15	
US	14	12	10	8-9	6	4	1	1-0											
US							B	C	D	E	F	G	H	I	J	K			P

EMBROIDERY AND TAPESTRY

It is high time that embroidery was rescued from the sexist, ageist backwater to which it has been consigned. Even in the 1920s it was considered a good pastime for both sexes and was much favoured by officers in the navy. With the right stitches and the right threads even the relatively unskilled can have a lot of fun, and produce some attractive results – think of the peasant embroideries of Mexico and India. Embroidery with colourful threads is a great wet afternoon pastime for children from the age of 8 onwards. And it does a lot to make them neat-fingered – a Victorian virtue, but one worth having.

Crewel Embroidery

Embroidery can be done on any fabric, from the finest silk or lawn to heavy linen, but it is seldom worth spending time on it unless the material is a good quality natural fibre. Whatever the fabric, you will get a much better result with far less effort with an embroidery frame. The easiest to use are those which have a stand, or clamp on to a table, but even the simplest frame will pay dividends. Place the fabric over the smaller ring, put the larger ring on top, tug the fabric until it is smooth, but not unduly stretched, then tighten the upper ring.

The big divide in threads is between wool and cotton – silk is rare now. Wool wears better, but only suits the heavier fabrics. And **stranded cotton** is much more versatile. It's soft and silky and its six fine strands can be separated. So you can use a single thread for the finest stitches or all six for chunky work, or combine strands of different shades. It suits any fabric, and crewel needles numbers 5 to 8, according to the number of strands. The finer the needle the better

★ If the thread gets twisted let it hang down with the needle on the end and it will untwist.

★ To thread a needle with any springy thread, such as wool, fold it over the needle. Press it between finger and thumb as you draw it off the point of the needle – then thread this flattened loop through the eye of the needle.

★ If you prick yourself and drop blood on your work, chew a small ball of white cotton and use the saliva-filled ball to dab off the blood immediately. It should leave no stain, if you do this quickly.

Copying a Design
● The easiest way to acquire a design is to buy a transfer, place it face down on the fabric, pin it carefully in position (centre it if necessary) and iron it with a fairly hot iron.
● You can place dressmaker's carbon paper on the fabric, pin the design over and trace simple outlines with a tracing wheel.
● You can trace any design on tracing paper, then enlarge or reduce it by the square method given below. Once it is the right size the easiest way to trace a complex design on to light-coloured fabric is to go over the design in black ink. Then place it on a sheet of glass. Fix the fabric carefully over it. Then shine a light up so the design will show through clearly and you can draw it onto the fabric with a pencil or special pen.
● To enlarge or reduce a design draw a grid of lines over it. Take a fresh sheet of paper, the right size for your final work and draw a grid of the same number of squares on this. Then copy the design from one to the other, copying the position of each line and shape in relation to the lines and squares of the grid.

Addresses and suggestions for further reading are at the ends of chapters.

Copying
a Design

French Knot

Embroidery Stitches

Start with a small knot underneath, and finish by taking several stitches into the threads on the underside, or weaving the thread a suitable distance through them before cutting it.

Chain stitch makes quite substantial lines. Bring the thread up to the right side and take a stitch as shown. Pull the needle through, above it so that the thread forms an elongated horseshoe.

Lazy daisy is an easy stitch for making small flowers. Make a stitch as shown, and pull the needle through, so the thread forms a loop round it. Then push it down, so a stitch straddles the end of the loop. Bring the needle out at the base of the next petal and repeat.

Lazy Daisy

Chain Stitch

French knots are used as the stamens of flowers. With the needle pointing *up* the thread, wind it several times round. Then push the needle through the fabric, close to where it came out, tighten and pull it through.

Satin stitch is hard to do well and always needs an embroidery frame. The thread can lie either straight across or at any angle. But the stitches must be perfectly parallel and close together, so no fabric shows.

For long and short satin stitch the next layer of stitches can either mesh irregularly into the bottom of the row above – or butt exactly on to them – according to whether you want a defined line or delicate shading.

Great subtleties are possible if you use your threads cleverly. You can also start by running stitches in the opposite direction to make a padded effect.

Basic Satin Stitch

Long and Short Satin Stitch

Stem stitch is used for lines of stitching. Keep the thread always to the same side of the needle, and make the stitches all the same length.

Stem Stitch

Tapestry *(canvas embroidery, needlepoint)*

Let me say straight away that it is quite incorrect to use the word tapestry for what I am going to write about. Tapestry is a woven fabric picture, such as a Gobelin tapestry, not one sewn with a needle on canvas. But everyone I know calls the canvas type 'tapestry', not the correct names – canvas embroidery or needlepoint. So tapestry I shall call it.

Canvas

The best canvas is called double thread and its threads

hold their positions with a minimum of distortion; it also allows you to use tramming if you wish. Of the single thread canvases 'interlock' is the most stable. Ordinary canvas has a tendency to pull out of shape with handling and is best kept for small tapestries which can be quickly done.

Each type of canvas comes in a variety of gauges still based on the inch – so 7 has 7 stitches to the inch. Choose the gauge to suit the object. Chair seats normally use gauges 10 to 14, whereas a handbag needs a fine canvas such as a 17-gauge. You need a piece at least 10 cm (4 in) longer and wider than the design.

To stop canvas fraying at the edges, when you start sewing, make a turned-in hem, of about 1 cm (½ in), and machine it all round. Draw the exact outline of the canvas on a large sheet of white blotting paper before you start to sew – and keep the blotting paper for blocking.

Copying a Design

Canvases with the designs painted on them are undoubtedly the easiest to work, but you can copy any design you like. Either copy the design on to graph paper, and work from the graph, counting stitches, or trace the chart by putting the design under the canvas and drawing on the threads with a canvas-marking pen (sold by needlework specialists). If you wish to paint in the colours use thinned acrylic paint not oils – oils will slowly rot an unprimed canvas.

Yarn

Four ply tapestry wool is ideal for medium gauge canvas, or 2 ply crewel wool, which you can use double or single, according to the gauge of the canvas. There is also 2 ply Persian wool and perle or stranded embroidery cotton.

The amount of thread needed varies with the stitch and the canvas size, but as a rough guide Coats suggest the following quantities, using tapisserie wool on double thread 10 gauge canvas.

	Per 10 m skein	Per 13.7 m skein
Tent	29 rows × 30 stitches	39 rows × 30 stitches
Trammed tent	22 rows × 30 stitches	30 rows × 30 stitches
Half cross	38 rows × 30 stitches	52 rows × 30 stitches

Frames

You may be able to get away without a frame, but large ones will distort too much. You can buy special rectangular frames for the job – but they are expensive. To fit canvas on a frame sew heavy tape top and bottom of medium or light canvas. Mark the centre in each edge and attach it accordingly to the instructions for the frame working from the centre of each side. Adjust the frame so the canvas is taut.

A less expensive option is to buy the type of frame made for stretching canvas for paintings, or use an old picture frame, which lets the tapestry just fit within the opening. Match the mid points of the sides of both the frame and the canvas, and attach it top and bottom and then at both sides with drawing pins. Then work away from these centre points keeping an even pull.

Whatever the frame, make sure the canvas is perfectly stretched before you start sewing or the tapestry will never look right.

Needles
You *must* use a blunt-ended tapestry needle in a size which will slip through the canvas without dragging.

Starting and Finishing
Every stitch is done in two movements – down through the canvas, then up through the canvas – and the thread pulled right through on each. Always try to make a downward stitch where there is already some yarn in a hole, as an upward movement roughs it up.

Start with a knot on the *right* (top) side about 3 cm (1½ in) from where you need the thread – the knot can be cut off later when some other stitches have secured the thread leading to it. Then bring the thread up where you need it. When you finish that thread or section bring it to the right side a short distance from the stitching and leave an end until the under-thread has been sewn over. If there is no room run it through the thread underneath, once vertically and once horizontally.

Where colours mingle have a different needle threaded with each, and keep them at the front of the work until you need them. Then run the one you need through the back to where you need it.

Stitches
Tramming is making a series of very long stitches along each row, on the right side of the work, to provide padding over which the tapestry stitches are worked. This makes a tapestry far more hard-wearing, but you can only do this on double mesh canvas. The tramming should match the colour which will be over it and lie along the centre of the close pair of threads. Bring each new tram up through the last square of the one before – then there are no dips where the ends of two threads meet – and make it no more than 4 to 5 cm (1½ to 2 in) long.

Half-cross stitch, on the right side, looks like tent stitch but, as the thread travels a shorter distance on the back, it is less firm. So this should be worked on double thread canvas, or interlock.

Tent stitch (or *basketweave*) uses a considerable amount of thread but wears and covers well – which is why it is the basic stitch for most tapestry.

Upright Gobelin is a stitch which can be worked over 2, 3 or 4 threads – provided the thread is thick enough not to leave gaps on the longer versions.

Order of Work
It is always tempting to start with the bit one likes best, but the correct order, to ensure clear shapes, is first the veins and outlines, then the motifs, then the background.

Half-cross Stitch

Tent Stitch

Upright Gobelin

Blocking a Finished Tapestry

A tapestry always needs to be blocked before being made into the finished item. Take a board about 10 cm (4 in) longer and wider than the tapestry. Cover it with the blotting paper on which you drew the outline of the canvas. Then tack the tapestry face downwards on it with drawing pins, about a thumb width apart, stretching it carefully to the size of the original outline (if necessary snip the selvedges slightly to allow for stretch). Damp it well with a sprayer and leave until completely dry – unless the instructions say otherwise. Not easy – so you may prefer to have it done professionally (see page 415).

KNITTING

Ancient and soothing, knitting allows you to relax, to save money and watch television all at the same time. It is also blessedly easy, and even someone with two left thumbs can produce *something* which will be a pleasure to wear, if only a straight scarf in a stunning yarn. Complete beginners should see below.

It pays to read knitting patterns with a critical eye. The methods they choose are often those which are quick to explain, rather than those which give the best results. Often little changes, which would improve the finish, need to be made right at the start – like knitting up the first part of a front band with the ribbing.

If things go wrong and you can't make it work, write to the company – big ones have very helpful advisory services.

Alterations

Altering a pattern isn't hard, but careful where you do it. Before changing a shaped section draw it out on graph paper, one square to a stitch, showing the increases or decreases. Then you can see the best place to add or subtract, without spoiling the shape. If the alteration will affect a seam draw both pieces.

To alter a pattern to fit a slightly different size use a larger or smaller needle (see Tension, page 401). But, to make a big change you need more stitches. This is tricky and takes experience.

When making a child's garment, which you may need to enlarge later, plan ahead. Sleeves are easier to lengthen if you knit down from the top. You can even knit them (and the body) on circular needles, so you have no seam to unpick. This is how jumpers were knitted for centuries in certain parts of Britain. For lengthening either unravel from the bottom, pick up the stitches and knit the extra you need; or cut it at some point, undo a row, then knit on from the unpicked edge and graft the new knitting to the old (page 400). Either method shows least if you put a band of contrasting colour at the join.

Beginners

Knitting is very easy. Any pattern is only made by combining knit stitches and purl stitches. And what looks like gobbledegook on paper will make total sense when you start doing it, provided you go one step at a time. The ideal yarn is a mohair in a stunning colour. Its fuzziness will conceal any unevenness in the knitting, and your pleasure in its colour will keep you going.

Putting stitches on the needle – casting on – is the hardest part for beginners, so if possible get someone else to cast on and do the first couple of rows. If you can't, turn to casting on (page 397), use method 1, which is very easy. Continental knitting is undoubtedly fastest, so, why not start with the faster method? Try knit stitch, then purl. When you can do both, you can knit. For your first garment, choose a textured wool knitted on fairly large needles. It won't take an eternity to finish and from there on it's pure pleasure.

A *left-handed* beginner needs to sit *facing* the person who is teaching them. Then their movements are a mirror image of the teacher's. But constantly having to re-interpret patterns, because they are working in the opposite direction, can get confusing, so it is often better to learn the Continental style of knitting (below) instead. This also gets over the disadvantage of the twist of the yarn being made for right-handed knitting.

The Continental Method

Continental knitting is extremely fast. The needles are held as illustrated and the yarn comes up between the little finger and ring finger of the left hand, across the backs of the three fingers, and once round the first finger. For either plain or purl, the right-hand needle goes through the loop on the left and the needle tip hooks the yarn back through the loop. The trick is to keep the yarn neither too slack nor too tight, by holding it with the little finger, and to keep the right wrist flexible.

The Continental Method

Almost every country has a different way of holding the wool. If it ends up over the top of the first finger and is controlled by the others suit yourself.

The English Method

The needles are held as illustrated. The yarn goes once round the little finger of the right hand, under the middle two fingers, and over the first finger. When knitting a stitch the right hand slides forward, winds the yarn round the needles, then grips the right needle between thumb and forefinger as it hooks the yarn through the loop. It feels very awkward until you relax.

The English Method

Knit Stitch

This is the most basic stitch. * With the wool on the far side of the work, you push the right-hand needle away from you, through the nearside of the loop at the tip of the left needle. Take the yarn under the right needle and up between the two needles. Hold the yarn tight and twist the right needle so it pulls that yarn through the stitch as a loop, then slide the last stitch off the left needle. Repeat from * for each stitch.

Knit Stitch

> For the Continental method the needle movement is the same, but you use your *left* hand to position the wool.

Purl

To purl, have the yarn at the nearside of the work. Then push the point of the right-hand needle through your side of the stitch on the left needle, with the point travelling to the left. Take the yarn over the top of the right

Purl Stitch

needle, down between the two needles and pull it tight(ish). Then tilt the point of the right needle so it hooks the wool backwards through the stitch on the left needle, and at the same time slide that stitch off. (Continental – page 396.)

General Knitting

Bands and Borders

If a garment has a ribbed welt, and needs ribbed bands up the front, it is neatest to cast on and knit the stitches for the band when you do the welt. Then slip the band stitches on to a safety pin, to knit up later. Work both bands at the same time (using 2 balls of wool). Then, when you make a button hole on one side tie a piece of yarn to the same row on the other, for perfectly positioned buttons.

Button Holes

You need to buy the buttons before making the button holes or you may not be able to find ones which fit.

For a basic button hole, with the slit in the direction of the stitches, knit up to the row on which it will start, then across to where you want it to come. Slip the remaining stitches in the row onto the right needle without knitting them. Join a small ball of yarn to the edge of the knitting. Then knit back with this. Switch to the main ball, repeat so a slit is created where you switch balls. When the button hole is long enough, work across the width of the band using the main ball.

A beautifully neat button hole can be done if you knit a band with a facing. Work to the start of the hole * and break off your yarn, leaving a long end. Join in a contrasting colour – leaving long ends and work across the button hole stitches. Break off the yarn. Join in the main colour ** and knit to the matching hole in the facing. Repeat from * to **. When the facing is folded back, match the contrasting yarn marking the button holes, pull out this yarn and graft (page 399) the front and back sections together, top and bottom.

Button Hole Knitting

★ Yarn is dyed in batches. Two different dye lots may look the same in balls, but look very different knitted up. Buy all the yarn you need at the start – the shop may sell out of your dye lot by the time you need some.

Casting On

Different methods of casting on need to be used according to the result you want. But use a slip knot to put the first loop in the needle, and leave a long end which you can use for sewing up later.

It is often a good idea to cast on using needles a size or two larger than you will use for the knitting. Even so, casting on can be uncomfortably tight to knit. A good trick to prevent this is to place a slim needle beside the main needle, then cast on to both needles. (Stop the needles slipping with a twist of sticky tape near the knobs). Then slip out the extra needle and your stitches will be comfortably loose.

The *thumb method* is too sloppy for most edges but it creates stitches which are easily picked up later. You just knot a loop of yarn round the needle and then repeatedly make a loop with your thumb and pick it up on to the needle.

Thumb Method of Casting On

For the *twisted thumb method* turn the loop right round, so the needle goes into what was the front of the loop. This makes a neater, but rather elastic edge, which can be used before ribbing. The stretchiness is an advantage with yarns which lack give, such as cotton or metallic thread.

When two needles are used the basic method is to knit a stitch, using the initial loop, slip it on to the needle, and knit the next one into that – and so on. A neater edge is given by *double casting on*. Knot yarn round the left needle. Slip the right needle through the loop, knit a stitch and slip it onto the left needle. * Slip the right needle *between* the last two stitches, knit a stitch and slip it on to the left needle, making it comfortably loose. Repeat from *.

Casting Off

Casting off is a job which it is easy to do with a sigh of satisfaction and indecent haste – which can lead to trouble later. Think about the job casting off will do on the garment. Will it need to stretch to let a head into a small neck? Or must it stop a shoulder seam stretching under the weight of a heavy sleeve? Different situations need different approaches, but the basic points are these.

- Cast off on a knit row, if there is one.
- When casting off in a series of steps, slip the first stitch to reduce the stepped effect.

- If you need stretch, use a needle 1 to 2 sizes larger.
- If you don't want firmness or a defined line, where an edging starts, stitches can be slipped on to a holder – to be picked up later, and not cast off at all.

Casting Off

For *basic* casting off, knit the first two stitches, * put the tip of the left needle into the first and lift it over the second, off the end of the needle, and drop it. Knit another stitch and repeat from * to the end of the row. On the last stitch cut the yarn so there is enough to sew up the seam, and slip it through the final loop.

For *stretched basic* start exactly as for basic, but when you lift one stitch over the other keep it on the left-hand needle while you knit the next stitch, and *then* drop it. Hanging on to it like this has the effect of stretching the loop and makes it less likely to have a tight edge.

★ Circular knitting can be done on a circular needle or on 4 double-pointed straight ones. The latter are the most practical for small circles, the former for large ones.

★ Keep tabs on the position of the 'seams' for increasing or decreasing. So, slip a loop of ribbon, or a safety pin over the needle, at the point where they should be. When you reach that point again transfer the marker up to the new row.

★ If a circular needle feels stiff at first put it in an airing cupboard or warm it in a basin of hottish water, and dry quickly, before casting on.

Dealing with Several Colours

The secret of handling *vertical stripes* is to wind several balls and use one for each stripe. At the junction between one stripe and the next, pass one yarn over the other, linking them neatly together. This technique will result in neat checks with no loops of yarn behind.

On Fair Isle and similar patterns simply carry the yarn along the back for 4-5 stitches, without linking it into the knitting. This is called *stranding*. It's very easy but be careful. It's too tight it takes all the give out of the knitting. If it's too loose you catch your fingers in it when putting on the garment.

In *weaving* the spare yarn is taken across the top of the yarn being knitted, at each stitch, so it is woven along the back. It's the best method to use if the yarn has to travel more than a few stitches along the back. In any garment the two methods can be used according to the situation. The old Fair Isle knitters would even use two methods of knitting at once, holding one colour in the right hand, English style, and the other in the left hand to knit Continental style. Anything is possible, so long as it works.

Addresses and suggestions for further reading are at the ends of chapters.

Knitting Stripes

Stranding

Decreasing

Decreasing is done by knitting two stitches together. You will usually get the best results by doing it one or two rows in, as it's easiest to sew up an edge which has a single line of knitted stitches. But first, decide where the decrease will look best. Annoyingly, stitches knitted together always lean to the right. When you want a left-sloping decrease, slip one, knit one and pass the slipped stitch over. If several decreases need to be made in a row knit 2 together at even intervals.

Decreasing

Dropped Stitches

It's worth checking both sides of your work frequently for dropped stitches. If you have dropped one it can be picked up with a crochet hook, for a few rows, so it looks like knitting. Put your crochet hook through the loop at the base of the ladder, hook it onto the 'bar' of the ladder just above and pull it through the loop. Repeat to the top. (Use the same system to repair ladders in heavy

Crocheting Up Dropped Stitches

tights, but suit the size of the crochet hook to the thickness of the yarn.)

Elastic

Yarn with little elasticity, like acrylic, cotton and mohair, will quickly lose its shape on ribbed sections and become baggy. You can prevent the problem by knitting in shirring elastic as you knit the yarn. Use a stranding technique (see left) to run it along the back, catching it in every couple of stitches. Or thread it through at the back of the work with a tapestry needle afterwards. You can do this to bought sweaters, preferably before bagging has begun. You can also buy ready made 'strips' of shirring with several rows linked by a fine web – which could speed up the de-bagging of an old jumper.

★ Odd ends of yarn, from joins, should just be threaded on a tapestry needle and woven neatly into the back of the garment, near the seams.

★ If a few stitches need to be held while others are knitted a nappy pin makes a good holder.

Garter Stitch

This is the easiest stitch of all, as every row is in knit stitch. It has a lot of stretch. So, when it is used as a border to other knitting, some patterns suggest using needles one or two sizes smaller. Check the first row – it often looks much better on one side than the other – and choose the better side for the right side.

Grafting

Grafting is a very easy way of sewing two stocking stitch

The needle follows the arrows for the next steps 2 3

sections together, so they seem to have been knitted as one. But it can only be used if their final rows have not been cast off. Lie your sections edge to edge. Thread a blunt-ended tapestry needle with knitting yarn and slip the last two stitches off each needle. Then follow the illustration carefully, so you sew together the matching stitches from each needle. The yarn follows the meandering path it would in knitting. Pull the yarn through carefully so that the 'tension' of your sewn row is exactly the same as in the knitted rows to either side.

Grafting can also be used to join basic ribbing. The easiest way is to graft the knit stitches on one side then on the other. First divide the stitches, on each piece of knitting, so every plain stitch is on one needle and every purl on another.

Increasing

If a number of increases must be made in a row, divide the number of stitches in the row by the number of increases to find how often you should increase one. Then they will spread out evenly across the row. If a large increase is needed above a welt it will look better if you do half of them in a row after the ribbing and the other half in the next row.

There are two ways of increasing. The basic method is to knit into the front of the stitch and, without lifting the stitch off, knit into the back of a stitch. Then slip it off. The other is, on a knit row, to bring the yarn forward under the needle, then pass it to the back *over* the needle before knitting the next stitch. This extra yarn is then treated like a new stitch on the next row. This is used above a hole.

Interesting Facts

There are a number of easy ways of producing fancy effects to jazz up an ordinary pattern. But the more elaborate the stitch the more yarn you use, the stitch also alters the size of the garment. So check your tension using the stitch you plan to use.

Bobbles come in every shape and size, but for a very simple bobble, on a knit row, work until the position for a bobble. * Knit into the front and back of the next stitch 4 or 5 times before slipping it off. Work alternate knit and purl rows on those stitches for 4 rows. With the purl side facing you lift all the stitches over the end one in turn. ** Continue the original row. On each bobble repeat from * to **.

Cable looks impressive but is quick and easy. It can be done with three strands as a proper plait, or with two as a twist. For a twist using 6 stitches slip the first 3 stitches on to a short double-pointed cable needle (the same gauge as the main needles), put this in front of the work or behind, according to the direction of the twist you want. Work 3 more stitches, with your main needles then knit in the stitches from the cable needle. Continue as before until the next twist is needed. A three strand plaited cable uses the same method with 3 groups of stitches and, every so many rows, one of the groups is slipped on to the cable needle and put either in front or behind, to give the over and under of a plait. The overs

and unders can be made often, to produce a tight twist or plait, or a loose one. And the number of stitches involved varies from 2 to about 12.

Cable

Eyelet holes for ribbon to be threaded are made by knitting two together wherever you want a hole, passing the yarn over the needle and to the back again, and knitting on from there to the next hole. On the next row the yarn over the needle is also knitted – so you get back to the same number of stitches.

Joining Yarn

It seems inelegant but the strongest way of joining yarn is to knot it on to the old yarn at the edge of a row. Finish off the ends when you sew up.

With shaggy yarn which won't show an extra strand just *overlap* the two ends, by at least 15 cm (6 in) and carry on knitting. This is not as strong as the knotted method and on big stitches yarn could pull loose with wear. You have to judge whether it will hold firmly.

Splicing works for slightly rough yarns or fluffy ones, but is bad on smooth ones. Unravel the last few inches of yarn, so the strands are separated, and do the same to the end of the new yarn – the larger the needle, the farther you must undo, but 15 cm (6 in) is average. Overlap the two yarns, spreading the strands and matching the strands. Cut through these pairs of strands at different points so the junctions are staggered – long, middling and short. Bring all the strands together and twist them into a single strand, and knit immediately.

★ To check if an end of yarn is enough for a row stretch it across the row and back three times. That much should knit a row using a basic stitch. For fancy stitches allow more.

★ To avoid losing your place in a pattern use markers. A kirby grip slid down the edge of a paper pattern does well. Safety pins, or contrasting yarn tied in, can mark crucial points in the knitting itself. For example, you often find instructions like 'knit 20 more rows and then cast off'. Marking the start means that if you forget to turn the counter you aren't lost.

★ When two parts need to match exactly knit both at the same time – using two balls of wool on the same needle. It is far more satisfying to come to the end and know you have done two fronts, than to face doing yet another, and the match is exact.

Addresses and suggestions for further reading are at the ends of chapters.

Knitting Needle Size Equivalents

mm	GB old	US
2	14	0
2 1/4	13	1
2 1/2	–	–
2 3/4	12	2
3	11	–
3 1/4	10	3
3 1/2	–	4
3 3/4	9	5
4	8	–
4 1/4	–	6
4 1/2	7	7
5	6	8
5 1/2	5	9
6	4	10
6 1/2	3	10 1/2
7	2	–
7 1/2	1	–
8	0	11
9	00	13
10	000	15
		16

Moss Stitch (Seed Stitch)

For moss stitch knit 1, purl 1, knit 1, purl 1 across every row, just as in rib. But in moss stitch a knit stitch comes above a knit stitch, and a purl above a purl – producing a series of tiny bumps.

Picking Up Stitches

First mark off the area into halves, quarters and even eighths. Small safety pins make the best markers – ordinary pins fall out or split the yarn. Then divide the number of stitches to be picked up by the number of sections marked off. With 72 stitches to pick up you would mark the knitting off into eighths and pick up 9, evenly-spaced stitches ($72 \div 8 = 9$) in each section. This gets an even result every time.

Use a needle 1 or 2 sizes smaller than you will use for knitting up the stitches. Hold the edge of the knitting firmly, insert your needle just below the line of casting off. Wind the yarn round the needle, as if knitting, and tilt it up through the hole carrying the loop of yarn with it. Repeat. (If you just pick up loops from a cast-off edge you get awful results.)

Ribbing

Basic ribbing is, knit 1, purl 1, repeated on every row, with an even number of stitches. So a purl in one row always has a knit above it in the next, and vice versa.

Rib welts and cuffs are usually knitted on needles two sizes smaller than the rest of the garment. The basic stitch can be varied by alternating more stitches (e.g. knit 3, purl 3) but such changes affect the size of the garment – check your tension.

Stocking Stitch

This was originally used for stockings – just as garter stitch was used for garters. It is simply a row of knit stitches, followed by a row of purl stitches, repeatedly.

Tension (Gauge)

Tension testing is infuriating. Just when one is longing to get going on some new knitting it stops you. But, over a whole garment someone who knits very tightly or very loosely can change the size by several inches without adding or subtracting a stitch. So failing to check the tension imperils the whole project.

Patterns normally say how many stitches and how many rows are allowed to a given measurement. Knit a square several stitches larger than the measurement given. Put a line of pins down one row and along another and measure from these with a ruler. If there are fewer stitches to the measurement than the pattern says, change to a smaller needle. If there are more stitches change to a larger needle. Either way, keep knitting squares until you get a perfect result. If you do change needles remember to change the needles for the ribbing by the same number of sizes.

★ If you have to unravel work, thread a needle, smaller than the ones you are knitting with, through every stitch in the first correct row below the fault. Then you can quickly unravel back to that point without dropping a stitch.

Yarns

Yarn manufacturers want to sell yarn, so naturally they say their yarns *must* be used to make up the patterns. The truth is that what matters is that the tension is right. If, by adjusting the needle size, you can make a square with the same number of stitches to the cm (in) as the tension the fit will be the same. Obviously, this is most easily done if you buy a yarn of the same thickness as the one given but small changes can work very well.

If you have trouble getting interesting yarns **Patricia Roberts** (page 415), whose designs often use lovely colours and textures, runs a mail order service. So does **Colourway** (page 415), which has mail order knitting wool and patterns.

If you buy yarn in skeins not balls, put two dining-room chairs back to back, stretch the skein around them. Wind the yarn round and round several fingers, about a dozen times. Remove it, hold the little bundle between thumb and fingers, so the next winding will go *across* the first lot and *over* your fingers. Keep turning the ball so the yarn winds first one way then another – and always *over* your fingers. This prevents the spring being stretched out by tight winding.

★ Before starting to knit with a ball drop it in a small plastic bag, pull the end of yarn out through the neck and put an elastic band loosely round the opening. This keeps it clean, and stops it rolling about the floor.

★ Yarn which has been knitted up is usually too crinkled to knit with. To smooth it out, make it into a long skein by winding it round the back of a chair, and secure it in several places with loops of yarn. Dip this into lukewarm water, squeeze gently and hang it up to drip dry looped over the neck of a rust-proof metal coat-hanger.

Machine Knitting

It is impossible to cover machine knitting here because of variations in machines. But there are knitting machine clubs and classes all over Britain which practised knitters can join and where beginners can ask advice about buying a machine. Your local library may be able to tell you about them, or see page 415.

Making Up

The first thing to do is check that you made the pattern pieces correctly with no faults or dropped stitches. Most knitting then repays some preparation. Some you can just smooth with your hands, others need blocking and pressing. Whatever the method, knitting should be handled *lightly*. Pressing heavily can make a new garment look flat and tired, before it's even worn, and ruin a raised design. Only you can judge the resilience of your yarn and pick the best method to use.

Blocking is pinning knitting to the perfect size and shape. You need an ironing board or padded table (an old blanket covered with a sheet on a kitchen table is ideal). Place the knitting wrong side up, and very carefully pin it to shape and size, measuring and being careful not to pull it crookedly. Insert long tailoring pins, at an angle, at very frequent intervals down the edge (too far apart will give the scalloped edge sometimes used for decorating shawls). Place them between the stitches, not into the yarn itself, or they will damage it. Then use one of the options below and leave the piece pinned out until it is *completely* dry.

● Damp it with a plant sprayer and just leave it.
● Place a damp cloth over it and press it *lightly* with a warm iron – not for acrylics, raised patterns, or fluffy wools.
● Hold a steam iron a few millimetres above it and spurt the steam on to it – not for acrylics or silk.
● Wet a towel with hot water, wring it out *very* well, and lie it on the knitting while still warm. Then remove it when the yarn has absorbed the moisture and flattened with the weight.

Sewing Up

Before sewing up mark long seams in halves and quarters with safety pins between the stitches. Match these, plus any stripes, when joining up the seams.

Use a blunt-ended tapestry needle for the sewing and, if possible, sew the seams with the ends of yarn left when casting on or off. When you have to start a new thread secure it with several small stitches. If the yarn is too bulky cut several lengths, and separate the strands to make threads of a manageable thickness. Then damp these, twist them firmly and leave them to dry.

Seam Styles

Choose the style of seam to suit the result you want. A long loose coat may need a loose seam to prevent it looking puckered as the garment stretches. But a tight sweater needs firm seams which won't gape as the garment is stretched.

Oversewing is the easiest method and good for ribbing, and wherever you want stretch. Pin the two layers of knitting together, like hands praying. Then oversew, matching row to row. Pull it comfortably tight and it will open into a perfectly flat seam.

For *backstitching* place the pieces as for oversewing but make a seam, one or two stitches in (See Backstitch, page 387). This is the firmest seam. Use it to give firmness to a shoulder seam, for example.

In *invisible seaming* place the pieces side by side with a right side up. Then sew through the loops to either side, as illustrated, drawing the two sides together. This has more give than backstitch and usually produces a neater finish than oversewing.

Invisible Seam

For a straight shoulder seam with no decreases the best method is a *knitted seam.* For this you end the shoulders by slipping the stitches on to a stitch holder. To finish and join them you put each on to a needle, so the needles both face the same direction. Then knit a row taking a loop from each needle at each stitch, and casting off the stitches you make as you go along.

Knitted Seam

Addresses and suggestions for further reading are at the ends of chapters.

KNOTS

I first realized the benefits of knots when I was on the television programme 'Pebble Mill at One'. A researcher and I were knotting grass round an egg for dyeing at Easter. Exasperated at her grass repeatedly coming undone she asked me the knack – the knack was a reef knot. She said that was the most useful thing she'd learnt in ages. So here is a selection of the most useful knots for everyday situations.

★ Pushing through a loop, not an end, in the last stage of many knots makes them easy to undo.

★ If you are ever using rope, a useful rule to remember is that twice the thickness gives 4 times the strength – provided both ropes have the same structure and composition.

Reef

This is the basic knot for tying together two bits of string (tape or whatever) which are the *same* thickness and will have *equal stress* in opposite directions. But it is a dangerous knot to use if the stress will be unequal.

Hold one end in each hand. Go left over right, and under. Right over left, and under. Pull tight.

Sheet Bend

This is useful when you need to join two bits of string of different thicknesses.

Fold the end of the thicker rope into a loop. Feed the thinner rope up through the loop, round the back of it, then under itself. Pull it tight.

Fisherman's Knot (Water Knot)

Another knot for joining two lengths of unequal thickness. Not as elegant as a sheet bend, but it works – provided it isn't asked to stand too much strain.

Place the two ropes side by side. Knot each end as illustrated. Pull tight.

Slip Knot (Noose)

The most basic, and useful, is the slip knot. Make a folded end. Pass the short end over the other, round under it, then down through its own loop.

Sheepshank

Pull ends evenly in each direction

If you go camping and guy ropes keep slipping, which you don't want to cut, you may be glad to know this. I certainly have been.

Round Turn and Two Half Hitches

A useful knot for attaching a rope to a ring in a wall – to tie up a washing line, or a horse.

Clove Hitch

A very easy knot for hitching a rope on to a post. Where you can't drop it over the end you can thread it round to form the same shape, but this is harder.

Lashing

Useful to link two garden canes together. Start with a clove hitch. Wind rope round the front of cross bar, behind the upright, across the front of the other side of the cross bar, and back behind the upright. Repeat several times, pulling it tight. Then wind the rope tightly several times round the ropes, passing between the upright and the cross bar. Tuck the end of the rope under a secure loop and pull tightly.

PATCHWORK

Patchwork has something for everyone. It is so simple a child can do it, but at its best it can be a folk art. And there is something extraordinarily touching about old quilts in which stitchers have patiently created loveliness out of the scrap fabric of their lives. A really fine old patchwork is a revelation, which could make you itch to start one. There are some good examples in *Patchwork* by Avril Colby (page 415).

Unlike embroidery, in which you can only take stitches of a reasonable size, you can make patchwork pieces in any size you like. Use big, slap-happy pieces for a quick bedspread for a child, create a fabric mosaic of minute fragments, with years of patient labour. And you can either sew it gently by hand or whizz simple shapes together with a machine. The skill lies not so much in the sewing, as in the design you create with the shapes and colours of the fabrics.

Assembling the Templates

The fabric patches are supported and shaped by paper or cardboard backings. You can buy metal templates for cutting these out. But to make any size and shape you want you only need a protractor, a pair of compasses and a ruler. Even if you day-dreamed through maths lessons patchwork geometry is child's play on graph, or squared, paper especially. Once you have drawn a shape make a master template on firm cardboard for cutting out. For the papers, cut exactly round it, being careful to have sharp corners, but cut the fabric pieces 1 cm (½ in) larger, all round.

Square

There's no need to back square patchwork pieces if you are going to machine them. Mark the template outline with a pencil or tailor's chalk, cut out and machine squares together into strips. When you have several strips, iron the seams open and machine the strips together. If you put half squares at the ends of alternate rows you stagger the seams and get a wall effect which conceals slight inaccuracies. Oblongs can be treated the same way, and both are great for quick quilts for a child's bed.

Five-Sided Figure – Pentagon

- Draw the lines and circle as shown.
- Centre a protractor where the lines meet and mark 36

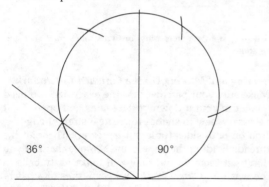

degrees. (Have its bottom black line on top of the line along, and the line up its middle on the upward line. Then read round to find 36 degrees.)

- Draw a line from that dot to where the other lines meet at point A.
- Open the compasses to *exactly* the length from A to where that line crosses the circle, at B.
- *Keeping that measurement*, put the compass point where the line crosses the circle and make another mark as shown. Repeat this, round the circle and draw lines, joining them.

Six-Sided Figure – Hexagon

This is one of the most successful shapes and you can vary it with internal triangles and diamonds. It is also very easy to make.

- Use a pair of compasses to draw a circle.
- *Keeping them open to the same extent*, put the point on the circle and draw a curve across it where the pencil touches.

- Move the point to where that mark crosses the circle and make another mark farther on, as above.
- Repeat this until you have 6 marks, then join them.

Seven or More Sides

Figures with more than six sides fit together less well and you need to fill gaps with other shapes. Draw them as for five-sided shapes. To find the angle you need, divide 180 by the number of sides you want. So for an eight-sided figure, 180 divided by 8 = 22.

Fabric

The nicest patchworks are surely those in which you can pick out family fragments with nostalgia. But family scraps are fewer than they were, and remnants can be expensive. The answer is to scavenge. Beg scraps from the rag trade in your nearest town – if such exists – or raid jumble sales. They sometimes sell garments in lovely fabrics as rags because a single indelible stain has made them unwearable – but you need to ask as such 'rags' won't be on show.

Almost any fabric can be used, but, apart from log cabin designs, it is easiest to work with similar weights and, on the whole, jersey and man-made fibres look wrong. New washable fabrics *must* be pre-washed – to avoid later shrinkage – and ironed flat before use. This includes any backing fabrics, lining and interlining.

★ It makes it a lot easier to find the next piece you need if you put each shade in a different plastic bag.

Preparing the Pieces

Most patchwork experts say you should use paper, the weight of heavy notepaper, to support the pieces and give them their shape. I find it crushes too easily, so I prefer thin cardboard, the weight of postcards. Card *must* be used for fragile fabrics such as velvet, silk and glazed cotton, which would have needle marks if you tacked them on to paper.

For paper backings you tack right through both the paper and the right side of the patch. For card you just draw the fabric together on the back with long stitches. Either way, if the shape of the piece allows, have the grain running the length of the piece.

Design

Part of the fascination of patchwork is that it has layer upon layer of design, like Chinese boxes which go one inside the other. Do leaf through books like those given on page 415 for inspiration before you embark on your own designs. Then, once you start planning a patchwork with coloured pens on graph paper, you may find the planning almost as pleasurable as the sewing. There is also a lot of pleasure in an informal patchwork which you create at random. Either way, you can be certain that what you make will be unique – and when else can you be sure of a world first?

Sewing Patchwork Together

For sewing two backed shapes together put the two pieces, right side to right side, and use a whipping stitch. Match your thread to the fabric, in both colour and type and use a fine needle.

Log Cabin

In log cabin patchwork, instead of using backing papers, measured strips are sewn on to a foundation square 15-38 cm (6-15 in), in the order illustrated, using a fine running stitch. Its effectiveness depends entirely on the skill with which you plan and position the squares. A design takes a lot of forethought. But using a foundation fabric means you can mingle fabrics of different weights, such as silk and velvet, in a way which would be unsatisfactory in other patchwork. Open and smooth each strip carefully away from the centre, pin it down once it is attached, and tack round the outer edge of the last strips.

When all your squares are finished mark the template size in pencil on the back material, so you can sew exactly down the lines. Then hand sew them together or use a machine.

★ Use fine, stainless steel pins; ordinary ones may rust and leave stains.

Trimming and Making Up the Finished Patchwork
- Make sure your patchwork is the exact size you need – you can't cut it down or the seams will open. So, if necessary, sew in shapes to create a straight edge.
- Iron on both sides (unless it is velvet). Then cut the threads holding the papers and remove them. If you don't get them all out they will make nasty balls in the wash. In *Oliver Twist*, Dickens writes of a patchwork quilt which 'rustled' – did thrifty Victorians leave the paper in, to add insulation? If so, they must never have washed the quilts.

Interlining and Lining

Make up cushions, and similar items as you would any fabric, but a bedcover may be better interlined. This gives it a slightly padded look which suits some patchworks admirably, and at night gives extra warmth.

For interlining use an old blanket or a soft, washable interlining. Cut or seam this to the right size with flat seams, then tack the quilt to it carefully. Use long lines of tacking from side to side in each direction, making sure the quilt lies perfectly smoothly.

The lining can be any pre-washed fabric and there are three ways of joining it – (1) and (2) are fine for thin work, but (3) is best if the interlining is thick.

1 Pin and tack the two wrong sides together, turn the edges in towards each other, so they match, and sew two rows of fine running stitches round the very edge to join them.

Addresses and suggestions for further reading are at the ends of chapters.

2 Pin the two right sides together, and machine or back-stitch round the edge, leaving a big enough hole to turn the 'bag' inside out. Then sew up the hole.

3 Start like (**1**) but, instead of turning in the edges, bind them with long strips of fabric. At the corners make a diagonal fold and sew it flat by hand. Machine or use running stitch along the edge of the binding on the upper side, then fold it over the edge and hem.

Knotting

The patchwork, its interlining and lining need to be held together. Patchwork used to be quilted on, but an easier way to join the three layers is the knotting method used on the 'stobbed' quilts of County Durham in the nineteenth century. To do this take a very short stitch through all the layers. Leave the ends long, tie a reef knot and cut the ends to 1 cm (½ in). You can make these ties either in the centre of patch pieces, with the ends on the right side – or invisibly on a seam with the knots on the wrong side. And you can use matching thread, or a decorative one, such as twisted embroidery thread like Anchor perle cotton.

Knotting Method

SOFT FURNISHING

The great thing about making soft furnishings is that it only demands a few, very basic techniques and is nothing like as fiddly as making clothes. Anyone with a sewing machine and a little patience can do it. This section provides the key facts you need to know.

Bear in mind that most furnishing fabric is 120 cm (47 in) wide and some is 136 cm (53½ in) wide. It is prudent to ask whether it is washable or 'dry clean only' before you buy it. Then, having bought it, write to the retailer and ask what shrinkage can be expected and how you should keep it clean. File the reply with the bill and a sample of the fabrics. This may sound calculating, but if the curtains on a large window shrink, several hundred pounds may have been wasted.

Rods and Tracks

Before deciding what curtains or blinds to have, it is worth looking at the tracks which are now available. Some of the unexpected options are – brass rods which bend round bay windows complete, spring-loaded rods

to hold up net curtains, tracks for Austrian blinds which incorporate cord holders – and there are even devices which will open and shut your curtains by remote control. Many of the companies also supply ready-made blinds or curtains. If your local shops don't have a good selection some of the big mail order houses do (page 217)

Blinds

Blinds fit into even the smallest space, and can make the most constricted window look attractive, whereas curtains squashed into tight alcoves can look as if they are playing sardines.

Austrian Blinds

Austrian blinds are particularly good for improving a window which isn't quite as high as it should be, as they look prettiest when only half-drawn up. Hanging them some way above the window, so the upper edge is not quite exposed, makes it look longer.

The ruched swags of Austrian blinds have a period air reminiscent of silk frocks, so they look particularly good in glazed fabrics, which catch the light on the folds. But any lightweight curtain material can be used, and they can be unlined or lightly lined.

The blind needs to be twice the width of the space it will fill, plus seam allowances of 1.5 cm (⅝ in) each. For a very full swag, make it two and a half times the width. It looks best slightly longer than the window (say 20-46 cm, 8 to 18 in extra), plus seam allowances and extra inches if the heading stands up, so that a ruched section covers the bottom even when fully let down.

Ideally have a frill either along the bottom, or right round. For luxury, two in contrasting colours and slightly different lengths. You need:

● pencil pleat tape – a fairly deep pencil pleat usually looks best

● plain narrow tape and rings, or Austrian blind tape which has ready-made loops to run the cord through

- cords to draw the blind up
- a special track or single curtain track, plus screw-in rings to carry the cords which draw up the blind
- a cleat or wedge to hold the blind string in position.

★ Before buying a blind kit check the contents carefully: in some the pencil pleat heading is shallow and would not suit some windows.

Making the Blind with a Lining

1 Measure and cut out the material and any lining to exactly the same size. If necessary, seam lengths of fabric together (see Curtains, page 410) but for blinds place a full width in the centre and add equal amounts to either side. Press the seams open.
2 Make and gather the frill (page 413).
3 Pin it on the right side of the main fabric, matching the raw edges.
4 Pin the lining on top – right side to right side. Machine round a seam's width in from the edge, as if making a bag. Trim the gathered seam allowance.
5 Turn the 'bag' right way out, press it to get sharp edges to the seams. Then smooth it face down so that the back and front are perfectly matched with no wrinkles. Tack it like this.
6 Fold over the top 1.5 cm (⅝ in) and pin the heading tape across the top, as on page 411.
7 If you are using plain upright tapes and hand-sewn rings, sew the rings on, 15-20 cm (6-8 in) apart, spacing them exactly.
8 Position the vertical tapes. The maximum effective width for a swag, as it hangs, is 30 cm (12 ins) So: if the blind is twice the width of the window, the tapes should not be sewn on more than 61 cm (24 in) apart. If the blind is two and a half times the width of the window, the tapes must not be more than 76 cm (30 in) apart. The spacing also depends on what figure will evenly divide into the width of the window. Place the first ring or loop of *every* tape 6 cm (2½ in) up from the bottom. Tuck the top under the heading tape and turn the bottom 1.5 cm (⅝ in) under.
9 Machine across the heading tape, then up each side of the upright tapes. Draw the heading to the final

width, and insert curtain hooks. Then thread the cords through the filaments or rings, tying each neatly to the bottom one.
10 Set up your track and space the cord holders to match the position of the tapes. Hang, running the cords through.

You can adjust the way the blind falls by shortening some strings in relation to others. Then tie all the strings together, or attach them to a ring – with the blind fully let down – and have a single-cord coming down the side to a cleat.

Unlined Austrian Blinds

Omit steps 3 and 4. Instead, pin a matching bias binding across the bottom of the frill. Then sew on the binding with the frill. Trim the seam allowance on the frill, fold the bias over it and hem it to conceal the raw edge. Press in the sides allowance and conceal it under the side tapes.

★ Weighting the edge of the blind with curtain weights can improve the hang.

★ Where an ugly window really needs concealment use an Austrian blind in the centre and have a swagged pelmet and false curtains to cover the frame.

Roller Blinds

These are the thriftiest, and easiest, window coverings of all. You can make all kind of elaborate bottoms, but they are just adaptations of the basic version which follows. You need: a roller mechanism, a batten for the bottom, a cord and cord holder.

Establish the width of roller which will fit in your window. The blind must be the width of the roller plus 5 cm (2 in). The length is the total of: the measurement round the roller + the length from the bottom of the roller to sill + the material you need to fold up at the bottom 3 cm (1¼ in).

Making

- Fold up the bottom, right side to right side, by the amount you have allowed and machine the side seams just under 2.5 cm (1 in) in. Turn and press.
- Oversew the sides, turn in and herringbone flat.
- Stitch across the pocket to take a batten and across the top to make a tunnel the right size for the roller. Insert the roller and hold the fabric in place on it with drawing pins.
- Open one side seam enough to insert batten. When it's in, screw on the cord holder and cord.
- Roll the fabric round the roller and twist the spring catch in the roller before placing it in the holders.

Roman Blinds

Roman blinds are usually lined, but if the fabric is fairly stiff they need not be. The top has no heading but is attached with strong Velcro to a small shelf. Make them the width of the window, lining them like an Austrian blind, but with a battened bottom – like a roller blind. Use upright tapes and cords, as for Austrian blinds, about 30 cm (12 in) apart.

Addresses and suggestions for further reading are at the ends of chapters.

Box Pleats

Triple Pleats

Pencil Pleats

Curtains

Very often the difference between a stunning window and a dull one isn't the cost of the fabric; it's the way it is used. The variations are endless but look at the windows in the context of the whole room.

Curtains can be used to create optical illusions. Taking curtains right across the width of a room can make it seem much wider. If the room is too low, curtain the windows individually, using them to create a series of vertical lines. If the window is narrow for its height you need enough track to either side to give an impression of a wider window and a dreary window can be given interest by simply framing it charmingly.

Headings

For a hidden heading you only need a very basic Rufflette tape to gather the fabric evenly. For a more elaborate heading the major effects produced by heading tapes are those on the right, but tapes can also produce smocked and ruffled effects, and there are translucent tapes, for lace and net. There is also a Rufflette tape which allows you to make the curtain and its lining separately and link the two with the curtain hooks. This won't give the same hang as lining in the usual way, but it could be used to put protective lining on a very sunny window. It also means shower curtains can have a fabric exterior and a detachable waterproof lining – so they need not be dreary.

Headings using tape are undoubtedly the easiest to sew, but for a luxury look you need a heading about 13 cm (5 in) deep and most aren't made to that width; also tape is machined on – which shows on the front and slightly spoils the effect. So the most professional finish is given by making the heading by hand.

Measuring Up

It is the width of the track, *not* the size of the window, which decides how wide the curtains must be and the length will depend on where you place the track.

The track always needs to be wider than the window – unless, of course, it is pinioned between two walls.

Normally, if a window is about 90 cm (3 ft) wide, the track needs to stick out 15 cm (6 in) beyond the window *at each side*. If the window is wider you will need proportionately more or the curtains will look too squeezed together when drawn back. Also bear in mind that curtains without pelmets usually stand a little away above the rail, and those on rods usually hang slightly below it.

Curtains need to be *generous*. Whatever the heading, they can't be less than twice the width of the track and to look really good need to be two and half times the width. But check the heading tape instructions – some only work if the curtain is a certain multiple of the track length. To find out how much fabric you need first establish the total length you will need for a finished curtain. The sum is this:

distance from rail to where you want it to end	+
depth of hem	+
allowance for turning in the upper edge 2.5 cm (1 in)	+
the length of the pattern repeat	+
depth of the heading (unless they will hang by its top edge)	+
allowance for shrinkage	+
Total length	

★ Most fabric manufacturers say there can be up to 5 per cent shrinkage. That means curtains 2 m (6 ft 7 in) long, could shrink 10 cm (4 in). Also see page 186.

Multiply the length of a curtain by the number of widths of fabric you need to make the curtains wide enough, adding a 6 cm (2½ in) turning at each side of each curtain. Then calculate, and add on, the extra material for a pelmet.

Lining and Interlining Curtains
Lining makes curtains hang better, improves the insulation and protects the curtain fabric from the ravages of the sun, which might fade it in streaks on the folds, and make it fall apart far sooner. Use the measurements for the curtains, bar any allowance for pattern. Choose a good quality cotton sateen or investigate insulated lining. It usually looks best if all the windows have the same lining material.

Interlining not only gives curtains a softly luxurious look but also acts as insulation. So interlined curtains pay for themselves in lower heating bills.

There are several different kinds of interlining. The best is bump, domette is next, and even a cheap interlining is better than none. But interlinings aren't washable, so only interline curtains which will be dry cleaned. Buy the same quantity as for lining.

★ On washing, the curtain fabric and lining material may shrink by different amounts. If you plan to wash curtains, wash both fabrics to shrink them, before cutting out.

Cutting Out Curtains
Spread out a full curtain's length of fabric before cutting. Professionals use a vast table. Lacking that, spread it out on the floor, on one of the big plastic sheets which most DIY shops sell. And the golden rule is check everything twice before you cut or sew.

1   Decide where you want your pattern to come. Some very bold patterns look odd if they are incomplete at the bottom of a curtain.
2   Measure the length you need, positioning it to get the pattern where you want it. Mark it on the right side – first making sure it is perfectly flat and straight. *It is essential for the fabric to be cut straight across,*

not at a sloping angle or the curtains will never hang properly.

3a If there is no pattern to match just cut the remaining lengths by measuring.
3b If the fabric has a pattern, place the cut length beside the one you are about to cut. Match the pattern *exactly*, pinning it at key places, then mark the cutting lines. And do this for *each* length. Cut out the lining and interlining to the same size.

Sewing Curtains
Pin and sew the seam lengths 1.5 cm (⅝ in) in from the edge, exactly matching any pattern (see above). Any part widths must come at the outer edge of each curtain. Put small cuts at intervals down the selvedges, as you go, so they don't pucker. Sew the lining in the same way.

★ Try out your stitch length on two spare bits of fabric, face to face. Too tight a stitch will create a gathered seam; too loose will look home-made.

★ Having pinned velvet sew it immediately or the heads may impress dents in the pile.

> For unlined curtains follow the steps below, ignoring all references to interlining and turn in and hem the edge. For curtains lined but not interlined ignore all references to interlining.

1   Iron all the seams open (unless fabric can't be ironed). Doing it at this stage makes a difference.
2   If the interlining needs to be seamed use a simple overlap.
3   Spread the curtain out face down. Place the interlining on it, so the top and sides match and both layers are totally smooth and lying straight. Pin together about 30 cm (1 ft) from the selvedge edge, and turn the interlining back almost at that point and lock stitch. Smooth, pin and repeat at 60 cm (2 ft) intervals, making the last one only 30 cm (1 ft) from the edge. (Make sure the two layers stay perfectly matched at the top.)
4   Cut off the top 2.5 cm (1 in) of interlining. Turn the top of the curtain over the edge of the interlining and tack it, folding in the corners as shown below – 6 cm (2½ in) in from the side – and trimming the excess interlining at the angle.

> This is the point at which professional curtain makers mitre the bottom corners and sew the hem. But to do that you need to be 100 per cent sure that you have every measurement correct and that you won't change the level of the heading tape. The order below allows for error and mind changing.

5   Treating the curtain and interlining as one, turn the side in 6 cm (2½ in). Herringbone this to the interlining using a fairly long stitch (see page 382) and catching both layers of the fold-over, but leave the

sides unhemmed to twice the probable depth of the hem. If there is no interlining just herringbone the curtain fabric.

Lining the Curtain

6 Turn in one side edge of the lining by 2.5 cm (1 in) and iron the fold. Make little cuts in the selvedges at intervals. Mark a chalk line down each folded-in side of the curtain 4-5 cm (1¾-2 in) from the edge. Pin one folded edge of the lining down the chalk line and hem it to the curtain. Leave the bottom loose, as on the curtain itself.

7 Smooth the lining across the curtain, pinning the top, lock stitch to the interlining in the same way as the interlining was attached. Turn in the far edge of the lining and hem it to the chalked line of the curtain.

8 Pin the header tape just below the edge and 2.5 cm (1 in) beyond the curtain at either end. Undo and knot the strings on the wrong side at a point just inside the width of the curtain at the central edge as shown. Fold the tape end under just inside the curtain edge. At the other end pull out the strings from the surplus on the *right* side and turn the end under. Make sure there is room to machine without sewing over the strings.

Fastening the Strings on
Heading Tape

9 Machine up one end of the tape, along the upper edge, and half way down the far end. Then machine down the first end, along the bottom edge, and up the far end. Draw up the heading and insert the hooks not less than 10 cm (4 in) apart.

Pulling Up the Strings

Making the Hem

10 Pin the curtain and interlining together, slightly above the bottom, making sure neither pulls the other. Turn a little of the interlining back and lock-stitch the two layers together.

11 Hang the curtains, decide the hem, pin and re-check. Fold in each corner on a diagonal where the hem line meets the side fold. Iron this and cut along interlining at the fold. Fold it all back into place. Pin down the loose sections of the side-turnings making sure the angled corners create neat mitres with the hem. Herringbone the hem and loose sides. If it isn't interlined, hem carefully so the stitches won't show.

12 Fold the bottom of the lining in towards the curtain so the lower edge is about 5 cm (2 in) above the bottom of the curtain. Fold in its top edge, press, and machine. Finally, hem the loose sections of the lining edges.

★ Ideally weight the curtain by stitching a lead weight, like a button, on to the interlining at each seam in the curtain fabric and at each corner. Or run bead-style weights right along the bottom, securing them at intervals.

Make sure the heading is perfect and hang the curtain. If you are not hanging it from a pelmet board, push the last hook into the ring from the window side, so it curls the edge of the curtain around.

★ For the best hang, adjust the folds carefully and tie strips of fabric round the curtain to hold the folds together – but not crushed – for 24 hours.

Headings without Heading Tape

If you don't want to use heading tape, the top of the curtain can be lined with buckram which is sold for this in various widths. After step 3, tack it in place along the top and tack the interlining and curtain over it. Then omit 4, 8 and 9 and hem the top of the lining to the curtain. Mark out the pleat positions by measuring them – allowing about 4 inches flat between each triple pleat. Machine the basic pleat in place, on the right side, and fold and sew it in the triple pleat by hand. Finally, hem-stitch a strong tape along the back where the pin-ended hooks will stab in.

Shortening Curtains

Much the easiest way to shorten curtains is to measure them carefully and cut off the excess from the top, then attach a new heading tape. Having drawn a cutting line tack all the layers together very carefully right across the curtain before you cut.

Pelmets

Pelmets divide into hard and soft. In deciding which to use bear the maintenance costs in mind. A soft pelmet can be washed or sent to the cleaners. To get a hard one clean may mean calling in professionals to deal with it.

The size needs to be related to the length of the curtains. A pelmet of less than 15 cm (6 in) looks skimpy; long curtains need considerably more, and the side-drops of elaborate pelmets usually need to be one third the length of the curtain.

Supporting a Pelmet

Some companies make pelmet rails which are linked into the curtain rail. It is probably best to attach substantial pelmets to a shelf which can also carry the curtain rail. A piece of 1 cm (½ in) pine, 15 cm (6 in) deep, supported on L brackets is ideal for the shelf.

Hard Pelmets

1 Design the pelmet you want, cut a pattern in newspaper, and check that it looks right on the window. Don't feel limited to simple shapes, you can do anything that suits the window.
2 Draw the shape on ¼ in ply and cut it out, with side pieces that will cover the sides of the shelf.
3 Seam some interlining, with flat seams, to cover it, plus about 10 cm (4 in) each way. Seam the pelmet material with a full width of fabric at the centre and extra width added to either side – if the shape you have chosen demands it.
4 Use sticky-backed carpet tape on the board to hold the side pieces at right angles. Cover with interlining – cutting slashes if you need to fit it round curves – and use a staple gun or Copydex to attach the fold-over firmly. Let any glue dry.
5 Iron the fabric for the pelmet. Repeat the procedure for the interlining, so it is nicely taut and the design is not pulled out of true. Pull it, pin it and look at the right side before slashing the fixing. Fix with Copydex or a staple gun. Carefully glue on any braid trimmings.
6 Cut out a lining to the shape of the pelmet plus 2 cm (¾ in) all round. Machine a strip of velcro along the top edge, just below the turning allowance. Pin the lining on to the wrong side of the pelmet, turning in its edges, and hem it in place, using a curved needle if need be.

Assembly

Glue the other half of the velcro firmly on to the edge of the shelf above the window.

Screw the curtain rail in place half way back on the board, so the curtains won't brush the pelmet.

Screw two ring screws into the board at each side very close to the wall – to take the end curtain hooks and make sure there is no draught between the window and the curtain.

When the glue is dry, hang the curtains. Then press the velcro of the pelmet firmly against the shelf. It should hold perfectly but you can put a small nail through the side flaps close to the wall.

Soft Pelmets

Soft pelmets are miniature versions of curtains so they must be twice the width of the track. Even an unlined pelmet can have an interesting heading tape, and it is simply made like a very short curtain.

The pelmet is made like a curtain but the lower edge is finished differently. For a pelmet either seam the lining on at the lower edge and fold it up the back to the top, before making the heading, or line it like a curtain, tack the lower edges together and bind them decoratively.

The easiest way to make elaborate soft pelmets with a lot of shaping was devised by a friend in Cambridgeshire. Cut the pelmet shape out of a piece of newspaper with no allowance for gathering. Place it on top of a piece of paper twice its width, which has a long straight edge at the top. Draw vertical lines on the pelmet pattern at 5-cm (2-in) intervals. Cut carefully up each line and space the 'pelmet' out across the under paper, with its upper edges against the top edge. Create precise 5-cm (2-in) gaps between each of the 'slices'. Stick it carefully to the paper underneath and cut it out.

Curtain Ties

There is no magic formula for ties: just use a tape measure to loop the curtains back and see what length you need. They will take more fabric than you might expect and you should allow for this when buying.

← Interlining

Net Curtains

Net curtains need to be twice the width of the space they will fill. In length they should be the length of the window plus about 18 cm (7 in) for the hem and extra for the top – see the steps below.

Cut out and seam with French seams, having the selvedges at the outside, so they need no side hems.

To hang them on a rod or wire, turn in the top by 2.5 cm (1 in), and by an inch again, pin and iron it. (If you want a frill above the rod make these turn-ins longer). Machine along the bottom edge of this hem. Then make another row of stitches higher leaving enough room to push the rod or the looped end of the wire through without effort.

To hang them on a rail, turn in the top 1 cm (½ inch). Attach transparent heading tape as for curtains (page 409).

Hang the curtains and decide on the depth of hem you need. Take the curtains down and fold the bottom edge up by *half* the depth of hem you need. Iron in the fold. Fold it again by the same amount, so the raw edge touches the fold. Press, pin, and machine in place.

Addresses and suggestions for further reading are at the ends of chapters.

Loose Covers

Loose covers aren't hard to make, but they do take a great deal of time and patience. For instructions on making them it would be hard to better those given in the *Which* book on page 415.

Choose a fabric which will take a good deal of wear, such as a heavy cotton, linen union or rep. The rule-of-thumb guide for how much fabric an armchair will need is 5 times the height of its back. But *don't buy* by this; just use it to decide what price of fabric you can run to.

The following measurements are a slightly better guide to how much fabric you will need. They are based on fabric 122 to 137 cm (48 to 54 in) wide, but do remember that if you have a pattern you will need considerably more and that quite small differences in key dimensions could mean that you require more fabric than is suggested.

Without back cushions in the shape illustrated

	armchair	2-seater sofa	3-seater sofa
Seat depth	86 cm (34 in)	86 cm (34 in)	86 cm (34 in)
Back height	80 cm (31 ½ in)	80 cm (31 ½ in)	80 cm (31 ½ in)
Back width	77 cm (30 in)	142 cm (56 in)	191 cm (75 in)
Fabric	7 m	10 m	13.5 m

With back cushions

	armchair	2-seater sofa	3-seater sofa	wing chair
Seat depth	92 cm (36 in)	92 cm (36 in)	92 cm (36 in)	87 cm (34 in)
Back height	82 cm (32 in)	82 cm (32 in)	82 cm (32 in)	114 cm (45 in)
Back width	75 cm (29 in)	150 cm (59 in)	198 cm (78 in)	91 cm (36 in)
Fabric	9 m	14.5 m	16.5 m	6.5 m

Cushions

Cushions can be made by anyone with a sewing machine and cutting-out scissors. For the most basic, you just measure the cushion, across the top from seam to seam. Then cut two sides each 4 cm (1½ in) bigger, in each direction, than the cushion. Put them right side to right side, and machine 2 cm (¾ in) in from the edge, leaving one side half open in the middle. Clip the corners, as on page 389, then turn the cover inside out and iron it. Ease the cushion in and sew it up. If you want a zip opening put it in first; and sew the other sides as above.

For a piped cushion you need a good deal more fabric and cotton piping cord. Boil the piping cord for 5 minutes and dry it well or it may shrink when cleaned. Create bias strips of fabric 6 cm (2 ½ in) wide (see page 380) and sew them over the cord.

Pin the two layers of the cover together, with the piping between them, so that the seam lines match. When you are almost where you started, cut each end of the piping cord so it overlaps well. Pull the casing off it a little way and seam the two ends to fit the size of the cushion. Cut the strands of the cords to stepped lengths, twist them together and bind them firmly with cotton. Close the casing round this and tack into place.

Before sewing the cushion you need to fix the cord to one side of the cover where you will have the opening. Then machine round the rest of the cover with a zip foot, right up against the bulge of the cord. Trim, turn right side out, insert the cushion and hem the opening neatly together. A frill is put round a cushion in just the same way.

Frills

All frills are made the same way.

- A good frill must be twice as long as the measurements of whatever it will be attached to.
- In deciding the depth of a frill err on the side of generosity. Even a frill on a pillow looks skimpy if less than 8 cm (3 in) deep.
- Most frills need to be made with a double width of fabric, plus hem allowances, so that the fold is the outer edge of the frill.

By folding, find the half, quarter and other subdivisions of its length, until you have it marked into manageable sections. Fold and mark the edge of whatever you will attach it to in the same way, and match the marks.

★ For a frill with a machine-hemmed edge you machine a thin double hem first.

Round Tablecloth

These have become almost too popular, but their great virtue is that they allow you to create a table out of nothing more expensive than a few chunks of supporting wood and a sheet of ply. But the tablecloth costs more than you might think. For example a table 91 cm (36 in) across and 76 cm (30 in) high takes 8 metres of plain 137-cm (54-in) wide fabric.

To make your pattern, stick together a number of sheets of newspaper until you have a sheet rather larger than the cloth you will need. Fold this in half and then into a quarter. Take a long piece of string and tie a pencil to one end. Measure along the string, from the pencil, the distance from the floor to the table top, plus half the width of the table. Push a drawing pin through the string at this point. Push the pin through the folded corner of the newspaper, and hold the pin firm. Then stretch the string to its full length and mark a quarter of a circle. Cut round this pencil mark with the paper still folded.

Before cutting out the cloth decide on your hem. Circular hems are hard to sew neatly. There are several other options.

● Bias binding – cheap, easy.

● Fringing of some kind – expensive but stylish.
● Braid – fairly expensive but effective.
● A wide bias strip of some contrasting or toning fabric. Very effective but takes time and fabric.
● A lining, so you make the two as a bag and turn it inside out. Heavy on fabric unless you have an old sheet looking for a home.

Use the paper to cut the fabric for the tablecloth. (Remember the circle has no allowance for seams or hems.) For the most luxurious effect put an undercloth of curtain interlining under the tablecloth.

Bed Linen

It is very easy to make attractive bed linen and you can save a fortune doing so. I buy sheets in attractive colours in the sales and just seam them into something more interesting. The more expensive shops often have king sizes in the sales which are ideal.

Duvet Covers

The most basic duvet cover is made just like the basic cushion cover on page 413, except that you either sew ties (made from the fabric or matching straight tape) along the opening in the foot or sew on a strip with ready-made poppers. Either way, you can finish it in under an hour. For a more decorative cover add contrasting strips of fabric, wide broderie Anglaise strips with ribbon threaded through or put a deep frill right round the edge.

Valance and Frilled Bedcover

For a valance, cut out and, if necessary, seam up fabric to the size of the surface of the bed base plus 2 cm (³⁄₄ in) seam allowance all round. Cut strips of fabric the depth of the bed base plus 2 cm (³⁄₄ in) seam allowance at the top and 5 cm (2 in) for the hem. Treat these as for frills and seam to the base.

A bedcover with an edge that is gathered from surface level can be made in the same way as the valance. You just increase the length of the frill. Attach to the top – with the pattern side facing the other way – a section twice the pillow's measurement from front to back and 26 cm (10 in) wider, at either side, than the bed.

USEFUL ADDRESSES AND BOOKS

Crochet

Sally Harding, *Crochet Style*, Windward – a book that includes Tunisian crochet if you are curious about it.

Pauline Turner, *Creative Design in Crochet*, Batsford – dated designs, but a wide range of stitches and techniques.

Starting Crochet – a Coats booklet from Coats stockists.

Dressmaking

Clothkits, Freepost P.O. Box 2500 Lewes, Sussex BN7 3ZB Tel: 0345 900200, sells ready-cut and printed clothes by mail order; most are for children.

Useful Books

Ann Ladbury, *Dressmaking with Basic Patterns*, Batsford.

Ann Ladbury, *Fabrics*, Sidgwick and Jackson – an A-Z of fabrics and how they behave when sewn.

Embroidery and Tapestry

Embroiderers' Guild, Apartment 41, Hampton Court Palace, East Molesey, Surrey KT8 9AU Tel: 081 943 1229 M£M, M, G, Lib, A, promotes embroidery, has a small museum, and sells books by mail. (P.392)

The Royal School of Needlework, Apartment 12a, Hampton Court Palace, East Molesey, Surrey KT8 9AU Tel: 081 943 1432, will stretch, mount and make up and mend items of tapestry (canvas embroidery), embroidery and bead work. It no longer has a shop but has a mail order service. (P.392)

RSN Mail Order, Little Barrington, Burford, Oxon OX18 4TE Tel: 0451 844433, has an excellent range of materials and equipment and an illustrated catalogue (CC). Classes B. (P.392)

Dunlicraft Ltd, Pullman Road, Wigston, Leicester LE8 2DY Tel: 0533 811040, has a list of stockists (sae). (P.392)

Coats, do inexpensive booklets covering most aspects of needlecraft. For stockists contact **Coats Consumer Services**, Patons Crafts, McMullen Road, Darlington, Co. Durham DL1 1YQ Tel: 0325 381010.

Useful Books
Batsford Encyclopaedia of Embroidery Stitches, Batsford.
Thérèse de Dillmont, *The Complete DMC Encyclopaedia of Needlework*, Running Press (USA) – despite Edwardian illustrations, an embroiderer's bible. A book for enthusiasts.

Knitting

Brother Knitting Machine Division, Jones & Brothers, Shepley Street, Audenshaw, Manchester M34 5JD Tel: 061 330 6531, runs a telephone advice service for its own machines. It has a list of tutors and classes throughout Britain, and of knitting-machine shops which stock their machines. (P.402)

Colourway, 112a Westbourne Grove, London W2 5RU Tel: 071 229 1432, has an interesting and original range of wools. (P.401)

Patricia Roberts, 60 Kinnerton Street, London SWIX 8ES Tel: 071 235 4742, has original designs and wools in lovely colours. (P.401)

Useful Books
Hugh Ehrman ed, *Designer Knitting*, Century Hutchinson – highly original designs.
Shelagh Hollingworth, *Knitting and Crochet for the Physically Handicapped and Elderly*, Batsford – hard-to-find old-fashioned patterns like fingerless gloves.
Michael Pearson, *Traditional Knitting*, Collins – a fascinating history of British traditional patterns with guidelines for recreating them.
Debby Robinson, *The Encyclopaedia of Knitting*, Michael Joseph – a first-rate book on techniques.

Knots

Bigon and Ragazzoni, *The Century Guide to Knots*, Century – covers vast range of knots.

Patchwork

Quilters Guild, Dean Clough Business Park, Halifax, W. Yorks HX3 5AX Tel: 0422 347669 – is an international guild for increasing the understanding of patchwork, quilting and appliqué. You may only join if you do one of these. M&M, M, L, Lib, workshops, Young Quilters 5-18. (P.404)

Useful Books
Avril Colby, *Patchwork*, Batsford.
Alice Timmins, *Patchwork Technique and Design*, Batsford.
Fine Patchwork and Quilting, Odori.

General

Fred Aldous Ltd, P.O. Box 135, 37 Lever Street, Manchester M60 1VX Tel: 061 236 2477, has lampshade-making items and for a wide range of crafts.

Jacobs, Young and Westbury Ltd, Bridge House, Bridge Road, Haywards Heath, Sussex RH16 1VA Tel: 0444 412411, has the essentials for lampshade-making, chair caning, or restoring rush seats.

Pointnorth Ltd, 16-18 Newry Fawr, Holyhead, Anglesey, Gwynedd LL65 1LB Tel: 0407 760195, has all the frabrics for making soft luggage, tents, groundsheets and so on, plus waterproofing and the zips and fasteners to go with them, and even patterns.

Russell & Chapple Ltd, 23 Monmouth Street, London WC2H 9DE Tel: 071 836 7521, sells a most unusual range of items – artists' canvasses and wooden stretchers, bunting, webbing, boat and car covers, stage cloths and druggets, plus hessian in good colours for walls or cheap curtains. Shop or mail order.

Useful Book
Which? way to make soft furnishings, Consumers' Association, Hodder and Stoughton.

Things Mechanical

Bicycles • Cameras • Car Buying and Selling • Car Driving • Car Care and Maintenance • Computers

BICYCLES

My own relationship with bicycles ended when a pedal irreplaceably parted company from the ancient frame of the secondhand two-wheeler I had bought as a sixth-former. I would never have looked closely at a bicycle again had not my succession of children required bikes of every type and size, right up to a multi-gear racer. It is to my, now adult, son – whose hobby it is – that I owe most of the information in this section.

Buying a Bicycle

Children's Bicycles

The ideal time to learn to ride a bicycle is when very young, and the best place to buy it is a bicycle shop rather than a toy shop. There are still traditional cycle shops where they take pleasure in guiding a child up through the stages of bicycle riding, and make sure it has the right bike for its size and ability. Such a shop is well worth searching out, and the men in it are usually good at telling the child how to care for the bicycle too – which may be more effective than words from parents.

Ideally, children start with tricycles. Even at this stage there are differences. Good tricycles have ball bearings at the main moving parts, such as the headset where the front wheel turns; cheap ones don't. The cheap ones go perfectly well; the snag comes if they have to be repaired. Those without ball bearings may be impossible or expensive to put right. As tricycles fairly seldom need repairing it's a gamble which is the better option.

From tricycles the next stage is a small bike, with large tyres and a pair of outrider wheels splaying out from the back wheel as stabilizers – so the bike won't easily fall over. It should be possible to remove the outriders when they are no longer needed. Children like the achievement of riding without the stabilizers as soon as possible, but taking them off before the child is steady will just give you the job of mopping up rather more grazed knees.

Small-wheeled bicycles are usually needed until a child is about 12 years old and at every stage the bicycles should be given a critical look. According to those in the business, there's a lot of rubbish around in junior bikes. There are also seductive bicycles which may not be the best ones for the job. For example, children tend to fall in love with the brilliantly marketed BMX bicycles. They are fun for messing about on but aren't designed for flat ground.

Adult Bicycles

The big divide in adult bicycles is between small wheels (20 in or under) and large wheels (around 27 in). Within the large-wheeled group there is a steady gradation from heavy basic bikes to light sporty ones.

The big disadvantage of small wheels is that you have to work harder to go at any given speed. This makes them a poor choice for long distances and for hilly country. The plus side is that the slow speed and small wheels make them easy to use in tight situations, such as heavy traffic.

The greatest advantage of small-wheeled bicycles is that there are fold-away models which can be kept in a flat or carried in a car. There are also ones which collapse even more and can be carried as hand luggage. Before buying any folding bike it is advisable to scour the latest tests on them, in *Which* and in cycling magazines, and check the reports on the folding mechanisms.

Buying Secondhand

Bicycles seem like a natural secondhand buy. They can be, but there are basic precautions which need to be taken:

- Be suspicious of secondhand sports bikes which have been used for over 2 years. The gearing is likely to be very worn and this is expensive to put right. But it isn't easy to recognize worn gearing unless you have seen it before.
- Rotate the wheels while looking at them edge on, so the far side seems to disappear behind the nearside. Then rotate them. If the far side doesn't stay invisible the wheel is buckled and a bad buy.
- Check the brakes: they shouldn't need to travel very far before gripping – to sell a bike with defective brakes is illegal.
- Look at the side view of the line of the main column from handlebars to front wheel. The upper part of the 'fork' holding the wheel should be in line with the column itself. If it isn't the bike has crashed and could be weak elsewhere.
- Check the paint of crossbars near where they join the uprights. Vertical cracks in the paintwork, or rust, also suggest a crash has damaged the frame, which is potentially dangerous.

Care and Maintenance

Bicycles must have a certain amount of care and maintenance if they are to remain safe. A bike which has been out in the rain should be dried with a cloth before being put away, and if it is being used much it should be checked once a week. The most essential points to check regularly are the brakes.

Brakes

Make sure the rim of the wheel is free of oil and grease, otherwise the brakes won't work. Use spirit to remove any oil or grease you find, but keep it off the tyres. After that there are three parts to having safe brakes:

1 Is the pad correct for the wheel rim?
   With new bikes this is no problem, but you do need to be careful when buying replacement pads and check those on a secondhand bike. Most brakes work by pressing against the rim of the wheel and not all brake pads suit all rims. Having the wrong brake pad may not show in the dry, but in the wet it can be dangerous. Leather pads are bad for aluminium wheel rims but ideal for steel rims. The other possibility for steel is a special composition.
2 Is the pad in good condition?
   Pads need to be replaced when worn by half their full thickness. They are easily replaced but if one end of the shoe which holds them is closed, put it to the front so the block doesn't slide out. Make sure it is positioned so it will pull against the rim not the tyre.
3 Does the cable need adjusting?
   Most brakes work on cables which go down to levers which operate the brakes. As the brakes start to wear you can tighten them by taking up the slack in the brake cable. You do this by turning the barrel screw at the end of the cable housing.

Chain

Since the chain communicates your energy to the wheels it's more important than it looks. It must be kept clean and well oiled, and if it has been used over salted roads it needs to be cleaned immediately or it may seize up.

How often you need to remove and clean it varies with the use. If you do a lot of serious cycling it could be every two weeks; if you only use it an average amount then every couple of months will be enough. On a hub-gear or single-speed bicycle the chain will undo at a spring clip which you can open with a twist of a screwdriver. But you need a pin extractor to undo one of the links on the chain of derailleur gears.

Having removed the chain, use meths, paraffin or petrol and a small scrubbing brush to get off all the old oil and dirt. Replace the chain on the bicycle and rub it well with a light multipurpose oil, such as 3 in 1, on a cloth, back-pedalling as you do so.

If a chain breaks it can be repaired with a chain riveting tool. With derailleur gears the spring-loading will adjust the tension. With other bicycles you need to adjust the position of the wheel until there is about 1.5 cm (½ in) of play at the mid-point.

Gears

The most basic type of gear is the hub gear with its 3 to 5 ratios enclosed in the hub of the wheel. As they aren't exposed, you don't have to do anything about them unless they go wrong. But if they do go wrong take them to an expert as they are hard to put right. You can, however, make minor adjustments, and will probably need to. To stop gears slipping when you change gear you can re-set them by selecting the middle gear, then undoing the lock nuts beneath the cable connector. When the end of the indicator rod is precisely level with the axle you tighten the lock nuts and the adjustment should be correct.

Derailleurs look more complicated, but are far more amenable to DIY. By shifting the chain between notched discs of different sizes, it can give between 5 and 21 gears, but the most basic adjustment is to tighten the central bolts on the control levers from time to time. More important is to adjust the tension of the cable – especially if you have removed the back wheel. To adjust it you loosen the anchor bolt on the gear changer, pull the cable through and re-set the adjustment screws on the top of the changer until it moves easily from one gear to another. (Note: one screw adjusts the setting for top gear, the other the setting for bottom gear.)

Handlebars and Saddle

These adjust by undoing a quick release lever, or a bolt. Having undone the nut, tap the bolt lightly with a hammer to release the stem. If an old bike is severely stuck try turning the seat or handlebars sideways rather than pulling. Failing that, put penetrating oil round the joint and leave it.

Tyres

Tyres must be kept at the right pressure to steer safely, but you don't need a gauge to keep them correctly pumped. Anyone with a reasonable grip can do it by feel, once they have felt them at the correct pressure. When not in use for any time, bicycles should be hung up with the tyres slightly deflated, so the weight isn't carried by the tyres. Check the tyres regularly for anything which might puncture them. If there is a puncture:

1 Turn the bicycle upside down.
2 Remove the wheel from the bicycle. (With a derailleur you need to put it in gear on the smallest sprocket first.)
3 Lever the tyre off with a tyre lever or a strong teaspoon handle. *Don't* use a screwdriver as it may rip the inner tube.
4 Remove the inner tube. If you can't see or hear the puncture, inflate the tube and slowly rotate it through a basin of water. You will see bubbles coming up from the hole.
5 Dry the tube and mark the puncture site with chalk.
6 Roughen the area round the hole with glass paper.
7 Choose a patch which will fully cover the hole and spread a matching area of tyre adhesive (*not* ordinary glue) round the hole.

8 When the adhesive is almost dry press the patch on firmly.

9 Wipe off any surplus glue and let it dry completely.

10 Dust over the patch with French chalk to stop it sticking to the tyre.

11 Pump up the tube. Test the repair in water, then deflate it.

12 Check, inside and out, that nothing is in the tyre which could cause another puncture; and that the spokes aren't sticking up on the wheel rim.

13 Push the valve through the hole in the tyre, and slip the inner tube into place before pumping it up.

14 Replace the tyre on the wheel, levering it carefully so as not to pinch the inner tube.

Oiling

To get the maximum efficiency from your bike you can buy special oils for every part of a bicycle – if your interest and pocket allow – but a light multipurpose oil will do the job quite well enough for the average bicycle.

Oiling Points for a Bicycle

3 speed hub gears

Saddle

Brake lever

Handle bars

Frame

Wheel bearing

Derailleur gears

Chain

Pedal

Addresses and suggestions for further reading are at the ends of chapters.

If a bicycle is being used all the time it needs to be oiled as follows:

- Pedals – monthly
- Wheel hubs – monthly
- Gears – monthly
- Brake stirrups – monthly
- Headset and bearings – a light oil monthly (some need only a touch, some quite a bit; check with your manual or a bicycle shop). Turn the bicycle upside down to do this or the oil may drip onto the tyres.
- Brake cable – light oil occasionally.

Fitting the Bicycle to the Rider

For safety, a bicycle must be the right size for the rider. But the less good bicycle shops try to sell children's bicycles by the age of the child. It may be a rough guide but children don't always come in standard gauges. So the actual size of the child is a much better guide. You may need to be firm with the shop about this. When my 12-year-old son was pushing 6 foot, one shop insisted that a 12-year-old must need a child's bike.

To allow for growth you need to buy the biggest bicycle the child can manage. This means that with the seat fully down they should be able just to touch the ground securely with their feet on each side. If you want to buy a bicycle as a surprise you can pretend you are measuring up for trousers.

A rough guide if you see them near a bike they like is that the cross bar of a boy's bike (or the equivalent point on a girl's) should be just below crotch level when they stand beside it.

Adjusting a Saddle

For both children and adults the saddle should be adjusted so the leg is fully stretched when the arch of the foot is over the pedal at its lowest point. The handlebars should then be adjusted to give a comfortable position.

In adjusting the seat and handlebars, there should be *not less* than 8 cm (3 in) of handlebar stem, or seat pillar, inside the column.

Safety

Carrying Children and Luggage

The basic safety rule when carrying children or luggage on a bicycle is not to carry more than half your own weight, or it will be dangerously unstable. For a child's seat alone, fitted on the rear, the weight limit is only up to 20 kg (45 lb) and the seat needs to be carefully attached and guards fitted to prevent a child's fingers getting caught in any part of the bicycle.

Visibility

Cyclists need to do everything possible to make themselves visible. Unless they also drive a car, they seldom realize how easily bicycles blend into the background when a motorist is mainly watching for larger vehicles. A big danger is wearing dark clothing. Reflective diagonal bands, and arm and leg bands all increase visibility and you can now buy some with small lights on.

Reflectors on the wheel spokes make a bicycle more visible from the side, and a sticking-out reflector makes it easier to see from behind. And, when buying cycling clothing, choose colours which show up in bad weather and in the dark.

Protection

A good crash helmet protects the skull but leaves the ears clear so you can still hear traffic. It should have a hard plastic shell and a strong foam inner lining. Look for a BS number to be sure it has been tested and approved.

Cycling Proficiency

There is a national cycling proficiency scheme which is run by the **Royal Society for the Prevention of Accidents** through local Road Safety Officers. Children from the age of 9 can be given training and road safety tests plus lessons on bicycle care. Contact the address on page 444 if you want to know the name of your nearest centre and your council hasn't been able to help.

Theft

Many hundreds of thousands of bicycles are stolen every year, so it is worth taking a few preventive measures.

Note all the details of your bicycle, so it can be identified by the police if it is stolen. In addition to the colour, model and make, there should be a maker's serial number on the frame somewhere. This is vital.

Park it where lots of people are passing, and put the chain through both wheels and the frame. (This deters thieves from stealing parts or sawing through the chain.) Alternatively, use one of the U-shaped shackle locks. These are made of hardened steel and are very effective. They are more expensive than chains, but some carry a year's insurance. As the insurance element in the price is considerably cheaper than most independent insurance, this makes them an especially good buy for those who can't put their bike on a household policy. But the insurance may only cover loss incurred *when the lock was in use* and you may need to *prove* that it was used. Not easy.

Tools

For basic care and repairs, you need a puncture repair kit, 2 to 3 tyre levers, allen keys, a multi-size spanner, chain riveting tool (unless the chain is super-link) and pliers.

CAMERAS

This section is for those who are wondering about buying a camera, and for those who have one and are not sure how it works.

Buying a Camera

There are basically three types of camera on the market:

1 Cartridge load cameras in which almost everything is

automatic and the film comes in a cartridge, so you don't have to fiddle about.

2 Compact cameras in which most functions are automatic, but you load a normal 35 mm film.

3 Single lens reflex cameras, known as SLR cameras. These use 35 mm film and although you can often control most of the functions by hand, many modern ones offer automatic options and have built-in extras such as flash, a zoom lens or autowind.

The choice of camera depends entirely on what type of person you are and what you want to do with it. There is no camera which is 'best'. Nor is it reasonable to say that a beginner should start with a very undemanding camera, with a cartridge load, and then move on to something more exacting. Some total beginners would love to be able to take pictures with so little thought; others would hate the lack of flexibility.

If you simply want to be a 'point and press' photographer – as they put it in the trade – then there are any number of cartridge and compact cameras on the market which can produce good pictures with little or no thought.

However, before buying one, do consider what you may want to do with the camera. An automatic is fine for happy snaps on the beach or in the garden. But automatic cameras do have some limitations, so only buy one if you can either afford to replace it with a more versatile camera when you need to, or if you are sure you will never want any of the options it lacks.

When choosing an SLR camera a key point is that some are 'aperture priority' – so you select the aperture setting and the camera selects the shutter speed (both explained below). Others are 'shutter priority' – which is simply vice versa. Some let you select both. The first essential, when buying a camera, is to find your preference between aperture priority or shutter priority. The range is constantly improving, so check out any reports in *Which* magazine and read the magazine *Which Camera* before talking to local dealers. Prices are also variable and can be judged by advertisements; the mail order camera company on page 445 is also a good yardstick. There is no disadvantage in buying at the cheapest price for that model, as the guarantee will be the same whatever the price.

Cameras Explained

The modern camera seems to have passed into the realms of space-age technology, but it is really exactly as it was in the nineteenth century: a box containing film and a hole which lets light onto the film to record an image.

Films vary in the amount of light they need to create a picture. Those which need very little light are called fast films; those that need a lot of light are called slow.

However complex a camera may look, the first thing to get right is the amount of light reaching the film. Without that there is no picture. Two things decide how much light reaches the film:

● the size of the opening letting in light (the aperture)
● the length of time light enters for (the shutter speed).

If you are a 'point and press' photographer with an automatic camera, both the size of the opening (aperture) and the time it stays open (shutter speed) are set for you. If you have an SLR camera you may be able to choose the opening (aperture) or the shutter speed, or both.

As you would expect, the two interact. So if you increase the hole, you can let light enter for a shorter time yet still get a picture. So long as you increase one

The Working Parts of a Camera

Film advance lever
Accessory shoe
ASA Film speed dial
Light meter switch lever
Rewind crank
Shutter release button
Rewind release lever
Shoulder strap eyelet
Self timer
Aperture ring
Focusing ring
Lens

Addresses and suggestions for further reading are at the ends of chapters.

as you reduce the other, and vice versa, the situation – so far as light is concerned – will always balance out (just as 2 + 4 = 4 + 2).

Automatic cameras may judge the light for themselves and decide on the size of the opening and how long the shutter should be open. On some other cameras there may be simple settings, so you set it for a sunny day, a cloudy day or flash.

Shutter Speed Range

On most SLR cameras the range of shutter speeds is from a 1000th of a second, to 1 or 2 seconds, and there is also a 'B timer'. When set on B timer the general rule is broken and the shutter stays open for however long you hold down the shutter release button.

The shutter speed controls the length of time the film is exposed to the image. What I've said above makes it sound as if it doesn't matter whether you have a fast shutter speed and a large opening (aperture) or vice versa. That is true if you just want to get *an* image on the film. But to get a *good* image you need to balance the two to suit the situation. This is really very simple.

Fast Movement

If a photograph is being taken of a fast moving object, such as a bird or a racing car, then a fast shutter speed is needed to 'freeze' the subject and prevent it blurring. This obviously demands a wide opening (aperture) to give the film enough light.

But suppose you wanted a slight blur, to show its speed. Then you would have the shutter speed slightly slower, so the car moved past the camera while it was still open. With a slower shutter speed you would then use a slightly smaller opening (aperture).

A racing car is an extreme example, but the same would be true of capturing a child running or playing, or even the fleeting expression on someone's face – though the speed could be slower, so the shutter could stay open longer and the opening (aperture) be smaller.

When Close Up

Movement also counts if you want to get very close to something. A flower which is barely trembling in the breeze will look perfectly stationary at most speeds if you photograph it from several metres (yards) away. But the closer you go the more any swaying will show on the picture, and if you plan to fill the whole frame with a single bloom you will need a fast shutter speed to cut out both the tremble of the flower and camera wobble. Here again fast speed will go with a large opening (aperture).

Shutter Speed and Light

If the light is poor, and whatever you want to photograph is not moving quickly (or – preferably – not moving at all) a slow shutter speed can be used. But below a 60th of a second even a slight unsteadiness in the hand will make the picture lose its sharpness, so it is wiser to support the camera on something steady. This doesn't have to be a tripod. Many photographers take excellent pictures, in very low light, by just resting a camera on a wall or a car (with the engine off and nobody moving inside it).

It is the combination of shutter speed and aperture which form the final exposure that will achieve a crisp, light-balanced photograph.

What the Size of the Opening (Aperture) Does

The examples above demanded a particular shutter speed, and the size of the opening (aperture) had to follow from that. But it doesn't have to be like that: the size of the opening also gives different qualities to a picture.

Light Effects

We may think of light as a single entity, but it isn't really like that. For example, if a child is sitting with her back to a window the amount of light behind her will be far greater than the amount on her face. If you simply focused the camera in her direction and adjusted the f-stop by the reading on your light meter (which is what an automatic camera would do) she would come out as a silhouette against a nicely photographed background. To photograph her face you would need to set the f-stop (see below) for the light *on* her face. So you would either take a reading by going close to her or take an overall reading and then open up by one and a half to two f-stops. Then she would be properly exposed and the background would probably be rather bleached – which can be very effective.

Effects on Focus

Whenever a camera is pointed at anything it is focused on a particular point (automatic cameras which have 'autofocus' will automatically focus on the first object which occupies a major part of the picture; other cameras have to be focused – see page 423). The point which is focused on (and everything to right and left of it) will look perfectly sharp and clear in the picture. How clear everything else will look depends on the size of the opening (aperture). The rule is:

- the smaller the opening (aperture) the greater the range of distances, behind and in front of the point of focus, which will look crisp and in focus.
- the larger the opening, the more hazy things will look which are behind or in front of the point of focus.

In a non-automatic camera the size of the opening (aperture) is controlled by turning a ring on the lens which is marked in f-stops. The more you close the opening (aperture) the larger the number of the f-stop and each f-stop allows in half as much light as the previous one. The distance which is in focus at any f-stop is called the depth of field.

Pros and Cons of Different Depths of Field

When you use a large f-stop, giving a small depth of field, you have to be far more precise in your focusing, or your subject may be out of focus. But once you get that right the subject will stand out sharply against a softly blurred background – which can be very effective.

If you use a small f-stop, giving a large depth of field,

much more is in focus, so you can get away with less precise focusing and do it faster. The penalty is that your main subject may look more of an also-ran, as everything else will be just as clear. It is points like this which make the mysterious difference between a 'snap' and a photograph.

The size of the opening (aperture) isn't the only thing which affects the range of distances that will be in focus. Two other factors play a part: how close the subject is to the camera, and the type of lens you are using. The closer a subject is to the camera, the less depth of field at any f-stop. Different lenses operate within a different range of f-stops and also have different depths of field at the same stops. So, if you focus a standard 50 mm lens, and a 28 mm wide angle lens and a telephoto lens on the same point, and choose the same f-stop the depth of field will vary considerably.

Depth of Field

Above: How different f-stops affect the amount of light entering the camera. The higher the f-stop the greater the depth of field.

Below: How different lenses affect the depth of field. The figures at the side in feet (metres) show the depth of field for each lens.

Film

How It Works

Film works by capturing light in microscopic particles called silver halide which are embedded in a gelatin to form what is called an emulsion. Colour slide film (also called 'reversal') produces both slides and excellent prints. In theory, colour print film will also produce colour slides and black and white prints. In practice,

amateurs can seldom get slide quality from it. So using slide film usually gives more options.

The larger the particles, the more sensitive they are to light. So fast film uses larger particles than slow film. In the past, if you enlarged two photographs, taken on different speeds of film, the larger particles of the faster film used to give the enlargement a grainy look. However, technical improvements mean that films as fast as ISO 400 now have as fine a grain as ISO 100 used to have, and only with much faster film will graininess be a problem. So this old disadvantage of using fast film has largely gone.

Film Speeds

Film speeds are now shown as two sets of figures like this: 125/22° – the first is the ASA number for cameras using ASA speeds, the second is the DIN number for cameras using DIN speeds.

These are called ISO speeds and an ISO speed is always referred to in terms of the number before the slash. So an ASA 125 and an ISO 125 are just identical 'roses' by other names. The main ISO numbers used by amateurs are these:

ISO 50   Film for studio work.
ISO 100 A very fine-grained film for good light.
ISO 125 A film for most conditions.
ISO 200 A very useful film which allows you to get pictures even in rather poor light. It can be used with a wide range of shutter speeds and apertures.
ISO 400 This allows you to take fast moving objects with a fast shutter speed, so you freeze the action, or possibly even take shots indoors without a flash. It's ideal for places like temples and art galleries where photography may be allowed but flash is banned. But not all cameras can be set to handle this speed of film in bright sunlight. Before buying it check that a camera has a fast enough shutter speed and small enough aperture.

Very fast films, such as ISO 400 and 1000, are widely available and these can be ideal for very low light conditions or capturing extremely fast action.

In choosing film remember that a long lens cuts off some of the light, making it easier to use a very fast film in bright light. But, whatever the ISO, film such as Kodacolor Gold, which is tolerant of errors makes it easier to get good results. And Kodak will now transfer slides or prints on to a CD which will allow you to show them on your television, via a special TV CD player. They can also be shown on a computer screen, if your computer can run CDs of this kind (see page 440).

Film Care

Film dislikes heat and humidity. If you buy professional film it should be kept at below 13°C (50°F). Amateur film is more tolerant and accepts room temperatures, but it still dislikes hot sunlight and if you are taking a film or camera to a hot beach or picnic it is best to keep it in an insulated bag (see page 424).

Addresses and suggestions for further reading are at the ends of chapters.

Flash

Using flash allows you to take pictures when the light is too low for the film you are using. Angle the flash so it bounces off some light surface – such as a white ceiling – and down onto your subject. You don't have to be a demon mathematician to spot the point it needs to bounce off.

Flash can only operate within a limited range. This is 1.2 to 5.5 m (4 to 18 ft) with a normal lens and works best within 2.4 to 3 m (8 to 10 ft), though it will go closer with certain close-up lenses. Objects closer to the flash will look paler than those farther away, so the differences in distance shouldn't be too great.

How to Use a Camera

Inserting Film

For cartridge cameras you just insert the film according to the handbook. With 35 mm you must insert the tongue of the film in the spool to the right and then pull the film spool back to slot in place, so the film stretches across the back of the lens. (Don't worry about this bit getting light on it.) Now use the wind-on lever on the top of the camera to wind on as for 2 exposures. With some cameras you may need to press the shutter button, as if taking a photo, between each wind on, or they will not wind on. Make sure the holes in the film nestle nicely over the little 'cogs' sticking up inside the camera. Then shut the camera. Now wind on *twice* more, looking at the top of the camera on the side where the main film spool is. There is a rewind knob there which will turn if the film is going through properly – as you turn the lever at the other end of the camera. If it doesn't turn open the camera and sort the film out. By winding the film on 4 times you don't lose money. There should still be the correct number of exposures, but by skimping it the film may slip and the whole reel be wasted.

Setting the ISO/ASA

Some modern cameras automatically read a code on the film (called a DX code) which tells them the speed of the film, in which case you needn't make any adjustments at this stage. But most cameras need to be set to operate with the speed of film you have bought. Look for a knob marked ASA or ISO (it doesn't matter which as they are both the same film speed by another name). Set the knob so the number indicated matches the ISO/ASA speed written on the box of film. Sometimes it doesn't say ISO: it just has a figure like 100, 200 or 400 written on it.

Setting the Exposure

On a simple camera this may be done automatically or you may have to judge whether the light is bright or dull, and set it to sun or cloud. Don't go by whether there *are* clouds. It can be cloudy but quite bright – especially if water, snow or white buildings are reflecting the light.

With an SLR camera you will need to check the light meter and turn the ring on the lens to the right f-stop (see page 422), or adjust the shutter speed, bearing in mind the points on pages 420 to 422. If in doubt, on an average day, with a moderately fast film set the shutter speed to 125. This is fast enough to minimize the effects of wobbling hands or any slight movement by your subjects.

Focusing

Simple cameras may give you a choice of close-in (indicated by a head and shoulders silhouette), a few feet away (figures full length) or at a distance (indicated by trees or mountains). Set the control to whichever position is most similar to what you want to photograph.

SLR cameras can have various types of focusing, but the most common is a split field. To focus with this look through the camera and try to look at something (in your picture) with a line in. Turn the focusing ring on the lens until the line is perfectly straight.

Lenses

One of the great advantages of an SLR camera is being able to change lenses. It adds a whole new dimension to taking photographs if you can pop on a wide angle lens to capture a sweep of scenery or use a zoom to 'get close' to people and animals which would be camera-shy. Most camera shops have a choice of good quality lenses, and if you are going to change lenses it is worth having as good a one as you can afford.

Lens types vary in two ways: how wide an angle of picture they capture, and the distance from the subject at which they operate well. The standard lens offered with most 35 mm cameras is 50 mm. This lens captures the scene very much as the eye would see it. It operates from about half a metre to infinity.

From 50 mm downwards there are the wide angle lenses. These allow you to take in more in all directions. So they are useful for landscapes. The disadvantage is that, in capturing more of the scene than the human eye they distort perspective.

Any camera with a standard lens can work at a distance as close as 1.2 m (4 ft). To get closer, for example to take flowers or insects, you need a macro lens designed to produce sharp pictures with very little distortion when very close to the subject. There are zoom lenses with macro facilities but these are seldom as good as a pure macro.

From 50 mm upwards (e.g. 110 mm, 200 mm to the extreme of 3,000 mm) there are the telescopic and caterdioptric lenses which enable you to capture that lion you daren't get close to, in daredevil pictures which look as if you did (to all but an expert eye). The zoom is the most flexible lens as it allows you to alter the point of focus very quickly, which is perfect when taking anything in motion, so wildlife and sports photographers tend to use these. A 70 or 80 to 210 mm lens is one of the most useful and most widely sold.

Since these lenses exaggerate the closeness of the subject they will also exaggerate camera shake; you therefore need to have the shutter only open for a short time if you possibly can. The rule of thumb is that to avoid camera shake the slowest shutter speed you can use is the number closest to the focal length of your lens (but not less than it). So:

Focal Length	Shutter Speed
50 mm lens	60th of a second
80 mm lens	125th of a second (from 60 to 125 may seem a big gap, but no speed closer to it is above 60)
200 mm lens	250th of a second
400 mm lens	500th of a second

Problem Solving

Blank film It probably failed to go through the camera. (see page 423).

Bleached and pale pictures Over-exposure. Either you had too slow a shutter speed or the aperture was open too wide. Another possibility is that this was a faster film than the previous one and you forgot to change the film speed to the new ISO (ASA/DIN) setting.

Blobs on the picture You either got something in the way of the lens (such as your fingers) or the lens is dirty.

Blurred picture Either the camera wobbled or the picture was out of focus.

Streaks on the first few shots You pointed the film cassette at the light when loading or unloading it, and a little light got through the slit.

Taking Better Snaps

The rules for taking expert photographs are rather different from those for taking snaps. The following hints are for snaps, not art work.

★ Get in close to your subject. Whatever you are taking should almost fill the frame – a picture of a whole house seldom means much; a shot of a stunning door (or face) can be great.

★ Don't get people to pose. It's far more interesting to catch them unawares with typical (or odd) expressions than to have a row of heads facing the camera.

★ Don't take every picture standing up or sitting on a chair. Try other levels for a change. Children often look better from lower down.

★ Don't be so busy looking at the subject of the photograph that you don't see the curious post in the background seeming to stick out of the person's ear or the dog doing something unmentionable by Granny's foot.

★ If you want to get pictures of people, be patient. Pretend to take pictures until they get tired of paying attention to you and start behaving normally; *then* photograph them.

★ Don't feel you always have to have your back to the light. That makes your victims face the sun, and screw up their eyes; side lighting is usually more effective and kinder.

When You Go on Holiday

● Check the camera over at least a week before leaving.
● Buy spare batteries – sizes which seem standard in Britain may not be obtainable in some countries.
● Buy plenty of film (unless you are sure it is cheaper at the airport or where you are going).
● As heat can seriously affect film, keep it cool. If you will want to take your camera about in a hot climate, put it and your film (plus books but *not* swimming things) in one of the insulated cooler bags supermarkets sell for frozen food and picnics. *Make sure you don't tuck in anything liquid which might spill on the camera.*
● Keep sand and dust off the camera and *never* open the back when dust or sand are blowing.

Don't let film go through X-ray machines if you can avoid it. The faster the film, the greater risk that it will be harmed by X-ray equipment in airports. Some airport equipment may be safe for film, but a lot isn't – whatever they say. So, if you want to have anything to show for your trip, keep all your films – used and unused – at the top of your hand luggage and take them out before the luggage is X-rayed. The more often film is X-rayed, the more likely it is to fog, so if you are touring you may need to get some processed *en route*.

CAR BUYING AND SELLING

The Cost of Buying

A car is probably the most expensive thing you will ever buy – apart from a home. So, before buying one it's as well to tot up the real cost – it comes to a lot more than just the price. To get an idea you need to add up the figures for the following on the car you have in mind:

● the depreciation (an average family car loses about £1,000 to £1,200 of its value in its first year)
● the interest on the money you borrow (or interest not earned if you take money out of the bank and pay cash)
● insurance
● road tax
● servicing
● petrol – miles x price (an average motorist drives 10,000 miles a year)
● parking
● replacement cost of tyres
● an annual MOT test if the car is over 3 years old
● special clothing for a motorcyclist.

Add up the figures you get and divide your answer by the number of miles of motoring you expect to do and you will have the cost per mile – you may find it would be less expensive to take a taxi each time.

★ The figures for a motorbike shouldn't be so daunting, but before buying a motorbike check that the law allows you to buy the type you covet – the post office has a leaflet on this.

New v Used

The moment you take delivery of a new car it becomes a used car and is worth less than you paid for it (unless it is a rare car in enormous demand). The steepest drop in value in the first year is for cars at the top and bottom ends of the price range, but even an average family car can lose over 15 per cent of its value in the first year.

With a used car you get a cheaper car, but you risk buying a car which will have the problems associated with its age and may also have been worn by bad driving and poor maintenance. Some cars are far tougher than others and will give fewer problems in their old age. So the type of car you want is an important factor in choosing whether or not to buy secondhand. Similar comparisons apply to motorbikes.

Buying New

When buying a new car or motorcycle you pit your intelligence and judgement against millions of pounds' worth of seductive advertising and brochures. You only get good value if you are forearmed against the blandishments of both, with a knowledge of exactly how well any car lasts, as well as performs. The research is easy. *Which* magazine, from the **Consumers' Association** (page 692), does reports on family cars each month (there is no longer a separate *Motoring Which*), plus an annual *Car Buying Guide* which includes user reports from 25,000 people. Back copies should be in your public library. The **AA** (page 445) has road test reports' on most cars, which are free to members, and good motoring magazines also have reports and tables of new car prices.

If you can pick your timing, buy either early in the year or just after the registration letters change – then the car seems new for longer and you get a better price when you sell.

Comparing Makes
To get the best out of any reports it helps to have a system, such as listing the points you want to look at and writing beside them the facts for each model you are interested in. Here's a useful 12-point checklist of the basics:

1 petrol consumption – town and touring (and grade of petrol)
2 depreciation (some cars hold their value better than others)
3 cost of insurance (the cost rises with the category and it isn't just sports cars which carry a premium)
4 suitability to your type of driving – speed, parking etc
5 number of doors – for young children you need child locks or only 2 doors
6 boot capacity and ease of carrying shopping or luggage
7 cost and frequency of servicing
8 ease of getting servicing done near you
9 maximum speed
10 time taken from 50 to 70 mph (this is usually a realistic figure, whereas 0 to 60 mph tends to be much less so)
11 the real cost of the car, on the road
12 the details of the manufacturer's warranty.

In theory, all the usual legal protections apply to a car as much as to anything else. But in practice, though you can get a company to replace a faulty chair; it is well nigh impossible to get a faulty car totally replaced. So the poor owner is faced with a series of battles over individual repairs. It therefore pays to buy a reliable make – however much fun a car is, it's no fun off the road.

If you do have trouble with a car, and the dealer isn't giving you much joy, get on to the manufacturer. He has a reputation to maintain.

Prices
The car industry has been plagued by over-production for years now. So discounts are rife, as are extras like special deals on servicing – for example, car loans while yours is in dock. But don't buy an amazing bargain without checking out the model – it may be a car which has been given the thumbs-down by a lot of people.

Part Exchange – Pros and Cons
You will usually get a better price by selling your car privately than you will by trading it in. You can then talk down the price of the new car by playing one dealer off against another. However, it is illegal to misrepresent the condition of goods you sell, so if you know the car has a fault it may be best to sell it to a garage, as they may be less put off than an individual. (See also Selling, page 428.) Some companies may offer to help you finance the purchase. See Consumer Law before you accept the offer.

Taking Delivery
On delivery of a car or motorcycle you should be given:

● the pre-delivery inspection checklist – make sure that all the points on it have been properly checked, and no defects found
● the manufacturer's warranty
● the handbook
● the vehicle registration documents (log book).

Buying a Car Abroad and Importing It

Car and motorcycle prices in Britain used to be inflated compared to those on the Continent, and there used to be a clear case in favour of buying abroad. Whether this is worthwhile now depends on the model, the relative strength of the two currencies and how good a deal you can strike – in 1987 the saving averaged 15 per cent to 20 per cent. But you need to be meticulous in your research. Here are some checkpoints:

● Check out the company and choose an established dealer; pick the wrong one and you may well lose your money – they die like flies.
● Check every detail of the specifications in that country. You *can't count on a model having the same ones as it would in Britain*. The name is no guarantee.
● Read the small print about price increases.
● Check that the warranties will be valid in Britain.
● Check the details of the delivery date.

The **AA** (page 445) can provide information on importing and registering a car and the **Consumers' Association** publishes an 'Action Kit – Importing Your Car' which tells you everything you need to know. It is well worth getting. Mistakes in this field can cost you dear.

★ If you want to buy or sell a special registration number, companies such as **Elite Motors** deal in them, and the DVLA (page 445) has a monthly auction.

Buying Secondhand

About 4 million used cars change hands in Britain each year, and it's estimated that one person in ten is dissatisfied with their purchase – that's 400,000 disappointed people a year. If you don't want to be one of them you need to look into any secondhand purchase very carefully.

Preparing to Buy

The first thing to do is put yourself in a bargaining position by talking to the manager of a garage which services cars of the type you plan to buy. Discover its most common faults, and how much it costs to put them right. Make a note of every price so you have something to show a would-be seller when you haggle over the price.

A vehicle must be covered by insurance before you drive it. If you already have car insurance, a phone call to your broker should give you immediate cover so you can test-drive cars. If you aren't insured, arrange cover with a broker before you go out to see a vehicle, so you can insure it in a hurry if you decide to buy.

Dealers

If you use a dealer, for a new or a used car, pick one which is a member of the Society of Motor Manufacturers and Traders (SMMT), **Retail Motor Industry Association**, the Scottish Motor Trade Association Ltd (SMTA) or the Motorcycle Retailers Association (see page 445).

● Dealers must make a pre-sale inspection of the vehicle and give you a checklist of faults they find. Those faults are your responsibility, unless the dealer agrees to put them right. But it is illegal to sell the vehicle if the faults make it unroadworthy.
● Code dealers must check the vehicle's mileage.
● Any claims made must by law be true – but get them in writing anyway – there are liars in this industry as in any.
● A dealer may offer a warranty – but check what it covers and for how long.

However, a car bought from a dealer is unlikely to be a bargain; the same car from an owner-driver should be quite a bit cheaper. If you read the small print you may find the advantages of some dealers' guarantees may not be what they seem at first glance.

Auctions

Auctions are risky for the inexperienced, because you can't drive the car or have it inspected by an expert –

and people can, and do, use auctions to sell loads of junk. They may also be used to sell reborn wrecks.

Despite that, auctions can also produce bargains if you really know about cars, and auctioneers are much better to deal with than you might expect. However, your legal protection when buying by auction is limited, because auctioneers may legally opt out of many of the usual sellers' obligations (see page 447). Read the small print in the auction catalogue and on any notices which are up. The rule is *caveat emptor* – buyer beware.

Buying Privately

A vehicle bought privately, through an advertisement or a computer contact, is often the best buy. Car or motorcycle magazines, local papers and *Exchange and Mart* are all good sources of advertisements, and you can also buy by computer (see page 428). However, some of the consumer protection laws don't apply to private sales. A vehicle sold privately need only be 'as described', and this attracts cowboys who pose as private sellers. To protect yourself against these:

● Scan the columns for the same phone number cropping up for more than one car.
● Be suspicious of any number you can only ring between very limited hours (they are probably manning a phone box).
● Don't let anyone bring the car round to you – they may be concealing their true address, and will afterwards melt into the night with your money, leaving you with a dud car.
● Watch for trade terms like 'All good' appearing in 'private' advertisements.
● Make sure the seller's name is in the log book – and distrust any excuses.
● Don't think an MOT is any guarantee of roadworthiness. Cowboys switch licence plates, so a good car is tested while bearing the number plate of the heap of junk they plan to sell you. Then they switch back the number plate so that the bad car appears to have an MOT.

★ If you find a good buy try to pay cash and use this to bargain the price down – most people are tempted by a thick wad of notes.

Checks from Professionals

Even the most honest seller may be unaware of hidden faults in a vehicle, so you can't even buy from your grandmother without risk. It is well worth getting an AA or RAC inspection first, and protecting yourself legally by agreeing to buy it only 'subject to inspection'. Inspection costs money, but it could save you a great deal more. If the seller seems reluctant to have it inspected they probably have something to hide, so leave it alone.

If the inspection shows up faults – but the car is still worth buying – get the seller to lower the price by whatever it will cost to put the faults right. But don't feel that having had it inspected you are committed to buying. You aren't – unless you make some commitment in words or writing. A cheaper and quicker check – though less thorough – is an MOT. If it doesn't pass you will have avoided buying a dud, and if it passes you know it's roadworthy – for the moment, though it may have non-MOT faults which will soon cause problems. If you tell the centre why you are having it tested they may be prepared to tell you about such faults as well.

Checking a Car Yourself
Before you get to that stage, there are a number of checks which should tell you whether it is worth having tested. First, check the car's log, insurance, MOT and service history (see page 426 for phoney MOTs) – a careful owner should have every receipt. As a precaution, telephone the previous owner and ask who they sold it to and whether it was in any accidents. Then go over the car itself. The Association of British Insurers (page 542) sells a video showing how to check out some of the following points.

Checking the Bodywork
One of the most common causes of cars failing the MOT is rust. Nowadays faults like that can be far more expensive to put right than problems in the engine. So first check for rust, or damage to the body. If it has been patched up and resprayed it will show, unless it was very professionally done – in which case the chances are they didn't spray over rubbish.

- Look carefully at the paint surface against the light. If it has a faintly orange-peel look it has been resprayed.
- Meticulously check all surfaces which aren't painted – including inside the engine; most resprays leave paint traces *somewhere*.
- Go over the surface of the car with a good magnet – where it fails to cling the body-work has been filled, probably after rust. Beware.
- If you don't have a magnet tap carefully over every inch and listen for a change of sound.
- Get under the car and look for rust there too – if you can. And lift the carpets and look for rust under them. Be suspicious of carpet which has been glued down and of areas recently undersealed: both may conceal rust. Rust underneath is costly and dangerous.
- Look for rust on the headlamp reflectors, on some cars a new pair could be expensive.
- Check the chromework for cracks.
- Inspect the join between the bumper and the chassis. If the bumper supports are bent or cracked the car has been in a crash, and could give dangerously at the next impact.
- Don't necessarily be put off by a small dent – it should take money off the car's value but it won't fail you an MOT, and it tells you that the car is honest, not patched up, or, at least, not recently. Just in case it was done earlier it is still worth checking over.

Checking the Interior
- Look hard at the mileometer. If it has been reset the numbers may not be perfectly in line.
- Look at the pedals. On a car which has really done 30,000 miles or under there shouldn't be much wear on the accelerator or the brake.
- Look at the dent in the driver's seat. Unless the owner is very heavy, a car with genuinely low mileage shouldn't show much wear.
- Check that all the seat belts work. Most belts can't be mended and have to be totally replaced – not cheap. And a faulty belt could make it illegal to drive or carry a passenger.

Checking the Mechanisms
- Go round and press the car down to bounce it. If the shock absorbers are in good condition the car will bounce up and rapidly become still. With worn shock absorbers the car bounces for longer. (Try bouncing a new car in a showroom first, so you know how it should behave).
- Before starting the car, open the bonnet and feel the engine. If it is warm the chances are that there are problems they are trying to hide by warming it up first.
- Look at the oil on the dip stick. If it is very dirty the car has been poorly maintained. If it is very thick it may have been filled with thickener to stop rattles in worn crankshaft bearings (often called the big ends). Run your finger round the inside of the hole where the oil goes in – if you feel a muddy substance Fullers Earth has been used to thicken the oil. It means the seller is a tricky customer: avoid the car.
- Look in the radiator: any sign of oil in there means trouble.
- Run the car with the radiator cap off – if there are large bubbles the head gasket may have gone – that could be expensive.
- Start the engine and then look at the exhaust. Blue smoke shows the car is burning oil. This could mean worn piston rings, worn valve guides or that it needs a re-bore – all quite costly.
- With the engine running, cover the end of the exhaust firmly with a *thick* cloth. You should feel pressure build up and then the engine should stall. If it doesn't the exhaust probably has a fault. (NOTE On cars with a powerful engine the exhaust will be hot, and this is not a trick to try with valuable or classic cars with delicately tuned engines.)
- Check the tyres – including the spare tyre. Tyres which are generally worn are just old (try to adjust the price accordingly). But tyres which are more worn on the inner or outer edges suggest problems. The tracking could be out – quite cheap to put right – or the king pins or the wheel bearings may be faulty – both expensive.
- Get someone to work the lights – including the brake lights – one by one, while you check if they work.
- Beware of cars with an engine number which doesn't look quite as it usually does. It may have been ground off and restamped. Thieves buy wrecks to get their papers and then doctor a stolen car to make it fit the credentials. They also buy two wrecks – one ruined at the back, the other at the front and join them together.

This is called 'ringing' in the trade, and these cars are clearly to be avoided.

- Find a large space and turn the car on full lock once in each direction, listening carefully – on rear wheel drive cars it will show up any noises in the differential in the rear axle. On front wheel drive cars the constant velocity joint will be noisy.
- On a straight flat *deserted* road check the steering and brakes. To do this set the car on a straight course and take the hands just off the wheel. It should keep perfectly straight unless the road has a heavy camber. Then brake gently. If it pulls to one side the brakes are either incorrectly balanced or the discs are worn. Discs can be expensive to replace, as you must always replace both sides at once.

The Formalities of Purchasing Secondhand

Before buying a secondhand car look at the log and check that the seller is the registered owner. If he or she isn't, be suspicious and ring the previous owner before any money changes hands. Possessing the registration documents is *not* proof of ownership.

When you pay for the car, *get a signed and dated receipt*, and take the car but leave your name and address.

The seller should keep the log book while any cheque is cleared. Then he or she should tear off the portion at the back, on which notification of change of ownership is given, and send it to the DVLA at Swansea, and send that portion of the registration documents to you. When you get them you too fill in a section of the documents and send the whole document to the DVLA address given on the slip – be sure to use the right postcode or it will go to the wrong department.

Selling a Car

If you want to sell a car the options are the same as when buying, but there are some basics to remember:

- If the car isn't fully paid for get the finance company's permission before you attempt to sell.
- Time spent cleaning the car first will pay handsomely.
- Smokers should banish the smell of smoke, or non-smokers may not buy.
- Have the following ready to show any buyer – log book (vehicle registration certificate), MOT certificate and, if needed, service record book or receipts showing the servicing.
- The law on not misrepresenting something you sell applies to you too. If you say it has new brakes, or low petrol consumption and it hasn't you can be prosecuted. So, if the buyer asks for facts to which you don't know the answer, say you don't know – don't invent anything.
- Don't forget to notify the DVLA (see above) that the car has been sold – or the police may be knocking on your door if the new owner is a hit-and-run driver.

Advertising a Car

You are likely to get the best price by advertising, but you need to make sure that you neither break the law nor get ripped off by a dishonest buyer. So here's a quick check list for safety:

- Know the law on selling secondhand goods (see Law) and keep it.
- Don't let a prospective buyer drive the car unless you have *seen* that their insurance covers them to drive your car (you don't want a claim on *your* policy).
- Don't let a prospective buyer drive your car without you (and take a friend too if you're a woman and the buyer is male).
- Don't part with the car until you have cash in hand or have cleared the cheque through the bank. (I know I said something different in car buying – but whichever you are doing you need to protect *yourself*.)
- Know the going price for similar cars and price it appropriately.
- When the deal is done give the buyer a receipt and ask him or her to sign a paper saying they have bought the car 'as seen and inspected'.

Several guides to secondhand car prices can be bought at newsagents and the prices in *Exchange and Mart* are also a useful guide. But no printed price should ever be taken as gospel; cars can sometimes fetch more, and often a lot less. The condition of the car is one factor and so is the season. Coupés, for example, will fetch much more in spring than in autumn.

Buying and Selling by Computer

Cardata (page 445) is the computerized marriage bureau of the secondhand car world, matching sellers with would-be buyers all over Great Britain. It costs a good deal more than the average advertisement in the press, but they will advise you and put the car into an auction at much less than the usual percentage fee if it doesn't sell through them, and offer various perks as well. It may also be a good way to find a type of car which isn't easy to track down – and there is no charge to a buyer.

Selling by Auction

This is likely to bring in the least money but it is a way of getting rid of a car in a hurry, or disposing of one well past its best. But remember, it is illegal to sell a car which is not roadworthy without making this clear.

You usually put the car in on the same day as the auction or the day before, and most auctions charge a small flat fee and then take a minimum commission which is a percentage of the sale price (there may also be a maximum commission). You can set a reserve price, below which you don't want the car to be sold, but a high reserve could leave it on the shelf. Be sure to check the terms of the auction house before leaving your car.

CAR DRIVING

Car Hire

You can hire vehicles of every type, from Rolls-Royce to lorries. Opening times for car hire companies are usually limited to standard business hours, except for branches at places like airports. Just look up 'Car hire' in the Yellow Pages and ring the local offices of a hire company. Anyone who hires will have to pay a deposit which will be forfeited (at least in part) if the car is damaged. Before accepting it check it thoroughly with a company representative and *both* write down any faults, such as marks and scratches.

Children in Cars

By far the safest place for a child is the back of a car, and even if the adult in the front is wearing a seat belt *it isn't safe for a child to be held on that adult's lap.* If an accident happened the shock of even quite a slow-speed impact would fling the adult's arms wide open – however hard they tried to hold tight – and let the child be flung through the window.

Wherever it sits, a child should, by law, be in a special car seat or use a suitable restraint. Being light, a child is more easily flung about than an adult and, if there's a crash, a child becomes an unguided missile, smashing through the windscreen and on to the road – possibly into the path of on-coming traffic. If there are adult belts in the rear seats you can buy booster cushions which raise a child high enough to use them safely in its middle years. Babies should be carried in carry cots, and carry-cot restraints should be used. The **Royal Society for the Prevention of Accidents** (page 444) and the **Department of Transport** (page 694) have leaflets showing the safest way to do this. Toddlers are safest in special car seats with a safety harness, and when they weigh 18 kg (2½ stone) they need a child's seat belt. Adult seat belts are suitable only for children over 12 years old.

Disabled Drivers

Some car manufacturers – such as Ford – give a big discount to anyone registered disabled. Others, such as Volkswagen, only give discounts to those receiving a mobility allowance. The best way for a disabled person to buy a car really depends on their circumstances. There is a scheme run by **Motability** (page 446) which allows disabled people to use their mobility allowance to buy a car on hire purchase, provided it meets certain criteria. It's useful for those who would find it hard to get a loan from any other source. But it charges interest at commercial rates, and you may be able to negotiate a better deal elsewhere – especially if you are not totally dependent on the mobility allowance. There are also leasing schemes which can be very attractive. Information on these, and on much else, can be obtained from the **Disabled Drivers' Association** (page 445).

Insurance – see the Money section

Learning to Drive a Car

To learn to drive you must have a provisional licence, which you get by filling in a form from the post office and sending it to the DVLA address given on the form. (The provisional licence for a car lasts until you are 70.) On a provisional licence you can only drive a car insured

for a learner driver (see Money) and you must have a qualified driver with you.

Professional Instruction

Driving schools can be found in Yellow Pages and every professional instructor must be qualified and have a coloured sticker on his or her windscreen saying Department of Transport Approved Instructor. All instructors have to be approved, and your lessons are only as good as the teacher concerned. So you may do as well, and save money, by asking around and finding a particular individual who is good, rather than by opting for a big name. Motorcyclists must also have instruction now.

Learning Privately

If someone is learning, or practising, on a private car it must have a white plate 18 x 18 cm (7 x 7 in) front and back, carrying a red L, 10 x 9 x 4 cm (4 x 3½ x 1½ in). They must also be accompanied by a qualified driver.

Applying for a Test

You should have been sent a booklet about the driving test when the DVLA sent you your provisional licence. But if you need to obtain it write to **Customer Enquiries – Drivers** at the, DVLA (page 445).

The forms for applying for the driving test are in post offices. How far ahead you need to apply varies with the area; so ask locally. But you may take the test anywhere you choose – it doesn't have to be where you live – provided you send your application and fee to the appropriate Driving Standards Agency. They are listed under Transport, Department of, in telephone books, and your local Agency can give you the addresses of those more far-flung. So, if you want to take your test where only cows will challenge your right to the road you can.

The usual delay on getting a test is 3 to 4 months, but you may get tested sooner if you will take a cancelled appointment at short notice.

★ Don't take the test in an automatic car or you will only be licensed to drive solo in automatics. For other cars you would need another driver beside you.

Motorcycling

Motorcyclists *must also* now be trained by an approved instructor, and obtain a certificate of competence from him, before they may legally drive on the road alone. They can get the addresses of training centres from the **British Motorcycle Federation** (page 445) or the **Royal Society for the Prevention of Accidents** (page 444).

Motorcyclists without a full driving licence may only drive on the road with a certificate of competence (see above) which must be kept with their provisional licence. These only allow them to drive a motorbike of up to 125 cc (50 cc if aged 16). The certificate lasts 3 years; however, a motorcyclist's provisional licence only lasts 2 years. If they exceed that time there must be a gap of a year before another provisional licence is obtained. So the test should be taken within that time, and if illness or absence abroad prevents this, surrendering the licence gives you the right to claim the balance of unused time when you wish to.

Problems with Licences

If your driving licence is lost apply for a duplicate on a form from the post office and pay a small fee. Telephone queries about driving licences and vehicle licences should be made to the DVLA (page 445).

Advanced Motorist's Test

If you haven't been convicted of a serious traffic offence for 3 years and drive any motor vehicle, or a motorbike of over 200 cc, and think you could be an ace driver, it may be worth taking the Advanced Motorist's Test. If you pass and join the **Institute of Advanced Motorists** (page 445) you may be able to get up to 20 per cent discount on your car insurance, plus discounts from some car hire companies. But these advantages only apply while you remain a member of the Institute and you cease to be a member if your licence is endorsed for a serious motoring offence.

The Institute will put you in touch with the nearest local group which helps people prepare for the test, so you are examined locally by the Institute's examiners.

Learning to Control Skids

Most serious road accidents involve loss of control or a skid, and some motor racing circuits run courses on how to handle these. Some use a skid pan but others use cars equipped with a device which can simulate ice, grease or water by variably reducing the grip of the wheels – and the device happily makes a roll-over impossible. If you would like to attend such a course I suggest you write to your nearest motor-racing circuit and ask if they have one. Failing that, write to a circuit like Silverstone, near Towcester, Brands Hatch, near Sevenoaks, or to Goodwood. But it may pay to compare the prices and the time you get for your money – it can vary dramatically.

Motoring Organizations

Whether it is worth joining a motoring association or not depends very much on the reliability of your car and how much you will use the subsidiary services: some have a lot more to offer than just a breakdown service. They don't all work on the same basis. With **National Breakdown**, **Mondial** and **Europ Assistance** (pages 445-446) membership covers the *car* for any number of drivers, and they vary on their charges for further cars; the other two clubs cover the *drivers* for any car they drive, and a husband or wife may take out associate membership. They also vary in their strengths and weaknesses. The **AA** and **RAC** (pages 445-446) offer lots of services like car inspections and route planning, whereas a company like Mondial has none of these but its forte is its medical emergency service when travelling overseas.

With any organization, you need to choose the type of membership which suits your needs; some cover only rescue, some repairs and others include breakdowns within a mile of your home. This latter can be important. I once had a car which only seemed to break down when parked overnight – and, foolishly, the one cover I didn't have with my motoring organization was 'home start'. So check exactly what is required.

Saving Fuel

It's amazing how much petrol can be saved without doing anything very dramatic. Start with the car. For optimum saving:

- Use the recommended tyre pressure.
- Use the correct oil at the right level.
- Have a clean carburettor which is correctly adjusted.
- Have the timing of the engine set correctly.
- Use the right grade of petrol for the car.
- Don't carry unwanted weight – garbage in the boot, mud under the wheel arches, an unused roof rack.
- The car uses most petrol when on choke so:
  move off as soon as you start up
  park the car so you can move off easily
  push the choke in as soon as you can.
- Drive in top gear as much as possible.
- Don't suddenly speed up or slow down; do everything gently.
- If stuck in a jam turn off the engine.

Starting Problems

- Silence or a faint clonk on turning the key indicates a flat battery (see page 432).
- Engine turns but fails to fire indicates a damp distributor (see page 433) or no petrol.

Weather Problems

Deep Water

If you have to drive through water which is higher than the exhaust the secret is to keep up your acceleration from start to finish. While you accelerate the pressure from the engine forces the fumes out of the exhaust and stops the water going in. But the moment you slow down water will be sucked in and you will stall. Test the brakes, when it is safe to do so, as soon as you are clear of the water, and keep depressing them slightly to dry them out.

Fog

Fog creates optical illusions as well as limiting the visibility, therefore you can't see if someone ahead is stopping. So:

- Leave a far bigger gap than usual between you and the car in front.
- Use your headlights or fog lights, whenever visibility is under 100 m (110 yd).
- Clean your headlights, windscreen and rear lights when safe parking can be found.

Slippery Conditions

The secret of driving on snow is gentleness. Treat all the controls as if they were made of glass and avoid any

Addresses and suggestions for further reading are at the ends of chapters.

sudden movements. If you find the back of the car is swinging turn your wheel *very gently* in whichever direction the back is going. So if it swings out to the left, turn the wheel slightly to the left. But don't overdo it – overcorrecting a skid can put the car into an uncontrollable spin. Equally, front-wheel-drive cars will tend to understeer, and go straight on at corners. So lift the accelerator and wait for the grip to improve.

Safety Points

● On ice, stopping distances can be up to 10 times more than usual, so keep your distance. On a normal motorway you should be able to count to 2 seconds between the car ahead passing an object and you passing the same object – on ice you should be able to count to 20.

● When you need to brake don't try to do it in one movement, but pump the brake gently up and down (smartly called 'cadence braking', and useful in heavy rain too). Only brake when travelling in a straight line.

● Go steadily in deep snow; slowing down can suck snow into the engine and stall it, and it may be impossible to start.

● *Don't* lower the tyre pressure to give a better grip – that is an old-fashioned technique which doesn't work with modern radial tyres.

● Fit chains for long journeys on snow and ice.

● When travelling in very bad weather carry food, drink, blankets (a space blanket is a good idea too) and a shovel – even in Britain marooned drivers die. If you do get stuck the AA advise you to
   – tie something bright to the highest point of your radio aerial
   – *Stay in your car*
   – beware of running the engine if the snow is blocking the exhaust or the fumes will enter the car and be fatal.

● If a car seems to be dragging, the handbrake may be frozen to the rear wheel. Do not continue driving until this has thawed as, even if you release the brake lever, the brake shoes may be stuck to the drums.

● When moving off on a slippery road put the car in second gear, and let the clutch out slowly to reduce wheel spin.

★ If you can't get a car key into a frozen lock keep warming the key with a lighter or match just before you put it in.

★ Put vaseline on the front of lights to stop the snow sticking.

★ When you scrape snow or ice from a windscreen wipe it over with methylated spirits straight afterwards – being a spirit it won't be in a hurry to refreeze. But don't let meths get on the paint of classic cars.

Weather and Road Information

If you need to know the weather forecast for any area you can telephone the Meteorological Office Weather Centres (page 446), though they don't give information on the roads themselves. If you are planning to cross the Channel or the North Sea you may find it more useful to talk to the Coast Guard service (page 446). Coast Guards can tell you the forecast, say how the wind direction is affecting their particular stretch of sea, and the tides and weather for yachtsmen and scuba divers.

Motorway Information

The **AA** (page 445) produces a free leaflet on its information lines. You don't need to be a member to use them, you just pay a higher rate for the phone call. They cover traffic and road conditions in each region of Britain, plus a Continental road watch. But if you want a forecast or the likely conditions for channel crossings you will find the phone numbers of Coast Guards and Meteorological offices on page 446.

CAR CARE AND MAINTENANCE

Basic Cleaning

● If anyone in the family suffers from car sickness it may help to go over the whole interior, from time to time, with an **anti-static spray** to stop the build-up of static electricity.

● **Chrome** is best cleaned with a branded chrome polish such as Solvol Autosol – avoid wire wool which can scratch it permanently.

● **Upholstery** and **carpets** should be vacuumed (the most convenient way is to use a small battery cleaner such as the Dustbuster). Most car fabrics can be shampooed with a good upholstery shampoo. But, if a stain has penetrated the underlying foam, don't expect to remove any smell.

● **Vinyl** and **rubber** can be renovated extremely effectively with a product made by STP which goes by the odd name of 'Son of a Gun'!

● **Leather** should be cleaned with saddle soap (unless otherwise instructed).

● One of the safest and most effective cleaners for **windows** is a tablespoon of ammonia in 500 ml (1 pt) water – but keep this off the paintwork. Rub insects off with one of those ball-like nylon saucepan cleaners that look knitted, but don't let the central metal clip scratch the window. If you need to clean a windscreen while away from home use wet newspaper – the printing ink helps remove the traffic film.

● **Paintwork** should be cleaned with washing-up liquid and water and polished with a high quality resin wax. Really dirty paint can be cleaned with a product called T-cut, but this can only be used very occasionally as it removes a layer of paint with the dirt. Using Brasso instead works, but it is too abrasive to get really good results.

DIY Maintenance and Servicing

The rising cost of servicing makes car DIY ever more tempting. There are car maintenance classes at many Local Education Authority evening classes and some garages and dealers also do them. But before you get too optimistic about the amount of servicing you will be able to do, check with someone who knows your type of car. Modern cars are becoming more and more difficult to service yourself, as they may need highly specialized equipment. Even so, there are a number of basic jobs which anyone can do with ease on most cars, although I strongly suggest keeping well away from the brakes. A car which won't start is a nuisance; a car which won't stop is a disaster.

You can buy manuals which tell you how to service almost every make of car. Autodata, Autobooks, and Haynes all produce them – and the Haynes manuals are particularly good. Also the spares departments of dealers usually sell the service manuals for their cars. But some makers ban their sale to the public and, as they are written for experienced mechanics, they can be perplexing if you aren't.

Battery Filling
Most modern batteries are sealed units which need no attention, but older ones need regular topping up with distilled water – sold at chemists and motor shops. If your battery doesn't show how much water it needs make sure the plates are covered by a couple of millimetres.

★ Strained through a handkerchief, to remove debris, the water from defrosting your fridge is perfectly good distilled water for car batteries.

Battery Reviving
When a battery is so dead that turning a key doesn't produce even a 'clonk' it may be past help. But if you can raise a faint 'clonk' the battery of a non-automatic car can usually be revived. There are two methods. The first can only be used for a non-automatic; the second can be used on both automatics and non-automatics.

1 For a bump start:
   a switch on the ignition
   b put the car in 2nd gear (not 1st, 3rd or 4th)
   c take off the hand brake
   d press down the clutch and keep it down
   e get the car moving (pushed or downhill)
   f when it is rolling bring up the clutch and the engine should fire.

Once the car engine is firing you must keep it turning over until this has charged up the battery. If it stalls you may have to start all over again, so keep it gently revving if you have to stop.

2 If you have a pair of jump leads:
   a Put a car with a live battery within jump lead reach of the flat battery – but don't let the two cars touch. Each battery has a pair of 'knobs' on it, usually with plastic covers. Remove the covers and look for the + and – signs by them.
   b If there is any doubt about the strength of the working battery, start the engine of that car.
   c Connect each end of the red lead to the positive + 'knobs' on each car. Hold them by the insulated handles and DON'T touch the car body with the end of the lead.

   d Attach each end of the black lead to the negative – 'knobs'.
   e Start the car with the faulty battery. As soon as it fires you can uncouple the jump leads, but keep the engine running – revving it slightly if it sounds weak. Then immediately take the car for a drive for at least 20 minutes – preferably without using anything which needs electricity (radio, lights, wipers) – to recharge the battery before switching off the engine.

Not only is it impossible to bump start or tow start an automatic car but they are also tricky to tow. Some manufacturers set strict limits on the distance and speed that an automatic car can be towed without damage so do check the manual first.

> Most car batteries have the same volts, but not all give out the same amount of power. So a low-powered car may not be able to start a high-powered one, though revving the weaker engine very hard may help. Also if you set up the jump leads and leave the small car's engine running for a while it may boost the other battery.

Buying Tools
Good tools are expensive and there is no point in buying even one until you know what jobs you want to do and have checked which tools are needed. Most jobs on modern cars can be done with 11 mm, 13 mm, 15 mm and 17 mm spanners, and on older cars with $7/16$ inch, $5/8$ inch and $1/2$ inch ones. It is usually cheapest to hire tools which are rarely used – Yellow Pages list hire shops.

> Don't even consider doing anything which needs you to get under the car unless you have a proper tripod axle stand and know exactly where to position it for safety. Bricks, wood blocks, jacks and so on may look secure but all of them can collapse and people are killed every year because of this. And always have a car on level ground when working on it.

Changing a Tyre
This is very easy:

1 Get out the spare wheel and check it's inflated (there's no point in proceeding if you put it away flat and forgot to repair it) then put it close to the flat tyre.
2 Double check that the handbrake is fully on.
3 Put bricks or some other blocks under a wheel on the good side of the car.
4 Lever the hub cap off the flat tyre with the end of a screw driver.
5 Loosen the wheel nuts (anticlockwise) with a wheel brace – the old-fashioned sort with a U-shaped kink

Addresses and suggestions for further reading are at the ends of chapters.

is useful for the less brawny, as you can stamp on the U if arm force isn't enough.

6 Put the jack in the correct position for your type of car. Not all makes are the same but it will be under the edge of the side – your manual will say where. On soft ground you need to put something firm under it. Make sure it is standing firmly. Then jack up the car – lifting it high enough to let you insert a non-flat tyre afterwards.

7 Remove the wheel nuts – put them where you won't lose them (the hub cap is dodgy; if you step on the edge it will catapult them everywhere).

8 Remove the wheel and put the spare one in its place (you may need to raise the car higher with the jack, as a fully inflated tyre may be larger than you thought).

9 Screw on all the nuts as tightly as you can, working on diagonal pairs.

10 Let the jack down and replace the hub cap.

Damp Distributor

In wet weather some cars are prone to get damp in the distributor. When this happens the engine turns over but it won't fire. The distributor is easily recognized as it has several thick leads joined to it at slightly cone-shaped junctions. To dry it out undo the clips which hold the top on, and either spray WD40 inside or blow it dry with a hair dryer, on an extension lead. Sounds unlikely, but it works. If necessary, dry under the lead junctions too.

★ With an old car which is vulnerable to cold and damp, it is easiest to start it if you have put a blanket under the bonnet overnight. In this case it is ESSENTIAL to leave a corner of blanket sticking out where you can't miss it: leaving it in while driving could cause a fire.

Electrical Parts

If any electrical part stops working look for a broken fuse and replace it, with one of the same amps. Some fuse boxes have labels showing the function of each fuse. But many cars have sequence wiring which means that if a fuse for one part goes, another part may cease to work too. On my Honda, for example, fusing the windscreen wipers immobilizes the windows. If the same fuse blows twice, for no good reason, have the wiring checked; there is probably a fault and that could cause a fire. If a light stops working it is probably a bulb. These are easy to replace.

Fan Belt

It's a good idea to check that the fan belt is taut whenever you check the oil. A loose fan belt will allow the engine to overheat and will stop the alternator working properly, so the battery won't recharge.

The old trick of replacing a broken fan belt with a nylon stocking does work – if you can get it on (engines aren't designed like they used to be) but it will get you to the nearest garage, though no further.

Oil Checking

The oil should really be checked once a week. If it gets too low the engine wears faster, and will eventually seize up. When the engine is cool, pull out the dip stick (it usually has a finger loop), wipe off the oil at the base, push it fully in again, withdraw it and check the level. It should be just below the line marked as 'max'. If it needs topping up (and it won't tip in tidily) but you have no funnel, roll up some thick paper into a cone and pour it in down this.

Oil Changing

Oil needs to be changed at least every year. To do it yourself first get a suitable container – larger than the contents of your oil tank. (Buy a Bell Drainer Can which holds 8 l (14 pts) if you plan to do this often).

1 Run the car to warm it up and make the oil runnier.

2 Put the container in place.

3 Undo the drainage plug on the sump and let the oil drain fully into the container.

4 Replace the drainage plug and refill.

If you bought your oil from a garage it may dispose of the old oil. If you bought it (often more cheaply) from a discount shop you should take it to the container for such things in the local authority dump. If it is thrown away anywhere else it can cause contamination.

The filter needs changing rather less often than the oil. On most cars it is a job for a garage, as it can be very tough to remove.

Overheating Engine

If a light on your dashboard doesn't tell you the engine is overheating, your nose should. If you smell something odd, stop and check. If it seems to be overheating DON'T be tempted to remove the radiator cap – the steam it releases will scald you. Leave the engine open and wait for the radiator and engine to cool, *then* look. If the water is low, top it up slowly with lukewarm water to avoid too sharp a change of temperature. If the metal hasn't warped with the heat, all should now be well.

Rust

Rust is one of a car's biggest enemies. And salt is the biggest rust creator. After a cold spell, when salt will have been on the roads, give the car a hose down underneath as well as on top. (Check the brakes afterwards by trying them out when you aren't needing them.) Also lift the carpets and unblock the vent holes in the floor. Whether it is worth having a car rust-proofed really depends on what protection the manufacturer has given the car, how often you are prepared to hose down the underside and whether you live near salt sea air. Wherever you live, don't cover a car in a plastic cover or tarpaulin; this stops air circulating and creates ideal conditions for rust.

Rust in the bodywork can be treated, but you need to let each stage dry out completely before starting the next. So start when you have a series of free evenings or weekends.

1 Use a wire brush and wire wool to remove as much

rust as possible, using finer and finer wire wool as you get deeper in.

2 Apply an effective rust treatment such as Trustan, according to its instructions.

3 Allow that to dry completely before applying a filler, such as Isopon.

4 When this has dried completely use a fine sandpaper, and then a flour paper (see below) until it is perfectly even.

The secret of a good finish is to use 3 *thin* coats of spray-on car primer – allow each to dry according to the instructions before applying the next. Use flour paper (the finest grade of sanding paper) to give this a key. Then spray on 3 to 4 *thin* coats of top coat – allowing it to dry between. Don't try to cover exactly the same area with each spray – uneven spraying prevents an edge being created. Make the final coat *slightly* heavier than the others. Then let the paint dry for several days. When it is *totally dry and hard* go over it with T-cut to smooth out any speckles. Finally polish it up.

Scratched Paint

Clean the scratched area well and wipe the scratches with white spirit to remove any oily grime. Use a very fine artist's brush to apply several layers of paint to the scratches, letting the paint dry very thoroughly between each coat. For this start with 4 parts of thinner to 6 parts of paint and gradually reduce the thinner on each coat. When the top coat is totally dry T-cut the area and polish it.

Tyres

The correct tyre pressure is more important than it may seem. The right pressure opens up the tread so its edges grip the road – just what you need in the rain. So it pays to make regular checks and adjust the pressure for heavy loads if your tyres need it – but read your manual to see whether they do need extra pressure and, if so, how much.

There are no fixed rules; it all depends on the tyres – which is one reason why it is important to stick to the tyres the makers recommend.

Incidentally, it is illegal to carry a spare tyre which is not fit for use – for example, with too little tread.

★ Some handbooks have the tyre pressures in obscure places. Having found the pressures, make life easy for yourself by writing them on a sticky label and putting it somewhere convenient, like the glove locker flap.

Water

Water needs weekly checks in summer – it should be almost up to the top. Anti-freeze with corrosion inhibitor must be used all year for cars with aluminium cylinder heads. On other cars add antifreeze before the coldest weather starts – it doesn't have to be removed when the weather warms up. However, it must be chosen to suit the make of car – the wrong one can rot the pipes.

★ Be warned, if you have a high-tech car and a cellular phone is installed badly it can interfere with the electronic systems which control functions like the braking and ignition. So cellular phones need expert installation.

Professional Servicing and Repairs

It is tempting to suppose that, so long as a car goes, all is well with it. Unfortunately, this is a dangerous and expensive view. Regular checks are needed to keep the car safe and prevent unnecessary wear.

Most manufacturers recommend different types of service at different intervals. Their spacing is dictated not just by the design of the car but by the built-in ageing speeds of components like oil and spark plugs. Stop-start town driving is toughest on a car and makes regular servicing doubly important. On modern lean-burn engines spark-plugs usually need attention at around 10,000 miles, and the best lubricating oils need changing after 16,000 to 20,000 miles, so these will set the interval of the shortest service.

Most new cars have a warranty which covers parts and labour for the first year. The mileage may be limited or unlimited, but certain parts, such as tyres, won't usually be covered for fair wear and tear and you will have to pay for basics like oil. Also, this warranty may only be valid if you use an approved dealer and make no changes to the car.

By law garages must use reasonable care and skill and charge an appropriate price. There is also a code of practice established between the Office of Fair Trading and the major motor trade organizations given on page 445. If you go to one of their members they should follow the code. Even so, it pays to take precautions that the work is correct and that bills don't soar. Personal recommendation is the best guarantee of a good garage. Failing that, there may be an advantage in using a garage which is a member of one of the trade associations listed on page 445 – though some very good small garages do not belong to them. Wherever you go, you can protect yourself against problems with the following steps:

● At services, agree what will be done, and leave your telephone number and ask them to contact you, and get your approval, before doing anything more than that. This puts a brake on creative servicing.

● For anything more than a service give the garage a written list of what you want done and ask for a *written* estimate covering parts, labour, and VAT.

● Before you leave your car get a definite indication of when the car will be ready, and tell them when you will be collecting it.

● Ask if the work or parts are guaranteed. (Companies following the motor trade's code of practice must guarantee repairs for a stated mileage or time.)

● Get a detailed invoice.

● Under the **VBRA** code of practice (see page 445) if work has to be done again because the first lot was unsatisfactory the car's guarantee period must be extended by however many days it is off the road this second time.

If you aren't happy with the work the steps to getting things put right are these:

Addresses and suggestions for further reading are at the ends of chapters.

a Complain to the manager or garage owner at once, in writing using recorded delivery, and try to get things put right then and there.

b If you can withhold payment until you are satisfied do so – but write to them saying that you are only withholding it until the job is done properly.

c If you have to pay, when you know you aren't satisfied, give them a letter saying you are not satisfied with the work and that you make the payment 'without prejudice' – and keep a copy of the letter. This wording means that your payment doesn't harm your right to take legal action if necessary.

d If the garage refuses to put things right get free advice from a CAB, Consumer Advice Centre or Trading Standards (Consumer Protection) Department, or use your motoring organization to help you. And if it is a dealer get on to the manufacturer – the SMMT (page 445) has the address.

e If you used a garage which belongs to one of the organizations listed (on page 445) ask for their help.

f If the garage is not a member of such an association taking the matter to court is the final option.

If there is a major problem and you plan to take legal action it may be worth getting an independent inspection from a motoring organization. They may also be able to give you free legal advice and even representation (see under Law). Or, you can use the complaints and conciliation service of one of the organizations on page 445 if the garage is a member.

Theft Prevention

It is a nuisance for thieves if a car's windows are marked with its registration number as it makes it harder to disguise. You can now buy kits which allow you to etch the number on to the glass. Some are small electric drills; others are etching fluid, and some companies will etch it for you. So it's worth asking about.

Theft is also far less likely if you avoid parking in side streets, always lock up and leave nothing tempting in full view – apart from the car, that is. But a practised thief can enter a car in seconds. Happily, alarms are getting better all the time. Some of the most sophisticated only react to disturbance *inside* the car – so bounce-off-the-bumper parkers don't set them off. At the other end of the scale, there are devices, like the Krooklok, which prevent a car being driven away but don't stop thieves taking the radio. The price range is from several hundred pounds to under £10. But my favourite story is of the man who found an imitation snake curled up on the passenger seat a most effective deterrent.

COMPUTERS

Computers should never have acquired the exalted status they now have. Fascinating and invaluable as they are, even the most advanced have less brain power than a three-year-old. They do, however, score on single-mindedness. The three-year-old uses its brain not only to think but also to do tasks like seeing, hearing and running about, which need incredibly rapid and sophisticated electro-mechanical interactions – we too run on electricity. But the computer just sits there and sends spacecraft to the moon or re-organizes the world banking system – which is very much easier. That's why the space fiction dream of robot servants pandering to our every whim is still, alas, a long way off. It's also why nobody needs to be daunted by them.

To use a computer you don't need to have a clue how it works; you can drive it in blissful ignorance, just as you can a car. But knowing the basics lets you use it with more flexibility and makes you feel like the boss. It also helps you to know what to look for when buying.

Don't let the jargon bother you – it isn't even the same from country to country. To misquote *Alice*, the computer boffins 'only do it to annoy because they know it teases'. So you'll find computer jargon full of little jokes; for example, half a byte (a unit of measurement, pronounced bite) is called a nibble, and the mechanism which carries information is called a bus.

What a Computer Can Do for You

I have been in love with my personal computer for several years now. Seeing my devotion to the thing, people are always asking me if they should buy one. The answer is 'yes' *if* you want to do one of the things which a computer does well. Here are just some of the jobs it can potentially do in the family, or in a home-based business if it has the necessary equipment and programs.

● Make it easy to change any written text around, correct mistakes, rewrite it, cut words, and then print out a perfect copy, as if you had never made a single error.

● Check what you have written against its own dictionary, and point out any mistakes in spelling or grammar.

● Provide multiple copies of anything you write, without the expense of photocopies and hold copies of letters in memory, so you can refer back to them without the clutter of paper copies.

● Run educational programmes for children or adults – an increasing feature of 'open learning' programmes.

● Rapidly do any kind of mathematics, from balancing the family budget to high-flown calculations.

● Create a spreadsheet, evaluate stocks and shares, or give a profit forecast.

● Allow you instantly to look at any information you have saved on it; no more riffling through drawers or filing cabinets.

● Store names and addresses (or any other facts) as on a card index system, and *instantly* find the one you want.

● Print out address labels for everyone in a particular category – say those you want to send a Christmas card to, or all your contacts in America.

● Draw and print out graphs and diagrams needed for work or school.

- Play games, ranging from innocent games for children to the most risqué sex quizzes from California, plus unbeatable chess.
- Hold encyclopaedias, complete with examples of pictures by the painters and recordings of famous speeches and music, which it can play just like a normal CD player (some systems have full CD sound quality).
- Hold interactive books, which you can read, print out, and write into.
- Control the editing of home videos.
- Let you create invitations, or leaflets which look professionally printed.
- Send faxes and take dictation.
- Dial up phone numbers, and keep a note of who it rang when.
- Control a big-screen display at a talk or demonstration.
- Display your photographs at full screen size.
- Play music

That is just an idea of what they do. To appreciate fully the pleasure of using a computer, and the speed and ease it can bring, you must feel for yourself how swiftly it lets you add up a long column of figures, draw a graph or alter a sentence.

Hardware, Software and Peripherals

There are three aspects to using a computer – the hardware, the software and peripherals. The hardware is anything you can see, and kick – the screen, printer, keyboard and the control unit with its chips and disk-drive. The software is the program which tells the computer what to do, and you mainly buy it on a floppy disk. Peripherals range from essentials like printers to luxuries like scanners.

They are often created by different companies. The hardware gets all the publicity, the software is the important part and the role of peripherals is growing. Without software the hardware (the machine) is like a severely brain-damaged person – it may be alive but it isn't able to do anything. When we touch something hot a message goes to our brain and it instantly tells the muscles to move away from the heat. In the same way, if you touch a key which means you want to print, the software picks up the message and tells the computer hardware to start printing.

Buying a Computer

Paradoxically the best advice on buying a computer is *don't*. The best starting point isn't the computer, it's the software (see above). Without software a computer is as useless as a car without an engine – but two different programs, which seem to do exactly the same things, can need computers of very different levels of power (see page 437).

So first pick the software you plan to use. Reviews in computer magazines are a good starting point and I have mentioned some useful programs on page 442. But they are *only* a starting point. A program can have as many tricks as a circus monkey yet fail to do the things

which you need most. Or it may only do them in a way which doesn't suit *you*. And the whole point of computers is that they should make life easier *not* that we should bend over backwards to adapt to them. So why not make a check list of what you want a program to do, in order of priority, ask around until some programs come close to it, then try them out.

Some manufacturers will send demo disks, which you can try on a friend's machine. Failing that, computer shows are a great chance to test programs and see how they suit you. But do try them yourself. Demonstrators can make any program look good by just picking the jobs it shines at.

Then, *before you buy the software* find a computer which has enough speed and memory, and the right add-ons, to handle it efficiently.

An important point here is that software uses the 'or better' principle. If, for example, a program needs a 386 machine (see page 437) it will work on faster ones too. And a program that needs 1 Mb of RAM will be even happier with more. So, as programs are getting more memory-hungry and needing greater speed, you may want to buy rather more speed and memory than you need immediately.

If you check out computers at a show you will find some which aren't in any shops, for this industry majors in direct selling. Some direct marketing companies offer good computers at attractive prices. But beware: good-looking computers can be assembled, in a back bedroom, from ready-made parts. This means anyone can set themselves up as a 'computer manufacturer' and offer computers with great specifications at bargain prices, plus a 3-year warranty. But the quality control may be nil and the warranty will be worthless if the company goes bust.

Magazines such as *Computer Buyer* and *What PC* have reviews and detailed tables. But even a glowing review may not guard against trouble. Most magazines are concerned with the *product* not the company's bank balance – and a boffin may create a great product, but be hopeless at running a company. So it might be wisest to buy from a company which is a member of the **P.C. Direct Marketers Association** (page 446) which vets its members, and requires them to keep its code of practice. It's a young organization, so that isn't a huge safeguard, but it's a start.

Unfortunately, buying through a dealer isn't always safer. A lot of those who once sold used cars seem to have found better pickings in the computer industry. And even good dealers may be staffed by young men with more enthusiasm for computers than knowledge of what they need to do in the real world. So although there *are* good dealers you may need personal recommendation to find one.

Best of all, before buying anything, find a good computer consultant, such as **Swift Computers** (page 446), who will give honest advice – a little money spent on good advice could save you wasting a lot on a bad buy.

Finally, unless you are a computer buff (or know a tame one), make sure the computer and software

Addresses and suggestions for further reading are at the ends of chapters.

companies will provide support if you have a problem – and ask whether it is free. Some companies offer free support for ever, others for the first year, others not at all.

Computer Types

Computers can be divided into a series of groups, although the lines between them are becoming increasingly blurred as smaller and smaller machines become more and more powerful.

The largest are the **mainframes**, used in places like NASA. Then come **mini-computers** which, despite their name, pack enough power to run a factory. At the other end of the scale are **pocket computers** by companies like Psion and Sharp. These may be hardly larger than a pocket calculator yet have memories able to hold thousands of addresses and some can link into standard databases and spreadsheets held in desktop machines. The snag is, many will only run their own programs. So you might have to remember one set of commands for one of these and another set for your PC.

PCs (personal computers) sit in the middle and can be used for anything, from a game to writing a letter or running a small business. Within them are three broad categories: notebooks, laptops, and desktops.

Notebooks are smaller than a sheet of A4 paper, while laptops are usually around A4 in size. But both types are portable, run on batteries or mains, and should accept international voltages. Best of all, huge advances in technology mean that they can now be as fast, and store as much data, as most hunky desktop machines. Canon has even pioneered laptops with built-in printers. And some laptops are designed so parts unclip, like Lego bricks, allowing you to make them even more powerful still as new developments come along. Useful, in this fast changing industry.

Neat, powerful, and easy to stow away, a good laptop or notebook computer is ideal for the home and they also seem set to replace bulkier machines in many offices. However, they can have disadvantages. They vary widely in the number of hours they can run on batteries. The screens are always smaller than free-standing screens and, as I write, those with really good colour screens are pricey and, since very fast machines create a lot of heat, companies aren't rushing to install the ultra-fast chips in them. Also, though laptops usually have good keyboards, those on notebooks can be too small for comfort. However, you can overcome screen and keyboard problems by linking a notebook or laptop to a free-standing screen and full-sized keyboard: all you need are the right cables.

Desktops are what they sound like: larger models designed to go on a desk – though the control unit can often be put under it – and they come in separate parts, not one compact unit. This gives you the freedom to position the screen and keyboard to suit yourself – but you can't put one away in a hurry.

IBM Compatible or Non-compatible
Among both portable and desktop PCs the big divide is between IBM compatible machines, and non-IBM compatibles. Non-IBM compatibles, such as Apple and Amstrad, are popular but IBM compatibles are currently the major players.

'IBM compatible' is a term for a machine which can run any program written for an IBM PC – which is almost any major program. Non-IBM compatibles, run either programs designed for them, or their own version of the programs which run on IBMs. But problems arise if you want to transfer documents from an IBM compatible to a non-IBM compatible – or vice versa. It will either be impossible, or you may need extra software to allow the transfer. So, if you want to bring work home try to match your office machine.

However, when you choose a machine it isn't simply a matter of whether a computer will run a particular program but of whether it will run it well (see Software page 440) and here the issues are power, speed and RAM (see below).

Picking Power
Computers have numbers indicating their power, just as cars do. The main power behind a computer is its microprocessor or chip. Annoyingly, different makes of non-IBM compatible number their chips differently. However, a single numbering system is used for those in IBM compatibles – although sometimes there is an 80 in front. As I write 386s (or 80386s) are the standard workhorses, 486s are the mainstream and 586s are the top end. However, the fastest chips are now being given names instead of numbers, and these vary with the makers.

Within each number band there may be SX and DX versions. DXs are the more powerful. But there is no benchmark for these letters, so one company's SX could be as powerful as another's DX.

Picking Speed
A key speed to look for is clock speed. This is given in Mhz (megahertz) and tells you how many instructions the microprocessor can execute in a second. In theory the higher the Mhz the swifter the machine.

I would find a machine running at under 25 Mhz too slow for anything except a game. But how fast a computer works depends both on the type of chip and on the Mhz *combined*. So a 25 Mhz 486 should be faster than a 25 Mhz 386. And on a task like massive number-crunching, performance will also depend on whether the machine has a special maths co-processor chip. Most 486s have them built in, 386s usually don't, but they can sometimes be added – though you won't need one for school homework.

Also, it's no good the computer doing its job like greased lightning if you can't see the results on screen. So the screen must be able to change fast enough to keep up – this is called the screen refresh rate and is measured in Hz (hertz).

The final factor in how fast a computer performs is the size of its RAM (page 438) and how the software uses it. A big RAM is to a computer what an almost traffic-free road is to a car – it lets it get a move on. But for real speed, with or without traffic, a car needs a driver who can use the road to the full. The computer equivalent is software, such as DESQview (page 441), which can make other programs use the computer's RAM to best advantage if expertly installed.

The Control Unit
The control unit in a desktop is the box of works to which all the other parts are linked by cables. If the keyboard, printer and monitor are the arms and legs of the machine, the control unit's box is its body, filled with vital organs. In a notebook or laptop, however, the limbs and body are in one case, like a hibernating tortoise.

The Microprocessor
The key 'organ' in the control unit of a PC is the microprocessor (or CPU – Central Processor Unit). This is the biggest chip in the computer, and is the brains of the machine. It performs mathematical and logical functions at almost the speed of light. It is also the middle man which allows information to be held in memory, or sent out to the screen or printer. The better the microprocessor, the more powerful the machine.

Until fairly recently microprocessors were only able to handle 1 unit of information (8 bits) at a time. Now most PCs can handle 2 units (16 bits), and 4 unit (32 bit) machines are the ones to buy if you can. For the more bits it can handle at once, the faster the computer. But, microprocessors are still rather primitive, and their abilities are limited to logical or mathematical functions which are wired in and unchangeable. The thinking robot is still a long way off.

The Memory
Several 'organs' in the computer are sometimes called memory. If a computer has a hard disk, all your programs and all the letters and documents you create are stored on it. So it is sometimes called the memory. But when computer buffs talk of 4K of memory, for example, they usually mean the main memory or RAM (Random Access Memory). K stands for Kilobytes and a byte is enough memory to hold a single character. So 4K of RAM can hold four thousand characters at a time (e.g. four thousand letters of the alphabet).

The RAM is the kitchen into which the computer brings the ingredients of the program so it can cook up what happens on screen, or elsewhere. With a really big RAM it can get everything at once and work really fast, with a smaller one it will fetch different ingredients of the program at different times. This is much slower and can make it impossible to run a program at all, but adding extra RAM is *very* easy, but you must pick the right type for your machine.

Unfortunately, the DOS software (page 441), which most PCs use as the cornerstone program, limits the amount of RAM which can easily be used. This slows things down needlessly. So operating environments (page 441) like Windows, DESQview and OS/2 use an extended memory manager to get at the parts of the RAM which DOS fails to reach.

Another form of memory is ROM. This holds the instructions for starting up the computer and it can't be erased. There are also special versions of ROM, such as PROM and EPROM, which can hold programs and CD-ROM (page 440). ROM stands for Read Only Memory, which means you can get information out of these types of memory but you can't put in anything new.

The Disk Drive
The disk drive is an electro-mechanical device which spins the disk, and allows a magnetic head to record files on to it or read programs or other data off it. Most PCs have IDE disks but for big databases a faster SCSI disk may be better. You need two disk drives, so that you can copy data from one to the other – either twin drives for floppy disks (see below), or a hard disk plus a drive for a floppy disk. Portable computers may save weight by having an external floppy drive, linked with a cable And some allow you to remove the hard disk, so if your computer is stolen all your private data doesn't go with it.

Hard Disks and Floppies
There are two categories of disk: hard disks and floppies. Programs are supplied on floppies and you also need blank floppies on which to store anything you create on the computer. They come in three sizes: 5 1/4, 3 1/2, and 2 inches, with 3 1/2 the most widely used. They can hold anything from 360Kb to 2.88 Mb according to their density (the density of their magnetic coating) and whether they are single or double sided. But a typical double-sided, high-density 3 1/2 can hold 1.44 Mb (that's 1.44 million letters of the alphabet – or other characters). Your computer dictates what size and type you can use but high density drives can format, read and write high and low density disks.

The hard disk is actually several disks in a stack, each with a large storage capacity, able to run at many times the speed of a floppy disk. So all your programs, and all the work you do, can be permanently stored on it ready to run whenever you switch on. Whereas, with floppy disks, the programs have to be loaded in each time you start up, which makes switching from one type of program to another very tedious. If you can afford it, get a computer with a hard disk of about 80 Megabytes (Mb) of memory or more – the larger the better. For although, in theory, you can upgrade to a bigger hard disk, in practice it is very disruptive.

> Both hard disks and floppies work within disk drives. By convention if there is a hard disk, it is called the C drive, whereas floppy drives are normally called A and B. In performing tasks like copying a document from a hard drive to a floppy, A, B or C are used like postal addresses. So the command tells the computer to copy from C to A, for example.

Keyboards

Computers always have a QWERTY keyboard, like a typewriter, plus various other keys. But there is no standard keyboard. Manufacturers can give you any number of extra keys they please and some even omit the £ sign – so it pays to check them out. The most generous ones copy the enhanced IBM keyboard which has 101 keys, but others may only have 84 keys. For most purposes that is enough but for complex tasks the number of keys can make a difference. For they are used to tell the computer what to do and are controlled by the software. So when doing accounts a key may add a column of figures, but in a graphics package it may select a colour.

If you consider buying a notebook computer the other point to check is whether you really can touch type on it. A very small one, which seems fine when tested with a few fingers in a showroom, can be hand-aching after an hour's typing. The pressure on space may also mean that certain function keys are missing. Usually it is the extra block of numbered keys normally found at the right of a keyboard. However, on a good machine, these will either be available as a separate keypad – which may cost extra – or some of the alphabet keys may convert into a number pad when necessary. In which case you will see coloured figures on the front faces of some of the keys.

The Mouse, Trackball or Pen

In all Windows programs and some DOS programs (see page 441) you can tell the computer what to do by simply pointing an on-screen arrow at a command button. You control the arrow through a mouse, trackball or 'pen'. With a mouse or trackball the arrow moves as you roll a large 'ball bearing' in them. A 'pen' looks like a normal pen but moves the pointer by interacting with a special pen-sensitive screen as it moves across it. Having reached the command, you just click a button on the mouse, trackball or pen, to tell the computer to take action.

This speeds up some tasks and slows down others. But there are some things which can't be done without them, and games and programs run under Windows rely heavily on them. They are also essential for drawing curved lines in graphics packages – and here the pen is by far the best. As I write, pen programs are still in their infancy but they can already let you tick lists and input handwriting as handwriting. And, since computers can be trained to recognize handwriting, some computers will now let you write on the screen and will then translate your writing into typing. This is a tool of the future and you may want to consider pen compatability when buying a computer – if you can afford it.

> A mouse seldom works unless it is plugged in when you start the computer. If you accidentally start up without it, and find you can't do a thing, don't worry. Just plug the mouse in, then press Ctrl Alt and Delete – all at the same time – and your computer should restart with the mouse working.

Printers

A printer does a double act with the computer and has its own computer chips which determine how it prints and what fonts (typefaces) it will do. So, having a font on screen doesn't guarantee that it will appear on paper. This interaction is worth checking when buying. You may also want to check how easy, and expensive, it would be to add extra fonts later. And, when you set up your system, you may need to fill in a form inside your word-processing program telling it which type of printer it will be linked to. But, unlike typewriters, computers don't print your words immediately. They hold what you write in memory until you want a printed copy then send the text down the wires to the printer.

There are four main types of printer: dot matrix, ink-jet, bubble-jet and laser. They vary in speed, quietness, print quality, the ability to do colour printing, the type of paper they take, whether they will print labels and envelopes and – most importantly – in the overall cost of printing a page.

Dot matrix printers have a group of tiny pins which thrust forward to create the shape of the letter as they hit a ribbon. The more pins the better the result. 24 pins give almost typewriter quality and the cost per page is usually low. But they seldom do colour printing, and are noisy and tend to be slow. Confusingly their speed is measured in characters per second (cps) whereas other printers are normally rated in pages per minute (ppm). For comparison, 40 cps roughly equals 6 ppm.

Ink-jets and bubble-jets squirt the ink out through microscopic nozzles, to give almost professional print quality for both text and graphics. Even quite inexpensive models may well do single colour printing and they can be remarkably quiet and swift, and some have a low cost per page.

Lasers manipulate magnetism to create fast, professional and even, perhaps, multicolour printing. But they are likely to have the highest cost per page and the fan which cools them can be tiringly noisy.

The Screen or Monitor

The screens (called monitors) vary hugely. At one end of the spectrum (and price range) there are monitors with colour rivalling a colour photograph and perhaps showing as many as a million shades. At the other end a basic colour monitor might show only 16 shades. There are also 'grey-scale' monitors offering various shades of grey and monochrome ones offering two colours – though not always black and white.

A good colour monitor is worth getting if you can – it is easier on the eyes and many games need the standard of colour provided by a VGA or super VGA colour screen. How clear the picture is will also depend on the number of 'dots' (pixels) which make it up. The more pixels the finer the picture. Flicker is another factor. A free-standing screen will have less flicker if it is what they call 'non-interlaced', but this doesn't apply to the flat screens on portable computers. On them the thing to look for is clarity at all light levels – and you can only judge that by eye.

Screens also vary in their refresh rate (page 437), and in their size and shape. Illogically most are wider than they are long – the landscape format – but, at a price, you can also get A4-shaped screens – portrait format. Either way the size is measured diagonally and screens of less than 9 inches can be constricting.

Bells and Whistles

There are an ever-growing number of bells and whistles which can be added to a computer to make it perform new and delightful tricks, or simply become better at what it is doing already. Below are just a few of them.

CD-ROM and Sound Cards

CD-ROM is a type of compact disk, which looks like a music CD. Like CDs they come with the information on them. They can carry as much data as 1,000 floppy disks, can't be erased, and will hold any kind of data from words to music and pictures. So they have become a new form of publishing, with an ever-increasing number of reference books being put out in this format. And Kodak can now put any types of photograph on to a CD-ROM for you – all indexed and numbered for easy access.

Most desktop PCs come with vacant slots into which you can fit CD-ROM players, and portables may be able to have one coupled to them. However, there are different kinds and they won't all play everything. Kodak's disks, for example, need a multisession XA Type 2 or better. So decide what you want to do with your CD-ROM and check the specifications you need before buying.

To play music from your CD-ROM you will probably need to fit your computer with a sound card too. These vary greatly in quality, and price, but you can now get sound cards which will enable you to play music from a CD-ROM at full CD quality. And perhaps, with a powerful machine and the right software, it may even be able to play to you as you work.

PCMCIA Slots and Cards

You can now get PCMCIA cards, only a little larger than a credit card, which slip into a special PCMCIA slot in the computer. In essence they carry extra memory. That memory is usually in the form of extra RAM or of instructions enabling the computer do a particular job. So, if your computer takes these cards, you can either use them to add to its hard-disk memory or use different PCMCIA cards to make it do different things. For example, one kind has a short telephone cable connected to it. When you plug that into a telephone socket, it lets the computer dial a call for you, or fax data straight down the line, without putting it on paper first.

However, not all computers will take these cards. Also they vary in thickness, so you must buy the right ones for the slot. Ideally, pick a computer which takes the latest version of these cards; the standards are improving all the time.

Modems

You only need a modem if you want your computer to talk to another down a normal telephone line. For example, it will let you transfer figures from your office computer into your home computer. A modem with 'Hayes compatibility' should work with most communications software. Look too for a good baud rate. This is the speed at which it sends information down the line. The faster it is, the lower your phone bill. However, two computers will only talk to each other if they too are compatible – and some have as big a communications gap as a Chinese and an Englishman. Also, it is illegal to use any modem which lacks BABT approval – so this isn't something to bring in cheaply from abroad. And remember, by opening your computer to input from the outside world you risk a virus entering and scrambling your programs. So you need to be extra careful in using two sets of back-up copies, alternately.

Scanners

Scanners should be the answer to the paper mountain: they look at an image and put it into the computer's memory banks. You drag hand-held scanners across the page, or lay the page on top of flat-bed ones. In theory, what you have scanned is put into a document and you can then manipulate it like any other document. In practice, some scanners have trouble reading small print and may leave out letters or words. Also the text may be difficult or impossible to manipulate once it is in your computer. So they are not yet the miracle they might be. If you need one, test every aspect before you buy it.

Software

'Software' is the term used for a computer program, sold on a floppy disk. The software is the brain of the computer. But it's the brain of a slave. You are the master and tell it what to do, the software decides the best way to do it, and the hardware does the work. Some people think that to run a program you have to know about programming. Far from it. That's the job of the people who made it. You use it as you would a record – switch on, put it in place and roll it.

There are four points to bear in mind when buying software.

1 **Will it run on your computer?**. That means is it the right type of computer and does it have enough RAM.
2 **Will it do what you want it to do?** This sounds very basic, but fast-talking salesmen can easily give the impression that any accounts package they have on offer will suit any kind of accounts, or that their word processing package will do what you want, when it will only do part of what you want. So first write a very specific list of everything you would like the software to do, then go through any piece of software *in detail*, testing it carefully.
3 **Will it do things in the way you want them done?** It's easy to be so delighted with the new box of tricks which a computer program offers that you forget to be critical. Different programs do the same things in different ways. Some ways are much more convenient than others – or may just suit the way your mind works.

Addresses and suggestions for further reading are at the ends of chapters.

4 Is it compatible with the industry standards? Being compatible is important: being well known isn't. The best-known programs aren't *always* the best. I wrote this book with a little-publicized British word-processing program, called LEX, because it could do things almost unheard-of in its competitors. Seven years later it still outshines the competition in many ways.

There are usually two parts of software, and these must work hand in hand and be compatible. The operating system tells the computer *how* to do the work, *in principle.* The applications program enables the computer to do a *particular* job, such as word processing or mathematics.

WARNING: If you use a pirated or a cut-price software it may carry a virus. A virus is a terrorist program, hidden within the main one, which will sabotage your software and gradually destroy or disrupt everything on your computer. Viruses are so sneaky that they can even get in if someone puts a document disk into your machine so as to print something out. However, MS-DOS 6 will check for viruses and so will special anti-virus programs.

Operating Systems

The operating system runs what you might call the internal office of the computer. All the other programs interact with it and are often bound by its rules.

- It organizes the filing system, and keeps an index of everything you create on the disk.
- It controls the movement of all data within the system, inputting it into the memory, for example, or directing it to the printer.
- It stops a faulty applications program from wrongly deleting data which you want saved.
- It may be able to free-up space on your disk by compressing the data.
- It also has various utilities which allow you to do jobs like copying a document from one floppy disk to another, or from hard disk to floppy, or deleting groups of documents.

While the computer is running, the operating system polices operations and does a double act with the applications program, alternating tasks – without you even knowing it. And each applications program is designed to work with a particular operating system.

The best operating systems tend to become standard – in their time – and be used by most of the popular machines and applications programs. Pocket computers apart, avoid applications using little known operating systems, they are unlikely to be any match for established ones.

This is where the divide between machines which are IBM compatible and those which are not shows (see page 437). IBM compatible PCs all run the same range of operating systems. MS-DOS (pronounced M S Dos and standing for Microsoft Disk Operating System) is the market leader for home computers, with the very similar DR-DOS trying to edge in. In contrast, non-IBM compatibles may run operating systems which are unique to them. This is fine with a company like Apple, which is so big that software houses produce applications programs to go with its operating system. But this is not true of all non-IBM machines. So if you buy a little-known non-IBM it may severely limit the range of programs you can use.

Going Gooey

Operating systems like DOS are sturdy workhorses and you can run a vast range of applications programs on them. However, it is fashionable to buy a second-tier operating system which lets you multi-task (page 444) and swap data between programs. These are often called operating environments. The best known of these is Windows which offers what is called a GUI – pronounced 'gooey' and standing for Graphical User Interface. This is a highly visual form of presentation in which you point to pictures on little 'buttons' to tell the computer what to do next. This may enchant you, or you may feel you've been put in kindergarten. And don't believe salesmen who say using Windows is intuitive. Like driving a car, it only feels intuitive *after* you have spent time learning it – and learning it is no easier than learning any other program.

If you have Windows on your computer it is up to you whether you buy, and run, DOS-based applications programs or Windows versions of them. And you can choose to run some programs on just DOS and others on Windows. The advantage of Windows versions of programs is that they look prettier and all use very similar commands. Windows also makes it easy to switch between programs and swap data or pictures between them. Which can make computer using more fun. But Windows can be too clever for its own good – or yours. To run it well you need a faster and more powerful machine than you do for DOS programs, and much more memory – and even then it will be slower on many tasks than DOS and be more likely to crash.

If you want the speed and sturdiness of DOS, with the multi-tasking and data swapping of Windows, you might look at DESQview. This also sits on top of DOS, lets you get into any program at a keystroke, multi-tasks and data swaps and maximizes the use of RAM. But it uses a word-based environment – in which a mouse is optional. It comes in three versions, so it can be run on a wide range of machines, including very modestly endowed ones. You can also run Windows within it. However, you may need a little help in setting it up at the beginning.

There are also operating systems which combine both tiers such as OS/2 and that of Apple. Both Apple and the more recent versions of OS/2 are automatically GUI and multi-tasking and both make good use of the computer's RAM. OS/2 will run both its own and DOS applications programs but is mainly found in offices. Apple normally requires Apple versions. Finally, there is the UNIX operating system widely used in offices since it allows networking. It remains to be seen which operating environments will come to the fore when 'Pen' computing (page 439) is widely used.

> WARNING: Some companies won't let you install their program without clocking in with them for a code – and won't let you install it on more than one computer without an extra fee. Annoying if you are a two-computer household. So this is a point to check.

Applications Programs

Applications programs are the software packages which allow you to use the computer for *particular* jobs such as word processing, doing accounts, creating graphs or playing games. At one time all the program-makers were looking to business for their profits. Now they have realized that home computers are a growth area. So the number of programs to suit family life is growing rapidly and they are both cheaper and easier to use than their ancestors.

For example, there are PIMs (Personal Information Managers) like Lotus Organizer, which looks like an on-screen filofax but will store hundreds of names and addresses and make your phone calls for you. And easy to use accounting programs, like Quicken, designed to run either household accounts or the finances of a small business, or club.

At the same time, the latest versions of programs designed for business use, such as powerful word-processing programs like Word or Ami Pro, or databases, such as DataEase or Alpha 4, are now remarkably flexible and easy to use. So you can easily design your own party invitations, or an elegant programme for a school play, or make a database of favourite wines, stocks and shares, or loved recipes – or avoid the chore of addressing Christmas envelopes by having the addresses on computer and just printing them out. There are also packages, such as Microsoft Works, which offer word-processing and database combined. And price competition is such that you can often find programs which used to cost over £300 being offered for under £100.

Information Programs

A computer can find and display images and references far faster than you could find them in a book. And it can let you interact with the information it finds for you. So it can be a great learning tool and there has been an explosion in reference books both on ordinary computer disks and on CD-ROM.

There are education programs ranging from basic maths to teach-yourself typing. There are also multimedia computerized reference 'books', such as the *Hutchinson Concise Encyclopaedia*, and specialized ones such as Orbits, which guides you through the solar system, or Babyworks, which tells you all about birth and the baby years – and helps you keep track of all the details of your baby's development. And even computerized maps which help you chart a route and tell you the distances and likely times. These are just some of the

tide of fascinating programs to be found. And they are not just a load of pretty pictures. Bodyworks, on anatomy, is being used by doctors to help them explain things to patients.

Utilities

Utilities are a division of applications programs which enable you to run your computer system more smoothly. For example, there are cheap utilities which display a menu of all your programs when you first switch on. And ones like PC Tools let you run through your documents, and check and erase them quickly and easily. Basically, if there's something you'd like to be able to do, there will be a utility for it.

Using a Computer

Getting Started with Floppy Disks

The golden rule is never work from the original, floppy disk, copy of your software. Take copies and work from those. Then if they get damaged you still have your program. Unfortunately, some companies are so worried about the threat of pirate copies being traded that they have made it impossible to take a copy of their program. Check this out before buying.

If a machine doesn't have a hard disk, the usual routine is to switch on and insert the operating system disk (such as MS-DOS) in one of the disk drives. Then press a key to transfer the program to the computer's memory (RAM). This is called booting up – from the term to pull yourself up by your bootstraps.

You then replace the operating system disk with an applications program disk, and press a key or type in a password to put the applications program into memory. The memory may take the whole program or take some and call on the rest from the disk when it needs to. Then a 'menu' will usually come up on the screen listing what the program allows you to do – for example, create or edit a document, or set the printing style. But before you choose you must usually put a document disk in the other disk drive. This is a formatted blank, or partly used, disk which will receive and store the documents you create (see page 443). You are then ready to go.

Getting Started from a Hard Disk

When you use a hard disk you only copy the operating system and the application programs on to the hard disk the very first time you use them. They are then permanently remembered until you erase them. So all you need to do is switch on and type in the name of the applications program you want to work from. You type it in straight after a C:\> which is often called the 'command prompt' in computer manuals. And, if you have an operating environment, such as DESQview or Windows (page 441) it can automatically enter those programs you switch on. If you have Windows but don't always want to use it, Microsoft will tell you how to set up the system so you don't automatically go into it.

When you use the correct exit procedure the work you have been doing is automatically transferred from the computer's memory chips to the hard disk, and stored there until you erase it, or on to a disk in your second disk drive.

Backing Up Your Disk

There are all kinds of housekeeping jobs which can be done with just the operating system (e.g. MS-DOS). The most important of these is making a second copy of any work you do. Good machines and disks are remarkably reliable but they do have their off moments. They can lose a document, or a whole disk can become unreadable. So it is vital to keep a second copy of everything you do. These are called 'back-ups'. Making one is just a matter of telling the computer you want to copy a disk. The exact command varies with the operating system you are using.

Some commands will allow you to add documents to a disk which already has some on, others will copy over any existing documents on the receiving disk. So it pays to read the manuals carefully and pick the right command. You can also execute these commands from within an operating environment, such as Windows. Ideally, use two floppies on alternate days, or both each day. Then, if one is faulty you have lost little or nothing. If you have no hard disk your program will automatically save your work onto a floppy in your second drive whenever you 'Save' it. Using two disks on alternate days again cuts your chances of loss if a disk is faulty.

A floppy can't hold the entire contents of a hard disk. So when taking back-up copies from a hard disk on to floppies you can either copy them by a certain category, such as documents created that day, and keep taking a new disk for each group of documents. Or you can copy everything and wait for the computer to prompt you to give it a new disk.

Dealing with Disks

The blank floppy disks which you buy normally need to be set up ready to take data (formatted) through an instruction from the operating system. The instruction will be in the manual. But beware, formatting erases anything which used to be on that disk. So if you have a hard disk and are formatting a floppy be sure to name the right disk drive.

Both hard disks and floppies are (invisibly) divided into sectors – like a slice through an orange. At first the computer puts the documents you create neatly into the sectors. But, as you erase work, spaces are left. The computer uses these up too. So it may start by putting a document in one sector, run out of space there and put the rest of it into some other. If you are working on floppies or have a very full hard disk, you may find that when you run through a long document there may be an occasional pause before the next page comes up; this is probably because the computer is having to scan several sectors to find it. When that happens use the operating system to reorganize the documents neatly into sectors and speed things up. But beware of cramming any disk to the brim.

A document on a disk needs what I think of as 'turning space' and, like an oil tanker, it needs slightly more than its own length to 'turn' in. So if you want to create a document some 10,000 bytes long you must have more than 20,000 bytes free. This is rarely a problem with hard disks but it is something to be aware of with floppies.

Tips on Computer Use

Naming Documents and Directories

Whatever your software or hardware, think carefully about what you need from your computer before you start to use it. How quickly it will find and display the information you store greatly depends on how you organize things. Anything you create on a computer must have a name before you can store it. Your operating system and applications program combine to dictate how you may name files or documents. To make life easy think, from the start, about the kinds of writing, maths or pictures you will want to store and decide on some naming conventions. This will make it easier to find things again. Your manual will tell you how many characters a name may have and after it will be a full stop and a short suffix. Some programs add this for you. Others let you choose your own – in which case you can also use this to sort one type of document from another. For example, putting .ltr on all letters, and .hom on homework.

Better still are directories. These are a series of names, divided by a \ which let you divide your work into a series of groups. You apply them to your documents as you name them. For example, you might call all documents first by the year when you wrote them (making it easy later on to select old documents for storage on a disk); you might also want to distinguish between documents created by yourself and those created by your partner, and each of you might want to distinguish between business letters (to banks and so on) and private letters. So the name of one letter might look like this:

94\John\bus*loan.ltr*

while another might go down a different directory path and look like this:

94\Susan\pri*mother.ltr* – typing 'pri' takes less time than 'private'.

The difference between the name of a letter (which is in italics above) and its directory path, is that you can give a document any name you wish. But directory paths first have to be set up in the operating system (easy if you follow the manual). You then apply them, in different combinations, to group documents together. You can think of them as filing cabinets, since they allow you, at a later date, to look at all the documents of a certain type. This makes it far easier to find a document within the system. For, even if you have forgotten its precise name you will know the type of document it was and can therefore tell the computer which directory to look in. This means it will retrieve it faster from a hard disk, and if you use floppies you can back-up different directory types on to different disks, also speeding access.

Databases

Salesmen sometimes make out that all databases are the same. They aren't. For a start there are two main kinds: relational and non-relational. A standard non-relational database is like a card-index system on computer, except that you should be able to search for 'cards' in far more ways. A relational database, such as Alpha 4, Dataease or Access, allows you to divide your facts up into a number of separate sub-databases, then combine these when you want to. So you could keep the addresses of club members in one database and the subscription details in another, then combine the two when you want to send out reminders to those who haven't paid.

Good databases of either kind can be adapted to take any kind of information you want. However, they don't all do everything you might want and vary greatly in how easy they are to tailor to your personal needs, so it is worth checking them thoroughly before buying. For example, some don't allow a free text field – which would be essential for recipes or notes about books you had enjoyed. Also some make it impossible to lengthen a field or add a new one without disrupting any data you have already entered. Which can make a database a bad buy unless you have a handy crystal ball with which to determine your future needs. That said, those which don't let you add fields later often compress the data, which may be vital if your hard disk is small.

Disk Labelling

Obviously every disk must be labelled to show its contents. A useful tip is to write on the main copies in red and on the back-ups in black. Then you can instantly tell which is which and there is far less risk of accidentally erasing documents by copying the back-up on to the main disk when you mean to do the reverse. And, if you have a lot of disks, covering different topics, use a different colour to label each type.

★ One of the most useful adjuncts to all this technology is an elastic band. Put one *loosely* round each disk (*in* its sleeve), from top to bottom, as soon as you make a back-up copy. That way all the disks with new work on will have missing bands, and you know instantly which ones to back-up. But don't leave the bands on so long that they perish on to your disk.

Service Contracts and Guarantees

Any computer should come with a year's guarantee. If it doesn't you should wonder why. After that you may be offered a service contract. These can be very expensive, but anyone covered by a contract usually gets attention the day they phone, while those without it may wait a week or so. So, if your computer is vital to you, a contract may be worthwhile whatever the price, and there may be two ways of cutting its cost. They may reduce the price if you agree to take the computer to them and collect it afterwards, or you can take a slight risk and only take out a contract for the two parts of a computer which go wrong most often – the printer and the disk drive. Some software suppliers have a free helpline service; others expect you to pay so much a year for this support. Check this when buying any program.

Terms Used in Computing

Baud rate the speed at which a modem can send sound waves, carrying computer data, down a telephone line. 300 baud (obscurely known as V21) is about 300 words a minute and 1200 baud (V23) is about 1,200 words a minute.

BIOS basic input output system: the most basic layer of program and it is built into the computer
Boot load the piece of software which starts the computer up after switching on.
Compress means store data without wasting disk space.
Cursor a small patch of light which shows the point of the screen where you are working.
Data anything you create on the computer, whether writing, mathematics or drawings.
Debug correct errors in a program (strictly for the experts).
Edit change and correct a document which has been created and held in the computer's memory.
Field a segment of information in a database. For example, a name would be one field, a phone number another field.
Index the list of documents which have been created, which is held on the disk of the applications program.
Multi-tasking is when a computer does two jobs at once, e.g., sends data to a printer while you edit another document on screen.
Network two or more computers linked by cables **and** software so they all use the same database, diary, etc.
Update an instruction sometimes used to change data which is already on the disk. For example, you call an address to the screen, change it, and 'update'. The machine then erases the old address and puts the new one on the disk instead.

USEFUL ADDRESSES AND BOOKS

Bicycles

British Cycling Federation, 36 Rockingham Road, Kettering, Northants NN16 8HG Tel: 0536 412211 – NB for cycle racing and cycling clubs. Handicaps, such as blindness, via the Tandem Club Liaison Officer. Racing only from 12+. M£L-M, B, E, Rg, Ins, HD, sae. (P.416)

Cyclist's Touring Club, Cotterell House, 69 Meadrow, Godalming, Surrey GU7 3HS Tel: 0483 417217 – has useful Information for touring in the UK and overseas. M£L-M, M, L, E, EI, T, HD, Ins, routes. (P.416)
Royal Society for the Prevention of Accidents, Cannon House, Priory Queensway, Birmingham B4 6BS Tel: 021 200 2461, runs cycling classes for children. (P.419)

Useful Books
Bicycle Magazine does regular reviews of bicycles.

Richard Ballantine, *Richard's Bicycle Book*, Pan – a guide to all you need to know about bicycles.

Photographic

Bonus Film Express P.O. Box 100, Borehamwood, Herts WD6 2AZ Tel: 081 953 9911, develops and prints.

Bonus Photo (address as Bonus Film Express) – is a different company in the same business.

Kodak Limited, Consumer Services, P.O. Box 66, Station Road, Hemel Hempstead, Herts HP1 1JU Tel: 0442 61122, offers help and advice on all aspects of photography, and does good leaflets on topics like how to take pictures or process your own film.

Techno Mail Order Shop, 9 Hampton Farm Industrial Estate, Hampton Road West, Feltham, Middx TW13 6DB Tel: 081 898 9934, is the mail order arm of a chain of specialist photographic shops with good prices. (P.420)

Useful Books
Julian Calder and John Garrett, *The 35 mm Photographer's Handbook*, Pan.

John Hedgecoe's Photography Course, Mitchell Beazley.

Cars and Motorcycles

Buying and Selling
AA (see below). Telephone 0345 500600 for details on importing a new car for yourself. (P.426)

Cardata Tel: 081 882 8888 9 am-9 pm weekdays or until 4 pm at weekends for computerized car finding. (P.428)

DVLA auctions special number plates: for the monthly brochure Tel: 0792 782508. (P.426)

Elite Motors, P.O. Box 1, Bradford on Avon, Wilts, also deals in special number plates. (P.426)

Complaining
Retail Motor Industry Association, Conciliation Service, 9 North Street, Rugby CV21 2AB Tel: 0788 576465, operates the same code of practice as the SMMT (see below) and offers a similar service for both cars and motorbikes. (P.426)

The **Motorcycle Retailers Association** is a division of the Retail Motor Industry Association and complaints about its members go to the same address. (P.426)

Society of Motor Manufacturers and Traders Ltd (**SMMT**), Forbes House, Halkin Street, London SW1X 7DS Tel: 071 235 7000, is primarily for the benefit of its members, but has a consumer affairs department which administers the motor industry code of practice, which covers both new car sales and work under warranty. It offers a free conciliation service and, if no conciliation is possible, it offers arbitration – which the customer must pay for. There is usually no appeal against the arbitrator's decision. (P.426)

Scottish Motor Trade Association Ltd, Customer Complaints Service, 3 Palmerston Place, Edinburgh EH12 5AF Tel: 031 225 3643, operates the same code of practice as the SMMT and offers a similar service, but mainly deals with complaints about servicing and repairs of both cars and motorbikes. But it does not handle complaints about new cars. (P.426)

Vehicle Builders and Repairers Association (**VBRA**), Belmont House, 102 Finkle Lane, Gildersome, Leeds LS27 7TW Tel: 0532 538333 – members of this association follow a code of practice for body work only. If they also do other repairs they are not within the code. It deals with complaints in a similar way to the SMMT. (P.434)

Motoring Organizations
Auto-cycle Union, Miller House, Corporation Street, Rugby, Warwicks CV21 2DN Tel: 0788 540519, covers all types of 2- and 3-wheel motorized sport, G, all ages from 6, send 9x6 in sae for starter pack of Inf.

Automobile Association, Fanum House, Basingstoke, Hants RG21 2EA Tel: (Head Office) 0256 492004, (Motoring Holidays) 0256 493878, (Insurance Freephone) 0800 444 777. (P.430)

British Motorcyclist Federation Rider Training Scheme, P.O. Box 2, Uckfield, East Sussex TN22 3ND Tel: 0825 712896. (P.429)

The Camping and Caravanning Club Ltd, Greenfields House, Westwood Way, Coventry CV4 8JH Tel: 0203 694995 – M£M, M, G, HD, Ad, Ins, Disc, A, foreign touring service, Ins, sae. Sites, club for 12-17.

The Caravan Club, East Grinstead House, East Grinstead, West Sussex RH19 1UA Tel: 0342 26944 – M£M, L, Ins, sites, foreign touring service, courses, breakdown service.

Disabled Drivers' Association, Ashwellthorpe Hall, Ashwellthorpe, Norwich NR16 1EX Tel: 0508 41449 (10 am-4 pm), campaigns on all aspects of mobility and welcomes disabled non-drivers. Some companies give members useful concessions. M£L, M, G, L, Adv, Inf, H, Ins. (P.429)

DVLA, Customer Enquiries – Drivers, Swansea SA6 7JL Tel: 0792 772151 for *driving* licence queries, 0792 772134 for those regarding *vehicle* licences. (P.429)

Europ Assistance, Sussex House, 58-62 Perrymount Road, Haywards Heath, W. Sussex RH16 1DN Tel: 081 680 1234. (P.430)

Environmental Transport Association, The Old Post House, Heath Road, Weybridge, Surrey KT13 8RS Tel: 0932 828882, offers breakdown rescue to its members but its profits go to campaign for better public transport.

Institute of Advanced Motorists, 359 Chiswick High Road, London W4 4HS Tel: 081 994 4403, runs advanced driving courses. M£L, M, G, B, Ins. (P.430)

Mondial Assistance, Leon House, 201-241 High Street, Croydon CR0 9XT Tel: 081 681 2525. (P.430)

Motability, 2nd Floor, Gate House, West Gate,

Harlow, Essex CM20 1HR Tel: 0279 635999, runs a car-buying scheme for the disabled. (P.429)

National Breakdown Recovery Club, P.O. Box 300, Leeds LS99 2LZ Tel: 0800 800 600 (Admin), 0800 400 600 (Breakdown Freefone). (P.430)

RAC Motoring Services, RAC House, M1 Cross, Brent Terrace, London NW2 1LT Tel: 081 452 8000, breakdown 0800 828 282. (P.430)

RAC Motor Sports Association Ltd, Motor Sports House, Riverside Park, Colnbrook, Slough SL3 0HG Tel: 0753 681736 – for all motor sports, from cars to karting. Link for local clubs.

Weather Information

Meteorological Office

Aberdeen	0224 210574
Belfast	08494 22339
Birmingham	021 717 0570
Bristol	0272 279238
Cardiff	0222 397020
Glasgow	041 248 3451
Leeds	0532 451990
London	071 836 4311
Manchester	061 477 1060
Newcastle	091 232 6453
Norwich	0603 660779
Nottingham	0602 384092
Plymouth	0752 251860
Southampton	0703 228844

Coast Guard

Dover	0304 210008
Harwich Thames	02556 75518
Falmouth	0326 317575
Solent	0705 552100
Liverpool	051 931 3341
Pentland (re Orkneys)	0856 873268

Computers

Alpha Software Corporation, Suite 113, The Computer Complex, City Business Park, Stoke, Plymouth PL3 4BB Tel: 0752 606881, sells the Alpha 4 database by mail. (P.442)

Computer Bookshops Ltd, 50 James Road, Tyseley, Birmingham B11 2BA Tel: 021 706 1188 sells an immense range of computer books by mail, including ones from America.

GuildSoft Ltd, Suite 110, City Business Park, Stoke,

Plymouth, PL3 4BB Tel: 0752 606200, sells Bodyworks, Babyworks and other information programs by mail. (P.442)

PAPST Plc, Freepost, Andover, SP10 3BR Tel: 0264 333388, sells thermostatically controlled computer-cooling fans, so reducing computer noise.

PC Connections Direct, Unit 15 Hardmans Business Centre, New Hall Hey Road, Rawtenstall, Lancs BB4 6HH Tel: 0706 222988, sells multimedia equipment and information programs.

P.C. Direct Marketers Association, P.O. Box 48, Royston, Herts, SG8 6JS. (P.436)

Quarterdeck Office Systems UK Ltd, Widford Hall, Widford Hall Lane, Chelmsford, Essex CM2 8TD Tel: 0245 496699, has details of DESQview. (P.441)

Swift Computers, 8 Swift Street, London SW6 5AG Tel: 071 731 4192. (P.436)

Useful Books

Computer Works – a computer program which gives you a guided tour of how computers work, from GuildSoft.

Ron White, *How Computers Work*, PC Computing – clear text and illustrations make this book a gem – even Granny would understand a computer after a browse in it but it is about the workings, *not* about how to *use* a computer.

PC Self-Assembly Manual and *PC Upgrade Manual*, tell you, in plain English, how to build your own computer and up-grade it. But they also take the worry out of up-grading *any* computer – for example, by adding sound cards, CD-ROM or more RAM. By post from Olympian Computer Systems, Technopark, Ashley Road, London N17 9LN Tel: 081 880 4222.

Philip Margolis, *Personal Computer Dictionary*, Hutchinson.

Dan Gookin and Andy Rathbone, *PCs for Dummies*, IDG Books.

Michael Groh, *DOS for Non-Nerds*, NRP.

Bryan Pfaffenberger, *I Hate DOS*, QUE.

The 'Dummies', 'Non-Nerds' and 'I Hate' books are 3 different series. Each series has books on PCs, DOS and Windows which give you the essential know-how on how to use a PC or these programs in an informal, highly American way, complete with dire cartoons. The fast food of the computer book industry: useful when you're in a hurry – and the chips are good.

Law And The Legal System

Consumer Law • Criminal Law • Divorce and Separation • Driving and Vehicle Law • Employment Law • Family Law • Household Law • Legal Aid • The Legal System

Britain operates not one legal system but several. There is one law for England and Wales (which allows Wales special rules over such things as pub opening hours), and there are different systems for Scotland and Ireland.

The biggest divide of all is probably between England and Scotland. No act of Parliament prior to 1707 has any force in Scots law – unless it has been re-enacted since. Historically, through its links with France, Scottish law is linked to Roman law in ways in which other British law is not. Since a great deal of law is based on the precedents of decisions made by previous courts, this leads to considerable differences between Scottish laws and those in the rest of Britain.

These historic differences, in turn, affect how Parliament drafts legislation for Scotland. So, for example, the law contained in the 1980 Housing Act, which allowed council tenants to buy their own property, had to be separately drafted for Scotland to allow for the differences in property law in the two countries.

Parliament can pass two separate acts, but it is unfortunately impractical to write here the two or three separate legal sections which are needed to do justice to Ireland and Scotland, as well as to England and Wales. I therefore apologize to my readers from both nations for having included less of their law than I would have wished. Unless specific reference is made to Scotland or Ireland, readers in those countries should assume that the law in their part of Britain may be different.

Finally, a word of warning: this section doesn't pretend to be a comprehensive guide to law. Instead, it is designed to provide a broad portrait of how the law operates in the areas which most affect people's daily lives, so that when they approach a lawyer, or an advice centre, they will already have some feel for what they can expect and what their rights may be. But details which could be vital in a particular case have had to left out. On top of that, law changes fast and new laws will have been enacted since this was printed. So, inevitably, some of the facts here will be out of date by the time you have read them. *Anyone planning to do anything which could have legal consequences – such as writing a will – or intending to take any kind of legal action, should not take what they find here as gospel, but should consult a lawyer.*

You don't need to have deep pockets to get legal advice. There are lawyers in most of the organizations given at the end of this chapter and many of the charities concerned with special issues in other chapters have lawyers able to advise on their field. Between them these organizations also produce a wide range of useful leaflets and booklets giving legal facts in laymen's terms.

CONSUMER LAW

Buying and Selling

Every time we buy something we are making a verbal contract which has two parts. The first part is our offer to buy the goods at a given price; the second part is the shopkeeper's acceptance of our order or verbal agreement to sell them to us. Once both halves are completed, there is a binding contract and we cannot change our minds without risking penalties (such as compensating the shopkeeper), nor can the shopkeeper decide he or she wants to raise the price. With mail order goods the company only accepts the order when it *posts* the acceptance, so the customer is free to cancel the order up to that point. At an auction the acceptance is when the hammer comes down – so if you want to back out speak up *fast* before it strikes. All this means that either side can sue the other for breach of contract and the seller cannot make a customer accept substitute goods. The customer is entitled to her money back if goods aren't what was agreed or ordered. However you buy, the legal implication is that the goods are not defective in any way. If they are, see Quality and Safety on standards of goods, below.

Shopping

Sellers' Obligations
There are two different aspects to the law regarding the sale of goods – criminal offences and civil offences.

Criminal offences are prosecuted by officials like the police or (more often) the Trading Standards Officers; for civil offences the consumer herself has to sue. In practice, where a case might fall into either category Trading Standards Officers may try to lighten their own work by insisting it is a civil offence. It is illegal to:

- display misleading prices,
- describe either goods or services falsely,
- display prices which are not genuine.

The clause on prices in the latest act covers not only goods but also services, accommodation and facilities. Goods with 'reduced from' notices must have been on sale at the higher price for 28 days during the past 6 months. But, since it is up to the prosecution to prove this was *not* the case, this is not as strong as it sounds. Vague signs saying things like 'up to 50 per cent off' or 'up to £15 off are also illegal under the 1979 Bargain Offers Order – though even quite reputable shops use them. But if you think any retailer has broken these laws report it to your local Trading Standards Officer, at your council.

Quality and Safety

The sale of new or second-hand goods, and the servicing related to them is covered by a whole range of acts. However, nobody should be too confident of the protection given by these laws. The Chairman of the National Consumer Council has described current consumer legislation as 'leaking like a sieve'. What's more, the law distinguishes between goods and services. So the protection you get if you spend £500 on a holiday (a service) may not be the same as you get if you spend £300 on a cooker. However, the following are the key points on goods (and directly related services). They must:

- 'correspond with their description' (this applies to both labels and sales talk)
- be of 'satisfactory quality'
- be 'fit for the purpose' they are sold for
- be reasonably safe, having regard to all circumstances.

The description clause also applies to second-hand goods – so be careful what you say when selling your car. And, although charities may sell second-hand toys without the CE mark, the toys must meet the usual safety standards.

Deposits

If you see something you like in a shop and put a deposit on it, to hold it while you look elsewhere, it could be expensive. Deposits placed on goods are usually taken to be a legal contract to buy them. The only way round this is to ask the person who accepts the deposit to give you a receipt saying that the deposit is returnable if you decide not to purchase. The same rule applies to services, but in either case it doesn't hold if the supplier of the goods or services fails to deliver in a reasonable time.

Credit Notes

The law doesn't recognize credit notes. If a customer has not accepted the goods he is entitled to a cash refund. If the goods have been accepted, then he will only be entitled to damages. So a credit note can be either a bad deal or rather a good one.

Ordering

If you order goods you may give a date by which you must receive them, and if they don't arrive by that time you can refuse them. If you don't give a date companies still have a legal obligation to deliver within a reasonable time. How long is 'reasonable' will vary with the goods, but 28 days is used for many situations. If goods are slow in arriving you may write to the seller and say that if they have not come back within a certain time you will want your money back.

Refusing to Serve a Customer

Anyone supplying goods or services may refuse to serve any customer, provided the refusal is not on grounds of race or sex.

Stolen Goods

If you accidentally buy stolen goods you aren't guilty. If you buy goods you know, or believe to be, stolen, it is a crime punishable by imprisonment.

Auctions

Auctions are not governed by all the usual rules. An auctioneer *can* refuse to be responsible if goods are faulty, but must say so in the catalogue or on a sign. However, in some cases, it can be challenged.

Business Purchases

All the rules above apply if you 'deal as a consumer' (i.e. not for business purposes) and buy goods of the type used for private purposes. The rules for buying for business purposes may be different.

Buying in Your Own Home

There are special rules if you agree to buy anything while in your own home. Provided the goods cost more than a certain price (£35 as I write) they apply whether a salesperson turns up uninvited or makes an appointment first. Having agreed to buy, or having paid for and accepted goods, you have a 7 days 'cooling off' period in which you may change your mind, cancel the contract and get your money back. So, *the instant* you change your mind tell the company by phone. Note whom you spoke to. Then write saying you confirm your change and name the person you spoke to on the phone. Either use a fax office and ask someone there to read the letter you send, or ask the post office to give you proof of posting, so there can be no argument about whether you told them within the 7 days.

Postal Selling

The Unsolicited Goods and Services Act 1971 says that if you are sent goods you have not ordered you may ignore the invoice and keep the goods. If the company fails to collect them in 6 months they become yours. Alternatively, you can write to the sender and say the goods were not ordered and suggest they collect them – if they don't the goods belong to you within 31 days.

A more subtle version is to send leaflets inviting you to inspect a book, or something similar, for 14 days before paying. You order it, and when it arrives you are legally bound to pay for it or return it in 14 days. The company gambles on you either forgetting to return it in 14 days, or being reluctant to pay the postage on the heavy item. But if you do send it back get a proof of posting slip from the post office.

Pyramid Selling

Pyramid selling, in which you buy goods from an organization and act as agent for it, selling them directly or through other people, can easily lose you money. Literature put out by such organizations must now warn you of the risks and, if you agree to act as an agent, they may not take more than £75 from you in the first 7 days. You can change your mind within 14 days of signing on and get all your money back when you return the goods. The contract must also explain how to opt out later on. Even so, be wary. Some of these companies are dangerous despite the law. And some claim they are *not* pyramid ventures when they are – in all but name. The DTI's Consumer Affairs Division (page 694) has a free leaflet on your rights and the risks. It is worth reading it before agreeing to act for such a company.

Telephone Selling

There are dubious techniques like sugging, in which someone makes out that they are doing simple market research; they then try to sell you something. It is not illegal but if you can find out the company's name and address report it to the **Market Research Society**. It is against the society's code of conduct and if a member is engaged in it the Society can penalize them. But there is no redress if you have been conned.

Hire Purchase and Credit

If you buy on hire purchase the goods don't belong to you until you have made the final payment. So it would be illegal to sell them. This fact must be printed in the contract which you sign. But, if you buy on credit, the goods belong to you immediately.

Whichever way you buy, the company must tell you the cash price of the goods, the rate of interest and the total price *with* the interest. This may well be in writing on a label or on the contract – so read both carefully.

The Consumer Credit Act 1974 in some circumstances makes the supplier of credit carry part of the liability for goods meeting the standards outlined above. This means that if you use a credit card, bank loan or HP to buy goods which turn out to be faulty you may be able to sue those companies – but the sum must be over £100 and under £30,000. This may sound crazy but it could be useful if a supplier goes bankrupt, so it is usually worth buying large items on credit.

Cancelling an Agreement

Customers can change their minds up to the point when the company approves their application for credit. Those who sign the agreement at home have the usual 'cooling off' period (page 448). If you cancel the agreement within the legal period you should get all you money back bar a £3 fee.

If part-exchange was involved you should get the goods back in unchanged condition within 10 days. Failing that, claim the trade-in value, in cash. You must also keep the company's items in good condition – if they have already been delivered and allow them to be collected, but you don't have to return them physically. (See also Buying in Your Own Home, page 448.)

A credit agreement cannot be cancelled once it is in force; an HP agreement can. But you can only cancel an HP agreement if you have paid all the payments up to half the credit price of the goods, and the goods are in good condition. To cancel you simply notify the company and return the goods. But you lose all the money you have spent up to that point, and if the goods are not in good condition you can be liable to pay for their drop in value.

Debt

If a customer gets behind on HP payments the company can reclaim the goods. But first they must give the customer 7 days' notice in which to pay. If you have paid a third, or more, of the credit price, they cannot reclaim the goods without a court order. (See also page 506.)

Early Payment

If you pay off the whole amount early you should pay less than the credit price, because interest charges are related to the amount of time for which the money is borrowed. Sort this out before paying it off.

Extortionate Interest

If the interest rate is 'extortionate' you can ask the courts to reduce it. But in deciding whether it is extortionate the courts will look at all the circumstances: a high rate is not always an extortionate rate.

Licensed Lenders

There are plans to change the law on lending but, as I write, to lend money a company must be licensed by the Office of Fair Trading (OFT). If the company isn't registered it is committing a criminal offence, and any agreement is not legally valid – so you don't have to pay it a penny. However, the lender can apply to the OFT for a validation order. This order gives a lender the right to obtain repayments under the agreement. However, the OFT can impose certain conditions. Equally, a court can alter the terms of the agreement and the interest rate. If you want to check if a company *is* a registered lender, for a tiny fee the OFT will tell you. It can also tell you the latest rules on lending.

Refusal of Credit

If any company refuses to give you credit – when they allow credit to other customers – it may be because they

---

Law changes: this is guidance not gospel. Consult a lawyer before any decision.

have checked with a credit reference agency and been told that you are a bad risk.

If you know of no reason why anyone should think this, there is a set sequence which may enable you to put the record straight. *But the timing is crucial.*

1 Within 28 days of the shop denying you credit, ask for the name and address of the credit reference agency they used.
2 The shopkeeper must supply this within 7 days – not to do so is a criminal offence.
3 In reasonable time write to the agency in question and ask for a copy of the file on yourself (there will usually be a small fee).
4 The agency must send the file (if they have one) within 7 working days.
5 You then tell the agency which points are incorrect and ask for them to be altered or removed.
6 The agency has 28 days in which to tell you what it proposes to do.
7 If you are not happy with what they propose you have 28 days in which to send a note of up to 200 words, which must be put on your file, giving your views on the sections you object to. If the agency does not agree to put this on its files you can appeal to the Director General of the OFT. There is a heavy fine for agencies which are unreasonable in their reaction.

> Credit reference agencies used to damn *everyone* who lived at a particular *address*, if just one of them was a bad credit risk. This is no longer allowed. But, they may damn everyone in a *family* if just one member of it is unreliable. However, they must give you a clean credit record if you prove to them that your finances are not linked to that person's. The Data Protection Registrar has a leaflet on all this.

Hiring

In England, Wales and Northern Ireland anyone hiring goods has virtually the same rights as someone buying them. In Scotland there are implied terms under common law which consumers should check before hiring.

Codes, Guarantees and Exclusions

If a company breaks the code of practice of its trade association this may put right on your side. But the code of practice may not be identical with the law. In that case, it is usually best to try to settle the matter by first pointing out to the firm that it is breaking the code of practice, and say that you will take the matter up with the trade association if they don't satisfy you. If necessary, ask the trade association to sort it out. It may suggest taking the matter to arbitration; this is not the same as arbitration in a court. So discuss these options with a CAB or Law Centre.

Exclusion Clauses

Sometimes organizations put up notices which claim they are not responsible for all kinds of things. Some-

times these are genuine warnings to remind people of how the law stands; sometimes they are utterly false exclusion clauses with no basis in law. For example, you may see notices saying that a company is not responsible for any death or injury suffered by someone on their premises. In law they *would* be responsible if the death or injury was due to their negligence, and no amount of notices can alter this. This also applies to 'no refunds' notices on sale goods. In these circumstances, they can refuse a refund if you just change your mind, but if the goods are faulty in any way the notice doesn't absolve them of their legal liability. There is, however, a grey area regarding damage to your goods while in someone else's care – such as a car in a car park or a coat on a restaurant coat rack. Whether you get compensation for loss or damage will largely depend on whether it was reasonable to expect them to take better care, in the particular circumstances.

> When someone is buying for business, not therefore as a consumer, shopkeepers are allowed to insert various exclusion clauses and these should be looked for.

Guarantees

All goods and services must, by law, reach certain standards and perform for reasonable periods of time. Guarantees can add to the obligations of a company in relation to its goods and services, but they can never reduce a company's obligations below those set out by the law. Guarantees which promise the earth are suspicious – the company may be planning to vanish before they are called on to fulfil those great promises. However, exclusion clauses may be valid if the buyer is not 'dealing as a consumer' (see page 448).

Despite that, if something breaks down while under guarantee there is no set time limit in law within which the manufacturer, or their agent, must come and put things right. In law they are expected to act within a 'reasonable' time – but a court might think a delay reasonable which a mother of young children with an unusable washing machine might find intolerable. (See also manufacturers' and retailers' codes of practice, opposite.)

Services not Related to Goods

'Services' covers not only obvious services like car servicing but also such things as holidays. As with goods, the major protection is given to private customers 'dealing as a consumer'. Therefore, if a company agrees to perform a service for a given price there is an implied contract between you, just as there is when the purchase of goods is agreed (page 447). Under this contract you have a right to expect certain things.

● The contractor will use the right materials for the job. This means right in both type and quality.

Addresses and suggestions for further reading are at the ends of chapters.

- He will do a satisfactory job using 'reasonable care and skill'. (Trade associations often have established standards of what is reasonable. So it may be safest to use one of their members.)
- The job he does will be the job you asked him to do. (You don't want him to make a lovely job of taking down the wrong wall.)
- He will take care of your goods (e.g. not scratch your car in servicing it).
- The job will be done 'within a reasonable time'. Reasonable can be a touch elastic, so if you need the job done by a certain date make that very clear right at the start – preferably in writing.

If someone fails on any of these clauses they are in breach of contract and you should be able to claim damages.

Broken Appointments

If you break an appointment with someone supplying a service and so cost them money (e.g. fail to turn up at the dentist) they are entitled to charge you. Equally, if you are taking time off work to wait for the washing machine serviceman, tell the company when you book and ask them to be punctual. Then if he turns up in the afternoon when booked for the morning you can claim a nominal sum for the cost of your time and any phone calls you made to his company to trace him. The best way is to knock it off the bill when you pay it, and make clear why you are doing this. The company may try to sue you for the difference but it is very unlikely.

Charges

When the contractor does a reasonable job you should expect to pay a 'reasonable amount'. If a company tries to charge more than a *similar* company would charge it is not 'reasonable', and you are not bound to pay it, nor need you pay for work you did not ask to be done (unless it would have been impossible to do the work which was ordered without this extra work). This applies only when charges have been agreed in advance.

If you agree a price in advance you have to pay it, even if you later discover that it is daylight robbery. Equally, if a company gives you a firm quote it is binding on both sides. If the painter finds the job takes twice as long as he planned, that is his problem: he can't charge you extra. However, if you are given an estimate it is only a guideline to the final cost. So it is wise to accept the estimate in writing and say clearly if any extra work needs to be done, or if, at any point, the work seems likely to exceed the estimate by more than £x (whatever sum you wish) the contractor must get your approval before continuing.

Forgotten Goods

If you forget goods (such as dry cleaning) and leave them with a company for a long time the company should write and remind you. As this is a hassle most have a notice or clause in the agreement they have with you, saying that if goods are not collected within so many months they will be sold. They are entitled to do this. So if you take your tiara to be cleaned, tell your family where it is – accidents do happen and you could die before you can collect it.

Hiring Goods

Hired goods are expected to be in a safe condition. The small print in the hire contract may say the company isn't liable if the equipment kills or injures someone. This disclaimer isn't worth a jot. If the injury was because the equipment wasn't working perfectly (e.g. an electrical fault), rather than due to your negligence, the company is liable. Even so, some lawyers say you should check the small print of any hire contract and delete clauses which you don't think reasonable. But those who hire goods are expected to take reasonable care of them.

Hotels and Holidays

If you book a holiday, in Britain or abroad, through a travel company, you may be protected by the EC Package Travel Directive. This covers not just package tours but many other travel and holiday situations. If it doesn't cover your case and the hotel was a disaster the two travel-industry trade associations ABTA and AITO may be able to help you. For these and the EC law see page 689. Failing that a law centre can advise you on whether you would have a case in the small claims court.

If you booked a hotel in Britain yourself it is a legal contract and the following rules apply:

- It is legal for hotels to charge a deposit in advance, and they can keep at least some of it if you fail to cancel and don't arrive.
- If a hotel accepts your booking but has no room when you arrive you can claim compensation. They also have a duty to accommodate you without a booking, if they have room and you aren't drunk, shabby or otherwise inadmissible. But this doesn't apply to small establishments and guest houses.
- The prices, plus VAT, must be displayed near the entrance or in reception.
- If you cancel you may be liable for damages or lose your deposit.

For your obligations to pay the bill see Restaurants (page 455); the difference is that a hotel can retaliate by keeping your belongings, though you will be glad to hear they must not keep your car or your horse. So if you find yourself at a Fawlty Towers, lock your luggage in the car *before* you argue the bill with the manager.

Taxis

Taxis can be one of the thorniest services. But, alas, they *are* within their rights to sail by with the For Hire sign alight and laughing at you. It is only when they are stationary that they must accept a passenger (traffic lights don't count). They can only charge what is on the meter when within the meter area (the radius varies with each city) but they can negotiate any fare they like outside that limit – provided they do it at the start.

In London there are special rules. If they stop to pick you up they must accept you as a passenger provided:

The law in Scotland or Northern Ireland may be different.

● you aren't asking them to go outside the Metropolitan Police District,
● you aren't tasking them to drive for more than an hour or 20 miles,
● there are no detours to pick up other passengers.

When Things Go Wrong

When goods or services are unsatisfactory complain to the company which supplied the goods – not the manufacturer. The retailer, in turn, has a claim against the maker. And if they were a gift, the *buyer* must do the complaining. If a fault in the goods causes damage or injury see below.

If the wrong goods are delivered to you, and you do not 'accept' them in the legal sense, or if the goods do not meet the rules on quality and safety (see page 448) and are judged defective, you can reject them and get your money back. In the latter case, you may also be entitled to compensation for any losses or expenses incurred. You do not have to take a credit note instead. However, if you have accepted the goods you may only be entitled to damages. So a credit note can be less than you are entitled to or rather more, according to the situation.

Many of your rights in law depend on the issue of whether you have 'accepted' the goods. The law would say you have accepted them if:

● you say you have accepted them,
● you keep them for long enough to imply you have accepted them,
● you do something which implies you own them (e.g. security mark them with your postcode).

Once you have accepted goods you lose your right to reject both them and the contract. But you still have a right to compensation for any breach of the terms of the contract. In either case, you are able to claim damages for any defective state. But beware of those delivery notes some firms ask you to sign which say that the goods are 'received and in good condition', when you haven't had a chance to inspect, let alone try them. You may be 'accepting' the goods in law. So sign the note, but cross out the bit about good condition and write 'subject to inspection' instead.

Liability for Injury or Death

Under the Consumer Protection Act 1987 the manufacturer, importer or 'own brander' of a product became liable for death, injury or damage to personal property worth more than a set sum, caused by defective goods. This clause covers electricity, gas and water as well as goods. And under the Act it is no longer necessary to prove negligence when you sue them.

Where to Get Help

If you ask the company concerned to put things right, and it doesn't, there are many sources of help and advice.

If you have used a trader who belongs to a trade association you may be able to get that trade association to take the matter up. In some cases, although your remedy isn't with the manufacturer, it may be possible to persuade a manufacturer to lean on a dealer. Failing that, contact the Trading Standards Officer on your local council (or the council where the goods were bought).

Law Centres, CABx and some independent advice centres will advise you and have very readable leaflets on consumer law put out by the OFT. You may be able to take the matter to the Small Claims Court and get a legal remedy. Failing that don't ignore the clout of the consumer programmes on radio and television. Anyone can write to them. (See also **Which Personal Service**, page 496)

Conveyancing and Property Buying

A house or flat is the biggest purchase most people ever make. By law an estate agency must give you its written terms of business before it handles your property. It must also declare any interest (fact) which might affect its dealings. And it is a criminal offence for it to describe the property inaccurately to buyers. However, that *doesn't* mean that it must tell buyers about faults: just that it mustn't say things which aren't true. So in any property description watch for points which *aren't* mentioned: they may be the bad points.

Incidentally, the law gives *no compensation* to the buyer of a property which has been misdescribed, it just punishes the agency. And if a seller does a DIY sale, with no estate agent, he is not bound by the same rules on accuracy at all.

> **WARNING: If you buy abroad, *but sign the contract in the UK*, you can change your mind within 14 days, with no penalty. If you *sign* in any other EC country, you have only 10 days' grace. But no deposit can be taken until after that. Outside the EC you may well have no protection at all.**

It is perfectly legal for someone to sell you property which is falling apart: property is sold 'as seen'. So it is wise to have a surveyor's report (page 221) and ask the seller about any guarantees on the property – it may have been treated for damp or dry rot under a guarantee scheme. When there isn't a run on property a surveyor may look at the place *before* you make an offer but, when things are being snapped up, that delay can lose it.

Gazumping

In a rising market, choose a conveyancer who does a lot of this kind of work. There is always a risk that the seller will accept a better offer while your conveyancing is being done. This gazumping is legal right up to the moment when contracts are exchanged. So speed counts, and a solicitor who doesn't do a lot of conveyancing may be too slow. So there is less chance of you losing your dream home.

To DIY or Not to DIY

Whether it is wise to do your own conveyancing will depend very much on the situation. A leasehold flat will have leasehold clauses which might benefit from a legal eye (though they might not). A new property needs clauses in the contract about the quality of the finished work, which a non-lawyer might find hard to draft.

Any property may have some hidden complication, like an ex-wife's claim to it, which won't show until the investigations are underway. But, anyone can search the legal registers: checking petitions and receiving orders at the Land Registry or bankruptcy orders. And a seller can check that a buyer isn't bankrupt by checking with the Land Charges Department herself. So, when no snags occur, many people find DIY conveyancing of a registered freehold perfectly possible. Oyez sells the forms.

For safety, there should be a lawyer acting on the other side, and be prepared to hand the job over to lawyers and let them finish the job if an unexpected snag occurs – if you've done half the work you may be able to negotiate the percentage accordingly.

Registration of Property

In England and Wales there are two types of property – registered and unregistered. For centuries ownership of land or property rested on deeds which showed when B bought the house from A, then another deed would show when C bought it from B, and so on down the years. Hence the old need for deed boxes. Then politicians had the bright idea of keeping a register of who owned what, and there are now Land Registers for each area. The theory was that in due time every property in the land would be neatly docketed. They aren't. So the conveyancer may have to work with either system.

Any conveyancer must check to see the seller of a property is its rightful owner, and that the boundaries of the land are correct. The basic procedure is to complete a form asking the Land Registry to make a search. It then sends the results within a day or two. If the sale goes ahead the Land Registry must then register the new owner of the property, for a set charge based on the value of the property. DIY conveyancers can get heavily worded leaflets from the Land Registry on how to do it, but conveyancers do it for you.

> A new Transaction Scheme is trying to simplify, and speed up conveyancing through solicitors operating in new ways. For example, under it, the seller's solicitor may well do the search, in advance, and the buyer pay for it. (There are safeguards to ensure it is correct and up to date.) It can be cheaper as well as faster but, as always, it pays to shop around. For a list of solicitors involved in this scheme ring the **Transaction Scheme** number on page 497.

Freehold and Leasehold

A freehold property is totally owned by the present owner – who may or may not also occupy it.

A leasehold property is owned by one person while someone else has a lease (a form of licence) allowing them to live in it rent-free, apart from ground rent, for 1

to 99 years. And the price of the lease is related to how long the lease runs for. What follows is primarily for freehold property. Leasehold follows a similar pattern, but there are other checks on the clauses of the lease which need to be made. (See page 488 on Right to Buy.)

The Stages in Buying a Property

Whether the property is registered or not, the stages in buying a home go like this:

1 Make an offer through the agent, saying, verbally and in writing, that the offer is 'subject to contract' – or you might legally commit yourself to buy before you have the money to pay for it. By law, the agent must immediately tell the seller of your offer.

2 If the offer isn't accepted you negotiate until you and the owner agree a price. The agent may ask for a deposit but in law you don't have to give one. If you do, keep it nominal – and it must be returned to you if the sale doesn't go through, whatever the reason.

3 A solicitor is instructed to do the conveyancing, or you start yourself (it takes 1 to 6 weeks).

4 At the same time you start to arrange the mortgage.

5 When the mortgage is agreed and the conveyancing done, contracts are exchanged. It is legal for a seller to accept a higher price right up to this point, and there can even be a contract race in which several people try to get a property for the same price and whoever completes the legal and financial formalities and exchanges contracts with the seller gets the property. But from the moment contracts are exchanged the two sides are bound by law. On exchange of contracts 10 per cent of the purchase price is usually deposited with the solicitor.

6 A completion date is now set on which the whole transaction takes place and you become the owner.

> If you buy property at an auction the fall of the hammer signifies an exchange of contracts. So any surveys and checks should be done before then. You must also be able to pay the deposit then and there.

The Conveyancing

Conveyancing involves checking various facts about the property and transferring it into the buyer's name. It can be done by lawyers, estate agents, staff in banks and building societies, or by licensed conveyancers who specialize in conveyancing. These last can be found through the **Council for Licensed Conveyancers** (page 497), which will also deal with any complaints.

There are three issues in choosing a conveyancer: is she experienced enough to be fast, does she have the right training and professional indemnity insurance, and how much does she charge. Fees are a percentage of the price of the property – starting at about 1/2 a per cent. No small sum. So, since conveyancing is quite simple, you may choose to do it yourself. This is allowed too. But be very careful: a mistake could cost you your home. Oyez sells the forms you need. The *Penguin Guide to Law* covers it well, and Michael Joseph's *Conveyancing Fraud* is a step-by-step guide, written by a lawyer (page 497).

The legal steps in buying or selling a freehold property are as follows. For convenience they are written as if solicitors were involved on both sides.

> The company from which you intend to get a mortgage should be contacted when you start the conveyancing, then all the financial steps are going on parallel with the legal ones and neither (with luck) holds up the other. The mortgage company will use its own solicitor to check the vital facts about the property, but the buyer's solicitor is expected to keep the company informed and send it any documents (such as the evidence of ownership) which come from the seller's solicitor.

1 The seller's (vendor's) solicitor checks the documents on the property by either:
   ● looking at the deeds (usually held by the mortgage company)
      or
   ● seeing the land certificate (the Land Registry send a photocopy).

2 If everything seems correct, and the vendor does own the property, the vendor's solicitor draws up a draft contract and sends it to the buyer's solicitor. (Both the Law Society and Oyez publishing have standard forms for draft contracts.) The solicitor will also send a copy of the registration, if the land is registered, or of any restrictive covenants on an unregistered property.

> Write into the draft contract some agreement about reasonable access to the property between exchange of contracts and completion. Then you can measure up, and so on. Without this you have no right of entry until completion – even if the property is empty.

3 While this is going on the buyer and seller should agree on what fixtures and fittings are included in the purchase price. In law things which are permanently attached to the property should stay. But looks can be deceptive. So check.

4 The buyer's solicitor reads the draft contract and then:
   ● asks the vendor's solicitor about details like boundary fences, mains connections, tenants and formalizes agreement on fixtures and fittings;
   ● writes to the local council and asks about any council matters which could affect the property – proposals to develop the area, planning permissions granted in the past and so on (this is called a 'local search' and is done on a standard enquiry form);

   ● gets the buyer to sign a copy of the contract ready to be exchanged later.

5 Before contracts can be exchanged, and the buyer committed to the purchase, he or she should be happy about every detail of the following:
   ● the mortgage offer,
   ● the surveyor's report,
   ● the local authority search,
   ● the seller's answers to the questions put to him or her,
   ● the information on the ownership of the property.

   If there are problems in any of these areas – say the property is in the path of a proposed motorway and might be compulsorily purchased – this is the time to take back the offer and withdraw from the deal. But if nothing bad is revealed the contracts can now be exchanged.

6 The buyer deposits part of the purchase price (usually 10 per cent) either with the estate agent who arranged the sale or with the seller's solicitor. This money comes out of the buyer's pocket, not from the mortgage company and the buyer can always ask the seller to accept less than 10 per cent – at today's prices even 5 per cent is a sum few people would risk losing by suddenly pulling out. For if the deal is dropped now the buyer could forfeit the whole deposit. But the money is held on deposit by the solicitor or estate agent and doesn't go to the seller until completion.

> The buyer should take out insurance on the property (or it should be done by the bank or building society loaning the money). This should date from the moment contracts are exchanged. At that moment the buyer becomes liable if the whole place burns down. A seller would do well to keep his or her insurance up until completion as a double safeguard.

7 As soon as the money is deposited contracts can be exchanged. The buyer has signed one copy, the seller the other and they swap copies – usually through a solicitor. If the property is unregistered the buyer's solicitor will receive an 'abstract of title': copies of whatever document(s) prove the seller's ownership.

8 The buyer's solicitor checks any 'abstract of title', and asks any questions which arise from it. Or he gets the seller's permission to contact the Land Registry and check the legal ownership of the property – and asks any questions which arise from that.

9 The buyer's solicitor prepares the draft transfer which legally transfers ownership of the property, and sends it to the vendor's solicitors for approval. (It is only called a 'conveyance' if the land is unregistered.) If it's approved a smart copy of it is signed by the vendor (via the solicitor).

Addresses and suggestions for further reading are at the ends of chapters.

10 The seller's solicitor sends a completion statement to the buyer's solicitor saying exactly how much money remains to be paid. This will be the difference on the purchase price.

11 The buyer's solicitor checks that his or her client isn't bankrupt by getting a certificate to this effect from **the Land Charges Department**

12 Finally, the buyer's solicitor sends a form to the Land Registry (for a registered house) or to the Land Charge Registry (if it is unregistered) to check that while all this was going on nothing happened to alter the status of the house.

13 When the all-clear is given by those final enquiries, and the mortgage company is ready to produce the money, the deal can be struck. This is usually about three months after your first offer to the estate agent. The actual sale (completion) usually takes place in a solicitor's office. This is often the office of whoever is acting for the seller's bank or building society (if the seller is still paying off the mortgage). Bank drafts and the titles to the property are exchanged. The estate agent is told to release the keys and in nothing more dramatic than a flurry of paper the ownership of the property has changed hands.

Data Protection

You have the right to know what information companies and organizations hold on you on computer, and also in written medical records. The Data Protection Registrar (DPR) lists all registered data holders. Registered data holders must ensure their data is lawfully obtained and used, is accurate, has proper security and is available to the subject of the data. Although not all data holding has to be registered, check with the DPR before you even keep club membership records on computer – or you could be acting illegally. If you write to the DPR it will tell you what type of data any registered data holder may hold on you. If you then ask that data holder to send you the *actual data* it has on you, it *must* send it within 40 days. But, they may charge you £10 an entry – which could mount up if the organization has several branches with data on you (see also Refusal of Credit, page 449). If the data isn't correct you can ask for it to be put right and/or you can complain to the DPR. A company which fails to make corrections requested by the DPR commits a criminal offence. You can also ask the Crown Court for correction or deletion of the data or seek compensation via a court for inaccuracy or if damage (not distress) has been caused by the loss, or unauthorized disclosure of your data. The DPR (page 496) has good leaflets explaining all the details.

Drink

Licensing Hours

British law distinguishes between on-licences and off-licences – according to whether the alcohol is sold to be drunk on or off the premises. The permitted hours for premises with an on-licence, such as pubs are:

Monday to Saturday	11.00 am – 11.00 pm
Sundays, Christmas	12.00 am – 3.00 pm and
Day and Good Friday	7.00 pm – 10.30 pm

But licensees may choose to open for fewer hours, and licensing justices can alter the hours in their district to allow such licensees to open up to an hour earlier. However, if members of the public or the police can show that all-day opening causes disturbance or annoyance, justices can make a restriction order closing the premises from 2.30 to 5.30 pm. There are also special licences which let restaurants or clubs serve drinks in the afternoon or until later at night.

The licensing hours for off-licences are 8 am-11 pm from Monday to Saturday and the same as for pubs on Sundays, Christmas Day and Good Friday.

Measures in Licensed Premises

The quantities for draught beer and cider are $\frac{1}{3}$ or $\frac{1}{2}$ pt or multiples of the latter. At present wine can be sold in any measure the landlord chooses, but from 1995 it may only be sold in 125 and 175 millilitre measures. Spirits may be sold in measures of $\frac{1}{6}$, $\frac{1}{5}$ or $\frac{1}{4}$ of a gill or multiples of these *or* of 25 millilitres. But from January 1995 the gill measures will be abolished. The landlord must clearly display a notice saying which measure is being used. The exception is when three or more liquids are mixed together, which could explain the popularity of cocktails – among publicans. Carafes may only be offered in the following sizes:

metric: 250 ml, 500 ml, 750 ml, 1000 ml
imperial: 10 fl oz, 20 fl oz.

Food

Basically, food in shops and restaurants must be fit for human consumption and comply with a whole range of regulations. If food is off, contains anything it should not or does not contain what the label says it should, complain to the shop and get your money back. You should also complain to the manufacturer. Unfit food in shops and restaurants should be reported to the Environmental Health Department of the local council; and keep the evidence for him or her to see.

Restaurants

Restaurants are covered by the general clauses in consumer legislation and also by some rules designed just for them. The most important ones are these.

● They must display a notice outside, or immediately inside, their door giving the prices of food and drink, *and* any cover charge, *inclusive* of VAT. If they don't you can report them to the Trading Standards Officer. However, menus at the table don't have to show prices inclusive of VAT.

● Service charges must be displayed outside, like the other charges; if they aren't there is no need to pay them, and there is also no need to pay them if the service wasn't worth paying for.

● A restaurant doesn't have to admit you if you are not suitably dressed – even if you have booked.

The law in Scotland or Northern Ireland may be different.

- You are obliged to pay a restaurant bill, but if the meal was dreadful you can pay what you think is reasonable. Explain why and leave them your name and address. It is then up to the restaurant to sue you for the difference. Pay by cheque or credit card so you have evidence of how much you paid.
- If you book at a restaurant it can be a contract in law, and if you don't turn up you may be liable for a bill. One restaurant successfully sued for the loss when a large party booked and a small party turned up. On the other hand, it's more doubtful that a court will uphold your claim if you sue because the table you booked wasn't available.
- If your clothes are damaged by careless serving you can claim the cost of cleaning, or of a new garment if it can't be cleaned. They may also be liable for the loss of your property in their cloakroom – even if they have a notice saying they are not liable – provided they are clearly offering to look after it. A coat rack in the body of the restaurant may offer less protection.

Gold and Silver

Standards for Gold and Silver
Both gold and silver are normally mixed with other metals to make them stronger. The following table shows the usual international standards for the amount of other metals which may be added to gold, and the British standards for silver, in parts per thousand.

Proportions of Pure Metal

Jewellers normally talk about gold in terms of carats. But, in Britain, since January 1975, gold has had to be stamped with the amount of gold in parts per thousand, and this is common on overseas gold as well. Imported silver may also have its standard number stamped on it, but British silver carries a hallmark which tells you a great deal more.

Buying Gold and Silver
Anything sold in Britain as gold or silver has to be hallmarked to show it reaches the set standard. If it hasn't got a hallmark it can't be sold as such. But since 1975 it

has been legal for British gold and silver to be exported without a hallmark. The Middle Eastern and American tendency to value newness has meant that more and more silversmiths are exporting their wares unmarked – so no date mark betrays the 'shameful' fact that last year's silver is being used. So lack of a hallmark can't be automatically equated with poor quality.

Nor are hallmarks an absolute guarantee of the genuine article. Until the mid-1970s it wasn't illegal, in Holland, to mark silver and gold with fake hallmarks, and there was a cottage industry at the turn of the century doing just that. 'Dutch gypsy pieces' the London assay office calls them. Your only protection is to get a receipt, with the accurate description of the goods, giving the precise gold or silver standard of the article you are buying. Take no excuses; even a stall should be able to give a signed scrap of paper. You should then have legal redress if it turns out to be a lower quality.

Buying Overseas
Britain is one of the very few places to set official standards for items made from precious metals. Baltimore once had a hallmarking system, but its silver then became so popular that the other silver making centres ganged up and had it stopped. If you are buying abroad remember that in some places they sometimes use pure silver or pure 24-carat gold. Both are so soft you can bend them between your fingers, so they may seem inferior because of their very purity. But in other countries the proportion of gold or silver *claimed* for a particular item may be far higher than the actual content. Heaviness for its size is a characteristic of gold. So some sharp dealers in the Far East make fake designer label watches with lead centres, and cover them with a thin coating of what is laughably called '90-day gold' – because it wears off then.

There is no rule of thumb which will tell gold plate from solid gold (without scraping it) or, without chemical analysis, reveal how much other metal has been added. Even the colour of gold is no guide.

Hallmarks
The British hallmarking system, dating from 1300, is one of the world's oldest forms of consumer protection. By law, anything sold in Britain, and described as gold or silver, must be independently tested at one of four assay offices and stamped with a mark to show that it contains not less than a certain proportion of precious metal. Three different types of approved symbols fall within this system:

1 those used on items made in Britain,
2 that used on anything imported into Britain and stamped by a British assay office,
3 the mark stamped in certain European countries for export to Britain.

The mark you'll find most easily is the row of four symbols used for solid silver, made in Britain. To work out the date of a piece and where it was made you only have to decipher the mark from left to right.

Addresses and suggestions for further reading are at the ends of chapters.

Hallmarks

THE SPONSOR'S MARK with the initials of the person or firm which made articles

THE STANDARD MARK showing it is English sterling or Britannia silver

ASSAY OFFICE MARK showing which of the four assay offices tested it.

DATE LETTER showing the date it was marked.

The usual standard mark for sterling silver is

But this is the mark if it is made in Scotland

For Britannia silver the mark is the same for both England and Scotland but changed in 1975

Before 1975

After 1975

Until 1975 the four British assay offices all used different symbols for the same year – so to date a piece you first had to look up the assay office, *then* the date. On anything made since 1975 the date letter is the same for all four offices.

1975 was also a year of change for the standard marks on both British and imported gold and silver. The London Assay Office has a leaflet on hallmarking and the books listed at the end of the chapter will help you to decipher them.

EPNS and Gold Plate

These letters stand for electro-plated nickel silver, which means the article is not solid silver but a base metal plated with a thin layer of silver. But objects in EPNS can still have considerable value if they are very old or attractive.

Gold plate has no distinguishing stamp. Technically, it is very hard to plate an article with anything but pure gold – incredibly thin though that layer may sometimes be. So items which claim 9 carat plating may well be coated in something less than gold.

CRIMINAL LAW

In some families children learn the criminal law with their mother's milk. But for many it is a closed book. It shouldn't be. Ancient rights and civil liberties, such as habeas corpus, which are the pride of the British legal system, are enshrined here. But, like any rights, they only exist if they are used. So we should all know them.

Most of the time the police and the average citizen are on the same side. But mistakes can happen. You may think you will never be on the wrong side of the law, but few things are more distressing than to be arrested when innocent, and find yourself facing the full force of bureaucracy without knowing your rights. When that happens there is no one to help you and nowhere to read them up, and being a prisoner is more intimidating than you can imagine until it happens to you.

Arrest and Before

There is a set sequence of events if someone is thought to have committed a crime. Up to the point when someone is charged the police are free to decide that they have the wrong person, and let the matter drop. The order of events is this:

- questioning,
- arrest,
- questioning,
- detention,
- being charged.

In the Street – Stop and Question

The police may stop you in the street and ask you basic questions, such as your name and address. But you have an equal right to ask why they want to know. The police have to give a good reason for questioning someone – even if they only need a name and address. Whatever they say it is not a good idea to get into a debate with them about whether you are, or are not, connected with the offence they are interested in.

Though you are not obliged to stop or to give your name and address in these circumstances, the wisest course is usually to give it with as little fuss as possible. If you are innocent it does no harm, and if you are guilty they will find it out anyway. But some law centres say that while the police are taking down your particulars you should take down theirs – note the officer's number, which should be visible, and ask what police station he or she is from. A policeman who is simply doing his duty will have no objection to giving this, and with a policeman who is throwing his weight about it acts as a polite reminder that he is not above the law.

If the police then want to know more you have the right to refuse to answer any questions without a lawyer. And this is the wisest thing to do.

In the Street – Grounds for Stop and Search

Under the law a police officer may stop and search someone who is reasonably suspected of carrying:

- illegal drugs,
- firearms or other offensive weapons,
- protected plants, birds etc.,
- adjuncts to terrorism,
- stolen goods or instruments used in theft.

The 'reasonable grounds' must be more than just a hunch, and must apply to the *particular individual*. So even if 90 per cent of car thefts were committed by redheads, that would not be sufficient reason for stopping a redhead who was walking peaceably by.

The procedure for stop and search is laid down in a code of practice, though code lacks the power of law. It says that, before carrying out a search, if not in uniform a police officer must identify himself or herself by showing his or her warrant card (an identity card, not to be confused with a warrant for arrest) and the suspect must be told:

- the police officer's name and police station,
- the grounds for the search,
- the object of the search,
- that, having been searched, they can ask for a copy of the record of the search within a year.

In public, the police may only ask you to remove a coat or jacket and gloves. Further searches must be done in a van or police station. But – amazingly – if you are out of public view the police may go as far as a strip search (by an officer of the same sex) or even an intimate body search, *without having to arrest you first*. However, this can *only* be carried out by a doctor or nurse and on medical or police premises.

The aim of such searches must be to establish whether you are carrying class A drugs for sale or anything which might do harm to yourself or to others, and a police superintendent must authorize the search. However, under the 1984 Act the suspect is not *obliged* to give a name or address and the police may not detain someone in order to obtain a name and address. After the search the suspect must either be arrested or allowed to leave.

Questioning

In law, there is no such thing as 'helping the police with their enquiries'. You are either under arrest or not. If you aren't, you don't have to go to a police station or say anything (apart from giving your name and address). But if you are a vital witness and you refuse to cooperate you could be said to be obstructing the police.

The key point to remember is that, since the tortures of the Court of Star Chamber were abolished in the seventeenth century, a central rule of British justice has been *the right to remain silent*. Nobody has any obligation to say anything (especially if it would harm them) – before, during or after arrest. Only a lawyer can judge what can and can't be used in a court. So this right to silence should be used until your lawyer is present. This applies during general questioning as well as after an arrest. Most of all, lawyers advise that nobody should *ever* admit to a crime, since they may be ignorant of some vital defence which may be lost if they admit guilt to the police. So if the police want to question you, a lawyer's advice is:

- answer *no* questions, except for giving your name and address, until you have seen a solicitor,
- keep calm and polite,
- don't attempt to bluster, swear or bribe,
- if drunk or otherwise incapacitated, say *nothing* except your name and address until you recover.

Questioning of Children – see page 461.

Questioning the Mentally Ill and Mentally Handicapped

Everything above applies just as much to the mentally ill or handicapped as it does to other citizens. But, in addition, under the police code of practice mentally ill or handicapped people should not be interviewed or asked to make or sign a written statement in the absence of an appropriate adult, i.e.:

- the person responsible for his/her care or custody,
- the nearest relative,
- someone not in the police who is experienced in dealing with the mentally ill or handicapped,
- a responsible adult not in the police service.

One of those people should make sure that a lawyer is present before anything is said to the police.

Arrest

The rules on how the police should treat someone who has been arrested are partly laid down in acts of Parliament and partly in the police codes of conduct. When making an arrest a police officer must say that someone is under arrest and give the reasons for it – even if the reasons are obvious. They must say the well-worn words about the right to remain silent 'and anything you say . . .'. But, they don't need a warrant for most offences. There is a list as long as your arm of offences, such as smuggling, indecent assault and murder, which need no warrant. And the crime needn't even be serious. You can be arrested, without a warrant, for:

- refusal to (or failure to) take a breath test,
- obstructing a highway,
- being drunk and incapable,
- refusal to give a name and address when legally obliged to, e.g. after a car accident,
- assault,
- certain immigration offences.

On arrest you immediately have vital legal rights.

Your Rights on Arrest

- You can insist on seeing a solicitor in private. You can phone your own or the police have the phone numbers of duty solicitors, whose services are free. The duty solicitor may be the better bet as he will be up on criminal law, whereas your solicitor may not be.
- You can telephone a friend or relative or ask for someone to be told of your arrest.
- You can refuse to answer any questions.
- You may see a copy of the correct codes of police practice.
- You may keep all your pocket contents etc unless it could be used for escape.
- The parents of anyone of 16 years or less must be told if their child is arrested (page 461).

Those legal rights can be delayed only by a very senior officer, and then only in serious cases, for example, when access to a phone could allow other members of a gang to be warned. However, the police normally question anyone they arrest, and they may do so as much as they wish – even though you have no obligation to answer. That is their job; silence is yours. They can also search the place where they arrested you, plus anywhere that you live or have a business.

Unfortunately, one of the travesties of British justice is that they may also search you – even if, as in cases of refusing to take a breath test, the search could reveal nothing relevant to the crime. They may also take your fingerprints (however irrelevant) if you are over the age of 14, and, if they need to, may use reasonable force in doing this. But usually photographs and intimate body samples (urine, blood etc.) need written consent, and the samples must be taken by a doctor.

Detention
On arrest, the police must take you to the police station as soon as possible, and in most cases they can only detain you for 24 hours without charging you. For serious offences, such as murder, incest or manslaughter, senior officers can extend this to 36 hours. But they must give the reasons. Any extension is very rare, and can only be authorized by a magistrates' court – at which you can be legally represented. The maximum time you can be held without being charged is a total of 96 hours.

If the whole thing has been a dreadful mistake, or the police behave badly, you may be able to take a case against them for wrongful arrest, false imprisonment or assault. If need be they can be politely reminded of this.

Release has a 24-hour emergency advice line for those in trouble with the criminal law. And the Prisoners' Advice Service will advise prisoners on remand, or after conviction. And, as I write, a Prison Ombudsman scheme is planned by the Home Office.

Charging
The police should charge you as soon as they can. This involves an officer formally reading out the crime you are charged with and giving you a copy, plus a notice of your legal rights. For most offences you would then be released and only come before the courts some months later. But if the police want you to be remanded in custody (i.e. imprisoned until the trial), they can usually hold you until the next sitting of the magistrates' court. They then have to show that you might leave the country or repeat the offence. Your lawyer will argue for release on bail. If bail is granted it may involve finding sureties (people who undertake to pay money if you don't turn up for the trial) but usually there are more basic conditions, like checking in at a police station each week.

Assault

Assaults come under the Offences Against the Person Act 1861 and reflect those times – which means the law offers more protection than you might expect.

Common assault need not involve physical contact but normally covers any situation in which someone touches you in an unjustified way. So pushing and slapping are common assault. Common assault isn't a police matter, but you can take out a summons in a magistrates' court against someone who assaults you and that person can be fined, though courts don't like trivial cases. Unwanted sexual touching is indecent assault.

Actual Bodily Harm
Actual bodily harm covers an assault in which bleeding or bruising is caused. If it is reported to the police, an officer must take a full statement from the victim. If you are prepared to go to court and accuse someone of assault the police should arrest the person concerned. You don't need a witness, but it helps. Unfortunately, so few women are prepared to go to court about being beaten up by husbands and lovers that the police may be unsympathetic in such cases. But any woman who is prepared to use her rights can speak to a senior officer and demand the law be followed.

Defending Yourself
You may use 'reasonable force' in self-defence. The trouble is that nobody knows how much force is reasonable until the courts decide afterwards. Lawyers say 'use no more than you absolutely have to'. Many people believe that it is all right to use a weapon so long as it is not something *designed* to be a weapon. But, in law, *anything* can be considered to be a weapon if you use it as one. And if, in defending yourself with it, you injure someone, the fact that you were not carrying it for that purpose is not a copper-bottomed defence. In practice, the court's decision over whether your force was reasonable will be linked to the provocation, on both sides, and the relative power of the opponents.

If you are attacked make *as much noise as possible* and don't play fair – *go for the vulnerable bits immediately, and hard* – and the police recommend a personal alarm.

The law in Scotland or Northern Ireland may be different.

Many police authorities offer free instruction in self-defence.

Grievous Bodily Harm

Grievous bodily harm involves serious injury and is a police matter in the same way as actual bodily harm.

Personal Safety

From the press you would think that elderly women were the most frequent victims of attacks. In fact, some of the worst attacks are on young males, and I personally know of two incidents which resulted in young men, who were well able to defend themselves, being effectively castrated by the boots of gangs. So *nobody* should disregard personal safety. But it pays to seem confident – but not aggressive.

- Avoid walking alone after dark.
- Even with friends avoid dark alleys and lonely roads.
- On public transport keep with several other harmless-looking people.
- Don't wear jewellery where it shows.
- Remember drinking slows your reactions and makes you an easy target.
- Have your keys ready in your hand, so you can let yourself in quickly. If you hold them with the points sticking out through a clenched fist they also make an emergency weapon.
- If you have to walk alone, stick to the middle of the pavement and walk briskly, keeping alert to anything suspicious around you.
- Make life hard for bag snatchers by wearing shoulder bags diagonally, not swinging from your shoulder. And have the flap next to your body.
- Don't advertise the fact that you live alone: enter only initials and surname in the phone book and add an imaginary flatmate to name plates by doorbells.
- Don't invite peeping toms by dressing or undressing in sight of an uncurtained window.
- Keep a whistle and blow it into the phone if you get obscene calls.
- Don't drive with the door unlocked at night.
- Check the back seat before getting into a car at night.
- Keep a map so you don't have to stop to ask directions.
- Don't hitchhike or give lifts to strangers.
- When alone at night carry a personal alarm in your hand and be prepared to set it off.

The **Suzy Lamplugh Trust** (page 496) has excellent booklets giving more specific advice.

Bail

If someone is accused of a crime they can either be 'remanded in custody' – imprisoned until the trial – or released on bail. Since remanding in custody is imprisoning someone before they have been found guilty, this shouldn't happen unless there are good reasons for it. But in practice the system isn't always as good as it should be.

If a warrant is issued for an arrest the magistrate may put a note on the back saying the accused should have bail. In this case the police *have* to release the suspect after charging him, but without this they cannot do so.

Where there is no warrant it is up to the police whether they remand someone in custody or not. They can release them on 'police bail', but if the police refuse bail they must bring the prisoner before the magistrates within 24 hours (48 at weekends and public holidays). The magistrate must then grant bail unless the suspect has previously skipped bail, or the offence carries a prison sentence and any of the following applies:

- there are substantial grounds for thinking it will lead to another offence,
- there are substantial grounds for thinking the course of justice will be obstructed,
- there has been too little time to assess suitability,
- the case has been adjourned for a report to be prepared (e.g. a probation report).

If bail is refused the magistrate must give her reasons to the accused in writing. The accused will then be held in a remand prison and, although this is for 8-day periods, in practice these are constantly renewed until the trial. However, the accused can put forward changes of circumstances and, if bail is still refused, can appeal to the crown court.

Bail Sureties

There is no need for any conditions to be imposed or surety demanded, when bail is granted, but in practice they often are. It may just be reporting to the police every few days or surrendering a passport, but often two people are required to stand surety for an accused. The sureties agree to sacrifice a certain sum if the accused does not turn up at court when required. This money isn't held by the court meanwhile, but the court will check on the person's ability to pay if the need arises.

Burglary

The first rule on burglary is that if you suspect one – either in your own or someone else's property – phone 999. Don't feel you shouldn't bother the police – it is far less work for them if they can catch a burglar red-handed, and if it's a false alarm they understand. Unless you are very sure that you can tackle a burglar without danger to yourself, leave him alone. But note (in writing if possible) every detail which will help to catch him – his description, car or motorcycle number, and so on.

However, if you think you can safely grab a burglar and hold him, you can make a citizen's arrest for this, as for any other serious crime. All you need do is say you are arresting him. You can use reasonable force in doing this and the rules for reasonable force are the same as for defending yourself against assault, but you have more right on your side if someone has invaded your property.

Your local police station will usually have a crime prevention officer who will come and advise on ways of protecting your property from crime and will know about any neighbourhood watch scheme which you can join.

Addresses and suggestions for further reading are at the ends of chapters.

If the thief has flown with your valuables, you or your insurance company can, for a reasonable fee, put a picture or good description of them in *Trace* magazine, or on its database on optical disk. Both are consulted by the police and by legitimate dealers, so you may get your goods back.

Children and Crime

At all ages children have the same rights as adults (see page 457), and legal aid is more easily available. However, children under 10 cannot be prosecuted, though if they repeatedly behave illegally they may be taken into local authority care. Between 10 and 14 children can be convicted of crime, but only if the court can prove the child knew what it did was 'wrong'. For most purposes a child is a 'juvenile' until its 18th birthday, after which it is essentially an adult so far as criminal law is concerned.

The questioning of those between 10 and 18 is governed by a code of practice. The code of practice says that their parents must be told as soon as is practicable and that a child must not be interviewed, or asked to sign anything, except in the presence of:

● their parent or guardian,
● or a social worker,
● or a responsible adult who is not a police officer.

The adult concerned should *always* make sure a solicitor is there too. A child is not sufficiently protected if only a social worker is there: social workers are not legally trained in criminal law. The only time when the code allows the police to question a child without such adults being present is when some harm might result if there was a delay. Children's fingerprints can only be taken from the age of 14. If a child, or a concerned adult, is unsure about its rights, the Children's Legal Centre will give confidential advice.

The police must give bail to those under 14 unless they are charged with murder or manslaughter. And for those between the ages of 14 and 17 bail can only be denied if they are likely to break bail, defeat the course of justice, are charged with murder or manslaughter, or it is in their best interests.

What Can Happen to a Child
Children are tried in youth courts, which are special sections of magistrates' courts, unless the case also involves adults. In that case they will usually be tried with the adults, but sentencing will follow the juvenile pattern. The emphasis is now reforming under 18s within the community. A wide range of sentences can be passed by the courts but the major ones are as follows.

Police Caution
Police have discretion to let children off with a caution if they admit to the offence. But an innocent child should *never* admit to an offence just to avoid the embarrassment of a court case. In the long run the court case is far less embarrassing than a criminal record.

A curious side effect of a child being let off with a caution is that any victim of their crime may well lose the right to compensation under criminal law.

Absolute or Conditional Discharge
A child can be discharged without any strings attached. Alternatively, the court can leave the child unpunished on condition that it commits no more offences for a set period. If it does, it can be punished for the original offence, and the new one.

Bindover
The parents of juveniles can be told to ensure that the child will behave over a given period, the penalty for failure being a fine (surety) of up to £1000 if the child misbehaves.

Fines and Compensation
Children can be fined and told to pay compensation. And parents or guardians can be asked to pay fines and compensation imposed on their children.

Supervision Order
A supervision order appoints an official, such as a social worker or sometimes a probation officer, to 'assist and befriend' the child. And the order can last up to 3 years. Some supervision orders also have clauses about where the child must live and order it to take part in certain activities, have psychiatric treatment, or accept a night curfew.

Deferred Sentence
If a child can produce evidence that it is turning over a new leaf (for example, it is starting a job or a course) the court may decide to pass no sentence until several months have passed, so that it can see whether the child really has reformed – and make the sentence suit the new situation. The sentence is deferred in this way for a set period of time.

Attendance Centre Orders
A young offender may be ordered to spend a certain number of hours each week at an attendance centre, being instructed and kept occupied.

Community Service
This is community social work for up to 240 hours, and it can be imposed on 16- and 17-year-olds convicted of an imprisonable offence. If a child breaks the order it can be fined up to £1000.

Care and Custody
Taking a child away from its family is considered a last resort. However, at any age, if a child is likely to suffer significant harm through being beyond parental control, courts can make a care order placing it with the local authority. And harm includes being involved in certain crimes.

As I write there are also plans for Secure Training Centres for children aged 12-15 who don't respond to community methods. These are not yet law, but already children over 15 can be sent to a Young Offender Institution, for up to 12 months, for serious or repeated offences.

If someone aged 14 or over is convicted of any offence which could carry a sentence of more than 14 years for an adult (e.g., rape, arson) he can be sentenced, in Crown Court, to a term in custody – which can be as long as the maximum for an adult. And for manslaughter and murder this applies from 10 years old. The custody for Section 53 offenders is normally in secure accommodation run by the health service.

Drugs

To possess, use or sell even a very small amount of an illegal drug – such as cannabis, cocaine or heroin – is a criminal offence. It is also an offence knowingly to allow any prohibited drug to be kept or used on your property. So if friends smoke hash at your party you are committing an offence – unless you try to stop them. It is also illegal to sell even small quantities of drugs which can be misused, even if you got them from a doctor. New penalties are heavy and include seizure of property.

Drugs are divided into different classes. Trading in Class A – which is used for drugs like heroin – carries the heaviest penalties. But the legal classes are *not* an indication of the dangers of using those drugs. Some of those in Class B are extremely dangerous (see pages 583-585).

Rape and Indecent Assault

Despite its press coverage, rape is not a common crime. In law it is 'unlawful sexual intercourse with a woman who *at that time* does not consent to it' by a man who either knows she doesn't consent or 'is reckless as to whether she consents to it'. 'Intercourse' is defined as penetration, or near penetration, of the outer lips of the vagina by a penis. So a male cannot be raped, though he can be indecently assaulted.

Indecent assault is the term used when, without consent, parts of the body other than the vagina are entered by a penis. Or when the vagina or other parts are forcibly penetrated with objects. This is a serious offence.

Some women feel it cannot be rape if the man is a friend or relation, or an ex-lover. It can. A large proportion of rapes are committed by men whom the women know well. Even if a man has slept with a woman at some time *it does not* give him a right to force her to have sex.

The law now says that to have sex with a woman when she doesn't want it is rape – *even if she is your wife or your lover*.

Reporting Rape to the Police

If a woman wants to see a rapist brought to justice she should go to the police station, *ideally in the area in which she was raped, as soon as possible*, without washing or changing her clothes. Her appearance and all the physical traces left by the rapist are vital evidence. She is allowed to have a friend with her at the station.

What Happens at the Police Station

She will need to be examined by a doctor, to get evidence of the rape, but she may ask for it to be a woman doctor or her own GP. She will also have to make a statement to the police, but may ask to return and do this the next day. More and more police stations now have special homely rooms and female officers for rape cases. As they may need to keep the clothes she was wearing, they also provide others for her to go home in.

Officially, neither the police nor the courts are now allowed to ask about irrelevant sexual history (except in an appeal case). But old ways sometimes die hard. So, if they forget this, she should remind them of this rule.

Help and Support for Rape Victims

There are Rape Crisis Centres all over Britain offering free, confidential support and help to rape victims. If they are not in the phone book the **Rape Counselling and Research Project & London Rape Crisis Centre** (page 496) accepts calls from anywhere in Britain – reversed charge if necessary – and will give you the details of your nearest Centre, anywhere in Britain. Their people don't force victims to go to the police, but they will go with them if they want to, and also stand by them in a clinic or court. There are also Victim Support Schemes, which will send someone to be with a rape victim. The police will contact the nearest scheme if you ask them to.

> The medical examination at the police station does not test for pregnancy or venereal disease. There is a pill which can be taken after intercourse to prevent pregnancy, but it needs to be taken as soon as possible afterwards, within 72 hours at the outside (see In Health). A VD check is also wise.

Searches

Pretending to be a policeman is an easy way into someone's home. Even if someone is in uniform ask to see his or her warrant card: any genuine policeman should always carry one and should have no objection to showing it. It should carry the badge of the police district, a photograph, name and rank of the holder and a warrant number. It is just an identity document – a warrant for arrest is quite different.

Police Rights to Search

Police may enter premises either because a householder allows them to or because they have a search warrant. To get a warrant they must convince a court that a serious offence has been committed and that a search will produce evidence. They are only allowed to force themselves in without a warrant when arresting someone for an offence, searching after an arrest, preventing a breach of the peace, saving life or recapturing an escaped prisoner. But if a search is unjustified and unauthorized the police are trespassers, like anyone else, and can be ejected and sued. But to be justified doesn't mean that you have to be wanted for an offence, or even linked to one.

To get a warrant the police must convince a magistrate that they have been refused access or have been unable to communicate with the householder. Once the police obtain a search warrant the owner of the property has no automatic right to be told a warrant has been obtained or to be present at the search.

If the police want to search your home without a warrant they must explain the purpose of the search, tell you that you don't have to agree and that they may take away evidence. Landlords shouldn't usually permit searches of their tenant's property without a search warrant, and police shouldn't search on this basis.

Limits to Searches
What the police do during the search must suit the reason for it. So, strictly speaking, they can't search for *people* in drawers, but they can look in cupboards. However, the law now entitles them to take *any* evidence related to *any* offence if they think it might be lost, concealed or destroyed (and they may retain it for use in a trial); the exceptions are items:

● subject to legal privilege (e.g. solicitor's letters),
● excluded under the Act (e.g. medical specimens, journalists' confidential notes),
● used in a trade, profession or position of office.

After any search the officer in charge must make a record of the search which will be held at sub-divisional police stations. Warrants must be returned to the issuing court and can be seen by the householder for up to 12 months.

Searches by Officers of Customs and Excise
Customs officers can enter your business premises at any reasonable time and are allowed to inspect the areas used for the storage or supply of goods. If you are suspected of fraud, they may conduct a full search, similar to a police search, but first they must obtain a search warrant from a magistrate.

Vehicle Searches
Road checks can only be done by uniformed police, but the grounds for vehicle searches are the same as for people, and written information on the reasons for the check can be obtained in writing within 12 months. An unattended vehicle can be searched, but the officer must leave a note to say it has been searched, who has searched it and that an application for compensation for any damage caused can be made to the police station.

Sex and Sexual Abuse

Girls and boys under 16 cannot legally consent to sexual intercourse. And homosexuality is illegal between males unless both are over 21.

The sexual abuse of children involves sexual activities of *any kind* by an older person to a child, and is a criminal offence. Children who are concerned about adults who behave in a sexual way towards them can make a free phone call to **Childline** on 0800 1111 and talk to someone who will understand. They don't have to give their name or address unless they want to.

If an abuser is prosecuted the law now allows a child witness to give evidence from outside a courtroom, or for video recordings of earlier interviews to be used in evidence. And many victim support schemes (see below) have volunteers trained to support child witnesses. There is also a free information pack designed to help child witnesses and their parents or carers.

Child abusers who want help should ask their GP if they can see a psycho-sexual therapist; they should not be asked to explain why. A local Rape Crisis Centre may have the details of a local incest or child abuse group. A number of organizations which help those concerned about child abuse are also given on page 496. And the NSPCC sells leaflets designed to help child witnesses and their carers.

Theft

Theft is defined as dishonestly taking someone else's property and intending permanently to deprive them of it (i.e. not just borrowing). If you suspect someone has taken something you can report it to the police.

Shoplifting
Shops are becoming increasingly suspicious and many do spot-checks on whether people have receipts for their goods. They have no right to look into your bag without good grounds. The shop must prove that you didn't *intend* to pay for goods in your possession. So they seldom arrest anyone until they are out of the shop. But store detectives may take a change of department as suspicious enough. However, instead of prosecuting, more and more shops just ban suspected shoplifters from entering. This is perfectly legal but gives those wrongly suspected no chance to prove their innocence.

So, if you want to pick goods up and take them to a better light, avoid trouble by asking an assistant. If none can be seen, hold the goods high where all can see them. The elderly and absent-minded might find it safest to pin up their pockets, it is so easy to accidentally slip something into a pocket when you mean it to go in a basket but are thinking of other things.

Store detectives have no special powers of arrest. They are only making a citizen's arrest and you have all the rights given under Arrest on page 458. You don't even have to give the shop your name and address. You may also protest your innocence, and say you will sue the store for wrongful arrest if they pursue the matter.

Don't let them tempt, bully or persuade you into explanations if there is any risk of you saying the wrong thing. Stand on your rights, ask to ring a solicitor and say nothing. If they won't allow this, you can insist on going to a police station where they *must* let you see one (see Arrest, page 458). This is safest. **Crisis Counselling for Alleged Shoplifters** (page 496) will advise you too.

Victim Support and Compensation

Anyone who has been a victim of crime can get help and support from their local **Victims Support Scheme.** After certain types of crime the police automatically give the victim's details to the trained local volunteers who operate this scheme. But for immediate support ask the police for the number of the nearest branch. A member of the scheme will provide whatever support you need: visit you at home, go to court with you, help with replacing vital documents, such as pension books, or simply be a sympathetic ear. This is a free service which has government backing.

Members of the scheme will also advise on compensation. In theory, you can get compensation from criminals for loss and injury resulting from a crime of violence, theft or criminal damage. The reality is a little different. Compensation depends on conviction and *may also depend on you getting the police or prosecution to ask for compensation*. But, not all offenders get caught, and successfully convicted. Even when they are, the amount you receive will depend on what the offender can afford, and is often paid in instalments rather than a cheering lump sum. However, it is better than nothing. And, if you want it, make sure you tell the police and the court *before* any trial.

If you have suffered from a crime of violence you may also be eligible for compensation from the **Criminal Injuries Compensation Board**. However, there are set tariffs for different types of compensation, which may ignore individual circumstances. Also the Board will only consider the claim if:

● the compensation would be over a set sum,
● you reported the crime to the police *immediately*,
● you apply, in writing, within 3 years of the injury.

Those who lose a husband, wife, or child under the age of 18 because of crime may also apply for compensation. So may non-relatives who paid the funeral expenses after a death from crime.

Wildlife

The Wildlife and Countryside Act 1981 makes it illegal to:

● kill, injure, disturb, or take any protected species, such as badgers and red squirrels,
● pick or uproot protected plants, or uproot *any* wild plant.

The lists of specially protected species are long, and range from moths to dolphins. Birds are divided into four groups: pest species, sporting birds, specially protected species and the others. The pest species are:

collared dove, crow, feral pigeon, herring gull, house sparrow, great black-headed gull, jackdaw, jay, lesser black-backed gull, magpie, rook, starling, wood pigeon.

Only the pest species and sporting birds may be killed. All other birds are protected, and it is illegal to kill, injure or possess one, or to damage, destroy or steal from their nests.

As the lists in each category are long, the safest course is to harm nothing at all, and treat every plant and creature with consideration. Those who need to know the categories can obtain full details from the **Nature Conservancy Council** (page 693).

Witnesses

Although there's no legal duty, except in respect of terrorism, it makes sense to assist the police and report crime. If you offer to be a witness to a crime outside your area you can always give your evidence to your local police force, when the time comes. But you may have to go to court if the other side wishes to cross-question you, in which case your expenses will normally be paid.

Reporting Crimes
If you think theft is being committed:

1 dial 999 immediately – better a false alarm than an unreported crime,
2 note the appearance and distinguishing features of the criminal,
3 note the registration number and description of the vehicle used,
4 keep watching.

DIVORCE AND SEPARATION

Divorce

Divorce is never easy but the more reasonable the couple can be – and the more they can agree outside a court – the less pain they will probably suffer. Happily, the trend is towards a less confrontational approach to divorce. Some courts have mediators, a number of organizations now offer advice and mediation (page 498). Also the **Solicitor's Family Law Association** (page 498) has a database of solicitors dedicated to keeping conflict between their clients to a minimum, and the **Bar Family Law Association** has a similar list of barristers. Changes in the law have also reduced the risk of conflict. The Children Act has made it harder to use children as pawns. And decisions over support for the children has largely been taken away from the courts and given to the Child Support Agency.

If, however, it comes to a battle royal in court there is only one rule: God is on the side of the big battalions (those with top solicitors), and the most ruthless partner gets the best deal. Common sense, right and justice may scarcely come into it.

Couples who live together unmarried can often use the same mediation bodies as the married. However, they have special problems and may find it useful to read a booklet written by three women solicitors which spells out the legal side of such a liaison, and says how it can be made more secure. It is sold by **Twist, Taft and James**.

To divorce you *must* have been married 1 year or more and the marriage must be beyond repair – 'irretrievable breakdown' as the lawyers put it. There are five situations in which the court may judge that a marriage is beyond saving, and if one of these can be proved the divorce usually goes through – whether the other person wants it or not.

1 The couple have been living apart for 2 years (or more) and both want a divorce.

2 The couple have been apart for 5 years and one partner wants a divorce. Almost the only grounds for preventing such a divorce are if a woman can show that she would suffer severe hardship – which may be the case if the couple are elderly and funds limited.

3 The husband or wife deserted the other at least 2 years ago. Oddly, this is one of the trickier grounds as, among other things, it involves showing that the partner who deserted did so against the other's will, was not justified in leaving and regards the marriage as dead. Also, any separation order automatically changes it from desertion into separation.

> In 1, 2 and 3 'kiss and make up' periods are allowed to interrupt the years apart. But the rules are tricky. You can get back together as many times as you like during the 2 or 5 year period provided the *total* time, i.e. the occasions *added together*, does not exceed 6 months. But if they total more than 6 months you go back to square one and are not deemed to have been apart at all. Also, none of the time together is counted as part of the 2 or 5 years. So, if you get together for 3 months, during 2 years apart, you only qualify for divorce 2 years and 3 months after you first parted.

4 One partner has behaved in such a way that the other cannot reasonably be expected to live with them. This is a remarkably broad category. It covers such things as refusing to have children, physical and verbal abuse, drunkenness, drug taking, gross financial irresponsibility and mental illness resulting in impossible behaviour. But it can cover almost anything which the particular person involved finds intolerable, including quite minor sexual perversions, incessant whistling or even non-stop DIY.

5 One partner has committed adultery and the other feels he or she cannot continue the marriage. Courts are remarkably lax in the evidence they require of adultery – it is often enough to prove inclination and opportunity. But if adultery is admitted the courts don't usually hold this against someone in the arrangements over money and the children – although gross examples of adultery may affect the final settlement. The law also allows the couple to live together for up to 6 months (either as a block or in scattered weeks) after the last act of adultery, to try to make it up, without losing the right to divorce under this clause. The partner suing for divorce can ask the court to award costs against their partner and their lover.

Bringing the Case

When a marriage breaks down most people want to get the divorce over as fast as possible and put that part of their lives behind them. Natural enough, but not always wise. Even good solicitors tend to think of the immediate situation rather than discussing the ifs and buts which may affect the rest of their clients' lives. So you need to be feeling cool enough to think through every detail yourself extremely carefully. Decisions made at this time can affect the rest of your life – perhaps disastrously.

Anyone who is upset by the situation should take as long as they legally can and let the distress subside before embarking on the actual proceedings and agreeing to anything. In your desire to get shot of the whole business you may agree to terms which are not to your advantage. Nobody should assume that the terms are only temporary, because they are bound to marry again soon, or let their solicitor assume that – as they tend to with young and/or attractive women. Life isn't that predictable.

The Cost of Divorcing

You can now divorce without using a solicitor. For some couples it can be a cheap sensible option. It would be misleading to try to explain the procedure briefly, but any county court has a free booklet explaining undefended divorce and The Consumers' Association book on getting a divorce may also be useful. However, it is risky to try DIY divorce if a case is defended, if there are children, or if you want extra financial settlement.

Divorce is expensive – and the more the couple fight over the details, the more it costs. However, I cannot state too strongly that it is *essential* to have a solicitor who is experienced in divorce, and the best that you can afford. Cynical though it may sound, if you may ever want a divorce, start saving now. It is now hard to get full Legal Aid unless you are very hard up (see page 490). And if you do get it, it may be difficult to find a good lawyer who will work for the very low fees Legal Aid pays. Though this applies most in London and other major cities where legal fees are highest. So your chances of being well represented may depend on where you live.

When a divorce is granted the court issues a decree nisi; the decree absolute can be applied for 6 weeks later and is normally granted automatically. The divorce is then final and you should obtain a divorce certificate from the divorce registry or the county court which granted the divorce. This proves the divorce.

Arrangements for the Children

The Children Act has totally changed the approach to the arrangements for children after a divorce. Parents are encouraged to agree living and access arrangements for the children between themselves, with the help of conciliation services, the Court Welfare Service, Social Services, or their solicitor. If that fails, or they later disagree on other child-care issues, they can apply to the courts for one of the orders under Section 8.

The Children Act says court decisions *must* put the good of the children first – or what the court thinks is the good of the children. It gives children a right to have their wishes heard in decisions about them, and says the court may also base its decision on a welfare report.

Law changes: this is guidance not gospel. Consult a lawyer before any decision.

It also says parents have rights and are responsible for their children throughout their lives, regardless of whether they are married, separated or divorced.

Section 8 orders include:

- **Residence Orders** saying where the child should live, and can divide the time between the parents,
- **Contact Orders** say what contact a child should have with a parent it is not living with (an unmarried father may apply for this),
- **Prohibition Steps Orders** say a parent cannot do a particular thing, without the court's specific permission,
- **Specific Issues Orders** settle a disagreement over some aspect of upbringing (e.g., which school a child should attend).

Before the case is heard there may be an informal meeting, called a directions appointment. During this all evidence must be revealed in advance, and a timetable agreed for the proceedings. A court welfare officer may also be appointed to put the child's views if the child is unable to speak for itself. See also page 278.

Married parents share equal responsibility for decisions about the children, such as their schooling. A parent who is ill or abroad can appoint a relative or friend as stand-in on parental activities, while retaining basic responsibility for the child. And any signed, dated and handwritten document (not necessarily a will) is enough to appoint a guardian to take over parental responsibilities from a dying parent, after death.

Step-parents, grandparents and other relatives have no automatic parental responsibilities – even if the child is living with them. But anyone who is close to a child in need could, in principle, apply to the courts for a residence or access order.

Ceasing to Live Together

If a couple live together and have children the situation is a little more complex. The law gives an unmarried mother the legal responsibility for the children. So they will live with her and she will make all the decisions about them. However, the couple can make a legally binding agreement to share responsibility or an unmarried father can ask the courts to give him joint responsibility. But, whether he has it or not, an unmarried father is just as responsible for keeping his children as a divorced one (see below). And, if they have lived as married for some time, a woman may have financial rights as 'a common law wife'. A book on the legal side of living together has been produced by a law firm (page 498).

Money for the Children

By law an absent parent *must* now support his or her children. That applies whether the couple are married, divorced, separated, formerly lived together or produced a child after a single night. But most decisions on how much should be paid have, for rich and poor alike, been taken away from the courts and given to the **Child Support Agency** (page 498). Any lone parent applying for certain state benefits, will be referred to this Agency.

The Agency then works out how much the absent parent should pay out. Lone parents already on those benefits will gradually be contacted by the Agency and brought into the scheme.

Those not on state benefits, have two routes to fixing child maintenance. The two parents can either agree child support between them and, perhaps, have a legal agreement drawn up by a solicitor. Or they can ask the Child Support Agency to decide – via their local Benefits Agency.

The purpose of the Agency is to make absent parents maintain their children. So the Agency looks at the income and outgoings of each parent. It then uses a formula to calculate how much the absent parent should pay the parent with care (regardless of their sexes). It then supervises arrangements for the money to be paid over as suits the couple. It will also make sure the money *is* paid. So missing payments should immediately be reported to the Agency. It will pursue them and can have the money taken out of a pay-packet, by an employer, if necessary. It can also charge interest on late payments. And – if there is a risk that the absent partner may not pay – the Agency can collect the money and pass it on to the other parent.

The flip side is that if someone is on benefit and their ex is made to pay them £20, the benefit is cut by £20 – so they are no better off. It also sets a maximum payment. So, if your partner is wealthy you may also have to go to court to get more. The Agency charges each person not on benefit, for assessment; plus a yearly fee, each, for reassessment, and a further fee for collecting any money. And these fees can't be refunded by Legal Aid.

On money there are no firm rules and nobody should take what follows as any guarantee of what will happen: *every case is different*. But don't be optimistic about the outcome. Divorce is easy; living on the money you have afterwards seldom is.

Money for an Ex

The Child Support Agency is only concerned with money to support the children. So if you want maintenance for yourself from your ex, after divorce, you either have to agree it between you and, ideally, get a solicitor to draw up a legal agreement, or you must ask the courts to decide the sum.

The application for maintenance can be made when the divorce petition is filed, or those who are separated but not starting divorce proceedings can apply to the magistrates' or county court for a maintenance order. The magistrates' court is very much faster, but the procedure is a little rough and ready. Wherever you go, this is an area in which natural justice and common sense seldom enter the door. How much you have to live on – or pay out – may depend more on the skills of your lawyer than on the merits of your case.

The courts have enormous leeway in what they award, but in practice they usually play safe and stick to precedent. Traditionally courts have assumed that a woman needs less money than a man.

The courts look at the *combined* income of both people, then say what fraction each should have. So if a woman is working she may get very little indeed from her ex. What's more the courts seem very unaware that children need time and attention. So no allowance is made for the fact that to bring them up *and* work is to do two jobs not one. Indeed, recent legislation says that women should be encouraged to return to work or to re-train in order to support themselves, even when they are also bringing up the children. And the law is no fairer to men who are left holding the baby.

The new emphasis is on what lawyers call 'a clean break', in which a lump sum and/or property is awarded instead of maintenance. However, if there are children a 'clean break' is usually impossible. And accepting a lump sum, or property has disadvantages. It may prevent you from getting more money if your circumstances change (for example, through serious illness making earning impossible). Also, *if you are on Legal Aid*, unless the other side has to pay costs, Legal Aid will expect you to refund its aid out of any lump sum, above a set threshold, or out of the value of any property awarded to you (see Legal Aid). A lump sum can also remove your right to benefits. So people should think carefully before accepting this option. It suits some people very well, but not everyone. Keeping on a tenancy will depend on the terms of the tenancy, but a council house can usually be transferred from one partner to another on a court order.

Money on Re-marriage

The wife's right to maintenance *for herself* ends if she marries again, and a husband can even apply to stop maintenance if she lives with a man (though in both cases money for the children should continue). A husband can also ask the courts to reduce the maintenance because of a change of circumstances, for example because he wants to remarry and support a second family. Equally a wife can apply for the order to be increased, but the court will also look at the joint income of her and her ex-husband, so if she earns money to pay the bills while waiting for the case to come up, the courts can *reduce* the maintenance because she is earning more than she was when the maintenance was set – and this often happens. However, catch 22 is that failure to apply for an increase of maintenance, when you need it, can be taken as proof of being able to manage on what you get and make it harder to get an increase later.

Maintenance and Death

Maintenance ends on an ex-husband's death. So although the ex-wife and children can apply for a share of his estate, it is wise (and less costly) to have a legacy to her and the children written into a maintenance agreement in the beginning. It may also be worth including clauses related to insurance. For example, a husband could undertake to pay insurance for the children's education (which will cover school fees whether he lives or dies), or to insure his life, with his ex-wife receiving the proceeds if he dies.

Failure to Pay Maintenance

If a separated or divorced husband stops paying legally agreed maintenance the wife should immediately remind him, and send her lawyer a copy of the letter. If maintenance for the children isn't paid, report it to the Child Support Agency at once. If maintenance for an adult is in arrears a magistrate's court can be asked to make an 'arrears of maintenance' summons. If someone keeps on failing to pay up it can also make an 'attachment of earnings' order. The money is then taken straight out of their pay and given to the wife. But a woman on low maintenance and receiving benefit may need the court to make her maintenance payable to the DSS. Then she will get her money every week from the DSS whether the husband pays or not. But if a large sum is involved the court can issue a 'judgement summons'. Failure to pay after that carries severe penalties, including prison. The same applies if a woman is paying maintenance to a man.

Separation

Until divorce proceedings a husband is legally obliged to support both his wife and children. An informal separation in which the two simply live apart and agree matters, is civilized and thrifty. If you use a solicitor to draw up a formal separation deed remember divorce courts may use such deeds as the basis for future arrangements, so it is very important to make sure that no points are overlooked. For example, a wife should usually make sure she is paid maintenance – however little. If she renounces her right to it, in the deed, the courts may dismiss a claim for maintenance at the time of the divorce. And once a claim is dismissed by the courts she may *for ever* sacrifice her entitlement to it – even if her circumstances change dramatically. Equally, husbands should make sure there is a clause allowing the maintenance to be reduced if circumstances change – or he may never be able to reduce it. It may also pay to check the deed with an accountant before finalizing it, because the wording can affect the tax liability, even on the same sum. (This also applies to payments on divorce.)

When there are religious objections to divorce there can also be a judicial separation. There is no need to show a marriage has totally broken down.

Both types of formal separation remove sexual rights and remove desertion from the grounds for divorce.

Annulment

Annulments are statements that the marriage was never valid, so a Roman Catholic should be free to marry someone else (provided the Church accepts the annulment). The main grounds are bigamy, that no sex took place – sex *before* marriage doesn't count – lack of consent, mental illness, venereal disease, or pregnancy by another man at the time of the marriage. But children born in an annulled marriage remain legitimate, even if the marriage was bigamous – provided one parent did not know of the bigamy.

The law in Scotland or Northern Ireland may be different.

DRIVING AND VEHICLE LAW

Drivers tend to feel that most motoring offences are trivial matters. But the law sees many of them as criminal offences. Where they differ from other 'crimes' is that, where cars are concerned, the law isn't concerned with whether you *intended* to commit an offence, only with whether you did so. Luckily, only major offences are put into the criminal records.

For some driving offences the police must warn you there might be proceedings against you, either at the time or within 14 days or issue a summons within that time. (This does not apply if the offence played a part in an accident.) These offences are – ignoring certain traffic signs and police signals, most speeding offences, parking dangerously, careless or dangerous driving, or aiding and abetting such offences.

Failing to produce documents or take a breath test can be an offence in itself. However, drivers have no obligation to say anything which will be to their disadvantage in an insurance settlement or a court case and, if they are arrested, they have the rights given under Criminal Law, page 458.

Accidents

You *must* stop if you damage another vehicle, a person, certain animals, or anything attached to the land in which the road is situated. If you want to remember which animals you must stop for, the AA suggests the mnemonic 'How Can A Man Drive Past Galloping Sheep' – i.e. horses, cattle, ass, mule, dog, pig, goat, sheep. Allowing an injured animal – of any kind – to suffer unnecessarily could lead to a prosecution for cruelty. On stopping you must then give your name and address and the vehicle licence number (plus the name and address of whoever owns the vehicle, if *you* don't) to 'anyone who reasonably requires it'. If someone has been injured, or property damaged (including a car), you must also give your insurance details.

There is normally no need to report any minor accident to the police. But, if either side fails to meet all those requirements they must go to a police station in person, or to a constable, and report the accident as soon as possible – certainly within 24 hours – and produce any documents which they could not produce at the time. You have, however, 5 days in which to produce the insurance certificate. If the police come to the scene they may well prosecute for reckless or careless driving. The police are likely to require all the documents, as listed right, but in this case you have seven days to produce them.

What an accident costs you will depend on who is at fault. So say as little as possible, and write down as much as possible. However, not saying 'sorry' doesn't mean you have to be uncivilized. You can still express sympathy if you choose your words carefully.

In an Accident

DO	DON'T
Stop. Get the other car's licence number if it doesn't stop.	Don't move the cars, unless they are causing an obstruction, until you have sketched or photographed all the details of the scene.
Take names, addresses, car numbers and insurance details of everyone involved in the accident.	Don't attack or abuse the other drivers.
Ask witnesses for their names, addresses, and comments, or note their car numbers.	Don't apologize or admit guilt or blame.
Note the date, time and place of the accident, and the road widths.	Don't call the police unless you want everyone concerned breathalysed – which most forces do automatically. But if an ambulance has been called the police will come anyway.
Note *everything* that could have played a part in the accident – light, road signs, weather etc.	Don't make a statement to the police while you are still shaken up. What you say will be written down and may be given to the other side's insurance company. So just give them your name, address, car number, insurance details, driving licence and MOT papers. Then politely say you will make a statement later
Take precise notes of all damage or injuries to all concerned.	
Note the speeds everyone was travelling at.	Don't leave it to your insurance company to claim from whoever is to blame. Write yourself.
Note whether those in other cars wore seat belts.	
Note whether other drivers smelt of drink.	
As soon as you can, afterwards, write down everything that happened, *in detail*. Report the accident to your insurance company (there is usually a time limit of 7 days.)	

If you are involved in one of the accidents listed left and you neither stop and give details nor report it to the police it is an endorsable offence with 8-10 penalty points, a fine and possibly disqualification. For you to be 'involved in an accident' you don't have to be damaged. If your driving caused others to have an accident the law says you are still involved.

Addresses and suggestions for further reading are at the ends of chapters.

Careless or Dangerous Driving

The old offence of reckless driving no longer exists. Today's offences are 'careless and inconsiderate' driving and 'dangerous' driving – and they now apply to all mechanically propelled vehicles.

Careless and inconsiderate driving is driving without due care, attention, or reasonable consideration. And causing death by careless driving when under the influence of drink or drugs can cause 2 years disqualification, and up to 5 years imprisonment and/or an unlimited fine.

'Dangerous' means driving so as to risk injuring someone or seriously damaging property, *or driving a vehicle which is unsafe*. The penalties are a combination of disqualification, penalty points, imprisonment and/or an unlimited fine. And for 'causing death by dangerous driving' there can be up to 10 years imprisonment.

If you have been injured in an accident you can get free legal advice through the ALAS Scheme, page 499. Under it, member solicitors will give you a first interview free of charge. In it you can be told what chance you have of getting compensation and what the case might cost. This applies to accidents of *all* kinds, not just to road accidents.

Cycling Law

The law for cyclists is much the same as for other road users, and if they ignore a policeman's or traffic warden's signals, or disregard traffic lights or signs, they are in just as much trouble, and cyclists can now be tried for dangerous cycling. In some cases, parents can be heavily fined for faults in their children's bicycles. The list of offences includes:

- riding with defective lights – or allowing a bicycle to be used with defective lights – at night or in poor visibility,
- riding with defective brakes – or allowing a bicycle to be used with defective brakes,
- riding on the pavement,
- holding on to another vehicle,
- walking a bicycle through red traffic lights (though using a pedestrian crossing on foot is allowed),
- racing when not authorized,
- carrying a passenger (apart from a child in a seat),
- failing to give way to a pedestrian,
- selling or trying to sell a bicycle with poor brakes.

In addition, a bicycle must have a white light at the front and a red light and a reflector at the back if it is being used after dark. Offences can mean up to four-figure fines.

You can be convicted of careless or dangerous bicycling and of being drunk in charge of a bicycle – and the fines are heavy.

Drinking and Driving

Random breath tests are not allowed, but a police constable in uniform may stop any vehicle at random – for example, to check that it isn't stolen. Having stopped you for some other purpose, the officer can ask you to take a breath test if there is reason to suspect that you have taken alcohol. This also applies if you have committed a traffic offence while moving (not a parking offence) or been involved in an accident. There are several offences, one of which is being 'in charge' of a vehicle while unfit through drink or drugs.

If you are asked to take a breath test, you just blow into a small device and it gives a pass or fail result. If you pass, that will usually be the end of it. If you fail, it isn't evidence of an offence, so you will be taken to the police station and tested on a machine which gives your 'score' on a print-out which both you and the police officer must sign. You must then be given a copy, or sent one at least 7 days before any trial.

The police *must* take two readings on the machine at the station, and use the lower of the two. The legal limit is 35 micrograms of alcohol in 100 millilitres of breath, but the police *may* let you off with a warning if you have under 40 micrograms. If you have over 35 and under 50 micrograms, and the police intend to prosecute, you have a statutory right to have a blood or urine test as well, if you ask for it. You may take part of the sample to have it independently tested. If your breath registered over 50 micrograms you have no automatic right to such extra tests but they may sometimes be permitted. If these tests are done when you register under 50 micrograms their results are used in court and not the breath test's results. But if you registered over 50 in the breath test, that result is used and *not* any blood or urine tests – even if they are done.

Those who object to taking a breath test on the street, or cannot do so, will be arrested and taken to the station where they must then take a breath test. Those who cannot do this for medical reasons may be allowed a blood or urine test instead. If a medical problem would make it impossible to take a breath test it's wise to carry a doctor's letter stating the condition you suffer from. The legal limits for these tests are 80 milligrams of alcohol in 100 millilitres of blood, and 107 milligrams of alcohol per 100 millilitres of urine. You should be given part of the sample so you can have it independently tested if you wish.

Those disqualified for being 2½ times over the limit, or for refusing to be tested for alcohol, or have two drink-drive disqualifications in ten years, can now have their driving licence withheld until they have satisfied a board of medical examiners that they do not have a drinking problem and are fit to drive again. And, after this or *any* serious offence the courts can make you take an extended driving test to regain your licence.

Law changes: this is guidance not gospel. Consult a lawyer before any decision.

If you are convicted of drinking and driving, the magistrate has no choice but to disqualify you for at least a year. You can also be sent to prison and may have to pay a four-figure fine. And there isn't a get-out clause for those who will suffer hardship if they can't drive.

For a second offence within ten years the disqualification is for 3 years plus, possibly up to 6 months in prison, and/or up to £2,000 fine. (See also Careless and Dangerous Driving.)

How many drinks will put you over the limit depends on your size, weight, sex, health and how long you took to drink them. But you could be over the limit with only a glass or two. What's more, the police may prosecute *even if you are under the limit* if they feel your driving was affected by alcohol. They may also enter your home if you are a drink-drive suspect, especially if you have been in an accident involving injury to someone.

Incidentally, to be a 'driver' you must appear to have the intention of driving. This is a very grey area of law and intention can be widely interpreted. If you think you are too drunk to drive, don't decide to sleep it off in the car, the safest bet is probably to go home by taxi. However, the law is such that there is *nothing* I can tell you to do which will *guarantee* that you will not be prosecuted for drinking and driving if you have been drinking and came by car.

> Refusing to take a breath test is a serious offence in itself, and can lead to disqualification and a four-figure fine.

Drugs

Some medications may reduce driving ability as much as alcohol. By law you must not drive under the influence of *any* drugs which might affect your driving Check with your doctor whether it is safe to drive when taking any medicine. It is also an offence to drive having failed to notify the authorities of a relevant disability.

Though it isn't an offence to drive when ill, doctors have discovered that someone with flu makes driving errors very similar to those made when seriously under the influence of drink. So you could commit a driving offence because you were under the influence of flu.

Driving Licences

The ages for driving licences are broadly these:

- 16 – moped, invalid carriage, small tractor, small mowing machine
- 17 – motorcycle, car, large tractor, small road roller, commercial vehicle under 3.5 tonnes laden
- 18 – commercial vehicle up to 7.5 tonnes laden, trainee on a large goods vehicle (LGV)
- 21 – all other vehicles.

Anyone may apply for a provisional licence provided they can read a number plate at 67 feet in daylight – in glasses if they need them – and don't have any physical or mental disability which makes them unsuitable. Apply, using form D1 from a post office, to the DVLA address on the form. The provisional licence entitles the holder to drive a car if there is a qualified driver with her and learner plates are visible front and back. Learners on two-wheel vehicles are restricted as to what cc and weight they may ride and have a limited time to pass the two-part test (page 429). They should read the DVLA leaflet D100.

On passing the test your licence is normally valid until you reach the age of 70. It must then be renewed every 3 years. At any time you *must* admit to any health problems which might make you unfit to drive. Those with non-British licences, or an international licence, may drive for one year continuously, before having to take a British driving test. But someone who holds a licence from the EC, and certain other countries may be able to obtain a full British licence without taking a test.

If a policeman asks to see your licence you must either produce it immediately, or take it to a police station of your choice within 7 days – posting it won't do. Driving without a licence or while disqualified attracts a heavy fine plus penalty points.

Epilepsy

The rules on epilepsy are broadly these but check the details with the DVLA at Swansea (page 497).

Those who have had epilepsy may have a licence if they have been free of fits for 2 years or have had no fits *while awake* for the past 3 years. If they already have a driving licence when fits start it must be reported to the DVLA, in which case the licence will be withdrawn if fits occur while awake.

Insurance

As a motorist, you must at least have third-party insurance against your liability for injuries to other people and their property. Heavy fines are imposed for failing to do this, plus penalty points, and possibly disqualification. More extensive insurance is optional. Sometimes insurance only covers a particular driver in a particular car, but your policy may cover you to drive other people's vehicles. It may also cover other people to drive yours. Check with your insurer if you don't know which type you have.

> The **Motor Insurers' Bureau** is funded by insurance companies and pays for injuries to people and damage to property if the guilty driver was not insured. There is a maximum claim of £250,000 for damage to property, but injury claims are unlimited.

Addresses and suggestions for further reading are at the ends of chapters.

Lights and Horns

All obligatory lights and indicators have to be in working order all the time – even if you never drive after dark. They must be used from half an hour after sunset to half an hour before dawn, and there are fines for breaches of any of the following rules.

- Dipped headlights should be used by day if the visibility is very poor.
- Side lights and rear lights must be used at night where there are street lights.
- Dipped or full headlights must be used outside built-up areas at night.
- Fog lamps must be used when moving if visibility is seriously reduced but may not be used when stationary.
- Hazard warning lights may only be used when standing still.
- The rear number plate must be clean and illuminated.
- A reversing light must not exceed 24 watts and must have a European Approval mark if fitted after April 1986.
- There are strict rules on the exact position and colour of lights.
- Horns must not be used between 11.30 pm and 7 am.

A car may only be parked after dark without lights if:

- you are not within 10 metres of a road junction,
- you are parallel to the nearside kerb (except in a one way street) and as close as possible,
- the speed limit is 30 mph.

Motorcyclists

To ride a moped or motorcycle on the road you must now complete compulsory basic training (see page 429), however:

- a moped up to 50 cc can be ridden at the age of 16 on a provisional licence,
- a motorcycle can be ridden at the age of 17 on a provisional licence provided the motorcycle is under 125 cc, and its power is under 9 Kw.
- both parts of the motorcycle driving test must be passed before a motorcycle of over 125 cc, or more than 9 Kw.

The following regulations also apply to motorcyclists alone.

- Helmets are compulsory for both riders and passengers.
- It is illegal to carry a pillion passenger on a provisional licence.
- It is illegal to carry a passenger without footrests.
- It is illegal for a motorcycle to tow a trailer.

Parking

Parking offences are now civil, not criminal, offences. And parking administration is increasingly moving away from the police into the hands of local authorities. However, in London, a Parking Adjudicator has been appointed to handle appeals from motorists who feel they have been wrongly penalized. And the scheme is expected to go nationwide before long. She can only handle appeals after those to the authorities have failed. But, the authorities should automatically give motorists the adjudicator's address.

By a rather nasty quirk of the law, you can never assume that you have a right to park on a public road unless there is a notice to say you can. The absence of yellow lines doesn't mean a thing – you can still be done for obstruction. There could also be local zoning laws and not knowing about these is no defence. Dangerous

Parking Restrictions

Double yellow lines along the road – parking usually forbidden 7 am – 7 pm.

Single yellow line along the road – no parking 7 am – 7 pm on certain days.

Broken yellow lines along the road — restricted parking.

No parking ever not even setting down. Severe penalties for breaking these rules.

The law in Scotland or Northern Ireland may be different.

parking is liable to a fine, penalty points and, occasionally, disqualification, but most parking offences only attract a fine. However, the rules on when you *can't* park are these:

- double yellow lines along the road – no parking at any time (in practice)
- single yellow line along the road – no parking at certain times
- broken yellow lines along the road – restricted parking

Parking on a zig-zag by a pedestrian crossing is a serious offence, even if your car is only slightly over the end of them.

Bicyclists are not bound by the yellow lines, but they can still be prosecuted for a parking offence if their bicycle is on a traffic clearway, in a dangerous place, or on a footpath.

Penalties on Lent or Borrowed Vehicles

If someone borrows your car and commits an offence and you receive a 'statutory statement', complete it and give their name and address on the form. Also, get them to sign it before you return it, or you will be prosecuted instead. The exception is a hired car. Here, liability depends on the terms under which it was hired.

Clamps

You can be clamped for most parking offences and on private property. To get a car unclamped you must go to the clamping station given on your ticket, pay a substantial fine and return to your car and wait for the van to come and unclamp you. Then you must remove the car. If you don't go back and drive it off, you can be clamped a second time. In London there's the **Car Clamp Recovery Club** which will go and pay a fine or move the car, for a fee, and other cities may have similar companies.

Meters

Motorists may not feed meters to add to their initial time, even if that was under the maximum time, nor move their car to another meter in the same group. Staying on a meter after the set time attracts a fine ticket and so does parking elsewhere in the same area of meters. If you don't pay the fine within the set time or don't say you wish to contest it, whoever owns the registration documents will be given 21 days to pay the penalty or request a hearing. If he does neither he will be charged the penalty plus 50 per cent, and administration costs.

Penalties for Breaking the Law

For serious offences the courts may now seize the car. But conviction for most motoring offences means an endorsement, which is reported to the DVLA at Swansea, plus penalty points. If you total 12 penalty points for various offences in 3 years you automatically lose your licence for at least 6 months unless there are special circumstances. However, someone who has previously been disqualified in the past 3 years will lose their licence for a minimum of 1 year, and two disqualifications will make it a minimum of 2 years. Most offences have fixed penalty points, but some are at the court's discretion. So it can be worth putting your case to the court. Remember, disqualification takes effect immediately. You must not even drive the car home. Fines can also be imposed for all offences, though the courts seldom impose the maximum fine. Serious offences, involving risk to others, can land a motorist in prison.

Fixed Penalty Tickets

Fixed penalties have been standard for parking offences for a long time, but in 1986 their scope was widened. In situations where you would have been prosecuted before, you may now get a fixed penalty ticket. Basic tickets can be given by either a police officer or a traffic warden. Yellow tickets are given, only by a uniformed police officer, for offences such as speeding, for which a driving licence is also endorsed. You will either have to surrender your licence then and there or take it to a police station. If you are guilty you should pay the penalty within 28 days. If you were not guilty you can go to court. But just forgetting to pay is expensive: failure to pay within 28 days raises the penalty by half.

Registration Document (Log-Book)

This shows who is registered as having a vehicle, the 'registered keeper', and who has had it before. This is not always the same as who owns it. If you sell or buy a car, or change your name or address, you must notify the DVLA *immediately*. If you own a car and want to know who owned it before you, the facts can be obtained from the DVLA (page 497) which has the records of all registered keepers.

Road Tax

If a car is on the road, road tax has to be paid for it – even if the car won't go. The tax disc, from main post offices, must be displayed at the bottom corner of the windscreen on the nearside. The tax applies to that vehicle only, but if you sell the car before the time is up you can apply to the DVLA at Swansea for a refund – details are available from the post office. Late applications for road tax are always backdated unless the car was off the road the entire time.

Roadworthiness

MOT Tests

Any private car which has been registered for 3 or more years must have an MOT certificate. The police may ask to see it, but if your vehicle is not roadworthy an MOT certificate is not a defence.

It is now a very serious offence to drive a car which is not roadworthy (see Careless and Dangerous Driving) and the police can stop you driving such a vehicle on the spot. The police can stop a car *at any time* to check whether it is up to standard on tyres, lights, steering, brakes and other aspects which could affect safety, pollution or noise. But, unless the car has caused an accident, it may be possible for the inspection to be done some other time within the next 30 days.

- All brakes must work within set stopping times.
- The handbrake and steering must be properly adjusted.
- Windows must not be obscured, e.g. by dirt or stickers.
- Lights and reflectors must be clean and working.
- Horn, rear-view mirror, silencer, speedometer, windscreen-wipers, washers and seat belts must all be in good working order.
- The car must not be in a dangerous condition – bent metal could cut someone passing by.
- Any load must be secured so that it cannot be a danger or nuisance.
- Neither petrol nor petrol vapour may leak from the petrol tank – a suitable petrol cap is a must.
- Tyres must suit the vehicle and must have at least 1 mm of tread all over for motorcycles or 1.6 mm for cars, be correctly inflated, be of the same type on the same axle, and have no cut longer than 2.5 cm, or 10 per cent of the tyre width – whichever is greater.

Penalties for breaking these regulations range from a fine to penalty points and possible disqualification for dangerous faults. But some police forces have vehicle rectification schemes in which a minor defect must be put right within a set time and a form to that effect signed by an authorized tester given to the station.

Seat Belts

It is compulsory to wear seat belts in the front of a car except when reversing; and it is *illegal* for a child under 12 months to sit in the front unless 'suitably restrained by equipment suited to its age and weight' – someone's arms are not enough. If children between the age of 1 and 13 are in front and not wearing seat belts the driver can be prosecuted. Pregnant women and the disabled are not exceptions – unless they have an exemption certificate from a doctor saying they should not wear a seat belt for medical reasons. You can find other exemptions in the Motor Vehicles Regulations 1982.

Belts or restraints must be worn in the back if the car has them. For babies under 12 months this is a baby restraint; from 1 to 4 years old the restraint must suit the child's size and weight, or be an adult belt with a booster cushion; and from 4 to 14 it is either a child's restraint or an adult seat belt.

Speeding

The courts now accept evidence from certain automatic devices, such as cameras, as proof of speeding. But the police can only use an approved device and must serve you with a copy of their evidence 7 days before the hearing or trial. Up to 3 days before the trial you can ask for whoever signed the document to attend the proceedings. If they catch you by following you, the police must do so for 3/10ths of a mile.

The possible speed limits are 20, 30, 40, 50, 60 and 70 mph. If street lamps are under 200 yards apart the limit is 30 mph, unless you see some other speed sign. If the spacing is wider, or there are *no* lights, the limit is 70 mph on motorways and dual carriageways, and 60 mph on single carriageways, unless another speed is shown.

EMPLOYMENT LAW

The Trade Union Reform and Employments Rights Act 1993 gave employees new rights. For all the details ask your union or the Department of Employment.

Conditions of Work

The laws on conditions of work vary greatly with the job. Contact the **Health and Safety Executive** for those applying to a particular job, but in shops and offices the key points are these:

- The temperature should not be lower than 16°C (61°F) after the first hour – and there should be a thermometer with which to check this.
- There must be adequate ventilation (natural or by air conditioning) and no harmful fumes. As I write, 'fumes' doesn't yet cover tobacco smoke. But employers have a general duty to keep staff safe. The courts have already classed the effects of passive smoking (breathing other people's smoke) as an industrial injury. So EC laws say employers must now protect non-smokers from tobacco smoke in rest areas. And a government White Paper expects most workplaces to be non-smoking by 1995. Meanwhile the EC says *all* employers must also do a 'hazards assessment' of the workplace. Given the potential for lawsuits, it could be expensive for those who fail to class tobacco smoke as a hazard and protect non-smokers from it, if reasonably practicable.
- There should be enough space. However, if you want to know how the law defines overcrowding, I can only refer you to the Offices, Shops and Railway Premises Act 1963, which sets out the rules for shops and offices in this remarkable piece of prose:
The number of persons habitually employed at a time to work in such a room as aforesaid shall not be such that the quotient derived by dividing by that number the number which expresses in square feet the area of the surface of the floor of the room is less than forty or the quotient derived by dividing by the first-mentioned number the number which expresses in cubic feet the capacity of the room is less than four hundred.

The punctuation is theirs; the Department of Employment has been unable to explain the meaning.

> If you are starting up, or running, a business you can get free legal advice on any business related matter, during an initial interview. **Lawyers for Your Business** (page 497), which runs this scheme, has a list of member solicitors.

Contracts

An employee and employer are equally bound by any signed contract and a contract can often be negotiated before signature. So it pays to read the small print. By law an employee who works 8+ hours a week for one month has a right to receive a written statement of his terms of employment within 2 months of the start of employment. Among other things it should give the following:

● names – yours and the employer's,
● job title – not always a description of the work,
● pay-rate, how it is arrived at, and whether weekly or monthly,
● hours of work – hours a day, days a week, overtime,
● pension scheme – the details or how to learn them,
● sick-pay – rules on sick notes, what sick pay you get and for how long,
● the date of starting work,
● holiday entitlement – length and pay,
● notice – minimum period of notice to leave, on either side,
● discipline – any rules, and what happens if you break them,
● complaints procedures – whom you can complain to if you need to.

Dismissal, Redundancy and Leaving
This area is full of special exceptions, but most employees are entitled to written notice of the reasons for the dismissal. And, *unless your contract states better terms for notice*, the law on being dismissed or on giving notice to your employer sets the following rules. If you were employed:

under 1 month – no notice
1 month to under 2 years – 1 week's notice
2 to 12 years – 1 week's notice per year employed
over 12 years – 12 weeks notice.

However, any employer may give pay in lieu of notice and the more senior the position, the more notice is expected on both sides.

Since an act of 1993 employees have had protection against dismissal for exercising statutory rights or on grounds related to health and safety at work. If you think your dismissal was unfair, or too little notice was given, there are several things you can do. Talk to a union representative, or get the Department of Employment's free leaflets on your rights (page 693), or talk to the Equal Opportunities or Race Relations bodies (page 497) if it is relevant, or take your case to an industrial tribunal. If the dismissal is judged to be unfair you may get the job back, be given another job instead, or be paid compensation. And, dismissal isn't limited to telling you to go; if an employer's behaviour made it impossible for you to stay this may be considered dismissal.

Redundancy is usually fair dismissal – unless you were unfairly chosen for redundancy. But, if you have worked for an employer for 2 years, for 16 or more hours a week, or for 5 years, for 8 or more hours a week, you are probably entitled to redundancy pay. (Being laid off or put on short time may also entitle you to it.) This lump sum is based on your age, length of employment and pay, and you are entitled to a written statement of how it was calculated. If you don't get your entitlement you can go to an industrial tribunal *within 6 months*.

Time Off
Paid time off must be allowed for union activities. However, an employer has no duty to do that for civic duties. Nor is there any legal entitlement to holidays – although a court would normally expect an employer to follow the norms for the industry. (See also Maternity.)

Disabilities

The disabled quota says that, in a company employing 20 people or more, 3 per cent of the jobs must be given to those registered as disabled. Employers can be prosecuted for breaking this rule and can get exemption only if no suitable disabled person is available. However, if you feel you have been refused a job because of your disability, there is no route to redress, although Jobcentres will help with finding other employment.

Discrimination

It is an offence to treat someone unfavourably because of their race, colour, origins or sex. This means that an employer may not advertise a job in a way that bars any race or sex. Nor may jobs, promotion, housing and so on, go to people because they are (or are not) a particular race or sex. In interviewing people, questions may not be asked of a woman which would not be asked of a man – for example, do you intend to have babies? It is also illegal to treat any race or sex less well than another as regards goods and services, or to sexually harass them.

However, the law does not make *all* sexual and racial discrimination illegal. It is still legal to discriminate in all areas not specifically covered by the acts. For example, verbal abuse is not covered unless it is sexual harassment. And the law allows discrimination in certain circumstances. For example, racial and sexual discrimination are allowed in jobs in private houses (so nobody is obliged to have a male nanny or a female butler). Where sex or race is in itself a qualification for a job, discrimination is also allowed. So you *can* insist on a girl modelling women's clothes or a black actor playing a black part. Private clubs may also discriminate in some circumstances, and so may someone letting or selling part of a house in which they or a near relative live.

The equal pay law 1970 says that both sexes must receive the same pay for the same work, or for work of equal value.

If the acts are broken the person who has been discriminated against usually has to go to an industrial tribunal. A case related to sexual discrimination must be started within 3 months if it relates to employment, and 6 months for other areas. The Commission for Racial Equality and the Equal Opportunities Commission will advise, assist and perhaps represent you in court. And

Addresses and suggestions for further reading are at the ends of chapters.

both have forms on which the initial complaint can be set out, and booklets explaining the acts in detail. CABx, law centres and trade unions may also help. Cases not connected with employment can get legal aid and in some cases the commissions or trade unions may assist financially.

Industrial Tribunals

Industrial Tribunals are independent legal bodies set up to hear cases related to most aspects of employment. A senior barrister is chairman and there are two lay advisers who sit with him. Industrial tribunals cover such problems as:

- unfair dismissal,
- rights related to employment protection,
- redundancy pay and National Insurance payments,
- maternity rights,
- equal pay and conditions for women,
- sexual or racial discrimination,
- complaints relating to health and safety at work,
- rights to pay during lay-offs,
- lack of union notification regarding the transfer of undertakings,
- exclusion or expulsion from a trade union,
- certain aspects of compensation.

A Department of Employment leaflet (page 693) gives full details of what complaints can be heard by a tribunal and explains each stage. Read it before applying, as what follows is only a general outline of the procedure, as I write. For most cases, the application must be made within 3 months of the offence.

Application forms for a hearing by a tribunal are found in Jobcentres, unemployment benefit offices and CABx, and the latter may be able to help you with the application. Either the Equal Opportunities Commission or the Commission for Racial Equality may help with cases in their field. Applications should be sent to the **Central Council of Industrial Tribunals** (page 497), which will forward them to the right regional office. The system in Scotland is almost identical.

The Procedure
A copy of the application for a hearing is sent to whomever the case is being brought against and they receive a form on which they must say whether they will fight the case, and on what grounds. This form must be completed and sent in within 14 days – but if this was genuinely impossible a tribunal may accept it later. If it is not sent in at all you may not usually appear at the hearing, but you are still allowed to settle the case with the applicant before the hearing.

Most cases are sent to the Advisory Conciliation and Arbitration Service before the hearing, and through them a settlement may be reached without a hearing.

The Hearing
Notice of the date is given at least 14 days before and if either side is unable to attend they must tell the tribunal office immediately. A new date may be fixed if there is a good reason for it.

The procedure is informal but like that in any court. Each side may call witnesses and may question both their own and the other side's witnesses, and the tribunal may question all concerned.

Either side may put their own case to an industrial tribunal, but if they want someone to speak for them they can ask a trade union representative or a solicitor to do so. Anyone who needs a solicitor should get the leaflet 'Legal Aid for Civil and Criminal Cases', free from Jobcentres etc. (as above), since they may be entitled to it for the preparation of their case.

If whoever brings the case is not happy with the outcome he or she may appeal within 42 days provided there is a point of law which justifies this and, if necessary, can go on appealing right up to the House of Lords.

Maternity Leave and Allowances

A woman cannot be sacked because she is pregnant. If this seems like the reason for losing your job contact the Equal Opportunities Commission at once (see above).

Time Off
All women are allowed paid time off for antenatal care – even part-timers and those in new jobs. But they should tell their employers when they will need to be absent, and show them a certificate proving the pregnancy. However, time off to prepare for labour or parenthood isn't an automatic right. But refusing a woman time for them could be a matter for an industrial tribunal. If this is a problem talk to a law centre or CAB. Fathers have no statutory right to time off for the birth, but some employers make it part of the contract.

Alternative Work While Pregnant
If a woman can't do her normal work because she is pregnant (for example, it's too heavy for her) she has a right to be given another job which is more suitable, if it's available. But only if she has worked at least 8 to 16 hours a week for the employer for 5 years or more, or over 16 hours a week for 2 years or more. Not giving her such a vacancy is unfair dismissal.

Statutory Maternity Pay
Women can also apply for Statutory Maternity Pay (SMP). Key qualifications are:

- you have been employed with the company for at least 6 months by the end of the 15th week, before labour is due,
- you earned enough in the last 8 weeks, before entitlement, to pay full National Insurance contributions.

There is a flat rate, but if you have been with an employer for 2 years full-time or 5 years part-time you can get up to 90 per cent of your normal pay for the first 6 weeks. It is paid for:

	6	weeks before the birth
plus	7	weeks after the birth
also for	5	weeks before or after, or split between both periods

Total 18 weeks

The law in Scotland or Northern Ireland may be different.

To get it: write to your employers at least 3 weeks before you intend to stop work asking for SMP and enclosing your maternity certificate – Form MAT B1. *Write on time, even if you don't have the form*; late claims may be *too* late. Read the DSS leaflet on babies and benefits.

If the pregnancy lasts 24 weeks you are still entitled to SMP after the birth, even if the baby was stillborn. But you cannot take SMP from one employer after having started work for another.

Maternity Allowance

Maternity Allowance is paid at a flat rate per week to the self-employed and to those who lost out on SMP because of job changes. It is paid from 11 weeks before the birth and you can only claim it if you have been paying National Insurance contributions for 26 weeks out of 52 in the period ending 15 weeks before the baby is due. Claim it from 11 weeks before the birth from the social security office.

Women who are receiving certain benefits may be able to get a lump sum Maternity Payment before the birth.

Returning to Work After a Baby

From October 1994 women will get 14 weeks maternity leave, regardless of how long they have been in the job, provided they have notified their employers of their pregnancy and of the start of their leave 21 days before. Those who have worked for an employer for 2 years get longer leave after the birth. Before October 1994, the situation is that you can take up to 40 weeks' maternity leave (from 11 weeks before the birth to 29 weeks after), and then get your job back, provided *all* the following conditions probably apply. But do get proof of posting for the vital letters you have to send.

- The company employed 6+ people when you left.
- You have worked for that employer for at least 2 years by the start of the 11th week before the baby is due (5 years if you work under 16 hours a week).
- You work at least until the 12th week before the baby is due (i.e., whole working weeks, including Friday).
- You tell your employer *in writing*, 3 weeks before leaving, that you will be absent for the birth, but intend to return after it, and give the date the baby is due (if you suddenly stop work for medical reasons, write to the employer the instant you can).
- The employer may write to you from 7 weeks after the baby is due asking if you plan to return; in which case you must reply within 14 days or you lose your right to return.
- You must return within 29 weeks of the birth, having given at least 3 weeks' written warning to the employer of the date of your return. However, a 4-week period of grace is allowed on either side. So, if your employer isn't ready to have you back, your return can be delayed for up to 4 weeks. And if you are not well you can delay your return for that time – *with a medical certificate* – without losing your rights. But only one delay is allowed.

On Your Return

On returning, you must have the same pay and conditions as before – including any pay rises which have occurred in your absence – but not necessarily the same job. The time you were away from work may not count as part of your total time in employment when a pension is calculated.

If you don't know whether you will return, guard your options by following the procedure for keeping your job, but tell your employer the instant you decide you don't want it.

Patents and Copyright

Whether you personally are entitled to patent or register an invention or design depends on whether you created it as part of your work. If you did, then your employer owns the rights. If you didn't, you can ask for a patent or registration in your name.

A patent can be granted by the Patent Office for a new product or manufacturing process, or an improvement on an existing one, which is unknown in Great Britain or elsewhere. The patent gives the holder the sole right to make or sell his invention for up to 20 years from the filing of the patent application. But there are certain limitations on what can be patented. Fleming couldn't patent penicillin because it was a discovery, not an invention. But, ironically, the Oxford team which made it into a drug could. Nor need an invention work at the time of patenting: Whittle's jet engine couldn't work when he patented it, but it was capable of working *in principle*.

It is also possible to register the look of an article – for example, a greeting card or a new style of telephone – provided the design is new and original. Trade marks can also be registered.

Copyright covers written words or music, sound recordings, broadcasts, films, videos, photographs and computer programs. Once again, what you create through being an employee belongs to your employer. Freelance or non-work creations are yours. There is no registration. For 25-50 years, depending on the medium, these automatically belong to the creator. However, when selling such work say *in writing in advance* that you retain copyright and define what rights you give the other in exchange for payment. Otherwise it can look as if they are buying the copyright. It isn't essential to put the copyright mark © but putting it and adding your name and the date warns others not to take liberties. With important works go further: deposit a copy with a bank or solicitor or send yourself a copy of the work by registered post – and leave the envelope unopened.

For more advice on these issues and on performance rights contact the Intellectual Property Department of the DTI (page 694), the **Patent Office**, or the **Institute of Patentees and Inventors** (page 497). Incidentally, there is no copyright on a title or name – though it may be covered by trade mark law and nobody may use an

---

Addresses and suggestions for further reading are at the ends of chapters.

existing name to pass other work off as one and the same.

Pay

Since the Wages Act 1986 nobody has a *right* to be paid in cash. Whether payment is in cash or by some other method is something which the employer and employees must agree on. They must also agree whether it is weekly or monthly, and agree upon any fringe benefits – and there are no longer legal restrictions on payments in kind to manual workers.

All employees must be given itemized pay statements which show the total earnings, and all deductions such as tax and national insurance. In some jobs deductions may also be made if the employee causes losses (e.g. the till is short or something is broken). Normally, deductions for loss or damage can only be made if:

a they are written into the employment contract and the contract, or an explanation of it, was given to the employee before the deduction

or

b if the employee agreed to them in writing before they were made.

Any disputes which can't be resolved can be taken to an industrial tribunal within 3 months of the payment or deduction being made. Or of the last error in a series. An employee may also be able to take an employer to court for breach of contract. **Low Pay Unit** (page 698) may be able to advise you.

Sexual Harassment

If behaviour of a sexual nature is unwanted, unreciprocated and causes distress or serious embarrassment it may be illegal under the Sex Discrimination Act 1975. The Equal Opportunities Commission (page 497) is the main organization which advises and helps women with this problem. They like women to contact them fairly early on, but their general advice is this:

● tell the man to stop doing it – so he cannot claim that you wanted his attentions – and if possible do that in front of a witness,
● talk to your female colleagues about it – he may be doing it to everyone, but only when each of you is alone. It will be less distressing if you don't feel a sole victim and it is easier for a group of women to put a stop to it,
● keep a note of each incident, giving what happened and the date (don't rely on your memory; notes at the time are better evidence),
● if necessary, talk to your employer about it,
● if the harassment reaches a pitch which would be sexual assault it is a police matter, and the sooner it is reported to the police the better.

Trade Unions

When someone joins a union he becomes legally bound by the rules of the union – even though nobody may bother to show him the rule book. But unions cannot treat their members in a way which is clearly unjust, even if the rules permit it.

Closed Shop
There used to be situations in which those who didn't join the right union couldn't get a job in a particular company. Now this 'closed shop' is illegal. Nobody may be forced to join a union, either to get a job or to keep it. So, if you think you have been refused a job or dismissed because you aren't in a union you should complain to an industrial tribunal within 3 months. If unfair treatment is proved, you may receive substantial compensation. For dismissal for non-membership of a union is always unfair dismissal.

Elections
All members of the principal executive committee of a union must be elected by secret ballot and submit to regular re-elections.

Picketing
Picketing is legal provided it only uses peaceful persuasion to try and stop others entering the workplace. But this doesn't mean pickets may break other laws. They must not, for example, obstruct the highway, be intimidating in their numbers, or commit assault. And they may only be:

● employees,
● ex-employees who lost their job through the strike,
● full-time union officers of the relevant union representing those employees.

Strikes
● All union ballots to decide on strike action must now be secret ballots and members have a right to postal ballots.
● If you strike you lose the right to be paid and risk dismissal, and there may be no state benefits. Moreover, whether there is strike pay from the union usually depends on whether or not the strike is official, and on whether the union can afford to offer it.

FAMILY LAW

Abduction

It is a criminal offence to take a child under 16 abroad without the consent of the other parent or guardian – unless there is a court order allowing this. How easy it is to get a child back greatly depends on where it has been taken. Britain has treaties with some countries on this but not with others. So prevention is vital. If you think a child may be abducted get advice from **Reunite**, the **National Council for Abducted Children**. If you think it is *being* abducted, tell the police immediately and ask the Home Office to alert ports and airports. If a child has already been abducted, the **Child Abduction Unit** (page 498) of the Lord Chancellor's Department, and Reunite can advise and help you.

Abortion

In England, Scotland or Wales, it is a criminal offence for anyone other than a doctor, or a nurse under his supervision, to cause an abortion. But a pregnancy may be ended, before the 24th week (see In Health), if two doctors agree that:

1 the mental and physical risk to the mother and her existing children is greater if the pregnancy is continued than if it is ended

or

2 there is substantial risk that the child will be severely handicapped mentally or physically.

It is not essential to get the father's consent, but the parents of a child under the age of 16 should be consulted. In Northern Ireland abortion law is altogether stricter.

Artificial Insemination by Donor (AID)

As regards birth certificates and inheritance, a child born by AID is now treated as a child of the mother's husband, if he consented to the insemination, and any link with the donor ends. Unlike an adopted child, an AID child has no rights to trace its genetic father, and surprisingly the laws on marriage and incest apply to the child's legal father but not to its genetic one.

Birth and Adoption Certificates

A child's birth must be registered within 6 weeks (3 weeks in Scotland). To do this either parent simply goes to the Registrar of Births, Deaths and Marriages and gives them the details of the child and of both parents – no proof of the birth is necessary. However, if a child is illegitimate both parents must go along if both want their details to appear on the certificate, or the father must send a sworn testimonial. Otherwise the mother registers the birth and only her details appear.

> Babies are registered in the area where they are born. But this can be done via another office if it is more convenient. One nice quirk is that babies born on planes are registered via the Civil Aviation Authority and those born on ships via the Registrar of Shipping and Seamen in Cardiff.

To obtain a birth, marriage or death certificate apply to the Superintendent Registrar in the area where the registration took place. That way it costs only about half as much as from the General Register Office, and is usually much quicker. If you know the area you can find the address of its superintendent from that office itself. If you don't know the area you will have to apply to the **General Register Office** (page 498) but you can pay a reduced fee and search for it yourself. Either way, you need to give the person's surname, first names, date and place of birth, the fathers's names and the mother's name and maiden name. A certificate can be either short or long – the latter having more information and costing more.

Adopted Children's Certificates
Adopted people over 18 have the right to apply to the Registrar General for a copy of their original birth certificate which includes:

● their mother's (and possibly father's) name, and job,
● their date and place of birth,
● their mother's address at the time.

There is now an Adoption Contact Register which simplifies contact between those who have been adopted and all their blood relatives. Any blood relative can put their name on the register, for a fee, then if the adopted person tells the Register they are looking for their family, the blood relatives' details will be sent to them. However, the Register *won't* give an adopted person's details to the blood relatives. The register is operated by the General Register Office of the Office of Population, Surveys and Census. Forms are available from them (page 693) and **NORCAP** (page 317) will help and advise both parents and children. (See also below)

★ Those trying to trace a family tree can get a leaflet on what facilities are available from the **Office of Population Surveys and Census** (page 693; see also page 741).

Children

Much of the law on children was laid down in the Children Act. It gives new rights of appeal against court decisions. Also, amazingly, it took this act to put into law principles which most people would think common sense. Namely, that:

● in decisions about a child, the child's good must come first,
● in decisions about it, a child's wishes and feelings must be taken into account, as far as possible,
● courts should do nothing rather than to do something stupid (what a pity that law doesn't apply to governments too),
● service providers must listen to and work in partnership with children, and parents, or those with parental responsibility,
● those providing services for children 'in need' must not disrupt family life avoidably,
● the rights of parents of children in care must be protected,
● the courts and service providers must take race, culture and religion into account.

If the authorities fail to do these things they are now breaking the law and can be taken to court by the child, its parents or its carers. Many of the court orders which local authorities or parents can apply to the courts for come under Section 8 of the Act. Which is why lawyers talk of Section 8 Orders – and so will I. However, not all law affecting children is contained in this act.

Adoption
To adopt a child in Britain your home must be in Britain. This includes those who are not British but live here

permanently and British people temporarily overseas. Married couples adopt jointly but if a couple are just living together only one of them may adopt the child – and would keep it if they split up. Someone single may also adopt. Adoption gives adopters full parental rights and responsibilities for a child, and they must be over the age of 21. If you are related to the child or obtained it through an adoption agency you can obtain an adoption order once the child has lived with you for 3 months; otherwise it is 12 months. If you are considered suitable, and the parents don't veto the adoption, the court will make either an interim order or an adoption order. The adoption order makes you the adoptive parent immediately. The interim order means the child can stay with you for the next 2 years, but you must apply again for an adoption just before that time runs out. But, once an adoption order is through, the child is as much yours as if you had given birth to it (see also pages 273, 478).

Ages Which Matter

A child's rights and obligations increase steadily with its age, although in practice, until the later years, the parents usually act on the child's behalf and the obligation may be as much theirs as the child's.

There are no age limits relating to the following:

- the age at which a child may be left alone, or left to care for other children,
- complaining against discrimination because of race or sex,
- complaining against the police,
- gaining access to personal information covered by the Data Protection Act,
- choosing your religion – though parents can object,
- refusing medical treatment – but you cannot *consent* to it until a set age,
- opening a bank account – if the bank thinks you can handle it.

A full list of rights and duties at different stages in childhood can be obtained from the **Children's Legal Centre** (page 498).

Children in Care

If a child is suffering serious harm, or is likely to do so, or is beyond parental control, it can be taken into care, or placed under a supervision order. But the local authority needs an order from the courts first. If the authorities suspect a child is at risk, and parents won't give them access to the child, they can get an assessment order from the courts. This gives them the right to see and assess the child within 7 days – by removing it from home if need be.

If the authorities get a supervision order from the courts it can only be for 1 year. If they get a care order they must see that the child gets the right kind of care. And, unless a child, or its welfare, is at risk authorities *must* now let parents have reasonable contact with the children. (Pages 497-498 gives organizations which can help parents and children here.) If parents are unhappy about contact or how the child is being cared for they

can apply to the courts for orders to get a child back or get proper contact. So may step-parents, relatives and those with whom a child has lived for 3 of the past 5 years. Moreover, in theory, the authority doesn't take on parental 'rights and responsibilities' – those remain with the parents. However, the authority can say how far parents of children in care may use their 'rights and responsibilities'.

All that sounds fine. But, between the lines, a remarkable amount of power still rests with social workers, not all of whom are wise or experienced. The Law Society has set up a nationwide panel of solicitors who will act for parents and/or children in care cases, and are experienced in acting for them. Local advice centres may have the list or you can obtain it from the Care Panel Administrator at the **Law Society**. The organizations on pages 497-498 will also advise and help parents and children when care orders go wrong.

Accommodation (formerly Voluntary Care)

In trying to give more power to families the Children Act did away with the idea of voluntary care. Parents who, through illness or other reasons, can't look after their children for a while now ask their local authority to find their children 'accommodation'. The authority then puts them in a children's home or with foster parents. This no longer takes any rights away from the parents and the authority must try to place the children where the parent can easily visit them, and must agree reasonable access. The parents are also free to remove the children from accommodation at any time, without notice. This should remove the risk that a child who has been put with a local authority may be kept from the parents for ever.

Emergency Protection Orders

If the authorities, or the NSPCC, believe a child is being battered, abused, or neglected, they can quickly get an Emergency Protection Order from a court. This puts a child in care for up to 8 days, with a possible extension of up to 7 days. But, if parents weren't present when the order was made they can apply, within 72 hours, for it to be cancelled.

Wardship

Making children wards of court is a process by which the High Court gives all the parental rights to the court, so no decision about the child can be made without the court's permission. A child can be made a ward of court very quickly. But whoever asked for the wardship must apply for a preliminary hearing within 21 days; this decides whether the child should stay as a ward. If the application is not made, wardship ceases automatically. Parents can be legally represented in wardship proceedings.

Once a child becomes a ward of court it may live wherever the court decides, and the major decisions in its life must be made by the court. This lasts until it is 18 unless the wardship is cancelled by the court.

The law in Scotland or Northern Ireland may be different.

Corporal Punishment

The law allows parents to administer 'reasonable chastisement'. In practice this means that you can smack a child but not do anything which could injure it. So a clip round the ear – which could damage the ear – would be unreasonable, whereas a smack to the bottom might be reasonable – provided it was not too hard. It is a criminal offence to exceed the reasonable limit and corporal punishment in schools is illegal.

Education

LEAs must provide children from the age of 5 to 16 with education suited to their 'age, ability and aptitude' (often called the 'three As'). It isn't easy to *prove* that education fails to meet a child's needs – but parents can fight this in the courts if they feel their children are ill-served by the state system.

Parents must ensure that their children receive a full-time education which meets the 'three As' criteria. Allowing a child to play truant or keeping it at home to help is illegal. This doesn't mean that children must always go to school. But parents who educate their children at home must be able to show that the 'three As' criteria are being met, or they can be taken to court and their child placed under the supervision of an education welfare officer. The Children Act also says local authorities must inspect independent schools and make sure they safeguard the welfare of their pupils.

Dress and Discipline

All schools are allowed, within reason, to dictate how a child will dress and behave in school and on the way to and from school, and punish the child accordingly. Head teachers of state schools may prevent pupils attending school by suspending them, but may not expel them. (See page 296)

The only class from which parents have an automatic right to withdraw a child in a state school is Religious Instruction – if it differs from their beliefs.

Leaving School

Children may leave when they are 16, but they cannot leave instantly. Those born between:

- September and 31 January may leave at the end of the spring term,
- February and 31 May may leave at the end of May,
- June and 31 August may leave at the end of the summer term.

Fostering

If a parent places a child with someone not related to it, for more than 28 days, it is considered fostering. The local authority should be told if you intend to do this, as it may want to inspect the foster home. If a local authority wishes to put a child with foster parents it must, by law, place it within reach of its family, school and friends. It must also try to place it with a family of similar culture and religion. Parents who are not happy with fostering arrangements can get advice from the Family Rights Group, or Parents' Aid.

Grandparents and other Relatives

British law doesn't think of the whole family as a unit, nor does most social-work practice. It just thinks of parents and children. So grandparents and other relatives have no right of access to children after a divorce, or when they are in care. Nor will the authorities usually ask them to have them to stay when they need accommodation or fostering. However, the Children Act allows anyone who is close to a child to apply for a residence or access order.

Illegitimacy and Unmarried Fathers

A child is legitimate if the parents were married either at conception *or* at the time of birth (unless they were legally separated when the child was conceived). Illegitimate children can be made legitimate either by the parents marrying (which allows a new 'legitimate' birth certificate to be written), or the mother and her husband (who is not the father) can jointly adopt the child. Any adopted child is regarded as the legitimate child of whoever adopts it. Blood tests may be able to show a man is *not* the father of a child, but they cannot prove that a man *is* the father – because a lot of people have the same blood group – so all rights in relation to illegitimate children rest with the mother. However, fathers of illegitimate children must now support them. And, if a mother is preventing an unmarried father from seeing his children he can apply to the courts for an access order enabling him to see them.

> There are new tests using chromosomes which *can* effectively, prove a particular man is the father, but they are not normally available. See Child Poverty Action Group (page 480).

Nationality and Passports

The law on nationality changed in 1983. A child is now British if it is legitimate and one parent is British, or if it is illegitimate, with a British mother. In these cases it makes no difference if it is born outside Britain. It is also British if its non-British mother or married non-British parents are legally settled in Britain at its birth. If you think the Immigration and Nationality Department has made the wrong decision you can use the Immigration Appeals Advisory Service which provides legal advice and representation to those who have rights of appeal. Appeals can be made to the Immigration Appellate Authorities and reported to the Complaints Audit Committee, c/o the Home Office (page 694). If you simply want a passport, post offices have the forms and the addresses to send them to. The other details of nationality are highly complex and covered by leaflets from the **Home Office Immigration and Nationality Department**.

Sex

Sexual behaviour *of any kind* towards someone underage is illegal. A girl under 16 cannot consent to sexual intercourse but – despite the Gillick case – a doctor may advise her on contraception, without her parents' knowledge in certain circumstances. These include being unable to persuade her to tell the parents (or allow him to tell them), believing she intends to have sex anyway, and being convinced of her ability to understand the advice and its consequences. (See also page 281).

Step-Parents

Step-parents have no automatic rights over a step-child. This means that if the children are living with a mother and step-father, and the mother dies, the natural father may take the children away – even if he has not seen them or taken any interest in them for years. However, the step-parent can apply for guardianship or adoption or ask for a residence or access order from a court or ask for the child to be made a ward of court.

Death and What to Do

When someone dies there are a number of formalities which have to be observed quite rapidly. The DSS leaflet unit (page 693) has a free leaflet on what to do.

1 If organs have been bequeathed for donation the nearest hospital should be phoned immediately – kidneys must be removed within 30 minutes and eyes within 6 hours. However, most organs are only accepted from donors aged under 55 – though eyes are an exception.

> If a death has to be reported to a coroner his consent is needed before any organs can be donated. Also, in law, the body belongs to the relatives, not to the person who died. So if they object to the organs being taken or the body going to medical research they don't have to observe that part of a will.

2 The dead person's doctor must be told (unless they died in hospital).
3 If the doctor has seen the deceased within the past 2 weeks, or treated them during their last illness, he will normally give the relatives a free certificate stating the cause of death. Otherwise the death must be reported to the coroner who may order a post mortem.
4 The will must be found, and whoever is responsible for dealing with it must be contacted. (See Wills page 482.)
5 If the body has been left to medical research your nearest medical school or, for the south-east of England, the London Anatomy Office should be contacted as soon after death as possible. If the body is accepted by them they will send an undertaker to collect it. The medical school will then see to a funeral or cremation within 2 years, and invite the relatives to attend if they wish to.

> To find out about bequeathing your body to medical research, contact your nearest medical school or (failing that) the London Anatomy Office.

6 The will must be checked to see if a space has already been paid for in a graveyard.
7 A funeral director must be found and the arrangements made for the funeral – though the date cannot be fixed if the coroner has not yet issued a pink form (see also The Funeral, page 482).

Every death must be registered with the local Registrar of Births, Marriages and Deaths within 5 days, unless the death has been referred to the coroner. In this case, it cannot be registered until he issues a pink form. Police stations, post offices and other public bodies can give the address of the Registrar's Office and registration is a simple procedure if you take the right papers and information. These are:

- the deceased's full name (including maiden name) and home address,
- full details of date and place of birth, and sex,
- his or her occupation,
- the date of birth of the surviving husband or wife,
- the place and date of death,
- details of any state benefits they were receiving,
- the doctor's certificate of cause of death,
- the dead person's NHS card – if possible,
- any war pension order book – if applicable.

Whoever goes to the registrar will have to give their own details as the informant. The registrar then provides certificates registering the death and allowing a burial, plus leaflets on welfare benefits. The registration certificate then needs to be taken to the DSS office to obtain any widow's or other state benefit.

What Happens in Special Cases

If someone dies of an industrial disease, suddenly, in an accident, during an operation, or the cause of death is uncertain, the doctor *must* report the death to the coroner, who arranges a post mortem and possibly an inquest. Only after this will the coroner issue a certificate permitting the burial and allow the body to be taken away. He will also issue a death certificate which will either be given to the relatives or sent to the registrar. Deaths abroad must be registered according to the rules of that country and also with the British Consul there.

Extra Things to be Done

When someone dies a lot of ends need to be tied up and these are some of them.

- Tell any relatives or friends who ought to know.
- Tell the deceased's – bank
  - solicitor
  - insurance companies
  - credit card accounts
  - building societies
  - stock broker.

Law changes: this is guidance not gospel. Consult a lawyer before any decision.

- Return any pension book to the DSS.
- Apply for any widow's or other applicable social security benefits.
- Alter the insurance cover on the deceased's car if someone else is to use it.

The Funeral

The cost of a funeral comes out of the dead person's estate. Some banks and building societies will release money for this on production of the death certificate. State benefits may also be available, provided an application is made *before* the funeral is arranged. If there is too little money to cover the cost of the funeral, then the executors may be legally responsible for meeting the bills themselves.

It is up to the relatives to decide on cremation or burial. They have no legal obligation to carry out the deceased's instruction as to the type of funeral. A check should be made that no plot has been reserved in any graveyard – it may have been paid for in advance.

Before a burial can take place the funeral director must have either a registrar's certificate for burial or a coroner's order for burial, plus an application for burial signed by the executor or next of kin, and – if there is one – the deeds reserving a special plot.

For a cremation the funeral director also needs:

- cremation certificates from two doctors,
- a cremation certificate signed by the crematorium's medical referee,
- an application for cremation signed by the executor or next of kin,
- notification from the next of kin of what to do with the ashes,
- *if* the death was reported to the coroner, a coroner's certificate of cremation

Wills

Failure to write a will just puts money in the pockets of lawyers. If you don't make a will, your property won't go to the state – as many believe – unless you have no close relatives. Instead it will be divided among close relatives according to rules laid down in law, and your personal representatives will also be those the law decrees (depending what relatives you have). What the law dictates may not agree with your intentions at all, and needs more administration than a well-written will. So not writing a will gives money to lawyers, rather than to those you love.

Anyone in England, Ireland or Wales who is sane and over the age of 18 can – and should – make a will. (In Scotland the age is 12 for girls and 14 for boys – and the law on wills is rather different.)

If someone who is very old, or of variable mental state, makes a will, it is wise to have a doctor check that the person really knows what she is doing, make a medical note to this effect, and act as a witness.

★ A marriage usually revokes all previous wills, so make a new will as soon as you marry – or divorce.

Almost any high-street solicitor will advise on how to make a will. Charges vary, but if you shop around it shouldn't be expensive. If substantial sums are involved it may also be worth consulting an accountant, so that no more goes to the government on your death than really has to.

Of course, it is perfectly legal to make your own will and since the law changed in 1982 it has been a lot simpler but, even so, mistakes can be expensive and distressing for those whom you wish to benefit. If you want to save money on will making, the safest method is to read up the details in the books given on page 497. Then draw up a very correct draft will and take it to a lawyer for checking, then legal fees will be cut to a minimum. *But don't delay in making one. It is simply not fair to the rest of the family.*

> If you leave a husband or wife an unusually small proportion of the estate, the law allows them to apply to the court for a reasonable share, and they are likely to get it. But be warned, if you own property in France, French law governs it. So a man's parents or children inherit it, *not* his wife.

In writing a will, remember words do not mean the same things to lawyers that they mean to you and me. So a will which seems clear and concise to any ordinary mortal, may mean something totally different in law. What follows is only a rough outline of what a will requires. But it may make it easier to write the draft to take to a lawyer.

- It must be in writing (typed or hand-written).
- It must say that it is the last will and testament.
- It must give the *full* name of the person whose will it is – including the maiden name of a married woman.
- It should be dated and say it revokes all previous wills (even if there are none, this is a precaution).
- The first paragraph should appoint executors (see below), though you don't have to, and they may benefit from the will.
- The pages should be numbered.
- The lines should be spaced so there is no room to insert anything – which is why a will should *not* be written on a form from a stationer.
- It must be very precise. Give the full name of each person you want to leave anything to, if there could be any misunderstanding.
- If you name sums of money make it clear whether it is before or after tax.
- Remember inflation will reduce the value of lump sums. So it is wiser to divide the estate in fractions rather than actual figures.
- Be very specific. If you say you leave 'property' to someone it could mean several things. If you say 'my house 3 Acacia Avenue, SW13 and all its contents' there is no argument – but update this if you move.
- Have a final clause bequeathing 'everything else I

own', then there will be no problem over anything not disposed of.

- It must be signed *immediately under the bottom of the last page*, by the person making the will *in the presence* of two witnesses (in Scotland it may be unwitnessed if whoever is making it writes it entirely by hand and signs it).
- If there is more than one page the will maker and the witnesses should sign every page immediately under the bottom line.
- The two witnesses must be adult, sighted and traceable, and neither they nor their spouses may benefit from the will in *any* way – or the gift to them becomes invalid. So *never* witness the will of a relative. Witnesses must sign and give their name, address and occupation.
- Put it in a safe place, such as with a solicitor or the **Principal Probate Registry**, and tell those concerned.

> For safe keeping the Principal Probate Registry at Somerset House (page 497) will store your will. For a tiny sum they accept it and give you a certificate of deposit. Ask for their information on how to do it and do tell your executor where to find this – it will be far harder for them to get your will out without it.

Executors and Administrators to a Will

An executor (executrix – female) is someone who is appointed in a will, to act for someone after their death and see their wishes are carried out. They may recover their expenses or professional charges, for doing this job. But, if you are appointed as an executor and don't want to do it, you can write to the Probate Registry at Somerset House renouncing the role.

Appointing professionals – bankers, lawyers or accountants is seldom a good idea. They are often slow and charge large sums, *plus a percentage of the estate* – usually 1 to 2½ per cent. And banks can be the worst. If you appoint a sensible friend she can get advice from lawyers or accountants if it's needed. (And you can always put a note with the will telling your executor which lawyers or accountants are familiar with your affairs.) But if you appoint professionals as executors, and they are slow, inefficient or expensive, your loved ones are, frankly, lumbered with them.

If no executor has been appointed someone close to whoever died, usually a close relative, can apply to the District Probate Office or the Probate to Registry at Somerset House to act as administrator. If someone leaves very little the executor or administrator can divide it up, according to the will, without more ado. But usually either they, or a solicitor acting for them, must obtain probate. For this a form must be obtained from the probate offices above, completed, and returned with the necessary papers. Either those offices or the Lord Chancellors' Department (page 499) can send you a leaflet on obtaining probate.

Domestic Violence

The Public Order Act 1986 excludes family rows. So verbal assault in the family has no legal remedy – no matter how vicious it is. Physical assault is different.

> Since 1861 it has been a criminal offence for a man to hit his wife, just as it would be if a man beat up his neighbour. So the police have an *absolute duty* to prevent it happening – if necessary by putting the man in a cell for the night and prosecuting him. It is not correct for the police to say that they can't prosecute if a woman won't take a case against the husband. If they saw the evidence of physical attack that is enough. (See Actual Bodily Harm page 459.)

Unfortunately, the police often treat domestic violence as a special case. However, the courts do offer protection against domestic violence both for wives and for those living with a man but not married to him. A married woman has three options; a woman who is not married can only use the second.

1 A magistrates' court can make two types of order:
   a A personal protection order can be made if the court is satisfied that the husband or wife has used or threatened violence against their partner or one of the children, and feels the order is needed for their protection.
   b An exclusion order may be made, ordering the husband or wife to leave (or keep out of) the mutual home. For this there must have been violence (or threat of it) against the partner, or child, or the terms of a personal protection order must have been broken.
2 A county court can grant several different types of injunction, covering unmarried couples as well as those who are married.
   These can:
   order a partner to stop molesting the other,
   order a partner to stop molesting a child who is living with the applicant,
   exclude someone from the joint home,
   make one partner allow the other into a joint home.
3 If divorce proceedings have been started a divorce court can grant broadly the same two injunctions as a magistrates' court.

A woman can represent herself in these applications but it is probably safer to use a solicitor, and Legal Aid is usually available. Use a Law Centre, Women's Aid Centre (page 496) or CAB to find a solicitor who is experienced in cases of this sort and get support from your local Victim Support Scheme (page 496), if you need it. If an injunction is granted, then the solicitor should ask for a power of arrest to be attached. This will only be granted if actual bodily harm has been caused to the innocent partner or to a child and the court is satisfied that it is likely to happen again. But it means that if the

The law in Scotland or Northern Ireland may be different.

man breaks the injunction the police can be called to arrest him. Failing this, the woman has to go back to the court and show that the injunction has been breached – power of arrest may then be given, and further breaches of the injunction can mean prison.

Coping with Violence

Wife beating is a guilty secret which often condemns a woman not only to pain and fear but to shame and loneliness. There is no need for any woman to be ashamed or to feel alone. There are men who beat their wives among the richest and most educated as well as poorest and least able. Nor should a battered woman – or anyone else – believe the common idea that women who are battered must have asked for it and must enjoy it. People do not kick cats because the cats enjoy it but because the cat is weaker than themselves and they can get away with cruelty. Women get beaten up because physical weakness, financial dependence and anxieties about providing for the children trap them with men who are too immature to control their rage and violence, and feel free to break the law behind closed doors.

No woman who is being battered with words or blows should try to handle this situation alone, nor should she ask her children to keep it a secret; both she and the children need to unburden themselves. Being battered brings a woman's spirits so low that she may find it impossible to get away unless she finds support. She should contact her nearest refuge.

There are some 200 refuges for battered women around Britain which not only provide homes to which battered women and their children can escape but also offer a free telephone advice service. They all have different names, so you can't easily find them in Yellow Pages but the telephone exchange normally knows where they are. So ring directory enquiries and ask if they can give you the number of the nearest refuge for battered women. Or write to, or ring the 24-hour crisis line of Refuge (page 496). It has a list of all the refuges in Britain and will advise and take in women from all over Britain, not just from London.

If you are being battered you may fear that if you leave the man you will be penniless and homeless and have your children taken away from you. This isn't so. If you leave a violent man and have no income you will be entitled to social security benefits and you should have priority on a council house list.

Elsewhere in this book I say that a woman, splitting up from a man, should try to stay in the home and get him to leave. But with a violent man this is usually impossible and even dangerous. You should first get advice from a refuge; once you have found a place in one you can live in safety and use it as a base from which to find a new home. You only risk having children taken into care if you have nowhere to live while waiting for a council house.

Even if you feel you can survive the beatings it is a terrible ordeal for any child to have to hear, or see, a father beating a mother, and the fear and sense of impotence which this causes a child can scar it deeply.

There is no virtue in remaining in a relationship which causes a child such suffering.

Epilepsy

Some drugs used in the treatment of epilepsy are barbiturates included in the Misuse of Drugs Act. Epileptics using these drugs should carry a doctor's letter about their treatment which can be shown to the police if necessary.

Marriage

If an engagement is broken neither side has legal redress – not even for money spent for the wedding – but wedding presents should be returned. There can be problems if the couple has already bought a house together, and the best safeguard is to put in equal amounts and have it in their joint names.

As recently as 1929 the minimum age for marriage was 14 for boys and 12 for girls. Today it is 16 for both sexes, but under 18 the written consent of both parents must be obtained (or the consent of whichever has legal custody), except when this is not appropriate – for example, when one parent has deserted.

Who Can Marry Whom

The bars on who may marry whom are dictated not so much by blood ties as by a desire to prevent the social boat being rocked by seductions within the family. It therefore applies even to those people who are adopted or illegitimate, or, in some cases, have divorced and left the family. So, you may not marry your:

- brother/sister or half-brother/half-sister,
- uncle/aunt,
- nephew/niece,
- son/daughter,
- father/mother,
- grandson/granddaughter

However, there are some exceptions for relatives from a former marriage when no close blood links exist. But the rules are complex, so consult a solicitor.

Valid Marriage

A marriage is valid only if it has taken place in a registry office or in some other place licensed to register marriages – such as an approved church. Not all churches and temples are registered, and some religions have registered temples in Scotland but not in England. So it is always advisable to check the situation. When a place of worship is not registered a registry office wedding must take place before or after the religious ceremony.

The Effects of Marriage

If a woman adopts her husband's name she must get her bank account put into that name and the new signature authorized. But she doesn't have to take her husband's name. So she can continue to use a passport in her maiden name, or send it in to be changed, as she wishes. Nor does a British subject automatically change nationality on marrying a foreigner – though she may obtain

Addresses and suggestions for further reading are at the ends of chapters.

dual nationality. But marriage does change some financial facts.

- A man can be liable for his wife's debt on household essentials.
- If either dies without making a will, most of their possessions go to the other.
- State benefits change (and they may also vary when people live together as 'man and wife' without benefit of marriage).
- There is also an implied consent to a reasonable amount of sex – but see Rape, page 462.

However, it is no longer the case that one partner cannot be forced to give evidence, for or against, the other in a criminal action.

Mental Illness

There should be no fear that someone will be 'put away'. The 1983 Mental Health Act says that only those who are 'abnormally aggressive or seriously irresponsible' can be held against their will for any length of time. If a person needs treatment in hospital he is usually admitted as a voluntary patient and can leave at any time – even against the doctor's advice.

The official terms used are 'formal' (i.e. compulsory) admission or 'informal' (i.e. voluntary) admission. Compulsory admission always involves the evidence of at least one doctor, and the ease with which they can leave depends on the section of the act under which they were admitted. Briefly, the relevant sections are these:

Section 2. **Admission for Assessment,** at the request of the nearest relative or a social worker. The case must be reviewed every 28 days, and to appeal the patient must apply to the Mental Health Review Tribunal (MHRT) within 14 days of admission.

Section 3. **Admission for Treatment,** at the request of the nearest relative or an approved social worker for up to 6 months, renewable for a 6-month period, then annually. One appeal may be made to the MHRT in each period.

Section 4. **Emergency Admission,** at the request of the nearest relative or a social worker. Initially for 72 hours but up to 28 days more if two doctors agree.

Section 5. **Compulsory detention of voluntary patients,** while staff obtain a compulsory detention order. Sometimes the patient's nearest relative can persuade the doctors to make an admission voluntary, not compulsory, by offering to take responsibility for the patient should he or she leave the hospital.

Admission under 2 and 3 needs the written recommendation of two doctors. Controversially, section 4 only needs one doctor. Those compulsorily admitted must be told which section they were admitted under and given written information about appeals, legal aid and discharge. Legal aid is available for appeals to the Mental Health Review Tribunal (MHRT); but the patient can be represented by a friend instead of a lawyer. Relatives may also discharge a compulsory patient from hospital by giving 72 hours' notice that they are taking charge of them. The doctors can prevent this with a barring notice – against which the relative may appeal to the MHRT within 28 days.

If the objection is not to the fact of detention but to treatment during it, a complaint should be made to the Mental Health Act Commission for the region.

The mentally ill can be treated against their will. But there are limits. ECT, hormone implants and brain surgery require the patient's consent (unless he is incapable of giving it) and strict medical approval. The hospital concerned must give the addresses of the MHRT and the Commission to a patient or relative if asked. And Mind (page 589) will advise on the rights of the mentally ill.

Housing the Mentally Ill

The policy of 'care in the community' means there can be pressure on families to have the mentally ill living with them after discharge from hospital. *If the sick person is over 18, families have no legal obligation to take them in.* By law hospitals must assess the needs of the mentally ill before discharging them. The patient, relatives, health professionals and social services should then decide what accommodation and medical or nursing support is needed from social services, and a named individual should take responsibility for supplying this. Unfortunately, families aren't always consulted and professionals often assume people will automatically look after sick relatives.

So, if a close relative is admitted to hospital, and you don't want them to live with you again, make this *very* clear to the hospital professionals and to social services. Don't just tell them: put it in writing – and *do this well before discharge is expected.* You don't have to give a reason, the fact that you can't cope is enough. But if you have other reasons give them. It is the local authority which has a duty to find suitable accommodation, not you. If they fail to do that, contact the Complaints Panel of Social Services and *keep on* complaining up the ladder until you get results. Social services are under the local authority so include the head of the local authority and the Local Authority Ombudsman (page 694) if need be. Only when more people demand this will the true meaning of 'community care' be brought home to those who so glibly talk about it. Both Mind (page 589) and The Carers' National Association (page 323) will advise you.

Rights

Those being treated for mental disorders lose their rights in various ways. For example:

- their mail in and out can be stopped in certain circumstances – but no stop can be put on letters addressed to their MP, the Mental Health Review Tribunal and certain other public bodies,
- they may not serve on a jury (even if only under GP treatment),
- they may not vote if compulsory detained,

Law changes: this is guidance not gospel. Consult a lawyer before any decision.

● if they are not able to run their affairs anyone suitable may apply to the court to be a 'receiver' (which is essentially a trustee) of their property during the illness. If someone is appointed the patient loses almost all control of his or her financial affairs.

Missing Persons

If someone is missing, contact the police immediately. However, anyone over 17 (16 in Scotland) has a right to go missing. So even if they are found by one of the charities which trace missing persons they can prevent the charity from revealing their address – or even admitting that they have been found. However, some missing persons would prefer to be found. The **Missing Persons Bureau** (page 498) will try to trace the recent and long-term missing. The Salvation Army (page 317) will trace the long gone, and the Red Cross (page 592) will trace those missing abroad.

HOUSEHOLD LAW

Animals

Most dogs and other animals can be kept without a licence. However, to keep dangerous wild animals you need a licence from the local council. Also the Home Secretary can, at any time, name a breed of dog as dangerous. In which case owners must meet certain conditions and have a special licence from the Index of Exempted Dogs. The Index will tell you which dogs are currently listed.

Cruelty and neglect of an animal is illegal – and abandoning a dog is classed as cruelty. The owner can also be held responsible for its behaviour. If it runs into the road and causes an accident its owner may be sued. But for the owner to be held liable the court must also prove that reasonable measures were not taken to keep the dog under control. In the case of a dangerous animal, it isn't enough to take reasonable measures: if the animal escapes the owner is liable for any harm caused even if he did everything possible to prevent the escape. The same applies if an animal of a safe species is dangerous through temperament or special circumstances, and if livestock stray and damage someone's property. So, if your neighbour's cow munches your flower borders you could have a claim.

The law says that dogs must be kept under control, wear collars with the owner's name and address on public highways and not foul the footway. You can bring a private prosecution against owners who allow their dogs to foul the pavement, or worry poultry or livestock on agricultural land, and if a dog is deemed to be dangerous it can be put down. But a dog cannot be shot just for *chasing* animals, only for worrying or attacking them – or for attacking a human being.

Importing Animals
No creatures of any kind may be imported into Britain without an import licence from the Ministry of Agriculture, Fisheries and Food, not even your pets. For a licence write to the **Animal Health Division**, of the Ministry (page 694). Birds are usually allowed to be quarantined in the owner's home for 35 days. Almost all other animals have to be held for 6 months in a ministry-approved establishment (check with the Animal Health Division) and the owner pays for their keep. However, owners are allowed to visit their pets and may even ask for a kennels or cattery near where they live – if one exists. Anyone trying to smuggle in a pet is liable to an unlimited fine, and up to a year in prison, and the animal may be destroyed, or quarantined, or sent back to the country it came from.

Boundaries

Curiously, there is no *legal* obligation to fence your property or to maintain the existing fences, but you may be obliged to under the title deeds. The deeds usually say which fences belong to which house. If not, a fence usually belongs to whoever has the support posts on his side.

If a tree from a neighbour's garden has branches which overhang your garden you are entitled to cut off the branches at the point where they overhang. But they belong to the neighbour, and it is prudent to ask, in writing, whether he would prefer to chop the branches himself.

The same applies to tree roots, but tree roots present a far greater threat. They can invade water pipes and cause serious problems and the presence of a large number of roots under a house can, in dry seasons, take enough water from the soil to cause subsidence – especially with thirsty trees like willows. So, if a neighbour plants a tree close enough for the roots of the mature tree to threaten your house or drains alert him immediately, in writing, to the potential risks to your property. If you want to know whether it is close enough to cause damage, a rough guide is that trees' roots will stretch as far – in each direction – as the height of the full-grown tree.

Whether a tree owner is liable for damage caused by falling branches depends on why the branch fell. If it was rotten the owner should have noticed; if it was healthy but there was a gale it isn't the owner's fault.

Building

Planning permission is needed for developments of any kind – and the scope is very wide, ranging from change of use to modernization, conversion and some repairs. Those who don't get permission from the district council when they should have done can be made to restore the building to its previous condition – regardless of cost. However, the following can usually be done without permission – but *do check your particular situation*. There's no accounting for by-laws.

● Improvements within a building which do not extend it or change its use (e.g. most replacement windows).
● T.V. aerials.
● External maintenance – even if it changes the look of the building.

Addresses and suggestions for further reading are at the ends of chapters.

- Demolition – unless it is a listed building.
- As I write, you can usually build an extension, of no more than 15 per cent of the size of the house, or 70 cubic metres – whichever is greater. However, there are detailed rules about its height, how it affects roads, paths, neighbours, drains and so on. So do read all the rules before making plans.

Obtaining planning permission (or discovering that you don't need it) isn't the end of the story.

- If the property is mortgaged you may need approval from the mortgage company.
- If a party wall is affected you may need your neighbour's consent. (See also Trespass, page 490.)
- The alterations must not infringe your neighbours' rights to light.
- A lease may have restricting clauses.
- There can be restrictive covenants on a freehold.
- You may need approval, of sections of the work, under building or water board regulations.

Guns and Other Weapons

The law on guns was laid down in the Firearms Act 1968, with additional clauses on imitation weapons in the Firearms Act 1982. Breaking these laws risks both prison and fines. And if an imitation firearm is easily converted into a real weapon, and looks like one of the firearms mentioned below, the law on real weapons applies in all respects.

Someone under 14 may only use firearms in an approved club, or a shooting gallery, or use air-weapons within private land under adult supervision.

No type of gun may be bought under the age of 17. But this age group can be given or lent various guns, provided they have the necessary certificate from the police. Check with your local police.

The purchase and possession of air weapons is unrestricted after the age of 17. However, a shotgun needs a certificate unless the user is under instruction, or on private land with the owner of the land or an employee of the owner with an appropriate licence. And to purchase, possess or use rifles, pistols, revolvers, certain types of shotguns or certain 'dangerous' air rifles you must have a firearm certificate from the police. If the police refuse you can appeal, within 21 days, to the Administrator of the Crown Court.

Other Weapons

It is now illegal to sell or hire a crossbow to anyone under 17 and there are heavy penalties for doing so. And there are new, strict laws on the sale and carrying of offensive weapons, including certain 'martial arts' weapons which used not to be in this category.

Noise

The 1991 Environmental Protection Act strengthened the law on unwanted noise of all kinds, from barking dogs to grinding factories. It says local councils must investigate reasonable complaints and should make the noise cease or lessen. So every council should now have officials to deal with it. Before complaining to your council, write to the noise-makers asking them to stop it. If possible, get any neighbours who are equally annoyed to sign the letter too. If that fails, ask the Noise Control Officer in your council's Environmental Health Department to do something. For major noise problems she can issue a Noise Abatement Notice. If the noise doesn't then end within a set time either you or the council can take the matter to court. *The noisy can be sent to prison or face a five-figure fine.* A free Department of the Environment leaflet details the steps to take, and gives addresses you can complain to. You can also get advice from the Noise Abatement Society.

Telephone

It is illegal to use the telephone to make calls which are grossly offensive, indecent or menacing, and to cause annoyance, inconvenience or needless anxiety by such calls. But it isn't easy for a victim to *use* this law. So say nothing and hang up. This gives offensive callers less satisfaction than you sounding angry or upset. Or get a loud whistle and blow it straight into the mouthpiece of the phone and hang up – very nasty for the ears. Then report the calls to the police. British Telecom may also be able to help. But they advise women to go in the phone book by initials and surname only: first names, Miss, Ms or Mrs can attract such calls.

However, if the calls are from a particular person who is getting his kicks out of threatening you, think twice before changing your number. It is better to be threatened on the phone than in person – which could be the result if the telephone option is blocked.

Tenancy

The law relating to tenancy needs a book to itself. Act has been added to act, like children playing handstacking, with each one modifying, but not replacing, the last. With private landlords alone there are over sixteen different types of tenancy. They vary both with the clauses in the particular agreement, with the date they started, whether the place is furnished or not, whether the landlord lives in the same house – and the Acts in force at the time.

Most residential lettings since January 1989 have been assured tenancies. To be assured it must be the tenant's only, or main, home and be a 'separate dwelling'. Assured tenancies can be:

- indefinite tenancy – of no pre-set length,
- fixed tenancy – of a set length,
- fixed shorthold tenancy – a short set period of more than 6 months.

This last gives the landlord a guaranteed right to repossess the property after the set time. But to do that the landlord must meet precise legal requirements. These include using correct form at the *start* of the tenancy, and giving the right notice at the end. So it is vital for short-term landlords to get good legal advice *before* letting.

I warmly recommend to both landlords and tenants the Department of the Environment (page 693) housing booklets. Separate booklets cover the duties of landlords and tenants in different types of property and tenancy. They are free, clear, and give the basic laws in a nutshell. It's also worth talking to the Inland Revenue. To encourage room letting, as I write, rental income below a set sum isn't taxable. Here there is only space to sketch the main facts, not the multitude of special clauses. It is vital to talk to a lawyer before letting property, and it may be useful before becoming a tenant.

The key question for most tenants is whether they are protected by the Rent Acts. Much will depend on the terms of the written or verbal agreement between the landlord and tenant. However, they may well be protected if:

- they have absolute possession of part of the property – even a room,
- they are renting all or part of a home – as opposed to business premises,
- they do not receive meals or substantial services,
- the tenancy is not for the purposes of a job,
- it is not a holiday or company let,
- the rateable value of the rented property is within certain set limits,
- the rent exceeds two-thirds of the rateable value of the property,
- the tenant does not conduct business from the property,
- the landlord does not live in the same property (living in a separate flat in the same building may sometimes count as living in the same property and it needn't be the landlord's only residence).

The Acts may give complete or partial protection according to the circumstances, and there are also exceptions for those whose tenancies started before 1974. Before 1974 a key factor in whether a tenant was protected was whether or not the let was furnished. For lets started before that date the rules are rather different. So someone with an unfurnished flat in the same house as the landlord may well be protected if the let started before 1974.

Rent

Weekly tenants *must* by law be given a proper rent book. Council tenants must usually pay whatever the council asks, but they must be given 4 weeks' notice of increases. Councils also have a duty to police private tenancies, and if private tenants feel they are being overcharged they can ask the rent assessment committee (under Rent, in the telephone book) or Rent Tribunal (if the tenant has restricted protection) to decide what is a fair rent. First ask if there is a registered rent for the property. If there isn't, check the rents for comparable properties in the area by looking at the official register of rents – which is open to the public.

Once a fair rent has been registered, tenants may not be charged more – despite any agreement. If the rent officer sets a higher rent than they are paying, it can be increased only in stages over 2 years. With certain types of agreement it may not be possible to charge more even if the rent assessment committee sets a higher rent.

All that applies to most long-standing tenancies and also to the newer *shorthold* assured tenancies (see above) but *not* to other assured tenancies. In most assured tenancies agreed rents cannot be changed by the rent assessment committee. And the landlord may write into the initial agreement a mechanism for raising the rent periodically.

> There is no back-dating of rent changes. If the rent is to go up the landlord cannot recover the extra rent for preceding weeks, and if it is to go down the tenant cannot get a refund. The exception to this is if the landlord was charging more than a rent already registered with the rent officer – in which case tenants can be refunded up to two years' excess rent.

Right to Buy

A 1993 Act amended the 1987 Act on the issue of a tenant's right to buy. Now most long leaseholders have a collective right to buy the freehold of their building or to extend their individual leases. However, the scheme depends on at least two-thirds of the long leaseholders wanting to buy and having lived there for long enough. In some circumstances those with the lease of an entire house may also be able to buy it.

Eviction of Owners and Relations

The most important point is that *no one can be evicted from their home without a court order*. With council tenants this also applies to the husband or wife or (if the tenant dies) to any close relative who has lived in the property for the previous year. The same applies with private tenants, but relatives of the dead tenant need only have lived in the property for the past 6 months. Deserted spouses have the same security as the original tenant but on divorce, whoever is not the tenant loses the right to live there – unless the court specifically transfers the tenancy to that person.

Anyone who is being asked to move out or is being harassed by a landlord may be able to get help from the Tenancy Relations Officer on their local council. They should also take legal advice.

Eviction Orders

How easily a private landlord can get an eviction order will depend on the type of tenancy and the degree of Rent Act protection it gives. But the tenant must normally have at least a week's notice of the hearing. Common grounds for eviction are:

- serious rent arrears – which the tenant cannot or will not remedy,
- damage to the property or furnishings by the tenant or sub-tenant,
- the ending of employment which was a condition of tenancy,
- the use of the premises for illegal or immoral purposes,
- a major breach of the tenancy agreement,

Addresses and suggestions for further reading are at the ends of chapters.

- the owner needs the property for himself or his family – but the owner has to prove that without the property he will suffer more hardship than the tenant will in moving, and must normally have told the tenant, from the start, that he might need the property for himself,
- the neighbours have been caused considerable nuisance.

All those reasons apply whether the tenant causes the problem or whether someone for whom he is responsible causes them. In some circumstances, the following grounds can also be used:

- a member of the armed forces now needs the property back to live in,
- the property is a holiday home,
- the property is a retirement home – and needed to retire to – or is needed by a member of the owner's family after his/her death,
- the owner previously lived in it and needs to live there again, or has died and vacant possession is needed to sell the house,
- the tenant has allowed overcrowding,
- the tenant signed a shorthold agreement which is at the end of its term.

> Even when a landlord has a right to take over the property, to live in, there are strict rules on giving notice which the owner must keep to, or fail to regain possession.

Tenancy and eviction are, however, extremely complex areas of law, full of special clauses and exceptions. Both tenants and landlords should see lawyers. In particular, owner-occupiers who need to leave their home, but will wish to return should take good legal advice *before* letting. A lot depends on setting up the right type of tenancy in the right way, and giving the right warnings about your possible return, *right at the start*.

If an eviction order is granted the tenant usually has a set time in which to leave, though the order can sometimes be immediate. If a tenant fails to leave by the appointed date the landlord should ask the court bailiff to eject them – which will probably take another 2 weeks at the very least.

Leaving Voluntarily
If there is a fixed-term tenancy the tenant may be committed to paying rent to the end of the tenancy, even if she no longer wishes to live there, but when the tenancy ends the landlord does not have to have written notice of departure. In most *other* cases, the landlord must have written notice giving the date of departure. The notice periods vary with the tenancy.

Repairs and Improvements
In general, landlords have a right to enter their property to inspect it, having given 24 hours notice in writing. For in most tenancies a landlord must do certain repairs,

especially if a tenant asks for them to be done. But this is a tricky field: which repairs must be done by the landlord and which by the tenant depends on a host of factors – including the type of tenancy, its duration, when it started, the agreement and whether it is a proper tenancy or only a licence. (In general licensors do have less obligation than landlords to keep property in good repair).

Most tenancy agreements say which repairs must be done by the landlord and which by the tenant. The tenant only needs to do the repairs set in the agreement, or repair any damage he does. But a landlord usually has a duty to keep the structure and exterior, heating installations, baths, sinks and loos in good repair. The cost of this cannot be recovered through a service charge.

If a landlord has been told about necessary repairs, for which she is responsible in the tenancy agreement, the tenant can ask the county court for an injunction forcing the landlord to do them. The other remedy is for the tenant to get the repairs done himself and deduct the cost from the rent. This is legal, but the landlord may then try to evict the tenant for improper payment of rent and the tenant will have to prove he was justified in what he did. So it is very important first to make sure that the landlord *is* liable for the repairs – under your particular tenancy – and to keep ample proof that the repairs needed to be done and cost precisely the sum you have deducted from the rent. Alternatively, have the work done but, instead of deducting it from the rent, sue the landlord for the cost.

Where there is a health hazard or a lack of basic amenities – such as a lavatory – or such dilapidation that the place may be unfit to live in, the local authority has a duty to make the owner put things right. In practice, it may not be quick on the draw – as it could often mean finding money for a grant. If the authority fails to come and inspect the problem you can ask the magistrates' court to order it to do so. If it then fails to act talk to your local CAB or law centre, lobby your councillors and MP, and don't forget the power of the local media if the situation is really awful.

Usually a tenant cannot make improvements or alterations without the landlord's approval. But the landlord cannot refuse consent unreasonably. Equally, by law a tenant who makes certain improvements to a property, after April 1994, must be rewarded for them, by the landlord, on leaving the tenancy.

Management and Services
If a council wants to put the management of its property into outside hands the tenants can now oppose it and have a right to take on the management of their estate.

Some private tenancies allow landlords to make variable service charges for repairs, maintenance, insurance or management costs. However, tenants – or the secretary of a recognized tenants' association – then have a right to know how the charge is made up. They must also be consulted on major outlays and may inspect and take copies of accounts and receipts. And the landlord must hold any contributions to service charges in trust. The details of all this are more complex than I have space for, but are clearly explained in free Department of the Environment booklets (see page 693) which cover the rights and duties of landlords and tenants, in flats or houses.

Squatting

There are plans to make squatting a criminal offence. But, as I write, it is only trespass and you may not use force to get the squatters out. If they refuse to go, apply to a county or crown court for a possession order. This can be done within 5 days of your application, and the bailiff has to do the evicting – which can take a week or two but may take considerably longer.

Sublets and Sharing

Council tenants may take in a lodger, who lives as one of the family, but this must usually have council approval, or the sub-tenant can be evicted. If a private tenant sublets, the Rent Act protections (if they apply) normally pass on down, and may even pass to a sub-sublet. But much depends on the rights of the original tenant to sublet. Flat or house sharing isn't specially covered by the law. So sharers are usually considered to be sublets. One way round this is to make it a joint tenancy – which means the landlord has to approve both (or all) the tenants, and also approve any who replace them. But it can be argued that a landlord has appeared to approve a new tenant simply by accepting rent – even if the method of rent collection gives him no way of noticing the change.

Trespass

The law on trespass is odd. It is rude to walk into someone's property uninvited but it is not trespass. Trespass is refusing to leave or returning, after being asked to go. It is a civil, not a criminal, offence and forcibly removing someone could land you in the courts for assault. However, you can ask for police assistance and, if the offence is repeated, you can get a court injunction forbidding someone to trespass. They can then be fined or imprisoned if they continue. However, you cannot refuse a neighbour permission to enter your property to repair theirs. If you do, they can now get an order from a county court allowing them to enter. Though they must behave carefully and have to make good any damage as fast as possible.

LEGAL AID

What follows immediately below is the Legal Aid system for England and Wales. For Scotland and Ireland, see page 492.

Legal Aid is a means tested system of state grants for legal fees. Originally, it was designed to put legal advice within everyone's reach – regardless of income. It no longer does that, as many people have too much money to qualify for Legal Aid but far too little to pay today's soaring legal fees. Moreover, it doesn't cover all types of case. So it is no cure-all.

However, if you are getting certain state benefits you automatically qualify for Legal Aid – but not all benefits count. If not you will be means tested. This varies slightly between different types of case, or Aid, but usually looks at all money coming in from all sources, plus all savings and investments. This includes the surrender value of certain insurance policies, and items of value, such as jewellery, furs or antiques – but not your home, ordinary furniture, clothing or the tools of your trade. Against all this is set whether you are single or co-habiting, the ages of any dependants and vital outgoings such as rent, mortgage, council tax, or maintenance payments. However, each situation is different: so don't think you won't qualify just because a friend didn't.

There are several different types of Legal Aid: a fixed-fee interview, the Green Form Scheme, Civil Legal Aid, Criminal Legal Aid, and Duty Solicitor Schemes. To find a solicitor who will do Legal Aid work – and not all do – ask a local CAB or law centre, look in the Solicitors' Regional Directory in the reference library, talk to a charity which advises on related problems, (e.g., Victims of Medical Accidents), contact the Legal Aid Board (page 491), or look for the Legal Aid logo. In addition to Legal Aid you may be able to get a low-cost interview with certain solicitors to discuss whether you qualify for Legal Aid and have a case worth taking (see page 491).

A new scheme gives some solicitors Legal Aid franchises in certain fields of law. This doesn't mean that other solicitors in the area can't do Legal Aid work. But using a franchised solicitor may make it easier to get Legal Aid quickly.

The Sour Fruits of Success

If you win, and get or keep money or property, but don't get costs from the other side, you may have to repay all or some of the Legal Aid you had. This is called 'statutory charge'. However, if you gain a house which you need to live in you may not have to sell it to pay the lawyers. Instead, the Legal Aid Board may put a 'registered charge' on it. This means that when you want to sell the house you will have to repay the money you owe, plus simple interest. Even then, if you sell your house just to buy another you may be able to transfer the registered charge to the second house and continue to owe the money – and the, growing, interest.

This can make success decidedly bitter – unless you make allowances for it when deciding what terms are acceptable. However, there isn't a statutory charge on maintenance payments, various benefits, awards made by Employment Appeal Tribunals. Nor on half of any redundancy payment or on matrimonial property settlements under a certain, ridiculously low, value.

There is a Law Society scheme by which you may get a half-hour interview with a solicitor for under a set amount (£25 as I write) – and may sometimes be free. It is a voluntary regional scheme. So your local CAB or law centre should know if any solicitors in your area offer this service.

The Green Form Scheme

The Green Form Scheme has two parts. **Legal Advice and Assistance** covers most legal problems. Children are also covered and can sometimes apply for it in their own right. But parents usually apply on behalf of those under 16. For this scheme your means are assessed by the solicitor who helps you. But both your own savings and income *and* those of your partner are taken as yours – unless you are separated, or the dispute is with him or her, or there are special circumstances. But children are assessed in their own right and pensioners have different limits.

If you qualify you won't be asked to make any contribution. However, it only pays for a solicitor spending some 2-3 hours advising you, writing letters, getting a barrister's opinion or writing a case for a tribunal. That time is too short for most problems, but an un-franchised solicitor can't do more work than that without advance permission from the Legal Aid office. A franchised one can.

In some cases the Scheme can also cover **Assistance by Way of Representation (ABWOR)**. This is a solicitor preparing your case *and* representing you in most civil cases in the Family Proceeding's (Magistrates') Court, or in certain other cases, such as appeals to a Mental Health Review Tribunal. An un-franchised solicitor has to get permission for you to have Legal Aid for this, based on a form giving the merits of your case and your financial details. A franchised one can proceed without this. Either way you may have to make a weekly contribution from the time ABWOR is granted until the case ends.

A number of unions and solicitors belong to a scheme called Union Law. If your union is a member your first interview with any Union Law solicitor is free. But you can only get advice on matters *not* related to work. You find member solicitors through your union. (See page 473 for a similar scheme for businesses).

Civil Legal Aid

Civil Legal Aid covers the cost of a solicitor and, if necessary, a barrister preparing a case and going to court. And covers most courts and most civil issues, including appeals – but not libel, slander, coroner's courts or most tribunals. Even if you have too much money to qualify under the Green Form Scheme, it may be worth applying for Civil Legal Aid because the limit

could be different, and there may be no means or merit tests on some proceedings involving children.

You apply through a solicitor, who will help you complete the form. (The Advice and Assistance Scheme may pay him to do this.) Be very careful over this form. The decision on whether your case merits Aid depends on the details of your finances (as Green Form, opposite) and on whether you have *good grounds* for taking it and whether it is *reasonable* for you to get such help, is based on that form. But if they turn you down you may be able to appeal to the area committee. You can also ask them to review the assessment of your income if you disagree with it.

Legal Aid cannot be back-dated so only in special circumstances will a solicitor start work on a case before it is granted. But urgent cases can get emergency Legal Aid faster and a franchised solicitor can give it without getting permission. Either way you will be liable for the full legal costs, or an appropriate contribution, if it is afterwards found that you didn't fully qualify for Aid.

If your finances fall within certain limits you will have to make a monthly contribution to your legal costs from when you accept Legal Aid until you cease to receive it. This is adjusted if your income changes and Legal Aid is withdrawn if you don't keep up the payments.

Legal Aid For Criminal Charges

This only covers defence. You cannot bring a criminal private prosecution under Legal Aid.

Duty Solicitor Scheme

The Duty Solicitor Scheme covers the cost of being advised by a solicitor if the police question you about a criminal offence – at the police station or elsewhere. You can use a duty solicitor whom the police will telephone, or any other solicitor who is prepared to work under this scheme, and there is no means test on this. There are also duty solicitors at magistrates' courts, or on call, who will advise you free of charge under this scheme on your first time in court (on this case).

Criminal Legal Aid

If you are charged with a criminal offence you can get immediate advice under the Green Form Scheme (above) but you may need Criminal Legal Aid as well. It covers a solicitor or barrister preparing your case and representing you in court and is available from the initial proceedings, and possibly bail application, through any appeals. Your solicitor completes a form and sends it to the court, with details of your income and savings. The court then decides whether it is 'in the interests of justice' for you to have Legal Aid. So a lot depends on how well you put your case on the form.

If your funds come within certain limits the court may tell you to pay a contribution. This may be partly from income and partly from savings and the court can stop your Legal Aid if you don't pay it. So, if you have problems paying, tell the court immediately. Also tell them

The law in Scotland or Northern Ireland may be different.

if your income changes. However, if you are acquitted you will probably get your contributions refunded.

If the court refuses Legal Aid it must say why. You can then keep re-applying right up to the trial. Meanwhile you may still be able to use the Green Form Scheme to get some help with your case. In *serious cases*, if aid has been refused on merit, you can ask the Legal Aid Board's area committee to review your application.

Scotland and Ireland

Legal Aid in Scotland is very similar to the scheme given on page 490, but there are certain local variations. To get the details of Legal Aid in Ireland write to its law society. For Scotland contact the Scottish Legal Aid Board (page 499).

Overseas Legal Aid

If a British citizen needs legal representation overseas it may be possible, as certain countries are signatories to an international agreement. Under this you can complete a Legal Aid Application in Britain and the authorities send it to the equivalent Legal Aid organization in the country in question. You may then be able to get whatever Legal Aid is available in that country – if its officials feel you qualify for it.

THE LEGAL SYSTEM

European Court of Human Rights

Britain signed the European Convention for the Protection of Human Rights and Fundamental Freedoms. So British citizens have a right to appeal to the European Court of Human Rights if they are the victim of a breach of the rights set out in that convention. However, they can only apply if they have already appealed through each stage in the British legal hierarchy which is open to them, and their appeal must be made within 6 months of the last appeal decision. Written evidence is submitted, and from this the court usually tries to arbitrate without the case going to a court hearing. But it can go to trial if necessary.

The British Courts

Although England and Wales use one set of names for their courts and Scotland another set, there is always a strict hierarchy. This has two effects. First, it means that cases of different degrees of seriousness are tried at different levels. Second, it means that if there is an appeal against the decisions made in one court the appeal is always heard in the next court up the tree. Within some of the levels there are also divisions which specialize in certain types of case.

The hierarchy also varies slightly according to whether it is a criminal or a civil case. Acts of Parliament always say whether something is a criminal or a civil offence. For a criminal offence someone is almost always prosecuted by the state, whereas in a civil case one citizen sues another.

Courts in Scotland

In Scotland, the Courts of Session and the High Court of Judiciary are both facets of one Supreme Court, with the same judges acting in different capacities. However, the criminal court travels to several main cities, whereas the civil court does not, and there is no appeal from the criminal court to the British House of Lords, whereas you can appeal a civil case.

The Scottish system also includes specialized courts such as the Land Court; the Lyon Court and tribunals similar to those in England and Wales.

Small Claims – England and Wales

The 'small claims' procedure, operated by the county courts, is designed to deal with claims for damages. These can be for trespass, negligence, breach of contract and so on: for example, against a company which took your money and failed to do the work, or a dry cleaner that ruined a garment.

There are now no limits to the sum which can be claimed via the county courts, although complex cases may go to the High Court. However, if the sum is under a set level it normally comes within the small claims procedure which is usually heard by a district judge. The aim is to make the process quick and easy. So you may represent yourself or ask someone else (they needn't have any legal training) to be your 'lay representative' and speak for you, and you needn't use a solicitor. Your local court or CAB should have a range of leaflets explaining the details in plain English. However, the actual procedure can be surprisingly complex so it's usually wise to get some initial advice from a lawyer. If you need legal advice and are short of money some CABx have a lawyer who can advise on such claims, or use a law centre or the Green Form Scheme to get a solicitor's advice (see page 491). She won't, however, be able to represent you under this scheme.

Any claim must be made to the court in the area where the offence occurred – for example, where you bought the goods. The procedure, as I write, is as follows:

- You must give the court the key facts of your claim against the company or individual, in writing.
- You also have to complete a request form asking for the case to be heard.
- You then pay a plaint fee to the court, based on the sum you are claiming.
- The court then sends a summons to the other side.
- They may then decide to accept your claim and make you an offer.
- You then have 14 days in which to tell the court whether or not you accept the offer.
- But if the trader plans to fight your claim the court will arrange an informal 'preliminary consideration', which you have to attend, and tries to get the matter settled without the full court procedure.
- If the preliminary consideration fails the case goes to arbitration.

In the arbitration the case is heard by a district judge in private, not in a court, but you can take along a witness if you wish. Under the small-claims procedure each side must usually pay its own solicitor's fees – win or lose. So, if you aren't sure to win, consider keeping your claim to below whatever sum allows you to use the small claims procedure – then you don't usually risk paying for the other side's solicitor if you lose. However, the winner can claim expenses from the loser (e.g. the court fee, the cost of photocopying evidence for the court, phone calls, fares), so keep track of everything you spend and have this account with you – with receipts where possible – when you go to the last hearing. You may win.

Scotland and Northern Ireland
In Scotland there are two kinds of small claim: a small-claims procedure for the smaller claims and a summary-cause procedure for slightly higher ones. The rules on costs are slightly complex but Sheriff Courts have leaflets on the procedure. In Northern Ireland the procedure is much the same as in England but the terms are different and the threshold for small claims may not be the same. The Northern Ireland Court Service (page 499) has leaflets.

Jury Service in Scotland
In Scotland there are 15 jurors for criminal cases. For civil cases in Scotland and all cases in the rest of Britain there are 12. In Scotland a majority verdict is needed to convict someone.

Lawyers

In Scotland the legal system comes under the Lord Advocate; in the rest of Britain under the Lord Chancellor. Both are government ministers and senior members of the bar.

In the British system solicitors are the vital bridge between the public and the major courts. But, until recently, solicitors could only argue a case in county and magistrates' courts and in tribunals, and in their Scottish equivalents. Cases in higher courts had to be conducted by barristers. This is changing and some solicitors may now be allowed to argue a case in any court in the land. In addition, at all levels, from the magistrates' courts to an appeal in the House of Lords, anyone may do without lawyers and defend themselves, though the intricacies of the legal system make this far harder to do than you might suppose.

Finding a Lawyer
It is often important to choose a lawyer who specializes in a particular field. In court, using someone with experience in a particular field of law is often essential to win the case. And a firm which does conveyancing all the time is fastest, but may charge no more. To find a solicitor in Scotland, contact the Scottish Law Society. Elsewhere, look in the Solicitors' Regional Directory, which gives their specialities, which is in libraries, courts and town halls, or ask a CAB. Or, if you want a top firm, a book called *The Legal 500*, by John Pritchard, published by Legalease, lists them and gives invaluable facts. There is also Chambers and Partners Directory: *A*

User's Guide to the Top 1000 Law Firms and All Barristers' Chambers.

You can only use a barrister via a solicitor and she will usually recommend one, but in England and Wales you can pick one yourself from the book above or the increasingly informative Bar Directory (in public libraries).

Fees
In Scotland, many solicitors charge nothing for the first interview and they are allowed to advertise this fact. They may also take cases on a 'no win, no fee' basis. The Scottish Law Society publishes guidelines on fees but there are no guidelines in the rest of Britain and solicitors can charge anything they like. However, your local Law Society may run a scheme under which you only pay a token sum for an initial discussion with a solicitor. In addition, the Law Society in London runs a scheme which provides a free first meeting in accident cases of any kind. Also, the Law Society of Scotland has a scheme by which certain solicitors offer an initial free interview on certain topics, like housing. The Societies can put you in touch with participating solicitors and if you can't afford a solicitor in the usual way you may be able to use a Law Centre, which will offer free legal advice (your local library or CAB has the address), or get Legal Aid (page 490). Law centres are staffed by both lawyers and experienced non-lawyers and specialize in areas of personal law such as housing, welfare rights, juvenile crime, employment. They do not cover things like divorce, conveyancing or commercial work. The amount of help a centre gives varies from one-off advice to representation in court. The Law Centres Federation or your local library can tell you of your nearest law centre. Most operate on a walk-in basis, but those who are unable to get to a centre, for example because of illness, can ask for a visit.

Going to law is expensive. It's wise to check the hourly rate before you even make an appointment and then ask what the lawyer feels the case will cost if you go ahead. Precise figures may be impossible but you can set a limit and ask to be told when that much has almost been spent. Then you can decide whether or not to continue. But put all this in writing – then everyone is sure what has been agreed.

If you use a lawyer on a fee-paying basis and think you have been overcharged, you can ask a court to review and reduce excessive fees. Or, if there has been no court work, the Law Society will check that the fees are not excessive.

Complaints Against Lawyers
If your complaint to the lawyer fails, go higher. In Scotland, complaints against a solicitor should be sent to the Law Society of Scotland. In England and Wales, complaints against solicitors are dealt with by the Solicitors Complaints Bureau. It looks into complaints about delays in dealing with your case, failure to handle your money properly, dishonesty and other unprofessional conduct. It can arrange for shoddy work to be redone, enforce a refund of fees, make the bad solicitor pay for another to do the work properly, or even award compensation. It has a free leaflet on how to complain, or your CAB will help you. If a solicitor has been negligent

you may be able to bring a case against him, and obtain compensation. The Bureau can't help you directly on this but may tell you who can or put you in touch with a solicitor who will give you a free 1-hour interview in which to discuss the case.

Complaints against barristers for shoddy work or unprofessional conduct should go to the General Council of the Bar. It can admonish, fine, suspend, disbar or order fees to be refunded, but the client is not compensated. Also, you cannot normally take an action for negligence against a barrister for his actions *in* court but this immunity does not extend to work outside the court. In Scotland complaints go to the Dean of the Faculty of Advocates.

If you are dissatisfied with the response from those professional bodies, complain direct to the Legal Services Ombudsman (or the Scottish Legal Services Ombudsman), who oversees solicitors, barristers, and licensed conveyancers. Both have leaflets on their services.

Jury Service

To sit on a jury you must be on the voting register and have lived in Britain or the Channel Isles or Isle of Man for 5 years. And you must not have been a barrister, advocate, solicitor, police, clerical, prison or probation officer within the past 10 years. Nor may you have been sentenced to prison within the past 10 years – and those sentenced to 5 or more years in prison are disqualified for life, as are judges and JPs.

If someone who is ineligible or disqualified sits on a jury it is a serious offence punishable with a substantial fine. You can also be fined if you fail to go for jury service when summoned – and an employer who fails to release someone can be punished for contempt of court.

Payment for Service
Jurors are paid their travelling expenses, plus a laughably small sum for subsistence and loss of earnings.

Release from Jury Service
When called to a jury some professions such as midwives, MPs, vets, nurses, doctors, dentists and pharmacists can ask to be excused as of right. So can anyone who has served during the previous 2 years. You may also be excused for a 'good reason' such as exams, or a booked holiday. Whatever the reason, put it to the court as soon as you are called. If the officials do not excuse you, appeal to the judge. In an emergency, such as illness, a juror may be excused during the case and the trial may continue with fewer than 12 jurors.

Chartered Institute of Arbitrators
The Chartered Institute of Arbitrators deals purely with disputes on civil matters, which those concerned agree between themselves. For example, if you had a dispute with your builder you could agree to ask the Institute to arbitrate. You would get a *totally independent* judgement by a lay judge. And he or she would be both experienced and qualified in the field of the particular dispute and chosen and trained in arbitration by the Institute.

The purpose of arbitration is to settle disputes quickly and fairly without the cost of going to court. So many arbitrations are on the basis of written evidence alone, and any hearing has fewer formalities than a normal court.

There is usually a registration fee, and whoever loses may have to pay the arbitrator's fees and can be ordered to pay the fees for the other side. Many trade associations have codes of conduct for their members which offer this independent arbitration if you are dissatisfied with the treatment that a complaint has received. Different trade associations have different agreements with the Institute. But if you bring your case through a trade association it may bear most of the cost of the arbitration.

The arbitration schemes of most codes of practice allow only written evidence to be submitted, but some may allow a hearing or even an on-site inspection. In terms of speed, cheapness and ease, arbitration has much to offer, but anyone considering arbitration should be aware of the following facts:

- Arbitration is an alternative to going to a court, such as the Small Claims Court. The important difference is that the arbitrator's decision is *final* and both sides are bound by it; there is no appeal procedure – except in very rare circumstances. So you lose some of the rights of appeal which would exist if the case were heard in court.
- Even when the trade association subsidizes the cost of arbitration it could still run you into costs of three figures – just.
- Since all the evidence is likely to be in writing you get no chance to put your case face to face. This saves the time and possible upset of going to court, but unless you are very good at putting your points in writing (or get good help with it) most companies have an advantage over you, as they probably do have someone who is experienced in putting their case.

> WARNING: Some trade associations boast of arbitration schemes but they do not use the Institute's independent arbitration and their arbitrators may not be well qualified. Before relying on a code of practice, check that arbitration is by the Institute.

The Courts and Appeals System of England, Scotland and Wales

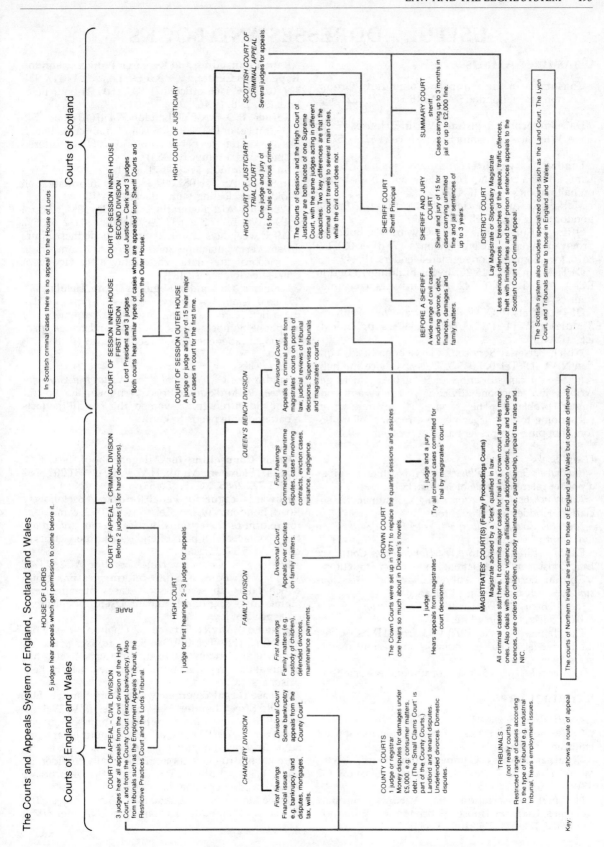

The law in Scotland or Northern Ireland may be different.

USEFUL ADDRESSES AND BOOKS

Consumer Affairs

Consumers in the European Community Group, 24 Tufton Street, London SW1P 3RB Tel: 071 222 2662. (P.205)

Data Protection Registrar, Wycliffe House, Water Lane, Wilmslow, Cheshire SK9 5AF Tel: 0625 535777. (P.455).

London Assay Office, Goldsmiths' Hall, 1-2 Foster Lane, London EC2 8AQ Tel: 071 606 8975, has a leaflet on hallmarking – sae. (P.457)

Market Research Society, 15 Northburgh Street, London EC1C 0AH Tel: 071 490 4911.

Office of Fair Trading (OFT), Government Building, Bromyard Avenue, Acton, London W3 7BB Tel: 081 269 8616, for information on registered lenders. (P.449)

OFT, Room 310c, 15-25 Bream Buildings, London EC4A 1PR Tel: 071 242 2858 answers consumer queries. (P.447)

OFT Leaflets, P.O. Box 2, Central Way, Feltham, Middlesex TW14 0TG Tel: 081 398 3405, supplies leaflets. (P.447)

Which Personal Service, 2 Marylebone Road, London NW1 4DF Tel: 071 935 3277, is an advice and help scheme you can subscribe to. It enables you to get written and telephone advice if you have any consumer problems. The service is separate from subscribing to the magazines, but reading *Which* before shopping can prevent a lot of problems. (P.452)

Useful Books
Bradbury's Book of Hallmarks, J. W. Northend – gives a pocket reference table of hallmarks.
The Which Book of Consumer Law, Consumers' Association, Hodder and Stoughton.
Touching Gold and Silver: 500 Years of Hallmarks, The Goldsmiths' Company.
Edith Rudinger, editor, *The Handbook of Consumer Law*, Consumers' Association, Hodder and Stoughton.
Gordon Borrie and Aubrey Diamond, *The Consumer, Society and the Law*, Pelican.
Judith Banister, *The Country Life Collector's Pocket Book of Silver*, Country Life.
The Hallmarking Act 1973, C43, from HMSO, gives all the details of changes in marks on precious metals since 1975.
350 Legal Problems Solved, Consumers' Association.

Criminal Law

Assault, Rape, Sexual Abuse and Violence
Childline 0800 1111 is a free helpline for abused children.
Criminal Injuries Compensation Board, Blythswood House, 200 West Regent Street, Glasgow G2 4SW Tel: 041 221 0945.
National Association of Victims Support Schemes, Cranmer House, 39 Brixton Road, London SW9 6DZ Tel: 071 735 9166. (P.483)

Rape Counselling and Research Project & London Rape Crisis Centre, P.O. Box 69, London WC1X 9NJ Tel: 071 916 5466 office, 071 837 1600 24-hour helpline, RC, L, B. (P.462)

Refuge, P.O. Box 855, London W4 4JF, Tel: 081 747 0133 (office) or 081 999 4430 is a 24-hour crisis line. It has a list of refuges nationwide and will help battered women find a refuge. (P.484)

Suzy Lamplugh Trust, 14 East Sheen Avenue, London SW14 8AS Tel: 081 392 1389, has information on avoiding or dealing with attacks. (P.460)

Women's Aid Federation, P.O. Box 391, Bristol BS99 7WS Tel: 0272 633494; Helpline 0272 633542 (staffed weekdays 10 am-10 pm – outside these hours an answering machine gives emergency numbers to call); coordinates nationwide refuges for victims of domestic violence. (P.483)

Women's Aid London Regional Office, Helpline 071 251 6537 (staffed weekdays 10 am-4.45 pm – outside these hours an answering machine gives emergency telephone numbers offering support and refuge space to women experiencing domestic violence. (P.483)

Useful Books
Sandra Horley, *Love and Pain: A Survival Guide for Women*, Bedford Square Press. Written by the director of the oldest refuge for women, this has all the facts a battered wife needs to know.

General
Crisis Counselling for Alleged Shoplifters, P.O. Box 147, Stanmore, Middx HA7 4YT Tel: 081 202 5787 or 071 722 3685, RC, L. (P.463)

Howard League for Penal Reform, 708 Holloway Road, London N19 3NL Tel: 071 281 7722, campaigns for reform of the criminal justice system and maintains contacts with both offenders and the victims of crime. M£5-17, M, sae.

Justice, 95a Chancery Lane, London WC2A 1DT Tel: 071 405 6018, is a law-reform pressure group which takes up some *serious* cases of injustice – mainly involving imprisonment. Useful publications on aspects of law.

Prisoners' Advice Service, 57 Chalton Street, London NW1 1HV Tel: 071 388 8586, advises prisoners and will sometimes speak up for them. It also has information on educational charities which help prisoners. RC.

Release (Legal Emergency and Drug Service) Ltd, 388 Old Street, London EC1V 9LT Tel: 071 729 9904, Mon-Fri 10 am-6 pm, emergency number outside those times 071 603 8654, offers a 24-hour emergency advice service on any legal emergency related to criminal or drug law. Its service is totally confidential and it has a list of solicitors all over the UK who are experienced in criminal law. RC.

Trace Magazine (and database), 33 New Street, The Barbican, Plymouth, Devon PL1 2NA Tel: 0752 228727.

Household Law

Council for Licensed Conveyancers, 16 Glebe Road, Chelmsford, Essex CM1 1QG Tel: 0245 349599. (P.453)

Index of Exempted Dogs, Chishill Road, Heydon, Royston, Herts SG8 8PN Tel: 0763 838964.

Land Charges Department, Drakes Hill Court, Burrington Way, Plymouth PL5 3LP Tel: 0752 779831. (P.453)

Land Registry (P.453), address on page 693.

Noise Abatement Society, P.O. Box 8, Bromley, Kent BR2 0UH, campaigns against noise of all kinds and assists members in their complaints against it. RC, M£L-H, L, B, F, E. sae for advice.

Oyez (**Legal Stationery**), 16 Third Avenue, Denbigh West, Bletchley, Milton Keynes MK1 1TG Tel: 0908 371111, sells legal forms for wills, conveyancing and so on.

Transaction Scheme, for easier conveyancing Tel: 071 320 5666 for a list of member solicitors. (P.453)

Useful Book
The Conveyancing Fraud is sold directly by Michael Joseph, 27 Occupation Lane, London SE18 3JQ Tel: 081 855 2404.

Motoring Law

Car Clamp Recovery Club, 20 Newman Street, London W1P 3HB Tel: 071 235 9901.

DVLA, Swansea SA6 7JL Tel: 0792 72151. (P.470)

Motor Insurers' Bureau, 152 Silbury Boulevard, Central Milton Keynes MK9 1NB Tel: 0908 830001. (P.470)

Parking Adjudication for London, 14 Buckingham Palace Road, London SW1W 0QP Tel: 071 630 0200, will decide about complaints of unfair ticketing. (P.471)

Useful Book
John Pritchard, *The Motorist and the Law*, Penguin – an A-Z of all you need to know in readable form.
See also Things Mechanical, p. 424.

Work-related Law

British Copyright Council, Copyright House, 29-33 Berners Street, London W1P 4AA, has a booklet on copyright and performance rights. (P.476)

Central Council of Industrial Tribunals (England and Wales), 100 Southgate Street, Bury St Edmunds, Suffolk IP33 2AQ Tel: 0284 76300 Freephone enquiry line: 0800 221111. (P.475)

Central Office of Industrial Tribunals (Scotland), St Andrew House, 141 West Nile Street, Glasgow G1 2RU Tel: 041 331 1601 8 am-5.30 pm (admin) 10 am-5.30 pm (court) – has a leaflet explaining the procedure. (P.475)

Commission for Racial Equality, Eliot House, 10-12 Allington Street, London SW1E 5EH Tel: 071 828 7022. (P.474)

Equal Opportunities Commission, Overseas House, Quay Street, Manchester M3 3HN Tel: 061 833 9244. (P.474)

Institute of Patentees and Inventors, Suite 505a, Triumph House, 189 Regent Street, London W1R 7WF Tel: 071 242 7812, assists inventors in furthering and patenting inventions and sends a bulletin of new patents, available for development, to industry. M£M, M, meetings (P.476)

Institute of Personnel Management, Camp Road, London SW19 4UX Tel: 081 946 9100, produces useful books on employment law.

Lawyers for Your Business, free legal advice on business matters. For a list of member solicitors Tel: 071 405 9075 or write c/o The Law Society. (P.473)

Maternity Alliance, 15 Brittania Street, London WC1X 9JP Tel: 071 837 1265, advises on maternity rights and on services during pregnancy and early parenthood. Also on pregnancy and childbirth issues. pressure group, L. (P.475)

Patent Office, State House, 25 Southampton Buildings, London WC2 Tel: 071 438 4700, has clear leaflets on all aspects of patenting issues. (P.476)

Special Commissioners for Income Tax, 15-19 Bedford Avenue, London WC1B 3AS Tel: 071 631 4242, hears appeals against tax assessments. This is usually after referral from the Revenue, but an individual may ask for a hearing.

Wills, Probate and Death

London Anatomy Office, Rockefeller Building, University College, University Street, London WC1E 6JJ Tel: 071 387 7850. (P.481)

Public Trustee Office, Stewart House, 24 Kingsway, London WC2B 6JX Tel: 071 269 7000, can be appointed to act as trustee, in a will, and administers estates and funds. It has leaflets on this and VAT Tribunals.

Principal Family Registry, Somerset House, Strand, London WC2R 1LP Tel: 071 936 7000 – has copies of all wills. The Safe Custody Clerk, **Principal Probate Registry**, Tel: 071 936 6997, looks after the storage, and release, of wills before probate. (P.483)

Useful Books
What to Do When Someone Dies, Consumers' Association.
Wills and Probate, Consumers' Association.
'What to Do After a Death', DSS leaflet no. 49, DSS (address on page 693).

Family Law

Child and Family Issues
A Voice for the Child in Care, 15 Wilkin Street, London NW5 3NG Tel: 071 267 5940. (P.479)

Advice, Advocacy and Representation Service for Children (ASC), Sickle Street Manchester M60 2AA Tel: 061 839 8442, helps and advises children on legal issues. (P.478)

Law changes: this is guidance not gospel. Consult a lawyer before any decision.

The Children's Legal Centre Ltd, 20 Compton Terrace, London N1 2UN Tel: 071 359 6251, provides a free, and confidential, Ad and Info service by letter or telephone (2-5 pm weekdays) for young people in England and Wales. It will also take enquiries from adults on issues concerning children, provided it is clear that the child involved would not object. (P.479)

Family Rights Group, Print House, 18 Ashwin Street, London E8 3DL Tel: 071 249 0008, offers advice and information, including the views of a solicitor, to those who have children in care or who are involved in child abuse proceedings. RC, M£M, vgL, vgB. (P.479)

General Register Office, St Catherine's House, 10 Kingsway, London WC2B 6JP Tel: 071 242 0262. (P.478)

The Joint Council for Welfare of Immigrants, 115 Old Street, London EC1V 9JR Tel: 071 251 8706, will advise and help those with immigration problems.

Justice for Children, 35 Wellington Street, London WC2E 7BN Tel: 071 836 5917. (P.478)

Missing Persons Bureau, Parkway House, Sheen Lane, London SW14 8LS Tel: 081 392 2000 – 24-hour helpline. It supports and advises and tries to trace the missing using streetworkers in London and media publicity. RC. (P.486)

National Association of Young People in Care, 8A Stukley Place, London NW1 8NJ Tel: 071 284 4793, offers advice and information for those in care. (P.479)

Parents Aid, c/o Hare Street Family Centre, Harberts Road, Harlow, Essex CM19 4EU Tel: 0279 452166, gives advice and help to families with children in care. (P.479)

Who Cares Trust, City Bridge House, 235–245 Goswell Road, London EC1V 7JD Tel: 071 833 9047, will help and advise a child in care and works to improve the system. RC, L, M. (P.479)

See also Adoption, pp. 273, 317.

Useful Book
The Police Act: A Guide for Young People, Children's Legal Centre.

Separation, Divorce and Child Support

Child Abduction Unit, Lord Chancellor's Department, 81 Chancery Lane, London WC2A 1DD Tel: 071 911 7127 free leaflet. (P.477)

Child Support Agency, P.O. Box 55, Brierley Hill, West Midlands, DY5 1YL Tel: 0345 133133 (information line). (P.466)

Divorce Branch, Family Proceedings Department, Somerset House, London WC2R 1LP Tel: 071 936 6000 – will supply copies of a decree nisi or absolute to anyone. (P.464)

Divorce Conciliation and Advisory Service, 38 Ebury Street, London SW1W 0LU Tel: 071 730 2422 (10 am-5 pm weekdays) – helps to sort out problems of the divorced and those approaching it. It helps them cope with its aftermath, and assists in practical difficulties. For example, separated or divorced

parents can sort out disputes regarding the children. The counsellors are not a substitute for a solicitor, but they can reduce the conflict. The service is confidential and those not earning may not be charged. (P.464)

Family Mediation Scotland, 127 Rose Street, South Lane, Edinburgh EH2 5BB Tel: 031 220 1610, will help separating parents agree arrangements for children. (P.465)

Family Mediator's Association, The Old House, Rectory Gardens, Henbury, Bristol BS10 7AQ Tel: 0272 500140, offers nationwide, non-adversarial approach to the problems relating to money, property and children, when married or unmarried partners split up. For a fee you get mediation by a lawyer or an experienced mediator.

National Council for the Divorced and Separated, 13 High Street, Little Shelford, Cambridge CB2 5ES Tel: 071 254 2080, gives companionship, support, and is interested in legal issues. The NCDS Trust may be able to assist in cases of hardship, RC, M£L, L, G, A, H, Ad, Inf, sae. (P.464)

National Family Conciliation Council, Shaftesbury Centre, Percy Street, Swindon, Wilts SN2 2AZ Tel: 0793 514055 9.30 am-2.30 pm, has local offices, which help couples resolve disputed issues after a marriage breaks down, especially those concerning the children. RC, useful L. (P.464)

Reunite, National Council for Abducted Children, P.O. Box 4, London WC1X 8XY Tel: 071 404 8356, helps and advises parents of abducted children. (P.477)

Reunite, P.O. Box 158, London N4 1AV is a support group for those whose children have been abducted overseas by ex-partners.

Solicitors Family Law Association, P.O. Box 302, Keston, Kent BR2 6EZ Tel: 0689 850227, is a group of matrimonial lawyers who feel it is better to keep conflict to a minimum in family law cases. They will put you in touch with members in your area. (P.464)

Other organizations for single parents are on page 318.

Useful Books
Living Together: You, Your Partner and the Law, the legal side of living together without marrying, by post from the law firm Twist, Taft and James, 3 The Quadrant, Coventry, CV1 2DY Tel: 0203 631632.
Which: Guide to Divorce, Consumers' Association.

Other Pressure Groups

Amnesty International, 99-119 Roseberry Avenue, London EC1 4RE Tel: 071 278 6000, campaigns for the release of prisoners of conscience and against torture and the death penalty.

Legal Action Group, 242 Pentonville Road, London N1 9UN Tel: 071 833 2931/2/3, works to improve legal services. Laymen representing themselves might find its books useful. Does not give legal advice but publishes a directory of legal advice and law centres throughout the UK.

Liberty (formerly **NCCL**), 21 Tabard Street, London

SE1 4LA Tel: 071 403 3888, lobbies the government and advises individuals on issues of civil liberty. Useful leaflets and books on a wide range of legal matters from maternity rights to nuclear power. M£M, L, B, sae.

Rights of Women, 52-54 Featherstone Street, London EC1Y 8RT Tel: 071 251 6577, is a feminist organization, campaigns and advises on women's rights.

Other Legal and Governmental Bodies

ALAS, free accident advice scheme Tel: 071 242 2430 or write c/o The Law Society for a list of member solicitors. (P.469)

Charities Commission's Central Register, St Alban's House, 57-60 Haymarket, London SW1Y 4QX Tel: 071 210 4477, has a leaflet on how to start a charity.

Chartered Institute of Arbitrators, 24 Angel Gate, City Road, London EC1V 2RS Tel: 071 837 4483.

Council on Tribunals, 7th Floor, 22 Kingsway, London WC2B 6LE Tel: 071 936 7045, is the advisory body for the government on tribunals and public inquiries. It will also look into individual complaints about the procedure of tribunals – but it is not an appeal body.

Court of Protection, Steward House, 24 Kingsway, London WC2B 6IX Tel: 071 269 7000.

European Court of Justice, BP 96, Plateau du Kirchberg, Luxembourg Tel: 010 352 43031, is concerned with disputes over the application of EC rules and regulations.

Faculty of Advocates, 11 Parliament Square, Edinburgh EH1 1RF Tel: 031 226 5071, is the professional body for Scotland's barristers (advocates).

General Council of the Bar (or Bar Council), 3 Bedford Row, London WC1R 4DB Tel: 071 242 0082, is the barrister's professional body, which maintains standards.

Home Office Immigration and Nationality Department (see Organizations, page 694).

Immigration Appellate Authorities, Thanet House, 232 Strand, London WC2R 1DA Tel: 071 353 8060, hears appeals an immigration decisions.

Incorporated Law Society of Northern Ireland, Legal Aid Department, Bedford House, 16-22 Bedford Street, Belfast BT2 7FL Tel: 0232 246441.

Judge Advocate General's Office, 22 Kingsway, London WC2B 6LE Tel: 071 430 5335, is the department which provides Judge Advocates for courts-martial.

Judicial Committee of the Privy Council is the final court of appeal from the courts in the former British dominions and colonies such as Australia, New Zealand, Malaysia and Jamaica.

Judicial Studies Board, 14 Little St James' Street, St James', London SW1A 1DP Tel: 071 925 0185, is in charge of training judges.

Lands Tribunal, 48-49 Chancery Lane, London WC2A 1JR Tel: 071 936 7200, decides issues relating to the cost of land compensation for compulsory purchase.

Law Centres Federation, Duchess House, 18-19 Warren Street, London W1P 5DB Tel: 071 387 8570, does *not* give legal advice. But it is the head office for law centres around Britain which do offer free legal advice. Some law centres also sell a range of publications.

Law Commission, Conquest House, 37-38 John Street, Theobalds Road, London WC1N 2BQ Tel: 071 411 1220, reviews law reform in England and Wales and often invites public comment when it publishes a consultation paper suggesting reforms.

Law Society, 113 Chancery Lane, London WC2A 1PL Tel: 071 242 1222, sets the professional standards solicitors must keep to and administers a compensation fund for those who suffer loss through defaulting solicitors. There is a similar fund in Scotland.

The Law Society's Hall, 26 Drumsheugh Gardens, Edinburgh EH3 7YR Tel: 031 226 7411, will deal with public enquiries. It cannot give legal advice but it will answer questions of fact and direct people to where they can find help. It also publishes clear, readable guides as to what to do in many common situations, such as when someone dies, or when buying a house.

Lay Observer, Royal Courts of Justice, The Strand, London WC2A 2LL Tel: 071 936 6000/6695, a non-solicitor who investigates complaints about how the Law Society has handled complaints against solicitors.

The Legal Aid Board Head Office, 5th & 6th Floors, 29-37 Red Lion Street, London WC1R 4PP Tel: 071 831 4209, will supply legal aid information, or give you the address of your area office. (P.490)

Legal Services Ombudsman, 22 Oxford Court, Oxford Street, Manchester M2 3WQ Tel: 061 236 9532.

Lord Chancellor's Department (address on p. 694), administers most of the legal system of England and Wales, bar certain tribunals which come under other government departments.

Northern Ireland Court Service, Windsor House, 9-15 Bedford Street, Belfast BT2 7LT Tel: 0232 328594, covers both the courts in Northern Ireland and the legal aid scheme. (P.493)

Official Solicitor to the Supreme Court, 81 Chancery Lane, London WC2A 1DD Tel: 071 911 7127, officially acts as guardian for children or those needing guardianship, and also monitors the cases of those admitted to prison for contempt of court.

Scottish Legal Aid Board, 44 Drumsheugh Gardens, Edinburgh EH3 7SW Tel: 031 226 7061. (P.492)

Scottish Legal Services Ombudsman, 2 Greenside Lane, Edinburgh EH1 3AH Tel: 031 556 5574.

Solicitors Complaints Bureau, Victoria Court, Dormer Place, Leamington Spa, Warwickshire Tel: 0926 820082, handles complaints against solicitors.

Money

Money Management • Debt • Insurance • Mortgages • Pensions • Savings • Stocks and Shares • Benefits and Grants • Tax and VAT

It is a great pity that money involves numbers. We deal with money in our pockets every day without a pause. But with larger sums the bogeyman of mathematics casts his shadow. As a result, money matters have a reputation for being hard to understand and best left to the experts. This is simply not so. Money matters are actually no more complicated than gardening or DIY. The real trouble is that a mystery has grown up around them and those in the money world have been allowed to develop a language which most of us simply don't know.

Don't let this put you off. If you ask for financial information from anyone, be prepared to ask for an explanation the moment they say anything you don't understand. Don't be afraid to reveal your ignorance. Ask, and keep on asking, until they put it in plain English. There is nothing to be said about money which can't be said in terms anyone can understand, and if the people you are consulting fail to do that it isn't you who is being stupid.

You need to be prepared to do this because never before has the ordinary consumer been faced with such a range of financial services, service companies and opportunities as he or she is today. And for almost every choice there is a pitfall. There are a few rules which could, however, help anyone to hang on to their money a little bit longer.

- Never rush into any financial decision.
- Always get as much professional advice as you can, from several sources – there is more free advice available in this field than in almost any other.
- Go to the reputable sources.
- If anyone telephones offering financial advice, don't even agree to talk to them. They are trained to persuade you to buy a particular type of financial product. You don't need financial advice from those who have an axe to grind.
- Beware of advertisements in newspapers. The law is now stricter than it was. But there are always loopholes. The better the company, the less likely it is to take out a small ad. Finding an adviser through a professional body is far safer.
- Beware of advertisements which offer to advise and help you with debts. Many of those who place such advertisements are really offering loans at much higher than normal rates, although, when they talk to you, it may not seem that way. Scores of people have

lost their homes by borrowing from such companies (see Debt, page 508).

- Before making any kind of financial decision, bone up on it. Have a look in this chapter. Read *Which* magazine – *Which* now has excellent financial sections each month. Listen to BBC Radio 4's 'Money-box', which gives first-rate information on personal finance. Read the family or personal finance sections of the newspapers. Check some of the books and leaflets I list. Never take any financial decision without checking the latest facts – the financial world changes daily.
- Don't forget that the managers of banks, building societies and other reputable organizations are sources of free advice.

★ Pause for thought before starting a family, and prepare your finances. A survey in the *Sunday Times* a few years ago found that it cost the average parent £66,000 to raise a child to the age of 18, and for many parents it is £164,000. And that doesn't include the difference it may have made to the mother's earning potential.

MONEY MANAGEMENT

Accounts

At one time the choice was simple: you had a current account at a bank for day-to-day money, and a deposit account as a back-up. Current accounts didn't pay interest and deposit accounts did. Today there are many types of account and almost every type of financial institution is behaving like almost every other type. So banks and building societies offer similar types of accounts and other financial organizations are in the running.

Looking after other people's money can be a highly profitable business, so each company tries to offer newer and better baits to lure new customers, especially students. Many current accounts now pay interest and there are numerous different types of deposit account, some of which offer the facilities of a current account – including a cheque book.

Accounts for Daily Money

A current account with one of the big-four banks isn't always the best place to put money for daily living. A building society could suit you as well, or better. Also some banks and building societies, such as the Post

Office based Girobank, are open longer hours, others offer better interest on accounts, or better perks or services to certain groups, such as students or small businesses. Some, such as the Royal Bank of Scotland, automatically transfer money between accounts to keep them in balance. Others, such as First Direct, offer 24-hour telephone banking, and many of them offer some banking by phone or computer link. But the hours, services and charges for telephone banking vary enormously. Ask too whether you just ring and talk to a human being or must route in via often irritating tones and get automated replies.

If you can keep more than one account in reasonable credit you might take the pick of the perks and benefits from several companies by splitting your money between several. A building society paying interest might, for example, be the best place to have a current account, but you might have another account in a bank with better loan facilities.

Before opening an account with any company, tell them your status (a student, for example). Useful questions to ask before opening an account are these.

- Do they pay interest on a current account? If so, are there charges for the account, or extra levies for using cheques?
- Have they any other accounts which pay interest and allow you to withdraw money by cheque?
- Do they offer free banking? If so, what sum must be in the account for services to be free? And would charges be made *the moment* you fell below that sum, or is there a period of grace?
- What is the limit of a cash-card withdrawal per day?
- How often can you have a free bank statement?
- What information does the bank statement give?
- How many branches do they have?
- Can you cash their cheques at any other banks without being charged for the service?
- Do they allow overdrafts? If so, up to what sum?
- What would an overdraft of £200 for 6 months cost in interest? (Giving a set figure for set months makes comparison easy.)
- Do they give loans, and if so what for?
- Will you get any perks if you open an account?
- How much do they charge for the following:
    (a) if you are in credit
    (b) if you aren't
    holding an envelope in safe keeping?
    holding a small box in safe keeping?
    a loan of £5,000 (and would other sums have another rate)?
    issuing travellers' cheques (if you travel)?
    issuing foreign cash (if you travel)?
    paying standing orders?
    bouncing a cheque?
    cancelling a cheque?
    arranging an overdraft?
    extra statements?
    credits and debits if you are overdrawn?
    direct debits?
    money from a cash dispenser?
    standing orders?
    financial services, e.g. buying shares?
- What standing charges are there?

Finally, do they have any services specially suited to you? For example, if you have trouble getting to a bank you may want one with a telephone service which will let you pay your bills from your home or office, or one which is open on a Saturday.

Savings and Deposit Accounts
In savings and deposit accounts you have an even wider choice than in current accounts. Every bank has several different types and, on top of that, there are all the building societies, and options like National Savings.

Some people say that as the interest rates only vary by a per cent or two it doesn't matter where you put your money. I disagree. It isn't worth constantly swapping from place to place. But it *is* worth choosing the best rate to start with – provided the account doesn't have any disadvantages which make it unsuitable.

The most likely disadvantages are that some accounts must be kept above a certain sum, and some need long notice of a withdrawal and/or make you lose months of interest on any money you take out before the end of a set time. So the key questions to ask about such accounts are these.

- What is the rate of interest?
- Is a minimum sum needed to open or maintain such an account?
- How much notice must you give before taking money out?
- If money is taken out, what interest is lost on it over what period?

Banking and Banking by Any Name

Many building societies now behave so much like banks that I shall use the word 'bank' to mean any organization that offers bank-like services. Either way, banking is like motoring: it is up to you to know the facts and to keep control.

Goodness knows how bank managers came to be elevated to the status of punishing father figures. A bank is a service industry – like a hotel. It looks after your money just as a hotel looks after you. So a bank manager can be regarded in much the same way as a hotel manager, not as someone who can tell you what to do. The same applies to anyone who offers banking services.

There is no point in banking with any bank because your family always has. Unless, of course, the family has such clout with that bank that it will let you borrow money more easily.

If your bank ceases to offer the services you want, or charges more than the next bank – *move your account*. You can even move an overdraft if another bank will take it on.

That said, bank managers have the power to grant or refuse loans and overdrafts. If you were a bank manager who would you rather lend to – a customer who ignored you until money was needed, or one who kept you informed of their success and treated you like a human being? So, cultivate your bank manager.

- Don't just visit him when there's a problem. Make sure you meet him (it is seldom a her) and get to know him. Give him lunch if it's appropriate.
- If you get a new job or promotion, write and tell him, and say what difference it will make.
- If you get a loan or overdraft, let him know what you have achieved with it and thank him.
- If you need money, go armed with the facts on why it's needed and the figures on repayment.
- Never run up an overdraft without arranging it with the bank. This shows you have things under control and it will cost less.

> If you are too ill to look after your affairs – or are going abroad – you can give someone else Power of Attorney by simply signing a form before witnesses. That person can then act for you and draw on your accounts. You can get the forms from **Oyez** (page 497) but it would be wise to get advice from a lawyer or Law centre before using one.

Cash Cards, Cheque Cards and Switch Cards
Bank and building societies usually offer customers a cash card which combines several functions on one card. Often it will act as cheque guarantee card, let you withdraw money from a cash machine, or pay a shop through the Switch system, which transfers money from your account straight to the shop's account. And, if you pay bank charges, it is usually cheaper to withdraw money by card than by cheque.

To get cash from your account by using a machine outside the bank you punch in a private number, called a PIN number. Increasingly the card from one bank can be used in many others. So these can be very useful. But there have been problems with money being taken from accounts by thieves who watched what number was punched in and used forged cards. So, under the latest banking code of practice, unless a bank can *prove* that you took the money, or were very careless with the card, you need only bear the first £50 of the stolen money; the bank bears the rest of the loss.

Never tell anyone your PIN number and *never* keep it anywhere near your card. If you can't remember it write it in a way which won't be recognized. Best of all, ask to choose your own PIN number (some cards allow this) and pick a number which means something to you but to nobody else. Like your mother's birthday, plus the number of the bus you take. Then you won't need to write it down. If it is lost, ring and *report it at once*. Then confirm this in writing the same day, saying what time of day you rang and giving the name of the person you spoke to. See also page 513.

Cheque Cards and Bounced Cheques
Having a cheque accidentally 'bounce' (be returned un-

honoured) is most embarrassing . But a bank need only pay out on a cheque if there is money in the account to meet the *full sum*. If you have £50 in the bank and write a cheque for £75 it needn't pay a penny (unless you have arranged for an overdraft). That even applies to standing orders and direct debits. So if you are overdrawn you could find a vital payment such as a mortgage being bounced and end up with real problems.

However, if you write a cheque and the person receiving it puts your cheque card number on the back of it, the bank *must* pay out – provided it is not more than the sum which the cheque card guarantees – even if you have no money in the bank. But the number must *not* have been written by you. However, a cheque card doesn't guarantee a forged cheque. (See also Stopping a Cheque, below.)

Another way to prevent vital payments bouncing is to use a bank which will automatically transfer money from your savings account into your current account, to keep it in credit. A few banks offer this service. But check the charges for it, they can be high.

Cash Cards Abroad
The trend is towards inter-bank deals which will allow you to use your British cash card to get money from cashpoint machines overseas. So this may be worth asking about when choosing a bank. But do ask about the charges per transaction; they vary enormously.

★ Keep a written record of when you use your card. It could be useful evidence if there is a problem.

★ Cash cards are no longer limited to being used in machines of the company that issues them. More and more companies are linking up. If you have a card, ask where you can use it.

★ The £50 limit on a cheque may now be raised if you apply for a card with a higher limit.

Cheques
There is an implied contract between a bank and its customer that the bank will honour the customer's cheques (if there is enough money in the account), obey the instructions and not disclose the customer's affairs to other people. Usually, if a bank pays out a cheque when it should not have done it is liable – for example, if a cheque needs two signatures and is passed with only one. There are, however, various rules which it is worth knowing:

- If a cheque card number is written on the back of a cheque, that cheque cannot be stopped.
- If you lose your cheque book and notify the bank immediately the bank is liable for any cheques forged. If you fail to tell the bank *you* are liable.

As soon as a bank knows someone is dead it stops all their cheques (this doesn't apply to a joint account). So if a husband is seriously ill and the wife is financially dependent on him it would be a good idea for him to give his wife a cheque for enough for her to live on for several months, and she would be wise to use it immediately to open an account in her name alone, and not tell the bank of the death until the cheque has been cleared. This may sound hard-hearted, but adding sudden poverty to grief is even harder.

Banks used to issue both uncrossed cheques (without tramlines) and crossed cheques without a/c payee only. Both were very unsafe. So crossed cheques, saying a/c payee only, are now standard. Only the owner of the cheque book can use such a cheque to get cash. In all other circumstances the cheque must be payed into the account of the person named on it (the payee). So, if it is stolen the thief won't make a penny from it. Many people also write the words 'not negotiable' on the cheque but banks say it has no legal meaning.

To open a crossed cheque (i.e. make it possible for someone to cash it) write 'please pay cash' between the tramlines and then sign it there as well as in the usual place. The payee can get cash for it at any bank if they can prove they are the person named. So if, for example, someone stole your wallet containing both an opened cheque and a credit card they could easily cash it.

However you write your cheques it is vital to note how much was paid, and to whom, on the counterfoil. Only then can you easily prove that you did pay a bill, or check that your bank statements are correct.

Banks won't honour cheques that are more than 6 months old but the person who wrote it is liable for 6 years. If you have a cheque over 6 months old keep a photocopy and return the original asking for a replacement.

Forged Cheques

Suppose you write a cheque for £20 and someone alters it to £120 and the bank pays out the larger sum. If you wrote the cheque carefully, so any additions had to look like additions, the bank was wrong to pay the money out on a suspect cheque and they should not take the extra money from your account. But if you left gaps which made it easy for the forger you would be to blame and they would be entitled to debit your account.

However, if your cheque book is lost or stolen and someone forges your signature the law says that your bank ought to know your signature. So, if it pays out, that is the bank's loss, not yours. This applies even if the cheque carries a cheque card number. However, you should notify your branch, as soon as you know the cheque book has been stolen. Monday morning is soon enough if you discover the loss at a weekend. If you are away and can't find the number of your branch phone the head office (pages 540-541).

Post-dated Cheques

If the date you put on a cheque is for some time in the future it is said to be post-dated. A bank will usually pay out money on, or after, the date on a cheque. This can be a convenient way of paying back money in stages. Post-dating a cheque is also useful if your account is low but you know money will come in on a certain date. But the person you are paying needn't accept it.

Stopping a Cheque

If a cheque has the bank guarantee card number on the back it cannot be stopped. If it doesn't, you can ask your bank not to pay the cheque and it *must* do as you say – unless it has already paid out the money – though it will probably charge you for doing so. It needs the instruction in writing but you can phone and ask for the cheque to be held until your letter arrives. If the bank pays out, when you have told it not to, it bears the cost.

Services from Banks

The range of services banks and building societies offer was transformed by the Financial Services Act 1986. Nowadays almost every imaginable financial service can be obtained from somewhere – though a bank won't always be the best place to get it.

Take insurance or unit trust advice, for example. By law banks and similar bodies must either sell only the financial products – insurance, personal equity plans and so on – of one company to which they are 'tied' or they must give you independent advice on what's best for you regardless of which insurance company or unit trust group supplies it. Most of the banks (and building societies) do not offer independent advice. (See also page 519).

Standing Orders

A standing order is a convenient way to pay regular set sums such as an annual subscription. You just give the bank details of how much should be paid, to whom and on what date, and they do the rest. This is usually done on a form provided by the company you are paying. There may or may not be a bank charge for a standing order – check.

★ It is very easy to forget about standing orders and go on paying out for magazines which are being sent to an old address. Banks do not always cancel them when you instruct them to. So keep a separate file with the letters which both start and stop them. Then your proof won't get lost.

Financial facts change daily, check the latest figures before making a decision.

> Did you know that if you get on a bus and only have a £10 note with which to pay the fare the bus conductor can't refuse to accept it? Nor may he or she get back at you by giving you change in dozens of small coins. If you only have the note and there isn't enough change, give your name and address and wait for the bill.
>
> Cash is legal tender and, by law, nobody may refuse to accept it in payment. But there are limits to what someone is obliged to accept in small coins. You can pay any amount you like in £1 coins but nobody has to accept:
> - more than 20p worth of 2p or 1p coins
> - more than £5 worth of 5p or 10p coins
> - more than £10 worth of 20p or 50p coins

Direct Debit
A direct debit is an arrangement whereby you give permission for a certain organization to make various charges directly to your account, and authorize the bank to pay them. This is convenient for paying regular bills monthly, for example. Unless you have free banking there is usually a charge for each direct debit, so it costs more than writing a cheque yourself. Only reputable organizations may directly debit an account, and if a mistake is made you should be refunded by the company or your bank.

Debit Cards
A debit card is really a cross between a credit card and a cheque book. You give the shop the card and it is handled like a credit card, but instead of being sent to a credit card company, the bill goes to your bank which takes the money out of your account within a couple of days. It can also be used to guarantee cheques and to withdraw money.

Sending Money Abroad
Posting a completed Eurocheque (from your bank) is cheap but slow and risks theft. Asking your bank to send the money by telex or mail transfer is safe, but usually takes 3-4 working days and the charges may be high both for sending and receiving. So those methods are best kept for large sums. However, some banks charge less to transfer to their own branches abroad, or to banks they have agreements with. But if speed is essential both Western Union and American Express do same-day transfers to most major cities – for a hefty price.

Complaining about Banks
If you have a complaint write to the manager of the branch concerned. If that fails write to the Customer Services Department at the head office. Then, as a last resort, there is the banking ombudsman.

The banking ombudsman is a lawyer appointed by a council and paid for by the major banks. His job is to sort out complaints by customers when complaints to one of these banks have failed to get results. He offers a free service as an impartial referee and he is in touch with other ombudsmen and where necessary he may refer a complaint on. You can get leaflets on this service by phoning, but complaints must be made in writing.

Making the Most of Your Building Society
Most building societies offer accounts very similar to those of banks. However, they may not offer all the same services and it can be surprisingly hard to do a simple thing like transferring money from your account to someone else's. Before using one ask all the questions you would ask of a bank (page 501) and see how it compares. You might also bear the following points in mind.

- The society which gives you the best deal on a deposit account may not be the one which gives you the best offer on a loan.
- Some societies sell travellers' cheques free of commission – saving you the 1 per cent charge.
- Several societies are linking up with travel companies to provide their savers with discounts – a plus.
- Several societies are joining large national networks of cash dispensers.

Borrowing Money

We are fast becoming a nation of credit junkies. 'Buy now, pay later' is the message many advertisements blare out. In fact it is almost impossible to live today without borrowing – even if it's only a mortgage. In the right circumstances borrowing can be a very good idea. However, it must be done with caution, and the terms of the loan checked very carefully.

Numerous banks, credit card companies, finance houses and even back-street money lenders will lend you money. They often suggest they are doing you a favour. They aren't. *You* are doing *them* the favour. Your interest rate is their profit. And if you think you have been charged excessive interest, talk to a CAB or lawyer. The courts can now rule on extortionate interest, but the best protection against those who charge such interest is not to borrow from them (see page 507).

Safer Borrowing
Before you borrow money check the following points.
- The APR (see page 511).
- Is the interest fixed for the whole of the loan period or will it change as interest rates change?
- Can you get tax relief on the loan? Where you get the money and what you spend it on can affect this. Ask the Inland Revenue.
- Will the lender be charging a fee for fixing the loan? Even a bank may charge for this.
- Over how long a period may the loan be repaid, and what other options are there?
- Does the lender want any security, such as your home or an insurance policy as a guarantee? See page 505 on the risks of using your home to secure a loan.
- Could you get better terms from any other source – have you *really* explored all the options?
- Is there a monthly or quarterly fee on that 'free' loan?

Addresses and suggestions for further reading are at the ends of chapters.

WARNING: Wives and live-in lovers should beware of acting as surety for money their partner borrows. Or of allowing such borrowing against a jointly owned home. Giving your consent *isn't* just a formality. If the business fails *you* will be liable for the debt – even if you are divorced by then. There are moves to tighten the law on the warnings a lender must give, and the rules surrounding such guarantees. But, as I write, once you agree to back *any* borrowing your partner may be able to increase the loan without telling you. Talk to the Independent Banking Advisory Service which advises on this. It is hard to say no. But it is even harder to become homeless if the business goes bust, or be lumbered with thousands of pounds of debt.

It is always hard to keep track of borrowing, but it pays to keep a strict check on it.

- Have a file for all papers related to any borrowing.
- Keep a note of each payment you make and get a receipt if it isn't by cheque.
- If you have problems about repayment, write letters and keep copies of the letters.
- If the money you owe is being collected from you, ask the head office if you would pay less if you took the money round yourself – there is sometimes a collection charge.
- When you have paid off a loan, ask for a statement in writing confirming this.

Your Rights

If you discuss a loan away from the offices of whoever is lending the money, *and* sign the agreement away from the offices, you have a right to a 'cooling off' period in which you can change your mind and cancel the agreement without penalties. You should be given a copy of any agreement you sign, and it ought to explain these rights. But you should also be sent a separate notice of your cancellation rights. From the day you receive this you have only a few days in which to cancel, so do tell them *the moment* you change your mind. Then immediately confirm *in writing* and make sure that you get proof of posting from the post office.

The government publishes **Consumer Credit Tables** which spell out the cost of loans of all sizes, with a range of interest rates, and for varied periods. The OFT (see page 692) has a leaflet telling you what tables cover which rates, and the tables can be bought from HMSO (see page 693). But your public library should have, or get, the table you need. These tables allow you to find the true APR on any agreement you enter into.

The OFT also produces a range of free, readable and very helpful leaflets on borrowing and debt.

If you decide to pay off your loan early, some lenders may make a charge for the interest they will lose by the debt being paid early. However, they are not entitled to *all* the interest you would have paid. In the Consumer Credit Act 1974 there is a formula for how much the lender may charge. A CAB or Money Advice Centre can give you the details.

Borrowing Money Against Your Home

One of the most dangerous ways to borrow money is to get a loan against the value of your home. For IF YOU FALL BEHIND WITH THE REPAYMENTS YOU MAY LOSE YOUR HOME TOTALLY. Don't be fooled by the wording. When anyone says it is a secured loan they *don't* mean *you* are secure: they mean *they* are. Secure is knowing that if you can't pay they can get their money by selling your home. They do give you any money left over from the sale after taking their capital and all the interest. But that will be meagre compensation for being made homeless. Many of the finance houses which offer such loans charge *extremely high interest rates* (though they may be worded to seem lower) and large brokers' fees may also be concealed in the agreement. Companies offering these 'second mortgages' must now make it clear that you may lose your home. But each year those who through illness and personal problems get behind with their payments tragically end up homeless.

If you can't meet any loan secured against your home don't panic. The moment you have problems, go to a local Money Advice Centre or a CAB, or talk to the manager of your building society or bank. Very often simply talking the matter over with someone else will let you see a solution. A reasonable company will usually extend the loan period. If it is a 'rip-off' company charging excessive interest it may be possible to get the interest reduced by going to court. But *don't wait*. Try to find a solution *before* they try to take your home.

The fact that the home is jointly owned by a husband and wife does NOT prevent a company from selling it to cover a debt taken on by only one of them. There are insurance policies which provide an income if someone becomes sick or is made redundant. Before using your home as security against a loan, it might be wise to take out a policy which would allow you to keep paying the interest on the loan if things go wrong.

Choosing Borrowing

A lot of people feel that borrowing is really rather bad. But borrowing has nothing to do with virtue and a lot to do with common sense. If prices are rising fast and it will be cheaper to buy something today, despite the interest on the loan, it is sensible to buy now, pay later. But if prices are stable and borrowing expensive, it pays to save up and pay cash. However, it is never wise to borrow more than you can pay back – *even if* you fall sick or lose your job.

Financial facts change daily, check the latest figures before making a decision.

★ It is illegal for anyone to accept a social security benefit book as security against a loan or debt.

Credit Unions

Credit unions allow the ordinary consumer to spit in the eye of all those who charge high rates on money. What happens is that a group of people get together and pay money into a central fund. Members can then borrow from this at a reasonable level of interest. As money in the fund gathers interest, the savers also get a yearly dividend.

To form a credit union people must have some common bond, such as all working for the same firm, living in the same street, or belonging to the same organization. There are strict rules on how such unions must be run. To find out more contact one of the Credit Union organizations on pages 542-543.

Free Money

The best borrowing of all is, of course, interest free, and there are more free loans than you might think. It is crazy to pay on the nail if credit will cost you nothing. Keep your money and use it to earn interest.

Some shops offer interest-free loans to buy goods in their sales, usually over 6-12 months. There really are no hidden snags – unless the prices are higher than elsewhere. The only cost is whatever your bank charges to service a standing order.

Using credit cards – but paying the bill *in full* before the 'pay by' date (see page 513) – can give several weeks' interest-free money.

Some stores have accounts which are interest free if you pay within a certain time. If you buy at the start of the month that's a month's interest-free money.

Mail order firms sometimes let you pay in stages at no extra cost Great if the prices are reasonable. But do ask in writing if it really *is* interest free. It isn't always clear in the catalogue.

> Do remember that free loans can be expensive if you time your repayments badly.

★ Although it *is* possible to get loans for free, be suspicious. If anyone doesn't want money on the nail there may be a snag. Look for the APR. If you can't find one, write and ask to be told the APR – by law you must be told the truth.

★ If you buy something on credit and it is faulty *don't stop paying*. If you fail your side of the bargain you could lose your rights. So pay while you complain.

Hire Purchase

If you buy on credit you own the goods even if you haven't paid off the debt. With hire purchase you don't own the goods until you have paid the whole sum. So you can lose them if you don't keep up payments. These will include interest and possibly hidden charges so ask for the APR *before* signing any agreement.

Loans v. Overdrafts

Loans can be obtained from a wide range of financial organizations, from reputable banks to disreputable money lenders, and the rates will vary according to whom you obtain one from, and also what type of loan you have.

A **personal loan** is usually more expensive than an overdraft, but is for a set time at an interest rate set the day you sign the agreement. If rates are rising this could be better than an overdraft. For overdraft rates change as interest rates rise. And you pay the rate at the time you pay back the money – not the time when you signed the contract.

An **ordinary loan** is also for a set time but the interest rate isn't fixed – the better deal when interest rates are falling.

Pawnbrokers

Pawning something is usually a very bad way to raise money. If you need money that desperately, how certain can you be that you will have the money to get your valuables out of hock before the pawnbroker has a right to sell them? Family fortunes have been thrown away by those who always thought they'd be able to get the next object back. Had the objects been sold they would have fetched many times as much and far less would have been lost.

If you do pawn something you should be given a paper telling you how you can get it back. Normally you must repay the sum in full by a certain date. If you can't, you must pay interest on the money, or lose the object you pawned. However, the pawnbroker doesn't have to insure the object. If it gets lost you have no comeback – and you still have to pay back the money.

Interest Rates on Borrowing and APRs

Some ways of borrowing money always cost more than others. So, although the following chart won't tell you exactly how much borrowing costs, it will let you compare the cost of borrowing money in different ways.

The APR ought to be called WICEY – What It Costs Each Year. For it should represent the *real* cost of borrowing the money for a year and includes not just the interest but also the other costs which are part of the loan, like brokers' fees. By law anyone lending you £15,000 or less must give the APR but there are some exceptions. Credit card companies and banks giving overdrafts are among them. But some APR's don't include all the charges they should.

The chart shows that getting a planned overdraft may be the cheapest option. But banks are no longer the only reliable places to get overdrafts. Some building societies and other forms of legitimate financial organizations are beginning to offer them. This means there is more and more competition. That should mean that they are fighting for customers and competing on interest charges, so shop around.

You don't *have* to borrow from your own bank or building society. You can borrow from any organization you wish.

Addresses and suggestions for further reading are at the ends of chapters.

The Comparative Terms of Borrowing

The table below DOESN'T use the current interest rate. For easy comparison it uses a base rate of 10%

Type of loan	Minimum	Maximum	Repayment time	APR	Comment
Planned Overdraft	nil	What your bank manager will permit	As agreed with bank manager, usually short	12.5%	Reasonable interest charges but heavy bank charges may not be in the APR.
Credit Card	nil	Your credit limit	Indefinite, if you pay the agreed minimum monthly	26.5%	An expensive way to borrow. Avoid it.
Gold Card	nil	Varies according to card, may be £10,000	Indefinite	13%	Good value and you aren't running up bank charges.
Bank Revolving Credit Schemes	£180-£300 depending on scheme	Up to 30 times your monthly saving, i.e. £50 a month saved lets you borrow £1,500 at a time	Indefinite	20%	More than an agreed overdraft, so why use it?
Store Revolving Credit Schemes (Budget accounts)	Around £100	Up to 30 times your monthly saving	Indefinite	35%	Very expensive, even more than credit cards. Avoid it.
Bank or Building Society Personal Loan	Usually around £300	Around £10,000	Within 1-5 years	20% (business loans cost less)	Usually marginally cheaper than a credit card but almost always more expensive than an agreed overdraft.
Personal Loan from a Finance Company (or Shop)	Usually several hundred pounds	Around £10,000	1 to 5 years	35%	Usually far too expensive, don't touch it with a barge pole.
Using your Insurance or Pension	Around £100 against your insurance plan, £1,000+ against your pension.	It depends on your policy. Check with the company.	May be taken from the sum due when the policy ends.	Variable	The cost is usually reasonable but it could seriously damage the long-term return on your insurance or pension plan.
Unplanned Overdraft	Nil	Until your bank says stop	To be agreed, usually short.	22.5%	*Much* more expensive than a planned overdraft. And there may be hidden extra charges.
Money Lenders	Any	What they feel like	As arranged	Often over 1,000%	Usually daylight robbery. *Avoid them.* They lead to trouble.
House Mortgage	Usually £5,000	A set multiple of your income	Usually around 25 years	11% over 20 years	Reasonable, usually a good buy but shop around for the best deal.

Financial facts change daily, check the latest figures before making a decision.

Revolving Credit and Budget Accounts

A budget account is also called revolving credit and it doesn't go round to your advantage. What happens is that you agree to pay a certain amount to the shop each month – like the old Christmas clubs. Then the shop allows you to spend more than you are paying in, raising your credit level each time you make a payment. The shop doesn't officially charge interest but it does make service charges. Those who have done the sums have found that those charges often come to even more than the interest on a credit card – and that itself is too high.

Budget accounts are a wonderful way for shops to seduce shoppers and boost profits. But *they are a very bad deal for the shopper*.

Refusal of Credit

If you are refused credit:

- always try more than one company
- ask why they are refusing you, although they are not always obliged to tell you
- be realistic about your ability to repay – you may be able to obtain a smaller sum.

Most companies use a computerized system of credit scoring, i.e. you must score several points for various factors (such as length of employment with current employer, income, length of time at a current address) and your total must be within an acceptable range.

Many companies use credit reference agencies to check your credit history. If you think you have been turned down on this basis see Law, page 449. If you think you have been refused credit because you are a woman this is illegal – contact the Equal Opportunities Commission (page 497).

Budgeting

Pick up almost any book on personal finance and the author will tell you to write down your income and expenditure and budget carefully. It is good advice – especially for anyone who is getting used to having an income for the first time. Arranging it in columns helps. Split up your possible expenditure into headings such as: food, drink, clothes, travel, entertainment, cigarettes, rent, heat etc., sundries. Then tot up each column at the end of the month.

I was blessed (and also cursed) with a Scots headmistress who used economics lessons to din it into us that the essence of money management was to make choices. We had to write down expenditure, then look at what we had spent our money on, and ask ourselves if we had really had as much value out of spending it that way as if we had spent it some other way. Then if the answer was 'no' she said we should try to stop spending money that way the following month. It was very good advice.

Budgeting for the Broke

It has to be said that all budgeting advice is best suited to those who have enough money and leisure to do it If one is really hard up, searching for the cheapest of everything, and doing every job the least expensive way absorbs so many hours in the day that there seems to be

no time to budget. What's more, if one does write it down, seeing how close one is to being broke, or how the debts are mounting, is deeply depressing. I have lived like that and anyone who simply can't face budgeting in those circumstances has all my sympathy. I couldn't either. That doesn't mean letting chaos reign. Some steps can be taken to make ends meet, if not exactly overlap.

- Work out what you can do without. A lot of spending is automatic. Stop buying the things you don't care about so you *can* buy those which matter to you.
- Try to be extra thrifty for a while and build up a small kitty, then use this to allow you to buy larger quantities of items like detergent which are cheaper in bulk. Small quantities aren't always more expensive, weight for weight, but they usually are.
- Only carry a cheque book or credit card if you know you have to buy a single expensive item which you have planned for. The rest of the time carry only enough cash to cover what you really need.
- Work out how much major bills will come to each month and transfer that much into a special account in the bank or building society and don't touch it for any other purpose.
- Buy fresh food in markets or in inexpensive butchers and greengrocers. Supermarkets are only good value for fresh food if you shop in the last few hours of Saturday, when they are marking food down. But their own brands are often best value for basics like detergents.
- Cut down on cleaning materials (see pages 155-156).
- Stop boosting chemists. The average healthy person does not need sticking plaster, antiseptic mouthwash, cough and cold medicines, laxatives, and so on. In Sickness explains why.
- Use energy carefully – see page 223.
- Finally, the most useful step I ever took was to adopt the policy that whatever it was I couldn't afford it. Only if I could convince myself – the following day – that something was totally *essential* would I allow myself to buy it. Making oneself take a day to think can make a lot of purchases much less appealing.

Debt

Few things are worse than owing money and feeling there is no hope of paying it off. But you aren't alone: there are people who can help you. More and more free Money Advice Centres and Debt Lines are springing up: ask your reference library. Many local Trading Standards offices run such centres and if there isn't one the CAB will help.

However, you may prefer to cope alone. I don't advise it. But if you want to, the first thing to do is face the problem. You may well feel frightened and simply want to put the bills in a heap, unopened, and pretend the whole nightmare isn't happening to you. Believe me, the worst part isn't the bills, it's what is happening in your head. You can't *really* forget a problem like that. Once you face it you will find that, however bad it is, the situation is less bad than you feel it is.

Addresses and suggestions for further reading are at the ends of chapters.

> Whatever you do, DON'T borrow more money to pay off old debts (unless a Money Advice Centre or similar unbiased adviser says it is the best course). And don't sell anything which you haven't fully paid for.

Step 1 Get the leaflet 'Debt, a Survival Guide' published by the OFT (a CAB should have it).

Step 2 Face the bills. The first thing to do is write to each company to which you owe money:

- say you have a problem with paying
- say that you are sorting out your finances
- ask them to give you a short time to do that

Step 3 Add up your income – pay, social security, pension, any other sources. Ask yourself whether you could get more money. Have you talked to the CAB about what state benefits you could get? If not, do so – whatever the social security office has said.

Step 4 Very carefully add up what you *must* spend each week to live – rent, council tax, heat and light, food, travel to work, essential clothing. Add up a separate list of how much you spend each week on items which you could live without, but like to have. Add the totals from these two lists together. If you take that figure away from your income, how much is left? If there is nothing left, look at the second list and decide what you could give up. It may be lousy to give up cigarettes and drink, if you enjoy them, but the worry of serious debt is probably worse.

If there is still nothing left even if you do without all luxuries, you MUST get outside advice – unless you can see a way to increase your income or cut your costs. A new head may see a solution you can't see.

Step 5 If you have some money over (even if only after doing without all luxuries), look at all your debts and how much you are expected to pay per week, month or year – if there is such an arrangement. Write two lists. In list A put those which must be paid to avoid losing your home or your heating – rent/mortgage, council tax, gas, electricity, or a loan secured against your home. Put all the rest in list B.

See how you could share out the spare money each week between the organizations on list A. (Leave a little for those in list B and do the same.) Make sure that those to whom you owe most get the most. It may mean each gets very little but at least they can see you aren't just ignoring them.

Step 6 Now write and give each of the companies or organizations these facts:

- your income per week or month
- your outgoings on absolute essentials (including a small sum for emergencies)
- your debt to them
- that you wish to pay it off
- how much you are offering to pay off each week. Also tell them *briefly* if there is some good reason why you got into debt (for example if you were ill or made

redundant). And ask the council, gas, and electricity about their schemes for helping people in trouble.

> *Make sure the sum you offer is one you can keep up.* It is better to offer a smaller sum and stick to it, than offer more and end up getting behind again. *Keep a copy of all letters you send and of all replies.*

Usually a company would rather have some money – however little – than go to the hassle of taking you to court or repossessing your furniture. Once they agree to your proposals, set up a system for paying. If you have a bank, see if the money can be paid automatically – if you won't be charged for this. If you are paid in cash, put the money to pay the debts aside – the instant you get it – into an account on which you don't get charged for putting it in or taking it out.

Once the system is running smoothly you can begin to work out ways to increase your income. There are always more ways to make money than there seem to be at first sight.

> WARNING: If you agree to act as 'guarantor' or to 'stand surety' for money someone else borrows it means that if they don't pay the money back you have to pay it in full, plus any interest they owe.
>
> If you don't agree to act as guarantor, or sign anything, you aren't usually liable for anyone else's debts. Not even those of your husband, wife or child (but see 'Borrowing Money Against Your Home' page 505).

Being Taken to Court for Debt
If a creditor threatens you with court you won't end up in a debtor's prison. That was in Dickens's time. Debt is not a crime: it is a mistake. And someone to whom you owe money must not harass or threaten you – with the law or with violence. If they do so, report them to the police or the Trading Standards Officer. People need a licence to lend money and they can have their licence taken away if they break the law.

You can get free legal advice from a law centre – your public library or CAB can tell you where to find one. Also solicitors who do legal aid work may be able to give you free advice (see page 490).

Don't wait for legal advice before dealing with papers from the court. Reply within a few days. If you admit to owing the money but need time to pay, you fill in an Admission form (if you haven't yet been through Steps 1 to 6 above, use them to help you fill in the form). If you deny owing all or part of the money, you fill in a Defence form.

The court normally decides that a certain sum must be paid to the other person each month. You *must* stick to that sum. If you can't do that because your situation changes you should *immediately* write to the court and ask for the amount to be changed. If you simply fail to make the payments the creditor can:

- ask for a bailiff to go in and take your property to the value of what is owed (he can't take your partner's property though)
- ask for an attachment of earnings, in which he is paid out of your wages or salary before you get it
- put a charge on your home. This means that if you fail to keep paying off the debt your home can be sold and the money taken from its sale. This can be done even if a home is jointly owned and only one person is in debt.

One way to avoid any of these may be to ask the court for an administration order. In this they look at your situation and work out what you should pay to whom and you then pay the whole sum to the court and the court pays the creditors. This can only be done if your debt is under a set figure.

> In Scotland different terms are used but the procedure is very similar.

Financial Calculations

The way in which interest rates are expressed doesn't always leave you much the wiser. The figures are all there but the real rates can seem oddly unrelated to those which appear on paper.

If the figures aren't totally clear, and you are planning to borrow or to invest, it is well worth working out exactly what the interest rates will really mean. This isn't hard. If you have a calculator it is just a matter of going step by step through one of the calculations below.

As even the mention of anything to do with maths can make some people's minds close up like a poked sea-anemone, I just want to clarify a few terms.

Percentages

The basic thing about percentages is that you pay, or receive, so much in every hundred. If you borrow £200 at 5% interest, you have to pay back £200 plus 5 interest for every hundred. So you pay back £10 in interest.

But that statement above was meaningless. The missing factor is time. And it's here that people can end up paying far more than they expect. If you pay 5% per annum on that £200, you obviously pay £10 a year. But if you pay 5% a *month* you could be paying out £10 × 12 = £120 a year *in interest*.

It is on this that it is easy for people to be caught out. Suppose you were desperately needing money to pay a bill, and your local money lender offered to lend you £300 at 16% interest a year. You hesitate, as the interest sounds high, and he says 'I tell you what I'll do, just for you I'll make it ½% a week'. Have you got a bargain? Would you have done better or worse if he had offered 2% a month? (Answers on next page.)

The answers there were based on simple interest, but

when compound interest is used – as it is in most business situations – what is owed can mount up remarkably quickly.

Borrowing – Compound Interest

Compound interest is the system used by most organizations which lend money.

With compound interest, if you can't, or don't, pay back money you owe, and don't pay the interest either, that interest is added to the basic debt. For the next time period you then pay interest on the initial bill *and* on the interest. This sequence of paying interest on interest can stack up month by month, making the total year's interest far bigger than the sum you first borrowed. If you ran up a bill for £100 and the interest rate was 10%, and you paid off neither at the end of the first month, the figures would look like this.

Month 2: Your bill was £100 at a monthly interest rate of 10%. You didn't pay, so £10 interest was added to £100 = you now owe £110.

Month 3: You didn't pay, so 10% of £110 was added to your bill = £11. This means your bill for month 3 is £110 + £11 = £121.

Month 4: If you don't pay it, 10% of £121 will be added on = £12.10. So your bill for month 4 is £121 + £12.10 = £133.10.

At this rate, if you keep on failing to pay the total bill you will owe £313.84 at the end of the year and £213.84 of that will be interest. Credit card companies charge in the same way and the sums mount up. Of course, if you have invested money and the interest keeps being added to the main sum (usually called the principal) it is very good news. The catch is that whereas money is often lent by big organizations on a basis of monthly compound interest, they usually *pay out* interest on a yearly basis.

Calculating Compound Interest on Investments

If you are investing money on a compound interest basis there is a formula for calculating how much your money will have grown by any year you care to name. The formula looks hard but taken step by step, with a calculator, it is easy enough. If the way it is written is unfamiliar, look up the Rules of Mathematics (in Facts and Figures) because the order in which you do the calculations makes a big difference.

P – stands for the principal, i.e. the sum you invest
R – stands for the annual rate of interest
n – stands for the number of years it is invested

The deposit grows to $P(1 + R)^n$ but as R is a percentage, you have to put it over 100 before you work with it:

$$P\left(1 + \frac{R}{100}\right)^n$$

So investing £100 at 10% p.a. for 3 years and compounding the interest goes like this:

$$£100\left(1 + \frac{10}{100}\right)^3$$

which gives $£100(1 + 0.1)^3$

which is £100 $(1.1)^3$.

Powers, i.e. the $(1.1)^3$, have to be dealt with first. $(1.1)^3$ is 1.1 x 1.1 x 1.1 = 1.331

So you have £100 x 1.331

So after 3 years the principal has grown to £133.10.

Calculating Simple Interest

With simple interest you only earn interest each year on the basic sum you invested – even if you don't take the interest out. So if you invest £100 (the investment is called the principal) at 10% you get just £10 interest each year, and after three years the £100 invested has only grown to £130.

To calculate the interest you will get by this method over a given period of years you use the formula:

$$\text{Interest} = \frac{\text{principal} \times \text{rate per annum} \times \text{period of years}}{100}$$

So in the example above, interest $= \dfrac{100 \times 10 \times 3}{100}$

So interest over 3 years totals = £30.

> Answers to the questions on previous page.
> Over a year the interest on £300 at 16 per cent a year = £48
> Over a year the interest on £300 at 2 per cent a month = £72
> Over a year the interest on £300 at ½ per cent a week = £78

The Annual Percentage Rate (APR)

When you are borrowing money, the interest you will pay on it is often quoted in ways which conceal the true amount which you will be paying (see page 494–495). Consumer legislation has made it compulsory for organizations like building societies and banks to quote you the Annual Percentage Rate – known as the APR – which is the true cost of borrowing over a year. But even reputable banks don't always include *all* their charges in the APR. So check the APR *and* ask about other charges. Also there can be some sneaky tricks to disguise APRs. A full-page advertisement in the national press by a mortgage corporation proclaimed:

Our rate is now 10.8%
(Typical APR 10.25%)

Anyone glancing quickly at that might suppose the APR was lower than the other rate: .8 looks less than .25. But they have left out the zero after the .8 – 10.80 is the real figure. To see just how different it is, apply these percentages to figures. Borrowing £60,000 at rate of 10.25% per annum would cost £6,150 a year. Borrowing £60,000 at rate of 10.80% per annum would cost £6,480 a year. A difference of almost £10,000 over 30 years. So it's wise to look at quoted APRs very carefully.

Mortgage Repayments

When you take out a mortgage whoever you borrow the money from should tell you, if you ask, precisely what the repayments will be each year. But interest rates change, and when they do it may be easier to work out the figures for yourself than to ask them to revise their figures. Those not mathematically inclined may recoil from the formula. They needn't. If they substitute their own figures for those I give, and follow step by step, it's just like walking up a hill: all you need to do is put one 'foot' in front of the other – and, with a calculator, the walking is being done for you.

The formula is:
The annual repayment =

$$P\left(1 + \frac{R}{100}\right)^n \times \left(\frac{\dfrac{R}{100}}{\left[1 + \dfrac{R}{100}\right]^n - 1}\right)$$

P stands for the sum borrowed – the principal
R stands for the annual rate of interest
n stands for the number of years the mortgage will run
Suppose you have a £40,000 mortgage so P is 40,000
borrowed at 12% p.a. so R is 12
with repayments spread over 30 years so n is 30
The first thing you do is replace those letters in the formula with the matching figure. This gives:

The annual repayment =

$$40,000\left(1 + \frac{12}{100}\right)^{30} \times \left(\frac{\dfrac{12}{100}}{\left[1 + \dfrac{12}{100}\right]^{30} - 1}\right)$$

First deal with the small fractions inside the brackets, i.e. divide each 12 by 100. This gives:

The annual repayment =

$$40,000(1 + 0.12)^{30} \times \left(\frac{0.12}{[1 + 0.12]^{30} - 1}\right)$$

Now do the additions inside the brackets. That gives:

Annual repayments =

$$40,000(1.12)^{30} \times \left(\frac{0.12}{[1.12]^{30} - 1}\right)$$

The 30s at the top right-hand corners of the brackets are powers. That means the figure in brackets needs to be multiplied by itself that many times. There are tables to give you the answer or you can keep pegging away on a calculator till you reach the answer – but I suggest you keep a note on paper of how far you have got; it is very easy to lose track. In this case it comes to:

Annual repayments =

$$£40,000 \times 29.96 \times \left(\frac{0.12}{29.96 - 1}\right)$$

Next take the 1 from the 29.96 in brackets, which gives you:

Annual repayments =

$$£40,000 \times 29.96 \times \left(\frac{0.12}{28.96}\right)$$

Financial facts change daily, check the latest figures before making a decision.

Divide the 0.12 by 28.96 and you get: 0.0041436

Annual repayments = £40,000 × 29.96 × 0.0041436

Next multiply 29.96 by 0.0041436. Since multiplying a number by anything less than 1 makes it smaller, you needn't be surprised that:

Annual repayments = £40,000 × 0.1241422.

Multiply these together and you find that

Annual repayments are £4,965.69.

Borrowing v. Using Capital

Anyone self-employed or running their own business may find themselves needing to buy a piece of equipment, or perhaps a car for business use, and wondering what is the best way to finance it. Should you borrow the money at the lowest rate of interest you can find? Or should you use capital which could otherwise be invested to draw interest? As the rate of interest paid to you is usually lower than the rate you pay out when you borrow, it looks at first sight as if the prudent course is to use capital. In fact, it isn't as simple as that.

The interest on the capital is probably taxable at the rate for *investment* income. But the money you pay in interest on a business purchase can usually be set against the taxation on *earned* income. So the cash benefits will vary according to the two rates of tax. The easiest comparison is to find the cost per year on each, once tax is allowed for, *at imaginary rates*, as follows:

In each case the cost allowing for tax =

$$S \times \frac{I}{100} 1 - \frac{T}{100}$$

Taking some imaginary figures it works like this.
S – stands for the sum you need to spend – say £4,000
I – stands for the rate of interest per annum – let's say you get 8% if the money is invested, but pay 10% on the money if you borrow it.
T – stands for the tax rates – suppose the interest if it's invested is taxed at 30%, you can set the interest paid on the loan against tax at 28%.

So, with these imaginary figures, *if you use capital*,

the real cost is $$£4,000 \times \frac{8}{100}\left(1 - \frac{30}{100}\right)$$

which works out as £4,000 × 0.08(1−0.3)

which becomes £4,000 × 0.08 × .7

Multiply these together and the annual cost of buying out of capital is shown to be £224.

But *if you borrow* the money the real cost is

$$£4,000 \times \frac{10}{100}\left(1 - \frac{28}{100}\right)$$

which becomes £4,000 × 0.1 (1−0.28)

which is £4,000 × 0.1 × 0.72

Multiply those together and the annual cost of borrowing is shown to be £288 a year.

With these imaginary tax and interest rates it still looks as if it is better to use capital. That isn't necessarily so. Even with both the interest and the tax rates stacked against borrowing, the difference in cost is only £64 a year and a fair proportion of this could be offset by capital growth if you invest your money wisely. Also, borrowing leaves your capital free for other things – like holidays, or medical emergencies – for which you'd be unlikely to get a loan or which you couldn't set against tax.

Paying with Plastic

Used wrongly, paying by plastic can be the road to ruin but it also has distinct advantages.

● You can use your card to order and pay by telephone.
● Used carefully, they give you interest-free loans.
● They may give consumer protection (page 513).
● You can pay overseas without the cost and hassle of changing money.
● It allows you to pay for goods costing more than the £50 backed by a cheque card.
● Charge cards have no pre-set spending limit so they are very useful in emergencies abroad when you might need to buy a plane ticket in a hurry.
● With some, you can pay money over and have an account in credit, then draw on this for cash when abroad without the hassle of traveller's cheques – and some pay you interest if your account is in credit.
● Some can be used to draw cash in banks or from machines – but watch the charges.
● Some of the perks may be appealing, such as discounts on travel or hotels, or private health insurance, or the use of a lounge at London airport.

Credit Cards v. Charge Cards

Credit cards and charge cards are often confused. **Credit cards** don't always charge you for having the card. They let you repay your debt slowly, and charge interest if you don't pay within a certain time. For example, some major companies such as National and Provincial still don't charge, as I write.

Charge cards always charge you for having them, and you must pay your bill *in full* when it arrives. If you don't, they make a 'late payment charge' which increases with time. This can make late payment even more expensive than failing to pay a credit card bill.

Access and Visa are credit cards, whereas American Express and Diners Club are charge cards. Although a charge card may be useful for the traveller, credit cards are accepted at more places than charge cards, and on the whole are perhaps better value than charge cards. However, charge cards may score on loans at good rates via gold charge cards (see page 507) – all gold cards are charge cards, not credit cards.

Access or Visa run all the credit card operations. But the banks and building societies which offer credit cards each set their own terms to customers. Even two cards offered by the same bank vary greatly in their initial charges, perks, interest rates and how fast you need to pay to avoid interest charges. So see who is charging what and what the perks and conditions are. When you apply you can ask for the credit limit you want.

Addresses and suggestions for further reading are at the ends of chapters.

★ Some credit cards, such as the National Provincial Visa, can carry your photo, for extra security.

Gold Cards

Gold, and other special, cards are issued by both charge card companies and banks – for a higher yearly fee. There may also be a joining fee in the first year. To get one you need to have earnings above a certain limit – but the limit may not be as high as you'd expect.

You get an automatic borrowing facility that is usually in five figures, immediate cash drawing rights of several hundred a day, plus an amazing range of perks from free annual consultation with a tax and investment consultant to lectures on antiques. But usually the most valuable perk is that the interest rate is so reasonable it could save you the cost of the card if you needed to borrow several thousand pounds.

How Cards Work

Credit and charge cards can be a blessing or a curse according to how you use them. Once you start using a card you will receive a statement each month saying what you owe. The blessing is that they can allow you interest-free credit for several weeks. The free loan works like this: you buy something on the first day you have the card. At the end of the month the card company sends you the bill. At the bottom it will give a date by which the minimum payment must reach them – usually some weeks from the date of the bill. So you pay weeks after you buy. During that time your money could be earning interest in a deposit account, so you could be *making* money on the deal. The trouble is that the loan is *only* free if you pay off the *whole bill* before that date.

If you leave *any* part of the bill unpaid, or even a day over the due-by date, interest clocks up alarmingly for you are immediately charged interest on the amount outstanding not just from the 'due-by' date but *from the date of the bill or from when you spent the money.*

> WARNING: If you draw cash with a credit card the charges on this *aren't* delayed until the 'pay-by' date. Some cards charge you interest on a percentage basis *from the date it appears on your statement* (i.e. almost immediately). Others don't charge interest but charge a single flat-rate fee (1.5% as I write), provided you pay in full by the pay-by date. If you don't, you *also* pay interest, as on any unpaid debit. So check the terms of your particular cards before using them to draw cash

Credit card companies may let debts go on mounting. You cannot rely on them to put a brake on your spending. So the great rule is *never spend more by credit card than you can afford to spend in cash* – then the money is there to pay the bill in full.

Charge cards are different. They expect you to settle your bill in full and may cancel your card if you don't pay up quickly enough.

How to Save at Cards

★ Pay your bill *in full* by 3 days before the last payment date – then you get maximum free credit and never pay interest.

★ If you might forget to pay your bill in time, pay it *the instant* you get it, but postdate the cheque to 3 days before the final payment date. It might be wise to attach a letter saying the cheque is postdated and asking them to hold it until the date.

★ If your credit card company refuses to take a postdated cheque, still postdate it and put the envelope where you can't miss it, and place a big note beside it saying 'Post on . . .' and a date a week before the money is due.

Interest Rates on Credit Cards

Failing to pay a credit card company is a *very* expensive way to borrow money (see page 507). In real terms the cost of borrowing on a card can be as much as *twice* the lowest bank lending rate. And some store cards which operate like credit cards charge interest at almost *three times* the lowest bank lending rate. *It is financial madness to borrow at such rates when you could almost certainly borrow more cheaply elsewhere.* Quite rightly, credit card companies have been strongly criticized by the National Consumer Council.

The Law and Your Cards

By law, if your credit or charge card is lost or stolen and used by someone else, you are only liable for the first £50 – though some companies set even lower limits. And from the moment you notify the company you cease to be liable at all. If you lose your card you should immediately report it to the police and the credit or charge card company – even if you aren't sure if it was stolen. The police have the card companies' phone numbers. Your card will then be cancelled and a new one issued.

By law, the credit card company has joint responsibility with the retailer for whatever you buy with the card, provided you spend above a certain limit. This can give you extra protection if the article you buy is faulty. Illogically, charge cards are *not* covered by that act, so they give no extra protection but some offer it voluntarily.

If a company has a sign up saying it takes credit cards it must not refuse them unless there is an equally large sign saying in what circumstances it refuses them. However, shops may legally give a discount for cash but charge the full price for card payments.

The Pinpoint System

This is probably the shape of things to come. You feed your credit card into a machine, tap in your PIN number and the machine lets you have the goods you want and the bill is automatically charged to your credit card.

Tips on Using Cards

★ Check all payment slips against your account.

★ Paying with cards when overseas saves you the commission on changing traveller's cheques. However, you could lose out in currency fluctuations. Visa payments in *any* foreign currency are first converted into dollars, then into sterling. Neither is done the instant you pay, so a time gap could lead to something costing more than you expected.

Financial facts change daily, check the latest figures before making a decision.

★ In some countries there is a trade in the carbons from between the layers of a credit card bill. Numbers can be read on them and used for telephone purchases or forging cards. When travelling it's wise to ask for your carbons.

★ Don't put cards in a safe deposit box in a foreign hotel. In some countries there is a roaring trade in forged cards, and they are easily 'borrowed' from a safe deposit.

★ On an expensive item it is sometimes worth using credit cards in reverse. Shops pay a percentage of every credit card sale to the card company; so if a shop takes credit cards say you'll pay cash if they discount the goods by 5% (most shops pay 3% to 7% to the card company so they gain by this and so do you).

Ready money will always command the best and cheapest of every article of consumption, if expended with judgement; and the dealer who intends to act fairly, will always prefer it.

Enquire Within, 1856

Shop Cards
More and more shops are offering cards. Confusingly some are run like charge cards and some like credit cards. Check whether interest will be charged if you fail to pay the account in full within the set time. The interest on some shop cards is daylight robbery.

There is no point in getting a store card unless you often shop somewhere, like Marks & Spencer or John Lewis, which doesn't take credit cards. The more cards you have, the harder it is to budget.

Most of all, avoid cards which ask you to pay money into an account in order to be allowed a loan later. These are really budget accounts with plastic trimmings (see page 507). If you have money to pay in anywhere, put it in a bank or building society which pays interest. Then you can spend it where you want.

Trust not him who seems more anxious to give credit than to receive cash. The former hopes to secure a hold upon you in his books; and continues always to make up for his advance, either by an advanced price, or an inferior article: whilst the latter (who takes cash) knows that your custom can only be secured by fair dealing.

Enquire Within, 1856

Switch Cards
Debit cards such as Switch are simply 'plastic cheque books'. The money is taken out of your account in a day or so. No credit is involved. See also page 504.

Protection Plans
There are several companies which offer 'protection' for your card. You pay a fee and let them have all your credit card numbers. Then if your cards are lost or stolen you just ring the 'protection' company and it notifies all the card companies. Those companies often benefit more than you do, as you are only liable for the misuse of a credit card up to a small set sum (see page 513).

However, frequent travellers may find it convenient to have just one number to contact 24 hours a day, especially as some of the companies will rush interest-free cash to a stranded client. There may also be key tags which will direct your keys back to you, if you lose them, via the protection company – safer than having your own address on them. You can also ask them to hold the numbers of documents, such as your passport, so if it was stolen you could just ring the company and ask for the numbers. Of course, all this suggests that you go round with the phone number of the protection company engraved on your heart. For how on earth would you find it out if everything was stolen in Bogota? American Express and Diners Club each have their own card registration service. For other cards see the companies on page 541.

PLANNING FOR TOMORROW

The 1986 Financial Services Act tried to prevent consumers being ripped off by dishonest advisers and set up Self-Regulatory Organizations (SROs) which authorize firms to advise on financial planning. SROs were supervised, in turn, by the Securities and Investment Board (SIB). Under this system financial advice can only be given by members of certain Registered Professional Bodies (RPBs), such as the Law Society, or by authorized firms, which SROs judged competent, honest and solvent. Unfortunately, as we have seen in the press, some dishonesty continued.

From mid-1994 all advisers on personal finance are under the Personal Investment Authority (PIA) or an RPB. These come under SIB and SIB should be able to tell you whether a firm is licensed to give advice.

The PIA has plans to tighten the rules. The snag is that by law those who advise and sell financial services (pensions, life insurance and so on) must either be 'tied agents' selling only one company's 'products' (often their own) or be totally independent. Few are independent.

In law any financial adviser must discover a client's circumstances and give advice in that *client's* best interests. But this need only mean choosing the most suitable product from *their* range of 'products'. And, both independent advisers and tied agents may get larger commissions and perks if they sell some products not others.

However, *all those who sell long-term products, such as life assurance, or pensions, must now tell you about such incentives to sell any product.* You are also entitled to know what proportion of your payments actually goes towards your pension, life insurance or whatever, and what proportion they take as commission. *So ask* – these are new rules and they might forget to tell you. And before using a tied agent, talk to several.

If a firm does not seem to act in your best interests, first complain to the PIA, or to the RPB given on the firm's papers. They are able to penalize the firm. You can also go to court for compensation – and even get the assistance of the PIA or RPB in this. However, if they fail to handle your complaint properly, ask SIB to take it up or use the investment Ombudsman. The SIB has leaflets on how the whole system operates and what the rules are.

Insurance

You can now buy insurance from a company belonging to any EC country and you can also buy non-life policies from Switzerland. To trade legally, companies must be officially approved in their own country and the DTI (page 694) can tell you if a company *is* approved. By law, you must also be given details of that country's complaints procedure when you buy the policy.

There are several key rules when it comes to buying insurance.

- Compare what several companies have to offer.
- See if buying direct, not through a broker would cost less.
- Read the small print *very* carefully.
- Having chosen a company, be sure you know *exactly* what it covers you for and what the terms are.
- Ask if there are any circumstances which would allow you any kind of reduced premium. There are often small clauses which you may already have met without realizing it, which would save you money. But look critically at clauses which give you a reduction – some are totally unrealistic.
- If you fail to tell the insurance company anything which *it* thinks is relevant to your insurance, your whole policy may not be worth the paper it is printed on. And you can't even get a refund. So include *every* fact that might interest them. And, if the broker fills in the form, check it before signing and see if all the facts are there. If you don't it's *you* not the broker who will suffer. And if something happens, after you take out a policy, which could alter your standing with an insurance company, write and tell them.

Even with the greatest care you may not be able to rule out all problems. Someone I know is locked in battle with one of the biggest companies in the land. He claims a lawn mower is a garden tool, they claim it is a vehicle and therefore not covered by a household policy.

Buying Insurance

You can buy insurance direct just by writing to the companies, or you can buy through a broker. It costs the same either way. Brokers advertise in Yellow Pages. But it's usually best to go to one who specializes in a particular type of insurance. You can get the names of specialist brokers in your area from the **British Insurance and Investment Brokers Association (BIIBA)**. Then ask several brokers to see what deal they can get you and insure with whoever does best for you.

You may be able to get an even better deal by searching hard yourself, but the advantage of brokers is that, if they are any good, they know not only which companies are cheap but also which pay up with decent grace. There's little point in getting a cut-price premium if getting the company to pay makes getting blood out of a stone seem easy by comparison. So do ask the brokers about this before deciding who *is* offering the best deal.

Claiming on Insurance

If you need to claim, act fast. If you claim too late you may get no money at all. How fast depends on what is insured, but it ranges from 24 hours to within several weeks. You needn't send in all the details immediately but do phone your insurance broker or the insurance company as fast as you can. Just say you will be claiming and why, and ask for a claim form. But make a note of the name of the person you speak to – as a precaution in case they forget to log your claim. If you don't feel up to phoning, someone else can do it for you. But the longer you leave it the less likely you are to get your money. The same applies if someone else will be claiming against you. *You* must tell your company as soon as you know this is happening. You must also take steps to see that the damage isn't made worse for lack of attention. For example, you should prevent rain coming in through a damaged roof. But keep the bills because you will need to claim for them.

With some types of insurance you can claim whether or not it was your fault. If, for example, you drop a lighted match on the upholstery and the house burns down you should still be insured for the house. Comprehensive car insurance also covers you even if you cause the accident. However, with some types of insurance your claim won't be met if you haven't taken 'reasonable care'. This applies particularly to losing things or having them stolen. But never assume you aren't covered. If your policy doesn't make it plain: put in a claim and see what happens: insurance is full of small print and for once it might work in your favour.

★ If something is stolen, here or abroad, always report it to the police and get documents from the police to prove you have done so. Otherwise you may have trouble claiming.

How fast the company will expect to receive the form varies with the type of claim. It's wise to write and acknowledge the form when you receive it. Also, ask the company how soon they need it back and whether you should start repairs and claim later. The more information you can give the better. If you are claiming on house contents and have valuations or receipts, send photocopies of them with the claim form. But, if the values are out of date, your claim should show the current replacement value of every item, plus what deduction you have made if your policy compels you to allow for wear and tear. Calculate this item by item, as different items have different life expectations. If something would normally last 10 years and it's 3 years old, you take 3/10ths off the current price.

If you can't face the job of claiming after a major disaster you can ask a loss assessor to do it for you. But he or she will probably charge a percentage of the sum you get from the insurance company (and you can't add the assessor's fees to your claim). Before taking on an assessor, get a written estimate of the likely fees. You can find an assessor through the **Institute of Loss Assessors**.

★ Keep a photocopy of your house inventory and of each of your insurance policies at your bank or some other place away from your home. You would need them after a fire.

Financial facts change daily, check the latest figures before making a decision.

Complaining About Insurance Problems

If you aren't happy with the way your insurance claim is being handled, first complain to your broker or the branch where you bought the policy. Then complain to the head office. If that fails, contact the regulatory body for the company in question. It must tell you which it is, and the addresses are at the end of this chapter.

You can't complain directly to a Lloyd's underwriter. But you can complain to the manager of the Advisory Department of **Lloyds**.

If all these fail there is the **Insurance Ombudsman Bureau (IOB)**. If the company is a member of the IOB he will investigate (free of charge) and make a decision which the company must follow if you agree. But you are free to reject his decision and take the matter to court. Or, if the other side agrees, to the **Institute of Arbitrators** (see page 499). If the company belongs to the Personal Insurance Arbitration Service (PIAS), not the IOB, you can only use PIAS with your insurer's permission. Any PIAS decision is binding – you cannot then go to court.

Car Insurance

It is illegal to drive any car unless it has at least third-party insurance. This must now provide the minimum legal cover not only in Britain and Gibraltar but also in all EC countries (although *what* you are covered for will vary in each country). It doesn't cover injuries to you, or to your car or theirs. So don't think an old banger only needs minimum cover. If you damage someone else's car it could cost you dear.

Within Britain:
Third Party only pays if you kill or injure someone (including your passengers) or damage someone's property (it doesn't have to be a car) while driving.
Third Party, Fire and Theft also gives cover if your car, or its accessories are stolen, or if it catches fire.
Comprehensive Insurance covers third party, fire and theft, and all accidental damage to your car.

The cost of car insurance varies hugely with the type of car, where you live, who will drive it (the fewer people, the cheaper), and the company you choose. A growing number sell direct to the driver, at very competitive prices, and some are known to deal with claims speedily (always a point to check). But shop around: ask for quotes from brokers, motoring organizations and the club for your make of car, too – if there is one. Also more and more companies offer reductions to people in certain categories: teetotallers, low mileage drivers, those in certain occupations, accident-free drivers, and so on. *Which* magazine reports on this make a good starting point for phone calls, and are in reference libraries.

A policy may also cover you to drive other people's cars, but before anyone else drives your car you should ask for their name to be added to the insurance if the insurance doesn't cover other drivers. This can be done – often at no extra cost – for even very short periods. This is where a good broker, who knows you, is useful. If you are changing cars you can also switch the insurance with just a phone call.

No Claims Bonuses

If you make no claims for a certain number of years most insurance companies give a 'no claims bonus' – they reduce your premium by a set percentage, for each year in which no claim has been made. The more claim-free years, the greater the reduction. However, you may lose part of it if you make any claim at all. Normally you go back 2 notches on the scale. So before claiming for a small sum check whether you will lose more in bonus than you are claiming. Some companies allow one broken windscreen a year without loss of bonus, and others allow you to insure against loss of bonus.

Health Insurance

Accident Insurance

Personal Accident Insurance is what it sounds. It pays if you have an accident in the course of your work and can't work. However, it may not cover you for accidents unconnected with work. So other cover is needed for those playing contact, or dangerous, sports. Most sports clubs offer insurance. But, in some policies, any lump sum for disablement will go to the club, to manage for you. This can save you losing state benefits but may not be ideal in other ways. So it's a point to check.

Dread Disease Insurance

Dread disease cover provides a lump sum at the time of diagnosis if you are hit by one of an assortment of diseases, including cancer or a heart attack, or if you die – for any reason – having made no claim. Permanent health insurance is normally a better bet.

Permanent Health Insurance

The rather ineptly named Permanent Health Insurance (PHI) provides an income each week if you fall ill and are unable to work. You can either be paid a fixed sum, set at the start; or you can agree a sum which is index-linked, so it increases with the cost of living. This last is the better bet.

Either way the payments will only start when you have been off sick for a certain period – which you set when you take out the policy. The shorter the waiting period the higher the premiums, but companies vary greatly in how short a waiting time they will allow. The cost also varies with your age and whether you agree to payments stopping at retirement age.

If you are employed, don't take out PHI without asking your employer how you are covered if you fall ill. Some policies taken out by employers reduce benefits if someone is getting money from elsewhere: dreadfully unjust, but it's allowed. Also check the tax position: whether PHI benefits are taxed may depend on who paid the premiums.

If you decide you want PHI, look at the policies of as many companies as possible and *do read the small print*. There can be all kinds of hidden snags. For example, some reduce what they pay if you get state benefits – and so on.

Addresses and suggestions for further reading are at the ends of chapters.

Private Health Insurance

A vast number of companies now offer health care insurance. Private health care has great advantages, but the standard of medical care doesn't *always* match the NHS. Nor will health care insurance always give cost-free care. It is usually full of limiting clauses, whose existence is obscured by purple prose, glossy brochures and glowing images. And key facts are often either left out or put in documents you may not even see till *after* you sign on.

So, compare policies very carefully looking for what *isn't* said. For example, most won't cover pregnancy and long-term illness, and some exclude out-patient treatment or those over a certain age. However, some do cover unconventional fields, like chiropractic treatment – if a doctor recommends it. This variation means there isn't a best buy to suit everyone. To find the best one for you, first work out your possible needs in detail, then read the small print of several policies and decide which suits your lifestyle and family. A married woman might want pregnancy cover but no sports cover; a bachelor the reverse. But I have yet to find an affordable policy which covers *every* type of care anyone might want.

Before buying also ask what would entitle you to a discount on the premium. Often being a member of a motoring organization or holding a certain credit card will get one – if you ask. Also group policies are often cheaper than individual ones and often allow wives and children to be included. So many professional bodies, unions and societies have cut-price schemes for members, or you may even be able to form your own group, for the numbers needed can be as few as three.

Most policies for those of 60 or over now qualify for some tax relief in the form of lower premiums. This applies even if the premium is paid for them by a friend or relative and covers couples if one of them has reached 65. But premiums go up sharply with old age.

To find the best buy either takes an immense amount of effort or needs a highly specialized insurance broker, such as the **Private Health Partnership**, familiar with the *whole* of this rapidly changing field. Few general brokers know it well enough.

Home Insurance (Building Insurance)

If you have a mortgage, the mortgage, company will suggest firms to go to for insurance. You may benefit from the buying power of the mortgage company. But not always, however; you have a right to check other insurers and, if you find a better deal, ask the mortgage company if they will accept it. However, if they do they may charge you an administration fee for the extra work. (See also page 454.)

Building insurance covers all buildings and outbuildings, plus most things which are fixed and part of the house and its grounds, including swimming pools, gates, walls, paths and drives. The cover includes most, but not all, of the accidents which could befall a home: flood, fire, subsidence, and so on. It also covers your liability to someone injured on your property because you didn't maintain it properly. So if a friend falls through your floor, you're covered.

The damage must, however, be *fully* caused by some specific trouble like a storm, gale or accident. If your floor was on its last legs anyway, insurers will only pay a token amount – and could pay nothing at all.

> If you are buying or selling your home there are strict rules as to who is responsible for insuring it at different stages and these vary between England and Wales, and Scotland. Check with your insurance company and make sure it is never uncovered and your responsibility.

Exclusion Clauses

Exclusion clauses may mean you can't claim if someone falls through your floor because of dry rot, woodworm and a whole range of similar problems which are specifically excluded. Nor can you claim the cost of the treatment and rebuilding they bring upon your head. And these are by no means the only items which a policy may exclude. So any policy needs to be searched for these traps.

Excess Charges

Policies may have clauses saying you pay the first £xxx of a claim of a certain type. Particularly when it comes to subsidence and landslip.

How Much to Insure For

The essential point to remember is that you insure to cover the cost of rebuilding the house – not its market value. The **Association of British Insurers** (page 542) issues a table to guide you, as rebuilding costs vary with the region as well as with the value of the house. They are based on square footage and most insurers have specimen tables showing the average square footage of various kinds and sizes of house. They are often adequate. Otherwise measure the width and depth of the house, and of all outbuildings, and find the area. Then multiply the area by the cost per square foot in your region. But if your house is unusual in any way you may do better to have the cost of rebuilding estimated by a surveyor. The Royal Institution of Chartered Surveyors can give you the name of someone suitable, and so can the Incorporated Society of Valuers and Auctioneers (pages 268-269).

> WARNING: One of the more astonishing injustices of the insurance system is that some policies pay out *nothing at all* if you haven't insured for the true value. Others pay out but, if you were under-insured by 20 per cent, they pay out your claim minus 20 per cent. Obviously rising costs can put any policy at risk of this unless it is index linked. *Read the small print very carefully* and go for index linking if you can.

Remember to check these points on any buildings policy.

- Are you covered for the cost of living elsewhere during repairs?
- What is the value of that cover (it's usually a percentage of the sum insured)?
- Are there any clauses whereby you pay the first £X on any claim? If so how much and on what aspects of the claim?
- Is it index-linked?
- Does it cover the cost of restoring the building to how it was or does it make it 'as new'?

If you are renting check whether the landlord is paying building insurance and what it covers internally. You may be responsible for insuring the rest.

House Contents Insurance
Insuring the contents of a house covers more than just theft or damage to the objects. It may also cover you if your china ducks fly off the wall and peck someone. Contents insurance should also cover a tenant for most types of damage to the building. Surprisingly this type of insurance may also cover personal liability. This is for damage you do to someone else or their property even if the accident isn't in the house. There are also a multitude of other risks it can embrace.

Because they can cover so many types of risk, and may depend on the security of your home, contents policies vary considerably in cost. So a good insurance broker is invaluable. Give her a list of the types of risk for which you would like to be covered, then ask her to suggest others. Decide a final list, and ask her to find companies which will give a good price on those risks. Then compare it with direct insurance by phone (page 542)

★ Insuring in a high risk area can cost many times as much as in a low risk one. But companies don't totally agree on what *are* high and low risk areas. Look for a company that doesn't rate the risk in your area too highly.

Exclusion Clauses
There are always exclusion clauses for fair wear and tear, revolution and war, and anything may cease to be covered if you take it out of the house. (So cameras and jewellery should usually be covered by an all-risks clause within the policy.) What's more, some policies have a clause whereby cover ceases if you leave the house empty for over 30 days, which could be disastrous if you go on long trips or might be away in hospital.

> WARNING: Each time you buy something new of value you should tell the insurance company in writing and ask them to check that your cover is sufficient or you could be under-insured. Most policies will have a clause that you have to give details of individual items above a certain value.

Types of Policy
You can choose between several types of policy.
With **indemnity** cover you don't get the full replace-

ment cost. Instead you get the value of the item, bearing in mind the loss of value because of its age and wear. (Depreciation is not applied to objects which don't depreciate or which rise in value – such as antiques.) This is a relatively inexpensive type of policy, but it can leave you heavily underinsured – so you lose out badly if some disaster happens.

With **replacement as new** cover you get the full cost of replacement. This is the most expensive type but the best. A cheaper version is to get limited new-for-old cover in which you only get full replacement if the object is under a certain age (often 2 years old).

If a policy covers you for **accidental damage** you will be covered even if it is your fault.

You can't always choose which to have, as some objects are only insured on an indemnity basis. But some companies offer mixed policies which allow you to insure some things on one basis, some on another. Also different policies set different age limits for 'as new' replacement. This is something to compare before buying insurance.

How Much to Insure For
There's no short cut to working out insurance. You have to list the contents in every room, including things of value which are out of sight, and tot up the value. You *must* insure everything, you can't decide that the sofa is too old to bother about. Some policies won't allow items of value to exceed a certain percentage of the policy – on the assumption that people don't *just* have valuable things to insure. Items of special value like jewellery and antiques must usually be listed and need a special valuation. If some items are on an indemnity basis ask about depreciation rules and value them accordingly.

In making the valuation, remember that the rules about being under-insured may apply (page 517). So an index-linked policy is safest.

★ In some policies items insured on an all-risks basis are not index-linked. Check this and adjust their insurance each year if the index-linking doesn't apply.

★ Photograph valuable paintings or objects and keep the photos in your bank (See Trace page 496)

> Before accepting money from an insurance company for a missing object, come to a written agreement that if it is found they will return it to you and you will refund their money. Otherwise it belongs to them and they may not even tell you if it is recovered.

Life Insurance
In the dim and distant past, life insurance was simply a matter of a group of people getting together, saving some cash, and the money in the kitty was paid to the family of whoever died that year. But, in the middle of the eighteenth century a mathematician called James Dodson set about devising plans that were linked to how long people were expected to live. And so today's life insurance industry was born.

Addresses and suggestions for further reading are at the ends of chapters.

Life insurance salesmen are known for being the sharpest in the business. Don't tangle with one unless you have researched the matter quietly first. Those who are tied agents (page 503) need only recommend the best policy *from the company they represent*, whereas independent advisers should give the client the *best* advice – not simply to recommend whichever company give them the best commission. Either may get the bulk of your first year's payment as commission but, as I write, need only reveal the commission they will be getting on any insurance which could be an investment. But this may change: so ask. Either way, they still have a vested interest in selling you *some* life insurance. But – do you need it? If nobody would suffer financially if you died, the answer is 'no'.

Don't let the terms life insurance and life assurance confuse you. Life assurance is the technical name for life insurance. As I don't like jargon I won't be using it.

Life insurance is very simple. You pay money every year and the company pays out if you die (or sometimes if you retire). It's a rather morbid gamble. The figures are geared to your personal life expectation. If you die young the company loses and you (in a sense) win. If you live long and pay long they win, you lose. But, as I write, no tax is saved on insurance premiums.

You can also take out life insurance on other people but, in case you were planning the perfect murder, there are limits to those whose life you may insure. You can't buy life insurance against the possibility of strangers dropping dead. You have to have an 'insurable interest', which is some legal or financial relationship which would justify you benefiting from the person's death. So it only covers marriage partners, children and employees. However, there are several types of life insurance.

> If you agree to buy life insurance and change your mind tell the company *at once*. A cooling-off period, on some types of insurance, allows you to change your mind, if you act fast.

Term Insurance

With term insurance you pay money to the insurance company *for a stated time* and if you die during that time your dependants get a cash sum tax free. You can choose how much will be paid at your death and how long you wish to pay the instalments. When you stop paying, the insurance stops, and if you have carelessly failed to die you get nothing for your money.

If you were a man aged 29 and wanted to buy a 20 year policy which would pay out £25,000 on your death, it would cost perhaps £6 a month at current prices, having risen sharply because of AIDS. A woman would pay slightly less, as women live longer than men.

Level term gives a set sum which is fixed when you take out the policy. You can also buy a level policy which, if the holder dies, gives a fixed tax-free income for a set period of time instead of a lump sum. **Increas-**

ing term means that if you drop dead in year 5 your family gets more than if you die in year 4. The steps are usually pre-set and the money could be a lump sum or an income for a set period.

One of the best options is **convertible term** insurance, which usefully gives you the same basic protection as the other term contracts, but allows you to turn your policy into a different kind of contract – one offering investment returns, for instance – you can do so, even if you are at death's door at the time. Insurers cannot 'load' your premiums or turn you down. But you must make your decision before the first policy ends.

Whole Life

With a whole life policy you pay life insurance until a set age or until you die. Then your dependants get either a lump sum or regular payments. The figures for these are set when you take out the policy and don't change. However, the policy can be bought 'with profits' or 'without profits' (see below). It will also have a surrender value if you want to cash it in, though doing that in the early days could mean you get back less than you pay in, as the broker's commission and setting-up costs come out of your early payments. This type of policy costs several times as much as a term insurance, but it does guarantee something for your money.

> Insurance is an important, complex, changeable and expensive business. It is worth reading the Office of Fair Trading's very good leaflets (page 496), and possibly those of the ABI, before you buy.

Endowment Policies

The system is that you pay premiums (monthly, quarterly, or annually) until a certain date, upon which you get a lump sum which was set at the start of the policy. If you die before the date, your family gets all the money which would have been paid on that date. Sometimes policies last for 10 years, but after that you can continue paying in money, or take your proceeds then and there. Within this there are two variations. A **with-profits** policy guarantees a minimum sum if you die very soon after taking it out, but that minimum will rise yearly as annual pay bonuses add up. And once insurers announce them, the bonuses cannot be withdrawn. This ensures that the contract's value builds up year by year. There is then a final bonus when the policy is due to end. Originally these bonuses were just the icing on the cake, but they can now be half the cake. The results vary sharply from one company to another, and the right life policy may give you twice as much as an insurer with a lacklustre record. In a **without-profits** (non-profits) policy only the agreed sum is paid. This last is usually a bad buy. Your money would have done more for you elsewhere.

Unit-linked Insurance

This is a curious creature: an insurance policy mated

with an investment fund. The money you pay is split, so part goes into buying units in an investment fund and the rest goes to pay for term insurance. However, a very small figure is usually set for the sum guaranteed by the insurance, and its value depends largely on the – unpredictable – value of the units at the end of the term. The payment can either be a lump sum or regular premiums.

What Happens if You Can't Pay

If you want, or need, to stop paying a life premium the policy will have a surrender value. But, as in war, there's not much joy in surrendering. Unless it has run more than half its time you are likely to make a loss – and that's on top of the value your money has lost with inflation.

A better option could be to ask the company to convert the policy to a 'paid up' basis. This means that it is frozen until it matures (i.e. until it would normally have paid out), they then pay less than they would have done on a fully paid policy but more than its surrender value would have been. There may also be the option of paying premiums again if your finances improve.

Travel Insurance

Don't assume that any automatic cover provided by your credit card will be sufficient – often it will only cover certain aspects of travel insurance. The cover you need depends entirely upon the value of what you're taking, the country you're going to and activities you intend to pursue while abroad. Shop around and *read the small print carefully*. Check that the cover for medical expenses, personal liability, lost baggage or money, and cancellation or curtailment is enough. You can't assume that any policy gives enough cover in all areas. And cover for emergency fly-back is essential unless the medical facilities where you're going are excellent. Also you are unlikely to be covered for active sports or hazardous activities so you need to take out special insurance for these.

★ Some policies only cover you for loss from the time you leave home until you land on British soil. So if your valuables are stolen just after landing in Britain you can't claim.

School Fees Insurance

School fees have shot up much faster than inflation over the past few years and sending a child to a fee-paying school can now cost more than buying a house. The easiest way to pay school fees is to take out an insurance plan, when the child is very young indeed, which will pay out a certain sum each year over a set period of years, after a set date. How much is paid out is entirely a matter of the type of policy and what is put in. So work out how much the fees are likely to cost by the time the money will be needed – allow for at least 10 per cent increase a year on current costs. The **Independent Schools Information Service (ISIS)**, (page 320) can give you the names of companies offering such policies. Or talk to the School Fees Insurance Agency.

Emergency Help

If you don't take out insurance early you can make last-minute arrangements. Banks have schemes for borrowing for school fees on terms which allow the money to be repaid over a long period. But you must also take out insurance which guarantees that the bank can't lose its money if you die.

If you already have life insurance you may be able to get a loan from the insurance company, against this policy, without it affecting your life policy, provided the loan is paid back. (See also Assisted Places page 299).

> Choose an educational insurance scheme which will allow you to use the money for something else if circumstances change. Eighteen years is a long time and a government might ban private education before then.

Mortgages

Mortgages are very simple. Instead of paying the full price of a home, you put down some of the money and ask the mortgage company to pay the rest. So you own it but the mortgage company has certain rights over it. You then repay the money on a monthly basis, plus interest on the loan. But if you don't keep up the payments, the mortgage company can sell your home and take back its share of the money plus the interest you owe. So don't spend so much furnishing or doing up your home that you can't meet the mortgage payments if you fall ill or lose your job.

Most mortgages are from building societies and banks and some give priority to account holders. But you don't have to save with a company to get a mortgage from it and, when offered a mortgage, remember: the company isn't doing you a favour. When you borrow from a financial institution – you pay, they gain.

What's more, surveys have shown that even advisers in banks and building societies often recommend whatever mortgage will give them the best commission – often an endowment mortgage. They may also make a tempting mortgage package depend upon you buying redundancy or household insurance from them, often at premiums far higher than they would be elsewhere. But these tie-ins aren't always made clear before you sign. So, in many ways, this is a rotten sector of financial services which needs a good clean-up. Meanwhile do a lot of shopping around and small-print reading. *Which* has done some good reports on mortgage snags and the leaflets and video from the **Council of Mortgage Lenders** cover the basic steps on buying a home and are in some public libraries.

The mortgage scene changes constantly. Besides the basics given below there are now unit-trust mortgages, interest-only mortgages and, for erratic earners, non-status mortgages.

★ Some companies offer employees the best terms of all. But do check what would happen if you wanted to leave the job before the mortgage was paid off.

How Much You Can Borrow

The percentage you can borrow on a mortgage varies with the economic climate. Often companies will lend you 80-90 per cent of the price.

The actual amount will depend on your income. But two incomes can be counted instead of one. You needn't be a couple, you could be friends of the same sex.

You can often borrow 2-3 times the main borrower's yearly salary, before tax. On a shared mortgage you can add on 1 × the second income. The repayment time is usually 5 to 25 years and, generally, the longer the time the more the total payment.

In deciding how much you can afford, don't forget that you also agree to pay interest – *at whatever rate the lender chooses*. This rate varies as general interest rates change. So be prepared to pay a higher rate than the one in force when you borrow. However, some companies sell mortgages at fixed rates. These are a gamble. If interest rates drop you lose, if they rise you win. Look hard at the political scene before choosing.

Those who would find it hard to pay full interest may be able to find an equity scheme by which less interest is paid but the mortgage company takes part of the profits when the property is sold. Or in which the mortgage company becomes part-owner of the property.

If you have problems paying a mortgage tell the mortgage company *at once*. You may be able to renegotiate the loan and pay smaller sums over a longer time. It is much better to ask for this than to fall behind on your payments.

Major Types of Mortgages

Endowment Mortgages

Mortgage brokers may try to push these. No wonder: they often get fat commissions on the premiums you pay for the insurance. It is often a bad buy.

With an endowment mortgage you take out a life insurance policy which will pay out the value of the mortgage exactly when the mortgage must be repaid. Meanwhile you pay monthly premiums for life insurance and pay interest to the mortgage company. Endowment policies are explained on page 519 and the fact that a mortgage is linked in doesn't alter the rules. You can use a with-profits policy or one without profits.

A **low-cost endowment** has cheaper premiums. This is a with-profits policy. But you insure for less than the full mortgage, gambling that the extra profits will pay the difference. If they don't, you have to find the balance out of your pocket.

The insurance premium is calculated on your age and fitness. The younger and fitter you are the less you pay. Once the premiums are set they stay the same until the end of the policy. The only exception is a low-start, low-cost endowment mortgage in which you pay less in the early years of the premium. This is geared to the young with low salaries but higher expectations – but the higher payments could be tougher to pay if a wife stops earning and children have to be paid for too. Don't rush into one without looking at the other possibilities.

Pros	Cons
You know your family will have a roof over their heads if you die.	You have to keep paying premiums even if you sell the house, pay the loan off and go abroad, or accept the surrender value.
You can transfer the endowment to a new home if you sell the first one, but see the cons.	When you want to sell one house and buy another you can't clear the first mortgage and start again as you can with a repayment mortgage.
When mortgage interest rates are under 10 per cent this system is a better buy than when they are over that.	If interest rates on the mortgage go up you can't renegotiate the mortgage to cover a longer period.
	If you fall on hard times the DSS may help with the interest on the mortgage but *not* with the premiums on the policy, whereas it may help with all of a repayment mortgage.

Repayment Mortgages

A repayment mortgage is a straightforward loan given for a set period of time. You then repay it month by month with interest. Your payments in the early years are mostly interest but, as the debt slowly drops, less of what you pay is mopped up by interest and a larger and larger proportion of the debt is paid off.

A repayment mortgage can be safeguarded with a mortgage protection insurance which will pay off the mortgage if you die. But it only pays out the amount needed to pay it off at that time. No extras, no bonuses. If you die the day you have taken out the policy it pays the whole lot, but if you die in the last year of the mortgage it pays out a few hundred. And if you don't die until the mortgage is paid it pays nothing. This is a cheap way of making sure a family isn't left homeless, and it can be taken out jointly if two people are paying towards the home. But premiums are higher for smokers.

Repayments on your main home qualify for tax relief (up to a certain value) and nowadays a system called

MIRAS is used. This stands for Mortgage Interest Relief at Source. What happens is that if you owe £150 a month to the mortgage company and should get tax relief of £50, you pay only £100 to the mortgage company and the Inland Revenue pays the difference. (Those are not real figures, incidentally, but real figures are untidy.) However, now MIRAS only gives relief on *part* of the tax you would have paid.

Pension Mortgages

This is very like an endowment mortgage except that the lump sum used to pay off the loan on the house is the one paid by a pension scheme. Appealing to high tax-payers, as you get tax relief on both the interest to the mortgage company and on the pension plan. However, there are snags.

- It is harder to move house.
- The loan period has to run until you retire.
- If any government decided to tax the lump sum paid as part of a pension you could be in trouble.

By paying slightly more you can also be covered if you are unable to pay the mortgage during periods of illness or when out of work. Rates for these policies vary, so do the terms: some will only cover interest up to a certain level, while others have no ceiling. With some you can't increase your cover without a new health check, with others you can. And some trades unions will offer members cover of this sort at competitive rates.

> There is no guarantee that any pension plan will be able to pay out a sum large enough to pay off the mortgage. It may be *expected* to but if there is a slump the value of a pension normally slumps too.

Shared Ownership and Housing Associations

Some local councils run shared ownership schemes in which you buy part of a home from a housing association, on a mortgage, and the council or a housing association buys the other part. You then rent the rest with an option to buy it when you can. The **Housing Corporation** (page 270), has details of housing associations which sell property or rent it out in the normal way.

Discount selling

Now that business is flat, some housebuyers are offered a scheme where you pay half the price of the house now and half in five years' time.

There are several big snags. You could lose half the house if you don't have enough income to raise a proper mortgage on it. Selling a complete house is tough enough, but selling half a house is impossible. And the property company decides what that other half of the house should cost in five years.

Pensions

There is no getting round it: pensions have about as much charm as a fly and carry a nasty reminder of im-

pending old age, the way a fly reminds of death and decay. However, your quality of life when old depends on taking the right action when young. Not just on how much you put in but on *when* it's put in. If you take a personal pension out at 30 you could get several times as much pension for your money as you will get if you start at 40 – so it pays to take action fast but carefully. For a pension is usually the biggest investment anyone makes in their life – even bigger than buying a home.

> A personal pension may be more vital than ever before. For, with people living far longer, there are growing doubts over whether the state can afford to keep on paying reasonable pensions. There could come a time when there are too many old, and young, supported by too few of working age.

National Insurance and State Pensions

So all embracing is the welfare state that it's easy to suppose one will get state benefits automatically, regardless of what one has paid, just as we get the Health Service. *This isn't so.* To get a state pension you must contribute to it. Everyone who reaches 16 is sent a National Insurance Number Card which should be kept safely as the number has to be given to any employer, or to the tax office if you are self-employed. It may also be needed when claiming benefits. The most important benefit which has to be contributed to is the state pension. The full basic pension is the same for everyone, but National Insurance Contributions (NIC) are in 4 classes.

Class 1 is an earnings-related payment by those employed.

Class 2 is a different flat rate paid by the self-employed.

Class 3 is yet another flat rate paid by those who choose to keep up payments even when they aren't working, for example, during a sabbatical.

Class 4 is a profit-related payment only for the self-employed, collected by the Inland Revenue.

Anyone who is employed and earns over a set sum must pay NIC, and their employer must also contribute. And Class 2 must be paid by the self-employed who earn more than a set amount per year. Class 2 and 3 can be paid by direct debit.

In return for a lifetime of contributions you get a basic state pension which can be drawn, as a right, at the pensionable age set by the state, provided they paid full NI contributions for 90 per cent of their working life. 'Working life' means from about 16 until a state pension would normally start. Those whose payments and credits don't add up to 90 per cent still get some pension but on a sliding scale according to how much they have paid in. If you have paid NIC for half your official 'working life' you get about half the basic pension. But if you have paid NIC for less than a quarter of your 'working life' you get nothing. Though some late payments can be made.

However, there are a host of special rules (see page

523). So *always apply for a pension* – even if you think you haven't contributed enough. The officials will soon say if you aren't entitled to it. And do remember there are special payments for those in special situations – widowed, with children, very old, and so on. So read the DSS leaflets.

Special Rules to Note on State Pensions

- If you were in full-time education between 16 and 18 it won't reduce your pension, even though you paid no contributions then. Pension status may also be protected during illness or unemployment when certain benefits are paid.
- The same goes for years spent at home, since April 1978, looking after children under 19 or the elderly or sick (called Home Responsibilities Protection – HRP). And from April 1988 it applied to SERPS (below) too. HRP also applies to the self-employed who paid full contributions before stopping work to look after someone.
- If a marriage ends in divorce a man or woman who does not remarry before pensionable age can use their ex's contributions to help them meet the conditions for a basic pension. Those divorcing after pensionable age can do the same.
- It is possible to backdate contributions for up to 6 years by paying the voluntary rate to cover unpaid years. Years as a student, when over 18, are counted as part of your working life even though no contributions are paid. Ex-students might find it worth their while making backdated payments to cover these years.
- Girls should be sure to pay at least one year's employed NIC. This establishes their right to home responsibilities protection if they then marry fast and stay at home with their children.
- A married woman who hasn't paid enough contributions can get up to 60 per cent of a single person's pension on the basis of those her husband paid, but she has to wait until *he* reaches retirement age and receives his pension.

The Self-Employed

The self-employed can only obtain the basic pension from the state, as their additional profit-related NIC payments don't count toward any extra pension. However, they can take out personal pensions – with any tax concessions they offer – just like anyone else.

Earnings and Pensions

The government has abolished all restrictions on what you can earn in the first five years after retirement. So your pension cannot be affected by what you earn.

SERPS – the Additional State Pension

SERPS sounds like a rather nasty disease but it stands for the State Earnings Related Pension Scheme. Under the scheme employees make an extra state contribution – scaled to earnings. (You have no choice as to how much this will be. If you pay SERPS you will pay exactly the same sum as everyone else with the same income.) Then, on retirement, you draw an extra pension linked to your earnings. The more SERPS you paid the higher your pension.

You can stay in the SERPS scheme or leave it. But if you opt out, you *must* either buy a personal pension plan instead or go into an occupational pension plan run by your company.

In or Out of SERPS?

The big question is – will you be better off leaving SERPS ('contracting out') or staying in? The answer is, it's a gamble with risks both ways. Governments can cut pensions as well as raise them. And, with more and more people living into ripe old age, there will be increasing pressure to do just that (though the growing power of the geriatric vote might prevent any government going too far). The government has already used carrots and sticks to get more people to move into personal pension plans.

A personal pension plan spares you the risk of being a victim of policy changes and comes with a bevy of tax concessions. But don't imagine that a pension plan is a rock solid investment. Money can only be paid out if the fund managers have made your money grow in the years before. That depends on the world economy as well as their skill. So when pension plans *guarantee* returns they tend to guarantee very small sums – often smaller than you would get with SERPS or a good company plan.

To encourage people to move out of SERPS the government will pay into the personal pension plan of anyone who leaves SERPS a rebate based on a slice of their earnings.

Reasons for Staying in SERPS	Reasons for Leaving SERPS
You know, more or less, what you will get.	You believe you can buy a better pension scheme for the same money.
You are middle aged and won't have time to build up a good personal pension. So SERPS offers more.	Your employer will definitely pay into your personal plan as much as into SERPS.
You don't want the risk of perhaps buying the wrong plan.	You get tax relief on your contributions. You don't on SERPS.
The charges may be high for taking out a personal plan (some money will certainly go in commission).	You can choose your own retirement age (within limits).
You don't like your pension depending on a fund manager and the economic climate.	You can switch between being employed and self-employed without it affecting your pension.
You are a woman and so have less time to build up a personal plan before retirement.	If you want to transfer your personal pension into a company scheme it may be possible to arrange this.
SERPS is indexed linked (at present).	

It will usually make sense for men over 45 and women over 40 to stay in SERPS, and for younger people to leave. But even if you leave SERPS you can always go back. It may be worth reading the DSS leaflets on the issue (page 541).

★ To find out how much SERPS pension you've built up so far, and what it is likely to be if you don't opt out, get the leaflet from a DSS office. You can also ask your local DSS office to give you a pension forecast on the basis of your contributions so far. Then you can see what you need to do to improve your final pension.

> The decision on SERPS is linked to whether or not you are well covered by a company pension plan. So read on.

Occupational Pension Plans

At one time a company could decide to 'contract out' of SERPS and make full-time employees join its scheme. Now joining a company scheme must, by law, be voluntary. So you can either join a company scheme or pick a personal pension scheme of your own.

Up to 15 per cent of your earnings can be tax free if they go into a pension scheme of any kind. But few employee contributions reach that 15 per cent. So, if you want to contribute up to that maximum you can do so either through Additional Voluntary Contributions (AVCs) to an occupational scheme or to a personal pension plan.

Pros of Company Schemes

There are two main kinds of company schemes.

1 The **final pay** type (sometimes called 'Defined Benefits'), under which the size of your pension is linked to your earnings. This is usually via a formula which takes account of both your final pay and the number of years you have been contributing. A good scheme would provide 1/60th of your final pay for each year you paid contributions. So 40 years of contributions to the company scheme would pay 40/60ths (i.e. two-thirds) of your final pay. So the older you are, the more valuable the company's contributions are – and early leavers still lose out.

2 In the **money purchase** type instead of being paid a sum set by a formula, the money paid in is invested and when you retire the money which has built up is used to pay you a lump sum and a pension. This method tends to be favoured by small companies.

Either kind may be 'contributory' (i.e. both you and your employer contribute to it) or 'non-contributory' (i.e. only your employer pays in). Contributions into both types attract valuable tax reliefs, so this is a cost-effective way of saving, and occupational schemes are index-linked by the state just like SERPS.

By law a company *must* contribute something towards an employee's pension, over and above paying its whack towards the basic state pension. It only has to pay into

one extra scheme, it can choose to pay into SERPS and into either a company plan, *or* an employee's personal pension plan. It may be prepared to put more money into one than another. So check what is on offer before deciding where to put your money.

> Every occupational scheme is different and has its own rules. But the trustees of a company scheme must, by law, keep you informed about both the scheme and your rights. If your questions about it aren't fully answered by your manager, pensions or personnel officer contact the **Occupational Pensions Advisory Service (OPAS)**. This government-backed body will help you through the maze and advise on problems with occupational and personal pensions. CABx have lists of its expert advisers all over Britain.

The Old Con of Company Schemes

There used to be a Dickensian system where only life-long loyalty to a single company guaranteed a decent pension. Happily, much has been done to change that. But some of the old rules may still affect certain sections of your pension.

Anyone who has contributed to a company pension scheme for 2 years or more, but leaves the job before reaching pensionable age, may either leave their money in the scheme or transfer its value to another pension scheme.

If you are in a Money Purchase Scheme and leave a job before retirement, and don't transfer your pension's value, your pension fund will keep growing until you reach pensionable age. If you are in a Final Salary Scheme, and left, or leave, after 1 January 1991 your pension will be partly protected against inflation.

> If you paid into a company pension, moved jobs, and lost track of your entitlement the Pensions Registry can help. It is a free governent service which will trace your missing pension. Ask OPAS (page 542) for the application form.

★ If you plan to change jobs negotiate your pension with the new employer before you accept the job. And, if you want to transfer the value of your current company pension into the new company's scheme, make sure they agree the figures as part of the deal, don't rely on general assurances.

The Pensions Ombudsman

The Pensions Ombudsman can investigate complaints of injustice by pension-scheme trustees or managers or – on pension matters – by an employer. He can also deal with disputes over facts of pension law. But he needs *evidence* of bad administration before he can act, not just suspicion.

Addresses and suggestions for further reading are at the ends of chapters.

> If a company goes into liquidation your pension should be safe. A company pension fund is normally administered as a trust and is not linked to the finances of the company. Ask the liquidators for the name and address of the trustee.

Personal Pensions

Since employees could have a personal pension, not a company scheme, every possible financial institution has got in on the act. The hard part will be finding good unbiased advice. A good accountant who is up on pensions could be the best bet. But whoever you choose make sure they are *independent*, not 'tied' (page 503). It's also wise to split your money between several pension schemes by different companies, so you spread your risks. Then have them mature at different times, so you spread your benefits.

The Society of Pension Consultants and the Association of Consulting Actuaries both have lists of firms whose staff offer unbiased pensions advice for a fee (the associations themselves do *not* offer advice). Until now such companies have tended to advise companies rather than individuals, so the fee schemes are still being worked out. But some plan to offer a reasonably priced computerized advice system.

In comparing the benefits of saving for your old age via a pension plan or by putting your money into some other investment, a key point is that your savings aren't tax-free, but the money you pay into a pension plan is. So, in effect, if the tax rate is 30 per cent the government pays about 30 per cent of any pension plan for you, which can't be bad. And you can turn part of your pension into a tax-free lump sum when you retire. The bad news is that you can't take the money out before you retire.

Types of Personal Pension Plan

A **deposit** plan keeps your money safe (but it loses value with inflation) and the pension you get depends on the interest rates when you retire. These deposit schemes may be fine if you are only two or three years off retirement, but rarely make sense for anyone else. However, many companies' AVC plans are tied to such schemes. That is why the right to pick the kind of extra pension plan to suit yourself is so important.

A **non-profits** policy is one which guarantees to give you a set pension no matter what happens. This sounds ideal but, as it gives the company no leeway for adjusting to the economic situation, the sum is likely to be set very low.

Unit-linked (or Managed Funds) pension plans which depend on the stockmarket, are quite risky. Some specialize in certain areas of investment. The safer schemes put money into a range of *different* investments – shares, property or government stock. But returns depend on how the financial markets are when you want to retire. If they are low you may have to postpone retirement until things look brighter.

In **with profits** plans the policy usually guarantees a small pension and/or lump sum topped up by extra money from the profits the company has (with luck) made on the money. You should do better than from a non-profits policy. For you will receive yearly bonuses, which cannot be withdrawn once given – although the insurers cannot guarantee their size. And there is normally a terminal bonus – of up to half the value of the contract – on the retirement.

All these schemes provide you with a lump sum. You can take some of it in the form of an immediate tax-free payment, but you have to turn most of it into a pension. Before investing in one check what your money will be invested in. Safe plans pick safe areas, such as government stock. They also spread the risk between different types of investment.

An **annuity** is often thought of as a pension: it isn't, it's a kind of insurance policy. You pay a lump sum to a company, which then guarantees to give you an income until you die. Some annuities are fixed – bad idea when interest rates are low – some are index linked. A man usually gets a higher income than a woman of the same age paying the same money – as men die sooner. It is one way of getting an income out of a lump sum paid out by a pension plan, or from the sale of a house which is too big for someone elderly. The lump sum belongs to the company.

Points on Buying a Pension

The quality of your pension – and therefore of your life in retirement – will depend on how good the pension plan is and on who is running it. Nobody should rush into buying a pension until they have looked at all the options and taken good advice. Never buy in a hurry, or buy the first you are offered.

- Compare several plans carefully and *look at the track record of the company* (see magazines listed on pages 542-543).
- Remember what matters is how insurers do against each other. When markets are booming, everyone does nicely. Compare a company's record with other insurers' success.
- Insurers must show you two different estimates of the pension you may get: one based on 8½ per cent growth a year, and the other on 13 per cent. But they are theory: no one can predict future growth.
- Ask how much any plan will cost you in commissions and other charges, especially in the early years.
- Ask if they can tell you what it will *really* be worth by retirement, allowing for 5-10 per cent inflation.

One of the key attractions of personal pension plans is that they will have tax relief at source. And the percentage you can put into a personal pension, tax-free, rises as you get older. The tax relief for employees uses the same system as MIRAS (page 522).

The rules for calculating the permitted contributions for the self-employed are complicated and you should consult an accountant if you need to know. At the end of this chapter I also give organizations and publications which will help and advise you.

Financial facts change daily, check the latest figures before making a decision.

Savings

Sarah Bernhardt was right when she said, 'Money isn't everything, but it's so good for the nerves'.

Almost everyone's ideal is to win, save up or inherit enough money to have a nice lump sum behind them: a nest egg for old age or a rainy day, or simply a nerve soother. To lack it is the emotional equivalent to living without an overcoat. The slightest draught of misfortune strikes doubly chill. So it is enormously important to put any savings or windfalls into the right hands.

Money ought to be working for you every minute of its life. If you have more money in a current account which doesn't pay interest than is needed to avoid bank charges, you are throwing money away. It ought to be earning you interest in a deposit account at least. Money that isn't earning is like a factory sitting idle.

If you would be wealthy think of saving as well as getting. The Indies have not made Spain rich, because her out-goes are greater than her in-comes.

Enquire Within, 1856

Savings v. Investments

Broadly speaking, there are two ways to place spare money.

1 Put it into a scheme which guarantees to let you have precisely the sum you put in – when you need it – and meanwhile provides interest that in most cases will fluctuate, in line with what is happening to rates generally. This is a way of saving.
The snag here is that although you can take out the money you put in, you may still lose because of inflation. If the rate of inflation is higher than the interest you are paid – or you don't have the interest added to the investment – the money you take out will have less buying power than it had when you put it in. So even if the figures are the same you have lost money. Of course, if interest rates are higher than the rate of inflation, and you have the interest added to your savings, your capital is safe *and* making money.
2 You can invest the money. You hope that the value of your money will go up and that rising dividends will boost it further. That may happen, but share prices can fall and dividends drop.

Somehow investment has a glamorous air and saving is a bit down-market. (Although one of the smartest investments for a millionaire is in National Savings Certificates.) Don't let that glamour fool you into the common delusion that if money is invested some excellent alchemy takes place and it always comes out larger than it was before. This simply isn't true. When you read the word 'investment' put 'risk' in its place and you will get a feel for the true situation. However, there is nothing wrong with risk if you can afford it. And – as in everything – there are degrees of risk. So the essence of placing money is to try to find the least risk with the most chance of either large growth or large interest.

Decisions Before You Place Your Money

Before you decide where to put your money, you need to think very clearly about what you want from it. This is a short checklist of points to consider – not in order of priority.

1 How much money do you want to place? (There may be a lower limit on how much you can place in a particular way.)
2 How long will you be able to leave the money without using any of it? (Some investments have set lives.)
3 If you might want to get at some of the money how much notice might you be able to give?
4 Do you want to be *sure* you get out at least as much as you put in, or would you be prepared to risk losing it in the hope that it would get bigger?
5 Do you want to build up any goodwill for future borrowing by placing the money with an organization from which you may later want to borrow (e.g. you might need a mortgage at some time)?
6 Do you want any income from the investment or are you prepared just to have capital growth or plough any interest back in?
7 What is your tax position? There is no point in having money in tax-free National Savings Certificates if you don't pay tax anyway. If you are not a taxpayer, you can now collect interest from banks and building societies in full – though you have to go through some formalities first.

Your answers to these questions should help you to decide which of the savings options on pages 527-528 should have your money.

The Rising Cost of Living

In planning for the future it's useful – and frightening – to see how the value of money has changed in the past. If you had £100 in 1914 you would need the sums given below to have the same buying power in the years which followed.

	£££		£££
1918	203.60	1964	502.70
1920	249.54	1966	546.85
1922	183.78	1968	587.39
1924	175.68	1970	658.56
1926	172.07	1972	772.07
1928	166.67	1974	977.48
1930	158.56	1976	1,415.32
1932	144.14	1978	1,775.67
1933	140.54	1979	2,013.51
1934	141.44	1980	2,375.68
1936	147.74	1981	2,657.66
1938	156.76	1982	2,886.49
no figures for 7 years		1983	3,018.92
1946	264.86	1984	3,169.37
1948	304.50	1985	3,362.16
1950	320.72	1986	3,476.58
1952	371.17	1987	3,620.00
1954	383.78	1988	3,798.20
1956	414.41	1989	4,094.59
1958	439.64	1990	4,482.88
1960	446.85	1991	4,745.05
1962	477.48	1992	4,893.60

I am indebted to the Central Statistical Office for these figures.

Addresses and suggestions for further reading are at the ends of chapters.

Some of the Savings Options and What They Offer

Investment	Maximum	Minimum	Interest	Tax	Charges	Duration	Notice	Comments
Building society or bank account paying interest	None	1p to many thousands, according to the account	Varies with the lending rate, the type of account and the company	Paid at basic rate by the account, *not* refundable	Usually nil	Any but you may need to give a few day's notice of withdrawal	The higher the interest the greater the penalty for sudden withdrawals	You can get at your money easily. A good place to keep funds for an emergency. Not *good for those who don't pay tax*. Check out the different types of account before placing your money.
Money market	None	Normally £10,000 but for money invested overnight £25,000–£50,000	Usually better than the best bank interest, but varies	Interest is paid gross	None	Subject to negotiation, often blocks of 7 or 31 days	The same as the duration	Banks put it on the money markets for clients. A short-term move to make money work between other investments.
National Savings Ordinary Account	£10,000	£10	Rarely changes but not high	First £70 interest tax free, all paid gross	Nil	Up to a week	Up to £100 on demand, the rest within about a week.	Tax-free money is always good. Also useful for high earners and those who are not taxable as none is deducted.
National Savings Investment Account (3)	£100,000	£20	Varies	Taxable but paid gross	Nil	1 month	1 month	Much better interest than a National Savings Ordinary Account. This could cancel out the tax advantage of the ordinary account not paying high tax.
National Savings Yearly Plan (2)	£400 a month	£20 a month	Guaranteed for 5 years	Totally free of income and capital gains tax	Nil	No interest if under 1 year, reduced interest under 5 years.	14 working days	Tax free and safe but your money is tied up for a year; otherwise you lose interest.
National Savings Certificates – Fixed Interest (2)	£10,000 but varies with each issue	£100	Fixed, guaranteed, and paid when you cash in the certificates	Totally free of income and capital gains tax	Nil	No interest if under 1 year, reduced interest under 5 years	8 working days	You can take out the money any time, but the interest rate goes up for each year you leave it in, peaking in the 5th year. After that it drops to a flat rate just below the peak.
National Savings Certificates – Index Linked (2)	£10,000 but varies with each issue	£100	Interest at least equal to rate of inflation, extra interest on cashing in.	Totally free of income and capital gains tax	Nil	as above	8 working days	Most attractive when inflation is high.
National Savings Income Bonds (1)	£250,000	£2,000	Variable but one of the highest paid by National Savings. Paid monthly	Interest paid gross but taxable	Nil	1 year (or some interest is lost)	3 months	Interest is paid monthly – useful for those needing a regular income from savings. But withdrawals only in multiples of £1,000.
Capital Bond (3)	£250,000	£100	Fixed but one of the best	Interest paid gross but taxable	Nil	1 year minimum (or no interest paid)	8 days	Gives a good interest rate if you can tie up a large sum for a longish time.

Financial facts change daily, check the latest figures before making a decision.

Some of the Savings Options and What They Offer (cont'd)

Investment	Maximum	Minimum	Interest	Tax	Charges	Duration	Notice	Comments
Premium Bonds*	£20,000	£100	Nil	Any winnings are totally tax free	Nil	Any	8 working days	When inflation is high you lose heavily as the money loses value. But at least ERNIE is a gamble where you get your stake back.
First Option Bonds (3)	£250,000	£1,000	Fixed for 12 months	Paid after standard rate tax	Nil	1 year or no interest	Cash 12 monthly or lose interest	
Children's Bonus Bonds (3)	£1,000	£25	Fixed for 5 years	Free of tax and CGT	Nil	No interest if cashed under 1 year. Less if under 5 years		Only buyable for those under 16. Must sell before 21. Very good rates.

There is also a National Savings option for the retired but, as I write, the details aren't yet decided.
* Lots of Premium Bond prizes are unclaimed. Main post offices have a quarterly list of prizes. Or, if you have moved, send your new address and Premium Bond numbers to National Savings' Blackpool address and they will check for winnings.

Spreading the Load

In general, if you have only a little spare money you should tuck it away as safely as you can, so at least the lump sum will be there, but this can be risky if inflation is high.

A second rule is that as soon as you have enough money to divide into sensible portions you should spread it between several forms of saving and investment with varied advantages and degrees of risk. What you lose on the swings you gain on the roundabouts.

National Savings

Most of the National Savings schemes can be bought over the counter of any post office but they can always be bought by post too.

On all matters related to premium bonds, or to buy or sell those marked (1) on the table on pages 527-528, contact National Savings' Blackpool office, for those marked (2) contact the Durham office, for those marked (3) contact the Glasgow office.

TESSAs

Both banks and building societies offer TESSAs (Tax-Exempt Special Savings Accounts). These are savings accounts on which the interest is tax-free, at the end of 5 years, provided you leave the money in the account for the allotted time and put in no more than the annual amount allowed by the government. A great way to save – unless inflation is high.

Alternative Investments

Alternative investments include art, antiques, stamps, coins – and indeed anything which someone tries to sell you on the basis it will rise in price. The only way to make money on these is to be very knowledgeable. As a general rule don't think of them as investments. Buy what you like and pay the amount of money you consider it is worth to you: any future rise in price is a bonus and if the price falls you have at least enjoyed it. Remem-ber you will not be earning any income from such an investment, so unless it increases in value by a percentage greater than the rate of interest you will be losing money on it every year. If you are offered a 'special' or 'limited' edition, check how many of the products have actually been made. Some of the objects and pictures offered in newspapers as 'investments' aren't even a decent gamble: you would be lucky to sell them for what you paid, let alone make money on them.

Stocks, Shares and Relations

Investing in the stock market is a gamble. But it's like pontoon: the skilled can win handsomely, the unskilled are more likely to lose, and even the cleverest can come unstuck. It is, however, infinitely more fascinating than any other form of gambling and if you have a few thousand *which you don't mind losing*, and enough time to follow the market, you can have a lot of fun.

The fascination lies in using your knowledge and your wits to decide which way a particular share will move. A company may have great profits today, and all the pundits may say its price is low for its potential. But does that necessarily make it a good buy? To decide you need to know about its future prospects and about the competition. For example, is its 'go-getting' managing director about to move elsewhere? Has a major competitor just brought out a product which could clean up? And so on.

You also have to be aware of national and international political events which may affect it, and the overall mood of the stock market. A crash can wipe pounds off the value of shares which had done nothing to deserve it. For example, ICI was £16½ (i.e. £16.50) at its peak and dropped to £9.37. Even when events are less dramatic, international affairs can still be a factor. A company may benefit from a drop in the price of oil, or suffer if there's a political coup in the country from which it gets its raw materials.

Addresses and suggestions for further reading are at the ends of chapters.

But even if you don't have any money to invest, following the market can be a spectator sport as good as watching horse racing. If you find that investing in shares directly is not for you, but you want to put some of your money where there is a bit of excitement, you can opt for a PEP or unit trusts (page 533) instead. You will still be investing in the market, but by proxy. But be wary of those who offer to teach you to invest in the stock market and make it easy. It is always dangerous ground for the small investors and in the 1987 crash it was the small investors who made the wrong decisions most often.

If you want to learn about the stock market you might find **ProShare** (page 543) useful. This government- and Stock Exchange-backed organization was created to tell the public about all aspects of share ownership, including employee share schemes. For a modest membership fee you get monthly guides to the market, visits to companies, seminars, and assorted perks.

Terms Used in Stocks and Shares

Assets and Liabilities
A company's assets include everything it owns which is saleable. The 'fixed assets' include not only obvious items like buildings, equipment and cars, but also valuable trade names and even goodwill. 'Current assets' is the term applied to the money it has in the bank, and any money due to it from goods or services already supplied, plus its stocks of raw materials. 'Liabilities' are the exact opposite and cover outstanding debts.

Bears and Bulls
The difference between bulls and bears may be obvious to everyone else. But it was only when I fixed it in my head that bulls charge forward and toss prices upwards, whereas bears shamble away, that I was able to remember that, in stockmarket terms, bulls are buyers (charging to get the shares they want) and bears are sellers (backing away from the shares they feel are not worth holding). Bulls are optimistic and bears are pessimistic. So when the market is said to be 'bullish' it means people feel prospects are good and share prices are rising overall. A bear market is the reverse.

Blue Chip
The term 'blue chip' is said to come from the colour of the highest chip in poker (a useful reminder that even blue chip shares are a gamble). It is applied to shares in the biggest companies in business: ICI, Sainsbury, the major banks and so on. But is big also beautiful? Not necessarily so. Blue chip shares command hefty prices, but they are not always fast moving. So if you need to sell in the short term you may not cover the broker's fees, even if the price has risen. Nor is it easy to spot when a rise is coming. These are the shares into which the big institutions put their money. They are better informed and faster on the draw than the private investor. So when good news is in the wind they get in, and thereby push the price up, before you know what is happening. Nor are blue chips always safe. They are not

likely to halve overnight but if you buy them at a high point in the market they could well drop considerably when the market falls.

Gilt-Edged Securities
When the government wants to raise money without increasing taxes it sells stocks on the stockmarket. The certificates registering the stock holders used to have gold edges so they came to be known as gilt-edged securities, gilts for short. Each stock has a face value of £100, and a set interest rate. It also has a redemption date on which the government will pay £100 to the stock holder. Each stock gets its name from these facts. So if the Treasury offers stock at 3 per cent interest for redemption in 1999 it will be called '3 per cent Treasury Stock 1999'. Most stocks pay interest twice a year and you can check the exact date in the Monday issue of the *Financial Times*.

You are stuck with the interest rate, but £100 is unlikely to be what you pay for them, and you can get your money back before the redemption date. But as an investment, gilts are really a gamble on interest rates. If interest rates rise after you have bought them, the stocks will earn you less than you could have got elsewhere, and the price of the stock will fall. But if interest rates fall after you have made your investment, you gain twice over. The fact that the government is due to repay most gilts at a particular date also has its impact on the price, which will gradually move upwards back to its starting point. There is one other point to watch. Gilts usually pay out the whole interest for each six-month period to whoever happens to be holding them when it is due. But just before the payment date, they go what the City calls 'exd'. If you buy them at that point, you miss out on the six months' interest that has built up.

In the late 1980s, the government introduced various 'inflation-linked gilts' where both the interest rate and the capital rise in line with prices.

You can buy gilts either through stockbrokers and banks or a form from the post office lets you buy gilts through the **National Savings Bonds and Stock Office** at Blackpool (see page 543). Buying stock this way will cost less than through a broker.

If you buy stocks from a stockbroker or direct from the Bank of England, which issues them, tax at the standard rate is deducted from the interest before it is paid to you. But if you buy through the National Savings Stock Register, interest is paid *without* deduction of tax – though you'll still have to pay it later if you are eligible. And, wherever you buy them, gilts are free from capital gains tax provided you keep them for one year. Though if you make a loss on them you can't set that loss against other capital gains.

Local Authority Loans
A local authority loan is rather like a gilt, but a local

authority is raising money instead of the government. You can lend money to any authority, get fixed interest on it and your lump sum back at the end of the time. In theory a local authority should be a safe investment, but today you never know. Even so, a local authority may give a good short-term return. And some banks or investment brokers may be able to place your money with a local authority for you.

New Issues

For the average investor the most important point about new issues is the opportunity they offer for stagging (see below). Shares can come on the market in three ways: offers for sale, placings and introductions. But stagging only really applies to the first of these.

An offer for sale can be made in two ways. In a fixed offer the shares are offered at a fixed price, and you apply for however many shares you want at that price. Normally you get the shares you ask for. But if the applications exceed the number of shares for sale, then the issuing house usually limits the number of shares which any one person can buy. In an 'offer for tender' a minimum price is set and those who want to buy the shares have to bid for them by offering figures above it. When the bids are in, a 'striking price' is decided and bids equal to, or above, are accepted and those below it rejected. In either case there is usually a short time lag between the closing date for applications and the first day on which these shares are traded in the stockmarket. Unsuccessful applicants have their cheques returned.

Offers for sale have to be well publicized in two national newspapers (one is usually the *Financial Times*).

If you want to avoid companies in certain fields, armaments, tobacco or whatever, the **Ethical Investment Research and Information Service** (page 542) will, for a fee, check your investments or supply a list of companies avoiding those areas.

New Issues and Stagging

Stagging is buying a new issue and selling it within the first few days of it being traded on the stockmarket. The great advantage of stagging is that you pay no broker's fees on the purchase and no stamp duty. So you can make a profit even on small sums. However, it is also possible to make a loss. So the wise stag waits until very near the closing date before applying and only applies if all the signs are good. Shares are not usually allocated on a first come first served basis, so there is no need to fear that you will lose your chance.

Penny Shares

The name penny shares seems to imply that all you need to make money on the stockmarket is a few pennies. This isn't the case. A penny share is a share priced on the stockmarket at under 20p (some purists say 10p). They are bought and sold in the same way as other shares. But there is a big difference between a share not costing a lot

and it being good value. Essentially there are four kinds of penny shares: those of weak companies which don't deserve more recognition, potential shells, weak companies about to undergo a shake up (which therefore have potential), and stable concerns which just have an abnormally large share issue.

Since you pay the standard percentage commission on the buying and selling it still isn't practical to invest small sums. Before you buy penny shares work out how much the share will have to rise, in percentage terms, to cover the cost of investing. And, as penny shares can take a long time to rise, include in your calculation the interest your money could have earned had it been invested elsewhere.

Placing and Introductions

Placings and introductions are much quieter affairs than new issues. A share price is agreed, and buyers then found, within the confines of the financial world. But placings can be very good buys, so it is worth discussing them with your stockbroker.

Rights Issues

When a company that is already traded on the stockmarket wants to raise more money it can do so by offering new shares for sale in a rights issue. To make them attractive these are usually offered at less than the current price of the company's other shares. The practice gets its name from the fact that existing shareholders have first rights to buy these bargains which they can then keep or sell at a profit.

Securities

This covers stocks and shares of all kinds.

Shells

A shell is a company which hard times have reduced to little more than a shell, despite its listing on the stockmarket. Having a stockmarket listing it may attract a thriving company which lacks this. For, like a hermit crab finding a home, the thriving company can back its operation into the readymade listing of the shell and so gain access to the advantages of the stockmarket for raising capital. So someone with shares in that shell will suddenly find they have a stake in a very going concern. Shells are the secret behind many of the big rises in the value of penny shares.

Stocks

The word 'stock' has two meanings, according to whether it is in the singular or the plural. In the plural it is used for securities which pay a fixed rate of interest, such as government stocks or gilts. But stock in the singular is used to refer to a deal in shares with flexible rates of interest. So you could say, 'I sold my ICI stock today', meaning you had sold your shares in ICI. The Stock Exchange, of course, deals in both stocks and shares.

A Toe in the Market

The only way to discover whether you have the time, energy and skill to play the stock market is to try it. But

Addresses and suggestions for further reading are at the ends of chapters.

you can do this without risking a penny. Read the financial press and pick a handful of shares which you think are good buys. Write them down (then you can't cheat) plus their price and the number of shares you would buy if you were genuinely investing. Then follow those shares, noting their movement on paper, for at least six months, 'selling' them when you think it wise and reinvesting the money. But when you 'sell' a share still follow it to see whether you sold at the right time.

At the end of six months check your 'profit' or 'loss' – remember that each time you 'buy' or 'sell' you have to deduct the stockbroker's fees, plus VAT, plus stamp duty. If you did well you might be able to do well with some real investments, but don't forget almost anyone can make money in a rising market but only the very well informed can do so in a falling one. So before you decide that you are a financial genius or dunce, compare the rise or fall of your shares with the overall performance of the market. For that is the only real measure of a share's success. Then compare what you would have made had you put the same money safely into a building society, bank or National Savings. Don't forget to allow for the tax you would or would not pay according to how the money made its gains. It's the sum *after* tax which is the fair comparison.

Reading Share Prices

Share prices are very easy to read once you know the jargon. But though the jargon is the same everywhere, there is no god-given law as to how newspapers divide shares up. So don't worry if the *Financial Times* has a share in one place and the *Wall Street Journal* has it in another. Companies pay to have their share prices put in the papers and hundreds of smaller companies just don't bother. The Stock Exchange has a complete list which any broker or bank will have. And the *Stock Exchange Official Year Book*, which should be in a good library, gives all listed companies.

The format for share price tables varies from paper to paper. Most try to divide companies into groups based on what they do, so if you know a company is a store or makes textiles, look under that heading. If you can't find it, try the miscellaneous column. This is a typical entry:

High	Low	Stock	Price	+ or -	Div Net	C'vr	Y'ld Gr's	P/E
70	27	Bigfoot Supershoes 5p	70	+4	1.5	2.7	3.1	14.6

The first two columns show you the highest and lowest prices at which that particular share has changed hands in the past year. Next you have the name, followed by the nominal (or par) value of the share – 5p – which is no longer relevant, so forget it. Then comes the average price at which Bigfoot Supershoes shares changed hands at the end of the previous day – but buyers paid slightly more and sellers got slightly less. The + or – shows the amount the price rose or fell during that day's trading, compared with its price the previous day. It rose 4p. When a share price stays the same this column is left blank.

After that come three bits of background information on the share. First the dividends: the 'Div Net' of 1.5 tells you the company paid out total dividends of 1.5p per share (after tax) in its last financial year. If the 1.5p had been preceded by a sign like a dagger pointing downwards it would have meant that the dividend rose that year. The C'vr tells you about the firm's ability to pay that dividend: the 2.7 tells you the profits were large enough to cover the dividend more than two and a half times. The 'Y'ld Gr's' is the gross yield, which is the rate of interest you'd get on your investment if you bought at today's price. That was found by dividing the price by the dividend before tax was deducted. In this case it is 3.1 per cent. Finally, P/E stands for Price to Earnings Ratio. The figure of 14.6 tells you that the present share price is more than 14 times as big as the net profits per share last year. A P/E can be high just because the whole stockmarket is booming, so you need to see whether it is high or low compared to other shares in its sector. If it's higher than average there has to be some reason why investors are interested in this share out of all proportion to its profits to date. And that is something which any would-be investor should look into.

> Never be tempted to buy if you get a call offering you shares quoted on overseas exchanges. The calls are illegal, but fraudsters, particularly in the Netherlands and Switzerland, rake in money each year and disappear. Don't get caught.

How to Buy Shares

You can only apply direct to a company or the Stock Exchange for shares, if they are new issues. Otherwise you can either pick your own stockbroker or use one through a bank, solicitor or accountant, or use an organization, such as a bank, which offers direct share dealing. Or use **ShareLink's** (page 543) telephone service for buying and selling shares: you may not get advice but the charges may be less than those of a stockbroker, and ShareLink offers expert written information on shares via ShareFinder.

Entering the Market with Care

There are now more ways to buy investments than there have ever been. But the ease with which you can buy investments through banks, building societies, shareshops, and so on, as well as stockbrokers, can fool one into thinking it's as safe as shopping at Safeway. Not so.

By law advertisements about investments shouldn't be misleading, and those who handle your money should act honestly. But there are crooks in every field. So only invest through a company which is registered with the **Securities and Investments Board** (**SIB**) (page 543). You can check registration by just ringing SIB. Registered firms should keep each client's money separate, and lay out their terms and responsibilities clearly. If, however, you have a complaint, first write to the firm itself. If that fails, contact the PIA (page 543) which should appoint an independent investigator to see justice is done. And if you have lost money through the fault of the firm you may be able to get it back through the Investors Compensation Scheme.

SIB produces a series of light-hearted but informative booklets on topics like how to spot investment cowboys, and how to get compensation. They are free and well worth reading. The Consumers' Association also has useful products in this field.

The Cost of Buying and Selling Shares

Before you buy consider how much will have to be paid in costs. Then work out how much the share would need to rise before you made any money after these have been paid. Brokers may charge what they please. So it really pays to choose carefully. Phone any firms you like the sound of, ask them if they handle your sort of business, and check their rates carefully. Then get them to send their prospectus and their latest newsletter giving investment advice.

When you buy shares brokers normally charge a percentage of the sum you are investing. They can charge what they like but 1-2 per cent isn't unusual and there is usually a fixed minimum. And you pay for selling as well as buying. On small sums they often charge a flat rate, either way, so when buying £1,000 worth of shares the charges might look like this:

Fee to stockbroker, for example	£15.00
VAT on broker's fee (only levied if he bought via another firm)	£2.25
Contract levy (flat rate on share deals of £1,000+)	0.80
Stamp duty on £1,000 at ½ per cent	£5.00
Total	£23.05

How does the cost of the actual share affect the calculation? As you see it's the *overall* sum you spend which decides the charges, but does the actual price of the share matter? In strictly mathematical terms the answer is no but, given the way the market operates, it is easier for a share to move up and down by 3 pence a day than by 33p. That's why penny shares have proved so popular. For example:

£1,000 invested in 200 shares at £5.00 each
To cover share costs need a profit of £23.05

This is a rise per share of $\frac{£23.05}{200} = 12$p per share.

£1,000 invested in 2,000 shares at 50p each
To cover share costs need a profit of £23.05

This is a rise per share of $\frac{£23.05}{2,000} = 1.2$p per share.

But you would need almost twice that rise simply to break even on the cost of both buying *and* selling because the same broker's charges apply.

What Happens if You Buy Shares

Buying shares involves remarkably little paperwork. When you buy shares you don't need to put your instructions in writing, you can simply telephone your broker. Millions of pounds' worth of shares are bought and sold on verbal contracts each day – and what you say is binding, you cannot change your mind.

When a broker receives your telephoned instructions he sends you a contract note giving the account day by which the money for the shares, plus any charges, *must* be with him. As electronic record-keeping is being introduced you are now expected to pay within 10 days and this may be cut to 5 days. Once the new CREST electronic system is fully working, share ownership will be recorded electronically and you will only get a share certificate if you ask for it – and there may be a charge.

Dividends on Shares

Shareholders receive a dividend certificate – this pays you a certain amount per share and will be in two parts. Tear the certificate in two and keep the part headed tax voucher because this proves the company has paid the basic rate tax for you. The other half should be paid into an account just as if it were a cheque.

In addition to dividends some shares offer perks. A hotel group may offer its shareholders discounts on rooms, a ferry company discounts on fares. It *isn't* usually worth buying a share for the perks but they're an amusing sideline.

Portfolios

If a lump sum has to be invested to create long-term income, you can hand the whole thing over to a broker to manage, provided it is large enough to be worth the stockbroker's time. Usually that means at least £50,000 and the bottom limit may often be a lot more. In those circumstances you give a stockbroker authority to buy and sell without asking you first; this is called a discretionary portfolio. Stockbrokers charge for moving money in and out of shares, which may be an incentive for them to buy and sell more often than is strictly necessary. By no means all brokers do this, but it can happen. So some people prefer to have the portfolio managed on the basis that they will be consulted about transactions – even though this prevents a broker reacting rapidly to market conditions.

If a smaller sum needs to be invested to bring in an income, for example if you are a widow, approaching a bank with whom you have a long-standing relationship may be a good idea. Their investment departments are familiar with situations of that sort, and can advise across a wider range of types of investments. They may also take more trouble for a valued client than would a stockbroker you had only just met.

Whomever you use, you don't have to take the first investment plan which is offered. The experts usually give free advice hoping they will reap the percentage profit when you place your money with them. So make this system work for you by getting free advice from several sources. Only place your money when you have compared the lot and decided who is offering you the best service.

Addresses and suggestions for further reading are at the ends of chapters.

Various Alternatives to Shares

If you don't want to choose your own shares there are several products where the experts make the decisions. But remember, experts can get it wrong and even a good track record is no guarantee of future performance.

Unit Trusts

Unit trusts get their name, first, because there is a trustee who is independent and who makes sure the fund managers do their job and don't run off with your cash and, secondly, because you buy units in a trust. The trust then makes investments jointly on behalf of all who buy units. So investing in a unit trust can give you a spread of investment. This provides some protection but not much: unit trusts rise and fall in value, just as shares do. If the trust is badly run, you can lose money even in a rising market.

Unit trusts now cover a far wider range of investments than used to be allowed. No longer is the division simply by country and type of company. Now there are securities funds which embrace both gilts and equities, other funds invest directly in property or in futures and options. Then there are warrant funds – which buy an option to purchase a particular share at a set time, funder funds which can invest both in other unit trusts and in the money market, and feeder funds which invest in other unit trusts in the same group or in pension funds.

Some of the new categories are too risky for new investors. But even if you invest in safe-seeming overseas shares there are three elements to the risk: the shares' performance, the economy and the value of that currency against the pound. So profit is not guaranteed.

You can buy unit trusts direct from the firms concerned. Just ring and say what you want to buy, it's very simple. Most are listed in the *Financial Times* with their phone numbers. Many financial journals give tables of unit trust performance, so does the *Unit Trust Yearbook*, which some reference libraries have. You will need to check the costs and charges yourself and, on risky funds, do take independent advice before investing.

You will see two prices in the press. You buy at the offer price and sell at the bid price. Each company sets its own minimum investment and may also make an initial charge, which could be 6½-7 per cent, plus an annual management charge. There are also proposals to introduce an exit charge. And one is already made when unit trusts are in a PEP. The **Unit Trust Association** (page 543) has more information on all this.

Large profits on selling unit trusts are subject to Capital Gains Tax and any income from the units is already taxed at the basic rate. But non-taxpayers can claim this back.

If you select your fund well unit trusts are a good way of dabbling in the stockmarket with small sums and, as many specialize in foreign shares, they are an easy way of investing in overseas stock markets, but they aren't good for a quick return as the charges are quite high. There are also huge differences between the performance and risk of different unit trust companies, so you need to pick your companies carefully.

Investment Trusts

Investment trusts are like unit trusts but are set up as a company, not a trust. They are all quoted on the Stock Exchange. So you can either buy shares in them in the usual way and pay the usual share-dealing charges (see Shares), or you can buy them through investment-trust savings schemes, which can be cheaper. The **Association of Investment Trust Companies** (page 542) can tell you about this. Either way a very small management fee is usually deducted from your dividends. The tax rules are the same as for Unit Trusts above and the *Daily Telegraph* and *Financial Times* give investment trust performance figures monthly.

Investment trust is a reassuring name, but don't be fooled. These aren't trusts and your money isn't safe. Their shares are as risky as any shares. In fact they are only for those who can afford to take a risk in the hope of a good return in the long term. The return can be very good, but the trust may rise and fall dramatically and if you sell through need, not choice, it is easy to lose. Invest in them only for the long term.

Personal Equity Plans (PEPs)

Personal Equity Plans are a government ploy to get people to invest in industry via a tax carrot. You can invest up to several thousand pounds each year in a qualifying general PEP (a bundle of investments based on investment trusts, unit trusts or shares), plus up to several thousand more each year in a single company PEP. Then *if* you make any money on these it is free of both income tax and capital gains tax. You need only keep the money in a PEP for one tax year, but setting-up charges can mean the tax incentive may be worth more in later years.

However, the money must go into a plan approved by the Inland Revenue – not into any old shares. Usually the PEP managers choose the investments, but some schemes do give you a say. PEPs are sold by banks, building societies, stockbrokers and so on. You can also buy PEPs by phone from the share-shop **ShareLink** which has a useful scheme whereby you can pay a small sum into a PEP each month, by direct debit. In choosing a PEP check the small print with great care, the charges vary greatly – and remember, PEPs are risky too.

Money Management magazine has details of how funds compare in performance. But any type of packaged investment is more expensive than investing by yourself. For you are paying for the skills of the fund manager. However, PEPs do offer small investors a good spread of shareholdings with the attraction of tax-free profits – if a profit is made.

Unlisted Securities Market (USM)

The USM is where up and coming companies, not ready for a full stock exchange listing, can first raise money by selling shares. To be quoted on the USM they only need to have traded for 2 years, so they are a big gamble. You may pick a winner, buy its shares cheaply and make a killing when it is launched on the main stockmarket – or pick one in an hour of glory which fades with the dawn.

Financial facts change daily, check the latest figures before making a decision.

The shares are bought just like any others, and the tax rules are the same.

GRANTS

Local education authorities pay course fees direct to the college. For living expenses, books and travel they can give students a termly mandatory or discretionary grant. However, grants no longer rise with inflation. Instead, extra funds are available as loans from the Student Loan Company (SLC). Loans will not normally be given to part-timers, those over 50, or to postgraduates unless qualifying in teaching. The DFE (page 693) has leaflets on the subject. So does the Education Department of the Scottish Office (page 694).

Students can borrow up to a set maximum each academic year, and may apply at any point during it. They should ask their college where to get the application form. The loan is interest free but the repayment must be to the same *value* as they borrowed, *allowing for inflation* – therefore more in real terms. And it must be repaid within 5 years from the April after graduation. However, low earners may defer repayment and the debt is not passed on to partners or parents.

★ Grants aren't intended to cover summer holidays but students who can't get work can apply for certain social-security benefits.

Mandatory Grants
Mandatory grants are ones the education department *must* normally pay to a student who takes one of the courses 'designated' by the Department for Education. They include those leading to a first degree, Higher National Diploma, or a teaching qualification, plus others – such as sandwich courses leading to qualifications equal to a degree. However, there are some curious exceptions: for example, the foundation year of an art degree doesn't qualify for a mandatory grant, and neither does a first degree through open learning.

There are 3 rates: one for those who live at home or choose to live in private digs; another for those living in hall and attending a London college or university; a third for those in hall or lodgings elsewhere.

Who is Entitled to Mandatory Grants?
There is no upper age limit on mandatory grants, they are open to anyone who attends a designated course and has lived in Britain for the previous 3 years. But those who have had to live abroad because of their own or their parents' work aren't usually disqualified.

In deciding a grant, capital is not assessed but income is. However, various allowances are set against gross income, and the cut-off point for obtaining a full grant varies with the number in the family. The main rules of assessment are simple.
- Usually the authorities look at the combined income of the student and his or her parents.
- If a student is over 25 when the academic year starts, the parents' income is not considered.
- If a student has been self-supporting for any 3 years, the parents' income is not considered.
- If a student has been married for at least 3 years before the course starts, the parents' income is not considered but the authorities assess the total income of the couple.
- If a student is married with a dependent spouse and/or child, the grant may be increased.

Above a certain ceiling the grant shrinks as the net income rises – though not on a £1 for £1 basis. But even a student who gets no grant at all for living expenses will still have her fees paid.

Discretionary Grants
A local education authority also has the power to give a discretionary grant for any non-designated higher or further education course except those leading to higher degrees. Getting such a grant depends on whether the local authority has the funds, whether you seem to deserve one, and on the suitability of the course. LEAs are unlikely to give grants to attend courses run by private establishments which are not accredited by the DFE. So make sure you apply for a well established and accredited course and muster good evidence to support your case.

Although degrees through open learning don't qualify for mandatory grants, a LEA can make a discretionary grant towards books or residential courses within the syllabus – for a first degree.

When and How to Apply for a Grant
It is vital to apply for a grant at the right time. You cannot apply before January if the course starts the following autumn. But in some authorities you should apply by March to be sure to have the money for the start of the autumn term. *Don't* wait to be accepted for a course. If you aren't accepted the grant is automatically cancelled. If you wait until you are accepted you will still get a grant, if you're entitled to it, but the money may not arrive until well into the first term – which is no fun.

> LEAs can refuse a grant totally if you apply too late. The latest date on which you may apply is the last day of the first term of a course.

You get a grant application form from a school or from the education authority of the area where you live – it's usually in the phone book under the name of the council, then under 'Education' within the council numbers. Application procedures vary, but there are normally three stages:

1 You fill in the application form and send it in.
2 If they think your course entitles you to a grant you are sent another form which they use to assess how much money you will get.
3 If you are offered, and accept, a place you complete a 'college acceptance form' and send it to the college. (If

Addresses and suggestions for further reading are at the ends of chapters.

your place depends on exam results, wait and send this part in only when you have the results.) The college then tells the local authority that you have definitely been accepted. Only after the authority has this in writing from the college will you get any money.

In addition to getting a loan, from the Student Loans Company, students in financial trouble can ask their college for money from the government Access Funds.

Other Sources of Money

Local authorities aren't the only sources of grants. Industry and various government departments – especially the armed services – have sponsorship schemes. Most of these are covered in the booklet *Sponsorship 19 . . .*, sold each year by COIC (page 323). Happily, an employer can sponsor a student by up to a tidy sum each year without it reducing the state grant. Alternatively, to study overseas, students may be able to get a grant from the country concerned. The Commission of the European Community (page 695) has the facts on EC schemes.

There are also educational charities and trusts which give grants for specific purposes, such as foreign travel to study a particular aspect of a course. On page 542 I give some directories which list them and say what each will support. They should be in reference libraries.

★ Tax rebates may be available against the cost of studying for NVQs and GNVQs.

BENEFITS

Many people lose out on benefits because they don't even try to claim them, and it is often the most deserving cases who go without. They are not gifts. They come from a rainy-day fund which you and your family paid into income taxes and national insurance.

There are dozens to be claimed. The DSS publishes free leaflets covering each benefit, plus a simple general guide to benefits. It lists the possibilities and names the detailed leaflets which cover each of them. It should be in post offices, social security offices and Citizens' Advice Bureaux, or ring the DSS freephone line or write to the DSS office (page 693). Or your post office has free stamped envelopes in which to send for free DSS leaflets. Some are only handed out if you have paid enough in national insurance (contributory benefits) but many don't depend on that. To claim most benefits, get a form from your post office. Fill it in, or go to your local social security office or Citizens' Advice Bureau and ask what benefits you might be entitled to and ask them to help with the forms. Some benefits are now open to the self-employed. But the able-bodied, not caring for dependents, who claim benefits because of lack of work, *must be seen to seek work.*

Under the new 'one stop shopping' system you should soon be able to obtain all types of benefits in one place. Also, being on one benefit will often open the door to others. But officials may not always tell you of *all* the benefits you could have – *so do ask*. If you disagree with what the officials decide to give you, ask if you are entitled to appeal. (In some cases you are, in others you aren't.) If you can appeal, be sure to write to your social security office *within 28 days of the decision*, and say you wish to appeal. The Citizens' Advice Bureau will advise you on this.

If officials have paid you less than you should have had, you are now entitled to full payment of the money owed you – dating right back to when the mistake was made.

★ Some benefits can now be paid straight into your bank or building society account if you ask for this.

> If you apply for a benefit within a year of being entitled to it you can get all the money you would have had during that year. But back dating of more than a year is only done in special cases. Sadly, not knowing you were entitled *doesn't* make you a special case.

Benefits for a Low Income or Unemployment

Before giving you most benefits the officials will look at your income *and* your savings. As I write, you get full Income Support or Family Credit with savings of under £3,000. Between £3,000 and £8,000 the rule is: the larger the savings, the smaller the benefits. With savings over £8,000 you may get no Income Support or Family Credit at all. But *do ask* as the figures and rules could change.

Income Support

Income Support is normally for those on low incomes, and those registered unemployed. While on it they can be employed, or self-employed, for not more than a set number of hours a week. The number of hours differ for those with or without children, and there are 3 types of Income Support:

● a low rate for the single and childless under 25
● a basic rate for everyone else
● dependent children premiums for those in special need, such as lone parents, the disabled or elderly (and they can earn slightly more without losing any benefit).

Being on Income Support opens the door to claiming some other benefits. A simple form for claiming Housing Benefit should be given to you. There is also a Residential Allowance for those in residential care. Your mortgage interest can be paid – if the mortgage isn't too big. And you should get Council Tax Benefit.

Family Credit

Family Credit (FC) is an income-related benefit for those in low-paid employment or self-employment, who have children. To get it you must meet *all* the following rules:

● you must have at least one dependent child
● one parent must work at least 16 hours a week
● you must not have more capital than the limits (see above)
● your total income must be below a set threshold.

Financial facts change daily, check the latest figures before making a decision.

FC is paid weekly at a post office or monthly into a bank or building society account and is normally given to the mother. It entitles the family to free NHS prescriptions, glasses, dental treatment and travel to hospital.

Unemployment Benefit

Unemployment Benefit is a contributory benefit (see page 535) paid to those who are out of work – but are able to work and actively seeking it. Take your National Insurance card and the P45 from your last employer to the social security office. The rate may vary because you are single, or married, or with the number of children you have. Payment starts 4 days after employment ends and lasts for 12 months.

Anyone made redundant after working for the same employer for 2 years (after the age of 18) may also be entitled to redundancy pay from the employer. The amount depends on the length of service, pay and so on, but the law sets minimum sums. A CAB can advise you.

Allowances for the Unemployed

Anyone who is unemployed may be entitled to an allowance from a Jobcentre when looking for jobs in other areas, or to help them with moving home to take a new job. Or they may get a retraining allowance.

Benefits for Illness, Disablement and Infirmity

There are benefits for the sick, disabled and infirm and for their carers. DSS leaflets (page 693) explain the full range of help on offer. But, as well as money to live on the disabled can now claim from the Independent Living Fund to help them live in the community. They can also get practical help and a special rail card. The range is too wide for me to cover here, and what someone gets will greatly depend on how their disability is classed. So, this is a complex area.

A CAB or DSS office should have the facts. But the **Disablement Income Group** (page 541), the Disability Alliance (page 541) and the Carers' National Association (page 323) are particularly good sources of information. It is also useful to talk to charities related to the disability as they are used to the special circumstances which may apply. Some benefits are only for those who have paid enough National Insurance contributions. However, not all have that limitation.

The disabled may also be able to get the standard benefits. For example Income Support (page 535) is also available for the sick and disabled whether they live at home or in residential care. There are extra payments to the disabled but the sum paid may be reduced if an attendance allowance is claimed.

Those who have been in-patients for more than a year may also be entitled to a loan from the Social Fund.

> The Department of Transport publishes a guide to transport for the disabled which should be in social security offices or free from the DoT (page 694).

Victims of Industrial Accidents

Victims of industrial accidents, or certain illnesses caused by work, have a set of benefits including special allowances for industrial injuries. Both trade unions and the Disablement Income Group should be able to advise you on these benefits.

> Any benefit may alter if you go into hospital or residential care. Equally, on leaving hospital there may be special help with fares, appliances or medicines. Ask the hospital social worker to advise you.

Child Benefit

Child benefit is paid tax-free for almost all children until they leave school, and single parents may be entitled to an extra sum on top.

Housing Benefits

If you find it difficult to pay your rent or local tax you may be able to get help from your council. This applies whatever other benefits you are or aren't getting, but doesn't usually apply to full-time students in college-owned lets.

Special Needs

Guardian's Allowance

A guardian's allowance is a tax-free weekly payment to anyone who takes an orphan into his or her family. It can be claimed whether or not you are the legal guardian and may occasionally be paid when only one parent is dead.

Maternity Benefits

If you stop work to have a baby and have paid enough NI contributions, you may be able to get a Maternity Allowance. The new rules are complicated, check the DSS leaflet *before* giving up work or you could lose this benefit. (See Law and the Legal System, page 475.)

If you are already receiving other benefits, such as Income Support, you can get a loan from the Social Fund to meet special needs. The snag is that money from the Social Fund is an interest-free loan which *must be paid back* over a set period. Also, the officials must choose who will and will not receive money – for only maternity and funeral payments may be claimed as of right. What's more, the fund has a limit. When the kitty runs dry there will be no money however good your case.

Under this scheme there are Budgeting Loans for those on benefits already, Crisis Loans for anyone in a serious crisis who is not on Income Support, and Community Care Grants to help someone cope in the community – after a long period in care for example. But savings of over £500 will affect the payments.

Widows' Benefits

There are three sources of potential money for a widow – widow's payment, widowed mother's allowance, and a widow's pension.

Addresses and suggestions for further reading are at the ends of chapters.

A **Widow's Payment** is a tax-free lump sum payable as soon as the husband dies, providing a woman was under 60, or her husband was not drawing a pension, when he died. It should be claimed within 12 months.

On top of that, the Widowed Mother's Allowance or the Widow's Pension are now paid from the time of the death, but these are contributory benefits (see page 535).

Widowed Mother's Allowance is still paid to those who are pregnant or have at least one child who fits the rules. Claim within 6 months or benefit may be lost.

Rules for the **Widow's Pension** create a sliding scale. A woman's age when her husband dies establishes *forever* the rate of pension she will receive. However, the pension is index-linked so the sums she gets will rise with the cost of living. Claim within 12 months.

Anyone whose husband died after 5 April 1979 should also be getting his entitlement to an earnings-related pension.

RENDERING UNTO CAESAR

Everyone is liable to tax from the cradle to the grave – and slightly beyond it. As the Chancellor of the Exchequer decides not only the rates of tax but what they will be levied on – and changes at least some of these in the budget each year – it isn't possible to give any tax guidance figures here. AND READERS SHOULD BEAR IN MIND THAT ALL THE FACTS IN THIS SECTION COULD CHANGE AT ANY TIME.

The biggest tax changes in recent years have been the introduction of separate taxation for husbands and wives and allowing bank and building society interest to be paid tax-free, to non-taxpayers. But, to get tax-free interest, non-taxpayers, such as many pensioners, must complete forms, from the Inland Revenue. There are two forms. One lets you reclaim tax already paid, the other stops a bank or building society taking tax off in future. Also, from 1996/7, taxpayers who receive returns will be allowed to calculate their own income from Capital Gains Tax, whether employed or self-employed. And self-employed tax is now based on the current year, not the preceding year.

Everyone has a duty to tell the taxman about any income or profit. Don't wait for the tax office to contact you. Not knowing the tax rules is no excuse for non-payment. Interest is now charged on late payments. There is, however, an exception. You can now rent out a room in your home without declaring the rent for tax – provided it comes to less than a set amount a year. But ask the Revenue what the latest tax-free limit of the Rent-a-Room scheme is before you leave rent undeclared.

That apart, you need to declare *all* sources of income, not just those which you believe to be taxable. If you have any income at all on top of a wage or salary you must ask the local tax office (under Inland Revenue in the phone book) for a tax return form to fill in. The tax year runs from 6 April one year to 5 April the next. So get a form when 5 April is past.

The Inland Revenue will help with straightforward factual questions – but they can't give advice on tax planning. If you are self-employed or a higher-rate taxpayer it will probably be worthwhile to consult an accountant. Anyone can set up as an accountant, *even if totally unqualified*, so do check you are dealing with someone from a reputable professional body. The Institute of Chartered Accountants in England and Wales or the Institute of Chartered Accountants of Scotland (see page 543) will send you a list of local accountants, but often the best course is to choose someone recommended by a friend or business acquaintance.

Since the budget of March 1992 there have been three rates of tax – a low rate of 20 per cent, a basic rate of 25 per cent, and a higher rate of 40 per cent.

> In cases of discourtesy, delay or errors over your tax, complain to your local office first. Then to the head or area office. If that fails ask the Revenue Adjudicator to look into your case.

Capital Gains Tax (CGT)

Capital Gains Tax is a tax on the profits made on the sale of most assets, such as shares, unit trusts, antiques, stamps or a second home. But you can set losses against gains. And among the gains you can make *without* any risk of paying CGT are profits made on the following:

- your main home – provided you have lived in the whole of it throughout the time you have owned it
- private cars
- pools or betting winnings
- an asset with a limited life (e.g. a horse)
- gilts sold after July 1986
- cash from an insurance policy
- household goods and personal effects sold below a certain price each
- cash from a Personal Equity Plan
- cash from shares in a Business Expansion Scheme which have been held for 5 years.

People worry more than they need about CGT. It is a tax that is only levied on the profits that provide a real boost to your buying power. For example, you don't pay tax on the whole of the difference between the cost of an item and the price you sell it for. A formula discounts any rise in value that is no more than the rise in prices generally (RPI) over the years you've owned it. And you may set losses in one area against gains in another.

After that each person is allowed tax-free capital gains up to a set sum, which is usually revised at each budget. Only the capital gains over that sum are added on top of your income and taxed. If your income is so low that you haven't used up all your allowances against income tax you *cannot* set these against your taxable capital gains.

★ If you make capital gains by selling your business, you can now get special CGT concessions by reinvesting in an unquoted company: so check with the Revenue.

Financial facts change daily, check the latest figures before making a decision.

Income Tax

There are two income tax systems for earned income running side by side. Both levy the same tax on the same amounts but the payments are paid at different times.

Pay As You Earn (PAYE) is the system by which an employer takes tax out of a wage or salary before it is paid to an employee. So the employer acts as tax collector for the Inland Revenue. First-time employees must fill in a form P46 to get their coding and National Insurance rights. But students doing temporary work can fill in form P38(S), which employers should have. This allows them to be paid without taking tax off.

Schedule D is for the self-employed. Under it, earnings are totted up at the end of each year. Allowable business expenses are then deducted – and what is allowable varies according to your occupation. Finally, you or your accountant send the sums to the Inland Revenue. But even if you use an accountant you are legally responsible for seeing that the figures are correct.

There are slightly complicated rules on how late someone may complete their accounts. Interest is now charged to those who are slow. There are also rules which allow tax to be spread over several years. On Schedule D you may choose the dates of your accounting year, which has considerable cash-flow advantages. These are especially useful when starting a new business. So the self-employed need a good accountant to guide them.

Unearned income is taxed at the same rate as earned income, and now that a married woman is taxed separately she may set her allowances against tax against her unearned income.

Taxable	Tax Free
perks and benefits if you earn over £8,500	pensions to those with gallantry awards
rent paid to you if in excess of the Rent-a-Room allowance.	most non-contractual compensation for loss of a job, up to £30,000
interest on accounts	interest on National Savings certificates
pensions	
profits from any business	interest on SAYE scheme
tips and Christmas boxes	the first £70 earned in a National Savings account
interest on shares	
maintenance payments under a court order – but the payer gets some relief	the lump sum paid out by a pension scheme up to a set limit

You have to declare all income from these sources, but in many cases tax will have been taken out before the money was paid to you. But not all income is taxable.

Unless you have arranged otherwise basic rate tax is taken out of most savings and dividends before you get them. But higher rate taxpayers may have to pay a higher rate on these too.

Husbands and wives are now treated separately on income from savings and investment. If you have income from a joint account, the tax office will normally assume that you have each had 50 per cent of the benefits.

Taxing Benefits

Often, what the DSS gives the Inland Revenue takes back. The position here tends to change. But organizations such as the Disablement Income Group (page 541) or a CAB can advise you.

Taxable	Tax Free
Retirement Pension	Maternity Allowance
Widow's Pension	Child Benefit (as I write)
	Attendance Allowance
Unemployment Benefit	Mobility Allowance
Income Support to strikers and unemployed	Family Credit
	Sickness Benefit
Statutory Sick Pay	Income Support if not on strike or unemployed
Industrial Benefit	Christmas bonus to state pensioner
Invalid Care Allowance	War Pensions
	Invalidity Benefit

Allowances Against Tax

A certain amount of income is allowed to be tax free. How much varies with your situation. Everyone, whether single or married, now gets a personal allowance, which rises at age 65 and 75. A single parent gets an additional allowance. A married man gets a married couple's allowance, which also rises at 65 and 75. If he dies his widow gets it in full for a year after his death. A couple may split the allowance between them by just telling the Revenue on a special form. However, it can no longer help you get tax off at your top rate. For the relief is fixed at 20 per cent. However, the age-related increases are reduced, on a sliding scale, if the elderly person has more than a certain income. There are also other allowances for special situations such as being a single parent, being blind, newly widowed and so on. All these allowances are usually changed at each budget. Your tax office will give you the latest rates.

Claiming Tax Rebates

If you have paid more tax than you should have done, write to the tax office and ask for a copy of the Notice of Assessment. This shows how your tax was calculated. If it doesn't agree with your figures, write quickly for a refund and explain why. You can claim up to six years after the error. You may also find that earnings or interest may have been paid to you after deduction of tax when you are not earning enough to be taxable. Non-taxpayers and those paying the lowest rate can also get rebates on interest payments from banks and building societies, which have been taxed. The Inland Revenue has numerous forms on which you apply for refunds but you can often apply with a letter.

★ If a parent gives money to a child who is unmarried and under 18 and the child invests it, any income from the investment is counted as the parent's income.

Tax on Pensions
The income from a pension of any kind is taxed as earned income. But there are generous rules regarding the lump sum which can be paid out from a personal pension or retirement annuity.

Tax and Changing Jobs
When you change jobs, your employer should give you a form P45. This shows the allowances you are due, so that your new employer can take over where the old one left off. If you do not hand it over to your new company, they will tax you as though you have no more than the minimal personal allowance.

Tax and Divorce
The budget of 15 March 1989 made big changes to the taxation of maintenance for ex-partners and children, which affect both the payers and the receivers. The precise rules vary according to whether the payments were set before or after that budget, so talk to an accountant or get the Inland Revenue leaflet which explains them. But, whatever your situation, *all* payments to ex-spouses and their children *must* be paid gross (with no tax taken off).

Understanding Payslips
Whether you are paid weekly or monthly, by cash, cheque or direct into your bank account, if you are employed you will get a payslip. This will show you how much you earned and, equally important, what has been deducted by way of National Insurance and perhaps an occupational pension scheme.

MR SMITH				ABC LTD		
NI No: FF 123456C	Tax Code: 242L	Pay By CHEQUE		Date: 31.12.87		Tax Period: M9
DESCRIPTION		UNITS DUE	RATE	AMOUNT	THIS YEAR	
1. BASIC PAY			1042.00	1042.00	9087.00	
3. PENSION CONTRIBUTION			− 25.00	− 25.00	−225.00	
5 BONUS			250.00	25.00	250.00	
			TOTAL TAXABLE PAY >>>	1267.00	9112.00	
INCOME TAX − PAYE				−287.55	−4968.30	
EMPLOYEE'S NI RATE A				−114.03	−821.61	
(EMPLOYER'S NI RATE A	132.40	TO DATE 953.98)				
			TOTAL NET PAY >>>	865.42	5322.09	

Starting from the top left-hand corner in the example you will find the National Insurance number and name. Moving along, you come to the tax code – that's the shorthand instruction to the employer telling him how much income tax should be deducted from the pay.

Every employer acts as an unpaid tax collector for the government. *It is very important to make sure your tax code is correct because otherwise the wrong amount of tax may be deducted.*

Anyone with a knowledge of the tax code, for example, would be able to tell that Mr Smith is under 65. That's because 'L' stands for someone receiving the personal allowance and under 65. If you want to know all the codes they are in leaflet IR34, from your tax office, but some of the other code letters are: P for a personal allowance for someone aged 65-74, and D for someone taxed at a higher rate.

On the slip there are details of the payment. In this case it's by cheque, which is common for small businesses, but large organizations often make payments directly to your bank or building society account.

There's also the date and the tax period. The tax year runs from 6 April to 5 April in the following year. So December is month nine of the tax year.

The first section is the taxable pay – sometimes called gross pay. This is the total earnings including bonuses before any deductions have been made.

Then come those nasty subtractions: income tax and National Insurance. You can check that you are paying the right amount of National Insurance – this will be affected both by the amount you earn and by any pension scheme your company runs. If it runs a scheme which replaces the government's earnings-related scheme, then there is a slight reduction in National Insurance contributions. Near the bottom there are the employer's contributions to Mr Smith's National Insurance. Finally, the crucial bottom line – the take-home pay, or net earnings.

Ways to Save Tax
Some of the legitimate ways to cut your tax bill include the following, but it's wise to take professional advice on which ones best suit your situation: some have disadvantages too.

● Buy your home with a mortgage – you can gain tax relief on the interest – but only on the first £30,000 you borrow.
● Contribute to a pension plan which gets maximum tax relief on contributions.
● If you are a higher-rate taxpayer, invest in National Savings Certificates – which are tax free.
● Take the maximum permitted lump sum from any pension plan when it pays out.
● Make gifts to reduce your tax bill on death.
● Claim all the allowances you may be entitled to.
● If your work takes you abroad, make sure you check the rules for reducing tax and abide by them.
● Make sure there is no mention of pay in lieu of notice in the terms of your employment. Payments written in are taxable, unwritten ones are tax free up to a certain level.
● Invest in a young company, under the Business Expansion Scheme (page 537).

Financial facts change daily, check the latest figures before making a decision.

- Give to charity through a 'Give as You Earn scheme'.
- A self-employed high earner or small business might save by becoming a limited company.
- Invest in an Enterprise Investment Scheme, giving tax relief at the basic rate up to a set sum.

Inheritance Tax

Inheritance tax is, in essence, the tax on whatever someone leaves when they die. It takes the place of Death Duties, Estate Duties and Capital Transfer Tax – all of which have been abolished – and covers the value of everything you own when you die.

You don't have to be very rich when you pay it. It is paid if the total sum left is £150,000 or more (in the 1993/94 tax year) at a rate of 40 per cent.

The only way to avoid this tax is to give away part of what you own while you are alive. There is now no limit to how much you may give away each year, but for the gift to avoid inheritance tax you must live for 7 years after giving it. Admittedly, once you have survived for three years, the potential tax bill goes down, and it gradually falls away until after seven years there is no risk of a bill at all. Even if you don't live that long the gift will only be taxed at its value when it was given, not when you die.

A vital point is that to count as a gift you may not continue to benefit from it. So you can't save tax by 'giving' your home to your children while still living there – unless you pay them the market rent and can prove you have done so.

Within those rules there are special exceptions. If you die in under 7 years of making any of the following gifts they will still not be taxable.

- You can give away up to £3,000 a year (1993-94).
- A husband and wife can give each other unlimited amounts and the 7-year rule will not apply.
- Gifts totalling up to £250 per person per tax year are not counted.
- Wedding gifts up to certain limits are not counted.
- Certain charitable and political donations are not counted.
- Gifts to the nation.

Council Tax

Council tax is based on the value of your home. In each area value bands, at a set date, have been established and all homes put into them. Those with homes in the highest bands pay the highest council tax. However, there are reductions for being a single occupier, for those with certain disabilities, and for having someone on a low income living with you rent free. There is also Council Tax Benefit for those on low incomes, which will meet all, or part of, the bill.

VAT

VAT is tax which uses businesses and services as tax collectors – including the self-employed. Anyone can register for VAT if they can show that they are trading. And if someone has earned or had a taxable turnover (*not* profits) above a set limit in the previous 12 months, they *must* register for VAT – quarterly figures no longer count.

The principle is simple. Someone who is registered for VAT adds VAT, at a set percentage, to every bill they charge to anyone else (unless the item is zero-rated). The VAT then has to be paid to the VAT office quarterly. But before it is paid, the individual who has collected it may deduct the value of all VAT she has paid on goods and services needed for her business. Or, if the VAT on purchases exceeds that on income, you can get a refund. These calculations used to be based on your invoice dates. Now, if your turnover is below a certain figure, you can do 'cash accounting'. Then you only account for VAT after you receive it.

You can choose the month ends on which each quarter's VAT falls due by writing to the registration department of your local VAT office. VAT offices are very helpful and their advice about what you can claim is free.

The book-keeping is easy and if you aren't a high earner you'll probably find it worthwhile to do it yourself. Your VAT form must be returned within a month of the end of the quarter. Later than that spells trouble. After two quarters in arrears you pay interest on an increasing scale from 5 to 30 per cent, according to the number of quarters for which you are late. And if you pull up your socks, then backslide, the interest will be at the rate you last paid. It stays at that rate for some while after you have reformed.

> If you can't get your form to the collection address on time, your local office will sometimes accept both it and your payment – but make sure you get a stamped receipt to show the date and place of payment.

If you are unhappy about a VAT (or Customs & Excise) decision, ask for it to be reconsidered. A departmental review should take place. If you are still unhappy, you can appeal to an independent VAT (or Duties) Tribunal.

USEFUL ADDRESSES AND BOOKS

Banking and Mortgages

Abbey National Building Society, Abbey House, Baker Street, London NW1 6XL Tel: 071 486 5555.

Alliance and Leicester Building Society, 49 Park Lane, London W1Y 4EQ Tel: 071 629 6661.

American Express Money Transfer Service, Tel: 071 930 4411.

Bank of Ireland, 34 High Street, Slough, Berks SL1 1BP Tel: 0753 517777.

Bank of Scotland, The Mound, Edinburgh EH1 1YZ Tel: 031 442 7777 or for Phoneline banking 7 days a week 0800 807777.

Banking Action Group, Park Gates, Leagram, Chipping, Lancs PR3 2GS Tel: 0995 61049, will advise on problems with banks and help with negotiations and litigation. Pressure group, Inf.

Barclays Bank PLC, 54 Lombard Street, London EC3P 3AH Tel: 071 488 1144.

Bradford and Bingley Building Society, P.O. Box 88, Crossflats, Bingley, West Yorkshire BD16 2UA Tel: 0274 554422.

Britannia Building Society, P.O. Box 20, Britannia House, Cheadle Road, Leek, Staffordshire ST13 5RG Tel: 0538 399399.

British Bankers' Association Information Department, 10 Lombard Street, London EC3V 9AP Tel: 071 626 8486, has the key facts on British banks.

Card Protection Plan (CPP), 198 King's Road, London SW3 5XP Tel: 071 351 4400, offers credit card protection. (P.514)

Clydesdale Bank, 30 St Vincent Place, Glasgow G1 2HL Tel: 041 248 7070.

Co-operative Bank, P.O. Box 101, 1 Balloon Street, Manchester M60 4EP Tel: 061 832 3456. For its 7 days a week telephone 'Armchair Banking' 0345 212212.

Council of Mortgage Lenders (formerly the Building Societies Association), 3 Savile Row, London W1X 1AF Tel: 071 437 0655, has information on home buying. (P.520)

Credit Card Sentinel (UK) Ltd, New Lane, Havant, Hants PO9 2NR – Freefone 0800 414717 in UK or reversed charges from anywhere in the world to 0705 471234. (P.514)

First Direct Bank, Arlington Business Centre, Millshaw Park Lane, Leeds LS11 0LT Tel: 0800 222 000.

Girobank plc, 10 Milk Street, London EC2V 8JH Tel: 071 600 6020 or for its Telecare phone service 0645 365 365. It does a special service for the deaf. Information from any post office.

Halifax Building Society, P.O. Box 60, Trinity Road, Halifax, West Yorkshire HX1 2RG Tel: 0422 333333.

Independent Banking Advisory Service (IBAS), Northview, North Fen, Somersham, Huntingdon, Cambs PE17 3HW Tel: 0487 843444/740742, advises on problems with banks.

Leeds Permanent Building Society, Permanent House, The Headrow, Leeds, West Yorkshire LS1 1NS Tel: 0532 438181.

Lloyds Bank PLC, 71 Lombard Street, London EC3P 3PS Tel: 071 626 1500.

Midland Bank PLC, 27-32 Poultry, London EC2P 2BX Tel: 071 260 8000.

National & Provincial Building Society, Provincial House, Bradford, West Yorkshire BD1 1NL Tel: 0274 733444 or, for its 24-hour, 7-day-a-week Telebanking 0800 919181.

National Westminster Bank PLC, 41 Lothbury, London EC2P 2BP Tel: 071 726 1000.

Nationwide Building Society, Nationwide House, Pipers Way, Swindon, SN38 1NW Tel: 0793 513513.

Office of the Banking Ombudsman (OBO), 70 Gray's Inn Road, London WC1X 8NB Tel: 071 404 9944. (P.504)

The Royal Bank of Scotland, 42 St Andrew Square, Edinburgh EH2 2YE Tel: 031 556 8555.

Standard Chartered Bank, 38 Bishopsgate, London EC2N 4DE Tel: 071 280 7500.

TSB Group plc, 25 Milk Street, London EC2V 8LU Tel: 071 606 7070 or ask your local branch about the round-the-clock Speedlink computer link service.

Western Union Money Transfer Service, Tel: 0800 833 833.

Yorkshire Bank plc, 22 Merrion Way, Leeds, LS2 8NZ Tel: 0532 441244.

Benefits and Grants

For Pensions, see page 542.

Contributions Agency, Newcastle-on-Tyne, NE98 1YX, administers National Insurance contributions.

Disability Alliance, 88-94 Wentworth Street, London E1 7SA Tel: 071 247 8776, publishes a handbook on disability rights giving all the vital facts on what the disabled and their carers have a right to. (P.536)

Disablement Income Group (DIG), Unit 5, Archway Business Centre, 19-23 Wedmore Street, London N19 4RZ Tel: 071 263 3981, is a pressure group and information source on benefits for the disabled. (P.536)

DSS Tel: 071 210 5240 for information on pensions and widows benefit.

DSS Free phone 0800 666555 for information on most benefits.

DSS Freephone 0800 882200 for information on benefits for illness or disability.

Office of the Social Security Commissioners, Harp House, 83 Farringdon Street, London EC4A 4DH Tel: 071 353 5145, hears appeals against entitlement to benefits after they have failed in an appeal to the Social Security Appeals Tribunal. But the Tribunal must grant leave to appeal to this body.

Scottish Office, Student Grants, Education Department, 4th Floor, New St Andrew's House, St James Centre, Edinburgh EH1 3TG Tel: 031 244 5823, publishes a guide to student grants.

SHAC (page 270) and **Child Poverty Action Group** (page 480), publish good booklets.

Useful Books
Charities Digest, Family Welfare Association.
Directory of Grant-Making Trusts, Charities Aid Foundation.
Grants for Students: a Brief Guide from the DFE.
Sponsorship 19.., lists student sponsorship opportunities each year. Sold by COIC, Room E405, Moorfoot, Sheffield, S1 4PQ Tel: 0742 594576.
The Grant Register, Macmillan Press

Insurance

Advisory Department, Lloyds, London House, 6 London Street, London EC3R 7AB Tel: 071 623 7100. (P.516)

The Association of British Insurers (ABI), 51 Gresham Street, London EC2V 7HQ Tel: 071 600 3333, has leaflets on insurance and pensions. (P.517)

British Insurance and Investment Brokers Association (BIIBA), 14 Bevis Marks, London EC3A 7NT Tel: 071 623 9043. (P.515)

Direct Line Insurance, Tel: 081 686 3313, offers insurance by phone, without using brokers, and aims to undercut usual prices. (P.518)

Institute of Loss Assessors, 14 Red Lion Street, Chesham, Bucks HP5 1HB Tel: 0494 782342. (P.515)

Insurance Brokers Registration Council, 15 St Helen's Place, London EC3A 6DS Tel: 071 588 4387 has the list of registered brokers.

Insurance Ombudsman Bureau, City Gate One, 135 Park Street, London SE1 9EA Tel: 071 928 4488. (P.516)

Personal Insurance Arbitration Service, 24 Angel Gate, City Road, London EC1V 2RS Tel: 071 837 4483. (P.499)

The Private Health Partnership, 8 Manor Square, Otley, West Yorks, LS21 3AP Tel: 0943 851133 is an insurance broker specializing in health insurance. (P.517)

School Fees Insurance Agency Ltd, Sfia House, 15 Forlease Road, Maidenhead SL6 1JA Tel: 0628 34291, specializes in school fees planning. (P.520)

Useful Book
As always, the OFT (p. 661) has good leaflets. So does the ABI.

Pensions

The British Pensioners and Trades Union Action Committee, Norman Dodds House, 315 Bexley Road, Erith, Kent Tel: 0322 335464, will advise and represent senior citizens and widows in disputes about entitlements.

The Industrial Society, (address on page 698) has information on pension rules.

The Occupational Pensions Advisory Service (OPAS), 11 Belgrave Road, London SW1V 1RB Tel: 071 233 8080, is a government-sponsored body which advises on problems with an occupational or personal pension. (P.524)

Pension Appeal Tribunal, 48-49 Chancery Lane, London WC2A 1JR Tel: 071 936 7034, hears appeals against DSS decisions relating to war pensions, the disabled, or widows and children.

The Pensions Ombudsman, 11 Belgrave Road, London SW1V 1RB Tel: 071 834 9144. (P.524)

Pensioners Voice, Melling House, 14 St Peters Street, Blackburn BB2 2HD Tel: 0254 52606, is a pensioners' pressure group on state pensions and can tell you where to get help.

Society of Pension Consultants, Ludgate House, Ludgate Circus, London EC4A 2AB Tel: 071 353 1688, can give you a list of registered *independent* pension advisers.

War Pensions Agency, DSS, North Fylde Central Office, Norcross, Blackpool FY5 3TA Helpline 0253 858858, can give you advice and leaflets.

See also **DSS** and **Scottish Home and Health Department** (P. 694).

Useful Books
Sue Ward, *Disclosure of Information to Pension Members*, The Industrial Society, clarifies the new rules about pension schemes, for employers and employees.
Your Rights for Pensioners, Age Concern.

Savings and Investments

Association of British Credit Unions, Unit 307, Westminster Business Square, 339 Kennington Lane, London SE11 5QY Tel: 071 582 2626. (P.506)

Association of Investment Trust Companies, Park House, 6th Floor, 16 Finsbury Circus, London EC2M 7JJ Tel: 071 588 5347, can tell you of stockbrokers who will deal in small quantities of investment trusts. And its information service gives performance figures. (P.533)

Association of Private Client Investment Managers and Stockbrokers (APCIMS), 20 Dysant Street, London EC2A 2BX Tel: 071 410 6868, represents most London stockbroking firms and has a brochure on those representing private clients.

Ethical Investments Research and Information Service, 504 Bondway Business Centre, 71 Broadway, London SW8 1SQ Tel: 071 735 1351, monitors company interests and can advise those who want to avoid companies in certain fields. (P.530)

Financial Intermediaries, Managers and Brokers' Regulatory Association (FIMBRA), Hertsmere House, Hertsmere Road, London E14 4AB Tel: 071 538 8860.

Investment Managers' Regulatory Organization (IMRO), Broadwalk House, 5 Appold Street London EC2A 2LL Tel: 071 628 6022.

Life Assurance and Unit Trust Regulatory Organization (LATRO), Centre Point, 103 New Oxford Street, London WC1A 1QH Tel: 071 379 0444.

National Federation of Credit Unions, Credit Union House, 102 Tong Street, Bradford, West Yorks BD4 6HD Tel: 0274 687692. (P.506)

National Savings, Boydstone Road, Glasgow G58 1SB Tel: 041 649 4555 or 041 636 2950 or recorded information 041 632 2766. Southerners can phone National Savings 071 605 9461 for information or 071 605 9483/4 for a recorded message. National Savings Freephone 0800 868 700. (P.526)

National Savings, Millburn Gate House, Durham DH99 1NS Tel: 091 386 4900 or 091 374 5023.

National Savings and Bond and Stock Office, Marton, Blackpool, FY3 9YP Tel: 0253 766151/715666, or recorded information 0253 723714 deals in both National Savings and gilts. (P.526)

National Savings, Financial Advisers' Liaison Officer, Charles House, 375 Kensington High Street, London W14 8SD, has a free publication on investing in National Savings. (P.526)

National Savings leaflets are in post offices and information is also on Prestel *50042; Ceefax page 223 and Oracle page 563.

Personal Investment Authority (PIA), 3/4 Royal Exchange Buildings, London, EC3V 3NL Tel: 071 929 0072. (P.531)

ProShare, Library Chambers, 13-14 Basinghall Street, London EC2V 5BQ Tel: 071 600 0984. (P.529)

Securities and Futures Association, First Floor, Cottons Centre, Cottons Lane, London SE1 2QB Tel: 071 378 9000.

Securities and Investment Board (SIB), Gavrelle House, 2-14 Bunhill Row, London EC1Y 8RA Tel: 071 638 1240, or to check the Register of Authorized Firms 071 929 3652. It has entertaining booklets on investment and its pitfalls, which are useful reading. (P.531)

ShareLink, Canon House, 25 The Priory Queensway, Birmingham, B4 6BS, is a telephone share-shop dealing in shares, PEPs and traded options by phone. Tel: 021 200 2242 to buy or sell shares, 021 200 4545 to buy or sell PEPs, or 021 200 4600 for the Sharefinder information service. (P.531)

Unit Trust Association, 65 Kingsway, London WC2B 6TD Tel: 071 831 0898, has a leaflet on unit trusts. Send a sae. (P.533)

Useful Books
Buying, Selling and Owning Shares Action Kit, Consumers' Association.
Christine Stopp, *More Shares for Your Money*, sponsored by the Association of Investment Trust Companies, Rosters.
Danny O'Shea, *Investing for Beginners*, Financial Times.
Financial Times and *The Times* review USM shares weekly.
Investors Chronicle Beginner's Guide to the Stockmarket, Penguin.
Money Management magazine has details of how PEPs compare.
Money Marketing Magazine; Money Management Magazine; Planned Savings Magazine; Make Your Pension Work, Rosters.
Rosemary Burr, *Guide to Personal Equity Plans 1988*, Rosters.

Several personal finance magazines concentrate on helping you plan your investments – although it is worth remembering a magazine is often written three months before it is published, so always check the rates, etc. are up to date: *Financial Times Magazine; Money Magazine; What Investment; Money Observer*.
The Guardian Money Guide.
Unit Trust Management, Money Management and *Planned Savings* are magazines covering unit trust performances.
Your Taxes and Savings in Retirement, Age Concern.

Tax, National Insurance and VAT

Contributions Agency, DSS Longbenton, Newcastle on Tyne, NE98 1YX Tel: 06431 56563 (a local rate call), handles queries on class 2 National Insurance. Other queries should go to your local DSS office. (P.522)

Institute of Chartered Accountants of England and Wales, Chartered Accountants Hall, P.O. Box 433, Moorgate Place, London EC2P 2BJ Tel: 071 628 7060. (P.537)

Institute of Chartered Accountants of Scotland, 27 Queen Street, Edinburgh EH2 1LA Tel: 031 225 5676. (P.537)

Revenue Adjudicator, 3rd Floor, Haymarket House, 28 Haymarket, London SW1Y 4SP Tel: 071 930 2292.

Other

National & Provincial Building Society, do a series of good guides to aspects of personal finance.

Official Receiver, 22 Martineau Square, Birmingham, B2 4UZ Tel: 021 233 4808, keeps the record of bankruptcies.

The Directory of the Financial Services Industry should be in reference libraries. It lists those offering every type of financial service.

Useful Books
Which Magazine, from the Consumers' Association (page 692) has excellent reports on money matters, often with valuable comparisons of companies.

In Sickness

A-Z of Ailments • Complementary Medicine • Medical Facts • First Aid • Social and Anti-social Drugs

In Sickness covers medical problems of every type. The first section is an A to Z of common illnesses and ailments. Then there are sections on medical terminology, on basic procedures like temperature and pulse taking, on the problems of drugs and sexually transmitted diseases, on disabilities, on infectious diseases and immunization, and on first aid. Both the information within each section and the sections themselves are arranged alphabetically – except on rare occasions when logic dictates otherwise.

The information is intended to help you to recognize when medical attention is needed, to provide basic home remedies for minor problems and to answer some of the questions which one can easily forget to ask a doctor. It also suggests other sources of information, help and support which may be valuable to the sufferer or to his or her family.

Some conditions seem to respond better to alternative treatments than to conventional ones, and many GPs now recommend alternative therapies for certain conditions. So the major branches of alternative medicine are explained.

Moreover, modern medicine is increasingly finding that health, like charity, begins at home and is placing new emphasis on prevention and on the need for patients to take an active part in their own recovery. So, both here and in the following section on health I have tried to provide the facts which could help people to prevent illness and to have more control over it when it does strike.

The information given here should never be used as a substitute for seeing a doctor. Before using any remedy in this book *always* discuss it with your doctor. Only a doctor can say what is safe for a particular person.

A TO Z OF AILMENTS

Aches

What all aches have in common is that basic home remedies often ease the pain. Hot baths and hot water bottles help, whether the ache is from a period pain, overworked muscles or some medical conditions (though inflamed areas need cooling – see Sprains). Research also shows that firm rubbing can block the sensation of pain, because the nerves concerned can only carry one message at a time – so if the rubbing keeps them busy the pain can't get through. Some hospitals now use electric massagers in pain control, but the power of the human hand should never be underestimated.

Acne and Other Spots

To squeeze or not to squeeze, that is the question. Ask any two doctors and they'll give two different answers – and they'll both be right. If you squeeze any spot with dirty hands you spread the infection. And if you squeeze a spot which isn't ready to burst, you will push the pus deeper into the skin, increasing the problem. So *no* squeezing in either of those situations.

But blackheads should always be removed while still small, and you can safely remove small spots, with heads ready to burst, provided you gently press them out straight after a bath, when heat has opened the pores, using *perfectly clean hands and nails* and a soft tissue. Swab with witch-hazel (from a chemist) afterwards in order to tighten and disinfect the stretched pores.

In acne there seem to be three combined causes. The male hormone, androgen (which both sexes make), stimulates the skin to produce more oils, the duct to the skin surface becomes blocked, forming blackheads and whiteheads, and – for reasons nobody understands – bacteria build up underneath and form very nasty spots which can cause permanent scars. But modern treatment can be very effective; so see a doctor and if necessary, ask to see a skin specialist. But basic care can make a difference.

● Wash the skin *very* well each day using a rough washing sponge or washing grains which rub off the dead surface layers of skin so the oils can seep out. Pat dry, preferably using kitchen roll – wiping and towels spread the bacteria.
● Eat a healthy diet – don't heap on the fats and sweets.
● Give up smoking.
● Use an anti-spot cream the moment a spot begins to appear.

Addresses and suggestions for further reading are at the ends of chapters.

● Keep the hair clean, so hair oil doesn't produce a spotty forehead.

Acquired Immune Deficiency Syndrome (AIDS)

The AIDS virus (HIV) destroys the body's ability to fight off other diseases. As it is usually impossible to pinpoint the date of infection, there are no hard facts on how long AIDS takes to develop. Some people may get a glandular-fever-type illness within the first year, but many may have no symptoms for several years. Once symptoms develop, 3 out of 4 die within 3 years of diagnosis, but nobody knows how long the virus can be carried without symptoms, and a symptomless carrier is as infectious as any other AIDS victim. For tests you need only contact your nearest hospital.

The virus is carried in the body fluids – especially blood and semen – but it usually enters the body when a break in the skin lets it into the bloodstream. It *can't* be breathed in, or enter through the pores. So AIDS cannot be caught by sitting near someone, working with them, or even by normal social touching, or from lavatory seats. And the virus is easily killed by heat or household bleach. You can catch it from:

Sex – all forms of penetration carry some risk, but anal intercourse is the greatest danger because the lining of the anus and rectum (back passage) is most easily broken.

Needles – unsterilized needles used for drug abuse, ear piercing, tattooing, acupuncture or medical injections (a problem in less developed countries).

Shaving – sharing razors with an AIDS carrier could transmit the disease from his cut to yours.

Toothbrushes – there is a slight risk that sharing these could spread AIDS, as gums often bleed; and there is a greater risk of hepatitis B.

Overseas blood transfusions – in Britain the blood is checked and the government says there is only 1 chance in 1,000,000 of getting AIDS this way. But travellers who need a transfusion in less developed countries run a serious risk.

Spilt blood – if infected blood enters a cut or scratch it could cause AIDS so, when in doubt, wear rubber gloves and throw away what you use to clear it up, and if you have to do first aid put a pad, such as a folded handkerchief, between yourself and any bleeding.

The high-risk groups for AIDS are homosexuals, drug addicts, prostitutes, those who may have caught it in Africa and severe haemophiliacs (who may, in the early days of AIDS, have been given contaminated blood products before they were treated to kill the virus – as they are now). In Europe and the United States male AIDS victims vastly outnumber females, whereas in Africa the numbers are fairly equal. This difference isn't fully understood but, clearly, anyone can get it, and the more sexual partners you have, the greater the risk of sleeping with a carrier. The symptoms are numerous and varied, but they include:

● swollen glands, for example in the neck or armpits
● great fatigue for no special reason
● a persistent temperature and night sweats
● persistent diarrhoea
● shortness of breath and a dry cough which won't go
● pinky-purple blotches on the skin like a bruise or blood blister
● loss of more than 10 per cent of body weight.

See also **VD**, page 564.

Allergy

Good horsemen have known for centuries that oats put a zip in sluggish horses, but make others develop skin problems and get silly. Yet the extent to which diet can affect human health is only beginning to be realized. The body can react badly to any substance it meets – in the air, in food, in drink or even in clothing. Almost any persistent health or mood problem may be due to an allergy. Common culprits include wheat, beef, milk products, caffeine, detergents, pets, feathers and certain garden plants and food additives.

Essentially, an allergy is the body's immune system over-reacting, and tests and avoidance can show which substances make it do this. If you think you have an allergy, and your GP isn't helpful, ask one of the organizations listed on page 587 where you can get expert help. Poor tests, badly interpreted, could just confuse the issue, and the government has warned about risks from desensitizing injections. In this field there are some unethical practitioners and inadequate testing laboratories, so choose carefully.

> Those allergic to medical treatments, such as penicillin, should carry a warning card or Medic-Alert bracelet (see page 547) saying so.

Alzheimer's Disease *(pre-senile dementia)*

This is a progressive disease, which can strike any adult, but affects 1 in 4 of the very old. It causes memory loss, and there may also be restlessness, loss of balance, irritability, over-reaction to stress and difficulty with basics like eating and dressing.

Nobody knows what causes it, but it can't be caught and there are physical changes in the brain, including marked loss of brain cells and unusual deposits of aluminium. There is no cure, but treatment may help and a sufferer should be registered as disabled, for entitlement to special benefits. Even so, sufferers are a great burden to their families and the future needs to be planned for: get advice at an early stage.

There is a growing body of evidence linking Alzheimer's Disease to aluminium. It is too soon to say what role it plays, at present it looks as if the cause could be exposure to high levels of aluminium *plus* an inability to stop the metal entering the brain – which may be inherited.

Cooking acid foods in aluminium pans, particularly with water containing fluoride, can dissolve the metal into the food, giving levels of aluminium up to 3,000 times those allowed in drinking water. Although there is no proof that this could cause Alzheimer's Disease it may be safest to avoid cooking in aluminium until there is proof that it *doesn't*.

Anaemia

If you have anaemia your red blood cells are inefficient, or in short supply. So too little oxygen reaches the body tissues and you easily become tired and breathless, and may have a very rapid heartbeat. But you can be anaemic and still have rosy-red cheeks. The paleness only shows in hidden places, like inside the eyelids.

Any slow insidious bleeding, for example from heavy periods, stomach ulcers or haemorrhoids, can cause anaemia. So can the extra demands of pregnancy and childbirth. But the most common cause is a poor diet. Lack of vitamin C makes it hard to absorb iron in the diet which is essential for making red blood cells. Lack of vitamin B12 and folic acid – found in liver and green vegetables – can also cause anaemia. But as there are other causes, those who think they are anaemic should see a doctor.

Anorexia and Bulimia

In anorexia it seems as if initial avoidance of food disrupts the body's mechanisms, setting up a vicious circle which causes loss of appetite and distorted thinking. Anorexics believe themselves to be fat, even when skeletal, and will lie outrageously about their food intake.

Starvation leads to loss of monthly periods, depression, severe constipation, dizziness and swelling of the face, stomach and ankles. Treatments vary. The main approaches are enforced eating and/or counselling or therapy. But recently people have also been successfully treated by adding zinc to the diet. This seems to restore the appetite and allow eating to begin again. This work is still experimental but there are good biochemical reasons for expecting zinc to help.

> The professor of organic chemistry who has pioneered this treatment says the dose should be based on a zinc taste test which shows the severity of the zinc deficiency. He also claims that, though 15 mg of zinc per day can safely be taken anyway, very much larger doses may be needed in many cases. This treatment should be discussed with a GP.

Bulimics may be a normal weight and seem happy but are caught in a compulsive cycle of bingeing and then purging or vomiting. This gradually disrupts the body's balance of mineral salts – which are vital for it to function normally – and there may be exhaustion, apathy and even coma and death. Bulimics often feel deeply ashamed and, whatever their outward appearance, may be exceedingly unhappy and depressed. Out-patient treatment, and joining a voluntary support group can help considerably. Meanwhile, bulimics should clean their teeth well after vomiting, as stomach acid rots the teeth. Zinc, as in anorexia, has been used successfully.

Appendicitis

The symptoms of appendicitis vary and are less precise in very young children than in older ones. They don't always have a stomach pain, but may have a high temperature, vomit and be irritable and off their food. Older children and adults are likely to vomit, have a stomach pain which starts around the tummy button, tenderness in this area if gently pressed, pain on coughing and a temperature of 37°-38°C (98.4°-100.4°F). In all ages there may also be a chest infection. ALWAYS CONTACT A DOCTOR IF YOU SUSPECT APPENDICITIS. Young children need *swift* medical attention – an appendix can burst dangerously in eight hours. But one type of food poisoning has similar symptoms.

Arthritis and Rheumatism

These terms have distinctly different meanings. Rheumatism is the pain caused by some 150 different rheumatic disorders in muscles, bones or joints, and affecting some 20 million people in Britain each year. Arthritis involves damage or disease in the joints. The most common forms are rheumatoid arthritis and osteoarthritis.

Rheumatoid arthritis is damage to the joint lining, which makes the smaller joints stiff and swollen. It mainly afflicts women and tends to start in their 30s and 40s. Osteoarthritis is the breakdown of the surface of the joints; it usually starts at about the age of 50, and particularly affects overworked joints – especially in the overweight.

The causes of these conditions are mysterious. Some, such as ankylosing spondylitis, rheumatoid arthritis, gout and osteoarthritis, seem to run in families. But the excess of uric acid which causes the acutely painful swelling in gout can be triggered by excess alcohol, especially beer, and by long use of diuretics. Fortunately, some forms clear up in a few years, others can be controlled with drugs, and reconstructive surgery can give mobility which once would have been impossible. Modern treatment tries to keep the sufferer mobile, and the joints should go gently through their full range of movement at least twice a day. This may be easiest when water is supporting the limb.

Some people undoubtedly find alternative medicine, such as acupuncture, chiropractic treatment or changes in diet, helps considerably. Others get relief from Balsona Ointment or Bengues Balsam, both of which contain oil of wintergreen, which is chemically a close relative of aspirin. This is also a field rich in folk remedies, such as copper bracelets, and my mother swears by a teaspoonful of honey and a teaspoonful of cider vinegar in hot water taken daily.

Asthma

About 1 child in 10 gets asthma and, although more than

Addresses and suggestions for further reading are at the ends of chapters.

half the children grow out of it, there are some 2 million asthmatics in Britain. The causes include allergies and viral infections, but asthma, hay fever and eczema tend to run in the same families, so there is probably a hereditary factor. Attacks may be triggered by exercise, suddenly breathing cold air, smoke, pollen, laughing or getting upset.

When we breathe in, the muscles round the tubes leading to the lungs normally tighten. During an asthma attack the tightening is exaggerated, so it feels like breathing in through a straw, causing coughing, wheezing, and distress. This happens very fast, and then the walls of the airpipe gradually become sore and swollen, and clogged with phlegm. Attacks often fade out untreated, but they need careful handling as they can be fatal. When someone has an attack:

1 Make sure they have taken their medicine and/or used their inhaler.
2 Stay calm and help them to stay calm and, if possible, avoid rapid breathing (gently distracting a child with a story may help).
3 Encourage them to sit with their arms resting on something slightly higher than their shoulders – this lifts the rib cage and makes breathing seem easier.
4 *Get medical help without delay if:*
   a the condition isn't improving in 15 minutes
   b breathing is exhausting them
   c they cannot stand up or speak more than a few words
   d they look blue
   e the pulse is more than 120 a minute.

Modern inhalers and drugs can control asthma very well. And if children take their medicines regularly, as prescribed, attacks can be prevented and they can live perfectly normal lives. But keep spare medication handy, and take sensible precautions like clearing the bedroom of dust and fluff and keeping smokers at bay.

A Medic-Alert bracelet can carry details of the wearer's medical condition such as epilepsy or asthma (see page 589).

Athlete's Foot and Ringworm

Athlete's foot is a fungal infection which makes the skin between the toes white, soggy, and uncomfortable. It can be caught wherever others go barefoot, and is worth curing fast, as it can spread to the upper thighs where it is most uncomfortable. Dry the area carefully after washing and use one of the powders sold for treating it. Wear cotton socks rather than man-made fibres and shake the powder into them before putting them on. Keep this up

for several weeks after the symptoms disappear to kill the last traces of infection, or the infection will return.

Ringworm is a fungus in the same family, but it starts as an itchy red rash anywhere on the body, and gradually becomes ring-shaped with a paler centre and a scaly surface. It can be caught from people and animals (dogs, cats, cattle) and needs medical treatment to stop it from spreading.

Back Pain

Back pain has many possible causes, but it isn't normal – at any age – and the earlier it is treated, the faster and more permanent the cure. If left to itself it may go away, only to recur, more severely, months or years later. Pain is often attributed to pulled muscles. But it is extremely hard to pull a back muscle and a more likely cause is a small displacement in the spine itself. Having been totally immobilized by back pain, and totally cured, I confess to a prejudice. One effective treatment, in many cases, seems to me to be offered by fully qualified chiropractors who use gentle manipulation to correct the offending bones. This is now recommended by some GPs. However, by no means all back pain would be treated by chiropractors. A number of back conditions do need conventional medical treatment.

To avoid back pain lift heavy objects carefully, bending the knees, keeping the back upright and lifting from the legs. And don't risk your back by trying to lift something too heavy for you without suitable help.

Bed Sores

Bed sores happen when someone, bedridden or chairbound, stays too long in one position. Pressure then cuts off the blood supply to a patch of flesh, which dies, forming an open sore. Prevention is much better than cure. Any reddening of the skin should be taken as a warning and the position changed. Putting a sheepskin pad under any pressure point helps (good pharmacists sell these) and there are now ripple beds and cushions which vary the pressure by circulating water under the patient (organizations for the disabled have the details).

Birth Marks

Mongolian blue spots are small blueish patches found on the lower backs of black and Asian babies, but they usually fade as the child gets older.

A port wine stain (capillary naevus) is a dark-red patch with a raised edge. It doesn't change, but some NHS hospitals now treat these with a laser. They vary in how well they respond and there may sometimes be scars, but many people prefer pale scars to a dark stain, and cosmetic camouflage can hide either (see In Health).

Salmon patches (sometimes called stork-marks) are pinky-red marks on a baby's forehead and eyelids and at the nape of the neck. They go in a few months.

A strawberry mark starts as a small red dot on the face which grows during the early months and becomes a raised red lump. It usually starts to fade in the second year and vanishes by the time the child is 5 or 6.

Bites, Scratches and Stings

Bites and **scratches** from animals should be washed thoroughly and treated with a mild antiseptic. Deep bites also need an anti-tetanus injection, unless the victim is properly immunized (see page 569).

Insect bites from ants, gnats and so on do no great harm. The best antidote is bicarbonate of soda in a little water. Moist soap is also soothing and so is fresh urine. (Not perhaps a nice idea, but at least you always have it with you.)

The best treatment for **nettle stings** is the age-old one of rubbing them with dock leaves, which usually grow nearby, but sage or mint will do instead.

Wasp stings are painful but seldom do much harm. To minimize the pain bathe them with vinegar. **Bees** leave their sting in the skin, so pull it out with tweezers, then bathe the sting with water and bicarbonate of soda. Remember: 'Vinegar for Vasps; Bicarb for Bees.' An ice cube on either sting will soothe it.

There is a rare condition, called anaphylactic shock, in which someone can react violently to a sting and become extremely ill, needing immediate medical attention. Take someone to hospital RAPIDLY if they show any of the following signs:

- swelling *away* from the site of the sting
- blueness of the skin and/or lips
- difficulty in breathing
- a rash or flushed face
- a rapid pulse
- collapse.

Boils

A boil is a bacterial infection in one of the pores. The area swells and fills with pus until it bursts. Keep a boil covered when near to bursting and hurry it along by applying a hot poultice. The best poultice is from a chemist, and based on magnesium, which draws out the fluid. Failing that, bread mashed with very hot water, squeezed out and placed between gauze which is then bandaged on can help – provided it isn't so hot that it burns. If a boil is very painful a doctor may relieve the pain by opening it.

Brittle Bones

There are two very different conditions which cause brittle bones.

Osteogenesis Imperfecta starts before birth and is sometimes inherited. In severe cases the bones are so fragile they fracture in the womb; in mild cases children may have several dozen fractures during childhood but live a normal life. Sadly, many are unable to walk, and repeated and inexplicable breaks have sometimes led to parents of such children wrongly being accused of ill treatment. It is incurable.

Osteoporosis has been called 'the silent epidemic': it will affect 1 woman in 3, and 1 man in 20 – and the figures are rising. Bones constantly shed cells and re-

place them with new ones. In osteoporosis too few are replaced. So, as people get older, the bones become small and fracture easily, and the bones in the spine weaken and crush painfully. More British women die of complications after hip fractures than of cancer of the cervix, breast and uterus combined.

Not all the risk factors are known but we need enough exercise and enough calcium in childhood and puberty to build strong bones. This regime must be continued. And after the menopause, or the removal of the womb or ovaries, or long-term cortico steroids, people need extra calcium, because hormone changes make its absorption less efficient (as does smoking, alcoholism and drug taking). People also need enough exercise, because without it the body doesn't renew bone so efficiently. Hormone replacement therapy (HRT) prevents and treats this condition and there are now other treatments that can stop the bones thinning. A bone density measurement – similar to an X-ray – can be used to check whether someone is at risk of osteoporosis. Ask the National Osteoporosis Society (page 588) about this. However, black people seem to be very much better at making bones than white people, so osteoporosis isn't their problem.

Bronchitis and Emphysema

Bronchitis attacks the air passages in the lungs. In acute bronchitis the sufferer has an irritating, dry and painful cough, and tightness in the chest, a temperature of 38°-39.5°C (100°-103°F), and may later cough up thick yellow, green, or blood-flecked phlegm. A healthy person will get over this in a few weeks without treatment, but chronic bronchitis is a long-standing problem causing breathlessness and a persistent cough. The more cigarettes a person smokes, the more likely they are to get this – and it can kill. Acute attacks can be treated with antibiotics, and those prone to it should talk to their doctor about having a flu vaccination, as colds and flu may trigger it.

Emphysema is when the lung tissue itself is damaged and becomes bad at transferring oxygen to the blood. It is linked to bronchitis and far more common in smokers. The lung damage of emphysema cannot be repaired, but those who stop smoking prevent greater damage, and if they stop before they get breathless, chronic bronchitis can be prevented. They should avoid cold, smoky or foggy air, get down to a normal weight and use hot drinks to help them bring up phlegm.

Cancer

Cancer is a fault in the mechanism which controls the development of body cells. So they multiply unchecked, forming a large growth in many cases (like an outsized internal wart) which gradually blocks the working of that part of the body. There are about 200 different types of cancer, and almost as many causes. But there have been dramatic improvements in treatment. Leukaemia in children can be cured in 50 to 75 per cent of cases, and cancers of the kidney, testicles and placenta are usually curable.

Addresses and suggestions for further reading are at the ends of chapters.

Recent developments in biochemistry have allowed cancer treatments to be more precise. At the same time, even in the bastions of conventional medicine, there has been a growing feeling that cancer may be related to the body failing to suppress it, and that this in turn may be linked to the mind as well as the body. Research shows that a positive attitude of getting on with life greatly increases the chances of defeating cancer. Organizations like the Bristol Programme encourage the patient to fight cancer through changes in lifestyle, diet and outlook as well as by medical means. Two books on these methods (page 588), written by former cancer patients, can help with the sense of isolation and distress that cancer brings. They also cover measures that may lessen the chances of cancer developing.

Bowel Cancer

Cancer of the bowel is less likely in those who eat plenty of fresh fruit and vegetables and fibre, and avoid excessive amounts of meat, fat and beer. The first symptoms may be alternating constipation and diarrhoea, blood in the stools and perhaps stomach pains. These can all have other causes but a doctor should be told. It may be treated by radiation, medicines or an operation to remove part of the bowel. If the cut ends of the bowel can't be joined, an opening is made in the stomach wall to replace the anus. This is a colostomy, and a disposable bag is attached to the opening to collect the stools. Afterwards the patient can live a normal life.

Breast Cancer

Breast cancer is the most common form of cancer in women, and the earlier it is caught the less drastic treatment need be. So every woman should be regularly checked by a doctor or check herself. Self-checking is taught at many local clinics. Checking the breasts at the same time each month, a few days after a period, is a first step to catching trouble early. These illustrations show how it is done.

Lie down with a towel under you and hunch your left shoulder up. Feel carefully for any lumps or other unusual signs at the top of your breast.

Raise your arm above your head and continue to feel around the breast, checking every part. Use your fingers rather than your palm.

Stand before a mirror with your hands above your head and look at your breasts closely for puckering or any other changes.

Continue to check the area right into your armpit. Then repeat these stages for the other breast.

- Does every part of the breast and nipple look normal – for you?
- Does every part of the breast and nipple feel normal – for you?
- Is the skin free from puckering?
- Is the skin surface its normal colour with no swelling, dimpling or puckering?
- Are the nipples free from any bleeding or weeping?

Any lump or abnormality should be seen by a doctor AT ONCE. Most lumps are *not* cancer, so your mind may well be put at rest. But if it is cancer, catching it early minimizes the treatment. Sometimes the lump can be checked by extracting a little fluid with a syringe; but sometimes a piece of tissue must be taken under general anaesthetic. In this case a woman may be asked to sign a form consenting to an immediate removal of the cancer if it is found. She does not have to consent, and should ask her doctor about the other options.

Breast Cancer Treatments

There is now a trend towards removing no more of the breast than is absolutely necessary, and treatment with radiation, chemicals or hormones may be used instead of or as well as an operation. There are three kinds of operation:

1 A lumpectomy is the removal of a small lump of breast containing the tumour and may change the breast very little.
2 A segmentectomy removes a larger section of breast, but shows relatively little on large breasts.
3 A mastectomy removes all the breast tissue, including the nipple, leaving the chest flat, and there is usually a curved scar towards the armpit. After the operation it will be tender and have pins and needles occasionally, and the arm and shoulder may be stiff.

Prostheses (falsies) are made to match every size and shape of breast, so people can swim and sunbathe without anyone spotting the difference. They are available on the NHS, and so are replacements – but some people prefer those sold privately.

Mastectomy isn't the end of everything: it's the beginning of life without cancer. Even so, it is hard to come to terms with losing part of one's body, especially when it is linked to one's identity as a woman, and it is better to talk about the sense of loss than keep smiling bravely. The Breastcare and Mastectomy Association (see page 588) can supply that need. And plastic surgery can often remake the missing breast if you wish.

Cervical Cancer

This cancer of the neck of the womb is probably caused by a virus transmitted during sexual intercourse. If so, the more a man sleeps around, the greater chance he has of passing it from one woman to another, and the more a woman sleeps around the greater her chance of meeting a carrier.

Regular tests are very important because cancer doesn't blossom overnight. Cells go through a stage when they are neither totally normal nor fully cancerous, and there are no symptoms. If a smear test finds them at this time they can be easily cured.

The smear test is nothing to worry about. A doctor slips a small wooden spatula into the vagina and brushes a few skin cells on to it. This only takes a moment or two and doesn't hurt.

One of the leading professional bodies in this field recommends that women have a cervical smear test every 3 years, from the first intercourse until they reach the age of 45, then every 5 years after that. But, ideally, a woman over 35 should have an annual check for diabetes, breast and other female cancers, with a smear test thrown in.

If tests show the cells are abnormal they can usually be burnt off *painlessly* with a laser, leaving tissue which quickly heals and is totally cured.

In 1 woman in 10 the abnormal area extends deeper into the cervix and a cone biopsy, which removes a section of the cervix, is needed. This is also done in more minor cases if a hospital has no laser. As it sometimes makes miscarriages more likely it is always worth checking whether the laser method can be used – and asking to have it at another hospital if necessary.

If cancer is established in the cervix it may be treated with radiation, medication or surgery. Surgery usually involves the removal of the womb (a hysterectomy). This is a major operation needing up to 2 weeks in hospital and 3 months of taking things easy. Sexual intercourse has to be avoided for at least 6 weeks after, and if the ovaries have been removed the patient may experience the symptoms of the change of life. Sex may also feel different, but the loss of the womb doesn't prevent orgasm and after this operation is over a very full recovery is possible.

Lung Cancer

Of the 158,000 people in Britain who die of cancer each year 1 in 4 has lung cancer – and 9 out of 10 of those are smokers. The earliest symptom of lung cancer is often a cough. Smokers may think this is simply a harmless smoker's cough. There may also be an ache in the chest either on coughing, or taking a deep breath or all the time. If examination reveals lung cancer it may be treated by radiation, with chemicals or by removing all or part of a lung. This still leaves enough to breathe with if the cancer is not too advanced but, by the time lung cancer is diagnosed, cancer may have invaded other parts of the body.

Skin Cancer

Skin cancer is increasing dramatically: it is now the second most common form of cancer in the UK, and it can kill. There are three different types. One type (melanoma) can spread to other parts of the body if it isn't treated. And the cases of melanoma are doubling every 10 years. Eight out of 10 skin cancers are caused by too much sunlight. People with naturally blond or red hair are most at risk, but all white people should seriously limit their sunbathing and use a high protection sunscreen. The typical symptoms are a new lump or sore which refuses to go away after several weeks, or a

Addresses and suggestions for further reading are at the ends of chapters.

change in the size or colour of a lump or sore which has been there for some while. Tell a doctor about these or about patches of skin of a different colour.

Most moles are harmless, but some can be cancerous. Consult a doctor if one changes shape or colour or bleeds. In 90 per cent of cases skin cancer can be cured by surgery, radiation or medicines if treated fast.

Happily, you can take action to prevent skin cancer. The most common cause is sunlight damaging the skin's DNA, so avoid getting sunburnt. Use a high-factor sunscreen, *which protects against both UVA and UVB light*, wear a brimmed hat and sun-block moisturizers and be very moderate in your sunbathing. It is *very* important that children aren't burnt. Even one incident of severe sunburn in childhood can make the risk of skin cancer as an adult *many times* greater. Even olive skins need a sunscreen of factor 8 or more and the fair or freckly skinned, who are most at risk, need factor 15 or more. However, not all the sunscreens block both A and B light waves. The medical organization MASTA (page 592) sells a sunblock, by mail and through BA travel clinics, which *does*. And the children's version is formulated so that you can tell if too little has been used to give proper protection.

Testicular Cancer

Cancer in a testicle is far more common than you might think and any unusual swelling, lump or pain in that area should be taken to a doctor at once. It is, however, usually one of the easiest cancers to cure. SOS (page 588) has a leaflet on self-examination.

Chilblains

When I was writing *Supertips to Make Life Easy*, a woman in Cambridgeshire wrote and told me that chilblains could be cured by bathing them with your own urine. When my daughter and I developed chilblains, we tried it. We both found it stops the itching almost instantly and that regular applications cure chilblains completely. But use it fresh. This is not the dirty remedy it may sound: if we can go around unbothered by a whole bagful of urine *inside* us a few drops outside are no great matter. Alternatively, go to your GP for medication.

Chlamydia *(Chlamydia trachomatis)*

This is becoming very common and needs immediate treatment, as it can block the fallopian tubes and make a woman sterile. It can also be transmitted to the unborn child, causing serious eye infections and sometimes blindness. Women's symptoms vary, and include pain deep in the lower abdomen, pain on intercourse or on urinating. A man may have a slight discharge and mild inflammation of the penis, and/or discomfort on urinating. But, in both sexes, there may be no symptoms at all. It can be cured, and anyone who has slept around or whose partner has should consider tests to check they don't have it – especially if they intend to become pregnant. Sexual partners need to be treated. See also **VD**, page 564.

Cold Sores

Cold sores are caused by a virus in the same family as the one causing genital herpes. So it is very important not to do anything which might transfer the infection to your own or someone else's genitals, and direct contact with the cold sore should be avoided. A sore starts as itching and tingling, then blisters form, which crust in a couple of days. It normally clears up in 10 days without treatment, but it may recur and a child can feel ill and miserable and need to drink through a straw because opening the mouth wider hurts. Some people find covering the cold sore completely with lip balm or vaseline speeds healing. But don't stick a finger which has touched the sore back in the pot. Cold sores may also lead to impetigo (page 559).

Constipation

Some people still think the bowels should move regularly at the same time each day. So they sit straining until they do. This shouldn't happen. The time to go to the lavatory is when nature urges, and the modern definition of constipation isn't failing to go every day: it is having hard stools which are difficult to pass – even if they are passed daily. On a balanced diet, with plenty of roughage and enough fluid, stools should be soft enough to pass quickly and comfortably. The body may produce several a day, or none for a day or so. The pause is no disaster, the body isn't a machine.

The main treatment for constipation is therefore a change of diet. But a temporary way to add roughage is by taking 1 to 2 dessertspoonfuls of bran (the plain kind sold by Boots, not Allbran) in yoghurt, cereal or stewed fruit. But there is some evidence that raw bran like this may make it harder for the body to take up calcium. So this should not be a regular practice.

Laxatives should only be taken occasionally, and be the mildest which work. Taking them too often can make the bowels lazy and increase the problem. Children can also get very constipated and may need such temporary help, though the important point is to find out why they are constipated.

Corns and Calluses

Corns and calluses are best prevented. So whenever a layer of hard skin forms, rub it well with a pumice stone at each bath. This can prevent a corn from developing. Banishing established ones may need a chiropodist but, unless you're diabetic or have problems with your circulation, try treating them carefully with a good corn-removing solution and corn plasters. Alternatively, bread soaked in vinegar and applied to a corn at night under a plaster will soften it. Meanwhile, take the pressure off the area with a circular corn pad, and stop wearing the shoes which are causing the corns.

Colds and Coughs

The classic runny nose, sore throat, sneezing and feeling of being below par can be accompanied by a temperature of 37.5°-38°C (99°-100°F) and these symptoms usually last 4 to 10 days. Opinions are divided as to whether colds should be ignored or taken to bed for a day or so. Doctors tend to favour the former, but some psychotherapists say mild infections like this can be the body's way of telling you to let up, and that failing to take the hint can lead to more serious illness. As we meet germs every day and only get ill sometimes this seems eminently logical.

There is no magic cure. The medicines which claim to stop the symptoms only do so for a short period, then they come right back. Decongestant drops have the same effect if used for more than 5-6 days (3-4 for a baby). But home remedies can do a lot. To make breathing easier put a few drops of oil of eucalyptus in a pudding bowl, pour on very hot water and sit with your head over this, with a towel forming a tent over the top so that you breathe in the vapour. Do this three times a day. For children, place the bowl in a washbasin, then if it spills it won't scald them. Rubbing some Vick on the chest will produce a vapour which will make breathing easier at night. So will a few drops of oil of eucalyptus on the pillow case. If babies have trouble feeding, gently clean out their nostrils with a cotton bud before meals. They also sleep more easily on their sides, though older children may prefer to be propped up.

Coughing

Coughing is a device for keeping catarrh off the chest and there is really no need to spend money on cough mixtures – many of which do very little. It is just as good to give plenty of hot drinks, adding a little glycerine (from a chemist) or honey to soothe the throat. Or put a teaspoon of the spice turmeric in a saucepan with a cup of milk, and bring to the boil. Sweeten this with sugar or honey to taste and drink it three times a day. This is an Indian remedy and cures coughs better than any other I know. Turmeric has a soft, almost scented, flavour (though when old it can taste bitter), but the brilliant yellow stains badly, so watch where you put it. The full effects won't be felt for three days, but the cough may improve before that, and it is just as good for bronchitis. In both cases it attacks the catarrh which causes the cough – though it only works on chest catarrh, and doesn't clear the head. Use steam inhalations as described for colds, as well.

Contact the doctor about the cough if:

- the cough lasts more than 10 days
- coughing produces yellow or green catarrh
- there is pain in the chest or shortness of breath
- coughing produces any blood
- the cough might be whooping-cough.

Flying with a thick cold can damage the ears as the air cannot get through the inner tubes to balance the pressure. Some ear specialists say people with heavy colds shouldn't fly, but if you *have* to do so ask your doctor for something to dry up the catarrh during the journey.

Cramp

Cramp is a painful and uncontrollable tightening of a group of muscles when lactic acid builds up in a muscle faster than the body can carry it away. This may be because an awkward position cuts off the blood supply, or because exercise makes the body produce more lactic acid than usual, or when there are extra demands on the blood supply, as in pregnancy. It is nothing to worry about. But don't swim for at least an hour after a heavy meal, especially if the water is cold: digesting food occupies the blood supply so it can't handle the lactic acid produced by swimming. This makes cramp a serious risk and people have drowned because of it.

A 'stitch' (rib muscle cramp) will go if you bend several times and try to kiss your knee; cramp in the foot will go if you turn your toes up, and so on. Massaging it afterwards will stimulate the blood supply and make the cramp less likely to return, and pregnant women who can't reach crampy insteps should roll their foot hard over a bottle. Some sports coaches advise drinking bicarbonate of soda in water before an event to counteract the acid. Those bothered by cramps could talk to their doctor about this.

Croup

Croup sounds like barking and is caused by a virus making the breathing tubes swell. It tends to happen at night to children under 4 years old. If they panic it aggravates the problem, *so be calm and reassuring*. Steam is the fastest way to relieve it. Just take the child into the bathroom and tell it you are going to make the cough better. Sit on the edge of the bath, holding the child upright on your knees, put the plug in and run the hot tap so the room fills with steam. (DO NOT put the child in the bath.) If there is no bath water boil up a kettle with the lid off and sit as near as is safe. Let the steam ease the coughing and then give the child a warm drink in little sips, *saying* that the drink will help. Once the croup is over a vaporizer lamp in the bedroom, until the infection goes, may stop a recurrence.

In most cases, croup fades with the steam. But, if the child has such difficulty in breathing that the lower ribs are sucked in at each breath and the skin looks blue, call an ambulance IMMEDIATELY.

Cuts and Grazes

Most cuts and grazes are nothing to worry about, and they don't need the treatment usually meted out to them. Nor should children see that adults are worried. Be reassuring, wash any dirt out under lukewarm running water, and gently remove stubborn grit with a clean handkerchief or cotton wool. Failing clean water, the victim should suck a graze and spit out any grit. If there is a lot of bleeding raise the cut above the head. Research shows it is best *not* to use strong antiseptics. They kill the body's defences against infection. It is far better to use a gentle, painless antiseptic like Savlon cream or witch-hazel. And if neither is obtainable, either honey or sugar will help to keep down infection, but don't use these where ants might be attracted.

Grazes tend to heal best when left uncovered – unless they are in a place which gets dirty. Cuts may need a bandage or sticking plaster. Whether one needs stitches or not will depend on its length, depth and position – a cut on the face may need stitches when one of similar size on a knee wouldn't, but if in doubt consult a doctor.

Try not to get young children used to sticking plaster on the slightest hurt. Once it becomes an essential part of making cuts better they may cry blue murder when it isn't available. One wise mother I know taught her child that a kiss and/or a nice drink of cold water were the big healers – and there are few places where you can't get either.

> There is often confusion between antiseptics and disinfectants. Disinfectants do kill germs, but they should NEVER be used on the human body, as some could cause chemical burns. Use them on the loo, not on you.

Cystitis

Cystitis is an infection of the bladder which causes an urgent and frequent desire to 'pee'. Urinating causes a burning sensation, and the urine may be flecked with blood. There may also be a fever and a pain low in the abdomen. It's mainly a female problem, because the bacteria which cause it invade from outside the body and women have a far shorter urinary tube for it to travel up. The bacteria can come from the anus. So women should make a habit of wiping from front to back, and if they indulge in anal intercourse the man should wash well before making love in any other way.

Most attacks can be cured with medical treatment. But at the first sign of any symptoms the following steps may stop an attack developing:

1 Drink ½ pint (285 ml) of water containing 1 teaspoon bicarbonate of soda (those with kidney or heart trouble should consult their doctor first).
2 After that, drink ½ pint of a bland, non-acid, non-irritant liquid every half hour – milk, weak tea, water, herb tea, etc., but *not* fruit juice or coffee. And repeat the bicarbonate of soda every 3 hours.
3 Take a mild pain killer if you need it.
4 Sit or lie down if you possibly can.

As the attack passes, ease up on the drinking but stay off acid drinks and make sure you drink 4 to 5 pints of bland liquid a day for the next week or two. Don't use sprays or douches in that area, they will aggravate the problem, and follow the suggestions on page 565 for hygiene.

There are two other causes of cystitis symptoms. One is bruising of the tube leading to a woman's bladder, caused by rough lovemaking, or intercourse before a woman is excited enough to produce lubrication (often called 'honeymoon cystitis'). In these cases, let the bruising die down and then re-start lovemaking more considerately. Also a small proportion of cystitis sufferers have nothing clinically wrong and cystitis may be a sign of anxiety or some deeper emotional or sexual problem. It will go only when they sort this out.

Diabetes *(Diabetes mellitus, or sugar diabetes)*

Diabetes is a breakdown in the mechanism by which the hormone insulin adjusts the level of sugar in the blood. So the amount of sugar in the blood, after meals, is far too high, too much sugar reaches the kidneys and they have to produce extra urine to handle it. The early symptoms are excessive thirst and excessive urine, coupled with loss of energy, loss of weight and possibly boils or thrush.

There are two forms. Insulin dependent diabetes starts in the young and thin and maturity onset diabetes mainly in the middle-aged, elderly, and overweight. There is no cure for either, but they can be controlled, and anyone with diabetic symptoms should see a doctor immediately. Proper control is important because diabetes can damage the walls of the blood vessels from the heart.

Control is by diet, plus possibly tablets or insulin injections. Treatment is less effective in the overweight, and the ideal diet is one which keeps the carbohydrate supply fairly steady. Once diabetes is under control diabetics need to eat regularly. This is especially important before driving because if the glucose balance suffers it causes faintness, sweating, headache, sickness, double vision, bad temper and – if not treated – unconsciousness. At the first signs of any of these symptoms a diabetic should take a sugary drink or glucose tablets.

Diabetics need to have regular eye checks and take care of their feet as they are prone to foot and eye trouble. They should carry a card saying they are on insulin, and declare diabetes on a driving application form and tell their car insurance company – but there should be no added premium.

The Stillbirth and Neonatal Death Society has a leaflet on how diabetics can prevent problems in pregnancy (page 642).

Diarrhoea

Diarrhoea is defined as loose watery stools several times a day, and is often attributed to a change in diet or climate. Doctors now dismiss this theory. Some foods, such as chillies, figs and prunes, can act like dynamite but, those apart, diarrhoea is caused by bacteria.

Many of the diarrhoea medicines sold across the counter are no longer approved of by doctors. The modern method is to give the bacteria nothing to feed on. So drink *plenty* of water, and *eat nothing*. The quantity of water is important as a lot of fluid is lost and there is a danger of dehydration, particularly in young children in a hot climate. The World Health Organization (WHO) recommends giving the following solution to help prevent this. In 1 litre (2 pt) of water put 1 flat (*not* rounded) teaspoonful of salt, and 5 to 8 teaspoonfuls of sugar or glucose, and give this little and very often. It is important not to give too much salt as young children can be harmed by it. A similar mixture is available in chemists and is called the mixture for Oral Rehydration Therapy (ORT).

If a baby has diarrhoea see a doctor the same day and meanwhile give plenty of ORT mixture in cool boiled water. Children over a year should only be given the WHO mixture in boiled water and must be taken to a doctor if it hasn't cleared up in 36 hours – or sooner if really unwell. Any child with pinkish stools should also see a doctor.

If you can't stick to just water, plain boiled rice dressed with lemon juice is the least harmful food. An old home remedy, which was given to my grandmother by a doctor, is to starve and drink fluids as above but drink port too. It works well, and Mexican tequila also seems effective. If diarrhoea lasts see a doctor.

Disabilities

The range of disabilities is so wide, and their problems so individual, that it's impossible to do justice to them here. The best sources of information and help are the charities concerned, and some of the major ones dealing with deafness, blindness and mental and other disabilities are given on pages 590–592. There are more and more excellent aids and electronic devices for the disabled, and it is well worth joining an appropriate organization to keep in touch with developments, and the special programmes on Radio 4 and television are good sources of information.

Ear Problems

The eardrum forms a barrier between the ear's outer tube and its inner workings, and problems can be roughly divided into those outside the eardrum and those behind it.

Otitis Media

The most common cause of earache in children is acute otitis media, in which an infection builds up behind the eardrum making it tight and painful. A child often has a cold at the time, and the pain tends to be worse at night because it is harder for the build-up to drain away when lying down. Sitting the child up for a while, to let the ear drain, and giving him or her paracetemol and a decongestant should help considerably. Placing a warm pad on the ear may also be soothing, but a doctor should be seen as soon as possible.

Glue Ear

Repeated infections can lead to a condition called 'glue ear' in which thick fluid collects behind the eardrum and gradually causes deafness – 20 per cent of children have

this at some time. It may cure itself but, if not, it can be cured by a minor operation which drains it away. Any child who has had earache more than once should be watched for signs of deafness, because it is remarkably hard to recognize its gradual onset. Children who become partially deaf (as my son did), may simply seem disobedient or may follow an instruction but get it oddly wrong (for example, 'take the cat outside' could be heard as 'take the cat upstairs'), they may do poorly at school or have temper tantrums. Hearing tests done in school aren't always sensitive enough to detect this sort of hearing loss. So, if a child has any sign of a hearing problem it should see a specialist immediately. Deafness in the early years at school is a handicap that takes a long time to overcome.

Minor Ear Problems

Loss of hearing can also be caused, at any age, by wax building up in the outer ear and a doctor can syringe this out. A boil in the tube of the outer ear is rather more painful and may need antibiotics. Young children may also get pain when they have something stuck in their ear. Unless it is very easy to remove, it may be best to let a doctor do it, rather than risk pushing it farther down.

Deafness

Specialists say that when talking to the very deaf one should use familiar words, and talk normally, but not too fast, facing both them and the light. Don't cover your mouth or smoke or eat. And treat them normally – they have ear trouble not brain trouble.

Adults often deny their growing deafness until they have lost a great deal of hearing. By then they may have lost the habit of listening, and of selecting the words they want to listen to from the host of background noises. It is then far harder to adjust to a hearing aid than it might have been when only a little deaf. Both children and adults should see a doctor *as soon as* there is a possibility of deafness. The sooner action is taken to cure or relieve it the better.

Tinnitus

Tinnitus is a condition in which strange, often ringing, sounds are heard. Sufferers sometimes think they are going mad, because the rest of the world can't hear the sounds. It is not a sign of madness; it is an ear problem which has a variety of causes, including excessive use of aspirin. It is not usually curable, but it may go and masking the noise can give relief. Ask the Royal National Institute for the Deaf (page 591) about this.

Addresses and suggestions for further reading are at the ends of chapters.

Eczema

Eczema produces rough, itchy, red patches which may weep, especially where the skin is soft, such as the backs of the knees or wrists. But it can affect any part of the body. It may come and go for no obvious reason, but it can't be caught and most often starts in infancy. It seems as if about half of those who have eczema may have an allergy, and cows' milk and eggs are common culprits. Often relatives have eczema, hay fever, asthma or dry skin. So, when these conditions run in the family, some doctors recommend breast feeding for babies, and careful attention to diet. It may also be worth avoiding food additives. More drastic dietary changes should only be made on a doctor's advice, and creams may be prescribed which help considerably. Keep the skin soft by avoiding soap and using emulsifying ointment for washing (a chemist will order it). Apply moisturizing cream afterwards – different creams suit different skins, as there are many types of eczema. There is growing evidence that some of them respond to alternative treatments, such as Chinese herbal remedies or Evening Primrose Oil. The National Eczema Society (page 589) has the facts.

Ninety per cent of cases improve during childhood, but eczema can also be an allergic reaction in adulthood, or be linked with varicose veins. Use pure soap for washing clothes, rinse garments very well and go for cotton which is often less irritating than wool or man-made fibres. Keep the nails short and clean, and scratch as little as possible (children may need mittens attached to the sleeves of their nightwear). *Most importantly*, sufferers could become seriously infected by contact with cold sores or impetigo, and must be kept away from anyone who has them. Very severe cases may qualify for financial help from the DH.

Epilepsy

Epilepsy affects about one person in 200 and has a variety of causes, but most epileptics are intellectually normal and lead perfectly normal lives, and some children grow out of it completely. However, anyone diagnosed as epileptic must tell the driving licence authority and may not drive for 2 years after the last fit. Fits can last from seconds to hours, and occur several times a day or only once in many months. What causes them varies greatly, but flickering light is a common trigger.

In a major fit (grand mal, tonic-clonic, or convulsion) there is usually no warning. Victims become unconscious and the muscles stiffen then relax, there are jerky movements, saliva may appear round the mouth, (blood-flecked if the tongue has been bitten) and they may wet themselves. Minor fits (petit-mal or absence) may be so slight that there is just a moment or two of blankness and clouded consciousness. Anyone who has fits of either type should see a doctor.

Epilepsy First Aid
- Get the sufferer away from hazards – sharp objects, fires etc.
- Put something soft under the head.
- Let the fit run its course without restraining movement.
- As soon as possible remove false teeth, check the airway is clear and place the victim in the recovery position (page 581).
- DO NOT put anything between the teeth – it could be bitten off and choke them – and don't put your fingers in their mouth.
- DO NOT give anything to drink until they wake FULLY.
- Gently loosen tight clothing round the neck.
- Only call a doctor if one fit follows another without a return to consciousness.
- Reassure them as consciousness returns.

Eye Problems

Grit and Eyelashes
If a piece of grit, or an eyelash, gets into an eye, fold a clean handkerchief into a point, and use this gently to wipe the particle away. To see where it is, pull the lower eyelid away with the eyes up, or pull the upper lid up with the eyes down. If nothing can be seen try leaning under a cold tap and running cold water over the eye. But DON'T use an eyebath; it could wash the particle farther back, and don't try to remove a speck which is embedded in the dark area of the eye. See a doctor as the cornea can be scratched. See First Aid (page 576) for chemicals in the eye.

Eyesight
Sunlight is a major danger to the eyes: the delicate inner workings of the eye age in proportion to the amount of light which hits them. So the more eyes are exposed to bright light the faster they age, and the younger the failing vision and cataracts of 'old age' develop. Eye specialists recommend using fully protective sunglasses but most fashion glasses are *not* protective enough. Look for really dark glasses in shades of brown, orange or yellowy green. The time to have an eye check – whether you have glasses or not – is when you notice a change. See also Blindness and Partial Sight, page 590.

Fainting

Fainting isn't something to worry about. It happens when, momentarily, too little blood reaches the brain, so the person loses consciousness, and looks pale. It is most common in adolescence, but can be caused by fear (the classic 'strong' man fainting at the sight of an injection), shock, standing immobile for too long (guards on parade), extreme fatigue and standing up suddenly when hot. When someone faints leave them lying down, and raise their feet higher than their head. Let them come round in their own time and stay lying down until fully recovered. There is no need to give smelling salts or any other treatment.

Genital Warts

A sexually transmitted virus causes warts in the genital

area up to 9 months after infection. They start as hard whiteheads but can grow to large, uncomfortable, warty masses. Unfortunately, women who have had them may have a higher risk of cervical cancer – but this may depend on the type of wart virus. So anyone who develops them should stop intercourse and get treatment to avoid passing on the risk. After having them, women need a cervical smear each year. See also **VD**, page 564.

Glandular Fever (*infectious mononucleosis*)

This virus infection is caught from saliva – which is why it is called 'the kissing disease'. Predictably, it is most common between the ages of 15 and 25, though you can get it at any age. It causes a temperature for several days, then a sore throat and infected tonsils, and the glands down the neck below the angle of the jaw may become swollen and tender. There may also be a fine red rash – particularly if the sore throat is treated with certain antibiotics. It is always worth seeing a doctor about these symptoms and checking that it *is* glandular fever. Some other medical problems have very similar symptoms, and it often takes a blood test to tell which is which.

The treatment is complete rest, gargling with a soluble pain killer when the throat is very painful, and eating soothing foods. A young child usually recovers in 2 to 4 weeks, but someone older can take far longer and they may feel weak, depressed and very easily tired for some months afterwards. It may also recur, though usually quite mildly.

Gonorrhoea

Gonorrhoea is the most common venereal disease, and probably the most widespread treatable infection in the world. A report in 1971 found it was the most common communicable disease in America after the common cold – and increasing. But it is more easily passed from a man to a woman than vice versa. The symptoms often start 2 to 10 days after infection. Men normally have a profuse yellow discharge from the penis, and a burning sensation on urinating – the French *chaudepisse* describes it well. If the anus is infected there may also be irritation and a discharge. Women may have discomfort on urinating, vaginal discharge, pain in the abdomen, occasionally aching joints and a fever. But many women, and some men, have *no* symptoms at all. It is infectious from the moment it is caught, not just when symptoms show. And in women the bacteria may be hard to trace, so most clinics do 2 tests on any woman who is a gonorrhoea contact.

It is easily cured, but needs rapid treatment, and every sexual contact must be seen too. Untreated, it can damage the reproductive organs of both sexes, and produce other major complications. Babies who contact the infection during birth can develop eye problems, and may occasionally go blind. Unfortunately, some overseas forms are becoming resistant to penicillin and need other antibiotics. See also **VD**, page 564.

Hay Fever (*Allergic Rhinitis*)

Hay fever is an allergic reaction which causes watering eyes and a streaming nose. The allergy is usually to pollen but the same symptoms are produced by allergy to substances like dust, pets and feathers. It is best to keep away from the substance which causes the reaction, but see a doctor; there are now safe and effective remedies for hay fever.

Headaches

Headaches aren't a problem; they are a symptom of a problem. The most common causes of headaches are tension, eye strain, back trouble or the start of an illness. Or it could just be a need for love and attention. If a child gets a headache try curing it with a long drink of cool water and a soothing head massage rather than with pain killers. Giving pain killers too readily can teach a child that the solution to every problem is found in a tablet. Logically it isn't a very big step from this to thinking that the answer to the pains of adolescence lies in drugs. That doesn't mean pain killers should never be given, but it is better if they are not a *first* resort, and better for children to learn that love and cherishing are also healers. Nor need this be limited to children.

When a headache is combined with other signs of illness any sufferer should be watched carefully and a doctor contacted if necessary. A doctor should also be seen if headaches occur regularly – but it could be worth having an eye check first.

Migraine

Migraine is described as the worst headache imaginable, often accompanied by nausea and distorted vision. Recent research shows it has physical, not psychological causes. Pain killers are less effective than usual, as the gut functions poorly during a migraine. Attacks can be triggered by various factors, including alcohol, chocolate, cheese and coffee, or hunger or lack of sleep. Oral contraceptives, high blood pressure, menstruation, bright lights, loud noises, and television are others. Some find taking feverfew – a herb which grows anywhere – helps. The **British Migraine Association** (page 589) has information on this and other measures. Help can also be got from the clinic of the **Migraine Trust** (page 589). At the *first signs* of the migraine sufferers should:

1 Take 3 aspirin *or* 2 paracetamol (unless they have other medications).
2 Eat something to speed the absorption of the medicine.
3 Lie down in a dark room and try to sleep.

> If you want to give blood for others your Regional Health Authority will have a centre. A reference library or CAB should have the address. More and more hospitals now allow people to have some of their own blood stored in the weeks before an operation. Then, if they need a transfusion, their own blood can be used. This may not be offered unless you ask.

Addresses and suggestions for further reading are at the ends of chapters.

	Men			Women		
		Naked Weight in stones and pounds				
Height (ft and in)	Average	Acceptable weight range	Overweight	Average	Acceptable weight range	Overweight
4 10				7 4	6 8 – 8 7	10 3
4 11				7 6	6 10 – 8 10	10 6
5 0				7 9	6 12 – 8 13	10 10
5 1				7 12	7 1 – 9 2	11 0
5 2	8 11	8 0 – 10 1	12 1	8 1	7 4 – 9 5	11 3
5 3	9 1	8 3 – 10 4	12 5	8 4	7 7 – 9 8	11 7
5 4	9 4	8 6 – 10 8	12 10	8 8	7 10 – 9 12	11 12
5 5	9 7	8 9 – 10 12	13 0	8 11	7 13 – 10 2	12 2
5 6	9 10	8 12 – 11 2	13 5	9 2	8 2 – 10 6	12 7
5 7	10 0	9 2 – 11 7	13 11	9 6	8 6 – 10 10	12 12
5 8	10 5	9 6 – 11 12	14 3	9 10	8 10 – 11 0	13 3
5 9	10 9	9 10 – 12 2	14 8	10 0	9 0 – 11 4	13 8
5 10	10 13	10 0 – 12 6	14 13	10 4	9 4 – 11 9	14 0
5 11	11 4	10 4 – 12 11	15 5	10 8	9 8 – 12 0	14 6
6 0	11 8	10 8 – 13 2	15 11	10 12	9 12 – 12 5	14 12
6 1	11 12	10 12 – 13 7	16 3			
6 2	12 3	11 2 – 13 12	16 9			
6 3	12 8	11 6 – 14 3	17 1			
6 4	12 13	11 10 – 14 8	17 7			

The table is based on the Metropolitan Life Insurance Tables and reproduced with the permission of the Royal College of Physicians.

Heart Disease

Heart disease covers a whole range of disorders, from inborn defects to those which develop later in life. Modern surgery can now work miracles but nonetheless, there is a limit to what medicine can do, and heart disease is Britain's biggest single killer. The heart has to beat 60 to 90 times a minute (3 million beats a month), which is quite enough to ask of it without putting it under stress. Yet many of those who die of heart disease have dug their graves with their own fingertips. Smokers under fifty are 10 times as likely to die of a heart attack as non-smokers of their age. Those who are overweight and eat the wrong diet also carry a greater risk. Spoilsport though it may seem, those who want to live to enjoy the other pleasures of life should stop smoking and keep their weight down.

Angina (Angina pectoris)

This is a painful cramp in the heart muscle brought on when the heart can't get enough oxygen from the blood. It happens after exercise, strong emotion, large meals or cold. It sometimes feels like severe indigestion, and occasionally it spreads to the left shoulder and arm, or the throat and neck. It shows that the heart is under stress and that an artery to the heart is narrowed either by a fatty lining or by a spasm.

There are several drugs which bring relief within about 5 minutes. If these fail surgery may sort out the problem. So someone with angina can usually live a perfectly normal life, but drivers must tell the driving licence authority in Swansea and their insurance company – or their insurance will not be valid. They need to learn to relax, and avoid overworking and excessive physical or emotional stress – though sex is allowed. They should also give up smoking, keep their weight down and eat a healthy diet.

Heart Attack (coronary thrombosis)

In a heart attack the blood supply to part of the heart is stopped. This can be because the artery has furred up, or because a clot of blood has blocked it, or when the wall of the artery splits. It causes severe pain in the centre of the chest, possibly spreading to the arms and neck, and perhaps lasting several hours. This leaves the patient unwell and exhausted, and part of the heart muscle may die (myocardial infarction).

The greatest risk of a repeat attack is in the days afterwards. If there is no recurrence within several years the risk of another is no greater than for anyone else. The current medical thinking is that after a heart attack people should live normally but *give up smoking*, get down to a better weight, eat sensibly and take gentle exercise. This includes sex after the first 6 weeks, provided it isn't too strenuous and doesn't provoke chest pain. The rules on driving are as for angina (page 557).

Heat Stroke and Sunstroke

Heat stroke and sunstroke are the same thing. The problem is that too much heat and sun upset the salt and water balance of the body. So the sufferer feels dizzy, feverish and sometimes sick, and may cease to sweat. The treatment is bed in a cool place, regular drinks of *very slightly* salted water, and sponging with tepid water. On rare occasions there may be high fever and even delirium. This needs IMMEDIATE medical attention in hospital.

Hepatitis

Hepatitis A is still a fairly common infection in Britain and is extremely common overseas. Hepatitis B is uncommon in Britain but quite common overseas.

Hepatitis A (often called infectious hepatitis) is caused by a virus which is most easily transmitted by the 'oral-fecal route'. For example, a carrier fails to wash after using the lavatory (the virus is in both faeces and urine), then handles food and you eat the food. Shellfish collected near a sewage outlet can also carry it, and so may primitive water supplies. Some 3 to 5 weeks after infection the victim has a fever, nausea, stomach ache and then jaundice – though in children it is often very mild and only 1 child in 10 who develops it gets the symptom of jaundice. The illness lasts at least 2 weeks and can go on for months, and sufferers are infectious from about 2 weeks before the symptoms start, until a few days after their onset. It is rarely fatal, but adults can be very ill for weeks and alcohol must be avoided for the next 6 months.

Hepatitis B (often called serum hepatitis) is a serious and sometimes fatal disease, and can sometimes lead to liver cancer. It is carried in the body fluids, especially in blood and semen, and must enter some break in the skin. It is caught in much the same ways as AIDS (see page 545), but it is far more infectious. The incubation period is 3 to 5 months and the victim usually feels below par and off food, and develops jaundice. The illness lasts about 6 weeks, but half of those who get it never have jaundice and many have no symptoms at all. Victims are infectious from several weeks before the first symptoms until several weeks after, and alcohol must be avoided for 6 months. A few people recover but remain infectious for up to 20 years; others are symptomless carriers. Immunization gives some protection and may be worthwhile when travelling in unsophisticated countries (page 572).

Hernia *(rupture)*

A hernia occurs when the wall surrounding one of the cavities of the body weakens at a particular point and allows an organ inside it to bulge through. Very young children can get hernias around the tummy button, but these usually right themselves within the first year.

By far the most common hernias are those in the groin, in which part of the bowel pushes through a weakness in the abdominal wall and bulges just under the skin. This is often provoked by a sudden strain on the area, such as when lifting a heavy weight, or even coughing violently. Normally it falls back when lying down, and is only mildly uncomfortable. The basic treatment is usually a support (truss) to push it back and hold it into position.

The only danger from a hernia is if the lump comes up and cannot be pushed back, and a doctor should be told immediately if this happens. In women the most common hernia is a hiatus hernia in which the abdomen presses up through a tear in the floor of the chest, and this is a fairly common cause of heartburn in pregnancy. But the same type of hernia can occur in men, particularly if they are overweight. In women it usually rights itself after pregnancy; in men the remedy is usually to diet. But any troublesome hernia may need an operation.

Herpes

Herpes is a growing problem. There are two viruses involved: HSV1 and HSV2. HSV1 usually causes cold sores, and HSV2 usually causes genital herpes – but each *can* cause either. See page 551.

Herpes starts up to 10 days after infection. The genitals tingle, ache and itch, and develop red spots which turn into small blisters, then into ulcers. These clear up in 3 to 10 days, though it may take 3 weeks in a woman having a first attack. The glands in the groin may swell and it can be painful to urinate. Sufferers can feel ill, shivery, nauseous and have a headache. They should take pain killers, and see a doctor. The symptoms go in a few weeks and some people never get it again, but others have it in cycles. An attack can be brought on by exposing the genitals to the sun – so nude sunbathing is out.

As first aid, apply ice cubes in a plastic bag at the first warning signs, and try to relax – this could stop the attack: ice during an attack reduces the pain. Herpes sufferers are most infectious during an attack (from first tingling to total healing), and should avoid sex, but even between attacks small quantities of the virus may be passed on. Some people are also symptomless carriers. So between attacks, or if someone could be a carrier, it is safer if the man uses a sheath, and an infected woman uses a cap and spermicide. A baby passing through the infected area, during birth, can become infected and suffer potentially fatal brain damage, so a Caesarian birth is needed. See also **VD**, page 564.

Hiccoughs

What almost always cures hiccoughs is drinking a teaspoon of neat vinegar.

Addresses and suggestions for further reading are at the ends of chapters.

High Blood Pressure *(hypertension)*

High blood pressure affects about 1 person in 5, and having high blood pressure increases the risk of heart disease, strokes and kidney disease. Someone who has high blood pressure at the age of forty is 30 times as likely to have a stroke as someone of that age with normal blood pressure. And the risk is increased if they smoke. Yet this problem usually has no symptoms and often goes unnoticed. Once detected, it can be treated with drugs and/or changes in diet and the risks reduced. The British Heart Foundation (page 591) has a leaflet answering queries about blood pressure and its treatment. But the best treatment is prevention:

● keep your weight down
● reduce the amount of saturated fat in your diet
● cut down on the salt in your diet
● some doctors also recommend eating more potassium
  – found in fruit like bananas – though this is controversial
● stop smoking
● take regular exercise.

Impetigo

Impetigo is a bacterial skin infection which spreads very easily, so sufferers must avoid touching others, and their towels, flannels and bedding must be kept completely separate. It starts as rather large blisters which dry into golden-yellow scabs. Doctors usually prescribe an antibiotic cream which clears these up quickly.

Indigestion

Drinking milk, to neutralize the acid, will usually relieve the discomfort of indigestion. But the early signs of heart trouble can sometimes feel very similar. If the symptoms persist see a doctor.

Heartburn
This is a burning feeling high in the stomach, just under the centre of the ribs, often with a little regurgitation. Half a teaspoon of bicarbonate of soda in a glass of water usually helps.

Wind and Gripe
An effective remedy is to drink a glass or two of port. Don't ask me why it works, but it does. Obviously this isn't good for babies. For them the best solution is a remedy which has been used in Poland for centuries – fennel water. Just steep a teaspoon of fennel seeds in a mug of boiling water until the water is cool enough for the baby to drink. Strain the seeds out and sweeten it to taste. It works because fennel, like all this family of plants, contains a substance which stimulates the intestines and makes them get rid of the wind. It can work far better than gripe water.

Influenza *(flu)*

The typical symptoms are achiness, a temperature and generally feeling below par. The cure is bed rest and reasonable doses of TLC (tender loving care). Flu will fade away in a few days. You can be immunized against it, but unfortunately the jabs need renewing each year.

Ingrowing Toe Nails

Ingrowing toe nails are better prevented than cured. If you are having problems, cut toe nails straight across, and don't wear shoes which are too small. Once one has developed it should be treated by a chiropodist.

Insomnia *(sleeplessness)*

Time drags at night and even waking for short periods can seem like hours. So you may start worrying that you will be too tired next day, tense up and stay awake even longer. Sleeplessness is annoying but it is *not* something to worry about. There are no rules for how much sleep the body needs, and if it gets too little one day it usually makes up for it another. The only time when it becomes a real problem is when pain, deep depression or anxiety interfere with the body's natural ability to do this. Then sleeping pills taken for a few days (*not* weeks) may break the cycle of sleeplessness, tension and more sleeplessness. But never *try* to go to sleep (the effort keeps you awake), instead use tricks to make it happen:

● Try to recognize the point when your body is ready to sleep, and go to bed then – however early it is.
● Do something which really relaxes you just before bed.
● Listen to the radio very quietly, close to you, in the dark (on headphones if you aren't alone in bed), abandoning all attempt to go to sleep and just relaxing. Ideally the radio should be the kind which turns itself off after an hour, then you won't be woken by the next loud music.

If you wake and can't sleep:

● Get out of bed and potter for a short while, letting yourself get a *little* bit cold. Meanwhile, make sure the bed is warm and cosy (switch on electric blankets, add hot water bottles). When you return to bed the warmth often brings a surge of relaxation and sleep with it.
● Read a book and enjoy the excuse to do so. If you read until morning you have still relaxed, but if your eyes feel sleepy stop instantly and turn off the light.
● Drink some hot milk laced with whisky. (Most effective for those who are not regular drinkers.)
● If worry and distress are going relentlessly round and round in your head, get up and *do* something. It doesn't matter whether you scrub the floor or garden at first light. Anything is better than lying there tense, worried and full of envy at the world of sleepers. The more active and satisfying the task, the more it will unwind the tension. If you feel tired later on don't feel guilty about lying down and sleeping. You worked when the rest of the world slept.

Jaundice

Jaundice isn't a disease; it is a sign of illness which involves yellowing of the eyes and face, and sometimes the whole body. The urine may also be dark and the stools pale. This shows that excess bile, from the liver, is entering the bloodstream. In a newborn baby the most common cause is an immature liver, and the baby usually grows out of it in 3 weeks, although babies can also have neonatal hepatitis, which takes longer to get over. In adults the most usual cause is infectious hepatitis (see page 558), but whatever the cause, it needs medical attention.

Kidney Disease

The kidneys are miniature purification plants which remove liquid waste products from the blood and get rid of them as urine. When the kidneys fail the waste is left in the blood and the sufferer essentially dies of internal pollution. This causes frequent urination – perhaps with blood in it (full kidney failure will have no urine output at all), pain at the waist level at the back, sometimes pain in the groin, and possibly a temperature and shakiness. It can affect any age, and the failure can be associated with high blood pressure or various infections. If a kidney fails the only treatments are dialysis, for 12 hours a day three times a week, on a machine, or a kidney transplant.

Anyone wondering about carrying a kidney donor card could talk to the **British Kidney Patient Association** (see page 589).

Meningitis

Meningitis is an inflammation of the membranes covering the brain, caused by either bacteria or viruses and different types of bacteria cause meningitis in different age groups. (Encephalitis, which is a separate viral disease, looks initially like meningitis.) All of them are probably caught by general contact, but there is no set incubation period, and the infection can be carried by someone with no symptoms. Anyone who develops it will have some of the following symptoms:

- general unwellness and irritability
- severe headache (often with vomiting)
- dislike of light
- temperature of 38.5°C (101°F) or more
- a rash of red spots
- confusion (not recognizing parents perhaps)
- a stiff neck – less common in young children (not to be confused with the stiff neck which goes with tonsillitis)

Some of these symptoms also occur with other illnesses, so they don't always mean someone has meningitis, but a doctor should be told *immediately* because, if it is meningitis, *swift treatment can be vital.* The sufferer will usually be admitted to hospital for tests, and may need 10 to 14 days there. Even those who are severely ill with meningitis can recover totally, but there can be brain damage, ranging from mild problems to serious disabilities.

Mental Illnesses and Problems

Mental illness broadly divides into neurosis and psychosis. Someone with neurosis is in touch with the real world and behaves like anyone else, but there may be some aspect of their life in which they are off key. For example, they may have a phobia, and be terrified of something which doesn't frighten others, or be deeply depressed. Whereas someone with psychosis loses touch with reality, either all the time or in patches. Psychotics may believe they are someone they aren't, or hear voices, or believe that people are getting at them. Psychosis is so varied it is impossible to cover all its symptoms and cures. But, if a relative you suspect is mentally ill refuses to see a doctor, or gets no real help from a GP, you may ask the GP to arrange for a home visit by a psychiatrist. Those who are severely depressed or have other mental problems they cannot handle may ask a GP to refer them to a psychotherapist, but the NHS facilities are limited and overstretched.

Depression

Nobody should be ashamed of being depressed. It is either a natural aspect of grief, or an illness which is treatable. It is normal to be depressed after a divorce or the death of a loved one. But, in today's rushing society, people may feel they should recover from depression faster than is really natural. Recovery from mourning should be expected to be a matter of many months, not weeks, and nobody should be afraid to let this depression run its natural course. In fact, trying to rush the pace or brighten up with anti-depressants is seldom the best route to a full recovery.

When there is no obvious cause for depression doctors often call it endogenous (meaning in-built). Most psychotherapists would say that such depression stems from buried grief and pain in the past. For example, someone sexually molested or battered in childhood may become depressed as an adult, or someone who did not allow themselves to mourn a death may become depressed many years later.

Real depression cannot be simply snapped out of, as people often suppose. It usually passes with time – but the time can seem endless. Activities giving companionship and a new interest can help. But for the sufferer to talk, again and again, about the causes of the depression helps most. People with depression need to be listened to and encouraged to find their own solutions, not made to feel yet more inadequate by good advice. This may need professional counselling as well as the support of family and friends.

Other types of depression can be caused by changes in the brain's chemistry. There is now evidence, for example, that manic-depression runs in families, and the inherited fault is likely to be chemical. Also, as light can affect the balance of important chemicals which regulate our moods, some people have winter depression, caused by the lack of light. The treatment is extra artificial light – the amount needed to cheer up some people is phenomenal but others respond to even a slight increase.

Tranquillizers, such as Valium and Librium, are widely prescribed by doctors to help people deal with anxiety and depression. Some people find that they help considerably, but those who take them should realize that they also tend to reduce mental alertness and make people less skilful at driving, rather as alcohol does, and they can cause both physical and mental dependence. They need to be used with care because, in addition to those dangers, large doses can be fatal, especially if combined with alcohol.

Unfortunately, recent research suggests that withdrawal problems can occur even from medically prescribed doses. The withdrawal symptoms vary, but they include nausea, insomnia, irritability and anxiety, panic attacks, shaking, loss of confidence and even agoraphobia (fear of going out of doors). These can make people feel that the solution lies in more tranquillizers, and the cycle is reinforced. It isn't easy to face up to the world without a familiar crutch – even if the crutch has become a handicap – but those who do it *do* return to normality and to a better life. However, this is still an area of medicine which is not fully understood; some doctors believe that tranquillizers are not addictive – but those who have experienced the ill effects of tranquillizers would say they are wrong. The best way to give up seems to be to come off tranquillizers little by little, with the help of a support group. The organizations on page 589 can help and advise.

Phobias and Anxieties

A phobia is an overwhelming fear of something which doesn't normally cause fear – or fear on that scale. Agoraphobia is fear of open spaces; claustrophobia is fear of being in small spaces. But people can be phobic about anything. Unlike general 'free-floating' fear or anxiety, a phobia is triggered only by one particular thing, and tends to produce blind panic – with all the physical symptoms that go with it. Most phobias can be successfully treated, and GPs may refer patients to a specialist clinic, but people can also help themselves.

When people get very anxious it can cause a tightening of the throat which makes it hard to swallow. Often this increases their anxiety because they think it is a sign of some serious illness. A visit to the doctor, and something to relax the throat, may solve that part of the problem.

Myalgic Encephalomyelitis *(ME, post-viral fatigue syndrome)*

This disease has only recently been recognized, and is still not fully accepted, although definite biochemical differences have been found in some diagnosed as having it. It seems as if the body fails to make the normal immune response to a virus infection so the sufferer is left with long-term after effects. The major symptom is extreme fatigue. Sufferers are exhausted by simple everyday jobs and find mental activity equally tiring. They feel continually unwell and 'fluey', and there may be pain in the muscles, swelling, soreness, loss of memory, and speech and eyesight problems. There is no cure for ME. Some people recover slowly but completely; others recover but have relapses, and in a few, it becomes chronic.

It looks as if ME is more likely to attack those who refuse to rest up during a viral illness. So ME is a good argument for bed rest, even if it *is* only flu.

Nappy Rash

The most common form of nappy rash is caused by bacteria changing the urine into ammonia, which burns the skin. So change the nappies often, wash the area clean each time, pat dry and apply a cream – such as zinc and castor oil ointment – which acts as a barrier to the urine. Thrush has very similar rash and needs special treatment. Any persistent rash should be medically checked. Rinse towelling nappies very well to avoid a build-up of detergent which can irritate any rash. Ideally, babies should spend as much time as possible during the day nappy-free. An old towel placed under them solves the problem.

Nosebleeds

The most effective way to stop a nose bleed is simply to pinch the nostrils very tightly together for about 20 minutes. But don't pinch a nose which is bleeding because of injury – it needs medical attention.

NSU and Friends

NSU (non-specific urethritis) is the best known of a group of puzzling problems all referred to by initials. They include NGU (non-gonococcal urethritis), PGU (post-gonococcal urethritis) and NSGI (non-specific genital infections). The symptoms may suggest a sexually transmitted disease – genital discharge, discomfort on urinating and perhaps a pain low in the stomach – but basic tests may fail to reveal a cause. This can be either because the culture methods aren't good enough, or because there is nothing there to form a culture. Nobody knows for sure and British and American experts disagree, but this is a developing field and many cases once regarded as unidentifiable are now attributed to chlamydia (page 551), or TV (page 564). The rest may not respond to treatment, but most clear up in time. However, the lack of any high-flown name doesn't mean such infections should be treated lightly – some women may be sterile afterwards. So men with suspicious symptoms should *not* have sex. See also **VD**, page 564.

Piles *(haemorrhoids)*

These are varicose veins of the rectum which cause itching, pain and even bleeding. The causes include constipation and straining on the lavatory, overweight and pregnancy and perhaps an inherited tendency. Treatment and more roughage in the diet can help.

Plastic Surgery

Plastic surgery for disfigurement of any kind can be obtained on the NHS. But not if the problem is too minor, or for cosmetic surgery. However, there are serious risks in having cosmetic surgery in some of the clinics which advertise in the press, as their doctors may lack the necessary qualifications or skills. The Medical

Advisory Service can give the names of reputable London plastic and cosmetic surgeons.

To keep bruising to a minimum during plastic surgery, give up spirits and smoking for a month beforehand. One top plastic surgeon advises his patients to take a 1 gram vitamin C tablet three times a day for a week before the operation to lessen bruising.

Pneumonia and Pleurisy

Pneumonia is an inflammation of the lungs. It can strike any age from tiny babies to the very old, and there are several different types. One of the most common is acute bronchial pneumonia, which has much the same symptoms as bronchitis. Children get a cold and cough, but with a higher temperature. An adult will have a severe cough and high fever, and there may also be pain in the chest. It can usually be controlled with antibiotics, but it may be complicated by pleurisy, in which the membranes encasing the lungs become swollen. This makes breathing very sore, but it usually clears up with the pneumonia. Medical treatment is essential.

Psoriasis

Psoriasis is an unpleasant skin problem which causes reddish patches covered with dry flaky white skin – which may or may not itch. It can start in childhood, but usually appears after the age of 14. It isn't infectious but, like eczema, it tends to run in families, comes and goes, varies in the area it covers, and increases with illness or emotional upset. Doctors can ease it with various ointments but there is no complete cure, and this is one of the few problems for which dermatologists recommended sunlight.

Sinus Trouble

The sinuses are spaces at the back of the nose. In acute sinusitis the tissue lining the sinuses becomes swollen, and full of catarrh, which presses painfully on the swollen tissue. The pain can reach across the forehead and along the cheeks and upper jaw. Use the steam and oil of eucalyptus treatment given on page 552 to ease it. Those who like herbal remedies can drink an infusion of a teaspoon of fresh or dried marjoram in boiling water 2 to 3 times a day while the sinusitis lasts and occasionally from then on. Any cold tea which remains can be sniffed up the nostrils. This is an old Austrian remedy which some sufferers find helpful but it works slowly. Severe sinus trouble needs medical attention.

Shingles

Shingles is a disease which strikes those who have had chicken pox in the past. It is most common in the elderly and the distinctive feature is that it only affects one side of the body. Usually an area becomes painful, then reddens and forms blisters which crust into scabs. Unfortunately, the pain may continue even after the skin has healed, and this is a disease which should always be seen by a doctor. These nasty symptoms are caused by the reawakened chicken pox virus, which has lain dormant in the body. Contact with chicken pox can cause this; the elderly should avoid those who have it.

Sore Throats and Loss of Voice

Most sore throats are caused by virus infections, they can't be cured with antibiotics. Most right themselves in 4 to 5 days, but see a doctor if a throat is getting worse after 2 days, or if there is earache, or the temperature rises above 39.5°C (103°F). Soothe with hot, sweet drinks with a teaspoon of glycerine.

If you have to talk the voice can be improved by gargling with neat whisky or with soluble aspirin in water. But don't give either to young children.

Tonsillitis

Children's tonsils are often plump and look swollen, even when perfectly well: this isn't tonsillitis. Tonsillitis starts as a sore throat, with pain on swallowing and you may be able to see the reddened tonsils with white spots on them. There may also be swollen glands at the side of the neck, and a child will be decidedly unwell with a high temperature. Children usually recover in less than a week, but you should still tell the doctor. Nowadays doctors seldom remove the tonsils unless a child has suffered repeated attacks of tonsillitis.

Don't try to make a child with a very sore throat or infected tonsils eat if it doesn't want to. Just give plenty of soothing and nourishing liquid, and see whether hot or iced drinks are more comfortable.

Splinters, Thorns and Spines

Splinters can often be pulled out with tweezers. Most thorns will ease out with a hot bath and a slight squeeze. If that fails sterilize a fine needle in a flame until it glows red, let it cool and then gently use the tip to pick open the skin over the splinter until it can be pulled out with tweezers. Bathe the area with witch-hazel afterwards. Sea urchin spines won't easily come out that way. Instead, cover them with a piece of paw paw or pineapple for a few hours. Both fruits contain enzymes which cause the skin to open up and allow the thorn to be squeezed or pulled out. Failing that, mix castor oil, as hot as the skin can stand, with flour and apply this under a bandage for 12 hours. The thorn should then come out easily.

Sprains

A joint can be sprained if it's suddenly forced in an unnatural direction, causing bruising and swelling. Put a cold compress on the swelling and immobilize it. An ideal compress is a pack of frozen peas. (Place a cloth between the pack and the skin.) Sprains shouldn't be tightly bandaged, but the less any sprain is used the faster it heals. One old-fashioned way to remind yourself of this is a loose bandage of stiff brown paper (hence the nursery rhyme about Jack going to bed 'in vinegar and brown paper'.) Sprains also seem to respond to sunshine. A bad sprain should be seen by a doctor.

Addresses and suggestions for further reading are at the ends of chapters.

Stammering

Nobody knows what causes stammering, but there are a number of speech therapy techniques which reduce it. See under Speech Problems (page 590). Speech therapy should be available on the NHS, but not all authorities provide it. Meanwhile, some stammerers find that they can sing without hesitation, even if they can't speak. Worth remembering if the police ask for your licence number and you can't say it.

Stress

Probably the most important factor is how people feel about themselves. Those who feel they have failed in some important aspect of their life or who lack, or lose, the circle of warm, caring relationships which family and friends normally provide, or lose a cultural or ethnic identity which they value, feel bad about themselves and are more prone to illness – especially stress diseases.

Happily, reducing stress is easier than you might think. An American insurance company found that if a wife simply kisses her husband goodbye each morning she increases his life expectancy. Patients given a little time and attention by their doctors get well faster than those who just get the medicine. And those who have pets to stroke are less likely to get ill. The message is that being more affectionate to those around you, and joining a club if you are lonely, could do you as much good as a lot of jogging (not that exercise isn't good too). But if you do feel awful let it *out*. A good cry, by either sex does more good than a drink or tranquillizers. Grief and tension, like bad food, are better out than in. And if you can get someone to hug you while you cry, do so. Human touch is one of the world's biggest healers and all too seldom used.

Stroke

Strokes are caused when the blood vessels of the brain get blocked or break open, damaging or destroying part of the brain. They range from a fleeting inability to speak, and a tingling sensation on one side of the body, to loss of consciousness followed by paralysis on one side. The effects depend on where the brain is damaged. Some people are left with restricted movement and speech but others recover completely, even from a major stroke, because, although damaged brain cells can't be replaced, other sections of the brain can learn to do their job. This only happens if the victim puts in a lot of work. The serious shortage of speech therapists means the family may need to do much of the speech work. (See page 590).

Strokes are three times as likely in those who smoke 20 cigarettes or more a day. The risk is also greater in diabetics and those who have high blood pressure. The contraceptive pill also slightly increases the risk of strokes in young women, especially if there is arterial disease in the family.

Stye

A stye is an infected pore on the rim of the eye. It doesn't last long or do any harm, so the best course may be to let it cure itself. But bathing it with diluted witch-hazel can be soothing and doctors can prescribe ointments to clear it up faster. A traditional cure – unlikely though it sounds – is to rub the stye several times a day with a gold ring.

Sunburn and Suntan

I once heard a woman invite a friend to 'come out and sunbathe'. 'You mean, come out and *age*,' her friend replied. And she was right. Tests have shown skin exposed to the sun gets old faster than uncovered skin.

Too much sun seriously increases the risk of skin cancer. Sunbathing should be limited and gradual. The nearer you are to the equator, the fiercer the burning rays – even if the heat is no greater. The rays are strongest between 11 am and 2 pm, regardless of temperature. So suit the protection factor of sunscreens to the time of day and place, not the heat – factor 6 is the recommended *minimum* for any white skin. On areas which stick out use a total sun block most of the time. Young children are especially vulnerable and they can even be burnt while swimming, so they should wear an old shirt in the water and a sun block on their face.

Cool sunburn down with a long cool shower, or by covering the area with a towel wrung out in cold water. Then soothe it, and put back some of the oils and moisture the skin has lost with an after-sun lotion. If you have none you can use rosewater mixed with glycerine or even milk, cream or yoghurt.

Syphilis

This bogeyman of sexual diseases is now relatively rare in most highly developed countries, where it is largely a problem of gays. But it is far more common in Africa, the East and even in some of the less sophisticated parts of Europe. It should be treated rapidly, before serious damage is done. In pregnancy syphilis causes miscarriage, stillbirth or a handicapped child. Like the AIDS virus, this bacterium enters the body through a break in the skin. The first symptoms, 1 to 12 weeks after infection, are a sore at the point of infection – penis, vulva, vagina, anus, mouth – plus swollen lymph glands. However, the sore may be inside the anus or vagina where it can't be seen.

The sore heals after 3 to 10 weeks, and the disease enters its second stage. The symptoms now include dark-red skin rashes, swollen glands, ulcers in moist areas of the body and flu-like aches and pains. These go after several weeks or months. The third stage, which is very rare in the West, may come many years later. It can cause appalling sores on the body, severe heart disease, paralysis and insanity.

When syphilis is latent, or in the first or second stage, it can usually be cured. But not all syphilis sufferers know they have it, as the initial sore may be hidden and the secondary symptoms can go unrecognized. Those who have syphilis are infectious all the time, not just when the symptoms show, but their infectiousness gradually diminishes after the second stage. See also **VD**, below.

Testicle Problems

It is *very* important that a boy's testicles are properly in place from babyhood. Sometimes they remain higher up in the body. If this happens he may grow up infertile. So, in the early months, feel both sides, in the bath with a warm hand – when cold, they may rise out of the scrotum. They should feel like two very small eggs inside the bag of skin. If either can't be felt, see a doctor. The earlier this is corrected, the better.

Sometimes the testicles can twist out of place and a boy may get a sudden severe pain low down in the abdomen, and pain in the testicle itself. See a doctor FAST. This is called torsion and it can cut off the blood supply to the testicle and damage it permanently.

Thrush *(Candida albicans)*

This is an extremely common female problem, but rarely occurs in men – and then only causes a slight soreness. You don't need to have sex to develop it. The culprit is an organism, similar to yeast, which lives in the bowels. It often develops after a course of antibiotics, which have killed the body's natural defences, and when the vagina loses its acidity after the menopause. Thrush has no serious consequences, but it causes a thick creamy-yellow discharge which dries to a powder, and the genitals feel very itchy and sore. It is easily treated by a GP and home remedies also work well. Cleanse the area with olive oil rather than water to soothe the itching. Then put a little plain (not fruit) yoghurt into the vagina with the finger tips or with the end of a tampon (removing the tampon after), and spread more yoghurt on the outside. Do this regularly and follow the rules in 'Hygiene' (page 565). If you get a prescription do complete the full course of medicine, or these organisms may become resistant to the treatment and very hard to get rid of. See also **VD**, below.

Travel Sickness

Research in America has shown that ginger is just as effective as most travel sickness pills, and it has the advantage of not making you sleepy. Eat crystallized ginger, or drink powdered ginger in hot water, sweetened to taste. The Chinese have for centuries drunk ginger tea after meals as a digestive, while in the Caribbean it has been used against morning sickness. So it could be worth trying it for either of these.

The build-up of static electricity in a car may be a factor in car sickness. Spraying the car thoroughly inside with an anti-static spray may therefore help. If queasiness starts, spit out the extra saliva that starts to gather in your mouth, and look ahead exactly as you would when driving.

Trichomonas Vaginalis *(TV)*

This is a very common vaginal infection (probably affecting 1 woman in 5 at some time) caused by a protozoon (an organism considerably larger than a bacterium or virus). In women it causes a thin, greenish, frothy, very smelly discharge and genital itching and soreness, which may even cover the inner thighs and buttock cleft. In men the symptoms, if any, are as for chlamydia (page 551). It is easily treated and both partners must see a doctor. See also **VD**, below.

Ulcers

Peptic Ulcers

These are thought to be due to stress and smoking. They usually cause stomach pains (often in the middle of the night), which may be relieved by drinking milk or taking anti-acids. Anyone who gets pain high in the centre of the stomach, just below the ribs – when hungry or full – possibly with burping or acid regurgitation should see a doctor, especially if the pain goes through to the back. Treatment is now very good and operations are needed far less often. This is one condition in which ancient and modern remedies can work hand in hand. It seems liquorice is still used alongside today's wonder drugs.

Mouth Ulcers

Occasional small mouth ulcers go in a few days without treatment. More severe, or repeated, ulcers should be seen by a doctor, as they can be a sign of illness.

Varicose Veins

Varicose veins are due to a weakness in the walls of surface veins. They start by showing too clearly through the skin, and gradually become twisted, lumpy and achy. As the action of the leg muscles helps push the blood round, the worst thing for varicose veins is standing still. Anyone prone to them should try to keep moving. It also helps to wear support stockings (on prescription) and raise the legs above the head whenever possible. If caught early enough, varicose veins can be treated with injections; they can also be operated on.

VD and Infections of the Sexual Organs

You will find each type of infection of the sexual organs under its name, and they are listed under sexual-organ infections in the index. Not all of them are passed on through sexual intercourse. And only those which *are* passed on that way are classed as VD (venereal disease). But some rules hold true for all of them. First, anyone who even *thinks* he or she may have a sexually transmitted (venereal) disease should stop all sexual activities and go to the 'Special Clinic' of a hospital for tests – there is no need to see a GP first. The clinics are listed under Venereal Disease in the telephone book.

Sex being a private matter, there is (AIDS apart) remarkably little data on which sexual practices are most

Addresses and suggestions for further reading are at the ends of chapters.

likely to transmit infection. So it is safest to assume that vaginal, anal and oral sex can all do so, though which is the most hazardous will vary with the nature and site of the disease.

It's no good thinking that you can tell the sort of person who would have VD. The patients in VD clinics look no different from those in an eye clinic. So the best protection is abstinence, the next best is a condom and a diaphragm is better than nothing. However, an IUD can actually increase the risk of infection. And how long any infection takes to show varies enormously.

You can – in theory – catch some sexual infections from lavatory seats. But the chances of two people both adopting the same (rather odd) position needed to bring the relevant bit of their anatomy in contact with the seat, *and* doing so in quick succession before the germs die in the cold, are *extremely* remote.

Hygiene

Women are especially vulnerable to minor infections because their genitals provide an ideal home for bacteria: warm and free from draughts, with plenty of body fluids to feed on – what more could a creature need? Our grandmothers knew better. Until the early years of this century women's knickers were open between the legs. Cooling the area prevents a lot of minor problems. Whenever possible, wear stockings or crutchless tights, with loose cotton pants – or no pants at all – and avoid tight-fitting trousers. That may sound impractical, unfashionable or indecent. But try wearing stockings, no pants and a fullish skirt round the house – you'll be surprised by how good it feels. And, when air-dried, moistness is not the problem you might think.

In its natural state the vagina's acidity is a good defence against bacteria. Excessive washing, or washing inside the vagina, removes this natural protection and makes infection more likely. This is counter-productive, as bacteria are far smellier than body fluids. A daily bath, plus an external wash after making love, if you wish, are quite enough. Vaginal sprays, deodorants and talcs and douches are totally unnecessary and even harmful – they *lower* the body's defences, and may also cause allergic reactions. Scented bath products should be used sparingly or not at all – too much can irritate the delicate tissue between the legs and create, or prolong, problems.

Men should wash the sexual organs regularly, including under the foreskin of the penis. But it is an old wives' tale that washing and urinating after intercourse prevent infection – they don't.

Foreign Bodies

Occasionally something gets lodged in the vagina and allows bacteria to build up round it causing a smelly discharge. Even a small tuft left from a tampon can do this. Check this out if there is a curious vaginal odour. Once the object is out the problem should end. If it doesn't or you can't get it out, see a doctor. However odd it is the doctor won't be surprised. One doctor I know had removed statuettes of Napoleon from three different people in one week.

Vomiting

Occasional vomiting is seldom anything to worry about. It can be caused by eating too much, by a virus infection or by drink. Some children also tend to vomit whenever they are unwell or even nervous. If anyone feels queasy encourage him to bend over, relax and let it come up. If they feel awful but can't vomit they should put their fingers in their throat and tickle their uvula (the little pink piece which hangs down above the throat). This usually does the trick and they feel a lot better, but if children are frightened stand behind them and support them gently and calmly. Rinse the mouth to remove the taste, avoid food that day and just drink liquid.

Consult a doctor if there is a stomach pain as well, a child has a temperature of over 38°C (100.4°F) or the vomiting lasts more than 24 hours. (See also pages 578 to 580 and under Food poisoning.)

Warts and Verrucas

Warts and verrucas (plantar warts) are both caused by a virus and often go away in time. Some anti-wart preparations may speed up the process and GPs can have them treated at a skin clinic. Doctors aren't agreed about whether covering a verruca stops the infection spreading. But it can't make it worse, so why not do it.

This is a great area for folk remedies. I even know of one skin specialist who 'bought' a patient's warts for sixpence – and they went. It certainly does no harm to try traditional remedies, but don't put plant juice on warts – some of the traditional anti-wart plants can cause skin cancer. For genital warts, see page 555.

Worms

Roundworms are not a common problem in Britain, but they can be picked up from the soil. The adults live in the gut, but the larvae move to the lungs, so they can cause problems in the lungs and in the stomach. They are a good reason to wash hands before eating.

Threadworms are very common, especially in school children. Itching of the anus (back passage opening) is the first symptom, and a check with a hand mirror may show tiny worms like white cotton threads. They may also be seen in the stools. The female worm lays eggs at the outside of the anus during the night. The worms tickle, so the sufferer scratches and eggs get under the fingernails – then go into the mouth when food or the mouth is touched – and are small enough to be breathed in. So some doctors treat the whole family together. Chemists sell effective treatments, but first get advice from a doctor.

Tapeworms can be caught from undercooked pork because the larval tapeworm lives in the pig's flesh. In humans it lives in the gut and takes nourishment from its host. Segments of tapeworm, like grains of rice, can sometimes be seen in stools. This problem is far more common in less developed countries.

Worms from Dogs and Cats

Toxocara canis (and *catis*) is a worm carried by dogs (and occasionally cats), which excrete the eggs. Small children who then crawl on soiled grass may pick up the eggs and transfer them to their mouth on eating. In a human the eggs develop into larvae which invade any part of the body – including the eyes and brain. Cases are fortunately rare, but infected children have been blinded and the damage can be fatal. So it is better not to let children play about where dogs are exercised.

COMPLEMENTARY MEDICINE

Complementary medicine covers all the approaches to healing which are not included in conventional medicine. In Britain more than 5 million people a year now use these therapies – and 1 in 10 are referred by their GP. But the training of practitioners who offer alternative therapy ranges from rigorous four-year full-time courses, similar to those of a conventional medical school, to brief postal courses and many have no qualifications at all. So anyone who uses any alternative therapy should take a hard look at the practitioner's qualifications: in the wrong hands even alternative therapies can be dangerous, yet referral by a doctor is not usually needed.

The most popular therapies are covered below, but anyone needing information on others can get the details from the **Institute for Complementary Medicine** (see page 592). It keeps a register of qualified practitioners in all fields, and is establishing standards for training. To find the branch of complementary medicine most suited to your problem and suitable practitioners in your area write to the British Register of Complementary Practitioners at the Institute's address.

Acupuncture

Acupuncture is an ancient Chinese treatment by which fine needles are inserted into the skin to influence the body's 'vital energy'. Practitioners believe this energy flows round the body along invisible channels and that when people are ill the energy is out of balance. So the aim of the needles is to correct the imbalance by stimulating or calming the flow at precisely the right points along the meridians. Treatments take about half an hour and are not painful like an injection.

Acupuncturists treat all kinds of conditions, ranging from headaches to addiction and strokes. They believe that, whatever the problem, putting the body into harmony can only do good. In France and Germany it is available under national health schemes. In Britain this is rarely so, but some health insurance schemes may cover it. But harm could be done by using it incorrectly; there are also risks from poorly sterilized needles – including AIDS and hepatitis. So it is unwise to go to anyone who is not fully qualified.

Chiropractic Treatment

Chiropractic treatment is more specific than many types of alternative medicine. It treats back and other pain arising from mechanical problems in spine and joints.

Nerves carrying messages to and from all parts of the body have to pass through the spinal column to join the spinal cord on their way to the brain. Chiropractors say that the normal alignment of the joints of the spine need only be fractionally altered to put pressure on vital nerves and cause not only back pain, but also pains such as headaches or sciatica which are not felt in the spine itself. Often pressure squeezes one of the discs between the vertebrae so it bulges (the mis-named 'slipped disc') and presses on a nerve, causing pain and immobility.

A fall, jolt or awkward movement can result in these problems, and so can the physical stresses of certain jobs. And, since nerves are extremely sensitive, very slight misalignments – which non-chiropractors may not detect on an X-ray – can cause pain. If a problem isn't treated muscles adapt, so a back problem may appear to go away when it has only been masked. This is why stress and tension will often trigger back pain, and also why it may come and go.

Treatment involves a careful diagnosis, often using X-rays. If a problem is found, precise manipulation is done with the hands to restore the back to normal. This doesn't hurt. I speak from experience – when I was crippled by back pain chiropractic treatment painlessly cured it in days. But a long- term problem will be harder to put right and a longer course of treatment may be needed. So it is always best to seek treatment soon.

There is often confusion between chiropractors and osteopaths. Both manipulate the spine, but chiropractors are more likely to use X-rays during the initial diagnosis: which could detect certain conditions which should not be manipulated. Chiropractors are also less likely to work on the soft tissue, and their manipulative technique is usually more precise. In Britain chiropractic treatment cannot be obtained under the NHS, nor on all private health insurance, unlike the case in North America, Switzerland and Denmark. A chiropractor should be a member of the British Chiropractic Association and have done a full-time four-year training at a recognized college.

Herbalism

Herbalists believe they can cure a wide range of conditions with plant substances alone. But they like to look beyond the immediate symptoms, to the body's total state. Each person is seen as unique and their aim is to restore 'balance and health' by helping the body to heal itself. They take an equally holistic view of plant remedies. Nature, they believe, has balanced medically active chemicals so that using a whole plant avoids side effects, whereas isolating a particular chemical is far more hazardous. Most medical chemists would not agree with that. But the skill of the herbalist is in knowing which plants are beneficial and which harmful.

Herbalism isn't available on the NHS, although some GPs are also herbalists.

Addresses and suggestions for further reading are at the ends of chapters.

Homeopathy

The idea behind homeopathy is that giving a patient minute doses of natural remedies will stimulate the body's own defence and healing mechanisms. Choosing the right remedy involves both diagnosing the condition, and the general physical condition and personality. So two patients with the same disease may be given different remedies. Most remedies are made from pure animal, plant or mineral sources, which are then successively diluted – until many doctors would claim that too little of the active ingredient remains to be of any use. However, homeopathy enjoys Royal patronage and it seems to work well for certain conditions, particularly colds.

There are five homeopathic hospitals in Britain, with both out-patient and in-patient facilities and homeopathy has always been recognized by the NHS. Ask the **British Homeopathic Association** (page 592) for the name of a properly qualified practitioner.

Naturopathic Medicine

Naturopaths see illness as something affecting the body, mind and spirit of the whole person. They believe the body possesses the power to heal itself, and that disease is the outward sign that the body is fighting against some block which prevents it from functioning as it should. So the aim of naturopathic treatment is also to find out why the patient became ill and try to prevent future illness. This involves educating the patient to take responsibility for his or her own health through correct diet, rest, exercise and hygiene, as well as using specific therapies to remove the block to good health. Diet, fasting, relaxation techniques, chiropractic and osteopathic treatment, exercises, homeopathy, electrotherapy, herbalism and hydrotherapy may all play a part in this. So practitioners qualified in other fields, such as osteopaths, may also practise naturopathy.

Osteopathy

Much of what I have written about chiropractic above applies to osteopaths. In both cases, a fully qualified practitioner will have done a four-year training which includes a considerable amount of basic medicine as well as specialist training. But the founder of osteopathy believed that the cures brought about by spinal manipulation were due to improved circulation of the blood, whereas chiropractors relate their treatment to the nervous system. Osteopaths also make broader claims for their treatment than chiropractors and usually believe it helps conditions which have no obvious link with the spine. This may be because they more often work on the soft tissues than do chiropractors.

Unfortunately, some osteopaths are fully trained, some are self-taught physiotherapists or masseurs and others are totally unqualified. Only members of a professional association should be consulted.

After a fall or whiplash injury it could be wisest to consult a practitioner who uses X-rays; then there is no risk of a fracture going undiagnosed.

Psychotherapy and Analysis

What distinguishes psychotherapy from other help for mental problems is that the treatment is purely talking. The patient may be depressed, afraid or have swings of emotion which seem to have no foundation. Psychoanalysis is a type of psychotherapy. It is usually longer and involves more frequent sessions than other forms of psychotherapy.

The patient sees the psychotherapist at regular intervals and talks about thoughts, feelings and memories. The aim is to allow the patient to understand the unconscious, as well as conscious, aspects of his or her feelings and behaviour, bring out what is happening inside them and realize how the roots of their behaviour have been formed. The therapist guides and questions, but does not tell the patient what to do. So it is a process of exploration, rather than advice. It is fundamental to psychotherapy that behaving in a new way will only work if the need for the old ways of behaving has gone.

The self-exploration may mean reliving memories which are distressing. So it can be important for the patient and psychotherapist or analyst to start with some rapport. See more than one for an initial consultation and choose whoever suits you.

Most sessions last 50 minutes, 1-5 times a week. Nobody can predict how long analysis will need to last. For some people it is 2 to 3 years, for others much longer.

One essential is that the analyst is properly trained and qualified but those who are well qualified don't normally advertise. So regard advertisements with suspicion. The professional organizations on page 589 will refer people to those who are properly qualified.

Spiritual Healing

Spiritual healing is not limited to any one religion or denomination, and those with no religious faith can still be healed – provided they are determined to get well. The healer may touch the patient, or practise absent healing, for the basic principle is that divine energy is channelled to the patient by the healer. The healer asks for the patient to be healed in whatever way is best for him or her. So the result could be a cure, but it might equally be giving someone the tranquillity to handle their condition. Of course, that isn't healing in the medical sense, but the test is not whether doctors rate it as healing, but whether patients do. And some certainly do.

Members of the **National Federation of Spiritual Healers** (page 592) work to a code of conduct which insists that diagnosis must be done by a doctor and that the healer must not countermand instructions or prescriptions given by a doctor. Nor may they ask patients to undress, or prescribe medicines. So healers should be told what medical treatment patients are having, and the doctor should be told about the spiritual healing, but it is not available on the NHS.

Transcendental Meditation

This is not a system of alternative medicine as such, and

those who teach meditation don't claim to be healers. I include it because there is now medical evidence that regular meditation reduces the mental and physical symptoms of stress. The GPs' magazine *The Practitioner* in 1987 said studies showed 'a consistent reduction in blood pressure' after meditation and 'meditation may be a promising clinical intervention technique for stress-related disorders ranging from fear of enclosed spaces ... to generalised anxiety, anxiety neurosis, back pain ... rehabilitation after myocardial infarct and bronchial asthma.' The article added that there have been reports of 'a number of cases of regression of cancer after intensive meditation in the absence of any orthodox treatment which could have accounted for the regression'. Remarkably high praise from a doctor and courses training doctors in meditation are now provided by the British Postgraduate Medical Federation.

There are numerous meditation techniques but one of the most widely available is transcendental meditation (TM). It is a useful technique for anyone who wishes to iron out the emotional creases which modern living puts into most of us. I have far more energy when I meditate than when I don't. Although TM has a certain amount of philosophy and semi-psychology (which you can take or leave), it does not have religious overtones, so you can practise it whatever your belief, or unbelief.

MEDICAL FACTS

Blood Pressure

There is no hard and fast figure which represents a 'normal' blood pressure, nor do doctors entirely agree on what is ideal. But somewhere between 110/70 and 125/80 is average for an adult — though some people with naturally low blood pressure may be closer to 100/60.

Blood doesn't circulate in an even stream, but in a series of spurts. So the pressure peaks in the blood vessels just after a heart beat and then ebbs until the next one. The two blood pressure figures represent the pressure when the force is at its peak and at its lowest. The stronger the arteries, the more they resist the force of the blood, and the lower the blood pressure. As you get older, and the elasticity arteries weaken, the figures tend to rise, but the lower figure should be under 90 until you are in your sixties.

Medicines

Analgesics

Government warnings have been issued against giving aspirin to children under the age of 12, except on medical advice. There is a rare, and possibly fatal, condition which aspirin can occasionally cause in young children. So children should be given paracetamol instead. Aspirin, paracetamol or neurofen are all suitable for adults. But – at any age – the soluble or specially coated versions of analgesics are safest: the ordinary tablets can stick to the lining of the stomach, and cause bleeding. Anyone who has to take analgesics regularly should see a doctor.

Antibiotics

Antibiotics are used to treat ailments caused by bacteria, but not those caused by viruses as viruses are not killed by them.

Doctors prescribe the amount of antibiotic needed for a course of treatment. Even if the illness seems to clear up before the medicine is finished it is important to keep on taking it. If you don't finish the treatment the remaining bacteria, which were the toughest to kill, may live on. This is how antibiotic-resistant bacteria are created.

Taking Medicines

Whenever any medicine is prescribed here are some questions which the patient ought to ask the doctor (as appropriate).

- Can I drink alcohol while taking them?
- May they make me sleepy?
- Is it safe to drive or operate machinery while taking them?
- Will they have any effect on the contraceptive pill? (Some stop it working.)
- Are there any side effects I should know about?
- Are there any over the counter medicines I shouldn't take at the same time?

Check precisely when any medicine should be taken. Some drugs need to be taken on an empty stomach (i.e. an hour before or after food), some must have food immediately before and after them, and others need to be taken straight after a meal. Some medicines won't work properly if you don't get this right. If you forget a dose don't just take a double dose next time: this could be dangerous – if the medicine is for a serious complaint ask a doctor or pharmacist what to do having missed a dose.

Temperature Taking

It is best to take a child's temperature in the armpit until he or she is about the age of 5. After that, a sensible, normal child can usually have it taken under the tongue, provided it knows the thermometer is fragile – though it's best for an adult to be there. For an accurate reading shake the thermometer to below normal by holding it firmly and giving several quick flicks of the hand, with a loose wrist. Keep the thermometer in place for 2 to 3 minutes, with the mouth closed, or the arm firmly against the body, so it has time to register fully.

It would be nice if I could tell you that below a certain temperature you didn't have to worry, and above it you had to ring the doctor. But temperatures aren't like that. Any fever shows someone has an infection, but the height of the fever *doesn't* show the seriousness of the infection because:

- some illnesses provoke higher temperatures, without being more serious
- some people get higher fevers than others without being any more ill

Addresses and suggestions for further reading are at the ends of chapters.

- young children run higher temperatures than older children or adults who are equally ill
- temperatures are often higher in the evening than in the morning
- the elderly can be quite ill yet have little or no temperature.

°C	°F	
40·6 –	– 105	Temperatures seldom go much above this.
40·0 –	– 104	A high temperature.
39·4 –	– 103	
38·9 –	– 102	
38·3 –	– 101	
37·8 –	– 100	
37·2 –	– 99	
37·0 –	– 98·4	The average temperature taken under the tongue but some people register a degree lower.
36·1 –	– 97	
35·6 –	– 96	
35·0 –	– 95	Below this temperature the patient has hypothermia.

By the law of nuisance small children fall ill at weekends, or near midnight, just when it is impossible to ring the surgery. In deciding if a child or adult is ill enough for you to telephone a doctor look at all the other indications of illness too. A very young baby may be really ill yet have no fever at all; equally, children can sometimes run quite high temperatures yet seem to be only a little poorly. In these cases the other symptoms would tell you not to go by the thermometer, and research has shown that mothers in particular are rather good at judging illness in their own children.

> If a young baby is listless and off its food contact a doctor, even if there are no other signs of illness. This is not the same as a fretful child who is off its food and is clearly teething.

Treating a Temperature

The traditional way of treating someone with a temperature was to put them to bed and keep them warm. However, some children under the age of 5 get convulsions

Immunization for Britain

No vaccine *guarantees* against an illness, but the following vaccines can give better than 90 per cent protection. The ages at which the injections should be given are regularly changed by the authorities. So discuss the latest possibilities with a GP or Health Visitor shortly after a baby's birth. Also discuss Vitamin K which is almost routinely given to newborns; there have been question marks over its safety.

Age	Disease	Method and Comments
Early days	Tuberculosis (BCG)	For babies born to high-risk families.
2 months	Diphtheria	Usually given in 3 doses with tetanus and whooping cough, second dose 1 month after the first, third dose 1 month after that. Mild feverish reaction is not unusual. A **booster** is usually given before the child starts school.
2 months	Tetanus	Basic course is 3 doses, timed as for diphtheria. A **booster** is needed at age 5 and at 15-19 years, also after an injury that could be infected – although not within 5 years of a previous booster. Any puncture wound or one in contact with soil carries a risk of tetanus if immunization is not up to date.
2 months	Hib (Haemophilus influenzae b)	This vaccine is now routinely given to babies to protect them against the most common form of bacterial meningitis. Given in 3 doses at the same times as Diphtheria and Tetanus, but by a separate injection.
3 months	Whooping cough	Basic course is 3 doses, timed as for diphtheria. Mild feverish reaction usual shortly afterwards and the arm may be sore and red. Extreme reactions are exceedingly rare. **Boosters** are not needed.
3 months	Poliomyelitis	Basic course is 3 doses, as for diphtheria. **Booster** at age 5 and at 15-19. Adults may need extra **boosters** if travelling to high-risk areas.
12-16 months	Measles, mumps and rubella (MMR)	This is a single-dose, combined vaccine. A slight fever and rash may occur 1 week after and last 2-3 days. Some get mumplike swelling 2 weeks after that. Other reactions are rare and should be reported to a doctor.
10-14 years	Rubella (German measles)	This single-dose vaccine is still given to those who missed the MMR and to adult women who lack rubella immunity and intend to become pregnant. But pregnancy must be avoided for 1 month afterwards.
10-14 years	BCG (tuberculosis)	One dose is normally enough. A reaction in 2-6 weeks on the site of the injection is normal. A light dressing can be used until the scab forms, but shutting out air may cause a large scar. Severe local reactions are possible.
Adults	Anthrax	Four spaced doses, plus annual **boosters** can be given to those who may encounter infected animal products during their work. Side effects are mild and rare.

Infectious Diseases

All the following diseases have some thing in common: the older you are when you have them, the worse they are likely to be. If you think someone has any of these illneses phone a doctor and explain the symptoms, and which illness he or she has been in contact with – the doctor will probably prefer an infectious patient to stay away from the surgery.

	Chicken pox (varicella)	German measles (rubella)	Measles
Incubation period	14-16 days	14-21 days	10-14 days
Cause	Virus	Virus	Virus
Symptoms	Separate red spots which each form a blister, then a crust, and itch severely. Moderately high temperature peaking about day 2 and lasting several days more.	A mild illness lasting about 10 days. Lowish temperature tends to peak on 6th day. There is a fine rash on about the 5th day. Adults may be far more ill and have severe joint pains.	Begins like a bad cold, and cough. After 3-4 days a slightly itchy red rash starts behind the ears, and spreads. Fever usually peaks on 4th day, and is often high. The eyes and mouth may be sore, light may tire eyes.
Infectious period	Starts the day before the rash appears, and lasts until all the scabs have totally dried up.	Starts several days before the illness begins, ends a week after the spots appear.	Infectious from several days before the rash, until 5 days later, or when the child stops being ill – whichever is later.
Treatment	Keep spots dry in early stages (e.g. no bath). Soothe with calamine lotion. Do not scratch off scabs or scars will be left. Antihistamine will ease the itching.	Usually so mild it may not even need bed rest. But stay indoors.	Consult a doctor and give complete bed rest in a darkened room. This is not an illness to take lightly.
Special features	See Shingles, page 562.	Keep away from women who might be pregnant. In the first 3 months of pregnancy this illness may cause abortion, or a deaf, blind or heart-diseased baby.	There can be complications such as ear, eye and heart problems. Tell the doctor if there are signs of these. Signs of deafness should be watched for afterwards.

	Mumps	Scarlet Fever	Whooping Cough (pertussis)
Incubation period	16-21 days	2-4 days	7-10 days
Cause	Virus	Bacterium	Bacterium
Symptoms	Starts with a moderate temperature. After 1-3 days glands below the ear and along the jaw swell painfully, on one side or both. A very sore throat and earache are common. If males get swollen balls tell the doctor immediately.	Sore throat, headache, moderately high temperature. Fine red rash starts in 12 hours and spreads.	Feel ill and cough and catarrh for 1-2 weeks. Then cough becomes severe, with a whooping noise between coughs and usually vomiting. This lasts 4-6 weeks, and takes a long time to go.
Infectious period	Starts several days before the symptoms. Ends when the swellings are down to normal.	Starts several days before the first symptoms. Ends when fully recovered.	Highly infectious from the first symptoms, until 3 weeks after the start of coughing.
Treatment	There is no specific treatment, but the swellings should go in 7-10 days.	Bed rest while fever lasts. Calamine lotion may soothe the rash.	A doctor may use antibiotics to relieve the whoop, but the main treatment is rest and soothing drinks.
Special features	Tell a doctor IMMEDIATELY if there is a headache, dislike of light or a stiff neck. Males who have this after puberty, and have swelling in both balls, may become permanently sterile. Those with mumps should keep away from men who have not had it. Occasionally deafness afterwards; watch out for this.		

Addresses and suggestions for further reading are at the ends of chapters.

when they have a fever. (This is more likely to happen if the temperature rises very rapidly and if fits run in the family.) So the latest nursing procedure is to bring the temperature down by giving paracetamol, *not* wrapping the child up or putting it to bed (unless it wants to be there) but sponging it cool with *tepid* water, leaving the water on the skin. I am assured that this won't give a child pneumonia. So this is probably the best course to follow with a young child, unless a doctor has advised otherwise.

However, some doctors believe that, like most of the body's reactions, a fever is a survival mechanism which helps to fight infection. They say, therefore, that although cool sponging may be soothing for adults and older children a fever should not be brought down with paracetamol unless it is uncomfortably high (40°C, 104°F).

Whether an adult or older child should go to bed or not is a matter of how they feel. If they want to be tucked up and warm let them. The body tends to know what it needs. Equally, if they feel more comfortable and cool out of bed they should come to no harm.

If a child does have a fit it will become unconscious and may go stiff and jerk strangely. Fits usually end in a few minutes, but stay with the child until it does to make sure it doesn't hurt itself, then ring your doctor.

The surface temperature, measured under the armpit, is about 0.6°C (1°F) lower than the temperature measured under the tongue or (as on the Continent) up the bottom.

If you find conventional thermometers hard to read there is now an 'Easy Read' thermometer which really is easy to read.

★ Most adults have a pulse rate of about 60 to 80 beats a minute, but top athletes have considerably lower rates.

Travel Care

Medical Agreements with Other Countries
Britain has agreements with a number of countries which allow British passport holders to use their health services. A DH booklet lists the countries covered, the free treatment you may be entitled to and how to obtain it or get costs refunded, and what immunizations you may need. You will find it in travel agents and post offices.

Within the EEC you can only use this concession if you have form E111, which you apply for by taking the form at the back of the DH booklet to a post office. If you leave in a rush you can, in theory, post the application for the E111 and ask them to send it to your overseas address – but they aren't geared for that.

If you don't have an E111 and find you need treatment, you can ask the health insurance authorities in that country to write to **DH International Relations** (page 592) and obtain the form for you.

★ These forms don't cover anyone moving to live in another EEC country, and they should apply to DH International Relations for details of their rights to EEC benefits.

★ Form E111 used to last for two years, it now lasts for ever – or until you have to give it to officials in another country to get treatment. If that happens you just get a new E111 before your next trip.

★ Take form SA30 with you when you go to a non-EEC country. Often you pay first then get a refund, the form tells you how to get it. Some countries need you to produce a passport; others want to see a driving licence or medical card to show you are *resident* in Britain. So take the necessary papers.

What You Get under these Agreements
In the EEC you are entitled to the same treatment as a national of the country. So in France we should get any free treatment a Frenchman would get and so on. It may be considerably less than you would get in Britain and the services usually cover sudden illness and accident; chronic illness may not.

In many other countries only certain medical needs are covered. For example, injuries from car accidents are not covered in some countries. On top of that, health scheme treatment may not be to the standard you are used to – and the cost of private treatment in some countries can be bankrupting. So it is never wise to assume that you don't need medical insurance.

If you do need treatment while away *tell* the medical staff that you wish to have it under their health scheme and have your passport with you.

Where to Get Advice
Any GP can give immunizations and prescribe anti-malaria tablets. But GPs get their information from government recommendations, which are likely to be out of date. In malaria there is a growing problem of drug resistance. So drugs which worked last year may not be safe this year. So it can be well worth getting up-to-the-minute information from the London School of Hygiene and Tropical Medicine. There is a recorded malaria information line on 0891 600350.

The London School of Hygiene and Tropical Medicine also validates information for a highly efficient service called MASTA, in which you fill in a form giving all your medical details, where you are going and the conditions. They then tell you the health precautions you should take. Charges vary according to the level of information you want. You can simply get basic information on advisable immunizations and antimalarial tablets, or have a general briefing on health precautions, or get a thorough run-down on all the health hazards in any area, how to prevent them, recognize the symptoms and treat them. This last could be invaluable to anyone travelling rough or doing VSO. Up to three other members of the family are covered at no extra charge and the advice is tailored to the medical histories of each person and to their age.

Apply to MASTA 2 to 3 months ahead; then there is time to get immunizations and they can give you the latest facts on local epidemics and drug-resistant malaria. Regular travellers can have a subscription service. MASTA also sells items like small sterile medical kits for countries where unsterilized needles carry the risk of hepatitis and AIDS. Forms by post from: **MASTA** (page 592). Or if you ring a premium price number and record the details of your trip, MASTA will send you advice computer-tailored to the date and location.

Protection Which May be Needed When Travelling

Travel in other developed countries usually has health risks similar to here and special precautions are seldom needed. But hot climates may foster diseases which are not found in Britain, and it is wise to check the water. In less developed areas, unhygienic conditions and food preparation increase the risks. There is also a big difference between the health hazards of staying in good accommodation, and of travelling rough. The immunizations which are advisable vary not only with the country but also with the circumstances of your visit. In addition, some countries may insist on evidence of certain vaccinations before you cross their borders. Three months before travelling abroad check whether any immunizations are needed.

The following table covers the most usual immunizations but get the latest information on what is needed where (see page 571).

	Cholera	Hepatitis A	Hepatitis B	Malaria	Polio
Immunization	2 injections not less than 1 wk apart	Injection (in) of immunoglobulin or a vaccine (vac)	2 injections of vaccine 1 mth apart, booster in mth 6	None. Take preventative tablets from 1 wk before *until 4 wks after leaving malaria area.*	Unimmunized adults need 3 doses each 4 wks apart, and those immunized may need a booster
Timing	2+ wks before departure	(In) just before trip (Vac) 2 months before	1 mth before travel	Order tablets 2 wks before travel	4 months (if 1st time), only days if booster
Reaction	Tenderness where injected, fever, headache	Nil	Soreness where injected	Nil	Very rare cases develop polio
Protection	50-60%	(In) prevents illness or (Vac) lessens severity	Very variable	90%	95+%
Duration of protection	6 mths	(In) 3 mths (Vac) 10 yrs	Perhaps 5 yrs	Only while tablets are taken	10 yrs
Other precautions	Avoid food or water which might be dirty. Low risk in reasonable tourist accommodation.	As typhoid	Avoid contact with blood, semen or saliva of potential carriers	Anti-mosquito spray on skin, knock down spray in rooms, covering clothes, mosquito nets	Nil
Incubation	Rapid	3-5 wks	60 days - 9mths or symptomless	12-30 + days	3-21 days
Symptoms	Sudden watery diarrhoea, vomiting collapse, rarely fatal	Fever, nausea, stomach ache, jaundice	Loss of appetite, slight stomach pain, nausea, possibly fever and jaundice. Rarely fatal.	Fever and sweating, then chills and shivering. In one form coma and possibly fatal shock. Fatal type increasing.	Headache, stiff neck and back, fever, stomach upset.
Treatment	No food, *plenty* of clean liquid with 1 flat tsp salt and 5-8 tsp sugar per litre (or ORT preparation, see page 537, from a chemist)	Drink no alcohol		Drink no alcohol	
Notes	Some countries need evidence of immunization 6 days – 6 mths before crossing their border. Not recommended for children under 1 year.	In children it may be mild with no jaundice	A new and costly vaccine. Usually only given to those at high risk, such as health care workers.	Malaria in pregnancy is a danger to both mother and child. And some key drugs used in prevention cannot be taken when pregnant or given to the very young.	Not usually given in early months of pregnancy

Addresses and suggestions for further reading are at the ends of chapters.

	Rabies	Smallpox	Tetanus	Typhoid	Yellow Fever
Immunization	2 doses 4 wks apart, booster 12 mths, and as needed thereafter	In 1980 the WHO declared the world free of smallpox. Immunization is no longer given.	Normally given in childhood. Boosters every 10 years.	3 types of vaccine: (A) 1-2 injections 4-6 wks apart (B) single short or (C) 3 daily oral doses	1 injection
Timing	5 wks before trip		Not critical	5-7 wks before departure	At least 10 days before departure, for certificate to be valid
Reactions	Soreness where injected, headache, muscle ache, vomiting, possible within 48 hrs		Rarely headache, lethargy	Soreness at injection, nausea, headache – worst in those over 35, and on repeat immunizations – lasts 36 hours	Possibly slight headache and low fever 5-10 days later
Protection	Some doctors say it prevents rabies, others that it enables a faster response to preventative treatment if bitten. Recommend it.		95+%	70-90%	Almost 100%
Duration of protection	3 months		Around 10 years	(A) 1-3 yrs, boosters (B) 3 yrs (C) 1 yr	10 yrs
Other precautions	Avoid bites, scratches or licks from *any* animals. If these occur wash the wound *fast and thoroughly* with antiseptic. Get IMMEDIATE medical treatment. DO NOT wait for symptoms.		Avoid getting wounds, and wash them well, use antiseptic	Avoid food, milk or water which could be contaminated with sewage or by flies	Against mosquitoes, as for malaria
Incubation	2-8 weeks normal, can be 9 days-2 years		4-21 days	Usually 1-3 weeks	1-5 days
Symptoms	The wound feels odd, fever, headache, followed by either paralysis and coma, or hallucinations and wild behaviour. Usually fatal unless treated *before* symptoms occur.		Violent contractions of the muscles	Vomiting and diarrhoea, possibly fever	Sudden fever, vomiting, prostration, jaundice, can be fatal
Treatment	**Get medical attention at once**		**Get medical attention at once**		**Get medical attention at once**
Notes	A relatively new immunization well worthwhile when visiting high-risk areas		Caught from the soil. Any skin puncture outdoors a risk. Keep immunization up to date in the UK and overseas.		Only available at special centres. Children under 9 months not immunized. Some countries require proof of immunization.

Some immunizations can only be given at special centres and even these may not carry all the vaccines. Check that a doctor or clinic has what you need before going.

Some travellers, needing blood transfusions or injections while overseas, have caught AIDS. It is not always easy to know whether blood is or is not adequately checked for AIDS but be prepared for the worst.

- Know your blood group and agree mutual blood transfusion with a fellow traveller, of the same blood group, who seems unlikely to have AIDS.
- Take a kit of sterile medical needles (from MASTA, page 592) to countries where they might not be sterilized.
- Ask your doctor to prescribe Haemocell (a blood substitute, which can be used instead of a blood transfusion) to take with you, and take enough to last while you are flown to the nearest good medical centre. It comes in small packs, needs no special storage conditions, and will last the duration of an average trip.

General Precautions

It's easy to be unduly alarmed about hygiene and the risk of illness in strange countries. But being ill abroad can really spoil a trip. So judge which of the following precautions are needed and err slightly on the side of caution, but without seeing germs in every corner.

- Wear covering clothing – malaria is not the only disease carried by biting insects.
- Wear covering shoes – against ticks, bugs, hookworms, scorpions, etc.
- Do not enter fresh water (except swimming pools) – some exceedingly nasty conditions (e.g. bilharzia or liver fluke) can enter through the skin.
- Cover all wounds with plaster – some flies lay eggs in human cuts.
- Take a torch to countries which may have nasties underfoot, or wild animals in the bushes.
- Don't use scent or wear bright clothes in tropical countries which have stinging insects – they like both.
- Ask about possible hazards. Don't be embarrassed about seeming ignorant. Things aren't always the way common sense suggested – for example, some tiny African scorpions are far more poisonous than some large ones.

Serious Illness or Death

If you need to come home lying down, the airline has no obligation to transport you in that position unless you pay for the extra seat space. Such costs should be covered by holiday insurance. If you die while abroad you return as freight, in which case the airline may refund to your estate the difference between freight and passenger charges either as an obligation or as a favour depending on the type of return ticket.

FIRST AID

First aid seems like the kind of thing which would be commonsensical and stay very much the same. In fact, even common sense isn't static and first aid is constantly changing and improving in the light of new developments. What follows is the very latest thinking in the field – so don't be surprised if it isn't what you've learnt. Experience has shown that some old techniques were none too safe.

In an Accident

In a serious accident which could have damaged the spine or internal organs NEVER MOVE THE PATIENT unless it is vital to get him or her out of greater danger. *Moving someone with a spinal injury can cause life-long paralysis.*

Never give injured people food or drink – especially not alcohol – as it may make it difficult for doctors to give an anaesthetic.

The order in which to act:

1 Prevent any further danger – e.g. turn off the electricity in electrocutions (page 577).
2 If the patient isn't breathing give artificial respiration (below).
3 If there is no pulse (pulse taking, page 578) give heart massage (page 578).
4 Treat any bleeding, starting with the worst (page 575).
5 If they are unconscious make sure the airway is clear and place in the recovery position (page 581).

Meanwhile, if possible, get someone else to dial 999 for help, and ask for Ambulance. When alone, take action needed to save life, as above, then call an ambulance.

Artificial Respiration

WORK QUICKLY. Check for false teeth, and remove them. Also, check the airway for any obstruction. Feel whether the tongue has fallen back and blocked the throat – if so pull it forward. Tilt the head back and a gasp of air may go in. If not, use one of the following methods to get breathing started.

Method 1 – Mouth-to-mouth Resuscitation

1 Put the patient on her back.

2 Tilt the head well back so the chin sticks up.

3 Open her mouth. Take a deep breath yourself.

4 Hold her nose shut and place your mouth firmly over hers.
5 Blow out steadily (not too much for a young child or baby)
6 Raise your head; breathe in – looking to see that the chest is now falling.

Repeat once, ensuring the chest is fully inflated, quite quickly, then check that the pulse can be felt.

If it CAN – continue steps 1 to 6 at normal breathing speed until she is breathing or help comes.
If it CAN'T – give heart massage (page 578).

Chemists sell a tube which allows you to give mouth-to-mouth resuscitation without placing your mouth on the other person's. If you don't have one and really can't stomach mouth-to-mouth, use the Holger Nielson method below.

Method 2 – Holger Nielson method (*less effective than 1*)

1 Put the victim on his front.
2 Place his arms with elbows bent and head resting on hands.
3 Kneel above the head.
4 Press firmly down on the back, breathing out yourself (for timing).
5 Take hold of each of the victim's elbows and raise them, lifting the chest slightly (breathing in yourself).

Repeat 4 and 5 three times, then check the pulse (see page 578). If it can be felt continue. If it can't give heart massage (see page 578).

If necessary, treat for unconsciousness (page 580).

Bleeding

If there is severe bleeding ACT FAST. Clean hands are best, but dirty hands are less harmful than no action at all. Arterial blood is bright red and its loss must be stopped RAPIDLY. Since AIDS, first aid instructors recommend putting a clean cloth, such as a handkerchief or scarf between the blood and your hand.

> When something (knife, pen, etc.) is stabbed deeply into the flesh DO NOT REMOVE IT. Removal could cause fatal bleeding.

● If bleeding is on an unbroken limb raise it above the heart – blood moves more slowly uphill.
● If the blood is from a place which can safely be pressed, pressure will help stop the flow. Press cuts together or, on a larger injury, apply a pad of dressing and press.
● First aid experts no longer recommend applying a tourniquet to shut off the blood vessels. Bandages intended to stop blood flowing out through the injury can very easily block off the blood vessels carrying

vital blood *back* to the heart, and this is *more* dangerous than the blood loss through the wound.

● Don't remove bandages to see how an injury is doing, this will slow down the good work. If blood oozes through, place a second pad on top.

● After treating bleeding *always* wash your hands well – the victim could carry a blood-borne disease.

Burns – Chemical

1 Rinse the area immediately, and *very* thoroughly, under running water. A few chemicals are activated by water. Try to check the container rapidly to make sure the chemical is not one of these. If it is, an alternative treatment may be given.
2 Remove any clothing containing the chemical.
3 Rinse again and get medical help.
4 If the chemical is in an eye rinse it IMMEDIATELY, AND VERY WELL, under a running tap (see above). DO NOT use an eye bath; it washes the chemical back into the eye.

Burns – from Fire

1 Smother the flames on burning clothes with any thick material – towel, blanket, jacket – pressing it close enough to keep air from the flames. (Don't worry about bits of fabric stuck to the skin.)
2 Put the injury immediately under cold, running water

or plunge it into a container of cold water, or – failing those – place a pad soaked in cold water over the burnt area. Leave the injury under cold water for at least 10 minutes. (It may hurt more but it *is* doing good.) Containers and pad will warm up, so keep adding fresh cold water.

> Plunging the whole body into a cold bath could increase the shock. Only plunge the burnt area.

As the body holds heat for a long time, so the cold water treatment helps even if it is not applied until 20 to 30 minutes after the accident.

3 Get medical attention if:
   a the burn is on a child and larger than a 50p piece;
   b the skin is charred or white;
   c burns are deep or cover much skin.

Be prepared to treat for shock (page 580) and give any burnt person frequent sips of tepid sweet water – this is doubly important with children.

4 Remove anything tight, if this can be done without further injury – rings, watches, shoes etc. – as the burnt area will swell. Don't try to remove any fabric which may have stuck to the burns, leave that to the professionals.
5 DO NOT apply lotions, creams, butter OR ANYTHING ELSE to the burns. Despite the folklore *none* of them helps and some may make medical treatment far more difficult and painful. Just cover the burn *lightly* with a *very clean* cloth such as a clean handkerchief, table napkin or pillow case – not a paper tissue or cotton wool as these will stick to the burn.

Chest Injuries

If an injury makes a hole in the chest there is a danger of air getting in and compressing a lung. Cover the wound IMMEDIATELY with a pad under your hand and bandage it as soon as possible to make it as airtight as you can.

Choking

Coughing is designed to remove whatever is blocking the throat. If coughing fails:

1 Try to have the victim's head down or hang a child downwards over your knee. Give 4 firm slaps between the shoulder blades. *Time the slaps to their coughs*; slapping as they breathe in could make them inhale the object. This could be dangerous.
2 If this fails, a small object like a fish bone may be dislodged by eating bread.

If the choking is serious and could endanger life use the following treatment – but do not use it for mild choking as it can cause internal injuries:

1 Get behind the person.
2 Place your fist thumb-side against the lower chest of the victim *just* below the centre of the ribs.

Addresses and suggestions for further reading are at the ends of chapters.

3 Cup your other hand over this and give a sharp pull inwards. Repeat several times.
4 Forcing the breath out suddenly like this should force the object into the mouth. Remove it quickly, before it can be breathed in again. If unconsciousness occurs give artificial respiration (page 574).

Drowning

If the body can be *briefly* held head down to drain any water, do so. Then apply artificial respiration (page 574).

> Children can recover completely from surprisingly long periods under cold water. Keep trying to get them breathing, even if it seems unlikely that they will recover.

Electrocution – Domestic Current

1 If possible switch off the current.
2 If you can't turn off the current DON'T touch the victim directly, or with anything which could conduct

electricity (e.g. metal). Using something made of wood (e.g. broom or chair), push the source of the electricity away from the person or vice versa. Rubber is another good protection against electricity, so wearing rubber gloves or pushing your arms down wellington boots is a safeguard.
3 Once separated from the electricity give whichever of the following is needed in this order:
artificial respiration (page 574)
heart massage (page 578)
burns treatment (page 576)

Then get medical attention – there can be a sudden collapse hours later.

Electrocution – High Voltage

> DO NOT try to rescue someone electrocuted by a high voltage such as a pylon or some factory supplies. It can reach out and 'grab' you if you get too close. Stay two normal room widths (18 m) away.

Fractures, Broken Bones and Dislocations

The signs of a break or fracture or dislocation are any of the following:

● the area looks out of shape
● there is swelling
● loss of normal movement below the point of the injury
● considerable pain.

> Whenever treatment under an anaesthetic may be needed DO NOT give *any* food or drink: it could delay the treatment.

Dress any open wound with as little disturbance as possible, and keep the patient warm. If the injury is to the skull or body DO NOT move the injured person (unless to save them from greater danger); get an ambulance to them. Keep them warm while it comes. DO NOT REMOVE ANY HARD HAT IF THERE IS RISK OF A HEAD INJURY.

If the injury is to arm or collarbone use a triangular bandage or scarf, or a buttoned-up coat to support the limb. If necessary, take stress off the bone by supporting it with a splint – a whole newspaper rolled tightly is effective. If bending the arm is painful bandage it to the body in any position which relieves the pain.

Splint a broken leg to immobilize it completely, using anything to hand that is wider and longer than the limb

you need to immobilize – a plank is ideal. Tie this to the leg firmly but not too tightly, avoiding ties at the site of the injury. Unless it is clearly a very minor injury call an ambulance. Failing that, bandage the two legs together, so one bone supports the other and take the victim to hospital.

Frostbite

Frostbite must warm *slowly, without rubbing*. Remove anything tight or wet. Cover the frostbite with something warm and dry, or warm it with the body – tuck fingers under an armpit.

Heart Failure

Taking a Pulse
If you suspect heart failure take the pulse. To do this rest your fingers (not your thumb) lightly on the underside of the victim's wrist just below the base of his or her thumb. You should feel a slight beat in the area between the bone and the tendon. *Don't press too hard* or you will block off the beat – practise on yourself. If there is no pulse ACT FAST.

1 Put the patient on his or her back.
2 Place the heel of one hand on the lower half of the breastbone (it runs down the centre of the chest).
3 Put the heel of the other hand on top with the fingers pointing in the *same* direction. Interlock the fingers. (This stops the lower fingers digging down into the chest.)
4 Repeatedly press down VERY HARD and FAST. Count 1 and – 2 and – 3 and – as you do it. Repeat 15 times, then give 2 breaths (page 574).

Once the heart is beating, check the breathing and treat that if necessary (page 574).

Forget the television series in which people doing heart massage press gently. It isn't easy to massage a heart through bone, and it is not unusual for correct heart massage to break a rib. Which is why you should never do it unless it really is necessary – but better a broken rib than dead.

Hypothermia

Hypothermia is a state of such great cold that it stops the body functioning. In conditions of extreme cold, such as icy water, anyone of any age can get it. But in normal life babies are at special risk because they have a large surface area from which to lose heat in relation to their total volume. The elderly are also vulnerable because in old age awareness of temperature changes becomes less acute – as eyesight does – and so they may not realize they are getting too cold. The symptoms are:

● the body is very cold
● adults look white, but a baby may be pink
● the pulse and breathing are feeble
● the victim is dozy, or unconscious.

Call medical help fast. While it comes:

1 remove any wet clothing
2 wrap the patient lightly in warm dry blankets or substitutes. DO NOT apply heat such as hot water bottles or electric blankets (if appropriate, cuddle them to share your body heat)
3 warm the room
4 DO NOT give alcohol; give warm – *not hot* – drinks if the victim is conscious.

Poisoning

There are a lot of false and dangerous ideas about poisoning. Forget what you have heard or seen on television. The action first aid experts recommend is this:

1 Watch the victim all the time; the conscious may become unconscious, the unconscious stop breathing.
2 Wipe the mouth area well, in case they have taken a chemical which burns. Then, if the patient isn't breathing, use artificial respiration (page 574).
3 If the patient is breathing but unconscious, place in the recovery position (see page 581) – then ring for an ambulance. Keep them warm.
4 If conscious, find out what has been taken then ring for an ambulance and tell them what the poison was.
5 If the poison is a corrosive substance such as an acid or strong alkaline, DO NOT MAKE THE VICTIM SICK – *these are more dangerous coming up than in the stomach.* Instead give drinks of milk, or water to dilute the poison and soothe. Examples include:

petrol	bleach
white spirit	cleaning fluids
polishes	turpentine or turps substitute

Addresses and suggestions for further reading are at the ends of chapters.

6 Do not try to get rid of the poison by making the victim sick – unless a doctor advises it. Even poisons which could be brought up with relative safety do not act instantly, and will not be totally vomited by any first aid method. So give drinks of milk or water to dilute the poison and get proper medical attention FAST. One of Britain's top poisons units also recommends two products which use harmless activated charcoal to absorb the poison. Either can safely be taken, even by small children, and will help to stop the poison entering the bloodstream, so they are well worth keeping in any medicine cabinet. They are Carbomix and Medicol, and are obtainable from good chemists.

> Neither mustard nor salt should be given to make someone sick. Salt is particularly dangerous as high doses of salt are themselves poisonous – especially to children. *Children have died because parents gave them salt and water, though the poison they took would not have killed them.*

7 When the ambulance comes, give the attendants all the details of what has been taken, including whatever bottle or container held the poison, plus a sample of vomit.

The numbers of the major **poison information centres** are as follows:

Belfast 0232 240503	These numbers are for
Birmingham 021 554 3801	doctors: DO NOT
Cardiff 0222 709901	phone them unless you
Dublin 0001 379966	have a serious
Edinburgh 031 229 2477	emergency and cannot
Leeds 0532 430715	get local medical advice.
London 071 635 9191	A NEEDLESS CALL
Newcastle 091 232 1525	COULD BLOCK THE LINE
	WHEN IT IS URGENTLY
	NEEDED.

Poisonous Plants

The following plants, which are often found in the wild, in gardens or as house plants are poisonous. If you think someone has eaten one of them, see above. Just how ill someone would be after eating one of these plants would vary with the amount which was eaten and the age of the eater. Young children are more easily poisoned than adults. How the poisons are presented is another factor. Some plants have poisonous juices which you encounter by just breaking a leaf or stem; others may have their most severe poison locked up inside a seed whose hard casing would take some determined chewing. The risk of poisoning also varies according to whether the plant looks inviting and tastes good. A child is far more likely to eat an attractive berry – especially if it looks like a familiar fruit – than leaves, and anything which tastes dreadful will not be eaten for very long – and many of them do taste vile.

If you have any of the following plants in your home or garden there is no need to get unduly alarmed. Just make sure that no one eats them or, in some cases, gets the juice on the skin. But children should be taught, from very young, that they do not pick or eat *anything* they find growing unless they have checked with you. This is particularly important if they ever see adults picking food from a garden, allotment or hedgerow: to a toddler blackberries and deadly nightshade are very similar. I emphasize 'anything' because many children like nothing better than to do the forbidden. So, if you point out the very poisonous plants in a garden, and tell them not to eat them, those will be the first ones they sample. But if you have children who are not able to learn to be cautious it may be necessary to remove poisonous plants from the garden. Be careful how you do it: don't load branches into a car and drive to the local dump. In the enclosed space of a car the fumes given off by the broken leaves could land you in hospital.

When making a barbecue in the wild, be sure that you recognize the wood you take for the fire or for skewering food. Even troops on survival training have been poisoned by carelessly skewering sausages on innocent looking, but highly poisonous shrubs.

Reactions to Poisonous Plants

★★★ extremely poisonous and possibly fatal
★★ very poisonous but rarely fatal
★ extremely unpleasant symptoms but not fatal
Assume *all* parts are poisonous unless otherwise stated.

Plant		Symptoms
Black Bryony (*Tamus communis*)	★★	vomiting, diarrhoea, also sap blisters skin
Castor Oil Plant (*Ricinus communis*)	★★★	vomiting, sweating, rapid pulse, weakness and collapse
Cherry Laurel (*Prunus laurocerasus*)	★★	headache, vomiting, dizziness, low blood pressure, dilated pupils, unconsciousness
Cowbane/Water Hemlock (*Cicuta virosa*)	★★★	dizziness, vomiting, unconsciousness, violent convulsions, coma
Cuckoo Pint (*Arum maculatum*)	★★	sore throat, diarrhoea, irregular pulse, coma
Deadly Nightshade (*Atropa belladonna*)	★★	vomiting, diarrhoea, convulsions, coma
Death Cap Mushroom (*Amanita phalloides*)	★★★	start after 6 to 24 hours, pain, vomiting, intense thirst, weak pulse
Foxglove (*Digitailis purpurea*)	★	nausea, weakness, rapid pulse, seeing yellow haloes round objects
Hemlock (*Conium maculatum*)	★★★	dilated pupils, lowered temperature, difficulty in moving, fluctuating pulse, rapid breathing, stupor
Henbane (*Hyoscyamus niger*)	★	nausea, dizziness, difficulty breathing, confusion, rapid pulse

Plant		Symptoms
Holly (*Ilex aquifolium*)	★	stomach pain, vomiting, diarrhoea
Laburnum (*Laburnum anagyroides*)	★★	stomach pain, vomiting, drowsiness, fever, rapid pulse, coma
Lily of the Valley (*Convallaria majalis*)	★★★	stomach pain, vomiting, cold clammy skin, delirium, coma, possibly death
Monkshood (*Aconitum napellus*)	★★★	burning mouth and throat, stomach pain, vomiting, intense thirst, headache, coldness, paralysis, convulsions, delirium, coma
Leopard Lily, Dumb Cane (*Dieffenbachia*)	★	extreme swelling of lips and tongue, pain
Oleander (*Nerium oleander*)	★★★	stomach pain, vomiting, diarrhoea, rapid pulse, dizziness, coma
Pokeweed (*Phytolacca americana*)	★	stomach pain, vomiting, diarrhoea, dizziness, exhaustion
Privet (*Ligustrum vulgare*)	★★	stomach pain, vomiting, diarrhoea
Rhubarb leaves (*Rheum rhaponticum*)	★	stomach cramps, vomiting, weakness, reduced blood clotting, liver and kidney damage
Thorn Apple (*Datura stramonium*)	★★	dry mouth, nausea, dilated pupils, loss of co-ordination, drowsiness, delirium, coma
White Bryony (*Bryonia dioica*)	★	diarrhoea, copius urine, also skin irritation
Woody Nightshade (*Solanum dulcamara*)	★★	vomiting, stomach pain, distressed breathing, flush, exhaustion
Yew Tree (*Taxus baccata*) not the red flesh of the berry	★★★	vomiting, stomach pain, fever, drowsiness, stiffness, often death

The following plants are also poisonous:

Lupins	Daffodil bulbs
Buttercups	Hyacinth bulbs
Potato – leaves and stem, and green sprouting tubers	Poinsettia
	Members of the spurge (euphorbia) family
Broom	Meadow saffron
Marsh Marigold	(*Colchicum autumnale*)
Water Iris – Yellow Flag	Snowberries
Bluebells (Wild Hyacinth)	Ivy
	Rhododendron
Christmas Roses (Hellebores)	Dog's Mercury
	Ragwort
Wood Anemone	Daphne mezerium
Mistletoe	Buckthorn

All fungi should be regarded as poisonous unless you are experienced in telling which is which.

Shock

In shock the heart slows down and the victim becomes cold, pale, drowsy and possibly unconscious. It can be fatal, and needs medical attention. To avoid it:

1 Keep the patient warmly covered – DO NOT give hot water bottles. If it is safe to do so (page 574) get warmth under as well as over them.
2 Loosen any clothing which might hinder breathing.
3 If the injuries allow it (page 574) raise the feet higher than the head.
4 DO NOT give food or drink – it could cause vomiting.
5 Be reassuring and calm – even when seemingly unconscious they may be able to hear what you say.

The reason why hot water bottles must not be used is that they draw blood to the surface, away from other organs which need it.

Snakebite

Forget the stories about cutting open snakebites, sucking them and applying tourniquets. With the British adder the biggest danger is shock. Reassure the bitten person that adder bites are NOT fatal, and keep them calm. Move the bitten limb as little as possible (the more it is moved the more the poison will spread). Wash the bite or wipe it clean. Put a pad over it and bandage it firmly. Immobilize the limb as if it was broken and get the person to hospital. Give paracetamol or aspirin to relieve the pain.

> Always avoid contact with snakes in the wild, but don't assume all snakes are out to get you. Most avoid encounters with man and retreat at the vibration of footfalls, and some even shyly hide their head in their coils if surprised. However, this is not true of all of them. The black mamba, for example, has a reputation for aggression, and can rear and strike at a distance of up to two-thirds of its total length.

For most foreign snakes the treatment is the same – but get the victim to medical treatment FAST. The venoms of some tropical snakes work very rapidly, and try to get a good description of the snake as treatment varies with the type. With bites from certain highly poisonous types overseas there may be a need to apply a tourniquet. Before travelling in wild areas check the best first aid for those you may encounter.

Unconsciousness

If someone is unconscious and you *know* there is no injury put them in the recovery position; this prevents the tongue falling back into their throat and allows blood, saliva or vomit to flow out without choking them.

Addresses and suggestions for further reading are at the ends of chapters.

It is most easily done by two people, with the victim on their back.

1 Remove anything from front pockets which might be hard to lie on.
2 Turn the head towards you.
3 Place one arm so it is folded across the chest.
4 Place the arm nearest to you by the victim's side.
5 Lift the leg on the side of the bent arm, cross it over the other one and bend the knee.
6 As the leg goes over roll the hips and shoulders with it – turning the casualty *towards* you.
7 Adjust to the position illustrated.

St John Ambulance Association and the **British Red Cross Society** (page 592) both run courses in first aid all over the country. Your nearest course can be found from the local branch in the phone book, or failing that contact head office. **St Andrew's Ambulance Association** (page 592) runs training courses in first aid in Scotland. For further information see *The First Aid Manual* (page 592).

SOCIAL AND ANTI-SOCIAL DRUGS

Some people may be surprised, or even affronted, to see smoking, drinking and gambling set alongside heroin and cocaine in a section on drugs. The grouping is scientific rather than critical. The *Collins English Dictionary* defines a drug as 'a chemical substance taken for the pleasant effect it produces' – which fits all of them, except gambling, very nicely. Gambling joins them because its thrill makes some people just as high as some drugs – which is not surprising, since extreme excitement makes the body produce chemicals very similar. All drugs share the ability to dominate those who enjoy them, to a point where they may be very hard to give up. Nor is there any neat line here between 'drugs' such as heroin and cocaine and more respectable substances like alcohol and tobacco. The heavy drinker who gives up alcohol may not suffer the withdrawal symptoms which are attendant on giving up heroin, but it can certainly be much harder than giving up a soft drug like marijuana. Finally, all drugs share the fact that even the mildest can make the user sacrifice friends and family to the need for them.

Those who feel this last statement isn't true of smoking should consider that every year families all over Britain suffer the grief of losing fathers, mothers, sons, daughters and grandparents prematurely, from diseases directly caused by smoking. What greater sacrifice is there?

Everyone however has the right to choose how to live their own life. This chapter is simply a route map to help people see the road they are on, and to provide signposts to where those who would prefer to go in a different direction can get help.

Alcohol

Alcohol is so much the socially accepted drug of the Western world that it is hard to think of it as a drug – let alone a harmful one. But it is. More young people die as the result of alcohol than from all the illegal drugs put together, and overall, in Britain and the United States, it is the third most common killer. By the year 2000 the World Health Organization predicts that alcohol may be the *biggest* killer in the industrial world, causing more deaths than cancer or heart disease.

It is not just alcoholics who are at risk. Vulnerability varies, and the young, the elderly and women are all rather more easily harmed by it than the average man. That doesn't mean men can drink without ill effect: 1 man in 5 admitted to hospital has an alcohol-related problem. It causes liver damage, high blood pressure, stomach problems, depression, damage to unborn children and personality changes. Yet alcohol consumption is rising.

Amounts of Alcohol
People generally think of spirits as strong, and beer as relatively weak. But we drink small measures of whisky and big glasses of beer, so the amount of alcohol consumed hardly differs. In alcohol content 1 glass of wine = 1 vermouth = 1 small sherry = 1 single whisky = ½ pint ordinary strength beer or lager.

The Health Education Authority (see page 587) uses units of alcohol to measure safe levels for drinking.

Units a Week

Men	Women	Level	Advice
up to 21	up to 14	low	Try never to exceed this.
22-35	15-21	moderate	Your chances of accidents and health damage increase.
35+	21+	high	Danger zone; cut down now, or you risk liver damage.

Drinking and Driving
The official facts are these:

● Driving ability can be affected by even 1 to 2 units of alcohol in the bloodstream.
● It takes one hour for each unit of alcohol to wear off.
● 10+ units during an evening could make you unfit to drive the next morning.

One unit =

single measure of spirits

small sherry

glass of wine

two-thirds can of ordinary beer

one-half pint of ordinary beer

one-half can of export beer

two-fifths pint of export beer

one-third can of strong ale or lager

one-quarter pint of strong ale or lager

one-third pint of ordinary cider

one-quarter pint of strong cider

one-quarter can of extra-strength beer or lager

one-fifth pint of extra strength beer or lager

- Tests with racing drivers have shown that drink made them far *more confident* of their ability to drive an obstacle course – but far *less good* at driving it. See also Law and Driving, page 469.

Drink alters the way the brain works and affects judgement, self-control, reaction time, memory and personality. When driving or operating machinery the most dangerous of these changes is in reaction time and judgement. Where relationships are concerned, the change to the personality is the killer. Most drinkers are their worst selves in their cups. But, as alcohol affects the memory, they may never know just how badly they have behaved. So they feel angry that others in the family aren't being as loving as they expect, and take refuge in more drink. This cycle breaks marriages and alienates children.

Those who become dependent on alcohol don't do so overnight: in some people it takes 5 years, but in most it takes 10 to 15 years. During that time most of them think they are just normal drinkers 'like everyone else'.

Women have less water in their bodies than men. So there is less to dilute the alcohol, and they are more easily harmed by it. A woman who drinks 8 units of alcohol a day is 36 times more likely to get liver disease than a man drinking the same amount. With the trend of women drinking more the number of women dying of liver disease has risen steadily. It is now 6 times more common than it was 20 years ago.

It is best not to drink when pregnant. Drink can get through to an unborn baby and harm it, and there is very new evidence which suggests that too much alcohol at the time when a baby is conceived may possibly cause abnormalities in the child.

There are NHS treatment centres, and increasing numbers of private clinics, which help people with alcohol problems. A GP can refer people to either. The organizations on page 593 have the latest information.

Warning Signs

Experts say these are some of the signs that alcohol may be getting a hold on someone:

- a need to have alcohol always available
- looking forward to drink as something they need to pep them up
- drinking playing an important part in their life
- having to increase the intake of alcohol to 'feel good'
- irritability if anyone else discusses their drinking
- feeling sick, irritable, having the shakes, sweating regularly in the morning or the middle of the night.

Gambling

The compulsion to gamble can be as strong as the compulsion to take drugs, is accompanied by the same delusions of being in control of the problem and is just as destructive. Wins just stimulate the urge to win more; losses – however serious – produce an urge to win them back. Normal, reasonable behaviour is steam-rollered by the compulsion and, thanks to fruit machines, even children as young as 8 years old are becoming hooked on gambling. For organizations to help gamblers overcome the urge to gamble, see page 593.

Smoking

Smoking is addictive – as most smokers who have tried to give up realize. But perhaps the greatest proof of its addictive power is that people continue to smoke despite the overwhelming evidence of the harm it does. The two harmful elements are tar, which condenses out of the smoke on to the lungs, and the poisonous gas carbon monoxide. Filter tips yield less tar but *more* carbon monoxide than other cigarettes. Research has *failed* to show that smoking low tar cigarettes is always much safer than other brands.

Effects on Those who Smoke

In its 6 years the Second World War killed only *half* as many British people as have been killed by smoking in the last 6 years. Of the 40,000 who die each year from lung cancer, 9 out of 10 are smokers. The younger someone starts smoking, the more likely he or she is to get lung cancer. That is only the tip of the iceberg: consider the following facts.

- Smokers are twice as likely to get cancer of the bladder as non-smokers.
- Nine out of 10 who die from chronic bronchitis and emphysema are smokers.
- A smoker is 2 to 3 times more likely to have a heart attack than a non-smoker.
- Smoking while taking the contraceptive pill more than doubles the risk of a stroke or heart attack, compared to non-smoking pill takers.
- Smoking may cause abnormalities in sperm which lead to infertility.
- Smokers get the menopause 2 to 3 years earlier than non-smokers.
- Smokers are 3 times more likely to die in middle age – unless they give up before 30.

Addresses and suggestions for further reading are at the ends of chapters.

- Smokers are impotent more often than non-smokers.
- Smoking also increases the risk of cancer of the mouth, larynx and windpipe. It may also be linked with cancer in the pancreas, kidney and cervix.
- Of every 1,000 young British smokers on 20 cigarettes a day:

  1 will be murdered
  6 will die in road accidents
  250 will die from smoking.

Effects on Non-Smokers
Those who breathe the smoke from the cigarettes of others are smoking passively.

- Sizeable amounts of nicotine and tar (two harmful elements in cigarettes) are found in the blood and urine of non-smokers who have been with smokers in a poorly ventilated area.
- Those who work for years in a smoky atmosphere suffer measurable lung damage.
- Non-smoking women may have an increased risk of lung cancer if their husbands smoke, or if they work among smokers.

Unborn babies and children are harmed by their parents' smoking. In all cases the more the adults smoke, the greater the likely harm to the child.

- A baby is more likely to be miscarried if its mother smokes.
- Babies of smokers are far more likely to be stillborn or to die in the first week.
- Children whose mothers smoked 10 or more cigarettes a day throughout pregnancy do less well at school.
- Children whose mothers smoked 10 or more cigarettes a day throughout pregnancy are more likely to develop cancer.
- Children under one year old are twice as likely to have serious chest complaints if both parents smoke

---

Giving up Smoking
The key to success is really wanting to give up. But the following methods can help:

- Make the first day without a cigarette a special day.
- Change your routine to cut out the events you associate with smoking.
- Find something else to do with your hands and/or mouth: sip water, chew gum, knit, carve wood – anything. If it's eating, make a bag of peeled carrots or washed celery each morning – not sweets.
- You may get no side effects, but if you do get irritable or depressed, start coughing or get stomach upsets be aware these *will* pass in several weeks – and they prove how much harm the cigarettes were doing you.
- Save up the money you would have spent on cigarettes for something you would really enjoy – or save

your cigarette money for your favourite charity and see how quickly it mounts up.
- Learn relaxation or meditation techniques and use them when the craving starts.
- If you smoke a cigarette, don't feel defeated; give up again from then on.
- Remember over 9 million people have beaten the habit, and you are as good as any of them; so you can do it.

Health Education Offices and Community Health Councils, listed in the phone book, have information on clinics and self-help groups for those who wish to give up. See also page 593.

Soft Drugs and Hard Drugs

Each drug has its own particular effects, and people differ in their reactions. Generally, the lighter the body weight, the greater the effects. Also the more psychologically fragile someone is, the greater the risk of being pushed over the brink, even if other taking the same drug are affected very little.

Despite this, drug reactions do have some common characteristics. When 'high', users normally feel they are at their best – more relaxed, wittier, happier and more able to cope with those around them. To the observer the reverse is usually true: even relatively sociable drugs seem to put a distance between the users and non-users. Their reactions seem off-key and, being caught up in the distorted events of their own mind, they become unresponsive to other people's moods and needs. Anyone who has been teetotal at a drinks party has experienced a version of this phenomenon.

Teenagers and Drugs
One of the problems for parents and teachers is that most of the symptoms of drug taking mimic the behaviour of normal adolescence. Any parent whose child has reached its twenties without it ever being moody, irritable, depressed, over-confident, ill-washed, selfish, sleepless, insensitive to others, constipated, over-energetic, apathetic, late, off his or her food or obsessed with music, is either a very unobservant parent or has a very unusual child. Yet these can be the symptoms of drug taking.

Adults need to think very carefully before accusing a child of taking drugs. If the real problem is just adolescence, an accusation may produce the reaction of 'I may as well be hung for a sheep as a lamb' and push them into drug taking. So watch out for confirmation first – unusual tablets, capsules or powders, cigarette papers (if the child doesn't usually roll his or her own) or even needles or syringes or skin and hair looking lifeless. Meanwhile, try to find out if anything else is causing the symptoms – a child who is worried about something, or unwell, will also be moody, irritable and apathetic. This can also be the time to read up or talk to organizations which deal with drug problems and learn more about what you can do if drugs *are* being taken (page 593).

Unfortunately, there is no easy way to get an adolescent to admit to anything – let alone something illegal.

But the adult who can *ask* a child calmly and caringly about the possibility that he or she may be taking drugs is more likely to learn the truth than someone who accuses. This means planning the moment carefully and not letting yourself be pushed into suddenly reacting to the child's behaviour. If drugs *have* been taken, try to find out how much, which ones, and why. Then discuss the future. Things need to be kept in proportion. A child regularly taking heroin has a serious problem, but a child experimenting with pot may be going through a passing stage – albeit an illegal one.

Such discussion isn't easy. Adolescents don't like talking about their lives. Equally a child's drug taking often makes adults feel rejected and furious. But it may be easier to handle if we take stock of our own drug taking first. Most of us take drugs of some kind, to keep others company or to make life more bearable or more enjoyable – the very reasons why adolescents take them. Our drugs are pain killers, sleeping tablets, tranquillizers, drink or cigarettes. Even if the first three are on doctor's orders, we all know that drink does us little good and that cigarettes are killers.

So shouting at adolescents for following the example which the adult world has set them is likely to be unproductive – however much we may feel like it. If *we* don't use our 'drug taking' as a route to understanding how they feel the risk is that *they* will use it to make us look foolish. They know that, as killers go, pot doesn't begin to compete with cigarettes. But they probably underestimate the risks of other drugs and the danger of one illegal drug leading to another, if those around them are taking them.

Common Hazards
People sometimes talk about drugs as if the slightest brush with them inevitably leads to addiction and death. This is simply not the case. But drugs do have risks attached to them which those who experiment with them tend to underestimate and the hazards involved *cannot* be judged by whether or not the law classes them as type A drugs. Some type B drugs are just as dangerous as those which are classified as type A.

First, the effects can be unpredictable, because the strength naturally varies from batch to batch, and sellers add impurities to increase their profits. Even if the strength doesn't vary, individual differences in people still mean that there is no totally 'safe' dose. So there is *always* a risk of an experience getting out of control and causing distress, or possibly overdose. And even in the 'right' dose drug effects may not always be pleasant. People take drugs to make them feel better but, in reality, drugs strengthen the mood you are in. So if someone is feeling worried, depressed or aggressive, these feelings increase.

Most drugs reduce physical control and concentration and slow down reaction times, even though the user may feel alert and totally in control. So it can be dangerous to drive, use machinery or even cross a road. The emotions are affected in a similar way, and regular use can distort the user's view of the world to a point where it harms emotional development and the ability to

function normally and have normal relationships. Drugs can also affect basic body functions. Amphetamines, for example, reduce the normal renewal of calcium in the bones, which could later lead to osteoporosis (see page 548), and both amphetamines and heroin play hell with the menstrual cycle and may stop it completely. In this situation girls should realize that they can still get pregnant and should not stop using contraceptives. In pregnancy there is also a risk of harming the baby, who may receive the drug through the mother's bloodstream. Drug users tend to have premature, underweight babies, and babies can experience withdrawal symptoms after birth.

Since the body adapts to drugs, this means the user needs more and more to get a buzz. In drugs that create dependence the body or the mind learns to 'need' that drug, and without it the user feels very ill. The cost can be disastrous for his or her lifestyle. Moreover, when combinations of drugs are used to get the desired effect it creates complex and unpredictable chemical interactions in the body, which are extremely dangerous and can be fatal. There are added risks from injecting drugs: it is more addictive and there is a greater danger of overdose, and sharing used needles causes infections such as abscesses, gangrene, hepatitis B and AIDS.

Coming Off Drugs
Relatives and friends may find it helpful to bear in mind that addiction is an escape from reality. So users may not know the truth, let alone tell it, and promises are often not remembered, let alone kept. The key to coming off drugs is the desire to do so. When someone really wants to give up, even the most addictive drug can be defeated, with help.

The first stop is the family doctor, but not all family doctors are experienced in this field, so it may be better to go to a specialist out-patient clinic. In-patient treatment is also available in some areas. Meanwhile it is safest to come off the drug gradually, and this will lessen the unpleasant symptoms of withdrawal. One useful trick is the slimmer's ploy of 'allowing' yourself the drug, but each time you feel like taking it, you tell yourself you will have some, but not until a little later. In that way you cut down the total amount taken in the day.

Once off drugs former users need other satisfactions in their lives to help them stay off and to give them a new focus and source of relationships.

Recognizing Drugs and their Effects

Amphetamines (speed)
Amphetamines and other stimulants – sometimes described as the poor man's coke – are available in several forms. In the 1950s and 1960s they were often prescribed for depression, but are rarely used now. They are relatively cheap and easy to get and much used by teenagers, especially at weekends. The most common is amphetamine sulphate, a white or brown powder, which is sniffed or injected, small white tablets and capsules are also available. They speed up the body, raise the heart and breathing rate and widen the pupils.

Addresses and suggestions for further reading are at the ends of chapters.

People become confident, energetic, bouncy, giggly and wakeful, and lose their appetite. The effects last 3 to 4 hours and it can take the body several days to recover.

As the body's energy runs down, the 'up' feelings can change to irritability, restlessness and extreme hunger, followed by depression and exhaustion. Tolerance can develop, and heavy use may cause heart problems, delirium, panic, hallucinations and feelings of persecution which can develop into a psychosis from which it may take several days to recover. With most teenagers speed is just a phase, but some youngsters take it compulsively and even inject it – which is particularly dangerous.

Cannabis (marijuana, pot, dope, hash, grass, gear, ganja, black)

Cannabis comes in two forms. One is a hard, dark-brown resin. The other looks rather like tobacco but is greener, sometimes seedy and less well chopped. It is smoked either in a pipe or in a cigarette paper, sometimes mixed with tobacco, but it is also brewed or put in food. The smoke smells distinctly herbal, and the strength is very variable, though resin is usually stronger than grass. The effects last from 1 hour to several, depending on the strength.

Cannabis distorts the sense of time and produces an exaggerated awareness of the world around. Some users become talkative and giggly, others withdraw. But not all its effects are pleasant: those who are feeling low, or are unused to it, can experience panic and distress. There are no obvious effects the next day, and almost no danger of overdose or physical dependence. But smoking it can aggravate both chest complaints and existing mental problems, and excessive use causes lethargy and loss of drive.

Cocaine (coke)

Cocaine is a fine white powder which is a powerful stimulant. It is usually sniffed (snorted) off paper through a tube, but it can be injected (sometimes mixed with heroin) or tucked into the inner lip. Occasionally it is smoked (freebasing), which produces a sudden rush similar to injecting. Its effects are like those of amphetamines, but the much greater feeling of well-being, and loss of sensitivity to pain or fatigue, make it far more likely to lead to dependence. As the effects peak after 15 to 30 minutes, the dose may have to be repeated every 20 minutes to maintain the effect. Large doses, or too many repeats, can make people extremely agitated, anxious and paranoid, and may cause hallucinations. With frequent, heavy use the effects become increasingly unpleasant. Initial euphoria is replaced by restlessness, extreme excitability, nausea, insomnia and weight loss, then later by paranoia. But giving up cocaine usually cures these reactions and there are no physical withdrawal symptoms.

Regular use destroys the membranes inside the nose (and in time the division between the nostrils). So, even when they aren't high, regular users may sniff frequently. In rare cases excessive doses can kill through heart failure.

Crack

Crack is cocaine which has been refined and concentrated, then mixed with bicarbonate of soda to form a hard cake. But, contrary to popular belief, the refining doesn't free it from impurities. It is sold as tiny rocks which are vaporized into smoke with a match. It engenders the same euphoria as cocaine, but gives an instant 'rush' as high concentrations reach the brain within 10 seconds. Its other attraction is that inhaling smoke seems more 'normal' than sniffing powder or injecting, so those who might reject other forms of drug taking find crack acceptable. However, it is rapidly addictive both physically and psychologically and the ill effects are both unpleasant and dangerous. Regular use makes it increasingly hard to get a 'high' while its biochemical effects on the brain cause chronic depression, withdrawal and paranoid reactions. It can also cause high blood pressure, strokes and fatal brain seizures or heart failure.

Ecstasy and Fantasy

Ecstasy comes in capsules or as a powder. It is a hallucogenic modified amphetamine, and is swallowed or smoked. Its effects start 20–60 minutes later and may last 4 hours. They include enlarged pupils, brief nausea and sweating, a dry mouth, raised blood pressure and heart rate, and loss of appetite. The user feels serene and euphoric and wants to touch everything. Afterwards the user feels very tired. It is psychologically but not physically addictive and dangerous for those with heart problems. Fantasy is very similar.

Heroin (smack, skag)

Heroin is a fine white or brown speckled powder made from the milk of the opium poppy. The fumes are usually inhaled after heating it on silver foil ('chasing the dragon'), but it can also be sniffed, injected, and occasionally smoked. Using it for the first time may cause nausea and vomiting, but habitual users feel more alert. Like all opiates, it depresses the activity of the nervous system, so the blood vessels dilate (making the user feel warm and drowsy); reflexes like coughing are suppressed and the user begins to feel detached and content, free from pain, desire or stress. A heroin user may seem drunk and dopey to an onlooker. Gradually larger and larger doses are needed to produce these effects, and long-term users cease to feel good and need it even to feel normal.

Regular use produces both physical and psychological dependence, and withdrawal symptoms are similar to flu – aches, shaking, sweating, shivering, sneezing, yawning and muscular spasms. These start 8 to 24 hours after the last dose and usually last 5 to 10 days. In the short term it leads to constipation and loss of concentration, sex drive and appetite. And there is always a risk of infection if it is being injected.

Hypnosedatives (downers, blues)

These are prescribed drugs used to calm people down or to make them sleep – such as Tuinal, Seconal and Nembutal. But they are among the most dangerous drugs to misuse, and are the most dangerous of all if injected. Most are sold as coloured capsules. They damp down the nervous system in the same way as alcohol. Small doses make people just feel relaxed, but larger doses slur the speech and make them clumsy and prone to extreme emotional reactions and mental confusion. The effects last 3 to 6 hours, depending on the dose.

Heavy users are vulnerable to bronchitis and pneumonia, and large doses may cause unconsciousness and death. There is a constant risk of overdose, as the difference between a 'pleasurable' and a fatal dose is very small. Even a few barbiturate pills can be fatal and the dangers are increased if they are combined with alcohol. They cause both physical and psychological dependence, and the withdrawal symptoms include irritability, faintness, nausea, twitching, delirium and sometimes convulsions. There may be lasting brain damage. Sudden withdrawal can be fatal, so coming off must be medically supervised.

Ice

Ice is a crystal form of methylamphetamine and looks much like its name. It is usually smoked via a tube. The user is extremely energetic and wakeful and may feel able to work better, but lacks appetite and becomes fidgety and anxious, and may react violently to frustration. Extreme tiredness follows and ice can cause paranoia delusions, and chemical changes in the brain similar to schizophrenia. The delusions may last for months – even after giving it up – and some doctors say it may take only one smoke to become addicted.

Ketamine (super K, vitamin K, green)

Ketamine is increasingly used as a party drug. Sold as red/white capsules, gold/white capsules, plain white tablets or a white powder, the effects take 30 seconds to 20 minutes to show, depending on whether eaten, sniffed or injected. It both numbs the body (it is used as an anaesthetic for animals) and causes hallucinations. Users may hear voices, see visions and feel they are flying – and think these hallucinations are real. But, feeling no pain, they may not realize they are getting hurt. The heart speeds up, and they may become aggressive and sensitive to light and sound. There may also be vomiting, nausea, slurred speech and vision, loss of muscle co-ordination and temporary paralysis. Too much can cause heart failure; and long-term use may cause brain damage, psychological dependence, psychosis and loss of contact with the real world. (Vitamin K is a slang name. It is *not* Vitamin K.)

LSD (acid)

Lysergic acid diethylamide is a very potent synthetic chemical which causes hallucinations. It is sold through drops on blotting paper, stamps or lumps of sugar – which are all sucked – and also as tiny coloured tablets. The trip starts within 30 to 60 minutes, peaks in 2 to 6 hours and fades in about 12 hours. The hallucinations range from the ecstatic and mystical to the very unpleasant. They may be accompanied by panic, disorientation and depression. While high, the user may seem either over-excited or deeply withdrawn, and may need reassurance on the way down. There is no physical dependence, prolonged psychological reactions are rare and deaths from LSD overdose are unknown. But heavy use can create acute confusion and ideas of persecution, and on occasions the hallucinations have proved fatal.

Magic Mushrooms (psilocybin)

These mushrooms grow wild in Britain and elsewhere and are also sold dried on the black market. Eaten in large quantities they produce much the same effects as LSD, but, unlike LSD, there may be euphoria and often nausea, vomiting and stomach pains. The effects start within 30 minutes, peak after 3 hours, and last 4 to 9 hours. They can cause bad trips, for which reassurance and support may be needed, but there are no withdrawal symptoms, and there is no physical dependence. A major risk lies in confusing these mushrooms with poisonous ones. Curiously, it is illegal to cook or dry them for eating, but not illegal to eat them raw – though the effects are no different.

Other Opioids (dikes, 118s)

A range of red, white or parti-coloured tablets, capsules and ampoules which are used clinically but sold on the black market. They have effects, and risks, similar to heroin.

Smart Drugs

I can find no evidence that the drugs sold to improve memory and performance do what they claim. But there have been reports that they can do lasting damage.

Solvents

The solvents used in glues, paints, lighter fuel, hair spray and so on produce effects similar to alcohol, and some children increase the effects by sniffing them inside a paper bag. Users behave as if they are drunk, and an overdose can cause unconsciousness, vomiting and, occasionally, sudden death from heart failure or suffocation. Repeated sniffing produces a hangover, pallor, fatigue, loss of concentration and depression, and there are often spots round the mouth and red rings round the eyes. Glue can be addictive but physical dependence on solvents is rare. Heavy long-term (10 years) misuse, however, can permanently damage the brain, and there is a *very* great danger in getting high on the propellants in aerosols by spraying them into the mouth: they can freeze the throat, causing instant suffocation and death. Since 1985 it has been illegal to supply solvents to those under the age of 18 if misuse is suspected.

Temazepam

Temazepam is a tablet or capsule prescribed to relieve anxiety. Drug abusers may find ways to inject it. They may suffer from light-headedness, confusion, skin rashes, visual disturbances and, with continued use, blood disorders, jaundice and dependence. It can interact dangerously with alcohol.

Tranquilliser addiction, see Depression, page 560.

Addresses and suggestions for further reading are at the ends of chapters.

USEFUL ADDRESSES AND BOOKS

General

Action for Sick Children, Argyle House, 29-31 Euston Road, London NWI 2SD Tel: 071 833 2041, has campaigned for parents to be able to be with children in hospital and for emotional needs of children to be considered. M£L, M, G, L, B, Ad, Inf.

Association of Parents of Vaccine Damaged Children, 2 Church Street, Shipston-on-Stour, Warwicks CV36 4AP Tel: 06086 61595, Ad and Inf on compensation when children are damaged by immunization, sae.

The British Medical Association, BMA House, Tavistock Square, London WC1H 9JP, TEL: 071 387 4499, working party reports may be bought by the public.

Carers' National Association (see page 323), Inf, Ad, support for those looking after others at home through age or illness.

Chartered Society of Physiotherapy, 14 Bedford Row, London WC1R 4ED Tel: 071 242 1941.

College of Health, St Margaret's House, 21 Old Ford Road, London E2 9PL Tel: 081 983 1225 has written information on aspects of health and illness. They also speak for the consumer in the NHS.

Contact a Family, 16 Strutton Ground, London SW1P 2HP Tel: 071 222 2695, helps families of children with special needs of all kinds – from allergies to disabilities. Also publishes a directory of 200 helping organizations and/or support groups. RC, helpline.

Health Education Authority. (P.582)

Hospice Information Service, St Christopher's Hospice, 51-59 Lawrie Park Road, London SE26 6DZ Tel: 081 778 9252, can tell you where to find a hospice for the seriously ill.

Intractable Pain Society, Association of Anaesthetists of Great Britain and Northern Ireland, 9 Bedford Square, London WC1B 3RA Tel: 071 631 1650, is mainly for the medical profession but will give the address of a local NHS pain clinic to anyone with incurable pain. L.

Medical Advisory Service, 10 Barley Mow Passage, London W4 4PH Tel: 081 994 9874. Ad (5pm-10pm) on how to obtain all types of medical services, both NHS and private, and how to get in touch with organizations that help with specific problems. RC.

The **NHS** 0800 free helpline on page 693, has some information on illnesses and will explain medical jargon.

Patients' Association, 18 Victoria Park Square, London E2 9PF Tel: 081 981 5676/5695 advises patients on their rights and campaigns on their behalf. Has a directory of organizations for most medical conditions RC, M£3, S, F&F, L, B, HD, sae.

The Health Education Board for Scotland. (P.640).

See also **National Council for Voluntary Organizations** (P.692).

Useful Books
Concise Medical Dictionary, Oxford.

Dr Barrington Cooper, Dr Laurence Gerlis, *A Consumer's Guide to Prescription Drugs*. Hamlyn.

The DH Publications Unit, No 2 Site, Heywood Stores, Manchester Road, Heywood, Lancs OL10 2PZ, has full range of free information leaflets, including a good one on services for women, and donor card. Freephone 0800 55777.

The Health Address Book (1,000 addresses), Patients' Association (above).

A-Z of Ailments

Allergy

Action Against Allergy, (AAA) 24-26 High Street, Hampton, Middx TW12 1PD RC, M£L, S, CS, O, F&F, L, B, F, EI, G, A, HD, send large sae for information and telephone rota. (P.545)

The Coeliac Society, P.O. Box 220, High Wycombe, Bucks HP11 2HY Tel: 0494 437278, has inf on allergy to gluten, B, L, V, F. (P.545)

Hyperactive Children's Support Group, 71 Whyke Lane, Chichester, W. Sussex PO19 2LD Tel: 0903 725182, M£L, CS, F&F, L, B, G, HD, diet sheets, sae. (P.545)

National Society for Research into Allergy, PO Box 45, Hinckley, Leicester LE10 1JY Tel: 0455 851546, will direct to ethical practitioners in this field and away from dubious ones, sae. RC, M£L, S, CS, O, F&F, M, L, B, G, HD. (P.545)

Useful Books
Dr Jonathan Brostoff and Linda Gamlin, *The Complete Guide to Food Allergy and Intolerance*, Bloomsbury.

Dr H. Morrow Brown, *The Allergy and Asthma Reference Book*, Harper & Row.

Amelia Nathan Hill, *Against the Unsuspected Enemy*, from Action Against Allergy (above).

Mary Steel, *Understanding Allergies*, Consumers' Association.

Alzheimer's Disease

Alzheimer's Disease Society, Gordon House, 10 Greencoat Place London SW1P 1PH Tel: 071 306 0606, RC, M£L optional, F&F, M, L, B, G, T, sitting service, Ad, sae. (P.545)

Anorexia and Bulimia

Eating Disorders Association, 44 Magdalene Street, Norwich NR3 1JE Tel: 0603 621414, national information centre on anorexia and bulimia. RC, M£L, S, CS, O, F&F, doctors, nurses, M, L, B, Rg, G, sae. (P.546)

Useful Books
Professor D. Bryce Smith and Liz Hodgkinson, *The Zinc Solution*, Century Arrow.

Maureen Dunbar, *Catherine*, Penguin – a mother's story of her child's anorexia.

Arthritis and Rheumatism

Arthritis Care, 18 Stephenson Way, London, NW1 2HD Tel: 071 916 1500, free helpline 0800 289170, RC, M£L, S, CS, O, F&F, M, L, B, EI, G, A, H, C, Inf, welfare, groups for all ages. Embraces rheumatism and lupus. (P.546)

Arthritis and Rheumatism Council, P.O. Box 177, Chesterfield, Derby S41 7TQ Tel: 0246 558033, funds research and has a wide range of free leaflets on the different forms of these illnesses. (P.546)

National Ankylosing Spondylitis Society, 5 Grosvenor Crescent, London SW1X 7ER Tel: 071 235 9585, helps sufferers cope with their condition. RC, local physiotherapy, M£L, M, G, A, Ad, V, TR. (P.546)

Asthma

National Asthma Campaign, Providence House, Providence Place, London N1 0NT Tel: 071 226 2260, RC, M£L, S, F&F, M, very helpful, L, B, G, A, sae. (P.546)

Back Pain

National Back Pain Association, 31-33 Park Road, Teddington, Middx TW11 0AB Tel: 081 977 5474, Ad, Inf, RC, M£M, S, CS, O, F&F, M, L, B, EI, G, A, sae. (P.547)

Brittle Bones

The Brittle Bone Society, Ward 8, Strathmartine Hospital, Dundee DD3 0PG Tel: 0382 817771, RC, M£L, L, Ad, sae. (P.548)

The National Osteoporosis Society, P.O. Box 10, Radstock, Bath BA3 3YB Tel: 0761 32472, RC, M£L, M, L, Ad, sae. (P.548)

Cancer

Breastcare and Mastectomy Association (BCMA), 15-19 Britten Street, London SW3 3TZ Tel: 071 867 1103 (helpline), 071 867 8275 (admin), RC, S, EI, L, T. Concerned with *all* breast cancer treatment, not just mastectomy. Inf and support throughout and mastectomy aids. (P.550)

The Bristol Cancer Help Centre, Grove House, Cornwallis Grove, Clifton, Bristol, Avon Tel: 0272 743216, offers alternative holistic approaches to cancer. (P.548)

British Association of Cancer United Patients (BACUP), 3 Bath Place, Rivington Street, London EC2A 3JR Tel: 071 613 2121, RC, M£M, Inf line, excellent free L. (P.548)

British Colostomy Association, 15 Station Road, Reading, Berks RG1 1LG Tel: 0734 391537. Inf, Ad, free L, support from others with a colostomy. (P.549)

Cancer After-care and Rehabilitation Society (CARE), 21 Zetland Road, Redland, Bristol B56 7AH Tel: 0272 427419. (P.548)

Cancer Relief Macmillan Fund, Anchor House, 15-19 Britten Street, London SW3 3TZ Tel: 071 351 7811, RC, nursing homes for the seriously ill, grants and nurses for those at home. (P.548)

Cancerlink, 17 Brittania Street, London WC1K 9JN Tel: 071 833 2451, RC, S, CS, O, F&F, G, L, Inf and emotional support for those with cancer and those who care for/about them. Self-help groups throughout the UK, sae booklet on complementary approaches. (P.548)

Hospice Information Service, St Christopher's Hospice, Lawrie Park Road, Sydenham SE26 6DZ Tel: 081 778 9252, has information on hospices throughout Britain. (P.548)

Hysterectomy Support Network, 3 Lynne Close, Green Street, Orpington, Kent BR6 6BS Tel: 081 856 3881, M£L, S, M, G. (P.550)

Leukaemia Care Society, 14 Kingfisher Court, Venny Bridge, Pinhoe, Exeter, Devon EX4 8JN Tel: 0392 64848, RC, S, F&F, M, Res, Inf, support grants, H. (P.548)

National Association of Laryngectomy Clubs, Ground Floor, 6 Rickett Street, London SW6 1RU Tel: 071 381 9993, umbrella for local clubs throughout Britain. L, Ad, EI, Inf, B.

Save Our Sons (SOS), Tides Reach, 1 Kite Hill, Wooton Bridge, Isle of Wight PO33 4LA Tel: 0983 882876 (evenings best), Inf, Ad, L, for men and boys on cancer of the testicles, sae. (P.551)

Tenouns Cancer Information Centre, 142 Whitchurch Road, Cardiff CF4 3NA Tel: 0222 619846, offers S, B, L, V, F, telephone helpline weekdays 0222 691998. (P.548)

Women's Nationwide Cancer Control Campaign (WNCCC), Suna House, 128-130 Curtain Road, London EC2A 3AR Tel: 071 729 4688/1735. Helpline 071 729 2229 gives inf on breast and cervical screening and advice and support. (P.549)

I don't have room for all the bodies which might help you with advice and support on each type of cancer, or which give other support, but the **Cancer Relief Macmillan Fund** (above) has a free booklet 'Help is There' which lists them.

Useful Books

Penny Brohn, *The Bristol Programme*, Century.

Rachael Clyne, *Living with Cancer* Thorsons.

Harriet Copperman, *Dying at Home* John Wiley & Sons.

Shirley Harrison, *New Approaches to Cancer*, Century.

Understanding Cancer of the Breast, from BACUP (see above).

Diabetes

The British Diabetic Association, 10 Queen Anne Street, London W1M 0BD Tel: 071 323 1531, RC, S, CS, F&F, M, very good L, B, V, E, G, A, T, C, recipes, children's club, sae. (P.553)

See also **The Stillbirth and Neonatal Death Society** (page 644) for how diabetes can present problems in pregnancy.

Diarrhoea

National Association for Colitis and Crohn's Disease, 98a London Road, St Albans, Herts AL1 1NX Tel: 07278 44296, general information on inflammatory bowel diseases only. RC, S, O, F&F, M, L, G, A, sae. (P.553)

Eczema

National Eczema Society, 4 Tavistock Place, London WC1H 9RA Tel: 071 388 4097, RC, F£L (but general enquiries welcome with a large sae) S, CS, O, F&F, M, L, B, G, T, inexpensive Inf pack and the facts on alternative treatments such as Chinese herbs. (P.555)

Epilepsy

British Epilepsy Association, Anstey House, 40 Hanover Square, Leeds LS3 1BE Tel: 0532 439393 RC, S, CS, F&F, L, B, T, sae. (P.555)

National Society for Epilepsy, Chalfont Centre for Epilepsy, Chalfont St Peter, Gerrards Cross, Bucks SL9 0RJ Tel: 0494 873991, RC, S, CS, O, F&F, L, B, V, CI, T, C, sae. (P.555)

Medic-alert Foundation, 12 Bridge Wharf, 156 Caledonian Road, London N1 9UV Tel: 071 833 3034, provides warning bracelets engraved with the name of the sufferer's medical condition (e.g. 'epileptic' or 'diabetic'), plus a 24-hour emergency number which has access to computerized details on their problem and the dosage of any regular medication. (P.547)

Heart Disease

The British Heart Foundation, 14 Fitzhardinge Street, London W1H 4DH Tel: 071 935 0185, has excellent fact sheets on many heart conditions, the risk factors and their treatment. RL, S, CS, F&F, L, B, sae. (P.559)

Coronary Prevention Group, Plantation House, Suite 5/4 D&M, 31-35 Fenchurch Street, London EC3M 3NM, has inexpensive booklets on heart disease prevention. (P.557)

Kidney Disease

The British Kidney Patient Association, Bordon, Hants GU35 9JZ Tel: 0420 472021/2 RC, M£L, S, O, F&F, CS, L, H, T, Ad, Inf. (P.560)

Useful Books
Stewart Cameron, *Kidney Disease: the Facts*, Oxford University Press.
Elizabeth D. Ward, *Timbo – A Struggle for Survival*, Sidgwick & Jackson.

Meningitis

The Meningitis Trust, Fern House, Bath Road, Stroud, Gloucestershire GL5 3TJ Tel: 0453 751738, offers information and support, 24-hr helpline: 0453 413344. (P.560)

Mental Problems

British Association for Counselling, 1 Regent Place, Rugby, Warwicks CV21 2PJ Tel: 0788 578328 has free information on counselling services throughout Britain, both by individuals and through varied organizations. Some have low fees for those unable to pay more; sae. (P.560)

British Association of Psychotherapists, 121 Hendon Lane, London N3 3PR Tel: 071 346 1747. (P.560)

Depressives Associated, P.O. Box 5, Castle Town, Portland, Dorset DT5 1BQ offers support, contact, Inf for sufferers and relatives. (P.560)

The Institute of Psycho-analysis, 63 New Cavendish Street, London W1M 7RD Tel: 071 580 4952/3/4, has a list of Freudian psychoanalysts. (P.560)

Mental Aftercare Association, Bainbridge House, Bainbridge Street, London WC1A 1HP Tel: 071 436 6194, has a database on residential services and housing for those who have had mental problems. (P.560)

The National Association for Mental Health (Mind), 22 Harley Street, London W1N 2ED Tel: 071 637 0741, RC, M£L, S, F&F, M, G, Rg, A, Ad, Inf, L, B, Res, carers. It also has the details of other mental health organizations. (P.560)

The National Schizophrenia Fellowship, 28 Castle Street, Kingston, Surrey KT1 1SS Tel: 081 547 3937 – M£H, M, G, L, B, Ad, Inf.

Phobic Action, Claybury Grounds, Manor Road, Woodford Green, Essex 1GA 8PR Tel: 081 559 2551, helpline 081 559 2459, RC, L, TR, Inf, sae essential. (P.561)

The Phobics' Society, 4 Cheltenham Road, Chorlton-cum-Hardy, Manchester M21 1QN Tel: 061 881 1937, helps those with *any* anxiety disorder. RC, M£L, S, F&F, L, G, Inf, Ad, pressure group. (P.561)

Samaritans, 10 The Grove, Slough SL1 1QP Tel: 0753 532713/4, is a free confidential service listening to the problems of those in despair. Branches throughout the UK listed in the telephone book, or write or call. Excellent book list, sae appreciated. (P.560)

SANE, 5th Floor, 120 Regent Street, London W1A 5FE Tel: 071 494 4840, offers help and support to those with mental problems, and to their families. 24-hr Saneline is 071 494 4840. (P.560)

Society of Analytical Psychology, 1 Daleham Gardens, London NW3 5BY Tel: 071 435 7696, has a list of Jungian analysts.

See also the **Association for Post-Natal Illness** (depression). (P.642)

Useful Books
Lindsay Knight, *Talking to a Stranger – A Consumer's Guide to Therapy*, Fontana.
Dorothy Rowe, *Beyond Fear*, Fontana.
Ruth Hurst Vose, *Agoraphobia*, Faber & Faber – by a former sufferer.

Migraine

British Migraine Association, 178a High Road, Byfleet, Surrey KT14 7ED Tel: 0932 352468, RC, M£L, B, L, Inf, sae. (P.556)

City of London Migraine Clinic, 22 Charterhouse Square, London EC1M 6DX Tel: 071 251 3322 is a specialist clinic (Dr) treating people from all over Britain. Emergency help, without referral, for anyone struck by a migraine while in London but its hours are limited, ring first. RC. (P.556)

The Migraine Trust, 45 Great Ormond Street, London WC1 3HZ Tel: 01 278 2676, RC, S, CS, F&F, Dr (to visit clinic), M, L, B, G, A, sae. (P.556)

Myalgic Encephalomyelitis (ME)
Myalgic Encephalomyelitis Association (ME), Stanhope House, High Street, Stanford-le-Hope, Essex SS17 0HA Tel: 0375 361013, RC, M£M, F&F, M, group support, Inf, Ad. (P.561)

Psoriasis
The Psoriasis Association, 7 Milton Street, Northampton NN2 7JG Tel: 0604 711129, RC, M£L, M, L, Ad, Inf. (P.562)

Speech Problems
Action for Dysphasic Adults, Canterbury House, 1 Royal Street, London SE1 7LL Tel: 071 261 9572, Ad and Inf to dysphasic people, carers, the public and professionals. RC, S, F&F, M, excellent leaflets, free help, M£L sae. (P.563)

Association for all Speech Impaired Children (AFASIC), 347 Central Markets, London EC1A 9NH Tel: 071 236 3632/6487, helps parents to obtain speech therapy for children with any kind of speech problem. M£L, G.A, Inf, B, pressure group. (P.563)

The Association for Stammerers, St Margaret's House, 21 Old Ford Road, London E2 9PL Tel: 081 983 1003 may also be able to advise on how to find help. (P.563)

The College of Speech and Language Therapists, 7 Bath Road, Rivington Street, London EC2A 3DR Tel: 071 613 3855 – can provide names of both private and NHS speech therapists in any area. (P.563)

Communilink, 37-39 Station Road, New Milton, Hants BH25 6HR Tel: 0425 272226 matches patients with suitable private speech therapists, sae. (P.563)

Foundation for Communication for the Disabled, 25 High Street, Woking, Surrey GU21 1BW Tel: 0483 727848.

Stroke
The Stroke Association, CSHA House, 123-127 Whitecross Street, London EC1Y 8JJ Tel: 071 490 7999, referal to stroke clubs, Ad rehabilitation schemes, RC, S, O, E&F, M, I, B, V, F, E, G, Res, sae. (P.563)

Venereal Disease (VD) – and Sexual-Organ Infections
AIDS and HIV freephone helpline 0800 282445. (P.545)

The Haemophilia Society, 123 Westminster Bridge Road, London SE1 7HR Tel: 071 928 2020 RC, L, B, M. AIDS and HIV information.

Health Line – recorded tel inf on AIDS: 081 681 3311

The Herpes Association, 41 North Road, London N7 9DI Tel: 071 607 9661, M£L, S (and partners), M, G, B, L, A, 24-hr helpline: 071 609 9061. (P.558)

Terrence Higgins Trust, BM/AIDS, 52 Gray's Inn Road, London WC1X 8JU Tel: 071 831 0330; helpline: 071 242 1010 (3pm-10pm). RC, Inf, support, referral, befriending for AIDS victims. (P.545)

TVTS Helpline: 071 728 1466 (2pm-4pm Wed-Fri and 8pm-10pm Fri-Sun). (P.564)

Useful Books
David Barlow, *Sexually Transmitted Diseases: the Facts*, OUP.

Disabilities

Blindness and partial sight
British Wireless for the Blind Fund, Gabriel House, 34 New Road, Chatham, Kent ME4 4QR Tel: 0634 832501, supplies radios and radio cassettes and TV sound receivers, free to the registered blind aged 8+.

Royal National Institute for the Blind (RNIB), 224 Great Portland Street, London W1N 6AA Tel: 071 388 1266 – Britain's largest organization for the blind, deaf-blind and partially sighted. RC, S, CS, O, F&F, M (braille), L, B (braille and Moon), Lib, E, EI, G, Rg, A, C, HD, TR (talking books), special accommodation, educational advice and units, holidays, rehabilitation courses, braille music, wireless provision, numerous benefits and concessions, employment and business advice, housing service. Also a massive list of UK organizations for visually disabled people. Ring and ask, sae.

Sense (National Deaf-blind and Rubella Association), 11-13 Clifton Terrace, London N4 3SR Tel: 071 272 7774 – RC, M£L-Vol, S, CS, F&F, M, G, V, Ad, Inf, L, B, holiday programme, education service, further education establishments, some long-stay accommodation, grants.

Deafness
British Deaf Association, 38 Victoria Place, Carlisle, Cumbria, CA1 1HV Tel: 0228 48844 (Vistel) is for those born deaf. RC, S, CS, O, F&F, M, L, B, V, E, G, A, T, C, HD, sae. (P.554)

Hearing Concern, 7/11 Armstrong Road, London W3 7JL Tel: 081 743 1110/1353 – offers help and information for those who gradually go deaf. RC, F£L, S, CS, M, very good L, B, E, G, A, T, C, sae. (P.554)

National Association for Deafened People, 103 Heath Road, Widnes, Cheshire WA8 7NU (no phone), caters only for those who become very deaf prematurely, not those born deaf. RC, M£L, S, F£F, M, L, B, E, A, C, sae. (P.554)

National Deaf Children's Society, Family Services Centre, Carlton House, 24 Wakefield Road, Rodwell, Haigh, Leeds LS26 0SF, W. Yorks Tel: 0532 823458, RC, CS, F&F, M, G, Inf on all aspects of child deafness. (P.554)

Royal National Institute for Deaf People (RNID),

105 Gower Street, London WC1E 6AH Tel: 071 387 8033, excellent help and information source for all kinds of hearing disorders, including tinnitus. RC, S, F&F, L, B, E, EI, Lib, communication courses, residential care, directory of hearing problem organizations, large sae. Also runs Typetalk, which translates speech in writing and vice versa, so a hearing person can communicate with a deaf person by phone. This is a 24-hr international service. (P.554)

There are many other organizations, drama groups, sports associations and so on. See the *Directory of Organizations for the Deaf and Hard of Hearing*, published by the Charities Aid Foundation (48 Pembury Road, Tonbridge TN9 2JD) or the similar list from the RNID (above).

Mental Disabilities

Down's Syndrome Association, 155 Mitcham Road, London SW17 9PG Tel: 081 682 4200, RC, M£H-Vol, F&F, G, Rg, M, Ad, Inf, L, B, V, Ed, education adviser, resource centre.

National Autistic Society, 276 Willesden Lane, London NW2 5RB Tel: 081 451 1114, runs schools and centres for the autistic and offers life-long care, and also does research. RC, M£L, F&F, M, G, B, L, Ad, Inf, parent-to-parent contacts.

Royal Society for Mentally Handicapped Children and Adults (MENCAP), 123 Golden Lane, London EC1 0RT Tel: 071 253 9433, RC, M£Vol, S, CS, O, F&F, Dr, M, L, B, V, E, G, A, T, C, HD, sae.

Varied disabilities

Association for Research into Restricted Growth, 61 Lady Walk, Maple Cross, Rickmansworth WD3 2YZ Tel: 0923 7707591, RC, S, M, G, L, Inf on specialists in this field and sources of clothing.

Association for Spina Bifida and Hydrocephalus, 42 Park Road, Peterborough, Cambridgeshire PE1 2UQ Tel: 0733 555988 – RC, S, CS, F&F, M, G, B, L, C, HC, Ad, support, welfare grants.

The Association of Crossroads Care Attendant Schemes Ltd, 10 Regent Place, Rugby, Warwicks CV21 2PN Tel: 0788 573653, runs a scheme whereby care attendants will stand in, to give carers a break. This is a free service and will include the elderly if they have any illness.

Association of Disabled Professionals (Hon. Secretary), 170 Benton Hill, Horbury, Wakefield Road, W Yorks WF4 5HW Tel: 0924 270335, fosters employment of disabled people in the professions. RC, M£L-M, S, F&F, Ad, Inf, pressure group, sae.

British Limbless Ex-service Men's Association, Frankland Moore House, 185/187 High Road, Chadwell Heath, Essex RM6 6NA Tel: 081 590 1124 – welfare for members and their widows, residential and convalescent homes, events to rehabilitate amputees, advises and assists on pensions and allowances. Also for ex-service women, will advise non-service amputees. RC, M£ optional, S, O, F&F, M, L, B, E, Rg, Res, A, C, HD, sae.

British Polio Fellowship, Bell Close, West End

Road, Ruislip, Middx HA4 6LP Tel: 0895 675515, RC, M£L, S, CS, F&F, M, O, G, Ad, Inf, EI, Res, grants, holiday homes.

British Society for Music Therapy, 25 Rosslyn Avenue, East Barnet, Herts EN4 8DH Tel: 081 388 8879, has information on how music can help a wide range of problems and can suggest therapists.

Carematch, 286 Camden Road, London N7 0BJ Tel: 071 609 9966, is computerized matching of young physically handicapped with suitable residential care. Free service, but they cannot inspect the homes, only say what is available. RC.

Contact a Family, 16 Strutton Ground, London SW1P 2HP Tel: 071 222 2695, M£L, F&F, M, Ad, Inf, links parents of children with special needs. Publishes a directory of charities and self-help groups for all conditions affecting children – in most reference libraries, updated often.

Dial (National Association of Disablement Information and Advice Lines), St Catherine's Hospital, Tickhill Road, Balby, Doncaster DN4 8QN Tel: 0302 310123, gives free advice by phone, letter or visit on most aspects of disability.

Disability Scotland, Princes House, 5 Shandwick Place, Edinburgh EH2 4RG Tel: 031 229 8632, the voluntary body linking all Scotland's voluntary organizations for those with disabilities. Free enquiry service on equipment, facilities, access, clothing and employment.

Disabled Living Centres Council, c/o **Traids**, 286 Camden Road, London N7 0BS Tel: 071 700 1707, has details of centres all over the UK where aids for the sick and disabled can be seen.

Disabled Living Foundation, 380/384 Harrow Road, London W9 2HU Tel: 071 289 6111, covers almost every aspect of coping with most handicaps and disabilities, and the problems of old age. RC, S, CS, O, F&F, L, B, E, EI, Rg, HD, list of centres throughout UK where aids can be tried out.

In Touch, 10 Norman Road, Sale, Cheshire M33 3DF Tel: 061 905 2440, supports and links parents children have mental handicaps or rare disorders. RC, M£L.

Invalid Children's Aid, 10 Bowling Green Lane, London EC1R 0BD Tel: 071 253 9111, gives professional support and advice, school, centres, for chronic physical and mental disorders of all kinds. RC, M£M, CS, F&F, G, E, B, Res, sae.

The Leonard Cheshire Foundation, Leonard Cheshire House, 26-29 Maunsel Street, London SW1P 2QN Tel: 071 828 1822; offers residential care, all over the UK. Mainly to physically disabled younger adults, also to mentally handicapped adults and children, and discharged psychiatric patients. Local groups run family support services.

Lets Face It, 10 Wood End, Crowthorne, Berks RG11 6DQ Tel: 0344 774405, helps those with facial disfigurement.

The Multiple Sclerosis Society, 25 Effie Road, London SW6 1EE Tel: 071 736 6267; helpline 071 371 8000, RC, M£L, S, F&F, M, L, B, Ad, support, research.

Muscular Dystrophy Group of GB and NI, 7-11 Prescott Place London SW4 6BS Tel: 071 720 8055, RC, S, CS, F&F, G, L, B, Rg, Ad, Inf, EI, some grants, M – free on request, research, advises on genetic counselling.

National Listening Library, 12 Lant Street, London SE1 1QH Tel: 071 407 9417, books on cassette by post for those with any handicap which prevents them reading (but the blind should contact **RNIB** instead).

Parkinson's Disease Society, 22 Woburn Place London WC1H 0RA Tel: 071 383 3513, RC, M£Vol, S, F&F, M, G, B, L, supports research, sae.

Royal Association for Disability and Rehabilitation (RADAR), 25 Mortimer Street, London W1N 8AB Tel: 071 637 5400 – has over 400 affiliated organizations offer wide range of services and activities. Vast range of publications on all aspects of living as a disabled or handicapped person, correspondence courses, RC, C, E, L, A, sae welcomed.

The Spastics Society, 12 Park Crescent, London W1N 4EQ Tel: 071 636 5020, RC, S, CS, F&F, M, L, B, V, E, T, Th, Ed, F, G, Rg, A, C, HD, assessment, therapy, counselling, sports and leisure activities.

Spinal Injuries Association, 76 St James' Lane, London N10 3DF Tel: 081 444 2121; RC, M£L, S, CS, F&F, M, L, B, EI, G, A, T, Inf, link service HD, confidential welfare service, care attendant agency, holiday facilities, sae.

See also **Disablement Income Group** and **Disability Allowance** (page 544); **SPOD** (P.644).

Useful Books
The Department of Transport a door-to-door guide to transport for the disabled, which should be in Social Security offices.

Ann Darnborough and Derek Kinrade, *A Directory for Disabled People*, published by **RADAR** (above)

First Aid

The British Red Cross Society, 9 Grosvenor Crescent, London SW1X 7EJ Tel: 071 235 5454, offers first aid courses, nursing courses for those nursing someone at home, clubs, holidays and escorts on transport for handicapped and elderly, loan of nursing equipment, and cosmetic camouflage. Free international tracing service for lost relatives. L, sae. (P.581)

St Andrew's Ambulance Association, 48 Milton Street, Glasgow G4 0HR Tel: 041 332 4031, offers training courses in first aid and home nursing in Scotland. (P.581)

St John Ambulance, 1 Grosvenor Crescent, London SW1X 7EF Tel: 071 235 5231, runs classes in first aid all over Britain. Plus other varied services. (P.581)

Useful Books
The First Aid Manual, Dorling Kindersley – the first aid bible produced jointly by the Red Cross and St John Ambulance – regularly revised.
Poisonous Plants of Britain and their Effects on Animals and Man, HMSO ref book 161.

Complementary Medicine

The British Acupuncture Association and Register, 34 Alderney Street, London SW1V 4EU Tel: 071 834 1012/3353 keeps a register of fully qualified practitioners. (P.566)

British Chiropractic Association, 29 Whiteley Street, Reading, Berks RG2 0EG Tel: 0734 757557, Inf, sae. (P.566)

The British Homeopathic Association, 27a Devonshire Street, London W1N 1RJ Tel: 071 935 2163 (P.567)

British Naturopathic and Osteopathic Association, 6 Netherhall Gardens, London NW3 5RR Tel: 071 435 8728 – £1 and a large sae obtains a list of members; there is also an outpatients' clinic. (P.567)

Institute for Complementary Medicine, P.O. Box 194, London SE16 1QZ Tel: 071 237 5165 – keeps a register of complementary practitioners in the UK. (P.566)

National Federation of Spiritual Healers, Old Manor Farm Studio, Church Street, Sunbury-on-Thames, Middx TW6 6RG Tel: 09327 83164. (P.567)

National Institute of Medical Herbalists, 9 Palace Gate, Exeter, Devon EX1 1JA Tel: 0392 426022 – large sae for list of qualified practitioners. (P.566)

Transcendental Meditation, information from TM Freepost, London SW1P 4YY; freephone 0800 269303. (P.567)

Useful Book
Ruth Lever, *Acupuncture for Everyone*, Penguin.

Travel Care

British Airways Medical Centre, 156 Regent Street, London W1 Tel: 071 439 9584 weekdays 8.30am-4.30pm – appointments preferred – immunizations, E and Ad re health precautions; other BA clinics nationwide. (P.571)

Thomas Cook Ltd, 45 Berkeley Street, London W1A 1EB Tel: 071 408 4157 – offers a walk-in service 8.30am-5.30pm weekdays, Saturdays by appointment, giving immunizations, and advice on malaria. (P.571)

International Relations (DH), Hannibal House, London SE1 6TE Tel: 071 972 2000. (P.571)

MASTA, Keppel Street, London WC1E 7HT Tel: 071 631 4408 or ring 0891 224100 (premium-priced line) for a print out. (P.571)

Useful Book
Dr Richard Dawood, *Travellers' Health*, OUP (paperback).

Social and Antisocial Drugs

Accept, 724 Fulham Road, London SW6 5SE Tel: 071 371 7477 – advises on giving up drink. (P.581)

Adfam National, 1st Floor, Chapel House, 18 Hatton Place, London EC1N 8ND. Tel: 071 405 3923 National helpline for the families and friends of drug users; RC, F&F, L, G, A. (P.581)

Al-anon Family Groups, 61 Great Dover Street, London SE1 4YF Tel: 071 403 0888 (10 am-4pm), 890 self-help groups for relatives of problem drinkers. The Al-teen section helps teenagers who have an alcoholic relative, RC, F&F, L, B, G, sae. (P.581)

Alcoholics Anonymous, P.O. Box 1, Stonebow House, Stonebow, York Y01 2NJ Tel: 0904 644026, has helplines and self-help groups for those with alcohol problems. Local groups listed in phone directories. RC, S, CS, M, L, B, G. (P.581)

Alcohol Concern, 275 Gray's Inn Road, London WC1X 8QF Tel: 071 833 3471, has a directory of all related organizations and will refer people to local centres. (P.581)

ASH (Action on Smoking and Health), 109 Gloucester Place, London W1H 3PH Tel: 071 935 3519, has Inf on smoking and rights of non-smokers, Ad on giving up, referral to sources of help, sae and/or donation. (P.582)

Dawn, 30-31 Great Suttom Street, London EC1V 0DX Tel: 071 253 6221, L, Inf, for women with alcohol, tranquillizer and drug problems, sae. (P.581)

Families Anonymous, 650 Holloway Road, London N19 3NU Tel: 071 281 8889, helps families and friends of drug abusers. RC, F&F, L, B, G, sae.

Galsworthy Lodge, Priory Lane, Roehampton, London SW15 5JJ Tel: 081 392 1238, one of a group of private units operating the Minnesota Programme for in-patients with drink or drug problems. GP, S, F&F. (P.581)

Gamblers Anonymous, P.O. Box 88, London SW10 0EU Tel: 081 741 4181, is like Alcoholics Anonymous (above). **Gam-Anon** (at the above address) helps anyone related to a gambler. (P.582)

Narcotics Anonymous, P.O. Box 1985, London N19 3LS Tel: 071 351 6794 (helpline); 071 281 9933 (inf on meetings). Lists self-help groups for ex-addicts. (P.584)

Parents of Young Gamblers Tel: 021 443 2609. (P.582)

SCODA (Standing Conference on Drug Abuse), 1-4 Hatton Place, London EC1N 8ND Tel: 071 430 2341/2. RC, CS, F&F, L, B, large sae for a list of local clinics and services.

Turning Point, New Loom House, 101 Back Church Lane, London E1 1LU Tel: 071 702 2360, RC, S, F&F, G, Rg, C, residential rehabilitation projects for those who have had drink, drug or mental problems. Inf, Ad, telephone 'druglines', industrial advisory service re employees with those problems, sae.

UK Forum for Gamblers, 11 St Bride Street, London EC4A 4AS Tel: 071 353 2366, gives advice and help. (P.582)

See also Release (page 496) for advice on legal problems.

Useful Books

A Great and Growing Evil: the medical consequences of alcohol abuse, the Royal College of Physicians, Tavistock.

The booklet 'Emergency Aid in Schools' covers first aid for drink and drugs, from **St John Ambulance Association** (page 592). Pamphlets on giving up drugs and on helping drug takers can be obtained from **ISDD** (at SCODA address above) or from **DH Literature Line** (page 695) and local Health Education Units.

In Health

The Baby-Making Business • Contraception • Pregnancy • Infertility • Sexual and Marital Problems • Menopause – Change of Life • A Healthy Diet • Dental Health • Looking After the Face and Body

THE BABY MAKING BUSINESS

Puberty

Nobody really knows why the changes start, but puberty usually begins two years later in boys than in girls and no two people develop in exactly the same way. It is certainly tough to be the only flat-chested girl in the class, or to have friends shaving when you haven't a vestige of a hair. But nobody need worry if his or her timing is different from other people's or if things happen in a different order; that is perfectly normal.

The first changes are unseen alterations in the balance of hormones – the chemicals which make the body changes take place. After that, people often have sudden spurts of growth, and most girls start to round out over the hips, become slimmer at the waist and lose that pot-bellied little girl look. The hair on the head sometimes gets darker, and becomes curlier, or straighter. It may also become greasier as the hormones produce more oil – which is why spots are one of the hazards of the teens.

Girls' nipples get bigger and darker and the breasts begin to grow – often in fits and starts. They vary greatly in size, shape and even the position on the chest, and often one is slightly larger than the other. In both sexes, body smells alter and become stronger, and body hair starts sprouting on the fleshy mound over the pubic bone, between the legs and later under the arms, also on the chests of some boys. With these changes come new feelings and experiences. A girl's nipples become sensitive and sexual feelings may come when she touches them. This is perfectly natural.

There are also big changes in the genitals. The boy's penis begins to grow and his balls (scrotum) get bigger and drop lower. On girls the tightly-closed fleshy pads (the labia majora – literally big lips) between a girl's legs open out to reveal the tiny, but very sensitive, bump of the clitoris at the front where these 'lips' meet. Then further back are revealed the labia minora (little lips) and the entrance to the vagina, mid-way between the anus (back passage) and the urethra (urine opening). Stories make so much of the existence of a hymen, which has to be broken on first making love, that girls who look

at this area in a mirror may be surprised to find that the hymen is only a small ring of tissue at the entrance to the vagina. It can be so thin that it is almost transparent or up to 2 mm thick. It is often broken by girls and women inserting tampons.

Advertisements give the impression that to keep the genital area clean women need to use all kinds of douches, sprays and deodorants. This is totally untrue and just a ploy to sell products. Nature has arranged things so that the fluid of the vagina contains exactly the right balance of chemicals to keep it healthy. The outer area needs regular washing. But to wash inside the vagina or spray the area with deodorants just upsets the balance of nature and invites trouble.   Periods – a loss of blood from the vagina – usually start in girls about two years after the first signs of puberty. This is usually around the age of 12, but it can be anytime between the ages of 10 and 17. They are often erratic at first but they gradually settle down to about once a month (see page 595). A boy finds his voice may alter suddenly from his high-pitched boyish one to a deeper, more adult, tone. Disconcertingly, this comes and goes from day to day. And while his voice is breaking he also has what doctors call 'nocturnal emissions' – which means that he spurts a creamy liquid (seminal fluid) from his penis while asleep. The body is just practising for when he will make love.

Unfortunately, the hormones which cause these physical changes also have a strong effect on moods. Formerly reasonable pleasant children often become withdrawn, depressed, irritable, noisy, defiant and arrogant. Worst of all, they tend to think it is the rest of the world which is getting it wrong. Hormones are a kind of mind-changing drug, which the body produces, and adolescents should know this (and realize that adding other drugs will just confuse the issue). It isn't always easy for an adolescent to handle the moods which hormones produce, and putting up with them can be pretty hard on everyone else, but, unfortunately, growing older is the only cure. So both sides just have to keep reminding themselves that it *will* pass. They may be surprised to find how well they get on once the hormones stop moaning.

Masturbation

From early childhood most children enjoy touching the

area between their legs. But even those who don't may find that in adolescence it becomes tender and itchy, so when they touch it they discover a rather pleasant sensation results. With a lot of touching and stroking the sensation may suddenly reach a climax and then fade (a boy also releases a spurt of liquid). The climax is an orgasm and the activity which leads to it is masturbation.

Because the genitals are so closely linked to the tubes for excreting and urinating some people think the genitals themselves are dirty and bad, and not to be touched. And all sorts of stories have been told about how people who touch themselves do damage and become ill. This is total nonsense.

Far from being immoral, touching and getting pleasure this way is very good preparation for both giving and receiving sexual pleasure from the opposite sex – which is an important part of a happy marriage. So nobody should be ashamed or worried about it. It can be far more than that. Masturbation is the dry ski slope of sex, where a boy can practise creating and controlling his own excitement, and a girl can learn what arouses and what checks arousal, so that when the time comes both can make love with more sensitivity. For it is very hard to understand other people's sexual needs unless you understand your own. Sexuality – like driving – takes practice and learner drivers are best without passengers.

Menstruation (Periods)

It's a pity menstruation has acquired bad names, like 'the curse', for it is not the problem such names suggest. What happens is that a complex chain of instructions from the hormones tells the ovaries to release an egg each month. While it travels slowly down the fallopian tubes the womb prepares a good home for a potential baby, thickening its lining and gaining more blood vessels. If the egg isn't fertilized within 14 days of its release the body realizes it has prepared the womb to no purpose. So the hormone levels change, making the new womb lining peel away and dissolve, releasing blood as a period. During the next 14 days or so the body ripens another egg ready for the whole cycle to start again. The hormones which control the cycle also affect the way in which water is stored in the body. So, in the early stages of a period, women often put on weight and feel bloated and swollen, and the breasts may be larger and rather tender.

The ripening time isn't always exactly 14 days so, although most periods come every 28 days, the cycle is seldom totally regular. Equally, some people have small periods lasting only 3 days, others heavy ones lasting 7 days. Even in the same person they may vary considerably from period to period. We aren't machines. Our body reacts to every aspect of our lives – feelings, diet, exercise, work, even our companions. (Nuns often menstruate in unison.) When deeply upset, for example, periods may suddenly stop for a while, or become very heavy. In fact, doctors are only just realizing just how much emotions affect a woman's rhythm, and how often female problems occur when something else – like their marriage – is going wrong.

Myths about Periods

False	True
Periods are dirty.	A healthy person's blood is one of the cleanest fluids – if it wasn't there would be no blood donor scheme.
Periods are smelly.	Fresh blood has almost no smell but bacteria love to live on it. The bacteria produce the smell. Normal washing and frequent changing banish it.
You shouldn't have a bath during a period.	You certainly should. It is failing to have a bath which makes periods smelly.
It is dangerous or unwise to wash your hair during a period.	Nonsense. Washing the hair has no link to periods at all, good or bad.
You can't do active sports or swim during a period.	You can do what you normally do. Tampons make swimming no problem – but don't swim where there are sharks, they are drawn to the blood. (No joke – women have died this way.)
During a period women should not cook or they will contaminate food.	An idea based on ancient ignorance and folklore. No harm comes to anyone if women cook during a period.
Sexual intercourse should be avoided during a period.	There is no health reason for avoiding sex. Some couples do; some don't. It's a personal choice. But, as the cervix is less tightly closed sexually transmitted infections are more easily caught (see also Diaphragm, page 599).
Tampons (internal sanitary towels) can only be used by non-virgins.	Anyone can use them and they are by far the neatest form of towel.
Tampons are dangerous as they can get lost in your insides.	No chance. The vagina is a short tube like the finger of a rubber glove, with no exit at the far end. The cervix which comes into it is far too small for a tampon to enter (see illustration, page 600).

False Ideas about Periods

Over the centuries the fact that periods come and go so mysteriously and uncontrollably, with bleeding but no wound, has led to all kinds of superstitions. Superstitions die hard, and odd ideas about periods persist, though it is high time they were abandoned.

Period Pains

A period is not an illness; it is just part of the body's functioning, like the heart beating or the lungs breathing, and for many women it is just as easy and unnoticeable. Unfortunately for others it isn't. There isn't one neat cause of period pains, there are different causes in different people. In young girls the hormones may be poorly balanced (the body is still learning its new role) and cause crampy pains in the womb, and there may also be nausea, diarrhoea and a headache. The mind also plays a part. A girl who is afraid of growing up or upset (perhaps at the beginning of term or before exams) is far more likely to have a painful period. It can also be a matter of temperament. Some people of both sexes tend to express their anxieties through pain of some kind. The pain is real, but the cause is emotional, and such women are more prone to get period pains.

Period pains can also possibly be caused by very small problems in the spine, and I have found that chiropractic treatment cures them totally (see page 566), but it may not do this for everyone. Equally, a friend of mine suffered so badly with pain that, in her twenties, she booked to have a hysterectomy (removal of the womb) despite the fact that she wanted children. Luckily, before the operation, she was told about vitamin B6, took it and the pain was cured. But this is a treatment to discuss with a doctor as it could be harmful if not used correctly. And, as B6 reduces the body's magnesium, it is a good idea to eat magnesium-rich foods, such as nuts, cereals and seafood, while taking it.

With most period pains you need only take it easy (if you can), put a hot water bottle where it comforts, and take a pain killer if necessary. But if pain occurs regularly see a doctor. There are various disorders of the womb which can make periods heavy and uncomfortable, so it is worth having a check-up. Claire Rayner's book *Woman* (Hamlyn) has a useful section on these.

Pre-Menstrual Tension (PMT) and Pre-Menstrual Syndrome (PMS)

Most women are not at their best in the week before a period, and many feel tense, irritable, depressed, bloated, forgetful, 'headachey' or generally low. Objective tests show women drive less well and perform less well in exams at this time. The reasons for this are still a mystery.

As the hormone changes make the body retain more fluid it may be that the fluid which cushions the brain increases, causing enough pressure to alter the emotions. Some specialists find it helps to prescribe a drug which lowers the fluid levels in the body. Others recommend vitamin B6 (see Period Pains, above). Research at St Thomas' Hospital suggests oil of evening primrose, which contains gamma linolenic acid, is effective – if costly. You can get it in health food stores. Some people need only 250 mg a day; others need as much as 500 mg three times a day. If you try it, start low and only work up if necessary. Another possible treatment is hormone therapy, but this is still controversial.

Diet is also a factor. Salt makes the body retain fluid. A low salt diet helps, as does avoiding caffeine in tea or coffee, for caffeine greatly increases tension. A diet with less junk food, less sugar and less alcohol, but more raw foods and more fibre can also help. If you have dandelions include some leaves in salads, for dandelion makes the body hold less water.

CONTRACEPTION

Contraception is a subject with almost as many myths as facts. And the myths are dangerous.

Myth	Truth
You can't get pregnant the first time you make love.	You can – and many do.
You can't get pregnant standing up.	It makes no difference. Sperm can swim uphill.
You can't get pregnant with clothes on.	Yes you can. Clothes are no protection.
You can't get pregnant making love during a period.	You can, sperm can live 5 days in the vagina.
You can't get pregnant if the penis never enters the vagina.	You can. If semen spills on to the area outside the vagina the sperm can find their way into it and up to the womb.
You can't get pregnant if the man withdraws before orgasm	You can, very easily. Some semen often leaks well before orgasm.
You can't get pregnant if you are breast feeding.	You may be less likely to get pregnant if you are breast feeding *very* frequently. But, while breast feeding, a woman can release eggs before her periods return.
You can't get pregnant if you don't have an orgasm.	You certainly can. The world population would be a lot smaller if orgasm was needed.

Addresses and suggestions for further reading are at the ends of chapters.

Those are only some of the myths. There's another mythology about other, more effective, types of contraception. So the main ones are listed below. It is hard to be precise on effectiveness rates as they can vary with the sexual frequency and carefulness of the user. So all of them should be taken as approximate.

Sterilization – Male (vasectomy, 3 failures in 1,000 men)
The tubes carrying the sperm from the testicles to the seminal fluid (the liquid released when a man 'comes') are cut. This takes 10 to 15 minutes under local anaesthetic but, as some sperm are already part of the way down the tube, sterility isn't immediate. Other forms of contraception are needed for the next 20 or so ejaculations, until tests show the semen is sperm-free. A man's masculinity and sex drive are unaffected and, as sperm are only a tiny fraction of a man's seminal fluid, nobody notices any change.
Disadvantages: Normally, the tubes cannot be rejoined to restore fertility, though this may sometimes be possible. It should only be used if a man is *sure* he will never want (more) children. However, it is sometimes possible to store semen before the operation.

VASECTOMY

Sterilization – Female (Less than 1 failure in 100)
The fallopian tubes, which pass the egg down to the womb, are cut or closed, under general anaesthetic, during a 24-hour stay in hospital. Occasionally they heal together on their own, but cutting is usually more certain than clipping. Another contraceptive is needed until after the first period following the operation.

STERILISATION

Disadvantages: Usually there are no side effects. But it is normally impossible to restore fertility (though this can depend on how the tubes were closed). So it is only for those who will NEVER want more children in future.

If You Forget – contraception AFTER unprotected sex
If someone has had intercourse without using a contraceptive, pregnancy can usually be prevented if she acts *fast*. The first method is two doses of a special pill prescribed by a doctor. This treatment *must* start as soon after as possible, and at the latest within 72 hours of intercourse. This is usually effective but makes some women vomit and is not suitable for everyone. It is a one-off method and *not* a regular means of contraception.
  The other method is the fitting of an IUD, which stops the egg attaching to the womb. Again it should be done as soon as possible, but up to 5 days after intercourse. Once there, it can remain as a permanent method of contraception. But IUDs don't suit everyone (see IUDs, page 588).

Injected Contraceptives (99% effective)
An injection of hormones which stop the woman producing an egg lasts 8 to 12 weeks according to which type is being used. It is only available from doctors and – though it sounds the ideal option – the possible ill effects should be thoroughly discussed first as you will be stuck with them for 3 months.
Disadvantages: Some women have fewer periods and no problems, but others may get heavy bleeding or irregular spotting, back pain or depression. It may take up to a year to regain normal fertility after the injections are stopped. There may also be other risks. So it could be wise to opt for other methods – if you can use them.

INJECTABLE CONTRACEPTION   THE PILL

The Combined Pill (99% effective)
This type of pill combines two hormones – oestrogen and progestogen – which stop the woman releasing an egg. There are lots of different brands, each with its own balance of these hormones and its own advantages and disadvantages. But it is important to take some

contraceptive pills in the correct order or they won't work. Being on 'the pill' is convenient and may reduce the risk of some pelvic infections and of rheumatoid arthritis, and can also relieve pre-menstrual tension.

Disadvantages: This method is not suitable for lifelong use. Contact lens wearers may have problems. Some women may have nausea, headaches, tiredness, sore breasts, depression or increased weight with some brands. A pill which suits one woman may not suit another. There is also a small risk of blood clots which can block a blood vessel and cause a stroke or heart attack. The women at greatest risk are those over the age of 35, the very overweight, smokers and diabetics. Also doctors do not usually recommend it for those with high blood pressure, strokes or heart disease in the family nor for women who themselves suffer from heart disease, migraine, cancer, depression or herpes.

Both Pills

They may not work if you vomit or have diarrhoea – either can make you lose the pill before the hormones have time to work. Other medicines and drugs can interfere in the same way. So always check this possibility before taking any medication. It may be wisest *not* to take the pill when bedridden or with a leg in plaster, so discuss this with the doctor. It is essential to see a doctor every 6 months or if you have any unusual symptoms.

The Mini Pill (97-98% effective)

This 28-day pill uses only progestogen and may be less likely to produce problems with blood clotting or high blood pressure. But it *must* be taken at the same time each day – ideally in the early evening.

Disadvantages: There is a high risk of pregnancy if even one pill isn't taken within the set 3-hour time-slot. If you miss the time-slot keep taking it but use another contraceptive for 7 days. It is less effective than the combined pill and offers less protection against ectopic pregnancy (pregnancy somewhere other than the womb). There may also be an increased risk of ovarian cyst – though this is not yet proved.

Intra-Uterine Device (IUD; IUCD or coil, 96-99% effective)

IUDs are a range of devices which are inserted by a doctor sliding them up the birth canal, when tightly folded. Then they open out in the womb and react with its lining so that an egg can't attach itself. For some women an IUD is the ideal contraceptive – trouble free and unobtrusive. Made of plastic and copper, it can stay in place for 2 to 5 years and should normally be removed by a doctor. IUDs are best for those with children – especially if they intend to have no more.

Disadvantages: Some women get a pain and heavier periods; there can also be bleeding for a while after fitting. It is possible (though rare) to become pregnant with a coil in place. If a period is very light or late see a doctor AT ONCE. There is an increased risk of ectopic pregnancy (other than in the womb) – which can be dangerous. Also pelvic infection, which can cause infertility, is more likely with an IUD, especially if a woman has several partners. Any IUD user who has low abdominal pain, a vaginal discharge or pain after sex should see a doctor immediately, especially if there is a fever. Anyone who has *ever* had a sexual infection of any kind should tell the doctor before an IUD is fitted.

Condom (sheath, rubber, French letter, Johnny, 85-98% effective)

This is a thin rubber tube, like a long balloon, which is rolled over the length of the erect penis, so that the sperm are caught within it. It must be put on before the penis even touches the area round the vagina (most men trickle long before they 'come' and the sperm released that way can travel into the womb from outside the vagina). The big advantage is that condoms can be obtained from any chemist and it protects against sexually transmitted diseases. It is now vital to wear them in all but the most faithful sexual relationship.

But, since the sheath isn't the best way to stop a baby, the young and fertile should use another form of contraception as well.

Disadvantages: It can slip off; some men find it makes the penis less sensitive; sheaths have to be bought whereas most other contraceptives are on the health service. Also, some women find the interruption of the man putting one on may hinder orgasm. This is less likely to happen if she can put the sheath on him while he continues to excite her.

I.U.D.

THE CONDOM

Addresses and suggestions for further reading are at the ends of chapters.

Diaphragm or Cap plus Spermicide *(98% effective)*

A circular device of arched rubber with a flexible rein-forced rim. It is pushed high up in the vagina well before sex, blocking off the entrance to the womb, and stays in place for at least 6 hours afterwards. It must be coated with sperm-killing cream, and more cream should be squeezed into the vagina before making love again. Vaginas vary in size, so a doctor or nurse must choose the size, and this should be checked every 6 months, after weight gains or losses of 3 kg (7 lb) or more, and after childbirth, miscarriage or abortion. There are no side effects. It is not noticeable during lovemaking. Also it may be a protection against cancer of the cervix, and you can have sex during a period without leaking.

Disadvantages: The risk of forgetting to have it with you when you need it, and the spermicide tastes somewhat unpleasant. Also the effectiveness varies with the user. Careful users find it very effective; careless ones less so.

THE CAP OR DIAPHRAGM

Sponge *(unpredictable effectiveness)*

A man-made sponge, containing sperm-killing chemicals, which can be put high in the vagina up to 24 hours before intercourse. One size fits everyone and it can simply be bought at a chemist. It can stay in place throughout a love-making session – no matter how often intercourse occurs, but must remain in place for 6 hours afterwards and be thrown away on removal.

Disadvantages: Some authorities claim 75 to 91 per cent effectiveness, but one gynaecologist gave sponges to 7 women and all 7 became pregnant. It cannot be used during a period, and some women are allergic to the spermicide.

'Natural' Methods *(safe period, sympto-thermal rhythm method, variable effectiveness)*

The old joke '"What do you call people who use the rhythm method?" Answer: "Parents!"' isn't entirely true. But effectiveness rates for 'natural' methods are tricky. A leaflet by the Family Planning Association says, 'However careful you are, unplanned pregnancy occurs more often with this method than with any other method of contraception.' However, it also says the sympto-thermal method, correctly used, can be 80 to 98 per cent effective. This method uses a woman's daily temperature, and a number of other physical signs, such as day-to-day changes in her vaginal mucus, to decide when the egg is released. The advantages are that there is no interference with the body's chemistry and no side effects. However, women do not have textbook body changes. So these methods must be carefully taught and systematically used.

Disadvantages: Natural methods take care, and considerable self-control. For, since sperm can live in the vagina for up to 5 days, intercourse has to be avoided for more than half of every month. Also, irregular periods, disruptions through travel or illness, or the use of pain killers which lower body temperature can all reduce the accuracy. And, the so-called rhythm methods, which simply rely on avoiding intercourse at the mid-point between two periods, will have nothing like the success rate of the sympto-thermal method.

Femidom *(female sheath, 95-98% effective)*

Made of stretchy transparent polyurethane, the femidom looks like a vagina-sized thin polythene bag. One bendy plastic ring holds the top high in the vagina, close to the cervix. Another soft ring lies just outside the vagina's entrance, to stop it slipping in as the man enters. It is good news on several counts. It feels far less noticeable, to both people, than a condom. It gives women a way to protect themselves against diseases which are caught through sex. Also, it can be put in an hour or so ahead if you want, so using it needn't interrupt lovemaking. Being very lubricated, it has a special advantage for those with anxieties about dryness. And – unlike the condom – there is no risk of spillage as the penis softens, so the man can come out at leisure.

Disadvantages: Some women find it wrinkles up if the outer ring isn't held at critical moments. Also, a careless man could slide in beside it, instead of *inside* it. Either leaves you unprotected. So it has to be used carefully.

THE SPONGE

The next contraception to come on the scene seems likely to be a progestogen implant that will work like the pill but last for 5 years.

Contraceptive Advice and Help

Contraceptive advice and contraceptives are available free on the NHS to British residents (though GPs can't prescribe condoms). This applies to both sexes, whether single or married, and to everyone over the age of 16. It is available from NHS clinics all over the country, and from private clinics. You can go to your own GP – or, if you prefer, you may ask to see a different GP. Clinics are listed under 'Family Planning' in the phone book. A chemist, social worker, health visitor or midwife should have the address, or contact one of the organizations on page 640.

PREGNANCY

Preparing for Pregnancy

Responsible mothers often change their lifestyle once they know they are pregnant – giving up smoking and drinking, and taking more care of their diet. But, if you think about it, it's odd to make this change several weeks after the baby has been conceived, but to allow the embryo to bear the brunt of these things during the early weeks when it is, in some ways, at its most vulnerable. Logically, the time to change one's lifestyle is well before conception.

Any woman who might become pregnant, even by chance, should be tested for immunity to German measles – parental memories can be faulty. Those who aren't immune should be immunized *at least* 3 months before they intend to become pregnant. German measles in pregnancy can lead to severe mental and physical handicaps in the child. As some venereal diseases may be symptomless, a VD check is also advisable.

Radical as it may sound, there is also a strong argument for *both* partners improving their diet and giving up alcohol and smoking (page 581), and checking for hazards in the work place of both. A man is making sperm all the time, and smoking, drinking, drugs and environmental pollution can all damage the sperm and increase the chance of miscarriage or abnormality.

Farmers only mate a cow with a bull which is in prime health – so isn't it slightly odd that we often take less forethought for our children than a farmer would take for a calf? Several organizations (page 640-642) offer excellent advice on health care before and during pregnancy. This is also a good time to research the best hospital for the birth (page 602).

It is also wise to test for toxoplasmosis before and at regular intervals during pregnancy. In most of mainland Europe pregnant women are given monthly tests, but some British doctors only test for it if the woman asks them to. Toxoplasmosis is normally a mild, flu-like infection, but if a woman gets it while pregnant she needs swift treatment to prevent it from blinding, handicapping or even killing the foetus. Cats are major carriers and, once excreted, the infecting parasite will live in earth for 14 months and be caught by livestock. Eating rare meat, or handling raw meat and failing to wash, risks infection. So does handling cat litter. Wear rubber gloves for cleaning cat litter and strong gloves for gardening. Cook or wash thoroughly any vegetables with soil on. Incidentally this is not to be confused with toxicara catis (page 565). Those who have had it before pregnancy are immune and there is no risk to the foetus.

Fertilization to Birth

Fertilization

The facts about human conception are quite extraordinary. Whatever lubricious magazines suggest, the average man ejaculates less than a teaspoonful of semen, but it carries some 400 million sperm, each about a five-hundredth of an inch long. Once in the vagina the race is on for the fastest, strongest sperm to get to the egg and fertilize it. Speed is vital for, after about fifteen minutes, the semen thins and the sperm can be killed by the natural acids of the vagina. Only 10 per cent make it to the welcoming, alkaline environment of the womb.

Sperm must travel about 9 inches, up the cervix and along to the other end of the fallopian tubes. Tadpole-like, they swim with their tails, helped by minute hairs

The Organs of Conception

Oviduct

Ovary

Uterus (womb)

Cervix

Vagina

Prostate gland

Sperm duct

Urethra

Testis

Penis

Addresses and suggestions for further reading are at the ends of chapters.

and small contractions inside the womb. It's survival of the fittest and only a small proportion of them manage this 45-minute Himalayan climb. Those that do, live on the sweet juices in the fallopian tubes for up to 72 hours while they wait for the egg – if it isn't already there.

On meeting the egg – which is vastly larger than them – they crowd round it, producing between them a substance which breaks down its outer layer and allows just one sperm to enter; the rest then fall away and die. If 2 separate eggs have been released they will each be fertilized and produce non-identical twins.

Deciding the Child's Sex

Conception itself doesn't happen until the fertilized egg is implanted. But, long before this, the 23 chromosomes of the sperm, which carry the genetic characteristics from father to child, link with the mother's 23 chromosomes in the egg to make one complete human cell. In some sperm the 23rd chromosome is a Y, in others it is an X. If an X-type sperm enters the egg it makes a girl; if a Y-type wins it's a boy. The complete 46-chromosome cell starts growing almost immediately, dividing and sub-dividing, making 2 cells, then 4, then 8, doubling in size at each division.

Implantation

It takes about a week for the fertilized egg to travel down to the womb. By the time it attaches itself and joins its own minute blood vessels to the mother's massive blood supply it has 64 cells. She is now pregnant, and her body is already releasing a pregnancy hormone – which tests can detect – but she hasn't yet missed a period. There are some 266 days to go before the birth – but to calculate when a baby is due count 280 days from the first day of the last period.

Ectopic Pregnancy

Occasionally cells implant on the way down the fallopian tube. Very rarely they even go the wrong way, and move out of the top of the fallopian tube and implant outside the reproductive system altogether. These are ectopic pregnancies, and are usually ended because they can cause serious complications. Some of the fallopian tube may have to be removed but the ovary is usually left, and a woman can have other perfectly normal pregnancies with eggs from the other tube.

The Vital Early Weeks

Between implantation and week 13 the cell will multiply and change to create almost all the human organs. These early weeks are crucial to the development of the baby. While the limbs and senses are forming they can be damaged if the mother takes certain drugs, or has infections like German measles, or even runs a high temperature. The range of infections which can disrupt a pregnancy is probably quite wide, so mothers need to keep away from anyone unwell, and any infection needs prompt treatment. But medicines of any kind should only be taken when really necessary and on doctor's orders.

Weeks 5 to 6

The baby floats in liquid inside a transparent bag (the amniotic sac) which cushions it until birth. It grows from 2 mm long to 6 mm long and the limbs begin to form. Gradually the chest and stomach cavities and the head and brain are formed, and the spine and nervous system develop.

Weeks 7 to 8

By the end of the 7th week the limb bulges have become arms and legs, with the first signs of fingers and toes. The heart begins to work, and the liver, kidney and lungs have developed – but don't yet work. The head grows rapidly, developing eyes, holes for nostrils, ears and a jaw. The body gains shoulders, the limbs develop joints, and genitals can be seen. But the baby is only as long as a finger joint (22 mm).

Weeks 9 to 10

The foetus looks more like a baby. Eyelids now cover the eyes, the nose and mouth develop fast, and the feet and hands have fingers and toes – though still webbed. The umbilical cord becomes complete and the placenta – the liver-like pad attaching the umbilical cord to the lining of the womb – is developing fast. The baby is definitely moving. It is as long as two joints of its mother's finger (4.5 cm) and weighs less than a Christmas walnut.

Weeks 11 to 12

Though only as long as a finger (5 to 6 cm) and weighing no more than a fat prune (10g), all the main organs have formed and most are starting to work. The face is clearly human, the genitals are growing fast, and the details of the body are almost complete. From now on the foetus is far less vulnerable to outside factors which could damage it.

Weeks 13 to 14

At 13 weeks the mother is three months pregnant and the main risk of miscarriage is over. The womb has enlarged and can just be felt as a soft bulge above the pubic bone. The baby is about 7.5 cm long and has developed a neck. Its head can move, and some mothers may begin to feel movements – though many can't. By the 14th week the baby is fully formed. Now it must grow.

Week 16

Like the apes from which we descended, the baby begins to grow a layer of downy hair all over the body (lanugo) – plus eyebrows, eyelashes and head hair. It is now about 15 cm (6in) long, and weighs about 135 g (almost 5 oz).

Week 20

It begins to move quite vigorously, and almost every mother can feel it. So can fathers if they put a hand on the still small bulge. This was once thought to be the time when life was 'breathed' into the baby and it got its soul.

Week 24

The organs are mature enough for the baby sometimes to survive briefly outside the womb if aborted or miscarried.

Week 28
From this week the baby is said to be viable – able to live without the mother.

Week 32
The baby is totally formed and can open its eyes. Its skin is covered with a greasy substance, called vernix, which protects the newly perfected skin against the water it lies in. But it is still only about 40 cm (16 in) long and weighs about 1.5 kg ($3\frac{1}{2}$ lb). It is getting ready to be born. By now half the babies lie head down.

Week 36
It is about 46 cm (18 in) long. If born at this stage it has a better than 90 per cent chance of surviving. Now the baby usually moves lower in the pelvis. People say the head has 'engaged' or the baby has 'dropped'.

Week 40
In theory, time to be born, but in practice perfectly normal babies may be early or late, as they will be as adults, so they may be born any time between 38 and 42 weeks. The average weight is about 3.2 kg (7 lb).

Medical Attention in Pregnancy

Pregnancy tests, on a sample of urine, by GPs or NHS clinics are free. Once pregnancy is confirmed a woman needs to have regular check-ups to see that all is going well, and paid time off work must usually be allowed for these. Check-ups are usually monthly until the 32nd week, then fortnightly until 36 weeks, and weekly after that. There are several options on how this is done.

1 If the baby is to be delivered at home, or in a nursing home, the GP who will deliver it may do all the check-ups himself, perhaps with the help of a midwife.
2 If a baby is to be born in hospital the GP usually refers the mother to the nearest one and she goes there for her check-ups.
3 Sometimes a GP does the ante-natal care in the early months and the hospital handles the later months and the birth.
4 Some areas have ante-natal clinics which may save a long journey to a hospital.
5 Those having their baby privately will see a GP or consultant – whichever will be delivering the baby.

Choosing a Hospital
If a woman would prefer a different hospital from the one her GP suggests she may ask to be referred there. If her GP doesn't agree she may still book into the hospital she wants – but she needs to book in early or it may be too full to take her. So it pays to research the local hospitals *before* getting pregnant and find out their policies on childbirth so you can book the instant you need to. *Choosing a hospital which does things the way you want is important.* Once under the care of a hospital you only have limited rights to insist on what you want and, in practice, demanding anything once in labour is almost impossible. Here are ten points you may want to check:

1 What is the policy on inducing labour?
2 What positions do women give birth in?
3 What types of anaesthetic are available?
4 Is the father allowed to be present *all* the time?
5 Do they always shave and give enemas?
6 What is the policy on episiotomies?
7 Do babies stay with their mothers?
8 Are babies put to the breast straight after birth?
9 What is the policy on breast feeding?
10 May mothers breast feed on demand?
11 Do they allow water births?

Home Births
A woman has a right to choose to have her baby at home. The NCT and AIMS (page 641) have information on this. In certain circumstances a home birth is risky, but Holland, which has one of the highest proportions of home births in the developed world, also has some of the lowest figures for babies dying during or soon after childbirth. The truth is that in Britain what makes home birth statistics look bad is that planned home births are often lumped in with data on women who concealed their pregnancy and delivered the baby themselves and/or those with problems who were booked into hospital but never reached it.

Many doctors feel that first babies should be delivered in hospital. But if you had no trouble with your first labour there is probably no reason why you should not have the second, third and possibly fourth baby at home. (The risks begin to rise at the fifth birth and it may be wiser to go to hospital.) The advantages of a home birth can be considerable. It is much easier to relax and this alone makes labour easier, you can get to know your baby without the pressures of hospital routines or the risk that some nurse will foil your attempts to breast feed or leave the child crying when you want it comforted, and there is no risk of the baby picking up a hospital infection. There is also less disruption for your other children.

Some GPs do home deliveries, and so do some private gynaecologists, in which case they may have a midwife who works with them. But in law it isn't essential to have a doctor for a birth, a midwife is considered sufficient. If you need a midwife your local health authority has a statutory duty to provide one. So write to the Director of Midwifery Services in your health authority and ask to be provided with one. The alternatives are to obtain a private midwife through an agency (page 641) or the Independent Midwives Association (page 641).

Body Changes and Problems in Pregnancy

Soon after conception a hormone is released which causes periods to stop. This is just the first of many changes which hormones cause during the 9 months. The hormone gives the body more elasticity. The skin on the breasts and stomach stretches more easily, and the gristly cartilage which links various bones in the body softens a little, so the pelvis can open slightly for the baby. The womb also stretches and grows new tissue. Quite early on the nipples darken and swell, and the breasts develop as they grow new tissue to make milk.

Unfortunately, not all body changes are beneficial. The softer tissues are less efficient and constipation, piles and varicose veins can result (see Diet, below). Some people also develop moles or freckles or darker patches of skin where it is exposed to the light, especially strong sunshine, and frequently in a line from tummy button to pubis. On the other hand, some people find their skin is better than ever, and positively glow. The hair may gradually alter – sometimes being glossier, sometimes greasier – and it can even change colour quite considerably. Mood swings are also common and emotions become so changeable that even a well-balanced woman can find herself suddenly tearful. She may also become victim to excessive worries about the baby. This is perfectly normal and isn't a sign that something is wrong with it.

Backache
When you consider how, during pregnancy, an extra couple of stone are carried amidships, with most of the weight dragging on the small of the back, it isn't surprising that many women get backache. Even a perfect back can ache, but if a woman has any specific back problems it's wise to get them sorted out before she becomes pregnant (page 547).

The best relief for normal aching in pregnancy is to stand as little as possible, and, when you have to stand, avoid letting the weight simply hang. You can't pull your stomach in, but you can tuck in your bottom. Supporting the weight with a pregnancy girdle can also help – even if you wouldn't be seen dead in one at any other time. Try to take plenty of rest and to lie down for at least half an hour each day.

Giddiness
As the mother breathes for both herself and the baby heavy demands are put on the oxygen-carrying red cells in her blood and she may feel faint or giddy and become anaemic. Doctors often prescribe folic acid to correct this. Neither the faintness nor the folic acid are bad for the baby.

Morning Sickness
Nobody should *expect* to feel sick during pregnancy. Pregnancy isn't an illness and you don't *have* to feel ill. In fact, 50 per cent of women never feel sick at all. However, the other 50 per cent do. As this is mainly in the early months of pregnancy, when the biggest changes are happening in the body, there may often be biochemical reasons for this. Each woman has her own pattern; some feel awful in the morning, some at night, often it only lasts a few months but in some it lasts throughout pregnancy. Avoid things which make it worse – some people, for example, find the smell of coffee disastrous. Get enough rest: everything is harder to bear when tired. This is easier said than done, but one of the things a woman needs to learn in pregnancy is to be a little gentle with herself.

Miscarriage
There is no need for a pregnant woman to be so afraid of a miscarriage that she wraps herself in cotton wool. She should steer a middle course between behaving as if ill and fragile and carrying on so much as usual as to be downright daft. Normal exercise is fine. But this is not the time for moving furniture, falling off horses or exerting any sudden strains on the body, especially at times when a period would normally be due – for this is when miscarriages most often occur. And smokers have more miscarriages than non-smokers.

If any bleeding occurs in pregnancy it could be the start of a miscarriage and the doctor should be phoned immediately. About 1 pregnancy in 7 miscarries. The causes vary: the mother's body rejecting the 'foreign body', the placenta not establishing its role properly, an inefficient cervix, problems with the uterus or severe illness or shock. But it can also be the body rejecting an imperfect foetal cell which would have made a handicapped baby.

For most women a miscarriage is the loss not of a foetus but a baby, and their grief needs all the understanding of those around them. It is all too easy to blame oneself, and feel as humiliated as a man who is impotent, for having failed in a basic female function. Understandable as these feelings are, there is no need for them, and another pregnancy will usually be fine, although it is hard to feel confident of this at the time. Changes in diet and lifestyle may help next time; see the organizations on page 642.

Sex in Pregnancy
Neither intercourse nor orgasm normally causes miscarriages, and pregnancy needn't interrupt people's sex lives – though the positions may have to change as the bulge grows. But if a woman is prone to miscarry a doctor may advise her to avoid sex for the first 3 months and when periods would have been due. This is mainly to avoid the guilt a couple may feel if they have sex and then lose the baby. For even if making love didn't cause the miscarriage they will probably think it did.

Toxaemia *(pre-eclampsia)*
Toxaemia is the most common and most dangerous complication of pregnancy. It is a condition in which the body stores more fluid than usual (e.g. in puffy ankles), blood pressure rises and protein is found in the urine. It is more likely to happen if the mother is especially tired or tense, and a high salt diet may possibly contribute to it. Doctors may recommend inducing the birth early. This is because toxaemia reduces the blood supply to the placenta, on which the baby depends, and it can have serious consequences for both mother and child. Whether induction is needed or not will depend on the severity of the toxaemia, but mothers who don't want to be induced can ask whether it is really necessary. **Action on Pre-eclampsia** (page 641) has the details.

Diet in Pregnancy

There's a good word in the computer business – GIGO.

It stands for garbage in garbage out. That is, what you get out is only as good as what you put in. The pregnant woman is feeding both her body and her child's. This doesn't mean she has to go along with the old wives' tale of needing to eat enough for two. But it does mean it is doubly important to have a good diet.

Foods to avoid in pregnancy

Garbage food isn't the only problem. Some foods can also carry elements which could damage the unborn child. Women who are pregnant or planning a pregnancy should avoid foods which might carry the infection listeria. These include soft, mould-ripened cheeses, such as Brie, Camembert and some blue-veined cheeses, and pre-cooked chilled foods. If such foods can't be avoided they should be heated very well indeed, preferably in a normal, not a microwave, oven. Undercooked fresh meat should also be avoided both because of toxoplasmosis (page 641) and the risk of salmonella. And, while extra folic acid B vitamin is recommended to lessen the chances of a child with certain handicaps, too much vitamin A could be harmful. To avoid an excess of A, the government advises pregnant women to avoid liver and liver products, and get medical advice before taking extra vitamins.

The **Centre for Pregnancy Nutrition** has a helpline offering up-to-date advice and several other organizations also give advice (page 641). The **Health Education Authority** (page 640), and its Scottish equivalent, will also send you free leaflets on healthy eating in pregnancy, if you ask. And **Food Sense** (page 694) has one on food safety. These are also issues to discuss with your doctor.

Unfortunately, researching the effects of women's diets on their babies is a long and complicated business. So there is a lack of hard data on how much a baby is affected. But some people are convinced that hyperactivity, and even major personality disorders, may be caused by the effects of certain substances – especially additives (page 40) – taken by the mother during pregnancy. Whether that is so or not it would certainly be very odd if the ill effects of a bad diet on adults did not apply even more strongly to the far more vulnerable foetus.

Prospective mothers should avoid:

pâté, ham	tinned foods
junk foods	instant packet foods
dehydrated foods	man-made drinks
caffeine	undercooked meats
liver in any form	alcohol
additives	

The foods to eat instead are:

fresh fruit	fresh vegetables
fresh meat (not liver)	(especially spinach &
rice	broccoli)
nuts	fresh fish
cereals	dried beans
pasta	well-cooked eggs
milk products (but *not* soft, mould-ripened cheeses)	
frozen foods (without dubious additives)	

It's also a good precaution to adopt a high fibre, low sugar diet so as not to encourage piles by constipation, and for her to get enough calcium (page 625). If there is risk of lead or high levels of chemicals in the tap water a pregnant woman should also avoid drinking it if she can – these may get through to the baby, and lead is bad for the brain. Use bottled water or a water filter jug, such as the Crystal, which removes a proportion of such metals. Avoid alcohol, not just in pregnancy but from the time you intend to conceive: excess alcohol at ovulation may cause abnormalities in the baby. Don't smoke or take drugs, not even ones from the chemist, unless a doctor says you need them. You should also talk to your doctor before taking extra vitamins or iron.

Two other changes can be useful. For centuries the Chinese have given up salt during pregnancy, because salt makes the body retain more fluid. As retaining unwanted fluid is one of the problems and hazards of pregnancy this makes sense and is easier than you might think. Another ancient practice is drinking raspberry-leaf tea. If taken regularly, it seems to work on the womb and make labour easier. Some otherwise conventional doctors believe in it and, after three remarkably short labours, I personally swear by it. Many health-food shops sell raspberry leaves and you just infuse a spoonful in boiling water and drink a cup or two each day, like ordinary milkless tea. But, like all unusual substances, it should not be taken in the first 4 months.

★ Sheep and lambs and sileage may carry an infection that can make women miscarry or cause damage to a baby. So avoid them when pregnant and go to a doctor immediately if you feel at all unwell having been in contact with them.

> Smoking in pregnancy greatly increases the risk of a baby dying at or soon after birth.

Tests during Pregnancy

Women may now be offered a number of tests during pregnancy to check that the baby is normal. Screening with ultrasound is fairly routine for everyone. But other tests are usually only offered to certain women. This is because there are three possible reasons for having them.

1 Women who are in a general 'at risk' category may be routinely screened. For example, screening for Down's syndrome in the babies of those over the age of 38 (35 in some areas), since the risk of having a Down's child increases with age. But, even at the age of 45, the risk of having a Down's baby is still only about 1 in 50.

2 Women who have a special risk of having an abnormal child will be tested to check the baby doesn't have a particular abnormality

3 A positive result in one test may be followed by other tests to double check it.

So don't expect *all* the tests below to be offered to everyone.

Detecting Abnormalities

At one time tests in pregnancy could only detect a narrow range of abnormalities. Now, they can pick up many more – though they will only find the abnormalities they look for, and the looking is selective. So having negative result does not *guarantee* a normal baby – though it makes it extremely likely. Nor does one positive test *always* mean the baby has problems. It may take more tests to be sure.

Only a handful of tests are used, but this is now a sophisticated area of medicine and the samples obtained from the mother can be subjected to numerous different screening procedures.

How Soon the Results Come

With a test such as ultrasound scanning the results are

The Main Types of Test

Name	When Taken	How	Purpose	Advantages	Drawbacks
AFP Blood Test and Triple Test	16 to 18 weeks	A little blood is taken from the mother, as in any blood test.	To indicate whether the baby could have spina bifida or any other defect of the spinal cord. The Triple Test can also check for Down's syndrome.	It sounds a warning, through a test which is simple to apply and gives quite quick results.	These tests look for raised levels of 'markers' in the blood, but some of these levels can also be altered by twins or by diabetes, or if the pregnancy is farther on than the mother calculated. So more tests may be needed.
Amnio-centesis	16 to 18 weeks	While 'looking' into the womb with a scanner, doctors choose a place where the baby isn't lying and insert a needle through the wall of the abdomen into the uterus, at that point, and draw off a little of the fluid in which the baby floats.	To detect a wide range of abnormalities including Down's syndrome, spina bifida and certain blood disorders.	Women who could not bear to have an abnormal child can abort it if they choose. It also reveals the sex of the child – if the couple want to know.	The sample of fluid from any one woman is only tested for a narrow range of defects. So, although a negative result usually means that the baby is fine, it does not *guarantee* a normal baby: the baby could have a defect for which the fluid was not tested. A very small proportion of positive results are incorrect. In about 1 woman in 100 to 200 the test causes a miscarriage.
Chorionic villus sampling (CVS)	8 to 10 weeks	Particles of the placenta are usually taken through a tiny tube inserted up the vagina and cervix.	It can detect many defects including Down's syndrome, and various inherited blood diseases found by amniocentesis, but not spina bifida.	The test can be done early in pregnancy and doctors have results quite quickly. So if an abortion is needed it can be done early in pregnancy when it is safer and less hard for the woman.	This test seems to cause more miscarriages than amniocentesis.
Ultrasound	Usually routinely at 16 to 20 weeks. Occasionally twice: once to date the baby and later to see how well it is.	Sound waves are sent into the womb which bounce off whatever they encounter and produce pictures on a screen. The strength of these waves can be adjusted to give more detail if an abnormality is suspected.	To check the development of the baby and get an accurate date for its birth. It also shows whether there are problems like the placenta lying across the cervix (which could complicate labour) and detects abnormalities in the baby, such as heart defects or other structural defects.	If it detects a defect there may be no need for amniocentesis. It also reveals twins (or more) and many mothers rather enjoy 'seeing' their baby.	The results can be inaccurate. Close to 16 weeks it is very good at telling the baby's age, but less good at picking up defects. Close to 20 weeks it is good for picking up defects but less good for dating. Around 18 weeks may be the ideal time. There is no evidence to suggest that ultrasound has any ill effect on the baby. But long-term ill effects cannot be entirely ruled out however unlikely.

Name	When Taken	How	Purpose	Advantages	Drawbacks
Doppler ultrasound	During pregnancy or during labour.	High intensity sound waves are sent into the womb through the mother's abdomen.	To monitor the baby's heart and make sure it is alive and well.	Heart defects are detected early, giving an opportunity for abortion or babies with weak hearts may stand a better chance as if an emergency operation may be needed at birth the hospital can be ready.	Nobody knows how upsetting the sound may be for the baby. The mother has to lie on her back, which may be uncomfortable and is not the best position for blood flow to the baby during labour.
Foetal blood sampling	From 18 weeks to the end of pregnancy.	Uses the same procedure as amniocentesis, except that a small sample of blood is taken from the umbilical cord, which links the baby to the placenta.	To test for some chromosomal abnormalities and blood and metabolic disorders after scanning has suggested they may be present.	It can be used to detect some of the same abnormalities as amniocentesis, but the results come back much faster. This saves waiting and may make abortion possible at a stage when it is easier for the mother.	There is a slightly greater risk of miscarriage than with amniocentesis, but this test is being used more and more and in the most practised centres the difference in risk is not very great.

there at once, but some analyses take time. So a mother may have to wait several weeks for certain tests following amniocentesis. Waiting weeks for the results is very hard on the parents, but some procedures simply cannot be hurried, and the delay does not mean that something dreadful has been discovered. A late result could be either negative or positive – just like any other.

Choosing to Have a Test

These are tests a woman *can* have; not tests she *must* have. Some doctors don't so much offer tests as tell the woman they want her to have them – or even that she will be having them. It's understandable that a busy doctor should word things this way, but this is not what is meant to happen and, as one leading doctor in the field put it, 'is to be deplored'.

Any test should be explained and the mother asked if she would like to have it. If not, she should ask for an explanation. If the doctor's explanation isn't enough the couple can ask to discuss the test with someone else. Most hospitals which do these tests have access to a genetic counsellor to help parents in this way. Once they understand the pros and cons of a test, it is up to them to decide whether or not they want it.

These tests should not be dismissed lightly, but a woman has a legal right to refuse to have any of them at any stage, and if the tests show that a baby is abnormal she and the father are free to decide whether they will or will not have it aborted. Equally, if a woman is not offered a test she wishes to have, she should ask the doctor whether she can have it, and discuss the pros and cons.

Preparing for Tests

Even with a routine test like ultrasound, which is looking for other things besides abnormality, there is always a risk of discovering the baby is not normal. Some doc-

tors believe couples should think about and discuss this, before any test is even offered, and decide whether they would want an abortion if something was wrong. Some may prefer to have no tests and go through pregnancy not knowing; others may want to know if a child is handicapped so they can prepare for it, and may want these techniques used to give it the best possible chance. Either way, it is better for all if the doctors know the parents' views from the start.

Abortion

If pregnancy is risking the life of a mother, or tests show that a baby is severely abnormal, doctors may recommend an abortion. Equally, a woman who does not wish to continue a pregnancy can ask her GP to refer her for an abortion, or she can go to one of the organizations given on page 641. Either way, an abortion should be done as early as possible.

The methods used vary according to how far pregnancy is advanced and this is always measured from the first day of the last period. (See also Law, page 478).

1 Up to 9 weeks RU 486 can be given as tablets and pessaries to cause a miscarriage.
2 Up to 12 or 13 weeks it is possible to insert a thin tube into the womb and remove the foetus by suction.
3 Up to 18 or 19 weeks abortion can be by a process called D & E (dilatation and evacuation) which is essentially the same as a D & C (see page 607).
4 After 18 weeks drugs are given which cause premature labour. This is like labour at full-term, except that it produces a baby too young to live.

The number of weeks at which each of these can be done is only approximate, as each organization or hospital sets its own limits. Abortions can only be performed up to the 24th week if the mother's life is in danger or the baby is abnormal. And not many abortions are done after 20 weeks.

Addresses and suggestions for further reading are at the ends of chapters.

Emotions

The moral issues which surround the ending of pregnancy are beyond the scope of this book, but there are also emotional factors.

Abortion is often seen as an easy option. For some women it may be. But for many it is a deeply distressing experience from which they may take months to recover. Even those who have no desire for a child, or who become pregnant through rape, may suffer deeply. And for anyone who wants to be a mother (even if not by that man), ending a pregnancy, even in its earliest stages, runs clean against her deepest needs as a woman. Those who accept an abortion, after discovering that a wanted child is abnormal, have the added burden of going through a labour which can only end in the loss of a wanted child. This loss can then be made more bitter by the fact that a late abortion causes the mother's breasts to fill with milk for the dead child.

This means there is maybe a deep sense of bereavement and intense grief, often coupled with feelings of guilt. Even the knowledge that the child was severely handicapped and might scarcely have survived birth, or have suffered terribly, may not blunt these emotions. And the woman can find them doubly hard to bear because the hormones which affect her moods have been disturbed by ending the pregnancy. This means that those who have lost a child through an abortion need not only good medical attention, but also loving support and comfort from everyone around them for some time afterwards, and a chance to talk about their feelings. For a grieving mother, or father, to bottle them up is to ask for depression later.

Devastating as an abortion may be, many people feel that some pregnancies have no 'good' solution. Women who put out for adoption a baby whom they cannot care for, or cannot love because it is the result of rape, may suffer just as deeply as they would have done from an abortion.

Risks

When a full D & C is needed there is the risk of physical complications which can occur in any operation. There is also a slight risk that a complication could lead to infertility. Anyone considering an abortion should realize that to have one without proper medical supervision can lead to complications which make it impossible to have children later. Backstreet and DIY abortions are very dangerous.

Preparing for Labour

Giving birth to another human being is one of the biggest things anyone can do in their lives. Because it is so important conflicting schools of thought have grown up about it. At one end of the spectrum, some doctors distrust nature and use every high-tech device at their disposal to organize, monitor and anaesthetize the birth. At the other, some natural childbirth fanatics insist that childbirth is a natural and deeply emotional event which *must* have no intervention and no pain killers if the mother is to experience the full joys of childbirth.

In their enthusiasm for the naturalness of birth, authors of books on natural childbirth invariably seem to depict women giving birth stark naked. You may like to know that it is by no means essential. It is for you to choose.

Many expectant mothers are either determined to have their baby naturally at all costs, or pooh-pooh preparation for childbirth and swear they will just have an epidural and leave it to the doctors.

Either way, the mother could be in for a shock. Epidurals don't always work, nor can anyone guarantee that the labour won't be too fast to set one up. Equally, although a totally natural and unaided labour can offer a great deal, nobody can promise that everything will go smoothly, or that the sensations of a particular labour won't be too tough to handle. So, to go into labour with a rigid view of how it will be is to invite disappointment in what should be the least disappointing event of your life.

I am all in favour of natural childbirth, but the most important thing about labour is not that you do it one way or another way, but that you give birth to a healthy baby. Going into labour is a journey into unknown territory: like walking alone down a dark street in an area you don't know. If you walk down it relaxed and confident that you can cope, not expecting mugging but knowing you can fight back if anyone tries it, you are far less likely to be a victim. But if a mugger does attack, you would be crazy to feel you were failing if you shouted for aid or accepted help. The same is true of labour. You shouldn't *expect* problems or intolerable pain, and should go into it confident that you know enough to cope with the sensations which will assault you, but if you are unlucky enough to have problems there is no failure in accepting help. Even if you need a general anaesthetic you won't miss the most satisfying moment. That moment is when you first see the baby, and hold in your arms the miraculously independent and whole human being whom you and your partner have created.

That, of course, means that every mother should go to ante-natal classes and learn techniques for coping without anaesthetics – even if she intends to be drugged up to the eyebrows. Understanding what is happening and learning good techniques for coping with the quite overwhelming sensations it produces can make labour a far easier experience and greatly reduce the pain, and will see some women through to the end without anaesthetics, even if the rest move on to anaesthetics when they feel it is right. Many hospitals run good classes but if you prefer private classes the National Childbirth Trust (see page 641) runs them: book *the instant* you are pregnant.

Fathers Attending Births

Fathers may be expected to attend the birth and they can be an immense help and support to their partners. There are very few times when a modern husband can take on the role of his wife's defender and champion, but this is one of them. A woman is at her most defenceless when in labour and it is easy for her needs to get steamrollered under hospital procedures or be misunderstood because the staff on duty have changed. The father can see this doesn't happen, and should be able to provide far better comfort and support than a stranger – however well qualified and caring. He can also be of practical help – the benefits of back rubbing, and similar help, in labour can be immense. However, fathers may be best able to handle the situation if they have attended some classes first.

Water Births and Gentle Births

Many women report that giving birth in a birthing pool reduces labour pains and makes birth much easier. So many more are choosing to have their babies that way. A portable birthing pool can be hired for use at home or in hospital – if the hospital agrees – and some hospitals have their own pools. The **NCT** (page 641) has a leaflet giving useful information on waterbirths, including the addresses of hirers, and how to find a midwife who favours them.

It is also worth reading books by Michael Odent (page 641), and finding ways to make the birth as peaceful as possible. It is bound to be stressful for a baby. How would you feel if you encountered bright light, cold air, and sharp sounds for the first time all at once? But at least you can make it less stressful if you discuss with your doctor how gentleness and quiet can be part of the event.

Labour

In theory, labour occurs 280 days after the first day of the last period. But most babies are early or late. In the last twenty years there has been a dramatic increase in the number of labours which are started artificially. This can be best for both mother and child, but it isn't always. There are 'inducing doctors' just as there used to be 'hanging judges', and induced labours can be harder to cope with than those nature produces. The best way to avoid an unnecessary induction is to avoid such a doctor – so ask.

For all the wizardry of modern medicine doctors still don't know what makes labour start naturally. Labours don't all start the same way, even in the same woman. But one of three things always happens and the other two follow during the first stage.

1 a 'show' (a slightly blood-stained discharge) from the vagina;
2 the bag of waters cushioning the baby bursts and liquid floods out;
3 contractions begin.

Eating in Labour

Having tantalizingly gone into labour with my first child just as I was serving Christmas dinner, I remember vividly the old-fashioned rule that you couldn't eat a morsel once labour started. This was because eating before a general anaesthetic is dangerous. But very few women need a general anaesthetic and if they do it is seldom in the early stages of labour. So the new thinking is that a woman can eat what she feels like – in moderation – *in the early stages.*

First Stage Contractions

In films a woman who goes into labour immediately starts groaning and grimacing and promptly gives birth. This is artistic licence. The start isn't usually as painful nor the result so swift – nor is it always as long and awful as some 'old wives' like to make out. The truth is that labours vary hugely, and no two are alike – even in the same woman. What's more, some people are naturally good at handling stress and discomfort and take it in their stride, while others fall apart under it. So two identical labours would feel quite different to women at opposite ends of that spectrum.

The contractions of the first stage open the cervix (neck of the womb) and pull it out of the way, much as you'd prepare a sock to put your foot in. The contractions usually start weakly with big gaps between and gradually get closer and stronger, and some women even get practice contractions occasionally long before the start of labour itself. Contractions are just what their name suggests – muscles tightening. Try clenching your fist *as hard as you possibly can* for 30 seconds, and imagine that sensation inside your stomach – that's roughly the feel of it.

What Contractions Feel Like

The average labour is 10 hours, but it can be considerably shorter or longer. But that doesn't mean hours of agony. Early contractions are usually no more painful than clenching your fist, and they last under a minute and only come every 20 minutes or so. They gradually increase in length and strength and come more and more frequently. Some women would not define the sensation as pain, and for some they feel more like a massive orgasm (some of the same muscles contract in orgasm) than like normal pain. That's not as much fun as it sounds. Imagine having an overwhelming orgasm every two minutes for an hour or two and you get some idea of how exhausting labour can be. Any muscle which is worked hard in a way it isn't used to can ache enormously (backache is a common feature of the first stage too) and the worst part is you can't stop and rest from this abdominal marathon. Not surprisingly there comes a time when one tends to get irritable.

However, some women do have very severe pain. The chances of this are greatly increased in those who are untrained and frightened and therefore tense up against the contractions, setting up an internal war between opposing sets of muscles, but this isn't always the reason. You can have a painful labour even when previous labours have been easy.

In the early stages there is no need to sit down (unless you want to) – let alone lie down. But use each contraction to practise whatever exercises you have learnt for controlling it. You may feel like walking about, but doing it aimlessly creates tension. The early hours can drag, so do something constructive – clean the house, do some gardening, or cook and freeze food for later. When you feel like sitting have something really absorbing to do – a book you long to read, or a tape of some favourite music (plus Walkman, so you can take it to hospital), or a video film you can watch at home. But don't do as I did and leave your packing for hospital until you need to leave – by then bending may be impossible.

Help and When to Seek It
A woman often reaches a stage when it feels 'right' to go into hospital and she should act on this feeling. Failing that, medical authorities say any of the following indicate that it is time to go in:

- loss of fresh blood (not the same as the 'show' – see page 608)
- the waters breaking
- contractions coming every 10-15 minutes
- the contractions getting much longer and stronger.

Hospital Procedures
I spent the whole of my first pregnancy in a blue funk about the trivia of childbirth – the enema and shaving. In fact, neither are essential and many hospitals have now abandoned both practices. In those that like to give an enema the doctor may agree to you being given a suppository to insert yourself, if you ask well before labour. If your hospital hasn't abandoned shaving you can ask if they can keep it to a minimum.

Pain Killers
You are entitled to refuse pain killers during labour or to ask for the type you would prefer – though a doctor may have good reasons for not giving it. It is best to discuss the options with the doctor during an ante-natal check-up and not wait until labour, when you may be too busy to talk. It is also worth talking to other mothers about the effect pain killers had on them, and their babies. Whatever you opt for, do remember that no pain killer is 100 per cent certain to work, not even an epidural. The major options are these:

Anaesthetic	Possible Disadvantages
Entonox often called gas and air is given through a face mask. It makes you feel slightly woozy and dulls the edge of the pain	No known ill effects for mother or baby, but those who find breathing exercises helpful may lose their timing and feel out of control.
Pethidine is injected. Some women find it kills the pain and they float; others find the pain is there but seems farther away.	If given too late in the first stage the woman may have trouble pushing and the baby may be 'floppy', have difficulty breathing and be slow to suck. This can make breast feeding harder.
Epidural injections are given into the back near the spinal cord and most of the sensation in the lower part of the body is blocked. There should be no pain at all and a well-managed epidural will allow the mother to feel the baby emerging. But the effects of epidurals can vary.	Some women have a severe headache and bladder problems for a short while after. The labour may be longer and the baby is more likely to be delivered by Caesarian section or forceps. In *very* rare cases, it has permanently paralysed the mother.
Transcutaneous electrical nerve stimulation is a new system by which small pads are attached to the back which receive tiny electrical pulses from a battery-operated box the mother can carry about. The pulses stimulate the body's own pain-killing chemicals and also interfere with the passage of pain signals to the brain.	The big advantage is that there are no side effects for the mother or baby. In one trial 60 per cent of women found it helpful and felt it did reduce the pain. But opinions are divided on its effectiveness and it cannot be used when heart monitoring is needed.

Positions for Labour
Some hospitals allow a mother to adopt almost any position she wants, others insist on a certain position. Some methods of monitoring the progress of labour make movement almost impossible. In most cases, the doctor decides the position, not the mother – though you can always try persuasion – if you are up to it.

The Second Stage
Once the cervix is open the second stage starts, and lasts 20 minutes to an hour, with contractions about every 2 minutes. A quick vomit may be the start. Then an overwhelming desire to push downwards comes in waves. Women always used to go through this stage on their backs, but more and more doctors now allow women to do what feels right for them – whether standing, sitting or lying, though some anaesthetics make this impossible.

The baby is pushed down until the head presses on the mouth of the vagina. The skin should stretch, but it can tear, so some doctors or nurses then make a small cut (an episiotomy) instead. There is now medical evidence that this is not the advantage it was once thought to be. However, some hospitals still do it routinely rather than risk a tear – as tears are seen as bad practice. So discuss it with your doctor before labour. If you don't want one tell *all* the medical staff, then they will only do it if it can't be avoided. In either case, ask (at the time) for the stitches to be left with long tails, then they won't prick as you sit on them, (a tip some doctors tend to overlook).

Twins in the Womb.
This picture illustrates the position of twins in the womb.

Problems

If labour is not going smoothly doctors may, at any stage, decide it is safest to intervene. This may simply be helping the baby out in the normal way, or it may mean having a Caesarian section – in which a small cut is made above the pubic hair and the baby taken out – under local or general anaesthetic. Some women feel they have failed if they need such help. This is totally untrue. Some babies just don't adapt to the normal exit and that is no fault of the mother or the baby.

The Third Stage

The afterbirth – the placenta (and remaining umbilical cord) – has to be expelled. The womb contracts to push it out and to reduce the bleeding where it separates from its wall (though some bleeding usually lasts for 6 weeks). Ideally the baby should be put to the breast as soon as it is breathing easily. It will instinctively suck and nature is so well organized that the sucking stimulates a hormone which makes the womb contract. This helps the afterbirth to be expelled. Usually these contractions can hardly be felt, but in the early weeks of breast feeding they can occasionally be so strong that a mild pain killer is needed.

Problems at Birth and After

Premature Babies

A premature baby may have to be put straight into an incubator to give it the conditions it needs to survive. This can be very hard for the parents who are longing to hold it, but a good hospital will try to give them as much contact as the child's condition allows. Parents who use every chance to be with their baby will grow closer to it even if they can't hold it. But it can be frightening to have the responsibility for taking home a baby who has been frail, so support and advice from the organization **Nippers** (page 642) can be very useful.

A 'Breech Baby'. This baby is the wrong way up for a normal birth and a doctor will try to manipulate it into the correct position.

Stillbirth and Neonatal Death

Sadly some pregnancies result in a child who dies at birth or soon after. Legally a stillbirth is a baby born lifeless after 24 weeks of pregnancy. Doctors also use different terms according to when a child dies. A neonatal death is when a child dies within one month of birth, perinatal death is when a child dies just before labour, during labour or within 7 days of birth.

The grief and sense of loss which the parents experience are, unfortunately, not always understood. But the depth of grief can be frightening. If the child had some handicap there may be the added burden of guilt (however unnecessary) and the confusion of relief that it will not suffer or burden the rest of the family. These feelings can be hard to handle and nobody who loses a child should allow people to jolly them into putting a brave face on it, or feel ashamed if it takes a long time to get over the loss. Grief is just as natural as pregnancy, and those who let themselves mourn will recover more completely.

Many now feel that if parents see and say good-bye to the dead child, and have a chance to give it a name and a burial in a place they choose, the grieving is easier to handle in the end. Although hospitals may offer to 'dispose of' the child, parents have a right to ask for other arrangements.

Cot Deaths

Cot deaths are now called SIDS (Sudden Infant Death Syndrome) and are when a seemingly healthy baby, during its first year, is suddenly found dead when it was thought to be sleeping. Nobody quite knows why this happens, but several factors have been found which put a baby at risk. They are – having a mother who smoked or took drugs during or after pregnancy, or the baby getting over-heated, sleeping on its stomach or not seeing a doctor when unwell. However, babies who are breast fed for the first six months are *less* likely to die in this way.

Addresses and suggestions for further reading are at the ends of chapters.

Unfortunately, as the death has no known cause the coroner must be notified and in some areas the police will talk to the parents. This is routine procedure and does not mean the parents are being accused of anything, though it may be very upsetting.

Post-natal Depression

Most mothers get depressed and tearful a few days after the birth – the baby blues – but feel better in a few days. But for a few it lasts longer and is far more severe, and there may be anxiety and panic as well as dislike of sex. During pregnancy huge changes take place in the levels of key hormones – an upheaval equivalent to going through adolescence in 9 months flat – and the body has to swing back to its normal hormone levels after the birth. Research shows that the brief baby blues – like adolescent dumps – are caused by these hormonal changes. Why long-term depression sometimes follows childbirth is less clear, but some doctors feel certain hormones *stay* out of balance and successfully use hormones to correct this, although others disagree and prefer to use anti-depressant drugs.

Restoring your Figure

Post-natal exercises are the very last thing one feels like doing in the weeks after a baby is born, but they are worthwhile. Most important of all are those for the pelvic floor as this can be weakened by childbirth. Among other things, this can lead to an annoying condition called stress incontinence – a formal name for the fact that you can't help peeing slightly if you cough, lift a heavy weight or do anything else which puts pressure on that area.

It is important to do the right exercises in the right way both during and after pregnancy or they could do more harm than good. A few hospitals have physiotherapists specializing in obstetrics and gynaecology, and you should ask your doctor about this.

INFERTILITY

Anyone who has followed the exploits of Henry VIII knows that for centuries women took the blame for infertility. It was thought self-evident that a man who managed erection, penetration and orgasm was fertile. But potency and fertility are different and in fact men and women suffer equally from both infertility and low fertility, with sperm defects or problems being the biggest single cause in men.

Infertility is usually defined as failure to conceive within 12 months and it affects about one couple in six. Sometimes the causes are simple – excess weight, too much drink, tobacco or marijuana, or even the man wearing tight pants. Other causes may include the following.

- Incomplete intercourse or using the wrong opening (not as rare as you might think).
- The woman washing immediately after intercourse. This lowers the chances of conception (but it is not a contraceptive).

- Infertility after coming off the contraceptive pill. It can take a while to regain full fertility.
- Illness and anaemia.
- Infection of the cervix.
- Too little moisture in the woman for the sperm to travel (this may be treatable with hormones).
- Blockage of the fallopian tubes so the egg can't reach the womb. (Scars left by the venereal infections (page 564) are unfortunately an increasingly common cause of this.)
- The woman's body reacting to the sperm as if they were germs and making a chemical which kills them. This is not easy to treat but it can be done.
- Recent research suggests that women who are too thin find it harder to conceive.
- A hormone imbalance causing the woman to release immature eggs or no eggs at all – surprisingly the periods can be normal while the eggs are not. In the past, boosting the hormones to cure this led to women having six babies, but now the risk of a multiple birth is far less.
- A woman's subconscious feelings may affect whether she conceives or not – which is why it is not unusual for pregnancy to follow an adoption.

Infertility in Men

The man plays some part in infertility in about half the cases. Sometimes he is the infertile partner; sometimes his low fertility combines with his wife's problems to make conception harder. The causes of male infertility include illnesses – such as mumps in the testicles during or after puberty, injury to the testicles, a block in the ducts carrying the sperm or a low sperm count. Some causes of male infertility can be treated; some cannot. But when a husband is seriously infertile some couples find a very happy solution in AID (see below).

Secondary Infertility

Secondary infertility is the term used when a couple have managed to have one child, but don't seem able to conceive another. Surprisingly, this is the case for as many as half the couples troubled by infertility. The tests and remedies are the same as for a totally infertile couple.

Increasing your Chances

When the problem is due to a low sperm count the chances of pregnancy may be increased by making love at just the right time. The **Catholic Marriage Advisory Council** (page 640) (predictably) excels in this field. And there are a number of testing kits which allow a woman to know exactly when she is ovulating.

Artificial Insemination by Donor (AID)

AID can be used when a fertile woman has an infertile husband, or one who carries a hereditary disease which he should not transmit. For AID a nurse or doctor inserts into the entrance to the womb semen from a donor who has been checked for good mental and physical health. Once pregnancy is achieved it proceeds as normal, though sometimes it takes several inseminations to achieve pregnancy.

AID is a solution which takes a bit of thinking about. But in Britain over 2,500 babies are conceived this way each year, and the AID parents I have talked to have had great joy from their babies. (See also Law, page 478). AID is available in a number of NHS hospitals, and is also offered by the **British Pregnancy Advisory Service** and the **Pregnancy Advisory Service** (page 641) together with infertility counselling.

Artificial Insemination by Husband (AIH)

A man who is about to have a vasectomy or some medical treatment, which could damage his sperm, such as those for cancer, can have some of his semen frozen and stored (at some storage cost) against the day when he wants a child. In due course his wife can then be artificially inseminated with his sperm (as in AID) – this is called AIH. Unfortunately, this isn't always plain sailing. Semen is test frozen before storing and a small proportion of men are found to have semen which just won't stand up to freezing. And even if the semen stores well, some women who have no trouble conceiving through intercourse just don't conceive by artificial insemination. Finally, though sperm certainly keep for years, their exact life is a little speculative as the technique of freezing hasn't been around all that long. Both PAS and BPAS can advise on AIH (page 641).

In Vitro Fertilization

Nowadays there is also increasing use of techniques for fertilizing a woman's egg outside her body – usually with her husband's sperm – and then putting the fertilized egg into the womb to begin an otherwise normal pregnancy. This is the method for the so-called test tube babies.

SEXUAL AND MARITAL PROBLEMS

At one time all sexual problems were thought to be psychological, but there is now evidence that some sexual difficulties may be linked to the body's chemistry. When this is so, the problem can sometimes be cured by purely physical treatment, but unfortunately the tests which are needed to establish such physical problems are not widely available.

When the problem is psychological the prospect is also very good. Sex therapy is one of the most successful areas of therapy, and it's possible for a therapist to bring about real change remarkably quickly, and make a great deal of difference to those involved. This is not an area in which therapy can only be obtained from psychoana-

lysts and psychiatrists. They have a role in some psycho-sexual problems, but there are excellent sex therapists among those with other backgrounds.

Sources of Help

For marital problems the main source of help and advice is **Relate** (National Marriage Guidance Council), and there is also a **Catholic Marriage Advisory Council**. These not only have counsellors who deal with general marital problems, but also people specially trained in psycho-sexual counselling, and you can ask to see either. You can find the local branches of either organization in the telephone book – usually under 'Marriage' or 'Catholic' – or through the head office addresses on pages 640-642. The **Jewish Marriage Guidance Council** (page 642) is purely for general marital and family problems.

In many parts of Britain it is hard to find a sex therapist other than those involved in marriage guidance, but GPs and Family Planning Clinics may be able to refer you to someone in your area. Alternatively, you can write to the **Association of Sexual and Marital Therapists** (page 642) which can refer you either to individuals who offer therapy or to clinics, and the clinics are often on the NHS. The **British Association of Psychotherapists** (page 589) or the **Institute of Psychosexual Medicine** (page 642) also have the names of sex therapists. Both associations cover trained sex therapists drawn from a number of disciplines – psychology, psychiatry, marriage guidance and so on – whereas the Institute is the professional body for medical doctors trained to help sexual problems, some of whom may offer help on the NHS.

Handicapped Sex

The sexual difficulties of the handicapped and disabled are the special province of **SPOD** (page 642), which provides advice and information by phone or letter. Sometimes it can also put people in touch with professional counsellors, in their area, if they wish for face-to-face counselling. This is basically a free service for both the disabled and their partners, but those who want longer-term individual counselling may be able to obtain it through SPOD on a fee-paying basis. The leaflets and books available through **MENCAP** (page 591) may also be useful.

Homosexuality

There are numerous 'Gay Switchboards' which offer information and advice to homosexuals, of either sex. They are listed in the telephone book under 'Gay', 'Homosexual' or 'Lesbian'. Londoners, or those unable to find their local number, can contact the London switchboard given on page 642, which is a national information source.

It is run entirely by homosexuals and keeps a nationwide list of switchboards, clubs, support groups, medical centres and other organizations related to homosexuality. There is a similar line purely for lesbians, but its hours are far more limited.

Addresses and suggestions for further reading are at the ends of chapters.

MENOPAUSE – CHANGE OF LIFE

Strictly speaking, the term 'menopause' means 'end of periods' and refers only to the point when periods stop; the term 'climacteric' means the time before and after periods stop. However, most lay people use menopause for the surrounding time, during which related changes take place. Periods usually stop at about the age of 49 – but 46 in smokers. But the change isn't always sudden, and the age isn't certain. Women vary widely in the symptoms they experience in the time around the menopause. Some have symptoms for as long as 5 years before their periods stop, or up to 5 years after. Others have symptoms for only months both before and after, and some have no problems at all.

What happens is that the ovaries cease to function properly and so the oestrogen level falls. This in turn effects an interaction with the pituitary gland, and it is these changes in body chemicals which cause the unpleasant symptoms. Because the ovaries play a key part in these changes, women whose ovaries are removed for any reason also experience a change of life which, being more sudden, can also be more severe.

Periods can become erratic, or suddenly heavy. There may also be hot flushes, when blood suddenly surges to the skin surface giving a fierce burning sensation, like all-over blushing, which the woman fears everyone can see (though if she goes to a mirror she will realize it hardly shows). With the flush may come sweating, nausea and all the symptoms of panic. The panic is only caused by hormones interacting and giving the body a sudden shot of adrenalin – the hormone which makes us act fast in emergencies. But it may also make her breathe too fast and bring on other symptoms, such as giddiness, pins and needles and cramps.

The symptoms go fastest if she relaxes and reminds herself that it is just the body playing tricks. It often helps to stand still, relax and take steady, slow and fairly deep breaths – thinking about the breathing – then, when calm, to run cold water over the pulse point in the wrists.

★ If she can't control her breathing an old, and effective, trick is to breathe into a paper bag until the symptoms go.

Physical Changes During the Menopause

As the hormone levels change the skin loses its bounce and elasticity – so, alas, lines become more obvious. The female hormone levels are no longer high and may not be enough to counteract the male hormones which all women have, so hair may appear on the chin and upper lip, muscle tone is reduced and the vagina produces less lubricant during sex (KY jelly isn't the only solution – see right). The vagina also becomes less acid, and so more vulnerable to genital infections. So, although the more sex a woman has at this time the better her hormone balance will be, promiscuity carries greater risks. At the same time, hormone changes make the body less efficient at taking up calcium (page 625) and more is needed in the diet.

Mental Changes near the Menopause

A symptom which is often overlooked is difficulty in remembering things: usually little things, like appointments or what shopping is needed. Infuriating, but not the start of madness or senility. It ends when the menopause ends – and if it affects someone seriously, it can be treated.

There can also be swings of emotion rather like you get in adolescence, with depression and tearfulness striking out of the blue. The fact that the menopause often arrives just when children have left home and a marriage is rather tired may not make it any easier.

Help with the Hormones

There are creams containing oestrogen which can be used both to lubricate the vagina and slow down its ageing. As a proportion of the oestrogen in these creams is also absorbed into the body as a whole, they can't be used if someone has a condition which would be badly affected by it. There is also Hormone Replacement Therapy (HRT), in which the woman's hormones are boosted to the levels they were at when she was younger. This has been much vaunted as the answer to menopausal problems. Some doctors rate it highly, and many women find it an enormous help. But there are certain medical conditions which may make it unwise, and it has not been used for long enough for all its possible risks and side effects to be known. Even so, it may be helpful during a bad patch, and allow those whose menopause results from an operation to be eased into it more gradually. On the plus side there is some evidence that it protects against coronary thrombosis and osteoporosis (page 548).

There are now a number of clinics specializing in the problems which are linked to the menopause, and if your doctor isn't getting to grips with your problems you can ask to be referred to one.

Self-help in the Menopause

Some women feel randier than ever during the menopause and, barring promiscuity, they should make good use of it. Sex is nature's way of keeping the hormones in balance. Some American research suggests that women who have sex fairly frequently maintain their female hormone levels for longer, and have fewer menopausal problems. Yoga exercises, which not only keep the muscles in trim but also stimulate the glandular system of the body, are another way to soften the blows of time.

A good diet, and learning to relax (see Transcendental Meditation, page 567), also helps. It is also vital to have some real source of interest and satisfaction. The woman who has nothing to absorb her except her own symptoms is sure to notice every one of them.

Male Menopause

Although this term is bandied about, men can't have a menopause because there are no periods to stop. However, some men in their late 40s, 50s and 60s do have other symptoms very similar to those women experience. They have night sweats, lose muscle power and go off sex, and some even have a measurably low level of male hormones. But this only happens to a small percentage of men and the cause is not known.

Men usually retain their fertility all their lives and the sperm remain perfectly normal. But the ability to get, or maintain, an erection often lessens with age, as the body tissues lose their general elasticity and the blood flow becomes less efficient.

A HEALTHY DIET

Diet for Babies and Children

Breast Feeding

Some books say women should make up their minds in good time about whether they want to breast feed or not. I disagree. If someone is sure they want to breast feed that's fine. But to decide against it before you have the baby is a pity. How one feels about breast feeding is part of how one feels about oneself and one's own body. Few people emerge from giving birth feeling quite the same as they did before. So, whatever your reluctance, it may be wise not to make up your mind too firmly about not breast feeding until you have the baby in your arms. And, as putting a baby to the breast the instant it is born is the best way to get the placenta to detach, even those who are opposed to breast feeding may experience a baby suckling and discover it is very different from what they expected.

Those who do want to breast feed should tell the hospital beforehand but be prepared for the fact that everyone around them may not make it as easy as it should be. In the hospital there may be nurses who do unhelpful things like giving the baby bottle feeds when is should have been brought to the breast, or give strict advice which ends up making feeding harder than it need be. There is no expert quite so dogmatic as one who has only book learning.

There are, however, some excellent nurses who offer every support to the breast feeding mother. Some of them work as breast feeding counsellors. It may help to talk to one before going into hospital, so you have the confidence to handle any problems. The NCT or **La Leche League** (page 642) may be able to put you in touch with one.

★ Research has shown that, in Western countries, the more educated a woman is, the more likely she is to breast feed.

Advantages for the Baby

- Breast milk is perfectly balanced to give a baby *exactly* what it needs to grow. Powdered milk formula is only close to what it needs.
- Breast milk is easier to digest than formula.
- There is less risk of the baby developing an allergy.

- Breast feeding gives a baby antibodies which protect it from infection, like flu, measles and polio, especially in the early weeks.
- Breast feeding is cleaner – it carries no risk of infection from a poorly sterilized bottle. (Babies don't develop the stomach acids to kill germs in food until they are several months old.)

Establishing Breast Feeding

The size of a woman's breasts, or her nipples, are no guide to her ability to breast feed. So nobody should decide they won't be able to. Try to start the baby at the breast within the first 48 hours as that is when the baby establishes its sucking habits most easily. If it can't be put to the breast it can still learn later, but it will be harder.

A baby should be given *no bottles at all* in the early days of breast feeding so as to stimulate the breast milk to come in. Tell nurses in hospital that you don't want your baby to be given any bottles and that you want it brought to you each time it seems hungry. Otherwise they may give it a bottle to let you rest.

Colostrum

The first sign that the breasts are preparing to make milk may be a thick yellow substance called colostrum which sometimes leaks from the breasts in the last weeks of pregnancy. It is all the breasts produce for the first day or so. Colostrum contains everything that a baby most needs in the first days of life, especially antibodies which protect it from infection. If a baby is put to the breast whenever it wants it, it won't need any other feeds, and its regular sucking is exactly what is needed to help the body to produce milk. Only let it suck for a couple of minutes at a time in the first few days, so the nipples get used to it. A newborn baby may want to feed every couple of hours in the first week or two.

Even a mother who doesn't want to breast feed might consider letting her baby have the colostrum for the first few days, to give it those protective antibodies.

The First Milk

Almost every mother worries that she won't be able to produce enough milk. The great thing to remember is that *the body creates milk to meet the demands of the baby*. The more a baby demands the more the body makes. So the more often a baby is put to the breast in the early days, the sooner the breast milk will start flowing. During this time the mother should simply try to relax as much as possible and just enjoy and get to know her baby.

The milk starts to come in 2 to 4 days after the birth. At first it is mixed with colostrum and looks rich and creamy, later it becomes thin and watery. No one need ever worry that their milk is too thin and not good enough for the baby. This is one thing the body *always* gets right. Human milk is naturally watery looking, but it is very nourishing. Even if a mother is starving, nature will deprive the mother's body rather than let breast milk go short of what the baby needs. And, like colostrum, human milk contains antibodies which protect a baby against infections such as whooping cough, diarrhoea and flu.

Addresses and suggestions for further reading are at the ends of chapters.

Helping the Milk Come In

The first thing to do is to stop worrying that it won't. It's as natural for it to come as it was for the baby to grow once you'd conceived it – and there wasn't any trouble with *that*. The basics are very simple.

- Let the baby suck as often as it wants.
- Get as much rest as you can – including an afternoon rest if you can make time.
- Have a good diet (pages 621 to 628).
- Have at least six pints of liquid a day – and put a glass of something beside you when you start the feed.
- When feeding practise any relaxation you learnt before childbirth and think of milk flowing.
- Don't go on the pill as it can reduce the amount of milk you make, and some of the hormones get into the milk.
- Start with the right breast at one feed and the left at the next, and so on.
- If there is milk left in the breast after the baby has finished express it into a sterilized jug in the early days and keep it in a sterilized bottle in case your own supply runs short later in the day. (If it hasn't been used by the evening freeze it in a sterilized container in case you are ever called away suddenly and a feed is needed.)
- If a baby refuses the breast it is probably because it can't breathe. Check if its nose is bunged up.

Demand Feeding

Since the breasts make milk in response to the baby's sucking it obviously helps the milk supply if babies are fed whenever they ask for food. But some people are afraid that letting the baby have food whenever it asks for it will make it spoilt and difficult.

Over the past fifty years opinions have see-sawed over whether babies should be fed to a timetable or when they cry. The logical solution seems to be to look at nature. Every animal which is suckled feeds whenever it wants and the fields of Britain are not littered with spoilt foals and fox cubs, nor are jungles filled with spoilt gorillas. With a small stomach and inexperienced digestion a baby, like all young animals, needs to be fed little and often. This is not the baby being naughty or demanding, nor are you spoiling it. There comes a time when children *do* get demanding but it is not for months. So, feed it as soon as it cries. Or, better still, feed it if it looks restless, *before* it cries. That teaches it that it doesn't need to cry to get attention (a good lesson for later). Babies do not need to cry to expand their lungs, as some believe. And if anyone says you are spoiling the baby you can point out that women fed on demand for centuries without the slightest evidence that it produced nations of spoilt children.

A newborn baby will usually need at least 6 feeds a day but in one survey a quarter of the babies wanted 8 feeds or more. As the weeks go by the feeds will gradually space themselves out. Nature has so well arranged it that, by then, the breasts will produce what milk is needed with far less frequent stimulation.

Babies are very variable in how many feeds they need.

Don't expect your baby to conform to any baby book or do what any other baby does. It has its own pattern which is right for it. However, at about 6 weeks old many babies are ready to give up the feed they have at around 2 am. If the baby is gaining weight well and is not small for its age, you could try offering it a bottle of warm boiled water at this time instead. Some babies get bored with waking up for boiled water. If your baby doesn't get bored or starts waking earlier in the morning go back to feeding it – it needs it.

Timing

The main thing a mother needs to know about timing breast feeds is – *don't*.

If nature had designed all breasts to give milk at the same rate and all babies to take it at the same speed she would have made all breasts look alike and all babies have the same faces. Differences in speed are as natural as differences in looks. And any woman who has breast fed several children, as I have, will be able to tell you that each child has its own speed, even on the same pair of breasts.

Keep the baby on one breast until it seems tired of it. Then give it the other one. Research shows that the milk a breast produces in the first few minutes of each suckling is less rich than the later milk. So switching breasts too soon can mean a baby has to drink more than is comfortable, to get the nourishment it needs.

You don't have to take it off the breast just because it has finished eating. A baby enjoys just being at the breast and feeling it in its mouth, and, as it gets older, will start patting and pushing it. This is perfectly legitimate play: the breast is a child's first toy, its mother's skin its first real encounter with the textures of the world. It is learning through her body.

This means that the end of any feed is a good time to talk to a baby and get to know it.

Nipple Care

- Avoid washing the nipples with soap (and you don't need to wash before and after a feed).
- Some nipples get sore and can develop problems if sucked too long. If yours begin to get uncomfortable shorten the sucking time.
- Keep them as dry as possible – in the air if you can.

Engorgement

In the early days, the breasts can become so full of milk that they become hard and hot and painful. This is called engorgement.

If you feel the breasts getting very full, feed the baby *before* it becomes too painful. If this is impossible, squeeze out some breast milk by hand by pressing the breast rhythmically with a finger and thumb just behind the edge of the nipple. It helps the milk to come out if you imagine it flowing as you do this. Let enough flow to relieve the pressure but don't go on too long or you will just stimulate production. Then soothe the breasts with ice packs. Bags of frozen peas are ideal, but ice cubes in plastic bags are thriftier.

Pain when Feeding

Some women find breast feeding is perfectly easy and comfortable from the start. Others find it uncomfortable to start with but it becomes comfortable with time. Try varying the way you hold the baby, so it doesn't always chomp on the same bit of the nipple – lying down, or with its feet going back under your arm are good variations.

If it has been comfortable and becomes painful you should get a doctor, health visitor or breast feeding adviser to see what is going wrong. There are many reasons why it could hurt. If the cause is a lump in the breast and you feel as if you have flu see a doctor as soon as you can. You may have a blocked duct, mastitis, or an abscess which need prompt treatment. The breast-feeding books and organizations listed on pages 641-642 are useful sources of information and help.

Supplementary Feeds

It is always good to have a bottle and some formula in the home, just in case an emergency makes it impossible to feed a baby. As babies often dislike switching to a bottle teat it is a good idea to get a baby used to a little milk from a bottle from time to time – using expressed breast milk or formula – from early on. (But not before breast feeding is well established.) A bottle can also be used to supplement a feed if a baby is hungry and the breast milk has clearly finished. But, until the milk is well established, this should only be done *after* a feed, not instead of one.

Weight Gain

Breast feeding mothers often worry about whether their baby is getting enough to eat. The best guide is its weight. If it is gaining weight fairly steadily it is getting enough, however short or few its feeds.

Babies don't usually gain weight in the first week, but once feeding is established they gain fairly steadily, though the amount varies slightly according to their birth weight. On average a baby gains:

up to 2 months – 4-5 oz (110-140 g) a week
2-6 months 2-3 oz (55-85 g) a week.
By 6 months a baby will normally have doubled its birth weight.
By 12 months it will usually be 3 times its birth weight. But don't expect a baby to meet these figures to the dot, week in week out. Some variation is normal.

It used to be thought that a fat baby was the ideal baby. But it has been found that those who are overweight as babies are more likely to be fat adults (with all the ills that flesh is heir to). Nowadays, they are chubby, not rolling in fat. The two big causes of babies being overweight, which you should guard against, are mixing more formula with the water than the manufacturers recommend, or giving sweet foods. Both are bad for the baby for other reasons beside fatness and are best avoided.

It's a good idea to have the baby weighed each week at a clinic. As babies aren't all born the same weight there isn't a right weight for a baby at a certain age. What matters is steady growth and weight gain (see above). If a baby is not gaining enough weight you should talk to a doctor.

Weaning

There are no rules about when to stop breast feeding. Most babies would like to go on nursing until well over 6 months old, and may even like it for far longer. Some women enjoy feeding until a child is long past its first birthday. Others want to stop well before 3 months are up.

But if a mother suddenly stops feeding, her breasts will become engorged and painful and the baby will be suddenly disappointed. Instead, let a baby have half a feed on a bottle (the first half – when it's eager), then half on the breast. Start doing this with just one feed, then with two and so on. Once this is established, cut out the breast entirely for one feed, then for another and so on. Exactly the same principle applies to weaning from bottle to cup.

Whether a baby *can* be shifted from breast to bottle or from bottle to cup or solid food is not the only issue. The breast or bottle are a major part of its pleasure in life. It is not just a matter of getting nourishment, it is the sensation of the whole business that it enjoys. Think how important our meals are and how deprived we would feel if someone decreed that, in future, we were to get our balanced diet through tablets taken with water three times a day. The day wouldn't be the same at all, would it? Yet we have all kinds of other pleasures to enliven our day which a baby doesn't have. To a baby the experience of the breast or bottle must be much more important than the experience of eating is to us, and it is unfair suddenly to take it away.

If a baby slowly switches from breast to bottle it can usually get a lot of satisfaction from the bottle, even if it prefers the breast. But it will get nothing like the pleasure if it is switched to a cup. So the fact that it can drink from one at about 6 months should *not* be the signal for depriving it of all the delicious sensations of sucking.

Often a child will want an evening feed by breast or bottle well after its first birthday and there is nothing wrong with that. You may also find that if it is unwell or especially tired a chance to suck may be a great comfort. This is totally natural. Don't worry if your child still enjoys a bottle long after other children have given up. It doesn't mean it's backward; it just means you are tolerant.

Bottle Feeding

A newborn baby's digestion is tailor-made to use breast milk. Cows' milk is very different in its richness and in the minerals it contains, so a tiny baby simply can't digest it. So the DH experts on child nutrition now say cows' milk shouldn't be given for the first year. If it isn't being breast fed a baby should be given a powdered milk formula made from cows' milk which has been treated to make it as close to human milk as possible. Only use those which say 'modified' on the container. Best of all look for those saying 'humanized' as these are the very closest to human milk. Unfortunately, they are also the most expensive.

Addresses and suggestions for further reading are at the ends of chapters.

From 6 to 12 months a baby can be put onto a formula made for the older baby. But these richer formulas should *never* be given to babies under 6 months old as they will strain their kidneys.

★ Mothers who think their babies are allergic to milk should consult their doctor. Babies should not be switched to a non-milk formula without a doctor's approval.

★ Most teats have rather small holes which make a bottle harder work than a breast. Enlarge the hole *carefully* with the tip of a darning needle heated to red hot in a flame. The hole should be large enough to allow a steady series of drops. But have a spare teat or two to hand in case you get it wrong. If the stream is too rapid the baby can choke – so be careful.

Keeping Bottles Clean
Until a baby is 6 months old bottles and teats must be sterilized. They should be rinsed after use and washed in clean soapy water, with a brush kept just for this, to remove *all* trace of milk. They should then be kept in a sterilizing solution when not in use, so should any spoon or jug used for mixing the formula. Whoever makes up the feed should wash their hands well, then remove the bottle and the teat from the liquid, fill it *without* rinsing them, and place the teat on the bottle without touching the part the baby will suck.

The sterilizing solution should be one specially made for babies' bottles and should be changed daily. But don't expect it to make a bottle safe to use if it is badly washed. The fats in milk can prevent the chemicals in the sterilizing solution from working at all.

★ If you run out of sterilizing fluid just boil the bottle and teat for at least 25 minutes in a pan of water.

Making Up a Bottle
Put the recommended amount of formula in the jug or bottle. Pour on the correct amount of boiling water (or use water which has boiled and cooled if the instructions say cool or cold water must be used). Put the lid on the bottle with the teat pointing inwards, and shake the bottle until it mixes. Put it in the refrigerator or a bowl of cold water to cool. Or stir the jug until the formula is mixed, pour it into several bottles, cap, and put them into the refrigerator.

★ Standing bottles in a plastic box in the refrigerator will stop them being knocked over.

When a baby is on formula it should *only* be mixed to the strength recommended on the container: more is *not* better, it is harmful.

Bottled water can contain mineral salts which would strain a baby's kidneys. However, it may be a good idea to use water which has been through a purifying jug (page 604) that will remove some of the chemicals and metals, but it will still need to be boiled.

Giving Bottle Feeds
Babies tend to prefer slightly warm milk, but it does them no harm to have it at room temperature. However, germs breed very happily in milk, so made up bottles shouldn't be left sitting in the warm for longer than an hour. Equally what hasn't been taken at the end of a feed should be thrown away.

WARNING: A microwave may seem the ideal way to warm a bottle but it may not be the same temperature right through. If you want to use a microwave always shake the bottle before testing it for temperature.

Before giving a bottle to a baby shake a few drops onto the inside of your wrist to check it's not too hot. It should be *just* warm. Undo the cap a half turn, so air can get in as the milk flows out, or the milk won't flow. Hold the baby in a half-sitting position and have the bottle tilting down towards the baby's mouth, not level.

★ If the baby doesn't open its mouth stroke the cheek nearest you with the end of the teat and it will open and root for it.

● Younger children can feel very left out with their mother sitting feeding a baby again and again. For some feeds try letting them feed the baby. They can sit on your lap and have a cuddle, while they cuddle and feed the baby. The safest place for this is a big bed – so no harm comes if the baby isn't held too securely.
● A young baby should never be left alone with a feeding bottle – it could choke and suffocate.

Burping and Posseting
Babies vary in how prone they are to wind. Just hold it upright against your shoulder, and gently rub its back (don't pat it firmly or it may vomit). Even with gentle handling, a baby may 'posset' (i.e. bring up part of its feed). This is nothing to worry about; lots of babies do it, and you can easily spot the difference between vomiting and posseting.

When to Feed and How Much to Give
Some people try to make feeding very regimented, giving feeds at regular intervals and giving the same amount at each feed, or taking the same time on each feed. This is just to make a rod for your own back. It also seems to assume that a baby is either a machine or very, very stupid – which is a poor basis for your relationship with it. We all feel more hungry on some days than others, and more hungry at certain times of the day. Babies are just as varied. When a baby seems hungry offer it a bottle straight away (page 615). Just let it drink for as long as it seems to want to. If it hasn't had enough it will either ask for another meal sooner, or drink more next time. You may want to guarantee it won't yell for food when you are out. The fact is you can't, and you can waste a great deal of time trying to force food down it. It is much better to take a bottle with you in case it does cry.

At first, babies need a lot of small feeds — usually under 3 to 4 ounces a feed in the first 6 weeks. From then on most babies begin to find their own routine, taking less and less interest in certain feeds as they have rather more at each of the others. They usually take about an extra ounce per feed per month. So let the baby guide you.

However, if you know it's nearly time for it to get hungry and you want to get a feed out of the way, offer it a bottle. If it will drink, fine. If it won't there's no way you can make it, so don't try.

> If a doctor prescribes a vitamin D supplement for a child *it must only have the recommended dose*. A little is good. Too much can do harm.

Introducing a Mixed Diet

Amazingly, some mothers give babies solid food in the first weeks of life. This is not a good idea. When babies are very young their bodies have not yet developed the enzymes needed to get the goodness out of anything except milk. Nor are their kidneys able to get rid of extra salt in the way more mature kidneys can. Giving solid foods to a very young baby, when its body isn't ready, could harm it.

Babies vary slightly as to when they are ready to start mixed feeding, but the timing recommended by a DH report is as follows:

- Most babies can begin a mixed diet at between 4 to 6 months old.
- Some babies are ready to start at 3½ or even 3 months old.
- All should start a mixed diet before 8 months old.

Ordinary foods are added while the baby is still on baby milk, and it is recommended that:

- sugar should not be added to a baby's solid food or bottle
- salt should *not* be added to a baby's food as its kidneys cannot cope with it
- extra vitamins should be given from 1 month onwards and up to 2 years old, or preferably 5. (Clinics supply these.)

Drinks Other than Milk
What the recommendations boil down to is that *unsweetened water is the best drink you can give your child between meals*. They don't need vitamin C drinks; it is better for them to get that vitamin in drops without the sugar. Up to 6 months water should be boiled. Bottled water may have too many minerals so it may be an idea to use a filter jug to remove some of the chemicals, boiling the water afterwards.

Approaching Mixed Feeding
Solid food gives a baby two new experiences: a totally new flavour (which must be most surprising) and a food which needs a new tongue action before it can be swal-

lowed and doesn't trickle conveniently towards its throat. At first keep one of these new experiences to a minimum by making the purée very runny by stirring in mixed formula, boiled water or breast milk.

Most mothers start with a baby cereal. Baby rice is now thought to be best because it looks as if some babies become allergic to gluten (which is in flour, bread, and most cereals) if given it too early, and rice has no gluten. For this reason bread and biscuits should not be given until the baby is 6 months old.

There is no evidence that cereal is the best food to start with, but it may be the one most like plain milk, and therefore least likely to be rejected. But don't think a baby is rejecting food just because a lot comes out. It can't get the tongue action right at first, so a lot *always* comes out. Just scrape it off its cheeks and pop it in again. Once it gets used to the feel of spoon food it will make it very clear when it rejects something. If it dislikes a food miss it out for a while. Babies tend to know the foods which don't agree with them.

Home-Made Food v Bought Baby Foods
There are no rules which say home-made food is better than baby food or vice versa. It depends which foods you buy and how you cook them.

> When a mother gives her baby food she is also giving her love. It can be hard not to feel hurt when a baby spits the food out and turns its head away from the proffered spoon. You can remind yourself that the food is being rejected not you. Try not to make meals a battleground as this can pave the way to food fads later.

Making Baby Food
- Choose the freshest fruit and vegetables — they have more vitamins.
- Cut them up small so they cook quickly — long heat destroys vitamins.
- Cook them with as little water as possible then goodness isn't lost in the water.
- Stop cooking them *the moment* they are soft enough to purée.
- Use any cooking water to thin the purée.

If you cook enough for the whole family you will all benefit from the extra goodness of cooking this way.

★ Keep baby food in a refrigerator once made or opened, transferring tinned food into some other container. Don't feed the baby directly from the container. It is safest to throw away what isn't eaten after 24 hours.

★ For thrift, sterilize an ice cube tray, and when you make or open baby food put enough for one meal in each ice cube section. Pop the tray in a new plastic bag and freeze it. Then less is wasted.

★ Many baby rusks contain sugar. Check their packets and choose one which has no sugar or as little as possible. And don't give babies sweet biscuits.

Addresses and suggestions for further reading are at the ends of chapters.

Tips for Starting Mixed Feeding

● Only introduce one new food a day. Then, if it disagrees with your baby, you will know.

● Make the food into a smooth purée: check for lumps: they can choke a young baby.

● Give puréed food on a teaspoon, *never* in a bottle.

● At 6 months you don't need to sterilize the cup and spoon you use, but you should wash your hands before preparing the food.

● Start with ½ to 1 teaspoon – but don't try to put it all in at once. Give it *before* the breast or bottle feed.

● Food which is puréed looks much less than food in lumps. Don't worry if a baby seems to eat very little. The figures below right are only guidelines. If your baby wants less (or more) that's fine.

● Don't try to force a baby to eat more than it wants. Babies may be young but they aren't stupid: they don't starve themselves. They know how much food they need better than you do.

● Once a baby is eating one food try to give two different foods a day at different feeds.

● Build up gradually until by 1 year the baby is eating almost normal meals, at your mealtimes, plus a bottle or breast if it wishes at other times, or drinks of water.

> You may be thinking that the human body needs salt and wondering what will happen to the baby if you don't add any. It does need salt but salt occurs naturally in almost all foods.

Foods the Very Young Have Problems With

Not to be given under 1 year	Foods some children react to
Eggs	Cheese
Honey	Pork
Bovril or Marmite (too salt)	Tomatoes
Smoked meat or fish (too salt)	Strawberries
Salted meat or fish (too salt)	Citrus fruit
Shellfish	Peanuts
Coffee or tea (children don't need stimulants)	Shellfish
Alcohol	
Dried fruit (too sweet and a child may choke)	
Nuts (often salty and a child may choke)	
Chunky peanut butter (a child may choke)	
Oily fish	
Sugary foods	
Fizzy drinks	
Fruit with seeds	
Sweets or chocolates	
Unripe or acid fruit, such as rhubarb (possible indigestion or diarrhoea)	
Liver	

Both the baby and its digestion need to get used to new foods in easy stages. If it starts mixed food a little late don't suddenly put it on to the food for that age. And do read the tips before using the chart.

Eating wheat products early in life can cause some children to develop an allergy. So bread, biscuits and other wheat products should only be given after a child is 5-6 months old.

Children under 5 *must not* be put on the very low fat diet adopted by some adults. In the first year a child grows faster than at any other time outside the womb. To grow they need far more calories for their size than adults do.

Age	What You Can Give When
6 weeks	baby rice (see page 618)
4 months	Steamed, boiled or microwaved fresh carrots, cauliflower, green beans, potatoes. Mashed bananas, stewed dessert fruit such as pears, apples (see page 618). Give ½-1 teaspoon before a breast or bottle feed at one or two of its meals, each day.
5-6 months	Include egg yolk, plus a wider range of vegetables and fruit, meat broth. Also rusks when wanted. A baby can have a total of about 3-4 teaspoons of food a day divided between 3 meals. Give breast or bottle afterwards and for other feeds.
6-7 months	Include puréed meat of all types, beans and lentils, white of egg, fish – with *all* bones removed, cottage cheese, grated cheese in other food, yoghurt, porridge. Simply build up the variety and give milk by breast, bottle or cup afterwards and for other meals.

> If the baby is already used to purées, its food can be a little coarser from now on. If not, keep to purée a little longer.

9-12 months	Most ordinary food, if not too fatty. Not sweetened drinks or other sweet foods.
1 year	From now on a baby can eat small amounts of ordinary family meals. Salt and extra sugar should still be avoided as much as possible. (It could benefit the whole family to cut down on these – see page 620.) Food should be cut into tiny pieces and the baby can begin to feed itself.

WARNING: In the past few years there have been cases of young children, in normal well-off families, being admitted to hospital because they were under-fed. Believing that a low-fat diet was healthy, their mothers put them on to skimmed or semi-skimmed milk and only gave them small amounts of other fats. *The low fat diet was never meant for young children.*

Half the calories in human milk come from fat. So babies are 'programmed' to grow on a relatively high fat diet. The fat they most need is found in milk. Like a cake, fat is made with several different ingredients which can't be seen. Those in milk are ones the body uses to build cells and which are important for other aspects of growth. A child should have 1 pint (500 ml) of ordinary pasteurized milk a day – or its equivalent in cheese or yoghurt.

Feeding Itself

You don't need to buy special bent spoons and forks for a baby to learn to feed itself, an ordinary teaspoon is fine. A baby will tell you when it wants to try this by holding your hand or grabbing the spoon. If it wants to feed itself let it. Attempts to be independent are worth encouraging, so praise it. Don't worry that quite a lot will go anywhere *but* in its mouth. When it flags you can always offer it some more. If a baby doesn't try to feed itself by about 8 months let it have the food in front of it with a spoon in for a minute or two while you are 'busy' in the same room. Or, if it's old enough, it may prefer to eat finger foods like bananas or bread.

A baby is learning all the time. The *feel* of puréed food is a totally new experience and it will want to discover the sploshiness of food by sploshing. This is not naughty. It is good – the baby is using its intelligence to learn what the world is like. However, in doing so it may look perfectly revolting and make a dreadful mess. So I strongly recommend feeding a baby in a low chair which sits on the floor, rather than a high chair from which it can spread the food in a wider arc and be a most off-putting sight at meal-times.

Some people will feel this deprives the child of a role in family meals. Maybe. But a baby won't think it's bad being below the table (particularly if it has never known any different) and there are other times when it can be part of the scene. Babies can dominate meal times too much, when adults and other children need attention too. (And there's no risk of the baby toppling out if left alone for a moment – but see below.) There also comes a time for a toddler to give up being so messy, but it will often continue just to get attention. Below the table it has no such incentive, and joining adults and any older children at table is a great reward for civilized behaviour – when it can manage it. It also means that once elevated to table status, a badly behaved child can be put back in the 'baby chair' on the floor – where it can't show off with bad behaviour – which it won't like at all.

A table full of people can be a marvellous audience and few toddlers can resist playing havoc at a meal sooner or later, and some try it regularly. If you have a suitable remedy, like this, it is very useful.

A baby or toddler should never be left alone while actually eating: it can choke.

Diet in Childhood

Starting a child on solid food is much more than a matter of just giving it nourishment. The food a child eats when very young sets the pattern for its eating later in life. The types of flavours it learns to enjoy will probably be the ones it returns to for comfort even as an adult. When most of us were babies giving sugary foods was a sign of love, and it can be difficult to abandon that idea. But developing a sweet tooth can mean no teeth at all: most people need dentures in old age, and a horrifying proportion have them by the age of 18. Sugar also plays no small part in the fact that half those over 50 are overweight – and few of them thank their mothers for it. So, if we really want to do our children a favour, we should tell ourselves that sugar may taste lovely but it isn't loving.

Not buying sweets, cakes, biscuits, canned and bottled drinks, and packets of snack food frees a lot of the family budget to buy food that *is* good for you and tastes a lot better, which means that treats can take the form of out of season fruit or a better cut of meat or fish – so teaching your child to turn to good food when it wants comfort in later life. The British Dietetic Association's report says the following:

- Once solids have been introduced, and the child is on a mixed diet, milk, lean meat, poultry, fish, eggs, cheese, fruits, vegetables, and cereals – preferably of the wholegrain type – should form the major dietary sources of nutriments and energy.
- Sugary foods should continue to be limited.
- Fried foods and high fat foods such as chips, pastry, fatty meat products and crisps should be limited or reserved only as occasional foods rather than for everyday. (The right fat is good, but not all fat is the right fat.)
- If children want to eat between meals they should be given milk, fruit, or bread: not sweets or fatty foods.

★ Even on a good diet not every child grows normally. Effective treatment means early treatment. **Child Growth** (page 642) has information.

Fibre and Young Children

There has been very little research on the right amount of fibre for a young child. What is known is that they need a balanced diet in order to get the full range of vitamins and minerals. For that they need to eat several different fruits and vegetables at some time in a week, and a whole grain cereal or wholemeal bread. Once they can cope with it, leave the skins on most fruit and vegetables: it saves you work and it does them good. That way they will get enough fibre anyway.

Addresses and suggestions for further reading are at the ends of chapters.

Food Fads

The great thing to remember is *never* to worry or fuss if a child refuses food. Otherwise it will learn to use food refusal to get attention.

If a child, of any age, dislikes a *new* food don't try to persuade it to eat it. Stop offering it that food at that meal, and *without fuss* offer something else – even if it is only milk. Don't offer the disliked food again for days, weeks, months or years – according to the age of the child. Children's palates change, what they loathe at a year they may love at 2.

If a child just goes off a familiar food let it. We do. But don't try to make something *nicer* to cajole it into eating. If you could turn down cod and get smoked salmon wouldn't you think you were onto a good thing? If it refuses something in a main course it can always fill itself up on everything else, and if it has had enough main course, doing without pudding will do no harm. Do this so that it's not *you* making the child go without food as a punishment but simply the child choosing not to eat, so it doesn't.

The lesson a child needs to learn is that it has a right to choose what it eats, and you are not going to try to push it about, by anger or persuasion. But it also needs to learn that it can't push you into cooking special things to pander to its likes and dislikes. This applies whether it is a toddler or considerably older.

Sometimes, children restrict their diets to quite bizarre combinations: one child I knew would only eat fish fingers and chocolate. If this happens the chances are that the child is enjoying your reaction. Behave as if you totally take its behaviour for granted and have *no* desire for it to change. This is much easier said than done. The following may help the situation.

- Let it have the food it wants, without comment, and don't even offer anything else.
- Talk to your doctor *without* your child, so he can reassure you that the lack of variety for a time won't harm it.
- Get the doctor to prescribe, or recommend, some vitamin and mineral tablets you can give the child so you *know* it is not going short of those. (Give similar suitable tablets to the whole family – then the child won't feel you are worried about it.)
- Don't let it overhear you saying you are worried or upset by its behaviour.
- If the child is old enough (even a 3-year-old can get something out of a cupboard), let it get as much of its own meal as it is able to. You can be busy making the other family food and just ask it to help you by doing its own. *Praise* the way it does it, and ask for its help next time. If it can manage (even badly), gradually shift the responsibility for its food away from you and onto the child. If the battle was really a power struggle you are putting the power to make what it wants into its own hands – and transferring your attention away. It also makes it easier for the child to sneak new foods into its diet without the loss of face involved in asking for them.

★ Milk is such convenient nourishment that it's a nuisance if young children go off it. If they liked it before and aren't allergic to it try simply adding safe food colouring. Sometimes they are just bored with white milk and green milk through a straw will be bolted down.

Unhealthy Food

There is a stage when children seem to crave the very foods which are least nourishing. You offer them gourmet cooking and they complain that they aren't having Bloggins Bursting Burgers. If they learnt to like good food when younger this is a phase. Let it ride. It will do no harm if some meals in a week would make a dietician weep.

Vegetarians and Vegans

In general, vegetarians need to be careful that their children eat enough high protein food (pulses and so on). Other vegetables and cereals are filling and a small child can become full on them without taking enough calories for normal growth. They should discuss their child's need with their doctor.

> People are not identical, nor are their needs. What follows is based on dietary reports by the medical profession, but it is not meant to be a substitute for discussing diet changes with your doctor, and following his or her recommendations. Major changes in diet should only be made with medical approval.

A HEALTHY DIET

The body needs energy, fibre, certain fats, about 10 vitamins and 20 minerals. If you eat when hungry you will get enough energy, so the question is how to get enough vitamins, minerals and fibre.

Having found out roughly how much we need of each I decided to construct the perfect diet. So I sat down with the latest scientific analyses and, after hours of arduous calculation, I had it. I'd hoped for a revelation. There was none. The list was precisely what my grandmother had always told me to eat – a little meat and fish, some dairy products and cereals, some vegetable oils and plenty of varied fresh fruit and vegetables. The good old balanced diet. The only modern touch was that added sugar and salt simply didn't appear because they contain nothing the body needs which it won't get from other sources.

The message for a healthy diet is: eat everything which is natural, eat it in varied ways so it tastes delicious – both raw and cooked if appropriate – and eat everything in moderation. The rest of this section is simply an explanation of why that is true. However, you are unlikely to get a balanced diet through eating a wide range of processed and manufactured foods. As I write I have ringing in my ears the words of one of the most noted authors on the subject of diet who, on hearing that I was writing about it, told me firmly, 'Don't tell them about nutrition; tell them about good food.'

Some people say a good diet is too expensive. It needn't be if you buy what is in season and keep to the cheaper cuts of meat and fish. In processed food you are always paying for the labour as well as the food: with fresh food you aren't. The real problem with a healthy diet isn't the cost, it's the rethinking.

Why Variety is Important

We tend to think of each food as adding to our total diet rather like pieces in a jigsaw puzzle. It isn't quite like that. Foods interact to make it easier (or occasionally harder) for the body to use the goodness in them. Some substances can't be used at all unless those from other foods are there. So, the more varied your diet, the better the chances of foods helping each other, and the maximum amount of goodness getting into the blood.

Variety is also good because vitamins and minerals are often absorbed better from one source than from another. So, for example, iron from meat is very well absorbed, but less than 5 per cent of the iron you eat in vegetables will get in your blood.

About Digestion

Before food can do us good it has to work its way through a series of extraction chambers.

1 Down the gullet from mouth to stomach is a 3-second chute.

2 Stomach juices containing an enzyme and hydrochloric acid then get to work on it.

3 How long food stays in the stomach varies with the emotional state of the eater and the type of food. Rice goes through fastest, fats and pasta go slowly: 2 to 4 hours is average.

4 Next it travels through the small intestine being bombarded with body chemicals to get the goodness out of it.

5 The goodness is absorbed through the walls of the intestine into the bloodstream, while the debris is shunted to the bowel.

The journey takes 1 to 7 days depending on what was eaten. A high fibre diet passes through fastest.

The 1856 *Enquire Within* recommended 'feeding' those who were ill with a nourishing enema of beef tea – which just shows how little the digestion was understood in those days. What a waste of good broth.

Indigestion

Indigestion happens when food isn't digested so it ferments, causing gas and discomfort. This can happen because of the nature of the food, or the nature of the eater. I believe there is also a wind-producing bacterium. But this is a personal theory which is totally unproved.

Calories You Need Each Day

Officially Britain has gone metric and works in kilojoules not calories. 1 calorie (also called a kilocalorie) = 4.2 kilojoules. A calorie is a measurement of the amount of energy food will provide.

The number of calories someone needs varies with the amount of energy they use and with their age, size, and sex, but this is how many calories the experts recommend for the average person on an average day.

Age	Girls	Boys	Age	Men	Women
1 yr	1100	1200	18 - 34 not active	2500	2000
2	1300	1400	18 - 34 fairly active	2900	2100
3-4	1500	1560	18 - 34 active	3350	2500
5-6	1680	1740	35 - 64 not active	2400	2000
7-8	1900	1980	35 - 64 fairly active	2750	2100
9-11	2050	2280	35 - 64 active	3350	2500
12-14	2150	2640	55 - 75 not active	2400	1900
15-17	2150	2880	75 + not active	2150	1680
			Pregnancy		2400
			Breast feeding		2750

What Foods Are Made Of

Carbohydrates

These are sugars and starches. Both provide energy, but any surplus is changed into body fat. We get starch from potatoes, rice, cereals, pulses (peas, dried beans) bread, biscuits, cakes, pasta.

Sugars include – glucose, fructose, lactose, sucrose and maltose. Any of those on a label is sugar by another name – so are corn syrup, and corn syrup solids. Sorbitol and mannitol are related to sugar but are absorbed more slowly, which makes them suitable for diabetics. But saccharine, aspartame and acesulfame K are not even related.

Sugar provides no vitamins or minerals. Even brown sugar, which is less refined, has only a trace of minerals. So, it isn't much better for you. Treacle and golden syrup contain iron and calcium, but not a lot.

Sugar encourages the bacteria which rot teeth and you get used to it and gradually add more and more – so building your calorie load (and probably your waistline too). It has been claimed that it increases the risk of appendicitis, heart disease and bowel cancer, but this is not certain.

The average person eats about 46 kg (100 lb) of sugar a year – about 110 g (4½ oz) a day. NACNE (National Advisory Committee on Nutrition Education) recommended halving this to about 20 kg (44 lb) a year. A BMA report recommends that sugar intake should be cut from 18 kg (40 lb), to 11 kg (24 lb) per person a year. That's about 4 teaspoonfuls a day. Easy if you eat fresh food, and give up sugar in tea and coffee, but very hard if you eat processed foods. Many processed foods are sugar-loaded. Even savoury foods such as tinned soup, ketchup, pickles, salad dressings and even peanut butter.

Addresses and suggestions for further reading are at the ends of chapters.

Fats and Oils

An old Dutch saying is:

Eat butter first, and eat it last
And live till a hundred years are past.

and, according to Paracelsus, the Greeks used to present newly weds with a 'pot of butter, which they esteem the foundation of their lives'. Today's newly weds might think it a less happy omen. But few foods are surrounded by more confusion and misinformation than fats and oils.

Since word got around that saturated fat could cause heart trouble the media story which has emerged is that butter and animal fats are saturated fats and therefore bad, while margarine and vegetable oils are unsaturated fats which are good. The truth is rather different and a recent survey showed that in trying to buy what is good for them many people are getting it wrong.

The animal versus vegetable distinction is not valid. Duck fat, for example has much *less* saturated fat than many brands of margarine, while coconut oil has *twice* as much saturated fat as butter. What's more, there aren't two types of fat, there are three: saturated, mono-unsaturated and polyunsaturated. All fats and oils contain all three types; it's the proportions which matter.

No two tables agree exactly. On margarine and animal fats I have used figures given by the Ministry of Agriculture, Fisheries and Food.

One study showed that out of 27 brands of margarine a quarter of them had more saturated fat than beef and half had more saturated fat than pork. It pays to read the labels.

> What are saturated fats? Essentially, it's a case of hydrogen strikes again – not the hydrogen bomb but the hydrogen bond. Fats are made of atoms bonded together. And the difference between saturated, mono-unsaturated and polyunsaturated fats lies in the number of hydrogen atoms which are bonded to the carbon atoms of the fat. The more hydrogen atoms are bonded in, the greater the hydrogen saturation is said to be. Hence saturated fats. The difference between monounsaturated and polyunsaturated is simply in the number of bonds which are used to hold the atoms together. Polyunsaturates are more firmly bonded.

How Saturated Is Your Food?

Fats and Oils	Satur %	Mono %	Poly %	Vit E mg per 100g
almond oil	5		95	
beef fat	41	47	4	
butter	68	23	4	
chicken fat	30	45	20	
coconut oil	89	8	2	1.6
corn oil (maize)	13	25	58	73.2
duck fat	29	57	13	
herring oil	22	56	20	
lamb fat	52	41	5	
lard	44	44	9	
mackerel	20	49	20	
margarine – hard	39	47	10	
margarine – soft	30	41	26	
margarine – 'polyunsaturated'	17	27	52	
olive oil	14	73	12	5.1
palm oil	45	45	9	78.5
peanut oil	15	53	30	37.0
pork fat	35	42	15	
rapeseed oil	4	24	25	57.6
salmon oil	27	42	26	
sardine oil	20	57	20	
sesame oil	14	40	43	
safflower	9	13	74	80.0
soya	14	24	60	95.8
sunflower	12	33	58	54.6
tuna oil	19	41	38	
turkey fat	36	27	34	
walnut oil	8	15	75	

Fat Intake Recommendations

The big dietary issue is, how much fat should we eat? In Britain the average person eats about 40 per cent of their daily calories as fat.

The government *Manual of Nutrition* suggests only taking 35 per cent of calories as fat. While the report by COMA (the Department of Health's Committee on Medical Aspects of Health) suggested no more than 33 per cent and NACNE recommended cutting it to no more than 30 per cent of total calories (10 per cent saturated fats, 20 per cent unsaturated fats).

The Case Against Fat

There is no doubt at all that fat is a high calorie food which makes it very easy to put on weight. And being overweight makes people more prone to a whole range of diseases. So there is a strong case for keeping the intake of fat moderate. And *all* fats are high in calories, whether saturated or unsaturated.

The argument against *saturated* fat concerns cholesterol. The body gets cholesterol in two ways: it takes it in through food, and it makes it in the liver. It looks as if saturated fat increases blood cholesterol levels, while eating polyunsaturated fats lowers it (monounsaturated fats have no effect either way).

Those who recommend lowering our fat intake believe that raised levels of cholesterol cause heart disease, and that reducing the nation's fat intake would reduce the toll taken by it. This is, however, not the open-and-shut case many people believe. In fact, there is a serious division in the ranks of both doctors and dieticians. Some eminent members of these professions question whether the evidence against saturated fat justifies the recommended cut-backs.

If the case is not proven, the question is – how can we hedge our bets until the scientists get it sorted out? The answer is surely to avoid going to extremes. If you eat a lot of saturated fat (see page 623) you may want to cut back, and/or substitute polyunsaturated fat for some of it (see page 623). If you eat almost no saturated fat you might consider increasing it slightly – in some studies in which saturated fats were sharply cut deaths from heart disease went down, but those from cancer went up. Paracelsus said, 'The dose makes the poison', and there can be a risk in taking anything in excess – even good advice. But if you start manipulating the fats in your diet you may like to consider the following:

● There is some evidence to suggest fish oils may protect against heart attacks.
● There is beginning to be evidence that vitamin E may help to protect against heart attacks. There is most vitamin E in whole grains, in certain cooking oils (see page 628) and in eggs.
● The seed oils contain 'essential fatty acids', which the body must have to work properly.
● Some experts say butter may be better for you than margarine. To make a consistent product, most margerines are filtered, bleached and deodorized, then emulsified, coloured and flavoured with an alarming variety of chemicals, then hydrogenated to make them become solid. So eating margarine is just adding yet more chemicals to the chemical load you are already carrying. They say that those who want to cut down on saturated fat should simply use less butter, and if necessary use unsaturated oil for more of their cooking.

There is growing evidence that most margerine may not be as good for you as you may think. In making it, processes are often used which convert the healthy unsaturated fats, such as sunflower oil, into hydrogenated fats. Some research suggests that hydrogenated fats may be bad for the arteries. So, if you are avoiding butter, look for the new breed of non-dairy spreads, such as Superspread, which say they contain *no* hydrogenated fat.

> Young children should not be put on a low fat diet (see page 620)

Fatty Delights

Food is for pleasure as well as nutrition and the individual virtues of the various fats and oils deserve more consideration than they get. They are not tasteless mediums for cooking in, as water is, each has its own special flavour which suits some dishes but not others. A simple carrot salad sprinkled with sesame oil can be excellent, anointed with corn oil it can be very unappealing; potatoes roasted in duck or beef fat are delicious, cooked in lard they are more ordinary. Equally, each has different keeping qualities and smoking points, and different properties as a cooking medium. If we are going to be eating less of them, there is a case for getting the most enjoyment out of what we do eat.

Fibre

Fibre is a carbohydrate which the body cannot break down and use, and until about 1969 most experts said fibre was useless. Then a doctor discovered that cancer of the bowel, and several other diseases, were almost unknown in parts of Africa where a high fibre diet was eaten. Research soon began to confirm that fibre could help prevent, or relieve, a whole range of conditions.

Fibre is whatever is toughest in a plant, often its skin but sometimes part of its flesh too. That is why high fibre food produces big soft stools which are easy to pass, but it does a great deal more than just prevent or cure constipation.

● By keeping the bowels moving high fibre stops one kind of bad breath.
● Increasing the amount of fibre *from pectins* – in apples and other fruit – lowers the levels of cholesterol in the blood.
● Increased fibre is recommended for diabetics.
● Those with healed duodenal ulcers may be less likely to have more if they eat a high-fibre diet.
● It has been suggested that speeding the passage of waste products through the colon lowers the chances of any harmful substances damaging, or being absorbed through, its walls.
● Fibre helps to prevent piles.
● Eating enough fibre may prevent diverticular disease. It also relieves it.

However:

● If you suddenly increase your fibre intake you may get wind and very loose stools until your body gets used to it; so a gradual change is better.
● Fibre reduces the absorption of certain minerals, such as calcium, iron and zinc. So the intake of these should be increased.
● As fibre holds water those who switch to high-fibre diet should drink more liquid.

How Much Fibre is Good

The average Britisher eats about 20 g a day. The recommended level is at least 30 g and Passmore and Eastwood (in their diet textbook, *Human Nutrition and Dietetics,*) say up to 50 g a day will do no harm. But they add: 'Enthusiasts who pour large quantities of bran on their food gain no benefit from the excess and expose themselves unnecessarily to hazards, known and perhaps unknown.'

The British Medical Association report, *Diet, Nutrition and Health,* says, 'Dietary fibre should be derived from [natural] foods and *not* [my italics] from either dietary fibre preparations or from foods to which fibres are specifically added.' It adds that fibre intake should be increased by eating more whole grain products.

Bran can reduce the body's ability to use other nutrients, especially when raw. But if you eat whole wheat which contains both bran and calcium the fact that bran lowers the percentage of calcium your body takes in should be balanced by the extra calcium the grain gives you.

Addresses and suggestions for further reading are at the ends of chapters.

★ A high fibre diet saves time: scrub potatoes don't peel them; don't peel cucumber; eat fresh fruit rather than puddings; and eat them with their skins on.

Fibre Content of Food

The list shows milligrams of fibre per 100 grams.

Food	Fibre mg per 100g
Dried apricots	24
Haricot beans	7
Dried figs	19
Spinach	6
Puffed wheat	15
Sweetcorn	5
Weetabix	13
Celeriac	5
Shredded wheat	12
Butter beans	5
Frozen peas	12
Broad beans	4
Wholemeal pasta	10
Broccoli tops	4
Blackcurrants – raw	8
Leeks	4
Muesli (typical)	7
Lentils	4
Raspberries	7
Blackberries	7
Oatmeal	7
Baked beans	7
Brown rice	varies
Wholemeal bread	varies

Some high bran cereals and cornflakes contain very large amounts of sodium and chloride (essentially salt). Compare the levels in these four cereals.

	Sodium	Chloride	Fibre per 100g
All bran	1670mg	2440 mg	26.7 g
Cornflakes	1160 mg	1780 mg	11 g
Puffed wheat	4 mg	50 mg	15 g
Shredded wheat	8 mg	53 mg	12 g

(Figures from McCance and Widdowson's *The Composition of Foods*, HMSO)

Protein

Protein is found in milk, eggs, meat, fish, cereals and pulses. The quality (i.e. usefulness) of any protein depends on its ability to supply the body with essential amino acids. As the various amino acids complement one another, and different proteins have these acids in different amounts, the best diet is one which combines several types of protein in a single day, or even a single meal, especially as the body has no way of storing them from day to day.

Just how these amino acids are used at different stages in the human life is still under research. But it is known that certain ones are needed for children to grow; that is why milk is an important food for young children (page 614).

Calcium in the Diet

The importance of calcium in the diet has only been recognized fairly recently. It is used in the functioning of muscles, nerves and certain hormones and enzymes but most of all in building bones. There are 4 possible stages to its use.

1 From birth to the age of 20 builds strong bones and teeth.
2 In adults it maintains the constant renewal of the bones.
3 When pregnant or breast feeding a woman needs calcium for two; if she eats too little the baby takes it from her bones.
4 From middle age onwards it is still needed to replace the bone structure, but the body is less efficient at absorbing it – especially in women.

Lack of calcium makes the bones slowly weaken, becoming more likely to break and much harder to mend. It can also make bones crumble – causing the painfully stooped backs of old age.

The body excretes large amounts of calcium daily and a healthy diet must put back more than is lost. It is also important that it is absorbed (see below).

People are now taking less calcium than they used to, possibly because of low fat diets. Those who cut down on fat should not give up milk, which is the richest and most usable form of calcium (see page 44). And, they should make sure they get enough vitamin D, and enough protein; both are needed for the calcium to be used by the body (see above).

Opinions vary as to just how much calcium we need. The levels recommended by the DH are among the lowest in the world, and some British experts feel they are far too low. In America they recommend about double the DH level. Lack of calcium causes osteoporosis (see page 548). The National Osteoporosis Society advises on calcium intake.

Recommended Daily Calcium Intake in mg

	DH	Other UK experts
children under 9	600	600-850
adolescents 9-14	700	1100
adolescents 15-17	600	1100
adult of 18+	500	800
pregnancy & breast feeding	1200	1000-1500
women over 40	500	1000-1500

Even the best figures cannot be exact. As with all the essential food elements, the amount which is taken up by the body is affected by whether the rest of the diet helps or hinders its absorption.

Factors Which Affect Calcium Absorption
Without vitamin D in the diet calcium cannot be absorbed properly. During middle age hormone changes in women make calcium absorption inefficient. So from then onwards women need to take more in order to put the same amount into the bones. The factors which help calcium absorption are vitamin D in sunlight, oily fish, eggs, liver, butter/margarine, yeast, unskimmed milk. Also, daily exercise of any kind and lactose in milk. The factors which hinder calcium absorption are smoking, alcohol, inactivity, uncooked bran, laxatives, coffee, lack of protein, some medication, hormone changes in middle-aged women.

Amounts of Calcium in a Typical Helping
milk (see page 44)

yoghurt	5 oz	270 mg
cottage cheese	4 oz	60 mg
hard cheeses (like cheddar)	1 oz	220 mg
sardines (with bones)	2 oz	220 mg
broccoli and other greens	4 oz	30-76 mg
beans (baked, butter etc)	4 oz	45 mg
peanuts, almonds, brazils	2 oz	34 mg
apricots, dates, figs (roughly) 2 oz		52 mg

N.B. 1 oz = 28.35 grams

★ It is sometimes claimed that too little calcium can cause period pains. Keeping calcium levels up could carry a bonus for those troubled by them.

The Role of Minerals

We seem to need about 20 different minerals: some we take in quantity; some have only a tiny trace in the diet (called trace elements). Only some of their roles and interactions are understood, but most are only needed in very small amounts and too much can be poisonous.

Minerals	Role	Major Sources
Calcium (Ca)		see above
Iron (Fe)	Making red blood cells which carry oxygen. Lack causes anaemia	Meat especially liver, eggs, apricots, pulses, wholemeal bread, spinach. Absorbed well from meat, poorly from vegetables
Magnesium (Mg)	Vital for all body cells, and the work of enzymes which create energy from food. Present in bones	Most foods, especially wholemeal bread, cheese, fish, vegetables, milk
Phosphorous (P)	Strengthens bones and teeth. Allows energy in food and vitamin B to be used	Plentiful in most foods. Deficiency unknown
Potassium (K)	Used in body cells. Vital for muscles (heart). Interacts with sodium	Most natural foods
Sodium (Na)	Keeps the body's water balance. Needed by muscles and nerves	Most foods, especially eggs, celery, milk, meat, fish
Trace Elements		
Chromium (Cr)	Probably enables the body to use glucose	Black pepper, liver, wholemeal bread
Cobalt (Co)	Needed for creating blood and maintaining nerve cells	Only used as part of vitamin B12 – page 628
Copper (Cu)	Enables body to use iron, needed for some enzymes to work	Liver, shellfish, meat, bread
Fluorine (F)	Strengthens teeth and bones	Tea, fish bones, water with fluoride
Iodine (I)	Vital for the thyroid gland	Sea food, milk, meat, eggs
Manganese (Mn)	Used in making bone and cartilage	Tea, nuts, spices, whole grains
Selenium (Se)	Needed by an enzyme in the blood	Fish, meat, cereals
Molybdenum (Mo)	May strengthen teeth and excess may cause gout	Plants
Zinc (Zn)	Wound healing, activity of many enzymes, DNA repair possibly appetite	Oysters, cheese, milk, beef, chicken, eggs, grains

Addresses and suggestions for further reading are at the ends of chapters.

Sodium and Chloride

Salt is sodium chloride, a combination of sodium and chlorine. Many doctors (though not all) think that people should limit their salt intake, and that too much salt can lead to high blood pressure. There is less agreement on what represents a suitable amount for an adult. A major committee in the United States opted for 3 g a day. A British Medical Association report recommends that we bring our average intake down from 12 g a day to 9 g.

The most compelling argument is surely that man did not evolve with a salt pot in his hands. So it would be logical to assume that the human body is geared to run well on naturally occurring salt rather than needing additions to food. Evidence suggests that some people are more vulnerable to excess salt than others – but no one can tell who is and who isn't.

In cutting down on salt the major step is to stop eating processed foods. Stick to fresh meat, fish and vegetables, fruit and frozen foods. High salt levels are not limited to food which you would expect to find salt in, such as crisps and bacon. Watch out for salt, sodium or chloride on the label.

> It may also be useful to keep up your potassium intake. Salt and potassium do a double act which controls the way the body uses water and it looks as if potassium may be able to counteract the effect of sodium.

Vitamins

I think ascorbic acid [vitamin C] is fundamental; it is involved in the simplest processes of which life is built.
Szent Gyorgyi, Nobel Prize winning researcher 1978

The more research is done on the substance, the more intriguing it appears. Thus there is a nagging suspicion that there is a very important use for the vitamin and we are just not smart enough to see it.
A. L. Tappel on vitamin E 1973 – and the mystery still exists

Vitamins are one of the great discoveries of this century but we are only beginning to understand what they do, and huge research projects are in progress to discover their roles in a whole range of diseases – especially cancer.

Very often their role is to enable some kind of food stuff to be converted into a form which the body can use. So the lack of certain vitamins can make the goodness in other foods unusable.

The big divide is between vitamins which dissolve in fat and those which dissolve in water.

Fat Soluble	Water Soluble
Vitamin A Vitamin D Vitamin E Vitamin K These are not easily destroyed but, as most can be stored in the body, there is risk of overdosing.	Vitamin C Vitamin B family These are destroyed by: long-cooking, alkali (*don't* put bicarb in cooking water), long storage, leaving food standing in water (e.g. peeled potatoes) too long.

As we don't totally understand what vitamins do, the recommended levels are very hazy. I have used British figures, unless only those from the USA were available. Every country sets recommended intakes, but no two countries agree on every one. For example, Sweden and Germany both recommend twice as much vitamin C as the British authorities suggest.

★ A survey in 1985 showed that 90 per cent of people have diets low in key vitamins and of iron.

★ To eat more salads made of really varied vegetables, and dress them with a little oil high in vitamin E would be a major step forward in any diet.

The Role of Vitamins and Adult Daily Requirements

The following chart gives the recommended daily amounts of vitamins for adults in either milligrams or micrograms. A microgram is one-thousandth of a milligram. But our needs vary during our life. Babies often need less of many vitamins and adolescents more. But all children need the vitamins which fresh food provides. The higher figures in the chart below usually apply to the young and/or active, especially males. The requirements of babies and children vary greatly with age and health so always check with your doctor before giving extra vitamins to your children. During breast feeding the vitamins a woman eats provide the baby with its vitamins too. So it is particularly important to have the whole range. More vitamins are needed when breast feeding than at any other time. The old need more fibre to prevent constipation, and more vitamin D if they don't spend so much time in the sun.

Vitamin	Normally	Pregnancy	Breast Feeding	Uses	Sources	Lost Through
Vitamin A Retinol (micrograms)	750	750	1200	Night vision, healthy skin, hair and mucus membranes. Can prevent cancer in animals — may do so in man. Excess can be poisonous.	Fish oils, liver*, kidney, dairy products, eggs, orange fruit and vegetables and dark-green vegetables. An average diet gives plenty.	High temperatures, light, air, copper or iron.

Vitamin	Normally	Pregnancy	Breast Feeding	Uses	Sources	Lost Through
Vitamin B1 Thiamin (milligrams)	0.8-1.3	1	1.1	Vital to the enzyme system and in breaking down carbohydrate into energy. Shortage may cause fatigue, irritability and anxiety. Excess excreted.	Many foods, especially grains, pork, peas, rice, potatoes, nuts, wheatgerm.	Heat, alkaline, leached in thawing. Absorption reduced by alcohol.
Vitamin B2 Riboflavin (milligrams)	1.3-1.6	1.6	1.8	Growth. Maintenance of various tissues. Lack gives tired 'gritty' eyes.	Liver*, kidney, dairy products, eggs, meat. Milk easily loses it in sunlight on a doorstep. Those on the pill need more, so do smokers and drinkers.	Light – 50% lost in two hours of sunlight.
Vitamin B Niacin Nicotinic Acid (milligrams)	15-18	18	21	Releases energy from food. Linked to lung enzymes. Lack causes severe skin conditions.	In many foods, especially liver*, kidney, meat, whole grains, pulses, brewers yeast, peanuts. Some forms in cereals need alkalis to become usable by the body e.g. bicarbonate.	
Vitamin B Folic Acid Folate Folacin (micrograms)	300-400	300-400	300-400	Assists cell division. Shortage causes anaemia. Surplus stored in liver.	In many foods especially liver*, broccoli, spinach, cabbage, runner beans, oranges, wholemeal bread, nuts, bananas.	Much lost in water and in long cooking.
Vitamin B6 Pyridoxine (milligrams)	2-2.2	2.6	2.6	Metabolism of amino acids from protein. Helps make red blood cells. Doses over 10 mg can be harmful.	In many foods especially meat, fish, eggs, grains and some vegetables.	Oral contraceptives reduce its uptake, so more may be needed.
Vitamin B12 (micrograms)	3	3	3	Cell division, especially in bone marrow. Lack causes anaemia. Maintains myelin coating in nervous system. Excess is stored in the liver.	Only occurs in meat, fish, eggs and dairy produce. Liver richest source (but see page 95). None in vegetables.	Dissolves in water. Heavy smokers (20 a day plus) need 40% more than non-smokers.
Vitamin C Ascorbic Acid (milligrams)	30	60	60	Present in all body tissues. Aids healing of skin and bone, may be needed for iron absorption. Vital for connective tissue. Stress and cold increase the need for it. Unknown role in adrenal gland and other functions not yet understood.	Almost entirely in fruit and vegetables especially blackcurrants, green peppers, sprouts, broccoli, mangoes, cauliflower. Deficiency not uncommon in Britain.	Very easily lost by storage, heat, cooking in water.
Vitamin D Cholecalciferol (micrograms)	sunlight	10	10	Vital for bones to grow and for calcium to be used to make them strong. Too little leads to bone softening and rickets. Too much is poisonous.	Fish liver oils, herrings, salmon, liver*, made by the skin in sunlight. Dark skins need more sunlight for this than pale skins.	
Vitamin E (milligrams)	8-10	8-10	8-10	Animals short of E show disorders in every system of the body. Role in man uncertain but probably key. May lessen risk of heart disease. Seems to lower blood cholesterol.	Vegetable oils especially wheat germ and sunflower, grains, eggs.	
Vitamin K (micrograms)	40	40	40	Makes blood clot. Too much can cause anaemia.	In most vegetables especially spinach, cabbage, cauliflower and our body can make it.	Antibiotics reduce Vitamin K production.
Pantothenic Acid (milligrams)	3-10	3-10	3-10	Releases energy from fat. Stops rats going grey but no evidence it does this in people.	Most foods, especially grains and pulses.	
Biotin (micrograms)	300	300	300	Lack causes fatigue, depression, nausea, loss of appetite and the skin becomes dry. Positive role not certain except for using fat.	Liver*, kidney, eggs.	

* Liver provides many vitamins but please see page 95 on its safe use.

Addresses and suggestions for further reading are at the ends of chapters.

Slimming

Extra weight puts a strain on the heart, and makes you far more prone to a whole range of diseases. However, medical opinion is against sudden crash diets. The more faddy and extreme the diet, the greater the risk that you will deprive yourself of vital nutrients without which your body will not be able to process even those you are getting, and such imbalances can make you seriously ill. If you do decide to keep your expansion within limits, talk to your doctor first.

Incentives to Dieting

To diet successfully the whole of your mind has to be doing it, if you need to convince one half of your mind that the other half is talking sense, here are some ways to do it.

1 Work out how much heavier you are than you ought to be, then fill a rucksack, or suitcase, with that amount of weight and carry it everywhere you go for a whole day.

2 Stand in front of a full-length mirror and take off your clothes little by little. At each stage look at yourself from the front, the back and the side in a good light.

3 Try on some garments from the time when you were your right weight.

4 Next, find yourself some incentive to keep at it. For example, buy a coveted garment one size too small.

Dieting Methods

Whatever anyone says, you can't change the way the body works. The easiest way is to think of it as a steam engine. Instead of shovelling coal into our steam engine we shovel in food. The body burns up the food to produce the power it needs to keep going, just as the steam engine burns coal. This is why food values are measured in calories – a calorie being a unit of energy.

Unfortunately, if it is given more fuel than it needs for the work in hand it stores it as fat, ready to be used on some other day when there is less fuel than the work demands. A great system in the days when primitive

Calories in Food per 100 g (4 oz)

Food	Cal	Food	Cal	Food	Cal
Bacon, grilled	393	Cabbage, raw	22	Pineapple, canned in juice	46
Beef, average cooked	225	Cabbage, boiled	15	Plums	32
Chicken with skin, roast	213	Carrots, boiled	23	Prunes, dried	161
Chicken (no skin), roast	148	Cauliflower, boiled	9	Raspberries	25
Duck with skin, roast	339	Celery	8	Rhubarb, cooked with sugar	45
Duck meat only, roast	189	Courgettes, raw	29	Strawberries	26
Fish – white, baked	77	Cucumber	10	Sultanas	250
Fish – white, fried	235	Leeks	24	Almonds	565
Fish – herrings	251	Lentils, cooked	99	Coconut, desiccated	604
Fish – trout	135	Lettuce	12	Peanuts	570
Ham	166	Mushrooms, raw	13	Biscuits – chocolate	524
Kidney – pigs', fried	202	Onions	23	Digestive	471
Lamb, roast	266	Parsnips	56	Bread – white	230
Liver – lambs', fried	237	Peas, frozen, boiled	72	Bread – wholemeal	215
Pâté, average	347	Peppers, green	14	Cake – rich fruit	322
Pork chop	332	Potatoes, boiled	76	Cake – chocolate with butter icing	500
Sausages – beef, cooked	267	Potatoes, chips	234	Jam tarts	368
Sausages – pork, cooked	317	Potatoes, roast	150	Porridge	374
Tongue	293	Spinach, boiled	30	Rice (approx)	350
Turkey with skin, roast	189	Sweetcorn, canned	85	Spaghetti (approx)	330
Brie	300	Sweet potato	91	Chocolate – milk	529
Cheddar cheese	406	Tomatoes, raw	14	Cocoa powder	312
Cottage cheese	96	Turnips, steamed	14	Coffee – instant powder	100
Cream – double	447	Watercress	14	Coffee – ground infused	3
Cream – single	195	Apples	46	Curry powder	325
Eggs, boiled	147	Apricots, dried	182	Drinking chocolate	366
Eggs, fried	232	Bananas	76	Honey	288
Yoghurt – low fat natural	65	Blackcurrants	28	Jam	262
Yoghurt – low fat fruit	89	Cherries	47	Ketchup	98
Custard	118	Dates, dried	248	Peanut butter	623
Butter	740	Figs, dried	213	Pickles – sweet	134
Lard	892	Grapes	63	Sugar – white	394
Margarine, average	730	Grapefruit	22	Tea	0
Oil for cooking, average	899	Mango	59	Beer	37
Aubergine	14	Melon	23	Spirits	222
Avocado pear	223	Oranges	35	Wine – typical white	89
Runner beans, boiled	19	Peaches	37	Cider – typical	43
Beetroot, boiled	44	Peaches, canned in syrup	87		
Brussels sprouts, boiled	18	Pears	41		

man never knew when the next elk would pass by; but a bore with a supermarket round the corner.

The good news is that eating less fuel than we need will force the body to draw the energy it needs from our fund of fat, and we will just as surely lose weight.

Whatever wrapping is put round them, these facts are central to the success of every diet ever invented.

The Calories You Need

Health experts recommend the following calorie levels for slimming.

Man: to lose 1 lb a week eat only 2,300 calories a day
        to lose 2 lb a week eat only 1,700 calories a day
Woman: to lose 1 lb a week eat only 1,500 calories a day
        to lose 2 lb a week eat only 1,000 calories a day

That weight loss of 1 to 2 lb a week may not sound dramatic, but if you diet gradually you change your eating habits and the weight is more likely to *stay* off.

The Snags of the High Fat Diet

Because calories are what count you can diet on *anything* – beer, cream cakes, doughnuts, baked beans, chocolate, cheese, coconuts, cabbages – or even, if you're a cannibal, kings. But there are snags to dieting on high calorie foods. First, you may lack vital vitamins and minerals needed for health (so you may look and feel lack-lustre). Second, the higher the calories of any food, the *less* you must eat to keep below your fuel needs. So it takes a great deal of self-control. For example: to take in 1,000 calories you could eat just:

> 4½ oz (125 g) cream cheese *or*
> 2½ buttered crumpets *or*
> 5½ oz (160 g) milk and nut chocolate *or*
> 8 rich biscuits *or*
> 2 lb (1 kg) smoked haddock *or*
> 12 cucumbers *or* 14 oranges
> 16 apples *or* 16 lettuces

On half that amount of fish in a day, plus lettuce and cucumber salad, you would be amply full, but on 2½ crumpets you'd be decidedly peckish.

The figures in the table on page 629 were taken both from the Ministry of Agriculture Fisheries and Food **Manual of Nutrition** and from the 4th revised edition of McCance and Widdowson's **The Composition of Foods** (HMSO).

The No-Diet Diet

If you normally eat a very well-balanced diet then the best way to lose weight is probably to eat slightly less of everything, and little by little the weight should come off. Try to get up from every meal feeling slightly hungry.

However, it may be easiest to diet by changing your eating pattern entirely and only eating low calorie foods, so you can create feasts and still lose those pounds.

The Diet That's a Feast

If you look at the calorie list on page 614 you'll see you can eat a vast amount of vegetables before you begin to approach your calorie limit. They don't have to be raw, but the best feast of all is raw vegetables because they take time to eat and bulk out the stomach, leaving you feeling nice and full for some time afterwards. So try a salad diet. The salads I'm talking about are delicious concoctions of every vegetable imaginable. Avoid the higher calorie salad items like avocados and tomatoes.

For dressing use freshly ground black pepper, a sprinkling of Maldon sea salt and some lemon juice or plain low fat yoghurt.

The Whole Meal

After your salad have a smallish portion of grilled or roasted meat or fish, or any plain protein that the rest of the household is having, provided it isn't fried or fatty. If you feel like something sweet afterwards make it a piece of raw fruit with no extra sugar.

For the rest of the day allocate yourself 2 slices of wholemeal bread, and half a pint of skimmed milk. Have no sugar, and avoid alcohol, squashes, mixers and fresh fruit juice – all packed with calories.

> Even with half a pint of milk a day you may run low in calcium. Ask your doctor whether you should take calcium tablets.

★ If you are a nibbler choose some vegetables you like eating raw – such as celery or carrots and prepare a bag of them in the morning.

Keeping Up the Burn

Only keep to a strict diet for three days. Then have two days of eating normal meals in smaller quantities than usual, so you neither lose nor gain. (This means keeping off sweet snacks and drinks.) Then go back on the diet for three days more – and so on. Research has shown that when the body is short of food for any length of time it changes into a different 'gear' and learns to make far better use of what it is given. So, if you diet hard without a break, it actually makes it harder to lose weight.

Weighing Yourself

It's hard to lose weight unless you have scales to show you the pounds you are shedding. I find by far the most effective are the new electronic ones which allow no self-deception in unambiguous dulcet tones, 'Your weight is 19 stone 3 pounds' – or whatever it happens to be. Weigh yourself at the same time of day each time and wear exactly the same clothes, if you can't be naked.

★ Take a long hot or cold calorie-free drink.

★ Chart your drop in weight day by day, but don't expect it to drop evenly *every* day. It is normal to have slight ups and plateaus, as well as downs.

★ Never have serving dishes on the table while eating.

★ Carry that loaded suitcase mentioned on page 629 whenever you feel yourself weakening.

Addresses and suggestions for further reading are at the ends of chapters.

★ *Most important of all:* if you break your diet don't feel a failure and give up totally. A slip is a slip, accept that you are human and get on with dieting from that point on.

★ Never eat while standing up.

★ Only let yourself eat in one room of the house.

DENTAL HEALTH

Children's First Teeth

A child's first teeth are already in the jaw bone at birth. The first tooth cuts through at about 6 months – some sooner, some later. The other 19 will appear before the child is three.

The order in which Teeth usually Appear

Children often become fretful and flushed. Rubbing the bump where the tooth is coming through with a clean finger usually helps a lot. Teething rings also help, especially those filled with liquid, which can be refrigerated to soothe with coldness. But don't put all problems down to teething. It should never make the child ill. And *don't* comfort the child between meals with a sweetened drink – not even if it has 'health drink' written on the bottle. Any sweetness in a bottle just encourages the bacteria which are waiting to eat into the baby's lovely new teeth. The same goes for sweetened comforters.

Children's Second Teeth
The second teeth usually start coming through when the child is 5 to 7 years old and they keep on coming until adulthood.

Cleaning the Teeth
The time to start brushing is when the first tooth comes through. The sooner you start, the sooner the baby gets used to it. Use a soft, very small toothbrush with the child on your lap and its head cradled in your arm. Brush up and down rather than across the teeth, and do the inside surface as well as the outside. Until it is old enough to spit do without toothpaste, but use fluoride toothpaste when you can, and clean the teeth twice a day from then on – especially last thing at night. Once the teeth have been cleaned the child should not have food,

drinks (apart from water) or liquid medicine, as they will all give the tooth decay bacteria a new feast to work on during the night.

Until the age of 8 or so children aren't thorough enough to do their teeth alone. When they do take over the job, occasionally use a disclosing tablet (most chemists sell them) which will (briefly) stain any badly cleaned patches a lurid colour and show a child which bits they haven't cleaned. Children usually find it fascinating and it is much easier than just nagging.

★ If you are ever out of toothpaste, salt makes a very good substitute.

Decay

Teeth decay when bacteria which live in a thin coating of plaque on the teeth have a chance to feed on sugar and change it into acid. The acid then dissolves the teeth. Each time we eat or drink something sweet the bacteria create acid for about one hour afterwards. So a child who eats about one sweet every hour bathes his or her teeth in acid for a whole day, and children's teeth are especially vulnerable.

Dental Checks

The first dental check is needed at about 2 to 2½ years old. However much you hate dental treatment yourself, don't let the child know. Say the dentist is going to count the child's new teeth – and tell the dentist, in front of the child. Then the dentist can take your cue.

How often dental checks are needed varies with the person, and dentists themselves are not totally agreed. But a child or teenager usually needs a check-up every 6 months, and an adult once a year.

Gum Disease – Gingivitis and Periodontis (*pyorrhoea*)

Most adults have gum disease to some degree, and more teeth are lost because of it than from any other condition. The cause is a sticky film of bacteria forming on the teeth. This attacks the junction between teeth and gums. The rim of the gums then loosens, making access easier for the bacteria, and providing a pocket for food debris. Finally the bacteria attack the bone holding the teeth in place.

> Warning signs: a coating you can see or feel on the teeth; red or swollen gums; bleeding from the gums on brushing them; pain or soreness; a certain type of bad breath.

Prevent it by very thorough brushing, at least once a day, and by cleaning between the teeth with dental floss and/or special soft wood sticks such as 'Interdens', plus regular dental checks and descaling. For plaque which is left on the teeth hardens into calculus (tartar) which is hard to remove. Pregnancy and certain illnesses lower resistance to gum trouble, so more frequent checks are necessary, but I am assured that it is not infectious. So the kissing doesn't have to stop.

> If a child's tooth is knocked out act fast – you may be able to save it. Rinse any dirt off it in lukewarm water swiftly and pop it in the pocket of your cheek (or get the owner to do that if she or he is old enough not to swallow it). It has to be kept moist and at mouth temperature and teeth don't mind alien saliva. Get the tooth and its owner to a dentist in 1 to 2 hours. If the root isn't fully adult it should be possible to put it back.

Orthodontics

Teeth can be crooked or badly placed for a lot of reasons. Orthodontics is the work of persuading the teeth to move into better positions. It used to be thought that orthodontic work couldn't be done in adulthood, but in America women in their thirties are to be seen in braces – and with beautifully straight teeth afterwards. But it is quicker and easier when done in childhood: talk to a dentist about it as soon as you see the teeth aren't looking good.

This treatment is available on the NHS provided the dentist feels it is clinically necessary, and there is no hard and fast definition of what 'clinically necessary' means.

★ To deal with bleeding after a tooth extraction rinse the mouth with a solution of a dessertspoonful of salt in a tumbler of warm water. This cleans the socket and removes the taste of blood without interfering with the natural healing.

★ If the jaw aches after an extraction wrap an ice cube in a handkerchief and press it to the cheek. The cold both numbs the pain and reduces any bruising.

LOOKING AFTER THE FACE AND BODY

Skin and body care are often looked upon as mere fripperies. Some people certainly get through life perfectly well without ever introducing their skin to anything more cosmetic than a bar of soap. That, however, does not suit everyone and it has been discovered that looking good contributes far more to someone's sense of well-being than has been appreciated. This means that when people feel that they look good they are more likely to look after their health and even to recover more quickly from illness. So beauty and relaxation are, in their own ways, important factors in health.

The Body

Beauty care starts at the toes, not at the neck. After all, it's the people we really care about who see the whole of us. Even if we aren't all shaped like Marilyn Monroe or Robert Redford the surface can at least be good to touch.

Rough Dry Skin

Few people have skin as smooth as a baby's, but there are plenty of cures for the roughness which adults are heirs to.

A long-term solution to dryness is to rub liquid paraffin (the laxative from a chemist, not the kind used for fires) all over the body before getting into a bath. Let your skin absorb the oil in the heat of the bath for a while before washing in the usual way. Do this at each bath when the skin is dry, or several times a week when it isn't. It can produce velvety results, especially if you combine it with the bumpy skin prevention below. But to clean the bath you will need the method on page 157.

> *Don't* oil the soles of the feet or use oil before showering – you could slip.

Bumpy Skin

I'm not talking here about the under-the-skin bumps of cellulite but about the goose-pimple bumps *on* the skin. To prevent them, wash with a loofah at each bath. But, if you already have bumps, set to work with soap and a pumice stone. They won't vanish in one go, but a week or two should cure them. After the bath smooth on skin lotion.

Scars

Rubbing vitamin E cream on potential scars has long been said to be a cure. Doctors now say that it's the rubbing – and not the vitamin – which stimulates the skin to heal better. It is a technique well worth using if a scar might form.

Stretch Marks

Stretch marks can occur anywhere that the skin is stretched by excess weight, and cannot be removed. The most annoying are those across the stomach as a result of pregnancy. As they are partly caused by hormone changes people dispute whether they can be prevented. I think that it's certainly worth a try. Avoid excessive weight gain, cut out salt to keep down the fluid gain, and start preventive measures on the skin. Stretch marks occur more easily on dry skin, so give any area which is liable to be stretched a daily massage with a rich hand or body lotion such as one based on cocoa butter. To this add a little wheatgerm oil, as the vitamin E it contains seems to help skin to renew itself.

Broken Veins

When fine spiders' webs of broken veins appear on the legs, as part of the early stages of varicose veins, they can be removed by injections – though NHS doctors are unlikely to bother with this cosmetic treatment.

A small spider of blood vessels on the face is called a naevus and it can usually be removed permanently.

Addresses and suggestions for further reading are at the ends of chapters.

Face Facts

It may sound a curious thing to say, but the most important thing about making-up is getting to know your face. You may think you know what you look like, but very few of us really do.

A face is like a river, always the same and yet always changing: our health, our moods, our diet and the amount of sleep we get are reflected in it, as surely as clouds in water. So we each have many faces, not one.

A shade of lipstick or eyeshadow which looks wonderful on Monday can be a disaster on Tuesday after a late night. To look her best every woman needs to take a few moments to *look honestly* at her face as it is *that day*.

The other factors in looking good are diet, exercise and skin care. Unless we get all four right we are painting make-up on to a badly prepared canvas and it will show. But if you decide to eat better, sleep more and revise your beauty routines don't expect your face to be like new the next morning. Skin is remade from the bottom layers upwards, to replace what flakes off the top. It will take *at least* three weeks before those layers reach the surface and show even the first sign of improvement.

Sleep and Diet

It is only during sleep that our body can give its undivided attention to feeding and remaking the cells of our skin. Of course, it will make new skin cells whatever happens, but somehow they don't seem to look as good.

How much sleep is enough varies from person to person. You can only let your body guide you, but if you've become used to very little, yet feel tired, you will need to re-educate it little by little.

Diet is also important. The body will chug along on almost any food. But it needs a whole complex of vitamins and minerals to work at its best. Nobody should expect to stay looking good on a poor diet any more than they would expect to get the best out of a Rolls Royce if they ran it on 2-star petrol.

Smoking and alcohol both affect the amount of vitamins which are available for skin renewal. By tightening the fine blood vessels smoking also reduces the amount of oxygen which reaches the surface of the body, so making it function less well. As a result smokers have sallower, spottier skins than non-smokers and develop lines measurably sooner. Alcohol gives skin a coarser, slacker texture and can produce the venous and swollen nose of the heavy drinker on either sex.

Cleansing

Make-up is best removed with a cream cleanser – which will remove both dirt and make-up. Whether it's basic cold cream or the most expensive cleanser, it will do the same job. Apply it with upward strokes (gravity pulls the face down quite enough without us helping it) and massage it into the make-up. Then remove it with clean cotton wool and repeat. It's amazing how much comes off the second time.

★ If you want to feel extra fresh you can now splash your face with warm water. Those with a high colour should avoid using very cold or very hot water on the face; either will increase the

problem. So will temperature extremes in sauna and steam baths, or skin tonics with alcohol in them.

If You Have to Wash

If soap upsets your skin you can use a soap-free washing cream. The big cosmetic companies make expensive ones but you can wash just as well with emulsifying ointment which is a fraction of the price. Dermatologists recommend it for people who can't take soap – such as those with eczema – so the pharmaceutical counter of most chemists will produce it if you ask. It's a thick cream which you apply to a wet face, lather up like soap and rinse off. It leaves the face feeling perfectly clean but with none of the dryness of soap.

Open Pores

For an oily skin, with no tendency to broken veins, put boiling water in a bowl in a wash basin, and lean over it with a towel over your head so all the steam is trapped under it. When the face is thoroughly hot and the pores are open any blackheads can be very gently pressed out *with well scrubbed fingers*. Then wipe a slice of lemon all over the open pores and leave it to dry. Finally rinse the face with tepid water.

Face Packs

Face packs can be as varied as cakes – and contain many of the same ingredients. A pack by any good cosmetic company will do the job, and the ones which peel off afterwards are appealing, but you can easily cleanse and tighten the skin by applying simple home-made mixtures provided you remember the rule that anything which disagrees with you as a food is likely to disagree with your skin too, and that food put on you should be as fresh as food put *in* you.

For cleansing and tightening use a mixture of plain yoghurt and Fullers Earth (from a chemist) – the earth absorbs the grease while the yoghurt nourishes and tightens. One famous French beauty of the last century swore by a mixture of strawberries and cream – without the sugar, of course. This does have a tendency to slide off the face unless you keep very still, but the astringency of strawberries certainly tightens the skin and refreshes it.

Whatever the pack, rinse it off with very cool water and pat dry.

★ If you go swimming both salt and chlorine are equally bad for the skin. Rinse them off with cool water and cleanse, tone and moisturize the skin as soon as possible afterwards.

Exfoliation

Exfoliation is a smart word for removing the top layers of skin. You can buy washing grains which are just rough enough to rub off rather more of the surface than washing would remove. These can be excellent for skin. But most are not for fine dry skin.

There are also more drastic forms of exfoliation which go as far as peeling the upper layer of skin off with chemicals. It is said that this allows new young skin to grow. Anyone who is considering such harsh treatment would do well to discuss it with more than one beauty therapist.

Toning

You might think that the best toning lotion you could get would be a gleaming bottle from a big cosmetic company. Not so. Many branded ones contain alcohol which is positively bad for sensitive skins, especially black skins, very fair Celtic skins and those with a high colour. But you can tone with cosmetic rosewater from a pharmacy counter. Use the rosewater neat or mix it with witch hazel (which is a mild odourless antiseptic extracted from a shrub). For a normal skin try one spoonful of witch hazel to three of rosewater. The witch hazel is especially good for greasy skins and those with a tendency to spottiness, so for that type of skin increase the proportion of witch hazel – but don't expect it to scotch full-blown acne.

For dry skins add a little glycerine (also from a pharmacy), as glycerine has the ability to hold moisture in the skin. Suit the proportions to your skin.

Nourishing

Just how much skin can or cannot be fed is debatable, but it is certainly worth applying an oil or cream at night – at worst it will protect it from the drying effect of the atmosphere. To feed your skin you don't need to confront your nearest and dearest with a face like a lard bag. A rich moisturizer which sinks invisibly into the skin is all you need or, better still, use a vitamin A or vitamin E cream or oil. Both vitamins are said to help the skin restore itself. Do include your neck; it too is exposed to the elements. The old saying is, 'A woman is as old as her hands and her neck', and in these face-lifting times it was never truer.

Moisturizer

The face, neck and hands are the only parts of our bodies we expose to the elements day in day out. And if they can take the water out of clothes on a washing line they must be doing just the same to the skin. Of course, some people who never use moisturizer reach old age none the worse for the lack of it – but no one can know how their skin will weather, until it's too late. So if you don't want to end up looking like a Cox's Orange Pippin apple after long storage you should wear moisturizer on your face and neck every day, whether or not you use other make-up.

The effectiveness of different moisturizers *may* be related to the price, but if any cream could be scientifically proved to be much more effective than all the rest the fact would be advertised in bold letters on its packing and splashed across the women's press: that hasn't happened. So buy whatever suits you.

Moisturizer and Sun Block

There is now ample scientific evidence that sun is bad for skin. It creates what are called 'free radicals' – skin saboteurs which damage it internally, speeding up the skin's ageing and reducing its bounce and elasticity. In fact, strong sunlight hitting the skin is equivalent to a classroom of schoolchildren jumping on a sprung mattress. Worse still, sunlight affects the cell's biochemistry and causes skin cancer. Even among the British, who get little strong sun apart from summer holidays, the incidence of skin cancer is rising dramatically in the generations who have sunbathed. In summer sunshine your moisturizer should contain a total sun block. See also page 563.

Concealer

One make-up artist who teaches the general public says concealer is the most under-used make-up of all. It's a very dense form of foundation which you apply to small areas where something needs to be blotted out. It works equally well on spots, blemishes and on shadows under the eyes, and lightens the effect of long lines bracketing the sides of a mouth. Choose one slightly lighter than your skin, and towards beige rather than pink. Apply it with a fine brush, working it to nothing at the edges. Properly blended in it should be invisible. It can be used with or without foundation – and more men use concealers than you might think. (For covering major marks see Cosmetic camouflage, page 637.)

★ Be very careful how you apply it if you have bags under your eyes. If you put it *on* the bags it will highlight them and make them look bigger. It must only go on the shadow *under* the bag.

Foundation

If nature didn't give you a perfect complexion having the correct foundation correctly applied is *the* most important part of make-up. If it isn't right you won't look good whatever else you do.

Choosing Foundation

Whatever the publicity machines of the big cosmetic companies imply, foundation should be the same colour as your skin: keep changing it to suit fashion and you risk looking like a doll with its neck a different colour. That doesn't mean there is only one shade which is right; hardly any make-up is *exactly* the colour of skin. So there will be several similar shades which look like your skin when you apply them – and some may be more flattering than others. You may even find that to get a good match you need to mix two together. They usually mix best if they are the same type – both liquid or both block – but they don't need to be the same brand.

When looking for the right shade the golden rule is not to be fooled by the lights in the shop where you buy it.

Only buy what looks good in *daylight*, and buy one that is no heavier than is necessary. A good foundation looks and feels light but gives as much coverage as you personally need. And there *are* foundations which block out even the reddest veins yet look natural – they just take a bit of finding.

★ If you can't face shopping for foundation with no make-up on get several of the little plastic cylinders which camera film comes in (photographic counters usually have empties) and ask the sales girls to put a test dab of the foundations you like in each so you can take it home to try. But do label them as the dabs go in or you'll be none the wiser.

Addresses and suggestions for further reading are at the ends of chapters.

Applying Foundation

No professional make-up artist would dream of applying foundation with anything except a moist sponge – and it really does give much the best finish. Wet the sponge and then squeeze it *very* hard in a tissue to remove all the excess water. Apply the foundation with it, working from the middle of the face outwards. If you have a good skin you can even use it simply to cover small blemishes or excess rosiness; it doesn't have to be wall to wall – provided nobody can spot where it ends. Don't forget the neck. Foundation needs to shade to nothing under the jaw line.

★ To take a little foundation down the upper part of the neck without it showing and to blend it away to nothing, mix a little with your moisturizer as you apply it.

Powder

Fashions for powder come and go. Its great advantage is that it helps foundation to stay on. So, if powder isn't out of fashion use it. Unless you have very dark skin, choose a colourless translucent powder. (For films, television or photography beware of those with a sparkle – they can make you look as if you are sweating.) Take some on a clean puff, knock the surplus off on your hand and then apply it all over, pressing it lightly into the foundation – but not dragging at it. Then brush off every loose particle with a big soft brush.

★ Some make-up artists say older women with fine lines under the eyes should avoid powdering this area at all; others say the big secret is to brush every extra atom out of the creases – it may depend on the powder. So, if time has added a tracery, try both ways and see what suits you.

Blusher

Blusher tends to be over-used or not used at all. The point about blusher is that red creates optical illusions. When I learnt theatrical make-up, from a splendid old pro, he showed us how colouring something red makes it seem more prominent than it would be if it were flesh colour. (This is one reason why the Chinese, who have none of the rosiness of Europeans, seem to have flatter faces.) So by putting a redder tone on the cheekbones, we make the bone structure seem stronger and more prominent. This adds essential definition to a face, but needs a light hand or it creates a clownish look.

Blusher should never be a feature *of* the face, it should only bring out the features *in* the face. So choose a blusher only a few shades darker than your skin tone. Take some up on a large brush – use the sort that looks like an artist's brush but with a very big head. Brush most of it off on the back of your hand, and smile. Then apply it to the outer part of the bulge, working it very lightly in a pear shape, along the cheekbone, to *slightly* wider than the eyes.

★ If you put too much on blot it and powder over to kill the colour.

★ If you aren't wearing foundation, powder the area before applying blusher or it will cling too brightly on any oily patches.

Eyes

Most people regard eye shadow as eye colouring, look for a 'pretty colour' and apply it. There is more to it than that. In fact, there are two totally different aspects to using eye make-up – eye shaping and eye colouring. And the first is the most important.

Eye Shaping

Most eyes are a fairly similar shape and size. Where they differ greatly is in the shape of the sockets. So the object of eye shaping is to use light and shadow to sculpt the area around the eyes, improving the shape and concealing any faults. To do this you don't need dramatic colours; in fact, it is much easier to work with milk chocolate tones, or browny-grey ones, and these suit almost any eye colour. Use a fairly fine brush, rather than the applicators the cosmetic houses supply.

Big eyes are almost always beautiful, and the illusion of size can be created by having enough space between the brows and the lashes. To make this area seem larger apply a highlighter to the bone just under the outer half of the eyebrows. Or apply a light eye make-up base over the whole lid and up to the eyebrows – a good base does double duty by helping the eyeshadow to stay on and prevent it creasing.

Once you have created the space you can begin to shape the eye with light and shadow. There are no fixed rules for how to do this, but with most eyes the aim is to make them look bigger and wider than they really are. So avoid shading heavily near the nose or you will make them seem closer together. Try to imagine your ideal eye and how the shadow would fall on it, and try painting those shadows on your lids. Then imagine where the highlights would come and paint those on. Finally blend the edges of the light and shadow together so nobody would know where either began or ended. Few people's eyes are symmetrical so don't try to apply the shading in exactly the same way on both eyes. Instead, look at them from a slight distance and shade them to *look* the same.

★ If you find it hard try reversing the process. Imagine you are trying to make yourself up for a stage part in which you have to look old, or tired, or ugly. Then make-up for that part. You will discover what you *mustn't* do and from there it is far easier to see what should be done.

Once you have the eyes shaped you can decide whether or not to use a colour. If you do, don't apply one colour all over or you will kill the effect you have just created. Instead use touches of several colours, which blend well, to recreate the basic shading.

The tones should be chosen to go with your skin shade, and with the lipstick you plan to wear. Olive tone skins look great with lipsticks which lean towards coppery tones, and with brown, golden or sludgy green eyeshadow. Pinker toned skins look better with pinker toned lipsticks, and eye-shadows in greys, silver, light gold and certain blues (though blue is much harder to wear than grey). Seductive as glittery shadows may be, flat colours are far easier for most people to wear.

If you are lucky enough to have a mid-toned skin you

may be able to lean either way – wearing blues and greens, greys and browns with equal success. But most people have a smaller range of shades which really show them off at their best.

The young can use spectacular colours with great effect – if they apply them well – but, unfortunately, spectacular colours get harder to wear with every year. Basically a face is a very small place, and it doesn't look its best when it's too ornamented. We may not think of lines as ornamental but each one adds a new 'busyness' to the face, until there comes a point where quite enough is happening in it without bright colours as well.

★ If you want a slightly dramatic look at times when eyeliner is out of style try using a *very* fine brush to put minute dots of liquid liner right in the base of the eyelashes. The dots should be invisible, but the eyes should have an extra something.

Eyebrows

The face has two frames – the hair and the eyebrows. The hair frames the whole face but it is the eyebrows which frame its most important feature – the eyes. If the eyebrows aren't right the picture just isn't set off properly. It is currently fashionable to leave the eyebrows looking unplucked and have them brushed away from the eyes but slightly shaggy. Fine, if it suits you – and thin highly plucked brows now look ridiculous – but most eyes have less space between them and the brows than is ideal. So a *little* judicious plucking *under* the brows at the outer half opens up the eyes and makes them seem much larger. Eyebrows can be shaggy but still have a defined shape, and hairs growing down the lid do nothing for anyone.

The best way of darkening the eyebrows isn't to use an eyebrow pencil because, being hard, it forces you to draw on the skin. A far more natural effect is achieved by brushing a little block mascara onto the hairs of the eyebrows, or by using a soft eyeshadow to colour them – an eyeshadow pencil is ideal. Avoid black, unless you are genuinely raven-haired; a soft brown gives as much definition and looks more natural. Finally comb the hairs away from the eyes, and – if you don't want a shaggy look – smooth the comb along the upper edge.

Mascara

Mascara should be the last item of make-up you apply. There are basically two kinds – one kind smudges when wet, the other smudges on oil. (There is also a third kind, which manufacturers don't admit to, which smudges whatever you do.) When using the oil-smudge type avoid taking moisturizer and foundation close up to the eyes. To apply mascara neatly just pull your chin in and hold the mirror high while doing the under lashes. Then tilt your head back and hold the mirror down for the upper ones. Brush it on in the direction the lashes grow – a sideways movement will make them clump together and, as Raymond Chandler put it, look 'like miniature iron railings'. For a thicker effect without iron railings apply mascara lightly to both sides of the upper lashes. If any do clump together comb them apart with a tiny eyelash comb before the mascara dries.

Tired or Sore Eyes

Two easily made eye-packs are slices of cucumber or cold tea bags (old used ones which have been in the refrigerator). However, I'm told tea may not suit some skins – and if it doesn't suit yours don't use it. Whatever you use, lie down and relax (see page 640). If your eyes are tired the rest of you probably is too.

Lips

It's easy to envy the model girls their lovely mouths. The truth is most of them don't have them. They simply redraw the lines to achieve perfection, and anyone can do the same. Vast changes in outline look silly on the young and only create the look of an ageing vamp on an older woman: but you don't need vast changes. It's amazing how much difference can be made by drawing the lips *slightly* fuller or narrower or curvier than nature intended. Experiment in private; it's a skill which takes practice but it's well worth practising.

★ Keep soft lip and eye liners in the refrigerator for a while before sharpening them, then they will break less easily.

If you use foundation take it right over the lips, so you have a blank canvas to start on. Hold the mirror so you can see your entire face and imagine your ideal mouth. Then see how close you can get to it without it being obvious. It needs to be a combination of the mouth you have, the mouth which would best suit your other features and the mouth which is in fashion – for mouth shapes do change. Start with a lip pencil and only fill in with lipstick when the outline is right.

★ To check whether the upper lip line is even on both sides pull your chin in and hold the mirror above the mouth. To check the bottom lip line do the reverse – stick your chin out and hold the mirror low.

To be unobtrusive the lip pencil can match the lipstick. But if very pale lipsticks are in vogue, using a slightly darker liner can prevent that vague amorphous look which pale lipstick gives. If you want a more dramatic mouth a darker liner can be used with a medium-toned lipstick. Equally, by night or for photographs, I have seen a paler liner or even a *minute* line lighter than the foundation used to give the illusion of a strong lip angle. But be careful with this or it can look decidedly odd. Whatever the shade, blot the pencil before applying the lipstick.

★ To prevent lipstick creeping into any, otherwise invisible, lines in the upper lip: outline the lips with lip pencil, blot with tissue. Powder over the line. Brush off the excess powder, and apply the lipstick keeping just *inside* the lip line. This works better than most special products designed to stop lipstick creeping – and it costs nothing.

The Shades of Lipstick

Different shades of lipstick can make an enormous difference to the look of a mouth. Nothing makes a small mouth look smaller and meaner than a really dark lipstick, whereas the same mouth with a lighter tone can look a perfectly normal size. In the same way big mouths can look like cushions when painted pale pink.

Addresses and suggestions for further reading are at the ends of chapters.

There is also the matter of age. The very young and beautiful can get away with almost any shade – but the rest of the population needs to be wary of extremes. Very pale tones can look too baby-doll after a certain age and dark tones are hard and ageing. This doesn't mean the over-25s have to ignore fashionable colours. When deeper tones are in fashion they can be softened by applying a light shade first, then the dark one, and finishing with a glosser. Then the darkness has some life to it. When very pale tones are 'in' you can do the reverse and put a mid-tone underneath.

★ When buying lipstick try the shades out on the pads of your fingers. They are pinker than the back of your hand and you will get a better idea of how it will look on your lips.

★ There's never any need to be stuck with a lipstick shade. With a lip brush you can mix several together. You can even put the stubs in a plastic container in a low microwave and melt them to make a totally new colour.

★ If you find the acid in your skin turns lipstick bluer than it should be, you can minimize this effect by putting foundation base over the lips before the lipstick.

> Any scent can react with sunlight to cause ugly dark patches on the skin. So it should not be applied before sunbathing nor should scented skin lotions be used before going in the sun.

Colour Counselling

A friend of mine rang me one day to say her life had been revolutionized: she had been to a colour counsellor and discovered what colours of make-up and clothes really suited her. She has been looking twice as attractive since. The international organization which offers colour counselling is **Colour Me Beautiful**, 56 Abbey Business Centre, Ingate Place, London SW8 3NS Tel: 071 627 5211. There are representatives all over the UK, but – and it's a *big* but – they pay to be trained by the organization and then essentially have a franchise to operate the scheme. This means that there is no guarantee that all the operatives have a real flair for the job.

Cosmetic Camouflage

To cover up a heavy mark on the skin takes make-up with more density than the usual foundation. But there are several ranges on the market designed to do just that. So almost any skin blemish, anywhere on the body, can be camouflaged with the right technique. As many of these cosmetics are waterproof, you can even swim with confidence.

If you want to find a beauty therapist trained in this kind of work the association given on page 642 will put you in touch with one. In addition, the British Red Cross have a cosmetic camouflage service. Their representative will visit patients in need of this while they are in hospital and show them how to use make-up to cover marks and disfigurements – as it is possible to disguise marks without leaving the skin looking made up. The service is available to both sexes, and to children. Patients are only given this help after referral by a doctor, but anyone who needs it may ask his or her doctor to refer them.

Most of the companies which make these special cosmetics will supply samples, for a small fee, so you can try them out at home. Some of the major manufacturers and distributors of cosmetic camouflage are given on page 643 and some products can be obtained on a NHS prescription or through a hospital pharmacy. A word of warning though. To achieve perfect camouflage you need to blend several shades together to produce one which exactly matches your skin, and then apply it with considerable skill so as to minimize any problems in the texture of the disfigured area. This is a skill which anyone can acquire, but very few people will have it the first time they try to apply the make-up. To get good results you may need either a lot of practice or a lesson from an expert – or both. You may need to experiment to find a brand which suits you.

Feet and Legs

Most feet are like a pair of ancient retainers working away below stairs with never a thank-you. They benefit from being given a good scrub to stimulate the circulation. After scrubbing, rub down every bit of dry skin with a pumice stone, or it may crack painfully on the heels or turn into nasty corns on the toe joints. If the skin is hard and dry rub some glycerine on at night.

Chiropodists say people shouldn't treat corns at home with bottled chemicals in case they let the acid damage normal skin around the corn. Instead they advise using a pumice stone to remove the first signs of a corn forming or to rub it down if it has already formed. This isn't a job which can be done in one session. Do, meanwhile, apply a corn ring to remove the pressure when in shoes. You can also try the old-fashioned remedy of soaking some bread in vinegar and putting this on the corn under a plaster. It isn't so strong it will damage the skin, but it will make the surface of the corn a lot easier to rub off.

Tired Feet

The most basic treatment for tired feet is to remove not only your shoes but your socks, stockings or tights as well. Feet weren't designed for footwear and they benefit from going barefoot for part of the day.

If the feet are tired soak them for 5 to 20 minutes in a basin of warm water containing a handful of salt. Wiggle your toes as you sit, to undo the cramping effect of shoes. Next, lie on your back and put your feet up the wall. Having your feet above your head will rest all the veins in your feet and legs which have been under pressure from walking, standing and tight footwear.

Hands

The counsel of perfection is to put handcream by each basin and apply it every time you wash them. Failing that, at least try to spare them the worst assaults by household products. There is no substitute for rubber gloves. Most of the products used for such jobs are made to strip off grease – and they are even more effective on the delicate natural oils in the skin.

★ When about to do a job which will push dirt up under the nails scratch them into vaseline or lanolin so the grease gets well under the nails and prevents the dirt embedding.

Rough Hands

When the skin is roughed up by jobs like decorating and gardening handcreams don't smooth it. Much better is an old-fashioned remedy given to me by a man who was forever tinkering with cars. Pour into a cupped hand a teaspoonful or so of cooking oil. Add a teaspoonful of granulated sugar. Then rub the mixture *very* thoroughly all over the hands for about 2 minutes. Then rinse the mixture off and dry. It works because the sugar acts as very gentle sandpaper rubbing off all the little rough corners of skin, while the oil softens the skin and lets the sugar slide enough to do its job painlessly.

At night apply a few drops of neat glycerine or a mixture of glycerine and rosewater to keep the hands (or body skin) soft. If they are very chapped, apply lanolin cream as well and put on cotton gloves to stop the lanolin getting everywhere. (A few people are allergic to it, so if you get any reaction stop using it.)

Smelly or Stained Hands

By tradition, finger bowls always contain a slice of lemon. This is because lemon removes smells from the skin. So if you are doing a smelly job it's useful to keep an odd wedge of lemon to rub over the skin afterwards. Failing that you can rub them with vinegar, salt or dry mustard. Each removes a slightly different spectrum of smells. Whatever the smell, don't wash your hands in hot water: the smell penetrates the skin more deeply.

Lemon is almost as good for stains on the hands as it is for curing smells. It needs to be rubbed on and left to act as a bleach. For nicotine stains the only solution is hydrogen peroxide. Chemists sell it in different strengths. Ask the chemist to advise you on how much you should dilute the one he sells, to make it safe for your hands.

Nails

Manicurists sometimes take clippers to the cuticles. This is not a good idea. The cuticles are there to protect the nail bed. In time it can also produce a thickened edge to the skin around the nail which is most unattractive.

If the cuticles really grow too far over the nails try a tip recommended by the Body Shop: soak the finger tips for 30 minutes in a mixture made from 2 tablespoons of egg yolk, 2 tablespoons of pineapple juice and 1/2 teaspoon of cider vinegar. Then gently push the cuticles back with an orange stick.

Scissors may fracture the nail layers as they cut through them, so it is better to shorten them with an emery board. It should be rubbed from the sides towards the middle – not used like a saw, because sawing to and fro overheats the nail and makes it more likely to break later. So does a metal file. But even the most careful filing won't prevent some nails from breaking because

nails reflect our general state of health. If they keep breaking the cause is likely to be an unbalanced diet or some kind of strain.

If you improve your diet and reduce the strain don't expect strong nails in a trice. They take about 6 months to renew themselves.

★ Toe nails should be cut straight across; angling them down at the corners risks very painful ingrowing toe nails.

★ Nails stained with vegetable juices can be bleached with lemon juice, but the best way to whiten nicotine-stained nails is to scrub them with smoker's toothpaste regularly.

Hair

Hair is one of those curious substances which, like ivory, is both dead and delicate. In more than one detective story the murderer is caught because he shows traces of arsenic in his hair – having fiendishly built up an immunity to it and then administered it to both himself and his victim. These revelations appear in the hair because it is fed by the blood supply and everything we eat and drink is reflected in it. So the first step to beautiful hair is a good diet.

To look its best it also needs to be treated gently. Mild shampoos are better than harsh ones, gentle brushes better than scrapers, and most hair looks better with conditioner. Apply the conditioner to the ends of the hair, not to the roots; it's the hair which has been exposed to the elements for longest which most needs its soothing touch.

Bleaching

The idea that gentlemen prefer blondes has an ancient history: it is said that the prostitutes of ancient Rome were required either to dye their hair yellow or to wear a blond wig. The bleaches they used were probably horrific, but hair can be made fairer quite gently. To lighten fair hair gradually without the harshness of bleach, infuse camomile flowers (as for camomile tea) and pour the mixture over the hair as a last rinse.

Alternatively, pour dilute lemon juice all over your hair before going in the sun, or draw strands of hair through a wedge of lemon to get a streaked effect. Using lemon and sun is not good for the hair. But then neither is bleach – and lemon is the milder of the two.

Be very careful about trying to bleach hair suddenly with strong peroxide. If hair has any undertone of red – and a lot of brown hair does – peroxide can turn it pure carrot. If this happens don't assume you can just blot it out by dyeing over it. Get professional advice: some dyes turn it green.

★ If you have already made the mistake of using strong peroxide on your hair – which can be most unpleasant for the skin – neutralize it with a strong solution of bicarbonate of soda and water.

DYEING THE HAIR – It may be stated once for all that this practice is decidedly injurious. It may fail altogether in producing the desired result; it is never unattended by a certain amount of unpleasant circumstances, and frequently with evil results.

Enquire Within 1856

Addresses and suggestions for further reading are at the ends of chapters.

★ An infusion of sage leaves used as a final rinse will reduce the greyness of hair which is just beginning to go grey.

Conditioners

One reason why conditioner improves the look of hair is that it restores its acid/alkali balance. But, if you don't want to use bought conditioner, a touch of vinegar in the last rinse helps to remove the alkalinity of the soap and makes the hair shine. You can also infuse a few sprigs of fresh rosemary in boiling water and when it has cooled pour it over the hair. This also leaves the hair shiny and manageable, and smelling perfectly delicious. If you don't have rosemary but have nettles in reach, use them instead. You won't smell as sweet but there is the bonus that nettles help prevent dandruff.

Dandruff

Dandruff is a condition in which dry flakes of skin fall from the hair in excessive amounts. It's nothing new, though the cures of the past could well have been fatal. One seventeenth-century recipe for preventing it includes among its ingredients old wine dregs, cyanide and vitriol. It probably has more than one cause and is linked to both a bacterial infection and to stress, possibly also to a lack of vitamin B.

The first step, if you think you have dandruff, is to rub the scalp regularly with witch hazel and to switch to a mild medicated shampoo. This should deal with the infection. At the same time improve your diet and get more vitamin B.

However, not all dry flaking skin is dandruff, so if you think you have dandruff but it doesn't respond to a medicated shampoo quite quickly you should see a trichologist. There are some conditions which look like dandruff which need expert treatment and could lead to hair loss if they aren't treated properly.

★ To cure dandruff: age. The over-60s don't get it.

Dry Hair

Sun, salt, chlorine, heated rollers, hair dryers, bleaching and perming can all individually – let alone combined – wreak havoc with the condition of the hair. To have healthy hair keep all of them to a minimum. If you must use heated rollers put a layer of tissue between the roller and the hair to lessen the damage.

It was a West Indian mother of a pupil of mine who taught me that if hair does become dry and tired one of the best treatments is coconut oil. It is remarkably effective. Rub it well into the hair, wrap a hot towel round it and leave it for several hours (or smother the pillow in towels and go to sleep on it). Then shampoo the hair as usual. The hair will look shiny and restored and not at all oily. If you find yourself with dry hair on a Mediterranean holiday use olive oil in the same way.

For dull dry hair, when you haven't time to oil it, beat up an egg and massage it well in. Leave it a few minutes, then rinse off with almost cold water – unless you want scrambled hair. This can also be used instead of conventional washing if you run out of shampoo.

Hair Loss

Hair loss can be caused by illness, pregnancy, stress, sudden weight loss, certain types of medical treatment (such as some cancer therapies and certain drugs), the menopause and an hereditary tendency to baldness. But a growing range of products claim to treat it. So see a trichologist.

Baldness may not simply be an hereditary tendency. It looks as if the male hormone androgen is bad for hair growth. This hormone is produced in greater quantities when either sex is under stress. So those who push themselves will increase their chances of hair loss. It is interesting that hair loss among women in highly competitive jobs is an increasing problem.

There is also a condition called *alopecia areta* in which bald patches appear randomly on the scalp. The precise causes of alopecia are unknown but in most cases the hair starts to regrow 1 to 2 years later.

Unwanted Hair

Unwanted hair is one of the most unmentionable of beauty topics. As a result most women who have hair in the 'wrong' places feel they are uniquely blighted. But anyone in the beauty business will tell you it is one of the most common problems of all. Hair can grow absolutely anywhere it shouldn't be, so no misgrowth is uniquely embarrassing.

Plucking

For small areas, such as the eyebrows, or a slight excess on the bikini line, plucking is probably easiest. Numb the area with an ice cube, or by stretching the skin very tightly, before you pluck. But DON'T pluck hair out of a mole (see page 640).

Shaving or Waxing

Larger areas, such as the legs, can be waxed or shaved. Some experts say that shaving doesn't increase the hair growth. Many women disagree. Experience suggests it is coarser and thicker after shaving, whereas after waxing it seems to regrow a little less each time. But be warned: both professional and DIY hot waxing carry a risk of burning if it isn't done carefully, and this is one of the most common causes of claims against beauty therapists.

Depilatories

Cream depilatories are usually effective but they may not suit some skins. Also they should only be used in the areas of the body recommended by the manufacturers.

Electrolysis

Electrolysis can permanently remove areas of unwanted hair from almost any part of the anatomy. It involves passing an electric current into the area of the hair root, to kill the root. Using a fairly strong current will kill most strongly growing hair at one session. But it can produce soreness and scabs. On the delicate skin of the face there is a special risk that if these scabs are knocked off they will leave a scar. The alternative is to have a far weaker current, which may take several treatments to remove the more stubborn hairs, but is far less likely to cause scabs. The right current is a matter of judgement so it is important to have it done by someone who is both qualified and experienced. And if you get any bad reaction at all, have no more done. UNDER NO CIRCUMSTANCES risk trying to do it yourself (see below).

Unwanted Hair in Moles
Moles with hair in present a special problem. They should not be plucked and can only be treated with electrolysis if you have a doctor's approval. This is because certain kinds of moles can be the beginning of cancer, and interfering with such moles could spread cancerous cells to the rest of the body. However, most moles are perfectly healthy and a doctor can tell whether a mole is healthy or cancerous. If your doctor gives the all-clear for electrolysis, there is a chance that it will not only remove the hair but cause the mole to vanish too.

Relaxation

If you need to relax in preparation for something which makes you tense, such as making a speech, use the trick actors have used for generations. Close your eyes, drop your shoulders and breathe slowly and deeply for a few minutes. Make it very slow and calm, and concentrate all your attention on your breathing. You will soon be far calmer than you were.

It works because the body and mind work as one. Slow breathing and calmness go together. When you feel calm you automatically breathe more slowly. But equally, when you behave in a calm way, and breathe slowly, it tricks the body and tells it the crisis is over, so it can stop producing all the chemicals it jets into the bloodstream in an emergency. It's those fight or flight chemicals which hype us up to a point of tension which may be too much for the situation.

You don't have to be doing anything special to try this technique. You can use it to unwind before going to sleep or on the journey home at the end of a hard day, but, like anything else, it takes practice.

Eye Relaxation
This is a good way to rest a little if your eyes are sore and tired. Put your elbows on a table in front of you, with your hands up at eye level. Rest your closed eyes on the heels of your hands, with the rest of the hands supporting your forehead. Then think black and 'see' the black getting blacker and blacker. Stay like this for as long as you feel like it. Your eyes will feel odd when they first come back to the light, but they should be refreshed.

Bath Relaxation
Those who believe in aromatherapy claim that if you use the right aromatherapy oil it will make you relax. Certain herbs and smells do seem to have a relaxing effect, and herbs have been used in baths for centuries. If you have no special oils but do have a herb garden try throwing a sprig or two of rosemary in the water as the bath is running.

Finally, for really in-depth relaxation, there is meditation – see page 567.

The International Vegetarian Handbook lists companies that make beauty products without testing them on animals.

USEFUL ADDRESSES AND BOOKS

General Health

Brook Advisory Centres, 153a East Street, London SE17 2SD Tel: 071 708 1234, have centres in many towns and cities for under 25s. Offering advice on safer sex, pregnancy test if a period is overdue, free birth control, abortion and counselling on sexual and emotional problems. RC, optional M£M, L, B, V, tapes, E, HD, sae appreciated.

The Catholic Marriage Advisory Council, Clitherow House, 1 Blythe Mews, Blythe Road, London W14 0NW Tel: 071 371 1341, will advise on 'natural' methods of contraception and offers marriage counselling at branches nationwide. (P.611)

Family Planning Association Information Service (FPA), 27-35 Mortimer Street, London W1N 7RJ Tel: 071 636 7866, has free information on contraception, fertility, menstrual and menopausal problems. RC, optional M£L, P, L, B, V, E, Rg, Cl, HD, sae.

Health Education Authority, Hamilton House, Mabledon Place, London WC1H 9TX Tel: 071 631 0930, information leaflets on many health issues – for both sexes – from diet to contraception and pregnancy.

Health Education Board for Scotland, Woodburn House, Canaan Lane, Edinburgh EH10 4SG Tel: 031 447 8044, has useful free leaflets on keeping healthy and also on coping with many health problems – obtainable from Local Health Boards. *Well Woman – A Guide to Woman's Health* is especially good.

Society of Chiropodists, 53 Welbeck Street, London W1M 7HE Tel: 071 486 3381, has a register of qualified chiropodists.

Many organizations related to medical conditions advise on diet. So do some of those related to pregnancy and breast feeding. See also Food (P.123-124)

Useful Books
Your Health: A Guide to Services for *Women* – free from the NHS via freephone 0800 555777 – has information on advice lines and common female problems.

Your Greatest Guide to Calories, Slimming Magazine – on manufactured food.

Infertility

Issue, 509 Aldridge Road, Great Barr, Birmingham B44 8NA Tel: 021 344 4414, covers all aspects of childlessness including adoption, fostering and a list of clinics for AID, AIH and other methods of conception. RC, M£M, S, M, L, B, self-help support, G, A, Ad, Inf, telephone counselling, sae. (P.611)

See also **British Pregnancy Advisory Service** and **Pregnancy Advisory Service** (below).

Women's Health, 52-54 Featherstone Street, London EC1Y 8RT Tel: 071 251 6580, RC, M£L (optional), M, L, B, Ad & Inf related to infertility and clinics treating it, self-insemination and pelvic inflammatory disease and other issues. Also on aspects of abortion. It runs a database of self-help groups. (P.611)

Useful Book
   Joseph Belina and Josleen Wilson, eds, *The Fertility Handbook*, Penguin

Contraception and Abortion

British Pregnancy Advisory Service, Ansty Manor, Woolten Warren, Solihull, W. Midlands B95 6BX Tel: 0564 793225, offers pregnancy tests after 7 days late, abortion, contraception, post-abortion and sterilization, sexual counselling in some branches, all on a fee-paying basis but at lowest possible cost. RC, branches in many major cities. (P.612)

Life, Life House, Newbold Terrace, Leamington Spa, Warks CV32 4EA Tel: 0926 421587; (hotline) 0926 311511, is a pressure group opposed to *all* ending of pregnancy, even the post-coital pill. Helps women avoid abortion by advising on accommodation, welfare, adoption.

Lifeline, 14 Beech Road, Reigate, Surrey RH2 9LR Tel: 0737 221428, offers alternatives to abortion. Its branches, in major cities, offer free pregnancy testing, plus counselling and practical information where necessary. It also counsels on miscarriage, stillbirth and menopausal problems.

National Abortion Campaign, The Print House, 18 Ashwin Street, London E8 3DL Tel: 071 923 4976, is a pressure group to retain abortion rights.

Pregnancy Advisory Service, 11-13 Charlotte Street, London W1P 1HD Tel: 071 637 8962, offers pregnancy testing, abortion help and advice, post-abortion counselling, birth control, AID, cervical smear tests, all on a fee-paying basis. (P.612)

Women's Health (see Infertility above).

Preparing for Pregnancy

Foresight (The Association for Preconceptual Care), 28 The Paddock, Godalming, Surrey GV7 1XD Tel: 0483 427839, RC, M£L, S, F&F, L, EI, G, Inf on diet and all other factors, for both sexes, that can affect the chances of a healthy baby. (P.600)

The Maternity Alliance, 15 Britannia Street, London WC1X 9JP Tel: 071 837 1265, RC, M£M, S, F&F, M, leaflets on health care before and during pregnancy, including one for a man who wants children, and maternity rights, sae. (P.600)

Pregnancy and Childbirth

The Association for Improvements in Maternity Services (AIMS), 24 Iver Lane, Iver, Bucks SL0 9LH Tel: 0753 652781, campaigns for better treatment of women during pregnancy and labour. M£L, M, L, Inf, support and Ad. (P.602)

Association of Radical Midwives, 62 Greetby Hill, Ormskirk, Lancashire L39 2DT, is committed to a more caring attitude to midwifery, less intervention, more choice for mothers, and more concern for what birth means to the parents. L, sae. (P.602)

The Centre for Pregnancy Nutrition, Department of Obstetrics, University of Sheffield, Clinical Services Centre, Northern General Hospital, Herries Road, Sheffield S5 7AU Tel: 0742 424084 (helpline), will give advice to anyone on diet and food safety in pregnancy. Their advice is based on all research in English to date. (P.604)

Independent Midwives Association, 65 Mount Nod Road, London SW16 2LP, a small association of private midwives who offer a start-to-finish service for those wanting home births. (P.602)

National Childbirth Trust (NCT), Alexandra House, Oldham Terrace, London W3 6NH Tel: 081 992 8637, runs ante-natal classes all over Britain, preparing for childbirth without fear (book early). Ad, Inf on all aspects of childbirth, including water births. Free breast-feeding advice, post-natal support via other mothers. RC, M£L, M, L, B, E, G, A, maternity mail order, sae. (P.607)

Toxoplasmosis Trust, 61-71 Collier Street, London N1 9BE Tel: 071 713 0663, advises on avoiding and testing for toxoplasmosis – which doctors will do on request. L, send A4 sae. (P.604)

Useful Books
   Dr Peter Huntingford, *Birthrights*, BBC.
   Sally Inch, *Birthrights*, Hutchinson.
   Sheila Kitzinger, *The Experience of Childbirth*, Penguin; *The New Good Birth Guide*, Penguin – useful reading before signing on with a hospital; *Freedom and Choice in Childbirth*, Viking.
   Frederick Leboyer, *Birth Without Violence*, Mandarin.
   The NCT, *Pregnancy, Birth and Parenthood*, OUP.
   Michel Odent, *The Nature of Birth and Breastfeeding*, Bergin & Garvey.
   Vivienne Parry, *The Antenatal Testing Handbook*, Pan.
   Dr Barbara Pickard, *Eating well for a Healthy Pregnancy*, Sheldon Press.

Problems During and After Pregnancy

Action on Pre-eclampsia, 16 Greenways, Abbots

Langley, Herts WD5 0EV, sells a paperback explaining the facts on this condition, which may also be called toxaemia. RC, C, L. (P.603)

Association of Chartered Physiotherapists in Obstetrics and Gynaecology, Garrelloch, 1 The Cottages, High Street, North Scarle, Lincoln LN6 9EP, will put you in touch with those who supply leaflets on physiotherapy exercises for use after various conditions including childbirth, if your hospital can't help you.

Association for Post-Natal Illness, 25 Jerdan Place London SW6 1BE Tel: 071 386 0868 has a nationwide network of volunteer supporters, who have been through post-natal depression themselves. RC, membership free, S, F&F, L, B, G, sae. (P. 611)

Foundation for the Study of Infant Deaths (FSID), 35 Belgrave Square, London SW1X 8QB Tel: 071 235 1721, offers support and advice for bereaved parents by letter, telephone and by individual befriending RC, L, B, M.

Miscarriage Association, c/o Clayton Hospital, Northgate, W. Yorks WF5 9XG Tel: 0924 200799, RC M£L, S, F&F, L, Support groups, B, Inf on prevention. (P.610)

Nippers (National Information for Parents of Prematures), c/o Sam Segal Perinatal Unit, St Mary's Hospital Praed Street, London W2 1NY Tel: 0934 733123 gives help with the physical and emotional problems of a premature baby, practical information on clothes, equipment etc. M£L, M, L, B. (P.610)

Stillbirth and Neonatal Death Society (SANDS), 28 Portland Place, London W1N 3DE Tel: 071 436 5881 helpline 071 436 7940, has support groups for the bereaved, plus experienced befrienders, information on new preventive measures. RC, Opt, M£L, S, F&F, M, L, B, Lib, G, sae. (P.610)

Twin and Multiple Births Association (TAMBA), 59 Sunnyside, Worksop, Notts Tel: helpline: 0732 868000 (evenings and weekends), supports and advises those with twins – or more – and also covers such matters as adoption or the death of a twin. M£L, M, G, A, Ad, L, B.

Useful Books
Katherine Dalton, *Depression After Childbirth* – a very readable book though not every doctor agrees with her conclusions.
Glover and Hodson, *You and Your Premature Baby*, Sheldon Press.
Anne Oakley, Helen Roberts and Dr Anne McPherson, *Miscarriage*, Fontana.
Hank Pizer and Christine O'Brian Palinski, *Coping with Miscarriage*, Norman & Hobhouse.
Barbara Whiteford and Margie Polden, *Post-Natal Exercises*, Century – written by gynaecological physiotherapists.

Baby and Toddler Care

Baby Milk Action, 23 St Andrew's Street, Cambridge CB2 3AX Tel: 0223 464220, has information on the limitations of baby formulas. (P.616)

Child Growth, 2 Mayfield Avenue, London W4 1PW Tel: 081 994 7625, has advice and information on growth norms. (P.620)

La Leche League, BM 3424, London, WC1N 3XX Tel: 071 242 1278 – free help to women who want to breast feed. M£L (if you wish), M, L, B, G, Tel.Ad, visits. (P.614)

Mothercare Ltd, Cherrytree Road, Watford, Herts, WD2 5SH Tel: 0923 233577, offers the Mothercare range of maternity and children's gear.

NCT Maternity Sales Ltd, Burnfield Avenue, Glasgow G46 7TL Tel: 041 633 5552 sells leaflets and hard-to-find maternity items like nursing bras.

The **NCT** (page 641) also offers advice and support.

Useful Books
Simon and Joanna Blackley, *Feed Your Children Well*, Penguin.
Norma Jane Bumgarner, *Mothering Your Nursing Toddler* (only from **La Leche**, above – for those who wish to prolong feeding).
Maire Messenger, *Breast Feeding*, Century.
Penny and Andrew Stanway, *Breast is Best*, Pan.

Sexual and Marital Problems

Association of Sexual and Marital Therapists, P.O. Box 62, Sheffield S10 3TL. (P.612)

Catholic Marriage Advisory Council – see p. 582.

Institute of Psychosexual Medicine, 11 Chandos St, London W11 9DE Tel: 071 580 0631. (P.612)

Jewish Marriage Council, 23 Ravenshurst Avenue, London NW4 4EL Tel: 081 203 6311 offers counselling on all relationship problems and runs local groups and courses on social skills. Crisis line: 081 203 6211. (P.612)

Lesbian Line, BM Box 1514, London WC1N 3XX Tel: 071 251 6911 within limited hours. (P.612)

London Lesbian and Gay Switchboard, BM Switchboard, London WC1N 3XX Tel: 071 837 7324 (24 hrs 7 days a week). (P.612)

Pastels, 36 Newmarket, Otley, W. Yorks LS21 3AE Tel: 0795 661463, gives support and advice for the straight partner of gays, transsexuals and transvestites. (P.612)

Relate, Herbert Gray College, Little Church Street, Rugby CV21 3AP Tel: 07885 73241, offers counselling on all relationship problems, both straight and gay. (P.612)

SPOD (Association to Aid the Sexual and Personal Relationships of People with a Disability), 286 Camden Road, London N7 0BJ Tel: 071 607 8851, L, B, telephone counselling. (P.612)

Body Care

British Association of Beauty Therapy and Cosmetology, 2nd floor, 34 Imperial Square, Cheltenham, Glos GL50 1GZ Tel: 0242 570284, will tell you where to find beauty therapists qualified in electrolysis, cosmetic camouflage and general beauty therapy. (P.637)

Boots (most branches), stocks Covering Cream make-up. (P.63)

Charles H. Fox, 22 Tavistock Street, London WC2E 7PY Tel: 071 240 3111, sells Dermacolour. (P.637)

British Dental Health Foundation, Eastlands Court, St Peter's Road, Rugby, Warks CV21 3PQ Tel: 0788 546365. (P.631)

Hairdressing Council, 12 David House, 45 High Street, South Norwood, London SE25 6HJ Tel: 071 771 6205 – the state registry for qualified hairdressers who have completed a set training and taken exams, but membership is voluntary. The council has a disciplinary committee to which you can complain. But, it can't, alas, get you compensation. So if you have a major problem go to you local Trading Standards Officer or to a Citizens Advice Bureau. (P.638)

Institute of Electrologists, 18 Stokes End, Haddenham, Bucks HP17 8DX Tel: 0844 290721, will put you in touch with someone qualified in electrolysis in your area, sae. (P.639)

Institute of Trichologists, 228 Stockwell Road, Brixton, London SW9 9SU Tel: 071 733 2056. Trichologists are trained to deal with every kind of hair problem. To find your nearest trichologist send a sae. (P.638)

The Make-up Centre, 26 Bute Street, London SW7 3EX Tel: 071 584 2188, is run by a make-up artist with 20 years' experience in films and making up the faces of the famous. She will make someone up and the shop also sells make-up ranges which are normally reserved for professional make-up artists. She will also teach how to use cosmetic camouflage. (P.637)

Flori Roberts, 158 Notting Hill Gate, London W11 3GQ Tel: 071 229 4224, sells camouflage and normal make-up especially suited to dark and black skins. (P.637)

Cupharma Ltd, 245B Hughendon Road, High Wycombe, Bucks HP13 5PN Tel: 0494 522114, sells the cosmetic camouflage Covermark by post. (P.637)

Useful Books
Joyce Allsworth, *Skin Camouflage*, Stanley Thornes.
The Body Shop Book, Macdonald.
Christina Probert, *Vogue Book of Beauty and Health*, Octopus.

PMS and Menopause

National Association for Pre-Menstrual Syndrome, 2nd Floor, 25 Market Street, Guildford, Surrey GU1 4LB Tel: 0483 572715 Helplines: 0483 572806 (day) 0959 24371 (night) – RC, M£L, support G, Ad, largely geared to the use of progestogen. (P.596)

Pre-Menstrual Tension Advisory Service and Women's Nutritional Advisory Service, P.O. Box 268, Hove, East Sussex BN3 1RW Tel: 0273 771366, gives advice, for a fee, on diet related to all female problems either by post or at clinics in London and Brighton. (P.596)

Useful Book
Dr Caroline M. Shreeve, *Overcoming the Menopause Naturally*, Century Arrow.

Animals

Bees to Tortoises, Terrapins and Turtles

Pet choosing, like marriage, is all too often done by falling in love. What it really needs is some good, old-fashioned matchmaking, in which each side carefully examines the other to see if it will meet its needs. Having an animal is a matter of give and take, on both sides, and nobody should go into the partnership without very clear ideas of what will be demanded and what will – and won't – be given in return.

In this chapter I have tried to give the basic information on the pleasures, pitfalls and needs of each of the popular domestic animals. Books and specialist societies are listed, wherever possible, to help you take your enquiries a stage further; other major animal organizations are given at the end of the chapter. Between them they provide a wealth of excellent leaflets – mostly free – which are well worth reading. You may fall in love with an animal, but there is no divorce – and a marriage of inconvenience can last a long time.

Basic Medical Facts

If first aid has to be given to any creature follow the basic rules given in In Sickness for people. The biggest problem with animals is shock, so it is most important to keep them warm, and calm. Also a *very* small blood loss can be a large proportion of a small animal's blood, so treat bleeding *rapidly*. If you lack antiseptics a mild solution of salt and water is a good cleanser.

Giving Tablets

If you have a dog which likes chocolates, as many do, the easy way to give it tablets is to push the tablet into the middle of a soft centre and pop it into its mouth.

Cats won't be fooled that way, and usually detect a tablet in any other food. If so, the only method is to tilt its head up, open its mouth and drop the tablet well in, then hold its mouth shut, with the chin pointing upwards, until it swallows. This is hard to do with a resistant and angry cat unless you adopt the right position. The easy way is to sit it on your lap with its back towards you, and its back legs gently but firmly between your thighs; you can then hold the front paws with one hand and use the other hand to give the tablet. Most animals will easily accept such handling if you do it confidently and without dithering.

Animals for Smallholdings

The **Agricultural Development Advisory Service (ADAS)** is the best source of information if you want to keep creatures like goats, pigs, poultry or even a cow. The regional ADAS offices are listed in the phone book under Ministry of Agriculture but, although the leaflets are free, they now charge for personal advice. They urge people not to take on livestock too lightly. Inexperienced neighbours may happily feed a cat while you take a holiday, but leaving them with chickens may not be so successful. If you can't track down your local **ADAS** office, the London office will direct you (page 658).

Bees

It is possible to keep bees in any quiet garden, including a suburban one – provided the neighbours don't object – and there is even an Inner London Beekeepers Association. But the best honey flows come when bees have access to heather, clover, beans, raspberries, sycamore or lime trees. The **Scottish Beekeepers Association** has a booklet (see page 659) which lists trees, shrubs and plants providing abundant pollen or nectar for bees – which could be planted by anyone who cares about these fascinating creatures. But keeping bees is not something to be undertaken lightly, as the hive requires skilled and systematic attention. I strongly recommend anyone considering this hobby to read *Teach Yourself Beekeeping* (see page 659). Join an adult education class on beekeeping and/or a local beekeeping association. It can also be useful to talk to people at the National Honey Show, which the **British Beekeepers Association** (see page 658) organizes each October at the Porchester Hall, in London.

Buying Bees

Bees from a member of a local association are adapted to the weather in your area. But there is a risk that an amateur could sell ill-tempered or diseased bees. So ask for a written undertaking that they are disease-free. Alternatively, buy from one of the dealers advertising in beekeeping magazines. There are really two kinds of worker bee: summer bees and winter bees. Summer bees only live about 6 weeks, whereas those born in August and September live right through to the following spring.

The hive needs a site which is sheltered and faces south, with no overhanging trees or dampness. Avoid placing it within the magnetic fields of high tension electricity cables as bees become aggressive.

Some hives may yield no honey at all, others as much as 200 lb, but the average is 30 to 40 lb. To obtain this you need to supply the hive with about 50 lb of sugar as winter feed. So honey is not the bargain it might seem.

> Be careful what you wear near bees. Bees are angered by red, dark-blue or black clothing and may also be upset by woollen garments if they become entangled in them. Nylon also seems to irritate them – perhaps because of the static electricity.

Birds

Birds may seem like trouble-free pets, undemanding and contained. This isn't necessarily the case. All birds are gregarious and it is cruel to keep them singly unless you are prepared to spend all day with them yourself. Parrots, in particular, need constant attention throughout the day, and resort to feather plucking when bored. Some also need a new branch to gnaw daily, and many indulge in raucous screeching, loud enough to disturb the neighbours. Some can also become very attached to one person and may live as long as a human and all birds litter the floor with seeds and feathers. So the general rule is: the smaller the bird, the smaller the problems.

Many are bred in Britain, but some of the exotic birds are captured in the wild and transported in horrific conditions. To buy any which have suffered this fate is to encourage cruelty to animals. So check a bird's origins before buying.

It is safest to buy from a specialist shop or breeder. The signs which indicate a healthy bird are: preening, standing on one leg, alertness, bright eyes, a clean vent unstained with droppings and a plump breast. Hollows felt beside the breast bone could be due to illness. If you want a bird to talk buy it young. A budgerigar should be 6 to 9 weeks old, and at this age should have no white ring round the eye; the dark lines or flecks in the feathers should come down to above the bill, and the dark spots on the throat shouldn't be well defined.

Cages

If a bird is deprived of flying its muscles waste away and it is unlikely to be happy. As birds fly horizontally, having enough width and length is far more important than the height. The *minimum* sizes of cage *per bird* are as follows and you should try to give them more.

Bird Type	Height		Width		Length	
Budgies, canaries, finches	30	x	30	x	60 cm	(1x1x2 ft)
Cockatiel, love birds	60	x	60	x	90 cm	(2x2x3 ft)
Small parrots	60	x	90	x	90 cm	(2x3x3 ft)
Large parrots	60	x	90	x	120 cm	(2x3x4 ft)
Macaws	60	x	120	x	120 cm	(2x4x4 ft)

See the table on page 646 for bird lengths.

Wall cages which are large enough are advertised in some of the specialist bird magazines. It's important to avoid anything which might injure the birds, such as wrongly spaced bars which could catch a bird's head. Parrots need 16-gauge wire (not the standard 19-gauge) on tougher supports, well encased in wire on the inside. Perches, preferably of chemical-free washed branches, should be of varied diameters (within the bird's grasp) so it doesn't get sores from always gripping with the same part of its feet. Small birds like finches need pot plants to perch on too. The cage must be put out of direct sunlight – or birds overheat – and away from draughts.

Softbills, like macaws, are messy and need their cages cleaned daily; others every 2 days. Line the floor with newspaper which can quickly be removed. The cage needs to be thoroughly scrubbed and disinfected every 2 weeks.

Care

They are creatures of routine and so they are happiest when feeding and cleaning follow a predictable pattern. They need 9 to 12 hours' sleep, according to the season. Erratic hours and staying up late can make them tetchy and neurotic. They also need the sunlight; use a special bulb which compensates for this.

Birds need a daily 'bath' – some like to nestle in damp plants; others like to splash in a shallow dish, and the larger parrots often like to be sprayed with a plant sprayer – or even to shower with their owner.

It is also good for birds to be allowed to fly freely in the house. But, before releasing them, vet the room for hazards – they don't know they mustn't go near the vacuum cleaner or into cooking pots or down lavatories, and may bang into windows unless the curtains are closed.

Entertainment

Birds are naturally active and like to have things to play with and sound is also important to them. Birds left alone will often be happiest with the radio quietly on. But even with plenty to do a caged bird may get bored, distressed or sexually frustrated. The result is usually feather plucking, but occasionally they will take to compulsive eating or chronic egg laying. Sometimes a mate is the solution, but even so some birds can't stand captivity.

Feeding

All birds need water constantly and like to feed morning and evening, as they would in the wild. Dr Axelson's book (see page 659) gives the food needs for each species. The basics are these. Good quality bird seed mixtures are sold for parrots, canaries and budgerigars. Those of in-between sizes, such as parakeets, can be given some budgerigar food and some parrot food. Birds (especially parrots) also need fresh food each day – fruit or green vegetables cut in pieces can be left in the cage. But be sure to wash them well – birds are not as tolerant of chemicals as we are. Mung beans, soaked and sprouting (but mould-free) can also be given to larger birds, and chickweed is good if there are no chemical sprays on it. A cuttlefish bone hung in the cage provides the calcium they need, and a vitamin supplement must be given on some fruit to avoid vitamin D deficiency. They also need grit occasionally, or the food cannot be digested in the gizzard: the larger the bird, the larger the grit.

Softbills, like mynah birds, are fruit and insect eaters and need the proprietary food designed for them, supplemented by fruit such as peeled apple in half-inch chunks or seedless grapes. Insects can be provided for softbills by obtaining mealworms or by putting in their cage sprays of garden plants carrying aphids – provided no chemicals have been used.

Health

A major threat to birds is dirty air. They may get breathing problems if kept near smokers, drying paint or aerosols of any kind, and also from kitchen smells such as burning fat or the fumes from non-stick pans.

Some birds carry almost invisible mites. Using a proprietary spray immediately after purchase should get rid of the problem.

It is normal for birds to moult, dropping old and damaged feathers and replacing them with new ones. Some do it once a year, some twice a year and it can take several months, during which they may constantly preen the new feathers and stop singing. This is perfectly normal, but they are more vulnerable to chilling and illness at this time and will benefit from quiet and a good diet.

The signs of a sick bird are abnormal droppings, loss of appetite, listlessness, soiled or matted feather around the nostrils or difficulty in breathing. Some experts say all birds should be taken to a vet 3 to 4 times a year for a health check and a nail (and possibly beak) trim – nails have blood vessels in so they need careful cutting. When carrying the bird outside, cover the cage with a blanket and pre-warm the car in cold weather.

Birds which are newly imported, or have been in contact with imported birds, may develop a disease called Parrot Fever (chlamydiosis, psittacosis or ornithosis). This is not common but it can be transferred to humans and is occasionally (if rarely) fatal. It is, therefore, wise

to avoid putting one's mouth close to a bird, and to wash after handling and cage cleaning.

Talking

Among the birds available in Britain canaries win as singers, and the Roller is the best variety. They sing best if there are two male birds *each in a separate cage*. To stand a good chance of teaching a bird, like a budgerigar, to talk, you need a young bird on its own. A budgerigar bought at 6 weeks old should start after 5 to 6 weeks. Some find that if the bird is put in an empty cage, and this is covered with a cloth while the bird is talked to for just 10 minutes a day, it will talk far sooner. Start with one word or short phrase. Once that is mastered gradually introduce new words and phrases, including perhaps your address or phone number, in case the bird ever escapes. Don't put a mirror in its cage until it has learned to talk or it will just twitter to its alter ego.

Whatever bird you have, don't shout at it or let it hear you shouting. Birds will copy anything and if you shout so will they. If this advice comes too late Dr Axelson gives a cure for shrieking in his book (see page 659). In the list below the best talkers are star-rated – ★★★ being the best talkers. Of course, it varies from individual to individual: some birds are brighter than others.

Bird	Talking Ability	Life Span in Years	Length
Budgerigars	★★★	6-8 (but sometimes to 20 years)	20 cm (8 in)
Cockatiel	★	10-14 (but sometimes to 30 years)	31 cm (12 in)
Cockatoos	★	25-45 (but sometimes to 100 years)	31-67 cm (12-27 in)
Love birds	★	10-14 years	14 cm (5 in)
Macaws	★	up to 60 years	30-100 cm (12-40 in)
Mynah birds*	★★★	up to 25 years	30-45 cm (12-18 in)
Parrakeets	★	10-15 years	13-36 cm (5-15 in)
Parrots	★	20-70 according to type	25-52 cm (10-21 in)

* (Greater Hill variety only)

A newly acquired bird can be as bewildered as a small child in a new school. So give it time to settle into a new home in peace. Let it get used to you gradually; and talk to it quietly as you offer it its regular food. Do this so it has to come to you to get it. Once it eats happily from your hand you can begin to stroke or scratch it gently on the head and chest, keeping every movement slow so the bird is never startled. Most birds will try to bite in the early days, or with strangers, and the largest ones can remove a nasty chunk of flesh or part of a finger, so don't allow small children near large birds. Never hold out one finger for a new bird of any size to hop on to – it's a nice beakful. Instead hold out your hand, palm down, with the fingers together, while talking gently and catching its attention with a movement of the other hand – and if necessary wear thick protective gloves at first. If it does bite, *never* hit it or it will become scared and redouble its attack next time. Just put it in its cage immediately and leave the training for that day. When it is tame you can begin to teach it to talk.

Cats

We probably owe today's felines to the ancient Egyptians, who 3,000 years ago domesticated them to keep down the rats and mice in their grain stores. It is even said that the word 'puss' derives from Basht (pronounced Pasht), the Egyptian cat goddess. But it was the Romans who introduced cats to Britain, and much prized they were. By the ninth century a mouser was valued at two pennies – a sum which, given 1,000 years of inflation, makes today's pedigree pussies a bargain.

Buying

Before falling in love with some adorable kitten take stock of what it will be like as an adult cat. Long-haired cats need daily grooming if their coats are not to mat into painful hair balls. Siamese are decidedly noisy, and Burmese have a penchant for climbing – curtains included. So a plain moggy may be a better bet for most households. And before taking on a cat remember that it could live for at least 14 years.

To find a young cat ask your local vet for a good source, go to a show and find a breeder whose animals you like, or write to a cat society for information on breeders offering a particular kind. As with all animals, look at the parents to see what the offspring will be like. A kitten can leave its mother when over 8 weeks old, but get a diet sheet from the breeder so it can eat what it is used to, at first.

If cats are neutered there is nothing to choose between males and females in affection, but it is a great joy, and education, for children to experience one litter of kittens, *provided they can be found good homes.*

Food

Cats need a varied diet of cooked or raw meat and fish to stay healthy, with quite a lot of fat or fish oil to provide enough vitamins A, D and E. Most cats prefer food at room temperature and usually eat about 200 g (7 oz) of meat or fish a day, in two meals. Kittens and cats which are growing, pregnant or feeding babies need larger and more frequent meals. All cats need clean water.

Offer kittens a little cow's milk as soon as they are 2 to 3 weeks old, and begin to add a little minced meat and cereal soon after. So by 8 weeks they are weaned and on four meals a day. Give them a very varied diet so they won't be faddy.

Branded cat foods usually provide a balanced diet, but dog foods (which cats often enjoy) have too much vegetable and cereal to be used regularly. Most cats also like about a quarter of a pint of milk a day – though some do better on milk and water. Non-milk drinkers need a calcium supplement until they stop growing. If a cat is fed on dry food it is essential that it drinks plenty of liquid or it may develop bladder problems.

Grooming

Long-haired cats need daily grooming, with a good quality metal comb, to stop the hair matting. First sprinkle on grooming powder or unscented baby powder, leave it for 10 minutes to absorb any grease, then comb it out systematically.

Health

The three most dangerous infections are rabies (outside the UK), feline enteritis and cat 'flu'. The last two are easily picked up by any cat allowed out, and enteritis is usually fatal. So kittens should be vaccinated against both, at about 3 months old, and given regular boosters as your vet recommends. If boosters have been missed make sure a cat has one before moving to a new area or going into a cattery, and also if there is an epidemic. Good catteries won't accept cats without a certificate of recent vaccination.

House Training

A kitten quickly learns to be clean. Start with a shallow box of cat litter close to its box, and if it seems about to 'go' pop it on it. If you have a garden, start taking the kitten outside first thing in the morning and at intervals during the day. If it performs out there praise it warmly. But if it makes a mess indoors don't punish it – it won't understand. Just clean it up and eradicate the smell – cats home in on any place where they smell previous use. So, ideally, keep kittens away from carpeted areas until they are trained. But the easiest way to clean up solids is with a flat scraper like a wallpaper stripper.

Housing

The ideal home for a cat is a cardboard box lined with scrunched-up newspapers and an old jumper. It keeps out the draughts and can be burnt if the cat gets fleas, but cats are nocturnal and, if it is safe for them to be out at night, they enjoy it.

Mating

The breeding season for a queen (female) can be all year, peaking in spring and autumn. She will become increasingly restless and start crying. If kept in she may even try to jump from a high window, go off her food and spray urine in the house. She will only mate when fully on heat. Cat societies can often recommend suitable mates, but unmated moggies will quickly find their own.

A cat pregnancy takes about 65 days. Some get morning sickness and vomit occasionally. Make sure she has extra food and enough calcium. Some can get all they need from milk, but those which can't digest it need a calcium supplement.

In week 7 she may start looking for a warm dark place to give birth. Provide one or she may well use your cupboard. Get a cardboard box large enough for her to stretch out fully and line the base well with newspapers. Then place the box on a sheet of plastic and more newspapers somewhere warm and quiet. When about to give birth she may refuse food and perhaps vomit. Have a litter tray near the birth box in case she needs it.

Many like to be alone during labour; others need their owner. Sometimes the first thing out is an empty sac – this is quite normal – and the kittens may emerge head or tail first, each encased in a thin sac. The mother should lick the sac off. Having bitten through the umbilical cord she usually eats the membrane, cord and placenta. These are rich in hormones and are thought to encourage her milk.

Human intervention shouldn't be needed. But if a cat strains for a long time, with the kitten half in half out, you may need to take hold – with a piece of towelling – and gently help on the next contraction. If the cat fails to lick the membrane from a kitten you can wipe it clear, and stroke the kitten into breathing. Do this near the mother's head so she can finish the job and eat the placenta – there is no rush to cut the cord. But if things go seriously wrong and the cat is in distress call a vet.

To check the sex of a kitten press gently near the genital area – on males a penis will emerge, but not when they are very young.

Moving with a Cat
Cats often get more attached to places than to people, and need time to get adjusted to a new home. You need to keep them indoors for a few days and give them time to learn that the new home is now the source of food and comfort, or they could stray.

Neutering
Male kittens are sexually mature at 6 to 8 months and will start looking for a mate. They will mark out their territory, by spraying their strong-smelling urine all round your home. It is one of the hardest smells to eradicate, so get a tom neutered at 5 to 6 months old.

Female kittens don't start 'calling' for toms until about 10 months old, but some breeds can be precocious and call long before it would be safe for them to have kittens. Cat contraceptives are advisable, as a frustrated female can make herself ill and become infertile by calling for a longed-for tom. Vets usually neuter a cat at 6 months old, but it can be done after she has had kittens. As a general anaesthetic is used, the cat must not eat for 12 hours before.

Parasites
Worm treatment should come from a vet and, as fleas can infect a cat with worms, the cat should be treated for these at the same time. Vets can now provide tablets which make the fleas die when they bite the cat. Or use an aerosol. The easiest way to apply it is to spray it on to cotton wool and wipe this over the animal as if you were stroking it. Burn the bedding at the same time and spray the rooms with a long-acting insecticide from a vet.

See also Toxoplasmosis Trust, page 641.

Opinions vary on the effectiveness of flea collars and there is a danger that tree-climbing cats will catch them on a branch and hang themselves.

When You Go Away
The best place for a cat is at home, and pet sitters are provided by some agencies. But if it has to go to a cattery the **Feline Advisory Bureau (FAB)** (page 659), runs a Boarding Cattery Approval Scheme and will send a list of approved catteries. Inspect any cattery before booking. Even approved ones may have changed hands since the last inspection. Catteries should provide food, warmth, shelter, genuine care and thoroughly clean conditions. Outdoor catteries are healthier than indoor ones, and cats from different households should be housed separately to prevent infection. If a cattery is inadequate report it to the local Environmental Health Officer *and* to FAB if they approved it.

Dogs
At first sight there seems to be a dog to fit every family. This isn't quite the case. Dogs are demanding: even tiny ones need careful training and regular exercise. 'Going walkies' may be enchanting on long summer evenings, but it is less delightful in driving snow. If you aren't prepared to feed and exercise it daily, for about 14 years, regardless of the inconvenience, don't buy a dog. The welcome companion to a woman at home looking after toddlers can be a bind when she wants to return to work. But if you decide to buy a dog here are some points to consider:

- Size isn't a good indication of how much exercise a dog will need – some small breeds, such as terriers, are very active.
- Long-haired dogs need daily grooming – have you time?
- Large dogs cost a great deal more to feed.
- All breeds need careful training and some can be dangerous if they lack discipline.
- Are you likely to be good at dog-training? If not, buy one you can manhandle when fully grown.
- Some breeds have in-bred health problems – especially very small and very large dogs.
- Dogs which need clipping run up bills with their hairdressers.
- What other animals are in the house? I include small children here. In guard dogs and hunting dogs, like Dobermanns and German Shepherds, the fighting instinct is not far below the surface. Others have a slower fuse with toddlers.

It's true that having a dog to pet will help keep down your blood pressure, reduce your risk of heart attack and make you recover from illness more swiftly. But the strain of a large dog in the average house or flat can practically *give* you high blood pressure. It is also very bad for the dog to be captive in too small a space. So the

Sunday Times asked experts on dogs to name their top six for town living. They were:

1 Cavalier King Charles Spaniel
2 Dachshund
3 Chihuahua
4 Yorkshire Terrier
5 Pekinese
6 Miniature or Toy Poodle

Buying a Dog

Many of the qualities of a dog depend on the character and health it inherited. So one sure way to get a good dog is to buy a puppy from a friend who has a bitch of good health and character, which had an equally reliable mate.

Another good, if expensive, source is a pedigree dog from a specialist breeder. **The Kennel Club** or **Dog Breeders Associates** (see page 659) will send you a list of breeders for any breed.

Taking pity on an animal from a market stall, pet shop or dogs' home is the least reliable way to get a good animal. Though many lovable creatures end up in such places, it is often a route to disappointment. These animals may carry infections and, in some cases, unkind treatment may have made them nervous or aggressive. But some dogs' homes, such as Battersea, do have good dogs which have been rejected by callous owners.

The ideal age is 8 to 10 weeks, and the animal should seem in perfect health – bright eyes, moist nose, clean ears and no parasites or raw patches – and be alert, inquisitive and friendly to everyone, neither barking without provocation nor backing away. An independent animal which neither cowers nor advances may have a lot of character, but will not be so easy to train. Don't buy a dog which doesn't seem to like you – dogs tend to stick to their prejudices.

- Make your purchase conditional upon it being examined and given a clean bill of health by a vet. This is normal practice and nobody should be insulted. If the seller won't agree go elsewhere.
- When you pay you should be given: its pedigree, if it has one, its registration certificate, a diet sheet telling you what it eats, and how often to feed it, information on whether, and when, it was treated for worms, the dates and type of any preventive injections. If you don't get the papers, they shouldn't get the cheque.

The journey home will be frightening for the puppy, so prepare the car against puddles, and at home have ready a cosy box or basket, lined with something warm like an old pullover. Place the puppy in it immediately, so it has somewhere to belong; then let it explore from there. But don't let children maul or over-excite it. It may well howl the first night. Treat it as you'd like to be treated if you were frightened – a cuddle, a warm hot water-bottle (it's used to the warmth of other dogs), and a cheering tit-bit when it's quiet. But don't let it do things you won't want it to do later (like sleep in your bed). Training starts the moment it enters your home.

Exercise

Dogs need daily exercise (a marathon at weekends won't make up for 5 days cooped up), but don't take a puppy where other dogs have been until at least 2 weeks after it has been inoculated. A good play in a garden, where it can stop when tired, is better than a walk. Large dogs in particular, have soft bones and should not be walked too soon. Once a dog is grown, suit the exercise to its size and energy. Short-legged, or snub-nosed, dogs shouldn't be given long walks on hot days. And all dogs should be on a lead when there is livestock or game about.

Feeding

Good breeders provide a diet sheet for a puppy. Stick to it for 2 weeks. But get the puppy used to all kinds of flavours and gradually switch it from minced meat to chunks.

Puppies need food little and often and each meal should be the amount the puppy will eat in 10 to 15 minutes.

2 to 4 months	*Breakfast:* minced or tinned meat + dry dog meal
	Lunch: cereal and cow's milk
	Tea: cereal and cow's milk
	Supper: as breakfast, and time it for an hour before bedtime to encourage the puppy to open its bowels on its bedtime walk.

3 to 7 months	Cut out the 'teatime'.
7 to 12 months	Cut down to two meals a day by dropping the mid-day feed, but it can still have milk and cereal as part of another meal.
12 to 18 months	Drop the milk and feed it once a day.

On average a young dog needs about ½ oz meat for every pound of its body weight, while a full-grown dog needs only about ⅓ oz. Beef can be raw, other meat cooked. Dogs also need cereal in the form of biscuits or meal, or toasted wholemeal bread, plus some cooked vegetable matter. Small bones, especially poultry, are dangerous, but raw marrow bones are excellent – unless the dog is so big it can even splinter these. A diet of fresh food usually needs added vitamins, but most branded dog foods have vitamins already added – check this on the tin. There should always be clean water out for a dog – cow's milk can cause diarrhoea in adult dogs.

Dogs should be fed from their own bowls and not from plates used by humans, and their bowls should be washed up separately. There is a small and avoidable risk of catching worms or disease from dogs.

Health and Grooming

Regular brushing with a suitable dog brush, or combing with a smooth, toothed, metal comb, is better for a dog than frequent bathing. Any washing must be with a dog shampoo which won't irritate the skin.

Inoculations against a number of infections are usually given at 10 to 12 weeks, but the timing depends on weaning. So check earlier with a vet. Make sure a booster is given before a dog goes into kennels or moves to a new area.

A healthy dog is alert and active, with bright eyes and a glossy coat (if its type permits), and its temperature (taken up its bottom, not under its tongue) is 101° to 102°F (38.5°C). Illness needs swift attention from a vet. Some diseases are fatal, even with modern drugs; others, like distemper, are highly infectious, and some can be given to humans.

There is more to dog **first aid** than can be covered here, but it is really very like human first aid (see In Sickness) except that an animal in pain may bite. If necessary, prevent this by tying something round its nose. The **British Veterinary Association** (page 658) has a free leaflet on first aid for dogs and cats.

Most dogs get **fleas** or **lice** at some time and they are easily recognized. The treatment for both is tablets, flea powder or aerosol. Treatments must be every 4 to 7 days for at least a month to be effective, burning the bedding at each treatment.

Mites are too small to see but may cause mange or ear infections, and one type can be given to humans – take a dog to the vet even for mild skin problems. All dogs and cats in a house should be treated at the same time, as mites get passed around.

Roundworms are usually in puppies from birth and stools free of worms are *not* a proof that the dog is worm-free. Worm the puppy at 2, 4, 6, 8, 12 and 16 weeks old, then every 3 months, especially if there are young children in the house. Eating the eggs of dog round-worms (*Toxocara canis*) can be dangerous. The larvae can travel through the human body and into the eyes, causing blindness. As the eggs are in dog faeces (droppings), children playing where dogs have been are most at risk. **Community Hygiene Concern** (page 659) has leaflets on this and recommends regular worming every 3 months.

Tapeworms can be caught from fleas which carry the eggs. Segments of tapeworm may show, like grains of rice, in the stools or near the dog's anus. A vet will prescribe and it usually takes several treatments to kill them.

Ticks look like rather faded baked beans. They must *never* be just pulled off or the head will remain in and cause infection. First make them let go by painting them (but not the dog) with surgical spirit, meths or paraffin. Cover the dog with flea powder to kill any unattached ticks.

Holidays

A Herald Holiday Handbook, called *Pets Welcome*, lists establishments which welcome pets. It also gives boarding kennels and catteries, and these are also listed in the Yellow Pages. But some pet sitter rates compare favourably with boarding two animals. If you have to board pets do inspect the place before you book, and book well in advance. The best places get booked up and the worst you wouldn't put a louse in.

House Training

A young puppy has a very limited ability to control itself and can't go through the night without wetting. Let it sleep where an accident won't be a disaster. Make a habit of putting it outside whenever it wakes up, after any great excitement, and after food, and praise and pet it lavishly if it performs – even accidentally – in the right place.

If it looks about to go take the puppy straight outside (stay with it so you can praise its achievement). Say 'no' firmly if you catch it doing it indoors – and growl for good measure. It will learn in a few weeks. But it is pointless to get angry or smack a young puppy or rub its nose in it after the accident has occurred: it hasn't got the brain to link the mess or puddle with the making of it. That method won't teach it to be clean, but it will teach it to distrust you.

Pregnancy

Bitches can only conceive when 'on heat' (in season). This usually happens twice a year and lasts about 3 weeks. Special sprays may make a bitch less seductive, and there are now pills which remove the bitch's appeal to males. But if you want puppies, mate her when the discharge becomes clear. During mating dogs are anatomically locked; forcibly separating them can harm both animals, and the act itself can take 5 to 60 minutes.

There are no pregnancy tests for dogs, but a vet can often tell at 4 weeks and pregnancy lasts about 63 days. The mother needs milk and some jelly from boiled-up

Addresses and suggestions for further reading are at the ends of chapters.

bones, plus extra food in the last few weeks, and a vet should check her.

Make a birth-bed with a warm blanket, and get her used to it well before the birth – you don't want her to choose your bed. When the puppies are due, line it with newspaper and let her get on with it. Puppies may come every half hour or with a gap of an hour or so. If she fails to lick the membrane from a puppy's head you may need to break it and rub its chest to get it breathing. Break the umbilical cord with your nails – it bleeds less than a smooth cut – about 2 inches from the puppy, but don't tug or you could cause a hernia.

Bitches seldom need assistance. So only call a vet if:

- the puppies are overdue by 2 days
- she has strained for 2 hours without producing a puppy (first or other)
- a puppy is stuck half in, half out, and a gentle pull hasn't helped
- she is very excitable
- something else seems abnormal.

Spaying and Castration

Most male dogs are routinely castrated to prevent straying and fighting. Some people favour doing it at 6 months. Other breeders and trainers say that doing it at a year old allows the dog to develop its adult character in a way which it may not if its hormone balance is altered before this. A castrated dog is usually less aggressive and more obedient and affectionate.

If puppies aren't wanted many vets recommend spaying bitches to avoid unwanted pregnancies, or 'female problems' in old age. The surgical risk is slight – but it does exist. Vets differ in the age they do the operation, but some claim that if a bitch is spayed after her first season she is less likely to have incontinence problems. If they are not spayed, dogs stay fertile all their lives.

Training

Training a dog is easy. The hard part is training yourself. You can't vary from day to day; you always have to follow the rules and be entirely consistent.

Dogs are pack animals. Your family becomes its pack and it will feel safe and happy if it knows its place in the pack – as a bottom dog who obeys. Dogs are most devoted where they are most obedient – a devoted undisciplined dog is a contradiction in terms.

1 Use *exactly* the same command words *every* time (not 'sit' one day and 'sit down' the next).
2 Always say the word *first*, then help the dog to obey it (e.g. press its bottom down); then the word will gradually trigger the action.
3 Teach the formal commands – heel, sit, stay, come, lie – one at a time, only introducing a new one when another is well learnt. By 8 to 9 months it should come when called, walk well on a lead and stop what it is doing on the word 'no'.
4 At first let it know you are *delighted* if it even begins to get it right. Keep repeating the *same* words of praise (e.g. 'good dog') and *follow* them with petting. Then the dog associates 'good dog' with the reward of your pleasure, and the words themselves slowly become a reward. Gradually become more demanding until you only reward immediate obedience.
5 Punish bad behaviour *instantly* (see punishments below): the dog must learn to associate bad behaviour with something bad *immediately* happening to it, and say 'no' as you punish. Then 'no' becomes linked to the idea of punishment. But don't use any other words which might muddle it – 'bad dog' and 'good dog' sound too alike. And don't use its name when punishing. If you want it to come when called it mustn't link its name with punishment.
6 Remember dogs don't discriminate. If you love your Alsatian jumping up and licking your face when you get home, and reward it for doing so, don't expect the dog to work out that smartly-dressed women, frail old ladies and tiny children will not welcome the same treatment.

Once you are clear about the rules you want it to obey you *must* win *every* time. Dogs don't respect pack leaders who don't. Nor do they respect those who fly off the handle. If 'no' doesn't work, stop the dog doing what it shouldn't by using only as much force as is necessary. Your advantage is psychological not physical. As punishment, don't hit it with a newspaper; do as dogs would – growl at it, hold it by the scruff of the neck and shake it hard (the hardness being adjusted to the size and strength of the dog) or glare into its eyes or, if necessary, tap it firmly on the nose with two fingers (using an open hand to hit a dog makes the start of a pat look like the start of a slap and confuses the animal). If it's on a slip lead jerk it – just enough for the size of dog. Banishment is another punishment.

> Dogs can die if they are left in a car in the sun with too little air. The windows must be left open a crack so cool air can come in, and while the car is still they need some water.

Frogs, Toads and Relatives

Frogs and toads have different images: frogs are seen as attractive, smooth, moist-skinned creatures and toads as ugly, lumpy, dry-skinned ones. Although true in Britain, worldwide the distinction fails to stand up. So, many scientists refer to both as frogs, and so shall I.

Frogs lead a double life: first in water, then on land. As ponds have been infilled and ditches ploughed out, they have increasingly lost the water they need for breeding. The Great Crested Newt and the Natterjack Toad are already rare enough to be protected, and there are moves to have them all protected. Anyone planning to collect frogs' spawn or frogs should first take advice on whether there are enough frogs in that particular area for it not to matter, and on which types are protected. Most counties have a Naturalists' Trust or a Natural History Society which can be found through the public library and will be only too glad to advise you; or you can read up the restrictions in the Wildlife and Country-side Act. If in doubt don't take any spawn.

If you take a little spawn it deserves careful treatment. Put it in rainwater or pondwater, not chlorinated tap water. As the tadpoles hatch from the eggs, they need algae to eat, so add plants or objects which have algae on. Christopher Mattison's book *The Care of Reptiles and Amphibians* recommends lightly-boiled lettuce or flaked fish food. But be careful not to overfeed tadpoles; rotting food fouls the water and kills them. As they grow, their appetites increase and they need more protein – or they will eat each other to get it. Finally, as the legs sprout, their appetite reduces but they need something on to which they can climb to get air; they must also have a diet which includes small flies and white worms (from tropical fish dealers). If well fed they may be sexually mature in 6 weeks and ready to be released into the wild, or a garden pond, to start the extraordinary cycle all over again.

Gerbils and Jirds

One of the little-known secrets of the pet world is that most gerbils aren't really gerbils at all: they are jirds. Gerbil is a blanket term used to refer to about a hundred different species. These include true gerbils, jirds, fat-tailed rats and other small rodents related to voles and lemmings. They are all about half-way in size between a mouse and a rat, with long tails. True gerbils, or *Tatera*, have a long-nosed ratty look, whereas jirds have shorter noses. In either case, they make excellent pets, clean, disease-free and tame – though they are not ideal for very young children.

It is the clawed jird, *Meriones unguiculatus* (sometimes called the Mongolian gerbil), which is most often found as a pet, but the slightly larger Libyan Jird and the Indian Gerbil are also sold. To find which you have, check its feet: jirds have furry soles, gerbils don't; and Libyan Jirds have white claws, while Clawed Jirds have black claws. They are happiest in pairs and, if you don't want to breed, two males or two females will live together provided they are from the same litter and have grown up together. For breeding, the pairs need to be of the same species.

When tame, they will run into an outstretched hand; otherwise pick them up by the tail *close to the body* – but never farther down or the skin may pull off. But they shouldn't be over-handled and, as they are very active, they must be held over something so there can be no long fall.

Provided they are kept in clean conditions, don't eat too much fruit or vegetable matter and have a good diet,

they should have few problems and may live to 5 years old.

Breeding
Start matchmaking when the couple are under 4 months old, so they mature together and are less likely to fight. If mates introduced as adults start fighting they should be separated at once and reintroduced another time, but once mated they mate for life. A litter of 4 to 8 is usually born 22 to 25 days after mating, and a female can have several litters a year. The male can remain in the nest, but the female may abandon or destroy the young if she is disturbed by people. The babies open their eyes after 3 weeks or so and wean themselves naturally at 4 weeks. As the mother can mate immediately after giving birth the young may then need to be removed to make room for the new arrivals. At about 4 months the males may need to be separated to prevent fighting. This tendency to produce numerous litters can give you an awful lot of babies to find homes for each year.

Feeding
A good hamster mix from a pet shop feeds them well, or you can make your own mix from peanuts, flaked maize, wheat, sunflower seeds and spray millet. To either you need to add pieces of apple, carrot and green vegetables to give them vitamins and moisture. They also like the occasional treat of meat or a live mealworm or two, and there must always be a drinking bottle filled with water.

Housing
As these creatures live in desert areas they like to burrow out of the sun. So, though they can be kept in a cage, it may be more interesting to use an aquarium, at least 51 cm (20 in) x 46 cm (18 in), with the top covered with wire. You can then construct a little cave out of stone and clean dry sand and watch them underground. If they are in a cage give them a deep layer of sand, and plenty of unprinted shredded paper or hay in which to burrow and nest. They also like a few twigs to climb and to gnaw, as their front teeth grow extremely fast. The ideal temperature for them is above 5°C (40°F) and below 20°C (70°F); damp and draughts are harmful. As their droppings are dry and odourless, cages need only be cleaned out once in three weeks.

Guinea Pigs

Though descended from the wild cavies of South America, guinea pigs have been kept as pets for hundreds of years, and vary greatly in size, colour, and coat length. There are three main sorts: the kind with short smooth hair, those with long straight hair – such as the Peruvian – and the Abyssinians with short hair in rosettes. Their needs vary slightly, so ask about them before you buy. Whatever the kind, choose a lively young animal with no scars or wounds.

Guinea pigs need to feel secure. So handle them calmly, using two hands until they are used to you, or their wriggling may lead to a fatal fall.

Breeding

It is quite easy to get cross-bred guinea pigs to breed, but pure breds are harder. Females can be mated at 6 months old and pregnancy lasts 9 to 11 weeks. A mother may have 2 to 3 litters a year, and is able to mate again on the day she has just given birth. So if you don't want a production line keep males and females apart. Babies are born furry and adorable and can be weaned at 3 weeks on to the same food as adults. What's more, males are so oversexed that they may start mating their mother if you don't remove them.

Feeding

Guinea pigs *must have* plenty of vitamin C every day. They need fresh green vegetables, like lettuce, cabbage or dandelions, hay, root vegetables, such as carrot or raw beetroot, and a handful of guinea pig mix. They also need constant fresh water in a heavy dish or drinking bottle. They aren't usually inclined to overeat, so let them guide you on quantities unless they begin to get fat.

Health

Healthy guinea pigs can live for 7 years, but 3 years is average. They tend to fight, and scratches may turn into abscesses, so it is worth cleaning them with a mild antiseptic such as you'd use on a human cut. Mites and lice sometimes trouble them and need to be treated with an insect powder recommended by a vet. It is also important not to let them become very fat or they may die suddenly, especially if they are pregnant. Penicillin is also fatal to them – but not all vets realize this.

Housing

They can use an outdoor cage during the summer, if it is out of sun and wind, has stilts against the wet and a waterproof roof. But some need to be indoors in winter, so check the hardiness of any guinea pig before you buy it. A single animal needs a hutch about 60 cm (2 ft) long, by 45 cm (18 in) wide and high, with about a third partitioned off for sleeping and 18 mm (¾ in) wire mesh across the front. A family group of three females and one male needs a hutch twice as long. Put paper on the floor and cover this with 2 ½ cm (1 in) of wood shavings, then add hay for bedding. The bedding should be changed daily if there is no separate sleeping quarter, or weekly if there is. (Don't use sawdust: it gives them breathing trouble.) In summer guinea pigs enjoy having a wire run on a lawn, provided they are well protected from larger animals and the lawn has not been treated with chemicals.

Hamsters

Hamsters were domesticated in this century, and make excellent pets provided you buy the Golden Hamster – which is not always golden. Their only disadvantages are that each one needs a separate cage and they tend to sleep by day and rush about at night. Choose a lively animal, in good condition, with no scars or scratches, and 8 to 10 weeks old. Either sex makes a good pet, but you can tell which is which by looking at their hind quarters: males have an elongated rump, whereas females have a rounder one. Females also have two rows of teats from about 8 days old.

Handle hamsters very carefully. In the early days, before they are tame, hamsters may need to be picked up gently by the loose skin at the back of the neck. But as soon as possible get them used to cupped hands. Handle them while sitting on the floor – if they fall more than 23 cm (9 in) they may be killed.

Breeding

Before breeding hamsters, think whether you have the space. You need separate cages to keep old from young and male from female or they will fight. They can breed at only 6 to 8 weeks old, but the female (doe) should be 3 to 4 months old before she is mated. She is most likely to be broody in the summer and will be in season every 4 to 5 days, but mating needs to be watched carefully as you may have to separate them if they fight. They should also be separated straight afterwards. A litter of 4 to 7 naked young will be born 15 to 18 days later. Their eyes open and they start eating dry oatmeal after about 5 days and chopped greenstuff after 10 days. However, they should not be handled at all for over 2 weeks. Segregate them at 4 to 5 weeks to stop them from fighting – even siblings scrap.

Food and Drink

Hamsters need to be fed once a day – ideally in the evening – and will thrive on pellet seed preparations made for rats or mice. But they will eat almost anything, and some people claim they do well on a firm, crumbly, chopped-up mixture of left-over meat, fish, eggs, vegetables and biscuits. But they also need mixed grains and fresh green and root vegetables. Avoid oats in the husk, as the pointed tips can pierce a hamster's cheek pouches. If they are fed at the same time each day they become tamer, but only give them enough food for one day or they will store it, and it will become mouldy and unhealthy. They like water from a bottle hanging in the cage and can have milk occasionally.

Health

Hamsters get fewer fleas and lice than other rodents and should not get ill if properly fed and housed. They live 3 to 4 years. Treat any problems as for guinea pigs or gerbils.

Housing

As the rule for hamsters is only one hamster per cage, they are not as easy to house as some other rodents. They need a strong house which will resist their large teeth. Many hamster pens are too small, for they like to climb and move about a lot, especially at night. Each one needs a separate cage at least 60 cm (2 ft) by 30 cm (1 ft) and 30 cm (1 ft) high, though there is no need for a separate sleeping section. The cage can be in plastic, metal or wood, but metal tends to be cold and if wood is used it must be strong hardwood at least 2 cm (⅝ in) thick, painted inside with non-poisonous hard gloss paint, and protected on tempting edges with metal strips. A thick floor covering of wood shavings and a supply of fresh meadow hay or shredded white paper (from pet shops) for bedding is all a hamster then needs. Don't use sawdust, newspaper, feathers, cotton wool or artificial fibre bedding as they can cause health problems.

Keep them at an even temperature of 18° to 21°C (65° to 70°F), away from draughts and direct sunlight. For when the temperature falls below 5°C (40°F) they may go into a coma, and seem dead. If this happens revive them in a warm place and offer warm sweet milk.

They are remarkably clean creatures, and will learn to leave their droppings in one place if you put a flat container there and give them the idea by putting some of the soiled litter on it when you clean the cage. Clean the whole cage out once or twice a week, but remove wet patches daily.

Horses

Owning a horse is a major undertaking, needing more than an ability to ride. Only someone who will be totally committed should take a horse on. Care and exercise can take at least 3 hours a day – *every* day. It is one thing to help a friend muck out a stable on a summer's day, and quite another to do the job, twice a day, week in week out – especially with the temperature below freezing, and everyone else in the warm. They also cost more to keep than any other animal.

Horses also require more detailed information than I have space for but the organizations and books on page 660 will help you. Anyone wanting to buy a horse should first talk to other owners, read books on the subject and gain practical experience in horse care – it could just change their mind. There are also courses in stable management which are well worth taking before a horse is purchased. And someone with spare land who simply wants to own a horse may get a great deal out of giving a retired horse a good home.

Lizards

Buying

Lizards are increasingly popular as pets, and should live for about 5 years. But far too many die young because of improper care, and some are too delicate to be kept in captivity at all. Their needs are very varied. So do check on their special needs before you buy. Some won't drink from a dish, but only sip water sprinkled on plants in their environment – which gives you the role of rain-maker. Worst of all – some eat lizards of other species if they are kept together. This range of needs makes it hard to generalize about their care, but there are certain needs they all have in common.

Feeding

Most lizards adore eating spiders, as well as many insects and a wide range of other foods. They like bran-fed mealworms (which are often fed to them), but these contain too few vitamins and minerals and too little calcium unless they have been on a special diet. Varied fruit, vegetables and insects should be offered, plus multi-vitamins and powdered cuttlefish bone and, of course, water. The larger lizards, in particular, benefit from the extra vitamins and minerals in tinned cat or dog food. They may also accept a small whole mouse. But not all their likes are so distasteful – it seems iguanas have a penchant for rose petals.

Housing

The right temperature is vital, for it dictates the rest of their behaviour and in the wrong temperature they cannot thrive. Most lizards thrive at 25° to 30°C (77° to 84°F) and need a lamp to bask under and a cooler place to retire to.

Being active creatures they easily entangle themselves in wire mesh and become injured, so a glass aquarium (correctly called a terrarium), with enough room for them to run around, is the best home. As most lizards are wall climbers, it needs a firmly attached perforated lid too. Cover the bottom with newspaper or cardboard, for ease of cleaning, and then give them a good layer of earth or sand. Other details should be adjusted according to the species. Study, and try to mimic, their natural habitat; tree climbers should have twigs to climb and those which bury themselves in the sand should have sand. Like any creature, they must be kept clean if they are to stay healthy.

Mice and Rats

Mice and rats are often considered dirty creatures. Wild ones are disease-carriers, but a cleanly-kept caged mouse or rat is no dirtier than a rabbit or a hamster, though they do have a strong smell, especially if you fail to clean them out regularly or give them the wrong diet.

If you intend to exhibit get advice from the relevant society (see page 660) on which type to choose. The best rat or mouse to buy is one which looks alert and lively

Addresses and suggestions for further reading are at the ends of chapters.

and whose coat is in good condition. If you want a happy mouse, get it a friend of the same sex. When choosing a rat pick a female – they're less smelly than males – but avoid the wild Brown Rat: it may carry disease.

To find the sex of rodents you need to compare several. The anal-genital distance is greater in a male than in a female. But don't press around hoping to extrude a penis and confirm your diagnosis – as you could on a rabbit or kitten: it won't work.

Breeding

Rats reach maturity at 2 months, mice at 6 to 7 weeks. Rats can produce 6 litters a year, but it's best to delay the first pregnancy by separating the sexes, and separate them again during pregnancy. This lasts 17 to 22 days in mice, and 20 to 22 days in rats, and the mother may produce from 6 to 16 young. The baby mice can be taken from their mother at 3 weeks, rats at 4 weeks.

Feeding

Ready-mixed rat and mouse food gives a balanced diet, or you can make your own mixture of oats and other cereals. These animals also need green foods such as lettuce, chickweed and rose hips and haws, fruit according to the season, biscuits and bread in a little milk and table scraps. Give the food at night and remove any that isn't eaten by the morning. But avoid cheese, it makes them smelly; and provide a constant supply of water.

You can buy water bottles which hang upside down on the cage or fix a piece of very narrow metal tubing, in a small cork, in the neck of a medicine bottle and hang this up.

Handling

Mice need gentle handling. Don't grab them; lift them by grasping the tail near the base, and then place them on your hand. Rats are too heavy for this; so grasp them round the middle, with your thumb and first finger beneath their chin. Handle both creatures calmly, even tame ones may bite if you startle them.

Health

Mice don't need grooming, but children enjoy polishing their coats by stroking them gently with a piece of silk – a trick which is just as good for smooth-haired dogs. Treat fleas with a powder recommended by a vet. Sores can be cured by adding arrowroot to the diet and applying a skin ointment from your vet. A healthy rat may live 3 years, a mouse slightly less.

Housing

Rats are very active and need a cage 75 x 50 x 45 cm (30 x 20 x 18 in). But two mice are happy in a standard mouse cage 46 x 25 cm (18 x 10 in) and both creatures need play wheels and things they can climb. Metal or strong plastic are the best materials for rat cages as these can't be gnawed through and don't absorb the smell of urine. Mice are best in a wooden cage, as plastic cages attract condensation, which is bad for them. Mice also need to be indoors, away from damp and draughts, but

cover any cage ventilation holes with wire mesh – believe it or not, a mouse can squeeze through a hole only a third of an inch across. Both creatures need plenty of sawdust or wood shavings in their cages to mop up the urine, and the cage must be completely cleaned 1 to 3 times a week, and scrubbed out every month.

Rabbits

Rabbits which get used to being petted when young make good pets and seem to enjoy company. I knew some that loved to watch the television, and sat so close the family had to watch it between their ears. The more a rabbit is handled when young, the more friendly it will be. Lift it carefully, and *never* by the ears. There are several different types of rabbit, each kind having its own advantages and disadvantages. Ask about these before you buy. For example, Rex get very large and may weigh 3 to 4 kg (6-8 lb), English Lop have excessively long ears which are easily damaged by children, and Angora need careful daily grooming.

Feeding

Water must always be available, and an upside down bottle with a metal tube to drink from is ideal. Rabbits will eat as much green food as you care to give them, plus any root vegetables except raw potatoes. But to keep a rabbit happy include a handful of hay in the morning (or have a hay rack in the hutch) and pellets of meal – oats, wheat, barley or sunflower seeds – in the afternoon. They also appreciate cooked potato peelings or wholemeal (not white) bread toasted or mashed with milk.

Food should be stored away from the hutch, and leftovers cleared up so as not to attract rats or mice. Rabbits must *not* be overfed: folds of fat may become raw and attract flies whose maggots will then eat into the animal. This also happens if their rump is unclean.

Health

One of the advantages of rabbits as pets is that they seldom get ill, but they do have an odd habit of eating their night droppings. This is perfectly normal. If rabbits get parasites *don't* use an insect powder based on DDT, get a safer one from your vet. If there is ear canker it also needs veterinary treatment.

Housing

The hutch must be about 1 m (1 yd) long and 60 cm (2 ft) wide for one rabbit, or half as big again for two, with a sloping waterproof roof. The wire front should be ½ inch mesh – if it's larger they can put a foot through and cut it on the wire. About a third of it needs to be enclosed for a sleeping compartment and the whole hutch must be safe from foxes, and even dogs and cats. Cover the floor with sawdust and bed the sleeping compartment with hay, changing it whenever it is soiled. Whenever possible rabbits should be allowed out for a run – preferably on grass. They are not solitary animals, so if you can't keep 2 give them the company of people or other pets. If keeping several choose females, as bucks may fight.

Pregnancy

Does can become pregnant 10 times a year and produce 4 to 8 young in a litter. Keeping the sexes apart is the only birth control. To mate them deliberately take the doe to the buck, not vice versa or there will be territory squabbles. Pregnancy averages 31 days and the doe needs to be alone and to have extra food and materials she can use for a 'nest'. She also needs considerably more food while feeding her young.

Snakes

Snakes are in some ways perfect pets: silent, clean, deliciously silky to touch, and requiring food very infrequently. But one must face certain facts before buying this ancient symbol of wisdom. First, most snakes feed almost entirely on other live animals. In captivity they may be persuaded to eat dead food, but it can't be counted on. Even then, you may need to kill the food yourself and give it to the snake while it is still warm and – preferably – kicking. Second, they are expensive to care for properly and need special attention. Finally, most snakes manage to escape from their cages – so if you'd mind one underfoot think again. You also need to consider your responsibility under the Dangerous Wild Animals Act.

Obviously, no sane amateur is going to buy a poisonous or semi-poisonous snake. But even those snakes which lack venom in the fangs have venom in their saliva – not strong venom, but it can produce ill effects in certain people. This means that even the least poisonous snake needs careful handling and that you should only buy from a responsible and knowledgeable pet dealer who can advise you about this. The London Zoo suggests looking in *Exchange and Mart* for a snake dealer who also deals in equipment and books.

Feeding

Snakes must always have fresh water available, as they may refuse to drink stale water, and they must not be overfed as this shortens their life and affects their fertility. Don't handle them for several hours after they

have eaten and, if you have several, separate them for feeding.

How often they must eat varies with the type and their individual preference, and the details can be found in the books listed on page 660. Once a week is average for a medium-sized snake, like a Garter Snake, but some can go much longer. Favourite foods vary with the species, but baby hamsters, mice, guinea pigs and rats are usually popular, though some prefer fish. It is kindest to kill the creature yourself, but if you can't bear to do this, stay and watch the snake kill and eat its dinner. If it doesn't go for the creature quickly the snake may be the one that gets bitten. When live animals can't be obtained snakes will usually eat raw fish, especially if you wiggle it to make it look alive. When about to change their skin it is natural for most snakes to refuse food and for their eyes to look milky, but they are very hungry afterwards.

Health

To know whether a snake is well you need to observe its feeding and excreting patterns. If these are abnormal, or it vomits, something is wrong. But don't worry if a snake doesn't seem to sleep: it just sleeps with its eyes open.

Housing

Snakes need cages to suit their size. The minimum is a rectangular cage about 50 cm (20 in) by 50 cm (20 in) by 100 cm (39 in). This can be a wooden cage or a lidded terrarium, and the bottom can be lined with wood shavings, or shredded newspaper, but earth may carry parasites. Try to mimic the snakes' natural habitat and include somewhere they can hide if they wish, as they tend to like privacy. The housing should be heated to about 24°-28°C (75°-80°F) for temperate species or 26°-30°C (77°-86°F) for tropical ones, with only a slight drop at night. If the temperatures are too low a snake will eat, but the digestive enzymes won't work and the food will remain undigested and make it ill.

Scrupulous cleanliness is essential if snakes are to stay healthy. Remove large droppings as soon as possible and clean the cage thoroughly with Milton disinfectant every 2 to 3 weeks. Snakes have an excellent sense of smell, although curiously they smell with their tongue. To avoid being bitten when cleaning out the snake's house wear rubber gloves and put something strong-smelling – such as alcoholic spirits – on the gloves. The snake will then avoid your hand.

Tortoises, Terrapins and Turtles

Toothless and gentle, these creatures are living fossils, far older than the dinosaurs, and almost unchanged in 100 million years. In the wild many live as long as a man, and longer, but it is rare to find any British family with a tortoise which has survived more than a few years. So to keep a tortoise in the average family is, essentially, to kill it, and their popularity as pets has helped to make European tortoises an endangered species. The Wildlife and Countryside Act of 1981 made it illegal to import these. Some are now bred and sold in Britain, but many are imported from America, and may need far warmer

Addresses and suggestions for further reading are at the ends of chapters.

conditions than can easily be provided. Terrapins may carry salmonella bacteria, which cause food poisoning, and transfer them to humans. So neither could really be called an ideal pet.

A fall could fatally break their shell, so they must be handled with great care. The shell must never be painted or pierced as it is a living part of the creature. If necessary, a label can be attached with a *small* dab of superglue.

Feeding Tortoises
Tortoises are often put in a garden and left to fend for themselves. Although European tortoises may munch your greenery this is *not* all they need, and some are unlikely to survive such treatment. They usually eat about 1 to 1½ cups of varied meat and vegetables a day, with more vegetables than meat – and they may enjoy cat or dog food. Try them on green vegetables (well washed because of chemical sprays), carrots, sweetcorn, bananas and non-poisonous weeds – dandelions are a great favourite. Leave them to munch slowly, but throw fruit away before it becomes overripe or they will get stomach upsets. To stay healthy they also need direct sunlight and extra calcium and phosphorous in their food.

Feeding tortoises early in the morning makes them less prone to stray, and if you always choose the same place and time they will learn to arrive there on the dot. If you call them, or make some other noise each time before you feed them, they will even learn to come when called. When kept indoors give them 3 meals a day to mimic their natural browsing. Put the food on a clean piece of ground – they are not designed for eating off dishes. Water should always be available, and they love to paddle in hot weather, so a shallow dish sunk in the ground doubles for drinking and bathing, but only give them a little water or they drown.

Tortoise – Health
Most tortoise problems need a vet, but if they get a cold keep them at 18 to 21°C (67°F) until they get better, and treat ticks as for ticks on dogs (page 650). Cuts should be cleaned, smeared with Savlon and covered with a plaster or flies may lay eggs in them.

Hibernation of Tortoises
When the temperature drops in autumn and a tortoise slows down and eats less, it is ready for hibernation. Put it in a box at least a foot cubed, with plenty of shredded paper, dry leaves or litter, but not woodwool as this could cut it. Then fix wire over the top and put the box in a garage or garden shed – provided there are no rats or mice – until the spring. Check it weekly; if it wakes

too soon, keep it indoors until the weather is warm. On waking, its eyes may be sticky and need bathing with 1 teaspoon of boracic acid (from a chemist) in 5 teaspoons of water. It may also need lots of water and some vitamins, such as Abidec, to stimulate its appetite, and if it seems slow to get going put it in *shallow* lukewarm water and splash the water over it. However, some American tortoises do not hibernate.

Housing Tortoises
A tortoise can wander in the garden, if there are no poisonous plants around, or be given a large run – though it may well burrow out of either. It also needs a waterproof wooden house with space to move about in. This must be made with a doorway allowing for growth. The underside needs battens to keep it off the ground, and the ramp up to the door should have some anti-slip device, like strips of wood attached in a V. David Robinson's book (see page 660) has detailed instructions. A litter of shredded newspaper inside is better than straw, which can cut a tortoise, or hay, which grows fungus when damp. The house must be cleaned out regularly. At night, or when the temperature is below 15°C (60°F), they should be brought indoors and put in a pen well-lined against droppings.

Sexing a Tortoise
To tell the sex of a tortoise look at the undershell. In a female it curves slightly outwards; in a male it curves inwards. Males also have longer tails. Mating and breeding are well covered in David Alderton's book (see page 660).

Feeding Turtles and Terrapins
Terrapins like ¾ of meat to ¼ of vegetable or fruit. Finely chopped fresh fish or meat (without fat, and not liver or heart), tinned tuna fish or sardines, earthworms, mosquito larvae, mashed berries or tiny pieces of tomato are all suitable. Sprinkle a little cod liver oil, for vitamins, and ground cuttlefish bone on all the food or their shells will weaken from lack of calcium. Feeding them in a separate bowl avoids polluting the aquarium and cuts down the cleaning, though a lettuce leaf can be floated on the water for browsing. A bunch of aquarium plants is also a good idea.

They will only eat if the temperature is right. If cold they withdraw into their shells and refuse to eat or, having eaten, are unable to digest their food and become ill. Feed young ones daily, when the temperature has been right for some hours. Those 13 cm (5 in) or over only need food 3 to 4 times a week; and only offer what they can eat in 15 minutes. Include a few drops of Vionate vitamin supplement each week: lack of vitamin A can lead to a fatal infection.

Turtle and Terrapin – Health
Terrapins can suffer from colds, pneumonia, eye infections and fungus infections. The fungus shows as a halo in the water round the terrapin, and immersing in a solution of 1 teaspoon of salt to each cup of water for 15

minutes a day may cure it. Other conditions are best seen by a vet as terrapins are delicate creatures.

Housing Turtles and Terrapins

These need an aquarium giving slightly more than a cubic foot per creature. Put 2.5 to 5 cm (1 to 2 in) of coarse aquarium gravel in the bottom, and a water depth twice the creature's length from head to tail. Keep it at 23° to 29°C (75° to 85°F) with a heating element. As basking is their delight, they need a flat stone, under a lamp, to climb out on to. Like all reptiles, turtles cannot adjust their body temperature. So they depend totally on the environment and must have a temperature of 29° to 34°C (85° to 92°F) by day. You can buy ready-made aquarium lids complete with a light fitting, and an ultraviolet bulb should be used to give them 8 hours of 'sunlight', but switch it off at night.

Sudden temperature changes harm them. Get the water temperature right, then float the plastic bag you bought them in on the water for 30 minutes, so it takes on the same temperature. Then release them in the tank. A dirty aquarium causes sick terrapins, so the tank must be cleaned every 2 days, unless it has a filter. With a filter it need only be cleaned 3 times monthly. But never empty the water by first sucking it up a tube – there is a risk of salmonella poisoning.

USEFUL ADDRESSES AND BOOKS

Many of the animal organizations have no fixed address, but rove as the secretaries succeed each other. If you can't trace an organization, the **RSPCA** or **BVA** (see below) may have the latest address. The **Charities Aid Foundation** (page 214) publishes a *Directory of Organizations for the Protection and Welfare of Animals* which may be in your public library – but, as with this book, things may have changed while it was being printed.

General Organizations

Abbot Bros, Thruxton, Norwich, Norfolk, NR4 0QJ Tel: 0362 850220/850309 do an unusual service sending mail order animals such as lop-eared rabbits or tame ferrets by train.

Blue Cross, The Animal Hospital, 1 Hugh Street, London SW1V 1QQ Tel: 071 834 4224, provides free veterinary care for the animals of those who can't afford a vet. By appointment only, with evidence of inability to pay. Branches also in Hammersmith and Wandsworth, RC.

British Small Animal Veterinary Association, Kingsley House, Church Lane, Shurdington, Cheltenham, Glos GL51 5TQ Tel: 0242 862994, can suggest vets knowledgeable about small animals.

British Veterinary Association (BVA), 7 Mansfield Street, London W1M 0AT Tel: 071 636 6541 – book series on pet care. (P.650)

National Association of Private Animal Keepers, c/o D. H. Keeling, 13 Pound Place, Shalford, Guildford, Surrey GU4 8HH Tel: 0483 37547, advice and information for family pet keepers and professionals, sae.

People's Dispensary for Sick Animals (PDSA), Whitechapel Way, Priorslee, Telford, Shropshire TF2 9PQ Tel: 0952 290999, runs centres which give free treatment to sick pets and wildlife, and neuter male cats, when their owners are unable to pay fees. Vets displaying a PDSA Auxiliary Service sticker also do this. 24-hour emergency service. Take proof that you are receiving state benefits or rebates. Busy Bees Club for children with pets. M£M, M, G, L.

Pet Health Council, Thistledown Cottage, 49 Main Street, Sewstern, Grantham, Lincs NG33 5RF Tel: 0476 861379, leaflets on pet health and health risks to humans. It also has a database of over 80 pet-related organizations. It is partly funded by the pet-food industry. 24-hour helpline.

Royal Society for the Prevention of Cruelty to Animals (RSPCA), The Causeway, Horsham, West Sussex RH12 1HG Tel: 0403 264181 – animal clinics and welfare centres. RC, M£free, M, L, G, F, V, B, charts, junior membership and magazine.

The Wild Life Hospital Trust, 1 Pemberton Close, Aylesbury, Bucks HP21 7NY, Ad and Inf – on caring for injured wildlife if your vet can't help, including a hedgehog helpline.

Wood Green Animal Shelters, Highway Cottage, Chisell Road, Heydon, Royston, Herts SG8 8PN Tel: 24-hour helpline 0763 838329. These shelters take in any animal from a mouse to a horse if it needs a home and sells the animals to good homes. It also runs the **National Pet Register**. Pets registered on this get a unique tag to wear and are put on a computer database so, if they stray, they can be traced to you.

Useful Books
Black's Veterinary Dictionary, A.C. Black.
Francis Hunter MRCVS, *Before the Vet Calls*, Thorsons Ltd: a book of homeopathic first-aid for pets.
Geoffrey P. West (ed.) *First Aid for Pets*, A.C. Black.

Animals for Smallholdings

Agricultural Development Advisory Service (ADAS), Noble House, Smith Square, London SW1P 3HX Tel: 071 238 5632. (P.644)

Useful Book
David Mackenzie, *Goat Husbandry*, Faber.

Bees

British Beekeepers Association, National Agricultural Centre, Stoneleigh, Coventry CV8 2LZ Tel: 0203 696679 – Rg, G, A, L, B, HC, Ad, tours. (P.644)

Scottish Beekeepers Association, 44 Dalhousie Road, Kilbarchan, Strathclyde PA10 2AT Tel: 0505 72680 – M£5, M, L, B, F, G, A, Ins, sae. Special facilities. (P.644)

Useful Books
An Introduction to Bees and Beekeeping, Scottish Beekeepers Association.
Frank Vernon, *Teach Yourself Beekeeping*, Hodder & Stoughton.

Birds

The Avicultural Society, Bristol Zoological Gardens, Clifton, Bristol BS8 3HA – M£M, M, A, advice, use of library at the Linnean Society, also open to non-bird owners, sae. (P.646)

The Budgerigar Society, 49-53 Hazelwood Road, Northampton NN1 1LG Tel: 0604 24549 – M£L, M, G, Rg, L, B, shows, sae. (P.646)

The National Council for Aviculture, 87 Winn Road, Lee, London SE12 9EY Tel: 081 857 4208 – M£L, G, Ad, the linking body for a mass of societies covering individual species. (P.646)

The Parrot Society, 108b Fenlake Road, Bedford MK42 0EU Tel: 0234 358922 – M£L, includes junior members 8-16, M, I, will recommend vets for birds. (P.646)

Royal Pigeon Racing Association, Reddings House, Reddings Road, Cheltenham GL51 6RN Tel: 0452 713529 – keeps the records of racing pigeons, supplies rings, supervises racing, age 8-10+ upwards, free booklet for children, M£L, G. (P.648)

Useful Books
David Alderton, *Looking After Cage Birds*, Ward Lock.
Jim Allcock, *A Pet Bird of Your Own*, Sheldon Press.
D.V. Belding, *Racing Pigeons*, Saiga, 1 Royal Parade, Hindhead, Surrey GU26 6TD. The same publisher also has books on ornamental wildfowl, and on domesticated ducks and geese.
Dr R. Dean Axelson, *Caring for Your Pet Bird*, Blandford.

Cats

Cats Protection League, 17 Kings Road, Horsham, West Sussex RH13 5PP Tel: 0403 65566 and 0403 61947 – RC, cat welfare, with cat shelters and a placing system finding good homes for cats. (P.647)

Feline Advisory Bureau (FAB), 1 Church Close, Orcheston, Nr Salisbury, Wilts SP3 4RP Tel: 0980 620251. (P.648)

The Governing Council of the Cat Fancy, 4-6 Penel Orlieu, Bridgewater, Somerset TA6 3PG Tel: 0278 427575 – Inf on local clubs and shows, L. (P.647)

Useful Book
James Allcock, *A Pet Cat of Your Own*, Sheldon Press.
Bradley, Viner, *The Cat Care Manual*, Stanley Paul.

Dogs

Community Hygiene Concern, 32 Crane Avenue, London N8 Tel: 081 341 7167. (P.650)

Dog Breeders Associates, 10-13 Heathfield Terrace, London W4 4JE Tel: 081 742 7442. (P.649)

Dogs Home Battersea, 4 Battersea Road, London SW8 4AA Tel: 071 622 3626 cares for and sells to good homes dogs which have been abandoned or neglected. (P.649)

The Kennel Club, 1-5 Clarges Street, London W1Y 8AB Tel: 071 493 6651 and 071 493 2001. (P.649)

Useful Books
The Kennel Club, *Illustrated Breeds Standards*, Bodley Head – useful guide to what to look for in any breed.
James Allcock, MRCVS, *A Pet Dog of Your Own*, Sheldon Press.
John Holmes, *The Family Dog: its choice and training*, Century Hutchinson.
John Palmer, *Training Your Dog*, Salamander.
Trevor Turner B. Vet Med, MRCVS, *How to Feed Your Dog*, Century Hutchinson.
Robert C. White MRCVS, *The Care of the Family Puppy*, Century Hutchinson.
Manual of Canine Behaviour, British Small Animals Veterinary Association.

Farm Visits

See **National Farmers Union**. (P.124)

Frogs

Michael J. Tyler, *Frogs*, William Collins Pty, Sydney, from libraries only.

Gerbils and Jirds

National Mongolian Gerbil Society, 93 Somerville Drive (2-R), Mount Florida, Glasgow G42 9BJ – M£L, M, G, shows, sae. (P.652)

Useful Books
David Alderton, *A Pet Keeper's Guide to Hamsters and Gerbils*, Salamander.
Chris Henwood, *Love Your Gerbil*, Foulsham.

Guinea Pigs

The National Cavy Club, Olney Park Cottage, Yardley Road, Olney, Bucks MK46 5EJ Tel: 0234 712023, covers guinea pigs of all kinds. (P.652)

Useful Book
Isabel Day, *Guinea Pigs*, Hamlyn Pet Guides.

Hamsters

British Hamster Association, P.O. Box 825, Sheffield S17 3RU (no phone). (P.653)

Useful Book
Chris Henwood, *Love Your Hamster*, Foulsham Press.

Horses

Association of British Riding Schools, Old Brewery Yard, Penzance, Cornwall TR18 2SL. Tel: 0736 69440. (P.654)

Bransby Home of Rest for Horses, Bransby, Saxilby, Lincoln LN1 2PH Tel: 0427 788464 – cares for old and sick horses, donkeys and mules. (P.654)

British Horse Society (and the Pony Club), British Equestrian Centre, Stoneleigh, Coventry, Warks CV8 2LR Tel: 0203 696697 – covers both riding and carriage driving through numerous affiliated clubs and branches. Pony clubs for under 21s. Riding schools are inspected and given the BHS 'seal of approval'. M£L-M, M, L, F, V, A, Inf, B, E, EI, HD – see below, sae preferred. (P.654)

British Equine Veterinary Association, Hartham Park, Corsham, Wilts SN13 0QB Tel: 0249 713170. (P.654)

British Show Jumping Association, British Equestrian Centre, Stoneleigh, Coventry, Warks CV8 2LR Tel: 0203 696516 – M£L-H, M, A, Ins. (P.654)

The Donkey Breed Society, Manor Cottage, South Thoresby, Alford, Lincs LN13 0AS Tel: 0507 480520. (P.654)

The National Pony Society, Brook House, 25 High Street, Alton, Hants GU34 1AW Tel: 0420 88333 – for pony breeders. (P.654)

Riding for the Disabled Association, National Agricultural Centre, Stoneleigh, Coventry, CV8 2LY Tel: 0203 696510. (P.654)

Useful Books
Brian Giles, *Safety with Horses*, Stanley Paul (paperback).
Susan McBane, *Your First Horse*, Stanley Paul.
Gillian McCarthy, *Horse Feeding*, David & Charles.
C. Vogel B Vet Med, MRCVS, *Horse Ailments and Health Care*, Ward.

Lizards

Joan Palmer, *Reptiles and Amphibians*, Blandford – covers the special needs of each type of lizard.
Robert G. Sprackford, *All About Lizards*, THF Publications.
R. H. Wynne, *Lizards in Captivity*, THF Publications.

Mice and Rats

National Mouse Club, Ansteys Lea, Clay Lane, Marton, Winsford, Cheshire CW7 2QE Tel: 0606 883331. (P.654)

The National Fancy Rat Society, 71 Groome Court, Regency Walk, Croydon CR0 7UT Tel: 081 777 3762. (P.654)

Rabbits

The British Rabbit Council, Purefoy House, 7 Kirkgate, Newark, Notts NG24 1AD Tel: 0636 76042 – M£M, G, A, shows. (P.655)

Useful Books
David Robinson, *Encyclopaedia of Pet Rabbits*, THF Publications.
Care for Your Rabbit, the RSPCA official guide, Collins.

Snakes

Klaus Griehl, *Snakes, Giant Snakes, and Non-Venomous Snakes in the Terrarium*, Barron Educational Series, New York.
Christopher Mattison, *The Care of Reptiles and Amphibians in Captivity*, Blandford.
Joan Palmer, *Reptiles and Amphibians*, Blandford.
Mervin F. Roberts, *Snakes*, THF Publications Ltd – mainly on constricting snakes.

Tortoises, Terrapins and Turtles

The Association for the Study of Reptilia (ASRA), c/o Richard Allen, P.O. Box 73, Banbury, Oxon OX15 6RE Tel: 0993 823006 – M£L, M, G, A, Lib. (P.656)

British Herpetological Society, c/o The Zoological Society of London, Regents Park, London NW1 4RY Tel: 081 452 9578. (P.656)

Useful Books
David Alderton, *Tortoises and Terrapins*, Saiga (paperback).
C. Mattison, *The Care of Reptiles and Amphibians in Captivity*, Blandford Press.
David Robinson, *Tortoises, Turtles and Terrapins*, Bartholomew (paperback).

Organizations

Consumer Bodies • Government • Media and the Arts • The Medical Services • The Police • Religious Faiths • Services • Travel and Transport • Work-Related Organizations

CONSUMER BODIES

Citizens Advice Bureaux (CABx)

Citizens Advice Bureaux are among Britain's most useful institutions. Their role is to make sure nobody fails to get their entitlements because they don't know their rights, or are unable to fight their own case. CABx offer a free, and confidential, service in which they explain social security entitlements, help people make complaints against public bodies of all kinds, show them how to cope with financial problems and assist with legal problems. How far they can go in helping with a problem depends very much on what it is. They will guide a desperate battered wife through the legal steps needed to get her legal protection, but they can't hold someone's hand right through a divorce.

You can phone – or visit them – with or without an appointment and when the team at a Citizens Advice Bureau don't know the answer, they can always tell you where else to go. They also carry the leaflets and explanatory pamphlets put out by government departments and quangos. CABx are founded by local authorities, and listed in the phone book under Citizens Advice Bureau.

Federation of Independent Advice Centres

There are independent advice centres all over the country which offer free advice on a wide range of problems, such as benefits, housing and discrimination. Unlike the CABx they are funded from a range of sources, and they often specialize in certain issues or sectors of the community, such as the disabled, single parents or some ethnic group. They may take on in-depth work on particular cases, and some centres will even represent people in tribunals. Although you may find them in the 'Advice' section of some telephone directories, such as Thompsons, there is no general name under which you can look them up in an ordinary phone book. To find your nearest one, ask your public library, or contact the address on page 692.

National Consumer Council (NCC)

The National Consumer Council is financed by govern-ment and its members are appointed by the Secretary of State for Trade and Industry, but otherwise it is entirely independent. It represents the interests of consumers in every area, from goods and services to the health service, public transport and amenities like gas and water. The Council does *not* help with individual complaints but reports to governments on faults in services and legislation, and lobbies them for improvements. This means that, although it will not deal with your particular problem, you can write and tell the Council if there are flaws in the system about which the NCC should lobby the authorities.

Money Advice Centres

The Money Advice Association is an independent organization. Its role is to supply the name of your nearest Money Advice Centre which will give advice on serious personal financial problems, such as debt, if you have been unable to find it through your local CAB.

Office of Fair Trading (OFT)

The Office of Fair Trading is a government organization looking after the interests of consumers. It approves the codes of practice of trade associations, alerts the Monopolies Commission to potential monopolies, and is the body to which Trading Standards Officers report. It also publishes excellent free leaflets on consumer rights – available from CABx, *not* direct from the OFT.

If you think a company has broken any consumer law (see Law) ask the Trading Standards Officer, at your local council, to look into it: the OFT doesn't deal with individual complaints. However, the OFT does like to be told if a code of practice is not being properly applied.

GOVERNMENT

The European Community (EC)

The European Community (EC or Common Market) has 12 member states. The founding 6 – France, Germany, Italy, Belgium, Luxembourg and Holland – signed their agreement in 1957 and formally united in 1958. Britain, Denmark and Ireland then joined in 1973, followed by

Greece in 1981, and Spain and Portugal in 1986. It is the largest trade bloc of its kind in the world and has special trading relationships with many African, Caribbean and Pacific countries.

Council of Ministers

The Community is run by the Council of Ministers. It creates all major EC legislation, and its laws are binding on EC members. The major work is done by the specialist ministers from the various departments of state, such as the Minister for Agriculture. They stand up for the interests of their countries, and each country has a voting strength, on the Council, proportional to its size. Major issues demand a unanimous decision, but minor ones can be passed by a majority. The presidency of the Council passes to a different member state every 6 months, and the heads of the various governments also meet at 6-monthly intervals.

European Commission

The Commission has 17 members, appointed for a 4-year term by agreement between the member governments. Unlike the members of the Council, they are sworn to uphold the interests of the *whole* Community and ignore their national interests. The Commission's job is to see that the EC rules are kept. It is also the policy planning body which makes proposals to the Council. The only way members can be removed from office is by a motion of censure, on the entire Commission, from the European Parliament.

European Parliament

The members of the European Parliament were voted in for the first time in 1979. There are 81 British members (MEPs), elected for 5 years, from candidates put forward by the political parties, most of whom are not already MPs at Westminster. The elections are held in each country according to its own electoral system. So, in Britain, MEPs are elected on a majority vote from constituencies which embrace several Westminster ones. Anyone can get the name and address of their MEP from their local library and may write to him or her direct.

In the European Parliament MEPs belong to party groups, according to their political complexion, regardless of national boundaries. They meet once a month and debate issues and sit on special committees in much the same way as they would in the House of Commons. Commission proposals are submitted to the European Parliament for an opinion before decisions are taken in the Council. And the Parliament and the Council have joint powers in deciding the ill-fated EC budget.

Economic and Social Committee

This is a large committee made up of representatives of employers' organizations, trade unions and special interest groups. It has to be consulted on a wide range of EC aims, but it operates purely in an advisory capacity. In theory, it can be lobbied via one of the groups represented on it – in reality, this is hard.

Financing the EC

The EC budget is now a portion of VAT revenue and of the Gross National Product (GNP), plus import levies. It is mainly spent on regional policies and on the Common Agricultural Policy (CAP). Income and expenditure have to balance but this doesn't always happen, so extra payments from member states occasionally have to be agreed.

How the EC Affects Us

The major influence of the EC is through common policies agreed by the members and incorporated into our legislation. These policies cover almost every area of life, and are agreed by The Council of Ministers in the EC. A directive is then issued telling the national governments the date by which they must make that policy into law. Our government *must* obey the directive – whether MPs like it or not.

Our Rights in Relation to the EC

Both houses of the British Parliament have scrutiny committees which examine proposed EC legislation, and British ministers are answerable to Parliament for their actions in the EC Council of Ministers. Anyone who wishes to lobby or protest at EC proposed legislation can approach: (a) his or her MP, (b) the relevant minister, (c) a member of the European Parliament, (d) the relevant commissioner at the European Commission. The **Commission of the European Community** will provide information on the Commission's policies and on EC laws.

Parliament

The two, unequal, sections of Parliament – the House of Commons and the House of Lords – are officially headed by the Queen. She therefore opens each session in October or November and lays out the government's intended policy in the Queen's Speech – which is actually prepared by the Prime Minister's Office.

House of Commons

At a general election about 650 Members of Parliament are elected – one for each constituency. The party with the greatest number of MPs forms a government by its leader appointing a cabinet of about 22 senior ministers, plus 80 or so other ministers. The majority are from the Commons, but some can be from the Lords. The leader of the largest defeated party appoints an equivalent 'shadow cabinet'. Ministers and shadow ministers sit on the front seats on their sides of the House. All the other MPs are known as back-benchers.

The Public and Parliament

In theory, the role of an MP is to represent the views of his constituency in Parliament, and every citizen has the right to contact his MP on any issue he feels strongly about. An MP can also take up a constituent's case with certain authorities outside Parliament. The best way to reach an MP is by letter to the House of Commons, or by visiting one of the 'surgery' sessions which most MPs hold. But any constituent may simply turn up at the

Addresses and suggestions for further reading are at the ends of chapters.

House of Commons, fill in a green card and give it to a doorkeeper, who will find the MP, if he is in the House. The MP usually meets the constituent in the central lobby – hence the term 'to lobby'. There is also an unwritten rule that constituents must reach other MPs through their own MP, and not contact them directly.

Ministers are an exception to this rule: anyone may write to any minister, and may even ask to see him or her. Alternatively, they can ask their MP to deal with a ministry. An MP usually writes to the minister and can also raise the matter in the House at Question Time or in an Adjournment Debate.

The Structure of a Ministry

Each ministry is usually headed by a Secretary of State, and under him come one or more Ministers of State, and one or more Parliamentary Under Secretaries of State. Each has special responsibility for an area of the ministry's field, and one of them usually sits in the Lords – though this is not essential.

Acts of Parliament

Changing things is the very life-blood of politicians and the main instrument of change is an Act of Parliament. An act starts life as a bill – a draft law – and it then has to come before both Houses of Parliament in a set sequence before it can be made law. It is during this sequence that members of the public, who have noticed flaws in the bill, can point them out to their MP and ask him or her to take them up. So it's useful to know the sequence. It is even possible for an MP to press for an amendment very late in the day, via a member of the Lords. Most bills start in the Commons and the pattern is as follows (when a bill starts in the Lords the process is exactly reversed).

At the **First Reading** the Commons is formally notified that a bill of a certain name is being introduced. There is no debate. The bill is then printed and available to the public, through **Her Majesty's Stationery Office**.

The **Second Reading**, at which the bill is explained and the minister cross-questioned, is usually several days later. If a majority of the House are then in favour of the bill it goes to the Committee Stage. But it may be voted out.

In the **Committee Stage** a small group of MPs go through it clause by clause, agreeing to cuts and improvements. They are usually selected because they know something about the subject of the bill and all parties are represented in about the same proportions as in Parliament. The altered bill is then printed.

The bill then goes to the **Report Stage** and is presented to the Commons and debated by MPs, who have a chance to make further changes.

In the **Third Reading** the bill comes before the Commons. It has to be accepted or rejected as it is. If the Commons reject it, that is the end of it. If it is accepted it goes before the House of Lords.

In the Lords the bill goes through exactly the same stages as it did in the Commons, except that the Committee Stage is the whole of the Lords, not just a small group, and changes can be made in the Third Reading.

If the Lords have made no changes the bill can go straight to the Queen for Royal Assent. But, if changes have been made, the bill must go before the Commons first. Once a bill receives Royal Assent it becomes an act, and is law, but it may not come into force straight away.

MPs' Attendance at Parliament

MPs have considerable freedom, but each party uses a system of 'whips' to let MPs know whether they need to attend. A whip is a document giving the business of the day. If a section is underlined once they should try to attend. Two underlinings mean they should either attend or 'pair' with a member of the opposition who also agrees not to be there. A three-line whip, with three underlinings, is an emergency and every MP is expected to be there unless actually dying. This system is administered by the Chief Whip for each party.

House of Lords

The House of Lords has about 1,178 members, consisting of hereditary peers, life peers created by the Queen, the 26 most senior archbishops and bishops, and a group of judges. Some, however, may never go there. Until 1958 there were no women in the Lords, but there are now more women there than in the Commons. The Lords divide along party lines, and the same whip system applies. But, with no constituents to offend, the Lords can afford to be more controversial. Some of the most progressive legislation of the last 20 years owes much to this chamber.

The House of Lords has five main activities:

1 It is the supreme court of appeal in legal cases. These appeals are only heard by a specially appointed group of law lords, not by the whole House, and about 70 cases are brought before them a year.
2 It is a forum for debates – which may or may not have any influence on the rest of Parliament.
3 It can originate legislation – which is then passed through both Houses.
4 It considers and amends bills which have started in the House of Commons.
5 It questions the government on its activities. It has a special role in relation to bills on issues which affect only one or two people. If you need a bill to be brought you first have to find a peer or peeress to sponsor it. Obviously, it is a good idea to lobby a peer or peeress who is already in sympathy with the topic. A run through Dod's *Parliamentary Companion* should help here, and any member of the House of Lords may be approached in writing by a member of the public.

Visiting Parliament

Parliament sits for about 37 weeks a year, taking holidays (known as recesses) for 4 weeks at Christmas, 1 week at Easter, 1 week at the Spring Bank Holiday, and a summer recess from early August to October. The House of Commons usually sits at 2.30 pm on Mondays, Tuesdays, Wednesdays and Thursdays, and at 9.30 am on Fridays. A normal sitting may last until after 10 pm.

The House of Lords sits at 2.30 pm on Tuesdays, Wednesdays and Thursdays and 11 am on Fridays.

The best way to watch the Commons in session is to write to your MP, about 6 weeks in advance, asking if he or she can obtain a ticket for you (maximum two tickets) and giving a selection of dates. This lets you watch Question Time – which is often the liveliest part of the proceedings. If you simply queue outside St Stephen's entrance, you get in later. You queue in the same way to watch the Lords. The queues are shortest on Fridays, because the sitting ends at 3 pm.

Parliamentary Ombudsman

If you have suffered as a result of injustice by a department of central government, such as the Department of Social Security or the Inland Revenue, you can ask your MP to take your case to the Parliamentary Ombudsman (page 695). The Ombudsman investigates and, if an injustice is found, can instruct the department to make amends either by apologizing or by making an appropriate payment. You cannot take your case to the Ombudsman yourself, it *must* go via an MP, but you can get an information leaflet direct from his office.

Political Pressure Groups

Britain is rich in pressure groups. Every conceivable viewpoint seems to have one and they seem to me to be some of our most useful organizations. However, the only thing to be said about them, in a book like this, is what they press for and where they can be found. So you will find many of them among the useful addresses on page 695, rather than here.

Many other organizations, concerned with such issues as consumer rights, medical problems and disabilities, and legal issues, also act as political pressure groups. You will find them under the relevant sections of this book and at the ends of appropriate chapters.

Political Parties

Political parties are hard to summarize and easy to misrepresent. What follows is taken entirely from information supplied by the parties themselves, and the quotes are their own words.

Communist Party – see Democratic Left

Conservative Party

The Conservative Party stands for 'personal freedom', 'free enterprise', 'the rule of law'. It favours a strong defence policy, believing NATO and nuclear weapons have a vital role in preventing war and that British forces must be capable of operating effectively both within and outside Europe. It also claims to be a party which cares for every sector of society regardless of class, colour or creed. There is no fixed membership subscription and, though industry does contribute to it, most of its funds come from subscriptions and from money raised by constituents.

Democratic Left

Although some splinter groups still use the word 'communist' in their name, the main Communist Party of Great Britain is now called the Democratic Left, with a slightly different manifesto. It is still anti-capitalist, and favours a state-planned economy with a high degree of equality, but the call for a 'revolutionary transformation' has been removed and there is no longer an obligation to convert others to the 'faith'.

Green Party

The Green Party wishes to promote an economic system which does not exploit resources or people and emphasizes locally based work and finance – without multinationals or big banks – so that people's needs may be met without 'damaging each other or the planet'. It is strongly unilateralist. It would leave NATO, close all foreign military bases in Britain, remove all nuclear, chemical and biological weapons from British forces, and encourage other European countries to follow suit.

Labour Party

The main aims of the Labour Party stated in Clause 4 of the constitution are 'to secure for the workers . . . common ownership of the means of production, distribution and exchange, and the best obtainable system of popular administration and control of each industry or service' and 'to co-operate with the General Council of the Trades Union Congress, or other kindred organizations, in joint political or other action . . .'

Although it would work within NATO and now favours multilateral, not unilateral, disarmament, it opposes the modernization or deployment of short-range and tactical nuclear weapons within NATO.

Only a small proportion of the party's funding comes from the members. In recent years between 78 per cent and 86 per cent of the party's total income has come from trade-union affiliation fees, and some candidates are directly funded by a union.

Liberal Democrats

The Liberal Democrats were formed in 1988 when the Liberal Party merged with most of the Social Democratic Party. This party is committed to a mixed economy in which prosperity is fairly shared and the global environment protected. It wants to introduce proportional representation, freedom of information and a bill of rights. Internationally it believes in Britain playing a full part in the EC, NATO, the UN and the Commonwealth. But it aims for the demilitarization of East-West relations, substantial reductions in both conventional and nuclear forces, the inclusion of Britain's nuclear weapons in negotiations and a reduction in defence spending. It is funded almost entirely from private subscriptions and local fundraising.

Plaid Cymru

Plaid Cymru means 'Party of Wales' and it was founded in 1925 to work for self-government for Wales by peaceful means. It would like to see the restoration of the Welsh language, and Wales under an independent democratic socialist government, which would play a part in world affairs through the United Nations. Its policies are broadly socialist, decentralist and environmentalist. The funding is entirely from members of the party.

Scottish National Party

This claims to be a moderate left of centre party. It stands for self-government for Scotland, and greater decision making within its local communities. Having gained independence, it would also like to renegotiate Scotland's conditions of entry into the EC. It is dedicated to unilateral nuclear disarmament and the removal of all foreign bases from Scottish soil.

Social Democratic and Labour Party

This is a socialist party, formed in 1970, which aims to produce peace in Northern Ireland, by democratic means, and works for 'Irish unity based on the consent of the majority'.

Ulster Democratic Unionist Party

The stated objectives of this party, led by Ian Paisley, are to 'smash Sinn Fein' and 'annihilate the IRA'. It is fiercely Protestant, and wants to maintain Northern Ireland's position as part of the United Kingdom.

Ulster Unionist Council

Originally formed in the struggle against 'Home Rule' as a coalition of Liberals and Conservatives, this party is dedicated to remain British and *not* uniting with the Irish Republic. But it wants to see less direct rule from England.

Government Departments and Bodies

One seasoned campaigner claimed that the great advantage of the British system of government was that there was so much confusion and overlap that on any issue he could approach at least a dozen different departments. The addresses of those departments are on pages 693-694; defining which does what to whom is more than there is space for – but we all know who pays. I wish you luck in approaching them.

Local Government

The relationship between central and local government is essentially the same as between husband and wife in an old-fashioned marriage: central government says what should be done; local government does it. Central government handles the broad issues – defence, international affairs. Local government deals with those which affect our daily lives – health, education, welfare, parking, libraries, consumer protection. But, true to the marriage simile, it does so within constraints placed by the appropriate department of central government, which ultimately holds the purse strings. So, predictably, local government has second-class status.

Administration

A local authority is, in theory, the epitome of government by the people for the people. Its policy is decided by local councillors who are elected from those in the area. Their work on the council is virtually unpaid and is done in their free time from other jobs. Provided they stay within the law, local authorities can more or less run themselves as they wish. However, since the 1960s local politics have become dominated by party politics and the decisions of councillors increasingly made along party lines.

Councillors oversee the authority, but the day-to-day work is done by full-time staff and supervised by local government officials.

Financing Local Government

Local authorities are among Britain's largest land owners, shareholders, and employers, and the budget of the Greater London Council *alone* was, in its day, larger than that of many nations. The income comes both out of national taxes and from money raised locally, through the council tax. Of these old local rates used to be the most important, but now more than half the money spent by local councils is from government grants, out of taxes, applying the Robin Hood principle of funding the poorer boroughs out of taxes paid by those in richer ones.

The Structure and Role of Local Authorities

The structure of local authorities in Britain is changing as I write and the final form is yet to be decided. Major cities apart, there is at present a tiered system, which varies slightly in Scotland. At the top come county councils; below them are borough councils or district councils, which have almost identical roles; then town or parish councils.

London

Since the abolition of the Greater London Council (GLC) the London Residuary Body has been giving back to the London boroughs the powers which belonged to the GLC. Essentially they have the powers of county and borough councils combined. The City of London is not a borough but a separate corporation, with similar powers.

Large Cities – England

City areas like Liverpool and Manchester are under city councils which have the powers of both county and borough councils. In many cases these councils link with other authorities, in the same region, to form joint authorities for administering services like fire-fighting and the police.

Scotland

- Regional Councils – similar to county councils.
- District Councils – much the same as borough councils in England and Wales
- Community Councils – very similar to town or parish councils.

Grievances, Complaints and Suggestions

Local libraries have lists of local councillors, with their home addresses and phone numbers, which can be used if you want to discuss any local issue or make a complaint. How much a councillor can, or will, do is very variable but, at the very least, he or she should be able to help you pinpoint the level of local government you need to complain to.

Every town hall should have an officer who deals with complaints. Start with him or her, or with the chief officer of the department in question. Failing that, try the chairman of the relevant committee or sub committee. If you still get no joy, *and have suffered personal injustice*, go to the Local Government Ombudsman (see below). If local authorities break the law they can also be taken to court, but most problems aren't on that scale.

Another route is to complain to your MP, who probably has experience on a local council and can help you through the maze. Also, certain local authority schemes must be approved by a government minister before they are implemented, and can be halted by a minister if he objects. If your complaint falls into one of these categories, complain to the appropriate minister either directly or via your MP. Such areas include planning, housing, education, the appointment of senior officials, such as chief constables, and the making of by-laws.

The Local Government Ombudsman

There are three local government ombudsmen who cover the whole of England between them, and one each for Scotland and Wales. They offer a free service dealing with complaints in connection with any local authorities – except town or parish councils, which are not under any such supervision. They also cover certain other public bodies. These are listed in a free booklet which you can get from a CAB, from your local council, or from the Ombudsmen's Offices.

Before approaching an ombudsman you *must* try to resolve the problem yourself. So, if you have a grievance against one of these organizations your first move must be to complain to them directly. If you are still not happy, ask a councillor to take up your complaint – the local library has a list of councillors. If this produces no result send your written complaint to the local ombudsman.

The local ombudsmen are concerned with *injustices* created by what these organizations do, or fail to do. You cannot take a complaint to them just because you don't like what has been done, and the ombudsmen can only deal with something which occurred after 1 April 1974. There are also a number of other situations they may not handle, so it is best to get their leaflet first (see above). Your complaint will be investigated and you may be asked for more details. If they find the complaint justified they contact the organization concerned and encourage it to put things right. But, unfortunately, the ombudsman cannot insist it does so.

Voting for Local Councillors or MPs

To vote you must be over the age of 18, be a British subject (or a citizen of the Irish Republic) and have your name on the electoral register of your local council. You can check the draft list in a public library in early December and notify the Electoral Registration Officer of the council, before 16 December, if your name is not there. The people not allowed to vote are those in prison for more than a year, those detained in psychiatric institutions, and (in Parliamentary elections) peers.

Proxy votes, in which you appoint someone to vote for you, are only allowed to those working outside Britain (e.g. servicemen).

Postal votes are allowed if you cannot go to the polling station for the following reasons:

- Illness or incapacity (a doctor or nurse must vouch for this)
- Work which prevents you (e.g. long-distance lorry drivers)
- You have moved to a new area and are not yet on the electoral register there (this only applies in Parliamentary elections)
- You are engaged in religious observance on that day.

Enquiries about both proxy and postal votes should be made some weeks before the election. And neither type of vote is allowed for those who are away on holiday.

Those entitled to vote are sent a numbered polling card, shortly before the election, telling them which polling station to vote at. They simply take this with them and place an X by the name of the candidate they prefer. Whichever candidate gets the most votes wins.

MEDIA AND THE ARTS

Advertising

Advertisements are controlled by both laws and codes. For example, they must not break the Race Relations Act, infringe copyright or libel someone. Also, there is the British Code of Advertising Practice (BCAP), agreed among all those involved, which applies to all printed advertisements – in newspapers, magazines, on posters, on documents put through your door – and to those in the cinema, on video, and on viewdata services (excluding Oracle). It also covers the use of personal data in direct marketing.

The code is regularly reviewed and amended, in line with public feeling, and copies of it are available in libraries and Citizens Advice Bureaux. Basically, in addition to being legal, an advertisement must be:

- decent (i.e. it must respect accepted UK standards of propriety)
- honest (i.e. it must present facts clearly and not exploit consumers' lack of knowledge or experience)
- truthful (in all respects it must be accurate, unambiguous, not exaggerate or omit relevant facts)
- safe (i.e. it should not show or advocate dangerous behaviour)
- socially responsible and harmless to children (i.e. must contain nothing which could harm people

physically, mentally or morally, or exploit their credulity)
- fair (i.e. not make unfair comparisons with competitors, or denigrate them, or exploit the goodwill of a trademark).

Under the code on personal data, a mailing list may not be sold without those on it having a chance to have their details removed or corrected. And if you ask where an organization got your address, you must be told. There is also a British Code of Sales Promotion Practice (BCSPP) which covers promotional lotteries, competitions, and so on.

Complaints

The **Advertising Standards Authority (ASA)**, which is indirectly funded by the industry, but independent of it, handles all complaints about breaches of either code, except those on radio and television – which are dealt with by the Independent Television Commission and the Radio Authority (see page 668).

Complaints to the ASA should be made in writing, ideally with a copy of the advertisement or exact details of where and when it appeared. If its council feels a code has been broken, the advertiser is asked to withdraw, or amend, the advertisement, and agree not to repeat the offence. If this fails, either the media are asked to block the advertisement or misleading advertisements can be referred to the OFT and a legal injunction obtained. Equally, if personal data is repeatedly misused in direct marketing, the Royal Mail may revoke its contract with the company. Details of complaints, both upheld and rejected, are given in an ASA bulletin. Reading it you'll find even well-known companies make totally false claims.

The ASA has a useful leaflet on the do's and don'ts of complaining. However, the ASA only deals with the *content* of advertisements. If you have problems with the product itself, complain to the maker, or to a Trading Standards Officer.

The Arts

The arts, like almost every other area of British life, have a surfeit of administrative bodies. At the top there is the **Arts Council**, through which government money is channelled to Regional Arts Boards and arts organizations. Money is also channelled into them by local councils, the British Film Institute, and the Crafts Council. Some companies also sponsor arts projects. To find out which, contact the **Association of Business Sponsorship for the Arts**. These organizations may award grants and bursaries to individuals. Your local reference librarian should know the bodies for your area. But applications usually have deadlines and most of the money goes to arts groups – especially those which are charities.

The **Charities Commission** (page 692) can tell you how to register your organization as a charity. It can also tell you how to check whether any organization which claims to be a charity really is one.

British Broadcasting Corporation (BBC)

The BBC is established under royal charter, licensed by the Home Secretary and funded by licence fees paid by the public, and must present audited accounts to Parliament. The powers of the BBC are vested in 12 governors, mainly from outside broadcasting, appointed by the Queen in Council, on the recommendation of the Prime Minister. But the powers are exercised by a permanent staff headed by the Director General. In Scotland, Wales and Northern Ireland responsibility for the policy and content of BBC programmes is shared with their National Broadcasting Councils, each headed by a BBC governor and staffed by BBC appointees. A series of advisory councils also cover different subjects and areas.

Ceefax from the BBC

Ceefax is a large news and on-screen information and entertainment service, obtainable on any television with a teletext decoder, and offers up-to-the-minute news, and financial, travel and consumer information. It also gives subtitles to an increasing number of TV programmes (for those with hearing problems).

Complaints and Queries About BBC Programmes

If you want to complain about anything you don't like on the BBC ring Television Centre, Broadcasting House or Bush House, as appropriate. An information officer will note your complaint, and a daily log of complaints is passed on to the heads of departments. If you want a reply to a complaint write to BBC Viewers and Listeners Relations at White City (page 696) which handles both radio and television. From there your comment should be referred to the programme-makers.

Frequencies

The frequencies on which different services are transmitted vary with the transmitter which relays them. If you have a RDS radio it will automatically tune to the best FM frequency for your location. It is ideal for car radios and will also let traffic flashes from other frequencies butt in on your main programme to warn you of hazards. BBC Engineering publishes booklets listing all domestic radio and TV transmitters and advising on reception. They can be obtained from **BBC Engineering Information**. Devotees of the World Service, who want to know transmission times, can subscribe to BBC Worldwide (see page 696).

Publications

BBC products, such as books and language courses, are available from booksellers, and also from BBC bookshops near Broadcasting House, Television Centre and Bush House or by mail from the BBC Bookshop.

Radio Weather Forecasts

The usual weekday times for general forecasts on Radio 4 Long Wave are 06.03, 06.55, 07.55, 08.58, 12.55, 17.55, 21.59, 00.27; for shipping forecasts, they are 05.55, 13.55,

17.50, 00.33. Warnings of dangerous conditions – fog, icy roads, etc. – are broadcast at short notice on all networks.

SOS Messages

Free messages seeking relatives of anyone *dangerously ill* are transmitted, after medical confirmation of the emergency. The broadcast is made once only, either before the 07.00 or 18.00 news. Requests to Broadcasting House in London, Glasgow, Cardiff or Belfast.

Tickets for BBC Programmes

Anyone may ask for free tickets for any BBC show which has an audience. Apply in writing 6 weeks before the date, giving the type of show you want and the ages of any children in the party. But be warned – many shows are recorded months before transmission, so your favourite may not be available. Send a sae to the **BBC Radio** or **BBC TV Ticket Unit**.

Writing for the BBC

You may find it helpful to read the BBC publication 'Writing for the BBC'. Typed scripts (with a sae) should be sent to the Script Editor of the appropriate section – Radio Light Entertainment, Television Drama, or whatever. But scripts do get lost, so keep a copy yourself.

Cable Television

Cable television should soon be available to everyone in and around major towns. As the name suggests, the signal gets to your TV via a cable. So you need no dish. As cable can carry a huge number of channels, the franchise rules say the companies must offer all the major British channels plus any others they wish. There is a bias towards specialist channels and there is usually a monthly rental for the British channels plus a handful of others, with additional rental for extra channels. However, one of the main advantages is that the same cable can carry phone calls. And phoning by cable could be very much cheaper than using conventional phone lines. **The Cable Television Association** (page 697) has information on all aspects of cable.

Complaining About Broadcasts

The first route for complaints is to the editor of the programme or to the head of the company concerned. If that fails, and you feel a broadcast has infringed your personal privacy or treated you unfairly, complain to the **Broadcasting Complaints Commission**. It covers all sound, television, cable and British satellite programmes, including advertisements and teletext transmissions. But all it can do is tell the company to broadcast its finding and publish it in the press. It cannot insist on either an apology or compensation. And if you were asked to appear in a programme, and didn't make it clear to the programme's editor – from the start – that you didn't want to appear or expected a fee, you may get no sympathy.

However, if you feel that any radio or TV programme, including those on cable and satellite, has violated nor-

mal standards of taste and decency, or been too violent, the **Broadcasting Standards Council** can investigate and insist on its findings being made public on air or in the press.

Alternatively, if an independent radio or television company, or an advertiser, is at fault you may complain to the **Independent Television Commission** or the **Radio Authority**. They supervise independent radio and television companies which transmit programmes, including British satellite and cable TV. This means they regulate and licence programme companies and regulate advertising.

The **ITC** and the **Radio Authority** have a duty to ensure that the contents of advertisements meet the standards laid down by the Broadcasting Act and by various consumer acts. Also to see that advertisements unsuitable for children are not transmitted before 9 p.m., and that the number of minutes of advertising, per hour, do not exceed the legal limit. If the codes have been breached, the advertisement will be withdrawn.

If complaining to these authorities doesn't get results, the next step is your MP. You might also enlist the support of a suitable pressure group (see page 697), which will add its voice to yours. However, the Commission cannot control satellite programmes beamed in from abroad. On these, complain straight to your MP.

> When BBC or independent programmes offer helplines or follow-up leaflets the service is often provided by **Broadcasting Support Services**. **BSS** keeps fact sheets for some while after any broadcast, so it is always worth asking for the sheet you forgot to write in for. See page 697 for the addresses.

Local Radio

As stations tend to come and go it isn't practical to list them, but the BBC and Radio Authority will supply a list of their respective local stations. Some, such as Capital Radio, offer a wide range of local services.

Press Complaints

If you have been wronged by something printed in a newspaper, magazine or periodical, you should complain to the editor. You may also complain in writing to the director of the **Press Complaints Commission**, sending a copy of the offending article and of any correspondence between yourself and the paper. The Commission will investigate and can insist that the publication publishes the details of any judgement against it in a position of reasonable prominence. You can be asked to agree not to go to law if the editor accepts the Commission's investigation. A leaflet giving all the details on making complaints is available from the Commission. Alternatively, if you can afford it, you can take a publication which has broken the law to court – though not while the matter is also being dealt with by the Commission.

Addresses and suggestions for further reading are at the ends of chapters.

THE MEDICAL SERVICES

Patients' Charter

The Patients' Charter gives patients the right to a certain standard of service from the NHS. Key points are:

- that those working in the NHS must respect a patient's privacy, dignity and cultural needs
- that detailed information of local services must be available
- that, in Out-Patients, you must be seen within 30 minutes of your appointment time
- you should not have to wait more than 2 years for an operation

You also have rights regarding your medical records and over complaints (see below). To help the system work patients have been asked to keep their appointments or give proper notice if they can't. You can find out more about the charter or NHS services from the freephone line on page 695.

The National Health Service

The Department of Health, which set up the Patients' Charter, is under the Secretary of State for Health. Below that there are **Regional Health Authorities**. They allocate money to the District Health Authorities under them and are responsible for supervising fundholders and **FHSA** (below) and delivering NHS objectives. As I write, there are plans to change the role of Regional Health Authorities and also to enable District Health Authorities and FHSAs to merge.

However, the **District Health Authorities** are responsible for the hospitals and other medical services in their area – but not for **NHS Trusts**. Each District Health Authority usually has a **Community Health Council (CHC)** with members from both the local authority and voluntary organizations to bridge the gap between the public and the health service. Anyone may attend their meetings and, if you are having problems with the local health service, will give advice and help with complaints. In Northern Ireland the equivalents are District Committees.

NHS Trusts are independent organizations, within the NHS, which operate branches of the Health Service. There are ambulance-service trusts, hospital trusts and trusts covering care in the community. They are funded by the Department of Health, and each is run by a management committee, similar to the board of a public company, headed by a chief executive. They are answerable only to the Regional Health Authority and the Secretary of State.

Family Health Service Authorities (FHSAs) have replaced Family Practitioner Committees. They report to the Regional Health Authorities and most NHS general practitioners, dentists, pharmacists and opticians are under contract direct to them.

Joint Consultative Committees are the link between the District Health Authority and the local authorities in the same areas, and voluntary authorities are also included. Sub-groups within these committees cover particular problems such as the mentally ill.

The Scottish Health Service is under the **Scottish Home and Health Department**, which comes under the Secretary of State for Scotland. Scotland is divided into **Health Boards** which administer all levels of health care and have links to both local authorities and local Health Councils which play the same role as CHCs. **General Practitioner Committees** replace FHSAs.

Finding and Using Your Local Health Authorities

Health Service bodies are in the telephone book under the name of the region, district and so on. This can be confusing because health-service boundaries aren't usually the same as those of local authorities. However, the local reference library, your CHC or your GP's receptionist should be able to help.

The Health Service has a mass of detailed rules and regulations. But there is a freephone helpline (page 695) or the Consumers' Association book, *Patient's Guide to the National Health Service*, is invaluable here; and it's also worth getting a copy of the NHS Patients' Charter (page 695).

NHS Charges

NHS treatment from GPs and hospitals is free but there are charges attached to such things as prescriptions, dentistry, and glasses. However, not everyone need pay these charges, For example, those with low incomes, or on certain benefits, or with certain illnesses, or over or under a set age, or pregnant, may pay nothing at all for certain things, or pay a very reduced rate.

In some cases the charge will be dropped if you complete a form at the time, in others you will need to get a voucher from the Health Benefits Unit first. The leaflets and forms you need to use this system are in pharmacies, GPs surgeries or by post from the DH Literature Line (page 695). For example, G11 tells you how to get free glasses, D11 how to get free dentistry, and so on. There is even a WS11 for free wigs. But if you claim on the grounds of low income you may have to complete quite a detailed form on your income and outgoings.

General Practitioners

You may change your GP once without giving a reason. The best way to find a GP is through friends and neighbours in the area. Failing that, your local library, main post office, or CAB should have a *Medical List* giving the doctors in your area. Having found some who are conveniently close, you can check their sex, qualifications and other details in the *Medical Directory* in the reference library – letters after their names are explained in the abbreviations section of this book.

Before registering with a GP, go and see him. But *don't* take your medical card, or the receptionist may take it from you on arrival. If you don't like the doctor it is embarrassing to have to ask for it back, but if you do like him you can always post it.

Doctors often regard this as a one-way interview to

decide whether you will be accepted and may be suspicious if you have fallen out with your doctor. So if you are not moving home, it may help to have a good explanation ready. An acceptable reason is wanting a doctor of a different sex from the previous one. And you have a right to check on points which matter to you. GPs must now have leaflets giving the services they offer but ask the receptionist about points which aren't covered, for example:

- is it a group practice? In these, doctors usually stand in for each other when away, so you are always seen by someone you know, whereas in a solo practice the stand-ins may constantly change
- what are the surgery hours? (Saturday and evening surgeries are becoming less common)
- is there an appointment system?
- does he deliver babies – if you want a home delivery?
- does the doctor deal with contraception?
- Does the practice hold any preventive clinics, e.g. 'Well Woman'?
- Is he a fundholder?

> GPs who are fundholders manage budgets which they can spend on whatever services they think best for their patients. This can include having a complementary therapist working under them or buying hospital treatment outside their region if it is better or will shorten a patient's waiting time.

Registering with a GP
Don't feel you *have* to register with a doctor you don't like – you have a right to meet more than one before deciding. If you like the doctor, just send her your medical card to send to the FHSA for you. The Authority then registers you with the new doctor and notifies your previous one that you are no longer a patient.

If your doctor ceases to practise, you are automatically registered with his or her successor. If you don't want this, tell the FHSA within 14 days. The FHSA will also supply a new medical card if your old one is lost. A doctor can refuse to accept a patient or remove a patient from his or her list, and need give no reason. But if you can't persuade a doctor to accept you the FHSA will allocate one.

Prescriptions
Most people have to pay for their prescriptions, but there are many exceptions such as pensioners, those under 16, pregnant women, those who have had a baby in the last 12 months (even if it was stillborn), also those on low incomes and with certain medical conditions. A form from the Post Office gives the details.

Dentistry
The best way to choose a dentist is to ask around, and find someone who is known to be good at the sort of dentistry you want – whether it's treating children or

making dentures. Failing that, you can find one using the Dental List (see GPs, page 669). But if you can't find a NHS dentist your FHSA must find one for you. You can now sign on with a dentist as you do with a GP, but if you are not happy with any treatment you can go to another dentist for a second opinion.

If you don't sign on then, each time you start a new course of treatment you must make it clear to a dentist that you want to be treated on the NHS. You may be asked to sign a form and give your NHS number. The dentist must then give you a course of treatment on the NHS to make you 'dentally fit'. After that, the 'contract' ceases and next time you should go through the whole routine again. Make sure you get the dentist's agreement before you sit in the chair.

Dental Charges
Only in special circumstances is dentistry on the NHS free. Unless free treatment is agreed *before the dentist starts* and the right evidence of entitlement produced, you are simply charged a special scale of fees. Dentists can ask for payment before a course of treatment starts, and may also charge for an appointment a patient misses without notice.

Before certain work is done a dentist must get permission from the **Dental Estimates Board** (**DEB**). If permission is refused the dentist may appeal, to the FHSA, against the DEB decision within 4 weeks.

Emergency Dentistry
A local hospital or the police may know the number of any emergency dental service. If an NHS dentist sees you as an emergency out of hours there is no extra charge. But even if your dentist does NHS work, a stand-in on an emergency rota may not – so check.

Eye Treatment

Finding an Optician
You don't need to be referred by a GP to have your eyes checked, nor do you have to sign on with anyone, but you will be charged, unless you are exempt. Post offices, libraries and Yellow Pages all have lists of ophthalmic opticians and you can use whomever you wish.

Who Does What
The terms used in this field of medicine have been changing, so any of the following may be involved in eye treatment.

- A **dispensing optician** makes up spectacles.
- An **ophthalmic medical practitioner** is a doctor who treats eye diseases, tests eyesight and prescribes lenses.
- An **ophthalmic optician** tests eyesight, looks for eye diseases and prescribes lenses.
- An **ophthalmologist** (once called an oculist) is a senior doctor specializing in eye diseases and may also be an eye surgeon. You have to be referred to an ophthalmologist.
- An **orthoptist** treats children's eye problems, such as squints, and works under an ophthalmologist.

Addresses and suggestions for further reading are at the ends of chapters.

Other Services
You can ask for the following services via your Community Health Council or GP.

● **Chiropody** is provided mainly for the elderly, handicapped or disabled, pregnant women and school children. Some chiropodists will come to the home. Check the qualifications of the chiropodists before having treatment; the letters MChS or FChS are safeguards.
● **Day Centres** will care for, and feed, special groups. For example, the mentally handicapped or elderly.
● **District nurses** give care in the home and can provide certain aids and equipment, such as incontinence pads.
● **Health visitors** can call at the home and advise on baby care or the care of the sick or old. They also have information on equipment you may be able to get on the NHS.
● **Home adaptations** for someone handicapped or disabled may be partly paid for by the NHS, or provided by local authority social services.
● **Laundry services** are sometimes available for those in special need.
● **Meals on wheels** will provide a hot mid-day meal to the home.
● **Speech therapy** should be available both for children with speech problems, and for adult problems like stammering or speech difficulty after a stroke.
● **Transport** to and from hospital can be provided for those not able to use public transport or where suitable transport is not available.

Hearing Problems

> Hearing aids work best if you get one at the very start of deafness. People used to think that ears were like eyes: that just giving an aid would restore the lost faculty. This is NOT so. As deafness grows the parts of the brain which make sense of sound get less and less work to do – *and, like an unused muscle, they stop working. Once that happens they may never work properly again.* So it is very important to get an aid while all the brain pathways are still fit. And if both ears are deaf you should have *two* aids, like ex-president Reagan – one for each ear.

The NHS lends hearing aids, free of charge, supplies batteries and accessories, and sees to their servicing, but far more sophisticated ones are available privately. The **Royal National Institute for Deaf People (RNID)** (page 591) will test aids without charge, give free advice on deafness by post, and to personal callers, and show you their range of aids by appointment. It also has information on devices which make it easier to hear the telephone, listen to the television and so on, and these can be provided on the NHS if the local authority social

services decide you need them. Your family doctor will refer you to a consultant.

You don't need any referral to buy a hearing aid privately but to buy one without trying it first or getting medical advice could be a waste of money.

Patients' Rights
The key facts of the Patients' Charter are on page 669. On top of that the NHS constantly issues new guidelines. For example, these say that when children are in hospital their mental and emotional welfare must be provided for. So, unless there are overwhelming reasons to the contrary, close contact must be kept with their family, and young children should be nursed separately from adults or even adolescents.

Consent

> *Children under 16* can be treated in an emergency, without their parents' consent, if the parents cannot be reached or refuse consent to treatment which would save the child's life. Otherwise consent must be obtained from the parent or from the child if it is able to understand. However, a girl under 16 may obtain contraceptive advice provided the doctor is sure she understands what is involved, and has tried to persuade her to tell her parents.

Patients must consent to treatment, but consent can either be implied or expressed. If you go to a chest X-ray unit you imply that you agree to a chest X-ray. But if you are about to have an operation you must express consent by signing a form agreeing to it. The consent form names the operation and then has some general words that mean the doctor is free to do whatever else seems to be necessary to relieve the condition. Most people are happy to accept this wording. But if an operation might reveal a condition – such as breast cancer – which could be treated by surgery *or* by medication it isn't so easy. The doctor might choose surgery – since you are already on the table – but *you* might prefer medication. The answer is to tell the doctor how you feel *before* signing the form, and agree with him a change of wording which will leave the surgeon free to act in a sudden emergency but not to do anything you don't want.

Since the doctor you may agree this with won't necessarily do the operation, it is important to get this in writing, not just agree it in words. Some doctors and nurses may not like this, but it can be done, and there is no reason why anyone should sign away their rights over their own body. Nor do good doctors want them to. Private patients can insist on having a particular doctor to operate and they should cross out any wording which allows a change of doctors, except in an emergency. If doctors want you to accept treatment which is part of medical research they must explain it and get your permission. Ask questions and think very carefully before agreeing. You are free to say no and ask for other treatment.

Leaving Hospital

You may leave a hospital whenever you want – unless you are held under the Mental Health Act or have certain infectious diseases. But if you leave before the doctors advise it, you will be asked to sign a form saying you are no longer the hospital's responsibility. You don't have to sign it to leave, and it is best not to sign it if you have a serious complaint against the hospital.

Medical Records

Official medical records belong to the Secretary of State for Health. But the Medical Records Act gives you a right to see your medical records – written or on computer – unless your doctor thinks it will cause you harm or suffering.

Privacy

Whether you are seeing a GP or a consultant in a hospital, you have a right to privacy and can ask for medical students not to be present and refuse to be examined by them. If a doctor (or would-be doctor) examines or treats a patient without his or her consent it is assault and civil proceedings can be brought.

> A husband has *no* absolute right to be with his wife during labour or childbirth; it is at the consultant's discretion. So check the policy before booking a hospital. However, if any member of staff *physically* ejected a husband it might be assault. So, in practice, politely standing firm could work, as it can if a hospital refuses to let you be with a young child. However, the situation needs careful judgement. It is one thing to stand firm against hospital staff who are throwing their weight around, but it is quite another to get in the way of responsible staff carrying out vital procedures.

Donating Organs

Organs can only be removed after death if the donor gave written consent, or gave verbal consent in front of at least two witnesses. Also, whoever is 'lawfully in possession of the body' can authorize the organs' removal if, after reasonable enquiries, there is no reason to think the donor, or surviving relatives, would object. If someone dies in hospital the hospital is 'lawfully in possession of the body' until the relatives claim it. In practice, the relatives are almost always asked, but it is easier for everyone if those who want to give organs carry a donor card and tell their nearest and dearest, and if those *not* wishing to give them *also* carry a card saying so.

Confidentiality

Confidentiality is a difficult issue. In theory, the information on a patient's medical record can only be passed on if the patient agrees. In practice, doctors routinely pass it on to other health-care professionals. However, they should get the patient's consent before giving infor-

mation to organizations like insurance companies or prospective employers and don't normally reveal anything to a parent once a child reaches 16.

Mental Illness

If you feel a relative is mentally ill and the GP is failing to recognize this, you may ask for him or her to be seen by a consultant – if necessary in the patient's own home. And the GP should arrange this.

Complaining

You are entitled to complain to the NHS if:

- a service is not provided which should be provided,
- the standard of any service is not good enough,
- a rule of the Patients' Charter is broken.

But watch your timing. A formal complaint to a FHSA, hospital chief or other authority (see below) is only accepted if made within a set time. The time limit varies with the type of complaint. It may be extended if you were clearly unable to complain at the proper time – but don't count on it. Check the time limit with the Patients' Association. Then, get your letter to the authorities in time – *even if the people to whom you first complained have not replied*. If in doubt about which body to complain to, and with no time to find out, just send a copy to each one in the NHS pyramid. The Health Service is complex and it is important to send your complaint to the right person. In theory, you should start with the person concerned, then try that person's immediate superior. If you have to take it further the NHS freephone advice line can tell you whom to write to, or get advice from the Patients' Association.

The Patients' Charter says that complaints must be investigated and that you should get a full and prompt written reply from the chief executive of the health authority, or the general manager of the hospital. The basic procedures for each section of the health service are given below; your **Community Health Council (CHC)** (address from the phone book or reference library), local CAB or the Patients' Association will advise you. There are also DH leaflets, from the Department (page 693) or your health authority, giving practical advice. However, if a doctor has been guilty of serious misconduct, such as making sexual advances or being drunk, you should *also* complain to the **General Medical Council** (page 694). The right way to complain about improper conduct by other NHS staff varies greatly with the qualifications, so consult the Consumers' Association book (page 669).

The Sour Fruits of Success

If your complaint is upheld, the person concerned may be penalized. Some health authorities also offer redress. For example, compensation for loss of earnings if a hospital has cancelled a scheduled operation at short notice. But others will only refund any money you spent (e.g., on incorrect dentures) plus the cost of complaining – and you only get these if you ask the FHSA at the time. If a complaint is not upheld you can take it to the **Health Service Commissioner (Ombudsman)**. Leaflets, from a

DH office or CHC, give full details of all aspects of complaining.

Complaining About GPs, Dentists and Opticians

As I write, the time limit for complaining to your FHSA about treatment by a GP, dentist or optician is only 13 weeks after the treatment proves unsatisfactory (which for a dentist must not be more than 6 months after treatment). Complaints can now be made verbally, as well as in writing, and will be investigated by an FHSA from a different area (see also page 669). Those about a dentist's behaviour should go to the **General Dental Council**.

Complaints About Hospitals

The best time to complain is usually when the trouble occurs, and the best people to complain to are the staff involved or those senior to them. If you aren't getting the information you need about your illness or treatment, say so. Medical staff may use technical jargon not realizing they haven't been understood. But they will usually explain more clearly if you ask.

If you have a major complaint, write to the Hospital Administrator (the Chief Executive, for a hospital trust) or the District General Manager (ask the hospital for the address). As I write, patients, or their relatives, have a year in which to make a complaint. Your CHC will advise on these procedures. (See also the **Health Service Commissioner**, below.)

Complaining About Local Authority Health Services

The right person to complain to will vary according to which department organizes the service and whether the area is run by an NHS trust. Talk to your CHC and, if the medical routes fail to get results, complain to your local councillor, and/or MP.

Complaining About Mental Health Care

Most complaints in connection with the mentally ill are made like any other complaint against a hospital or medical staff, and relatives are allowed to complain on a patient's behalf. If these complaints fail they can be taken to the **Mental Health Act Commission**. **Mind** (page 589) will advise on making complaints about the care of the mentally ill or handicapped.

Complaining About Opticians

If an ophthalmic optician fails to give proper service, complain to your FHSA. If a dispensing optician is unsatisfactory complain to the **Association of Dispensing Opticians**.

Complaining About Other Disciplines

The methods of complaining about chiropodists, district nurses and others slightly outside the mainstream of the system vary, so ask your CHC or check the Consumers' Association book (page 669).

When Complaints Fail

If your complaints fail, contact your MP or write to the **Health Service Commissioner** (**Ombudsman**). The Commissioner can investigate complaints regarding Regional Health Authorities, District Health Authorities, Hospital Trusts, FHSAs, Boards of Governors and those individuals and areas of the Health Service under them. You should write giving details of what you are complaining about, of the health authority concerned, and the action you have so far taken, plus copies of any relevant letters. However, the Commissioner may not investigate complaints involving clinical judgement – for example, whether a particular treatment was appropriate, and only accepts complaints after your letters to the area authorities have failed.

When Legal Action is Needed

If complaints are upheld certain penalties may be imposed on whoever was at fault, but the patient usually gets no compensation or damages. In most cases, to get compensation, you must take the matter to court within 3 years, and the usual case is for negligence. Medical cases are complicated and expensive, so it is essential to get good advice before starting and *only* to use a solicitor who has handled medical negligence cases before. Your CHC or Citizens Advice Bureau will help and so will the **Patients' Association** (page 695) and the organizations listed on pages 694-695. They may also be able to put you in touch with others who have had similar problems, and tell you whether your case is eligible for Legal Aid. Vaccine damage is, however, a special case. There is an established procedure for compensating for damage caused by a routine childhood vaccination. Forms are available from the **Vaccine Damage Payment Unit** at the Department of Health.

If you are the victim of a medical accident **Action for Victims of Medical Accident** may be able to help you. This is an organization which gives preliminary advice to those who have suffered as the result of medical accident. This includes such things as misdiagnosis, failure to treat and incorrect treatment. It will both tell you how to use the NHS complaints system effectively and advise on how to go to law. Its lawyers will not take a case to court for you but they *will* advise on whether there is a case to be taken, and can put you in touch with lawyers experienced in this field. Send a brief outline of the problem when you write.

Private Medicine

The chief advantage of private medicine, over the NHS, is that with private treatment you can see a specialist of your choosing – instead of a succession of doctors, as one often gets on the NHS – and arrange the timing to suit you and your work. However, outside the NHS it is up to you to check that doctors are what they say they are. Surprisingly, it is legal for anyone to call himself or herself a doctor – if doctors are qualified they will be in the *Medical Register*, in your reference library.

You may straddle both systems. For example, an NHS doctor may be happy to deliver a baby in a private hospital. Equally, if you are with an NHS GP you can get a second opinion from a private doctor, or go for private health checks and screening, or have alternative medicine without it affecting your NHS status at all. You don't even have to tell your GP you are doing this – though, if another medical doctor treats you, he or she will normally notify your GP, even if you feel it is none of your GPs business.

Complaining About Private Treatment
One disadvantage of private treatment is that you are in a much weaker position if you need to complain, as there is no hierarchy to complain to. However, you do have the sanction of refusing to pay the bill (at the risk of prosecution) and private doctors rely on their patients recommending them to others. You can also complain to the **General Medical Council** (page 694) about improper conduct or go to the courts for compensation. See also Health Insurance, in Money.

Medical Agreements with Other Countries

Britain has agreements with a number of countries which allow British passport holders to use their health services. One DH form lists the countries covered, the free treatment you may be entitled to and how to obtain it or get costs refunded. Another shows what immunizations you may need. Both forms are in travel agents and DH offices.

Within the EC you can only use this concession if you have form E111, which you apply for on a separate form. If you leave in a rush you can, in theory, post the application for the E111 and ask them to send it to your overseas address – but they aren't geared for that.

If you don't have an E111 and find you need treatment, you can ask the health insurance authorities in that country to write to the DH Overseas Branch and obtain the form for you. However, you will need a different form from them if you go to **live** abroad.

★ DH Overseas Branch (page 693) has the details of how you can get free or subsidized health care abroad.

★ Form E111 used to last for two years, it now lasts for ever – or until you have to give it to officials in another country to get treatment. If that happens you just get a new E111 before your next trip.

★ Take form E111 with you when you go to a non-EC country. Often you pay first then get a refund, the form tells you how to get it. Some countries need you to produce a passport; others want to see a driving licence or medical card to show you are *resident* in Britain. So take the necessary papers.

What You Get Under These Agreements
In the EC you are entitled to the same treatment as a national of the country. So in France we should get any free treatment a Frenchman would get and so on. It may be considerably less than you would get in Britain and the services usually cover sudden illness and accident; chronic illness may not.

In many other countries only certain medical needs are covered. For example, injuries from car accidents are not covered in some countries. On top of that, health scheme treatment may not be to the standard you are used to – and the cost of private treatment in some countries can

be bankrupting. So it is never wise to assume that you don't need medical insurance.

If you do need treatment while away *tell* the medical staff that you wish to have it under their health scheme and have your passport with you.

THE POLICE

EMERGENCY – On most phones dial 999 – but on some mobile phones dial 112. Ask for police and be ready to tell them the phone number and exact address to come to. This gets a faster response than dialling the local police station.

The police are being reorganized but, as I write, there are separate police forces for each area of Britain. They come under the Home Office and are funded by both central and local government. Their boundaries are similar to those of local government. And each one has its own, independent, Police Authority made up of magistrates, local councillors and so on. The Authority controls the money and appoints senior officers – with the Home Secretary's approval. The Metropolitan Police is a special case: the Home Secretary is its authority.

Most police forces do a great deal more than catching criminals. A crime prevention officer will usually give free advice on the choice of locks and burglar prevention devices, and many forces run courses in self-defence, or cycling, or road safety classes for children. So ask your local station what extra services are available. It is in the phone book under 'Police'.

Each force is headed by a Chief Constable and both he and his senior officers are appointed by the Police Authority, with the approval of the Home Secretary.

Most police forces do a great deal more than catching criminals, and it is worth asking your local station about extra services they offer. There is usually a crime prevention officer who will give free advice on the choice of locks and burglar prevention devices, and many forces run courses in self-defence, or cycling or road safety classes for children. Your nearest station is in the phone book under 'Police'.

Complaints
If the complaint is about the behaviour of a particular officer, make a note of the number on his or her shoulder tab, at the time, and give it in your complaint. You can either complain in person at the police station in question, or you can write to the Chief Constable of the force concerned. If the incident was away from your home area, and you don't know which police force that would be, complain to your local Chief Constable, explaining where the incident occurred, and ask him to forward

your complaint. Alternatively write to the **Police Complaints Authority (PCA)** (page 693), which is a totally independent body staffed by people who have never been in the police. It is, however, purely concerned with disciplinary action. It cannot ensure you receive compensation.

The Authority will forward your complaint and, if it is about the police causing death or serious physical harm, the Authority will supervise an investigation by the police force. Either way, an investigating officer will be appointed and officers are likely to visit you to discuss the complaint. After investigations a report is filed with proposals for action. It is then up to the Authority to accept the report or take matters further – which, if there are allegations of criminal behaviour, can include asking the Crown Prosecution Service to consider prosecuting the policemen concerned.

If your property is damaged by the police and you want compensation, either you or your insurance company must make a claim, in writing, to the force in question. If you are wrongfully arrested, or injured by the police, you yourself make the claim. These claims can be made to the station in question, but on major matters it makes sense to address them to the Chief Constable. It is then up to the force in question to assess liability and either to agree to meet your claim or negotiate a compromise sum with you, or refuse to do anything at all. There seems to be no appeals procedure, but you can ask them to review their offer; try bringing pressure to bear through a letter to the Chief Constable personally, or by contacting local councillors who are members of the Police Authority. Your local library should be able to tell you who they are. You may also be able to get advice and support from local law centres and CABx. You could even go further and contact the Home Secretary, through your MP, but as I write there is no central body which will act as final arbiter between the police and a member of the public who is seeking compensation.

You can, however, seek compensation in the courts for wrongful arrest and/or imprisonment, and if a policeman is found guilty of criminal assault you can be compensated by the Criminal Injuries Compensation Board.

There are **Police Monitoring Groups** in many areas where relations between the police and the community are not smooth. Those who feel they are being victimized can talk to their local group – a local law centre can put you in touch.

RELIGIOUS FAITHS

The brief summaries here are not intended as a full introduction to these faiths but simply as a starting point towards understanding. The addresses of their organizations are on pages 695-696.

The Baha'i Faith

This faith started in 1863 when an Iranian, later called Baha'u'llah (Glory of God), announced he was the prophet of the unification of all religions. Since then it

has become one of the most widespread, but least known, faiths and has a growing British following. The central belief is the oneness of all mankind, and of all religions. For Baha'is believe that the prophets of all religions have, in turn, taught the basic truths about the one God, and added social laws suited to their period and country. They also believe that each successive prophet improves man's understanding of God. So Baha'is acknowledge the teaching of Moses, Zoroaster, Krishna, Buddha, Christ and Mohammad and see Baha'u'llah's teaching as an extension and refinement of their teachings. Equally, they expect other prophets to come in the future and extend his teaching.

Baha'is dedicate their lives to peacefully breaking down the prejudices and intolerance regarding race, class, country, sex or creed which divide man from man.

Buddhism

The Buddha was a nobleman born on the border of India and Nepal in the sixth century BC. Through meditation he achieved a new vision of the world, and set about teaching others to achieve this too. This ideal is a state of transcendent spiritual insight and awareness, coupled with intense love and compassion towards all living things, and inexhaustible mental and spiritual energy. The Buddha (the Enlightened One) emphasized that although a monk might find it easier to reach this state it was open to anyone.

Most Buddhists are vegetarian, but not all. Tibetan Buddhists, for example, found vegetables hard to grow and vegetarianism there is restricted to the deeply devout. Equally, though most Buddhists are teetotal, there are exceptions. Buddhist festivals, though usually set by the moon, vary from country to country and there are many forms of Buddhism in Britain.

Christianity

Christianity was started by a Jew, Jesus of Nazareth, as a movement within Judaism. His followers believed him to be the chosen one, 'Christ', which God promised to Abraham. It became a separate movement when the Jews failed to accept him, and after his death the apostle Peter led the small group of believers. Being based on Judaism, Christianity retained the teachings of Moses and other Jewish scriptures but the Christian Bible added the teachings of Jesus, as they were written down by his followers after his death, to form the New Testament or Gospel.

The key beliefs of Christianity were laid down in AD 481 when the bishops of the Christian world assembled and produced the Universal Councils. But by AD 325 the Nicene Creed had been established and it is still used, not only by churches in Britain but also by churches of the East, such as the Greek Orthodox.

Nicene Creed
(from the Alternative Service Book 1980)
We believe in one God, the Father Almighty, maker of heaven and earth, of all that is seen and unseen. We believe in one

Lord, Jesus Christ, the only Son of God, eternally begotten by the Father, God from God, Light from Light, true God from true God, begotten, not made, of one being with the Father. Through him all things were made. For us men and our salvation he came down from heaven; by the power of the Holy Spirit he became incarnate of the Virgin Mary, and was made man. For our sake he was crucified under Pontius Pilate; he suffered death and was buried.

On the third day he rose again in accordance with the scriptures; he ascended into heaven and is seated on the right hand of the Father. He will come again in his glory to judge the living and the dead, and his kingdom will have no end.

We believe in the Holy Spirit, the Lord and giver of life, who proceeds from the Father and the Son. With the Father and the Son he is worshipped and glorified. He has spoken through the prophets.

We believe in the holy catholic and apostolic Church. We acknowledge baptism for the forgiveness of sins. We look for the resurrection of the dead and the life in the world to come.

Although the creed may represent the beliefs which lie at the core of Christianity, each denomination tends to emphasize different elements in those beliefs, and some would add elaborations not found there.

Anglicanism – Church of England

This is the official Church of England which separated from the Church of Rome in the sixteenth century at the instigation of Henry VIII. This separation formalized a growing feeling in England that the absolute authority of the Pope was not acceptable.

The Church of England sees itself as a reformed part of Christ's universal Church, founded by St Peter. The key points of belief are the Trinity – of God, his son Jesus and the Holy Ghost, eternal life after death, and God's forgiveness of human sins through belief in Jesus Christ and through repentance. So it differs from other Christian Churches mainly in matters of organization. For example, it rejects the authority of the Pope in moral and doctrinal matters, but has a more structured hierarchy and form of worship than many Non-conformist Churches.

Admission to the Church is through baptism, which commits the individual to Christ. But each priest accepts a 'caring responsibility' for everyone in his parish, whether baptized or not, and this is most often expressed through marriages and funerals.

Baptists

There are various types of Baptist Church in Britain. Some are extremely strict and basically Calvinist. The main Baptist body is the Baptist Union. It has beliefs and practices very similar to the Congregationalists (see below), except that the Baptists returned to the New Testament baptism of total immersion in water to symbolize death and resurrection into a new life as a believer. As they hold that all believers are taken to God in the after-life, the emphasis is on hope.

Roman Catholicism

Roman Catholicism sees itself as the Church of Christ on earth, with the Pope being in direct succession to St Peter and acting as God's spokesman on earth. At every stage the Church is the vital mediator of God's will, love and forgiveness. In contrast with Churches like the Congregationalists, which place the emphasis on the individual, the Catholic Church places the emphasis on the Church itself and the priests have an important role as channels for God's forgiveness. The Church is 'the sacrament of God's salvation', the 'sign and instrument of the coming Kingdom of God'. It does, however, recognize 'sanctification and truth in other Christian communities which have a real degree of ecclesiality and are rightly called churches' – a statement which shows that the Roman Church also judges other Churches by their priestly hierarchy, not simply by their beliefs.

Christian Scientists

Christian Science was started by Mary Baker Eddy in 1879 to 'reinstate primitive Christianity and its lost element of healing'. The church takes the 'inspired Word of the Bible' as its 'guide to eternal Life' and regards the crucifixion and resurrection of Jesus Christ as the central events of history. A key belief is that God made man in his image – spiritual, good and eternal. Therefore mortal man is a false manifestation which must be outgrown through 'spiritual regeneration'. Christian Scientists believe in healing illness, fear, grief and sin through prayer, rather than through conventional treatment.

Congregational Churches

This Church started as a splinter group from the Church of England when, in 1662, some 2,000 clergymen decided to throw off the constraints of a Church governed by the state and form independent congregations. Two centuries later these independent churches formed a Congregational Union which sees itself as the most free of the Free Churches.

The Congregationalists base their worship on Jesus's saying that 'whenever two or three are gathered together' in his name God would be with them. So the Congregationalists have no hierarchy. The minister is ordained, but is part of that congregation, not a superior with a hot-line to God, and services are informal and Bible-based with no prayer book or formalized liturgy.

Methodist Church of Great Britain

Methodism was started by John Wesley, an Anglican minister, in the early eighteenth century, as a revivalist movement trying to take Christianity closer to its beginnings, when it carried a message of personal redemption. The name started as a taunt at the earnest group of Oxford students who joined Wesley in this.

Wesley's four key points, which are still fundamental to Methodism, all centre on salvation – that men can be saved from their sins, that they know they can be saved, that they can be saved utterly, and that this is achieved 'by grace through faith in the personal saving grace of Jesus Christ'.

Quakers – Religious Society of Friends

The movement was started in Britain by George Fox in

the mid-seventeenth century. Fox rejected the Church's emphasis on formalized services and argued for the importance of spiritual awareness in each human being. To the Church this was blasphemy. But he soon attracted followers who were equally dissatisfied with the strait-jacket they felt the Church then imposed.

Fox and his 'Friends' claimed that religious insight came from human experience, and an overwhelming awareness of the closeness of God and of the spirit of Christ within. They rejected the need for the Church and its priests as interpreters of the Bible and mediators between them and God. For them religion involved following Christ's teachings in daily life, rather than obedience to dogma. Quaker beliefs are still essentially the same.

Salvation Army
The Salvation Army was founded by William Booth in 1865 following the main tenets of the Christian Church.

They hold that the 'first parents' of man fell from innocence and that as a result 'all men have become sinners, totally depraved, and as such are justly exposed to the wrath of God'. Therefore repentance is necessary for salvation, and continued salvation depends on 'continued obedient faith in Christ'. They also believe in the immortality of the soul and the resurrection of the body. But prospects for the after-life are bleak for those who have not been saved – a general judgement at the end of the world in which the wicked will be endlessly punished and the 'righteous' eternally happy.

Unitarians
The origins of Unitarianism lie in radical thinkers like Erasmus, who in the sixteenth century questioned whether the Trinity – the idea of God as three persons, Father, Son and Holy Spirit – had any basis in scripture. At that time such questioning was blasphemy, and in Britain, this belief was illegal until 1813.

Today, their central belief is a 'reverence for life' combined with a search for individual truth. Most Unitarians follow the teachings of Jesus Christ without seeing him as the unique incarnation of God, and regard their reliance on him for salvation as being contrary to the need for individual moral responsibility. For, fundamental to Unitarianism is the belief that no *one* prophet, book or religious tradition possesses the whole and absolute truth, and that value can be found in all of them.

Hinduism

It is almost incorrect to talk about Hinduism as a religion. Hinduism is a way of life. Its origins are unknown, but some priests believe this philosophy grew up in India over 10,000 years ago. Hindus believe that there is one God, who may have different aspects. They also believe the soul travels through many incarnations and that the aim of life is to get rid of the bad qualities – like violence, selfishness and love of material things – in order to travel up the ladder of incarnation and eventually attain union with God. This state of blissful union

is called Nirvana, but the journey upwards is not inevitable. Bad deeds can lead to a Karma (destiny) of reincarnation at a lower level of being, such as an animal or a tree.

This belief in reincarnation means that all living creatures are thought to possess a soul, and even trees and rivers have something of the divine.

Hinduism developed differently in different regions. The oldest branch is Shaivism, from the south of India. In the north there grew up Vaishnavism, in which Vishnu is the supreme deity, but for the educated Hindu, Shiva and Vishnu are not opposing gods, but the same God seen from different angles.

At one time Hindus were vegetarian, but a great many of them now eat meat – but not beef. However, they must not eat meat for 24 hours before entering a temple, and must bathe after eating it. So, as Friday is the important day for attending the temple it is usually a vegetarian day, even for the non-devout. No dead creature may ever enter the grounds around a temple. Any woman should respect the rule that she must not enter a temple while menstruating.

Humanism

Since religion is about belief humanism is, in a sense, a religion. Its keynote is a belief in the power of mankind to work for a better life for everyone, and in man's absolute obligation to do so – if we are to have a society which is worth living in. Humanists believe there is a moral imperative which does not come from 'God', but from an acceptance of man's responsibility for the world around him. A responsibility which, logically, devolves upon him, as the most intelligent creature on the planet. To a humanist, the power for good is fundamentally the power of each individual. So each person is responsible for fulfilling his or her potential, both individually and to the world around them.

Islam

Muslims believe the Koran was revealed to Mohammad, in Mecca, by an archangel in about AD 610, and he dictated it to his companions. Unlike most other religions, Islam insists that its founder was a man, who was a mouthpiece for the one God, not semi-divine. The Koran speaks of the mercy of God, his absolute power, of the resurrection of the dead and judgement, and of the bliss of paradise for the good and the pains of hell for the wicked. It also lays down a framework of earthly law. In all its teachings the keynote of Islam is submission: submission to Allah (God).

The prophets listed in the Koran include Moses and Jesus Christ. However, Islam is thought to correct and purify the errors which have developed in both Judaism and Christianity. This means that both are seen as early stages in the route to the one God which is perfected in Islam.

The big division in the faith is between Shiite and Suni Muslims. This dates back to a dispute over who should succeed Mohammad. The Shiites believed that Mohammad's cousin, Ali, had to succeed him, whereas the Suni said that it was up to the community to choose the next leader and successfully selected Abu Backr, and from this seed complex philosophical differences developed.

Judaism: The Jewish Faith

The Talmud, the chief book of Jewish religious teaching and history, tells of a heathen who asked Hillel to teach him the whole of the Torah in the time he could stand on one leg. The sage replied: 'That which is hateful unto thee do not do unto thy neighbour. This is the whole of the Torah. The rest is commentary.' I am sure he was right – but there's a lot of 'commentary'. Strictly, the word 'Torah' is used for the five books of Moses but it is often used for the body of religious teaching, and 'Judaism' for the whole body of Jewish values – spiritual and secular.

The foundations of Judaism date back to Moses to whom the 'word of God' was 'revealed'. Central to the faith, as it developed, was that there was one God who demanded holiness, righteousness and justice from all mankind, and that this God was a loving and compassionate God who wanted men to both love and respect him. The other key beliefs were that a Messiah would come, that the dead would be resurrected, and that it was forbidden to make any 'graven image', or any manner of likeness.

SERVICES

Gas

British Gas

British Gas is a public company administered by a board and executive, and has responsibility for supplying gas, and ensuring its safety. Although it is divided into regions headed by regional chairmen, prices are set nationally and approved by the Office of Gas Supply. This body, headed by a Director General of Gas Supply appointed by the Minister for Energy, also authorizes new gas suppliers.

Complaints About Gas

If you have a complaint about gas write first to your local gas company – the address is on your gas bill or under 'Gas' in the telephone book. If that fails contact the **Gas Consumers' Council** (page 679).

> The 24-hour emergency service is under 'Gas' in your telephone book – for use if you think there is a gas leak.

Paying for Gas

- The cheapest way to pay for gas is to pay a quarterly bill based on the meter reading, and use cash or a cheque to pay.
- You can also buy stamps towards your gas bill, but

that means you are putting money into stamps which could be earning you interest in an account in a bank, building society or post office – so you lose money.

- You can also use gas budget payment schemes. In these the gas company estimates your year's bill, then you usually make twelve equal payments through the year. The difference in either direction is adjusted in the last bill.
- Gas slot meters mean you only use the gas you pay for. Some meters take a card, like a phone card, bought from a local shop. But most use coins and those in the meter are your responsibility. If they are stolen you have to replace them.

If you find it hard to pay the bill talk to the gas company immediately. The companies try to arrange payment systems which will make it easier for people in trouble, or advise them on how to get the social services to help with the bills. Special consideration is given to old people who cannot pay during the winter months, and there are 'pay as you go' schemes for those who find budgeting hard.

Paying Landlords for Gas

When tenants have a gas meter, or use gas paid for on a landlord's bill, landlords must not charge more than a resale price, set by the Office of Gas Supply. Your local gas showroom or Gas Consumers' Council can give you a leaflet with the permitted charges. As coins and gas units don't always match, a refund may be payable when the meter is emptied.

Modern meters show how many cubic feet you get for each coin they take. If the meter doesn't do this ask the landlord to have it changed for a modern one.

Reading a Meter

Gas meters show how many cubic feet of gas have been used. If you want to know what the bill will be, the easiest way is to obtain a free 'Gas Cost Calculator' from your local Gas Consumers' Council. If you don't have one, use the calculation given below.

- If your meter has a row of figures, like a mileometer in a car, read only the white figures.
- If you have dials only read the row with black hands. Write down the figure which each hand is on or has just passed, keeping the figures in the same order – from left to right – as the dials.

The difference between the final number now and the last time you read it will be the number of cubic feet of gas you have used. To convert this to therms you multiply it by what the gas board calls the 'calorific value' of your gas. This is on every bill, but is usually between 1008 and 1040 BTU (British Thermal Units). You then divide the answer by 1,000 and that gives you the number of therms you have used. Multiply that by the price per therm and you know the worst.

The standing charge for gas varies slightly from area to area if you have a credit meter (the usual kind). Then the therms are charged at a flat rate. On a coin-in-the-slot meter the standing charge is lower and the therms cost more for the first 39 therms, then the price per therm goes down.

★ The mathematics of that means that, for an approximate figure, you can take the figure you read off your meter minus your last reading.

★ If you find the calorific value on your bill is in megajoules, this is just a different type of measurement for the same thing. 37.6 megajoules = 1008 BTU and 38.8 megajoules = 1040 BTU.

> *Safety with Gas*
> If you smell gas or see a brown stain appearing on or around a gas appliance, call the gas company immediately and say you think there is a leak. They make no charge for the first 30 minutes spent making a supply safe. The old and handicapped who live alone may have free safety checks to their appliances once a year.

Installation and Servicing
To work safely and efficiently gas appliances such as boilers need regular servicing. The gas companies offer service contracts. Even if you don't take them up you can still use the emergency call-out service, if there is a leak. But, by law, you must make sure that the installation and/or servicing of any gas appliance is done by either a fitter from British Gas or by a member of CORGI (page 271).

Special Needs and Gas
If you have a disability ask to go on a Gas Care Register. Then, for example, meter readers will wait longer for you to get to the door. Or if you are blind or partially sighted, meter readers can have a special password, so there is no risk of you admitting someone who is not a genuine meter reader. Or you can use the talking bill service. Or bills can automatically be sent to a relative. There are also adaptors to help you use gas appliances safely despite disability or old age; these can include controls marked in braille. Some charities linked to particular handicaps also have information on specific aids or you can ask your local gas authority for a visit from the British Gas Home Service Advisor.

Gas Consumers' Council
The **Gas Consumers' Council**, was set up by Parliament to help consumers with problems and complaints regarding both the gas industry and gas-related companies. The Council is totally independent and champions the cause of consumers both with the industry and with government. It will also give free expert advice to any gas user, at any time. However, it only takes up complaints after your own complaints have failed, and though it can suggest and advise, it cannot force British Gas to take action.

Gas Otherwise
In addition to piped gas there are a large number of private companies supplying bottled gas to those not on the gas system. The largest of these is **Calor Gas Ltd**. Ring its freephone numbers (page 693) for an information pack on cooking and heating by bottled gas, on appliances suited to it and for details of your nearest dealer.

Electricity

Since privatization the electricity scene has had four parts: generating companies, distributing companies, a regulatory organization, and consumers. Powergen and National Power are the main companies generating electricity based on fossil fuels, and are totally independent of the government. Nuclear Electric, which runs all the nuclear power stations, is a curious hybrid: a state-owned Plc. In each area electricity is supplied to consumers by a separate public company with a subsidiary covering appliances and electrical contracting. Between them, the Regional Electricity Companies (RECs) own the National Grid and each is free to buy electricity from whichever generating company offers the best price – although it reaches them through a pooling system.

Most consumers buy from the RECs, but anyone using more than 0.1 of a megawatt of electricity, over any 3 months, may now buy direct from any organization with a supply licence – even if it's in Scotland and you are in Cornwall. And from 1998 any user can buy direct. Since 0.1 megawatt might be used by a large chain store or a housing estate, this could be a cost-saving opportunity worth looking into by schools or tenants' associations.

The regulatory body with the addresses of all the companies is the **Office of Electricity Regulation (OFFER)** (page 693). This licenses generating and supplying companies, and supervises the entire industry. It also deals with consumer queries and problems through regional offices in England, Scotland and Wales.

Electricity Charges
Two separate charges are made on every bill:

● the standing charge is for supplying the service and is the same however much electricity you use;
● the amount of electricity used is measured in units, and prices at a rate per unit. When the electricity companies make price changes it is the price per unit which alters.

Meter Reading
If any meter isn't read – for example, you are out when the reader calls – you get an estimated bill instead. Any inaccuracy will then be adjusted on the following bill, which can mean you suddenly get a whopping bill. But some boards let you send in your own reading and provide a card for you to do it on. There are basically three kinds of meter – dial, digital and those showing a special night rate. To read them:

● **Dial** – write down the figure indicated by the pointer on each dial, ignoring the red dial. If the pointer is between two figures write down the lower one. Don't forget that adjacent dials are numbered in opposite directions.

- **Digital** – write down the numbers shown, from left to right, ignoring the last figure shown as 0.1.
- **Digital with night rate**, for Economy 7 (white meter tariff in Scotland) – there are two rows of figures. Read the top row from left to right as for 'Digital' above to get the night rate units. Then read the bottom row in the same way to get the units at the normal rate.

Ordinary dial or digital meters clock up units at a single rate round the clock. The Economy 7 meter clocks up units at a far lower rate during 7 hours of the night, but at a slightly higher rate the rest of the time. Economy 7 meters are installed free, but the standing charge is higher than for general-purpose meters. It may be worth getting one if you often run major appliances overnight. But, if you don't, the higher day rate and standing charge can make them no economy at all. Your electricity company should have someone who will look at your bills and suggest the best meter for *you*.

Paying for Electricity
The person who applies for electricity to be supplied is legally responsible for bills being paid. So, whether sharing a flat, co-habiting, or married, beware of being the only one who signs that letter or you could be left holding the bill. If problems have been caused by the desertion of a partner who applied for the electricity, the company may pursue that person for the money.

Electricity companies need to get their bills paid promptly. They are usually able to advise you on ways to keep your bills down and offer varied schemes said to make payment easier for their customers. Ask your local company about these but beware – most involve paying in advance. So it could be wiser to budget for such bills by saving a regular sum each week or month, in a bank or post office account which pays interest. Those in financial difficulties should approach the company *before* they get behind with payments *and tell them of any special circumstances.*

Although they cannot disconnect for a bad debt on an appliance, companies have a right to cut off supplies if electricity bills, or security deposits, have not been paid. However, they say they will not disconnect old people *who are unable to pay* between 1 October and 31 March. And extra time may be given if Social Services have been contacted or if someone in the household is ill or handicapped in any way.

Electricity bills are normally sent out every quarter. But supply companies must have flexible payment schemes, or there are electricity stamps or slot meters – though a slot meter greatly raises your standing charge.

If you have difficulty in paying, tell your electricity supplier immediately and explain why. They may be especially understanding where people are old, infirm or very young.

Which Bit Do You Own?
All the wiring which supplies your electricity, up to and including the meter, belongs to the supply company and is its responsibility. Everything in your home, beyond the meter, is yours. But if you let your trees, for example, interfere with the cables you could be liable.

Complaints About Electricity
As with all complaints there is a sequence of moves.

1 First complain to your local supplier.
2 If that fails, approach the local branch of OFFER. It acts as the regional voice of OFFER's Director General and, through him, has power to enforce supply and settle disputes. But there is no procedure for appealing to OFFER's head office.

★ OFFER doesn't deal with complaints about appliances. Talk to your local Trading Standards Officer or a CAB.

★ OFFER covers economy and efficiency but there are also regional energy efficiency officers who come under the Department of Energy.

Postal Services

The Post Office is a financially self-supporting nationalized industry, directly responsible to the Department of Trade and Industry. Internally it is divided into several interdependent businesses run like subsidiary companies. This means that although the letter service and parcel post can all be used through a single post office, they are each run separately and have different area managers.

Every household should receive *The Post Guide* explaining Post Office services. If you haven't received one contact your local Post Office Customer Care number.

The basic weight limits are these – as I write:

- You pay extra on 1st and 2nd class letters weighing over 60 g.
- 1st class letters have no maximum weight but the maximum size is 610 x 460 x 460 mm inland or 900 x 900 x 90 mm by international mail.
- 2nd class letters may not exceed 750 g.
- On letters and postcards to the EC you pay extra for over 20 g.
- On other airmail letters and postcards you pay extra for over 10 g.
- The basic rate for surface mail to all overseas countries is for up to 20 g.
- Packets up to 2 kg can be sent at letter rate if they are not more than 60 cm (2 ft) long at any point. Printed matter has special rules.
- Parcels can weigh up to 20 kg, for most countries, and can be up to 1.5 m (5 feet) long.
- An international datapost service is available.

Proof of Posting
You can obtain proof of posting, for any letter or parcel, *free of charge* from main post offices and sub-post offices.

Dangerous Items
Nobody will be too frustrated by the fact that the Post Office specifically bans the sending of mustard gas through the post. However, some of the banned items, such as aerosols and paints, might not seem dangerous

at first sight, so the Post Office list should be consulted before sending anything unusual.

Recorded Delivery
Anyone can send a letter by recorded delivery, but only from a post office. However, all you get for the extra cost is a certificate of posting and an assurance that the Post Office will get a signature when they deliver it. You *don't* get any more compensation if it is lost than for an ordinary letter, and *no* compensation will be paid if you send money or jewellery this way.

Registered Letters
Any 1st class letter can be registered, at a post office, for an extra fee. The fee covers compensation: the more you might wish to claim, the higher the fee. Check how much compensation you would get – it may be much less than you would expect but, for *another* fee, the Post Office will arrange insurance if you wish. Any item to be registered must be sealed with sticky tape or glue, not just tied up, and any adhesive tape should have the sender's signature or initials across it.

WARNING: The Post Office delivers registered letters to the address, *not* to the individual the letter is addressed to.

Datapost
Datapost is a courier service for urgent mail and goods. The weight limit is 30 kg and only hazardous and high value items (gems, precious metals) are disallowed. The charge includes insurance against direct loss of the item and losses resulting from that. Collection is free and delivery is the next morning. For more information ask the operator for **Freephone Datapost** and check the value of the insurance.

Royal Mail Guaranteed Delivery
Guaranteed delivery ensures that if an item is received by a certain time it will be delivered the next day to any destination in the United Kingdom except the Channel Isles and the Isle of Man. The charge is 1st class plus a supplement. The Channel Isles and Isle of Man are covered by an Express Delivery service.

Parcels
Fragile articles must be packed so as to protect them adequately and labelled *Fragile with care* or *Do not bend* as appropriate, and *The Post Office Guide* has detailed advice on how to pack different types of objects. There is also a leaflet on sending food by post. Items of value can be sent by compensation fee parcel post, for which you pay an additional fee for insurance.

★ The Post Office will deliver printed unaddressed material to every household in a given postal area (e.g. a local business publicizing its opening).

★ A wide range of items may be sent to the blind free of charge provided they are within a limited size, wrapped according to

set rules and carry the words 'Articles for the Blind' on the outside.

Complaining About Postal Services
In theory, if the Post Office is to blame for something being lost or damaged in the *inland* post you are entitled to compensation – provided the object was properly packed, marked, and so forth. But you must have proof that it was posted, and compensation on anything sent by ordinary post is decidedly limited. Moreover, this does not cover money, in *any* form, or jewellery. For these there is only compensation if they are sent by registered post or by compensation fee parcel post (see above).

The first step is to contact your local Post Office Customer Care Unit. The address is available from your local office or under Royal Mail in the phone book. If it is a question of something failing to arrive, give the full details of the date and the time of posting and where it was going to. If there has been a serious delay, let him have the wrapper, if you can. But if you have received something in bad condition and will be claiming compensation keep the wrapper and the article, and complete and send in form P58, from the Post Office, as soon as possible. If you have suffered loss the Post Office is able to give you compensation.

If that fails, write to POUNC (see below), and ask them to take it up.

If you are still dissatisfied (or wish to bypass the step above) you take your claim for compensation to the Small Claims Court (page 492) or to the Chartered Institute of Arbitrators (page 499). You pay a small fee to apply to the Institute, but this is refunded if the decision is in your favour. However, the Post Office has limited legal liability for postal orders and items lost in overseas post, so you won't always get compensation for these even if the decision goes against the Post Office.

Post Office Users National Council (POUNC)
POUNC is a statutory body, set up under the Post Office Act 1969, but independent of the Post Office, with the additional councils for Scotland, Wales and Northern Ireland (addresses from POUNC). The Post Office has an obligation to consult them about policy changes. So write to these organizations if you dislike proposed changes in Post Office policy or charges. POUNC will also take up a personal complaint (see above) if you have failed to get satisfaction from the District Customer Services Unit. There are also some 160 local Post Office Users' Advisory Committees which may be able to help with complaints of a local nature but they have little power.

POUNC does not handle services such as the Girobank, Intelpost, or philatelic services – nor, oddly, Datapost or special delivery.

Red Star Parcels by Train
The Red Star parcels service is to be an independent company. As I write, it offers two options: either the parcel can be collected and delivered, or it can go station to station. On station to station it goes on the next train;

with door to door it gets there that day at premium rate, but takes 24 hours at the normal rate. Both are charged by weight, and neither is cheap.

The Telephone Industry

Privatization combined with technology has changed this industry totally. Since BT lost its monopoly the Department of Trade and Industry has licensed an ever increasing number of companies to offer varied telephone services. The **Office of Telecommunications (OFTEL)** (page 696) advises the government on granting licences, runs the numbering system, and supervises BT's prices – but there is no price control on other companies. It also has information on companies and services and an advisory committee for the disabled and elderly called DIEL. Finally, it can help if you have trouble with a phone company (see Complaints below).

To understand the telephone options now on offer it's useful to know a little about how the system works. And the more research you do before buying a phone, or installing a line, the better your chances of getting the best buy for you. OFTEL can give you the details of all the companies, so the latest facts are only a phone call away.

The Signals

Two key words are analogue and digital. Happily the difference between them is simple. To get from A to B your call has to be passed from place to place. Imagine the places as a line of people. Analogue transmission is like telling the message to the first person, who tells it to the second, and so on: the more people it travels via, the more it changes. In contrast, digital transmission is like recording a message on disc and asking the people to pass the disc from one to another: once in a transportable form (i.e. a digital signal) it stays unchanged however far it has to go. So, although good equipment can compensate for some of the changes in analogue signals, digital usually gives the best quality.

BT uses both analogue and digital technology in its system. So the real division comes in mobile phones. As I write, Vodaphone and Cellnet use analogue for their British mobile phone services. However, their Europe-wide GSM service, and the new Personal Communication Networks (PCNs) from other companies (see below) use digital signals. So analogue's future doesn't look bright.

How the Signals Travel

Basically there are now two ways a call can get into your phone:

1 via a physical link, such as a phone line or the cable that also carries TV,
2 via radio waves.

Within each there are two further options:

1 a cable or line can be either metal wires or fibre-optic cable
2 a radio signal can travel between transmitters or bounce off a satellite.

Fibre optics are fast, carry huge volume, and are free of interference. Wires are slower, carry far less volume and can be crackly. Earth-bound radio waves can be blocked by the landscape and may pick up interference. But satellite links are slow.

At present most calls use a combination of these. So a mobile phone might send a radio signal to a transmitter nearby, which sends it along a fibre-optic network, and up a metal wire into a home. But what is on offer is changing.

Telephones for Home and Away

At one time there were only a couple of phone networks to choose from. There was also a neat dividing line between fixed phones for the home and mobile ones for out and about – and the pricing made mobile phones a luxury. That is changing. New companies, such as **Energis** and **Ionica L3**, are coming on the scene to compete with **BT** and **Mercury** nationally.

At present you can link into Mercury (page 696) via the phone you use for BT. Provided it has a Mercury (or programmable) button you just pay Mercury's standing charge and set up your button. Then you can do some calls via BT and others via Mercury. Its advantages are that it offers cheaper long-distance and overseas calls than BT, and its itemized bills can let you see who made which calls. Whether it's worth having depends on how many long-distance calls you make.

As I write, nobody knows what edge the new companies will have, nor how you can get on their networks – but OFTEL will have the latest details for you. One way into them may be via TV cables. For many cable TV companies are – for a separate charge – using the spare capacity of the cable to offer phone lines. They usually do this via an existing telephone network, which could be one of the new ones. And, if a cable TV company brings fibre-optic cables right into your home the phone service should be extra clear – though *not* all cable lines *are fully* fibre optic.

Equally, you may not need a wire or cable. Ionica L3, for example, may soon be offering radio links to home phones. If you are near an Ionica transmitter this could make first-time phone installation faster, for there would be no cables to fit. However, I suspect that phones with wires will soon be obsolete. Mobile radiophones are neater, cheaper to run and wider ranging than they have ever been – though not necessarily all those things at once. But that will come.

Both Cellnet's and Vodaphone's analogue mobile systems have been trying to seduce the private market with lower charges. Competing with them are the low priced digital PCNs – standing for Personal Communication Networks. Mercury is offering one which will let you call, or receive calls from *anywhere* but you must be within the M25 to use the PCN. Hutchison Microtel is offering a nationwide PCN network – but you will need to be within the range of one of their base stations. These services have higher standing charges than a conventional phone but calls cost far less than on most mobiles. They also promise smaller handsets, clarity even indoors, and no eavesdropping.

Addresses and suggestions for further reading are at the ends of chapters.

Midway between two-way mobile phones and fixed phones are systems like the Rabbit. Away from home it claims to be a phone box in your pocket, allowing you to make outgoing calls *only*, anywhere within a set distance of a base station. But in the home, when coupled with a base unit, it links into the Mercury or BT system allowing you to make calls at their normal rates, but giving digital clarity on a mobile phone around the home.

At the luxury end is Vodaphone's digital GSM system which will let you dial and receive calls on a mobile phone, while anywhere in Europe, just as if you were at home.

Numbering
The whole basis of telephone numbering is changing. The additional 1 after the 0 in all British phone numbers in 1995 opens the door to using 2-9 in the same position. In the long term we may each have a tiny pocket phone and our own personal phone number, instead of the number belonging to the home or office. And even if we don't have personal phones, our home phones may soon be able to ring differently according to who the call is for.

In addition to personal numbers there are also a raft of numbers which have special prices attached. Mercury and BT offer the following, between them, and we can expect more from the new phone networks.

BT	What it means if a number starts with these figures
0800 or 0500	The call costs you nothing
0345 or 0645	You only pay for a local call, whatever the real distance
0374, 0385, 0802 0831, 0836, 0850 0860	These connect you to someone's mobile phone, or may belong to your own one. Ringing to or from these costs far more than calling a fixed number, but less than an information line.
0881, 0891, 0839, 0898, 0660, 0640, 0338, 0336,	These are information services or chat lines of various kinds. *At prime time you could pay over £2 for the first few minutes* – mounting steeply as you hold on.

BEWARE: on chat and information lines the extra high price rapidly adds up. However, there is a code of practice for such services. If you want a copy of that code, or think it is being broken, call or write to the secretary of ICSTIS (page 696).

Charges
There are several elements to charges. BT's connection charges vary according to whether a line is for a first-time user, or for an established user (even at another address), and there may be no charge if you take over a line within 24 hours of the previous owner. Once you have the initial BT socket you may install as many others

as you wish. There is a charge for BT installing them, but you can fit them yourself with a DIY kit, but BT makes no extra charge for you having them. Mercury is usually reached down BT's system, with no added installation cost but, as I write, the charges of other companies remain to be seen but some cable companies are charging rental for each extra socket. Most systems also have monthly or quarterly standing charges. But there may be reduced rentals for users in special categories.

In addition there are charges for BT's services, such as directory enquiries, or the time. These are now expensive but, as I write, BT charges the same price whether you ask directory enquiries for 2 numbers or 1 – provided they are both on the same call. And the blind and disabled can register for free directory enquiries by ringing 195 and the elderly or disabled can ask to be listed under the BT Protected Service Scheme under which they can name someone whom BT should contact if a bill is unpaid, so the phone won't be cut off if they are ill and in hospital.

Finally, call charges vary with the distance, the type of phone (see mobile numbers above), the time of day, the day of the week, and the telecommunications company you use. Also, on overseas calls peak and cheap times vary with the country you are calling. However, you are always charged for the length of time you talk. BT charges in whole units – rounding *up* to the nearest unit – whereas Mercury only charges for the actual *time* you talk – which can make Mercury cheaper on long-distance calls. BT's charges are in the front of phone books; other companies should supply a written tariff.

There may also be special offers, and special contracts. BT, for example, has a discount option for high users. Mercury frequently has special offers on calls abroad. There are also companies, like Swiftcall, which will route overseas calls from Britain via America at the cheapest US rates – which could be a saving if you had family there.

Both BT and Mercury have phone cards which allow you to make calls away from home and have the calls charged to your home bill; these can be used in certain countries abroad too. The snag with some of these cards is that the calls must be operator connected – which costs more.

Calls from public boxes can sometimes be made with coins but more and more need phone cards, sold in shops, or will take the phone cards above or credit cards.

★ A telemessage via the operator is delivered by post the next working day.

PHONING HOME FROM ABROAD: BT has instituted a system which allows a special code to be dialled from coin boxes in certain countries which will connect you straight to any British number you want. Another system connects you straight to a British operator (no more struggling with Japanese ones) when you want to make a transfer charge call. The telephone number for a leaflet is on page 696.

Equipment

Answering machines, computers, faxes, call-cost monitors, pay phones, video phones, and standard phones can all plug into your phone system provided they are BABT approved. There are also numerous devices and modifications for those who find the usual equipment hard to use, or need a special emergency service. The details are in a booklet from any BT office, or dial 100 and ask for Freephone Telecom Sales, or contact **BT Action for Disabled Customers** (page 696).

Although you can install as many sockets as you like, there is a limit to how many machines you can use on a domestic line. On telephones you will find a REN number – standing for ringer equivalent number. Domestic lines can only handle a total of 4 RENs. So, if you have 3 phones each with a REN of 1.5, giving a total of 4.5 RENS a fourth phone may not ring properly.

Information by Telephone

A growing number of companies provide information by telephone. As I write, there is no directory of such numbers – you must find them through advertisements. The best-known service is probably Prestel. This subscription service allows you to use your telephone to obtain facts on travel, finance and many other subjects via a specially modified television or a computer. You pay a quarterly subscription and calls are charged by length and time of day. Other companies provide information directly down the phone, from recipes and horoscopes to racing results or financial news.

The trade association for premium-rate information lines, other than sex lines, is the **Association of Telephone Information and Entertainment Providers**. It has a list of members which details the services they offer – without the numbers – however, most numbers are advertised in the press.

Repairs and Maintenance

Any BT fault which is reported to the engineers (dial 151) should be repaired by the end of the next day. If not you can claim compensation for every day it is unuseable.

Complaints

If you feel the bill is larger than it should be, don't pay the bill; ask to have it checked. Unfortunately, the company has no legal obligation to check your line within any set time, or under conditions comparable to those for the period of the bill – which can make nonsense of the whole procedure.

On a BT bill ring 150 (151 for a temporary fault) and complain to your local telephone manager then, on any major complaint, confirm your conversation in writing. If you get no satisfaction, contact one of the 4 national advisory committees for telecommunications given in the Consumer Advice section of your phone book. Alternatively, contact OFTEL. It can arbitrate in disputes between customers and any telephone company.

> If you use touch telephones and have a digital exchange you can use BT's range of network services. They will divert calls, tell you a second call is waiting, or enable you to block certain types of outgoing calls – such as foreign or long distance calls, or all calls bar those to the emergency services. You either pay a quarterly charge for each service or for a package of them.

Solid Fuel

The Coal Industry

British Coal

Being a nationalized industry, **British Coal** is directly responsible to the DTI. It controls mining and distribution of coal. It also promotes coal (and similar solid fuel, including smokeless fuel) to the general public through regional offices and nationwide showrooms (under British Coal in the phone book) and through leaflets. Its advisers will visit you, and suggest appliances to suit your needs. And its technical experts will help solve problems with existing fires and can recommend suitable contractors.

The **Solid Smokeless Fuels Advisory Service** (page 696) is sponsored by those who produce and distribute smokeless fuels and promotes their use through information and advice for the public. See also page 227.

The Domestic Coal Consumers' Council

The **Domestic Coal Consumers' Council** is Britain's oldest consumer council. It is involved in setting coal prices and is a source of information and advice. It will also take up complaints about coal merchants and put them to the Approved Coal Merchants Scheme, but it has no 'teeth' of its own. It advises customers who suspect short weight when coal is delivered to contact their local Trading Standards Officer immediately, so he can see what was delivered, or ask him to be present at the next delivery.

Approved Coal Merchants Scheme

The **Approved Coal Merchants Scheme** is designed to regulate coal merchants and make sure they give the public a reliable service. It is backed by British Coal, the Coal Merchants' Federation and the Domestic Coal Consumers' Council and, although some companies do sell imported coal, the NCB will only supply to 'Approved Merchants'. Approved coal merchants are meant to abide by a customers' charter which, for example, says merchants must:

● offer good quality fuel
● have it properly described

Addresses and suggestions for further reading are at the ends of chapters.

- write on the delivery ticket which coal he has supplied
- give the name and weight on any pre-packed fuel
- employ staff with a basic knowledge of solid fuel.

The scheme has regional officers who visit and approve a would-be coal merchant, and make spot checks after membership. If you are dissatisfied with British coal complain to the coal merchant. If that fails the **Approved Coal Merchants Scheme** (page 696) will try to ensure you get satisfaction.

> It is illegal to burn non-smokeless fuel in a smokeless zone.

WATER AND SEWAGE

In England and Wales

Since privatization, an assortment of independent companies have covered the supply of water and disposal of sewage in England and Wales. Some perform both roles, others only supply water. But, the **Water Services Association** is their trade association and has information on industry policy in general. The price any company may charge is now based on a formula which adds together the Retail Price Index and a factor called 'K' which has been set at a different level for each company. If your water comes from one of the water-only companies, you will receive two bills – one for water, one for sewage.

Complaining About Water Issues

By law each company must have a code of practice and a complaints procedure. So, if you have a complaint, tackle the company concerned. If that fails, most complaints should go to the OFWAT's Customer Service Committee (CSC). **OFWAT** is the **Office of Water Services**, the central consumer watchdog and monitors performance and prices. Its Director General is responsible directly to Parliament and can adjust the price-setting formula every 5 years, if it chooses. The CSC for your area is under OFWAT in the phone book and if it can't solve the problem it may refer it to OFWAT's Director General.

Complaints about drinking water can also go to the **Drinking Water Inspectorate**, which monitors the quality of drinking water nationwide, and comes under the **Department of the Environment** (page 693).

However, queries and complaints on river management, pollution control, flood prevention, sea defences, conservation, fishing and the use of water for sports and recreation in England and Wales should initially go to one of the regional offices of the **National Rivers Authority** (page 698). It was set up, during privatization, to handle these areas, and the addresses should be in your library.

Water Matters in Northern Ireland and Scotland

Privatization did not apply to the whole of Britain. In Northern Ireland all water functions still come under the Department of the Environment and in Scotland they are still under regional councils. So in Scotland your complaints should go to your regional council, and in Northern Ireland to the Divisional Office of the Department of the Environment and, if that fails, to the **Water Appeals Commission** (page 698). These bodies do *not* come under the office of water services.

TRAVEL AND TRANSPORT

Air Transport

The main body in this field is the **Civil Aviation Authority (CAA)**. It advises the government on aviation issues, monitors all aspects of air safety and regulates the aviation industry. This means that it runs air traffic control services, licenses airlines and air travel organizers, approves air fares, sets the standards for testing both private and commercial pilots and issues pilots' licences. In addition, it owns and runs aerodromes in the Scottish Highlands and Islands through its subsidiary, Highlands and Islands Airports Ltd.

For the airlines there is the **International Air Transport Association (IATA)** which is purely a trade association for airlines. Although it does claim to check the financial status of travel agents selling full-price tickets. While for the aviation industry as a whole there is the **General Aviation Manufacturers and Trades Association (GAMTA)**. This association looks after the interests of the aviation industry and has a code of practice and will investigate complaints against members although it has no formal arbitration scheme. If you need to get from A to B in a hurry – and have mislaid your private jet – this organization can give you the names of companies from which to hire one.

Representing you and me is the **Air Transport Users Committee**. This is a committee of unpaid members representing the general public, with a supporting secretariat. Its job is to look after the interests of consumers, and it covers every aspect of civil aviation, monitoring and advising on changes, and taking up complaints (see CAA). They supply various consumer leaflets.

Air Ambulances

GAMTA members include several air ambulance services. Most operate only when the sick person has insurance with fly-back cover, but **International SOS Assistance** (page 697) and **Europ Assistance** (page 697) will handle cases which lack insurance, provided someone will meet the bill. However, some conditions would be made far worse by the pressure changes of a flight and any organization is unlikely to agree to a flight until their medical team has all the facts. Often they can arrange for someone to be brought back by scheduled flight and provide doctors and nurses in attendance.

Compare prices and try to suit the plane (and the cost) to the degree of urgency.

Planes in a Hurry
If you need to fly somewhere in a hurry, **Air London International** (page 697) operates a round-the-clock, 7 days a week, worldwide air charter service. Or GAMTA, above, can give you the names of likely companies. Before you ring work out how you could guarantee to pay a substantial sum: the size most people would only pay in a serious emergency.

Complaints and Problems
When things go wrong contact the CAA. One of its objectives under the Civil Aviation Act 1982 is to 'further the reasonable interests of the users of air transport services'. However, if you have a complaint related to a British airline, go first to the **Air Transport Users Committee** (**ATUC**), which was set up by the CAA to represent consumers. ATUC may be able to get you redress, and possibly compensation. If that fails it may be possible to get compensation in the courts.

The CAA also issues the Air Travel Organizer's Licence (ATOL) to tour operators. Companies may only offer holidays with inclusive flights (i.e., what used to be called 'charter flights' until the EC changed the rules) if they have this licence, which gives the public a degree of protection. If an ATOL holder ceases to trade the CAA will bring home stranded holidaymakers or make refunds to those who have bought tickets but lost their flight. This applies both to specially chartered planes and to charter bookings on a scheduled flight. To claim, ask the CAA for a claim form. But it may not apply to seats you book just on a scheduled airline. Moreover, the fund only refunds basic costs; it won't compensate you for inconvenience or for losing a holiday.

Buses Outside London

Since the 1985 Transport Act the bus system has been revolutionized – for good or ill. Anyone may now run buses on virtually any route. Provided they show they can meet the MoT safety standards – they just register with the Traffic Commissioners for the region 6 weeks before they start the service (6 weeks' notice must also be given before discontinuing any service). As bus companies only choose to run profitable routes, councils fill in the gaps with subsidized bus services which are operated by private companies under contract. It is up to the companies whether they allow cross ticketing or have discount fares such as local travel cards and Explorer tickets. So ask. Unfortunately, nobody has a duty to provide information on where and when any buses run. However, some local authorities have a bus information service and the **Bus and Coach Council** (page 697) may have information on some services.

Complaints
Any complaint about buses should go to the company concerned. By law the company's name and address must be written on the side of its buses – usually near the door.

The **National Federation of Bus Users** (**NFBU**) (page 698) will take up complaints and advise you on your rights. If complaining fails, and the company is operating under licence to the council, you can complain to your local councillor or to the **Bus and Coach Council**. This is a trade association and has voluntary codes of conduct on such things as driving standards and handling customer complaints. It has a voluntary bonding scheme for members who offer coach tours, and if a member of the public has a grievance against a bonded company it will refer the complaint to arbitration – at the expense of those concerned. However, it has no powers over its members and no conciliation service. Bus companies are also vulnerable to bad publicity. So if one behaves really badly talk to the local media – or threaten to do so.

If it breaks its terms of registration – which the public have a right to see either at the office of the Traffic Commissioner or at the County Council – you can report it to the Local Traffic Commissioner. If a company breaks the safety regulations you can also report it to the Ministry of Transport.

If such complaints fail there is little you can do except go to court – if the case is suitable. However, CABx will advise you, and you may be able to get help from the National Federation of Bus Users.

Lost Property
Bus regulations oblige bus operators to check buses for lost property and notify the owner if an item with a name and address is found. They must also hold lost property for 12 months after finding it and keep a record of it. However, they may charge for returning your belongings, and throw away perishable goods after 48 hours.

London's Transport

London Transport (LT)
In 1863 the tunnels of today's Circle line between Paddington and Farringdon, carried the world's first underground train. But the roots of today's transport go back to the stage coaches of the eighteenth century and to London's first horse buses in the 1820s, later superseded by trams, started, ironically, by a Mr Train.

London's transport is about to change. **London Transport** (**LT**) used to supervise London Underground Ltd, London Buses Ltd and the Dockland's Light Railway. It set the routes and fares, and made sure they met the Department of Transport's guidelines. But, as I write, the docklands railway is already independent, although it accepts underground tickets, and the buses will soon be privatized. Initially, the private bus companies will operate London bus routes under contract to LT. So they will charge standard fares and accept LT passes and travelcards.

You can get free maps and information from LT information centres at major underground stations and at

Heathrow, and from LT's 24 hour Travel Information Service.

★ You can take a bicycle on the underground system, but not on all lines and not at peak times – so you need to check.

★ Dogs, other than guide dogs, are accepted on buses only with the approval of the conductor or driver.

Fares

On the underground fares are charged according to the zone, and on *ordinary* single and return tickets you cannot break your journey and keep your ticket, but on some other tickets you can. Ask about the following possibilities.

- Cheap day returns – issued on the underground after 9.30 am on weekdays, and any time during weekends and public holidays.
- Travelcards – take you from a London underground station to a British Rail destination outside London.
- The Visitor Travelcard – which can *only* be bought outside London – giving reduced fares on underground and on the entry to a number of London's sights.

> You need a photocard before you can buy or use a Travelcard (except a Day or Visitor's). Take a passport-sized photo to the ticket office to get one.

- Those with BR Senior Citizen's or Disabled Rail Cards can travel at a child's fare at the times given for cheap day returns.
- Refunds can usually be obtained on Travelcards if you are sick and off work.

Lost Property

LT *never returns* lost property, nor does the Docklands Light Railway. If the property has a name and address on it, a card is simply sent by LT saying it has been found. The **Docklands Railway** (page 697) keeps things a week and then sends them to LT's lost property office. To get it back you must claim it within 3 months. After that it is sold at auction by Greasby's.

If you have lost something on a train or bus, go to the manager of the first station you come to, or to the bus garage, and ask if it can be traced *immediately*. If your property can't be found, ask for a lost property enquiry form at a station or bus depot.

Once your belongings are in the system they cannot be extracted quickly. No enquiries about lost property are handled on the phone, but a recorded message (see page 697) will tell you the procedure. It involves writing to the Lost Property Manager, at **London Transport Lost Property Office**, or calling at that address between very limited hours on weekdays.

Complaints About Transport in London

The first complaint should go to the company concerned. The address of **London Underground Ltd** is the same as for **London Transport** (page 697). The address of any bus company should be on the side of the bus. That of the **Docklands Railway** is on page 697. If you don't get satisfaction complain to London Transport about any aspect of the transport system for which it sets the fares. But, if the buses become totally independent, LT may be unable to handle bus complaints – or may even be abolished.

If complaints through those channels fail, contact the **London Regional Passenger's Committee**. This represents passengers on all aspects of London's transport and also on the sections of British Rail within its area. Its area extends beyond London itself and covers an irregular circle around Aylesbury, Hitchin and Bishops Stortford, Gravesend, East Grinstead, Horsham and Windsor.

The committee looks at suggestions and complaints and makes recommendations to both the organizations themselves and to government. It also pursues transport issues with local government, and will back individuals in their complaints if it feels they are justified. However, it will only take up your case if you have tried yourself, and failed.

Railways

As I write, British Rail is directly under the Secretary of State for Transport, who sets standards and financial targets and has plans to privatize it – but nobody knows quite how or when. Already the major business decisions are made by several BR Business Directors, each covering different lines or aspects of the business. The plan seems to be that some of these will be offered for franchise and then, later, sold if the franchise experiment succeeds. I am told that only part of BR will be disposed of and that franchises will be bound by the Passengers' Charter and the BR code of practice – though the code of practice may change.

Code of Practice

As I write, the BR Code of Practice is this:

- You can get a refund on an unused ticket if you submit it within 28 days to a ticket office, travel centre or appointed travel agent, and explain why it is unused. For refunds on season tickets, hand them in with 7 days unused (3 days for a weekly ticket). (Exceptions are made for the ill.) There is a service charge unless it was BR's fault that you didn't travel.
- There are no refunds on lost tickets, but BR may replace a lost season ticket.
- If you leave property in Left Luggage or park on railway premises you may be able to claim compensation if the railway breaks the terms of the implied contract. Passengers are also entitled to refunds, of all or part of their fare, if BR's *self-chosen* standards of punctuality for the line are not met. This applies both to single journeys and the season-ticket holder's experiences over a period of time. But refunds are not given if the delays were due to such things as terrorism or exceptional weather.

Fares

The discounts and price variations on the railways need a tome in themselves as they can be local and seasonal, and vary with your circumstances. The rules are eccentric. For example, a London to Birmingham return used to be a different price from a Birmingham to London return. So the rule is *ask*. Who knows, you may get a discount for: being old, young, a student, a family, disabled, travelling on a certain day or at a certain time, or booking a set number of days in advance.

★ There are plans to make national concessions for the elderly, on public transport, valid throughout the EC. There will also be an international symbol to show museums, theatres and so on, which give the elderly cut rates.

> WARNING: If you don't buy a ticket and have to pay on the train it is likely to cost more. Also, if you travel in any part of a first class carriage you are liable to pay the difference between a Standard Class ticket and a First Class one. And if travelling on a season ticket you pay the *full* First Class fare – not just the difference.

Luggage and Other Items

There is a limit to how much luggage you may take on a train without paying extra. (It cost my daughter more to take her books to university by train than it would have done to hire a car.) The free limit used to be a matter of weight. Now you may carry two large items (e.g., suitcases) and one small item free, regardless of weight – is this sex discrimination I wonder? After that you should book on extra items, such as bicycles, in advance and will be charged per item 'per journey'. However, 'a journey' includes changes of train and special arrangements can be made for prams, pushchairs and wheelchairs.

Dogs pay half the Standard Class fare, but pets are only allowed in the passenger compartments if they don't annoy other passengers, and are never allowed in sleepers or dining cars (guide dogs travel free and are usually an exception). If muzzled or in suitable containers pets can travel in the guard's van.

For motor cycles and other two-wheeled vehicles with motors you pay a full Standard Class fare – and they are not allowed on certain trains, so it's best to check first. Passengers' bicycles travel free in the guard's van, except on certain trains – check before travelling.

Phoning for Information

Frequent British Rail users will increase their life expectancy by buying a timetable (there is also an international timetable). They come out each year in May and October. If, however, you are reduced to hanging on for one of those overburdened lines, remember they have a stacking system and take calls in order – so hold on or you lose your place in the queue. *There is no special number to ring in emergencies.*

Train Reservations

Seats can be reserved on most Intercity trains and on others indicated in the timetable. You can do this through travel agents or at major stations up to 3 months before. There is a small fee for reservations, but up to 4 seats can be reserved for the price of 1.

Complaining

If you have a complaint about any aspect of a passenger train service, keep your ticket. Then complain in writing, within 4 weeks, to the head of the line concerned – the address and phone number are in stations and timetables, and on trains. If you want compensation (apart from a refund) say so, and give all the details which justify it. It may help to check the rules governing BR. These are the Passengers' Charter, the Code of Practice, the International Uniform Rules and the Byelaws and Conditions of Carriage. The latter can be seen at booking offices, the Uniform Rules can be bought from HMSO, or seen in the office of the Claims Manager at Marylebone Station (or your library might get you a copy) and BR or the Ministry of Transport should be able to let you have the first two.

If you get no joy you can write to the appropriate Area Transport Users' Consultative Committee (ATUCC). BR officials may say you should take any complaint right up its hierarchy before going to an ATUCC. But the choice is yours. These committees were set up, by Parliament, to represent the interests of rail users. So they welcome complaints from those whose initial complaint has fallen on deaf ears. (You can also write to them if you are dissatisfied with any aspect of BR's services.)

If all else fails you can apply for arbitration by the Chartered Institute of Arbitrators (page 499). But this is not a free service, so do use the Consultative Committee first.

The final body you can turn to is the **Central Transport Consultative Committee**. This organization represents rail passengers – but has no link with buses. It is the co-ordinating body for the Area Transport Users' Consultative Committees and the London Regional Passengers Committee, and through the committee for Scotland also covers certain Scottish ferry services. The CTCC is formed by the chairmen of these area committees plus a number of outside members. The CTCC:

● monitors the policy and performance of BR's passenger services
● makes recommendations to British Rail and to government
● takes notes of complaints and comments from rail users

However, Parliament imposed certain limitations on it. It may not deal with individual fares or reductions in services. It *can*, however, deal with closures and the fare structure. So if you object to your local line being closed or feel the fare structure needs a rethink, this is the body to protest to.

Addresses and suggestions for further reading are at the ends of chapters.

Shipping

Passenger Shipping Association (PSA)

The Passenger Shipping Association is the trade association of companies running shipping lines. If you have a complaint about a shipping line, first take it up with the shipping line itself. If the issue is major and you want compensation *make sure that you put your case as well as possible and give all the evidence clearly.* If you get no satisfaction from the company and it has to go to arbitration, this first letter will be your evidence to the court of arbitration and it may be impossible to add further arguments later. If necessary, get a CAB or Law Centre to help you with this first letter, and keep copies of all correspondence.

If that fails, it may fall within the PSA conciliation and arbitration service. However, the service is only available if:

- You booked on the shipping line as part of an inclusive holiday with a ferry line, or it was a cruise or a fly/cruise holiday.
- You live in Britain and booked the holiday here.

You can use the PSA conciliation service by simply asking the shipping line to forward the written claim to the conciliator at the PSA. The conciliator is an independent solicitor who will consider the written evidence and advise on whether the company should compensate you (his or her fee will be paid by the shipping line). Neither side has to accept the advice.

If you still can't agree you can either take the matter to court (if appropriate) or ask the company to let you have a form to apply for arbitration with the Chartered Institute of Arbitrators (see page 499).

> If you are angry at, or an enthusiast of, any aspect of the transport system you may want to support one of the transport pressure groups described on pages 697-698).

Travel

Association of British Travel Agents

The **Association of British Travel Agents (ABTA)** represents the big travel agents and tour operators and its code of conduct has been agreed with the Office of Fair Trading. ABTA's code of conduct is as follows.

- Brochures should be clear, comprehensive and accurate.

> In the past, brochures have been optimistic, even fanciful, but an EC directive now makes it a criminal offence for a brochure to describe any aspect of a holiday in terms which are seriously untrue and sets rules for the degree of accuracy you can expect.

- ABTA members must absorb price increases of up to 2 per cent of the holiday price and you can cancel, without penalties, if a company adds a surcharge of 10 per cent or more.
- Companies may not pass any increased costs on to the customer in a surcharge in the last 30 days before the trip nor at any time after the final invoice has been sent to you. And may only do it before then if they can prove that it is necessary.
- Only in exceptional circumstances may a company cancel or make material changes to a holiday after the balance has been paid on it. And it must then give customers a chance to cancel and compensate them whether they cancel or not.
- Customers are entitled to compensation if a flight is delayed, or its time altered for a period which takes away a *substantial fraction* of the holiday and the delay was within the tour operator's control. (However, your travel insurance may cover recompense for long delays caused by such things as bad weather or strikes.
- Companies may not add a surcharge on hotel costs, because of exchange rate changes, less than 30 days before departure.
- If a hotel overbooks and notifies the tour operator, the operator must offer its clients the choice of equivalent accommodation or a full refund before departure. But there is no compensation for loss of holiday.
- If a hotel overbooks and it isn't realized until the client gets there, or if the tour operator overbooks, the operator must provide equivalent accommodation or compensation.

> The Code does *not* say that if flights are delayed passengers should be given meal vouchers, nor that they must be given a hotel room if a flight is delayed overnight. It is up to the airline. But, on a package tour, the tour operator should do everything reasonable to minimize customers' discomfort.

Company Failures

Under EC law any company offering a travel package must have financial protection. So it must either take out insurance or bonding, via a trade association, or put a customer's money in a trust account until after the holiday. Then, if the company goes bust, the customer's money can be refunded. A 'package', in this law, is not just a ready-made package. If a company supplies you with any two out of three possible elements of a trip, for business or pleasure, it counts as a package. The three elements are:

- transport
- accommodation
- a tourist service (e.g., a ski pass)

However, this law makes no provision for extra money to compensate for disappointment, loss of business and so on. For that you must seek compensation in the courts.

Complaints

If you are on holiday try to get the company's representative to put things right then and there. If that fails you may have a fight on your hands – so gather evidence.

- If it was something you can photograph (like peeling paint in a 'de luxe' hotel or a factory blocking a 'sea view') photograph it.
- If other holidaymakers are just as dissatisfied, or will witness to your problem, get their home addresses.
- Get the names of any members of staff who failed to put things right when you complained.
- Keep all proof of what you paid for the trip/holiday.
- Keep all bills for any extra expenses incurred because of the problem. For your own sake, be reasonable. If your 3-star hotel is overbooked and you have to find accommodation for yourself, get 3-star accommodation. If you go to a 5-star hotel instead, *you* will be meeting the bill – unless you can *prove* that every 3-4-star hotel in the area was totally full.

Once home, write to the customer complaints department at the tour operator's head office, giving details of what went wrong and saying what you would like them to do about it. *Keep a copy of your letter and of every piece of evidence you send them* and get the Post Office to give you proof of posting (free) when you send the letter. If necessary, also complain to the travel agent who booked you.

If you fail to get satisfaction write to ABTA with the facts and evidence. Its Consumer Affairs Service can advise you and it can heavily penalize companies which break its codes, and can tell you about arbitration by the Chartered Institute of Arbitrators (page 499). Moreover, if ABTA feels your complaint is justified, it will bear most of the cost of arbitration. The arbitration is based entirely on written evidence, so anyone who is not confident about writing should get help from a CAB.

ABTA will *only* act if it gets your complaint within 9 months of your return – unless your delay was unavoidable

ABTA only deals with complaints against ABTA members.

ABTA will not deal with complaints involving serious sickness or injury. For these you need legal advice. Go to a CAB or Law Centre if you have no solicitor.

Association of Independent Tour Operators

The **Association of Independent Tour Operators** (**AITO**) is the trade association representing many of the smaller, more unusual, travel companies. Its members must conform to the same EC rules as ABTA members, and must also keep AITO's code of practice and quality charter. Its members are far more interesting than its name suggests. Far from running guided tours, these companies mainly cater for independent travellers, and those who want something different. Often they spe-

cialize in holidays in a particular country or in a special aspect of travel – perhaps India, or great cities of the world, or French gites. Some also offer activities, such as weekends, or whole holidays, of wine tasting, painting or archaeology. And others have special concessions for certain arts festivals. Many will tailor a holiday to your personal needs – whether modest or super-luxurious. All this means they generally cater for the quality end of the market – though that doesn't mean they are necessarily expensive.

AITO (page 697) can send you a free directory of its members and their specialities. It also offers an inexpensive service for dealing with any complaints, using an independent arbitrator, and has its own bonding scheme.

WORK-RELATED ORGANIZATIONS

Advisory Conciliation and Arbitration Service (ACAS)

ACAS is an independent organization set up to improve industrial relations. These services are equally available to trade unions, employers and individual employees.

If you complained to an industrial tribunal about an infringement of your rights – say, unfair dismissal or unequal pay – the complaint would be passed to ACAS and one of its conciliation officers would try to sort the problem out before it reached the tribunal. The conciliation officer does not take sides, he simply helps the two sides to agree to a settlement which they choose themselves. The service is free, and anything said to a conciliation officer is strictly confidential. Equally, if either side wishes to refuse conciliation and simply goes to the tribunal it has a right to do so. There are ACAS offices in many major cities and you can approach them with queries about problems, such as employment rights, and redundancy, either in person or on the phone. Regional offices are in the phone book under 'Advisory'.

Certification Office

The full title of this organization is the Certification Office for Trade Unions and Employers' Associations, and it is the office of the Certification Officer. His (or her) job is to approve the way trade unions and employers' associations conduct certain aspects of their operations and see that they abide by certain rules. He approves union mergers and the ballot rules of trade unions in relation to political funds. He also runs the ballot refund scheme for postal ballots and holds the audited accounts for all unions and employers' associations – and allows the public to inspect them.

By law, if a trade union member feels the rules on the political funds have been broken, or that there has been a breach of the rules on the election of someone to the executive of a union, he should contact the Certification

Officer, who may investigate; however, his powers are limited. So if the election rules are broken the trade union member may also ask for an injunction in the High Court.

Low Pay Unit

The **Low Pay Unit** is an independent body which exists to help the low paid, through its regional offices. It will advise any individual who has a problem over pay, without charge, and put him or her in touch with other organizations which can help. It also campaigns for a minimum equal wage and sells a range of leaflets.

Confederation of British Industry (CBI)

The CBI is an independent organization representing British business. Its members include large businesses, small companies and trade and commercial organizations. Its policy is set by its ruling council and chairman, but a range of standing committees and regional councils, plus a Small Firms Council, bring their views to bear on decisions. It claims to speak for every sector of industry, and has close links with both the EC and Westminster. It also provides a specialist advice and information service, in a number of business fields, for its member companies including the self-employed and small businesses.

Industrial Society

The Industrial Society is both a campaigning organization and the largest independent business advice and training body in the UK. It tries to foster greater employee involvement, better leadership and communication throughout industry, and more productive industrial relations. Its members are employers, in companies of all sizes, and many of the major unions. It tries to achieve its ends by books, links with schools, conferences, courses all over Britain, an extensive business library, a telephone advice service on employing people, management advice and help on drafting documents, and a monthly newsletter covering changes in legislation which affects businesses. All those services are for members only but the cost of membership is reasonable and varies with the number of employees. In addition, it has schemes to help young people, who are not members, start up in business. It also has information on other agencies which will help in starting a business. Its publications list covers a wide range of work-related topics, from how to find a job, to successful retirement.

Institute of Directors

The institute is both a club and a pressure group for company directors, senior executives, sole proprietors and certain other business professionals. It aims to improve the industrial and economic climate, represent the interests of its members, bring the experience of business to bear on public affairs and help its members to become better business leaders. It has an information and advice service for members, and a research facility based on a business library with direct links to business databases and news services. It also runs a series of events aimed at bringing business people together, and offers short courses in business skills which are open to non-members.

Small Business Bureau

A pressure group linked to the Conservative Party, but useful for those involved in small businesses – and you don't have to be a Conservative to join. It has a limited information service, runs Europe's largest conference for small businesses, and incorporates Women into Business, which advises and assists women who want to make a career in business or run their own company.

Trade Unions and the Trades Union Congress (TUC)

There is no blanket description which fits all trade unions. To 'protect the interests of their members at work' is the most general aim, but each has created its own set of rules. Provided unions register with a government Certification Officer and do not break the Employment Act 1984, they can do as they like.

The most usual hierarchy is this: a workplace group is headed by a shop steward (though possibly under another name). The shop steward then represents his or her group of workers in a district committee. This committee, in turn, sends delegates to a regional body, from which the national representatives are then chosen. In some unions ordinary members, or their local representatives, play a more direct part in policy making at a national level. National policy decisions are usually made at an annual national conference and implemented by an executive committee.

It is illegal to force anyone to join a union. If you do join, however, the union is free to levy any subscription it wishes; you may also be asked to pay a political levy to support the political party the union leaders favour, usually the Labour Party. However, the decision to do so must be voted on by members every 10 years, so not all unions have such a fund. Also by law, individual members must be given the chance to opt *out* if they wish, and pressure must not be brought on them to pay the levy.

The shop steward or area representative will help employees with any problems related to pay and conditions. A union representative can also act on behalf of a member in an industrial tribunal. However, if your union representative fails to act properly on your behalf, or you are being unfairly treated by the union itself, you can approach the General Secretary of the union with your complaint – the TUC can supply the head office address.

Most trade unions are affiliated to the TUC, but they don't have to be. The TUC is governed by a General Council of about 50 union representatives. It is the official voice of the unions to the government, but only in very rare cases can the TUC act on behalf of an aggrieved individual.

USEFUL ADDRESSES AND BOOKS

General Organizations

National Alliance of Women's Organizations (NAWO) (see p. 316).

National Council for Voluntary Organizations, Regent's Wharf, 8 All Saints Street, London N1 9RL Tel: 071 713 6161, publishes *The Voluntary Agencies Directory* each year, listing over 2,000 organizations which offer help, advice and support with almost every problem, ailment or disability.

Scottish Council for Voluntary Organizations, 18-19 Claremont Crescent, Edinburgh, EH7 4QP Tel: 031 556 3888.

Useful Books
Congress Directory, National Consumer Council (paperback), embraces most organizations which bridge the gap between public and bureaucracy.

Central Office of Information, *Britain: An Official Handbook*, HMSO, covers most public bodies.

Advertising and the Press

Advertising Standards Authority (ASA), Brook House, 2-16 Torrington Place, London WC1E 7HN Tel: 071 580 5555. (P.667)

Press Complaints Commission, 1 Salisbury Square, London EC4Y 8AE Tel: 071 353 1248. (P.668)

The Arts

Arts Council, 14 Great Peter Street, London SW1P 3NQ Tel: 071 333 0100, can give you the addresses of the Scottish and Welsh Arts Councils. (P.667)

Association of Business Sponsorship for the Arts (ABSA), Nutmeg House, 60 Gainsford Street, Butlers Wharf, London SE1 2NY Tel: 071 378 8143. (P.667)

Charities Commission's Central Register (see p.499).

National Art Collections Fund, 20 John Islip Street, London SW1P 4JX Tel: 071 821 0404, helps retain works of art in UK. RC, M£M, M, A, private views, art tours, also under 30s group, sae.

Useful Book
British Performing Arts Yearbook, Rhinegold.

Consumer Bodies

Consumers' Association, 2 Marylebone Road, London NW1 4DF Tel: 071 486 5544.

Federation of Independent Advice Centres (FIAC), 13 Stockwell Road, London SW9 9AU Tel: 071 274 1839, can tell you where to find an advice centre. (P.661)

National Association of Citizens Advice Bureaux, Myddelton House, 115/123 Pentonville Road, London N1 9LZ Tel: 071 833 2181. (P.661)

National Consumer Council, 20 Grosvenor Gardens, London SW1W 0DH Tel: 071 730 3469.

Office of Fair Trading, Field House, Bream Buildings, London EC4A 1PR Tel: 071 242 2858. (P.661)

The Money Advice Association, Aizlewoods Mill, Nursery Street, Sheffield S3 8GG Tel: 0742 823165, has a list of centres which advise on money problems. (P.661)

Environmental Pressure Groups

Alarm UK, 13 Stockwell Road, London SW9 9AU Tel: 071 737 6641, advises on how to oppose road schemes.

British Association of Nature Conservationists, P.O. Box 14, Neston, S. Wirral, Merseyside L64 7UP, no phone – RC, M£M, M, some groups, sae.

British Trust for Conservation Volunteers, 36 St Mary's Street, Wallingford, Oxon OX10 0EU Tel: 0491 39766 – volunteers undertake conservation tasks all over the UK. RC, Opt. M£L, M, H travel paid, training for the unemployed.

Marine Conservation Society, 9 Gloucester Road, Ross-on-Wye HR9 5BU Tel: 0989 66017 – RC, M£L, booklet on beach conditions, sae.

Council for the Protection of Rural England, Warwick House, 25 Buckingham Palace Road, London SW1W 0PP Tel: 071 976 6433 – M£L, M-G.

Environmental Council, 80 York Way, London N1 9AG Tel: 071 278 4736. A forum for individuals and organizations working towards a sustainable future. It will advise anyone on environmental issues.

Fauna and Flora Preservation Society, 1 Kensington Grove, London SW7 2AR Tel: 071 823 8899, is dedicated to international wildlife preservation. M£M, M, meetings, talks, B, A.

Friends of the Earth, 26-28 Underwood Street, London N1 7JQ Tel: 071 490 1555 – RC, M£L, M, L, B, G covers conservation worldwide, workshops, sae.

The Green Alliance, 49 Wellington Street, London WC2E 7BN Tel: 071 836 0341, works to persuade each of the political parties to become aware of environmental issues by lobbying and information. Membership is by invitation only but the public can alert this organization to environmental issues which should be taken up with politicians.

Greenpeace, 30-31 Islington Green, London N1 8EX Tel: 071 354 5100, tries to prevent the destruction of the natural world. M£M.

London Wildlife Trust, 80 York Way, London N1 9AG Tel: 071 278 6612/3 – London wildlife surveys, conservation campaigning for threatened species. RC, M£LM, M.

National Playing Fields Association, 25 Ovington Square, London SW3 1LQ Tel: 071 584 6445, campaigns for the preservation and increase of open spaces and play facilities. RC.

The Open Spaces Society, 25A Bell Street, Henley-on-Thames, Oxon RG9 2BA Tel. 0491 573535, campaigns for the protection of all open spaces, such as commons, greens and public paths, RC, M£M.

Pedestrian's Association, 1/5 Wandsworth Road, London SW8 2XX Tel: 071 735 3270, campaigns for walkers' rights. At the same address is the **Ramblers' Association**, Tel: 071 582 6878, for those who enjoy walking. M£M, A, G, M, L, H, guides.

The Royal Society for Nature Conservation, The Green, Wickham Park, Lincoln LN5 5RR Tel: 0522 511616 – RC, M£L-M, excellent M, G, A, B, HD, weekends, Watch club for junior members, sae.

World Wide Fund for Nature (formerly World Wildlife Fund), Panda House, Wayside Park, Godalming, Surrey GU7 1XR Tel: 0483 426444, is devoted to conserving and protecting habitats, rainforests and wetlands, and promoting sustainable development whilst maintaining biological diversity worldwide. M£Var, A, Ad, E, Ed, F, G, Inf, L, M, RC, sae.

Gas and Electricity

British Gas, Rivermill House, 152 Grosvenor Road, London SW1V 3JL Tel: 071 821 1444, is the head office, but consumer queries should be addressed to the regional offices. (P.678)

Calor Gas Ltd, freephone 0800 626 626 for England and Wales or 0800 833 327 for Scotland. (P.679)

Gas Consumers' Council, Abford House, 15 Wilton Road, London SW1V 1LT Tel: 071 931 0977. (P.678)

Office of Electricity Regulation (OFFER), Hagley House, Hagley Road, Birmingham B16 8QG Tel: 021 456 2100. **OFFER** (Northern Ireland), Brookmount Buildings, 42 Fountain Street, Belfast, BT1 5EE Tel: 0232 311575. (P.679)

Governmental Bodies

Countryside Commission, John Dower House, Crescent Place, Cheltenham, GL50 3RA Tel: 0242 521381.

Crafts Council, 44a Pentonville Road, London N1 9BY Tel: 071 278 7700.

Forestry Commission, 231 Corstorphine Road, Edinburgh EH12 7AT Tel: 031 334 0303.

Health and Safety Executive, Baynards House, Chepstow Place, Westbourne Grove, London W2 4TF Tel: 071 243 6000.

HM Customs and Excise, New King's Beam House, 22 Upper Ground, London SE1 9PJ Tel: 071 626 1515.

Her Majesty's Stationery Office, P.O. Box 276, London SW8 5DT, and telephone orders are through 071 873 9090 (which has a queuing system), enquiries are on 071 973 0011.

Land Registry, 32 Lincoln's Inn Fields, London WC2A 3PH Tel: 071 405 3488.

Meteorological Office, London Road, Bracknell, Berks RG12 2SZ Tel: 0344 856655.

Office of Populations Census and Surveys (OPCS), The General Register Office, Adoptions Section, Smedley Hydro, Trafalgar Road, Birkdale, Southport PR8 2HH.

Police Complaints Authority (PCA), 10 Great George Street, London SW1P 3AE Tel: 071 273 6450. (P.675)

Scottish National Heritage, 12 Hope Terrace, Edinburgh EH9 2AS Tel: 031 447 4784.

The Nature Conservancy Council, Northminster House, Peterborough PE1 1UA Tel: 0733 340345, has been divided into separate bodies for England, Scotland and Wales. Their addresses can be found through this one. L, B.

Government Departments

Board of Inland Revenue, 22 Kingsway, London WC2 6NR Tel: 071 936 5843.

Department for Education, Sanctuary Buildings, Great Smith Street, London SW1P 3BT Tel: 071 925 9000. **Publications Despatch Centre (PDC)**, DFE Publications Centre, P.O. Box 2193, London E15 2EU Tel: 081 533 2000, will supply a list of free publications by the DFE. **DFE, Assisted Places Team**, Mowden Hall, Darlington, County Durham, DL3 9BG Tel: 0325 460155 for information on assisted places at public or private schools, or contact the Scottish or Welsh Offices.

Department of Employment, Caxton House, Tothill Street, London SW1 9NF Tel: 071 273 3000.

Department of Health (DH), Richmond House, 79 Whitehall, London SW1A 2NS Tel: 071 210 5963. **DH Overseas Branch**, Newcastle-on-Tyne NE98 1YX. (P.669) The **NHS freephone information and advice line**, 0800 665544 can give you information on local services, on the NHS in general plus some medical information.

Department of National Heritage, 2-4 Cockspur Street, London SW1Y 5DH Tel: 071 211 6000.

Department of National Savings, Charles House, 375 Kensington High Street, London W14 8SD Tel: 071 605 9300.

Department of Social Security, Richmond House, 79 Whitehall, London SW1A 2NS Tel: 071 210 3000; **DSS Newcastle Central Records Office**, Longbenton, Newcastle-upon-Tyne NE98 1YX; **DSS Leaflet Unit**, P.O. Box 21, Stanmore, Middx HA7 1AY. **DSS Leaflet Unit**, BA Storage and Distribution Centre, Manchester Road, Heywood Road, Lancs OL10 2PZ has free leaflets on benefits. **DSS**, Freepost (RCC2489), Horley, Surrey RH6 8BR Tel: 0345 825522 for a free guide to personal pensions. Freephone 0800 66655 with social security queries. Freephone 0800 882200 with disability benefits queries.

Department of the Environment, 2 Marsham Street, London SW1P 3EB Tel: 071 276 0900. **DOE Leaflet Unit**, Blackhorse Road, London SE99 6TT.

Department of Trade and Industry (DTI), 123 Victoria Street, London SW1 6RB Tel: 071 215 5000. **DTI Consumer Affairs Department**, 10-18 Victoria Street, London SW1H 0NN Tel: 071 215 5000, has free leaflets on consumer issues. **DTI Intellectual Property Department**, Room 4/5, Hazlitt House, 45 Southampton Buildings, London WC2A 1AR Tel: 071 438 4778, deals with copyright enquiries. **DTI Marketing and Information Directorate**, The Patent Office, Cardiff Road, Newport, Gwent NP9 1RH Tel: 0633 813535, for patenting information.

Department of Transport, 2 Marsham Street, London SW1P 3EB Tel: 071 276 0888.

Foreign and Commonwealth Office, Whitehall, London SW1A 2AL Tel: 071 270 3100.

HM Treasury, Treasury Chambers, Parliament Street, London SW1P 3AG Tel: 071 270 5238.

Home Office, 50 Queen Anne's Gate, London SW1H 9AT Tel: 071 273 3000.

Lord Chancellor's Department, Trevelyan House, 30 Great Peter Street, London SW1P 2BY Tel: 071 210 3000.

Ministry of Agriculture, Fisheries and Food (MAFF), 3-10 Whitehall Place West, London SW1A 2HH Tel: 071 270 3000. **MAFF Animal Health Division**, Government Buildings, Hook Rise South, Tolworth, Surbiton, Surrey KT6 7NR. **MAFF Food Sense**, London SE99 7TT Tel: 081 694 8862, has free MAFF leaflets on food topics.

Ministry of Defence, Main Building, Whitehall, London SW1A 2HB Tel: 071 218 9000.

National Radiological Protection Board, Chilton, Didcot, OX11 0RQ Tel: 0235 831600.

Northern Ireland Office, Whitehall, London SW1A 2AZ Tel: 071 210 3000 *and* Stormont Castle, Belfast BT4 5T. **Department for Education Information Service for Northern Ireland**, Rathgael House, Balloo Road, Bangor, Co. Down BT19 2PR Tel: 0247 270077.

Prime Minister's Office, 10 Downing Street, London SW1A 2AA Tel: 071 270 3000.

Scottish Office, Dover House, Whitehall, London SW1A 2AU Tel: 071 270 6744 *and* New St Andrew's House, St James Centre, Edinburgh EH1 3TD Tel: 031 244 1111. **Student Grants**, Education Department, 4th Floor, New St Andrew's House, St James' Centre, Edinburgh EH1 3TG Tel: 031 244 5823, publishes a guide to student allowances.

Scottish Education Department, Room 4/10, New St Andrew's House, St James' Centre, Edinburgh EH1 3SY Tel: 031 556 8400 or, on Scottish education for children with special needs, write to Room 209, 43 Jeffrey Street, Edinburgh EH1 1DN

Scottish Home and Health Department, St Andrew's House, Regent Road, Edinburgh EH1 3DE Tel: 031 556 8400, has leaflets on benefits of all kinds.

Welsh Office, New Crown Buildings, Cathays Park, Cardiff CF1 3NQ Tel: 0222 825111. **Education Department**, Information Division, Cathays Park, Cardiff CF1 3NQ Tel: 0222 825111, will send a list of its publications on education.

For **Parliament** see p.695.

Local Government

Association of County Councils, Eaton House, 66A Eaton Square, London SW1W 9BH Tel: 071 235 1200.

Association of District Councils, 26 Chapter Street, London SW1P 4ND Tel: 071 233 6868. Neither this nor the Association of County Councils is set up to deal with the public but they will advise on legislation and on the services you are entitled to expect from your council.

Association of Metropolitan Authorities, 35 Great Smith Street, London SW1P 3BJ Tel: 071 222 8100, represents the London Boroughs and the local authorities of many other big English cities, plus the City of London. Its committees are among the most powerful on the local authority scene.

Local Government Ombudsman for England, 21 Queen Anne's Gate, London SW1H 9BU Tel: 071 222 5622, is the head office, but there are also offices in Coventry and York. (P.666)

Local Government Ombudsman for Scotland, 23 Walker Street, Edinburgh EH3 7HX Tel: 031 225 5300. (P.666)

Local Government Ombudsman for Wales, Derwen House, Court Road, Bridgend, Mid-Glamorgan CF31 1BN Tel: 0656 661325. (P.666)

Useful Books
The Municipal Yearbook (in public libraries) lists every authority and gives a breakdown of their responsibilities.

Tony Byrne, *Local Government in Britain*, Pelican.

Medical Services

Action for Victims of Medical Accident, Bank Chambers, 1 London Road, London SE23 3TP Tel: 081 291 2793, sae appreciated, RC. (P.673).

Association of British Dispensing Opticians, 6 Hurlingham Business Park, Sullivan Road, London W1M 4AT Tel: 071 935 7411. (P.673)

General Dental Council, 37 Wimpole Street, London W1M 8DQ Tel: 071 486 2171. (P.673)

General Medical Council, 44 Hallam Street, London W1N 6AE Tel: 071 580 7642. (P.672)

Health Service Commissioner, Church House, Great Smith Street, London SW1P 3BW Tel: 071 276 2035 – Scotland and Wales have their own Commissioners (addresses from the above office). (P.672)

Mental Health Act Commission, Maid Marion House, 56 Houndsgate, Nottingham NG1 6BG Tel: 0602 504040. (P.673)

Patients' Association, 18 Victoria Park Square, London E2 9PS Tel: 081 981 5676/5695, advises on problems with the NHS and medical profession. RC, M£3, S, F & F, L, B, HD, sae. (P.673)

Vaccine Damage Payment Unit, Department of Health, Room 112H, North Fylde Central Offices, Norcross, Blackpool FY5 3TA Tel: 0253 856123. (P.673)

For a copy of the Patients' Charter write to **NHS Patients' Charter**, Freepost SE99 7XU, or the **Health Publications Unit**, Heywood Stores, Heywood, Lancs OL10 2PZ, or ring the **DH Literature Line** on 0800 555777.

But the **NHS Benefits Unit**, Sandford House, Newcastle on Tyne, NE2 1DB, handles enquiries about free dental care, spectacle vouchers and so on.

Parliament

Campaign for Freedom of Information, 88 Old Street, London EC1V 9AR Tel: 071 253 2445. The name says it all. RC, M£M, M.

Commission of the European Community, 8, Storey's Gate, London SW1P 3AT Tel: 071 973 1992. (P.662)

European Parliament UK Office, 2 Queen Anne's Gate, London SW1H 9AA Tel: 071 222 0411, provides general information on the EC.

House of Commons, London SW1A 0AA Tel: 071 219 4272.

House of Commons Public Information Office, 1 Derby Gate, London SW1A 2DG Tel: 071 219 4272.

Journal and Information Office, House of Lords, London SW1A 0PW Tel: 071 219 3107, has information on the Lords.

Parliamentary Ombudsman, Church House, Great Smith Street, London SW1P 3BW Tel: 071 276 2130/3000 (P.664).

Political Parties

Conservative Party, Conservative Central Office, 32 Smith Square, London SW1P 3HH Tel: 071 222 9000. (P.664)

Democratic Left, 6 Cynthia Street, London N1 9JF Tel: 071 278 4443. (P.664)

Green Party, 10 Station Parade, Balham High Road, London SW12 9AZ Tel: 081 673 0045. (P.664)

Labour Party, 150 Walworth Road, London SE17 1JT Tel: 071 701 1234. (P.664)

Liberal Democrats, 4 Cowley Street, London SW1P 3NB Tel: 071 222 7999. (P.664)

Liberal Democrats – Scotland, 4 Clifton Terrace, Edinburgh EH12 5DR Tel: 031 337 2314.

Liberal Democrats – Wales, 57 St Mary's Street, Cardiff CF1 1FE Tel: 0222 382210.

Plaid Cymru, 51 Cathedral Road, Cardiff CF1 9HD Tel: 0222 231944. (P.665)

Scottish National Party, 6 North Charlotte Street, Edinburgh EH2 4JH Tel: 031 226 3661. (P.665)

Social Democratic and Labour Party, Cranmore House, 611c Lisburn Road, Belfast BT9 7GT Tel: 0232 668100. (P.665)

Ulster Democratic Unionist Party, 296 Albert Bridge Road, Belfast BT4 5OX Tel: 0232 458597. (P.665)

Ulster Unionist Council, 3 Glengall Street, Belfast BT12 5AE Tel: 0232 324601. (P.665)

Political Pressure Groups

Campaign for Freedom of Information, 88 Old Street, London EC1V 9AR Tel: 071 253 2445. The name says it all. RC, M£M, M. (P.664)

Campaign for Nuclear Disarmament (CND), 162 Holloway Road, London N7 8DQ Tel: 071 700 2393, campaigns for unilateral nuclear disarmament. (P.664)

Electoral Reform Society, 6 Chancel Street, London SE1 0UU Tel: 071 928 1622, is a pressure group favouring a single transferable vote. (P.664)

Families for Defence, 6 Buckingham Gate, London SW1E 6JP, is a political pressure group against unilateral disarmament and for multilateral disarmament. (P.664)

The 300 Group, 3rd Floor, 19 Borough High Street, London SE1 9SA Tel: 071 357 6660, a cross-party group to help women to get into parliament, assists in building the necessary skills. M£H. (P.664)

Postal Services

Freephone Datapost, 0800 224466. (P.681)

Post Office Services, 148 Old Street, London EC1V 9HQ Tel: 071 490 2888. (P.680)

Post Office Users National Council (POUNC), Waterloo Bridge House, Waterloo Road, London SE1 8UA Tel: 071 928 9458. (P.681)

Religious Faiths

Baha'i Centre, 27 Rutland Gate, London SW7 1PD Tel: 071 584 2566. (P.675)

Baptist Union, P.O. Box 44, 129 Broadway, Didcot, Oxon OX11 8RT Tel: 0235 512077. (P.676)

Board of Deputies of British Jews, Woburn House, Upper Woburn Place, London WC1H 0EP Tel: 071 387 4044. (P.678)

British Humanist Association, 14 Lamb's Conduit Passage, London WC1R 4RH Tel: 071 430 0908. (P.677)

Buddhist Society, 58 Eccleston Square, London SW1 Tel: 071 834 5858. (P.675)

The London Buddhist Centre, 51 Roman Road, Bethnal Green, London E2 0HU Tel: 081 981 1225. (P.675)

The Catholic Enquiry Centre, 120 West Heath Road, London NW3 7TY Tel: 081 455 9871, or call at any presbytery or convent. (P.676)

Christian Science Committee on Publication, 108 Palace Gardens Terrace, London W8 4RT Tel: 071 221 5650. (P.676)

The Church of England General Synod, Church House, Great Smith Street, London SW1P 3NZ Tel: 071 222 9011. (P.676)

Congregational Federation, Congregational Centre, 4 Castle Gate, Nottingham NG1 7AS Tel: 0602 413801. (P.676)

Geet Bhaan Mandir, 107-115 Heathfield Road, Birmingham B19 1HL Tel: 021 554 4120/021 523 7797 for the branch of Hinduism called Vaishnavism. (P.677)

General Assembly of Unitarian and Free Christian Churches, Essex Hall, 1-6 Essex Street, London WC2R 3HY Tel: 071 240 2384. (P.677)

Highgate Murugan Temple, 200A Archway Road, London N6 5BA Tel: 081 348 9835, for Shaivism. (P.677)

Islamic Cultural Centre, 146 Park Road, London NW8 7RG Tel: 071 724 3363. (P.677)

The Methodist Church, 1 Central Buildings, Westminster, London SW1H 9NH Tel: 071 222 8010. (P.676)

Quaker Home Service, Friends House, Euston Road, London NW1 2BJ Tel: 071 387 3601. (P.676)

Salvation Army Information Service, 101 Queen Victoria Street, London EC4P 4EP Tel: 071 236 5222, sae welcome. (P.677)

Useful Books
The Baha'i Faith, Ward Lock.
Herman Wouk, *This is My God*, Fontana, on Judaism.
Mary Baker Eddy, *Science and Health with Key to the Scriptures*, on the Christian Science religion.
R.C. Zaehner, ed., *The Concise Encyclopaedia of Living Faiths*, Open University, takes an in-depth, philosophical look at most religions.
Rosemary and Jeremy Goring, *The Unitarians*, Religious, Moral and Educational Press.
Suzanne Haneef, *What Everyone Should Know About Islam*, Kazi Publications.

Solid Fuel

Approved Coal Merchants Scheme, Victoria House, Southampton Row, London WC1B 4DH Tel: 071 405 8218 or freephone 0800 181 351 (P.684).

British Coal Board, Hobart House, 40 Grosvenor Place, London SW1X 7AE Tel: 071 235 2020. (P.684)

Domestic Coal Consumers' Council, Dean Bradley House, 52 Horseferry Road, London SW1P 2AG Tel: 071 233 0582. (P.684)

Solid Fuel Advisory Service (SFAS), address as British Coal (above).

Solid Smokeless Fuels Federation, Devonshire House, Church Street, Sutton-in-Ashfield, Notts NG17 1AE Tel: 0623 550411. (P.684)

Telephone

Association of Telephone Information and Entertainment Providers, 3rd Floor, Russell Square House, 10-12 Russell Square, London WC1B 5LF Tel: 071 637 1696. (P.684)

BT Action For Disabled Customers, Room B4036, BT Centre, 81 Newgate Street, London EC1A 7AJ Tel: 0345 581456, local price charged all over the UK. (P.684)

BT: phoning home from abroad – for a leaflet Tel: 0800 800 852. (P.683)

Energis, 50 Victoria Embankment, London EC4Y, 0DE Tel: 071 936 5555 is offering a telephone network for homes and small businesses. (P.682)

ICSTIS, Third Floor, Kingsbourne House, 229-231 High Holborn, London WC1V 7DA freephone 0800 500 212. (P.683)

Ionica L3 Ltd, St John Innovation Centre, Cowley Road, Cambridge CB4 4WS Tel: 0223 42130 is offering a telephone network for homes and small businesses. (P.682)

Maritime Radio, BT, First Floor, 43 Bartholomew Close, London EC1A 7HP Tel: 071 583 9416 has information on its radiophone network designed for use on boats, with a special distress channel monitored by maritime rescue services.

Mercury, P.O. Box 49, Birmingham B1 1TE Tel: 0500 500194. (P.682)

Office of Telecommunications (OFTEL), 50 Ludgate Hill, London EC4M 7JJ Tel: 071 634 8700. (P.682)

For information on **BT chat lines**, ring 0800 800 898. (P.682)

Television and Radio

Anglia Television, Anglia House, Norwich NR1 1JG Tel: 0603 615151.

British Broadcasting Corporation (BBC), Broadcasting House, Portland Place, London W1A 1AA Tel: 071 580 4468. (P.667)

BBC Books, P.O. Box 234, London SE1 3TH Tel: 071 580 4468, sells books and computer software by mail order. (P.667)

BBC Engineering Information, White City, 201 Wood Lane, London W12 7TS Tel: 081 752 5040. (P.667)

BBC Radio, Broadcasting House, Portland Place, London W1A 1AA Tel: 071 580 4468. (P.667)

BBC Television, Television Centre, Wood Lane, London W12 7RJ Tel: 081 743 8000. (P.667)

BBC Viewers and Listeners Relations, White City, 201 Wood Lane, London W12 7TS. (P.667)

BBC World Service, Bush House, London WC2B 4PH Tel: 071 240 3456.

BBC Worldwide, P.O. Box 76, Bush House, Strand, London WC2B 4PH Tel: 071 240 3456.

Border Television, Television Centre, Carlisle CA1 3NT Tel: 0228 25101.

British Sky Broadcasting, 6 Centaurs Business Park, Grant Way, Isleworth, Middx TW7 5QD Tel: 071 782 3000.

Broadcasting Complaints Commission, Grosvenor Gardens House, 35-37 Grosvenor Gardens, London SW1W 0BS Tel: 071 630 1966. (P.668)

Broadcasting Standards Council, London SW1P 3JS Tel: 071 233 0544. (P.670)

Broadcasting Support Services (BSS), Tel: 081 992 5522; for BBC leaflets, write to P.O. Box 7, London W3 6XJ; for Channel 4 leaflets, write to P.O. Box 400, London W3 6XJ. (P.668)

Cable Television Association, 5th Floor, Artillery House, Artillery Row, London SW1P 1RT Tel: 071 222 2900. (P.668)

Carlton Television Ltd, 101 St Martin's Lane, London WC2N 4AZ Tel: 071 240 4000.

Ceefax, Room 7013, BBC Television Centre, Wood Lane, London W12 7RJ Tel: 081 743 8000. (P.667)

Central Television, Central House, Broad Street, Birmingham B1 2JP Tel: 021 643 9898.

Channel 4, 60 Charlotte Street, London W1P 2AX Tel: 071 631 4444.

Channel Television, Television Centre, St Helier, Jersey, Channel Isles Tel: 0534 68999.

GMTV Ltd, The London Television Centre, Upper Ground, London SE1 9LT Tel: 071 827 7000.

Grampian Television, Queen's Cross, Aberdeen AB9 2XJ Tel: 0224 646464.

Granada Television, Granada TV Centre, Manchester M60 9EA Tel: 061 832 7211.

HTV Wales, The Television Centre, Culverhouse Cross, Cardiff CF5 6XJ Tel: 0222 590590.

HTV West, The Television Centre, Bath Road, Bristol BS4 3HG Tel: 0272 778366.

Independent Television Commission, 33 Foley Street, London W1P 7LB Tel: 071 255 3000 (P.668).

ITN (Independent Television News Ltd), 200 Gray's Inn Road, London WC1X 8XZ Tel: 071 833 3000.

London Weekend Television (LWT), South Bank Television Centre, Upper Ground, London SE1 9LT Tel: 071 620 1620.

Meridian Broadcasting, Southampton SO9 5HZ Tel: 0703 222555.

National Viewer's and Listener's Association, Ardleigh, Colchester, Essex CO7 7RH Tel: 0206 230123, is the pressure group started by Mrs Mary Whitehouse. Anyone who objects to anything on TV or radio can write to her. The organization is Christian and anti-humanist. M£L. (P.668).

Radio Authority, Holbrook House, 14 Great Queen Street, London WC2B 5DG Tel: 071 430 2724. (P.668)

Radio Ticket Unit, BBC, London W1A 4WW Tel: 071 580 4468. (P.668)

Scottish Television, Cowcaddens, Glasgow G2 3PR Tel: 041 332 9999.

TV Ticket Unit, BBC, London W12 7SB Tel: 081 743 8000. (P.668)

Tyne Tees Television, Television Centre, City Road, Newcastle-upon-Tyne NE1 2AL Tel: 091 261 0181.

Ulster Television, Havelock House, Ormeau Road, Belfast BT7 1EB Tel: 0232 328122.

Westcountry Television Ltd, Western Wood Way, Langage Science Park, Plymouth PL7 5BG Tel: 0752 333333.

Yorkshire Television, The Television Centre, Leeds LS3 1JS Tel: 0532 438283.

Travel and Transport

Air London International Plc, Mack House, Aviation Court, Gatwick Road, Crawley, West Sussex LH10 2GG Tel: 0293 549555. (P.686)

Air Transport Users Committee (ATUC), 5th Floor, 103 Kingsway, London WC2B 6QX Tel: 071 242 3882. (P.685)

Association of British Travel Agents (ABTA), 55-57 Newman Street, London W1P 4AH Tel: 071 637 2444. (P.689)

Association of Independent Tour Operators (AITO), 133a St Margaret's Road, Twickenham, Middx TW1 1RG Tel: 081 744 9280. (P.690)

British Railways Board, Euston House, 24 Eversholt Street, London NW1 1DZ Tel: 071 928 5151. (P.687)

Bus and Coach Council, 52 Lincoln's Inn Fields, London WC2A 3LZ Tel: 071 831 7546. (P.686)

Capital Transport Campaign, 4th Floor, 42-44 De Beauvoir Crescent, London N1 5SB Tel: 071 249 4166, tries to defend and improve London's transport. (P.686)

Central Transport Consultative Committee (CTCC), First Floor, Golden Cross House, Duncannon Street, London WC2N 4JF Tel: 071 839 7338. (P.688)

Civil Aviation Authority (CAA), 45-59 Kingsway, London WC2B 6TE Tel: 071 379 7311. (P.685)

Docklands Light Railway Ltd, P.O. Box 154, London E14 0DX Tel: 071 538 0311, runs the docklands railway. (P.687)

Europ Assistance, Tel: 081 680 1234 (24 hour) emergency number. (P.685)

General Aviation Manufacturers and Traders Association (GAMTA), 26 High Street, Brill, Aylesbury, Bucks HP18 9ST Tel: 0844 238389. (P.685)

Greasby's Ltd, 211 Longley Road, London SW17 Tel: 081 672 1100, auctions lost property from BR and London Transport. Amazing items but no free catalogue. (P.687)

International Air Transport Association (IATA), Greener House, 66-68 Haymarket, London SW1Y 4RF Tel 071 839 2490. (P.685)

International SOS Assistance, Tel: 081 876 2929/392 1666 (24 hour) from anywhere to anywhere even China. Also referral to doctors in overseas countries. (P.685)

London Transport, 55 Broadway, London SW1H 0BD Tel: 071 222 5600. (P.686)

The London Regional Passengers' Committee (p. 000), **(LRPC)**, Golden Cross House, 8 Duncannon Street, London WC2N 4JF Tel: 071 839 1898. (P.687)

London Transport Lost Property Office, 200 Baker Street, London NW1 5RZ Tel: 071 486 2496. (P.687)

LT Travel Information Service, 071 222 1234 is a 24-hour personal enquiry service, 071 222 1200 gives recorded information on buses and undergrounds. (P.686)

National Federation of Bus Users (NFBU), 6 Holmhurst Lane, St Leonards-on-Sea, East Sussex TN37 7LW Tel: 0424 752424, represents bus users' interests to local and national government. It covers all bus services in England and Wales. M£M (individuals and groups), M, L. (P.686)

Passenger Shipping Association, 9-10 Market Place, London W1N 7AG Tel: 071 436 2449. (P.689)

The Railway Development Society, 48 The Park, Great Bookham, Surrey KT23 3LS Tel: 0372 452863, campaigns for the development and improvement of rail services. Its members are both individuals and local users' groups. M£M, M, Rg, A. (P.687)

Transport 2000, Walkden House, 10 Melton Street, London NW1 2EJ Tel: 071 388 8386, aims for more use of rail and water for bulk carriage, and better facilities for pedestrians, cyclists and public transport users. M£M, M, G, L, B. See also **Friends of the Earth**.

Water and Sewage

National Rivers Authority, Rivers House, Waterside Drive, Aztec, Almondsbury, Bristol BS12 4UD Tel: 0454 624400. (P.685)

Office of Water Services (OFWAT), Central City Tower, 7 Hill Street, Birmingham B5 4UA Tel: 021 625 1450. (P.685)

Water Appeals Commission, Park House, 87-91 Gt Victoria Street, Belfast BT2 7AG Tel: 0232 244710. (P.685)

Water Services Association, 1 Queen Anne's Gate, London SW1H 9BT Tel: 071 222 8111. (P.685)

Work

Advisory Conciliation and Arbitration Service, 27 Wilton Street, London SW1X 7AZ Tel: 071 210 3000, is the head office. Regional offices are listed in the phone book under 'Advisory'. (P.690)

Certification Office, 27 Wilton Street, London SW1X 7AZ Tel: 071 210 3734. (P.690)

Confederation of British Industry (CBI), 103 New Oxford Street, London WC1A 1DU Tel: 071 379 7400. (P.691)

Industrial Society, Peter Runge House, 3 Carlton House Terrace, London SW1Y 5AF Tel: 071 839 4300. (P.691)

Institute of Directors, 116 Pall Mall, London SW1Y 5ED Tel: 071 839 1233. (P.691)

Low Pay Unit, 29 Amwell Street, London EC1R 1UN Tel: 071 713 7616, gives information to those on low pay, and their rights.

Small Business Bureau, 46 Westminster Palace Gardens, London SW1P 1RR Tel: 071 976 7262. M£H, M, L, B, G, A. (P.691)

Trades Union Congress, 23-28 Great Russell Street, London, WC1B 3LS Tel: 071 636 4030, has a range of publications. (P.691)

Facts and Figures

Abbreviations • Alphabets • Astrology • Calendar Dates •
Clothing Sizes • Collective Nouns • Frequencies • Gems •
Historical Figures • Inventions and Discoveries • Names •
Roman Numerals • Temperatures • Useful Maths • Weather •
Weights and Measures

This section of the book may look like a rag-bag of assorted information. It is, quite deliberately, just that. Its aim is to answer the diverse, ill-assorted questions of fact which are raised in every household – whether the issue is how to decipher Roman numerals, signal SOS in Morse, or do long division.

ABBREVIATIONS

The vexed question, when it comes to abbreviations, is when to put full stops. At one time they were always put after an abbreviation in which the first part of a word or the first and last letters were used, as in illus. (illustration), Dr. (doctor) or Rd. (road). Full stops were also put between letters used to stand for the first letters of words – as in M.P. Then came the trend for pronouncing abbreviations like ASLEF as if they were words, so the full stops were gradually omitted. Now there is no one rule as to what is correct, but the modern trend is, increasingly, to leave full stops out unless this creates confusion. But even within any one dictionary there are contradictory uses, so it is really a matter for your own discretion.

@ at, as in 'at a certain price'

A1 or A-1 First class (Lloyd's Register of ships); first rate

AA Automobile Association; Athletic Association; Alcoholics Anonymous

AAA Amateur Athletic Association (referred to as 'the three As')

AAM air-to-air missile

A&M Ancient and Modern (hymn book); Agricultural & Mechanical

A&R concerning artists and repertoire (in the recording industry)

ABA Amateur Boxing Association; American Booksellers Association

ABC Australian Broadcasting Commission; American Broadcasting Company

ABM antiballistic missile

ABO the system for classifying blood; there are four types (A, B, AB and O)

AC alternating current; Air Corps; athletic club; before Christ (Latin: *ante Christum*)

ac used in prescriptions to mean 'before meals' (Latin: *ante cibum*)

a/c account; air conditioning (also A/C)

ACAS Advisory Conciliation and Arbitration Service

AC/DC bisexual (slang) – from the two types of electric current

ACE Advisory Centre for Education

ACGI Association of the City and Guilds Institutes

ACTU Australian Council of Trade Unions

ACW aircraftwoman

AD in the year of our Lord (Latin: *anno Domini*)

ad active duty

Ad hoc for this special purpose

Ad lib as much as you please (Latin: *ad libitum*)

ADP automatic data processing

AEA Atomic Energy Authority

AEC Atomic Energy Commission

AEU Amalgamated Engineering Union

AFA Amateur Fencing Association; Amateur Football Association

AFAM Ancient Free and Accepted Masons

AFB Air Force Base

AFC Association Football Club; automatic frequency control; automatic flight control

AGC automatic gain control

AGR advanced gas-cooled reactor

AH in the year of the Mohammedan calendar (Latin: *anno Hegirae*)

AHM Association of Head Mistresses

AI artificial insemination

AIA Association of the Institute of Actuaries

AICC All India Congress Committee – the national assembly of the Indian National Congress

AID Army Intelligence Department; artificial insemination by donor; acute infectious disease; Agency for International Development

AIDS Acquired Immune Deficiency Syndrome

AIF Australian Imperial Force

AIH artificial insemination by husband

ALU arithmetical and logical unit – computer jargon

AM Alpes Maritime; in the year of the world (Latin: *anno mundi*); Ave Maria; associate member

am before noon (Latin: *ante meridiem*)

AMA American Medical Association

anon anonymous

ANU Australian National University

ANZAC Australian and New Zealand Army Corps

ANZUS Australia, New Zealand and United States – defence alliance

A/O or **a/o** for the account of – used in accounting

AOB or **aob** any other business – as in timetable for a committee

AOD Ancient Order of Druids

AOH Ancient Order of Hibernians

APR annual percentage rate

APS American Protestant Society; American Peace Society; Aborigine Protection Society

APT advanced passenger train

AQ achievement quotient

AR Autonomous Region

ASA Amateur Swimming Association

ASE Amalgamated Society of Engineers

ASEAN Association of South East Asian Nations

ASGB Aeronautical Society of Great Britain

ASIO Australian Security Intelligence Organization

ASLEF Associated Society of Locomotive Engineers and Firemen

ASM air-to-surface missile

AST Atlantic Standard Time

ASTMS Association of Scientific, Technical and Managerial Staffs

AT or **at** automatic transmission

ATC air traffic control; Air Training Corps

ATV Associated Television

AU or **au** angstrom unit; astronomical unit

AUEW Amalgamated Union of Engineering Workers

AWOL or **awol** Absent without leave (Forces)

BA British Academy; British Association (for the Advancement of Science)

BAA British Airports Authority

BALPA British Airline Pilots Association

BAR British Auction Records

BBA British Beekeepers Association

BBC British Broadcasting Corporation

BC before Christ

BCG Bacillus Calmette-Guérin (anti-tuberculosis vaccine)

BCh/BChir Bachelor of Surgery – a fully qualified surgeon

B/D bank draft; bills discounted – commercial

BDA British Dental Association

be or **B/E** bill of exchange

BEF British Expeditionary Force

B/L, b/l, Bs/l bill of lading

BM Bachelor of Medicine

BMA British Medical Association

BMJ *British Medical Journal*

BO body odour; box office

B/O brought over – used in book keeping; buyer's option

BOA British Olympic Association; British Optical Association

BOAR British Army of the Rhine

BoT Board of Trade

BP British Pharmacopoeia

bp boiling point (also bpt); below proof – re alcohol

B/P or **bp** bills payable

BPC British Pharmaceutical Codex

bpi bits per inch – used of computer tape

BR British Rail

B/R or **br** bills receivable

BRCS British Red Cross Society

BRS British Road Services

BS precedes catalogue number of the British Standards Institution

bs balance sheet; bill of sale

BSI British Standards Institution

BSS British Standards Specification

BST British Summer Time

BThU British Thermal Unit

BTU Board of Trade Unit

bu bushel

B/W black and white – in photography

BWR boiling water reactor

BYO an unlicensed restaurant where you bring your own wine (Australian)

C Centigrade; Celsius; coulomb (electricity); Conservative

c about (Latin: *circa*)

© copyright

CA Chartered Accountant; chief accountant; Central America; consular agent; Consumers' Association

C/A current account; credit account; capital account

CAA Civil Aviation Authority

CAB Citizens' Advice Bureau; Civil Aeronautical Board (US)

CAF cost and freight

CAP Common Agricultural Policy – of the EC

c&b caught and bowled – cricket

C&G City and Guilds

C&W country and western

CARE Cooperative for American Relief Everywhere – charity federation

CARICOM Caribbean Community and Common Market – trade alliance

CARIFTA Caribbean Free Trade Area

CAT College of Advanced Technology

CB Citizens' Band – radio frequency

CB County Borough

cb centre of buoyancy – in boats etc.

CBC Canadian Broadcasting Corporation

CBD, cbd cash before delivery; central business district

CBI Confederation of British Industry

CBS Columbia Broadcasting System

CC County Council/Councillor; County Court; Circuit Court; Chamber of Commerce; Cricket Club

cc carbon copy; cubic centimetres; chapter

CD Civil Defence; Corps Diplomatique – visiting diplomat

cd cash discount

c/d carried down – in accounting

CD Acts Contagious Diseases Acts

CE Common Entrance – exam; civil engineer; chief engineer

CEGB Central Electricity Generating Board

CENTO Central Treaty Organization – for military and economic co-operation between Iran, Pakistan and Turkey

CERN Conseil Européen pour la Recherche Nucléaire – European centre for research into particle physics, based in Geneva

CET Central European Time – 1 hour ahead of GMT

c/f carried forward – book-keeping

CFE College of Further Education

CG Coast Guard; Coldstream Guards

cg centre of gravity; centigram

ch chain; chapter; chief; church

CI Channel Islands

CIA Central Intelligence Agency (US intelligence and espionage)

CID Criminal Investigation Department

CIF or **cif** cost, insurance and freight – included in quoted price

CM or **cm** Court Martial

cm centimetre

cml commercial

CMS Church Missionary Society

CMUA Commercial Motor Users Association

C/N, c/n or **cn** credit note

CNAA Council for National Academic Awards – degree awarding body

CND Campaign for Nuclear Disarmament

CNR Canadian National Railways

CNS central nervous system – brain and spinal cord

CO conscientious objector

Co county; company; the others

c/o care of

COD cash on delivery

C of C Chamber of Commerce

C of E Church of England (sometimes also CE)

C of S Church of Scotland

COI Central Office of Information

COM computer output on microfilm

com committee; commercial; comedy

COMECON Council of Mutual Economic Assistance – Eastern bloc alliance

Cons Consul; Conservative; constitution

cont continued; containing; contents; continent

CORE Congress of Racial Equality (US)

COSPAR Committee on Space Research

CP Command Post; Canadian Press; Communist Party; Common Prayer; Court of Probate

cp compare

cpd compound

CPR Canadian Pacific Railways

cps cycles per second

CPSU Communist Party of the Soviet Union

CPU central processing unit – computer technology

cr credit; creditor

cres crescendo

CRP Central Reserve Police

CS Chemical Society; Civil Service; Court of Session; Christian Science; Capital Stock

CSB chemical stimulation of the brain

CSC Civil Service Commission

CSE Certificate of Secondary Education

CSIRO Commonwealth Scientific and Industrial Research Organization (Australian)

ct cent; certificate; court

CTC Cyclists' Touring Club

CTO cancelled to order – in stamp collecting

CTV Canadian Television Network Ltd

CU Cambridge University

CUP Cambridge University Press

CUSO Canadian University Services Overseas – voluntary work

CWS Co-operative Wholesale Society

cwt hundredweight

D Democratic; Deus (God); Department

d date; penny; diameter; daughter; dose; dollar; drachma

D/A or **da** deposit account; documents for acceptance

DC direct current; District Court; District of Columbia

dc direct current

D and C dilatation and curettage – dilation of cervix and cleaning out of the uterus

DCH Diploma in Child Health

DCL Distillers Company Ltd

DCLI Duke of Cornwall's Light Infantry

DDT Dichlorodiphenyltrichloroethane – insecticide

DDS Dewey Decimal System – used in classification of library books

deb debenture

deg degree

del delegate

DFE Department for Education

DEW line distant early warning line – Arctic sensors of air attack

DF, D/F Direction Finding (or Finder)

DG thanks be to God (Latin: *Deo gratias*); Dragoon Guards

dg decigram

DH, D/H, DHC drop head coupé – car with removable roof

di or **dia** diameter

dig digest – i.e. book summary

dim diminuendo

Dip, dip diploma

div divide; dividend; division; divorce(d)

DIY, diy do-it-yourself

DJ, dj dinner jacket; disc jockey

dkg decagram

dkl decalitre

dkm decametre

D/L demand loan

dl decilitre

DLI Durham Light Infantry

DLO Diploma in Laryngology and Otology (ear, nose and throat)

DLO Dead Letter Office

DLP Democratic Labor Party (Australia)

dlr dealer

DM Deutsche Mark – German currency

dm decimetre

DMA direct memory access – computer term

DMS Diplomatic Management Studies

DMZ demilitarized zone

DNB Dictionary of National Biography

DNS Department for National Savings

D/O, do delivery order

DOA dead on arrival

DOD Department of Defense (US)

DOE Department of the Environment

DP Displaced Person

DPH Diploma in Public Health

DPW Department of Public Works

DR dead reckoning

Dr Doctor

dr dram; debit; drachma; debtor

DS *dal segno* – in music, meaning repeat from the mark

DSS Department of Social Security

DST daylight saving time

DTI Department of Trade and Industry

DTs delirium tremens – delirium caused by alcohol damage to brain

D/W dock warrant

dwt pennyweight

dwt deadweight tonnage

dz dozen

E East; energy; electro-motive force

e engineering

ea each

EACSO East African Common Services Organization

E&OE, e&oe errors and omissions excepted

EAROM electrically alterable read only memory – in computers

EC European Community

ECG electrocardiogram

ECOWAS Economic Community of West African States

ECGD Export Credits Guarantee Department – a government department providing facilities for UK exporters

ECSC European Coal and Steel Community

ECT electroconvulsive therapy – electrical stimulation of brain

EDC European Defence Community

EDP electronic data processing

EEC European Economic Community

EEG electroencephalogram; electroencephalograph

EFTA European Free Trade Association

Eg Egyptian

eg for example (Latin: *exempli gratia*)

ELDO European Launcher Development Organization

EMU, emu electromagnetic unit

ENE east-northeast

ENT ear, nose and throat

EP extended-play gramophone record

Ep epistle

ep in passing conversation (French: *en passant*)

EPA educational priority area

EPNS Electroplated Nickel Silver

eq equal; equation; equivalent

ERNIE electronic random number indicating equipment

ESN educationally subnormal – of below average intelligence

ESP extrasensory perception

ESRO European Space Research Organization

EST electric-shock treatment; Eastern Standard Time (US)

est established; estate; estimated; estuary

ETA estimated time of arrival

et al and others (Latin: *et alii*)

etc and so forth, and the others (Latin: *et cetera*)

ETD estimated time of departure

et seq and the following (Latin: *et sequens*)

ETU Electrical Trades Union

EURATOM European Atomic Energy Community – treaty by EC members

EV English Version (of Bible)

ex div without dividend

ex int without interest

F Fahrenheit; fellow; force; France

f forte – loudly in music

FA Football Association; Field Artillery; Fanny Adams

FAO Food and Agriculture Organization

FBI Federal Bureau of Investigation

FC Football Club

FCO Foreign and Commonwealth Office

ff fortissimo – music; folio, following pages or lines

FHC fixed-head coupé – coupé in which roof is not removable

FI fuel injection – of car

FIFA Fédération Internationale de Football Association

FI Flanders; Flemish

FM frequency modulation – radio receiving high frequency

FO Foreign Office

FOB, fob Free on board – i.e. free delivery to freight vehicle

FP, fp freezing point; fully paid

FPA Family Planning Association

fps feet per second; frames per second – photographic

frt freight

fs foot-second

fwd forward; front-wheel drive; four-wheel drive

G, g guilder; gauge; guinea

GA General Assembly

GATT General Agreement on Tariffs and Trade

GB Great Britain

GBH grievous bodily harm – legal

GCM, gcm greatest common measure

GCSE General Certificate of Secondary Education

Gdns gardens

GDP gross domestic product – a country's flow of goods and services during a year

GDR German Democratic Republic

gds goods

GG Girl Guides

GHQ General Headquarters

GMC General Medical Council

GMT Greenwich Mean Time

GNP gross national product – GDP plus overseas real earnings

GO general order

GP graduated pension; Gallup poll

GPI general paralysis of the insane

GPO general post office

GQ general quarters

gr wt gross weight

GS General Staff

gtd guaranteed

GTC, gtc goods till cancelled – on orders

HAC Honourable Artillery Company

Hb haemoglobin

HC House of Commons; Holy Communion

HCF, hcf highest common factor

hdbk hardback

HE high explosive

HEW Department of Health, Education and Welfare (US)

HF, hf high frequency

HG Home Guard

HGV heavy goods vehicle

HJ here lies (Latin: *hic jacet*)

HL House of Lords

HM headmaster; headmistress

HMS Her Majesty's Service; Her Majesty's Ship

HMSO Her Majesty's Stationery Office – publisher of government papers

HNC Higher National Certificate

HND Higher National Diploma

HO Home Office; head office

HP, hp horse-power; hire purchase; high pressure; Houses of Parliament

HQ headquarters

HR House of Representatives (US)

HT high tension

HV, hv high voltage

HW, hw high water

HWM high water mark

hyp hypothesis; hypotenuse

IAAF International Amateur Athletics Association

IAEA International Atomic Energy Authority

IAS indicated air speed

IATA International Air Transport Association

IBA Independent Broadcasting Authority

ICA Institute of Contemporary Arts

ICAO International Civil Aviation Organization

ICBM intercontinental ballistic missile

ICE Institution of Civil Engineers

ICFTU International Congress of Free Trade Unions

IChemE Institution of Chemical Engineers

ICJ International Courts of Justice

ID identification

ie that is (Latin: *id est*)

IEE Institution of Electrical Engineers

IFC International Finance Corporation

IGY International Geophysical Year

ILO International Labour Organization

ILS instrument landing system

IMechE Institution of Mechanical Engineers

IMF International Monetary Fund

IMinE Institution of Mining Engineers

IMunE Institution of Municipal Engineers

IND in the name of the Lord (Latin: *in nomine Dei*)

IUD intrauterine device – contraceptive in the womb

IPA International Phonetic Alphabet

IQ intelligence quotient

IR Inland Revenue

IRA Irish Republican Army

IRO Inland Revenue Office; International Refuge Organization

ISBN International Standard Book Number

ita, ITA Initial Teaching Alphabet

ITV Independent Television

JA joint account – in bank

JCR junior common room

KANU Kenya African National Union

KB King's Bench

KD, kd knock down – as in furniture which is sold in kits

KE kinetic energy

kg kilogram

KGB Soviet secret police

KKK Ku Klux Klan – secret anti-black organization in US

KO knock out

LA Legislative Assembly; Library Association

LAMDA London Academy of Music and Dramatic Art

LC letter of credit

LCM, lcm lowest common multiple

LD lethal dose

LDCs less developed countries

LEA Local Education Authority

LED light-emitting diode

LF low frequency

LH, lh left hand

lhd left-hand drive

LI Light Infantry

lit literary

LP long player

£sd term for UK currency before decimalization – pronounced as LSD

LSE London School of Economics

Ltd Limited Company

LV luncheon voucher

LW long wave, low water

LWM low water mark

M medium

M3 a fairly broad measure of the money supply which includes notes, coins, bank accounts and savings in the UK. M1 and 2 are narrower, excluding coins, notes and certain savings

MA mental age; military academy

MCC Marylebone Cricket Club

met meteorological

MF medium frequency – radio

mfd manufactured

mg milligram

MHz megahertz

MI Military Intelligence

MI5 Military Intelligence section 5 – British counter intelligence

MIDAS Missile Defence Alarm System

MIRV multiple independently targeted re-entry vehicle – i.e. missile

MIT Massachusetts Institute of Technology

mkt market

MLD minimum lethal dose

MLF multilateral force – nuclear

MLR minimum lending rate

MO, mo mail order; money order

MOD Ministry of Defence

MOT Ministry of Transport

MP Metropolitan Police; Mounted Police; Military Police; Member of Parliament

mp melting point

mpg miles per gallon

mph miles per hour

MRA Moral Rearmament

MRC Medical Research Council

MS, ms manuscript (plural Mss or mss)

MSG monosodium glutamate – food additive used to enhance flavour

Mt mount, e.g. Mt Everest

MV megavolt

MVD Ministry of Internal Affairs – Soviet police

MW 1 megawatt, medium wave – radio frequency

MY motor yacht

N north; National; Navy

n born (Latin: *natus*); noun; noon; number

NAAFI Navy, Army and Air Force Institutes – organized canteens

NALGO National and Local Government Officers Association

NAS National Association of Schoolmasters

NASA National Aeronautics and Space Administration

NATO North Atlantic Treaty Organization – defence alliance

NATSOPA National Society of Operative Printers, Graphical and Media Personnel – trade union

NB, nb note well (Latin: *nota bene*)

nb no ball – cricket

NBC National Broadcasting Company (US)

NBG no bloody good

NCB National Coal Board

NCCL National Council for Civil Liberties

NE northeast

neg negative

NERC Natural Environment Research Council

NF National Front

NFS National Fire Service

NFU National Farmers Union

NFWI National Federation of Women's Institutes

NG National Guard (US)

NGA National Graphical Association

NHS National Health Service

NI National Insurance

NIRC National Industrial Relations Court

NKVD Soviet police and secret police, 1934-43

nl not permitted (Latin: *non licet*)

NLC National Liberal Club

NLF National Liberation Front

NLLST National Lending Library for Science and Technology

nm nautical mile

NNE north-northeast

NNW north-northwest

NPA Newspaper Publishers Association

NPL National Physical Laboratory

nr near

NSB National Savings Bank

NSF, N/S/F not sufficient funds – banking

NSPCC National Society for the Prevention of Cruelty to Children

NSU non-specific urethritis – mild venereal infection

NT National Trust

nt wt net weight – weight without the packaging

NUAAW National Union of Agricultural and Allied Workers

NUGMW National Union of General and Municipal Workers

NUJ National Union of Journalists

NUPE National Union of Public Employees

NUR National Union of Railwaymen

NUS National Union of Seamen, or Students

NUT National Union of Teachers

NW northwest

NZBC New Zealand Broadcasting Corporation

O ocean

O & M organization and methods – work study

OAP old-age pensioner

OAS Organization of American States; Organisation de l'Armée Secrète – European settlers opposed to Algerian independence

OAU Organization of African Unity

o/c overcharge

OCAM Organization of French-speaking African States

OCTU Officer Cadets Training Unit

OD on demand – banking; overdraft – banking

ODM Ministry of Overseas Development

OECD Organization of Economic Co-operation and Development

OED Oxford English Dictionary

OEEC Organization for European Economic Co-operation

OFT Office of Fair Trading

OFTEL Office of Telecommunications

OHMS On Her Majesty's Service

OK expression meaning all right, fine, I agree

OMS Organisation Mondiale de la Santé (French: World Health Organization)

OND Ordinary National Diploma – qualification in technical subjects

ono or nearest offer – meaning offers of a lower price considered

OP, op out of print

OPEC Organization of Petroleum Exporting Countries

OR other ranks – military; operational research

OS outsize; Old School; Ordnance Survey

OST Office of Science and Technology

OTC Officer's Training Corps; over the counter – stock exchange

OU Open University; Oxford University

OUP Oxford University Press

ovno or very nearest offer – they won't accept a much lower price

P parking

p penny – since decimal coinage

PA personal assistant; press agent; Publishers Association; power of attorney; public-address system; personal appearance

pa each year (Latin: *per annum*))

PABX private automatic branch exchange – telephone system (also PB handling internal and external calls in a large firm)

P&L profit and loss

P&O Peninsular and Oriental – shipping company

p&p postage and packing – referring to the cost of these

Pat Off Patent Office

PAYE pay as you earn – system of tax deductions from earnings

PB Prayer Book; British Pharmacopoeia

pc post card; per cent; after meals – medicine (Latin: *post cibum*)

PD Police Department

pd paid

pdq pretty damn quick

PDSA People's Dispensary for Sick Animals

PE physical education; potential energy

PG paying guest; post graduate; parental guidance – film category

pg page

PGA Professional Golfers Association

PK psychokinesis

pkg package

pkt packet

pl place

PLA Port of London Authority

PLO Palestine Liberation Organization

PLP Parliamentary Labour Party

PLR Public Lending Right – authors' remuneration scheme

PM, pm after noon (Latin: *post meridiem*)

PN, P/N, pn promissory note

PNdB perceived noise decibel – sound measurement

PO Post Office; personnel officer

po postal order

POB Post Office Box

POE point of embarkation – military

pp pages; parcel post; past participle; privately printed; post paid

ppd prepaid; post paid

PPE philosophy, politics and economics – university course

PR Proportional Representation

pr pair; price; pronoun; to be inserted in the anus – medicine (Latin: *per rectum*)

PS postscript – note added after signature on a letter

PT physical training; physical therapy; pupil-teacher

pt pint; part; payment; point

PTA Parent-Teacher Association

PW policewoman

Q question; quarto

q quart; quarter; question

QARNC Queen Alexandra's Royal Army Nursing Corps

QB Queen's Bench – legal

QED which was shown or proved (Latin: *quod erat demonstrandum*)

ql as much as you please – prescriptions (Latin: *quantum libet*)

qm every morning – medicine (Latin: *quaque mane*)

QS quarter sessions

qv denotes a cross-reference (Latin: *quod vide*)

R royal

RAAF Royal Australian Air Force

RAC Royal Automobile Club

RADA Royal Academy of Dramatic Art

RAEC Royal Army Educational Corps

RAF Royal Air Force

RAFVR Royal Air Force Volunteer Reserve

RAM Royal Academy of Music

RAMC Royal Army Medical Corps

RAN Royal Australian Navy

R&B rhythm and blues

R&D research and development

R&R rest and recreation

RAOC Royal Army Ordnance Corps

RAS Royal Agricultural Society, or Astronomical Society
RATO rocket-assisted take-off
RAVC Royal Army Veterinary Corps
RC Roman Catholic; Red Cross
RCA Radio Corporation of America; Royal College of Art; Royal Canadian Academy
RCAF Royal Canadian Air Force
RCM Royal College of Music
RCMP Royal Canadian Mounted Police
RCN Royal College of Nursing; Royal Canadian Navy
RCO Royal College of Organists
RCP Royal College of Physicians
rcpt receipt
RCS Royal College of Surgeons; Royal Corps of Signals; Royal College of Science
RDC Rural District Council
RE Royal Engineers
REM rapid eye movements – in dreaming sleep
RFC Rugby Football Club
RGS Royal Geographical Society
Rgt regiment
RH, rh right hand
RHA Royal Horse Artillery
RI Royal Institution
RIBA Royal Institute of British Architects
RIC Royal Institute of Chemistry
RICS Royal Institute of Chartered Surveyors
RIP rest in peace – as on tombstones (Latin: *requiescat in pace*)
RM Royal Mail; Royal Marines
RMA Royal Military Academy (Sandhurst)
RNAS Royal Naval Air Service, or Air Station
RNLI Royal National Lifeboat Institution
RNVR Royal Naval Volunteer Reserve
RNZAF Royal New Zealand Air Force
RNZAN Royal New Zealand Navy
RoSPA Royal Society for the Prevention of Accidents
rpm revolutions per minute; resale price maintenance
RSA Royal Society of Arts; Republic of South Africa
RSGB Radio Society of Great Britain
RSJ rolled-steel joint – used to support building structures
RSL Royal Society of Literature
RSM Royal Society of Medicine

RSPB Royal Society for the Protection of Birds
RSPCA Royal Society for the Prevention of Cruelty to Animals
RSV revised standard version – of Bible
RSVP please reply (French: *répondez s'il vous plaît*)
RTR Royal Tank Regiment
RU Rugby Union
RV revised version – of Bible

S saint; Socialist; sea; senate; society; small
SA Salvation Army
SABC South African Broadcasting Corporation
SALT Strategic Arms Limitation Talks
SAM surface-to-air missile
SAYE save as you earn – deduction from earnings scheme
SCE Scottish Certificate of Education
SCR senior common room
SDP Social Democratic Party
SE southeast
SEATO South East Asian Treaty Organization
SERC Science and Engineering Research Council
sgd signed
SHAPE Supreme Headquarters Allied Powers Europe
SLADE Society of Lithographic Artists, Designers, Engravers and Process Workers – a trade union
SLR single lens reflex – type of camera
SNAKE EC scheme for harmonizing fluctuations in EC currencies
so seller's option; shipping order
SOP standard operating procedure
SPCK Society for the Promotion of Christian Knowledge
Sr Sister – religious
SRCN State Registered Children's Nurse
SRO standing room only; Statutory Rules and Orders
SS steamship; Schutzstaffel (protection detachment, i.e. originally Hitler's bodyguard)
SSW south-southwest
St street; saint; statute
sta station; stationary
suf suffix; sufficient

TA Territorial Army

TAVR Territorial and Army Volunteer Reserve
TGWU Transport and General Workers' Union
TM transcendental meditation
TPI Town Planning Institute
tr translated; trustee; treasurer
TT teetotal(ler); tuberculin tested
TTL through the lens – type of light metering on a camera

U category of film suited to all ages
UCCA Universities Central Council for Admissions
UDA Ulster Defence Association
UDC Urban District Council
UDR Ulster Defence Regiment
UGC University Grants Committee
UHF ultra high frequency
UN United Nations
UNCTAD United Nations Commission for Trade and Development
UNDRO United Nations Disaster Relief Organization
UNESCO United Nations Educational, Scientific and Cultural Organization
UNICEF United Nations Children's Fund
UNO United Nations Organization
UP United Press
USAF United States Air Force
USM unlisted securities market – for certain shares
USS United States Senate
USW ultrashort wave
UU Ulster Unionist
UV ultraviolet

V volt
VAD Voluntary Aid Detachment
V&A Victoria and Albert
var variety; various
VAT value-added tax
vb verb
VD venereal disease
VDU visual display unit – screen part of a computer
VLF, vlf very low frequency
VO very old – to imply brandy, port and similar are old
VSO very superior old – to imply brandy or port is twelve to seventeen years old; Voluntary Service Overseas
VSOP very superior old pale – shows brandy or port is twenty to twenty-five years old
VTOL vertical take-off and landing

W watt
WAAAF Women's Auxiliary Australian Air Force
WAAC Women's Army Auxiliary Corps
WAAF Women's Auxiliary Air Force
WASP white anglo-saxon protestant – slang for classy, white American
WC, wc water closet – lavatory; West Central – London postal district
WCC World Council of Churches
WEA Workers' Educational Association
WHO World Health Organization
WI Women's Institute
WL, wl water line

WLM women's liberation movement
WNP Welsh Nationalist Party
WNW west-northwest
WP weather permitting
WPB, wpb waste paper basket
WPC woman police constable
wpm words per minute
WRAAC Women's Royal Australian Army Corps
WRAAF Women's Royal Australian Air Force
WRAC Women's Royal Army Corps
WRAF Women's Royal Air Force
WRNS Women's Royal Naval Service
WRVS Women's Royal Voluntary Service

WSW west-southwest
wt weight
WVS Women's Voluntary Service

XL extra large

YHA Youth Hostels Association
YMCA Young Men's Christian Association
YMHA Young Men's Hebrew Association
yr year
YWCA Young Women's Christian Association

ZANU Zimbabwe African National Union
ZAPU Zimbabwe African People's Union
ZPG zero population growth

Ranks and Titles

If you need to know what the letters after someone's name stand for, or are generally curious, the following list covers those most commonly used. Among academic qualifications a bachelor is junior to a master, and a master junior to a doctor, and members of institutions are normally junior to fellows. Unfortunately, where titles are concerned it isn't possible to offer any neat rules, it's an immensely complex business with one order of knighthood being senior to another and different orders having different orders of seniority within them. On all

matters of precedence, from university degrees or monastic orders to dukedoms, the bible — which is even used by the honours department of 10 Downing Street – is Debrett's *Correct Form*. If you can't get hold of a copy, the *Daily Telegraph* information service (ring 100 and ask for custom call, the *Daily Telegraph* Information Bureau – there is a fixed charge for every query of £2.85 + VAT which will be automatically added to your telephone bill) will look up what you need to know. Other useful reference sources in this area are Debrett's *Peerage*, *Burke's Peerage*, *Who's Who*, and *Dod's Parliamentary Companion*.

AB Able Bodied Seaman
ACA Associate of the Institute of Chartered Accountants of England and Wales
ACP Associate of the College of Preceptors
ADC aide-de-camp
ADG Assistant-Director General
ADMS Assistant Director of Medical Services
AE & P Ambassador Extraordinary and Plenipotentiary
AFA Associate of the Faculty of Actuaries in Scotland
AFC Air Force Cross
AFM Air Force Medal
AGSM Associate of the Guildhall School of Music
AIA Associate of the Institute of Actuaries
AIC Associate of the Institute of Chemistry
AIG Adjutant Inspector General
AM Albert Medal, Master of Arts (US) (Latin: *Artium Magister*)
AMICE Associate Member of the Institution of Civil Engineers
AMIChemE Associate Member of

the Institution of Chemical Engineers
AMIEE Associate Member of the Institution of Electrical Engineers
AMIME Associate Member of the Institution of Mining Engineers
AMIMechE Associate Member of the Institution of Mechanical Engineers
AMInstCE Associate Member of the Institution of Civil Engineers
AMInstGasE Associate Member of the Institution of Gas Engineers
APS Associate of the Pharmaceutical Society
ARA Associate of the Royal Academy
ARCM Associate of the Royal College of Music
ARCO Associate of the Royal College of Organists
ARCS Associate of the Royal College of Science
ARIBA Associate of the Royal Institute of British Architects
ARMCM Associate of the Royal Manchester College of Music

ARSA Associate of the Royal Scottish Academy; Associate of the Royal Society of Arts
ARSM Associate of the Royal School of Mines
ASAA Associate of the Society of Accountants and Auditors
ASAM Associate of the National Society of Art Masters
ATCL Associate of Trinity College London (Music)
AVM Air Vice Marshal
BA Bachelor of Arts
BAgric Bachelor of Agriculture
BArch Bachelor of Architecture
Bart Baronet
BCh Bachelor of Surgery
BChD Bachelor of Dental Surgery
BCL Bachelor of Civil Law; Bachelor of Canon Law
BCom Bachelor of Commerce
BD Bachelor of Divinity
BDS Bachelor of Dental Surgery
BE Bachelor of Education; Bachelor of Engineering
BEd Bachelor of Education
BEng Bachelor of Engineering
BHy Bachelor of Hygiene

Addresses and suggestions for further reading are at the ends of chapters.

BLit Bachelor of Literature
BLitt Bachelor of Letters
BM Bachelor of Medicine
BME Bachelor of Mining Engineering
BMet Bachelor of Metallurgy
BMus Bachelor of Music
BPharm Bachelor of Pharmacy
BPhil Bachelor of Philosophy
BS Bachelor of Surgery
BSc Bachelor of Science
BSSc or **BSoc Sc** Bachelor of Social Science
Bt Baronet
BTh Bachelor of Theology
CB Companion (of the Order) of the Bath
CBE Companion (of the Order) of the British Empire
CEng Chartered Engineer
CF Chaplain to the Forces
CG Consul General
CGM Conspicuous Gallantry Medal (Naval)
CGS Chief of General Staff
CH Companion of Honour
ChB Bachelor of Surgery (Latin: *Chirurgiae Baccalaureus*)
ChE Chemical Engineer
ChM Master of Surgery (Latin: *Chirurgiae Magister*)
CIGS Chief of Imperial General Staff
CMG Companion of the Order of St Michael and St George
CO Commanding Officer
Cons Consul
CPC Clerk of the Privy Council
Cpl Corporal
CPO Chief Petty Officer
CPS (Latin: *Custos Privati Sigilli*) Keeper of the Privy Seal
CR (Latin: *Custos Rotulorum*) Keeper of the Rolls
CS Clerk of Sessions; Clerk to the Signet; Common Sergeant; Keeper of the Seal; Chartered Surveyor
CSC Conspicuous Service Cross
CSI Companion of the Order of the Star of India
CSO Chief Signals Officer; Chief Staff Officer
CVO Commander of the Royal Victorian Order
D Don (Spanish); Director
DA District Attorney (US)
DBE Dame Commander of the Order of the British Empire
DC Deputy Consul

DCB Dame Commander of the Order of the Bath
DCL Doctor of Civil Law
DCM Distinguished Conduct Medal
DCVO Dame Commander of the Royal Victorian Order
DD Doctor of Divinity
DDEng Doctor of Engineering
DDS or **DDSc** Doctor of Dental Surgery, or Science
DF Defender of the Faith
DFC Distinguished Flying Cross
DFM Distinguished Flying Medal
DG Director General
DHy Doctor of Hygiene
DIC Diploma of the Imperial College of Science and Technology
Dip or **dip** diploma
DipAD Diploma of Art and Design
DipEd Diploma in Education
DipN Diploma in Nursing (a senior qualification)
DLitt or **DLit** Doctor of Letters, or of Literature
DM Doctor of Medicine
DMD Doctor of Dental Medicine
DMus Doctor of Music
DO Doctor of Optometry; Doctor of Osteopathy
DObstRCOG Diploma in Obstetrics of the Royal College of Obstetricians and Gynaecologists
DPH Diploma of Public Health
DPhil or **DPh** Doctor of Philosophy
DPM Diploma in Psychological Medicine
Dr doctor
DSc Doctor of Science
DSC Distinguished Service Cross (Naval)
DSM Distinguished Service Medal (Naval)
DSO Companion of the Distinguished Service Order
DTh Doctor of Theology
DVM Doctor of Veterinary Medicine
E Earl
ER Elizabeth Regina – Queen Elizabeth
Exc Excellency
FAI Fellow of the Auctioneers' Institute
FBA Fellow of the British Academy
FCA Fellow of the Institute of Chartered Accountants
FCI Fellow of the Institute of Commerce

FCP Fellow of the College of Preceptors
FES Fellow of the Entomological, or Ethnological Society
FFA Fellow of the Faculty of Actuaries
FFPS Fellow of the Faculty of Physicians and Surgeons
FGS Fellow of the Geological Society
FIA Fellow of the Institute of Actuaries
FIC Fellow of the Institute of Chemistry
FIH Fellow of the Institute of Hygiene
FLA Fellow of the Library Association
FO Field Officer; Flying Officer
FoC Father of the Chapel – trade union official
FPS Fellow of the Philharmonic Society, or Philosophical Society
FPhysS Fellow of the Physical Society
FRCGP Fellow of the Royal College of General Practitioners
FRCO Fellow of the Royal College of Organists
FRCOG Fellow of the Royal College of Obstetricians and Gynaecologists
FRCP Fellow of the Royal College of Physicians
FRCPsych Fellow of the Royal College of Psychiatrists
FRCS Fellow of the Royal College of Surgeons
FRGS Fellow of the Royal Geographical Society
FRHistS Fellow of the Royal Historical Society
FRHortS Fellow of the Royal Horticultural Society
FRMetS Fellow of the Royal Meteorological Society
FRNSA Fellow of the Royal School of Naval Architecture
FRPS Fellow of the Royal Photographic Society
FRS Fellow of the Royal Society
FRSA Fellow of the Royal Society of Arts
FSA Fellow of the Society of Antiquaries
FSI Fellow of the Surveyors' Institution
FZS Fellow of the Zoological Society
GBE (Knight or Dame) Grand Cross of the British Empire

GC George Cross

GCB Knight Grand Cross of the Bath

GCIE Knight Grand Commander of the Indian Empire

GCMG Knight Grand Cross of St Michael and St George

GCSI Knight Grand Commander of the Star of India

GCVO Knight Grand Cross of the Royal Victorian Order

GG Governor General

GI soldier in US army, esp. an enlisted man

GM George Medal

GOC General Officer Commanding

GOC-IN-C General Officer Commanding-in-Chief

GP General Practitioner

GS General Secretary

GSO General Staff Officer

HBM His (Her) Britannic Majesty

HE His Eminence; His (Her) Excellency

HG His Grace

HIH His (Her) Imperial Highness

HIM His (Her) Imperial Majesty

HRH His (Her) Royal Highness

HRSA Honorary Member of the Royal Scottish Academy

HS Home Secretary

HSH His (Her) Serene Highness

HSM His (Her) Serene Majesty

IGM International Grandmaster (chess)

ISO Imperial Service Order

IM International Master (chess)

JA Judge Advocate

JAG Judge Advocate General

JP Justice of the Peace

KB Knight Bachelor; Knight of the Bath

KBE Knight (Commander of the Order) of the British Empire

KC King's Counsel

KCB Knight Commander of the Bath

KCH Knight Commander (of the Order) of Hanover

KCIE Knight Commander (of the Order) of the Indian Empire

KCMG Knight Commander of St Michael and St George

KCSI Knight Commander of the Star of India

KCVO Knight Commander of the Royal Victorian Order

KG Knight of the Order of the Garter

KH Knight of the Order of Hanover

KSG Knight of St Gregory

KStJ Knight of the Order of St John

KT Knight of the Order of the Thistle

Kt, Knt Knight

LAC leading aircraftman

LACW leading aircraftwoman

LCJ Lord Chief Justice

LCP Licentiate of the College of Preceptors

L/Cpl Lance Corporal

LDiv Licentiate of Divinity

LDS Licentiate of Dental Surgery

LittD Doctor of Letters

LJ Lord Justice

LL Lord Lieutenant

LLA Lady Literate of Arts

LLB Bachelor of Law (Latin: *Legum Baccalaureus*)

LLD Doctor of Law (Latin: *Legum Doctor*)

LLI Lord Lieutenant of Ireland

LLM Master of Civil and Canon Law (Latin: *Legum Magister*)

LM Licentiate of Medicine; Licentiate of Midwifery

LMRCP Licentiate in Midwifery Royal College of Physicians

LMS Licentiate in Medicine and Surgery

LMSSA Licentiate in Medicine and Surgery Society of Apothecaries

LP Lord Provost

LPS Lord Privy Seal

LRAM Licentiate of the Royal Academy of Music

LRCP Licentiate of the Royal College of Physicians

LSA Licentiate of the Society of Apothecaries

Lt Lieutenant

LtCol Lieutenant Colonel

LtComdr Lieutenant Commander

LtGen Lieutenant General

LtGov Lieutenant Governor

M Monsieur (French); Majesty

MA Master of Arts

MB Bachelor of Medicine (Latin: *Medicinae Baccalaureus*)

MBA Master of Business Administration

MBCPE Member of the British College of Physical Education

MBE Member of the Order of the British Empire

MC Master of Chemistry; Military Cross; Master of Ceremonies; Member of Congress

MCh/MChir Master of Surgery (Latin: *Magister Chirurgiae*)

MChD Master of Dental Surgery

MComm Master of Commerce

MCP Member of the College of Preceptors

MD Doctor of Medicine (Latin: *Medicinae Doctor*); Managing Director

MDS Master of Dental Surgery

ME Marine Engineer; Mechanical Engineer; Mining Engineer; Most Excellent

MEng Master of Engineering

MFH Master of Foxhounds

Mgr Monsignor

MGTI Member of the Gymnastic Teachers' Institute

MHA Member of the House of Assembly (Australian)

MHK Member of the House of Keys (Isle of Man)

MHR Member of the House of Representatives (USA & Australia)

MHy Master of Hygiene

MIEE Member of the Institute of Electrical Engineers

MIJ Member of the Institute of Journalists

MIME, MIMinE Member of the Institute of Mining Engineers

MIMechE Member of the Institution of Mechanical Engineers

MIMM Member of the Institute of Mining and Metallurgy

MIMunE Member of the Institute of Municipal Engineers

MINA Member of the Institute of Naval Architects

MInstCE Member of the Institution of Civil Engineers

MInstGasE Member of the Institution of Gas Engineers

MISTM Member of the Incorporated Society of Trained Masseuses

ML Licentiate of Medicine; Licentiate of Midwifery

MLA Member of the Legislative Assembly; Member of the Library Association

MLC Member of the Legislative Council

Mlle Mademoiselle

MM Military Medal; Master Mason

MM Messrs (French version)

Mme Mmes Madame, Mesdames

MNAS Member of the National Academy of Sciences

MNSPE Member of the National Society of Physical Education

Addresses and suggestions for further reading are at the ends of chapters.

MO Medical Officer
MOH Medical Officer of Health
MP Member of Parliament
MPhil, MPh Master of Philosophy
MPS Member of the Pharmaceutical Society, or Physical, or Philological Society
MR Master of the Rolls
MRAS Member of the Royal Academy of Science, or Asiatic Society
MRCGP Member of the Royal College of General Practitioners
MRCOG Member of the Royal College of Obstetricians and Gynaecologists
MRCP Member of the Royal College of Physicians
MRCS Member of the Royal College of Surgeons
MRCVS Member of the Royal College of Veterinary Surgeons
MRI Member of the Royal Institution
MRIA Member of the Royal Irish Academy
MRSA Member of the Royal Society of Arts
MRSL Member of the Royal Society of Literature
Ms title instead of Mrs or Miss
MS Master of Science; Master of Surgery
MSA Member of the Society of Apothecaries
MSc Master of Science
MTech Master of Technology
MtRev Most Reverend
MusB, MusBac Bachelor of Music (Latin: *Musicae Baccalaureus*)
MusD, MusDoc Doctor of Music (Latin: *Musicae Doctor*)
MusM Master of Music (Latin: *Musicae Magister*)
MVO Member of the Royal Victorian Order
MVS Master of Veterinary Surgery
MVSc Master of Veterinary Science
NCO Non-Commissioned Officer
NGO Non-gazetted Officer

NP Notary Public
OBE Officer of the Order of the British Empire
OC Officer Commanding
OL Officer of the Order of Leopold
OM Order of Merit
ORC Order of the Red Cross
OS Ordinary Seaman
OSA Order of St Augustine
OSB Order of St Benedict
OSD Order of St Dominic
OSF Order of St Francis
OSMA Order of St Michael and All Angels
P Prince; President; priest
PhB Bachelor of Philosophy (Latin: *Philosophiae Baccalaureus*)
PC Privy Councillor; Police Constable; Perpetual Curate
PhD Doctor of Philosophy (Latin: *Philosophiae Doctor*)
PM Prime Minister; Provost Marshal; Post Master; Paymaster
PMG Postmaster General; Paymaster General; Provost Marshal General
PO Petty Officer; Pilot Officer
PP Past President; parish priest
PPE Philosophy, Politics and Economics (a combined degree course)
PPS Parliamentary Private Secretary
Pr Prince
PRA President of the Royal Academy
PRIBA President of the Royal Institute of British Architects
PRS President of the Royal Society
PRSA President of the Royal Scottish Academy
PRSE President of the Royal Society of Edinburgh
QC Queen's Counsel
QM Quartermaster
QMG Quartermaster General
QMS Quartermaster Sergeant
RA Rear Admiral; Royal Academician
RD Rural Dean

RE Right Excellent
RGN Registered General Nurse (now the main nursing qualification)
RH Royal Highness
RHV Registered Health Visitor
RM Resident Magistrate; Registered Midwife
RP Regius Professor
RSA Royal Scottish Academician
RSM Regimental Sergeant-Major
RtHon Right Honourable
RtRev Right Reverend
RW Right Worshipful; Right Worthy
SAS Fellow of the Society of Antiquaries (Latin: *Societatis Antiquariorum Socius*)
ScB Bachelor of Science (Latin: *Scientiae Baccalaureus*)
ScD Doctor of Science (Latin: *Scientiae Doctor*)
SEN State Enrolled Nurse (the most basic qualification)
SG Solicitor General
Sgt Sergeant
SgtMaj, SM Sergeant-Major
SL Solicitor at Law
SMLonSoc Fellow of the London Medical Society
SRN State Registered Nurse
SSC Solicitor Before the Supreme Court (Scotland)
SSD Most Holy Lord (the Pope) (Latin: *Sanctissimus Dominus*)
ThB Bachelor of Theology
ThD Doctor of Theology
TRH Their Royal Highnesses
UKA Ulster King of Arms
V Viscount; Venerable; Vice (in title)
VA Vice-Admiral; Order of Victoria and Albert
VC Victoria Cross; Vice Chancellor; Vice Consul; Vice Chairman; Vicar Apostolic
VD Volunteer Officers' Decoration
VMD Doctor of Veterinary Medicine (Latin: *Veterinariae Medicinae Doctor*)
VO Victorian Order

Science Abbreviations

The Periodic Table

Dimitrii Ivanovich Mandeleev in 1869 discovered the periodic law which forms the basis of today's periodic table. But it was H.G.J. Moseley who, in 1913, realized the key to classifying the elements was not their mass but their atomic number – that is the number of positive charges in the nucleus. This set the pattern for the periodic table (page 710) in which the elements were arranged in order of their atomic number (1, 2, 3, 4 etc). For then certain properties keep recurring at regular intervals (or periods).

There is a dispute over the name of element 104 which is called either kurchatovium or rutherfordium – according to whether you belong to the East or the West.

Periodic Table of the Elements

Transition Elements Series

Element Key

atomic number
name
symbol
relative atomic mass

1
Hydrogen
H
1.00794

Period	Group 1 Alkali metals	Group 2 Alkaline earth metals																Group 3	Group 4	Group 5	Group 6	Group 7 Halogens	Group 8 Inert gases
1	1 Hydrogen **H** 1.00794																							2 Helium **He** 4.00260
2	3 Lithium **Li** 6.941	4 Beryllium **Be** 9.01218																5 Boron **B** 10.81	6 Carbon **C** 12.011	7 Nitrogen **N** 14.0067	8 Oxygen **O** 15.9994	9 Fluorine **F** 18.99840	10 Neon **Ne** 20.179
3	11 Sodium **Na** 22.98977	12 Magnesium **Mg** 24.305																13 Aluminium **Al** 26.98154	14 Silicon **Si** 28.086	15 Phosphorus **P** 30.97376P	16 Sulphur **S** 32.06	17 Chlorine **Cl** 35.453	18 Argon **Ar** 39.948
4	19 Potassium **K** 39.098	20 Calcium **Ca** 40.08	21 Scandium **Sc** 44.9559	22 Titanium **Ti** 47.90	23 Vanadium **V** 50.9414	24 Chromium **Cr** 51.996	25 Manganese **Mn** 54.9380	26 Iron **Fe** 55.847	27 Cobalt **Co** 58.9332	28 Nickel **Ni** 58.70	29 Copper **Cu** 63.546	30 Zinc **Zn** 66.38	31 Gallium **Ga** 69.72	32 Germanium **Ge** 672.59	33 Arsenic **As** 74.9216	34 Selenium **Se** 78.96	35 Bromine **Br** 79.904	36 Krypton **Kr** 83.80
5	37 Rubidium **Rb** 85.4678	38 Strontium **Sr** 87.62	39 Yttrium **Y** 88.9059	40 Zirconium **Zr** 91.22	41 Niobium **Nb** 92.9064	42 Molybdenum **Mo** 95.94	43 Technetium **Tc** 97.9072	44 Ruthenium **Ru** 101.07	45 Rhodium **Rh** 102.9055	46 Palladium **Pd** 106.4	47 Silver **Ag** 107.868	48 Cadmium **Cd** 112.40	49 Indium **In** 114.82	50 Tin **Sn** 118.69	51 Antimony **Sb** 121.75	52 Tellurium **Te** 127.75	53 Iodine **I** 126.9045	54 Xenon **Xe** 131.30
6	55 Caesium **Cs** 132.9054	56 Barium **Ba** 137.34	57 Lanthanum **La** 138.9055	72 Hafnium **Hf** 178.49	73 Tantalum **Ta** 180.9479	74 Tungsten **W** 183.85	75 Rhenium **Re** 186.207	76 Osmium **Os** 190.2	77 Iridium **Ir** 192.22	78 Platinum **Pt** 195.09	79 Gold **Au** 196.9665	80 Mercury **Hg** 200.59	81 Thallium **Tl** 204.37	82 Lead **Pb** 207.2	83 Bismuth **Bi** 208.9804	84 Polonium **Po** 209.9871	85 Astatine **At** 209.9871	86 Radon **Rn** 222.0176
7	87 Francium **Fr** 223.0197	88 Radium **Ra** 226.0254	89 Actinium **Ac** 227.0278	104 Unniliquadium **Unq** 216.109	105 Unnilpentium **Unp** 262.114	106 Unnilhexium **Unh** 263.120	107 Unnilseptium **Uns** 262											

Lanthanide series

57 Lanthanum **La** 138.9055	58 Cerium **Ce** 140.12	59 Praseodymium **Pr** 140.9077	60 Neodymium **Nd** 144.24	61 Promethium **Pm** 144.9128	62 Samarium **Sm** 150.36	63 Europium **Eu** 151.96	64 Gadolinium **Gd** 157.25	65 Terbium **Tb** 158.9254	66 Dysprosium **Dy** 162.50	67 Holmium **Ho** 164.9304	68 Erbium **Er** 167.26	69 Thulium **Tm** 168.9342	70 Ytterbium **Yb** 173.04	71 Lutetium **Lu** 174.97

Actinide series

89 Actinium **Ac** 227.0278	90 Thorium **Th** 232.0381	91 Protactinium **Pa** 231.0359	92 Uranium **U** 238.029	93 Neptunium **Np** 237.0482	94 Plutonium **Pu** 244.0642	95 Americium **Am** 243.0614	96 Curium **Cm** 247.0703	97 Berkelium **Bk** 247.0703	98 Californium **Cf** 251.0786	99 Einsteinium **Es** 252.0828	100 Fermium **Fm** 257.0951	101 Mendelevium **Md** 258.0986	102 Nobelium **No** 259.1009	103 Lawrencium **Lr** 260.1054

Addresses and suggestions for further reading are at the ends of chapters.

ALPHABETS

The Deaf and Dumb Alphabet

These deaf and dumb hand signals are included not only for those who would like to talk to people with these handicaps but also because I have fond memories of using them to signal across classrooms as a child, and I feel these little pleasures should not be lost.

The Modern Greek Alphabet

Printed Form	Handwritten Form		Name of Letter
A α	A	α	alfah
B β	B	β	veetah
Γ γ	Γ	γ	gamah
Δ δ	Δ	δ	deltah
E ε	E	ε	epseelon
Z ζ	Z	ζ	zeetah
H η	H	η	eetah
Θ θ	Θ	θ	theetah
I ι	I	ι	yeeotah
K κ	K	κ	kahpah
Λ λ	Λ	λ	lahmdhah
M μ	M	μ	mee
N ν	N	ν	nee
Ξ ξ	Ξ	ξ	ksee
O o	O	o	omeekron
Π π	Π	π	pee
P ρ	P	ρ	ro
Σ σ	Σ	σ ς	seeghmah
T τ	T	τ	tahf
Y υ	Y	υ	eepseelon
Φ φ	Φ	φ	fee
X χ	X	χ	khee
Ψ ψ	Ψ	ψ	psee
Ω ω	Ω	ω	omehghah

Pronunciation

Vowels

α	a as in park
ε	e as in bell
η, ι, υ	ee as in feet
o, ω	o as in spot

Consonants

β	v as in vain
γ	1) before α, o, ω, ov and consonants like the 'ch' in the Scottish 'loch' but voiced
	2) before ε, αι, η, ι, υ, ει, οι, y as in yellow
δ	th as in the
ζ	z as in zebra
θ	th as in thought
κ	k as in king
λ	l as in like
μ	m as in many
Nν	n as in never
ξ	x as in fix
π	p as in paint
P ρ	r as in road
Σ σ, ξ	1) before β, γ, δ, ξ, μ, ν, ρ, z as in zebra
	2) elsewhere, s as in sea
τ	t as in ten
φ	f as in four
χ	ch as in Scottish loch
ψ	ps as in dropsy

Morse Code

Morse code is essential not only for boy scouts but for all who have Walter Mitty dreams of being imprisoned in a good cause and tapping out courageous dying messages to the cell next door. The code of signalling devised by Professor Samuel Morse is now universally used. The complete alphabet is as follows:

A .—	N —.
B —...	O ———
C —.—.	P .——.
D —..	Q ——.—
E .	R .—.
F ..—.	S ...
G ——.	T —
H	U ..—
I ..	V ...—
J .———	W .——
K —.—	X —..—
L .—..	Y —.——
M ——	Z ——..

Figures are represented as follows:

International Code	Army Signalling Code
1 .————	1 .—
2 ..———	2 ..—
3 ...——	3 ...——
4 ....—	4 ....—
5	5 .
6 —....	6 —....
7 ——...	7 ——...
8 ———..	8 —..
9 ————.	9 —.
0 —————	0 —
. ...	; —.—.—. ? ..——..
, .—.—.—	: ———... ! ——..——

The Russian Alphabet

Printed Form		Handwritten Form	Name of letter	Pronunciation
А	а	𝒜 а	ah	a as in fatter
Б	б	Б б	beh	b as in boy
В	в	В в	veh	v as in victor
Г	г	Г г	geh	g as in get
Д	д	Д д	deh	d as in dog
Е	е	Е е	yeh	ye as in yes
Ё	ё	Ё ё	yoh	yo as in yonder
Ж	ж	Ж ж	zheh (soft z)	s as zh in pleasure
З	з	З з	zheh	z as in zebra
И	и	И и	ee	ee as in feet
Й	й	Й й	ee krahtkoyeh	y as in toy
К	к	К к	kah	k as in kitchen
Л	л	Л л	ehl	l as in leaf
М	м	М м	ehm	m as in man
Н	н	Н н	ehn	n as in not
О	о	О о	o	o as in pot
П	п	П п	peh	p as in pot
Р	р	Р р	ehr	r as in rabbit but slightly rolled, as in a Scots r
С	с	С с	ehs	s as in sit
Т	т	Т т	teh	t as in top
У	у	У у	oo	oo as in tool
Ф	ф	Ф ф	ehf	f as in food
Х	х	Х х	khah	kh as in ch of loch
Ц	ц	Ц ц	tseh	ts as in seats
Ч	ч	Ч ч	chah	ch as in chocolate
Ш	ш	Ш ш	shah	sh as in shop
Щ	щ	Щ щ	shchah	shch as in posh chips
Ъ	ъ	ъ	tvyordiy znahk	Ignore it – it is of historical interest only and never used in modern writing. It merely showed that the consonant before it stayed hard.
Ы	ы	ы	yehree	Similar to i as in sin but no English equivalent
Ь	ь	ь	myahkee znahk	This is a sign which softens the previous consonant by putting a slight y after it
Э	э	Э э	eh oborotnoyeh	e as in pen
Ю	ю	Ю ю	yoo	u as in universal
Я	я	Я я	yah	ya as in yard

ASTROLOGY

Chinese Astrology

According to the Chinese, every year belongs to an animal, and those who are born in that year have the animal's characteristics. Twelve animals occur in succession, and their qualities aren't always the ones the West would attribute to them, so don't worry if you find you're a pig.

Rat	1888	1900	1912	1924	1936	1948	1960	1972	1984
Buffalo/Ox	1889	1901	1913	1925	1937	1949	1961	1973	1985
Tiger	1890	1902	1914	1926	1938	1950	1962	1974	1986
Cat/Rabbit/Hare	1891	1903	1915	1927	1939	1951	1963	1975	1987
Dragon	1892	1904	1916	1928	1940	1952	1964	1976	1988
Snake	1893	1905	1917	1929	1941	1953	1965	1977	1989
Horse	1894	1906	1918	1930	1942	1954	1966	1978	1990
Goat/Sheep	1895	1907	1919	1931	1943	1955	1967	1979	1991
Monkey	1896	1908	1920	1932	1944	1956	1968	1980	1992
Rooster	1897	1909	1921	1933	1945	1957	1969	1981	1993
Dog	1898	1910	1922	1934	1946	1958	1970	1982	1994
Pig/Boar	1899	1911	1923	1935	1947	1959	1971	1983	1995

To know your Chinese animal sign find your date of birth and see what animal names that line. The snag is that the Chinese New Year begins at the first new moon after the sun enters Aquarius. It therefore falls on a different date each year – somewhere between 21 January and 19 February on our calendar. So those with birthdays at the beginning of the year take the sign of the year before. If you want to know the exact change-over date *Chinese Horoscopes* by Barry Fantoni (Sphere) has the answers, but they are too lengthy to give here.

Characteristics

Rat charming, quick-witted, loves company, spendthrift

Buffalo/ox calm, dependable, self-contained, a leader, but stubborn and inclined to shift blame on to others

Tiger thoughtful, strong, brave, dynamic and imaginative, but inclined to be rash and touchy

Cat/rabbit/hare methodical, cautious, comfort-loving, tactful and lucky, but also gossipy and moody

Dragon eccentric, self-confident, dynamic, perfectionist, highly sexed and loyal, but proud and incapable of routine

Snake attractive, sexy and wise, but can be possessive and conceited

Horse sociable and likeable, sporty, practical and logical, but can be prejudiced and intolerant

Goat/sheep harmony-loving, humorous, easy to get on with, but impressionable and easily lead

Monkey intelligent, fast-talking and good with figures, but insecure and sometimes superficial

Rooster hard-working, great organizers, punctual, competitive, but either very thrifty or very wasteful

Dog honest, loyal, idealistic, but a fault-finder who needs to be led

Pig well-mannered, industrious, domesticated, but obstinate, egocentric and bad at planning

Some Chinese marriage proverbs for these animals are:

- The sheep and rat are always at war.
- When the pig meets the monkey there are sure to be tears.
- The cock and snake are always at odds.
- When a dragon meets a rabbit good luck is shattered.
- The ox and tiger always quarrel.
- The cock and dog always end in tears.
- When a tiger meets a snake there is always battle.
- The horse fears the ox.
- The serpent with the hare gives supreme happiness.

But I wouldn't take them too seriously.

The Chinese calendar has a 60-year cycle in which your character and fate are thought to be influenced by the interaction of two cycles. These are the Ten Heavenly Stems and the Twelve Heavenly Branches, so the animals which represent the branches (see above) are only part of the picture. Those who want to know more or delve into the complexity of the two cycles can read the books on page 741.

European Astrology

Astrology has scarcely changed since Ptolemy's time, when in about AD 140 he warned that if Saturn was not tempered by Venus it could make men licentious, libidinous, practisers of lewdness, careless, and impure in sexual intercourse; obscene, treacherous to women . . .

It's odd to think that we send rockets to the moon yet still refer to star charts which grew out of a belief in all-powerful planet gods, and that some tycoons still place as much trust in astrology as did the kings of the ancient world. However, though Shakespeare's Cassius may have been right in saying. 'The fault, dear Brutus, is not in our stars, but in ourselves...' it is nonetheless amusing to see how our image of ourselves squares with our star sign. (See also the books on page 741.)

Here is a quick distillation of what a number of astronomers attribute to different star signs. But to know what astrologers really say the stars hold for you you need a proper star chart for the instant of your birth. For the truth is that the traits of your star sign are as close to astrology as an egg is to a soufflé.

ARIES
the Ram

DATE: 21 March-20 April RULING PLANET: Mars ELEMENT: fire
Aries are pushy, energetic go-getters who take on a challenge, think quickly and get things done. Though courageous, enterprising and highly-sexed, they are less good at considering the options (or the needs of other people) and at paying attention to details.

TAURUS
the Bull

DATES: 21 April-20 May RULING PLANET: Venus ELEMENT: earth
Bulls are pleasure-lovers with a thrifty and methodical streak. They love beauty, food and luxury, but they like to hold on to what they have. So they are seldom extravagant. They are affectionate and sensual but may get stuck in a rut and become possessive, boring and self-centred.

GEMINI
the Twins

DATES: 21 May-21 June RULING PLANET: Mercury ELEMENT: air
Geminis are adaptable, responsive and good at communicating. They are naturally resourceful wheeler-dealers, with a restless energy. But at worst they are shallow, cunning, and two faced in business and love.

CANCER
the Crab

DATES: 22 June-22 July RULING PLANET: Moon ELEMENT: water
Crabs are loyal, patriotic, imaginative and sympathetic. They are also moody, untidy and prone to self-pity. They like to protect and be protected and are inclined to be introverted and are happiest when surrounded by their loved ones.

LEO
the Lion

DATES: 23 July-22 August RULING PLANET: Sun ELEMENT: fire
At their best Leos are natural leaders, with warm, energetic personalities which command respect. They tend to be generous, broad-minded, and good organizers, and also sincere and sensual lovers. But they can be too power-loving and become opinionated and domineering.

Addresses and suggestions for further reading are at the ends of chapters.

VIRGO
the Virgin

DATES: 23 August-22 September   RULING PLANET: Mercury
ELEMENT: earth
Virgos are reserved (as befits a virgin), analytical and often clever. They are also discerning, methodical and thorough, but taken too far this precision and reserve makes some virgos into up-tight, over-critical worriers.

LIBRA
the Scales

DATES: 23 September-22 October   RULING PLANET: Venus   ELEMENT: air
Librans can spend so much time weighing things in the balance that they never make up their minds. But they are also charming, kind and able to create harmony and compromise, though secretly perfectionist. As lovers, they caress the mind more than the body and may lack fire, and they can be untidy and unreliable.

SCORPIO
the Scorpion

DATES: 23 October-22 November   RULING PLANETS: Mars and Pluto
ELEMENT: water
Scorpios tend to hide their true selves away, rather as a scorpion hides. But they have strong personalities which are intuitive, analytical and passionate. These qualities can become warped and turn into jealousy, vindictiveness and secretiveness.

SAGITTARIUS
the Centaur
with bow and
arrow

DATES: 23 November-22 December   RULING PLANET: Jupiter
ELEMENT: fire
The symbol stands for a man's intelligence combined with animal power and speed. Sagittarians are meant to be ambitious, freedom-loving, optimistic and deep thinkers; good at sport and sincere in love – if you don't tie them down. But they can be careless, tactless and have a playboy streak.

CAPRICORN
the Goat

DATES: 23 December-20 January   RULING PLANET: Saturn
ELEMENT: earth
Capricorns are self-disciplined, resourceful and cautious. They are great planners and take life rather seriously, working their way carefully to where they want to get. However, they can be unaffectionate, over-reserved, pessimistic and conventional.

AQUARIUS
the
Water-Carrier

DATES: 21 January-18 February   RULING PLANETS: Uranus and Saturn
ELEMENT: air
Aquarians are expressive, spontaneous, inventive and idealistic – even revolutionary. They are also artistic, friendly and unpredictable. The qualities may not add up to a faithful lover, but they are fun while it lasts. Some Aquarians go too far and become cranky and rebellious.

PISCES
the Fish

DATES: 19 February-20 March   RULING PLANETS: Neptune and Jupiter
ELEMENT: water
The least worldly of the twelve signs, Pisceans are very intuitive, emotional and creative. They are also highly compassionate, loving and sensitive to others, but they find it almost impossible to conform to any set patterns of living, and organization eludes them.

CALENDAR DATES

The year is still based upon religious calendars, which are in turn dominated by the moon and sun as they were in ancient times.

Christmas apart, the major dates of the Christian calendar are set in relation to Easter; and Easter is the first Sunday after the full moon following the vernal equinox of the northern hemisphere (sometime between 22 March and 25 April). The vernal equinox is the time when the position of the sun in relation to the equator is such that day and night are of equal lengths. (The Book of Common Prayer also contains a table showing how to find Easter.)

The Jewish calendar has twelve lunar months of 29½ days long, so the dates of religious festivals shift each year in relation to the Western calendar. Since the festivals are also linked to the seasons, adjustments are made every few years to ensure that they stay within the right seasons, so there is no predicting when they will occur.

The Muslim calendar dates from Mohammed's journey to Medina and also operates to a totally different set of dates from the Western calendar. What is more, the major Muslim festival of Ramadan happens in the ninth month of the Muslim year but cannot start until someone in that country sees the new moon. It last 27 to 29 days and ends in great festivities.

Exact Hindu dates are set for each year by holy men, with reference to the moon, and the process is slightly obscure to the layman. **Shap** publishes an annual booklet listing the exact dates of the festivals of the major religions and what they signify. *Whittaker's Almanac* gives the exact dates of movable festivals to the year 2000.

The dates for British Summer Time, when the clocks go forward and back, are regularly agreed with the EC. The Queen's official birthday is the first, second or third Saturday in June and is set each year by Buckingham Palace and approved by the Queen.

Epiphany	6 January
Candlemas	2 February
Septuagesima Sunday	Three Sundays before Ash Wednesday
Sexagesima Sunday	Two Sundays before Ash Wednesday
Quinquagesima Sunday	One Sunday before Ash Wednesday
St David's Day	1 March
Ash Wednesday	Wednesday before the 7th Sunday before Easter
Lent	Ash Wednesday to Easter Sunday
Quadragesima Sunday	First Sunday after Ash Wednesday
St Patrick's Day	17 March
Holi (Hindu Spring Festival)	March
Mothering Sunday	Third Sunday before Easter
Annunciation Day	25 March (but if this is Easter, then first free Monday after that)
April Fool's Day	1 April
Rama Navami (Ram's Birthday – Hindu)	April
Palm Sunday	Sunday before Easter
Holy Week	Sunday before Easter to Easter Sunday
Good Friday	Friday just before Easter
Easter	see introduction
St George's Day	23 April
Low Sunday	First Sunday after Easter
Rogation Sunday	Fifth Sunday after Easter
Pentecost/ Whitsunday	Seventh Sunday after Easter
Trinity Sunday	Ninth Sunday after Easter
Corpus Christi	Thursday after Trinity Sunday
Mayday Bank Holiday in Britain	First Monday in May
Liberation Day (Channel Isles)	9 May

British Spring Bank Holiday	Last Monday in May
Ascension Day	Forty days after Easter on a Thursday
Father's Day	Third Sunday in June
St Peter and St Paul	29 June (RC)
Salvation Army Founder's Day	2 July
Martyrdom of Bab (Baha'i)	9 July
Obon (Japanese spirit festival)	13-15 July
St Swithin's Day	15 July
Assumption	15 August (RC)
British August Bank Holiday	Last Monday in August
Festival of Hungry Ghosts (Chinese Buddhist)	18 September
Shubun No Hi (Japanese autumn equinox)	23 September
Michaelmas	29 September (C of E)
Navaratri/ Dassehra/Durga Puja (Hindu 9-day festival of Ram's victory over the demons)	October
Birth of Bab (Baha'i festival)	20 October
All Saints' Day	1 November (C of E/RC)
All Souls	2 November (C of E/RC)
Birth of Baha'u'llah (Baha'i)	12 November
Remembrance Sunday	Second Sunday in November
Divali Hindu festival of light	November
Thanksgiving Day	Fourth Thursday in November
St Andrew's Day	30 November
Advent	From the fourth Sunday before Christmas until 24 December
Christmas Eve	24 December
Christmas Day	25 December
Boxing Day	26 December

Law Terms

Hilary	11 January – until the Wednesday before Easter Sunday
Easter	Second Tuesday after Easter Sunday until the Friday before the Spring Bank Holiday (last Monday in May)
Trinity	Second Tuesday after the Spring Bank Holiday until 31 July
Michaelmas	1 October to 21 December

Addresses and suggestions for further reading are at the ends of chapters.

The **Parliamentary terms** are decided by the Leader of the House and the whips, according to parliamentary needs, at as little as two weeks' notice.

Cambridge University terms are set in relation to Easter. The system is so complex that even the vice-chancellor's department couldn't explain it. However, the actual dates for the next 10 years can be obtained from the telephone number on page 741. The Oxford system is simpler – but would take a page to define; the University of Oxford offices (page 741) will answer queries on future dates. Other university terms vary with the university.

CLOTHING SIZES

Clothing sizes are not as exact as you might suppose. It seems that different makers in each country use slightly different sizing and numbering. The following tables are therefore the most usual ones in the judgement of some of Britain's top clothing buyers.

Men's suits

UK/USA	32	34	36	38	40	42	44
Europe	42	44	46	48	50	52	54
Metric	81	86	91	97	102	107	112

Men's Shirt Collar

UK/USA (in)	14	14½	15	15½	16	16½	17	17½
Europe (cm)	36	37	38	39	40	41	42	43

Women's clothing

UK	10	12	14	16	18	20	22
USA	8	10	12	14	16	18	20
Europe	38	40	42	44	47	50	52

Hats

UK	5½	6	6½	7	7⅛	7¼	7⅜	7½
Europe	53	54	55	57	58	59	60	61

The National Cricket Association recommends a 4¾ oz ball up to the age of 14, and the following bat sizes for different ages.

Age	Bat Size
6+	3
8+	4
11+	5/6
13+	6/Harrow
14+	Harrow
16+	Full size

Shoes – Men's, Women's and Children's
Young children's shoe sizes are the same in America as in Britain. the following chart, for which I am indebted to Clarks Shoes, shows how the bands of measurements overlap in Europe, the UK and the USA.

Comparison of Shoe Sizes

Centimetres	Paris Points	English Sizes	US Women's Sizes	US Men's Sizes
11	16	1		
	17			
12	18	2		
13	19	3		
	20	4		
14	21			
	22	5		
15	23	6		
16	24	7		
17	25	8		
	26			
18	27	9		
19	28	10		
	29	11		
20	30			
21	31	12	15	5
	32	13		
22	33		25	15
23	34	1	35	25
	35	2	45	35
24	36	3	55	45
25	37	4	65	55
	38	5		
26	39	6	75	65
27	40	7	85	75
28	41	8	95	85
	42			
29	43	9	105	95
30	44	10	115	105
	45	11	125	115
31	46	12	135	125
	47			

Children's Clothing Sizes

Most manufacturers simply give an age for children's clothing sizes, but the following chart is an approximate guide to what measurements correspond to any age. Err on the large side. Other people's children are usually larger than you remember them, and your own will grow with purse-draining speed.

Children's Clothing Sizes

Age	Height (cm)	Chest (cm)	Waist (cm)
0-6 months	70	46	48
12 months	80	50	50
18 months	86	52	51
2 yrs	92	53	52
3 yrs	98	55	53
4 yrs	104	57	54
5 yrs	110	59	55
6 yrs	116	61	57
7 yrs	122	63	58
8 yrs	128	66	60
9 yrs	134	69	61
10 yrs	140	72	62
11 yrs	146	76	63
12-13 yrs	154	78	64

COLLECTIVE NOUNS

I am indebted to the Game Conservancy for the following list of old and charming collective nouns for birds and animals:

A shrewdness of apes
A cete of badgers
A sloth of bears
A singular of boars
A tok of capercailzie
A covert of coots
A paddling of ducks
A gang of elks
A business of ferrets
A skulk of foxes
A gaggle of geese (at rest)
A skein of geese (in flight)
A charm of goldfinches
A trip of hares
A sege of herons
A band of jays

An exultation of larks
A leap of leopards
A pride of lions
A tidings of magpies
A sword of mallard
A labour of moles
A watch of nightingales
A covey of partridge or grouse
A muster of peacocks
A flight of pigeons
A congregation of plovers
A bevy of quail

An unkindness of ravens
A building of rooks
A dopping of sheldrakes
A walk of snipe (at rest)
A wisp of snipe (in flight)
A murmuration of starlings
A pack of stoats or weasels
A herd of swans
A sounder of swine
A spring of teal
A company of widgeon
A trip of wildfowl
A fall of woodcock

FREQUENCIES

We tend to think of heat, light and radio waves as being entirely different from each other. This isn't quite true. Just as red, blue and yellow seem entirely different, but are all part of a spectrum of colour, so heat, light and radio waves are all part of an electromagnetic spectrum. They all consist of waves which travel at the speed of light. How they differ is in the length of those waves.

The greater the length of the waves (wavelength), the less frequently they occur in a given period – hence low frequency. Just as our ears can only hear part of the range of possible sounds, and therefore can't hear a dog whistle, so our eyes can only see a small central section of the electromagnetic spectrum. The fact that we can't see it all doesn't mean it isn't there. While dogs can hear both ordinary voices and a dog whistle, bees, for example, see many of the wavelengths we see and also ultraviolet which we can't see.

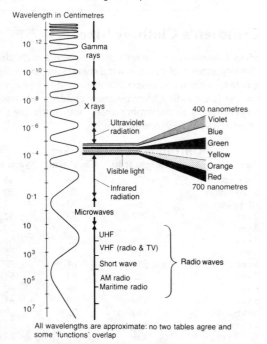

The Electromagnetic Spectrum

All wavelengths are approximate: no two tables agree and some 'functions' overlap

GEMS

Gems are classified by the form the crystals take – aquamarines, for example, are hexagonal – and by the way they refract light. In air light travels at 669,000,000 miles an hour, but in a diamond it slows down to 276,000,000 as the separate rays produce the brilliance in it.

Gems are measured in carats, a measurement which goes back to keration, derived from the Greek word for the carob beans which for centuries were used as weights. But gem carats are quite different from those used for gold. In gems a carat is 200 mg ($\frac{1}{5}$ g or 3.086 grains troy weight) so 5 carats are 1 gram. But, as even a 1 carat diamond is scarcely part of everyday trade, diamonds are usually referred to as pointers, so you may be offered a '10 pointer' or a '25 pointer'. A 10 pointer is one weighing 0.10 of a carat, and a 25 pointer weighs 0.25 of a carat.

Occasionally jewellers sell diamonds by carat *width*, as shown in the gauge below. So a stone which fits in the hole marked 3 could be referred to as '3 carats'. This is easily confused with weight, but a stone 3 carats wide may well be shallow and *weigh* much less than 3 carats. As the value of diamonds is by quality and *weight* – not width – make sure you ask what type of carat a jeweller is talking about and get the carat weight not just its width.

Pearls

Cultured pearls were first produced by the Japanese in the 1920s by inserting a bead made of mother of pearl into an oyster, which then coats it in pearl. X-rays can tell a natural pearl from a cultured one because they can detect the structure of mother of pearl on the inside. But, though natural pearls are usually more expensive than cultured pearls, they are both 'real' pearls because an oyster has formed both of them.

Addresses and suggestions for further reading are at the ends of chapters.

The twisted pearls sold as freshwater pearls, and sometimes called 'rice crispie pearls' are also real pearls but are made by mussels.

Pearls are usually sold by their diameter in millimetres – usually 3 mm to 9.5 mm – though larger pearls can be bought. Any size will vary in price according to its colour and lustre, with the pinker toned pearls costing most. When buying look at them in a good light and always try them against your skin. They look best against certain backgrounds and clever shopkeepers always show them against the colour which will flatter them.

★ To tell whether a pearl is real or simply a fake coated with a pearly substance rub it against the flat of your front tooth. If it feels smooth it's a fake, if it feels slightly rough it should be real. It's so well known in the trade that nobody turns a hair.

Hardness
In 1816 Friedrich Mohs developed a scale of hardness which is still used. The higher the numbers the harder the substance; anything can scratch a substance with a lower number – so the idea that only a diamond can cut glass is untrue.

Amber	$2 - 2\frac{1}{2}$	Quartz	7
Ivory (and finger nails)	$2\frac{1}{2}$	Topaz	8
Calcite	3	Sapphire	9
Window glass	$5\frac{1}{2}$	Diamond	10

Jewellers' Measures
1 metric carat = 200 milligrams
1 troy ounce = 155.52 metric carats

Troy ounces are not the same as standard ounces; a standard ounce is 28 g, but a troy ounce is 31 g. A standard gold bar weighs 400 troy ounces, though bars are sometimes made with 250 troy ounces.

Birth Stones

At one time much was made of birthstones for the qualities which were associated with them. Today they seem almost forgotten and the list somehow has an Edwardian flavour.

Jan.	garnet	purply-red	constancy
Feb.	amethyst	purple	sincerity
Mar.	bloodstone	green with red flecks	courage
Apr.	diamond	glassy	innocence and lasting love
May	emerald	green	success and hope
June	pearl	pearly white	health and purity
July	ruby	red	love and contentment
Aug.	agate	pale green	married happiness
Sept.	sapphire	blue	wisdom
Oct.	opal	white with coloured flecks	hope
Nov.	topaz	yellow, brown	fidelity
Dec.	turquoise	greeny blue	harmony

HISTORICAL FIGURES

Famous Artists

Artists are often known by either their first name or their surname alone. In this list the names are given in their correct order but those which are seldom used are put in () brackets. Where an artist is known by something other than his real name the real name is given in [] brackets after.

Phidias	c.490-420 BC
Praxiteles	active 390 BC
Duccio (di Buoninsegna)	AD1255-1319
Giotto (di Bondone)	c.1266-1337
Donatello [Donato di Niccolo]	c.1386-1466
Fra Angelico [Giovanni da Fiesole]	1387-1455
Jan van Eyck	c.1390-1441
Uccello [Paolo di Dono]	c.1397-1475
Roger van der Weyden	1399-1464
Luca della Robbia	c.1400-1482
Masaccio	c.1401-1428
Fra Filippo Lippi	c.1406-1469
Piero della Francesca	c.1416-1492
Andrea Mantegna	c.1428-1506
Botticelli [Sandro Filipepi di Mariano]	c.1440-1510
Hieronymus Bosch [Jerome van Aeken]	c.1450-1516
Leonardo da Vinci	1452-1519
Hugo van der Goes	active 1467-1482
Matthias Grünewald	c.1470-1528
Albrecht Dürer	1471-1528
Michelangelo Buonarroti	1475-1564
Giorgione [Giorgio da Castelfranco]	c.1477-1510
Raphael [Raffaello Sanzio]	1483-1520
Correggio [Antonio Allegri]	1489-1534

Titian [Tiziano Vecelli]	c.1490-1576	(Jean-Auguste-Dominique) Ingres	1780-1867	Vassili Kandinsky	1866-1944
Hans Holbein the Younger	1497-1543	(Jean Louis André) Théodore		Pierre Bonnard	1867-1947
Benvenuto Cellini	1500-1571	Géricault	1791-1824	Henri Matisse	1869-1954
Tintoretto [Jacopo Robusti]	1518-1594	(Jean-Baptiste Camille) Corot	1796-1857	Georges Rouault	1871-1958
Veronese [Paolo Caliari]	1528-1588	(Eugène) Delacroix	1798-1863	Piet Mondrian	1872-1944
Pieter Bruegel the Elder	c.1530-1569	Samuel Palmer	1805-1881	Maurice de Vlaminck	1876-1958
El Greco [Domenikos Theotokopou-los]	c.1540-1614	Honoré Daumier	1808-1879	(Constantin) Brancusi	1876-1957
Pieter Bruegel the Younger	1564-1637	Jean François Millet	1814-1875	Raoul Dufy	1877-1953
Caravaggio [Michelangelo da Maresi]	1573-1610	Jean-Désiré Gustave Courbet	1819-1877	Kasimir Malevich	1878-1935
				Paul Klee	1879-1940
Peter Paul Rubens	1577-1640	Gustave Moreau	1826-1898	Sir Jacob Epstein	1880-1959
Frans Hals	c.1580-1666	William Holman Hunt	1827-1910	André Derain	1880-1954
Nicolas Poussin	1594-1665	Dante Gabriel Rossetti	1828-1882	Fernand Léger	1881-1955
Gianlorenzo Bernini	1598-1680	Sir John Everett Millais	1829-1896	Pablo (Ruiz) Picasso	1881-1973
Anthony van Dyke	1599-1641	Camille Jacob Pissarro	1830-1903	Edward Hopper	1882-1967
Diego Velazquez	1599-1660	Edouard Manet	1832-1883	Georges Braque	1882-1963
Rembrandt [Harmensz van Rijn]	1606-1669	(James Abbot McNeill) Whistler	1834-1903	Maurice Utrillo	1883-1955
(Bartolomé Esteban) Murillo	1617-1682	Hilaire Germain Edgar Degas	1834-1917	Amedeo Modigliani	1884-1920
				Max Beckmann	1884-1950
Pieter de Hooch	1629-1684	Paul Cézanne	1839-1906	Oskar Kokoschka	1886-1980
Jan Vermeer	1632-1675	Auguste Rodin	1840-1926	Marc Chagall	1887-1985
Jean-Antoine Watteau	1684-1721	Claude (Oscar) Monet	1840-1926	Marcel Duchamp	1887-1968
Giovanni Battista Tiepolo	1696-1770	Pierre Auguste Renoir	1841-1919	Josef Albers	1888-1976
William Hogarth	1697-1764	Henri (Julian Felix) Rousseau (Le Douanier)	1844-1910	(Giorgio) de Chirico	1888-1978
Canaletto (Giovanni Antonio Canal)	1697-1768			Egon Schiele	1890-1918
				Man Ray	1890-1976
Joshua Reynolds	1723-1792	Paul (Eugène Henri) Gauguin	1848-1903	Max Ernst	1891-1976
Thomas Gainsborough	1727-1788	Vincent van Gogh	1853-1890	Sir Stanley Spencer	1891-1959
(Jean-Honoré) Fragonard	1732-1806	John Singer Sargent	1856-1925	George Grosz	1893-1959
(Francisco de) Goya	1746-1828	Georges Pierre Seurat	1859-1891	Joan Miró	1893-1983
Jacques-Louis David	1748-1825	Gustav Klimt	1862-1918	Henry Moore	1898-1986
William Blake	1757-1827	Edvard Munch	1863-1944	Marino Marini	1901-1966
Joseph Mallord William Turner	1775-1851	(Henri Marie Raymond de) Toulouse Lautrec	1864-1901	Mark Rothko	1903-1970
John Constable	1776-1837			Barbara Hepworth	1903-1975
				Salvador Dali	1904-1989
				Rex Whistler	1905-1944
				Francis Bacon	1909-1992
				(Paul) Jackson Pollock	1912-1956
				[Adolf] Ad Reinhardt	1913-1967
				Joseph Beuys	1921-1987
				[Andrew] Andy Warhol	1928-1987
				Frank Auerbach	1931
				Frank Stella	1936
				David Hockney	1937
				Anselm Kiefer	1945

Addresses and suggestions for further reading are at the ends of chapters.

Famous Composers

Guillaume de Machaut	1300-1377
Josquin des Prés	1440-1521
Thomas Tallis	1505-1585
Giovanni Pierluigi da Palestrina	1525-1594
William Byrd	1543-1623
John Dowland	1563-1626
Claudio Monteverdi	1567-1643
Jean Baptiste Lully	1632-1687
Arcangelo Corelli	1653-1713
Giuseppe Torelli	1658-1709
Henry Purcell	1659-1695
Alessandro Scarlatti	1660-1725
François Couperin	1668-1733
Antonio Lucio Vivaldi	1678-1741
Jean Philippe Rameau	1683-1764
Johann Sebastian Bach	1685-1750
Domenico Scarlatti	1685-1757
George Friedrich Handel	1685-1759
Carl Philipp Emanuel Bach	1714-1788
Christoph Willibald von Gluck	1714-1787
Franz Joseph Haydn	1732-1809
Wolfgang Amadeus Mozart	1756-1791
Luigi Cherubini	1760-1842
Ludwig van Beethoven	1770-1827
Carl Maria von Weber	1786-1826
Gioacchino Antonio Rossini	1792-1868
Franz Schubert	1797-1828
Gaetano Donizetti	1797-1848
Vincenzo Bellini	1801-1835
Hector Berlioz	1803-1869
Mikhail Glinka	1804-1857
Jacob Ludwig Felix Mendelssohn-Bartholdy	1809-1847
Frédéric François Chopin	1810-1849
Robert Schumann	1810-1856
Franz Liszt	1811-1886
Richard Wagner	1813-1883
Giuseppe Verdi	1813-1901
Charles Gounod	1818-1893
César Franck	1822-1890
Bedřich Smetana	1824-1884
Anton Bruckner	1824-1896
Johannes Brahms	1933-1897
Alexander Borodin	1834-1887
Camille Saint-Saëns	1835-1921
Georges Bizet	1838-1875
Modeste Petrovich Mussorgsky	1839-1881
Pyotr Ilyich Tchaikovsky	1840-1893
Antonin Dvořák	1841-1904
Arthur Sullivan	1842-1900
Edvard Hagerup Grieg	1843-1907
Nicolai Andreyevich Rimsky-Korsakov	1844-1908
Gabriel Fauré	1845-1924
Edward Elgar	1857-1934
Giacomo Puccini	1858-1924
Gustav Mahler	1860-1911
Claude Debussy	1862-1918
Richard Strauss	1864-1949
Carl Nielsen	1865-1931
Jean Sibelius	1865-1957
Ralph Vaughan Williams	1872-1958
Sergey Vasilyevich Rachmaninov	1873-1943
Arnold Schoenberg	1874-1951
Charles Ives	1874-1954
Maurice Ravel	1875-1937
Manuel de Falla	1876-1946
John Ireland	1879-1962
Béla Bartók	1881-1945
Zoltan Kódaly	1882-1967
Igor Stravinsky	1882-1971
Anton Weber	1883-1945
Arnold Bax	1883-1953
Alban Berg	1885-1935
Sergei Prokofiev	1891-1953
Arthur Honegger	1892-1955
Paul Hindemith	1895-1963
George Gershwin	1898-1937
Aaron Copland	1900
Sir William Walton	1902-1982
Sir Michael Tippett	1905
Dimitri Shostakovich	1906-1976
Olivier Messiaen	1908
Benjamin Britten	1913-1976
György Ligeti	1923
Pierre Boulez	1925
Hans Werner Henze	1926
Karlheinz Stockhausen	1928

Presidents of the United States of America

George Washington	Federal	1789
John Adams	Federal	1797
Thomas Jefferson	Republican	1801
James Madison	Republican	1809
James Monroe	Republican	1817
John Quincy Adams	Republican	1825
Andrew Jackson	Democrat	1829
Martin Van Buren	Democrat	1837
General William Henry Harrison	Whig	1841
John Tyler	Whig	1841
James Knox Polk	Democrat	1845
General Zachary Taylor (died in office)	Whig	1849
Millard Fillmore	Whig	1850
General Franklin Pierce	Democrat	1853
James Buchanan	Democrat	1857
Abraham Lincoln	Republican	1861
Abraham Lincoln (assassinated 14 April)	Republican	1865
Andrew Johnson	Republican	1865
General Ulysses Simpson Grant	Republican	1869
General Ulysses Simpson Grant	Republican	1873
Rutherford Birchard Hayes	Republican	1877
General James Abram Garfield (died in office)	Republican	1881
General Chester Alan Arthur	Republican	1881
Grover Cleveland	Democrat	1885
General Benjamin Harrison	Republican	1889
Grover Cleveland	Democrat	1893
William McKinley	Republican	1897
William McKinley (assassinated)	Republican	1901

Theodore Roosevelt			Franklin Delano Roosevelt			Lyndon Baines Johnson	
	Republican	1901		Democrat	1937	Democrat	1965
William Howard Taft			Franklin Delano Roosevelt			Richard Milhous Nixon	
	Republican	1909		Democrat	1941	Republican	1969
Dr Woodrow Wilson			Franklin Delano Roosevelt			Richard Milhous Nixon	
	Democrat	1913		Democrat	1945	Republican	1972
Dr Woodrow Wilson			Harry S. Truman	Democrat	1945	Gerald Rudolf Ford	
	Democrat	1917	Harry S. Truman	Democrat	1949	Republican	1974
Warren Gamaliel			Dwight David			James Earl Carter Democrat 1977	
Harding	Republican	1921	Eisenhower	Republican	1953	Ronald Wilson Reagan	
Calvin Coolidge	Republican	1923	John Fitzgerald Kennedy			Republican	1981
Herbert Clark Hoover			(assassinated)	Democrat	1961	Ronald Wilson Reagan	
	Republican	1929	Lyndon Baines Johnson			Republican	1984
Franklin Delano Roosevelt				Democrat	1963	George Bush Republican 1989	
	Democrat	1933				William Clinton Democrat 1993	

Kings and Queens of England

Saxon Line		*William II 'Rufus'*	1087-1100	*House of Stuart*	
Egbert	829-839	Henry I	1100-1135	James I	1603-1625
Ethelwulf	839-858	Stephen	1135-1154	Charles I	1625-1649
Ethelbald	858-860				
Ethelbert	860-866	*House of Plantagenet*		*The Commonwealth*	
Ethelred	866-871	Henry II	1154-1189	No monarch	1649-1660
Alfred 'the Great'	871-901	Richard I	1189-1199	Charles II	1660-1685
Edward 'the Elder'	901-924	John	1199-1216	James II	1685-1688
Athelstan	924-940	Henry III	1216-1272	William III	
Edmund I	940-946	Edward I	1272-1307	'William	
Edred	946-955	Edward II	1307-1327	of Orange'	1689-1702
Edwy	955-959	Edward III	1327-1377	and Mary II	1689-1694
Edgar 'the Peaceful'	959-975	Richard II	1377-1399	Anne	1702-1714
Edward 'the Martyr'	975-978				
Ethelred II 'the		*House of Lancaster*		*House of Hanover*	
Unready'	978-1016	Henry IV	1399-1413	George I	1714-1727
Edmund II 'Ironside'	1016	Henry V	1413-1422	George II	1727-1760
		Henry VI	1422-1461	George III	1760-1820
Danish Line				George IV	1820-1830
Canute	1016-1035	*House of York*		William IV	1830-1837
Harold I (died 1040)	1035-1040	Edward IV	1461-1483	Victoria	1837-1901
Hardicanute	1040-1042	Edward V	1483		
		Richard III	1483-1485	*House of Saxe-Coburg*	
Saxon Line (restored)				Edward VII	1901-1910
Edward 'the Confessor'	1042-1066	*House of Tudor*			
Harold II	1066	Henry VII	1485-1509	*House of Windsor*	
		Henry VIII	1509-1547	George V	1910-1936
Norman Line		Edward VI	1547-1553	Edward VIII	1936
William I 'the		Mary I 'Bloody Mary'	1553-1558	George VI	1936-1952
Conqueror'	1066-1087	Elizabeth I	1558-1603	Elizabeth II	1952-

Prime Ministers of Britain

Sir Robert Walpole was the first person who could be termed Prime Minister in anything like the modern sense, and party affiliations were very loose until about 1782. Cons = Conservative; Ind = Independent.

Sir Robert Walpole	Whig	1721	Duke of Devonshire	Whig	1756	Marquis of Rockingham		
Earl of Wilmington	Whig	1742	Duke of Newcastle	Whig	1757		Whig	1765
Henry Pelham	Whig	1743	Earl of Bute	Tory	1762	Earl of Chatham (William		
Duke of Newcastle	Whig	1754	George Grenville	Ind	1763	Pitt the Elder)	Tory	1766

Addresses and suggestions for further reading are at the ends of chapters.

Duke of Grafton	Ind	1767	Viscount Palmerston	Liberal	1855	David Lloyd George	Coalition	1916
Lord North	Whig	1770	Earl of Derby	Cons	1858	A. Bonar Law	Cons	1922
Marquis of Rockingham	Whig	1782	Viscount Palmerston	Liberal	1859	Stanley Baldwin	Cons	1923
Earl of Shelburne	Whig	1782	Earl Russell	Liberal	1865	Ramsey MacDonald	Labour	1924
Duke of Portland	Coalition	1783	Earl of Derby	Cons	1866	Stanley Baldwin	Cons	1924
William Pitt (the Younger)	Tory	1783	Benjamin Disraeli	Cons	1868	Ramsey MacDonald	Labour	1929
Henry Addington	Tory	1801	William Ewart Gladstone	Liberal	1868	Ramsey MacDonald	Labour	1931
William Pitt (the Younger)	Tory	1804	Earl of Beaconsfield (Benjamin Disraeli)	Cons	1874	Stanley Baldwin	Cons	1935
Lord Grenville	Whig	1806	William Ewart Gladstone	Liberal	1880	Neville Chamberlain	Coalition	1937
Duke of Portland	Tory	1807	Marquis of Salisbury	Cons	1885	Winston Churchill	Coalition	1940
Spencer Perceval	Tory	1809	William Ewart Gladstone	Liberal	1886	Winston Churchill	Cons	1945
Earl of Liverpool	Tory	1812	Marquis of Salisbury	Cons	1886	Clement Attlee	Labour	1945
George Canning	Tory	1827	William Ewart Gladstone	Liberal	1892	Sir Winston Churchill	Cons	1951
Viscount Goderich	Tory	1827	Earl of Rosebery	Liberal	1894	Sir Anthony Eden	Cons	1955
Duke of Wellington	Tory	1828	Marquis of Salisbury	Cons	1895	Harold Macmillan	Cons	1957
Earl Grey	Whig	1830	A. J. Balfour	Cons	1902	Sir Alec Douglas-Home	Cons	1963
Viscount Melbourne	Whig	1834	Sir H. Campbell-Bannerman	Liberal	1905	Harold Wilson	Labour	1964
Sir Robert Peel	Tory	1834	H. H. Asquith	Liberal	1908	Edward Heath	Cons	1970
Viscount Melbourne	Whig	1835	H. H. Asquith	Coalition	1915	Harold Wilson	Labour	1974
Sir Robert Peel	Tory	1841				James Callaghan	Labour	1976
Lord John Russell	Whig	1846				Margaret Thatcher	Cons	1979
Earl of Derby	Liberal	1852				Margaret Thatcher	Cons	1983
Earl of Aberdeen	Tory	1852				Margaret Thatcher	Cons	1987
						John Major	Cons	1990

Famous Writers

For use of round and square brackets in this list, see Famous Artists, page 719.

Homer *probably born between*	1050 and 850 BC	(Miguel de) Cervantes (Saavedra)	1547-1616	Voltaire [François Marie Arouet]	1694-1778
Sappho *probably born*	mid-7th C BC	Edmund Spenser	1552(?)-1599	Henry Fielding	1707-1754
Aesop	7th/6th C BC	Francis Bacon	1561-1626	Samuel Johnson	1709-1784
Aeschylus	525-456 BC	Christopher Marlowe	1564-1593	Laurence Sterne	1713-1768
Sophocles	496-406 BC	William Shakespeare	1564-1616	Tobias (George) Smollett	1721-1771
Herodotus	c.484-425 BC	John Donne	1572-1631	Oliver Goldsmith	1730(?)-1774
Euripides	480-406 BC	Ben Jonson	1572-1637	Edward Gibbon	1737-1794
Thucydides	c.460-c.400 BC	John Webster	1580(?)-1625(?)	(Johann Wolfgang von) Goethe	1749-1832
Aristophanes	c.448-388 BC	Robert Herrick	1591-1674	Richard Brinsley Sheridan	1751-1816
Plato	c.427-348 BC	Pierre Corneille	1606-1684	William Blake	1757-1827
Marcus Tullius Cicero	106-43 BC	John Milton	1608-1674	Robert Burns	1759-1796
Virgil [Publius Virgilius Maro]	70-19 BC	John Evelyn	1620-1706	(Johann Christoph Friedrich von) Schiller	1759-1805
Horace [Quintus Horatius Flaccus]	65-8 BC	Jean de La Fontaine	1621-1695	William Wordsworth	1770-1850
(Gaius? Cornelius) Tacitus	AD c.55-c.117	Molière [Jean-Baptiste Poquelin]	1622-1673	Sir Walter Scott	1771-1832
Dante Alighieri	1265-1321	John Bunyan	1628-1688	Samuel Taylor Coleridge	1772-1833
Giovanni Boccaccio	1313-1375	John Dryden	1631-1700	Jane Austen	1775-1817
Geoffrey Chaucer	c.1342-1400	Samuel Pepys	1633-1703	William Hazlitt	1778-1830
François Villon	1431-unknown	Jean Racine	1639-1699	Stendhal [Henri Beyle]	1783-1842
(Niccolo) Machiavelli	1469-1527	Daniel Defoe	1660(?)-1731	(Jacob Ludwig Carl) Grimm	1785-1863
François Rabelais	1494(?)-1553	Jonathan Swift	1667-1745		
		William Congreve	1670-1729		
		Sir Richard Steele	1672-1729		
		Alexander Pope	1688-1744		

(Wilhelm Carl) Grimm	1786-1859
(George Gordon) Lord Byron	1788-1824
Percy Bysshe Shelley	1792-1822
John Keats	1795-1821
Heinrich Heine	1797-1856
Alexander Sergeyevich Pushkin	1799-1837
Honoré de Balzac	1799-1850
Victor (-Marie) Hugo	1802-1885
Alexandre Dumas (father)	1803-1870
Alexandre Dumas (son)	1824-1895
George Sand [Armandine Aurore Lucile Dupin, Baronne Dudevant]	1804-1876
Hans Christian Andersen	1805-1875
John Stuart Mill	1806-1873
Henry (Wadsworth) Longfellow	1807-1882
Edgar Allan Poe	1809-1849
Nikolai Vasilevich Gogol	1809-1852
Alfred Lord Tennyson	1809-1892
Alfred de Musset	1810-1857
William Makepeace Thackeray	1811-1863
Théophile Gauthier	1811-1872
Charles Dickens	1812-1870
Robert Browning	1812-1889
Anthony Trollope	1815-1882
Charlotte Brontë	1816-1855
Emily Brontë	1818-1848
Ivan Sergeyevich Turgenev	1818-1883
George Eliot [Mary Ann Cross née Evans]	1819-1880
Herman Melville	1819-1891
Charles Baudelaire	1821-1867
Gustave Flaubert	1821-1880
Fyodor Mikhailovich Dostoevsky	1821-1881
Dante Gabriel Rossetti	1828-1882
Jules Verne	1828-1905
Henrik Ibsen	1828-1906

Count Lev Nikolaevich Tolstoy	1828-1910
Lewis Carroll [Charles Lutwidge Dodgson]	1832-1898
Mark Twain [Samuel Langhorne Clemens]	1835-1910
Algernon Charles Swinburne	1837-1909
Émile Zola	1840-1902
Thomas Hardy	1840-1928
(Etienne) Stéphane Mallarmé	1842-1898
Henry James	1843-1916
Gerard Manley Hopkins	1844-1889
Paul Verlaine	1844-1896
August Strindberg	1849-1912
Guy de Maupassant	1850-1893
Robert Louis (Balfour) Stevenson	1850-1894
Oscar (Fingal O'Flahertie Wills) Wilde	1854-1900
George Bernard Shaw	1856-1950
Joseph Conrad	1857-1924
Sir Arthur Conan Doyle	1859-1930
Anton (Pavlovich) Chekhov	1860-1904
Rudyard Kipling	1865-1936
W.B. (William Butler) Yeats	1865-1939
H.G. (Herbert George) Wells	1866-1946
John Galsworthy	1867-1933
Luigi Pirandello	1867-1936
Maxim Gorky [Alexei Maximovich Peshkov]	1868-1936
André Gide	1869-1951
Marcel Proust	1871-1922
(Sidonie-Gabrielle) Colette	1873-1954
G.K. (Gilbert Keith) Chesterton	1874-1936
Robert Frost	1874-1963
(William) Somerset Maugham	1874-1965
Thomas Mann	1875-1955
Hermann Hesse	1877-1962

P.G. (Sir Pelham Grenville) Wodehouse	1881-1975
James (Augustine Aloysius) Joyce	1882-1941
Virginia Woolf	1882-1941
Franz Kafka	1883-1924
D.H. (David Herbert) Lawrence	1885-1930
Alain Fournier	1886-1914
Siegfried Sassoon	1886-1967
Rupert (Chawner) Brooke	1887-1915
Eugene (Gladstone) O'Neill	1888-1952
T.S. (Thomas Stearns) Eliot	1888-1965
(John Ronald Reuel) Tolkien	1892-1973
e.e. cummings	1894-1962
Aldous (Leonard) Huxley	1894-1963
Robert (Ranke) Graves	1895-1985
F. Scott Fitzgerald	1896-1940
William Faulkner	1897-1962
Bertolt Brecht	1898-1956
Ernest Hemingway	1898-1961
Federico García Lorca	1899-1936
John Steinbeck	1902-1968
George Orwell [Eric Blair]	1903-1950
Evelyn (Arthur St John) Waugh	1903-1966
(Henry) Graham Greene	1904-1991
Jean-Paul Sartre	1905-1980
Arthur Koestler	1905-1983
Anthony Powell	1905
Samuel (Barclay) Beckett	1906-1989
W.H. (Wystan Hugh) Auden	1907-1973
Simone de Beauvoir	1908-1987
Anthony Burgess	1910-1993
Mervyn Peake	1911-1968
Albert Camus	1913-1960
Dylan Thomas	1914-1953
Tennessee Williams	1914-1983
(Alexander Isayevich) Solzhenitsyn	1918
Günter Grass	1927

Addresses and suggestions for further reading are at the ends of chapters.

INVENTIONS AND DISCOVERIES

3300 BC	the wheel	in Sumeria
250-226 BC	basic laws of mechanics	Archimedes
200-176 BC	concrete used for building	by the Romans
75-51 BC	glass blowing invented	Levant
46 BC	Julian (modern) calendar began	on Caesar's orders
AD 105	paper invented	China
232	wheelbarrow thought to have been invented	China
250	algebraic notation began	Diophanus of Alexandria
450-74	metal stirrup first used	horsemen of Asian steppe
467	earliest known sighting of Halley's comet	China
525-49	silk worms smuggled into Europe	from China
550-74	decimal notation began	India
575-99	first porcelain produced	China
751	earliest known printed book – Buddhist Diamond Sutra	in Korea
1042	first recorded use of movable type in printing	China
1138	first use of Arabic numerals in the West	on Sicilian coins
1167	first distillation of alcohol	Salerno
1190	first evidence of use of the mariner's compass in West	in De Utensibus
1232	first use of rockets in warfare	China
1276	first European papermill	at Fabriano – 'Italy'
1280-84	spinning wheel appears in West	from China
1289	convex spectacles first used	Roger Bacon – England
1315-24	first clock escapement	Western Europe
1315-24	development of guns	Western Europe
1377	first specific quarantine period recognized	Ragusa – 'Italy'
1408	first windmill to pump water	Holland
1455	first book in the West	Johann Gutenberg
1462	first watch	Bartholomew Manfredi – 'Italy'
1477	first English printing press	William Caxton
1515-19	coffee came to Europe	from Arabia
1520-24	chocolate came to Europe	from Mexico
1581	pendulum's motion understood	Galileo
1589	water closet invented	Sir John Harrington – England
1590	the microscope was invented	Zacharias Janssen – Holland
1621	slide rule invented	William Oughtred – England
1628	circulation of blood discovered	William Harvey – England
1644	barometer invented	Evangelista Torricelli – 'Italy'
1661	first definition of chemical elements	Robert Boyle – England
1665	experiments on gravitation	Sir Isaac Newton – England
1666	the prism invented	Sir Isaac Newton – England
1670	first minute hands on watches	unknown
1679	first pressure cooker	Denis Papin – France
1680	dodo became extinct	
1680	phosphorous matches invented	A. Hunckwitz
1690	first steam-driven piston pump	Denis Papin – France
1698	first steam pump engine	Thomas Savery
1714	first mercury thermometer with temperature markings	Gabriel Fahrenheit – Germany
1718	first machine gun invented	James Puckle – England
1720	first inoculation against smallpox	Lady Mary Wortley Montagu – England
1733	the flying shuttle invented for weaving	John Kay – England
1742	Centigrade scale developed	Anders Celsius – Sweden
1752	first lightning conductor	Benjamin Franklin – America
1764	Spinning Jenny invented	James Hargreaves – England
1769	first steam-driven car	Nicholas Cugnot – France
1776	first commercial steam engine	Watt and Boulton – England
1776	first submarine	David Bushnell

1777	circular saw invented	Samuel Miller
1779	first iron bridge	at Colnbrook-dale – England
1780	first fountain pen	Scheller
1782	first hot air balloon	Joseph Michel and Jacques Étienne Montgolfier – France
1784	shells invented	Henry Shrapnel – England
1785	seismograph invented	Salsano
1785	parachute invented	Jean Pierre F. Blanchard
1787	first iron ship	John Wilkinson – England
1792	gas lighting	William Murdock – England
1794	first telegraph used (Paris to Lille)	
1799	invention of bleach for cloth	Tennant and Mackintosh
1800	first electric battery	Alesandro Volta
1803	morphine discovered	Sertürner
1808	typewriter invented	Pellegrine Tarri – 'Italy'
1810	food canning started	Durand
1812	local analgesia by freezing	Baron Larrey – France
1816	stethoscope invented	Réné Laënnec – France
1821	the electric motor devised	Michael Faraday – England
1823	rubberized waterproof fabric	Charles MacIntosh – Scotland
1825	first passenger railway	George Stephenson – England
1826	the safety match	John Walker
1829	photographic processing perfected	J.N. Niepce and Louis Daguerre – France
1831	chloroform discovered	Guthrie and Jastus von Liebig
1834	forerunner of the computer designed	Charles Babbage – England
1835	Colt revolver patented	USA
1836	first propeller-driven ship	John Ericson – Sweden
1837	the Morse telegraph code	Samuel Morse – USA
1839	bicycle invented	Kirkpatrick Macmillan – Scotland

1845	patent for a pneumatic tyre	R. W. Thompson – England
1846	solid rubber tyres for cars	Thomas Hancock
1846	patent for a sewing machine	Elias Howe – USA
1849	safety pin	Walter Hunt
1850	first machine-chilled cold storage unit	James Harrison and Alexander Catlin Twining
1851	first practical sewing machine	Isaac Singer – USA
1854	first lift	Elisha Otis – USA
1856	first aniline dye – mauve	William Perkin
1858	first burglar alarm	Edwin T. Holmes – USA
1859	first sleeping car for trains	George Pullman – USA
1859	theory of evolution	Charles Darwin – England
1862	plastics discovered	Alexander Parkes – England
1866	theory of plant genetics	Gregor Johann Mendel – Czecho-slovakia
1867	dynamite invented	Alfred Nobel – Sweden
1869	DNA discovered	Friedrich Meischer – Switzerland
1873	barbed wire invented	Glidden – America
1876	telephone invented	Alexander Graham Bell – Scotland
1878	gramophone invented	Thomas Alva Edison – USA
1878	motorized tricycle	Karl Benz – Germany
1879	first electric light bulb	Thomas Alva Edison – USA
1879	first electric train	William Siemens – England
1885	first patent motorcycle	Gottlieb Daimler – Germany
1885	successful inoculation against rabies	Louis Pasteur – France
1886	first three-wheeler car patented	Karl Benz – Germany
1887	first four-wheeler car	Gottlieb Daimler – Germany
1888	first three-wheeler car ran	Karl Benz – Germany

Addresses and suggestions for further reading are at the ends of chapters.

1888	pneumatic bicycle tyres introduced	John Boyd Dunlop – Scotland
1891	first zip fastener	Whitcomb L. Judson
1895	safety razor	King C. Gillette – USA
1895	X-ray invented	W. K. Röntgen – Germany
1896	radioactivity from uranium discovered	Alexandre Becquerel – France
1898	discovery of radium	Marie and Pierre Curie – France
1900	first escalator	in America
1900	first loudspeaker	Horace Short – Britain
1903	Wright brothers' first flight	North Carolina, USA
1907	first electric washing machine	Hurley Machine Co – USA
1913	machine to measure radioactivity	Hans Geiger – Germany
1915	first tank used	Sir Ernest Swinton – Britain
1915	first fighter plane built	Hugo Junkers – Germany
1922	radar invented	Dr Albert H. Taylor and Leo C. Young
1924	first helicopter invented	Étienne Oehmichen – France
1926	first TV picture transmitted	John Logie Baird – Britain
1926	first 16-mm movie film made	Kodak – USA
1927	first electronic television	Philo Taylor Farnsworth
1928	penicillin discovered	Alexander Fleming – Britain
1931	the electric razor	Colonel Jacob Schick
1932	first nuclear disintegration	John Cockcroft and E.T.S. Walton – Britain
1933	discovery of polythene	ICI
1935	first parking meter	Carlton C. Magee – USA
1937	nylon created	Dr Wallace H. Carothers

1938	first practical ballpoint pen	Lajos Biró – Hungary
1939	first helicopter produced	Igor Sikorsky – USSR
1941	portable military bridge invented	Donald Coleman Bailey – Britain
1942	first atom split	Frédéric Joliot-Curie – France
1943	first electronic computer	Dr Alan M. Turing
1947	sound barrier first broken by an aeroplane	Major Charles Elwood 'Chuck' Yeager – USA
1948	first long-playing record	Dr Peter Goldmark
1948	semiconductors introduced	
1948	first transistor	John Bardeen, W. Shockley and W. Brattain – USA
1952	first atomic powered submarine	USA
1953	discovery of the structure of DNA	James Dewey Watson and F. H. C. Crick – Britain
1955	the hovercraft invented	Sir Christopher Cockerell – Britain
1956	world's first large-scale nuclear power station	at Windscale – Britain
1957	launch of first space satellite	by USSR
1959	first craft to land on moon (unmanned)	USSR
1960	laser invented	Dr Charles H. Towne
1961	first man in space	Uri Gagarin – USSR
1966	first plastic heart used	USA
1969	first men on the moon	Neil Armstrong and Edwin (Buzz) Aldrin – USA
1969	first supersonic passenger plane flown – Concorde	Britain and France
1975	Rubik cube invented	Professor Ernö Rubik – Hungary
1982	first successful artificial heart transplant	USA

NAMES

The origins and meanings of many names are highly debatable. Often a name seems to have cropped up in different places at much the same point in history and it's anybody's guess who started it. The following list does not pretend to be scholarly, but simply provides a useful checklist if you are trying to name a child, and gives a rough guide to some of the possible origins and meanings. Alternative spellings, short forms and diminutives are given with the name from which they stem. If you want to trace your family history, or the meaning of its name, or see if you are entitled to use a crest, the organizations which can help you are on page 741.

o/u stands for origin unknown
m/u stands for meaning unknown

Girls' Names

Abigail, *Hebrew*, father's delight
Ada, *German*, same as Edith, *q.v.*
Agatha, *Greek*, good
Agnes, *Greek*, chaste
Aileen, *Celtic* form of Helen, *q.v.*
Alexandra, *Greek*, helper of men
Alice, Alicia, *Old French*, m/u
Alison, pet name for Alice
Amabel, *Latin*, lovable
Amanda, *Latin*, fit to be loved
Amelia, *Old German*, m/u
Amy, *Latin*, a beloved
Andrea, modern from Andrew –
    manly, brave
Angela, *Greek*, from angel –
    messenger
Angelina, *Greek*, lovely, angelic
Ann, Anne, Anna, Annette, *Hebrew*,
    gracious
Annabel, *Latin/French*, lovable
Antonia, Antoinette, from Anthony
Arabella, *Latin*, a fair altar
Aurelia, Aureola, *Latin*, like gold
Aurora, *Latin*, morning brightness
Barbara, *Greek*, foreign or strange
Beatrice, *Latin*, making happy
Belinda, *Latin*, useful
Bella, *Italian*, beautiful
Benedicta, *Latin*, blessed
Bernice, *Greek*, bringing victory
Blanche, *French*, fair, white
Bona, *Latin*, good
Brenda, *Norse*, from the male Brand
Bridget, *Irish*, shining bright,
    strength
Bryony, climbing plant
Camilla, *Latin*, attendant at a
    sacrifice
Candida, *Latin*, white
Cassandra, *Greek*, a reformer of men
Catherine, Catharine, Katherine,
    Katerina, Kate, *Greek*, o/u
Cecilia, Celia, Cecily, Cicely, *Latin*,
    m/u
Charlotte, Carlotta, Carla, Caroline,
    Carol, *French*, from Charles, *q.v.*

Charmian, *Greek*, joy
Chloe, *Greek* a green herb
Christabel, *Greek/Latin*, beautiful
    Christian
Christine, Christina, *Greek*,
    belonging to Christ
Clare, Clara, Clarice, Clarinda,
    Clarissa, *Latin*, clear or bright
Claudia, *Latin*, lame
Clementine, Clementina, *Latin*,
    gentle
Colette, *French*, from Nicole
Constance, *Latin*, constant
Cordelia, *Latin*, warm-hearted
Cornelia, *Latin*, m/u
Cressida, *Greek*, daughter of the
    golden one
Daisy, Victorian pet name for
    Margaret
Daphne, *Greek*, laurel
Davina, *Scottish*, from David, *q.v.*
Deborah, *Hebrew*, a bee
Delia, *Greek*, from Delos
Denise, from Denis
Diana, *Latin*, Jupiter's daughter
Dinah, *Hebrew*, judged
Dorcas, *Greek*, a gazelle
Dorothea, Dora, Dorothy, *Greek*,
    gift of God
Edith, *Saxon*, happiness, a rich gift
Edna, *Hebrew*, pleasure
Elaine, Eleanor, Elinor, from Helen
Elizabeth, Beth, Betty, Betsy,
    Bessie, Elsie, Elspeth, *Hebrew*,
    oath of God
Emily, corrupted from Amelia
Emma, *German*, a nurse, industrious
Erica, from Eric
Esme, *French*, beloved
Esther, Heather, *Hebrew*, secrets
Ethel, *Saxon*, of noble birth
Eugenia, *Greek*, well-born
Eunice, *Greek*, fair victory
Eva or Eve, *Hebrew*, causing life
Evelyn, *Latin*, hazel
Fanny, diminutive of Frances, *q.v.*
Felicia, *Latin*, fortunate, happy

Felicity, *Latin*, happiness
Fenella, *Gaelic*, from white
    shoulders
Fiona, literary invention
Flora, *Latin*, flowers
Florence, *Latin*, blooming,
    flourishing
Frances, Francesca, Fanny, *German*,
    a Frank
Frederica, *Saxon*, abounding in
    peace
Gail, from Abigail
Gemma, *Italian*, a gem
Georgina, Georgia, Georgiana,
    from George, *q.v.*
Geraldine, *Saxon*, strong, spear
    power
Gertrude, *Old German*, from spear
    and strength
Gladys, *Welsh*, a fair maiden
Grace, *Latin*, grace
Hannah, *Hebrew*, gracious
Harriet, Henrietta, from Henry
Helen, Helena, Ellen, Ella, Nell,
    Nella, Nellie, Nelly, *Greek*, the
    bright one
Hilda, *Old English*, war and battle
Ida, *Saxon*, like a goddess, happy
Imogen, o/u
Iona/Ione, o/u
Irene, *Greek*, peaceful
Isabella, Ella, *Spanish*, fair Eliza
Jacqueline, Jacquetta, *French*, from
    Jacques
Jane, Jean, Jeanne, Joan, *Scots*,
    feminine of John, *q.v.*
Janet, Jeanette, little Jane
Jasmine, *Persian*, from the flower
Jemima, Gemima, *Hebrew*, dove
Jennifer, *Welsh*, from Guinevere,
    m/u
Jenny, pet name for Jane
Jessica, probably *Hebrew*, m/u
Joanna, Johanna, from of Joan, *q.v.*
Josephine, *French*, from Joseph
Joyce, *Latin*, sportive
Judith, *Hebrew*, praising

Addresses and suggestions for further reading are at the ends of chapters.

Julia, Juliana, feminine of Julius, *q.v.*

Juliet, *Italian*, diminutive of Julia

June, from the month

Justina, *Latin*, just

Karen, *Danish* form of Katherine

Kirsten, Kirsty, *Scandinavian*, Christine

Laura, *Latin*, a laurel

Lavinia, *Latin*, of Latium

Leila, *Persian*, dark-haired as night

Leitia, *Latin*, joy or gladness

Leonie, *Greek*, lion

Leslie, Lesley, *Scottish*, m/u

Lilian, Lily, *Latin*, a lily

Linda, *German*, m/u

Lisa, Liza, Lizzie, from Elizabeth

Lois, *Greek*, better

Lorna, invented for Lorna Doone

Louise, Louisa, *French*, from Louis, *q.v.*

Lucretia, *Latin*, a chaste Roman lady, light

Lucy, Lucinda, Lucia, *Latin*, from Lucius

Lydia, *Greek*, native of Lydia

Mabel, *Latin*, lovely or lovable

Magdalen, Madeline, *Syriac*, magnificent

Maia, Maya, *Latin*, exalted

Marcella, *Latin*, m/u

Margaret, Madge, Maisie, Maggie, Greta, Minnie, *Greek*, a pearl

Marina, *Latin*, of the sea

Marjorie, Margery, *French*, from Marguerite

Marlene, devised for Marlene Dietrich

Martha, *Hebrew*, lady

Martina, from Martin

Mary, Maria, Marie, Marion, Marilyn, Molly, *Hebrew*, bitter

Matilda, *German*, a lady of honour

May, *Latin*, month of May, or diminutive of Mary, *q.v.*

Melissa, *Greek*, a honey bee

Mildred, *Saxon*, speaking mild

Millicent, *Latin*, a sweet singer

Miranda, *Latin*, admirable

Miriam, *Hebrew*, exalted

Moira, Moyra, *Irish*, for Mary

Myra, *Greek*, grieving

Nancy, a form of Anne

Naomi, *Hebrew*, bitterness, consolation

Natasha, *Russian*, diminutive of Natalia

Netta, Nettie, forms of Henrietta

Nicola, *Greek*, feminine of Nicolas

Nina, *Russian*, diminutive of Anne

Nora, contraction of Honora

Olive, Olivia, *Latin*, an olive

Ophelia, *Greek*, a serpent

Pamela, invented by Sir Philip Sidney

Patience, *Latin*, bearing patiently

Patricia, feminine of Patrick, *q.v.*

Pauline, Paula, Paulina, from Paul

Penelope, *Greek*, a weaver

Philippa, *Greek*, feminine of Philip

Phoebe, *Greek*, the light of life

Phyllis, *Greek*, a green bough

Polly, variation of Molly, diminutive of Mary, *q.v.*

Priscilla, *Latin*, somewhat old

Prudence, *Latin*, discretion

Rachel, *Hebrew*, a lamb

Rebecca, *Hebrew*, a noose

Rhoda, *Greek*, a rose

Rita, short for Margaret, *q.v.*

Roberta, Robina, from Robert

Rosa, Rose, Rosie, *Latin*, a rose

Rosabella, *Italian*, a fair rose

Rosalie, Rosaline, *Latin*, little rose

Rosalind, *Latin*, beautiful as a rose

Rosamond, *Saxon*, rose of peace

Rosemary, o/u

Rona, Rhona, *Gaelic/Welsh*, m/u

Roxana, *Persian*, dawn of day

Ruth, *Hebrew*, friend

Sabina, *Latin*, sprung from the Sabines

Sally, form of Sarah, *q.v.*

Samantha, modern

Sandra, Sandy, from Alexandra

Sarah, *Hebrew*, a princess

Sasha, from Alexander (also for boys)

Selina, *Greek*, the moon

Serena, *Latin*, calm

Sharon, biblical place name

Sheila, *Irish* for Celia, *q.v.*

Sheena, Shena, *Gaelic* for Jane

Shirley, from the surname

Sibylla, *Greek*, a prophetess

Siobhan, *Irish* form of Joan

Sonia, Sonya, *Russian* diminutive of Sophia

Sophia, Sophie, *Greek*, wisdom

Stella, *Latin*, a star

Stephanie, *French*, from Stephen, *q.v.*

Susan, Susanna, *Hebrew*, a lily

Tabitha, *Syriac*, a roe

Tamsin, version of Thomasina

Tania, Tanya, *Russian* diminutive for Tatyana

Teresa, *Greek*, a gleaner

Theodora, Theodosia, *Greek*, given by God

Tracy, from Teresa

Una, *Irish*, one

Ursula, *Latin*, a she bear

Valerie, Valeria, *Latin*, m/u

Vanessa, invented by Swift

Venetia, possibly *Latin*, for Gwyneth

Vera, Vere, *Latin*, true

Verity, o/u

Veronica, *Latin*, true image

Victoria, *Latin*, all conquering

Viola, Violet, *Latin*, a violet

Virginia, *Latin*, chaste

Vivien, *Latin*, lively

Wendy, first used in *Peter Pan*

Winifred, Saxon, winning peace

Yvonne, Yvette, *French* diminutive

Zoe, *Greek*, lively

Boys' Names

Adam, *Hebrew*, red

Adrian, *Latin*, from Adria

Albert, *Saxon*, nobly bright

Alexander, Alastair, Alex, Sandy, *Greek*, defending men

Alfred, *Teutonic*, good counsellor

Algernon, *French*, bearded

Allan, Alan, Allen, *Celtic*, m/u

Ambrose, *Greek*, immortal

Andrew, *Greek*, manly

Angus, *Celtic*, excellent virtue

Antony, Anthony, Tony, *Latin*, m/u

Archibald, *German*, a bold observer

Arnold, *German*, strong as an eagle

Arthur, o/u

Barnaby, *Hebrew*, a prophet's son

Barry, *Irish*, spear

Bartholomew, *Hebrew*, the son of him who made the waters to rise

Basil, *Greek*, kingly

Ben, *Hebrew*, son

Benedict, *Latin*, blessed

Benjamin, *Hebrew*, the son of a right hand

Bennet, *Latin*, blessed

Bernard, *German*, bear's heart

Bertram, Bertrand, *German*, bright raven

Beverley, from beaver stream

Brendan, *Irish*, hill

Brian, Bryan, *Celtic*, strong

Bruce, place name

Byron, *Old English*, at the cowsheds

Caleb, *Hebrew*, a dog

Cary, *Old English*, place name

Cecil, *Latin*, blind

Charles, *German*, manly

Christopher, *Greek*, bearing Christ

Clarence, *Latin*, illustrious

Clark, from the surname

Claude, *Latin*, lame

Clement, *Latin*, mild-tempered

Clifford, from a place name

Clive, from the surname
Colin, *French*, from Nicolas
Conrad, *German*, able counsel
Constantine, *Latin*, resolute
Craig, *Old Welsh*, crag
Crispin, *Latin*, having curled locks
Cuthbert, *Saxon*, known famously
Cyril, *Greek*, commanding
Damian, *Greek*, tamer
Dan, *Hebrew*, judgement
Daniel, *Hebrew*, God is judge
David, *Hebrew*, well-beloved
Dean, o/u
Denis, Dennis, *Greek*, from
    Dionysius belonging to the god
    of wine
Derek, Derrick, Deric, Dirk, *Old
    German*, ruler of the people
Desmond, *Old Irish*, south of
    Munster
Dominic, *Latin*, of the Lord
Donald, *Gaelic*, proud
Douglas, *Gaelic*, dark grey
Duncan, *Celtic*, brown chief
Dunstan, *Saxon*, most high
Edgar, *Saxon*, happy hour
Edmund, *Saxon*, happy peace
Edward, *Saxon*, happy keeper
Edwin, *Saxon*, happy conqueror
Egbert, *Saxon*, ever bright
Emmanuel, *Hebrew*, God with us
Enoch, *Hebrew*, dedicated
Eric, *Anglo-Saxon*, kingly
Ernest, *Old German*, vigour
Eugene, *Greek*, nobly descended
Evan, *Welsh*, young warrior
Fabian, *Latin*, bean grower
Felix, *Latin*, happy
Ferdinand, *Old German*, from
    'journey' and 'risk'
Fergus, *Celtic*, manly
Francis, *Latin*, a Frenchman
Frederick, Fredric, *Old German*,
    from peace and ruler
Gabriel, *Hebrew*, the strength of God
Gareth, *Welsh*, high land
Gary, *French*, Gerard
Gavin, *Celtic*, hawk of battle
Geoffrey, Jeffrey, *Old German*, peace
George, *Greek*, a husbandman
Gerard, *Saxon*, spear power
Gideon, *Hebrew*, a destroyer
Gilbert, *Saxon*, bright as gold
Giles, *Greek*, a little goat
Glenn, *Celtic*, valley
Goddard, Godard, *Old German*,
    from God and hard
Godfrey, *Old German*, God's peace,
Gordon, *Scottish* surname
Graham, *Scottish* surname
Gregory, *Greek*, watchful

Griffith, Griffin, *Welsh*, m/u
Guy, *French*, a leader
Hamish, pseudo *Gaelic*, for James,
    q.v.
Harold, *Saxon*, a champion
Hector, *Greek*, a stout defender
Henry, *Old German*, house ruler
Herbert, *Old German*, from bright
    and army
Herman, *Saxon*, a valiant soldier
Horace, Horatio, *Latin*, m/u
Howard, recent, from the surname
Hubert, Hugh, Hugo, *German*, from
    heart and mind
Humphrey, *Old English* or *Old
    German*, m/u
Ian, *Celtic*, for John
Ingram, *Old German*, m/u
Isaac, *Hebrew*, laughter
Ivan, *Russian*, for John
Ivor, *Celtic*, Lord
Jack, pet name for John
Jacob, *Hebrew*, a supplanter
James, Jamie, Jacques, Jim, Jimmy,
    Old French, m/u
Jason, *Greek*, m/u
Jasper, Caspar, m/u
Jeremiah, Jeremy, Jerry, *Hebrew*,
    exalted of the Lord
Jerome, *Greek*, holy name
Jesse, *Hebrew*, wealth
Job, *Hebrew*, sorrowing, persecuted
Joel, *Hebrew*, acquiescing
John, *Hebrew*, the grace of the Lord
Jonathan, *Hebrew*, the gift of the
    Lord
Joscelin, Jocelyn, *Old German*, m/u
Joseph, *Hebrew*, addition
Joshua, *Hebrew*, a Saviour
Jude, *Hebrew*, confession
Julian, Julius, *Latin*, soft-haired
Justin, *Latin*, just
Keith, *Gaelic*, wood
Kenneth, *Gaelic*, leader of men
Kevin, *Irish*, comely birth
Kieran, *Old Irish*, black-haired
Kim, from Rudyard Kipling, used
    for either sex
Kirk, *Scottish* surname
Lambert, *Saxon*, a fair lamb
Laurence, Lawrence, *Latin*, from a
    town name, meaning crowned
    with laurels
Leonard, *Old German*, bold
Leopold, *Old German*, from people
    and bold
Leslie, *Scottish*
Lewis or Louis, *French*, famous
    warrior
Liam, *Irish* form of William
Lionel, *Latin*, a little lion

Llewellyn, *Celtic*, lightning
Lloyd, *Welsh*, grey
Lucius, *Latin*, shining
Luke, *Greek*, a wood or grove
Magnus, *Latin*, great
Malcolm, *Gaelic*, m/u
Manfred, *German*, great peace
Mark, *Latin*, a hammer
Marmaduke, *Saxon*, noble and
    powerful
Martin, *Latin*, martial
Matthew, *Hebrew*, a gift or present
Maurice, *Latin*, sprung of a Moor
Meredith, *Old Welsh*, lord
Michael, *Hebrew*, who is like God?
Miles, Myles, *Old German*, m/u
Morgan, *British*, a mariner
Nathaniel, Nathanael, Nathan,
    Hebrew, God has given
Nicholas, Nicolas, *Greek*, victorious
    over the people
Nigel, Neil, Neal, Neale, Niall,
    obscure – probably *Irish*
Noël, *Old French*, for
    Christmas-day babies
Norman, *French*, a North man
Oliver, *Latin*, an olive
Orlando, *Italian* form of Roland, *q.v*
Orson, *Latin*, a bear
Oscar, *Old English*, from god and
    spear
Osmund, *Saxon*, house peace
Oswald, *Saxon*, ruler of a house
Owen, *Old Welsh*, well-born
Patrick, *Latin*, a nobleman
Paul, *Latin*, small, little
Paulinus, *Latin*, little Paul
Percival, *French*, a place in France
Percy, *English*, adaptation of pierce
    eye
Peregrine, *Latin*, stranger
Peter, Piers, *Greek*, rock
Philip, *Greek*, a lover of horses
Phineas, *Hebrew*, of bold
    countenance
Quentin, Quintin, *Latin*, from
    quinctus – fifth
Ralph, contracted from Randolph,
    or Randal, Ranulph, *Saxon*,
    house wolf
Raymond, *Old German*, from
    counsel and protection
Reginald, *Saxon*, ruler
Reuben, *Hebrew*, the son of vision
Rex, *Latin*, king
Richard, *Saxon*, powerful
Robert, Robin, Rupert, Bob, *Old
    German*, fame
Roderick, *German*, rich in fame
Rodney, Somerset place name

Addresses and suggestions for further reading are at the ends of chapters.

Roger, *Old German*, from fame and
   spear
Roland, Rowland, Rollo, *Old
   German*, from fame and land
Ronald, *Old German*,
Rory, Roy, *Irish*, red
Rufus, *Latin*, reddish
Samuel, *Hebrew*, heard by God
Saul, *Hebrew*, desired
Sean, *Irish*, for John
Sebastian, *Latin*, man of Sebastia
Shamus, Seamus, *Irish* for James
Sidney, Sydney, from the surname
Silvester, *Latin*, born in the woods

Simeon, *Hebrew*, hearing
Simon, *Hebrew*, obedient
Solomon, *Hebrew*, peaceable
Stanley, from the place name
Stephen, *Greek*, a crown or garland
Stewart, Stuart, from the surname
Terence, *Latin*, m/u
Theobald, *Saxon*, bold over the
   people
Theodore, *Greek*, the gift of God
Thomas, Tom, *Hebrew*, twin
Timothy, *Greek*, a fearer of God
Titus, m/u
Tobias, Toby, *Hebrew*, God is good

Tristram, *Celtic*, a herald
Valentine, *Latin*, powerful
Victor, *Latin*, conqueror
Vincent, *Latin*, conquering
Vivian, *Latin*, lively
Walter, *Old German*, from rule and
   folk
Warren, *Old German*, folk name
Wilfred, *Saxon*, bold and peaceful
William, Bill, Willy, *Old German*,
   from will and helmet
Winston, family name in the
   Churchill family

ROMAN NUMERALS

Since Latin is a dead language publishers and film makers conveniently obscure their release dates by printing them in roman numerals, thereby leaving those unversed in Latin totally mystified. To frustrate this ploy here is how you decipher them.

Roman numerals are written with seven capital letters of the alphabet:
I = 1 V = 5 X = 10 L = 50 C = 100 D = 500 M = 1000

For most numbers the symbols are written in order of size, with the largest first, so they add up to the number intended.

   2 = II i.e. 1 + 1
   3 = III i.e. 1 + 1 + 1
   6 = VI i.e. 5 + 1
   7 = VII i.e. 5 + 1 + 1
   8 = VIII i.e. 5 + 1 + 1 + 1
  12 = XII i.e. 10 + 1 + 1
  15 = XV i.e. 10 + 5
  17 = XVII i.e. 10 + 5 + 1 + 1
  20 = XX i.e. 10 + 10
  35 = XXXV i.e. 10 + 10 + 10 + 5
  60 = LX i.e. 50 + 10
  75 = LXXV i.e. 50 + 10 + 10 + 5
 200 = CC i.e. 100 + 100
 600 = DC i.e. 500 + 100
 735 = DCCXXXV i.e. 500 + 100 + 100 + 10 + 10 + 10 + 5

Some numbers can't be made this way. So the other rule is, that if any letter has a smaller value than the one that follows it you subtract it from the one after it. So:

   4 = IV i.e. 1 taken away from 5
   9 = IX i.e. 1 taken away from 10
  19 = XIX i.e. 10 + (1 taken away from 10)
  40 = XL i.e. 10 taken away from 50
  90 = XC i.e. 10 taken away from 100
 900 = CM i.e. 100 taken away from 1000

For example, 1994 is written MCMXCIV.

TEMPERATURES

°C	°F	
100°	212°	*boiling point of water*
95°	203 °	
90°	194°	
85°	185°	
80°	176°	
75°	176°	
70°	158°	
65°	149°	
60°	140°	
55°	131°	
50°	122°	
45°	113°	
40°	104°	
39°	102°	
38°	100°	
37°	98.4°	*normal body temperature*
36°	96.8°	
35°	95°	
34°	93.2°	
33°	91.4°	
32°	89.6°	
31°	87.8°	
30°	86°	
25°	77°	
20°	68°	*warm weather*
15°	59°	
10°	50°	
5°	41°	
0°	32°	*freezing point of water*
−5°	23°	
−10°	14°	
−15°	5°	
−20°	−4°	
−25°	−13°	
−30°	−22°	

On average the air temperature falls 0.6° C for every 100 metres above sea level – hence the snow line on mountains.

Converting Temperatures

To convert Centigrade to Fahrenheit: multiply the temperature by 9, and divide that answer by 5, then add 32.

To convert Fahrenheit to Centigrade you do the reverse, in the reverse order. So you first *subtract* 32 from the temperature, then multiply the result by 5, and divide that answer by 9.

Or – if you prefer formulae:

$$C \text{ to } F = \frac{(temp \times 9)}{5} + 32$$

$$F \text{ to } C = \frac{5(temp - 32)}{9}$$

If you forget which version produces which result remember 32 °F = 0 °C. So you can test one version of the formula on one of these figures and see if it comes out right.

Centigrade temperatures are the same as Celsius and Kelvin. In some parts of Europe where the term Celsius is used, Centigrade is a measurement of angle – worth bearing in mind with doctors overseas, if you don't want them to mistake your inclination.

USEFUL MATHS

It's a pity mathematics is often seen as an unconquerable mountain. It shouldn't be. It *can* be rarified and hard, but few people climb Everest and in its early stages mathematics is just a useful game in which the rules never change: 2 and 2 always make 4. In an uncertain world that is really rather reassuring, and some of the patterns numbers form have a decided charm. Before you dismiss the idea as crazy take a look at this:

1×1	=	1
11×11	=	121
111×111	=	12321
1111×1111	=	1234321
11111×11111	=	123454321
111111×111111	=	12345654321
1111111×1111111	=	1234567654321
11111111×11111111	=	123456787654321

Mathematics is full of curious patterns and though that palindrome may not be useful I hope it will convince you that numbers can have their own unexpected charm.

Nobody should feel insulted by the simplicity of what follows, as much of it is written to make it easier for parents, and other adults, to help children, or for children to read up alone. But I hope that if anyone who is teaching a child, turns to these pages for the rules of maths, they will also turn to the section on teaching children (page 288). It is not so much *what* you teach a child that matters, but how you teach it. The right facts given in the wrong way will run from the mind, as easily as rain runs off stone.

Getting to Grips with 10

The basis of our mathematical system is that figures have *two* meanings. The first comes from the *quantity* they stand for: 5 means five apples, cars, people or whatever. The second meaning comes from their *position* in relation to other numbers. We arrange numbers in columns. One column tells us about single figures (units), the next about tens, the next about hundreds, the next about thousands and so on. So the 5 in 50 means 5 lots of ten because it is in the column devoted to tens, in 500 it tells us how many hundreds there are. Those columns increase in value as they move to the left, with each column being ten times as large as the previous one.

Obvious perhaps, but it can be overlooked that the rule also holds good in reverse: Moving from left to right on the chart below, each column is made by dividing the previous one by 10. Divide 10 by 10 and you get 1, divide 1 by 10 and you get one-tenth, and so on through the whole range of decimal fractions.

Notice that whole numbers are separated from fractions by a dot (point) in the line. This always stays still as a fence dividing one field from another and the numbers move across it as you multiply or divide them (although people talk about moving the point when what they mean is that they move the figures).

millions	hundred thousands	ten thousands	thousands	hundreds	tens	tens or units	decimal point	tenths	hundredths	thousandths	ten thousandths	hundred thousandths	millionths	ten millionths
1	1	1	1	1	1	1	•	1	1	1	1	1	1	1

Addition

The tens rule applies to every move in basic maths. So when you add

```
  7
+ 3
 10
```

you have written it to show you have one ten and no spare units.

Subtraction

Subtraction is the most commonly misunderstood process in basic maths, and the first one children get muddled by. One of the most muddling methods is that in which you borrow and pay back. It gets the right answer, but doesn't relate to the real situation. So, if you are helping children, it is best not to use that method, as it can make it harder for them to understand what numbers are really about. A better method to use is borrowing without paying back. Children can grasp it very quickly if you make it concrete with some objects.

Before a child can even begin to do sums with borrowing, he or she must be totally confident about what numbers mean. So, if there's any doubt about this, spend time letting the child set up groups of tens and groups of ones using small objects like beans or Lego. So 52 is five groups of ten and two ones. (The term 'units' can be muddling and it is clearer to talk about '2 ones'.) Once a child sets them up correctly every time, try taking away simple numbers, say 25 – 12, or 34 – 21. Once simple subtraction with beans or Lego is going well you can move on to borrowing.

If the sum is: 23 – 15 or 23
                          – 15

set up two heaps of Lego each with 10 pieces in, and establish that 2 in the tens column means *two lots of* 10. (This idea of numbers in the tens column standing for groups of ten is the really important thing for a child to grasp, so still use that phrase all the time.) Then set up a heap of 3 pieces to the right, to represent the 3 ones.

Young children like owning things. So make the 23 pieces theirs, and say you are coming to take away 15 of the pieces for yourself. Show them that you can't take 5 when there are only 3 there. So you have to use one of the tens. Do this by moving a group of 10 to sit above the 3.

Take 5 from the 13 – using the Lego – and let the child count up how many it has left from the 13. Explain that taking away 15 means taking away one lot of 10 as well as one lot of 5 and take the heap of 10 away. So the child can see it has 8 left.

Repeat this, with you owning the heaps and the child taking 15 away. Once sums like this have been mastered with just beans or Lego it is time to do it on paper too.

Try this process, from the top, with different combinations of numbers, using bricks each time. Even better, use tiny sweets and let the child eat them if it gets the sum right. Bad for the teeth but good for the memory, and the teeth can always be cleaned afterwards. The same principle can be applied to borrowing from the hundreds column, but here you point out to the child that borrowing one lot of 100 is the same as borrowing ten lots of ten (easy to demonstrate with beans if you have enough of them).

Fractions

Basic fractions are those in which the two numbers are put one above the other with a line separating them. So $\frac{1}{2}$ and $\frac{1}{4}$ are basic fractions.

The top number is called the <u>numerator</u>
the bottom one is called the denominator.

The denominator tells you how many pieces you *need* to make one whole. The numerator tells you how many pieces *there actually are*.

So, if you cut a cake into 4 pieces each piece is one $\frac{1}{4}$. The 4 tells you that 4 pieces make a whole cake. The 1 is one bit of those 4.

Fractions in which the top number is smaller than the bottom number are called proper fractions. So

$$\frac{5}{6}, \frac{7}{10}, \frac{9}{35} \text{ and } \frac{125}{150} \text{ are proper fractions.}$$

Fractions in which the top number is larger than the bottom one are called improper fractions. So

$$\frac{15}{6}, \frac{32}{10}, \frac{48}{35}, \frac{165}{150} \text{ and } \frac{100}{90} \text{ are improper fractions.}$$

Improper fractions can also be written as a whole number and fraction combined. For example,

$$\frac{15}{6} = 2\frac{3}{6} \text{ and } \frac{100}{90} = 1\frac{10}{90}$$

The names don't matter but the rules of handling the fractions do. They are very simple.

Adding and Subtracting Fractions
To add two fractions you have to make the denominators (bottom numbers) the same. You do that by multiplying the top and bottom of each fraction by the bottom number of the other.

$$\frac{1}{2} + \frac{7}{9} \text{ can be converted to } \frac{1 \times 9}{2 \times 9} + \frac{7 \times 2}{9 \times 2} = \frac{9}{18} + \frac{14}{18}$$

This is the same as $\frac{9+14}{18} = \frac{23}{18}$

Subtraction is just the same except that in the final stage you take away.

Multiplying Fractions
This is really easy. You just multiply the two top numbers together and the bottom two together.

$$\text{So } \frac{1}{2} \times \frac{7}{9} = \frac{1 \times 7}{2 \times 9} = \frac{7}{18}$$

Dividing Fractions
To divide one fraction by another you simply do a rather neat trick and turn the second fraction upside down. Then proceed as for multiplying. (Don't worry about *why* it works – it takes a bit of explaining – but it does.)

$$\text{So } \frac{1}{2} \div \frac{7}{9} = \frac{1}{2} \times \frac{9}{7} = \frac{1 \times 9}{2 \times 7} = \frac{9}{14}$$

Multiplication

The easiest multiplication of all is by 10. Suppose you need to multiply 137 by 10. You know that each column to the left is ten times larger, so all you need to do is move each figure one column to the left to get the answer. So 137 × 10 becomes 1370 (you put a 0 in the gap to keep the columns right).

Multiplying by 100 is really multiplying by 10, and then by 10 again, so the figures move two places to the left and you fill in the gap between the last figure and the point with 0s. So 137 × 100 becomes 13700 (you fill in the gaps with two 0s).

Or if you need to multiply a number by, say, 70 you can multiply by 7 and then by 10. So 70×55 is most easily calculated as:

55
×7
385 multiplied by 10 = 3850

You can use the same system for 700×55 except that you'd multiply by 100 at the end, and therefore add two 00s to the answer, making it 38500. The method works for multiplying by 20, 40, 80 or 300 or any other number ending in a zero. So 4.25×100 becomes 425.0 which is written as just 425 because points are only used if there are figures to their right.

Obviously, to multiply by 1000 you move the figures *three* places to the left. (Notice that the number of columns the figure moves is always the same as the number of zeros in the figure you are multiplying it by).

Since division is the opposite of multiplication to *divide* by 1000 you do the opposite. So you move the figures three places to the *right*.

So   137 divided by   10 becomes   13.7;
and   137 divided by   100 becomes   1.37;
and   137 divided by   1000 becomes   .137.

The decimal point has been put in to show which column each figure belongs in. There is an invisible point after every whole number but it is only shown if there are figures to the right of it.

A table of answers for multiplication by other numbers is given below. For long multiplication without a calculator you just need to apply the table, keeping the columns right. Always write a long sum down so the tens come under the tens and the hundreds under the hundreds and so on.

So 3472×37 is written as

```
   3472
  × 37
  24304
  10416
 128464
```

First multiply each of the top numbers by 7, starting at the right. When any figure is more than 9 you write down the unit and carry the tens into the answer in the next column. Whichever column it happens in you always carry ten.

Having multiplied 3472 by 7 you now multiply 3472 by 3. The vital point is that when multiplying you always start by writing your answer *under the figure you are multiplying by*. So, in this sum, the answer for multiplying by the 7 starts under the 7 and the answer for multiplying by a figure in the tens column (the 3 here) starts under the tens column. Finally you add the two results of the multiplication together.

The same holds good for multiplying by hundreds or thousands. So a longer multiplication looks like this.

```
    1987472
×      2145
    9937360
    7949888
    1987472
   3974944
 4263127440
```

So $145.87 + 43.12$ is

```
  145.87
 + 43.12
  188.99
```

And $189.43 - 37.01$ is

```
  189.43
 - 37.01
  152.42
```

Multiplication and Division Table

For those who have forgotten their tables and their calculator:

	2	3	4	5	6	7	8	9	10	11	12	13	14	15
2	4	6	8	10	12	14	16	18	20	22	24	26	28	30
3	6	9	12	15	18	21	24	27	30	33	36	39	42	45
4	8	12	16	20	24	28	32	36	40	44	48	52	56	60
5	10	15	20	25	30	35	40	45	50	55	60	65	70	75
6	12	18	24	30	36	42	48	54	60	66	72	78	84	90
7	14	21	28	35	42	49	56	63	70	77	84	91	98	105
8	16	24	32	40	48	56	64	72	80	88	96	104	112	120
9	18	27	36	45	54	63	72	81	90	99	108	117	126	135
10	20	30	40	50	60	70	80	90	100	110	120	130	140	150
11	22	33	44	55	66	77	88	99	110	121	132	143	154	165
12	24	36	48	60	72	84	96	108	120	132	144	156	168	180
13	26	39	52	65	78	91	104	117	130	143	156	169	182	195
14	28	42	56	70	84	98	112	126	140	154	168	182	196	210
15	30	45	60	75	90	105	120	135	150	165	180	195	210	225

Addresses and suggestions for further reading are at the ends of chapters.

To find the answer when two numbers are multiplied together go down the column headed by one of them until you come to the row belonging to the other. So 13×11 is 143.

To divide one number by another go down the column for the smaller number until you find the row for the other number. The answer will be where the column and row meet. So 98 divided by 7 = 14.

If you can't find the exact number in the table take the next number smaller than it and take it away from the number you are looking for. So 100 divided by 7 = 14 remainder 2

Decimals

Adding and Subtracting Decimals
To add or subtract decimals you just put the points under one another and treat the numbers just like any others (page 732), applying just the same rules.

Multiplying Decimals
The basic multiplication is the same as for other long – or short – multiplication (see page 733), and while you do the multiplication you ignore the points.

So 12.25×1.7 can be written as

$$
\begin{array}{r}
1225 \\
\times\ 17 \\
\hline
8575 \\
1225 \\
\hline
20825
\end{array}
$$

You then look at the original numbers which you multiplied together, and see how many figures were after the decimal point *altogether*. In this case there were two (.25) in one case, and one (.7) in another. So altogether there were 3 numbers after the decimal. This tells you that you must place the decimal point in your answer 3 figures in, counting from the right.

So 20825 becomes 20.825

Dividing Decimals
To divide decimals you have to convert the one you are dividing by into a whole number. This is easily done by just multiplying it by 10, or 100 or by whatever is needed (see page 733). So if the sum is $8147.25 \div 2.7$ you first multiply 2.7 by 10 to make it 27.

To keep the two parts of the sum in balance you *must* then multiply the other number by 10 too.

So $8147.25 \times 10 = 81472.5$

Then you can divide 81472.5 by 27 using the ordinary rules of long division. (See right.)

Decimal Places
The farther to the right you go with decimals, the smaller the fraction they represent. Unless you are calculating something of infinite fineness, it isn't worth bothering with these tiny amounts. So, for most purposes, you only need answers to one or two decimal places. This simply means you only write down that number of figures to the right of the point. But always check the figure to the right of them. If it is 5 or larger you increase

the figure to its left by 1, if it is under 5 you do nothing. This is called rounding up. So 564.13596 to two decimal places may seem to be 564.13 *but* as the 3 is followed by 5 the correct answer is 564.14

Similarly, in both decimals and non-decimals an answer may be needed to a certain number of 'significant figures'. Obviously, a number is more significant (important) the bigger it is. So the farther to the left a number is, the more significant it is. This means that in picking out significant figures you start from the left.

Suppose you are asked for 4828.04 to four significant figures. You'd take the four left-hand figures and drop the rest = 4828. Easy.

But suppose you were asked for 4828.04 to three significant figures? The answer is *not* 482. What you actually do is replace any non-significant numbers to the left of the point (in this case an 8) with 0s. And if the left-most of the numbers you drop is 5 or greater you increase its significant neighbour by 1. In this example the left-most figure is 8. So 4828.04 to three significant figures is 4830. But 4828.04 to two significant figures would be 4800 as the 2 which was dropped was smaller than 5.

Long Division

Long division without a calculator is tedious, but not hard. This is one case where there is no choice but to just do the steps without thinking too hard about the mathematical realities.

Suppose you need to divide 15965 by 52.

$$
\begin{array}{r}
3 \\
52\overline{)\ 15965} \\
-\ 156 \\
\hline
3
\end{array}
$$

Working from the left, find the first number that 52 can be divided into. It won't go into 1, or into 15 but it will go into 159. Work out how many times it will go, on a bit of scrap paper. i.e.

$$
\begin{array}{r}
52 \\
\times\ 3 \\
\hline
156
\end{array}
$$

$$
\begin{array}{r}
30 \\
52\overline{)\ 15965} \\
-\ 156\downarrow\downarrow \\
\hline
365
\end{array}
$$

Put a 3 above the 9 of 159, and write 156 under the 159 and subtract it. That leaves 3.

$$
\begin{array}{r}
307 \\
52\overline{)\ 15965} \\
156\downarrow\downarrow \\
\hline
365 \\
-\ 364 \\
\hline
1
\end{array}
$$

Now bring down the 6 from the upper line. 52 can't go into 36, so put a 0 in the top line and bring down the 5. 52 will go into 365; a quick calculation shows it goes 7 times.

$$
\begin{array}{r}
52 \\
\times\ 7 \\
\hline
364
\end{array}
$$

$$
\begin{array}{r}
307.01 \\
52\overline{)\ 15965.000} \\
156\downarrow\downarrow \\
365\downarrow\downarrow\downarrow \\
-\ 364 \\
\hline
1\ 0\ 0 \\
-\ 52 \\
\hline
480
\end{array}
$$

Put 7 in the top row and put 364 under 365 and take it away.

For most purposes the answer 307 remainder 1 will do. But if you need to be fanatically accurate just put a point after the figures and keep on dividing bringing down a zero each time. etc. etc.

Binary

The tens system isn't the only one possible, it's just the one mankind found convenient (having ten fingers). Computers, having switches instead of fingers, don't find it convenient. So their creators chose to work in the binary system – so-called because instead of each column being ten times as big as the one to its right it is just *twice* as big.

thirty twos	sixteens	eights	fours	twos	units
1	1	1	1	1	1

So instead of 11 standing for 1 lot of ten and 1 unit, it means 1 lot of 2 and one unit – in other words 3. And 111, stands for one 4, one 2 and one 1 – that's 7 to you and me. You add or subtract just as with tens, but using the values of the columns given above.

Percentages

Discounts

The situation in which percentages are most often encountered is when discounts are offered. To calculate a percentage discount on a price divide the price by 100, and multiply the answer by the percentage discount being offered. So a 12 per cent discount on a bed costing £499 goes like this: $499 \div 100 = 4.99$

$$4.99 \times 12 = 59.88$$

So the 12% discount is worth £59.88. Take that away from the original price of £499 and you find the bed is reduced to £439.12.

Percentages as Part of a Price

This is how to find a percentage element of a price – for example, the VAT element.

1 Add 100 to the percentage VAT (or whatever other percentage you need to calculate). Say 15 (VAT) + 100 = 115.
2 Divide the price by this figure.
3 Multiply the result by the original VAT (or other) percentage.

So, with VAT at 15%, the calculations to find the VAT element on a car costing £10,500 would be:
$$15 + 100 = 115$$
$$£10,500 \div 115 = £91.304347$$

The last four figures (4347) are fractions of a penny and may not seem worth writing down, but don't get rid of them, they make a difference to the final answer.

$$£91.304347 \times 15 = £1369.5652$$

So the VAT is £1,369.57 (to the nearest penny). The price is £10,500 − £1,369.50 = £9,130.43 without VAT.

Percentages Added to a Price

This is how you do the calculation to increase a price by a given percentage.

1 Divide the price by 100: this gives you 1 per cent of it. (See page 732 for the quick way to divide by 100).

2 Multiply that answer by the percentage.
3 Add the result to the original price.

To increase £110.67 by 23% the calculation is this:
$$£110.67 \div 100 = £1.1067, \text{ which is } 1\%$$
$$£1.1067 \times 23 = £25.45$$

So the price + 23% is £110.67 + £25.45 = £136.12.

Converting Fractions to Percentages

Fractions are converted into percentages by multiplying them by 100.

As a fraction always means that you divide the upper figure by the lower one to get an answer in simple figures, 100 can be written as $\underline{100}$. So to convert ³/₅ to a percentage:

$$\frac{3}{5} \times \frac{100}{1} = \frac{3 \times 100}{5 \times 1} = \frac{300}{5} \qquad 300 \div 5 = 60\%$$

The same rule applies with decimal fractions.
So 0.35 becomes $(0.35 \times 100)\% = 35\%$

Converting Percentages into Fractions

Percentages are converted into fractions by dividing them by 100.

So $12\% = \frac{12}{100}$ $20\% = \frac{20}{100}$ $75\% = \frac{75}{100}$ and so on.

To make large fractions more manageable divide both the top and bottom by any number which goes exactly into *both*. So $\frac{12}{100}$ can be divided by 4

$$\frac{12 \div 4}{100 \div 4} = \frac{3}{25}$$

> In any calculations in which a percentage is one of the figures it *must* be converted into a fraction in this way. You *can't* just drop the % sign, as you might drop a £ sign, and tack it on at the end of the calculation. Doing that would give the wrong answer.

Positive and Negative Numbers

Positive and negative numbers are extremely simple to understand if you use a method my daughter learnt from a brilliant maths mistress at her school who had that rare knack of making the obscure perfectly obvious. The system is called heaps and holes. Think of a positive number as a heap. So + 7 is a heap 7 cm (or 7 in) high.

Now think of a minus number as a hole the same size. So − 3 is a hole 3 cm (or 3 in deep).

Therefore, if the sum was − 3 + 7 you could use a heap of 7 cm high to fill in a hole of − 3 cm deep and you'd be left with 4 cm above the ground so 4 is the answer.

But if the sum was 3–7 you would put the 3 cm into a hole 7 cm deep and still leave 4 cm unfilled. So the answer would be −4.

Addresses and suggestions for further reading are at the ends of chapters.

In the same way, the tricky concept of (−2)+(−2) is bound to be two holes each 2 cm (or whatever) deep – which is the same as one hole 4 cm deep. So the answer is − 4.

The other thing to remember is that the + or − always belongs to the number which follows it. So provided you keep each sign firmly attached to the number it belongs to you can switch the order of the numbers to make it easier to do the sum. It is often easier, for example, to gather up all the plus numbers then deal with all the negative ones.

Powers

Powers are shown as a small figure at the top right-hand corner of another figure, or a bracket. They indicate the number of times the number they are attached to must be multiplied by itself. 2^2 is called 2 squared. It means there are two lots of 2 which must be multiplied together.

So $2^2 = 2 \times 2$ which is 4, and $3^2 = 3 \times 3$ which is 6.

And $5^3 = 5 \times 5 \times 5$ making 125

$7^3 = 7 \times 7 \times 7$ which is 343

And $10^{10} = 10 \times 10 \times 10 \times 10 \times 10 \times 10 \times 10 \times 10 \times 10 \times 10$, so $10^{10} = 10,000,000,000$.

There are books of tables which give you the answers for calculations of this sort. But you can just as easily do the maths on your calculator provided you keep track of how many times you have multiplied.

There is also a short cut which can be useful: 2^6 is the same as $2^2 \times 2^4$ i.e. 2^6 is $2 \times 2 \times 2 \times 2 \times 2 \times 2 = 64$ but 2^2 is $2 \times 2 = 4$ while 2^4 is $2 \times 2 \times 2 \times 2 = 16$. And $4 \times 16 = 64$

Notice that if powers *add* together to make the power you want to calculate the answer by *multiplying* their products together.

Rules of Geometry

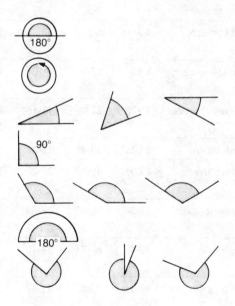

180°	a half circle
360°	a circle
less than 90°	an acute angle
90°	a right angle (square corner)
greater than 90°	an obtuse angle
180°	a semi-circle
greater than 180°	a reflex angle

The angles inside a triangle total 180°.

The angles inside any figure with 4 sides total 360°.

The circumference of a circle (measurement right round) is worked out by the formula 2(π)r. r = radius – the measurement from the centre of a circle to its edge.

$\pi = 3.142$ or $\dfrac{22}{7}$ (approximately).

The area of a circle is $\pi \times r^2$

Signs and Symbols

In maths signs and symbols often show not only what you have to do but the direction in which you have to do it. We all know 6–3 means you take the 3 from the

6, and not the 6 from the 3. The other rules of direction are just as simple, but it is important to get them right.

+ add
− subtract (i.e. 6–3 means take 3 from 6)
× multiply
a . on the line, not raised as in decimals, also means multiply 4(5+2) is the same as $4 \times (5+2)$ and means the numbers inside the brackets are multiplied by 4, but the calculation inside the brackets must be done first.

÷ divide; $\dfrac{6+8}{7}$ means the 6 and 8 are added then divided by 7.
> means 'is greater than'. So an elephant > a mouse, and 56 > 3.
< means 'is less than'. So an elephant < a castle, and 15 < 60.

≥ means greater than or equal to. So one dog ≥ another dog.
∞ means infinity
≈ means approximately
: means 'is to'
∴ therefore symbol – means therefore
∵ because symbol – means because
√ square root symbol means square root. The square root of a number is the one which multiplied by itself makes that number.

So 2 is the square root of 4 (i.e. $2 \times 2 = 4$) and 10 is the square root of 100 (i.e. $10 \times 10 = 100$)
() {} [] – brackets like these indicate that the calculations inside them need to be done before any numbers outside the brackets are brought into the action. If there are brackets within brackets start inside the innermost pair.

WEATHER

Beaufort Scale of Wind Force

Force	Wind Type	mph	kph	knots	Effect on Land and Sea
0	none	0-1	0-2	0-1	Smoke rises vertically. Sea like a mirror
1	faint breeze	1-3	2-5	1-3	Smoke drifts but wind vane stationary. Sea slightly rippled
2	light breeze	4-7	6-12	4-6	Wind felt on face, leaves rustle, vanes move. Sea has wavelets
3	gentle breeze	8-12	13-20	7-10	Wind extends light flag, twigs move. A few white horses on sea
4	moderate breeze	13-18	21-29	11-16	Raises dust and loose paper, small branches move. Small waves, more white horses
5	fresh breeze	19-24	30-39	17-21	Small, leafy trees sway. Moderate waves, some spray
6	strong breeze	25-31	40-50	22-27	Large branches move. Telegraph wires whistle. Umbrellas a problem. Large waves with foam crests, extensive spray
7	moderate gale	32-38	51-62	28-33	Whole trees in motion. Hard to walk against the wind. Sea heaps up and foam blows with the wind
8	fresh gale	39-46	63-74	34-40	Twigs break off trees. Walking difficult. Moderately high waves of greater length, streaks of blown foam
9	strong gale	47-54	75-87	41-47	Slight structural damage. Chimney pots and slates blown off. High waves, blown foam begins to limit visibility
10	whole gale	55-63	88-102	48-56	Trees uprooted and major structural damage. Very high waves and sea white with foam. Worse visibility
11	storm	64-75	103-120	57-65	Widespread damage. Rare in Europe. Exceptionally high waves, can mask medium-sized ships from view. Bad visibility from blown foam
12	hurricane	75 +	120 +	65 +	Very great damage – typical of revolving storms in the tropics. Air filled with foam, sea totally white, very bad visibility

Addresses and suggestions for further reading are at the ends of chapters.

Shipping Forecast Areas

For those who go to sea and those who, like me, are bemused by the shipping forecast.

Published by the Met. Office with brochure 'Weather Services For Shipping' January 1993

WEIGHTS AND MEASURES

Capacity

UK Imperial

8 fluid drachms	=	1 fluid oz
5 fluid ounces	=	1 gill
4 gills	=	1 pint
2 pints	=	1 quart
4 quarts	=	1 gallon
2 gallons	=	1 peck (only used for dry goods)
4 pecks	=	1 bushel (only used for dry goods)
8 bushels	=	1 quarter (only used for dry goods)
31½ gallons	=	1 barrel
2 barrels	=	1 hogshead
36 gallons	=	1 bulk barrel

American pints and gallons are not the same size as British ones. (See page 111 for measurement in US cups.)

Metric

10 millilitres	=	1 centilitre
100 centilitres	=	1 litre
1,000 millilitres	=	1 litre
100 litres	=	1 hectolitre
1,000 litres	=	1 kilolitre

Conversion Factors

1 fluid ounce	=	28.4 millilitres
¼ pint	=	142 millilitres
1 pint (UK)	=	568 millilitres
1 quart	=	1.136 litres
1 gallon	=	4.546 litres
1 litre	=	2.1134 pints US
1 litre	=	1.7598 pints UK

Circular and Angular Measures

60 seconds (")	=	1 minute
60 minutes (')	=	1 degree
30 degrees (°)	=	1 sign
45 degrees (°)	=	1 octant
60 degrees (°)	=	1 sextant
90 degrees (°)	=	1 quadrant
4 quadrants	=	1 circle
12 signs	=	1 circle

Conversion Factors

Multiply number of	by	to obtain equivalent number of
inches	25.4	millimetres
	2.54	centimetres
feet	30.48	centimetres
	0.3048	metres
yards	0.9144	metres
miles (land: 5,280 ft.)	1.609344	kilometres
miles (UK sea: 6,080 ft.)	1.853184	kilometres
miles (international nautical)	1.852	kilometres
sq inches (in²)	645.16	sq millimetres (mm²)
	6.4516	sq centimetres (cm²)
sq feet (ft²)	929.0304	sq centimetres
	0.092903	sq metres (m²)
sq yards (yd²)	8361.2736	sq centimetres
	0.836127	sq metres
acres	4,046.86	sq metres
	0.404686	hectares (ha)
	0.004047	sq kilometres (km²)
sq miles	2.58999	sq kilometres
cu. inches (in³)	16.387064	cu centimetres (cm³)
UK pints	34.6774	cu inches
UK pints	0.5783	litres
UK gallons	4.54609	litres
US gallons	3.785	litres
cu feet (ft³)	28.317	litres
cu feet	0.028317	cu metres (m³)
UK gallons	1.20095	US gallons
US gallons	0.832674	UK gallons
ounces, avoirdupois (oz)	28.3495	grams
ounces, troy (oz tr)	31.1035	grams
ounces, avoirdupois	0.9115	ounces, troy
pounds avoirdupois (lb)	453.59237	grams
	0.45359	kilograms
short tons (2,000 lb)	0.892857	long tons
	0.907185	tonnes
long tons (2,240 lb)	1.12	short tons
	1.01605	tonnes
millimetres	0.03937	inches
centimetres	0.3937	inches
centimetres	0.03281	feet
metres	39.3701	inches
metres	3.2808	feet
metres	1.0936	yards
metres	0.54681	fathoms
kilometres	0.62137	miles (land)
kilometres	0.53961	miles (UK sea)
kilometres	0.53996	miles (international nautical)

Multiply number of	by	to obtain equivalent number of
sq millimetres	0.00155	sq inches
sq centimetres	0.1550	sq inches
sq. metres	10.7639	sq feet
sq. metres	1.19599	sq yards
hectares	2.47105	acres
sq kilometres	0.3861	sq miles
cu centimetres	0.06102	cu inches
litres	61.024	cu inches
litres	0.0353	cu feet
litres	2.1134	US pints
litres	1.7598	UK pints
litres	0.2642	US gallons
litres	0.21997	UK gallons
hectolitres	26.417	US gallons
hectolitres	21.997	UK gallons
hectolitres	2.838	UK bushels
hectolitres	2.750	US bushels
cu metres	35.3147	cu feet
cu metres	1.30795	cu yards
cu metres	264.172	US gallons
cu metres	219.969	UK gallons
cu metres	6.11026	UK bulk barrels
grammes	0.03527	ounces, avoirdupois
grammes	0.03215	ounces, troy
kilogrammes	2.20462	pounds, avoirdupois
metres quintals (q)	220.462	pounds, avoirdupois
tonnes	2,204.62	pounds, avoirdupois
tonnes	1.10231	short tons
tonnes	0.984207	long tons

Approximate Conversions

Miles to kilometres: multiply by 8, then divide by 5
Kilometres to miles: multiply by 5, then divide by 8
Square metres into square yards: add one fifth
Acres to hectares: multiply by 2 and divide by 5
Hectares to acres: multiply by 5 and divide by 2

Distance

Imperial

12 inches	=	1 foot
3 feet	=	1 yard
5 ½ yards	=	1 rod, pole or perch
4 rods (66 ft)	=	1 chain
10 chains	=	1 furlong
5,280 feet	=	1 mile
1,760 yards	=	1 mile
8 furlongs	=	1 mile

Metric

10 angstroms	=	1 nanometre
1,000 nanometres	=	1 micrometre
1,000 micrometres	=	1 millimetre
10 millimetres	=	1 centimetre
100 centimetres	=	1 metre
100 metres	=	1 hectometre
1,000 metres	=	1 kilometre
10 hectometres	=	1 kilometre

Approximate Equivalent Distances

1 inch	=	2.5 cm
1 foot	=	30 cm
1 yard	=	91 cm
1 mile	=	1,609 m
1 centimetre	=	0.4 in
1 metre	=	3 yd 3 in
1 kilometre	=	1,093 yd
1 kilometre	=	almost ¾ mile

Nautical Distance

6 feet	=	1 fathom
100 fathoms	=	1 cable length
6,080 feet	=	1 nautical mile
1 international nautical mile	=	1,852 metres

Old British Currency

Until February 1971 British currency was pounds, shillings and pence which were abbreviated to £ s d, from the Roman coins Libra, solidus and denarius.

4 farthings	=	penny (1d)
2 half pennies (½d)	=	1 penny
12 pennies (12d)	=	1 shilling (1s)
4 threepenny pieces (3d)	=	1 shilling
2 sixpences (6d)	=	1 shilling
2 shillings (2s)	=	1 florin
2 shillings and sixpence (2/6)	=	1 half crown
5 shillings (5s)	=	1 crown
10 shillings (10s)	=	1 half-sovereign
20 shillings (20s)	=	1 pound (£1)
1 pound (£1)	=	1 sovereign
1 pound 1 shilling (£1 1s)	=	1 guinea

Paper Measures

Writing and Drawing Paper

24 sheets	=	1 quire
480 sheets	=	1 ream
20 quires	=	1 ream

Printing Paper

516 sheets	=	1 ream
2 reams	=	1 bundle
5 bundles	=	1 bale

Weights

Imperial

437½ grains (gr)	=	1 ounce
16 drams (dr)	=	1 ounce
16 ounces (oz)	=	1 pound
14 pounds (lb)	=	1 stone
28 pounds	=	1 quarter
8 stone	=	1 hundredweight
4 quarters	=	1 hundredweight
2,240 pounds	=	1 ton
20 hundredweights	=	1 ton

Addresses and suggestions for further reading are at the ends of chapters.

Metric

1,000,000 microgrammes	=	1 gramme
1,000 milligrammes	=	1 gramme
1,000 grammes	=	1 kilogramme
100 kilogrammes	=	1 quintal
1,000 kilogrammes	=	1 tonne

Approximate Equivalent Measures

1 ounce	=	28 grammes
1 pound	=	454 grammes
1 stone	=	6.3 kilogrammes
1 cwt	=	50.8 kilogrammes
100 grammes	=	3½ ounces
200 grammes	=	7 ounces
1 kilogramme	=	2 pounds 3 ounces
1 tonne	=	just under 1 ton

Conversion Factors

1 ounce	=	28.35 grammes
1 pound	=	0.4536 kilogrammes
1 gramme	=	0.035 ounces
1 kilogramme	=	2.204 pounds

> Under the Weights and Measures Act 1963 the rod, pole or perch, quarter (capacity), bushel, and peck are no longer legal measures. The old apothecaries' measures with their quaint drachms, scruples and grains have also passed into history.

USEFUL ADDRESSES AND BOOKS

Astrology

Useful Books

Derek and Julia Parker, *The New Compleat Astrologer*, Mitchell Beazley.

Lori Read, *How to Read Hands*, The Aquarian Press–for those with an interest in palmistry.

Theodora Lau, *The Chinese Horoscope*, Arrow.

Suzanne White, *The New Chinese Astrology*, Pan.

Genealogy

Association of Genealogists and Record Agents, 29 Budgens Close, Horsham, W. Sussex RH12 5RU Tel: 0403 63119, can tell you how to obtain the services of a professional genealogist.

Federation of Family History Societies, 5 Mornington Close, Copthorne, Shrewsbury SY3 8XN Tel: 0743 65505 – M, B, G, Ad, sae.

Guild of One Name Studies, Box G, 14 Charterhouse Buildings, Goswell Road, London EC1M 7BA, links those researching a particular surname – it could be yours.

Institute of Heraldic and Genealogical Studies, School of Family History, 72-82 Northgate, Canterbury, Kent CT1 1BA Tel: 0227 768684, runs correspondence and short residential courses on how to trace coats of arms and family history.

Society of Genealogists, 14 Charterhouse Buildings, Goswell Road, London EC1M 7BA Tel: 071 251 8799 – M£H, B, access to the society's collection of parish registers and directories.

Useful Book

Leslie Dunking, *The Guinness Book of Names*, Guinness Superlatives.

General

Cambridge University – for term dates telephone 0223 337733. (P.717)

Gemmological Association of Great Britain, St Dunstan's House, Carey Lane, London EC2V 8AB Tel: 071 726 4374.

Oxford University – for term dates telephone 0865 270001. (P.717)

Shap Working Party on World Religions in Education, 7 Alderbrook Road, Solihull, West Midlands B91 1NH.

BIBLIOGRAPHY

Many of the books which form part of the bibliography are recommended in the relevant chapters. The rest are as follows.

David Alderton, *Looking After Cage Birds*, Ward Lock, 1982

John Arlott (ed.), *Oxford Companion to Sports and Games*, Oxford University Press, 1975

Peter Arnold (ed.), *The Complete Book of Indoor Games*, Hamlyn, 1981

Denis Arnold (ed.), *The New Oxford Companion to Music*, Oxford University Press, 1983

British Dietetic Association, *Children's Diets and Change*, 1987

British Medical Association, *Diet, Nutrition and Health*, 1986

Stefan T. Buczacki and Keith Harris, *Collins Guide to Pests, Diseases and Disorders of Garden Plants*, Collins, 1986

Stefan T. Buczacki, *Gardeners' Questions Answered*, Collins, 1985

James R. Busvine, *Insects and Hygiene*, Chapman & Hall, 1983

Pamela Carmichael, *The She Book of Cats*, Ebury Press, 1983

Collins English Dictionary, Collins, 1973

The Concise Oxford Dictionary, Oxford University Press, 1982

Robert Dearling (ed.), *Guinness Book of Musical Facts and Figures*, Guinness, 1976

Department of Health and Social Security, *Present Day Practice in Infant Feeding*, HMSO, 1983

Diagram Group, *Official World Encyclopedia of Sport and Games*, Paddington Press, 1979

Margaret Dibben, *The Guardian Money Guide*, Collins Willow, 1986

Directory of British Associations, C.B.D. Research, 1986

Alexandre Dumas, *Dumas on Food*, trans by Alan and Jane Davidson, Michael Joseph, 1979

John and Peter Filbey, *The Astrologer's Companion*, Aquarian Handbooks, 1986

Maureen Foster, *Preserved Flowers*, Pelham, 1973

H.W. Fowler, *Dictionary of Modern English Usage*, Oxford University Press, 1965

Frohne & Pfander, *Colour Atlas of Poisonous Plants*, Wolfe Medical, 1984

A.R. Gennaro (ed.), *Blakiston's Gould Medical Dictionary*, McGraw, 1979

Brian Giles, *Safety with Horses*, Stanley Paul, 1985

Glanz, *Mosby's Medical and Nursing Dictionary*, Mosby, 1985

William R. Gondin and Edward W. Mammen, *The Art of Speaking Made Simple*, W.H. Allen, 1975

Conal Gregory, *Caterer's Guide to Drinks*, Northwood, 1979

James M. Haig, *The Householder's Guide to Plumbing*, Stanley Paul, 1984

Maurice Hanssen, *E for Additives*, Thorsons, 1986

Arthur G.L. Hellyer, *The Amateur Gardener*, Collingridge, 1972

Norman Hickin, *Pest Animals in Buildings*, George Godwin, 1985

Betty C. Hobbs and Diane Roberts, *Food Poisoning and Food Hygiene* (5th edition), Edward Arnold, 1987

Ingrid Holford (ed.), *Guinness Book of Weather Facts and Feats*, Guinness, 1977

James Holgate and David Coulter, *Speak with Confidence*, Stanley Paul, 1974

Angela Hollest and Penelope Gaine, *Parties for Older Children*, Piatkus Books, 1986

Derek Hull and Derek I. Johnston, *Essential Paediatrics*, Churchill Livingstone, 1980

Investors Chronicle, Financial Times Business Publishing Ltd, London

Hugh Johnson, *World Atlas of Wine*, Mitchell Beazley, 1977

Felicity Lawrence, *Additives: Your Complete Survival Guide*, Century, 1986

Margaret Leach, *Freezer Facts*, Forbes Publications Ltd, 1975

Jeff Mayo, *Teach Yourself Astrology*, Hodder & Stoughton, 1981

Susan McBane, *Keeping Horses*, Collins, 1986

Susan McBane, *Your First Horse*, Stanley Paul, 1985

R.A McCance and E.M. Widdowson, *The Composition of Foods*, HMSO, 1978

Diane McCrea, *Opening the Floodgates*, London Food Commission, 1987

The Macdonald Guide to French Wines, Macdonald, 1988

Norris D. McWhirter (ed.), *Guinness Book of Answers*, Guinness, 1978

A.G. Mears, *The Right Way to Speak in Public*, Elliott Right Way Books, 1987

Mims Magazine, Medical Publications Ltd, London

Ministry of Agriculture, Fisheries & Food, *Manual of Nutrition*, HMSO, 1985

Ministry of Agriculture, Fisheries & Food, *Poisonous Plants in Britain and Their Effects on Animals and Man*, HMSO, 1984

National Consumer Council, *Consumers and Credit*, 1980

The New England Journal of Medicine, Massachussetts Medical Society, Boston, Mass.

Maureen O'Connor, *A Parent's Guide to Education*, Fontana, 1986

Derek and Julia Parker, *A History of Astrology*, André Deutsch, 1983

David Parlett, *Penguin Book of Card Games*, Penguin, 1979

R. Passmore and R.A. Eastwood, *Human Nutrition and Dietetics*, Churchill Livingstone, 1986

The Practitioner, Morgan-Grampian Ltd, London

David Robinson, *Tortoises Including Turtles and Terrapins*, Bartholemew, 1976

David Rubenstein and David Wayne, *Lecture Notes on Clinical Medicine*, Blackwell, 1976

W.E. Shewell-Cooper, *Soil: Humus and Health*, David & Charles, 1975

Felicity Taylor, *How to Invest Successfully*, Kogan Page, 1983

W.A.R. Thomson, *Black's Medical Dictionary*, Black, 1984

Alan Titchmarsh, *Down to Earth Gardening*, Ward Lock, 1984

Alan Titchmarsh, *How to be a Supergardener*, Ward Lock, 1988

United Kingdom Bartenders' Guild, *International Guide to Drinks*, Century Hutchinson, 1988

Update: The Journal of the Post Graduate Practice, Siebert Publications Ltd, Guildford

Frank Vernon, *Teach Yourself Beekeeping*, Hodder & Stoughton, 1986

Caroline Walker and Geoffrey Cannon, *The Food Scandal*, Arrow, 1986

Derek Walters, *Chinese Astrology*, Aquarian Handbooks, 1987

The Which? Guide to Your Rights, Consumers' Association, 1981

Michael Wright and Sally Walters (ed.), *The Book of the Cat*, Pan, 1980

INDEX

Main references are shown in **bold type**; references to illustrations are in *italic*.

National Council for Civil Liberties (Liberty) 499
National Council for Industry Training Organizations 322
National Council for One-Parent Families 318
National Council for the Divorced and Separated 498
National Council for Vocational Qualifications 306, 322
National Council for Voluntary Organizations 692
National Council of Industry Training Organizations 310
National Cricket Association 717
national curriculum **294**, 297
  and GNVQs 305
National Dairy Council 124
National Deaf-blind and Rubella Association (Sense) 590
National Deaf Children's Society 590
National Eczema Society 124, 555, 589
National Educational Guidance Initiative 311, 320
National Extension College 309, 323
National Family Conciliation Council 498
National Fancy Rat Society 660
National Farmers' Union 124
National Federation of Bus Users 686, 697
National Federation of Credit Unions 542
National Federation of Gateway Clubs 316
National Federation of Painting and Decorating Contractors 269
National Federation of Roofing Contractors 228, 269
National Federation of Solo Clubs 318
National Federation of Spiritual Healers 567, 592
National Federation of Women's Institutes 316
National Fireplace Council 271
National Foster Care Association 274, 317
National Fruit Centre 379
National Gardens Scheme 377
National Grid 679
National Health Service 587, 669, 694
  cosmetic camouflage and 637
  fees/charges 670
  NHS Trusts 669
  private medicine and 673-4
  sex therapy on 612
National Heritage 216
National House Building Council 230, 269
National Information for Parents of Prematures (Nippers) 642
National Inspection Council for Electrical Installation 222, 272
National Institute of Adult Continuing Education 310, 321
National Institute of Carpet Fitters 184, 215
National Institute of Medical Herbalists 592

National Insurance **522-3**, 541, 543
  amount payable 539
  backdating contributions 522-3
  card 522
  contributions 522
National Library for the Handicapped Child 320
National Listening Library 592
National Marriage Guidance Council (Relate) 318, 612, 642
National Mouse Club 660
National Newspaper Mail Order Protection Scheme Ltd 206, 217
National Organisation for Adopters and their Parents 273, 317, 478
National Osteoporosis Society 548, 588
National Pet Register 658
National Playing Fields Association 692
National Pony Society 660
National Power 679
National Radiological Protection Board 694
National Record of Achievement 294, 305
National Rivers Authority 685, 698
National Savings 501, 526, 528, 542-3
  accounts, tax on 538
  Bonds and Stock Office 529, 543
  certificates 526, 539; tax on 538
  different types compared 527
  saving with 527
National Schizophrenia Fellowship 589
National Society for Epilepsy 589
National Society for Research into Allergy 587
National Society for the Prevention of Cruelty to Children 274, 319, 463
National Stepfamily Association 286, 318
National Supervisory Council for Intruder Alarms 229, 271
National Toy Libraries Association 317
National Trust 216, 218, 377-8
National Trust for Scotland 378
National Union of Townswomen's Guilds 316
National Viewers' and Listeners' Association 697
National Vocational Qualifications 304, **305**
  and Youth Training 311
  tax rebates 535
National Women's Register 316
nationality, law 480, 484-5, 499
NATO 664-5
natterjack toad 651
Natural Parents Support Group 273, 317
Natural Pest Control Ltd 379
nature 342, 692
Nature Conservancy Council 230, 464, 693

naturopathic medicine 567, 592
nausea
  and tranquillizer withdrawal 561
  cardomom for 82
  food poisoning 55
  ginger for 84
nautical distance 740
Navarra (wine region) 151, 152
NAWCH see Action for Sick Children
NCB 278, 317
NCCL (Liberty) 499
NCMA (National Childminding Association) 287, 319
neatsfoot oil
  in sharpening tools 265
  to clean leather bindings 157
neck, skin care 634, 635
nectarines 64
needlepoint **394-6**
  cleaning 170
  repair 215
needles
  darning 381
  hand sewing 388
  knitting 401
  tapestry 395
  threading 381, 388
needles (hypodermic)
  AIDS from 545
  sharing 584
  when travelling abroad 574
needlework see embroidery; patchwork; sewing
negative numbers 736-7
neglect of animals 486
neglect of child 319
  emergency protection orders 479
negligence
  and exclusion clauses 450
  and insurance 515, 517
  medical 673
negotiations 541
Neighbourhood Energy Action 271
neighbourhood watch 460
neighbours
  and eviction order 489
  boundaries, law 486
  building works and 487
  right of entry 490
Nembutal 585-6
neo-natal death **610-11**, 642
net
  sewing 381
  washing 194
net curtains
  buying 186
  making 412
  washing 194
  see also curtains
nettles
  as hair conditioner 639
  for dandruff 639
  stings 548
Network Scotland Ltd 323
neurofen 568
neurosis 560
neutering, cats, free service 658
new baby
  problems 274
  step-children and 285, 286

new homes, hotline 230
new issues (shares) 530
New Zealand wines **148-9**, 154
Newspaper Society 206, 217
newspapers 692
  announcements 8
  complaints about 668-9
  education sections 295
  lonely hearts columns 342
  mail order 206
  new share issues in 530
  to clean windows 163
NHBC 230, 269
NHS see National Health Service
nicene creed 675-6
nicotine, removing stains
  from hands 638
  from nails 638
  from paint 248
nicotinic acid 628
night, personal safety 460
nightshade, deadly 579
nine men's morris 332
Nippers (National Information for Parents of Prematures) 642
nipples, care of during breastfeeding 615
nitrogen (fertilizer) 359
nits, control of 210
no-diet diet 630
no claims bonus 516
'nocturnal emissions' 594
noise
  and children's sleep 284
  checks on cars by police 472-3
  law 487
Noise Abatement Society 487, 497
non-gonococcal urethritis 561
non-smokers, effects of smoking on 582-3, 593
non-specific genital infections 561
non-specific urethritis 561
non-stick pans, cleaning 172
nonconformist church wedding 11
noodles 78-9
NORCAP 273, 317, 478
North Atlantic Treaty Organization, political parties and 664-5
Northern Ireland
  District Committees (health) 669
  education 694
  legal aid 492
  legal system 126, 499
  political parties 664-5
  small claims 493
  water supply 685
  see also Ulster
Northern Ireland Court Service 499
Northern Ireland Office 694
Norwegian lobster 51
nosebleeds 561
notebook computers 437
  typing onto 438-9
notepaper, choice of 36
notes, cards for 37
notice
  by employer 474
  pay in lieu 539-40